THE ENCYCLOPEDIA OF
GLOBAL POPULATION AND DEMOGRAPHICS

THE ENCYCLOPEDIA OF
GLOBAL POPULATION
AND DEMOGRAPHICS

IMMANUEL NESS

Brooklyn College, City University of New York

JAMES CIMENT

New School University

FITZROY DEARBORN PUBLISHERS
CHICAGO • LONDON

British Library and Library of Congress Cataloging-in-Publication information is available.

ISBN 1-57958-180-3

First published in the USA and UK 1999

Printed by Maple-Vail, Binghamton, NY
Composition by Westchester Book Composition, Danbury, CT

For more information about Fitzroy Dearborn Publishers, see:
www.fitzroydearborn.com

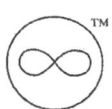

Contents

Acknowledgments vii

PART ONE: ESSAYS

1. Introduction to Demography 3
2. Demography, Resources, and the Environment 13
3. General Population and Vital Statistics 23
4. The Demography of Families and Households 33
5. Demography and Cultural Identity 43
6. The Demography of Labor and the Economy 55
7. The Demography of Migration 64
8. The Demography of Transportation
   and Communications 74
9. The Demography of Health Care and Education 81

PART TWO: TABLES

How to Use the Tables 93
Table Bibliography and Sources 97
1. World Data, Graphs, and Tables 101
2. The Regions of the World: Data, Graphs
   and Tables 105
3. The Countries of the World, Statistical Tables
Afghanistan 135
Albania 138
Algeria 141
Andorra 146
Angola 148
Antigua and Barbuda 153
Argentina 156
Armenia 161
Australia 164
Austria 169
Azerbaijan 173
The Bahamas 176
Bahrain 180
Bangladesh 184
Barbados 189
Belarus 193
Belgium 197
Belize 201
Benin 205
Bhutan 209
Bolivia 212
Bosnia and Herzegovina 216
Botswana 219
Brazil 223
Brunei Darussalam 229
Bulgaria 232
Burkina Faso 236
Burundi 239
Cambodia 243
Cameroon 246
Canada 250

Cape Verde 256
Central African Republic 260
Chad 264
Chile 268
China 272
Colombia 278
Comoros 282
Congo, Democratic Republic of (Zaïre) 285
Congo, Republic of 289
Costa Rica 293
Côte d'Ivoire 297
Croatia 301
Cuba 305
Cyprus 310
Czech Republic 314
Denmark 318
Djibouti 322
Dominica 325
Dominican Republic 328
Ecuador 332
Egypt 336
El Salvador 342
Equatorial Guinea 346
Eritrea 349
Estonia 352
Ethiopia 356
Fiji 362
Finland 366
France 370
Gabon 376
The Gambia 379
Georgia 383
Germany 386
Ghana 392
Greece 396
Grenada 400
Guatemala 403
Guinea 409
Guinea-Bissau 413
Guyana 416
Haiti 419
Honduras 422
Hungary 426
Iceland 430
India 434
Indonesia 440
Iran 446
Iraq 452
Ireland 457
Israel 461
Italy 467

Jamaica 473
Japan 479
Jordan 485
Kazakstan 489
Kenya 494
Kiribati 500
Korea, (North) 502
Korea, South, (Republic of Korea) 505
Kuwait 511
Kyrgyzstan 515
Laos 519
Latvia 522
Lebanon 526
Lesotho 530
Liberia 533
Libya 536
Liechtenstein 540
Lithuania 543
Luxembourg 548
Macedonia, Former Yugoslav Republic of 552
Madagascar 556
Malawi 560
Malaysia 564
Maldives 568
Mali 571
Malta 575
Marshall Islands 579
Mauritania 582
Mauritius 586
Mexico 590
Micronesia, Federated States of 596
Moldova 598
Monaco 602
Mongolia 605
Morocco 608
Mozambique 614
Myanmar 618
Namibia 622
Nauru 626
Nepal 629
Netherlands 633
New Zealand 639
Nicaragua 643
Niger 647
Nigeria 651
Norway 656
Oman 660
Pakistan 664
Palau 670
Panama 672
Papua New Guinea 676
Paraguay 680
Peru 684
Philippines 690
Poland 696
Portugal 702
Puerto Rico 706

Qatar 710
Romania 713
Russian Federation 719
Rwanda 725
Saint Kitts and Nevis 729
Saint Lucia 732
Saint Vincent and the Grenadines 735
San Marino 738
Sao Tome and Principe 741
Saudi Arabia 744
Senegal 749
Serbia and Montenegro (Yugoslavia) 755
Seychelles 761
Sierra Leone 765
Singapore 769
Slovakia 775
Slovenia 779
Solomon Islands 783
Somalia 786
South Africa 789
Spain 795
Sri Lanka 801
Sudan 805
Suriname 809
Swaziland 813
Sweden 816
Switzerland 822
Syria 826
Taiwan 832
Tajikistan 835
Tanzania, United Republic of 839
Thailand 843
Togo 849
Tonga 853
Trinidad and Tobago 856
Tunisia 860
Turkey 864
Turkmenistan 870
Tuvalu 873
Uganda 875
Ukraine 879
United Arab Emirates 884
United Kingdom 888
United States of America 894
Uruguay 900
Uzbekistan 904
Vanuatu 908
Venezuela 911
Vietnam 917
(Western) Samoa 923
Yemen 926
Zambia 930
Zimbabwe 934

Bibliography 939
Index 943

Acknowledgments

The authors are grateful to the many individuals who made this project a success. In particular, we received valuable guidance and help from officials, librarians, and researchers at the United Nations and its member agencies, who provided valuable material, assistance, and direction for the gathering of our reference and data sources. In researching and writing this encyclopedia, we received invaluable help from Clare Newman, who helped us with the enormous task of organizing the tables and assembling the data. We would like to thank Evelyn Fazio, who saw the need for such an immense work on the state of humanity at the turn of the century, for advising us on the content of these volumes. On the production side, we would like to thank Angela Piliouras for managing this project by coordinating the copy editors, graphic artists, printers, and the authors. We also thank Aud Thiessen for her suggestions, and Esther Clark for helping to organize and prepare the manuscript for production.

Immanuel Ness
James D. Ciment

Part One

Essays

Section 1

Introduction to Demography

THE NUMBERS TELL THE STORY

The numbers in this reference tell a story or, more accurately, two stories. The very title of this resource, *The Encyclopedia of Global Population and Demographics*, offers a clue to these narratives. The term *demography* come from two Greek words: *demo* (people) and *graph* (written record). This book, then, offers a written record of humanity—specifically, of human population.

The stories are alarming. The first concerns a species that has increasingly overcome the causes of death, and is paying the price for its selective achievement of growth. It is no secret that the population of planet Earth is increasing at an awesome and, perhaps, even unsustainable pace for one very simple reason. Death increasingly has been delayed, especially among the young, the vulnerable, and the potentially fertile, because of improved diet, better awareness of personal and public hygiene, and advances in medicine. At the same time, births continue to increase, particularly in the less economically developed and less-educated societies.

The consequences of this dichotomy are already evident, as seen most concisely in the timeline graph on page 4. In the ten thousand years from the discovery of agriculture to the beginnings of the industrial revolution, the human population increased from about 15 million to 800 million, that is, roughly doubling every fifteen hundred years.

Between 1750 and 1945—when World War II ended, and the great medical and farming advances of the postwar era began—the world's population doubled every 122 years. By the end of that period, the total had swelled to some 2.5 billion. In the fifty-five years since then, it has doubled, totaling nearly 6 billion people

For anyone concerned about the future of the planet and the future of humanity, the upward line shown in the graph appears as frightening as a nuclear mushroom cloud, and potentially as destructive. Not surprisingly, the best book ever written on the subject of demography was entitled *The Population Bomb*.

The second story told by the essays and tables in this book relates less to the quantity of human beings on Earth and more to the quality of their lives. Specifically, the enormous amount of resources consumed by the so-called first, or developed, world has an inordinately heavy impact on the planet's environment as well as on humanity's ability to nourish itself, since part of the high-consumption life-style of developed-world residents includes the consumption of meat—cultivation of which requires far more land than does a vegetarian diet—and excessive use of water.

Equally troubling is the fact that most developing world inhabitants and governments are busily striving to move toward developed world standards of living; a goal that is understandable—given the misery in which much of the world's population lives and the ubiquity of developed world–controlled mass media, with its high-consumption messages and imagery—albeit destructive.

In *The Population Explosion*—Paul and Anne Ehrlich's sequel to Paul Ehrlich's *The Population Bomb*—the authors offer a simple equation to calculate the effects of the high-consumption standard of living currently enjoyed by the de-

3

veloped world and aspired to by the developing world: (Environmental) impact = population × affluence × technology, or I = PAT. (Although the definition of "affluence" is relatively straightforward in the equation—referring, roughly, to level of consumption—defining technology is a bit trickier. The authors are referring not to the amount but to the type of technology: Heating bath water with an oil burner has a greater impact on the environment and depletion of resources than doing it with solar panels.)

Thus, while this equation can be used to calculate hundreds of permutations of the environmental impact of the various elements, the equation inherently yields two basic messages. Small rises in population in high-consumption societies—such as the United States—have disproportionately large impacts on the environment, as do relatively small hikes in the level of consumption in high-population societies such as China.

As awareness of environmental stress and wealth disparities between developed and devel-oping nations have increased in the past thirty years, theorists have tended to cast the central villain in the demographic narrative as either the prolific developing world or the overconsuming developed world.

In fact, there are more than enough "villains" to go around because of the many subplots in the demographic narrative. Deforestation—a particularly urgent environmental problem—illustrates this point. The well-publicized fires in Indonesia in 1997 are now widely believed to have been caused by the burning of rain forests by Indonesian and multinational corporations seeking cheap timber and land (largely to supply products to developed world countries—in this case, Japan). The denuding of forests in the Himalayan foothills—which is less publicized because it is less immediately catastrophic—has been caused by the astronomical population growth among small farmers in India and Nepal.

Of course, environment degradation is just one—albeit perhaps the most important—effect of rapid population growth and unsustainable

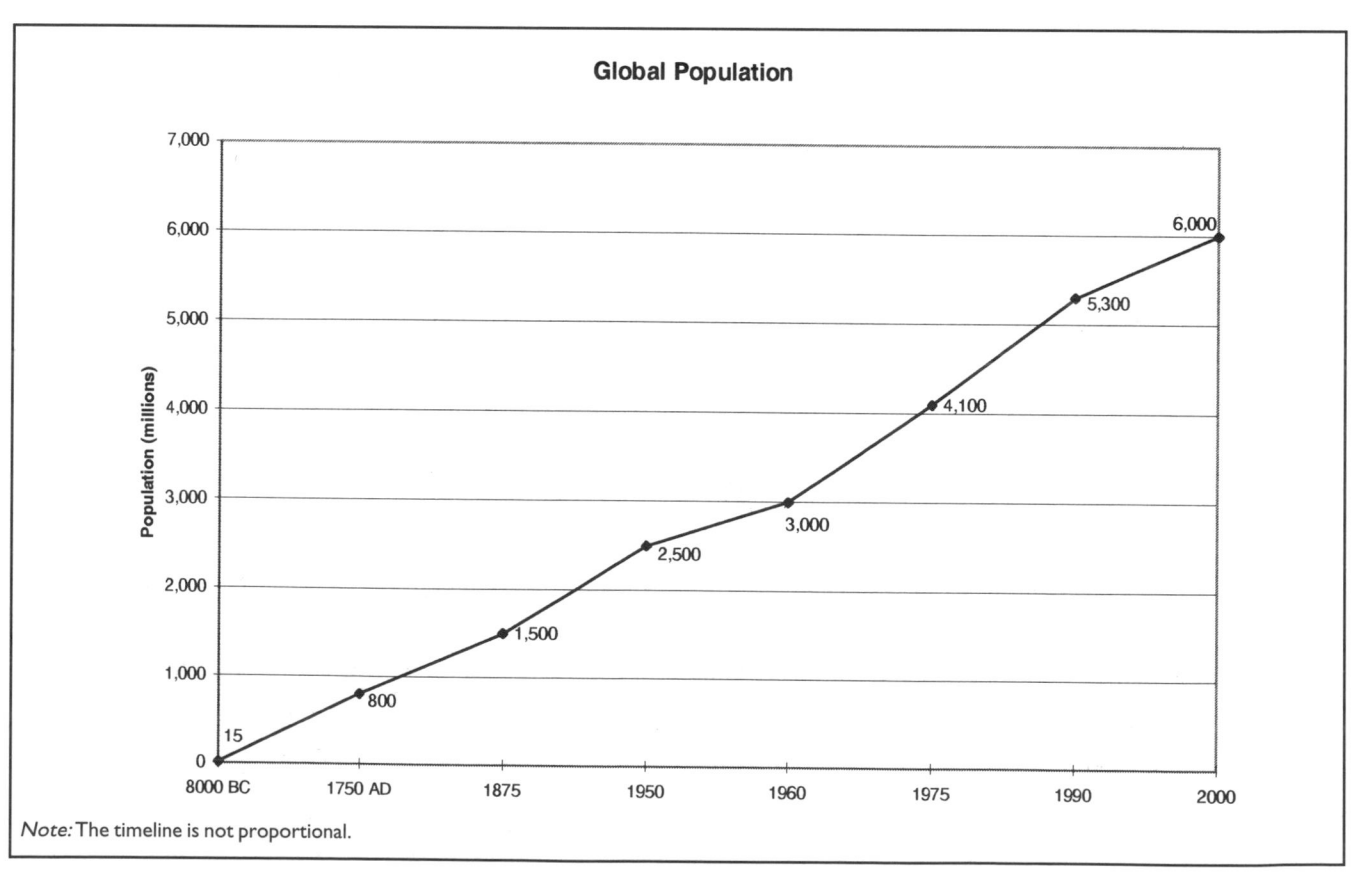

Note: The timeline is not proportional.

levels of consumption. Other issues include public health and hunger. As is true of so much else concerning the demographic narrative of recent decades, the story of public health and hunger is full of multiple ironies, the most obvious of which is the fact that the very gains made in recent years in medicine and agronomy have come to backfire on themselves. That is to say, these public health and agronomic advances have contributed to explosive population growth, which, in turn, undermines the gains already made. The overcrowding caused by the drop in birth rates often leads to public health problems and hunger.

Heavy consumption in the developed world offers the same implicit ironies, as the case of air conditioning makes clear. Because it emits (until recently) large amounts of freon and requires the burning of huge amounts of fossil fuels, air conditioning contributes to both global warming (and thus to hunger, in that global warming is widely believed to increase the likelihood and severity of drought) and ozone depletion (a documented public health problem in the form of increased cases of skin cancer)—two reasons to remain indoors and use even more air conditioning.

Political instability is yet another, even less understood effect of overpopulation and overconsumption. The struggle between the Palestinians and the Israelis offers a relevant case. One of the most important, but least-publicized, disputes between the two sides to this conflict concerns water—specifically, the large aquifer beneath the West Bank that is tapped by both Israelis and Palestinians. Each blames the other for its gradual depletion. The Israeli government argues that explosive population growth among the Palestinians is to blame; Palestinian authorities claim the problem lies in the heavy water-consumption patterns of Israelis.

Finally, as with any tale, the demographic narrative can be understood only if we take several steps back from it to examine the model within which it exists and the terms by which it is conveyed. In other words, the demographic narrative exists within a dominant model that says population growth is bad and economic growth is good. Now that communism has been vanquished on the world stage, the dominant model remains an essentially capitalist one, shaped by experts from the developed world and its dominant institutions like the World Bank: Endless growth is both positive and essential. (Of course, that is not to say that the socialist bloc did not develop its own model also stating that expanding economic output was always good.)

But this model is increasingly being challenged on two fronts. First, the environmental movement has forced people and governments to reconsider humanity's relationship to its planetary home. If endless population growth is unsustainable, how can endless growth in consumption be any different? In other words, can we have limitless growth of any kind on a planet with finite resources?

The second and more nuanced challenge to the existing model comes from the more radical population experts of the developing world: It is not so much economic growth per se that is unsustainable as its unequal distribution among the world's peoples. By means of the exploitative economic order, dominated by developed world–based multinational corporations and enforced by the various international lending and aid agencies, developing-world societies have no choice but to pursue economic agendas that further impoverish their own people.

In Colombia, for example, highly productive farmland has been taken from peasants and given over to plantations that supply cheap flowers for developed world countries, especially those in North America. In other words, various parts of Colombia are experiencing a shortage of land for growing food that has little to do with the country's growing population. Moreover, the displaced peasantry inevitably flocks to urban areas, causing public health problems in the areas to which they migrate. Thus, in many poorer countries (except in certain selective and obvious cases like overcrowded Bangladesh), it is not overpopulation alone that is destroying environments and leading to the degradation of human life, but rather the exploitation of the resources and labor of those societies to support developed world consumption patterns.

At the same time, both developed-world environmentalists and developing-world demographers have been challenging the terms in which the dominant demographic and economic narrative of recent decades is conveyed. Take, they say, the most important conventional measure of economic progress—gross domestic product, or the total value of goods and services created by a nation-state. Environmentalists say it masks the true costs of economic growth by ignoring or devaluing that growth's impact on the environment and human health. For example, if a country burns more petroleum for transport, heating, or industry, this is measured as economic progress, while the health problems (rising rates of respiratory disease, for instance) and environmental costs are dismissed or underestimated.

Developing-world demographics add an additional spin by pointing out that much of the cost of economic "progress" is borne by the more poverty-stricken societies on Earth or by the poorest and least-represented elements within a given nation-state. Because they have inadequate access to health care, they are more likely to suffer from the effects of increased air pollution. Moreover, they suffer the consequences without gaining the benefits. While the tiny middle and upper classes of developing-world societies gain increased mobility from the burning of hydrocarbons for transportation via automobiles, the poor do not. The same pattern operates on a global scale, as countries that are low consumers of hydrocarbon suffer from the effects of increased consumption of petroleum worldwide—in the form of global warming—while gaining few if any of the benefits of burning those hydrocarbons.

Finally, both developed-world environmentalists and developing-world demographers point out that the very category of measurement—the nation-state—offers a flawed statistical view of reality. As the former point out, exploitation of the natural environment creates effects that do not respect borders and thus must be considered in a global context. Regionwide droughts, partly caused by global warming, are felt in the American Midwest and the African Sahel alike (though, of course, the human costs to the latter—where

inhabitants exist much closer to the margins of life—are far greater).

For developing-world critics of the dominant model, or paradigm, the nation-state as a standard of measurement is flawed for two reasons. First, this conception often lays the blame in the wrong place for the human degradation caused by overpopulation and environmental destruction and does so in several ways. It fails to recognize the powerlessness of developing-world governments in the face of pressure from pro-export multinational corporations and international lending institutions. It ignores the fact that many unpopular developing-world governments—which fail to serve their own people's needs—are essentially kept in power by the same multinational institutions that are exploiting their societies (or have been trained to think in terms conducive to those institutions by being educated at developed-world universities and business schools). Finally, the use of the nation-state as the standard of measurement masks critical internal differences within that country. What does it mean when a country like Chile, for example, boasts rising income levels at a time of increasing polarization of wealth?

This encyclopedia both succumbs to these shortcomings and attempts to overcome them. Like any compendium of statistics, this work includes tables that rely on existing sources of data, which both emphasize standard measurements of economic progress and catalog them by nation-state. At the same time, the nine essays in Part One analyze those numbers based on the critique offered by both developed-world environmental leaders and developing-world demographic experts.

Before turning to these contemporary debates, let us, then, begin with a history of demographic ideas or theories.

A HISTORY OF DEMOGRAPHIC DOCTRINE AND THOUGHT

Pre-Malthusian Thinkers

Since ancient times, philosophers have considered the two basic questions of demography:

What causes population growth or decline, and what are the consequences? Their thinking clearly emphasized the latter. The Western tradition, at least, has usually attributed population growth or decline to forces beyond human control and comprehension—an act of the gods pleased or displeased by human individual and group behavior.

Because of the isolated nature of early civilization and the vast open spaces in the world, until modern times those considering the consequences of population change obviously lacked a global perspective. Thus various societies examined the question only in light of their own immediate circumstances. In his work *The Laws*, Plato wrote that a healthy society should place a greater importance on the quality of life than on the quantity of lives. Given the lack of space and fertile land in ancient Greece, this perspective should not be surprising nor should the more expansive Roman government's emphasis on population growth policies.

In the early Middle Ages, the prevalent philosophy was the opposite of that of pro-growth Roman doctrine. The collapse of ancient civilization and the barbarity of life in the Dark Ages led early Christian thinkers to emphasize the relative unimportance of life in this world. If God and the afterlife were the ultimate reasons for life in this world, then removing oneself from the needs and desires of this world was a human duty. Thus, St. Augustine argued, procreation was a less godly path than abstinence.

As in so much else, the late medieval thinker Thomas Aquinas contradicted early Christian thought, contending that marriage and procreation were as godly a path as celibacy. Aquinas's thinking on the subject prefigured Protestant thinkers who believed that the individual's achievements in this world foretold his or her existence in the next. Procreation, like hard work, was a means of achieving a more godly order on this Earth as well as a place in heaven, two objectives that were no longer seen as mutually exclusive.

As one might expect in such a religious age, secular thinkers reflected sacred ones. The first great school of political economic thought in modern times—mercantilism—emphasized the importance of expansion. Since a given political entity increased its power and wealth by capturing more resources—including human resources—population growth was only to the good. Mercantile thinking arose at a time when Europe was undergoing great physical expansion not only by expanding outward but by newly exploiting lands from marshes and forests through the power of commercial endeavor and as a consequence of growing population.

By the mid-eighteenth century, it was becoming clear that population growth often led to more human misery, especially as the movement to incorporate common land into commercial holdings spread—beginning in England in the seventeenth century and accelerating in the eighteenth century. The mercantilist notion that all growth—territorial, human, or otherwise—was good came into increasing disrepute among a group of thinkers known as the physiocrats.

The antimercantilist English economist Adam Smith came to the conclusion in the late eighteenth century that land—not people—was the source of wealth and power. Economic growth—through the better commercial exploitation of land and other natural resources—was a prerequisite for population growth. In fact, he argued, the two were always in natural harmony since population size was determined by demand for labor, which was, in turn, determined by the productivity of land. This was, of course, part of his overall assault on mercantilist political doctrine promoting economic direction by the state. Governments, he implied, should not have a doctrine of limiting population.

This was essentially a positive doctrine since it offered a conceptual path out of the dilemma that increasing population would necessarily lead to increasing misery. Taking this even further, scholars like the Marquis de Condorcet and William Godwin added technology to the equation. Scientific understanding, they claimed, would increase the productivity of land and thereby create increased wealth, which would lead to better education. As people became more aware of their situation, they would come to understand that limiting fertility promised them a way of ensuring that population growth never outstripped increased productivity. Indeed, Godwin believed that the first part of this equation—increasing productivity—was already occuring, but was masked from view by social inequities in which the few consumed more than the many.

Malthus and the Neo-Malthusians

All these thinkers were less concerned about how population grew or shrank—at least, in the real world—than about the consequences of that change. The Reverend Thomas Malthus, an English college professor, offered the first theoretical inquiry into the first basic question of demography. According to Malthus's theory—first published in 1798—humanity has two basic needs: to feed itself and to reproduce. Both, he said, were incontrovertible and unchanging.

Thus, as long as there was sufficient food, population would grow at a geometric pace, that is, it would constantly double. Food production, however, can grow only in arithmetic fashion since nature has been somewhat stingy in the availability of fertile land. "A slight acquaintance with the first," he laconically noted, "will shew [show] the immensity of the first power in comparison with the second." Given an unlimited source of food and unlimited space, he concluded, humanity "would fill millions of worlds in the course of a few thousand years." That it obviously doesn't, he said, was due to "positive checks"—those measures "whether of a moral or physical nature, which tend prematurely to weaken and destroy the human frame." Disease, war, starvation, accidents—what modern demographers refer to as "causes of mortality."

Seemingly fatalistic about increasing human population and the immiseration of life, Malthus offered a way out: "preventive checks," or limits on birth. Although current Malthusian believers condone various kinds of checks—such as contraception and abortion (infanticide is largely shunned in Western society, though it has been practiced in certain island cultures where land

limitations are most apparent)—Malthus advocated but one: "moral restraint," or abstinence.

Indeed, the willingness to accept contraception and abortion is the main difference between Malthus and his intellectual successors, for example, the Ehrlichs. In a chapter of *The Population Explosion* entitled "The Bang, the Whimper, and the Alternative," they argue that if humanity does not voluntarily employ such Malthusian "preventive checks," human nature or the natural world will impose "positive" ones. These include "the bang," a nuclear war caused by the tensions inherent in an overpopulated world (less likely with the demise of the Cold War or perhaps more likely with the current arms race on the Indian subcontinent) or "the whimper," a gradual collapse of our ecosystem.

Malthus was not very optimistic, citing the natural propensity to reproduce as almost impossible to overcome. Neither are today's neo-Malthusians, who offer a more sophisticated gloss on this idea. Human beings, they say, evolved brains and intellect best able to cope with immediate and proximate dangers, since they comprised the majority of the threats to continued existence during most of our prehistory. Long-term, less-immediate problems (most obviously, overpopulation), which are less discernible on a daily basis, are usually ignored.

To be fair, most thoughtful neo-Malthusians argue—as Malthus himself did, though it is rarely mentioned in discussions of his theory—that a redistribution of wealth and more social equity are prerequisites for implementing preventive checks on growth. The poverty caused by an unequal social order, Malthus argued, kept the masses ignorant of their own good—that is, of the necessity for "moral restraint."

Neo-Malthusians, with their eyes on the nuclear and environmental clock, note that continued high levels of consumption by developed world societies allow neither the time nor the motivation for "preventive" measures to take effect. Using the $I = PAT$ equation, they note that overconsumption may overwhelm the planet before the current demographic momentum (that is, population continuing to increase for a time after effective preventive measures take effect) can be stopped. In addition, they rhetorically ask, why should developing-world societies limit population growth at the behest of overconsuming developed-world countries?

Marxist and Neo-Marxist Perspectives

Both Karl Marx and Friedrich Engels essentially rejected many of the implications of Malthusian population theory, even if they did not discount the theory itself. In short, they had little quarrel with his idea that humanity grew geometrically through the constant impulse to procreate (though they saw no harm in birth control). Where Marx and Engels disagreed with Malthus was in the universality of his theory. Overpopulation, they argued, was a problem only where the social structure was incapable of handling it—specifically, in capitalist societies.

Marx and Engels believed that each society had its own population law. In capitalist societies, unchecked population growth led to poverty and want because the ruling class needed a surplus labor force in which to whip the working class into line. It was not that there were too many people in capitalist societies but that there were too many poor, a direct consequence of stripping land and control over the means of production away from workers. In fact, the very basis of the Marxist theory of surplus value bolstered their point since, in a capitalist system, workers always produced more value than they received in wages. If that was so, how could overpopulation be the cause of poverty?

Conversely, they argued, in socialist societies, overpopulation would not be a problem because its application of a "scientific" approach to humanity, new technologies, and the use of natural resources would guarantee that both population growth and production would grow in sync with each other and not at odds, as Malthus had argued. Philosophically, Marx and Engels dismissed Malthus's "vile and infamous doctrine" as placing blame on the poor for their own troubles, rather than on the exploitative owners of capital, where it belonged.

The leaders of communist revolutions in the twentieth century instituted policies that reflected these Marxist assumptions. This was the case in underpopulated Russia, as well as in densely populated China. As Mao Zedong argued in the 1950s, "a large population in China is a good thing. With a population increase of several fold we still have an adequate solution. The solution lies in production."

By the 1960s, the increasingly obvious need for birth control in many parts of the world led to a revision of Marxist theory concerning overpopulation. By the 1970s, Chinese officials were arguing that a rational socialist order required planning for population as well as for production. Other Marxist theorists returned to an old physiocratic idea, but with a twist. Condorcet, for one, believed that scientific reasoning would teach people to limit their reproduction for their own good, but socialist education would convince people to do the same for the good of society.

Two neo-Marxist schools of thought have reconsidered the idea of capitalism—not overpopulation—as the cause of human misery in a global context. Both Immanuel Wallerstein in his world system theory and the dependency theorists among Latin American scholars (considering things at a national and regional level) maintain that the inequities of the global economy—specifically, the exploitation of developing world populations by the developed world—are the cause of problems like hunger, war, and public health deterioration, which at first glance appear to be the direct outgrowth of overpopulation.

Indeed, these neo-Marxists argue that just as national capitalist economies maintain a surplus labor force—in order to hold down wages—global capitalism ensures that the developing world remains underdeveloped and therefore a source of both cheap labor and cheap resources. In short, then, overpopulation is not the cause of the continuing impoverishment of much of the world, but rather the result. Lower levels of education and health care induce couples to have more children to assure that some survive.

Table 1.1

Governments and Migration Policy

Country	Limitations		Groups	Political factors	Economic factors
	Immigration	Emigration			
United States	Discourage		Poor persons	Vote-getting issue	Loss of jobs
Israel	Encourage		Jews	Ethnic composition of state	
Brazil	Encourage		Skilled and moneyed		Develop country
East Germany		Discourage	All	Politically embarrassing	Loss of skilled workers
Philippines		Encourage	Young workers		Bring in revenue
Saudi Arabia	Encourage		Skilled		Necessary for running economy
Mexico		Encourage	Poor		Ease economic stress

Interestingly, on this last point, neo-Marxist thinkers share an outlook with certain secular and religious conservatives who argue that the world does not suffer from overpopulation. While the Catholic Church includes a strong critique of the inequitable global economic situation in its attacks on birth control policies, secular conservatives leave the economic question unchallenged, maintaining that increasing the number of human beings increases the number of human minds and thereby the possibility that new ideas will emerge to cope with the problems introduced by increased population.

SETTING POLICY: THE USES OF DEMOGRAPHY

Demography proves useful in many important fields, of which three of the most critical are business, politics, and social and infrastructure planning. For businesses, demography can be used to determine marketing and investment strategies, as well as better use of human resources within a given corporate structure. Politicians can use demographics to help design their campaigns, as well as project the likelihood of support for given legislative programs. These two uses of demography—though important—are not pertinent here. Social planning is, however. Obviously, it would be foolhardy for any institution or government to embark on any kind of

social and infrastructure planning without a consideration of the targeted population. To fail to do so is to guarantee one or both of the following outcomes: a program that fails to have the desired effect, or one that has a harmful effect. Social programs intended to provide health care, education, social services, transportation and communications facilities, and the like require a demographic analysis. Finally, there is the overall question of population growth and fertility itself.

International organizations like the United Nations and its agencies, such as the United Nations Population Fund, and international financial institutions, such as the World Bank, as well as many national governments, recognize the need for population policies. In most cases, this recognition leads to attempts at limiting growth, though, in some European countries with zero or negative population growth, population policies are often directed at increasing population growth or maintaining it at its current level.

Governments and institutions can implement population policies in one of three ways: by influencing mortality (or death), by influencing fertility, or by influencing migration.

Of the three, the first is the least acceptable politically, socially, and morally. No institution could openly advocate increasing mortality levels to produce drops in population. Still, this approach is not entirely taboo. Nongovernmental organizations and international agencies are often forced to make critical decisions about where to utilize scarce funds and resources. Like doctors in war or after natural disasters, they are forced to apply their skills, time, and energy on those cases that show the best chances of survival. This is known as triage and can lead to charges of covert racism when, for example, the world community chooses to send peacekeepers to a European country like Bosnia but not to an African one such as Rwanda, thereby condoning higher mortality rates in the latter.

Migration is a more palatable way of dealing with population problems, though one that often creates geopolitical problems. As a direct or even indirect social policy, migration is multifaceted. A government might want to limit its country's population growth by encouraging emigration or by discouraging immigration. Conversely, a government might encourage population growth by opening the country's gates to immigrants or by limiting emigration. Usually, but not always, limitations on immigration or emigration involve factors other than population growth and concern various population sectors. Table 1 offers some examples.

Ultimately, the most efficacious and widely used population programs involve efforts to limit—or, in rare cases, encourage—fertility. Fertility programs take three different forms: direct, indirect, and coercive. The most common—especially in developing countries where the population situation is most critical—are direct methods, such as spreading the use of contraceptives, educating the public in their use, promoting voluntary sterilization programs, or, in the case of some former members of the socialist bloc, providing cheap and easily obtained abortions. This latter policy was often an outgrowth of these planned economies' inability to produce and distribute enough contraceptive devices.

Indirect methods vary between those countries attempting to promote and those trying to discourage fertility. In some European countries suffering from low, zero, or negative population growth, governments actively encourage larger families by offering financial incentives, sometimes in the form of tax waivers and sometimes in the form of subsidies. In developing countries, indirect methods occasionally include economic incentives as well, but usually involve expanding educational resources. In recent years, for example, the United Nations has stressed the education of women as the best means of limiting fertility since educated women—aside from being more aware of contraceptive options—are more likely to see the benefits of smaller families. An even less direct method, supported by some, is simply the promotion of economic growth or, more usefully, economic growth and equity, which help limit fertility because better-situated families often have fewer children.

Coercive methods have been employed in the most desperate situations or, at least, in those countries where the government both perceives the need and has the capacity to implement such policies. The governments of China and Singapore are prime examples: They both use negative economic incentives—including fines and higher taxes—to discourage fertility. In addition, some experts' reports—denied by the Chinese government—claim that the measures have become truly coercive, in the form of forced abortions and sterilizations, particularly in the countryside. At the same time, the coercive policies of the Chinese government have had an unintended and unfortunate side effect. Since the government's population goal was the extremely ambitious zero population growth by 2000, single-child families were promoted as the ideal. The result was the infanticide of first-born children if they turned out to be girls, since sons are more highly valued in Chinese culture.

In short, as this book makes clear, the world faces a dual problem of the highest order. Citizens of developed countries continue to consume resources at an unsustainable pace, while citizens in many, though not all, developing countries continue to reproduce at unsustainable rates. Because they are resentful of developed-country lecturing and bitter over past and current exploitation, neo-Marxist, developing world–influenced population experts remain focused on the inequities of the global economic order. Because they are fearful that the environment's ability to function will be overwhelmed and the planet's capacity to feed its increasing numbers will be compromised (in addition, say third worlders, to having racist fears of the "dark" races overwhelming the Caucasians), neo-Malthusian, developed world–influenced scholars emphasize the need for population control in the developing world. As this work makes clear, both sides may be right.

FURTHER READING

Abernathy, Virginia. *Population Politics: The Choices That Shape Our Future.* New York: Insight Books, 1993.

Appleman, Philip, ed. *Thomas Robert Malthus: An Essay on the Principle of Population.* New York. Norton, 1976.

Ehrlich, Paul. *The Population Bomb.* New York: Ballantine, 1968; London: Pan, 1971.

Ehrlich, Paul, and Anne Ehrlich. *The Population Explosion.* New York: Simon and Schuster, and London: Hutchinson, 1990.

Lancaster, Henry O. *Expectations of Life: A Study in the Demography, Statistics, and History of World Mortality.* New York: Springer-Verlag, 1990.

Menard, Scott W., and Elizabeth Moen Mathiot. *Perspectives on Population: An Introduction to Concepts and Issues.* New York: Oxford University Press, 1987.

Neurath, Paul. *From Malthus to the Club of Rome and Back: Problems of Limits to Growth, Population Control, and Migrations.* Armonk, NY: Sharpe, 1994.

Sen, Amartya, and Martha Nussbaum, eds. *The Quality of Life.* New York: Oxford University Press, and Oxford: Clarendon Press, 1993.

Valentei, D.I., ed. *The Theory of Population: Essays in Marxist Research.* Moscow: Progress Publishers, 1978.

Weeks, John. *Population: An Introduction to Concepts and Issues.* Belmont, CA: Wadsworth, 1978, 7th edition, 1999.

Yaukey, David. *Demography: The Study of Human Population.* New York: St. Martin's Press, 1985.

Section 2

Demography, Resources, and the Environment

Almost everyone has seen a version of the political cartoon showing a long-haired, scragglybearded, doom-saying eccentric standing on a street holding a sign that reads: "The End Is Near." This show of unreasoning pessimism—this doomsday man—is usually an object of ridicule.

Yet, as we all know, there is a good deal of truth in his dark prediction. At the heart of the demographic problem facing modern humanity is a simple two-horned dilemma: how to ensure unending economic growth for an ever-increasing population on a planet with finite resources, and how to avoid burying ourselves in the endless waste that is an inevitable byproduct of this growth. This section examines both problems.

RESOURCE EXPLOITATION AND ENVIRONMENTAL POLLUTION

Through most of human history, it has been assumed that the Earth offered an inexhaustible supply of resources and, given the limited human population during most of that period, this was a reasonable assumption to make. But the commercial and industrial revolutions that began in Western Europe in the 1600s and 1700s, and spread to much of the rest of the world by the 1800s and 1900s, changed all that—the first by establishing an economic system requiring perpetual growth, and the second by developing the technology to sustain that growth through the ever-increasing exploitation of natural resources.

In their book *The Population Explosion*, Paul and Anne Ehrlich refer to what they call "the one-time bonanza," the fact that billions of years of geological history and hundreds of millions of years of biological history have deposited a vast treasure trove of resources for humanity to use, much like a balance in a savings account. The problem is that humanity, instead of living off the interest—that is, through the sustainable use of resources—is dipping deeply into the principal. Through overexploitation—caused by economic growth, consumption and rapidly increasing population levels—humanity is using up in decades what it took the planet hundreds of millions of years to create.

Two examples of these resources are petroleum and arable land. Humanity first began significantly to exploit the former of these about a century ago. Even the most optimistic estimate for existing and potentially recoverable reserves gives us no more than a hundred more years of exploitation, at currently expanding rates of use. That is, a resource that took nature hundreds of millions of years to accumulate will most likely be used up in two hundred years, a blink of an eye in geological time.

As for soil, it has been estimated by Lester Brown, an agricultural and environmental economist at the Worldwatch Institute, that every year some 25 billion more tons of topsoil are lost globally because of harmful agricultural methods than are being created naturally. The primacy of land to almost any discussion of resource depletion makes that a good place to start.

Land

Of the roughly 200 million square miles that make up planet Earth, approximately a third, or 60 million square miles, are land. Of this, about 33 percent is forest and woodland, 25 percent is meadow and pastureland, and 10 percent is arable (that is, land suited for intensive agriculture). The other 30 percent or so is icecap, tundra, high mountains, desert, and other lands incapable of sustaining more than minimal permanent human settlements.

It is estimated that at least 400 square miles of arable land are required to feed a population of 1 million, assuming that this population consumes a basic, vegetarian diet. Multiplying this figure by the roughly 6 billion people alive today, it can be roughly calculated that humanity requires 2.4 million square miles or approximately 40 percent of all arable land. At first glance, this would seem to imply that humanity could grow another 150 percent—to some 15 billion—before reaching the limits of arable land. Indeed, the 1988 anti–birth control Catholic encyclical, *Humanae Vitae*, argued that the world's arable land was capable of supporting 40 billion people.

True or not, this is based on several questionable assumptions, the first of which was the underlying insistence that all lands currently or potentially suitable for agriculture would stay that way. But approximately 2 percent of all land—much of it arable—is already paved over or used in some way to house or otherwise service humanity. Multiplying the population by a factor of twenty would obviously increase significantly the amount of land devoted to villages, cities, and other areas of human habitation.

In addition, there is the problem of desertification, a process by which arable land is rendered into unusable desert through climate change (greenhouse gas production, or carbon dioxide that traps the sun's heat in the atmosphere), overgrazing and soil compaction (too many animals in too small an area), erosion (poor

land management), salinization (making soil saltier through overdrilling of wells), and land poisoning (runoffs of industrial and agricultural chemicals). All of these, of course, are the direct result of either too many people in a given area or unsustainable agricultural practices.

According to the United Nations, over the past half-century, approximately 13 million square miles of arable land (four times the entire area of the United States) have lost one-quarter of their productivity, another 6 million square miles have lost half their productivity, and some 80,000 square miles (half the size of California) have been rendered entirely useless by desertification. Overall, approximately 250 million people—largely in the developing world—have been affected. Nor is this problem entirely new. Historians—often using texts from ancient philosophers—believe that much of the territory of Greece was made into semidesert by the overgrazing of goats thousands of years ago.

But what of moving to new lands, such as the forests or pasturelands that constitute nearly 60 percent of the land mass of the planet? Surely, this would offer humanity a virtually inexhaustible source of new lands to farm. First, this assumes that these lands are suitable for farming. But much of the pastureland is far too arid for agriculture, unless suitable irrigation is employed, which presents a problem of overexploitation of water resources (see the following section on water).

As for forests, many of them—particularly in the tropics—are not suitable for sustained agriculture. Belying their luxuriousness, many of these forests actually exist on extremely poor and thin soils that quickly lose their nutrients after a few years of farming. Deforestation is caused both by corporate economic exploitation—driven by the insatiable appetite for wood and paper in the developed world—and by rapidly expanding populations of small farmers in the developing world.

Moreover, deforestation has other negative effects on the land. The loss of forests can lead to serious erosion downstream in the short term—as the loss of root structure leads to rapid runoff, especially during heavy tropical down-pours—and global warming in the long term. Global warming occurs when carbon dioxide builds up in the atmosphere, trapping sunlight and heat in a phenomenon scientists call the "greenhouse effect." And, forests absorb massive quantities of carbon dioxide and produce oxygen in its place. Thus, deforestation leads to a build-up of carbon dioxide and, hence, global warming.

Ultimately, global warming may have a catastrophic effect on low-lying areas around the globe since, as the average global temperature increases, more of the ice at the poles melts. While it is difficult to predict an exact correlation between temperature increases and rising ocean levels, we do know that sea level was nearly 300 feet lower during the last ice age, when global temperatures were roughly 5 to 10 degrees Fahrenheit colder than they are now. Meanwhile, it is commonly accepted among climate experts that average global temperatures have risen about 3 degrees farenheit in the past 100 or so years of the industrial age. Whether this is part of a natural cycle or caused by the burning of fossil fuels by humankind is debatable, though most scientists believe human activity plays an increasingly significant role in global warming.

Rising ocean levels will permanently flood such heavily populated and agriculturally rich areas as Bangladesh, Florida, Rio de la Plata (Argentina), the Netherlands, the Nile Delta, and others (see the section on climate). Deforestation also leads to the mass extinction of plant and animal life, since forests—especially in the tropics—tend to sustain the highest number of species. The trend toward more rapid extinction of species can be seen in both the developed and developing world. In the former, this is largely due to pollution and, in the latter, to loss of habitat, though both causes are evident everywhere. A sampling of countries gives a sense of the scale of the loss. In tropical Cameroon, it was estimated in 1994 that some 62 individual species of animals alone were threatened; in arid Tunisia, 15; Arctic Canada, 43; temperate Chile, 91; is-

land-based Madagascar, 99; highly industrialized France, 109; and largely undeveloped Haiti, 26. Nor is species destruction a mere sentimental loss, confined to those who love nature. The extinction of an animal or plant species reduces the genetic resources of the planet, depriving humanity of potential life-saving drugs and other critical items. While there have been massive species die-offs at various times over millions of years, the current one is the first since the appearance of the human species 3 million years ago. And whereas past die-offs are believed to have had specific causes like changes in the sunspot cycle or asteroid impacts, the current die-off will go on and on until humanity changes its habit of spewing out ever greater quantities of carbon dioxide and destroying carbon dioxide-absorbing forests.

In short, to paraphrase President Franklin D. Roosevelt, in office during the Dust Bowl era of the 1930s, one of America's worst soil-based environmental catastrophes, a people that destroys its soil destroys itself.

Water

Although water covers about two-thirds of the planet's surface, most of it is unusable because of its salt content. Current desalinization techniques are both expensive and extremely energy-intensive. The costs in dollars and fuel make the process feasible only in countries where water is in very short supply and oil is plentiful—namely, the Persian Gulf countries. In short, humanity is—for the foreseeable future—restricted to existing freshwater sources.

In the United States, the world's largest agricultural country, water is being pumped out of the ground far more rapidly than it can be replenished. The Ogallala aquifer in the Midwest—the largest underground source in the country—is replenished at a rate of about 2 inches annually. But current pumping drops the level by as much as 4 to 6 feet a year. Because the Midwest is supplying much of the grain necessary both to feed many parts of the developing world and provide feed for cattle consumed in the developed world, aquifer depletion is expected to grow in coming years, especially if droughts, which many scientists believe are caused by global warming, continue.

Nor is the United States alone in the problem of aquifer depletion. China and India—the two most populous countries in the world—have reported major water shortage problems, despite recent flooding in the former. For example, the United Nations expects that by 2000 more than two-thirds of Chinese cities will face a water shortfall because of overpumping for agricultural purposes. (In general, roughly ten times the water is needed to irrigate crops in arid lands than is required for direct human use.) It is estimated by the U.N. that some 40,000 square miles of agricultural land in India are now suffering from water-poisoning and salinization, reducing its average productivity 20 percent.

The problem of depletion is thus accompanied by the danger of salinization. The pumping of aquifers—particularly those in low-lying areas—creates the risk that ocean water may seep in. Moreover, heavy irrigation tends to lead to salinization because, though required for many of the new high-yield crops developed in the "green revolution" of the 1960s and 1970s, it tends to waterlog land, causing natural salts in the soil to be leached out and carried into the aquifer.

In addition, chemical fertilizers—equally crucial to the new high-yield strains—have also entered many aquifers, along with industrial runoffs, poisoning them to the point that many may soon become unusable (see the section on food below). Deforestation also contributes to water shortages because the denuding of watersheds through timber operations or the clearing of lands for farming makes it more likely that rainfall will run off the land rather than sinking into it, thereby replenishing aquifers.

Energy

As anyone who has filled up a car's gas tank in recent years can attest, gasoline prices in the United States are low—the lowest, when adjusted for inflation, in the country's history. How can this be, just two decades after some of the worst peacetime shortfalls in recent memory?

There are several reasons: (1) conservation efforts and more efficient use of oil have helped keep demand from growing as rapidly as it might have; (2) high prices in the 1970s and early 1980s spurred oil companies to look for new sources, and they were very successful; (3) the price Americans pay at the pump does not reflect the true cost of the gasoline.

With regard to this last point, it is important to note that the price per gallon fails to factor in properly such related costs as defense (to protect overseas sources, primarily in the Persian Gulf); government subsidies to oil drillers, refiners, and shippers; or the environmental (global warning) and health (respiratory diseases) costs of burning gasoline. Thus, because oil and gas are so cheap, Americans have cut back on their conservation efforts and are consuming petroleum at an ever-increasing rate. In the single year from 1995 to 1996, sales at gasoline stations in the United States increased from $146 billion to $154 billion, or 5.5 percent. Lower gasoline prices lead to faster energy consumption in two ways: Drivers can maintain the total cost of their gas purchases, but consume more gas by using less-energy-efficient vehicles—such as the popular sport utility vehicles (SUVs)—and by driving more, car-pooling less, and not using mass transit.

Around the world, the story is the same. Between 1991 and 1994, in Africa, petroleum and coal imports increased from roughly 70 to 80 million coal-equivalent tons (that is, the amount of energy that can be obtained from a ton of coal); in North America imports increased from 761 to 916 million; in South America from 84 to 101 million; in Asia from 1.092 to 1.349 billion; in Europe (including Russia and former Soviet republics within Europe) from 1.528 to 1.727 billion; and in Oceania from 29 to 38 million tons. Yet, between 1990 and 1994, conservation policies and economic depression in many parts of the developing world helped maintain the per capita consumption of fossil fuels at roughly the same level (4,408 pounds per capita in 1990, compared with 4,385 pounds per capita in 1994). But because the world population grew some 500 million over that period, a billion more tons of fossil fuels were consumed in 1994 than in 1990.

A quick glance at the tables in this encyclopedia reveals one of the major reasons for this constantly increasing level of energy use. There is not a single major country—and virtually no minor ones—in which the number of private automobiles and commercial vehicles is not rising, often at a faster rate than population growth. (For a more detailed examination of these numbers, see Section 8: The Demography of Transportation and Communications.)

Nevertheless, energy prices continue to decline in much of the world because of newly discovered reserves of hydrocarbons. Indeed, every continent except Africa has seen increases in fossil fuel production. Between 1990 and 1994, production in North America increased from 2.999 to 3.236 billion tons; in South America from 493 to 561 million tons; in Asia from 3.270 to 4.017 billion tons; in Europe (including Russia and former Soviet republics within Europe) from 1.485 to 3.085 billion tons; and in Oceania from 240 to 261 million tons. (In Africa energy production fell slightly, from 739 to 732 million tons.) Overall, between 1990 and 1995, world energy output, including fossil fuel, wood, nuclear, solar, geothermal, wind, and other renewable sources, increased from 11.444 to 11.893 billion tons, or 3.9 percent, nearly equal to the rate of population growth. (The careful reader will note that the population growth rate outpaced the production growth rate by 1.6 percent in those five years. The majority of that population growth was in countries with low consumption of energy per capita, so while per capita use is going down, rapidly rising population means rapidly rising energy consumption, despite technology-created efficiency improvements and drops in energy use caused by economic downturns in the developing world.)

Ultimately, continued increases in energy production mean faster rates of fossil fuel depletion. Since the sources of these fuels, of course, are finite—indeed, expected to run dry before the end of the twenty-first century—the problem of overpopulation and overconsumption's impact on world energy sources is still with us, even if it does not seem as urgent as it did a couple of decades ago.

Food

The history of food production includes three great leaps in output. The first, of course, came with the agricultural revolution that began in the Neolithic era, about 10,000 years ago. Beginning in the Middle East and soon spreading to North Africa and South and East Asia—and later to Europe and the Americas—the agricultural revolution allowed humanity a much more predictable and bountiful supply of food than could be achieved by gathering natural food plants. Similarly, the domestication of livestock was a quantum leap over hunting in the supply of meat as well as in the introduction of dairy products.

The second great leap came with the commercial and industrial revolutions that began in Western Europe in the seventeenth century and had spread to much of the rest of the world by the twentieth century. By introducing the profit motive—first in the form of plantation slavery and later through free labor farms and eventually corporate food production—farmers had an economic incentive to continue increasing their output beyond immediate consumption. At roughly the same time, the industrial revolution led to urbanization and the growth of a nonagricultural workforce. The industrial revolution also had a more direct effect on food production, by introducing labor-saving devices for sowing, weeding, harvesting, shipping, and packaging foods in exponentially greater amounts than was possible before.

The third revolution—the so-called green revolution—occured in our own time. Beginning shortly after World War II ended, scientists in both developed and developing countries sought out particular strains of staple crops that seemed to prosper in certain climates. These crops were then scientifically bred to maximize output. Thus high-yield rice, wheat, corn, and other grains were developed to grow in the tropics and other regions where the population was growing rapidly. The spread of these crops was remarkably rapid. For example, in 1965 only 200 acres of high-yield variety (HYV) wheat was grown experimentally on a farm in the Philippines. By 1971, more than 50 million acres devoted to this hybrid were planted globally. The impact of new grain hybrids like HYV wheat cannot be overestimated. In India, for example, between 1965 and 1968 wheat production increased from 11 to 27 million tons.

Despite all these gains—critical to feeding burgeoning populations—both the industrial and the green revolutions have created problems. Both have made farmers far more reliant on nonsustainable energy sources, like fossil fuels, for their production. The new hybrids of the green revolution, in particular, require massive inputs of expensive and unsustainable petroleum-based fertilizers. In the Philippines, hybrid strains of wheat are estimated to require inputs costing fifty times more than those of normal strains. Not surprisingly, the cost of these inputs has made it more difficult for small farmers to compete and forced many to leave the land for urban areas, where they are transformed from food producers to consumers.

The use of green revolution crops also requires vast inputs of water and pesticides, since many of the hybrids are particularly vulnerable to drought and insect infestation. In addition to the enormous monetary costs involved, the heavy use of water and pesticides can destroy both soil and water supplies through salinization (see the earlier section on water) and poisoning. Moreover, the law of diminishing returns applies to fertilizer and pesticide inputs. It is estimated that a ton of additional fertilizer in 1950 increased grain output by 46 tons; by 1965, that figure had fallen to 23 tons; and by the 1980s, to just 13 tons.

Pesticides, of course, have their own built-in obsolescence. Insects quickly develop pesticide resistance since only the hardy survive the first years of a given pesticide's use. So, larger quantities are continually needed, especially with delicate hybrids. For example, in areas utilizing green revolution crops in the Philippines, the amount of pesticide use increased by a factor of

several dozen from the mid-1960s to the late 1970s.

Citing these problems, food experts are now placing their faith in what has the potential to become the fourth great leap in agricultural production: the "genetic revolution, " which involves the manipulation of the DNA in food crops. Genetic manipulation is nothing new. Throughout the ages, humanity has selected particulars strains of plants and animals for their productivity and other attributes. But the earlier attempts were based on what nature had already provided. By manipulating genes directly, scientists can now custom-design new breeds of plants and animals. For example, it is possible to create plants that are resistant to insects and drought.

The potential of genetic engineering is great, and so are the risks. Much work is being done on the manipulation of plants that consume nitrogen, a key nutrient in soil, to turn them into nitrogen producers. This involves rendering them less harmful to bacterias that live in nitrogen-producing plants. But the spread of such bacterias in formerly nitrogen-consuming plants is unknown and could lead to new strains of bacteria that could destroy crops.

In addition, genetically manipulated crops introduce some economic perils. Increasingly, the corporations developing the new seeds are patenting them. If these crops are patented, these companies—which, by the rules of economic behavior, must place profit-making first—will gain total control over new food supplies. Moreover, many chemical companies—which are heavily invested in genetic engineering—are developing strains that are more—not less—resistant to their herbicides and pesticides. Although this kind of genetic engineering increases profits, it also makes both producers and consumers of food ever more dependent on a few giant corporations. And because most of these corporations are based in the developed world, the developing world—with its rapidly growing population—will become ever more dependent for its food supply. (Even before this genetic engineering revolution, the world had become dependent on crops grown in the developed world. By 1980, just four countries—the United States, Canada, Australia, and Argentina, in that order—supplied virtually all of the world's grain exports.)

Finally, problems regarding the consumption of food exist in both the developing and the developed worlds. While rapid increases in population spell danger for food levels in the developing world, so does food waste and meat consumption in the developed world. It is estimated that Americans throw away approximately a quarter of the food they purchase or grow. At the same time, the enormous quantity of meat consumed by citizens of the developed world requires as much as ten times the grain, water, and other resources as a vegetarian diet. Worldwide about 40 percent of all grain is fed to animals.

Meanwhile, natural sources of foods are disappearing rapidly. Destroying rainforests for farmland may increase food production in the short term—though much of this is in the form of wasteful herding of cattle destined to be consumed in the developed world or by the elite of the developing world—but it limits the possibility of sustained harvests of natural forest foods. Similarly, world fisheries are being depleted by both overfishing and water pollution. According to the United Nations' Food and Agriculture Organization, 255 of the 280 major fisheries it monitored in the 1990s were considered heavily exploited or overexploited. As for pollution, China provides a frightening example. The discharge from industry, farms and cities of nearly 2 trillion gallons of domestic, agricultural, and industrial waste annually has destroyed most of the fisheries and shell-fisheries of the Yellow Sea, once a prime source of high-protein food. This destruction of fisheries is an inevitable outgrowth of China's race to industrialize, urbanize and increase its farm output through the more intensive use of pesticides.

Climate

The complex interaction of the different variables involved in economic production is most readily apparent in climate change. It is widely accepted in the scientific community that global temperatures have been increasing in the past several decades. The ten hottest years recorded in this century have all occurred in the past two decades. Global ocean temperatures have been rising on average about 0.2°F annually. Of course, because it is so volatile, climactic change does not occur evenly. Vast fluctuations, such as those caused in 1998 by El Niño—the shift of warm waters from the western to the eastern Pacific—occur from time to time, but the overall tendency has been toward a warmer world. Physically, warmer temperatures are more energy-intensive, producing greater disturbances in the atmosphere—largely in the form of devastating hurricanes, excessive flooding, or drought. The increasing severity of droughts both in the developing and developed world—notably in Africa and North America—in the past couple of decades may very well be a direct result of global warming.

In 1988, a Stanford University research team attempted to calculate the impact of global warming on world food production and supplies. The team set a base level of production in which average climatic conditions would allow food supplies to grow at a pace equal to population increases, roughly following the trend of the twenty-five years preceding the study.

But the report issued by the study team said that global warming would increase the number of major unfavorable climatic events—largely in the form of regional droughts—from one every 5 years to one every 3.3 years. With each event likely to cause a 10 percent drop in the upward trend of food production, it was estimated that future unfavorable climatic events in the coming century might cause the deaths of between 50 million and 400 million persons worldwide, though nearly all of these would occur in the developing world. This last prediction, they said, would be true regardless of whether or not the drought occurred there, since—as noted above—so much of the developing world has become dependent on grain exports from the developed world.

While the existence and effects of global warming are virtually beyond dispute, this is not quite the case when it comes to causes. Although a small minority of scientists insist that global warming is an entirely natural phenomenon, the vast majority agree that humanity's economic production and manipulation of the environment are factors. How large these factors are, however, is open to debate.

The most important contributor to global warming is the burning of hydrocarbon—oil, gas, coal—and other organic fuels—wood, peat, and manure. This burning causes the release of massive quantities of carbon dioxide, a naturally occurring element in the atmosphere. Indeed, carbon dioxide helps trap heat in the Earth's atmosphere by allowing sunlight to penetrate and then retain it, in the so-called greenhouse effect. Without carbon dioxide, the Earth's surface would be a lot colder than it is. But too much carbon dioxide means too much trapped heat, hence, global warming. Adding to the problem is deforestation. Plant life—through the process of photosynthesis—converts carbon dioxide into oxygen. Thus the destruction of the Earth's biomass (that is, the total mass of animal, bacteria, and plant life)—consisting largely of the clearing of temperate and tropical forests—means that the global environment is less able to absorb increases in carbon dioxide.

With regard to the production of carbon dioxide, the issue of developed world consumption patterns versus developing world population growth becomes especially acute. In 1992, the United States produced more carbon dioxide emissions (1.3 trillion tons) than the entire developing world combined, minus China. This fact has led many developing world environmentalists to cite overconsumption in the developed world as the main factor in global warming. That may be true at the moment, but slower economic growth and improving emission-control technology in the United States limited the increase in its carbon dioxide output to just 16 percent from 1983 to 1992. By contrast, in rapidly developing China—with its heavy emphasis on domestic but dirty coal supplies and more primitive emission control technology—carbon dioxide output over the same period increased from 455,215 to 728,161 million tons annually, an increase of roughly 60 percent. Nor is China alone. Output has increased proportionately by the same amount or more over the same period in countries as geographically and economically diverse as Nigeria (16,343 to 26,341 million tons), Malaysia (10,359 to 19,239 million tons), and Turkey (25,985 to 39,708 million tons).

Meanwhile, the reduction in the absorption rate of carbon dioxide emissions caused by deforestation is growing rapidly. It is estimated that in Central and South America, there is a loss of some 10,000 square miles of rainforest annually, or more than 10 acres a minute. Moreover, much of the rainforest is cleared for farming by slash-and-burn methods, releasing enormous—albeit one-time—quantities of carbon dioxide. Although the burning of forests is largely a tropical phenomenon, the systematic destruction of forests continues at an unsustainable pace in such temperate areas as the Pacific Northwest of the United States and British Columbia in Canada.

POLITICAL IMPLICATIONS

The depletion of global resources due to the consumerism of the developed world and rapid population increases in the developing world has enormous implications for political and economic stability worldwide. Recent events illustrate the tensions and conflicts ignited by the struggle for sources of energy and food. The most obvious example is the 1991 Persian Gulf War fought between Iraq and a coalition of twenty-seven countries led by the United States (but under the official aegis of the United Nations).

The crisis began with Iraq's invasion of Kuwait in August 1990. Saddam Hussein, Iraq's leader, insisted that Kuwait was illegally pumping too much oil from a field the two countries shared. Iraq, determined to pump more oil to earn revenues lost during a long-standing war with Iran, first asked, then threatened, and finally invaded Kuwait to obtain the oil. The world responded with a massive army that not only drove Iraq out of Kuwait but destroyed much of the former's military establishment and infrastructure. In response, Hussein's army set off massive oil-well fires in Kuwait, leading to one of the most serious environmental crises in recent years. But the disputes over energy sources need not always be global in scope. Ecuador and Peru have been fighting border skirmishes for years over a remote but disputed section of the upper Amazon basin that is reputed to contain signficant petroleum reserves.

Food resources, both natural and cultivated, can be a source of international and civil instability. North Atlantic states—including Canada and Iceland—have seized fishing boats owned by European nationals who were allegedly poaching in their territorial waters. Meanwhile, in the northeastern Pacific, the United States and Canada remain in a tense standoff over salmon stocks.

At the same time, disputes over food prices in many developing countries have led to riots, coups, and near–civil wars. The scenario follows a similar pattern in many places. The government of a developing country, usually located in a large metropolis, lacks credibility and support among the urban masses, usually because its institutions are weak, its officials corrupt, and its leaders repressive. To maintain civil order in the vulnerable cities, its leaders often subsidize the price of food and fuel, or pay less than market prices for produce from less politically explosive or influential farmers. When that is no longer economically feasible—and prices have to be raised—unrest and violence often break out, leading in some cases, such as most recently in Indonesia, to mass killings.

In several worst-case scenarios, food aid itself has become either a weapon or a hostage of war. In the Angolan and Sudanese civil wars of the 1980s and 1990s, rebels often forced military concessions from the government before allowing food aid to be brought into the famine-stricken areas under their control.

Many population experts say that in the future, political instability and civil and international conflicts might be triggered by famine on a regional, rather than a national, scale. This might happen if leaders use international tensions to distract their hungry citizens from internal problems or if governments attempt to seize the resources of their neighbors.

In general, there is little debate among scientists that humanity is having a significant impact on the global environment, though the extent and consequences of that impact are the source of great controversy. Meanwhile, policymakers in the developed and developing world exchange charges about who is more responsible for the human-based environmental damage—the citizens of the former, who consume far more resources and produce far more trash per capita, or the inhabitants of the latter whose numbers are doubling every thirty-five years.

The question, then, is not whether humanity will survive, but how. As a species, humanity will survive almost any environmental catastrophe, short of an all-out nuclear war, a possibility which has declined significantly since the end of the Cold War. But the quality of that life for the vast majority of the planet's inhabitants may continue to decline as the environment deteriorates. In addition, there is the very real possibility that great numbers of people in the most vulnerable famine- or flood-prone areas may be wiped out unless current trends toward ever-greater consumption in the developed world, and ever-greater population levels in the developing world, are not stopped and are ultimately reversed.

FURTHER READING

Arizpe, Lourdes, M. Priscilla Stone, and David C. Major, eds. *Population and Environment: Rethinking the Debate*. Boulder, CO: Westview Press, 1994.

Brown, Lester. *State of the World, 1989: A Worldwatch Institute Report on Progress Toward a Sustainable Society*. New York: Norton, 1989.

Coward, Harold G., ed. *Population, Consumption, and the Environment: Religious and Secular Responses*. Albany: State University of New York Press, 1995.

Ehrlich, Paul, Anne Ehrlich, and Gretchen Daily. *The Stork and the Plow: The Equity Answer to the Human Dilemma*. New York: Putnam, 1995.

Lindahl-Kiessling, Kerstin, and Hans Landberg, eds. *Population, Economic Development, and the Environment*. Oxford and New York: Oxford University Press, 1994.

Mazur, Laurie Ann, ed. *Beyond the Numbers: A Reader on Population, Consumption, and the Environment*. Washington DC: Island Press, 1994.

Myers, Norman. *Population, Resources, and the Environment: The Critical Challenges*. New York: United Nations Population Fund, 1991.

Piel, Gerard. *Only One World: Our Own to Make and to Keep*. New York: Freeman, 1992.

Salk, Jonas. *World Population and Human Values: A New Reality*. New York: Harper, 1981.

Tobias, Michael. *World War III: Population and the Biosphere at the End of the Millenium*. Santa Fe, NM: Bear, 1994; 2nd edition, New York: Continuum, 1998.

Section 3

General Population and Vital Statistics

There are several key demographic questions to be considered in this section: How many people is too many people? Have we reached that number yet? Are we going to reach it soon, or ever? Finally, is there such a number at all?

First, of course, there is a more neutral question to answer: How many of us are there? According to the last population estimate—calculated by the United Nations through mid-1995—there were 5.716 billion human beings on planet Earth. Assuming that the 1.6 percent annual growth rate for the first half of the decade continues into the second half, the population will have reached 5.995 billion by mid-1998 and surpassed the 6 billion mark sometime in late July. By the year 2000, the world's population is expected to reach 6.14 billion.

Numbers like this can sometimes be overwhelming. What does 6 billion mean? And what does 6 billion mean in the context of a planet with a surface area of roughly 60 million square miles? What does 109 persons per square mile—the average global density—imply? A few examples show that visual aids can be as treacherous as numbers in conveying the sheer quantity of human beings on the planet. Take the meaning of 6 billion, for instance. Stretched end to end, humanity would stretch from the Earth to its moon and back again a dozen times. That sounds like a lot. But standing side by side—with 4 square feet each—every human being on Earth could fit inside Rhode Island, the smallest of the United States.

HISTORY OF HUMAN POPULATION

The Long Term

As noted in the Section 1 of this encyclopedia, the rate at which human population has grown in the more than 10,000 years since the development of agriculture has increased rapidly, with the time span required for doubling dropping from roughly 1,500 years (at around the time of the industrial revolution) to about 35 years today. Indeed, if we go back even further in time, the change in the rate of increase becomes even more dramatic. If, as archaeologists tell us, the human species has been in existence on the planet for roughly 3.5 million years, then it took humanity millions of years to reach the estimated 8 million people living at the time of the agricultural revolution. Today, the world's population grows by 8 million persons every month. In other words, if an extraterrestrial visitor came to Earth, say 100,000 years ago, human beings would have represented a relatively minor life form of life in terms of quantity—the equivalent of, say, the chimpanzee today.

Still, there is something a bit misleading about growth rates and doubling averages. They make it appear that demographic expansion is consistent, over both time and space. But that is not the case. In fact, there have been several periods in which human population was able to grow dramatically faster than in others. The first of these great expansions occurred with the previously mentioned agricultural revolution. Agriculture, of course, allowed human beings to grow exponentially greater amounts of food than could be obtained by hunting or gathering.

Moreover, the process reinforces itself on an ever-greater scale. A steadier and greater food supply allows populations to become geographically stable, leading to the growth of cities, the development of classes of nonagriculturalists, and the steady advance of toolmaking and weaponry. At the same time, the development of agriculture requires a more ordered social structure. People live closer to one another. They acquire property, both land and personal. More rules, rule makers and rule enforcers are needed. More complex forms of government arise that can both organize and command greater internal human and nonhuman resources. The need for more land and other resources—including slaves— leads to military expeditions and conquests, often of less-advanced peoples. These are then incorporated into the existing political, economic, and cultural system, thereby expanding the realm of stable, agriculturally based economies and hence the number of human beings.

This process, of course, can and has been reversed from time to time in human history. The barbarian invasions of Rome after the year A.D. 400 and the Mongol conquest of China in the thirteenth century witnessed the triumph of more thinly populated nomadic pastoralists over more densely populated settled agriculturalists. Ultimately, however, while this may have resulted in a short-term breakdown of order and hence a drop in production and population, the long-term trend of increasing numbers of agriculturalists was not altered. Pastoralist invaders have almost always been assimilated into the existing agricultural society, not vice versa.

The second great spurt in human population occurred as a result of the scientific, commercial, industrial, and agricultural revolutions. Combined, the experimentation method of the scientific revolution (beginning in the seventeenth century), the more sophisticated modes of economic organization inherent in the commercial revolution (seventeenth century), the vast in-

crease in productive capacity created by the industrial revolution (late eighteenth century), and the enormous food bounties produced by the agricultural revolution (mid-twentieth century) have allowed far more people to meet their basic needs with far less effort in a far shorter period of time than was ever possible before.

Of course, these "revolutions" began in Europe and places where European settlers came to predominate (during the centuries noted in parentheses above)—and, thus, had their initial demographic impact there—before spreading to the rest of the world in the late twentieth century, as the following numbers reveal. For example, death rates—an excellent measure of a population's relative development profile—fell from about 34 to 18 per 1,000 persons annually in the developed world between the late eighteenth century and the first half of the twentieth century. That downward trend continued in the late twentieth century, falling by about half again to just 10 deaths per 1,000 persons. In the developing world, however, a very different pattern emerged. In the eighteenth century, the death rate stood at 37 per 1,000 persons, reflecting the fact that, before the great "revolutions" in science and commerce, the health and development profile of the now-developed and -developing worlds were roughly equal. But while the above-noted "revolutions" began having their impact on the death rates of the developed world over the next two hundred years, there was but a modest drop in the developing world—from 37 to 32 deaths per 1,000 persons—until those "revolutions" began to be exported. Thus only in the late twentieth century has the developing world seen a drop in death rates from 32 to 14 per 1,000 persons, bringing the developing world once again close to the levels enjoyed by the developed world.

The Short Term

Although Europeans and people of European origin were the main beneficiaries of the various "revolutions" described above, the ultimate demographic effect has been on non-Europeans, especially since the end of World War II. This has come about largely through the dispersion of more and cheaper machine-made goods, new agricultural methods and supplies, public health policies, and new medicines and medical techniques. Making all of this possible was the great economic boom of the postwar years. From roughly the late 1940s until the mid-1970s, the capitalist and socialist economies of both the developed and developing worlds experienced enormous growth, making it possible for individuals to improve their own lives and for governments to better the conditions of life for their citizens.

Economic growth and the expansion of social services—whether provided by the public or the private sector—had a major effect on population growth, particularly in the developing world for several mutually reinforcing reasons. First, improved diets led to healthier and more fertile mothers, helping raise the birth rate. Second, advances in public health and new medicines and medical techniques gradually—and, in some cases, rapidly—lowered death rates. As people lived longer, populations inevitably increased. Third, economic growth meant that families could afford to raise more children.

The result of all this has been a rapidly increasing population worldwide, as well as a rapidly rising rate of population growth. Thus the world's population grew from 1.96 billion in 1925 to 2.505 billion in 1950, an increase of some 545 million persons, or 27.8 percent. Between 1950 and 1975, the population expanded to 3.988 billion, an increase of 1.483 billion, or 59.2 percent. Finally, by 2000, the population is expected to reach 6.140, an increase of 2.152 billion, or 54.0 percent.

The fact that the absolute number of persons has risen more in the past quarter century than in the quarter century before it, while the percentage of growth has declined somewhat, is more than just a mathematical anomaly or contradiction (that is, the same growth from a larger base in absolute number always means a lower growth rate). It reflects a contradictory trend in the demographic profile of the past half century. On the one hand, the same factors that have contributed to population growth in the short run

begin to undermine that process in the longer run. This occurs in a variety of ways, both direct and indirect. To take one of the more direct ways, the same health facilities that a government builds to help extend lives—including both schools that teach hygiene and clinics that dispense medicines—are often the same institutions that can be and are used to spread knowledge of birth control methods. To take a less direct example, if better health care and diet increases the chances of a child reaching adulthood, parents who hope to have their surviving children provide for them in old age—a common practice in much of the developing world—will gradually realize that they do not need to have so many children. Moreover, economic globalization—the process by which manufacturing and commercial agriculture spreads to the developing world—tends to push people off the land. In cities, it is less advantageous to have large families. Economic modernization, too, plays a role. As economies become more sophisticated, education becomes more critical to success. Keeping children in school—as opposed to putting them to work—represents a financial drag on a family. So, parents make the decision to have fewer children. These developments have tended to occur in developed nations first, though they are increasingly spreading to the developing world.

Why, then, does the absolute number of persons continue to grow more rapidly even if the pace of growth is slowing? The answer relates to the above-mentioned mathematical anomaly and to something population experts call demographic lag. Demographic lag means that if a given population has a large number of births in one time period, a chain reaction is set off that takes several more time periods to work out. If, for example, country X has a massive increase in births during time period A, then its population of young persons of reproductive age is likely to swell in time period A plus fifteen to twenty years or so (depending on the age at which women tend to start having babies), even if the overall number of children born to each couple has decreased. This has been very typical of the past twenty-five years and is likely to continue at ever-diminishing rates for the next seventy-five years or so, as the bubble of children born during the 1950-1975 period begins to work its way up the age ladder.

Indeed, the slowing growth of the bubble is already noticeable. Between 1980 and 1995, the number of persons worldwide under the age of 15—that is, persons whose reproductive years are ahead of them—increased in absolute terms from 1.551 billion to 1.829 billion, implying a future growth in births; at the same time, however, the percentage of persons under age 15 worldwide dropped from 35 to 32 percent. In short, the bubble in the number of reproductive age persons is expanding, but at a slower pace, implying that at some point in the future, it will disappear.

There is also something that might be called the "cultural" demographic time lag. It was hinted at above in the statement concerning parental choice in the number of children. As noted above, when parents realize that their children are more likely to survive—or that fewer children mean a greater chance of economic success for both offspring and parent—they will have fewer of them. But it may take a generation for this result to become apparent to people. Hence, there is a lag between falling death rates and rising birth rates, resulting in accelerated population growth.

It is important to note here the differences between the developed and developing worlds. As noted above, a more modernized economy and society rewards families with fewer children, though it often takes a generation or two for parents to realize this. In the case of the developed nations of the world, however, it took more than a hundred years. That is, between the late eighteenth and the late nineteenth centuries—the height of the industrial revolution in Western Europe and North America—birth rates stood unchanged at 38 per 1,000 persons. In the developing world, on the other hand, there has already been a drop from 41 to 37 births per 1,000 in just the fifty years since the end of World War II, years roughly corresponding to the period in

which the effects of the European-initiated "revolutions" have begun to spread to much of the rest of the world. Why the difference?

First, the first century of "revolutions" in Europe coincided with a period of mass European migration. The opening up of new territories meant that almost as many agriculturalists were being created in European-settled overseas territories as were being destroyed in industrializing and urbanizing Europe. This opening up of new territories has no counterpart in the developing world. Second, the processes of industrialization and especially urbanization have occurred much more rapidly in the developing world. Finally, declining birth rates in the developing world have been affected not just by economic modernization but through the conscious efforts of national governments and international institutions, through the power of universal education and mass media. None of this occurred during the early period of economic modernization in the developed world.

REGIONS OF THE WORLD

An assessment of humanity's numbers would depend very much on where one looked. If it one looked in Bangladesh—which has a density of 2,165 persons per square mile—Earth might seem like a very crowded place. Looking at Australia—which has about 5 persons per square mile—would lead one to the opposite conclusion. Similarly, if someone stayed for a while, he might notice that people tended to have fewer children who lived longer in the temperate zones of the planet than was the case in the tropical parts of the world.

Indeed, in the previous sections much has been made of the differences between the developed and developing worlds. But this division of the world into two neat camps presents some problems. First, of course, is the definition of the terms themselves. What does it mean to call a country "developed" or "developing"? That question is clarified, in Section 6, The Demography of Labor and the Economy.

A second problem involves the categories or

designations themselves. If developed countries can range from relatively impoverished Portugal to extremely wealthy Switzerland, the gap among developing nations renders the term *developing* nearly meaningless. Developing countries can include relatively prosperous and industrialized South Korea, oil-rich Kuwait, struggling Mexico, and destitute Mozambique. Categories such as "newly industrialized countries" (NICs), for places like Singapore, and "fourth world," for many of the economically stagnant and undeveloped countries of sub-Saharan Africa, have been used to differentiate among the states of the so-called developing world.

More helpful than the general categories of developed and developing nations are regions and subregions. Regions roughly constitute the major continents: Africa, Asia, North America, Latin America (South and Central Americas, plus the Caribbean), Europe (including Russia), and Oceania (Australia, New Zealand, and the Pacific islands). Subregions are more precise yet, for these differentiate among such culturally, politically, and economically distinct zones as Eastern and Western Europe or the relatively prosperous countries of South America's "southern cone" (Argentina, Chile, and Uruguay) and the impoverished Andean countries (Bolivia, Peru, and Ecuador).

Africa

In many ways, Africa lags behind the rest of the world demographically. That is not to say that the rate of its population growth is slower. Quite the contrary: Africa represents the region with the fastest-growing population in the world. Between 1965 and 1995, its population expanded from 311 million to 728 million, an increase of 134 percent. This rapid increase—and its status as the region with the fastest-growing population—is relatively new. Between 1925 and 1950, the population in Africa grew from 153 to 219 million, an increase of 43 percent. During that same period, the population of Latin America grew 67 percent. But from 1965 to 1995, the rate of population growth in Latin America fell sig-

nificantly behind Africa's, though the population in Latin America was growing at the still-rapid rate of 69 percent. Other regions of the developing world provide an even greater contrast with Africa.

Indeed, Africa is the only major region of the world in which the rate of growth is still rising. In 1965, the population of the continent was increasing at the rate of 2.3 percent annually. Thirty years later that figure was 3.0 percent. Thus, it is expected that Africa—which had roughly the same population as North America in 1875 or Europe (minus the former Soviet Union) in 1975—will have almost eight times the population of the former and four times that of the latter by 2075.

Of course, Africa is not a monolith. There is the great divide of the Sahara Desert separating North Africa—which, culturally and economically, is more akin to the Middle East—from the rest of the continent, so-called sub-Saharan Africa. In North Africa, growth rates peaked in 1980 at 2.9 percent annually and have since fallen to 2.3 percent, a rate that is still higher than that of virtually any other region outside Africa. On the rest of the continent, growth rates continue to climb.

Several factors are causing this enormous growth. First, birth rates continue to be quite high at some 42 per 1,000 persons. Although this is a decline from the 46 per 1,000 of 1980, the drop is insignificant when compared to rates in most other regions of the developing world. Second, death rates have fallen dramatically in recent years, from 23 per 1,000 persons in 1965 to 14 per 1,000 in 1995. In effect, Africa has experienced the impact of the "revolutions" in science and commerce long after the rest of the world. Finally, there is the matter of population density. Despite its enormous growth rates, Africa is relatively underpopulated at just 62 persons per square mile, compared with roughly 280 in Eurasia. Indeed, Africa is both the second largest land mass and, next to Europe and Latin America, the continent with the highest proportion of land capable of sustaining large human populations. This has led many demographers—particularly African ones—to assert that Africa's problem is not too many people but too little development.

Latin America

Although much of Latin America shares linguistic and, to a limited degree, cultural roots in the Iberian countries (Spain and Portugal) that conquered the region in the sixteenth century, there are nevertheless dramatic differences of race, economics, and society (see Section 5, Demography and Cultural Identity and Section 6, The Demography of Labor and the Economy). Although the peoples of the southern part of the region are largely of European descent and the area among the most prosperous subregions of the developing world, the rest of the region is more ethnically and racially heterogeneous and is generally far less economically developed.

Still, there are some significant overall patterns in the demography of the region. Like North America and Africa, Latin America is relatively thinly populated, with just 60 persons per square mile. As in Europe, most of the continent is quite habitable. Even the high valleys of the Andean chain—located as they are largely in the tropics—support large populations. Overall, Latin America has seen its annual population growth rate drop significantly in the past thirty years from 2.8 percent to 1.8 percent, the most dramatic decrease of any major world region.

At the same time, Latin America's birth rate has declined from 41 to 26 per 1,000 and the number of persons under age 15 has fallen from 40 to 34 percent, a decrease attributable, say demographers, to more education and a reduction in the influence of the Catholic Church's anti–birth-control doctrine. Yet, despite all this, Latin America's population continues to grow rapidly in absolute numbers, a classic example of demographic lag. Thus, it is expected that Latin America's population will double to roughly 1.3 billion by 2075 before leveling off.

North America

After Europe, North America has the slowest rate of population growth of any major region of the world. Between 1965 and 1995, its population grew just 37 percent, from 214 million to 293 million. At the same time, its growth rate fell from an already low 1.5 percent annually in 1965 to just 1 percent thirty years later. Yet even this modest growth is misleading. Host to the second-largest number of immigrants annually—after Europe—its natural increase is barely above zero. (For more information on immigration, see Section 7, The Demography of Migration).

The region's slow growth rate is due primarily to low birth rates. In 1995, there were just 16 births per 1,000 persons, down nearly a third from 22 per 1,000 in 1965. At the same time, the death rate has stayed even at 9 persons per 1,000, reflecting the region's well-established health care system and nutritious diets. A second contributing factor is the age profile. With just 22 percent of the population under age 15, North America has the oldest population of any region in the world outside Europe. Unlike Europe, however, the region is thinly populated, with just 36 persons per square mile, though this low density rate is somewhat misleading since some 50 percent of the region consists of northern Canada and Alaska, where only a few million people live.

Because the rate of immigration is projected to slow due to stricter laws, the population of North America is expected to grow to only about 350 million by 2075, an increase of about 10 percent from 1999.

Asia

It is virtually impossible to speak of Asia as a unified region in any meaningful way. By far the most heavily populated continent, Asia is home to well over half of humanity. The largest continent in area, Asia can be divided into roughly four geographic and cultural zones: East Asia, Southeast Asia, South Asia, and Southwest Asia. (This does not include Siberia, the vast but sparsely populated northern third of the continent. Politically part of Russia, it was once included in statistics for the Soviet Union and is now lumped together with Europe.)

East Asia is the most populous of the subregions; its population in 1995 was 1.424 billion, up from 864 million in 1965, an increase of 65 percent. Although vast in area, at some 4.54 million square miles, it is quite crowded, with 313 persons per square mile. This, of course, varies from place to place within the subregion. Eastern China, the two Koreas, and Japan are intensely crowded, while western China is relatively underpopulated. East Asia's annual growth rate was already low in 1965 at 1.4 percent, and it has since dropped to 1 percent, largely as a result of China's strict one-child family policy. Thus the birth rate in the subregion has declined from 33 to 18 per 1,000 persons, roughly equivalent to the rate in highly developed North America. This is reflected in the rising age of East Asia's population, with the number of children under the age of 15 declining from 33 to 25 percent over the past thirty years.

South Asia, the second most populous subregion, presents an entirely different profile from East Asia's. Dominated by India and its relatively lax birth control efforts, South Asia has witnessed an increase in its population from 681 million in 1965 to 1.381 billion in 1995. At the same time, its annual population growth rate fell only slightly, from 2.4 percent in 1965 to 2.1 percent thirty years later. Even more densely populated than East Asia, with virtually no major part of the subregion uninhabitable, South Asia has a density of 332 persons per square mile, the highest of any major continental region in the world.

Like East Asia and South Asia, the subregion of Southeast Asia is dominated by a single state: Indonesia. With its population of roughly 200 million, Indonesia is nearly three times the size of its next largest neighbor, Vietnam. Southeast Asia, with some wealthy states and some rather impoverished ones, shows a wide range of economic conditions. Vietnam remains one of the poorest countries in Asia; Singapore is among the richest. Overall, however, the subregion has seen enormous economic growth in the past thirty years, which is reflected in its demographic profile. As a region, its annual population growth rate declined from 2.6 percent in 1965 to 1.8 per-

cent in 1995, while birth and death rates fell from 43 to 27 per 1,000 and 17 to 8 per 1,000, respectively, in the same period.

Southwest Asia largely overlaps the Middle East and is mostly made up of the Central Asian republics of the former Soviet Union. Southwest Asia has no single dominant state and has extremes of poverty and wealth, ranging from war-devastated Afghanistan to the oil-rich United Arab Emirates. Overall, Southwest Asia is an extremely rapidly growing region, where the population has increased 147 percent between 1965 and 1995, the fastest of any major subregion of the world. Indeed, as in Africa, the annual population growth rate is bucking international trends, although whereas in Africa this statistic has risen, in Southwest Asia it has remained the same. Ironically, the rapid increase in population has been evident in both the wealthy Persian Gulf countries and the poorer states to the north. Demographers believe that this is because the high income levels in the former derive from a rise in oil prices, which occurred rapidly and did not lead to a cultural shift toward smaller families.

It is expected that, while East Asia's population will increase by about a third over the next seventy-five years, the rest of Asia's population will more than double to exceed 5 billion by 2075.

Europe

If any region of the world can be said to lead the way in demographic change, it is Europe. From roughly 1700 to 1900, it remained the fastest-growing region of the world, if its emigrant population is included. But in the years since World War II, it has become the slowest- growing region of the world. Moreover, the population in many parts of the region is expected to remain stable or even decline in the coming century. This is especially true of Eastern Europe, where, in the wake of communism's collapse, health care and diets have deteriorated. These demographic problems are compounded by the fact that hundreds of thousands of Eastern Europeans have been emigrating to Western Europe, the United States, and Israel in recent years. Indeed, Eastern Europe had an annual growth rate of –0.1 percent in 1995, the only major region in the world whose population has declined. Birth and death rates reveal why this is happening. Whereas death rates increased from 9 per 1,000 persons in 1965 to 12 per 1,000 in 1995, birth rates fell from 17 per 1,000 to 12 per 1,000. So, although the natural increase is flat, outmigration produces a slight decline.

Western Europe presents a profile that is both similar and dissimilar to that of Eastern Europe. In Western Europe, the annual growth rate hovers just above zero, even though birth and death rates have nearly converged. Of course, this convergence did not occur because death rates are rising but because birth rates have fallen so dramatically. The population increase owes to in-migration, largely from the former colonies of West European powers or from Eastern Europe.

Thus it is expected that Europe's population will probably stabilize at about 800 million (including Russia) by the middle of the next century, up from about 727 million today.

Oceania

The world's smallest major region by both size and population, Oceania consists of three subregions: the tiny islands of Micronesia and Polynesia, scattered over millions of square miles of the Pacific Ocean; the medium-size islands of Melanesia off Asia and Australia; and the continent of Australia itself, along with the major islands of New Zealand. This difference is always noticeable first in the population densities of the various subregions. While the islands of Micronesia and Polynesia have some of the world's highest densities, Australia has perhaps the lowest of any major country in the world. Culturally, the three regions are quite distinct as well, with the former two among the middle rank of developing nations and the latter subregion a part of the developed world.

In Oceania the population rose from 17.5 million in 1965 to 28.5 million in 1995, an increase of 63 percent. The growth rate fell from 2.1 per-

cent annually in 1965 to 1.5 in 1995. The reasons for this growth vary in the different subregions. In the islands of Melanesia, Polynesia, and Micronesia, the growth pattern comes from high birth rates and falling death rates. In Australia, it derives from immigration, especially from Asia. Indeed, this rise in immigration to Australia and New Zealand was responsible for increases in the annual growth rates there from 1.2 to 1.4 percent between 1980 and 1995. It is expected that the population of Oceania will climb to about 52 million by 2075, an increase of roughly 85 percent.

PROJECTIONS

Population projections are tricky affairs. They must take into consideration such factors as improved health care and diet, which leads to lower death rates. At the same time, they must include factors—including higher educational rates, better economic conditions, and the implementation of family-planning policies—that tend to lower birth rates. Moreover, they must weigh which of these trends is most likely to prevail and to what degree. Finally, they have to account for all these factors and trends for the different regions of the world and then arrive at a global profile. As the recent history of U.N. demographic projections makes clear, it is easy to miscalculate.

Recognizing the hazards inherent in such a complex set of calculations—based as they are on projecting past trends into the future—most of the studies conducted by the United Nations have attempted to chart population changes along several variants. Known as low, medium, and high, these variants assume different weights for different variables. Will economic growth and urbanization have a greater impact on reducing the birth rate than improved access to health care will have on reducing death rates? And if this so, when will this shift occur? Simply put, low variants imply a slower rate of growth, high variants a rapid rate, and medium variants a rate somewhere in between.

During the great takeoff in developing world

population growth in the mid-1960s, for example, the United Nations predicted that the world's population would reach 7 billion by 2000. This high-variant projection was based on continued declines in death rates and a stable but high birth rate. The 7 billion figure was predicated on annual growth rates continuing their climb upward, reaching about 2.6 percent annually around 1990, then remaining stable. The medium variant, which predicted a global population of 6.5 billion in 2000, assumed that the rate of growth in 1965—roughly 2 percent annually—would continue through 1985, then fall to 1.7 percent by 2000. The low variant regarded 1965 as the peak, with the growth rate falling continually to about 1.3 percent annually in 2000, increasing the population of the world to about 5.9 billion by the end of the century.

By 1983, when another major U.N. population projection was done, population experts had the chance to reconsider the weight of the variables. Their most important changes concerned Asia. By the early 1980s, it had become clear that the heavily populated eastern half of the continent was undergoing rapid and sustained economic and urban growth—trends that were bound to lower birth rates substantially. At the same time, it became increasingly clear that the Chinese government had changed its position on population growth, reversing its earlier position favoring high birth rates. With its complex bureaucracy down to local and even neighborhood levels, Beijing could effectively implement family planning, particularly in urban areas. A final factor in the new projection calculations was the surprisingly sharp decline in European and Soviet birth rates.

Together these new variables led the United Nations to offer several new variants on population growth. In the new study, the high, medium, and low variants predicted a 2000 population of 6.36, 6.12, and 5.90 billion, respectively. As noted above, the world's population is now expected to reach 6.14 billion in 2000, very close to the median variant calculated in the 1983 study but significantly below the same variant in the mid-1960s projection.

More significantly, the 1983 study took the projections well into the future, calculating the population through the end of the twenty-first century. Here, the differences in the variants were remarkable, with the high, medium, and low predictions being 14.20, 10.19, and 7.52 billion, respectively. As in the calculations for 2000, the different variants assumed that virtually all the population growth would occur in the developing world. Indeed, even the high variant projected that population in the developed world would increase only about 70 percent, from roughly 1.10 billion in 1975 to 1.73 billion in 2100. At the same time, the high variant saw the developing world's population grow from 2.98 to 12.47 billion over the same period, an increase of 318 percent.

At its 1994 population conference held in Cairo, the United Nations offered its latest projections, using 1992 as the base year and projecting as far forward as 2025. According to the medium variant, the world's population would reach 8.472 billion in the latter year; again, most of the population growth would come in the developing world. While population in the developed world would grow from 1.225 to 1.403 billion—an increase of 14.5 percent—the developing world's population would increase from 4.254 to 7.069 billion, a jump of 66.2 percent.

Overall, population growth rates are declining throughout the developed and developing world, pushed downward by rising levels of education, income and urbanization. Over the past decade, the UN has gradually lowered its expectation for global population in 2000 from 7 to 6 billion, a 14 percent difference. The discrepancy reveals the difficulty in making population predictions, a difficulty that becomes more acute the further into the future the projection is made. In its most recent long-term prediction, the UN offered a high-variant prediction for the year 2150 of some 27 billion people worldwide and a low-variant of 3.6 billion. This immense difference reveals not only the difficulty in making such population projections, but the importance of individual decisions multiplied by billions. Indeed, the difference between the two figures comes down to every couple deciding to have just one extra child over the next 150 years.

FURTHER READINGS

Johnson, Stanley. *World Population, Turning the Tide: Three Decades of Progress*. Boston and London: Graham and Trotman, 1994.

Johnson, Stanley, ed. *The Earth Summit: The United Nations Conference on Environment and Development*. London and Boston: Graham and Trotman/ Martinus Nijhoff, 1992.

Jones, Gawin, ed. *The Continuing Demographic Transition*. New York: Oxford University Press, and Oxford: Clarendon Press, 1997.

Lutz, Wolfgang, ed. *Distributional Aspects of Human Fertility: A Global Comparative Study*. London: Academic Press, 1989.

———. *The Future Population of the World: What Can We Assume Today?* London: Earthscan, 1994, revised edition, 1996.

Piel, Gerard. *Only One World: Our Own to Make and to Keep*. New York: Freeman, 1992.

Preston, Samuel, ed. "World Population: Approaching the Year 2000." *Annals of the American Academy of Political and Social Science*, 510, July 1990.

United Nations. Department for Economic and Social Information and Policy Analysis. *Population Policies and Programmes: Proceedings of the United Nations Expert Group Meeting on Population Policies and Programmes, Cairo, Egypt, 12–16 April 1992*. New York: United Nations, 1993.

Section 4

The Demography of Families and Households

A BRIEF HISTORY OF THE MODERN FAMILY/HOUSEHOLD

Throughout history, the structure of the family has almost always been in transition. Sociologists believe that there is no one definition of the family that has been accurate across all time. To scholars of modern history, the great transition in family structure came with industrialization and urbanization, which began in England in the late eighteenth century. It then spread to parts of Western Europe and the northeastern United States in the early nineteenth century, enveloping most of the United States and Europe by the late nineteenth and early twentieth centuries. Finally it moved to many parts of the developing world—most notably East Asia and parts of the Middle East and Latin America—by the end of the twentieth century.

Industrialization and urbanization's impact on the family were extremely complex, making any summary of these developments an oversimplification. Nevertheless, it can be safely noted that these economic and geographic phenomena tended to shrink family size in two ways. First, these factors motivated parents to have fewer children. Second, they tended to replace extended families with nuclear ones—that is, families consisting of parents and children only.

Preindustrial families tended to be large and extended. They were large because they were centers of production and social welfare, that is, most families were farm families, which grew their own food, made most of the goods they used, and provided education, health care services, and charity for their members. Given these requirements, large and extended families made sense economically. Different members performed different tasks and resources were shared, which made for greater productivity and efficiency. Thus many families working as a single economic unit contained relatives of all generations as well as servants.

Moreover, death was a nearly constant companion of preindustrial families. Babies and young children often died of illness, making it essential for parents to have many children so that a few would survive to contribute to family production in the short term and provide for aging parents in the long term. Young and middle-aged adults were not immune to death either. It was quite common for parents—in particular, mothers in childbirth—to die before some or all of their children were fully grown. The presence of aunts, uncles, in-laws, and even grandparents within a single family unit helped guarantee the survival of children specifically and the family generally.

The advent of industrialization and mass urbanization changed. First, industrialization made it possible to buy cheaply many of the goods that were once produced in the home. Gradually, the family ceased to be a unit of production and became one of nurturing and comsumption. In an increasingly industrialized world, it made more sense to have fewer children, since the requirements of modern urban life put a premium on education. A child in school cannot work and thus becomes a financial burden—rather than an asset—for the family. Moreover, industrialization paid off in rising levels of health care and improved medicines, allowing more children to mature to adulthood. Similarly, the rise of the modern bureaucratic state—a by-product of industrialization and urbanization—led to social programs that took care of people in their later years of life, reducing the need for children to care for their aging parents.

Of course, this process was not evenly distributed across societies or even across classes within a single society. As noted above, the impact of industrialization and urbanization is only now affecting most parts of the world. Similarly, the modern family structure was first seen in middle-class families. Long after industrialization and urbanization had taken hold in America, for instance, many urban and rural poorer families continued to need children as contributors to family income and so could not send them to school. The uneven impact of industrialization and urbanization on the family is also seen in the developing world.

Before proceeding to a discussion of families in the modern world, we should define the terms used here. Demographers prefer the term *household* over *family* for several reasons. Households—that is, the community of people living under the same roof and sharing financial and other resources—are easier to measure statistically simply because they are concentrated in one place and usually have one (or sometimes more) householder(s) who is (are) legally responsible for the other members. Thus most censuses measure households and not families, since families are often dispersed geographically. And because families are dispersed—and so do not always share resources—family members living in different households may have radically different economic profiles. Therefore the term *householder* is used here.

Fertility measures the number of children born to each woman in a given society. One way of gauging fertility is to measure it for given time periods—usually a year—or for age cohorts, that is, over the course of a woman's reproductive life. These numbers can be arrived at three different ways. First, the crude birth rate can be analyzed. The crude birth rate is reached by dividing the total number of live births in a given year by the total population and then multiplying by 1,000. Another method, the general fertility rate, is found by dividing the total number of live births in a given year by the total number of women of reproductive age (usually 15-44), and then multiplying by 1,000. Finally, if actual birth statistics are unavailable or inadequate, there is the child–women ratio, in which the total number of young children (usually up to age 4) are divided by the total number of women of reproductive age plus 4 (usually 15-49) and multiplied by 1,000. The plus four is meant to factor in the possibility that a woman had a baby at age 44, who is now as much as five years old.

Because the crude birth rate is the most widely used by demographers and data-collecting institutions worldwide, this reference uses the crude birth rate as the standard of measurement.

FERTILITY AND CHILDBIRTH

As noted earlier, the term *fertility* is used to define the number of children born to each woman. There are two determinants of the level of fertility in a given society. The first is biological, that is, the physical ability to bear children, or fecundity. Since few women—especially in the developing world—are ever tested for their fecundity, demographers tend to use fertility—the actual bearing of children—as the prime measurement of a society's natural rate of increase. Nevertheless, some general guesses about the relationship between fecundity and fertility can be made. It is estimated that approximately 10 percent of all couples in the United States are infertile or sterile, that is, incapable of having children, whether the infertility lies with the man or the woman. Sterility varies by age, affecting about 2 percent of teenagers, and nearly 20 percent of those over age 40. Estimates in other developed countries indicate that the American rate is about average.

How can these figures be extrapolated to the developing world, where few estimates of fecundity exist? Two factors need to be considered. On the one hand, the generally younger age profile of developing countries means that there are more fecund women and men. On the other, however, poorer diets and health care may raise infertility rates. To what extent these two factors cancel each other out is impossible to say, but it does not matter much, since most reproductive decisions are made for social, not biological reasons.

The second determinant of fertility levels is social, chief among which is the use of contraceptives. Are the participants informed about contraceptives? Natural methods of birth control are, of course, almost as ancient as the family itself. They include natural abortifacients (natural medicines that cause women to abort fetuses), coitus interruptus (in which the man withdraws before ejaculating), and the "rhythm method," in which couples restrict their sexual intercourse to the less-fertile portion of a woman's menstrual cycle. These methods have been practiced by virtually all human societies.

Awareness of Western methods—including barrier methods (condoms, intrauterine devices, and diaphragms), surgical techiques (such as vasectomies for men or the tying of the fallopian tubes in women), birth-control pills, and, most recently, pharmaceutical abortifacients like the French drug RU-486—is prevalent in both developed and developing countries, albeit at different rates, though the majority of women in the developed countries are informed about most birth-control options.

In much of the developing world—as in the developed world before it—the idea that birth control is an option has been slow in coming, although it has become more widespread in recent years. Several conceptual obstacles had to be overcome first, prime of which was acceptance of the idea of planning or limiting families. Much of the developing world remains at an early phase in the transition toward industrialization and urbanization, so a large portion of

the population works on the land, where every child is a potential source of labor.

A second key obstacle to introducing birth control has often been the fact that women in developing countries have little decision-making power in the family. Because they have greater responsibility for the children and their well-being, women are usually more acutely aware of the changing economics of child-rearing and the need to have fewer children in an urban and industrial setting. Decision-making power is often tied to education and income, which are mutually reinforcing. Higher income usually means more education, and more education brings a greater awareness of the needs for a small family, a stronger commitment to limit births, and an awareness of birth-control options.

Even when their income does not rise, women often show lower fertility levels when their status changes as a result of urbanization. For example, they gain better access to education and an independent income, which often give women the confidence and the power to demand a say in marriage and family-planning decisions. They either postpone marriage, thereby limiting fertility by reducing the number of years in which the woman is likely to have children, or, after marriage, they insist on longer delays between children. The ability to earn an independent income also allows some women to forgo marriage—or remarriage after the death or divorce of a husband. Although the proportion of women in the developing world who forgo marriage remains small, it does have an impact on overall fertility rates by removing some women from child-bearing status.

Moreover, when urbanization removes them from traditional village society, where there is family and communal pressure to have many children, women can more readily assess the desired number of children on their own terms. Moreover, in cities, women are less likely to be as influenced by the church. Since most religions emphasize the benefits of large families, their absence in women's lives often leads to lower fertility rates. Finally, a newly urbanized woman often finds that she has more options in terms of education and income if she forgoes early or repeated childbirth.

It should now be clear that women are the key to fertility rates and that raising their social status—through access to education and, to a smaller extent, higher household income levels or independent sources of income for women—is the key to lowering those rates. Not surprisingly, given this dynamic, fertility levels in the developed and developing world differ dramatically. In the former, some industrialized countries are actually experiencing flat or even negative growth rates, while in most developing countries, fertility levels are only beginning to fall or level off. Thus, to understand the impact of economic modernization on fertility, it is important to examine both low- and high-fertility countries, beginning with the latter.

Theories of Fertility Reduction

Most developing countries have developed birth control and family planning policies, outlined in Section 1 of this book. The following discussion covers the two general theories of falling fertility rates.

The first such theory is based largely on economic criteria. Using the rational decision maker of classical economic theory—in this case, the parent who makes rational decisions based on complete information about the pluses and minuses involved in that decision—the economic approach to understanding fertility rates states that people will make the logical tradeoff of preferring higher living standards over large families. Knowing that having fewer children means that they and their child will lead better-quality lives, they will logically choose this option. Thus, as economies modernize and make smaller families the more rational choice, fertility levels drop accordingly.

The second general theory deals with the sociocultural bases of the decision to have children. The economic explanation for fertility levels, while logical by itself, fails to include this sociocultural aspect. The decision to have children can also be viewed as a rational one in social terms, motivated by ego gratification, the need to main-

tain a lineage, or obligations to extended family, community, nation, or religion. Thus fertility levels will drop only after such sociocultural needs are satisfied.

High-Fertility Countries

High fertility has both general social and immediate family causes. The social causes include the need for a given society to survive, as is the case for many indigenous tribal peoples. The survival imperative has been employed by some modern cultures as well. Both the Nazi regime in Europe and the communist government in North Korea incessantly propagandized about the need for and virtues of high fertility, and rewarded couples for having many children. Both believed that high fertility was necessary for their society to survive and ultimately triumph in struggles with other societies—Slavic Europe in Germany's case, South Korea in North Korea's case. Similarly, Palestinian leaders have advocated high levels of fertility in order to overwhelm the Jewish population of Israel and force the Israeli government to allow the Palestinians to form their own state. Indeed, for many years, the government of Israel has faced a demographic and political dilemma concerning the occupied territories. On the one hand, Israel considers itself a democracy. Absorption of the territories would require offering the vote to Palestinians. Their rapidly growing numbers would soon turn a Jewish state into a multicultural one. In other words, Israel appeared to be faced with a choice between its democratic and Jewish identities when it came to dealing with territories, a dilemma that has been partially eliminated by the move toward increased Palestinian autonomy in Gaza and the West Bank. While Israel has a low birth rate of 20.3 live births per 1,000—typical of an industrialized society—the occupied territories have some of the highest birth rates in the world—38.8 per 1,000 in the West Bank and 50.7 per 1,000 in Gaza in 1995.

As noted above, the need for children as laborers and for future security is an important factor in high-fertility societies, particularly where most people remain on the land. Thus it is not surprising to find that such largely rural African countries as Kenya (72 percent rural) and Tanzania (80 percent rural) have some of the highest fertility rates in the world: Kenya had 33.4 live births per 1,000 persons and Tanzania 41.3 per 1,000 in 1995. Moreover, as these societies have begun to urbanize, their birth rates have dropped.

For example, in Kenya, the percentage of people living in rural areas was nearly 85 percent in 1965. That same year, the birth rate was more than 55 live births per 1,000 persons. In other words, the percentage of people living in rural areas dropped by some 11.8 percent, while birth rates fell 39.3 percent. This indicates that the move from rural to urban areas provides only part of the explanation for falling birth rates. Much of the difference can be explained by the increasingly aggressive efforts by the government and by national and international non-governmnental organizations to expand birth-control use in the country. The prevalence of condom use, for instance, climbed from barely 8 percent of the population in 1975 to about 30 percent in 1990.

Other factors in high-fertility societies include rising social expectations and falling infant mortality levels. If parents can be convinced that their children are likely to live to adulthood, they become willing to reduce the number of children they have. Again, using Kenya as an example, life expectancy climbed from 40.5 years in 1965 to 55.6 years in 1995. From 1980 to 1985, the infant mortality rate fell from 80 per 1,000 live births to 55.3. Yet, as many demographers point out, there is a lag between rising life expectancy rates and lower birth rates because it can take as much as a generation before the realization sinks in that parents can expect more of their children to survive to adulthood.

This is especially true in places where women's status remains low. When infants' and children's mortality rates fall, it is often the women who are burdened with the problems of rearing a large family, including cooking, cleaning, and other household tasks. In poverty-stricken households, the man may be forced to recognize that he cannot support a large family. But in families where income is rising or already high enough to support many children, the traditional prestige attached to a man with many offspring is not offset by the difficulties of managing a large household since this burden falls primarily on the woman.

Another consideration in explaining high fertility rates in many developing societies is the widespread cultural preference for sons. Despite gains made in women's status in recent years, the preference for male offspring remains strong in many societies. This cultural bias is particularly strong in Asian societies, such as China and India. The desire for sons has contributed to female infanticide rates. Under China's strict one-child policy, some parents abandoned female infants if they were the firstborn, leading to a slightly higher number of boys than girls over the past two decades. In India, where there are no such restrictions on single families, the desire for sons leads parents to conceive until they have a boy, and then stop. This helps explain the fact that the country has one of the world's highest ratios of men to women: 1.08 men for every woman. (It should be noted that preference for male children permeates Western societies as well. When asked in a 1980s-era survey, five out of six potential American parents responded that if they could choose the sex of an only child, they would prefer a boy.)

Low-Fertility Countries

Much of the developed world falls into the category of low-fertility countries. As noted above, this drop in fertility rates has resulted from industrialization and urbanization, which have been taking place in Europe, the United States, and other developed nations for about a century. Indeed, aside from a brief rise in fertility after the end of World War II—an exceptional period known as the baby boom, in which a combination of cultural and economic factors led to a brief increase in the number of children born in the developed world—the size of the Western family has been shrinking steadily since the industrial revolution.

There are several key reasons for this, primarily the economic factors noted above. The modern requirement of a long educational period for children dictates smaller families for all but the small minority who have the means to support them. But economic factors do not suffice as an explanation; cultural factors are also critical. Greater prestige and higher status—not to mention a higher standard of living—accrue to those who are able to amass wealth. And by the time some aspiring couples have reached a higher income and wealth plateau, they may very well have passed their prime reproductive years. A variation on this theme existed in the communist bloc countries of Eastern Europe and the western parts of the Soviet Union as well. There, a perennial shortage of consumer goods and housing dictated smaller families.

The continuing drop in fertility rates—especially in the post–baby boom years of the 1960s through the 1990s—can be explained in terms of income and prestige. Because wages were stagnant in much of the Western world during this period, two incomes became necessary to attain higher incomes, usually by having both spouses work in paid employment. Women who work outside the home are more likely to have fewer children and to wait longer to have them, compared with those who do not work outside the household. Indeed, the expanding opportunities for women have introduced life options other than marriage and child-bearing and so have further dampened the fertility rates.

At the same time, the economic environment of the developed world has shifted jobs away from basic manufacturing in recent decades, just as employment has shifted away from the agricultural sector over the past century or two. The so-called postindustrial economies place a higher value on education and make postsecondary and even postgraduate degrees necessary for attaining higher income. To earn these degrees, both men and women must stay in school until well into their reproductive years, often delaying marriage and child-bearing.

HOUSEHOLDS

Urbanization and industrialization have transformed the modern household, first by making it smaller. Over the past century, households gradually shrank from large extended families to smaller nuclear families, beginning in what is now the developed world. In addition, the number of children living in each household has shrunk from an average of four or more in much of Europe in 1900 to fewer than two, and sometimes one, at the end of the century. As noted above, these trends are largely—though not entirely—the result of rational decisions made by citizens living in industrialized urban societies, where education is preferred over early childbearing; higher standards of living are enjoyed by smaller families; and, more recently, two incomes are needed to sustain a single household.

Sociocultural influences—including the increase in single-person households—have also affected the size of households in the developing world. As cultural pressures toward marriage have been removed in much of the developed world, many people now have the option to remain single throughout their reproductive years and, indeed, throughout their lives. Similarly, the easing of social pressures to bear children has led to the rise of childless families. Finally, the increasing acceptance of divorce as a legitimate cultural decision—and an easier legal choice—has caused many households to split into two, thereby reducing the average size of each household. The size of households in Europe, the United States, Japan, and elsewhere in the developed world has fallen significantly. Whereas, at the turn of the century, the average household in the developed world consisted of five or six persons, at century's end the average is closer to three.

All these factors, of course, are becoming increasingly evident in the developing world, though to varying degrees in different countries. The industrialization and urbanization of much of East and Southeast Asia have clearly led to a significant decline in the size of households there. In South Korea, for example, the average household size has decreased from 5.6 to 3.7 in just the past thirty years, reflecting that country's rapid shift to an economy dominated by the middle-class. But even where that shift to a middle-class society has not occurred, rising urbanization—which affects both economically vibrant and economically stagnant countries—has an impact, since urban families tend to be smaller than their rural counterparts. Thus, in Turkey, the average size of a rural household is 6 persons, while that of an urban household is 4.6, some 23 percent smaller.

The recent cultural changes in the Western world—the shift toward more single-person households and the rise in divorce rates—have been less apparent in the developing world, largely because cultural shifts usually follow economic change. Industrialization and urbanization often reduce traditional influences of family, community, and religion on the first generation to arrive in the city less than on their offspring, who are fully socialized to urban life.

So, while the number of children per household and the number of households with extended families have been shrinking in the developing world since the end of World War II, the number of single households and divorce rates have not risen to the same extent. For example, whereas both a developed country like Italy and a developing country like Jordan had comparable marriage rates in 1965—7.4 and 7.8 per 1,000 persons, respectively—Italy's has fallen to 5 per 1,000 persons, while Jordan's has risen slightly to 8 per 1,000 persons. Similarly, while a developed country like Canada has seen its divorce rate climb from 0.5 to 2.7 persons per 1,000 between 1965 and 1995—an increase of 440 percent—the divorce rate in Jamaica—equal to Canada's in the 1960s—remained roughly the same as that of 1995.

There has also been a marked trend toward more female heads of households. In this, unlike in divorce and marriage rates, the developed and the developing worlds are changing simultaneously. In countries as diverse economically and culturally as Namibia and New Zealand, the number of households headed by females—which almost always means there is no male adult in the household—now stands above 35 per-

cent. At the same time, in Iran, where Islamic culture holds sway, the rate is below 6 percent. Clearly, both cultural and economic factors are at play.

In the developed world, the explanation is largely cultural: the rising acceptance of divorce and the increased number of out-of-wedlock births. In Iran, the cultural pressure against—as well as the lack of economic options for—single women is critical. But what of Namibia? The high rate of female-headed households is related to high mortality rates among males, the large number of illegitimate births, and the widespread use of migrant labor in the country, which usually draws the men away from their families for extended periods and leaves the women to head the household. In short, then, the rise in the number of female-headed households has no single cause in Namibia. The reasons for female-headed households vary widely by society, though the number of such households is rising in most parts of the world.

AGE AND SEX STRUCTURES

Age

Changes in household size and composition are following a similar trend in both the developed and developing worlds, despite a difference in the pace of the changes, but the same cannot be said for age structures. An age structure is a snapshot of the number of persons in each age group, or cohort, of a society at a particular moment. Although these cohorts are sometimes distributed into segments as small as five years, demographers generally prefer to use three large segments: children or dependents (0-14); adults of working age (15-64), and older adults generally beyond working age (65 and up). (Readers in developed countries may find that the age when actual adulthood commences here seems early, but in many developing countries—even with the rise in educational opportunities—15 is the age at which many children begin to work.)

With respect to age structure, population experts generally distinguish three kinds of societies. A "young" society is one in which at least

35 percent of the population is under the age of 15 and less than 5 percent is over age 65; a "balanced" age structure refers to a society where 25 to 35 percent of the population is under age 15 and 5 to 10 percent of the population is over 65; an "old" society is one in which less than 25 percent of the population is under age 15 and more than 10 percent is over age 65. Most of the developing world falls into the first two categories, while virtually all of the developed world falls into the third.

Age structures are often pictured as pyramids, though this is not always the best way to describe the shape of age structures. A pyramid consists of bars representing each age cohort placed one on top of another. In "young" societies, the bulk of the people are represented in broader lower bars, which quickly taper off, forming a kind of pyramid. In "balanced" societies, the best description of the age cohorts might be a cone, in which a slightly larger base tapers off gradually. An "old" society might best be depicted as a column, in which the elderly and the young are roughly even.

The oldest societies are those of Europe, especially Western Europe, where modern medical techniques that extend life, combined with rapidly declining birth rates, produce populations in which the percentages of persons under age 15 and over age 65 are nearly equal. Italy, for example, has one of the lowest birth rates in the world—9.9 per 1,000 persons—and one of the oldest age structures—just 15 percent of the population is under age 15 and 17 percent is over age 65. East European countries, though also experiencing low birth rates, do not have quite as old an age structure because of rising death rates, in the wake of the collapse of communism and the social welfare network the communist governments provided. Russia has a low birth rate of 10.2 per 1,000 persons, but the declining life expectancy—now down to 63 years—means that the age structure, while still "old," is younger than that of Italy. In Russia, 21 percent of the population is under age 15, while some 12 percent is over age 65.

Countries with a moderate rate of population growth, such as the United States, offer what at first appears to be an age structure similar to Russia's. In the United States, some 22 percent of the population is under the age of 15, while 13 percent is over 65. The causes for this convergence of age structures, however, are very different in the two countries. Whereas in Russia declining life expectancy and falling birth rates explain the moderately old age structure, in the United States the causes lie in families with more children, especially among immigrants.

The "balanced countries" (a technical term, not meant to imply the ideal) include many of the newly industrialized and urbanized countries of East and Southeast Asia. In these regions, traditionally high birth rates are slowly being reduced by family planning programs, the economic decision making of parents, and changing cultural attitudes about families and children. At the same time, high death rates are being brought down through a combination of better diet and health care. Thailand, for example, has an age structure in which 25 percent of the population is under age 15 and 6 percent is over age 65. Other "balanced" countries include the more developed Latin American countries like Argentina, where 28 percent of the population is under age 15 and 9 percent is over age 65. A final group of "balanced" countries includes those that are less developed industrially but have advanced family planning programs. The most significant example of this group is China, where 26 percent of the population is under the age of 15, while 7 percent is over 65.

The "young" societies include virtually all of Africa, Southwest Asia, and tropical Latin America, though this last group has begun to slip into the younger end of the "balanced" group. To take three key examples: in Brazil 31 percent of the population is under the age 15 and 4 percent over 65, while in Nigeria and Iran 45 percent of the population is under age 15 and just 3 percent is over age 65. The key factor in "young" societies is continued high birth rates, since in many of these countries improved diet and health care mean longer life expectancy.

Both "old" and "young" populations present

problems for governments and social planners. In the case of the former, large segments of the population have moved beyond working age. Since this age structure is typical of societies—such as those in Europe or North America—in which social programs have replaced children and families as providers of care for the elderly, a political and economic dilemma arises: how to provide funds for the retired without draining the resources of those who are working through excessively high taxation. Young societies have the same problem, but in reverse: Large numbers of children tax the abilities of working-age people to support them.

Demographers measure the extent of these problems with what they call the "dependency ratio," the ratio of people of nonworking or dependent ages (under 15 and over 65) to those of working age. The ratio is calculated as follows: Japan, where 31 percent of the population is under 15 or over 65 and 69 percent is of working age, has a dependency ratio of 31/69, or .45. By comparison, in the Philippines, where 42 percent of the population is of nonworking age and 58 percent is of working age, the dependency ratio is 42/58, or .72. This means that an average working-age person in the Philippines has to support nearly three-quarters of a person more than his or her counterpart in Japan.

Of course, both societies face greater problems in the future. As Japan's population continues to age, its dependency ratio will rise. In developing countries like the Philippines, the future holds quite different and potentially more explosive political and economic problems. The increasing number of young persons means that jobs, housing, and other facilities must be created for the society to maintain current standards of living. And as these youths move into their reproductive years, they will flood the society with new children—even if they have fewer per family than their parents did.

Sex

Sex structures, like age structures, offer a snapshot of a society at a particular moment. The extreme differences among countries evident in age structures do not appear regarding sex structures, simply because, statistically speaking, there are only two "cohorts," male and female, which are normally evenly distributed. However, an evenly balanced sex structure can be skewed for several reasons. The first relates to women's status. If male children are valued more highly than female children, then human intervention may lead to a higher male to female ratio. As discussed above, India, which has 1.08 males for every female, illustrates this sex structure phenomenon.

The second is out- and in-migration. In general, males tend to migrate more often than do females. So, countries with high levels of out-migration have a higher ratio of females to males. El Salvador is a typical example, with a female-to-male ratio of 1.08. Conversely, countries that have high in-migration rates have higher male-to-female ratios among the younger age cohorts in which most immigrants lie.

Of course, one has to be extremely careful with these statistics, since most countries with high out-migration rates tend to be in the developing world, where life expectancy is shorter, while countries with high in-migration rates tend to be in the developed world where life expectancies are longer. This is important to keep in mind because women tend to live longer than men in all developed societies and in all but the poorest developing societies (exceptions being places where health care is so inadequate and birth rates are so high that many women die in childbirth). Indeed, the fact that women tend to live longer is the main reason women tend to outnumber men in the vast majority of countries.

Households have indeed changed dramatically over the course of the past 200 years, a period roughly corresponding to the birth of industrialization in England and its spread to much of the rest of the globe. Households have become smaller and more nuclear. But now a new phenomenon is occurring in the developed world and, to a lesser extent, in the more Westernized, urban sections of the developing world. With the rise of women's economic independence and the acceptance of alternative lifestyles—including lifelong single status and single parenthood—the household appears to be changing again, though the trend toward ever-smaller families continues.

FURTHER READINGS

Adepoju, Aderanti, ed. *Family, Population and Development in Africa.* London and Atlantic Highlands, NJ: Zed Books, 1997.

Bandarage, Asoka. *Women, Population and Global Crisis: A Political-Economic Analysis.* London and Atlantic Highlands, NJ: Zed Books, 1997.

Corson, Stephen, Richard Derman, and Louise B. Tyrer, eds. *Fertility Control.* Boston: Little Brown, 1984; 2nd edition, London, Ontario: Goldin, 1994.

Donaldson, Loraine. *Fertility Transition: The Social Dynamics of Population Change.* Oxford and Cambridge, MA: Blackwell, 1991.

Finkle, Jason, and C. Alison McIntosh, eds. *The New Politics of Population: Conflict and Consensus in Family Planning.* New York: Population Council, 1994.

Goldscheider, Calvin, ed. *Fertility Transitions, Family Structure, and Population Policy.* Boulder, CO: Westview Press, 1992.

Hartmann, Betsy. *Reproductive Rights and Wrongs: The Global Politics of Population Control and Contraceptive Choice.* New York: Harper, 1987; revised as *Reproductive Rights and Wrongs: The Global Politics of Population Control,* Boston: South End Press, 1995.

Moffett, George D. *Critical Masses: The Global Population Challenge.* New York: Viking, 1994; London: Penguin, 1995.

Niven, Catherine, and Anne Walker, eds. *Reproductive Potential and Fertility Control.* Boston and Oxford: Butterworth-Heinemann, 1996.

Quale, G. Robina. *Families in Context: A World History of Population.* New York: Greenwood Press, 1992.

Section 5

Demography and Cultural Identity

HISTORY OF STATES AND ETHNICITY

Nearly six billion in all, the human community often seems as if it were divided into 6 billion different subgroups. There are differences of race, ethnicity, language, religion, and culture, along with biological distinctions like sex and economic differences such as class. Laid over these differences is the nation-state. A relatively new phenomenon in human history, the nation-state has become the dominant political entity in the world today. But the nation-state and the various identities outlined above do not always correspond. And therein lies the problem of ethnic and cultural identity and ethnic and cultural conflict, two phenomena that have become especially acute in recent years as the basic global ideological division—Western capitalism versus Eastern communism— has largely faded away.

Julius Nyerere, the former president of Tanzania, well understood the dilemma as it pertained to Africa. He remarked that because Africa's borders were so absurdly drawn, they must remain unchanging. Nyerere's paradoxical statement revealed much about Africa's past and its present predicament. More than in other parts of the developing world, the national borders in Africa were drawn up in the late nineteenth century by European colonialists who took little notice of existing ethnic, religious, and linguistic settlement patterns. This ignorance is hardly surprising given the fact that the colonial borders—many of which became national borders after the wave of independence that

swept Africa in the 1960s—were drawn solely by Europeans, without consultation with Africans. The result of this practice was a collection of nations in which numerous ethnicities, religions, and language groups coexisted—often uneasily—within a single sovereign state. Despite these shortcomings, Nyerere believed, to disturb these borders might unleash endless wars in Africa.

The Middle East, another arena where Europeans did the border drawing—this time in the wake of World War I—found itself with a problem exactly the opposite of Africa's. Here, the Europeans—acting under the authority of the League of Nations, the predecessor of the United Nations—divided a single cultural, religious, and ethnic group—the Arabs—among many states. Arab historians believe this was done to ensure that no great post-independent pan-Arab state would challenge European hegemony. Of course, it should also be noted that some of the same problems of several ethnicities or religious groups in one state plagued the Middle East as it did Africa. In Iraq, for example, Shi'a Muslim Arabs represent more than 50 percent of the population, with Sunni Muslim Arabs and Sunni Muslim, non-Arab Kurds constituting the rest.

More than in other places in the world, in Africa and the Middle East, borders reflect an almost complete disregard for cultural divisions and unities. These regions are unique only in the degree that each state represents an artificial unit or place. Indeed, many of the states of the world—especially among the former communist

Table 5.1

Nation-States and Minorities (minority = at least 10 percent of the population)

Region	Total no. of countries*	Ethnic/racial minority	Language minority	Religious minority	No majority	No minority
Africa	52	16	4	8	29	4
Latin America/ Caribbean	34	15	2	6	4	12
North America	2	2	1	2	0	0
Asia	42	18	13	15	8	13
Europe	46	15	14	19	2	18
Oceania	14	3	0	7	2	5
World	190	69	34	57	45	52

* The number of different minorities does not correspond to total countries because many countries have more than one minority.

states of Eastern Europe and the Soviet Union—are home to multiple ethnic, religious, and linguistic groups, or, conversely, have larger groups broken up into different states. Even Western Europe, where the idea of nationalism first took shape, contains states with culturally divided polities. The very birthplace of nationalism—France—includes indigenous, geographically contained cultural minorities that believe they have a right to cultural autonomy.

South and East Asia and the Americas also consist largely of states with significant ethnic, religious, and linguistic minorities. In Asia, those states with large minorities include some of the biggest (India, Indonesia, and Iran), as well as smaller states such as Malaysia and Sri Lanka.

In the Americas, the mix of cultural, religious, and ethnic groups is the result largely of immigration or slavery. While the latter's legacy of racism leaves a heritage of ethnic bitterness in the United States, Brazil, and several smaller countries, immigration has blurred differences through what used to be called the "melting pot." Even with today's emphasis on cultural roots and identity politics, the power of assimilation—along with the fact that minorities in immigrant countries tend to be dispersed geographically—has helped eliminate the worst of irredentist, or separatist, impulses. The major exception to this is Canada, where a significant

French minority in Quebec seems to have opted for independence, even if the English speakers there continue to prevent a majority of Québécois from voting for separation from Canada.

Religions and Ethnic Edentity

A review of the world's religions reveals that a majority of countries today either have significant ethnic, linguistic, or religious minorities or are so divided that they lack a single cultural majority. Table 5.1 shows how many countries either have significant minorities (meaning at least 10 percent of the population) or so many minorities that there is no majority culture.

Of the 190 countries surveyed, only 52 had no significant ethnic, linguistic, or religious minorities. The regions with the highest rate of nonminority countries were Latin America and Europe. This should not be surprising, since Europe and Latin American represent regions where nationalism and the modern nation-state have existed for the longest time. At the other extreme—countries with no clear ethnic, religious, or linguistic majority—the largest number by far was in Africa. Some 56 percent of African countries do not have a single cultural majority and, of all the countries without a single cultural majority, 64 percent were in Africa. As for specific types of minorities, the most common worldwide was ethnic/racial. Some 36 percent of the countries in the world have significant racial or ethnic minorities, followed by 30 percent with religious minorities, and about 18 percent with linguistic minorities.

Ethnic, linguistic, and religious minorities can contribute greatly to the economic and cultural life of a country. Imagine American music without the influence of African-Americans or American food without the input of Asian-Americans. At the same time, the presence of minorities—as well as the lack of a majority culture—can create enormous political, economic, and social problems. Because ethnic identity is so heavily determined by history, it is difficult to generalize about the significance of ethnic minorities from one state to another and one society to another. Instead, a national and regional approach is required. The following section discusses the ethnic, religious, and linguistic composition of the various regions of the world, as well as selecting several representative or significant states from those regions for closer examination. The emphasis is on demography rather than culture; that is, on how demography shapes cultural minorities and majorities, and how cultural minorities and majorities, affect demography.

Africa

As noted above, African borders were determined largely by European colonialists, with little regard to existing settlement patterns. Almost all African states have minorities. These states can be divided into two rough groups: those in which there is no absolute majority, and those in which there are one or more significant minority groups. This represents a key difference in the histories of those countries since independence, as the following various country examples will show.

Nigeria

A British colony until 1960 and the most populous state in Africa, Nigeria consists of dozens of minor ethnic groups, as well as four major ones: the Hausa, the Fulani, the Yoruba, and the Ibo. The main division in the country falls along religious and geographic lines, however. The northern part of the country is dominated by the Muslim Hausa and Fulani; the southern half of the nation is mainly Christian or practices the trational faiths of the Ibo and Yoruba. The population is roughly 50 percent Muslim and 50 percent non-Muslim.

Rapid population growth in all parts of the country has meant that this ratio of Muslims to non-Muslims has not changed. However, the urban migration of the past thirty years has allowed the south's population to grow considerably at the expense of the north, since the country's major cities—including Lagos, its largest metropolis—are located in the south, as are the crucial gas and oil fields that generate the vast bulk of the country's revenues. This fact has only increased northerners' anxieties of southerners dominating the state.

In the first years after Nigeria's independence, the southern Christians governed the country. The northern Muslims felt excluded from the political and economic centers of power, although, under the British, the Muslims had been used largely as the colony's soldiers and police. This military tradition continued after independence, eventually leading in the mid-1960s to a coup by northern officers. This was followed by a secession by the Ibos in 1967 and the horrific Biafra secession war in which up to a million Nigerians died, most of them Ibo civilians. Fearing southern dominance ever since, the northern Muslim military elite has maintained an iron grip on political power to this day.

Rwanda

Rwanda, a former Belgian colony in the Great Lakes region of East Africa, has long been one of the most agriculturally fertile and densely populated parts of Africa. As of 1995, there were more than 670 persons living on every square mile of land. Because of the historically high density rates, the country developed a highly bureaucratic, monarchical system long before the arrival of European colonizers at the end of the nineteenth century.

Ethnically, the country has been divided into two main ethnic groups: the Tutsis and the Hutus. Although the origins of the former, a pastoral people composing 10 percent of the population, are unclear, they eventually came to dominate and subjugate the majority Hutus. But there has been much intermarriage and comingling of the two peoples, and in time they came to speak the same language.

When the Belgians came, they tended to favor the Tutsis. With their more angular features and warlike tradition, the Tutsis were seen as racially superior. Tutsis were made the local administrators and police of the colony. Upon independence, the Belgians handed power over to them. The Tutsis were quickly overthrown and subjected to nearly constant harassment from the government for thirty years, leading eventually to the infamous genocide of 1994, when Hutus murdered as many as 500,000 or nearly 80 percent of the Rwandan Tutsi population, until forced to stop by an invading Tutsi army from Uganda. These Tutsis from Uganda continue to rule the country.

Sudan

The largest country in Africa by area—nearly a million square miles—Sudan was ruled jointly by Great Britain and Egypt until 1956, when it gained its independence. Because of its huge size, Sudan straddled the line dividing Arab-dominated North Africa from black-dominated Central Africa. This division corresponded roughly to the country's religious and linguistic split between the Muslim, Arabic-speaking north and the Christian and animist south, where a variety of African languages were spoken.

Although Arabs composed only 40 percent of the population, they dominated the country's politics, since both the British and Egyptian administrators established more schools in the north. After Sudan's independence, the northern Arabs largely ignored the needs of the southern blacks. By the 1960s, this neglect had sparked a bitter civil war that has persisted to this day.

Latin America

Latin America has one of the most racially mixed populations in the world. Different races have intermarried and had children together to a much greater degree than in North America and Asia. Out of this Latin American mixing came two distinctive populations: the Spanish-speaking mestizo of mainland Latin America, who are mixed Indian and European, and the mulatto, who are mixed European and African. The mulatto are prevalent in Brazil and in the Spanish-speaking Caribbean islands. The descendents of European settlers have largely dominated the politics and business of Latin America.

Brazil

The largest country in South America in both geographic area and population, Brazil is the largest Portuguese-speaking country in the world. First settled by Amer-Indians tens of thousands of years ago, Brazil was colonized by the Portuguese beginning in the sixteenth century, and achieved full independence near the end of the nineteenth century. Outside the remote and barely settled Amazon region, most Amer-Indians quickly died out from diseases like smallpox and the measles because they had no immunities to the new illnesses introduced by Europeans.

During those three hundred years of Portuguese rule, millions of Africans were transported to Brazil as slaves, mostly to labor on the plantations in the central and northeastern parts of the country. Slavery was abolished near the end of the nineteenth century. Both during and after the time of slavery, however, there were few white females in these regions. The male white settlers often took African women as wives or had children by them without marriage. Meanwhile, by the late nineteenth and early twentieth centuries, the more temperate regions of southern Brazil were attracting European immigrants by the millions.

This dual influx of Africans in the north and Europeans in the south gives Brazil its complex racial makeup, in which 55 percent of the population is labeled white, 39 percent mulatto, and 6 percent African. Because of their tradition of racial intermixing, Brazilians claim that their society is much more racially tolerant than that of the United States, which has a somewhat similar racial profile. But Brazil has the most unequal distribution of wealth of any country in the world, and this inequality breaks down largely along racial lines, with whites far richer than mulattos and blacks.

Guatemala

The most populous country in Central America, Guatemala was part of Spain's American empire until the early part of the nineteenth century. As in other parts of Latin America, Spanish colonizers—most of whom were male—intermarried and interbred with the native population, creating a large group of mestizos. Yet in Guatemala, unlike other Latin American countries, a significant Indian population—many of them descendents of the Maya—survived in the Guatemalan highlands, where they maintained their own culture and language, even if they adopted Roman Catholicism. So, today, 60 percent of Guatemalans speak Spanish, while 40 percent continue to speak Mayan and other Indian languages. At the same time, virtually all Guatemalans, mestizo or Indian, practice Christianity, usually as Roman Catholics but increasingly as evangelical Protestants.

Despite their numbers, the Indians of Guatemala remained politically and economically powerless. Many of them were forcibly recruited to work the plantations of the lowlands—plantations owned by North American corporations and administered by Spanish-speaking mestizos or whites. When the Indians began to resist with a guerrilla movement in the 1970s, the army cracked down, conducting a brutal—some say genocidal—campaign against the Indians of the highlands. It is estimated that some 100,000 Indians, mostly civilians, were killed at the hands of the Guatemalan army in the 1980s.

Trinidad and Tobago

Trinidad and Tobago, twin islands at the southern end of the Lesser Antilles, has one of the most peculiar ethnic and religious profiles of any country in Latin America. First a Spanish, then a French, and finally a British colonial possession, Trinidad relied heavily on the population of African slaves who worked the commercial plantations. In 1833, Britain outlawed slavery and the plantation system collapsed. To revive it, planters came up with a plan to bring in tens of thousands of indentured servants from India, another British colony.

In 1962, Trinidad won its independence from Britain. Since then, the country's racial relations have exhibited a remarkable tolerance, largely due to the unofficial power-sharing arrangements in the country, in which the descendents of Asian Indians run the business sector and the descendents of African slaves administer the government. Although generally tolerant of each other, the two groups rarely intermarry or interbreed. Trinidad's racial profile reflects this complex history, with 43 percent of the population black, 40 percent Asian Indian, and just 14 percent mixed. The remaining 3 percent consists of whites and Chinese. Religious affiliation follows a similar division: Most blacks are Christian, and most Asian Indians are Hindu or Muslim. Tobago is almost entirely black and Christian, as there were few imported Asian workers because of limited plantation agriculture.

North America

The continent of North America consists of two countries: Canada and the United States. In many ways, these countries have similar ethnic profiles. Both were originally inhabited by indigenous populations; colonized by Britain; and eventually settled by waves of immigration from Europe and, more recently, Asia. But these similarities mask key differences. Canada never condoned slavery and so has few people of African descent. Moreover, its greater land area and smaller European population allowed native American Indian nations to maintain more cohesion. But, most important, Canada and the United States differ linguistically—the former being bilingual and the latter generally only English-speaking.

Canada

France was the first European country to settle Canada. But unlike the English colonists to the south, the French did not emigrate to the country in tremendous numbers. By the mid-eighteenth century, English colonists in North America outnumbered the French by more than ten to one. In the French and Indian Wars from 1756 to 1763, the English used their numerical superiority to conquer French Canada. Over the years, the English came to dominate the colony as a whole, both politically and economically. This was also true of the first hundred years of independent Canadian history, from the 1860s to the 1960s. Moreover, the waves of European immigrants who came to the country in the late nineteenth and early twentieth centuries adopted English as their primary language.

So, today, while only 40 percent of Canadians trace their origins to Great Britain, 70 percent speak English as their first language. Meanwhile, only 27 percent of Canadians trace their origins to France and roughly a similar percentage speak French as their first language. (A small percentage of Canadians speak native Indian languages.) But the French speakers are geographically concentrated in the province of Quebec. Beginning in the 1960s, they have agitated for independence. In recent referenda on the subject, the majority of French-speaking Québécois have voted for separation from Canada, but they have been unable to win an absolute majority because of the near-total opposition of English speakers in the province, including many of the newest immigrants from the Caribbean and Asia.

United States

America's current ethnic composition—and ethnic tensions—can be traced through its history. During the 1600s and 1700s, settlers poured in largely from Great Britain and Northern Europe, pushed back the native Americans to west of the Appalachian mountains, and imported hundreds of thousands of African slaves, primarily to the southern part of the country. At the same time, these so-called White Anglo-Saxon Protestants (WASPs) dominated government and business until the twentieth century.

In the nineteenth century, the country expanded westward to the Pacific Ocean, annexing nearly half of Mexico and confining the surviving native Americans to reservations. Meanwhile, slavery ended, but racist oppression continued against African-Americans. The nineteenth and early twentieth centuries also saw a massive influx of immigrants from Eastern and Southern Europe, China, and Mexico.

During the middle third of the twentieth century, immigration was reduced by legislation. But, at the same time, a massive migration of African-Americans from the southern to the northern portion of the United States occurred. Since the passage of new, more open immigration laws in the 1960s, a new wave of arrivals, this time largely from Asia and Latin America, has come to America's shores.

America's current ethnic profile reflects this history. African-Americans—two-thirds of whom are now in the northern United States and one-third in the southern part of the country—remain the largest minority group, composing about 12 percent of the population. But it is expected that they will be outnumbered by Hispanics early in the twenty-first century. As of 1997, Hispanics made up about 11 percent of the U.S. population, and Asians comprised another 4 percent. If current trends continue, people of European descent will make up less than half the population by the middle of the next century.

Asia

It is, of course, difficult to generalize about such a vast and heavily populated region as Asia, but several overall points can be made. Like Africa, Asia was heavily colonized or dominated by European imperialists in the late nineteenth and early twentieth centuries. But, unlike African states, most Asian states were further along on the road to nationhood upon the arrival of the Europeans, so colonial borders could roughly follow ethnic lines. In addition, many Asian states were empires of their own. Countries like China, India, and Iran housed numerous minority peoples within their borders.

Malaysia

Until the economic meltdown of 1997, Malaysia had one of the fastest-growing economies in the world, growing at an annual rate of 8 percent for more than a decade. Its per capita income in 1995 was $9,800, placing it in the top tier of developing countries.

This economic success has helped offset the ethnic tensions that once plagued the country. Malaysia's population for most of this century has been divided into roughly three groups. The native Muslim Malays make up roughly 60 percent of the population. Ethnic Chinese, who for hundreds of years have been settling in this country, which sits astride key trading routes in East Asia, compose about a third of the population. The remainder consists largely of Indians, brought by the British to work on plantations in what was called Malaya in the late nineteenth and early twentieth centuries.

Because the Chinese controlled much of the state's business, ethnic tensions built up between them and the more rural and impoverished Malays. Some of this tension took on religious overtones, as the Malays tried to legislate Muslim precepts into law. Gradually, a compromise has been reached between the two groups, giving Malays control of the government and, through affirmative action–type programs, better educational opportunities. Thus Malaysia has been able to avoid the anti-Chinese violence that recently erupted in neighboring Indonesia.

India

The second largest country in population in the world, India was born in a fire of ethnic violence. A largely Hindu region of the world through the early modern age, India began to come under the control of Muslim emperors by the 1500s. Particularly in the northern part of the country, millions of Hindus—largely from low castes, or inherited classes—converted to Islam over the next several centuries. By 1900—by which time the British had thoroughly colonized the region—roughly 30 percent of the subcontinent (including modern-day Pakistan and Bangladesh) was Muslim.

The British generally recruited Muslims to serve in the military and the police force. At the same time, the early independence movement was dominated by Hindus—a fact of some concern to Muslim nationalists, who demanded a separate state of their own. At the time of India's independence in 1947, Britain was forced by Muslim militants and politicians to divide the subcontinent into two countries, India and Pakistan. With this partition came violence. More than a million people of Hindu or Muslim descent were massacred simply for being in the sector predominantly populated by the other group. Some 15 million people were forced to migrate: Muslims to Pakistan, Hindus (and other non-Muslims) to India. Because of this mass migration, India's Muslim population shrank to about 15 percent, where it remains today. Meanwhile, tensions persist both between Pakistan and India, and between India's Hindu majority and Muslim minority, especially since the electoral victory of a Hindu nationalist party in 1997.

Israel

Unique among the countries of the world, Israel is not only a state of its citizens, but also a homeland for Jews around the world, who are granted immediate and automatic citizenship upon their arrival in Israel and their declaration of an intention to remain there. The Palestinians who left—or were forced out—during Israel's independence war in 1948–1949 are not permitted to return.

Israel is also one of the most ethnically heterogenous countries in the world. Twenty percent of its citizens are Arab (who are mostly Muslim, though a minority are Christian or Druze), and the 80 percent who are Jewish are racially and ethnically diverse, owing to the history of Jews in the twentieth century. There are four major groups of Jews worldwide, only one of which—those living in the Middle East—moved to the country early on. Most European Jews were killed in the Holocaust; most American Jews preferred to stay in the United States; and most Jews in the former Soviet Union were not permitted to emigrate (until the collapse of the Soviet Union. Since that time, however, many have left).

Not surprisingly, this complex mix of religion and ethnicity has dominated the country's history for all of its fifty years as a modern state. The conflict between Palestinian Arabs and Israeli Jews is well known. But there has also been the struggle for political and economic power between Sephardic Jews, who come from the Middle East, and Ashkenazi Jews, who come from Europe and the Americas. In only one area has Israel proved successful at dissolving differences: linguistically. It has been able to revive and disseminate the use of Hebrew as the language of all its people.

Turkey

Once at the core of the great Ottoman empire—which ruled the Middle East and southeastern Europe—Turkey's power ebbed in the face of the more aggressive British and Russian empires in the nineteenth century. The Ottomans, who sided with Germany in World War I, were utterly defeated and had their empire stripped from them at the conclusion of the war in 1918. Even the Anatolian heartland of Turkey seemed threatened with dismemberment.

But out of this disaster emerged Kemal Ataturk, a Turkish military officer, who was able to salvage the country by driving out the British and Greek invaders. Rather than opting for a multiethnic state, Ataturk and his successors—who rule the country to this day—brutally imposed a Turkish identity on all inhabitants. This was particularly galling for the Kurdish minority in the southeastern part of the country. The Kurds, who are heirs to one of the most ancient cultures in the world, compose about 20 percent of the population and are currently engaged in a guerrilla struggle for independence or cultural autonomy. But the military and political elite are unwilling to accept any further division of the country. Thus, the war in Turkish Kurdistan grinds on.

Europe

Europe is where both the modern nation-state and modern nationalism were born—the former as early as the fifteenth century in Western Europe, the latter a by-product of the French Revolution of the late eighteenth century. In the nineteenth century, the concept of the nation-state spread to Central Europe, and in the early twentieth century it moved on to the eastern half of the continent. But only with the collapse of the last great European empire—the Soviet Union in 1991—did nationalism finally triumph in Eastern Europe. Many European states are home to significant ethnic minorities—several of which have agitated politically or militarily for their independence.

Bosnia and Herzegovina

Until 1992—when its citizens voted for independence—Bosnia and Herzegovina constituted one of six provinces of the Yugoslav Federation. This federation and the territory in which it existed had a checkered history. Conquered by the Muslim Ottomans in the sixteenth and seventeenth centuries, portions of it were gradually annexed to the Austro-Hungarian empire or won their independence until, by the eve of World War I, the Ottomans had been completely driven out—not, however, before hundreds of thousands of Muslims from other parts of the Ottoman Empire had settled in the region, alongside thousands of local inhabitants who had converted to Islam. The effect of these conversions and settlements was a patchwork of Christian (both Eastern Orthodox and Roman Catholic) and Muslim communities in what would first become Yugoslavia and then Bosnia and Herzegovina.

Following World War I, the various parts of what would become Yugoslavia were united under Serbian King Peter to form the Kingdom of Serbs, Croats, and Slovenes. In 1929, the name was changed to the more inclusive Yugoslavia, which, in Serbo-Croatian, means Land of the Southern Slavs. During World War II, the territory was occupied by the Nazis and was liberated in large part by the communist partisans under Marshal Tito (Josef Broz), who used strong-arm tactics and economic stimuli to dampen the religious and ethnolinguistic rivalries. But after his death in 1980, the situation slowly began to unravel, and after the fall of communism in Eastern Europe in 1989, it finally collapsed.

Of all the former Yugoslav republics, Bosnia was the most divided religiously and ethnically. Eastern Orthodox Serbs and Bosnian Muslims each composed about 40 percent of the population, while Roman Catholic Croatians constituted 20 percent. The country was plunged into war as the local Serbs—backed by Serbia itself—tried to carve out an independent state. Only with the intervention of the North Atlantic Treaty Organization (NATO) in the mid-1990s was the war stopped. Tensions remain high however, and Bosnia is still provisionally divided into Serbian and Bosnian/Croatian sectors.

Northern Ireland (United Kingdom)

Often called the world's first modern European colony, Ireland was conquered by England in the late Middle Ages. Beginning in the 1500s and 1600s, the English government began to recruit Scottish people to settle in Ireland, as a kind of settler militia society, to maintain English control there. Most settled in what would become the northern six counties that now make up Northern Ireland, or Ulster. The settlers were Protestant; the indigenous inhabitants of Ireland were Catholic.

In 1916, the southern part of Ireland won its independence, but the north remained part of the United Kingdom. London argued that since 60 percent of Northern Ireland was Protestant—and preferred to remain British—Northern Ireland should remain part of the United Kingdom. Over the centuries, the English conquest and the Protestant presence led to a two-tiered society in Northern Ireland, with Protestants ruling over the Catholics. This led to bitterness, violence, and the outbreak of a civil war that has lasted from 1969 to the present.

Many observers believe that, given enough time, the Catholics—who tend to have larger families than the Protestants—will become the majority and

vote peacefully for amalgation with Ireland. But because of the poor economy, out-migration rates in the region remain high, and the majority of those who leave are poor and Catholic.

Spain

Ironically, although it was among the first states to form in Europe—the monarchies of Castille and Aragon merged in the late 1400s—Spain has also been home to some of the most vociferous ethnic minorities in modern European history. Two groups among these stand out: the Basques in the north and the Catalans in the northeast.

Brutally suppressed under the dictatorship of Francisco Franco from the late 1930s until his death in 1975, the movements for Basque and Catalan autonomy and independence have become quite potent since Spain's return to republican rule in the late 1970s. Both the Catalans and the Basques (who speak one of the most ancient languages in the world, one unrelated to any other in Europe) are culturally distinctive. But it may be their economic position that spurs on their ethnic and linguistic demands. Two of the most prosperous areas of Spain, the Basque region and Catalonia, do not want to be burdened by supporting the central government in Madrid or the poorer regions in the south.

Oceania

The smallest of the world's major regions in both population and land area, Oceania consists of two major Western-style countries—Australia and New Zealand—and several tiny island republics inhabited by Melanesian, Micronesian, and Polynesian peoples. In addition, several islands remain colonies of France (French Polynesia) and territories of the United States (American Samoa and Guam). All were once colonized by European or American governments, but only Australia and New Zealand became states settled largely by Europeans.

Australia

Initially settled by convicts from England, Australia continued to be largely a colony of Britain, even after independence in 1910. Most of its people—aside from the tiny minority of native Aborigines—came from the Great Britain, which dominated the country's culture. This began to change in the 1960s. First, there was Australia's involvement in the Vietnam War. Then came the rise of the Asian economies, which forged closer financial links between the two regions. And, finally, there has been a wave of Asian immigrants to Australia, who now outnumber the Aborigines four to one and make up almost 5 percent of the country's population. While this has produced a racist backlash among a minority of Australia's whites, most accept that the country must break its old but geographically strained ties with England and become more culturally and economically integrated with nearby Asia.

Fiji

Once an independent Melanesian kingdom, Fiji came under British rule as a protectorate in the late nineteenth century. Shortly thereafter, Britain began to import Indian laborers to work the commercial plantations of the islands. Gradually, the population of the two groups—the native Melanesians and the immigrant Indians—grew to be about even. During the first years of independence during the 1970s and early 1980s, the country was ruled by a consortium of Fijians and Indians. But, in 1987, Fijian nationalists in the army, angry about Indian control of the country's economy, overthrew the government and instituted programs aimed at improving the educational and economic opportunities of Fijians.

GLOBAL ISSUES

The demographic implications of ethnic, linguistic, and religious divisions are not confined to nation-states, as the previous survey of countries might imply. Demography and cultural issues can also be global. Since the fall of communism in the late 1980s and the subsequent end of the Cold War, cultural divisions seem to have taken precedence over ideological ones. Three of these cultural issues—(1) ethnic and racial, (2) linguis-

tic and cultural, and (3) religious—appear to be especially crucial.

Ethnic and Racial

Near the beginning of the century, the African-American sociologist W.E.B. Dubois pronounced that "the problem of the twentieth century is the problem of the color-line—the relation of the darker to the lighter races of men in Asia and Africa, in America and the islands of the sea." Despite the diversion of the Cold War—which pitted two white superpowers against each other—and the rapid decolonization of the developing world in the two decades after World War II ended, Dubois's remarks remain prescient. Euphemisms like "developed" and "developing worlds" or "first" and "third worlds" only partly hide the reality: With few exceptions, most of the wealthier countries of the world remain predominantly white.

This was not always so. Until the industrial revolution and the vast spread of European colonialism to Africa and Asia (the Americas, of course, were colonized and won their independence much earlier), the differences in wealth between what we now call the developed and developing worlds were minimal, as is reflected in birth and death rates. In the latter half of the eighteenth century, what are now the developed nations of the world had birth and death rates of 38 and 34 per 1,000 persons, respectively; what are now the developing nations had rates of 41 and 37 per 1,000, respectively. But the industrial revolution and the conquest of much of the world by Europe changed that. By the first decade of this century, the developed world had birth and death rates of 34 and 21 per 1,000, respectively, while the developing world had rates of 41 and 34 per 1,000.

The income and wealth ratios were even more sharply divergent. In the 1700s, it is estimated that the ratio of incomes in what are now developed countries to what are now developing countries was just three to two. Today, it is roughly ten to one. A 1998 United Nations Development Program study found that the world's richest 20 percent consumed 86 percent of all goods and services, half the energy, and nearly half the animal protein in the world. And despite the recent collapse of former white Soviet bloc countries and the rise of a few Asian economies and petroleum-rich, underpopulated countries in the Middle East, the divide between rich and poor remains largely a divide between whites and nonwhites.

Linguistic and Cultural

Classically defined, imperialism implies the political and economic control of one country by another. In so effecting this conquest, the imperialist power exploits the colony for cheap natural resources or labor and as a market for manufactured goods of the mother country. This was the model the British used in their global empire. And, arguably, this is the model—aside from outright annexation—that the United States has used to maintain its economic control over much of Latin America. Whether the United States is an imperialist power is more widely debated. Those who argue in the affirmative say that the only difference between the British Empire and U.S. economic hegemony in Latin America for instance is that, in the latter case, the region has not been annexed politically. Still, proponents of the so-called neo-colonialist argument insist that, through U.S.-based multinational corporations and U.S.-dominated international lending institutions like the World Bank and the International Monetary Fund, the United States is able to exploit natural and human resources, while dominating local markets for manufactured goods. Opponents of the neo-colonialist argument insist trade in the region is open and free, and that various other developed nations play as important a role as the United States does in the development of Latin American economies. Moreover, they insist that local elites—not foreign interests—have control over the political and economic decision-making process. More controversial is the definition of imperialism as a cultural offensive. Can it be called imperialism if one nation aggressively exports its cultural products—and, by implication, its language—to the rest of the world, especially if

the rest of the world can be said to accept it voluntarily? Clearly, one such country is the United States, which exports its film, fashion, TV shows, advertising, sports, music, and, most recently, its Internet to the rest of the world.

To critics of American cultural and linguistic hegemony, or dominance (though the basis for the linguistic hegemony of English was laid by British imperialists), the threat is to indigenous cultures and languages around the world. Nor is this division one between the developed and the developing worlds. Indeed, it could be argued that wealthier countries are more threatened by American cultural and consumer dominance because these are the countries with the higher disposable incomes to spend on cultural and consumer products. The most vociferous critics of American cultural dominance are high-income countries like France and Canada.

Moreover, linguistic issues continue to be interwoven with political ones in Africa. There, France—which once controlled a vast empire and still yearns for cultural dominance—has made the preservation of the French language on that continent a major pillar of its foreign policy. For example, in Rwanda, it has been argued by critics of French foreign policy, that France deliberately supported the genocidal Hutu regime because its leaders were francophones (or French speakers), while the Tutsi rebels—who were attempting to overthrow the government and stop the genocide—were English-speaking exiles from Uganda, a former British colony.

Religion

The collapse of communism and the great ideological struggle between East and West has led many political scientists to believe that the globe is being divided into great ethnocultural blocs, whose different values and interests place them at odds with one another. The most famous of these theorists is Samuel Huntington, who says that one of the sharpest differences between these cultural blocs is religion and the cultures influenced by religion.

Of course, this so-called clash of civilizations is nothing new. It was the basis for the millenium-long struggle between Christianity and Islam in the Mediterranean region, and for the conquest of the Americas by Roman Catholic and Protestant settlers from Europe. Nevertheless, the rise to political power of religious fundamentalists in India and Iran—as well as their increasing power in America, Israel, and some Arab and Asian states—is noteworthy and seems to bear out Huntington's argument. Critics, however, point out that religion remains a largely symbolic issue, a convenient political handle for struggles over old-fashioned economic privilege and political power.

CONCLUSION

It is often said that, with the end of the Cold War, humanity has entered the post-ideological age. No longer is the globe divided between capitalist West, communist East, and a developing world caught in the middle. The positive effects of this cannot be overstated. The simple fact that the threat of global thermo-nuclear war no longer hangs over humanity's collective head is enough for anyone to appreciate the demise of the old order.

But the fall of communism and the lifting of the ideological straitjacket has permitted ethnic and cultural minorities to voice and sometimes act upon their grievances against the dominant majority in nation-state after nation-state. Indeed, there has been a tendency to subdivide larger states into smaller and more ethnically homogenous mini-states. Sometimes this has occurred nonviolently—as in the case of Czechoslovakia—and sometimes it has led to war, as in the tragic case of the former Yugoslavia.

But there is a great irony in all of this. While these new culturally homogenous mini-states may provide a more politically stable and ethnically agreeable climate for their peoples, they may also be more economically vulnerable. That is because the trend toward mini-states has been occurring alongside a trend toward economic bigness. Multinational corporations, the global communications web, and the increasing power of international lending institutions are rendering the nation-state less important, with national governments facing decreased powers over their own economies. Ultimately, the struggle for cultural independence may be won even as the struggle for economic independence is surrendered without a fight.

FURTHER READINGS

Clarke, Angus, and Evelyn Parsons, eds. *Culture, Kinship, and Genes: Towards Cross-Cultural Genetics.* London: Macmillan, and New York: St. Martin's Press, 1997.

Driedger, Leo, and Neena L. Chappell. *Aging and Ethnicity: Toward an Interface.* Boston: Butterworths, 1987.

Goldscheider, Calvin, ed. *Population, Ethnicity, and Nation-Building.* Boulder, CO: Westview Press, 1995.

Herzfeld, Michael. *Cultural Intimacy: Social Poetics in the Nation-State.* New York: Routledge, 1997.

Huntington, Samuel P. *The Clash of Civilizations and the Remaking of World Order.* New York: Simon and Schuster, 1996; London: Touchstone, 1998.

Juergensmeyer, Mark. *The New Cold War?: Religious Nationalism Confronts the Secular State.* Berkeley: University of California Press, 1993; London: University of California Press, 1994.

Samarasinghe, S.W.R. de A., and Reed Coughlan, eds. *Economic Dimensions of Ethnic Conflict: International Perspectives.* London: Pinter, and New York: St. Martin's Press, 1991.

Szporluk, Roman, ed. *National Identity and Ethnicity in Russia and the New States of Eurasia.* Armonk, NY: Sharpe, 1994.

Van Horne, Winston A., ed. *Global Convulsions: Race, Ethnicity, and Nationalism at the End of the Twentieth Century.* Albany: State University of New York Press, 1997.

Wallerstein, Immanuel, and E. Balibar, eds. *Race, Nation, Class: Ambiguous Identities.* London and New York: Verso, 1991.

The Demography of Labor and the Economy

LABOR AND THE ECONOMY

The world economy at the close of the twentieth century would be unrecognizable to observers of the world economy in the 1950s and 1960s. At mid-century, the United States, Western Europe, Japan, and the Soviet Union were the leading industrial countries. Today the United States, Western Europe, and Japan are the leading economies of the world and the engines of global economic expansion. However, in these three regions, manufacturing employment has significantly declined as a share of their respective labor forces. There are two major causes for this decline: (1) technological advancements that have sharply reduced the demand for manufacturing workers; and (2) the relocation of manufacturing industry to developing countries where workers are paid significantly lower wages and environmental and workplace regulations are less extensive. Although these developed countries maintain high relative standards of living, they have lost much of their manufacturing industry to developing countries of the third world. In these developed economies, the vast majority of all workers are employed in the service, government, and trade sectors. Factories that once dotted the urban landscapes have been torn down. By 1996, the service sector contributed almost two-thirds of global gross domestic product (GDP). Although concentrated in the developed countries, the service sector is expanding to become a growing share of GDP in developing countries as well.

As developed countries have shifted from manufacturing to services, leading countries in Asia and Latin America have transformed their economies into industrial powerhouses. At the century's close, Brazil, China, Indonesia, Korea, and Mexico have larger shares of their labor force employed in the industrial sector than either the United States or Western Europe. In the past half-century, the Soviet Union, once considered one of the world's leading industrial powers, has declined and shriveled. By the end of the century, many factories of Russia and the Soviet Union's successor states and former socialist economies in Eastern Europe have closed. Although people have greater freedom to make their own economic decisions, the cradle-to-grave economic security provided by the planned economies has largely been eliminated by new leaders embracing neoliberal economic reform.

What accounts for this shift? The major force in this change is private industry's drive for greater productivity and profitability. The typical manufacturing facility at mid-century was the large centralized factory that produced and assembled every component of the final product sold on the consumer market. For example, the typical automobile producer was responsible for fabricating the steel, glass, and rubber materials into engines, transmissions, windshields, dashboards, radios, door handles, and all the other parts that went into the car that rolled off the assembly line. Today, automobile companies do not make most of the parts that go into the final product but contract out (or outsource) production to parts makers that typically pay their workers lower wages. Economists call this change in industrial product a shift from large centralized manufacturing to smaller-scale production facilities. Changes in the structure of industrial production—from centralized production to decentralized production and global competition from low-wage producers—have, in turn, lowered inflation-adjusted industrial wages in the developed economies of North America and Western Europe.

From Keynesianism to Neoliberalism

Keynesianism is an economic theory developed and elaborated by John Maynard Keynes (1883-1945), an English economist who argued that free markets are subject to periodic downturns and crises known as recessions and depressions. To curb the effect of these downturns, Keynes argued that it was necessary for governments to play a leading role in the economy by regulating the money supply and by spending public funds to create jobs and promote economic growth. In the 1950s and 1960s, most of the world's developed economies embraced this Keynesian economic strategy. While Keynesianism has many variations, from state ownership of key sectors of the economy to tinkering with the money supply, the model was put to use in virtually every country of the capitalist and socialist world.

However, in the 1970s and 1980s, Keynesianism was gradually superseded by what is commonly known as neoliberalism, an economic theory that advocates free capitalist markets with limited government intervention. Free marketers in academia and business leaders endorsed the neoliberal model, contending that government intervention was counterproductive because it artificially propped up weak economies. Increasingly, the neoliberal economic model was applied to developing countries in the third world.

By the early 1990s, after the collapse of the Soviet Union, the neoliberal model had virtually replaced the Keynesian model throughout the world. In country after country, national leaders were curtailing state ownership and participation in economic activities and opening their economies to greater global economic activity. Under the new economic regime, countries that want to attract foreign capital and investment are required to reduce and eliminate trade barriers that inhibit foreign competition. Moreover, national governments are required to reverse tariffs, regulations, and laws restricting money transfers from their countries. The formation of trade unions, which help prop up the wages of workers, is also discouraged because they are seen by national economic leaders as raising production costs and reducing economic competitiveness. For the last two decades of the twentieth century, national governments, with few exceptions, have sold off failing state-owned enterprises to domestic and foreign-owned investors. Many other countries have established stock markets that trade shares in private companies to investors throughout the world. Even China, which still calls itself communist, actively promotes private investment and ownership in its productive factories and resources.

What is neoliberalism's record thus far? Clearly freer global markets have produced tremendous profits for the powerful, the affluent, and the educated. Unleashing the free market throughout the world has made markets more responsive to the needs of consumers who can afford to purchase goods and services. However, as the twenty-first century approaches, the record of neoliberal reform seems to have raised more questions than answers for the economic future of all of humanity. In industrialized countries of the developed world, between the mid-1970s and the late 1990s, inflation-adjusted wages have fallen and basic social protections provided by governments have been withdrawn. Moreover, poverty has continued to grow throughout much of the world. Although many countries of the developing world would like to take advantage of increased foreign trade, their economies remain vulnerable to shifting raw material and commodity prices, as well as the vicissitudes of financial and capital markets.

Moreover, many developing countries pay significant shares of their national income to repay foreign debt, preventing them from dedicating economic resources to growth and development. Some poorer countries of Africa and Asia with a per capita GDP well below $750 a year use a majority of their national income to repay foreign debt. Thus, the economic record of developing countries over the past two decades is mixed. While some developing countries (notably Malaysia, Korea, and Indonesia) have experienced strong growth rates that have improved living standards, others (including those in sub-Saharan Africa, the Caribbean basin, Latin America, Oceania, and South Asia) have remained mired in poverty, with poor economic performance and declining living standards.

Although neoliberalism may rationalize markets and improve living standards for those who are already better off, much of humankind remains in abject poverty. In addition, the Asian and Russian economic crises of the late 1990s demonstrate that unregulated financial and capital markets may promote investment, but are more likely to aggravate the weaknesses of national economies and lead to severe economic slowdowns and even depressions. Indonesia, Malaysia, and other Southeast Asian countries that were celebrated as models of neoliberalism in 1997 were facing bankruptcy and economic collapse one year later. South Korea, which rapidly developed into one of the world's leading industrial powers through government-sponsored planning and investment in the 1980s and 1990s, was negotiating with international lenders for debt relief as the economy stumbled into a long recession.

The Decline of Organized Labor

How has the neoliberal model affected labor? In recent decades, governments have rolled back their regulations over labor markets. Deregulation and increasingly lax enforcement of statutory and administrative laws have permitted the entry, in both developed and developing countries, of new business competitors that are not complying with long-standing policies and rules

built up over the past century. The consequences for workers have been detrimental. Competition is leading firms to reduce production costs by ignoring laws and regulations governing wages, benefits, and working conditions. In previous decades, labor regulations protected most workers. However, in the deregulated economy, business profitability in general is enhanced by casting off government policies that provide standardized wage scales, government benefits, and safe working conditions. Today, calls for deregulation in developing countries are a customary response to globalization and capital flight. Until recently, deregulated labor markets were characteristic of underdeveloped countries. However, low wages, marginal labor, and informal economic activity have become primary features of urban centers in North America and Western Europe. Economists call labor deregulation "informalization"—meaning economic activities that are carried on outside the system of national regulations. By 1989, scholars were identifying the growth of informal labor markets in the United States and in Western Europe. In many cases, even large multinational corporations were depending on informal labor to produce garments, food, electronic goods, and other products for sale. Frequently workers were employed in sweatshops in both advanced and developing countries.

Many other workers who relied on stable jobs in manufacturing and service industries have seen their wages erode and working conditions decline. This decline is due in part to the weakening of labor unions, which have been a major force responsible for the improvement of wages and working conditions throughout the world.

Since the global economic decline in the 1970s, the number of low-paying jobs in the United States has grown, as has mass unemployment in Western Europe. Trade unions, which were first organized in the late nineteenth century in industrializing countries to protect worker rights, could not significantly curb the decline in wages. In the industrialized world, unions' weakness stems in part from labor's failure to organize marginal economic groups that are at the greatest risk of economic dislocation, including minorities, women, and immigrants. In Latin America (Guatemala, Mexico), East and Southeast Asia (China, Indonesia, Vietnam), and other countries of the developing world, independent trade unions have often been banned by national governments and labor leaders have often been arrested and imprisoned.

Despite these challenges to labor power, workers are organizing into unions in many countries throughout the world to fight for wage gains and improved working conditions. Major strike waves have challenged efforts by government and corporate leaders to initiate wage and benefit cuts. In the winter of 1995, French transportation workers waged a general strike that crippled the country and eventually led to the collapse of that country's conservative government. The following year, in South Korea, as the national legislature attempted to implement an austerity plan and to change laws so as to weaken labor, Korean workers in many industries went on strike to force the government to rescind the plan. In the United States, a revitalized labor movement is seeking to focus on organizing among minorities, the poor, and the working class.

From the mid-1980s to the mid-1990s, trade union density, or the share of nonagricultural workers who are members of trade unions, declined in most countries throughout the world (see Table 6.1). Trade union density has declined in sixteen of the twenty-one countries shown in Table 6.1, ranging from a 71.9 percent decline in union density in Bangladesh to a 56.2 percent increase in union density in Spain. Aside from Spain, the only countries to experience union density growth were South Africa (40.7 percent), the Philippines (24.1 percent), South Korea (4.7 percent), and Denmark (1.2 percent).

Economic Expansion and Poverty

The unprecedented expansion of the free market on a global scale in the 1980s and 1990s may have expanded international trade, but this growth has not reduced the human need and deprivation that stem from poverty. At the end

Table 6.1

Changes in Trade Union Density
(in ascending order)

Country	Year	Density	% Change
Bangladesh	1985-1995	4.3	-71.9
Kenya	1985-1995	16.9	-59.6
Portugal	1986-1995	18.8	-53.7
Argentina	1986-1995	25.4	-47.9
Mexico	1989-1991	31.0	-42.7
Austria	1985-1995	51.7	-29.2
United Kingdom	1985-1995	36.0	-27.2
Australia	1985-1995	28.6	-26.9
Egypt	1985-1995	29.6	-23.9
United States	1985-1995	12.7	-15.2
China	1985-1995	54.7	-7.8
Thailand	1985-1995	3.3	-7.4
Italy	1985-1994	32.9	-7.0
Japan	1985-1995	18.6	-4.0
Germany	1991-1995	29.6	-3.5
Canada	1985-1993	31.0	-0.6
Denmark	1985-1994	67.4	1.2
Republic of Korea	1985-1995	9.0	4.7
Philippines	1985-1995	18.4	24.1
South Africa	1985-1995	21.8	40.7
Spain	1985-1994	11.4	56.2

Source: International Labor Office, *World Labour Report: Industrial Relations, Democracy and Social Stability 1997-98.* Geneva: International Labor Organization, 1997.

of the twentieth century, about a third of the world's population is unable to afford everyday necessitities—food, shelter, and access to basic health care. Although economic wealth varies from one country to another, according to the World Bank, it is possible to calculate the percentage of a country's population that is living on less than $1 a day and $2 a day at 1985 international prices, adjusted for purchasing parity. These calculations produce a very disturbing picture (see Figure 6.1). Most states in Africa remain mired in abject poverty, with large portions of the population surviving on less than $2 a day. Of the twenty most poverty-stricken countries in the world, as measured by the percentage of the population surviving on the equivalent of $1 or less a day, fourteen are in Africa. Africa is home to the six at the top of that list: Guinea-Bissau (88.2 percent of the population defined as poor), Zambia (84.6 percent), Madagascar

(69.3 percent), Uganda (69.3 percent), Niger (61.5 percent), and Senegal (54 percent).

Abject poverty is not limited to Africa, but extends to every continent of the world. According to World Bank statistics, poverty remains high even in countries that have robust economies. About 43.5 percent of Brazil's population and 57.8 percent of China's population, among the most rapidly growing industrial powers in the world, survive on less than $2 a day. About 50.2 percent of all residents in India, the world's second most populous country, subsist on $1 a day or less, and 88.8 percent on less than $2 a day. In Latin America, about 40 percent of Mexico's population live on less than $2 a day, and in Guatemala, about 76.8 percent live on less than $2 a day and 53.3 percent live on less than $1 a day.

Although the causes of poverty are complicated, difficult to quantify, and varied, economic inequality and underdevelopment are the two factors that can be identified throughout the world. The distribution of income and wealth is critical in understanding poverty. Even in countries with a high per capita GDP, high poverty rates persist because of the unequal distribution and investment of income and wealth. Poverty is increasing because when a few people own and control most of a nation's wealth, many people have little access to economic resources. Thus, while the number of multimillionaires in China, Mexico, and Brazil has grown over the past two decades, the number of homeless, unemployed, and hungry has also grown. Moreover, populations in many poorer countries in Africa, Asia, and Latin America have become even more destitute as a result of their inability to gain access to capital to use in developing health care, housing, sanitation, educational institutions, and transportation.

An analysis of the twenty countries with the highest poverty rates shows that most of them also have low life expectancies, high infant mortality rates, low literacy rates, and high national unemployment rates. A clear distinction should be made between low per capita GDP and poverty. Although countries with the highest pov-

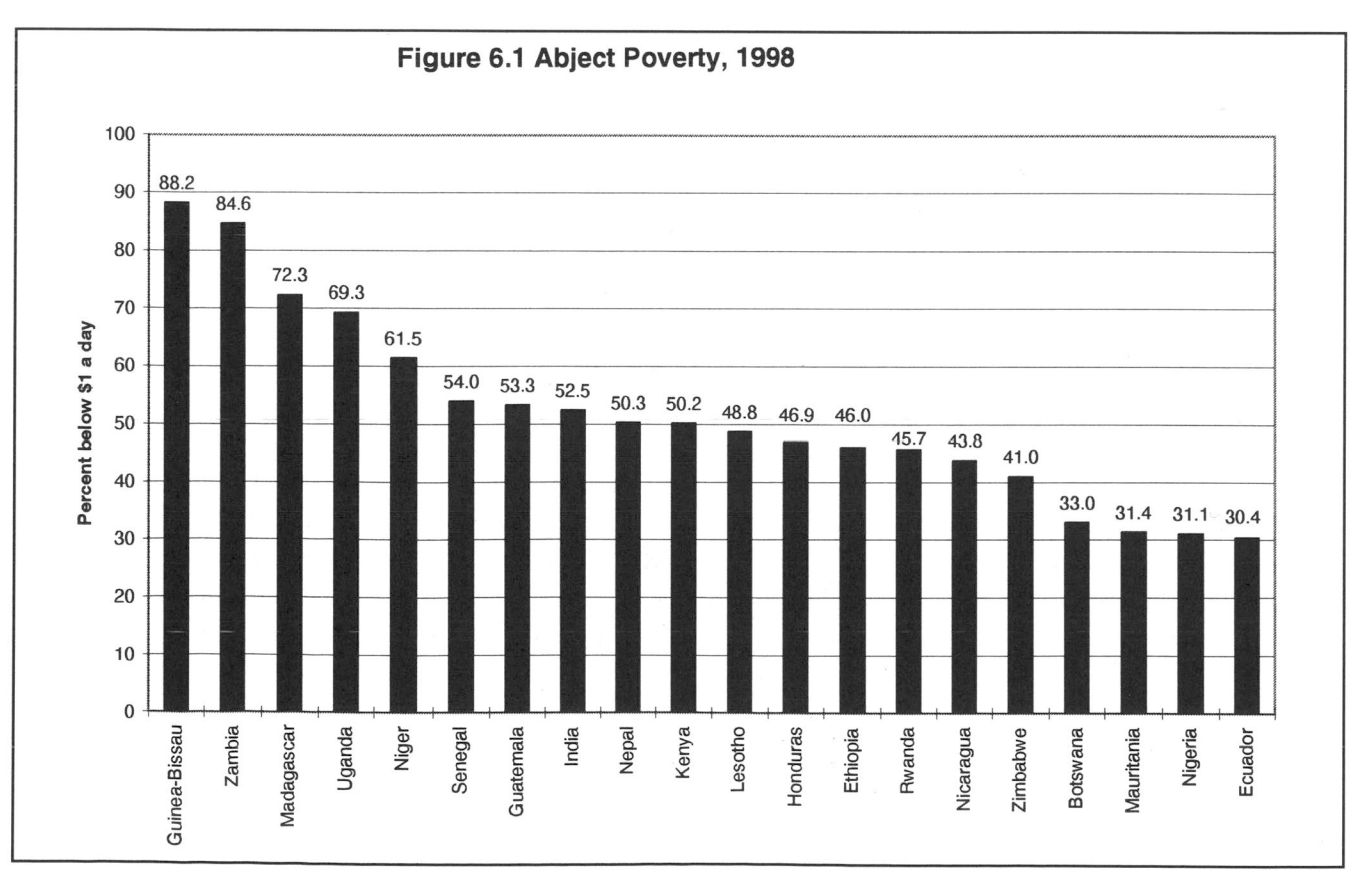

Figure 6.1 Abject Poverty, 1998

erty rates also tend to have low per capita GDP, certain countries have reduced poverty by redirecting resources to those in greatest need. Cuba, for example, which has weathered an American economic embargo for forty years since the 1959 revolution, ranks fairly high on most social indicators because of its more egalitarian distribution of wealth and income. Although much of its population is poor and does not have access to many commodities, Cuba continues to have a high life expectancy, low infant mortality, and a high literacy rate because of the country's effort to reduce income and wealth inequality.

REGIONAL ECONOMIES AT THE END OF THE TWENTIETH CENTURY

The world is significantly more integrated and interdependent than it was even a decade ago. This newfound global integration can be seen in the growth of regional trade blocs, the decline of global trade barriers, and the expansion of capital markets throughout the world. The decline in regional and global trade barriers, known conventionally as globalization, has important consequences for the fate of humanity. The following is a regional analysis of important economic and labor trends throughout the world.

North America

A major economic shift occurred in North America between the 1960s and the 1990s. As the United States and Canada changed from primarily manufacturing-based to service-based economies, Mexico went from being an agricultural producer to being a leading global manufacturer. By the end of the twentieth century, a larger percentage of workers was employed in manufacturing industries in Mexico than in the United States and Canada. Since the early 1970s, average wages have declined in the United States and income inequality has widened. Mexican, Central American, and Caribbean industrial workers, on average, are employed at a fraction of the wages and benefits of U.S. and Canadian workers. The poorer countries of the Caribbean

basin—the Dominican Republic, Guatemala, Haiti, Honduras, Nicaragua, and Panama—continue to depend on the export of agricultural commodities and raw materials for foreign exchange; most of their rural poor and new urban dwellers are living in poverty. After the Soviet Union suspended economic support for Cuba in 1991, the Cuban economy descended into economic crisis. Until 1991, Cuba benefited from substantial Soviet aid. After a "special period" of economic austerity, the country's economy has rebounded. However, the partial market reforms introduced have created greater inequality and jeopardized the country's socialist economy.

South America

Latin America's leading economies (Brazil, Venezuela, and Argentina) are among the most industrialized in the world, with large segments of their workforces employed in manufacturing. In the early 1980s, the region shifted from industrialization based on domestic production of goods from local markets that are produced abroad even if the foreign goods can be produced at lower cost (a term known as import substitution), to export promotion, which aims to expand exports of manufactured goods. Now a large proportion of manufacturing in Latin America is produced for export markets in North America and Western Europe. The export-oriented economies improved the national balance of payments in regional economies and eased a debt crisis in the region, which resulted from earlier policies that focused on the expansion of domestic markets. A second major development in the region has been the reduction in the high inflation rates that plagued the region during the 1980s. In Argentina and Brazil, the substantial reduction of double-digit rates of annual inflation in the 1990s has encouraged increased domestic and foreign investment. The high inflation rates of the early 1990s have been reduced as neoliberal economic reforms were instituted in countries throughout the region, including currency devaluation, privatization of state-owned industry, and reduction in public spending. In the 1990s, although

South America experienced intensified economic growth, the region became heavily dependent on exports. Brazil, the largest country in the region, remains heavily in debt to foreign lenders. South America, as a whole, is enduring high and growing levels of poverty and income inequality that are not being addressed by the individual governments. Despite these trends, Chile remains an economic success story in the region. The country's market-oriented economy has grown dramatically since the 1970s, significantly improving living standards for large segments of the population. Critics, however, argue that this growth has come at the cost of political repression and growing inequality.

Africa

Africa is the least developed populated continent in the world. Although significant differences exist among African countries, most of the population in Africa is mired in persistent poverty and destitution. With the exception of South Africa and perhaps Algeria, the region's leading exports are agricultural commodities, minerals, and natural resources, which provide limited foreign exchange with which to develop the continent. A significant impediment to economic growth in Africa since the 1960s is the persistence of insurrections, civil wars, and border disputes throughout the continent. On important economic measures, Africa is home to the poorest populations in the world. The continent has the highest poverty rates, the lowest per capita GDP, and the lowest level of industrialization. Moreover, the countries are heavily in debt to foreign lenders and must pay substantial proportions of national income to service foreign debt. The market reforms in Ghana, Tanzania and other countries of the continent have improved the capacity to export agricultural commodities and natural resources to Western Europe and North America. Although South Africa's economy is more economically advanced, the country's wealth is unequally distributed between an affluent European population and a poorer African population.

Asia

Asia is a continent of tremendous contrasts between economic development and underdevelopment. East Asia has been the center of economic growth and development. Since the end of World War II, standards of living in East and Southeast Asia have improved dramatically. By the 1980s, Japan, the economic powerhouse of the region, had become the world's second largest economic power after the United States. Japan's economic growth was stimulated by significant government investment in the private sector, a high savings rate, and an export-oriented economy. In the 1970s and 1980s, the Republic of Korea, Singapore, Taiwan, and Hong Kong duplicated this economic growth model with tremendous success. However, as wages have increased, international investors have been attracted to even lower-cost producers throughout the region—to Indonesia, Malaysia, and Thailand and, more recently, to China, the Philippines, and Vietnam. In the late 1990s, however, the region was suffering from a major financial economic crisis stemming from overspeculation that depressed most of the region's economies. Korea, Indonesia, Malaysia, and Thailand, facing default, were forced to negotiate debt relief with international lending institutions. The economic crisis threatened political stability throughout the region, and caused the collapse of a thirty-year dictatorship in Indonesia. In the late 1990s, governments fell in Korea and Thailand while Malaysia was in the throes of political crisis.

Beginning in the late 1970s, the Chinese government instituted capitalist economic reforms that have stimulated industrial growth and development. Although the country still calls itself a communist state, the private sector has expanded and developed as the state and collective sectors have declined. In the process, China has become a major exporter of industrial goods to North American and West European markets. Much of China's economic growth is concentrated in major cities. The growth of the capitalist economy has contributed to a widening income gap between a new affluent class and urban workers and rural peasants. Since the 1970s, the rural countryside, where a majority of the country's population resides, has stagnated and declined. Many of the new workers are undocumented migrants from rural areas who come to the cities in search of work. Rural poverty has grown dramatically in China since the 1980s as the government emphasizes urban development and neglects the countryside.

South Asia is not as economically developed as East and Southeast Asia. Although India instituted neoliberal market reforms in the early 1990s aimed at promoting private foreign investment, the economy remains primarily agrarian and undeveloped. The poorest major power in the world, India has one of Asia's highest poverty rates and a low per capita GDP of $1,500 a year. Much of India's population depends on subsistence agriculture. The country's burgeoning cities are overcrowded and beset by poor health and sanitation services, malnutrition, homelessness, and unemployment. India's market reforms have not penetrated significantly beyond a burgeoning high-technology sector in urban areas, due in part to limited access to capital and restrictive government regulations.

Although relatively more advanced than South Asia, Southwest Asia (including the Middle East, Afghanistan and the former Soviet Republics) is significantly less developed economically than East and Southeast Asia. The region's economic lethargy and underperformance are linked in part to political instability and military conflict in the region, including civil wars in Afghanistan and Lebanon, the legacy of the Iranian revolution, past conflicts between Iraq and Iran, the Persian Gulf War, and the persisting Arab-Israel conflict. Much of the region's economic wealth is concentrated in the oil-producing states (Bahrain, Iran, Kuwait, Oman, Qatar, Saudi Arabia, and United Arab Emirates). Labor shortages in the oil-producing states have encouraged large numbers of foreigners from poorer countries in the region to migrate to the region in search of employment. The largest economies in the region are Iran, Saudi Arabia, and Turkey.

Europe

Western Europe has an advanced industrial economy and a highly skilled workforce. Although Western Europe has endured a long-term economic downturn since the 1970s, it continues to have one of the world's highest standards of living. The economic downturn combined with growing global competition presents significant challenges to the region. In the 1990s, Western Europe has experienced high and persistent unemployment, due in part to growing global competition from low-wage producers in the United States, Latin America, East Asia, and Southeast Asia.

However, unemployment is mitigated by comprehensive social welfare systems in most countries of the region. In France, Germany, Scandinavia, and elsewhere in Western Europe, social protections (universal health care, unemployment insurance, family support) are significantly broader than in the United States. Efforts by national leaders to reduce national budgetary deficits in the 1990s by paring down social welfare programs have come under popular resistance. The creation of a single monetary unit, known as the euro, is expected to put additional pressure on governments to reduce budget deficits. Significant differences in wealth in West European (e.g., northern and southern Italy, eastern and western Germany) have intensified political conflicts in countries in the region.

In their efforts to move from state control to private market economies, Russia and Eastern Europe are undergoing serious economic turmoil. Many inefficient factories that were once supported by the state have been closed. Moreover, currency devaluation has severely strained the ability of emerging capitalist economies in Eastern Europe to service foreign debt. Since the collapse of the Soviet Union, the economies of Russia and the successor states have contracted, as inefficient factories have closed. In 1998, the Russian government, unable to stem the decline of the Russian ruble, defaulted on foreign debt. The economic crisis intensified political conflict and renewed calls for greater state intervention to protect and stabilize the economy. The Polish economy has rebounded from a period of economic decline in the early 1990s as it reorients its market economy from an Eastern European focus to Western Europe and North American markets. Although the Czech Republic and Hungarian economies have prospered in the post-Soviet era, the region as a whole has suffered from growing unemployment and higher poverty rates.

CONCLUSION

At the end of the twentieth century, the global economy faces opportunity, challenge, and uncertainty. Many countries have initiated economic reforms designed to reduce government bureaucracy and to promote the growth of investment and the expansion of free markets. The globalization of the world's economy has created tremendous opportunity for investors and speculators seeking greater profits through the development of new markets in developed and developing countries. However, many of these market reforms have at least initially taken a significant toll on the stability of traditional capital, industrial, and labor markets. In the former Soviet bloc and the developing world, populations endured long periods of economic crisis with high unemployment and inflation. Moreover, although urban centers have received greater investment, rural areas, where large segments of the world's population live, have often been ignored and face growing poverty. A major question in the twenty-first century is the degree to which governments will participate in managing markets through economic planning and regulation. With an uncertain future, there are many outlooks and perspectives on the economic future, ranging from those advocating the expansion of global markets to those favoring the return of national government regulation and planning. Which policies will ultimately be implemented? The future of the global economy, and by extension, the status of humanity, will rest on the direction of continued market growth or renewed government planning.

FURTHER READINGS

Aronowitz, Stanley. *From the Ashes of the Old: American Labor and America's Future*. Boston: Houghton Mifflin, 1998.

Block, Fred. "Postindustrial Development and the Obsolescence of Economic Categories." *Politics and Society*, 14, 1985.

Bluestone, Barry, and Bennett Harrison. *The Deindustrialization of America: Plant Closings, Community Abandonment, and the Dismantling of Basic Industry*. New York: Basic Books, 1982.

Brooks, David, and Jim Cason. "Mexican Unions: Will Turmoil Lead to Independence?" *Working USA*, March/April 1998.

Chomsky, Noam. "Power in the Global Arena." *New Left Review*, 230, 1998.

Davis, Mike. *Prisoners of the American Dream*. London: Verso, 1986.

Drucker, Peter F. "The Age of Social Transformation." *Atlantic Monthly*, November 1994.

Greider, William. *One World, Ready or Not: The Manic Logic of Global Capitalism*. New York: Simon and Schuster, and London: Lane, 1997.

Hayek, F.A. Von. *The Road to Serfdom*. Chicago: University of Chicago Press, and London: Routledge, 1944.

International Labor Office. *World Labor Report: Industrial Relations, Democracy, and Social Stability 1997-1998*. Geneva, Switzerland: International Labor Organization, 1997.

Kuttner, Robert. *Everything for Sale: The Virtues and Limits of Markets*. New York: Knopf, 1997.

Lindblom, Charles E. *Politics and Markets*. New York: Basic Books, 1977.

Miliband, Ralph. *Divided Societies: Class Struggle in Contemporary Capitalism*. Oxford: Clarendon Press, and New York: Oxford University Press, 1989.

Piore, Michael, and Charles Sabel. *The Second Industrial Divide*. New York: Basic Books, 1984.

Portes, Alejandro, Manuel Castells, and Lauren A. Benton. *The Informal Economy: Studies in Advanced and Less Developed Countries*. Baltimore, MD: Johns Hopkins University Press, 1989.

Schumpeter, Joseph A. *Capitalism, Socialism, and Democracy*. New York and London: Harper, 1942.

Sen, Amartya. *Inequality Reexamined*. New York: Russell Sage Foundation, and Oxford: Clarendon Press, 1992.

Wilson, William Julius. *When Work Disappears*. New York: Knopf, 1996: London: Centre for Analysis of Social Exclusion, London School of Economics, 1998.

Section 7

The Demography of Migration

DEFINITION OF MIGRATION

Since the origins of humankind, population movement from one geographic location to another has always taken place. Throughout human civilization, people have adapted to adverse environmental changes (for example, drought and floods) or social and political conditions (economic depressions, war, foreign occupation) by migrating to new localities that offer the opportunity to survive and prosper. Therefore, almost no ethnic or national group can justifiably claim to be the descendants of the original inhabitants of a region or country.

There are two types of migration: internal and external. Internal migration is the movement of people within the geographic boundaries of a nation-state, including population movement from one region of a nation-state to another, from rural areas to cities, and from cities to suburbs and rural areas. External migration is the movement of people across international boundaries of nation-states.

PUSH-PULL AND MIGRATION

Why do people move from one city, region, or nation-state to another? No single explanation can account for all forms of migration. However, historically, most demographers have embraced the push-pull theory as the most persuasive explanation for the movement of people across geopolitical boundaries. The push-pull theory, which emerged in the late nineteenth century, consists of two opposing arguments that lead to disagreement about the causes of migration.

Demographers who emphasize the push factor contend that migrants are forced by economic hardship from their impoverished regions of origin to new regions that offer greater opportunity for economic survival. Thus, although most people would prefer to stay in their home regions, economic catastrophe and disaster compel them to migrate to new locations that offer greater economic opportunity. Demographers who emphasize the pull factor argue that migrants are drawn to new areas by the opportunity for improving standards of living.

Two historical examples of migration, one drawn from eighteenth-century Europe and the other from the contemporary developing world, illustrate the push-pull factors causing migration. Since the seventeenth century, technical advancements in farming have reduced the need for peasant labor in the countryside. At the end of the eighteenth century, the emergence of capitalism brought about new social relations between feudal lords and peasants in England and much of Western Europe. Peasant economic survival in the rural countryside, where the majority of the population lived, became more difficult because of the growth of the enclosure movement, an activity that forced peasants off the estates and into the cities. The emergence of manufacturing industries in the burgeoning cities of Birmingham, Liverpool, and Manchester in the mid-eighteenth century spurred a greater demand for workers. The mass wave of migration from the English countryside followed the growing need for workers by manufacturers in the industrialized cities.

Although the life and culture of cities were clearly more dynamic and offered greater opportunity than the rural countryside, they were also sites of extreme poverty and exploitation. Newcomers to cities were exposed to overcrowded housing conditions and poor sanitation, which contributed to plagues and epidemics. The former peasants who went to cities in the millions formed part of the urban working class, forced by economic necessity and opportunity to work in factories and mills where occupational and health conditions were usually extremely dangerous. There were no laws regulating child labor, minimum wages, or working hours. The improvement of wages and industrial conditions for the new working class occurred only after the growth of a militant and politically influential labor movement in the nineteenth and twentieth centuries that demanded better working conditions, housing, and health care.

Migrants from developing countries in the late twentieth century face challenging social and economic conditions similar to those faced by English migrants in the eighteenth and nineteenth centuries. Peasants of developing countries are compelled to migrate to the cities as a result of economic necessity. As conditions erode in the rural countryside of developing nations, urban areas offer the possibility of survival and greater economic opportunity. For example, the stagnation and decline in the quality of life in the countryside in late-twentieth-century China has pushed many displaced peasants to migrate to the growing cities. Since unauthorized migration from rural to urban areas is illegal in China, these newcomers have few legal rights and little protection from economic exploitation.

Rural migrants regularly end up working as low-wage industrial employees and day laborers in the homes of middle class and affluent urban residents. In developing countries, the growth of cities and the decline of economic opportunities in rural areas have encouraged urban migration. As in eighteenth- and nineteenth-century Europe, new migrants from rural regions of developing countries are youths and young adults who have little opportunity for a productive life in the countryside. Although cities offer greater potential for improving living standards, migrant newcomers ordinarily endure years of destitution before they improve their living and working conditions. Migrants often reside in improvised and haphazard squatter communities on the fringes of big cities that lack adequate housing, sanitation, or health care. Those migrant workers lucky enough to find employment in factories typically put in long hours under adverse conditions for low wages. In many countries of Latin America, South Asia, and Southeast Asia, migrants are often adolescent girls employed in factories, sweatshops, and households as low-wage workers. Migrants from the developing to the industrialized world also endure poor living conditions and low-wage jobs.

THE DECISION TO MIGRATE

Although humans frequently move from place to place in search of gainful employment, the decision to move is not easy and has significant consequences for those who migrate, those who remain behind, and those who live in the areas to which the migrants go. In many cases, those who migrate are making a resolute statement that they cannot comfortably survive in their place of origin. Often when they move, they uproot themselves over a long period of time or even permanently from family members, homes, jobs, and culture (language, religion, ethnicity), usually for a harsh, often uncertain nomadic lifestyle somewhere else. At the turn of the twenty-first century, as many industrial countries close their borders to legal population movement, migrants are increasingly enduring extremely difficult and dangerous conditions, and often risk their lives in their trek to a new home. Thousands of migrants die each year from drowning, heat exhaustion, starvation, falls, vehicular accidents, and other injuries. Although migrants from less developed regions are needed as low-wage workers in industrialized countries, they are often designated as undesirable and illegal by those countries.

Upon arrival in a new location, migrants are almost always considered outcasts and faced with exclusion from the dominant culture. They must therefore adapt to significant changes in life-style or risk continuous isolation and extreme poverty. Even if migrants can earn relatively higher wages in their new location than at home, they almost always occupy the lowest rungs of the economic hierarchy, typically working at low-wage jobs shunned by those in the new area. In North America and Western Europe, migrants are employed as farm workers, housekeepers, nannies, low-level food service workers, construction workers, garment workers, and day laborers. Many migrant workers are employed in sweatshops, where working conditions are arduous, hours are long, and pay is low. Resident low-wage and unemployed workers often argue that migrants reduce wage standards and compete for scarce jobs, and so should return to their country of origin. Frequently, disreputable employers seize on the opportunity to hire low-wage immigrants who are afraid to assert their rights as workers. These employers are attracted to the enlarged pool of low-wage labor provided by migrant workers. Conditions are even worse in countries and regions with high concentrations of migrant workers, where labor regulations are ignored, wages and benefits are low, and working conditions are oppressive.

Migration often has harmful consequences for people left behind in the less economically developed regions and countries of origin. Those who are most likely to leave are the young, single, better-educated, and able-bodied, who can sustain the hardships associated with migration. Often, migrants are forced by necessity to leave destitute areas where traditional economies have been undermined by new political and social forces. For example, the decline of subsistence agriculture, privatization, industrial closures, and currency devaluation have made life extremely difficult for the peasants and working class of Latin America and the Caribbean, prompting many to leave for the United States and Canada. The migration of the able-bodied further drains the local economy of the young and educated. Many who are left behind are older residents, young children, and the less educated, who tend to be less productive than those leaving for greater opportunity. Nevertheless, migrant workers often perform an important economic function for their kin in their country of origin, as many send home a portion of their wages to help support their families.

ECONOMIC AND POLITICAL CAUSES OF MIGRATION

People migrate from one country to another for two basic reasons: (1) to seek economic opportunity, and (2) to cope with geopolitical change. Both forms of migration have important consequences for the countries migrants leave and the ones they go to. Economic migration typically includes population movement due to the inability to survive in one's country of origin and the possibility for gainful employment in the country to which one is relocating. Geopolitical migration results from changing government policies that restrict or encourage migration of segments of the population. It also flows from significant political change, including decolonization, independence, and the emergence of nationalist movements. Political migrants typically leave their country of origin because they feel unwelcome for reasons related to their identity. The four most important identity factors in migration, and thus the bases of potential discrimination in countries of origin, are nationality, religion, ethnicity, and political ideology.

Economic Factors: Disparity in Wealth Between North and South

Much of the cross-border migration since the end of World War II has been caused by inequality between the developed countries of North America, Western Europe, and East Asia and the developing countries of Africa, Asia, and Latin America. Economic inequality motivates migrants from the developing countries in search of employment to relocate in countries that have developed economies. In the 1960s and early 1970s, migration from the developing countries was encouraged by the developed world in response to the growing demand for foreign labor. However, in the aftermath of the economic decline in the industrialized economies since the mid-1970s, migration has been discouraged. In the 1980s and 1990s, restrictions and limits have been placed on legal immigration by developed countries. However, despite the legal and personal risks, and industrial government policies limiting the entry of foreign workers, migrants have continued voluntarily to leave their home countries.

Typically, migration is regional. Migrants from poorer regions in Africa and Southwest Asia travel to Western Europe for employment and send money to families in their country of origin. Migrants from less developed countries of the Arab world tend to travel to the oil-rich states of Kuwait, Saudi Arabia, and the United Arab Emirates in search of higher-wage employment. In Southeast Asia, Filipino and Indonesian migrants travel to the more affluent states of Brunei, Malaysia, and Singapore in search of work and economic opportunity. Immigrants from Latin America, the Caribbean, and East Asia form the majority of migrant workers to the United States. Figure 7.1 shows thirteen countries that experienced high rates of migration in 1995.

Although most jobs in countries receiving new migrants are low-wage positions that provide little opportunity for advancement (housekeepers, nannies, and fruit and vegetable pickers), migrants continue to come in large numbers, primarily because of the persistence and growth of poverty and income inequality in their countries of origin. Most migrants tend to be the young poor and working class, who have little opportunity for gainful opportunity at home. Figure 7.2 compares the out-migration levels of 1980 and 1995 in countries of the Caribbean basin. The growth in out-migration from Jamaica, Guyana, Grenada, Dominica, Cuba, Belize, Barbados, and the Bahamas was caused by increasing poverty.

Geopolitical Change and Realignment

A second cause of international migration is geopolitical change and realignment that leads to significant government policy shifts encouraging population movement. Typically, geopolitical change and realignment follow decolonization, independence, the emergence of nationalist governments, and the promulgation of poli-

cies that restrict or promote migration.

Status as a refugee is an important push factor in political migrations. Political refugees are typically forced to leave their country of origin to take refuge from danger or persecution. For example, during World War II, millions of Jews and other minorities fled Germany and Central European countries to escape Nazism, an ideology that advocated the extermination of Jews and other non-Aryan peoples. Although most of European Jewry was wiped out, many of those who survived migrated to North America, South America, and the Middle East. In the mid-1990s, the Bosnian civil war among Bosnian, Croatian, and Serbian ethnic minorities led to the extermination of hundreds of thousands of innocent civilians through a policy known as "ethnic cleansing." The war led to a mass exodus of refugees to safe havens in Europe. Also in the mid-1990s, in East Central Africa, the Tutsis, an ethnic minority in Burundi and Rwanda, fled to Zaïre, Tanzania, and Uganda to escape Hutu-led governments that persecuted them. Other refugees flee to escape military conflicts and wars that have spread to civilian areas. For example, during the 1990s, thousands of refugees from the Liberian civil war fled to nearby Sierra Leone. (See Figure 7.3.)

There are two types of refugees: those forced to leave under threat of persecution or death, and those who leave when military conflicts spill over into civilian regions. Refugees may be forced to leave because of their ethnic or religious identity (e.g., Armenians, Jews, Tutsis, Bosnian Muslims) or because of their political beliefs, which might be seen as threatening to the government. In the 1930s, communists and other opponents of Nazi Germany were forced to leave under threat of persecution. During the twentieth century, the number of refugees forced to leave their home under threat of persecution because of their identity has greatly increased and accelerated.

Independence and Decolonization

Geopolitical change and realignment has shaped the two leading waves of international migra-

Figure 7.1 Migration to Receiving Countries, 1995

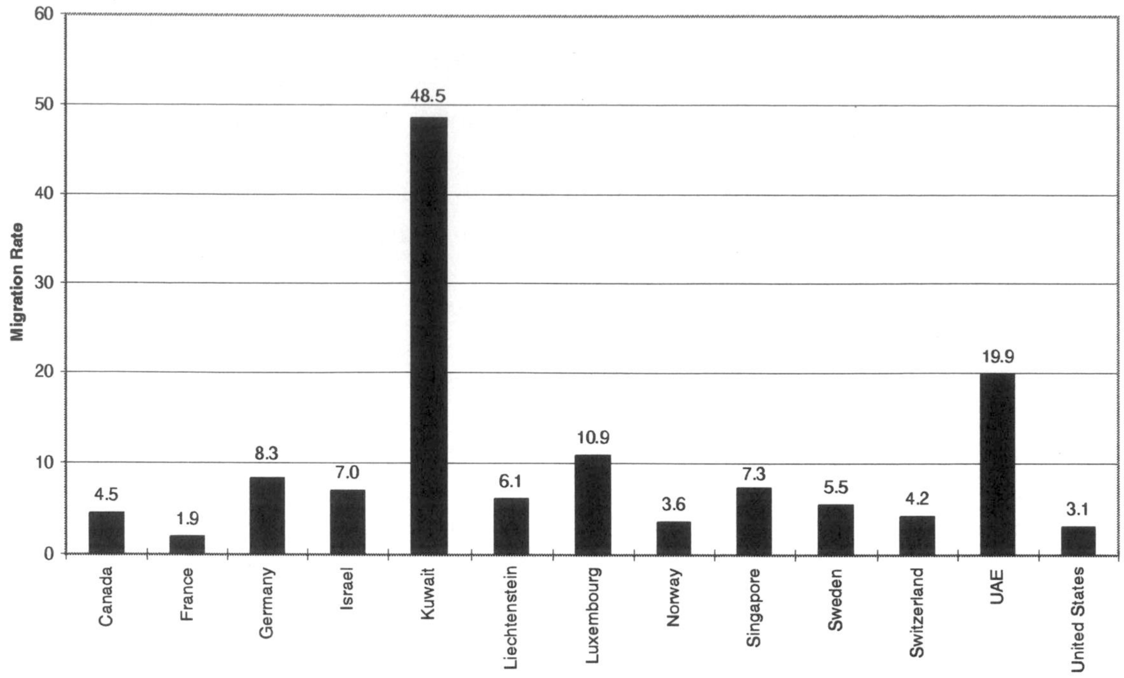

Canada 4.5
France 1.9
Germany 8.3
Israel 7.0
Kuwait 48.5
Liechtenstein 6.1
Luxembourg 10.9
Norway 3.6
Singapore 7.3
Sweden 5.5
Switzerland 4.2
UAE 19.9
United States 3.1

Figure 7.2 In- and Out-Migration in the Caribbean Basin, 1995 and 1980

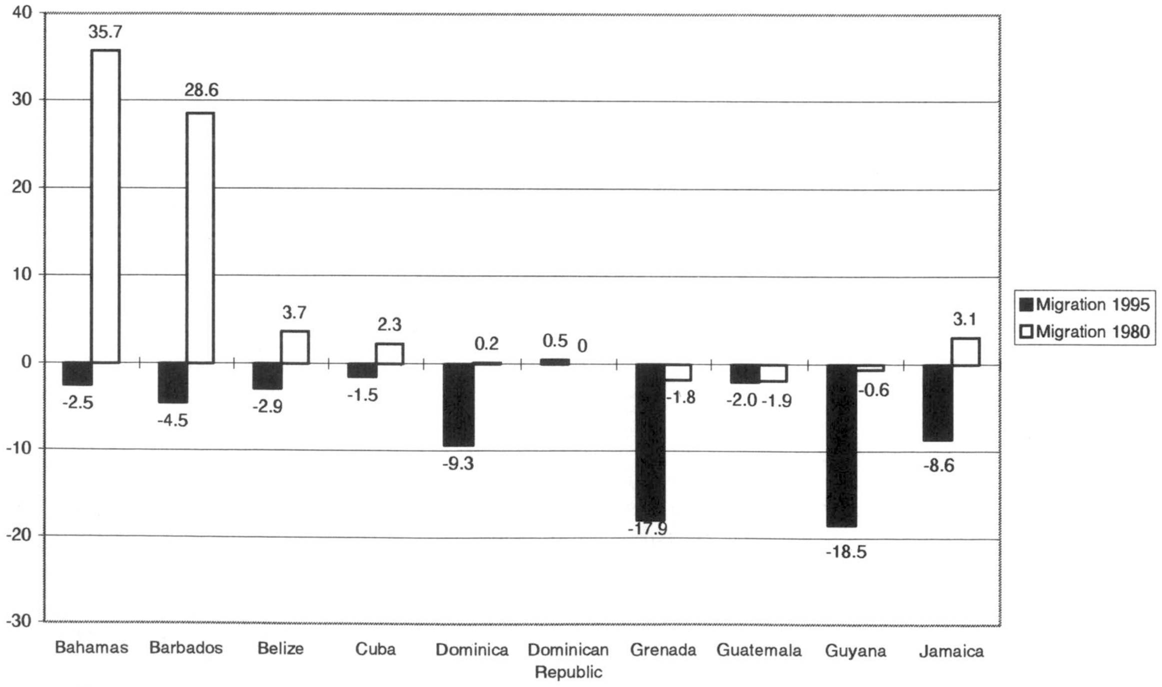

Bahamas -2.5 / 35.7
Barbados -4.5 / 28.6
Belize -2.9 / 3.7
Cuba -1.5 / 2.3
Dominica -9.3 / 0.2
Dominican Republic 0.5 / 0
Grenada -17.9 / -1.8
Guatemala -2.0 / -1.9
Guyana -18.5 / -0.6
Jamaica -8.6 / 3.1

■ Migration 1995
□ Migration 1980

Note: Migration rate represents persons leaving or entering per 1,000 national residents.

tion since the end of World War II. The first migratory wave, from the late 1940s to the early 1980s, followed the anticolonial movements in Africa and Asia that led to decolonization and independence. The independence movements forced European powers to relinquish control over colonial territories to national governments in Africa, Asia, the Caribbean, and the Pacific. After independence, settlers who had held political and economic power in the territory no longer felt welcome and many migrated to Europe. The three leading European powers that retained colonies in the developing world at the end of World War II were France, Portugal, and the United Kingdom. From the late 1950s to the early 1960s, hundreds of thousands of French nationals who had resided in Algeria and Vietnam for generations left for France. In the 1940s and 1950s, British citizens in India returned to England, as did British nationals in the 1960s and 1970s who had lived in Kenya and Zambia. In the 1970s, in the aftermath of the Portuguese revolution, expatriates living in Angola,

Mozambique, and Portuguese Guinea returned to Portugal.

The second leading wave of migration since the end of World War II followed the collapse of the Soviet empire in 1991 and the formal independence of the former Soviet republics in Eastern Europe and Central Asia. Many Russian nationals have lost their economic and political power in the new states that have emerged, and, since the 1990s, millions of Russian nationals residing in the former Soviet republics (as well as the Baltic states) have returned to Russia. By the early 1990s, Russian émigrés from the former Soviet Union represented one of the world's largest migrant populations. (See Figure 7.4.)

Government Policies

Government policies restricting and promoting population movement strongly influence the ebb and flow of migration. During the Cold War, the Soviet Union restricted population movement between East and West. The Soviet Union's poli-

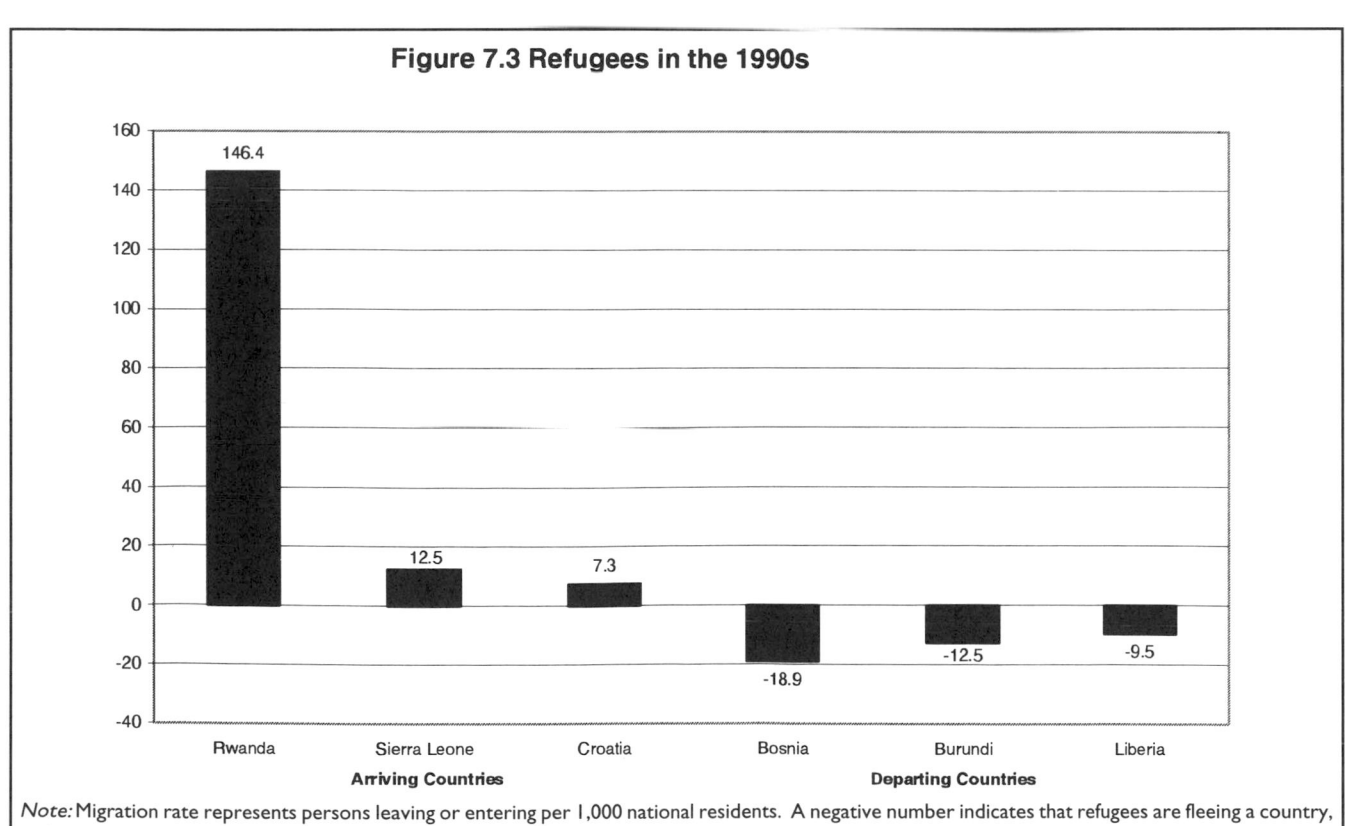

Figure 7.3 Refugees in the 1990s

Rwanda: 146.4; Sierra Leone: 12.5; Croatia: 7.3; Bosnia: -18.9; Burundi: -12.5; Liberia: -9.5

Arriving Countries / Departing Countries

Note: Migration rate represents persons leaving or entering per 1,000 national residents. A negative number indicates that refugees are fleeing a country, and a positive number indicates that refugees are entering the country.

cies restricting emigration were symbolized by the construction of the Berlin Wall, which divided Germany into two parts, separating East Germany, the Soviet zone of occupation, from West Germany, originally occupied by the United States, Britain, and France. During the Cold War, restrictions on migration were reproduced in Eastern European countries in the Soviet bloc. The policies preventing migration were motivated in part by both political and economic considerations. Migration restrictions from East to West were gradually relaxed during the 1970s and 1980s. In Eastern Europe in the late 1980s, the inability of Soviet bloc countries to control mass waves of undocumented migration caused by economic stagnation and the lack of democracy spurred the fall of communist-dominated regimes throughout the region in 1989. Restrictions on emigration to the West were lifted after the Soviet-dominated governments fell.

Paradoxically, most migratory restrictions in the post–Cold War era have been enacted by governments in North America and Western Europe, in an effort to limit the flow of potential immigrants seeking to escape economic uncertainties throughout the world caused in part by the globalization of production and rising unemployment. The growing disparity in wealth and living standards between industrialized and developing countries has led many migrants from the developing world to move in search of gainful employment. However, in the receiving countries, public support for unrestricted migration is declining and support for closing the borders to foreigners is increasing. Consequently, in the industrialized world, immigration policies are under review and new policies have been passed to dissuade and prevent migrants from entering.

REGIONAL MIGRATORY TRENDS

What are the primary regional migratory patterns at the turn of the twentieth century? Although the key global causes of migration are

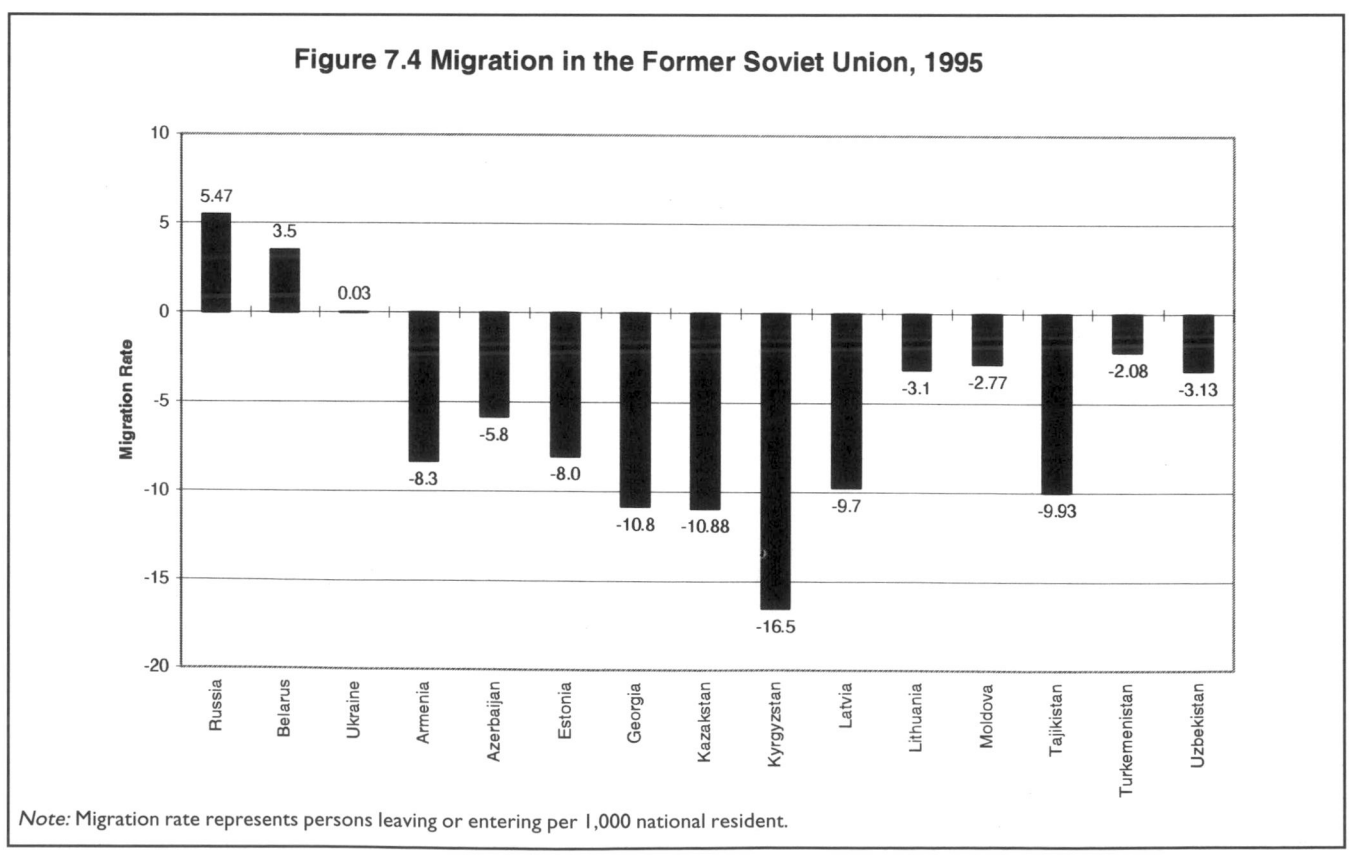

Figure 7.4 Migration in the Former Soviet Union, 1995

Note: Migration rate represents persons leaving or entering per 1,000 national resident.

economic need and geopolitical change, distinctive regional patterns of migration are themselves causing economic stress, political conflict, and policy shifts. The following is a summary of the key patterns in North America, Latin America, Africa, Asia, and Europe.

North America

During the 1980s and 1990s, migration to the United States and Canada continued to grow rapidly even as both governments reformed their immigration policies. During both decades, the United States enacted legislation curbing migration motivated by economic factors. By the early 1990s, the leading sources of migration to the United States, in descending order, were Mexico, Central America, the Caribbean, the Philippines, South America, China, Korea, India, the United Kingdom, Vietnam, Italy, and Germany. In addition, according to government estimates, in the early 1990s there were between 2 million and 3.5 million undocumented foreign nationals residing in the United States.

However, despite the passage of the 1986 Immigration and Reform Control Act, which sought to limit population movement to the United States, immigration from Latin America to the United States continued to grow. During the 1990s, immigration to the United States was restricted further by state and national governments, which instituted severe penalties for undocumented migration and narrowed the political and economic rights of immigrants who lacked either a green card (denoting their status as permanent residents) or citizenship. Government law discourages the immigration of those who require financial assistance and are too poor to survive without public support.

Canadian in-migration is determined by the Canadian government's estimates of the available government resources and financial capacity for absorbing immigrants. The three qualifications for legal migration are family reunification, refugee status, and financial status. Those immigrants that arrive with sufficient financial resources so they are not a burden on the state are more readily accepted. The primary sources of migration to Canada are Asia and the Pacific, Europe, the United States, and the Caribbean.

Latin America

Although Latin America was a major destination for immigrants from the late nineteenth century to the 1970s, in the past three decades the region has become primarily a source of emigration. After World War II ended, Argentina, Venezuela, and Uruguay were the leading destination countries in the region for migrants to and within Latin America. From 1970 to 1980, Latin America precipitously shifted from being a destination to being a source of migration: In 1970 the region gained a net 1.8 million migrants, but by 1980, the region lost a net 1.6 million residents because out-migration was greater than in-migration. Undocumented migration expanded rapidly in the 1980s and 1990s, in part due to legal restrictions placed on migration. The growth of rural and urban poverty in the region is a major reason migrants left for the more affluent United States and Canada. Moreover, migration has also increased in response to the rising cost of living and high unemployment throughout the region.

Asia

Asian countries are both sources and destinations of migration. The major reasons for the growth of migration are uneven economic standards and opportunities among countries in Asia. Moreover, as demand for skilled and semiskilled labor in Australia and North America has escalated, out-migration from Asia has increased steadily since the early 1960s. The Philippines, the Republic of Korea, China, and India are the leading source countries for immigration to Australia and North America. Although inter-Asian migration increased rapidly during the 1980s and 1990s to the newly industrialized countries (NICs) of East Asia and Southeast Asia, in the wake of the Asian financial crisis, the migratory flow has slowed and thousands of migrants have been sent back to their countries of origin. The economic misery may extend to Bangladesh, India, Nepal, and other countries that have depended on payments sent home by migrant laborers who have gone abroad for work.

In the last three decades of the twentieth century, political conflicts have produced major flows of refugees fleeing persecution and war. The two leading sources of refugees on the continent are in Southeast and Southwest Asia. Even though the war in Vietnam ended in the mid-1970s, large numbers of Cambodian, Laotian, and Vietnamese refugees still live in dire conditions throughout the region. The ongoing conflict in Afghanistan has produced nearly 6 million refugees, the vast majority of whom remain in Pakistan and Iran. Other sources of refugees in the region are China (Tibetans in India and Nepal), Sri Lanka (many now in India), Myanmar, or Burma (most now in Thailand), Israel (Palestinians in regional refugee camps and spread elsewhere throughout the Middle East), and Indonesia (refugees from the East Timorese and Irian Jayan regions now living in Papua New Guinea).

Africa

Africa has experienced two major waves of migration. The first wave of migration out of Africa followed World War II and the growth of the decolonization movement. Most migrants in this era were European expatriates who left the continent from the late 1950s to the 1970s, after the emergence of independent African states forced them out of positions of economic and social privilege under colonial regimes. The second major wave of migration in Africa has occurred in the postcolonial era, as a result of ethnic, political, and national conflicts and power struggles among countries in the region. Regional conflicts have produced millions of refugees throughout the African continent. Since the 1970s, ethnic conflicts, civil war, and political struggles have created mass migration and refugee crises in Angola, Burundi, the Democratic Republic of Congo (formerly Zaïre), Eritrea, Ethiopia, Liberia, Mozambique, Namibia, Rwanda, Sierra Leone, Somalia, Sudan, Uganda,

Western Sahara, and Zimbabwe. The growth of abject poverty throughout the continent increases pressure for migration to Western Europe and North America in search of improved economic conditions. In southern Africa, migrants from Mozambique, Zimbabwe, and other regional states have traveled to South Africa in search of work.

Europe

There were two major flows of international migration into Western Europe in the 1980s and 1990s—migrant workers and their families from southern Europe, Southwest Asia, and Africa who moved in search of greater economic opportunity, and East European emigrants from the former Soviet bloc. Since the economic downturn throughout Western Europe in the 1970s, government restrictions have been placed on legal immigration to the region. There is a growing sentiment against foreigners in West European countries, evinced by the growth of right-wing parties pushing for restrictions on the entry of migrants, particularly those from the Middle East and North Africa. But, as Europe's population ages, the region will need foreign workers, primarily to fill the menial jobs shunned by local workers. While foreign workers continue to migrate to the region, few have the opportunity eventually to become permanent residents or citizens. However, Germany and other governments are relaxing the most onerous of these restrictions.

CONCLUSION

In the coming decades, international migration is expected to continue to grow and become a major component of population growth and decline in nations throughout the world. Moreover, the causes of migration are increasingly more complex and more complicated than in previous periods. There is no such individual as a typical migrant. Some migrants leave their places of origin temporarily, others leave for longer periods, and still others leave permanently. Migration shapes and influences economic, political, and cultural conditions in both migrant regions of departure and arrival. Increasingly, global economic integration is contributing to greater interdependence between regions where migrants are leaving and regions where migrants are entering. Economic conditions in sending regions are often shaped by the ability of migrants living abroad to send money back home. Moreover, economic growth in countries where there are large numbers of migration are often dependent on the ability of employers to find low-wage or highly specialized workers who cannot be found locally. The growth of nationalism throughout the world at the end of the twentieth century also influences migratory patterns. As a result, migrants in large numbers are leaving countries where they no longer feel welcome and entering countries where they have a political and cultural affinity. Moreover, growing legal restrictions on official migration in many countries are limiting human rights of individuals who move for economic, political, or cultural reasons. Thus, although migrants continue to come and go throughout the world and to contribute to economic, political, and cultural vitality, at the turn of the century nationalist leaders are increasingly abridging their rights.

FURTHER READINGS

Macura, Miroslav, and David Coleman, eds. *International Migration: Regional Processes and Responses.* New York and Geneva: United Nations, 1994.

Sassen, Saskia. *The Global City: New York, London, Tokyo.* Princeton NJ: Princeton University Press, 1991.

United Nations. *1996 Demographic Yearbook.* New York: United Nations, 1998.

United Nations Centre for Human Settlements (HABITAT). *An Urbanizing World: Global Report on Human Settlements, 1996.* Oxford and New York: Oxford University Press, 1996.

United Nations Development Programme. *Human Development Report 1996.* New York: Oxford University Press, 1996.

United Nations High Commission for Refugees. *The State of the World's Refugees, 1993.* New York: Penguin Books, 1993.

World Bank. *Annual Report 1996.* Washington, DC: World Bank, 1997.

———. *World Development Indicators 1998.* Washington, DC: World Bank, 1998.

Zolberg, A.R. "The Next Waves: Migration Theory for a Changing World." *International Migration Review,* 23(3), 1989.

The Demography of Transportation and Communications

In the late nineteenth century, the pioneering French science fiction writer Jules Verne published his classic travel novel *Around the World in Eighty Days*. This story was meant in part to highlight the enormous progress humanity had made in taming distances. After all, roughly three centuries earlier, it had taken Ferdinand Magellan's fleet some three years to circle the globe. But the achievement of Verne's hero pales next to the strides made in travel in the twentieth century. Soviet cosmonaut Yuri Gagarin, the first human being in space, circled the Earth in less than eighty minutes in 1961, only seventy-odd years later.

It is, of course, a cliché to say that modern development in transportation and communications technology have shrunk the planet beyond the imagination of previous generations, but it is astonishing nevertheless. In the 1700s, it took months to cross the Atlantic in sailing ships; in the 1800s, it took weeks in steamships; in the first half of the twentieth century, it took just days in diesel-powered ocean liners; and in the second half of the century, it takes only hours in a transcontinental jet.

The achievements in communications are no less remarkable, if a bit different in kind. Since the invention of the telegraph in the 1830s, humans have been able to transmit data near the speed of light, providing virtually instant communication across vast distances. Because it is governed by the laws of physics, this speed cannot be exceeded. What has increased is the quantity and type of information, as well as the depth and reach of the communications network. A single telegraph message consisting of perhaps 100 individual bits of information moves near the speed of light, but requires several minutes to be transcribed. In contrast, using the most up-to-date form of written messages, e-mail, up to 56,000 bits of information can be transmitted in a single minute.

The benefits of these achievements are well known: instant transmission and reception of information, ease of travel, and the ability to sustain relationships across great distances. But the revolution in transportation and communications also has negative consequences: the ability to misinform and brainwash on a mass scale, the relentless drive toward a single dominant mass global culture and the destruction of local cultures, clashes of culture between tourists and native peoples, and the enormous environmental hazards caused by the burning of fossil fuels necessary for modern transportation.

TRANSPORTATION

Nearly all the forms of transportation in use between 1965 and 1995 were invented long before 1965: the automobile and airplane were invented at the turn of the century; railroads and fossil fuel–powered ships appeared in the first half of the nineteenth century. What is notable about the post-1965 era, however, is the sudden growth in the quantity and geographic spread of these transportation systems, and the impact this spread has had on societies throughout the world.

Motor Vehicles

No form of transportation has done more to revolutionize the movement of people and goods in the post-1965 era than motor vehicles—in particular, the private passenger automobile, the passenger bus, and the freight truck. This is especially the case with metropolitan and regional transport. If anything can rival the fantastic growth in the world's population and cities over the past thirty years, it is the increase in the number of motor vehicles. There are several reasons for this. First, growth in the number of human beings leads to a need for more transportation. Second, the rapid expansion of cities means that more people live at greater distances from their families and the sources of agricultural production. Third, although motor vehicle transport is not as crucial in international trade as freight-carrying aircraft and cargo ships, it does play a role in the globalization of the world's economy, serving as an intermediate link between smaller cities, outlying areas, and the major ports and air traffic hubs of the world.

Finally, there is the matter of prosperity. Higher disposable income in many developed and upper-tier developing countries means greater consumption of goods, which entails more transportation. Moreover, one of the key large consumer products purchased by newly prosperous individuals and families is the passenger car. Economists refer to a takeoff point for automobile purchases in the developing world, when an annual family income climbs to about 50 percent of the total purchase price of an automobile. In addition, experts also note that there is a kind of doubling effect at work: for every 1 percent rise in a country's per capita income, the number of motor vehicles tends to rise 2 percent. In view of these circumstances, it is not surprising that the overall number of vehicles is rapidly increasing in the developing world. What is more surprising is the rapid rise in the number of vehicles in the developed world as well, because of increases in the number of both commercial vehicles and passenger cars. Transformations in the production process in the de-

veloped world over the past thirty years have emphasized efficiency, primarily through maintaining lower inventories and "just-in-time" deliveries. This obviously means more goods in motion at any given time, hence the demand for more commercial vehicles. The increase in the number of private cars is due to prosperity—more two-car families—and the shrinking size of the household. As the number of single-person households or households led by a single breadwinner increases, so does the number of vehicles, for each of these smaller households requires its own car.

Table 8.1 shows the dramatic rise in the number of vehicles in key countries in both the developed and the developing world between 1965 and 1995. Several trends in the number of private cars are immediately evident. First, the greatest expansion has occurred either in newly industrialized countries like South Korea or in the former communist countries, like Poland, where economic, political, and cultural restrictions on automobiles were gradually lifted in the waning days of the communist regimes and were eliminated after those regimes fell.

Second, rapid expansion in private car ownership is seen in oil-rich states like Indonesia, Iran, and Nigeria, where the sudden increase in oil prices in the 1970s produced new wealth. In absolute terms, the greatest increases in private car ownership occurred in the developed world. Thus the increase in France from 1980 to 1995, for example, was just 35.3 percent, or 6.5 million passenger cars. In the more populous Nigeria, the increase was 393.5 percent for the same period, but this represented only 181,000 passenger cars.

Finally, the figures for the United States should be considered in terms of world totals. Living in what was easily the richest country in the world in 1965, Americans owned 53.6 percent of all the world's automobiles. Increasing incomes and consumption patterns in other developed countries reduced that to 37.4 percent by 1980. By 1995, with the rise of the newly industrialized countries of Asia, and with the removal of restrictions on automobile ownership in the former communist world, the percentage of the world's

Table 8.1

Passenger Cars in Selected Countries, 1965-1995

Country	No. of passenger cars (per thousand persons)			Percent change	
	1965	1980	1995	1965-1980	1980-1995
Brazil	1,140.8 (1.6)	8,004.6 (6.7)	8,098.4 (5.0)	601.6	1.2
Fiji	7.3 (1.8)	23.4 (3.9)	47.7 (6.1)	220.5	103.8
France	9,600.0 (17.8)	18,400.0 (34.5)	24,900.0 (42.7)	91.7	35.3
India	415.7 (0.1)	1,054.4 (0.2)	3,205.0 (0.3)	153.6	204.0
Indonesia	151.0 (0.2)	639.5 (0.4)	1,890.3 (0.9)	323.5	195.6
Iran	105.9 (0.4)	958.0 (2.8)	1,557.0 (2.4)	804.6	62.5
Nigeria	n/a	46.0 (0.1)	227.0 (0.2)	n/a	393.5
Poland	245.5 (0.8)	2,383.0 (6.8)	7,153.1 (20.4)	870.7	200.2
South Korea	16.3 (0.1)	249.1 (0.9)	5,148.7 (11.3)	1,428.2	1,966.9
United States	74,904.3 (38.1)	118,458.7 (52.3)	147,710.0 (55.4)	58.1	24.7
World	139,730.0 (4.2)	316,400.0 (7.1)	458,488.7 (8.0)	126.4	44.9

cars owned by Americans had been reduced further, to 32.2 percent.

The implications of this expansion in the number of motor vehicles for both the global and the individual countries' environments are staggering. Table 8.2 compares carbon dioxide emissions in 1992 over the levels in 1983 for the same countries listed in Table 8.1. The rise in carbon dioxide emissions—produced largely by motor vehicles, but also a by-product of various manufacturing processes—is the main cause of global warming, according to many scientists.

As Table 8.2 indicates, the general trend in carbon dioxide emissions is upward, though the pace varies in different countries because of differing rates of economic growth and the adoption of new technologies. The greatest increases are generally in countries with the highest increase in passenger car ownership, such as Nigeria and South Korea. But more environmentally friendly technologies also can play a role. Although the num-

ber of cars in Poland increased some 200 percent between 1983 and 1992, its carbon dioxide emissions actually declined because of the shift from highly polluting cars made under the communist regime to the cleaner cars either imported or made in Polish factories which employ advanced Western car manufacturing technologies. In France, the decline is due to both cleaner cars and the general stagnation of the economy, which results in less driving, as unemployed people will no longer commute.

Air Transport

As in the case of automobiles, the expansion of air transport has dramatically transformed the nature of long-distance passenger travel and trade. Table 8.3 shows the increase in passenger traffic by air from 1980 to 1995. As demonstrated in the table, the world as a whole and most individual countries have seen dramatic increases in air travel because of an increase in

Table 8.2

Carbon Dioxide Emissions for Selected Countries, 1983-1992

| Country | Carbon dioxide emissions (thousands of metric tons) | | Percent change |
	1983	1992	
Brazil	44,483	59,245	33.2
Fiji	196	194	-1.0
France	108,731	98,820	-9.1
India	118,457	210,000	77.3
Indonesia	30,981	50,378	62.6
Iran	36,904	64,268	74.1
Nigeria	16,343	26,341	61.2
Poland	114,445	93,311	-18.5
South Korea	38,517	79,103	105.4
United States	1,143,714	1,332,246	16.5

Table 8.3

Air Transport for Selected Countries, 1980-1995

| Country | Passengers (thousands) | | Percent change |
	1980	1995	
Bahamas	345	862	149.9
China	2,568	37,498	1,360.2
Egypt	2,028	3,538	74.5
Ghana	279	182	-34.8
Hungary	874	1,325	51.6
India	6,603	11,518	74.4
Peru	1,980	1,895	-4.3
Saudi Arabia	9,241	11,922	29.0
Spain	15,089	21,992	45.7
Thailand	2,459	11,405	363.8
United Kingdom	25,551	55,475	117.1
United States	295,281	513,756	74.0
World	748,978	1,225,067	63.6

domestic travel, tourism, and higher levels of migration. Each of the countries listed in the table has individual reasons for its own trends. The expansion in air travel among the Chinese is linked to China's opening toward the rest of the world in the 1980s, as well as its rapid economic growth. The rise in U.S. air travel relates to airline deregulation and falling ticket prices. The decline in Peru is attributable to its depressed economy and the drop in tourism because of political instability. Air transport levels in Ghana have fallen because of the economic recession that followed a decline in international prices for Ghana's tropical food exports, due to increased competition from other tropical countries and changes in tastes in the developed world (such as decreased consumption of sugar). The increase in air transport in the United Kingdom results from the country's new status as a transportation hub for Europe.

The rapid growth in air travel has had two lasting impacts regarding passengers. With respect to immigrants, there has not been an increase in numbers per se, since ships and railroads once carried millions of migrants to their destinations. Instead, migration and immigration by air have allowed many immigrants to go back and forth between their homeland and their newly adopted country.

Consequences that follow from this include increased money brought to the homeland as well as investment there by those who have emigrated. The impact on assimilation, however, is complex. On the one hand, the ease of travel and the ubiquity of modern communications have given people around the world common cultural references, such as a fascination with Hollywood film stars and rock and roll music, and a taste for Western products like Coca-Cola and McDonald's hamburgers. On the other hand, the ability to travel back and forth between the old and new countries may delay immigrants' assimilation to their new home country. (For more on transportation and migration, see Section 7, The Demography of Migration.)

With regard to tourism and travel, the increased accessibility of air transport has led to increases in both the number of persons traveling for vacations and the number and distances of their destinations. Nearly every major tourist destination has experienced a major increase in the number of annual tourists. Interestingly, the largest increases have been in countries that are either distant from the developed world (where most tourists originate) or not traditionally tourist-oriented. For example, the Maldives in the Indian Ocean hosted roughly 25 percent more visitors in 1994 than in 1990, while more accessible and traditional tourist destinations like Jamaica experienced an increase of 15 percent. Tourism levels are also related to political stability in the destination country and to fashion and economics in the country of origination. The recent trend toward "eco-tourism"—that is, tourism that is environmentally friendly and does not require ecologically unsound developments like hotels and resorts—may lead to more remote areas being opened up to tourists, though with less harmful impact.

COMMUNICATIONS

Even more than transportation, the world of communications has undergone a revolution of far-reaching proportions. As noted above, this has less to do with the speed of communications than with the quantity of information and entertainment that can be transmitted, the geographic scope of the modern communications infrastructure, and the different types of communication this infrastructure can support. The communications revolution involves the spread of one-way media broadcasting from a single point and received at many points (radio and television), two-way forms sending information from one point to another (telephones and faxes), and multiple sender and receiver forms (the Internet).

But before turning to electronic forms of communications, it is important to examine the extent of print media, which remain a key method of transmitting information.

Newspapers and Literacy

Although, at first glance, it would appear that the diffusion of print media, unlike radio and television, would increase with literacy, that is not necessarily the case, as seen in Table 8.4. Why not?

Perhaps, the most important reason for the simultaneous rise in literacy rates in developing countries and the decline in newspaper readership—the latter a factor in developed countries as well—can be ascribed to the rise of electronic media. Unlike newspapers, television and radio can provide information and entertainment

Table 8.4

Adult Literacy Rates, 1965-1995

Country	Newspapers per 1,000 persons*/ Adult literacy rate		
	1965	1980	1995
Argentina	148	142	143
	n.a.	94.0%	96%
Canada	227	221	204
	95%	96%	98%
China	19	34	43
	n.a.	56%	81.5%
France	245	192	205
	96%	98%	98%
Ghana	29	47	18
	26.7%	53.4%	64.5%
Guatemala	31	29	18
	38%	55.3%	55.5%
Malaysia	57	59	117
	n.a.	73.5%	83.5%
Pakistan	n.a.	12	6
	n.a	25.6%	37%
Poland	167	236	159
	n.a.	98.8%	98%
Syria	21	13	22
	40%	59.7%	71%

* Among daily and weekly newspapers sold on a regular basis.

without a distribution network. At the same time, as television and radio become more widespread, people choose to obtain their news and entertainment from a medium that is both more visually engaging and, after the initial purchase of the television set or radio, free of charge. Moreover, the younger population in much of the developing world does not have a strong newspaper reading tradition because it has grown up with radio and television. Thus, as the youth population rises, there are fewer newspapers sold per person, a phenomenon also seen in the developing world, though at a slower pace.

Television and Radio

The explosion in the number of radios and televisions—in both the developing and the developed world—has reduced the cost of reception and transmission equipment. At the same time, the size of this equipment has shrunk greatly, even as its power has expanded, allowing more of the world's poor to afford at least a radio; those with minimal discretionary income can even afford a television set. Table 8.5 records the increase in radio and television ownership between 1965 and 1995 for selected countries.

As noted in the introduction to the section on communications, the rapid spread of radio and television availability has both positive and negative implications. On the one hand, widespread radio and television ownership allows critical information to be broadcast to wide sectors of the population at low cost to governments and international agencies. As the United Nations has found, the level of awareness of contraceptive methods and sources rises with the level of radio and television ownership, particularly in countries with high rates of female illiteracy.

On the other hand, the potential for Western, and in particular American, cultural influence also rises with the extent of radio and television ownership, a trend that is evident in both the developed and the developing world. In 1989, the United States was the largest broadcaster of external radio programs, at some 2,374 hours per week. At the same time, nonlocal broadcasts dominated many of the world's television airwaves. As of the mid-1980s, some 38 out of 53 countries surveyed in the developed and developing world broadcast programs originating from other countries at least a third of the time. The highest rate in the world was found in Uganda, some 83 percent of whose programming came from outside the country, mostly the United Kingdom and the United States.

Telephones and the Internet

Although the cost of telephone equipment has fallen, the telephone remains a relatively expensive means of communications since, until quite recently, it required wiring over great distances. The enormous cost of building such an infrastructure put the cost of telephone ownership beyond the means of all but the richest citizens of the developing world. Similarly, high infrastructure costs made it too expensive to hard-

Table 8.5

Radio and Television in Selected Countries 1965-1995 (per 1,000 persons)

| Country | Radios/televisions | | Percent change |
	1965	1995	
Argentina	310/80	672/220	116.8/175
Canada	502/267	992/618	97.6/31.5
China	14/0.2	184/38	1,214.3/18,400
France	330/138	890/412	169.7/198.6
Ghana	83/0.1	269/16	224.1/15,900
Guatemala	n.a./13	68/53	n.a./307.7
Malaysia	49/7	430/151	777.6/2,057
Pakistan	6/0.1	88/18	1,200/17,900
Poland	190/70	439/298	131.1/325.7
Syria	382/14	257/62	-32.7/342.9

wire regions with low populations densities, since the overall cost would be shared among too few telephone subscribers. Thus, in many developing countries, telephone ownership and even access have been confined to the larger towns and cities. At the same time, the inefficiency of many nationally owned telephone monopolies has created long waiting lists for connection. Many experts claim that privatization will shorten such lists, but it will also raise the cost of connection, thereby restricting telephones by other means. Mobile, or cellular, telephones might offer a way out of bottlenecks of cost, reach, and technology.

As of 1995, however, cellular phones had yet to penetrate much of the developed world and most of the developing world. Thus, telephone ownership remains far behind that of radio and television, especially in the developing world. Moreover, telephone ownership is much more closely tied to rising levels of economic prosperity. In countries like Malaysia and China, rapidly rising incomes mean higher telephone ownership. In countries with stagnant per capita incomes like Canada, telephone ownership has remained flat, while in economically depressed Ghana, it has dropped significantly. The upsurge in France—where the economy also remains flat—is related to increased competition and lower prices. Table 8.6 shows the growth in tele-

Table 8.6

Telephones in Selected Countries, 1975-1994
(per 100 persons)

	1975	1994	Percent change
Argentina	7.8	14.1	81
Canada	57.5	57.6	0.2
China	0.2	2.3	1.005
France	26.4	54.7	107
Ghana	0.6	0.3	-50
Guatemala	0.8	2.4	200
Malaysia	2.5	14.7	488
Pakistan	0.3	1.6	433
Poland	7.5	13.1	75
Syria	2.4	4.9	104

phone ownership in 1994 over the level in 1975.

The Internet offers a way out of the foreign content dilemma of one-way broadcasting systems like radio and television. But Internet access requires a computer, which, despite rapidly falling costs, remains outside the reach of a large minority of the developed world and the vast majority of the developing world. Moreover, most Internet access still requires telephone wiring, presenting the same access and cost problems as those associated with telephones. As of mid-1997, out of some 90 million people with Internet access worldwide, about 67 percent were in North America and another 20 percent in Europe, leaving just 13 percent in the rest of the world, including Japan.

CONCLUSION

The revolution in communications technologies and the further development of the local, national, and global transportation infrastructures promises to have a deep impact on demographic trends. On the one hand, the ever-expanding reach of telecommunications means closer contact between peoples around the globe. Similarly, the expanding transportation infrastructure— and the lower prices it brings to the movement of goods and peoples—promises more abundance, more travel, and more migration.

At the same time, however, there are potential negatives to these developments as well. If, as cur-

rent trends seem to indicate, the telecommunications infrastructure comes under the control of a few multinational firms and developed nations, the flow of information and communications may be restricted. Those who control the media can influence the opinions of the world. The flow of information can become one-way—that is, toward the developed world. The Internet, of course, offers an alternative since, by its very nature, it is controlled by all who have access to it. The question remains, however, how long that access will be free to all.

FURTHER READINGS

Andersson, Åke, and Roland Thord, eds. *The Future of Transportation and Communication: Visions and Perspectives from Europe, Japan and the U.S.A.* New York: Springer-Verlag, 1993.

Button, Kenneth, and David Pitfield, eds. *Transport Deregulation: An International Movement.* New York: St. Martin's Press, and London: Macmillan, 1991.

International Energy Agency. *Transport, Energy and Climate Change.* London: Organisation for Economic Co-operation and Development, 1997.

Lundberg, Donald, and Carolyn Lundberg. *International Travel and Tourism.* New York: Wiley, 1985, 2nd edition, 1993.

Makimoto, Tsugio, and David Manners. *Digital Nomad.* New York: Wiley, 1997.

McLuhan, Marshall. *Understanding Media: The Extensions of Man.* New York: McGraw-Hill, and London: Routledge, 1964.

Nieuwenhuis, Paul, and Peter Wells, eds. *Motor Vehicles in the Environment: Principles and Practice.* New York and Chichester, West Sussex: Wiley, 1994.

Randall, Neil. *The Soul of the Internet: Net Gods, Netizens and the Wiring of the World.* London and Boston: International Thomson Computer Press, 1997.

Skovmand, Michael, ed. *Media Cultures: Reappraising Transnational Media.* New York and London: Routledge, 1992.

Theobald, William, ed. *Global Tourism: The Next Decade.* Oxford and Boston: Butterworth-Heinemann, 1994, 2nd edition, 1998.

Willis, William James. *The Age of Multimedia and Turbonews.* Westport, CT: Praeger, 1994.

Zacher, Mark W. *Governing Global Networks: International Regimes for Transportation and Communications.* Cambridge and New York: Cambridge University Press, 1996.

Section 9

The Demography of Health Care and Education

HEALTH AND HEALTH CARE

It takes little more than a quick glance at any statistical source, such as the tables in this book, to see the obvious global trend in health care and education. Simply put, humanity—with a few exceptions—is growing healthier and better educated with each passing decade. There are a variety of reasons for this trend. Growing economies mean greater tax revenues for governments to spend on health clinics and schools and higher incomes for families to use to pay for hospital and school fees. Growing urbanization means that people have more local access to education and health-care facilities. New medical and communication technologies have lowered the cost of health care and increased access to educational facilities through broadcasts and the Internet. Indeed, understanding the upward trend in global education and especially global health requires a multifaceted approach.

The demography of health care involves such related disciplines as medical sociology (the interaction of social institutions and forces on health), medical anthropology (non-Western health care and health care attitudes), medical geography (the spatial dimensions of disease and health care), medical economics (the financing of health care), and epidemiology (the course of diseases within a population).

Each of these components adds its own distinct contribution to the overall study of health care demography. Medical sociology—especially in recent decades—has helped establish the link between poverty and illiteracy, on the one hand, and the level of health, on the other. It also connects political institutions, political participation, and health. The field of medical anthropology has helped lead researchers to examine popular attitudes toward medicine—Western and non-Western—and a population's willingness and likelihood to avail itself of the two different medical traditions.

Medical geography examines a narrow but significant field: the spatial distribution of health care factors and health care provision. Medical economics, of course, looks into the links among economic development, class, and health care. How is health care financed? How is health care purchased? And which classes have access to it? Finally, epidemiology—a field that straddles the border between the health sciences and the social sciences—focuses on how various population measures of all kinds, from age cohorts to level of urbanization, explain the source, spread, and control of communicable and noncommunicable diseases.

Health Care Institutions and Influences

Health care institutions differ radically from one country to another, particularly between the developed and the developing worlds. In most developed countries, health care is provided by governmental or quasi-governmental agencies and financed through general government revenues. Most countries have small private health care sectors that provide elective procedures not covered by national insurance plans, as well as better conditions of health care, such as private hospital rooms. In the United States, unlike the other advanced industrial countries, health care is now provided largely through health maintenance organizations (HMOs), usually in the form of for-profit corporations financed jointly by employees and employers. In addition, the United States offers government health care for the elderly and, to a lesser extent, the poor. An estimated 40 million Americans are not covered by any private or government health insurance and are forced to rely on emergency rooms—which by law are required to treat all comers—for their primary care.

Developing countries almost always have less extensive and less well-financed health care infrastructures, with great variations in quality between rural and urban areas and among the different economic classes. Mexico's system provides a typical example. In major cities, modern, well-equipped clinics and hospitals with highly trained staff are available to the roughly 4 million members of the middle and upper classes with private health insurance. For employed urban workers, the government provides an adequate health care safety net through its Social Security program. But for casual laborers, the urban unemployed, and rural peasants, the Ministry of Health offers local clinics. Most of these clinics are underfinanced, and patients must wait long hours, provide their own supplies and food, and sometimes pay bribes to obtain treatment.

Other than the level of national economic development or an individual's finances, many factors—environmental, historical, geographic, demographic, cultural, political, and social—determine a person's health and the kind of health care he or she is likely to receive. Overcrowded housing, inaccessability of decent water and sanitation, and high levels of pollution are the chief environmental factors. Access to safe drinking water and adequate sanitation range from a low of 37 and 31 percent, respectively, in such sub-Saharan African countries as Mali; to 83 and 66 percent, respectively, in a midlevel developing country such as Mexico; to 100 percent and 96 percent, respectively, in a developed country like the United Kingdom.

Historical factors include how long a health care program has been in effect. Germany, for example, has had a nationalized system of health care of one type or another for more than a hundred years; Singapore instituted one in the past few decades, and many developing countries have yet to create a coordinated system. Cultural influences on the health care system include attitudes about prevention versus healing (Japan emphasizes the former, the United States the latter), the role of the family as caregivers (especially important in cultures with large extended families), and the influence of traditional therapies, which are especially common in developing countries. In addition, there are social factors such as levels of smoking and nutrition.

Health Care and Economic Development

Clearly, however, the main ingredient in assessing the quality of health care in a given population is the level of economic development. With few exceptions, a country's health care program can be assessed best by taking account of its per capita income to measure overall wealth, and its level of poverty to determine the distribution of national wealth. Table 9.1 shows the levels of per capita income, poverty, and infant mortality for selected countries in 1995.

As the table clearly indicates, the lower the per capita income, the higher the infant mortality rate. Rwanda, which has a per capita income of $400 (the lowest of the countries listed in the table), has the highest infant mortality, 118.8 per 1,000 live births. But per capita income alone does not determine overall quality of health. For example, Brazil, which has a per capita income level of $6,100, has a relatively high infant mortality rate of 57.7 per 1,000. The enormous disparities in wealth—as reflected in the high poverty rate of 43.5 percent of the population living on less than $2 day—are clearly a factor there. Thailand, which has a similar per capita

Table 9.1

Income, Poverty Levels, and Infant Mortality in Selected Countries, 1995

Country	Per capita income ($)	Poverty (percent)*	Infant mortality per 1,000 live births
Algeria	3,800	17.6	48.7
Brazil	6,100	43.5	57.7
Bulgaria	4,920	23.5	15.8
China	2,900	57.8	44.5
Côte d'Ivoire	1,500	54.8	91.7
Germany	17,900	0.0	5.6
Hungary	7,000	10.7	12.3
India	1,500	88.8	71.1
Jamaica	3,200	24.9	15.6
Kazakstan	2,700	12.1	63.2
Mexico	7,700	40.0	25.0
Rwanda	400	8 8.7	118.8
Thailand	6,900	23.5	33.4
United States	27,500	0.0	6.7

*Defined as living on $2 day or less.

income but roughly half the poverty rate, has an infant mortality rate of 33.4 per 1,000.

Political and institutional issues come into play as well. For example, the relatively extensive health care systems developed under communist regimes—now under pressure because of the financial chaos that has followed the transition to a market economy—have been able to keep infant mortality levels relatively low, despite falling per capita incomes and rising levels of poverty. Bulgaria—which has a per capita income just two-thirds that of Thailand and a similar poverty rate—has an infant mortality rate of just 15.8 per 1,000, well under the Thai level. At the high end of economic development, Germany and the United States provide a useful comparison. Although its per capita income is roughly two-thirds that of the United States, Germany has an infant mortality rate some 16 percent lower (6.7 per 1,000 live births), perhaps because Germany has an extensive national health care system and the United States does not.

This critical issue of health care provision becomes even more significant when health expenditures are considered. In 1994, the United States spent 13.6 percent of its gross domestic product (GDP) on health care, or $3,086 per person. By comparison, Germany allocated just 8.7 percent of its GDP, or $1,775 per person. At the same time, a developing country like Mexico expended only 4.0 percent of its GDP on health care, roughly $300 per person. When we compare expenditures and infant mortality rates, it becomes clear that both Germany and Mexico allocated their health care dollars far more efficiently than did the United States: Germany had a lower rate of infant mortality despite spending two-thirds as much per person, while Mexico spent roughly one-tenth as much and had an infant mortality rate only four times as high. Although this is a crude comparison, it shows that health care expenditures alone do not determine the overall quality of health care in a given country. The market-driven system in the United States often duplicates facilities, and the fact that large segments of the population lack health care insurance results in the need for heavy expenditures in post-illness care rather than in preventive care. In Germany, where all citizens are automatically covered and all health care costs are assumed by the government, the emphasis is on preventive care, since this is more economically efficient. As for Mexico, its low-tech approach—along with its extensive and closely knit families, which often provide basic health care to their own family members—means that each health care dollar goes farther.

This relationship between health care and economic development can be examined in even finer detail. For instance, there is a direct relationship among per capita income, poverty rates, and death rates, as well as a connection between economic development and the causes of death. Taking Thailand—one of the newly industrialized countries (NICs) of Southeast Asia—as an example, it is possible to see how rising incomes lead to the prevalence of different diseases. In 1965, the number one cause of death in Thailand was diarrheal diseases—31 deaths per 100,000 persons, usually among infants and the children—caused by poor sanitation and inadequate supplies of safe drinking water. This was compounded by both the country's tropical climate and its primarily rural living conditions, making it difficult for many people to travel to basic health care clinics.

By 1985, the number of deaths caused by diarrheal diseases had fallen to just 3 per 100,000 and they had become the sixth most common cause of death in the country. During those same two decades, heart disease— a health condition primarily of the elderly—had climbed from the number five cause of death in the country to the leading cause. In 1965, some 12 persons per 100,000 died of heart disease; by 1985, that figure had risen to 37 per 100,000. The life expectancy at birth rose from 56.1 years in 1965 to roughly 63 years in 1985. In other words, as childhood diseases like diarrhea were conquered, people lived longer, leading to higher rates of other medical conditions that affect older people, such as heart disease.

Not all health care statistics—particularly in the developing world—have been this positive. Indeed, while Thailand, until quite recently, experienced one of the fastest rates of economic expansion in the world, much of the developing world was experiencing stagnant growth and high foreign debt. In order to revive their economies and alleviate their debt, many of them have

had to accept harsh financial measures from their creditors, the major international lending institutions like the World Bank and the International Monetary Fund. One of the key demands of these institutions has been a contraction in public spending, including that on health care.

In the early 1980s, at the height of the debt crisis in the developing world, many countries were forced to shrink their health care sectors. Zambia, for example, spent 22 percent less on health in 1985 than it did in 1982. Bolivia cut its spending in this sector by 30 percent between 1980 and 1984. Moreover, the deepest cuts have come in those areas where hard currencies, such as dollars, are needed—for instance, in the purchase of medical equipment and pharmaceuticals. While Zambia's overall health care spending fell 22 percent over three years, its purchases of medicines dropped 75 percent over roughly the same period. Not surprisingly, diseases that had seemed to be eliminated from much of the developing world by the 1970s were reappearing: for example, yellow fever in Ghana and typhoid in Chile.

Geography and Health Care

Geographic considerations must be included in assessing the health care situation in a given country. As seen in Table 9.1, Kazakstan and Jamaica have per capita incomes that are fairly close ($2,700 and $3,200 respectively), though Jamaica's poverty rate of 24.9 percent is more than double Kazakstan's 12.1 percent. But whereas Jamaica is a small, evenly populated island (with a population density of 596 persons per square mile) where nearly everyone lives close to health care facilities, Kazakstan (16 persons per square mile) is a vast, underpopulated land where many live hundreds of miles from a hospital.

Clearly, geography determines access to health care and urban populations are more likely to be served by nearby facilities than are those in rural areas. But even this basic difference masks the complexity of the problem of geography and access to health care. In large countries in particular, health care facilities are not evenly distributed, even within rural areas. In India, for example, the relatively prosperous state of Punjab has roughly four times more hospital beds per capita in rural areas than does the impoverished state of Bihar. Moreover, in Indian states where the government has made rural primary health care delivery a priority, the differences with lower-priority regions are even more marked. In Kerala, where the communist-led government has expended large amounts of money, there is roughly one rural hospital bed for every 1,000 persons. In Madhya Pradesh, where the government's effort to provide more health care facilities in rural areas has been more fitful and underfinanced, the rate is one hospital bed for every 33,000 persons.

Urbanization and industrialization are also critical in the provision of and access to health care facilities. In Zambia, for example, the difference is noticeable. In territories along the rail lines that knit the vast southern African country together and are more heavily urbanized, there are more than 50 doctors per every 100,000 persons. In the more remote areas of the north and west, the rate is just 2 to 3 physicians per 100,000 persons. This pattern is repeated throughout Africa. For example, in Mozambique in 1990, while 100 percent of urbanites had access to some Western-style free health care, just 30 percent of rural inhabitants did. In Uganda and Morocco, the rates were 90 percent for urban and 57 percent for rural, and 100 percent for urban and 50 percent for rural, respectively.

Although urbanization is accompanied by more health care providers and facilities, it also introduces more health problems. The proportion of the developing world's population living in urban areas has increased greatly in recent decades, a trend expected to continue into the foreseeable future. In 1965, roughly 1 in 7 people in the developing world lived in cities; by 1995, roughly 1 in 3 did; and by 2025, it is expected that half the population in the developing world will be city dwellers.

Most of these urbanites will be desperately poor, living in overcrowded slums or shantytowns, with little safe drinking water and inadequate sanitation. Although urban rates of health generally tend to be better, there remain vast discrepancies among different sectors of the urban population. It has been estimated by some health care researchers that infant mortality rates in the poorer parts of major urban areas of the developing world can be from 4 to 10 times higher than those in the wealthier parts. (Of course, this is also true in many cities of the developed world; in New York City, for example, it is estimated that infant mortality rates in Harlem are 4 times higher than those in the more affluent sections of the city.)

History and Health Care Demography

The discrepancies in health care provision and the sorry state of public health can be understood in part by examining the political and economic histories of countries in the developing world. By the turn of the twentieth century, outside Latin America, most of the developing world had been colonized by European states, Japan, or the United States. To differing degrees, these colonizers failed to create either an adequate health care infrastructure or one that largely met the needs of the local European population and the indigenous elite. For the most part, this meant an emphasis on hospitals in urban areas or in areas of critical economic importance to the colonizer.

After the wave of independence that swept most of the developing world in the two decades following World War II, local elites—particularly in countries that failed to develop democratic institutions—often picked up where the colonizers left off. Many lavished their few resources for health care on urban areas, particularly in the form of modern, Western-style "prestige" medical centers. These were meant to serve the urban elites as well as indicate that the country had achieved a certain level of modernity. There were significant variations, however. Some countries—in particular those undergoing social revolutions like Cuba or Mozambique, but also democratic countries like India—emphasized numerous small health clinics in poor urban and rural areas. But these were exceptions to the rule.

Thus, in much of the developing world, health care provision—poor to begin with—was devastated by the economic crisis that hit many poor countries in the 1980s, when international prices fell for the raw materials they exported. Moreover, because of corruption and mismanagement, many of these countries were heavily in debt, some of which was incurred to build the "prestige" medical centers. When banks and international lending agencies began to impose austerity plans and privatization programs, the already precarious health care facilities in poor urban and rural areas deteriorated. Moreover, many superior city hospitals were privatized, forcing them to raise prices or reduce services offered to the poor at no cost or at subsidized prices. Most of the gains in health and health care in the developing world came in the early period of independence, from 1965 to 1980, and less so in the later era from 1980 to 1995.

AIDS/HIV and the Cultural Dimension of Health

Since 1981, when it was first mentioned in the medical journals, acquired immune deficiency syndrome (AIDS) has grown to pandemic, or global epidemic, proportions. By 1992, the number of people afflicted with the disease had climbed to 1.5 million worldwide and, by 1998, to an estimated 10 million. The number of those infected with the human immunodeficiency virus (HIV) increased to an even greater extent, from about 10 million carriers in 1992 to roughly 100 million in 1998. (Of course, the huge jump is attributable in part to better detection techniques and efforts, as well as to the increasing willingness of governments to admit that their populations are affected.)

The global distribution of the disease was not even, however. As of 1992, the vast majority of cases—some two-thirds—were in sub-Saharan Africa. Southeast Asia had about 10 percent, as did Latin America. The remaining 15 percent of the cases were in the developed world, largely in the United States and Western Europe. More than just geography was involved.

In the developed world, the disease was con-fined largely to male homosexuals and intravenous drug users, though more recently it has been spreading among African-American and Hispanic females. Extensive education campaigns among gay men in the developed world have lowered the rate of infection in that community, while the continued high use of intravenous drugs among blacks and Latinos has allowed the virus to cross over into the female population.

But it is in the developing world that the disease has taken the largest toll. In recent years, it has spread rapidly in Southeast Asia. There the problem has been caused by a lack of education, liberal sexual attitudes, and the prevalence of prostitution. In Africa, where many believe the disease originated, many experts blame urbanization for the massive spread of the disease. The breakdown of village culture—with its social restrictions and close-knit families—and the move to urban areas led many younger Africans to adopt the less restrictive ways associated with modern, Western-style life. Moreover, the disease tended to spread along lines of transport, as itinerant workers and truck drivers transmitted the disease from one urban area to another through sexual contacts with prostitutes.

Thus, today, the highest incidences of AIDS in Africa can be seen along the main transport routes of East Africa, from Uganda in the north to Zimbabwe in the south. In 1995, Uganda had roughly 48,000 official cases of AIDS out of a population of 20.2 million—a rate of 1 case for every 420 persons; Zimbabwe had 41,000 out of a population of 11.3 million—a rate of 1 case for every 275 persons. In West Africa, outside the main transmission route, the rate is much lower. In Cameroon, for example, there were just 5,375 cases out of a population of 14.3 million, a rate of 1 case for every 2,660 persons.

EDUCATION

The demographics of education involve three areas of inquiry. First is the impact of population and economic statistics—including age, sex, class, geographic distribution, and level of economic development—on various educational systems. Second are the demographics of the educational process itself: How many are enrolled in what kinds of educational institutions? Third is the impact of education on population statistics, including such key indicators as fertility, literacy, and employment.

Demographic and Economic Influences on Education

Educational levels have risen everywhere in the past thirty years, especially in the developing world. Along with the rise in health indicators, the increase in educational achievement is one of the more remarkable developments of the post–World War II era. The achievement is even more remarkable in light of the increase in the number of school-age children in most developing countries. In Brazil, for example, the population under the age of 15 climbed from 29 million in 1965 to more than 50 million in 1995; in Côte d'Ivoire, 1.4 million to 7.1 million; in India, 179 million to 324 million.

At the same time, these countries boasted substantial increases in the number of students attending school at various levels. In Brazil, where most children attended primary school, the advances were largely at the secondary level. In 1965, just 19 percent of the school-age population was attending secondary institutions; by 1995, that figure was 45 percent. In Côte d'Ivoire, substantial achievements were also made in secondary education, where the number of school-age children in such institutions rose from just 6 percent in 1965 to 23 percent in 1995. In India, the achievements have occurred at both the primary and secondary levels. In 1965, just 56 and 15 percent of all appropriate school-age children attended primary and secondary institutions, respectively; by 1995, those figures were 100 and 49 percent, respectively. (The rate at which school-age children attend a particular level of educational institution can be a misleading statistic since, in many developing countries, people outside that age group may also be attending. For example, the 100 percent figure for primary school enrollment in India in 1995 does not mean that 100 percent of all children between the ages

of 5 and 11 are attending primary school, since some of the students may be over the age of 11.)

What accounts for these achievements? First, there is the matter of expenditures. Throughout the developing world, governments have placed a great emphasis on education, since higher educational levels have been recognized as the key to economic development, better health, and slower population growth (see the section below on the influence of education on demographics). Of course, there is both a virtuous and a vicious cycle when it comes to education and economic development. On the positive side, in a country like Malaysia, rapid economic growth has meant more money for education and thus rapidly rising educational levels, which lead to better economic performance. On the negative side, declining economies have a direct impact on educational levels. In the case of Côte d'Ivoire, for example, rising international prices for Ivoirean exports like cocoa in the 1960s and 1970s allowed for more spending on education and thus for higher enrollment levels. Between 1965 and 1980, primary school enrollment increased from 60 to 75 percent of the school-age population. But the collapse of cocoa and other Ivoirean raw material prices in the 1980s had a direct impact on educational funding and, hence, on enrollment rates. By 1995, the enrollment rate at primary institutions in Côte d'Ivoire had fallen to 69 percent of the school-age population. This can only have a negative impact on the country's future economic development.

In addition to direct economic factors, there is the matter of urbanization. As in the case of health care, urbanites have a much better chance of receiving an education—even discounting for higher income levels—than those living in rural areas. Educational facilities are more geographically accessible in cities, and city schools in developing countries tend to be better financed than their rural counterparts.

Demographics of Education

As noted above, the level of enrollment in both primary and secondary schools around the world has increased greatly in the past thirty years, but the achievements represent a mixed bag. In the developed world (in both capitalist and communist countries), where primary and secondary education was nearly universal even in 1965, the real growth in enrollment has been at the tertiary level—that is, in colleges, universities, and professional schools. In France, for example, enrollment at tertiary institutions rose from 10.5 percent of university-age students in 1965 to 50 percent in 1995. Even in the lower tier of developed countries, the same held true. In Portugal, the rate climbed from about 4 percent to 34 percent over the same period. The same trend is noticeable in the former communist countries of Eastern Europe, despite the recent turmoil. In Romania, for instance, the rate of enrollment at tertiary institutions rose from roughly 7 percent of university-age students in 1965 to 18 percent in 1995.

In the developing world, the record is a bit less positive. At the primary and secondary levels, the biggest gains have come in countries with substantial economic growth. In Thailand, for example, the enrollment rate at secondary institutions increased from 12 percent of school-age children in 1965 to 55 percent in 1995. Economic growth was not the only criterion for expansion, however. Middle-tier developing countries that have not necessarily had rapid economic growth but have had relative political stability over the past thirty years have experienced improvement in their educational statistics. In Jamaica, for instance, the rate of school-age children attending secondary institutions climbed from 16 percent in 1965 to 67 percent in the 1980s. However, the declining economic fortunes of the island in the past couple of decades have led to stagnant growth in education. Between 1980 and 1995, the rate of school-age children attending secondary institutions remained roughly flat.

Even the poorest of countries have made substantial gains, although their low starting points mean that even substantial increases represent low enrollment. For example, in Guinea, where the per capita income is just $1,000 annually, the rate of school-age children attending primary institutions increased from 31 percent to 48 per-

cent between 1965 and 1995, while the rate at the secondary level rose from just 1 percent to 24 percent in the same period. In war-torn or politically unstable countries, educational levels remain even more stunted. In Mozambique, for instance, where anticolonial and civil wars have been raging almost continuously since the early 1960s, the rate of school-age children attending primary institutions has fallen continuously from 99 percent in 1965 to just 60 percent in 1995.

One trend, however, is beyond dispute. The number of female children, young people, and adults attending various educational institutions has risen, in both relative and absolute numbers. This is true for primary and secondary institutions in the developing world and for tertiary institutions in the developed world. This trend has been most marked in those regions that previously denied education to most girls and women. In South Asia, for example, the enrollment rate of school-age girls attending primary and secondary institutions rose from 32 to 43 percent between 1980 and 1990; in primarily Islamic North Africa, the rates are 50 and 67 percent, respectively. Proportionally, too, the gains are impressive. Whereas girls represented just 40 percent of all students in primary and secondary students in North Africa in 1980, that proportion had risen to 45 percent by 1989. Similarly, in South Asia, the proportion rose from 38 to 42 percent.

Meanwhile, in the developed world, the number of women attending universities rose both proportionally and in absolute terms. In Western Europe, roughly 50 women attended tertiary educational institutions for every 100 men in 1980; by 1990, there were roughly 90 women for every 100 men. In Eastern Europe, the figure went from 78 to 102. In other words, slightly more women than men were attending tertiary institutions in Eastern Europe in 1990.

The Influence of Education on Demographics

As noted above, as educational levels in a given country rise (or fall), they have a direct impact on the economic and demographic profile of that society. The link with economic development has already been discussed, but rising levels of education also have an enormous impact on population growth. According to the United Nations, women's fertility is in inverse proportion to their educational levels. Areas where women's illiteracy rates are high have the highest fertility rates. The states of North Africa and Southwestern Asia (or the Middle East), for instance, have an average female illiteracy rate of 56 percent. Fertility rates there stand at roughly 4.8 children per woman. In the countries of East and Southeast Asia, where female illiteracy rates average 23 percent, the fertility level is 3.2 children per female.

In addition to illiteracy, various educational levels affect fertility. For example, women with no education in sub-Saharan Africa have a fertility rate of 7 children each; with six years of education (roughly primary school), the fertility rate drops to 6.5. But from there, it declines steeply. Women in sub-Saharan Africa with 10 years or more of education (that is, secondary or tertiary) have an average of just 4 children each. Sub-Saharan Africa is unique only in the small drop associated with primary school levels of education.

In Latin America and the Caribbean, the difference between no education and a primary school education is 6.4 children for those women with the former and just 4.1 for those with the latter. Asia presents a different scenario. There educational levels matter less. The difference between women with no education and women who have finished high school—in terms of their average number of children—is 3.4 and 2.4. In Asia, it appears, overall higher educational levels for the population as a whole have had the biggest impact on fertility, in that they have lowered it for all women of all educational levels.

CONCLUSION

Despite substantial gains in the areas of health care and education in the thirty years between 1965 and 1995, there are nevertheless dark clouds on the horizon. In the developed world, demographic trends threaten to overwhelm health care facilities and undermine the political constituency for education. That is to say, as the population ages, it will require and demand increasing financial resources committed to health care. At the same time, an aging population means that there is a shrinking political consensus for adequately funding schools.

In the developing world, the problems are different, but even more acute. Here, rapidly expanding populations of young persons and steadily increasing populations of elderly threaten to overwhelm both health care and educational facilities. At the same time, the developing world remains mired in an economic slump that has affected even the best national performers in East and Southeast Asia. Ironically, the rapid economic gains made in these countries have been due in large part to expanded educational opportunities. Thus, the economic collapse in places like Indonesia and Thailand may be as self-perpetuating as the previous economic boom. That is, as economic resources dry up, so does educational funding. And with a less well-educated population, economies may suffer further.

FURTHER READINGS

Basch, Paul F. *Textbook of International Health.* Oxford and New York: Oxford University Press, 1990; 2nd edition, New York: Oxford University Press, 1999.

Grant, James P. *The State of the World's Children* 1993. Oxford and New York: Oxford University Press for UNICEF, 1993.

Lassey, Marie, William Lassey, and Martin Jinks. *Health Care Systems Around the World: Characteristics, Issues, Reforms.* Upper Saddle River, NJ: Prentice-Hall, 1997.

Phillips, David R., and Yola Verhasselt. *Health and Development.* London and New York: Routledge, 1994.

Pol, Louis G., and Richard K. Thomas. *The Demography of Health and Health Care.* New York: Plenum Press, 1992.

Roemer, Milton I. *National Health Systems of the World, Vol. 1, The Countries.* Oxford and New York: Oxford University Press, 1991.

————. *National Health Systems of the World, Vol. 2, The Issues.* Oxford and New York: Oxford University Press, 1993.

United Nations. Department for Economic and Social Information and Policy Analysis, Population Division. *Levels and Trends of Contraceptive Use as Assessed in 1994.* New York: United Nations, 1996.

United Nations. Department for Economic and Social Information and Policy Analysis, Statistical Division. *The World's Women, 1995: Trends and Statistics.* New York: United Nations, 1995.

U.S. Department of Education, Office of Educational Research and Improvement. *Education in States and Nations: Indicators Comparing U.S. States with the OECD Countries in 1988.* Washington, DC, 1993.

Part Two

Tables

How to Use the Tables

The tables in this encyclopedia offer a demographic profile of all the world's sovereign states (as well as Puerto Rico). The statistical information in the tables was gathered from various U.N. and other official publications. For a list of sources, see the bibliography immediately following this section. The authors have tried to simplify the presentation of statistical material as much as possible, through the use of consistent terms and comparable data. Still, the terms and data require some explanation. Below are explanations of some major categories, in the order in which they appear in the tables.

Note: Dates in parentheses correspond to data for years different from the ones listed at the top of the tables. For example, a datum in the 1995 column with a (91) after it means the datum actually refers to 1991. The term "rate" signifies the number per 1,000 residents.

GEOGRAPHY

AREA: Total area, including internal bodies of water.

LAND AREA: Total land area, excluding internal bodies of water.

COASTLINE: Total coastlines, including those on major internal seas.

CITIES: Population within city limits, *not* for entire metropolitan areas.

POPULATION

TOTAL: Total population at the end of the given year.

DENSITY: Number of persons living in a given geographical area.

ANNUAL GROWTH: Percentage growth of the population in a given year.

AGE COHORTS: Percentage of persons falling into the given age cohorts or groups.

MALE/FEMALE: Percentage of population by gender.

URBAN/RURAL: Urban statistics include people living in inner suburbs.

NET MIGRATION RATE: Persons leaving (emigrants) versus persons arriving (immigrants). A negative rate means more people are leaving than arriving.

IDENTITY

Where no percentages are given, the items listed are from largest to smallest. Where it says "official," the language listed is the language of government, and not necessarily spoken by a significant percentage of the population.

ETHNICITY: Refers to cultural and ethnic groups as defined by the national government.

LANGUAGE: Those who speak a given language as their primary tongue.

RELIGION: Includes practitioners and those who are born into a given faith, though they may not practice it. "Indigenous" refers to local faiths.

VITAL STATISTICS

BIRTH RATE: Births per 1,000 persons.

INFANT MORTALITY RATE: Deaths of babies in their first year of life per 1,000 babies born.

ABORTION RATE: Legally induced abortions per 1,000 live births.

LIFE EXPECTANCY AT BIRTH: Life expectancy for all persons.

MARRIAGE RATE: Marriages per 1,000 persons.

DIVORCE RATE: Divorces per 1,000 persons.

AVERAGE AGE AT MARRIAGE: Marrying ages, including persons who have married more than once.

DEATH RATE: Deaths per 1,000 persons.

HOUSEHOLDS

HOUSEHOLDS: Persons living within a single residence, including family members and others.

SINGLE: Households headed by a person who has never married.

MARRIED: Households with parents living at home.

WIDOWED: Households headed by a widow or widower.

DIVORCED: Households headed by a person who has separated or been divorced from his or her spouse.

ECONOMICS AND LABOR

GDP PER CAPITA US$: Gross domestic product (GDP); average income per person in 1995 dollars.

LABOR FORCE: Persons participating in the commercial economy. Excludes those who primarily rely on subsistence farming, fishing, hunting, or gathering.

AGRICULTURE: Persons engaged in agriculture, including farmers, pastoralists, and foresters.

MINING: Persons engaged in underground and surface mining, or quarrying.

MANUFACTURING: Persons working in the production of goods, including handicrafts.

UTILITIES: Persons employed in industries producing or providing energy, fuel, or water.

CONSTRUCTION: Persons involved in the construction of temporary and permanent buildings.

TRADE/FOOD/TOURISM: Includes persons in retail and wholesale trades, retail and wholesale food sales and distribution, restaurants, hotels, hostels, and other tourist services.

TRANSPORT/COMMUNICATIONS: Persons involved in the transport of passengers, the transport and storage of goods, and the provision or production of electronic and print communications and media, including newspapers and magazines; books; recordings; films and videos; telephone, telegraph, television, radio, and Internet service.

FINANCE/INSURANCE/REAL ESTATE: Persons involved in banking; securities; commodity exchanges; insurance of all types; and the buying, selling, and brokering of real property.

SOCIAL AND PERSONAL SERVICES: Persons involved in the provision of welfare, health, education, and personal services.

UNEMPLOYMENT: Percentage as determined by the national government. This does not include individuals who have given up looking for work and those who are not involved in the commercial economy. *Note: Official rates usually underestimate the number of people needing or wanting paid employment.*

UNION DENSITY: Percentage of the commercial workforce who are members of independent or government-run unions.

TRANSPORT

RAILROAD PASSENGER TRIPS: A statistic reached by multiplying the number of passenger trips times the distance times one million.

AIR PASSENGER TRIPS: A statistic reached by multiplying the number of passenger trips times 1,000.

PRIVATE CARS: Vehicles licensed for noncommercial purposes (excludes two- and three-wheeled vehicles).

COMMERCIAL: All vehicles—regardless of the number of wheels or axles—licensed for commercial use.

HEALTH AND HEALTH CARE

HEALTH CARE: Statistics concerning the provision of health care services.

ACCESS TO SANITATION: Percentage of persons living in housing with adequate sanitation, as defined by the United Nations.

MEASLES IMMUNIZATION: Percentage of children under 12 who have received at least one immunization against measles.

RATE OF PHYSICIANS: Number of physicians per 1,000 residents.

RATE OF HOSPITAL BEDS: Number of hospital beds per 1,000 residents.

HEALTH: Statistics concerning the health of a country's population.

LOW-BIRTH-WEIGHT BABIES: Percentage of babies born underweight, as defined by the United Nations.

CHILD MALNUTRITION: Percentage of children under 5 years of age who are not receiving an adequate diet, as defined by the United Nations.

SMOKING PREVALENCE: Percentage of persons who smoke tobacco on a regular basis.

TUBERCULOSIS INCIDENCE RATE: Sufferers from all forms of tuberculosis per 1,000 persons.

AIDS/HIV CASES: Persons afflicted with acquired immune deficiency syndrome (AIDS) or known to be infected by human immunodeficiency virus (HIV). *Note: All figures in the 1980 column are for 1993.*

TOTAL DEATHS: Persons dying from all causes in a given year.

EDUCATION

Note: Figures for this column may exceed 100 percent, because persons outside the school-age group considered may be attending school.

PRIMARY: Percentage of primary school-age children attending primary school.

SECONDARY: Percentage of secondary school-age children attending secondary school.

HIGHER: Percentage of young persons attending institutions of higher learning, including colleges, universities, military academies, and technical institutions.

FEMALES IN SCHOOL: *Note: Due to discrepancies in the sources, data in this section are defined in two ways. See immediately below.*

OF (OR IN) PRIMARY/SECONDARY/HIGHER: Percentage of school-age girls attending a given school level.

PRIMARY/SECONDARY/HIGHER: Percentage of school-age children and young persons who are female.

COMMUNICATIONS

RATE OF NEWSPAPERS: Newspapers sold on a regular basis (usually daily or weekly) per 1,000 persons.

RATE OF RADIOS: Radios owned per 1,000 persons.

RATE OF TELEVISIONS: Television sets owned per 1,000 persons.

Note: Metric Conversions

The following conversion rates are used in this volume:

1 square mile = 2.59 square kilometers

1 linear mile = 1.6 linear kilometers

Table Bibliography and Sources

The bibliography provides full citations for the information given in the tables that follow. The short citation in parentheses corresponds to the bibliographic sources given at the end of each table.

BIBLIOGRAPHY

Central Intelligence Agency. *The World Factbook, 1997–98.* Washington DC: Brassey's, 1997. (CIA, *The World Factbook,* 1997)

International Labour Office. *World Labour Report: Industrial Relations, Democracy and Social Stability.* Geneva: International Labour Organization, 1997. (ILO. *World Labour Report,* 1997)

Department for Economic and Social Information and Policy Analysis, Statistics Division. *1995 Demographic Yearbook.* New York: United Nations, 1997. (UN, *Demographic Yearbook,* 1997)

———. *1994 Statistical Yearbook.* New York: United Nations, 1996. (UN, *Statistical Yearbook,* 1996)

World Bank. *World Development Indicators, 1998.* Washington DC: World Bank, 1998. (World Bank, *World Development Indicators,* 1998)

TABLE SOURCES

Geography

AREA: CIA, *The World Factbook,* 1997

LAND AREA: CIA, *The World Factbook,* 1997

COASTLINE: CIA, *The World Factbook,* 1997

CITIES: UN, *Demographic Yearbook,* 1997

Population

POPULATION: UN, *Demographic Yearbook,* 1997, 1981, 1966

DENSITY: UN, *Demographic Yearbook,* 1997, 1981, 1966

ANNUAL GROWTH: UN, *Demographic Yearbook,* 1997, 1981, 1966

AGE COHORTS: UN, *Demographic Yearbook,* 1997, 1981, 1966

MALE/FEMALE: UN, *Demographic Yearbook,* 1997, 1981, 1966

URBAN/RURAL: UN, *Demographic Yearbook,* 1997, 1981, 1966

NET MIGRATION: 1995: CIA, *The World Factbook,* 1997; 1980, 1965: UN *Demographic Yearbook,* 1981, 1966

Identity

ETHNICITY: CIA, *The World Factbook,* 1997

LANGUAGE: CIA, *The World Factbook,* 1997

RELIGION: CIA, *The World Factbook,* 1997

Vital Statistics

BIRTH RATE: UN, *Demographic Yearbook,* 1997, 1981, 1966

INFANT MORTALITY RATE: UN, *Demographic Yearbook,* 1997, 1981, 1966

ABORTION: UN, *Demographic Yearbook,* 1997

LIFE EXPECTANCY: UN, *Demographic Yearbook,* 1997, 1981, 1966

MARRIAGE RATE: UN, *Demographic Yearbook,* 1997, 1981, 1966

DIVORCE RATE: UN, *Demographic Yearbook,* 1997, 1981, 1966

AVERAGE AGE AT MARRIAGE: UN, *Demographic Yearbook,* 1997, 1981, 1966

DEATH RATE: UN, *Demographic Yearbook,* 1997, 1981, 1966

Households

HOUSEHOLDS: UN, *Demographic Yearbook,* 1997, 1981, 1966

SINGLE: UN, *Demographic Yearbook,* 1997, 1981, 1966

MARRIED: UN, *Demographic Yearbook,* 1997, 1981, 1966

WIDOWED: UN, *Demographic Yearbook,* 1997, 1981, 1966

DIVORCED: UN, *Demographic Yearbook,* 1997, 1981, 1966

Economics and Labor

GDP PER CAPITA US$: CIA, *The World Factbook,* 1997

LABOR FORCE: UN, *Statistical Yearbook,* 1996

UNEMPLOYMENT: UN, *Statistical Yearbook,* 1996

UNION DENSITY: ILO, *World Labour Report,* 1997

POVERTY: World Bank, *World Development Indicators,* 1998

Transport

RAILROAD PASSENGER TRIPS: UN, *Statistical Yearbook,* 1996

AIR PASSENGER TRIPS: UN, *Statistical Yearbook,* 1996

PRIVATE CARS: UN, *Statistical Yearbook,* 1996, 1981, 1966

COMMERCIAL: UN, *Statistical Yearbook,* 1996, 1981, 1966

Health and Health Care

ACCESS TO SANITATION: World Bank, *World Development Indicators,* 1998

MEASLES IMMUNIZATION: World Bank, *World Development Indicators,* 1998

RATE OF PHYSICIANS: World Bank, *World Development Indicators,* 1998

RATE OF HOSPITAL BEDS: World Bank, *World Development Indicators,* 1998

Health

LOW BIRTHWEIGHT BABIES: World Bank, *World Development Indicators,* 1998

CHILD MALNUTRITION: World Bank, *World Development Indicators,* 1998

SMOKING PREVALENCE: World Bank, *World Development Indicators,* 1998

TUBERCULOSIS INCIDENCE RATE: World Bank, *World Development Indicators,* 1998

AIDS/HIV CASES: UN, *Statistical Yearbook,* 1996

TOTAL DEATHS: World Bank, *World Development Indicators,* 1998

Education

PRIMARY: UN, *Statistical Yearbook,* 1996, 1981, 1966

SECONDARY: UN, *Statistical Yearbook,* 1996, 1981, 1966

HIGHER: UN, *Statistical Yearbook,* 1996, 1981, 1966

Females in School

OF PRIMARY/SECONDARY/HIGHER: UN, *Statistical Yearbook,* 1996, 1981, 1966

PRIMARY/SECONDARY/HIGHER: UN, *Statistical Yearbook,* 1996, 1981, 1966

Communications

RATE OF NEWSPAPERS: UN, *Statistical Yearbook,* 1996, 1981, 1966

RATE OF RADIOS: UN, *Statistical Yearbook,* 1996, 1981, 1966

RATE OF TELEVISIONS: UN, *Statistical Yearbook,* 1996, 1981, 1966

I.

World Data, Graphs, and Tables

The world's population, distributed across six of its seven continents, as well as numerous large and small islands, is roughly six billion. The total area of the planet is 197 million square miles, with land masses accounting for about 30 percent of that. Most of the planet's land area is in the northern hemisphere, largely in the tropical and temperate zones. Following World War II, the global economy underwent a roughly 30-year period of sustained growth. Since the 1970s, the various regions of the world have experienced varying economic growth rates. While much of the developed and developing world went through sustained recession for 20 years, the Middle East and the Far East experienced rapid economic growth. In the 1990s, as the developed world appears to be coming out of recession, East Asia appears to be sinking into it. Still, in the past 50 years, the combination of overall economic growth, decolonization, and improved agricultural and health care practices have allowed the population to skyrocket, as death rates fell dramatically in comparison to slowly declining birth rates.

Population Growth Rates: World

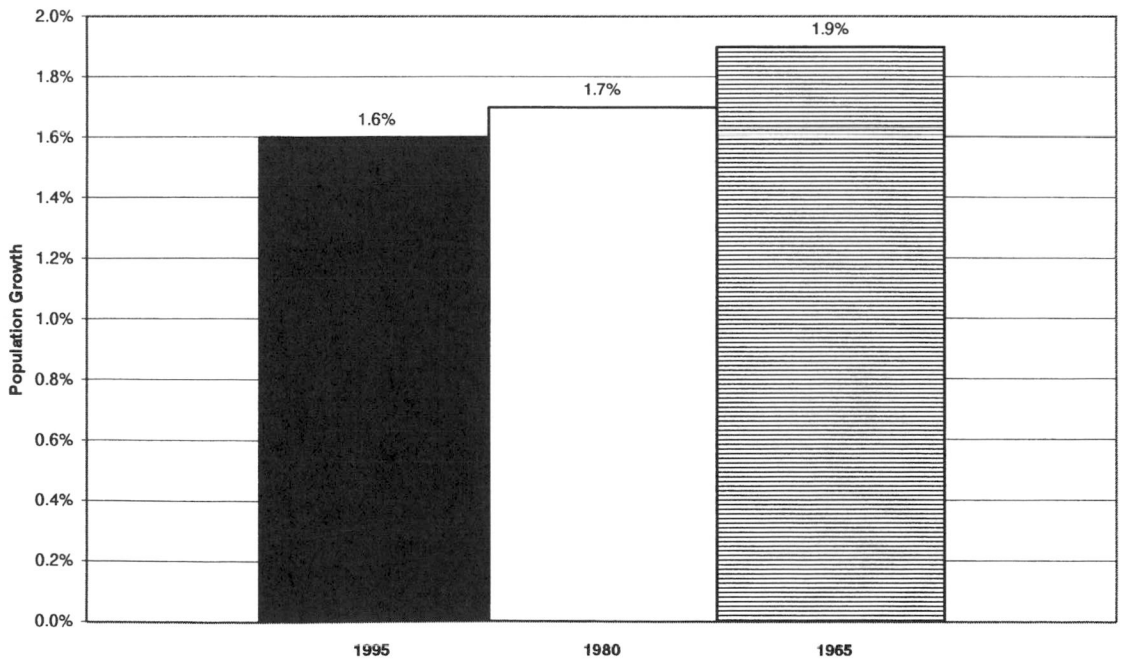

Population growth rates have been gradually coming down since 1965, but they remain high. To translate growth rates into doubling time, divide the annual growth rate into 70. Thus, a growth rate of 1.9 percent divided into 70 equals a doubling period of 36.84 years.

Growth in Population: World

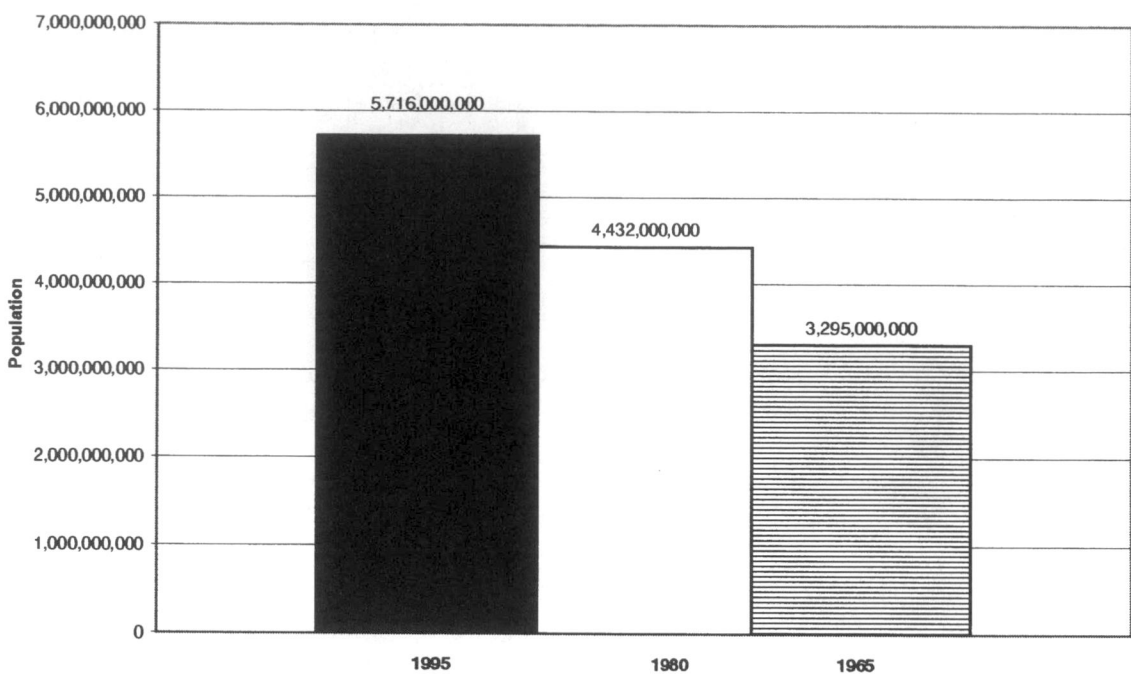

The time it takes the world's population to double has been rapidly getting shorter. While it once took millennia, and later centuries, doubling now occurs in decades. Though global population has not doubled since 1965, it is expected to do so shortly after the turn of the turn of the century.

Gender: World

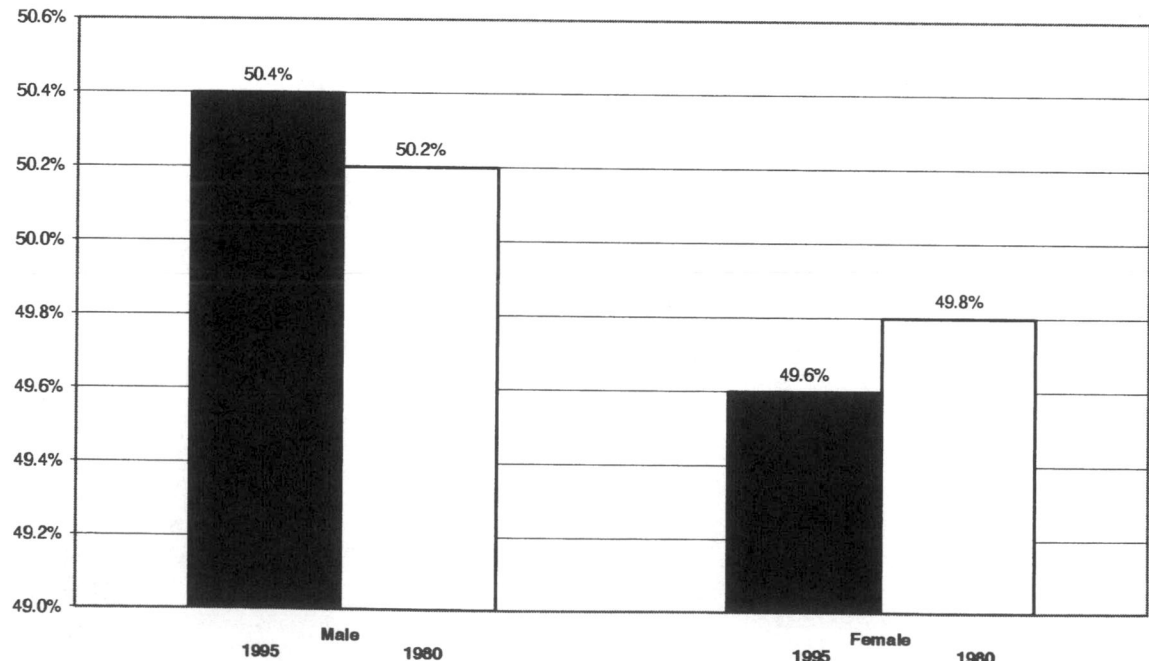

The rising percentage of males in the global population may be the result of birth control. That is, in many world cultures, boy children are valued over girl children. If parents decide to keep their families small, they may stop after one or two boy children, but will continue to reproduce even after they have a girl child or two.

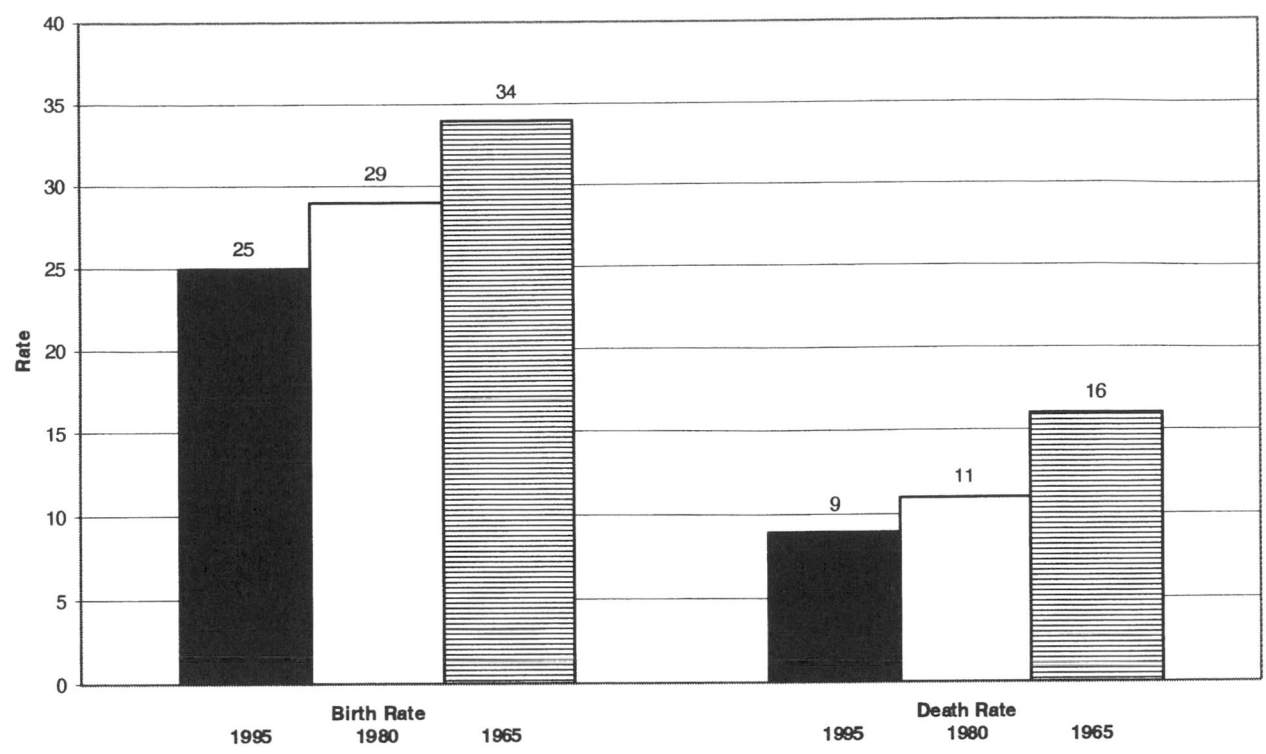

Birth and Death Rates: World

While the birth rate has come down by more than 25 percent since 1965, the death rate has fallen by nearly half. Thus, the gap between the two remains barely unchanged, promising further rapid population growth in coming decades, until the birth rate drops further.

	1995	**1980**	**1965**

GEOGRAPHY

	1995	1980	1965
AREA (square miles/kilometers)	196,938,990/510,072,000		
LAND AREA (square miles/kilometers)	57,505,791/148,940,000		
COASTLINE	222,500/356,000		

POPULATION

	1995	1980	1965
TOTAL	5,716,000,000	4,432,000,000	3,295,000,000
DENSITY (per square mile/kilometer)	109/42	85/33	65/25
ANNUAL GROWTH	1.6%	1.7%	1.9%
AGE COHORTS			
0–14	32%	35%	n/a
15–64	62%	59%	n/a
65 AND OVER	6%	6%	n/a

	1995	1980	1965
MALE	50.4%	50.2%	n/a
FEMALE	49.6%	49.8%	n/a

VITAL STATISTICS

	1995	1980	1965
BIRTH RATE	25	29	34
DEATH RATE	9	11	16

Source: CIA, *The World Factbook, 1997*; UN, *Demographic Yearbook, 1997*; UN, *Statistical Yearbook, 1996*.

2.

The Regions of the World: Data, Graphs, and Tables

AFRICA

Africa, the world's second largest continent, lies astride the equator surrounded by the Red Sea and the Indian Ocean to the east, the Atlantic Ocean to the west, and the Mediterranean Sea to the north. Largely ruled by Europeans until the 1960s—who did little to develop the continent except in areas that benefited the colonizers directly—independent Africa emerged onto the world scene burdened by a host of problems unfamiliar to other regions. First, its national borders had little correspondence to ethnicity, so that many different peoples were forced to live under one government. Second, much of its infrastructure was designed to serve foreign exploiters.

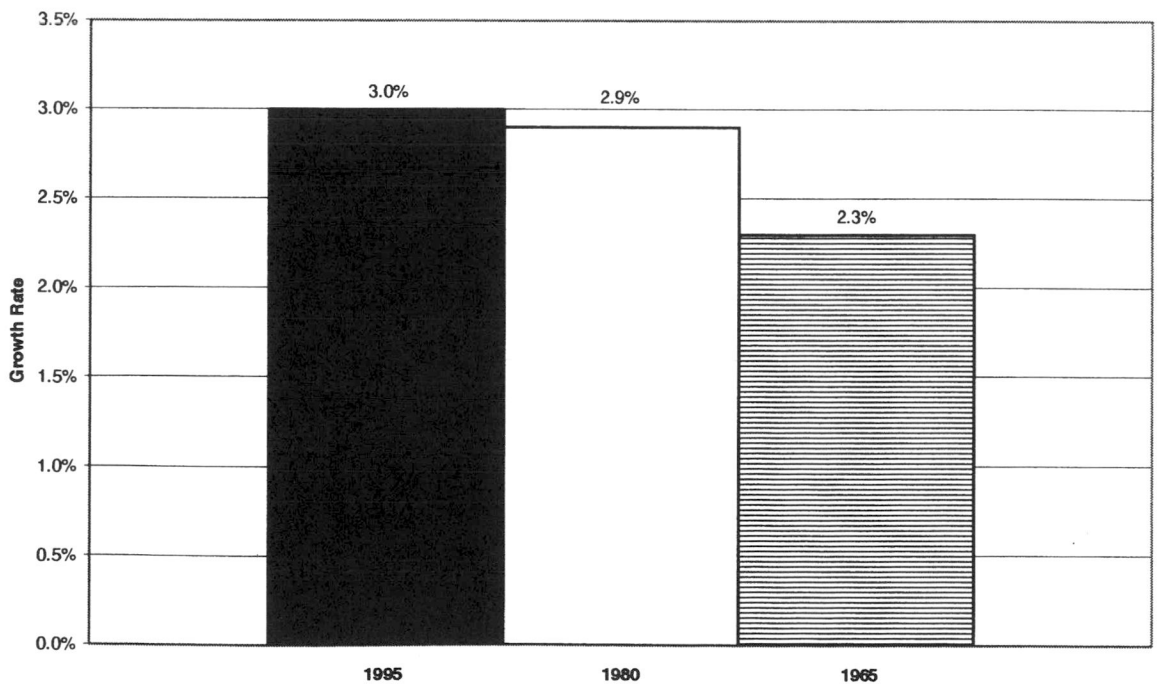

Population Growth Rates: Africa

Africa continues to buck the trends in global population. While all other continents have seen a falling rate of growth in recent decades, Africa's growth rate continues to climb. The key factor here is health care. Colonized by Europeans until the 1960s, Africans were unable to develop health care policies. Since then, independent African governments have made great strides in bringing down the death rates of their nations' populations.

Railroads, for example, usually connected mines or other sources of wealth with ports, rather than providing the continent with an integrated transportation system. Third, the colonizers did little to educate the people of the continent. Not surprisingly, given these handicaps, Africa has been plagued by war and underdevelopment for much of the past 30 years. Most of the world's poorest countries are located in Africa, below the Sahara Desert. (North Africa is often lumped together with the Middle East, or Southwest Asia, for reasons of culture and levels of economic and social development.) Still, recent trends are promising. More of Africa lives under democratic rule, and South Africa, potentially the economic powerhouse of the continent, is under black rule for the first time in its history.

Density: Africa

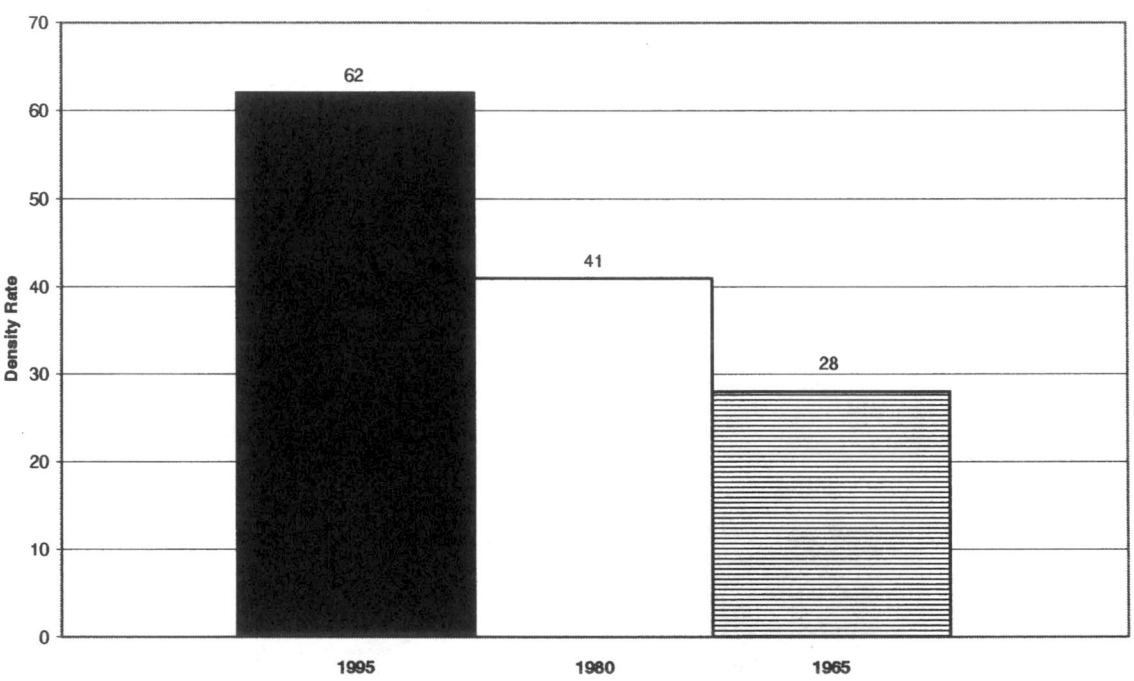

While the world bemoans rapid population growth in Africa, many African demographers and population experts are less concerned. They point to the fact that the continent—by world standards—remains less densely populated than some other areas, a legacy of slavery and colonialism. There is some truth to their claims. Compare Africa's density to that of Europe (minus Russia) and Asia.

AFRICA

	1995	1980	1965

GEOGRAPHY

AREA (square miles/kilometers)　　11,701,545/30,306,000

	1995	1980	1965
POPULATION			
TOTAL	728,000,000	470,000,000	311,000,000
DENSITY (per square mile/kilometer)	62/24	41/16	28/11
ANNUAL GROWTH	3%	2.9%	2.3%
AGE COHORTS			
0–14	44%	45%	n/a
15–64	53%	52%	n/a
65 AND OVER	3%	3%	n/a
MALE	49.9%	49.6%	n/a
FEMALE	50.1%	50.4%	n/a

VITAL STATISTICS			
BIRTH RATE	42	46	46
DEATH RATE	14	17	23

WEST AFRICA

GEOGRAPHY

AREA (square miles/kilometers)	2,369,884/6,138,000

POPULATION

	1995	1980	1965
TOTAL	211,000,000	141,000,000	98,000,000
DENSITY (per square mile/kilometer)	88/34	62/24	28/11
ANNUAL GROWTH	3.0%	3.1%	2.3%

	1995	1980	1965
AGE COHORTS			
0–14	46%	46%	n/a
15–64	51%	51%	n/a
65 AND OVER	3%	3%	n/a
MALE		49.6%	n/a
FEMALE		50.4%	n/a

VITAL STATISTICS

	1995	1980	1965
BIRTH RATE	46	49	50
DEATH RATE	16	14	27

EAST AFRICA

GEOGRAPHY

AREA (square miles/kilometers)	2,454,054/6,356,000

POPULATION

	1995	1980	1965
TOTAL	227,000,000	134,000,000	86,000,000
DENSITY (per square mile/kilometer)	93/36	57/22	36/14
ANNUAL GROWTH	3.0%	2.9%	2.4%
AGE COHORTS			
0–14	46%	46%	n/a
15–64	51%	51%	n/a
65 AND OVER	3%	3%	n/a
MALE	49.8%	49.3%	n/a
FEMALE	50.2%	50.7%	n/a

VITAL STATISTICS

	1995	1980	1965
BIRTH RATE	46	48	45
DEATH RATE	16	19	21

	1995	1980	1965

NORTH AFRICA

GEOGRAPHY

AREA (square miles/kilometers) 3,291,506/8,525,000

POPULATION

	1995	1980	1965
TOTAL	161,000,000	109,000,000	75,000,000
DENSITY (per square mile/kilometer)	49/19	34/13	23/9
ANNUAL GROWTH	2.3%	2.9%	2.4%
AGE COHORTS			
0–14	39%	43%	n/a
15–64	57%	53%	n/a
65 AND OVER	4%	4%	n/a
MALE	50.6%	50.5%	n/a
FEMALE	49.4%	49.5%	n/a

VITAL STATISTICS

	1995	1980	1965
BIRTH RATE	31	43	43
DEATH RATE	9	14	19

CENTRAL AFRICA

GEOGRAPHY

AREA (square miles/kilometers) 2,553,282/6,613,000

POPULATION

	1995	1980	1965
TOTAL	82,000,000	53,000,000	32,000,000
DENSITY (per square mile/kilometer)	31/12	21/8	13/5
ANNUAL GROWTH	3.1%	2.5%	1.9%

	1995	1980	1965
AGE COHORTS			
0–14	47%	44%	n/a
15–64	50%	53%	n/a
65 AND OVER	3%	3%	n/a
MALE	48.8%	49.1%	n/a
FEMALE	51.2%	50.9%	n/a

VITAL STATISTICS

	1995	1980	1965
BIRTH RATE	46	45	42
DEATH RATE	15	20	23

SOUTHERN AFRICA

GEOGRAPHY

AREA (square miles/kilometers)	1,032,819/2,675,000

POPULATION

	1995	1980	1965
TOTAL	47,000,000	33,000,000	20,000,000
DENSITY (per square mile/kilometer)	47/18	34/13	21/8
ANNUAL GROWTH	2.3%	2.8%	2.5%
AGE COHORTS			
0–14	38%	42%	n/a
15–64	58%	54%	n/a
65 AND OVER	4%	4%	n/a
MALE	48.9%	48.5%	n/a
FEMALE	51.1%	51.5%	n/a

VITAL STATISTICS

	1995	1980	1965
BIRTH RATE	32	39	42
DEATH RATE	9	11	17

Source: UN, *Demographic Yearbook, 1997*; UN, *Statistical Yearbook, 1996.*

ASIA

The largest continent on earth, Asia is surrounded by the Arctic Sea to the north; the Pacific Ocean to the east; Australia and the Indian Ocean to the south; and Europe, Africa, and the Mediterranean Sea to the west. With the largest population of any continent by a factor of nearly five, Asia is really several continents in one: East Asia (dominated by China), South Asia (dominated by India), Southeast Asia, and Southwest Asia (the Middle East and the former Central Asian republics of the Soviet Union). Each region presents a different profile to the world. East Asia and Southeast Asia, though still divided between countries calling themselves communist and capitalist, have—until the last couple of years—been experiencing rapid economic growth. This

growth has brought a host of other developments in its wake, including declining birth rates and better educational and health care services. Southwest Asia presents a mixed picture. While the rise in oil prices brought wealth to some countries of the Middle East—and, with that wealth, better education and health care—it left others behind. Plagued by continuing high rates of population growth and declining oil prices, the region is currently experiencing a prolonged slump. South Asia, though showing some signs of economic life, lags behind the other regions. Still, its dominant country—India—has managed to retain its democratic institutions through trying times.

Annual Growth: East Asia and Southwest Asia

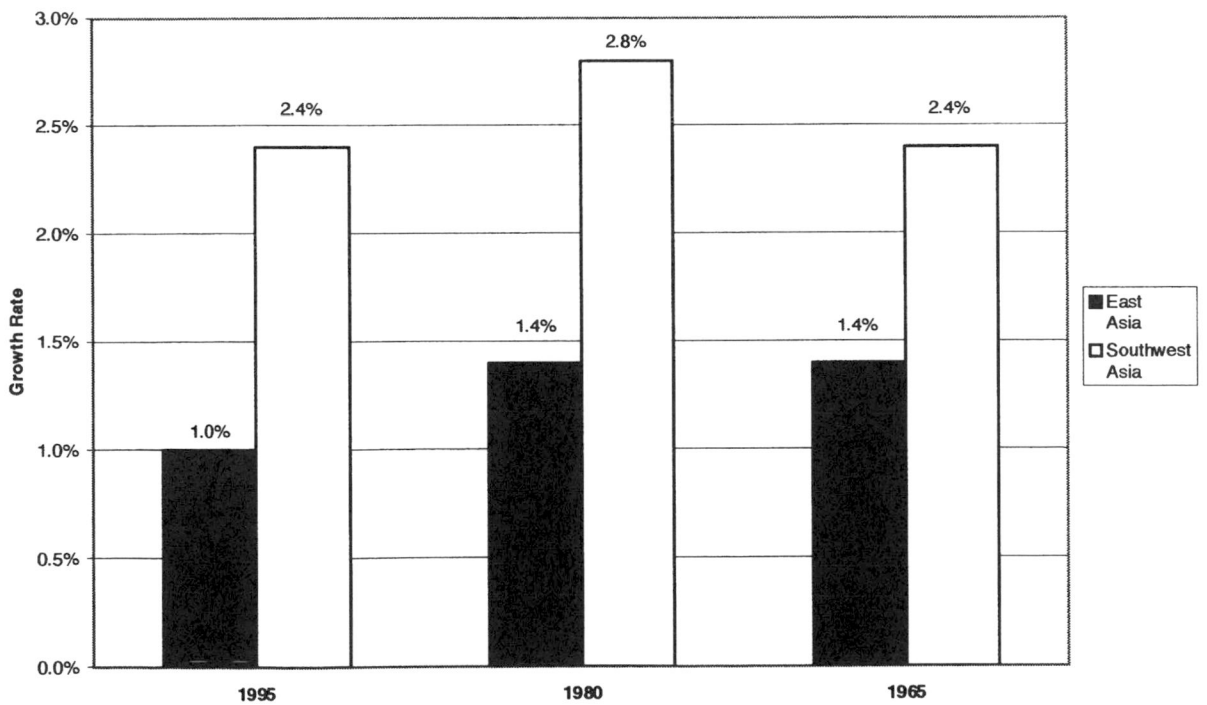

Asia is such an immense and varied continent, generalities about it are difficult to make. While East Asia—dominated numerically by China and its tough birth-control practices—has seen its growth rate drop significantly, Southwest Asia—roughly the Middle East and the former Muslim republics of the Soviet Union—has witnessed continued high growth rates.

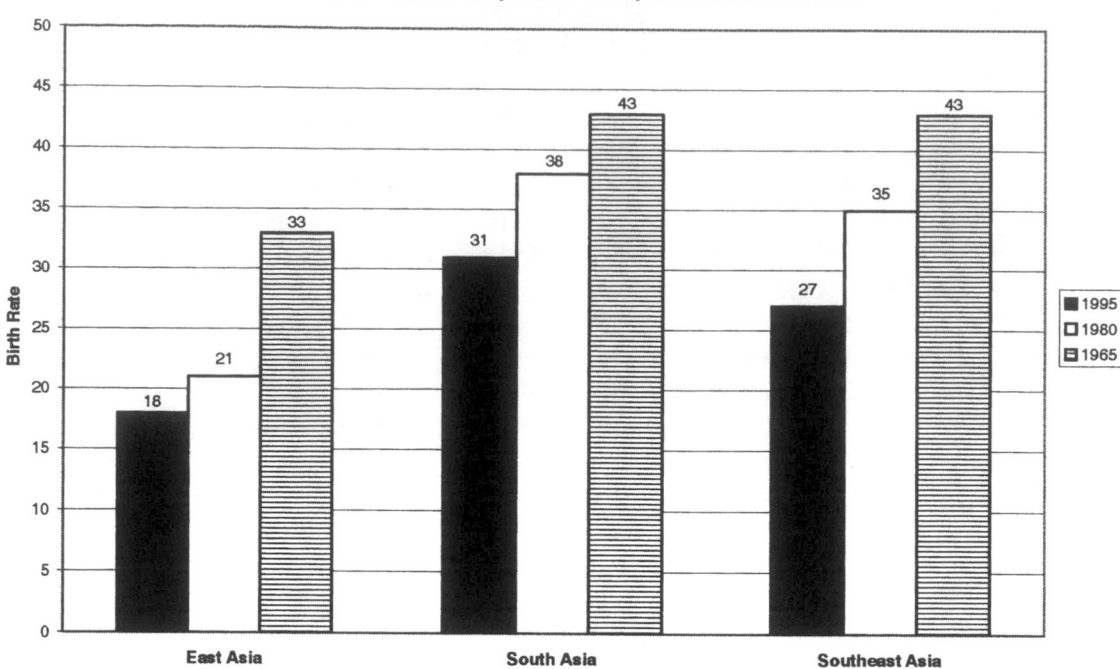

Birth Rates: East Asia, South Asia, and Southeast Asia

With its various regions, Asia presents several models for dealing with population control. In East Asia, China has imposed harsh pro-birth-control laws; in South Asia, democratic India has attempted to bring down the birth rate by education; in Southeast Asia, rapid economic growth is having an impact on birth rates.

ASIA

	1995	1980	1965

GEOGRAPHY

AREA (square miles/kilometers) 12,229,343/31,764,000			

POPULATION

	1995	1980	1965
TOTAL	3,458,000,000	2,579,000,000	1,830,000,000
DENSITY (per square mile/kilometer)	282/109	246/95	176/68
ANNUAL GROWTH	1.6%	n/a	2%
AGE COHORTS			
0–14	32%	37%	n/a
15–64	63%	59%	n/a
65 AND OVER	5%	4%	n/a
MALE	51.1%	51%	n/a
FEMALE	48.9%	49%	n/a

	1995	1980	1965

VITAL STATISTICS

	1995	1980	1965
BIRTH RATE	25	n/a	38
DEATH RATE	8	n/a	18

EAST ASIA[1]

GEOGRAPHY

AREA (square miles/kilometers)   4,541,313/11,762,000

POPULATION

	1995	1980	1965
TOTAL	1,424,000,000	1,190,000,000	864,000,000
DENSITY (per square mile/kilometer)	313/121	262/101	189/73
ANNUAL GROWTH	1%	1.4%	1.4%
AGE COHORTS			
0–14	25%	33%	n/a
15–64	68%	61%	n/a
65 AND OVER	7%	6%	n/a
MALE	51.1%	50.9%	n/a
FEMALE	48.9%	49.1%	n/a

VITAL STATISTICS

	1995	1980	1965
BIRTH RATE	18	21	33
DEATH RATE	7	7	19

SOUTH ASIA[2]

GEOGRAPHY

AREA (square miles/kilometers)   4,160,618/10,776,000

	1995	1980	1965
POPULATION			
TOTAL	1,381,000,000	944,000,000	681,000,000
DENSITY (per square mile/kilometer)	332/128	225/87	262/101
ANNUAL GROWTH	2.1%	2.2%	2.4%
AGE COHORTS			
0–14	37%	41%	n/a
15–64	59%	56%	n/a
65 AND OVER	4%	3%	n/a
MALE	51.5%	51.7%	n/a
FEMALE	49.5%	48.3%	n/a
VITAL STATISTICS			
BIRTH RATE	31	38	43
DEATH RATE	10	16	18

SOUTHEAST ASIA[3]

GEOGRAPHY

AREA (square miles/kilometers)   1,735,521/4,495,000

POPULATION

	1995	1980	1965
TOTAL	484,000,000	369,000,000	255,000,000
DENSITY (per square mile/kilometer)	280/108	212/82	148/57
ANNUAL GROWTH	1.8%	2.1%	2.6%
AGE COHORTS			
0–14	35%	40%	n/a
15–64	61%	57%	n/a
65 AND OVER	4%	3%	n/a
MALE	49.8%	49.9%	n/a
FEMALE	50.2%	50.1%	n/a

	1995	**1980**	**1965**

VITAL STATISTICS

	1995	1980	1965
BIRTH RATE	27	35	43
DEATH RATE	8	14	17

SOUTHWEST ASIA[4]

GEOGRAPHY

AREA (square miles/kilometers)   1,826,641/4,731,000

POPULATION

	1995	1980	1965
TOTAL	168,000,000	101,000,000	68,000,000
DENSITY (per square mile/kilometer)	93/36	57/22	39/15
ANNUAL GROWTH	2.4%	2.8%	2.4%
AGE COHORTS			
0–14	38%	42%	n/a
15–64	58%	54%	n/a
65 AND OVER	4%	4%	n/a
MALE	51.2%	51%	n/a
FEMALE	48.8%	49%	n/a

VITAL STATISTICS

	1995	1980	1965
BIRTH RATE	32	40	42
DEATH RATE	7	12	18

FOOTNOTES
1. Includes China, Japan, and the two Koreas.
2. Includes Bangladesh, India, Nepal, Pakistan, and Sri Lanka.
3. Includes all countries to the east of India, south of China, north of Australia, and west of the Pacific.
4. Includes the Middle East, Iran, Afghanistan, and former Central Asian republics of the Soviet Union.

Source: UN, *Demographic Yearbook, 1997;* UN, *Statistical Yearbook, 1996.*

EUROPE

Europe lies at the western extreme of the Eurasian land mass and is surrounded by Asia to the east, the Mediterranean Sea to the south, the Atlantic Ocean to the west, and the Arctic Ocean to the north. (Note that Europe is often considered to include all of Russia, which actually stretches across Asia to the Pacific.) Until the overthrow of East European communism in 1989 and the collapse of the Soviet Union in 1991, Europe was largely divided along a line that divided the capitalist West from the communist East. In the former, market economies boomed through the 1970s, before entering a period of prolonged economic slump. Despite high unemployment and slow rates of economic growth, the people in the region continued to enjoy some of the highest social indices and standards of living in the world. The southern parts of capitalist Europe have never been as prosperous as those to the north. In the East, there was also economic development through the 1970s, but not nearly as rapid. This region also enjoyed good health care and educational services, though its rate of consumption was below that of the West. The two regions do share one phenomenon: They remain the only regions of the world where population growth has approached zero and, especially in the East, actually begun to decline.

Birth and Death Rates: Europe

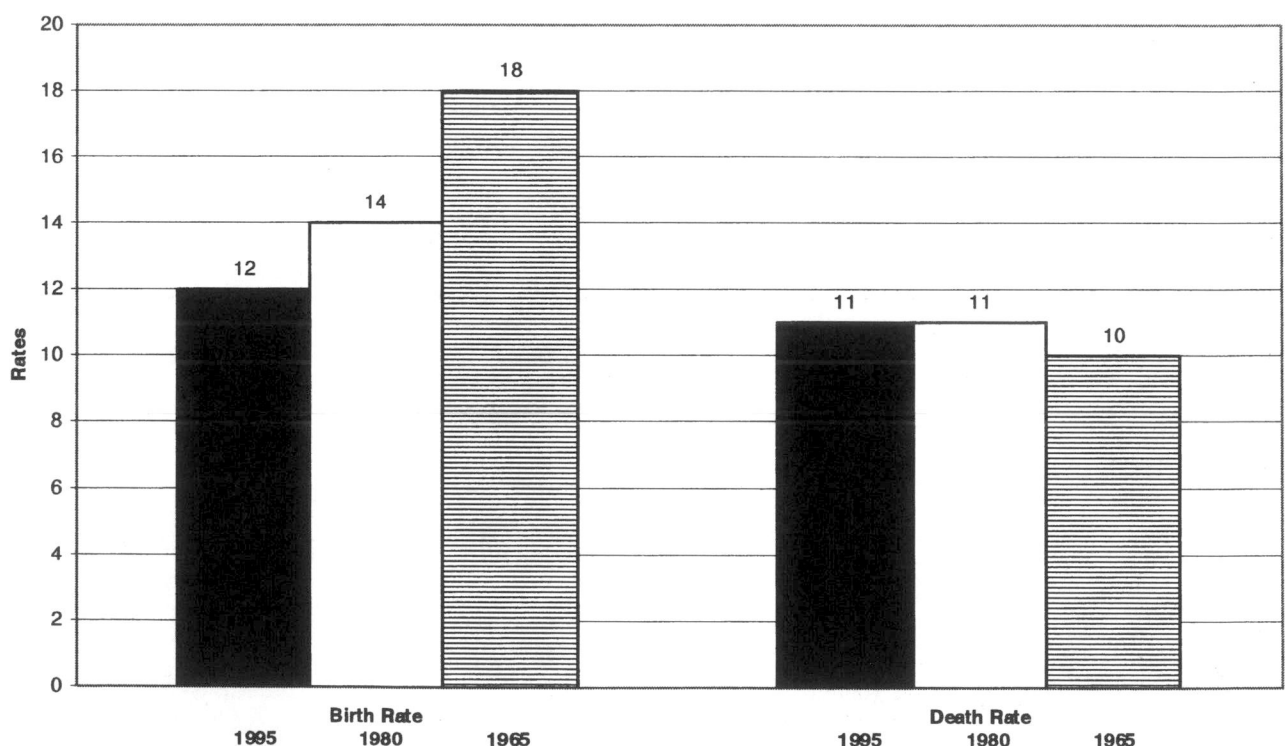

With its highly developed economies and small families, Europe has essentially achieved zero population growth as far as natural increase is concerned. Continued immigration from other regions of the world is now largely responsible for population increases.

Age Distribution: Europe

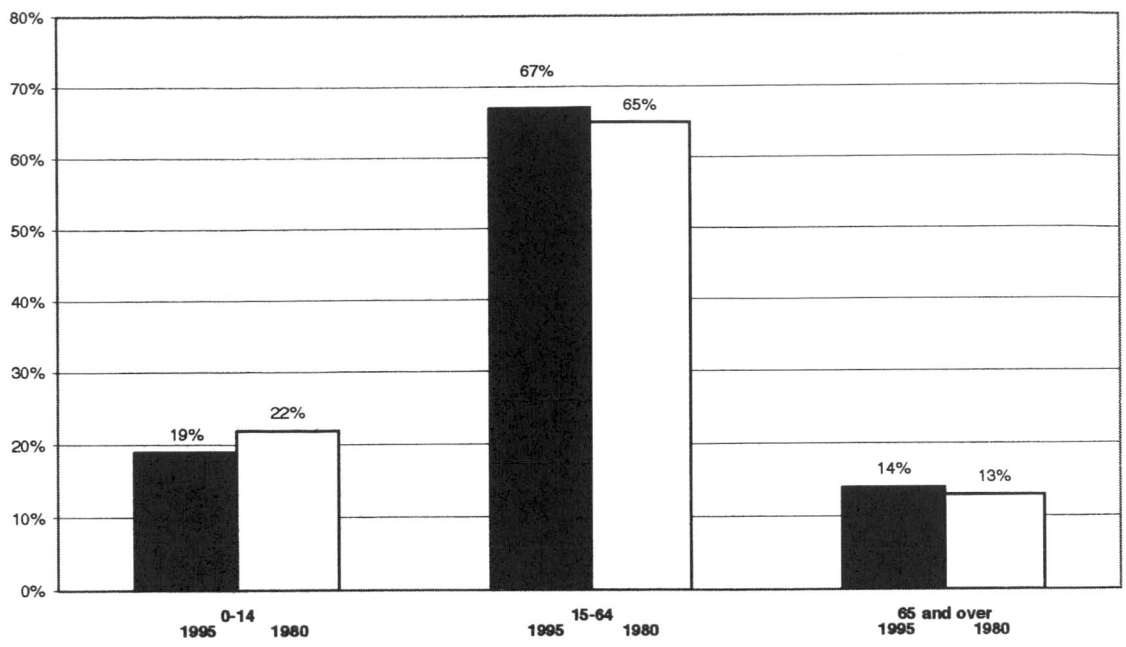

Because of declining birth rates and longer lives, Europe has the oldest population of any world region. In another 20 years, it is expected that the number of persons over the age of 65 will equal the number under 15.

EUROPE[1]

	1995	1980	1965

GEOGRAPHY

AREA (square miles/kilometers) 8,874,903/22,986,000[2]

POPULATION

	1995	1980	1965
TOTAL	727,000,000	484,000,000	445,000,000
DENSITY (per square mile/kilometer)	83/32	254/98	236/91
ANNUAL GROWTH	0.2%	0.4%	0.9%
AGE COHORTS			
0–14	19%	22%	n/a
15–64	67%	65%	n/a
65 AND OVER	14%	13%	n/a
MALE	48.3%	48.8%	n/a
FEMALE	51.7%	51.2%	n/a

	1995	1980	1965
VITAL STATISTICS			
BIRTH RATE	12	14	18
DEATH RATE	11	11	10

EASTERN EUROPE[2]

GEOGRAPHY

AREA (square miles/kilometers)   7,263,707/18,813,000

POPULATION

	1995	1980	1965
TOTAL	309,000,000	110,000,000	100,000,000
DENSITY (per square mile/kilometer)	41/16	290/112	264/102
ANNUAL GROWTH	−0.1%	0.7%	0.6%
AGE COHORTS			
0–14	21%	23%	n/a
15–64	67%	65%	n/a
65 AND OVER	12%	12%	n/a
MALE	47.4%	49.1%	n/a
FEMALE	52.6%	50.9%	n/a

VITAL STATISTICS

	1995	1980	1965
BIRTH RATE	12	18	17
DEATH RATE	12	10	9

NORTHERN EUROPE[3]

GEOGRAPHY

AREA (square miles/kilometers)   675,290/1,749,000

	1995	1980	1965

POPULATION

	1995	1980	1965
TOTAL	94,000,000	82,000,000	79,000,000
DENSITY (per square mile/kilometer)	137/53	130/50	124/48
ANNUAL GROWTH	0.3%	0.1%	0.7%
AGE COHORTS			
0–14	20%	23%	n/a
15–64	65%	65%	n/a
65 AND OVER	15%	12%	n/a
MALE	48.4%	48.8%	n/a
FEMALE	51.6%	51.2%	n/a

VITAL STATISTICS

	1995	1980	1965
BIRTH RATE	14	13	16
DEATH RATE	11	12	11

SOUTHERN EUROPE[4]

GEOGRAPHY

AREA (square miles/kilometers)	508,108/1,316,000		

POPULATION

	1995	1980	1965
TOTAL	144,000,000	139,000,000	123,000,000
DENSITY (per square mile/kilometer)	282/109	275/106	243/94
ANNUAL GROWTH	0.1%	0.7%	0.8%
AGE COHORTS			
0–14	17%	21.0%	n/a
15–64	68%	65.0%	n/a
65 AND OVER	15%	14.0%	n/a
MALE	49%	48.9%	n/a
FEMALE	51%	51.1%	n/a

	1995	1980	1965

VITAL STATISTICS

	1995	1980	1965
BIRTH RATE	11	16	21
DEATH RATE	10	9	9

WESTERN EUROPE[5]

GEOGRAPHY

AREA (square miles/kilometers)   427,413/1,107,000

POPULATION

	1995	1980	1965
TOTAL	181,000,000	153,000,000	143,000,000
DENSITY (per square mile/kilometer)	422/163	396/153	381/147
ANNUAL GROWTH	0.6%	0.1%	1.2%
AGE COHORTS			
0–14	18%	21%	n/a
15–64	67%	65%	n/a
65 AND OVER	15%	14%	n/a
MALE	48.9%	48.4%	n/a
FEMALE	51.1%	51.6%	n/a

VITAL STATISTICS

	1995	1980	1965
BIRTH RATE	12	12	18
DEATH RATE	11	12	11

UNION OF SOVIET SOCIALIST REPUBLICS (USSR)

GEOGRAPHY

AREA (square miles/kilometers)   8,649,421/22,402,000

	1995	1980	1965
POPULATION			
TOTAL	n/a	265,000,000	231,000,000
DENSITY (per square mile/kilometer)	n/a	31/12	26/10
ANNUAL GROWTH	n/a	0.9%	1.4%
AGE COHORTS			
0–14	n/a	24%	n/a
15–64	n/a	66%	n/a
65 AND OVER	n/a	10%	n/a
MALE	n/a	46.8%	n/a
FEMALE	n/a	53.2%	n/a
VITAL STATISTICS			
BIRTH RATE		18	22
DEATH RATE		9	7

FOOTNOTES

1. Statistics for 1965 and 1980 do not include the USSR (statistics for 1995 include both European and Asiatic areas of the Russian Federation; Eastern Europe designates all former communist countries, including republics of the former Yugoslavia and European republics of the former Soviet Union).
2. Includes European and Asiatic areas of the Russian Federation.
3. Includes Scandinavia and the British Isles.
4. Includes Iberia, Italian peninsula, and Greece.
5. Includes German- and French-speaking countries, as well as the Netherlands.

Source: UN, *Demographic Yearbook, 1997;* UN, *Statistical Yearbook, 1996.*

LATIN AMERICA

The southern half of the so-called New World, or the Western Hemisphere, Latin America lies to the south of North America, with the Atlantic and Pacific oceans to its east and west, respectively. It includes Central America (including Mexico), the Caribbean, and South America. It is also divided by economic development. While the nations of the southern cone (Chile, Argentina, and Uruguay) are relatively prosperous, the countries of Central America and the Andean Mountains are not. United by a common culture combining elements of Iberia (Spain and Portugal), Native America, and Africa (the latter especially prevalent in Brazil and the Caribbean), Latin America is the only significant part of the developing world that has been politically independent since the nineteenth century. Still, its history since 1965 has been troubling. Though it experienced substantial economic growth through the 1970s, most of the region was governed by military dictatorships. In many countries, these governments nearly bankrupted the economy, as they put the governments there into deep debt to first-world lending institutions. Since the 1980s, however, virtually all of Latin America has been liberated from dictatorship, though the economic problems created by the dictatorial governments continue to stifle growth. Latin America has also been making great strides toward developing its human potential, especially in the field of education.

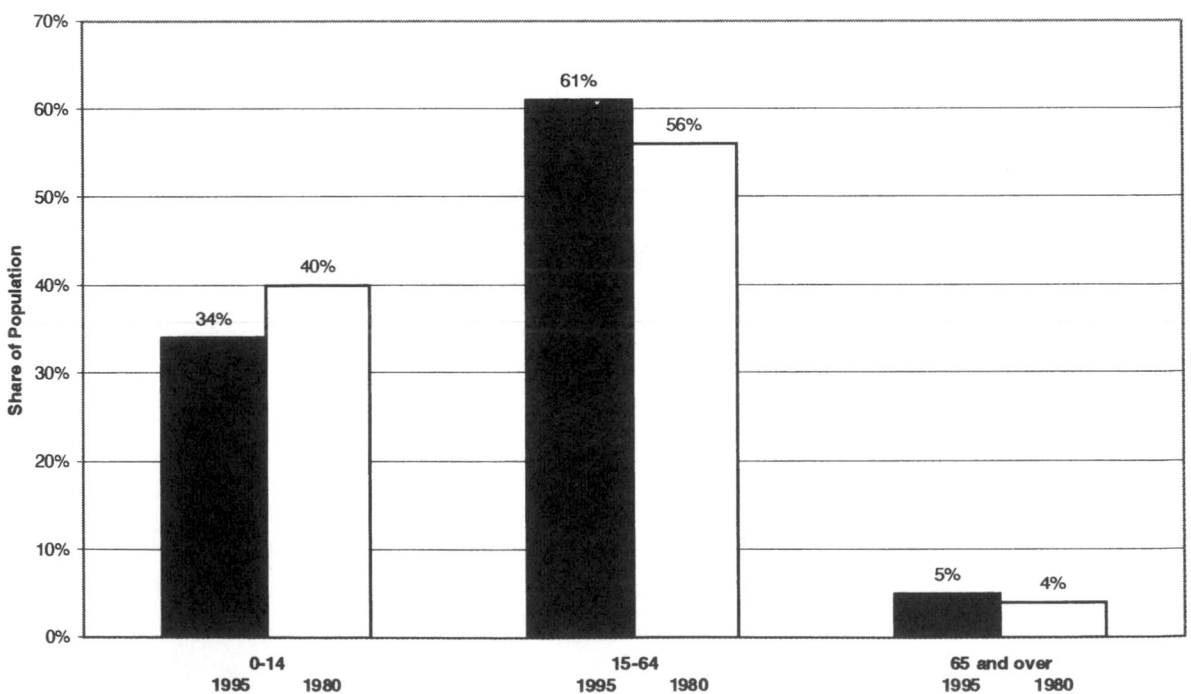

Age Distribution: Latin America

One of the key ways to predict future population growth is to examine age cohorts. If the number of young persons is on the rise, population is likely to grow rapidly. In Latin America, the percentage of persons under the age of 15 is falling, thereby promising slower growth rates in the coming century.

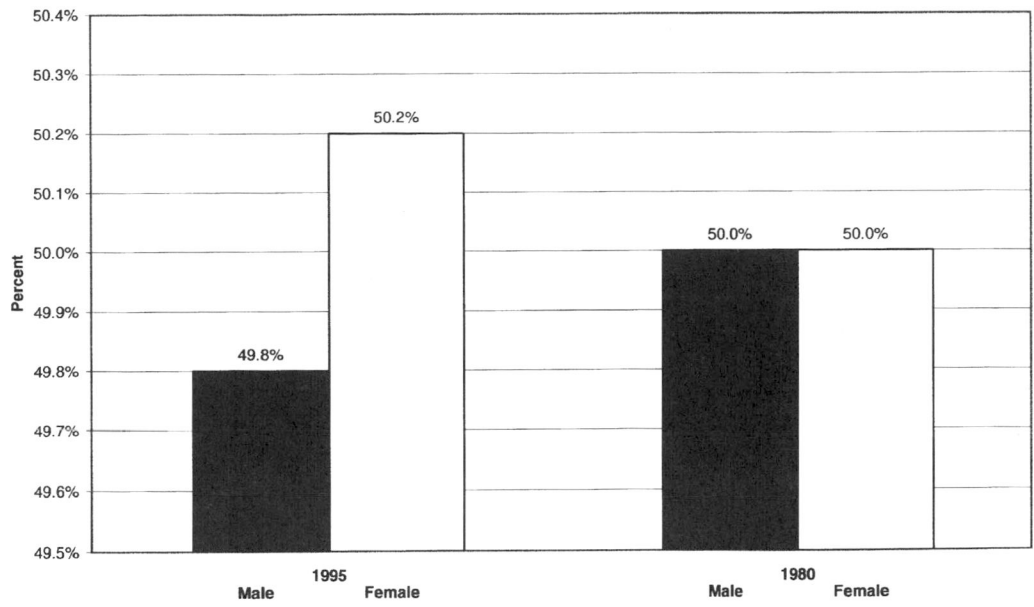

The growing percentage of females in the Latin American population reflects rising out-migration rates, since it is men who are most likely to seek educational and job opportunities by moving to other regions of the world, largely, in this case, the United States

LATIN AMERICA

	1995	1980	1965
GEOGRAPHY			
AREA (square miles/kilometers)	7,927,799/20,533,000		
POPULATION			
TOTAL	482,000,000	364,000,000	246,000,000
DENSITY (per square mile/kilometer)	60/23	47/18	31/12
ANNUAL GROWTH	1.8%	2.5%	2.8%
AGE COHORTS			
0–14	34%	40%	n/a
15–64	61%	56%	n/a
65 AND OVER	5%	4%	n/a
MALE	49.8%	50%	n/a
FEMALE	50.2%	50%	n/a

	1995	1980	1965

VITAL STATISTICS

	1995	1980	1965
BIRTH RATE	26	34	41
DEATH RATE	7	9	13

CARIBBEAN

GEOGRAPHY

AREA (square miles/kilometers)	90,734/235,000

POPULATION

	1995	1980	1965
TOTAL	36,000,000	31,000,000	23,000,000
DENSITY (per square mile/kilometer)	394/152	339/131	256/99
ANNUAL GROWTH	1.3%	1.8%	2.3%
AGE COHORTS			
0–14	30%	37%	n/a
15–64	63%	58%	n/a
65 AND OVER	7%	5%	n/a
MALE	48.6%	48.4%	n/a
FEMALE	51.4%	51.6%	n/a

VITAL STATISTICS

	1995	1980	1965
BIRTH RATE	24	28	38
DEATH RATE	8	9	14

CENTRAL AMERICA[1]

GEOGRAPHY

AREA (square miles/kilometers)	957,529/2,480,000

	1995	1980	1965

POPULATION

	1995	1980	1965
TOTAL	126,000,000	93,000,000	57,000,000
DENSITY (per square mile/kilometer)	132/51	98/38	62/24
ANNUAL GROWTH	2.2%	3.0%	3.5%
AGE COHORTS			
0–14	38%	45%	n/a
15–64	58%	52%	n/a
65 AND OVER	4%	3%	n/a
MALE	50.8%	50.5%	n/a
FEMALE	49.2%	49.5%	n/a

VITAL STATISTICS

	1995	1980	1965
BIRTH RATE	30	39	45
DEATH RATE	6	8	10

SOUTH AMERICA

GEOGRAPHY

AREA (square miles/kilometers)	6,879,923/17,819,000

POPULATION

	1995	1980	1965
TOTAL	320,000,000	240,000,000	171,000,000
DENSITY (per square mile/kilometer)	47/18	35/14	26/10
ANNUAL GROWTH	1.7%	2.3%	2.7%
AGE COHORTS			
0–14	33%	39%	n/a
15–64	62%	57%	n/a
65 AND OVER	5%	4%	n/a
MALE	49.7%	50%	n/a
FEMALE	50.3%	50%	n/a

	1995	1980	1965
VITAL STATISTICS			
BIRTH RATE	25	32	40
DEATH RATE	7	9	13

FOOTNOTES
1. Includes Mexico.

Source: UN, *Demographic Yearbook, 1997;* UN, *Statistical Yearbook, 1996.*

NORTH AMERICA

North America—the world's third largest continent—is surrounded by the Arctic Ocean to the north, the Atlantic Ocean to the east, the Pacific Ocean to the west, and Mexico and the Gulf of Mexico to the south. Consisting almost entirely of two highly developed countries—the United States and Canada—North America is the richest continent on earth, by per capita income. Long a home to immigrants from around the world, the continent's population represents a melange of distinct ethnic groups from around the world, as well as a tiny minority of native peoples. Until the 1960s, most of this population represented people of European and African (largely in the United States) descent. In the years since, the presence of people from Latin America and Asia have become more common. Indeed, it is expected that Hispanics will soon outnumber blacks to become the largest ethnic minority in the region. The North American economy, having almost entirely escaped the ravages of World War II, dominated the globe until the 1970s, when competitors in Europe and Japan revived. Following two decades of economic crisis, North America appears to be economically dominant again. Its population also continues to grow more rapidly than that of Europe, though most of the population growth comes from immigration.

Age Distribution: North America

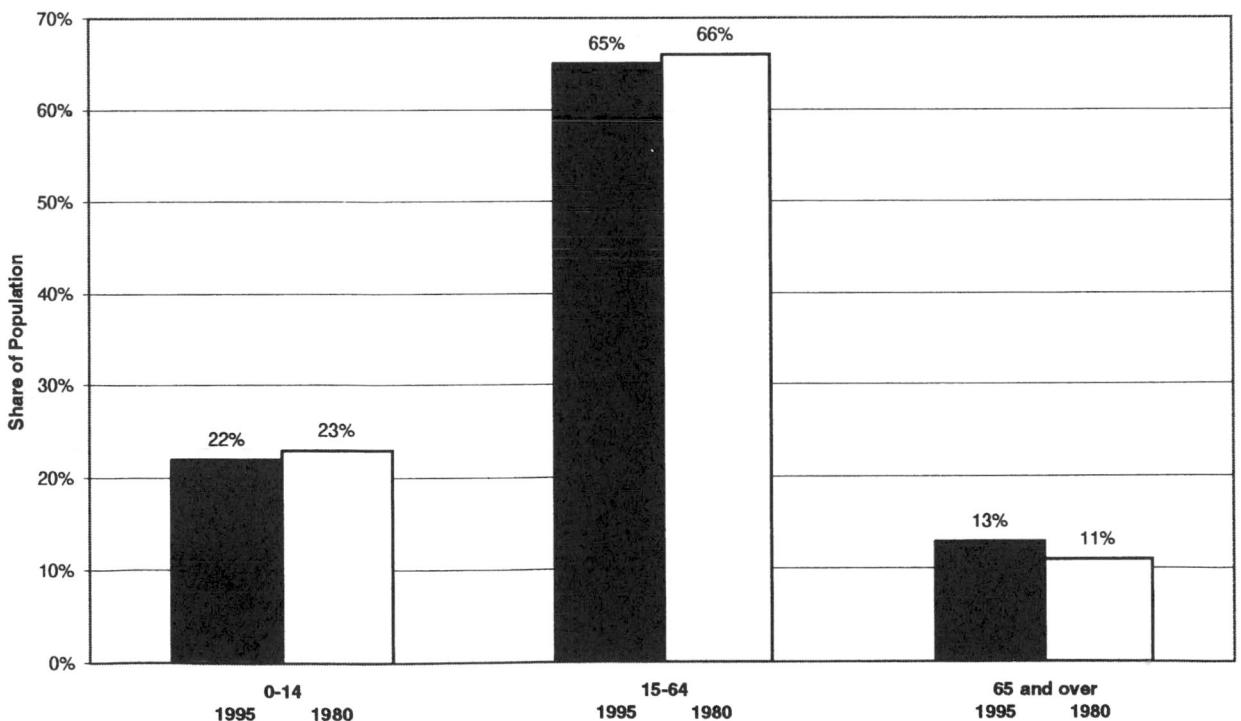

The aging population in North America reflects a phenomenon of developed nations. Better health care and falling birth rates mean more older people, along with strains on the economy caused by taking care of them.

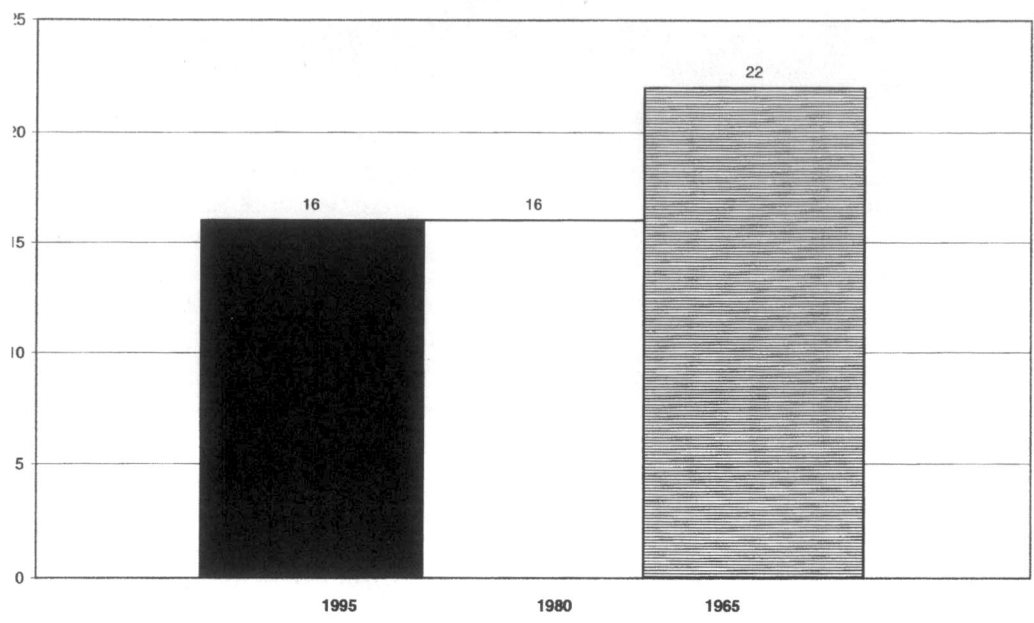

Birth Rate: North America

The birth rate graph reflects one of the most significant demographic developments in recent North American history—the baby boom. In 1965, the post–World War II reversal in declining birth rates was still being felt. By 1980, it had disappeared.

	1995	1980	1965

GEOGRAPHY

AREA (square miles/kilometers)   8,307,722/21,517,000

POPULATION

	1995	1980	1965
TOTAL	293,000,000	248,000,000	214,000,000
DENSITY (per square mile/kilometer)	36/14	31/12	26/10
ANNUAL GROWTH	1%	1%	1.5%
AGE COHORTS			
0–14	22%	23%	n/a
15–64	65%	66%	n/a
65 AND OVER	13%	11%	n/a
MALE	49%	48.8%	n/a
FEMALE	51%	51.2%	n/a

VITAL STATISTICS

	1995	1980	1965
BIRTH RATE	16	16	22
DEATH RATE	9	9	9

Source: UN, *Demographic Yearbook, 1997;* UN, *Statistical Yearbook, 1996.*

OCEANIA

The smallest region of the world by territory and especially population, Oceania lies in the southwestern Pacific Ocean, off the southeast coast of Asia. It consists of three distinct areas. The first and largest is Australia and New Zealand, a continent and series of large islands initially inhabited by Aborigines and Polynesians but eventually colonized and settled by European immigrants, who became predominant. In recent years, Australia has become a popular destination for Asian immigrants as well. Both countries developed economic and social profiles much like those in Europe and North America, with good social indices and high standards of living. Melanesia, consisting of large and small islands to the northeast of Australia and New Zealand, is the most impoverished part of Oceania. Most of its

people make their living through subsistence farming and fishing, and have social indices comparable to middle tier countries of the developing world. Micronesia and Polynesia are made up of hundreds of tiny islands scattered across immense stretches of the southern and western Pacific Ocean. Largely divided into newly independent republics or possessions of France and the United States, the people of Micronesia and Polynesia generally enjoy moderate standards of income and social indexes. While many of the people in this region also support themselves through subsistence fishing and farming, their national economies are heavily subsidized by tourism or, in the case of French Polynesia, revenues from the home country.

Birth Rates: Australia and New Zealand, and Melanesia

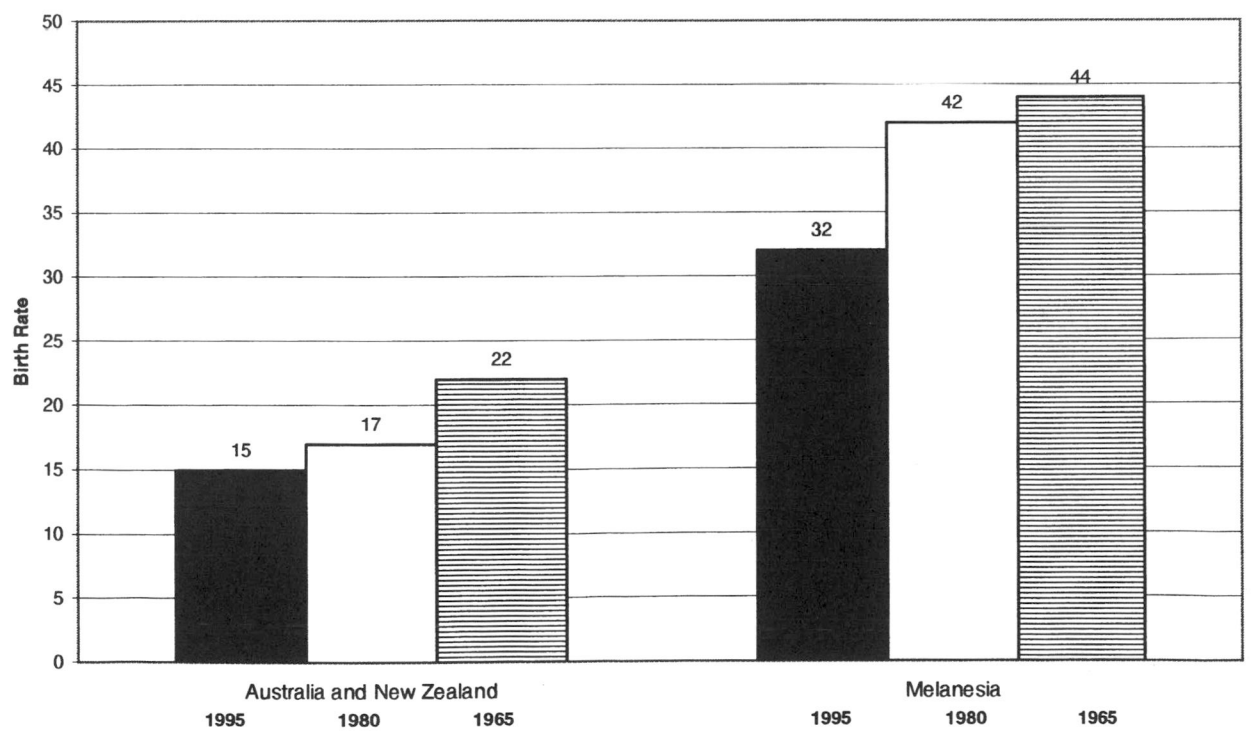

Like Asia, Oceania is highly diverse as a world region. Numerically dominated by Australia—a developed economy—it also includes the impoverished islands of Melanesia. Thus, while Australia and New Zealand have birth rates equivalent to those of North America, Melanesia has rates equivalent to those of South Asia.

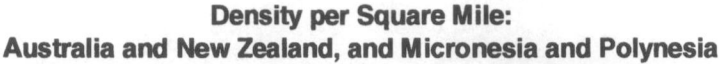

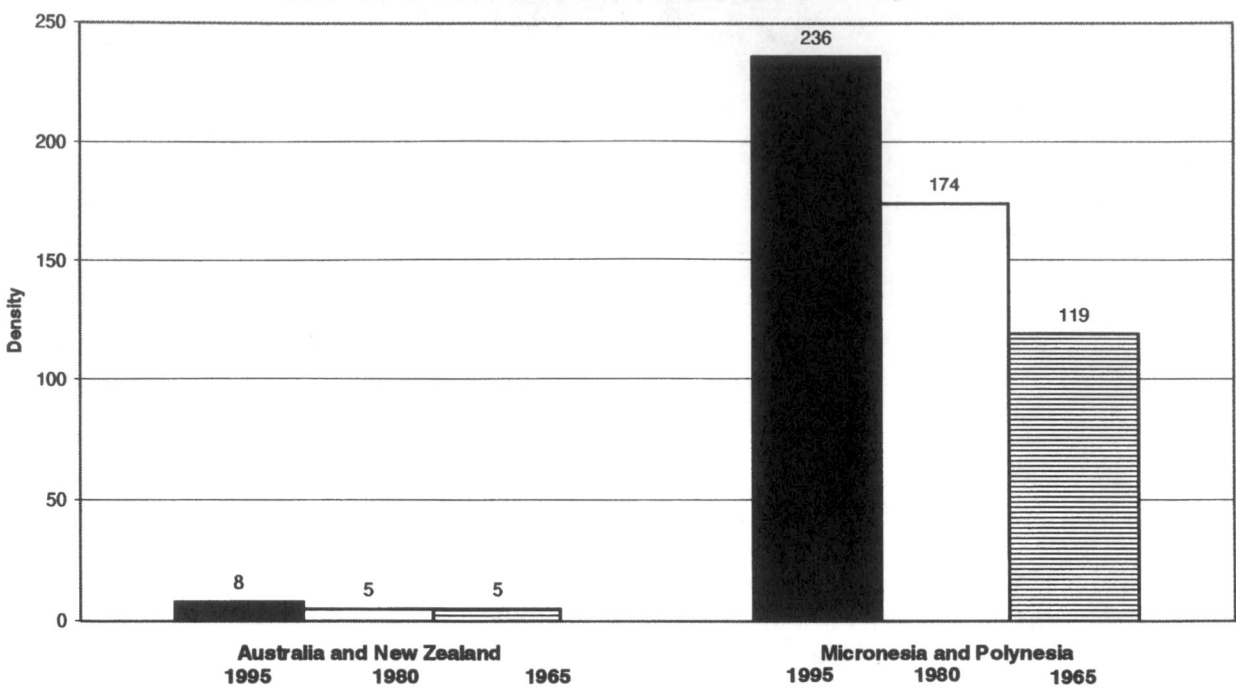

Density per Square Mile:
Australia and New Zealand, and Micronesia and Polynesia

Density rates for Oceania are as varied as birth rates. While Australia remains the least densely populated continent on earth (aside from uninhabited Antarctica), the tiny islands of Micronesia and Polynesia are among the most densely populated nations of the world.

OCEANIA

	1995	1980	1965
GEOGRAPHY			
AREA (square miles/kilometers)	3,296,139/8,537,000		
POPULATION			
TOTAL	28,500,000	22,800,000	17,500,000
DENSITY (per square mile/kilometer)	8.0/3.0	8.0/3.0	5.0/2.0
ANNUAL GROWTH	1.5%	1.5%	2.1%
AGE COHORTS			
0–14	26%	29%	n/a
15–64	64%	63%	n/a
65 AND OVER	10%	8%	n/a

	1995	1980	1965
MALE	50.2%	50.4%	n/a
FEMALE	49.8%	49.6%	n/a

VITAL STATISTICS

	1995	1980	1965
BIRTH RATE	19	22	40
DEATH RATE	8	9	10

AUSTRALIA AND NEW ZEALAND

GEOGRAPHY

AREA (square miles/kilometers)   3,082,625/7,984,000

POPULATION

	1995	1980	1965
TOTAL	21,700,000	17,800,000	14,300,000
DENSITY (per square mile/kilometer)	8/3	5/2	5/2
ANNUAL GROWTH	1.4%	1.2%	2.0%
AGE COHORTS			
0–14	22%	26%	n/a
15–64	66%	65%	n/a
65 AND OVER	12%	9%	n/a
MALE	49.5%	50%	n/a
FEMALE	50.5%	50%	n/a

VITAL STATISTICS

	1995	1980	1965
BIRTH RATE	15	17	22
DEATH RATE	8	8	9

MELANESIA

GEOGRAPHY

AREA (square miles/kilometers)   208,880/541,000

	1995	1980	1965
POPULATION			
TOTAL	5,800,000	3,600,000	2,500,000
DENSITY (per square mile/kilometer)	28/11	18/7	13/5
ANNUAL GROWTH	2.2%	2.7%	2.4%
AGE COHORTS			
0–14	39%	43%	n/a
15–64	58%	54%	n/a
65 AND OVER	3%	3%	n/a
MALE	50%	52.8%	n/a
FEMALE	50%	47.2%	n/a
VITAL STATISTICS			
BIRTH RATE	32	42	44
DEATH RATE	9	15	20

MICRONESIA AND POLYNESIA

GEOGRAPHY

AREA (square miles/kilometers)   4,633/12,000

POPULATION

	1995	1980	1965
TOTAL	1,100,000	800,000	550,000
DENSITY (per square mile/kilometer)	236/91	174/67	119/46
ANNUAL GROWTH	1.9%	1.7%	3.0%
AGE COHORTS			
0–14	40%	41%	n/a
15–64	57%	56%	n/a
65 AND OVER	3%	3%	n/a
MALE	50%	50%	n/a
FEMALE	50%	50%	n/a

	1995	1980	1965
VITAL STATISTICS			
BIRTH RATE	32	34	40
DEATH RATE	6	7	10

Source: UN, Demographic Yearbook, 1997; UN, Statistical Yearbook, 1996.

3.

The Countries of the World, Statistical Tables

AFGHANISTAN

Afghanistan is a landlocked country located in South-Central Asia, north of Pakistan, east of Iran, and south of the former Soviet Republics of Turkmenistan, Uzbekistan, and Tajikistan. The 250,000-square-mile (647,000-square-kilometer) country borders China on the extreme northeast. Since the country gained independence in 1919, its economic and social development has languished, primarily as a result of Cold War disputes between the West and the Soviet Union. Since the fall of the Soviet Union, the country has been racked by factional conflicts among competing adherents of Sunni Islam. Over the past decade, the military conflicts have produced millions of refugees. In part due to the long period of unbroken conflict, the country lacks basic necessities and health services, and is mired in abject poverty and neglect. In 1996, life expectancy at birth was 45.9 years in Afghanistan, significantly lower than in nearby Iran and Pakistan. The infant mortality rate was estimated at 163.4 deaths per 1,000 live births. The national economy is dominated by agricultural production. Only 20 percent of all Afghanis reside in urban areas.

	1995	1980	1965
GEOGRAPHY			
AREA (square miles/kilometers)	250,000/647,000		
LAND AREA (square miles/kilometers)	250,000/647,000		
COASTLINE	Landlocked		
CITIES			
CAPITAL	Kabul	1,424,400 (88)	
MAJOR CITIES	Kandahar	225,500	
	Herat	177,300	
	Mazar-I-Sharif	130,600	

	1995	1980	1965

POPULATION

	1995	1980	1965
TOTAL	20,141,000	13,051,058 (79)	n/a
DENSITY (per square mile/kilometer)	81/31	52/20	n/a
ANNUAL GROWTH	4.78%	2.6%	1.8%

AGE COHORTS

0–14	43%		
15–64	54%		
65 AND OVER	3%		

MALE	51%		
FEMALE	49%		

URBAN	20%	15.4%	n/a
RURAL	80%	84.6%	n/a

NET MIGRATION RATE	22.9	n/a	n/a

IDENTITY

ETHNICITY

PASHTUN	38%		
TAJIK	25%		
HAZARA	19%		

LANGUAGE

AFGHAN-PERSIAN (Dari)	50%		
PASHTU	35%		
UZBEK-TURKMEN	11%		

RELIGION

SUNNI MUSLIM	84%		
SHI'A MUSLIM	15%		

VITAL STATISTICS

BIRTHS

BIRTH RATE	43	48.1	n/a
INFANT MORTALITY RATE	163.4	181.6	n/a
LIFE EXPECTANCY AT BIRTH	45.9	37	n/a

	1995	**1980**	**1965**
MARRIAGES			
MARRIAGE RATE	4.6	n/a	n/a
DIVORCE RATE	0.9	n/a	n/a
DEATHS			
DEATH RATE	18.2	22.3	n/a

ECONOMICS AND LABOR

GDP PER CAPITA US$	$600		

TRANSPORT

	1995	**1980**	**1965**
JOURNEYS (by transport mode)			
AIR PASSENGER TRIPS (thousands)	238		
VEHICLES (thousands)			
CARS	35	n/a	12.8
COMMERCIAL VEHICLES	41	n/a	12.6

EDUCATION

	1995	**1980**	**1965**
SCHOOL AGE IN SCHOOL			
PRIMARY	n/a	36%	16%
SECONDARY	n/a	11%	2%
HIGHER	n/a	0.4%	0.2%
FEMALES IN SCHOOL			
IN PRIMARY	n/a	13%	5%
IN SECONDARY	n/a	4%	1%
ADULT ILLITERACY M/F	n/a	69.7/95% (79)	n/a

COMMUNICATIONS

	1995	**1980**	**1965**
RATE OF NEWSPAPERS	12	6	6
RATE OF RADIOS	118	75	n/a
RATE OF TELEVISIONS	10	3	n/a

Source: CIA, *The World Factbook, 1997*; ILO, *World Labour Report, 1997*; UN, *Demographic Yearbook, 1997*; UN, *Statistical Yearbook, 1996*; World Bank, *World Development Indicators, 1998*.

ALBANIA

Albania occupies a land area of 11,100 square miles (28,750 square kilometers) in Southeastern Europe, west of the Adriatic Sea and the Ionian sea. The country borders Serbia and Montenegro to the north, the former Yugoslav Republic of Macedonia to the east, and Greece to the southeast. The country's population of 3.25 million is dominated by ethnic Albanians, who compose over 95 percent of all residents. Large Albanian minorities live in nearby regions of Serbia and Montenegro, the former Yugoslav Republic of Macedonia, and Greece. In the Kosovo region of southern Serbia, ethnic Albanians have been wag-

ing a decade-long war for autonomy from the Serbian Republic. Albania was one of Europe's most isolated countries for most of the Cold War period between 1946 and 1991. As Albania's economy has opened to the West and reverted from state control to the free market in the 1990s, the country's population has suffered severe hardships, including astronomical rates of inflation and high unemployment. In 1997, the collapse of Albania's highly speculative capitalist market economy led to an economic depression, civil war, and mass out-migration of political and economic refugees.

	1995	1980	1965
GEOGRAPHY			
AREA (square miles/kilometers)	11,100/28,750		
LAND AREA (square miles/kilometers)	10,579/27,400		
COASTLINE (miles/kilometers)	226/362		
CITIES			
CAPITAL Tirane	244,153 (90)		
POPULATION			
TOTAL	3,249,126	n/a	1,626,315 (60)
DENSITY (per square mile/kilometer)	329/127	268/103	174/67
ANNUAL GROWTH	1.34 %	2.1%	3 %
AGE COHORTS			
0–14	34%		
15–4	60%		
65 AND OVER	6%		
MALE	51%		
FEMALE	49%		
URBAN	38%	33.6%	32%
RURAL	62%	n/a	68%

	1995	**1980**	**1965**
NET MIGRATION RATE	−1.17%	n/a	n/a

IDENTITY

ETHNICITY
ALBANIAN	95%		
GREEKS	3%		

LANGUAGE
ALBANIAN	97%		
GREEK	2%		

RELIGION
SUNNI MUSLIM	70%		
ALBANIAN ORTHODOX	20%		
ROMAN CATHOLIC	10%		

VITAL STATISTICS

BIRTHS
BIRTH RATE	22.2	26.2 (85)	34
URBAN BIRTH RATE	18.9 (91)		
RURAL BIRTH RATE	26.6 (91)		
INFANT MORTALITY RATE	49.2	86.8 (85)	86.8
LIFE EXPECTANCY AT BIRTH	67.9	66	64.9

MARRIAGES
MARRIAGE RATE	7.6	8.5 (85)	6.8
DIVORCE RATE	0.7	0.8 (85)	0.6

DEATHS
DEATH RATE	7.6	5.8 (85)	8.6

ECONOMICS AND LABOR

GDP PER CAPITA US$ $1,210

LABOR FORCE M/F (thousands)   494.1/356.4 (91)
UNEMPLOYMENT (official)   9.1%

	1995	1980	1965

HEALTH AND HEALTH CARE

HEALTH CARE

	1995	1980	1965
RATE OF PHYSICIANS	1.3	0.9	0.3 (60)
RATE OF HOSPITAL BEDS	3	n/a	5.1 (60)
MEASLES IMMUNIZATION	91 %		

HEALTH INDICATORS

	1995	1980	1965
LOW-BIRTH-WEIGHT BABIES	7%		
SMOKING PREVALENCE M/F	50/8%		
TUBERCULOSIS RATE	0.4		

EDUCATION

SCHOOL AGE IN SCHOOL

	1995	1980	1965
PRIMARY	87%	113%	84% (60)
SECONDARY	35%	67%	8% (60)
HIGHER	10%	8%	6.80%

FEMALES IN SCHOOL

	1995	1980	1965
PRIMARY	48%[1]	47 %[1]	75% (60)
SECONDARY	54 %[1]	59 %[1]	4% (60)

COMMUNICATIONS

	1995	1980	1965
RATE OF NEWSPAPERS	49	54	47
RATE OF RADIOS	177	150	47
RATE OF TELEVISIONS	89	36	0.6

FOOTNOTE
1. Percentage of students who are female.

Source: CIA, *The World Factbook, 1997;* ILO, *World Labour Report, 1997;* UN, *Demographic Yearbook, 1997;* UN, *Statistical Yearbook, 1996;* World Bank, *World Development Indicators, 1998.*

ALGERIA

Algeria is located in north Africa on the coast of the Mediterranean Sea, bordering Tunisia, Libya, Niger, Mali, Mauritania, and Morocco. Algeria has benefited from huge natural gas and oil reserves. However, the national economy has stagnated following the decline in world oil prices in the early 1980s, which has precipitated a national austerity program aimed at reducing government subsidies and economic assistance programs. The national economy is also burdened by onerous debt obligations to the International Monetary Fund and foreign banks. In 1992, the government refused to honor the results of elections that would have brought fundamentalist Muslims to power. This refusal led to a bloody civil war that has taken thousands of civilian lives. Between 1980 and 1995, the national birth rate fell from 42.7 births 28.5 births per 1,000 residents. Over the same period, life expectancy at birth increased from 59.9 years to 68.3 years.

Secondary Education

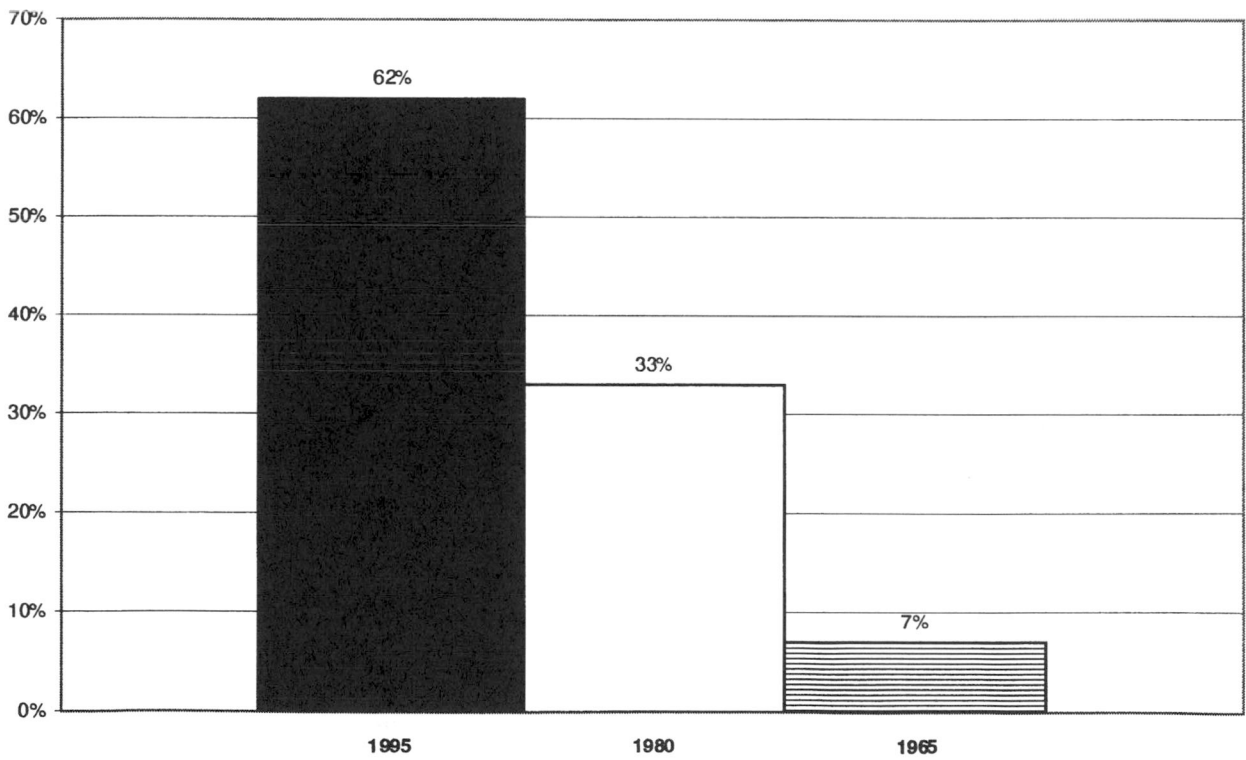

Rising levels of high school graduates are a testament to the resources the government has put into education since independence from France in 1962. However, rising graduation rates have not been matched by rising job opportunities. This is one of the sources of frustration that led to the rise of Muslim militancy in the country in the 1990s.

Private Cars

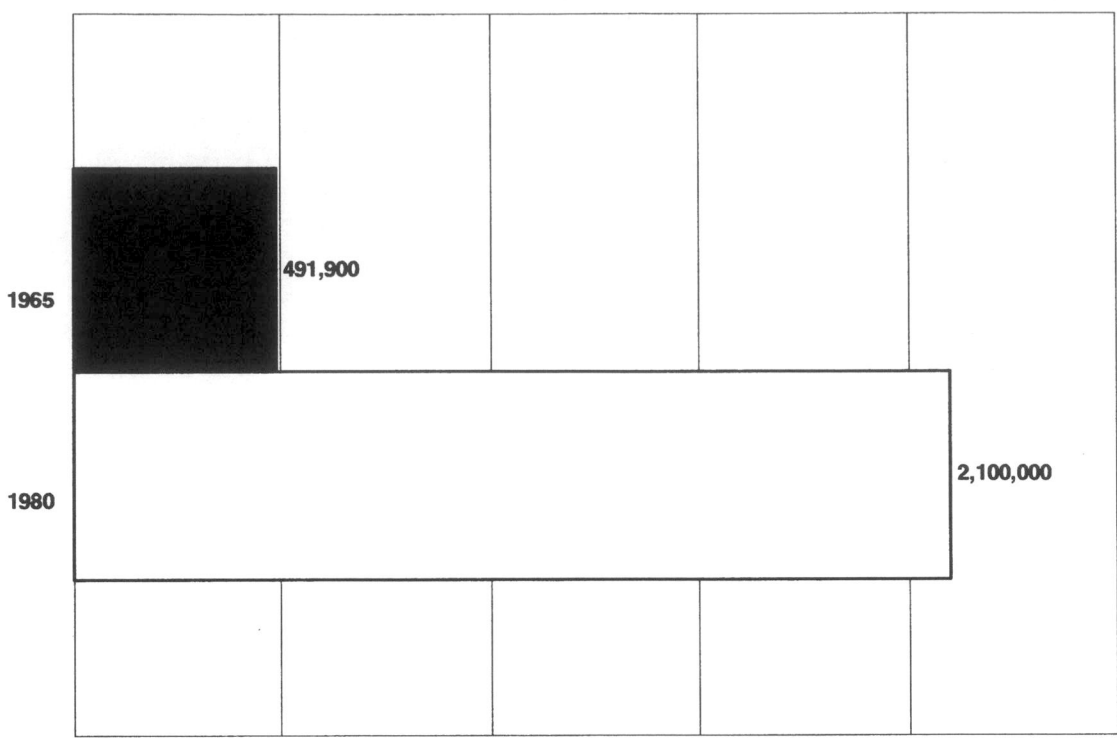

1965   491,900

1980   2,100,000

Massive increases in oil revenues in the 1970s raised living standards for a substantial minority of Algeria's population, a trend reflected in the rapidly rising rates of private car ownership during that period.

CHRONOLOGY

1962   Algeria wins independence from France after eight-year war.

1965   Socialist coup; Houari Boumedienne takes power.

1974   Rise in oil and natural gas prices brings new wealth to country.

1978   Boumedienne dies suddenly; replaced by close associate Chadli Benjedid.

1985   Collapsing oil/gas prices hit Algerian economy.

1988   Rioting over economic dislocations; army guns down hundreds.

1989   Government announces political liberalization.

1992   Army cancels elections that Islamic fundamentalists appear about to win; war breaks out between government and fundamentalists.

1996   New elections fail to end fighting.

	1995	1980	1965

GEOGRAPHY

AREA (square miles/kilometers) 1,093,336/2,831,740
LAND AREA (square miles/kilometers) 1,093,336/2,381,740
COASTLINE (miles/kilometers) 624/998

CITIES
CAPITAL Algiers
MAJOR CITIES Algiers — 1,740,461 (77)
Oran — 543485 (77)
Constantine — 378,668 (77)
Annaba — 246,049 (77)
Blida — 138240 (77)

POPULATION

	1995	1980	1965
TOTAL	29,183,032	16,948,000 (77)	12,101,994
DENSITY (per square mile/kilometer)	31/12	23/9	13/5
ANNUAL GROWTH	2.2%	3.10%	2%

AGE COHORTS

0–14	40%
15–64	56%
65 AND OVER	4%

	1995	1980	1965
URBAN	56%	40%	n/a
RURAL	44%	60%	n/a
NET MIGRATION RATE	2.2	−3.5	n/a

IDENTITY

ETHNICITY

ARAB	80%
BERBER	20%

LANGUAGE

ARABIC	85%
BERBER	12%
FRENCH	2%

RELIGION

SUNNI MUSLIM	99%

	1995	1980	1965

VITAL STATISTICS

BIRTHS

BIRTH RATE	28.5	42.7	n/a
INFANT MORTALITY RATE	48.7	88	n/a
LIFE EXPECTANCY AT BIRTH	68.3	59.9	n/a

MARRIAGES

MARRIAGE RATE	5.6	6.3	n/a
AVERAGE AGE OF MARRIAGE M/F	n/a	27.7/23.7	n/a
DIVORCE RATE	n/a	8.5	n/a

DEATHS

DEATH RATE	5.9	10.7	n/a

HOUSEHOLDS

NUMBER	n/a	3,283,409 (87)	n/a
AVERAGE SIZE	n/a	7 (87)	n/a

ECONOMICS AND LABOR

GDP PER CAPITA US$	$3,800		

LABOR FORCE M/F

AGRICULTURE	18/57%		
INDUSTRY	38/7%		
SERVICES	44/36%		

UNEMPLOYMENT (official)	23.8%		

POVERTY

UNDER $1/DAY	2%		
UNDER $2/DAY	17.6%		

TRANSPORT

VEHICLES

PRIVATE CARS	n/a	491,900	2,100,000
COMMERCIAL	n/a	91,000	251,500

	1995	1980	1965
HEALTH AND HEALTH CARE			
HEALTH CARE			
ACCESS TO SAFE WATER	n/a	77%	n/a
MEASLES IMMUNIZATION	69%	n/a	n/a
RATE OF PHYSICIANS	0.8	n/a	0.2 (60)
RATE OF HOSPITAL BEDS	2.1	n/a	3.1 (60)
HEALTH INDICATORS			
PREGNANT WOMEN WITH ANEMIA	42%		
LOW-BIRTH-WEIGHT BABIES	9%		
CHILD MALNUTRITION	10%		
SMOKING PREVALENCE M/F	53/10%		
TUBERCULOSIS INCIDENCE RATE	0.53		
AIDS/HIV CASES	217	138 (93)	
EDUCATION			
SCHOOL AGE IN SCHOOL			
PRIMARY	107%	94%	68%
SECONDARY	62%	33%	7%
HIGHER	11%	6%	0.7%
FEMALES IN SCHOOL			
OF PRIMARY STUDENTS	99%	86%	53%
OF SECONDARY STUDENTS	47%	26%	5%
ADULT ILLITERACY M/F	26/51%	42.7/68.3%	70.1/92%
COMMUNICATIONS			
RATE OF NEWSPAPERS	38	24	15
RATE OF RADIOS	236	197	12
RATE OF TELEVISIONS	79	52	n/a

Source: CIA, *The World Factbook, 1997;* ILO, *World Labour Report, 1997;* UN, *Demographic Yearbook, 1997;* UN, *Statistical Yearbook, 1996;* World Bank, *World Development Indicators, 1998.*

ANDORRA

The principality of Andorra is located in South-western Europe between France and Spain. The country is the size of a large city, occupying a land area of 174 square miles (450 square kilometers). Due to a large inflow of foreigners, Andorra's population grew twelvefold from 5,664 to 72,766 between 1954 and 1995. However, this population growth has moderated in the last de-cade because of a slow rate of natural growth. The leading ethnic groups in Andorra are Spanish (61 percent), Andorran (30 percent), and French (6 percent). Andorra has a vibrant economy with a relatively high standard of living. In 1996, Andorra's per capita gross domestic product was $16,200. Tourism and banking are the principality's leading economic sectors.

		1995	1980	1965
GEOGRAPHY				
AREA (square miles/kilometers)	174/450			
LAND AREA (square miles/kilometers)	174/450			
COASTLINE (miles/kilometers)	Landlocked			
CITIES				
CAPITAL	Andorra la Vella	n/a	16,151 (86)	n/a
POPULATION				
TOTAL		72,766	n/a	5,664 (54)
DENSITY (per square mile/kilometer)		389/150	199/77	62/24
ANNUAL GROWTH		3.0%	−0.30%	5.80%
AGE COHORTS				
0–14		16%	n/a	29% (66)
15–64		73%	n/a	61.9% (66)
65 AND OVER		11%	n/a	9.1% (66)[1]
NET MIGRATION RATE		22.3	n/a	n/a
IDENTITY				
ETHNICITY				
SPANISH		61%		
ANDORRAN		30%		
FRENCH		6%		

	1995	1980	1965
RELIGION			
ROMAN CATHOLIC	99%		

VITAL STATISTICS

	1995	1980	1965
BIRTHS			
BIRTH RATE	10.2	14.8	n/a
LIFE EXPECTANCY AT BIRTH	90.9	n/a	n/a
MARRIAGES			
MARRIAGE RATE	2	3.8	n/a
DEATHS			
DEATH RATE	2.9	4.1	n/a

ECONOMICS AND LABOR

	1995	1980	1965
GDP PER CAPITA US$	$16,200		

COMMUNICATIONS

	1995	1980	1965
RATE OF NEWSPAPERS	67	n/a	n/a
RATE OF RADIOS	206	194	n/a
RATE OF TELEVISIONS	367	118	90 (70)

FOOTNOTE
1. Age 60 and over.

Source: CIA, *The World Factbook, 1997;* ILO, *World Labour Report, 1997;* UN, *Demographic Yearbook, 1997;* UN, *Statistical Yearbook, 1996;* World Bank, *World Development Indicators, 1998.*

ANGOLA

Angola is located in southwestern Africa, bordering Zaire, Zambia, and Namibia. The 481,351-square-mile (1,246,700-square-kilometer) country lies on the coast of the South Atlantic Ocean. For much of the period since it received independence from Portugal in 1975, a civil war between the Angolan government and Union for the Total Independence of Angola (UNITA), an insurgent group, has destabilized the economy, wreaked havoc on the population, and obstructed national economic development. UNITA has continued to wage a guerrilla war against the national government, despite signing an agreement to end the conflict in 1994. Like many other African countries south of the Sahara, Angola has experienced rapid population growth in the last four decades of the twentieth century. Between 1960 and 1995, Angola's population increased from 4,840,719 to 10,342,899. National population growth increased from 1.7 percent in 1960 to 2.7 percent in 1995. In 1995, life expectancy at birth was only 46.8 years and the country had an infant mortality rate of 124.2 per 1,000 live births. The leading ethnic minorities are the Ovimbundu (37 percent), the Kimbundu (25 percent), and the Bakongo (13 percent).

Ethnic Groups, 1995

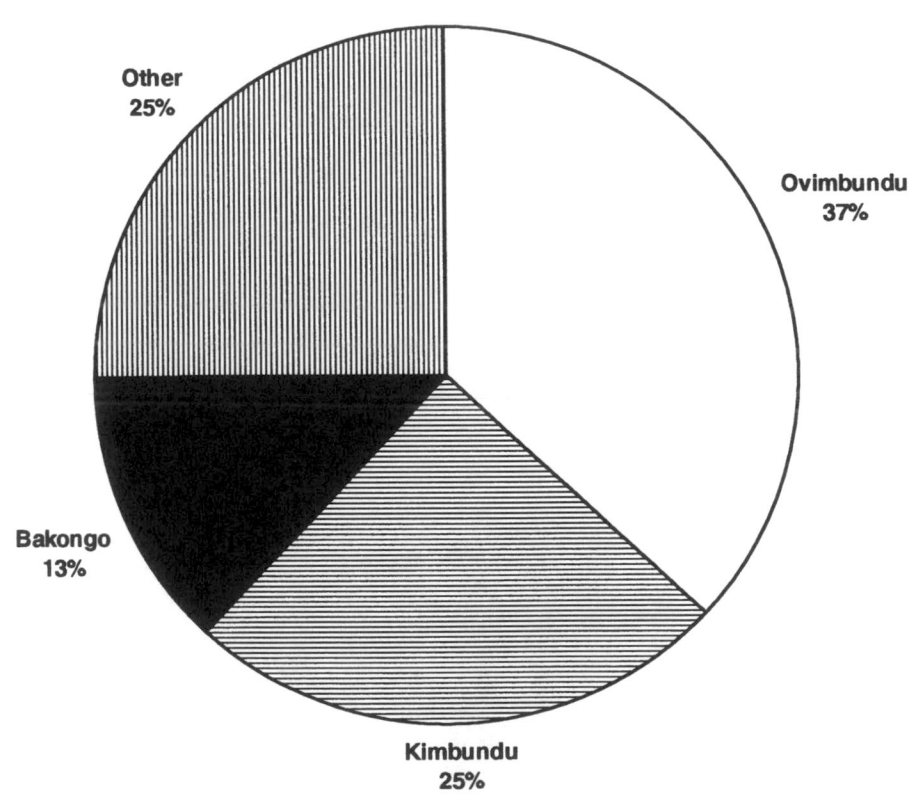

Since winning independence from Portugal in 1975, Angola has almost continuously been torn by civil war. While a host of factors have contributed to the fighting, the battlelines have often fallen along ethnic lines. Like many African countries, Angola is divided into several major ethnic groups.

Rate of Hospital Beds

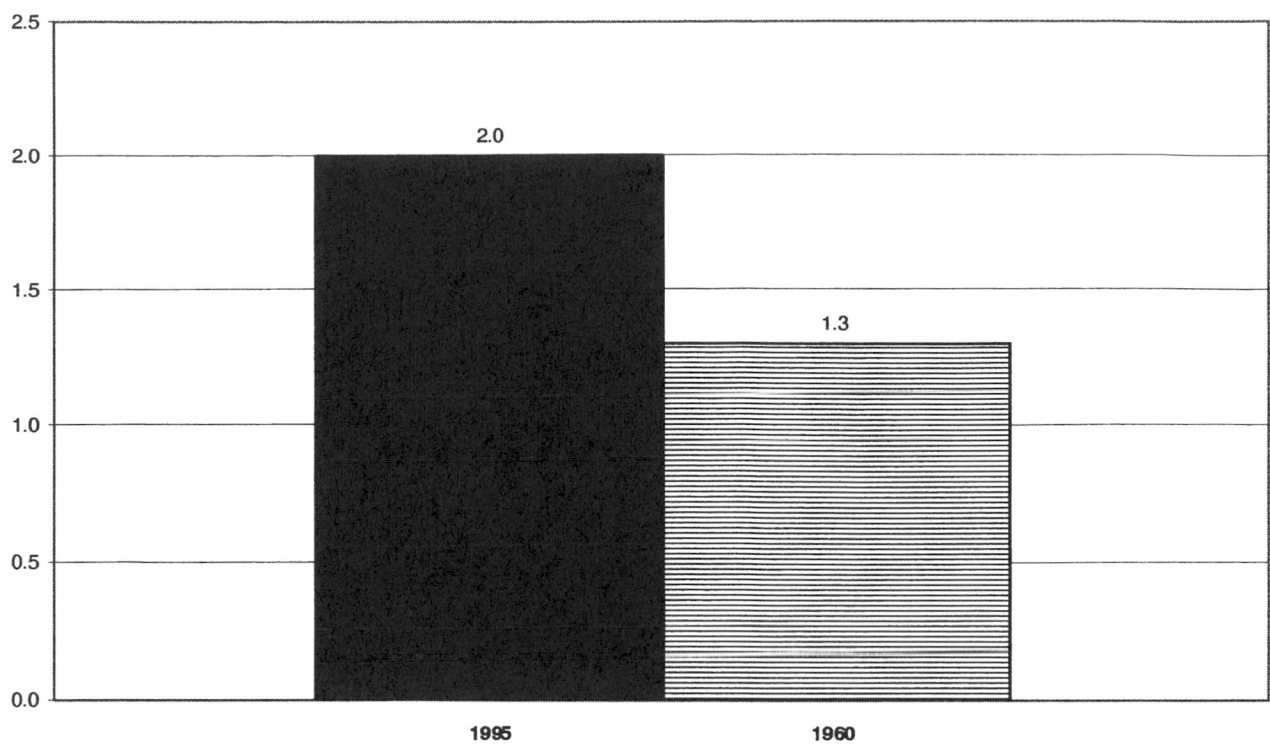

One of the goals of the rebel Union for the Total Liberation Movement of Angola (UNITA) has been the destruction of government-provided social services like health care, as reflected in the decline in hospital beds between 1965 and 1995.

CHRONOLOGY

1961	Uprising against Portuguese rule begins.
1974	Leftist coup ends pro-colonial dictatorship in Portugal.
1975	Angola wins independence from Portugal; war between liberation groups breaks out.
1979	Fighting between rightist rebel movement and leftist government is renewed.
1987–1988	South Africa invades; defeated by combined Cuban/Angolan forces.
1992	Government party defeats rightist rebel-led party in first national elections; rightist rebels return to fighting.
1994	Peace treaty signed, but fails to fully end fighting.

	1995	1980	1965

GEOGRAPHY

AREA (square miles/kilometers)   481,351/1,246,700
LAND AREA (square miles/kilometers)   481,351/1,246,700
COASTLINE (miles/kilometers)   1,000/1,600

CITIES

	1995	1980	1965
CAPITAL	Luanda	n/a	n/a	475,328 (70)

POPULATION

	1995	1980	1965
TOTAL	10,342,899	8,664,318	4,840,719 (60)
DENSITY (per square mile/kilometer)	23/9	18/7	10.0/4.0 (60)
ANNUAL GROWTH	2.7%	2.5%	1.7%

AGE COHORTS

	1995	1980	1965
0–14	45%	n/a	33%
15–64	53%	n/a	64%
65 AND OVER	2%	n/a	3%

	1995
MALE	52%
FEMALE	48%

	1995
URBAN	32%
RURAL	68%

	1995	1980	1965
NET MIGRATION RATE	−0.1	n/a	0.2

IDENTITY

ETHNICITY

	1995
OVIMBUNDU	37%
KIMBUNDU	25%
BAKONGO	13%

RELIGION

	1995
ANIMIST	47%
ROMAN CATHOLIC	38%
PROTESTANT	15%

	1995	**1980**	**1965**

VITAL STATISTICS

BIRTHS

BIRTH RATE	44.6	47.3	n/a
INFANT MORTALITY RATE	124.2	149	n/a
LIFE EXPECTANCY AT BIRTH	46.8	42	n/a

MARRIAGES

MARRIAGE RATE	n/a	4.5	n/a

DEATHS

DEATH RATE	17.7	22.2	n/a

ECONOMICS AND LABOR

GDP PER CAPITA US$	$700		

LABOR FORCE M/F

AGRICULTURE	65/86%		
INDUSTRY	14/2%		
SERVICES	21/13%		

TRANSPORT

JOURNEYS (by transport mode)
RAILROAD PASSENGER TRIPS

(millions of miles/kilometers)	76/122 (93)		
AIR PASSENGER TRIPS (thousands)	519 (94)		

VEHICLES

PRIVATE CARS	n/a	n/a	42,500
COMMERCIAL	n/a	n/a	17,500

HEALTH AND HEALTH CARE

HEALTH CARE

ACCESS TO SAFE WATER	32%		
ACCESS TO SANITATION	16%		

	1995	1980	1965
MEASLES IMMUNIZATION	32%		
RATE OF HOSPITAL BEDS	1.3	n/a	2 (60)
HEALTH INDICATORS			
PREGNANT WOMEN WITH ANEMIA	29%		
LOW-BIRTH-WEIGHT BABIES	19%		
CHILD MALNUTRITION	35%		
TUBERCULOSIS INCIDENCE RATE	2.25		
AIDS/HIV CASES	1,181	703 (93)	

EDUCATION

	1995	1980	1965
SCHOOL AGE IN SCHOOL			
PRIMARY	88%	174%	41%
SECONDARY	14%	21%	5%
HIGHER	1%	n/a	0.10%
FEMALES IN SCHOOL			
PRIMARY STUDENTS	n/a	47%	27%
SECONDARY STUDENTS	n/a	33%	4%
ADULT ILLITERACY	n/a	59% (85)	n/a

COMMUNICATIONS

	1995	1980	1965
RATE OF NEWSPAPERS	12	20	9
RATE OF RADIOS	29	21	16.5
RATE OF TELEVISIONS	7	4	0

Source: CIA, *The World Factbook, 1997;* ILO, *World Labour Report, 1997;* UN, *Demographic Yearbook, 1997;* UN, *Statistical Yearbook, 1996;* World Bank, *World Development Indicators, 1998.*

ANTIGUA AND BARBUDA

Antigua and Barbuda are in the Lesser Antilles, an archipelago bordered by the Atlantic Ocean to the east and the Caribbean Sea to the west. The country (including Antigua, Barbuda, and Redonda, a small island southeast of Antigua) covers a land area of 170 square miles (440 square kilometers). Since Antigua received independence from the United Kingdom in 1981, the country's economy has depended extensively on tourism from North America and Western Europe. Industrial development and new construction are tied heavily to the country's tourist sector. In 1995, per capita income was $6,600. Between 1960 and 1995, Antigua and Barbuda's population grew from 54,304 to 65,647, the vast majority of whom reside on the island of Antigua. Despite limited economic development, the country has a relatively healthy population. In 1995, life expectancy at birth was 73.6 years, comparable with developed industrialized countries.

	1995	1980	1965
GEOGRAPHY			
AREA (square miles/kilometers)	170/440		
LAND (square miles/kilometers)	170/440		
COASTLINE (miles/kilometers)	96/153		
CITIES			
CAPITAL	Saint John's	22,342 (91)	
POPULATION			
TOTAL	65,647	n/a	54,304 (60)
DENSITY (per square mile/kilometer)	386/149	n/a	352/136
ANNUAL GROWTH	0.8%	1.2%	1.6%
AGE COHORTS			
0–14	25%	n/a	43%
15–64	69%	n/a	53%
65 AND OVER	6%	n/a	4%
URBAN	36%		
RURAL	64%		
NET MIGRATION RATE	−0.1	n/a	2.4

	1995	1980	1965
IDENTITY			
ETHNICITY			
BLACK	n/a		
BRITISH	n/a		
PORTUGUESE	n/a		
LANGUAGE			
ENGLISH (official)	n/a		
RELIGION			
ANGLICAN	n/a		
OTHER PROTESTANT	n/a		
ROMAN CATHOLIC	n/a		
VITAL STATISTICS			
BIRTHS			
BIRTH RATE	16.8	15 (83)	30.4 (60)
INFANT MORTALITY RATE	24.4	7.7 (83)	45.4 (60)
LIFE EXPECTANCY AT BIRTH	73.6	70 (83)	62.5 (60)
MARRIAGES			
MARRIAGE RATE	5.4	2.4 (83)	3.7 (60)
DIVORCE RATE	0.7	0.4 (83)	0.4
DEATHS			
DEATH RATE	5.3	5.2 (83)	8.4
HOUSEHOLDS			
NUMBER	19,501 (91)	n/a	10,579 (46)
AVERAGE SIZE	3.1 (91)	n/a	3.9
ECONOMICS AND LABOR			
GDP PER CAPITA US$	$6,600		
UNION DENSITY	53.80%		

	1995	1980	1965

TRANSPORT

JOURNEYS (by transport mode)
AIR PASSENGER TRIPS (thousands)	1,000 (94)		

VEHICLES
ALL TYPES	15,100		

HEALTH AND HEALTH CARE

HEALTH CARE
RATE OF PHYSICIANS	n/a	n/a	0.3 (60)
RATE OF HOSPITAL BEDS	n/a	n/a	7.6 (60)

HEALTH INDICATORS
HIV INFECTION	45	34 (93)	

EDUCATION

SCHOOL AGE IN SCHOOL
PRIMARY	n/a	n/a	145% (63)
SECONDARY	n/a	n/a	96% (63)
HIGHER	n/a	n/a	0.80%

FEMALES IN SCHOOL
PRIMARY	n/a	n/a	160% (63)
SECONDARY	n/a	n/a	101% (63)

COMMUNICATIONS

RATE OF NEWSPAPERS	94 (90)	98	22
RATE OF RADIOS	425	279	70
RATE OF TELEVISIONS	369	262	28

Source: CIA, *The World Factbook, 1997;* ILO, *World Labour Report, 1997;* UN, *Demographic Yearbook, 1997;* UN, *Statistical Yearbook, 1996;* World Bank, *World Development Indicators, 1998.*

ARGENTINA

Argentina lies in southern South America, bordering the South Atlantic Ocean. Uruguay and Brazil are on the east, Bolivia and Paraguay are on the north, and Chile is on the west and south. The country covers a land area of 1,056,637 square miles (2,736,690 square kilometers). Along with Brazil and Mexico, Argentina has one of Latin America's most advanced economies, with a mature industrial sector. During the last decade of the twentieth century, the government of Carlos Saul Menem has introduced free market reforms and privatized state-run enterprises. Under President Menem's economic liberalization pro-

gram, inflation declined from double-digit levels. However, unemployment increased significantly, and by the mid-1990s, Argentina's unemployment rate exceeded 10 percent. In 1995, Argentina's per capita income was $8,100. Between 1960 and 1995, the country's population increased from just over 20 million to 34.7 million; however, annual population growth rates have declined from 1.6 percent to 1.1 percent. In 1995, Argentina's average life expectancy was 71.7 years at birth. The country has an infant mortality rate of 20.3 per 1,000 live births.

Infant Mortality Rate

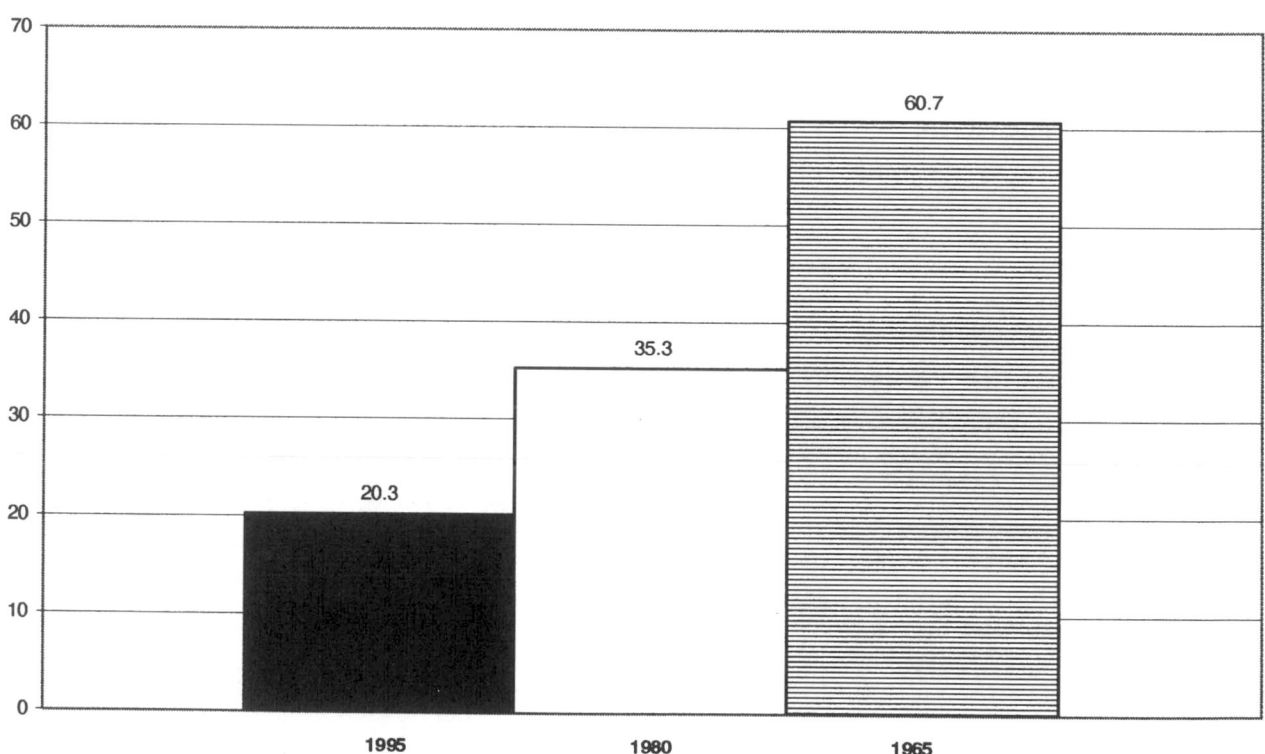

Falling rates of infant mortality reflect the growing health awareness of Argentinian mothers.

Life Expectancy at Birth

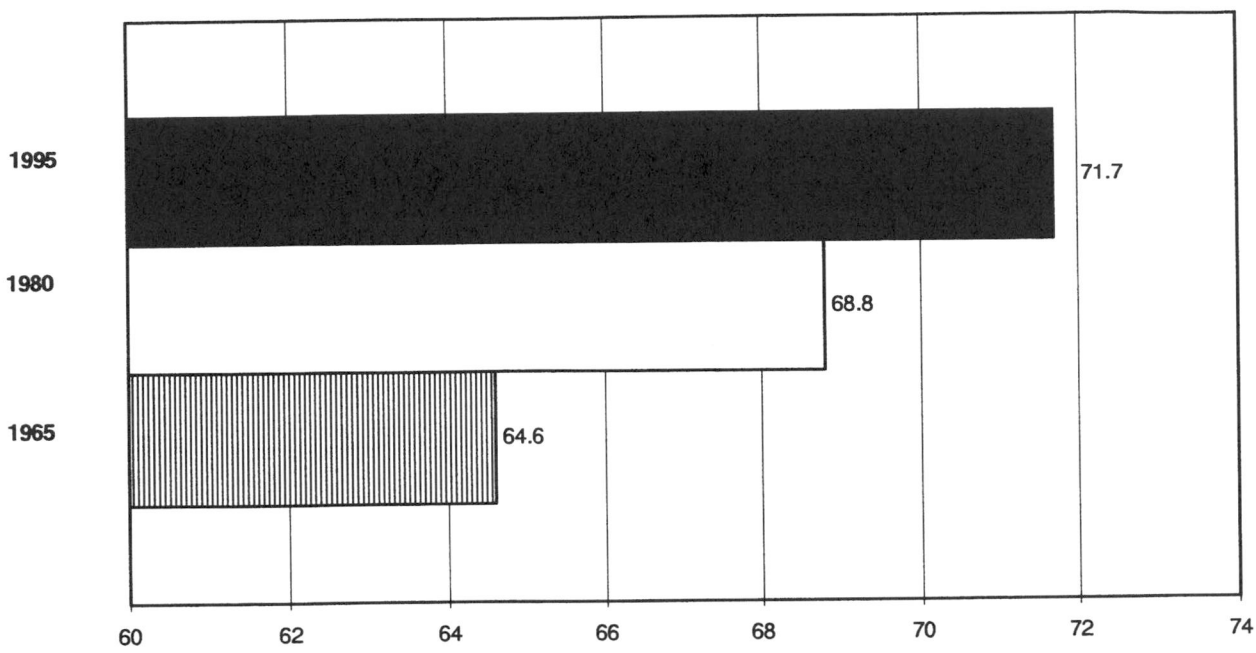

Gradually rising income and educational levels in Argentina over the past 30 years have translated into greater life expectancy.

CHRONOLOGY

1966   Military coup ends decades of civilian rule.

1974   Widow of Juan Peron takes power.

1976   Army ousts Peron widow after she fails to curb inflation.

1982   Argentina invades Falklands/Malvinas Islands; defeated by Great Britain in subsequent war.

1983   Military rule ends.

1989   Transfer of power from one civilian government to next.

1993   Major privatization campaign of state-owned companies accelerates.

	1995	1980	1965

GEOGRAPHY

AREA (square miles/kilometers)   1,068,397/2,766,890
LAND AREA (square miles/kilometers) 1,056,637/2,736,690
COASTLINE (miles/kilometers)   31,000/84,989

CITIES

		1995
CAPITAL	Buenos Aires	2,690,976 (91)
MAJOR CITIES	Córdoba	1,148,305
	La Matanza	1,111,811
	Rosario	894,645
	Moron	641,541

POPULATION

	1995	1980	1965
TOTAL	34,672,997	27,947,446	20,005,691 (60)
DENSITY (per square mile/kilometer)	31/12	28/11	21/8
ANNUAL GROWTH	1.1%	1.6%	1.6%

AGE COHORTS

	1995	1980	1965
0–14	28%	n/a	30%
15–64	63%	n/a	64%
65 AND OVER	9%	n/a	6%

	1995
MALE	49%
FEMALE	51%

	1995	1980	1965
URBAN	88%	83%	n/a
RURAL	12%	17%	n/a

	1995	1980	1965
NET MIGRATION RATE	0.2	n/a	3.6

IDENTITY

ETHNICITY

	1995
EUROPEAN	85%
MESTIZO/INDIAN	15%

LANGUAGE

	1995
SPANISH (official)	n/a
ENGLISH	n/a
GERMAN	n/a

	1995	1980	1965
RELIGION			
ROMAN CATHOLIC	90%		
PROTESTANT	2%		
JEWISH	2%		

VITAL STATISTICS

	1995	1980	1965
BIRTHS			
BIRTH RATE	9.4	23.7	23
INFANT MORTALITY RATE	20.3	35.3	60.7
LIFE EXPECTANCY AT BIRTH	71.7	68.8	64.6
MARRIAGES			
MARRIAGE RATE	4.6	6	6.6
AVERAGE AGE OF MARRIAGE M/F	225.8/23.3 (19)		
DEATHS			
DEATH RATE	8.6	8.4	9

HOUSEHOLDS

	1995	1980	1965
NUMBER	8,927,289 (91)	n/a	5,232,222 (60)
AVERAGE SIZE	3.7	n/a	3.7
FEMALE HEADED	22.3%		

ECONOMICS AND LABOR

	1995	1980	1965
GDP PER CAPITA US$	$8,100		
LABOR FORCE M/F			
AGRICULTURE	16/3%		
INDUSTRY	39/17%		
SERVICES	46/80%		
UNEMPLOYMENT (official)	10.1% (93)		
UNION DENSITY	25.4		

TRANSPORT

	1995	1980	1965
JOURNEYS (by transport mode)			
RAILROAD PASSENGER TRIPS			
(millions of miles/kilometers)	3,908/6,253		
AIR PASSENGER TRIPS (thousands)	6,460.00		

	1995	1980	1965
VEHICLES			
PRIVATE CARS	n/a	3,024,000	927,500
COMMERCIAL	n/a	1,334,00	625,800

HEALTH AND HEALTH CARE

HEALTH CARE			
ACCESS TO SAFE WATER	64%		
ACCESS TO SANITATION	89%		
MEASLES IMMUNIZATION	76%		
RATE OF PHYSICIANS	2.7	n/a	1.3 (60)
RATE OF HOSPITAL BEDS	4.6	n/a	6.3(60)
HEALTH INDICATORS			
PREGNANT WOMEN WITH ANEMIA	26%		
LOW-BIRTH-WEIGHT BABIES	7%		
CHILD MALNUTRITION	2%		
SMOKING PREVALENCE M/F	40/23%		
TUBERCULOSIS INCIDENCE RATE	0.5		
AIDS/HIV CASES	7,966	4,313 (93)	

EDUCATION

SCHOOL AGE IN SCHOOL			
PRIMARY	108%	106%	100%
SECONDARY	72%	56%	38%
HIGHER	38%	22%	10.9%
FEMALES IN SCHOOL			
PRIMARY	n/a	49%	101%
SECONDARY	n/a	64%	40%
ADULT ILLITERACY M/F	4/4%	5.7/6.4%	n/a

COMMUNICATIONS

RATE OF NEWSPAPERS	143	142	148
RATE OF RADIOS	672	427	310
RATE OF TELEVISIONS	220	183	80

Source: CIA, The World Factbook, 1997; ILO, World Labour Report, 1997; UN, Demographic Yearbook, 1997; UN, Statistical Yearbook, 1996; World Bank, World Development Indicators, 1998.

ARMENIA

Armenia is located in Southwestern Asia, bordering Azerbaijan, Georgia, Iran, and Turkey. It covers an area of 11,506 square miles (29,800 square kilometers). The country, which first received independence in 1918 from the Ottoman Empire, was subsumed as a socialist republic under the Soviet Union following World War II. In 1991, after the breakup of the Soviet Union, Armenia regained full autonomy. Armenia's economy fell into a recession after independence was achieved, due to the decline of state support for the industrial sector. Armenia also fell into a dispute with Azerbaijan over the future of Nagorno Karabakh, an Armenian enclave in Azerbaijan. The ethnic dispute with Azerbaijan has led to a chronic energy shortage and intensified the decline of Armenia's economy. The country has a life expectancy of 69.1 years and an infant mortality rate of 15.1 infant deaths per 1,000 live births.

1995[1]

GEOGRAPHY

AREA (square miles/kilometers)	11,506/29,800	
LAND AREA (square miles/kilometers)	10,96/528,400	
COASTLINE (miles/kilometers)	Landlocked	

CITIES		
CAPITAL	Yerevan	1,254,400 (90)
MAJOR CITIES	Leninakan	206,600
	Kirovakan	170,200

POPULATION

TOTAL	3,463,574
DENSITY (per square mile/kilometer)	326/126
ANNUAL GROWTH	0.02%

AGE COHORTS	
0–14	28%
15–64	64%
65 AND OVER	8%

MALE	49%
FEMALE	51%

URBAN	68.5% (92)
RURAL	31.5 (92)

NET MIGRATION RATE	−8.3

1995

IDENTITY

ETHNICITY
ARMENIAN	93%
AZERI	3%
RUSSIAN	2%

LANGUAGE
ARMENIAN	96%
RUSSIAN	2%

RELIGION
ARMENIAN ORTHODOX	94%
MUSLIM	3%
RUSSIAN ORTHODOX	2%

VITAL STATISTICS

BIRTHS
BIRTH RATE	16.3
URBAN BIRTH RATE	17.4 (92)
RURAL BIRTH RATE	22.9 (92)
INFANT MORTALITY RATE	15.1
ABORTION RATE	358.4
LIFE EXPECTANCY AT BIRTH	69.1

MARRIAGES
MARRIAGE RATE	4.6
DIVORCE RATE	0.9

DEATHS
DEATH RATE	7.7

TRANSPORT

JOURNEYS (by transport mode)
AIR PASSENGER TRIPS (thousands)	435

HEALTH AND HEALTH CARE

HEALTH CARE
MEASLES IMMUNIZATION	95%

	1995
RATE OF PHYSICIANS	3.1
RATE OF HOSPITAL BEDS	7.8

HEALTH INDICATORS

TUBERCULOSIS INCIDENCE RATE	0.4
TOTAL DEATHS	24,648 (94)

EDUCATION

SCHOOL AGE IN SCHOOL

PRIMARY	82%
SECONDARY	79%
HIGHER	49%

FEMALES IN SCHOOL

OF PRIMARY STUDENTS	50%

COMMUNICATIONS

RATE OF NEWSPAPERS	24

FOOTNOTE
1. Part of the Soviet Union in 1965 and 1980.

Source: CIA, *The World Factbook, 1997;* ILO, *World Labour Report, 1997;* UN, *Demographic Yearbook, 1997;* UN, *Statistical Yearbook, 1996;* World Bank, *World Development Indicators, 1998.*

AUSTRALIA

The Commonwealth of Australia occupies the entire continent of Australia, in Oceania, between the Indian and the South Pacific oceans. The country has an area of 2,967,896 square miles (7,686,850 square kilometers). It has a low density of 6 persons per square mile (2 persons per square kilometer). Most of the country's population is concentrated in five major metropolitan areas. While about 95 percent of Australia's population is of European descent, the growth in Asian migration is diversifying the nation's ethnic composition. Between 1965 and 1995, Australia's migration rate increased from 2.2 to 2.7 per 1,000 residents. The Australian economy is highly dependent on the export of raw materials and primary products, chiefly fossil fuels, minerals, and agricultural products. The country has strong social service and health care sectors relative to the region, contributing to a fairly high life expectancy at birth of 79.4 years.

Ethnic Groups, 1995

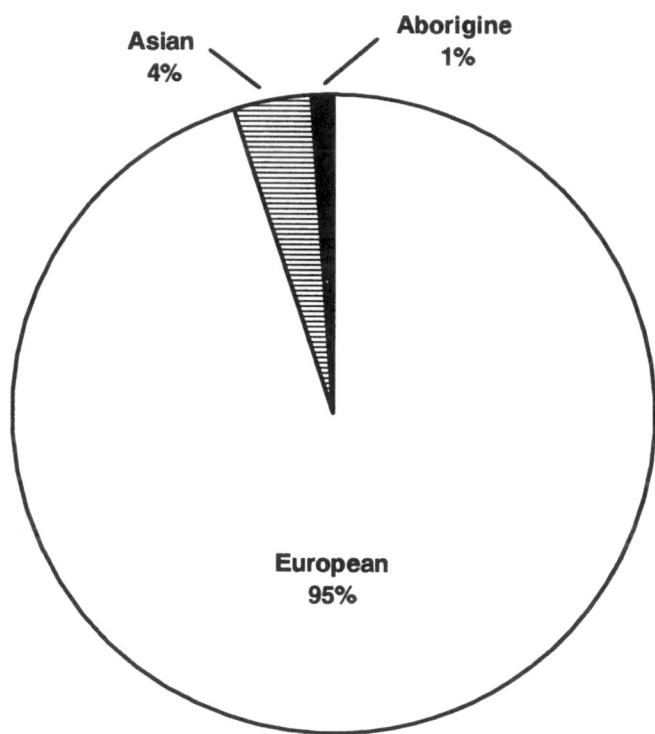

Always a haven for immigrants, Australia has lately seen the source of that immigration change. Whereas most immigrants came from Europe through the 1960s, a rapidly growing number have come from East and South Asia in recent decades, reflecting the country's shift from a European outpost to a Pacific-centered nation.

Net Migration

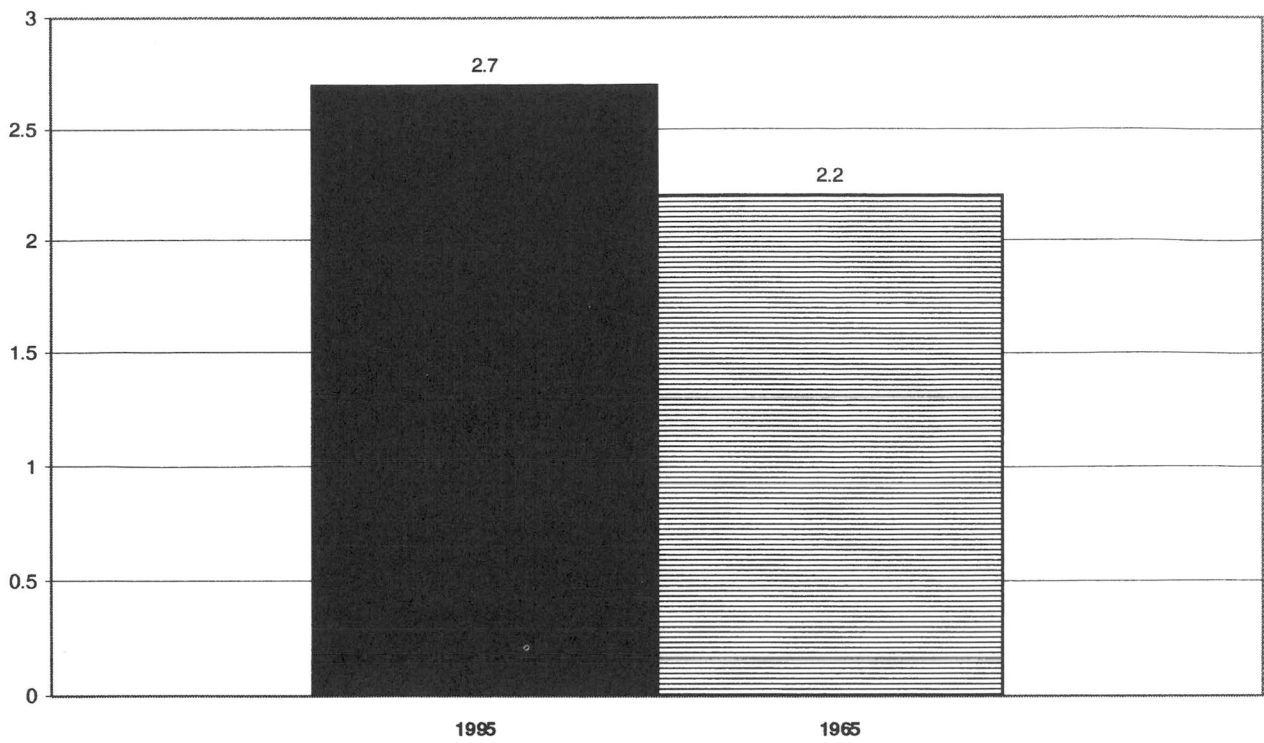

With just 6 persons per square mile, Australia remains one of the most underpopulated nations on the planet, though much of the country's territory is desert. This has led to consistently high rates of in-migration.

CHRONOLOGY

1965   Australia begins sending troops to Southeast Asia to help the United States and South Vietnam.
1972   Labour Party takes power.
1975   Liberal-Country coalition takes power.
1983   Radical Labour Prime Minister Bob Hawke wins national elections.
1988   Native aborigines protest Australian bicentennial.
1991   High inflation leads to ouster of Hawke government.
1998   Right-wing, anti-Asian immigration party wins seats in parliament.

	1995	1980	1965

GEOGRAPHY

AREA (square miles/kilometers)   2,967,896/7,686,850
LAND AREA (square miles/kilometers)   2,941,286/7,617,930
COASTLINE (miles/kilometers)   16,100/25,760

CITIES

		1995		
CAPITAL	Canberra	298,200 (93)		
MAJOR CITIES	Sydney	3,713,500		
	Melbourne	3,189,200		
	Brisbane	1,421,600		
	Perth	1,221,200		

POPULATION

	1995	1980	1965
TOTAL	18,260,863	14,576,330 (81)	11,540,764 (66)
DENSITY (per square mile/kilometer)	6.0/2.0	5.0/2.0	5.0/2.0
ANNUAL GROWTH	1.00%	1.40%	2%
AGE COHORTS			
0–14	21%	n/a	30%
15–64	66%	n/a	62%
65 AND OVER	13%	n/a	8%
MALE	50%		
FEMALE	50%		
URBAN	85%	85.7	n/a
RURAL	15%	14.30%	n/a
NET MIGRATION RATE	2.7	n/a	2.2

IDENTITY

	1995
ETHNICITY	
EUROPEAN	95%
ASIAN	4%
ABORIGINE	1%
LANGUAGE	
ENGLISH	99%

	1995	**1980**	**1965**
RELIGION			
ANGLICAN	26%		
ROMAN CATHOLIC	26%		
OTHER PROTESTANT	24%		

VITAL STATISTICS

	1995	**1980**	**1965**
BIRTHS			
BIRTH RATE	14	15 (84)	19.3
INFANT MORTALITY RATE	5.9 (94)	9.2 (84)	18.2
LIFE EXPECTANCY AT BIRTH	79.4	75.9 (84)	70.9
MARRIAGES			
MARRIAGE RATE	6.8	7 (84)	8.3
AVERAGE AGE OF MARRIAGE M/F	29.2/27 (94)		
DIVORCE RATE	2.7	2.8 (84)	0.7
DEATHS			
DEATH RATE	6.9	7.1 (84)	9

HOUSEHOLDS

	1995	**1980**	**1965**
NUMBER	n/a	n/a	2,781,945 (61)
AVERAGE SIZE	n/a	n/a	3.7 (61)

ECONOMICS AND LABOR

	1995
GDP PER CAPITA US$	$22,100
LABOR FORCE M/F (thousands)	4,545.4/3,375.2 (94)
AGRICULTURE	281.0/122.6
MINING	76.6/9.7
MANUFACTURING	811.5/294.5
UTILITIES	73.3/13.0
CONSTRUCTION	490.0/79.6
TRADE/FOOD/TOURISM	1,066.1/948.5
TRANSPORT/COMMUNICATIONS	384.2/126.5
FINANCE/INSURANCE/REAL ESTATE	537.5/488.7
SOCIAL AND PERSONAL SERVICES	800.1/1,278.1
UNEMPLOYMENT (official)	9.8 (94)
UNION DENSITY	28.60%

	1995	1980	1965
TRANSPORT			
JOURNEYS (by transport mode)			
AIR PASSENGER TRIPS (thousands)	26,816.0 (94)		
VEHICLES (thousands)			
PRIVATE CARS	8,209	5,800.60	2,894.2
COMMERCIAL	2,151	1,425.10	872.4
HEALTH AND HEALTH CARE			
HEALTH CARE			
RATE OF PHYSICIANS	2.2	1.8	1.4
RATE OF HOSPITAL BEDS	8.9	n/a	11.9
ACCESS TO SAFE WATER	95%		
ACCESS TO SANITATION	90%		
MEASLES IMMUNIZATION	n/a	68%	n/a
HEALTH INDICATORS			
SMOKING PREVALENCE M/F	29/21%		
TUBERCULOSIS INCIDENCE RATE	0.06		
AIDS/HIV CASES	6,442	5,006 (93)	
TOTAL DEATHS	126,692 (94)		
EDUCATION			
SCHOOL AGE IN SCHOOL			
PRIMARY	108%	112%	106%
SECONDARY	72%	56%	72%
HIGHER	n/a	25%	11.6%
FEMALES IN SCHOOL			
OF PRIMARY STUDENTS	49%	49%	50%
OF SECONDARY STUDENTS	49%	49%	49%
COMMUNICATIONS			
RATE OF NEWSPAPERS	265	323	373
RATE OF RADIOS	1,290	1,098	219
RATE OF TELEVISIONS	489	384	169

Source: CIA, *The World Factbook, 1997;* ILO, *World Labour Report, 1997;* UN, *Demographic Yearbook, 1997;* UN, *Statistical Yearbook, 1996;* World Bank, *World Development Indicators, 1998.*

AUSTRIA

Austria is located in central Europe, bordering Italy, Switzerland, Germany, the Czech Republic, Hungary, and Slovenia. The country has an area of 32,375 square miles (83,850 square kilometers). Persons of German and Austrian descent compose the vast majority (99 percent) of the nation's residents. In recent decades, the national birth rate has declined significantly, leading to a slow rate of growth. Migration accounts for a large share of the nation's population growth. In 1995, the country had a net migration rate of 3.3 per 1,000 residents. Austria is one of Europe's wealth-iest nations, with a high standard of living. In 1995, the country had a per capita gross domestic product of $19,000. The country has one of the most comprehensive systems of social protection in the world. A large share of the national economy is under the control of the state, and the national government provides one of the strongest social safety nets in the world. Like its counterparts in Western Europe, the Austrian government has come under pressure to cut budget deficits by reducing social benefits.

		1995	**1980**	**1965**
GEOGRAPHY				
AREA (square miles/kilometers)		32,375/83,850		
LAND AREA (square miles/kilometers)		31,942/82,730		
COASTLINE (miles/kilometers)		Landlocked		
CITIES				
CAPITAL	Vienna	1,750,000		
MAJOR CITIES	Graz	237,810		
	Linz	203,044		
	Salzburg	143,973		
	Innsbruck	118,112		
POPULATION				
TOTAL		8,023,244	7,555,338 (81)	7,073,807 (61)
DENSITY (per square mile/kilometer)		249/96	233/90	225/87
ANNUAL GROWTH		0.4 %	0 %	0.5 %
AGE COHORTS				
0–14		18 %	n/a	23 %
15–64		67 %	n/a	64%
65 AND OVER		15 %	n/a	13 %
MALE		48%		
FEMALE		52%		

	1995	1980	1965
URBAN	56%	55.10%	n/a
RURAL	44%	44.90%	n/a
NET MIGRATION	3.3	n/a	−0.2

IDENTITY

ETHNICITY

GERMAN-AUSTRIAN	99%		
CROATIAN AND SLOVENE	1%		

LANGUAGE

GERMAN	n/a		

RELIGION

ROMAN CATHOLIC	85%		
PROTESTANT	6%		

VITAL STATISTICS

BIRTHS

BIRTH RATE	11.2	11.5 (85)	17.6
INFANT MORTALITY RATE	5.5	11 (85)	28.1
LIFE EXPECTANCY AT BIRTH	76.5	73.7 (85)	69.3

MARRIAGES

MARRIAGE RATE	5.4	5.9 (85)	7.6
AVERAGE AGE OF MARRIAGE M/F	28.9/26.1		
DIVORCE RATE	2	2 (85)	1.2

DEATHS

DEATH RATE	10.4	11.8 (85)	12.5

HOUSEHOLDS

NUMBER	n/a	n/a	2,306,000 (61)
AVERAGE SIZE	n/a	n/a	3 (61)

ECONOMICS AND LABOR

GDP PER CAPITA US$	$19,000

	1995	1980	1965
LABOR FORCE M/F (thousands)	2,078.8/1496.6 (93)		
AGRICULTURE	129.3/117.2		
MINING	9.3/0.9		
MANUFACTURING	658.0/244.8		
UTILITIES	31.8/4.1		
CONSTRUCTION	280.7/25.1		
TRADE/FOOD/TOURISM	273.2/401.1		
TRANSPORT/COMMUNICATIONS	188.1/44.4		
FINANCE/INSURANCE/REAL ESTATE	133.7/131.6		
SOCIAL AND PERSONAL SERVICES	366.4/516.0		
UNEMPLOYMENT (official)	6.5 % (94)		
UNION DENSITY	36.60 %		

TRANSPORT

	1995	1980	1965
JOURNEYS (by transport mode)			
RAILROAD PASSENGER TRIPS			
(millions of miles/kilometers)	2,343/3,748.0 (94)		
AIR PASSENGER TRIPS (thousands)	9,384.0 (94)		
VEHICLES (thousands)			
PRIVATE CARS	3,479.60	2,247.00	789.7
COMMERCIAL	698.2	526.1	297.3

HEALTH AND HEALTH CARE

	1995	1980	1965
HEALTH CARE			
RATE OF PHYSICIANS	2.6	2.3	1.8 (60)
RATE OF HOSPITAL BEDS	9.4	11.2	10.8 (60)
ACCESS TO SAFEWATER	n/a	100	n/a
ACCESS TO SANITATION	100		
MEASLES IMMUNIZATION	60		
HEALTH INDICATORS			
LOW-BIRTH-WEIGHT BABIES	6%		
SMOKING PREVALENCE M/F	42/27%		
TUBERCULOSIS INCIDENCE RATE	0.2		
AIDS/HIV CASES	1,515	1,176 (93)	
TOTAL DEATHS	80,368		

	1995	1980	1965

EDUCATION

SCHOOL AGE IN SCHOOL

	1995	1980	1965
PRIMARY	101%	99%	105%
SECONDARY	104%	99%	69%
HIGHER	4.5%	26%	6.8%

FEMALES IN SCHOOL

	1995	1980	1965
OF PRIMARY STUDENTS	49%	49%	49%
OF SECONDARY STUDENTS	49%	49%	48%

COMMUNICATIONS

	1995	1980	1965
RATE OF NEWSPAPERS	398	351	249
RATE OF RADIOS	618	507	305
RATE OF TELEVISIONS	479	391	101

Source: CIA, The World Factbook, 1997; ILO, World Labour Report, 1997; UN, Demographic Yearbook, 1997; UN, Statistical Yearbook, 1996; World Bank, World Development Indicators, 1998.

AZERBAIJAN

Azerbaijan is located in the Transcaucasus of Southwestern Asia, bordered by the Caspian Sea on the east, Russia and Georgia on the North, Armenia on the west, and Iran on the south. The country occupies an area of 33,436 square miles (86,600 square kilometers). In 1995, it had a population of 7.6 million and a growth rate of 0.8 percent. Azerbaijan was a soviet socialist republic of the Soviet Union until 1991, when the Soviet Union collapsed and the country gained independence. People of Azeri descent compose the vast majority of the nation's residents (90 percent). Dagestanis (3 percent), Russians (3 percent), and Armenians (2.3 percent) are Azerbaijan's three leading minorities. In 1995, the country had an out-migration rate of 5.8 persons per 1,000 residents. The country has a birth rate of 22.3 and a death rate of 8.7 persons per 1,000 residents. Life expectancy at birth is 64.8 years. Although Azerbaijan is less economically developed than bordering states in the region, the country has extensive petroleum and natural gas reserves now under development and expansion.

1995[1]

GEOGRAPHY

AREA (square miles/kilometers)	33,436/86,600	
LAND AREA (square miles/kilometers)	33,243/86,100	
COASTLINE (miles/kilometers)	500/800	

CITIES		
CAPITAL	Baku	1,149,000 (90)
MAJOR CITIES	Giyandja	281,000
	Sumgait	235,000

POPULATION

TOTAL	7,676,953
DENSITY (per square mile/kilometer)	225/87
ANNUAL GROWTH	0.8%

AGE COHORTS	
0–14	32%
15–64	61%
65 AND OVER	7%

MALE	49%
FEMALE	51%

URBAN	56%
RURAL	44%

	1995
NET MIGRATION RATE	−5.8%

IDENTITY

ETHNICITY

AZERI	90%
DAGESTANI	3%
RUSSIAN	3%
ARMENIAN	2.3%

LANGUAGE

AZERI	89%
RUSSIAN	3%
ARMENIAN	2%

RELIGION

SUNNI MUSLIM	93%
RUSSIAN ORTHODOX	3%
ARMENIAN ORTHODOX	2%

VITAL STATISTICS

BIRTHS

BIRTH RATE	22.3
INFANT MORTALITY RATE	26.1
LIFE EXPECTANCY AT BIRTH	64.8

MARRIAGES

MARRIAGE RATE	6.4
DIVORCE RATE	1.6

DEATHS

DEATH RATE	8.7

ECONOMICS AND LABOR

GDP PER CAPITA US$	$1,480

LABOR FORCE M/F

AGRICULTURE	27/36%
INDUSTRY	35/21%
SERVICES	38/43%

UNEMPLOYMENT (official)	13.6 (94)
UNION DENSITY	75.40%

1995

TRANSPORT

JOURNEYS (by transport mode)
RAILROAD PASSENGER TRIPS
  (millions of miles/kilometers)   863/1,380 (94)

HEALTH AND HEALTH CARE

HEALTH CARE
MEASLES IMMUNIZATION   91
RATE OF PHYSICIANS   3.8
RATE OF HOSPITAL BEDS   10

HEALTH INDICATORS
CHILD MALNUTRITION   10%
TUBERCULOSIS INCIDENCE RATE   0.47
AIDS/HIV CASES   2
TOTAL DEATHS   54,921 (94)

EDUCATION

SCHOOL AGE IN SCHOOL
PRIMARY   104%
SECONDARY   74%
HIGHER   20%

FEMALES IN SCHOOL
OF PRIMARY STUDENTS   47%
OF SECONDARY STUDENTS   48%

COMMUNICATIONS

RATE OF NEWSPAPERS   59

FOOTNOTE
1. Part of the Soviet Union in 1965 and 1980.

Source: CIA, *The World Factbook, 1997*; ILO, *World Labour Report, 1997*; UN, *Demographic Yearbook, 1997*; UN, *Statistical Yearbook, 1996*; World Bank, *World Development Indicators, 1998*.

THE BAHAMAS

The Bahamas is an island archipelago located in the Caribbean, southeast of Florida and north of Cuba. The country occupies a total area of 5,382 square miles (13,940 square kilometers) in the Atlantic Ocean. The country's population increased from 136,368 in 1965 to 259,367 in 1995. Blacks compose a majority (85 percent) of the national population. In 1995, the country had a relatively high life expectancy of 72.5 years. The Bahamian economy is dependent on tourism from North America and Western Europe, which accounts for about 50 percent of the nation's gross domestic product. Compared to other regional states, the Bahamas had a high gross domestic product of $18,700 in 1995. Only 13 percent of the population resides in rural areas.

	1995	1980	1965
GEOGRAPHY			
AREA (square miles/kilometers)	5,382/13,940		
LAND AREA (square miles/kilometers)	3,888/10,070		
COASTLINE (miles/kilometers)	2,214/3,542		
CITIES			
CAPITAL	New Providence	n/a	
MAJOR CITIES	Nassau	172,196 (90)	
POPULATION			
TOTAL	259,367	223,455	136,368 (63)
DENSITY (per square mile/kilometer)	52/20	44/17	31/12
ANNUAL GROWTH	1.1%	1.90%	4%
AGE COHORTS			
0–14	28%	n/a	44%
15–64	67%	n/a	52%
65 AND OVER	5%	n/a	4%
MALE	49%		
FEMALE	51%		
URBAN	87%	75.3%	n/a
RURAL	13%	24.7%	n/a
NET MIGRATION RATE	−2.5	n/a	35.7

	1995	1980	1965

IDENTITY

ETHNICITY

BLACK	85%		
WHITE	15%		

LANGUAGE

ENGLISH	n/a		
CREOLE	n/a		

RELIGION

BAPTIST	32%		
ANGLICAN	20%		
ROMAN CATHOLIC	19%		

VITAL STATISTICS

BIRTHS

BIRTH RATE	18.7	22.2 (84)	32.6 (66)
INFANT MORTALITY RATE	27.3	22.9 (84)	36.5 (66)
LIFE EXPECTANCY AT BIRTH	72.5	66.6 (84)	n/a

MARRIAGES

MARRIAGE RATE	9.1	7.4 (84)	7.5 (66)
AVERAGE AGE OF MARRIAGE M/F	29.1/27.2		
DIVORCE RATE	1.2	0.8 (84)	0.1 (66)

DEATHS

DEATH RATE	5.7	5 (84)	7.1 (66)

HOUSEHOLDS

NUMBER	61,910 (90)	n/a	32,035 (63)
AVERAGE SIZE	4.1 (90)	n/a	4.1 (63)

TYPE OF HOUSEHOLD

SINGLE	25%		
MARRIED	43%		
WIDOWED	9%		
DIVORCED/SEPARATED	13%		

FEMALE HEADED	36%		

	1995	1980	1965

ECONOMICS AND LABOR

| **GDP PER CAPITA US$** | $18,700 | | |
| **UNEMPLOYMENT** (official) | 13.3% (94) | | |

TRANSPORT

JOURNEYS (by transport mode) AIR PASSENGER TRIPS (thousands)	862 (94)		
VEHICLES			
PRIVATE CARS	46,100	47,100	19,800
COMMERCIAL	11,900	8,000	3,500

HEALTH AND HEALTH CARE

HEALTH CARE			
RATE OF PHYSICIANS	n/a	n/a	0.5 (60)
RATE OF HOSPITAL BEDS	n/a	n/a	5.5 (60)
HEALTH INDICATORS			
AIDS/HIV CASES	2,101	1,389 (93)	
TOTAL DEATHS	1,538 (94)		

EDUCATION

SCHOOL AGE IN SCHOOL			
PRIMARY	n/a	n/a	106%
SECONDARY	n/a	n/a	42%
HIGHER	n/a	n/a	0.20%
FEMALES IN SCHOOL			
PRIMARY	n/a	n/a	105%
SECONDARY	n/a	n/a	46%

	1995	1980	1965
COMMUNICATIONS			
RATE OF NEWSPAPERS	133	157	113
RATE OF RADIOS	545	486	220
RATE OF TELEVISIONS	226	148	23

Source: CIA, *The World Factbook, 1997;* ILO, *World Labour Report, 1997;* UN, *Demographic Yearbook, 1997;* UN, *Statistical Yearbook, 1996;* World Bank, *World Development Indicators, 1998.*

BAHRAIN

Bahrain is an archipelago located in the Persian Gulf, east of Saudi Arabia and north of Qatar. The country covers an area of 293 square miles (620 square kilometers). Much of the country's terrain is desert. In the three decades between 1965 and 1995, the national population increased from 182,203 to 590,042. Ninety percent of the population resides in urban areas. Manama, located on Bahrain's north shore, is the country's capital and the largest population center. From 1980 to 1995, Bahrain's annual population growth declined from 3.8 percent to 2.3 percent. Bahrain's national economy is dominated by petroleum production and processing for export. The oil economy contributes to Bahrain's high per capita gross domestic product of $12,000. However, the country is dependent on stable oil prices. Frequent shifts in world oil prices in the last two decades of the twentieth century have subjected the economy to frequent and unpredictable changes. In 1995, the country had a net migration rate of 2.4 per 1,000 residents. Males compose a significant 58 percent majority of the country's population. Islam is the major religion. About 75 percent of Bahrain's population is Shi'a Muslim and 25 percent is Sunni Muslim.

	1995	1980	1965
GEOGRAPHY			
AREA (square miles/kilomters)	293/620		
LAND AREA (square miles/kilometers)	293/620		
COASTLINE (miles/kilometers)	100/161		
CITIES			
CAPITAL	Manamah	140,402 (92)	
POPULATION			
TOTAL	590,042	350,798 (81)	182,203
DENSITY (per square mile/kilometer)	2,186/844	1,738/671	837/323
ANNUAL GROWTH	2.3%	3.8%	1.4%
AGE COHORTS			
0–14	31%		
15–64	67%		
65 AND OVER	2%		
MALE	58%		
FEMALE	42%		
URBAN	90%	80.7%	n/a
RURAL	10%	19.3%	n/a

	1995	**1980**	**1965**
NET MIGRATION RATE	2.4	n/a	0.2

IDENTITY

ETHNICITY

BAHRAINI	63%		
ASIAN	13%		
OTHER ARAB	10%		

LANGUAGE

ARABIC	n/a		
ENGLISH	n/a		
FARSI	n/a		

RELIGION

SHI'A MUSLIM	75%		
SUNNI MUSLIM	25%		

VITAL STATISTICS

BIRTHS

BIRTH RATE	23.6	32.2	n/a
INFANT MORTALITY RATE	18	32	
LIFE EXPECTANCY AT BIRTH	74.3	67.4	n/a

MARRIAGES

MARRIAGE RATE	5.9		
AVERAGE AGE AT MARRIAGE M/F	28.4/25.6		
DIVORCE RATE	1.1		

DEATHS

DEATH RATE	3.3	4.5	n/a

HOUSEHOLDS

NUMBER	78,776 (91)		
AVERAGE SIZE	5.6 (91)		

ECONOMICS AND LABOR

GDP PER CAPITA US$	$12,000		

	1995	1980	1965
LABOR FORCE M/F (thousands)	104.0/11.8 (94)		
AGRICULTURE	0.9/0.3		
MINING	0.5/0.0		
MANUFACTURING	22.4/3.7		
UTILITIES	3.3/0.7		
CONSTRUCTION	33.0/0.3		
TRADE/FOOD/TOURISM	19.3/1.6		
TRANSPORT/COMMUNICATIONS	8.3/2.3		
FINANCE/INSURANCE/REAL ESTATE	5.0/1.6		
SOCIAL AND PERSONAL SERVICES	10.0/2.1		

TRANSPORT

	1995	1980	1965
JOURNEYS (by transport mode)			
AIR PASSENGER TRIPS (thousands)	1,151 (94)		
VEHICLES			
PRIVATE CARS	125,500 (94)	47,000	n/a
COMMERCIAL	29,400	18,400	n/a

HEALTH AND HEALTH CARE

	1995	1980	1965
HEALTH CARE			
RATE OF PHYSICIANS	n/a	n/a	0.5 (60)
RATE OF HOSPITAL BEDS	n/a	n/a	4.7 (60)
HEALTH INDICATORS			
AIDS/HIV CASES	28	15 (93)	
TOTAL DEATHS	1,695 (94)		

EDUCATION

	1995	1980	1965
SCHOOL AGE IN SCHOOL			
PRIMARY	n/a	104%	103%
SECONDARY	n/a	64%	33%
HIGHER	n/a	4.7%	1.7 (70)
FEMALES IN SCHOOL			
PRIMARY	n/a	97%	82%
SECONDARY	n/a	58%	21%
HIGHER	n/a	4.9%	2.2% (70)
ADULT ILLITERACY M/F	n/a	23.5/41.4% (81)	63.9/81.8%

	1995	**1980**	**1965**
COMMUNICATIONS			
RATE OF NEWSPAPERS	83	40	n/a
RATE OF RADIOS	553	360	494
RATE OF TELEVISIONS	430	259	71

Source: CIA, The World Factbook, 1997; ILO, World Labour Report, 1997; UN, Demographic Yearbook, 1997; UN, Statistical Yearbook, 1996; World Bank, World Development Indicators, 1998.

BANGLADESH

Bangladesh is located in southern Asia on the Bay of Bengal. The 55,598-square-mile (144,000-square-kilometer) country is bordered by India on the east, west, and north, and by Myanmar on the southeast. Bangladesh is one of the most densely populated countries in the world, with a rate of 2,165 persons per square mile (836 per square kilometer). The country received independence in 1971 following a civil war with Pakistan. However, the Bangladeshi government has experienced frequent internal political unrest and domestic turmoil for much of the period since independence. The high density often forces Bangladeshis to reside in regions susceptible to regular seasonal flooding. Frequently, water is polluted, intensifying sanitation problems and promoting communicable diseases. Residents who live near the Bay of Bengal suffer from cyclones and flooding during the summer monsoon season. Although Bangladesh's economic growth rate dropped from 2.2 percent in 1981 to 1.9 percent in 1995, the population increased from 87,119,965 to 123,062,800 over the same period. Nearly all the country's residents are of Bengali origin; however, 83 percent of the population is Sunni Muslim and 16 percent is Hindu. Due to the lack of economic development, the country's population is mired in a state of poverty. Most of the country's population is made up of agricultural workers who produce mainly rice and other grain products for personal use. In 1995, per capita gross domestic product was only $1,130.

Density

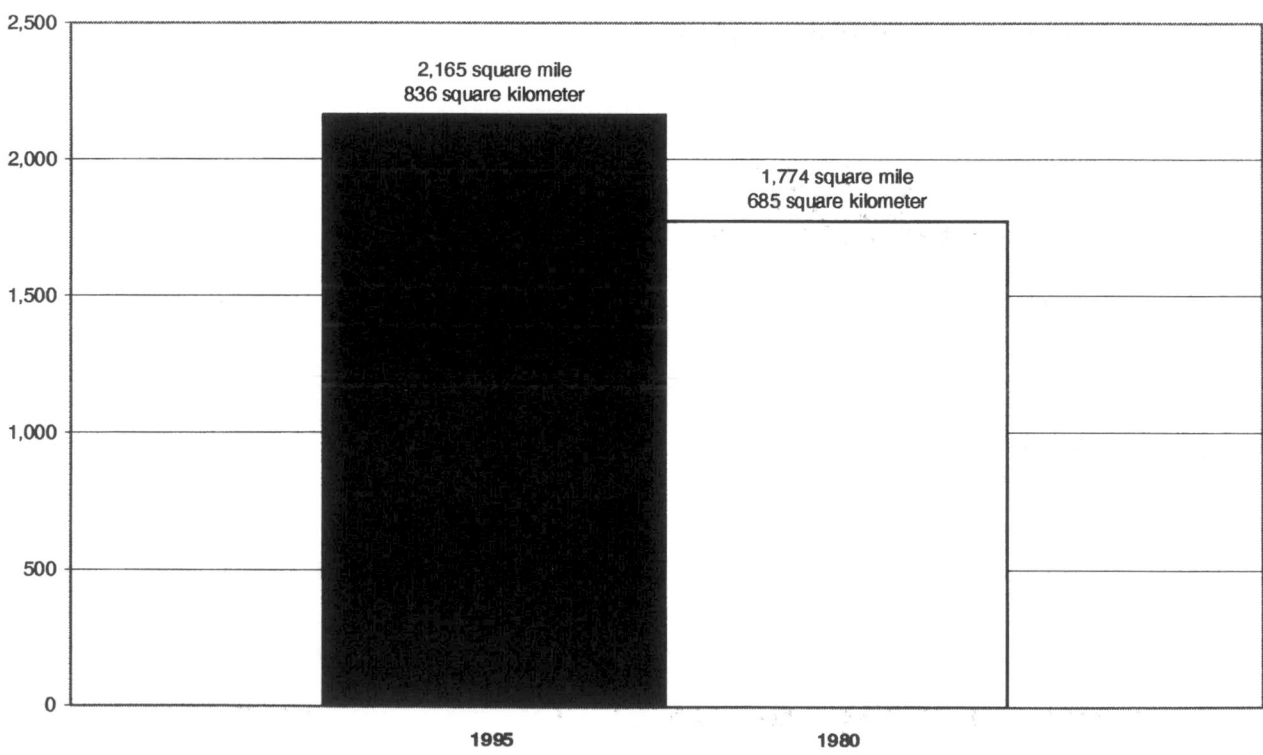

Since long before its independence from Pakistan in 1971, Bangladesh has been among the most densely populated countries on the planet.

Percent Urban

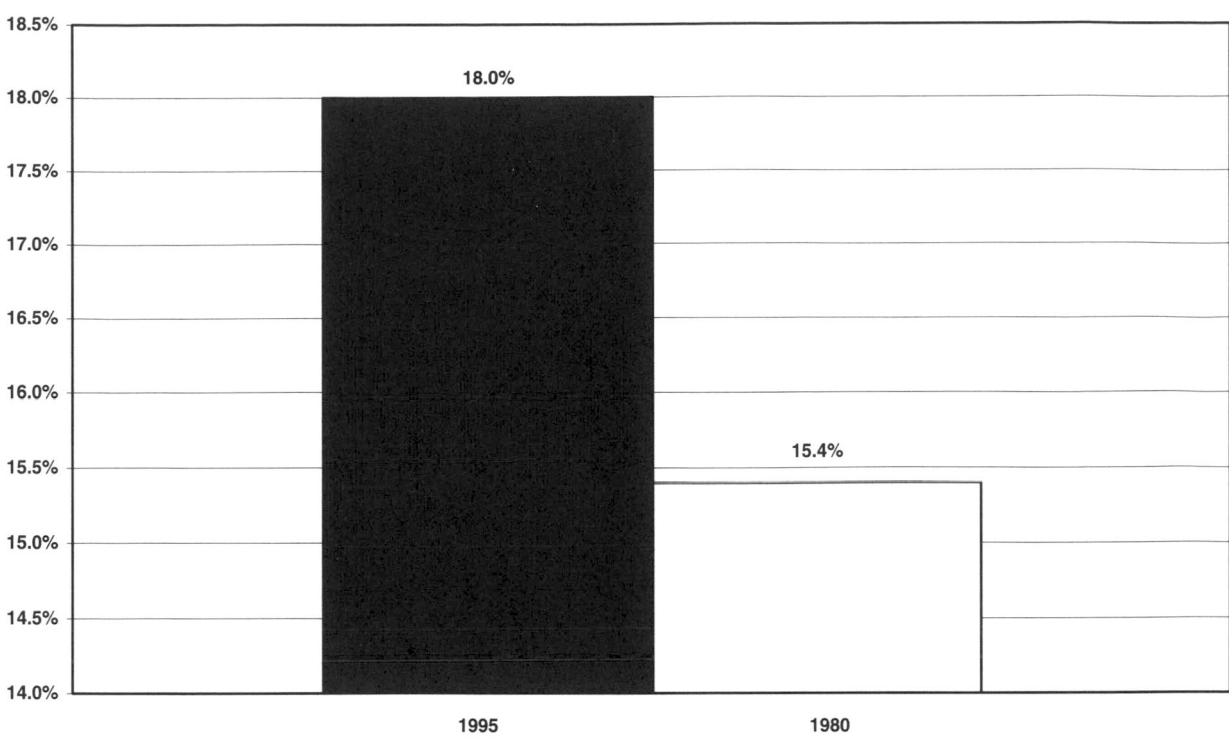

Like its giant neighbor India, Bangladesh has remained one of the most rural countries in the world. Despite the fertile delta land on which it lives, Bangladesh's rising population is causing reduced average farm size and setting off the beginnings of urban migration.

CHRONOLOGY

1971   With help from India, Bangladesh fights war with and wins independence from Pakistan.

1975   Military coup ends in assassination of country's first prime minister.

1979   Martial law lifted and democratic government reinstated.

1981   Prime Minister Ziaur Rahman assassinated.

1982   Military coup leads to renewed martial law.

1987   State of Emergency declared after antigovernment protests break out around country.

1991   Rahman's widow elected prime minister.

	1995	**1980**[1]

GEOGRAPHY

AREA (square miles/kilometers)	55,598/144,000	
LAND AREA (square miles/kilometers)	51,703/133,910	
COASTLINE (miles/kilometers)	363/580	

CITIES

CAPITAL	Dhaka	3,397,187 (91)
MAJOR CITIES	Chittagong	1,363,998
	Khulna	545,849
	Rajshahi	299,671
	Narayanganj	268,952

POPULATION

	1995	**1980**
TOTAL	123,062,800	87,119,965 (81)
DENSITY (per square mile/kilometer)	2,165/836	1,774/685
ANNUAL GROWTH	1.9%	2.20%

AGE COHORTS

0–14	39%
15–64	58%
65 AND OVER	3%

MALE	51%
FEMALE	49%

	1995	**1980**
URBAN	18%	15.4%
RURAL	82%	84.6%

NET MIGRATION RATE	−0.8%

IDENTITY

ETHNICITY

BENGALI	98%
TRIBALS	1%

LANGUAGE

BANGLA	n/a
ENGLISH	n/a

	1995	1980[1]
RELIGION		
SUNNI MUSLIM	83%	
HINDU	16%	

VITAL STATISTICS

BIRTHS		
BIRTH RATE	30.5	44.8
INFANT MORTALITY RATE	107.5	128
LIFE EXPECTANCY AT BIRTH	55.9	54.9
MARRIAGES		
MARRIAGE RATE	10.9	9
DEATHS		
DEATH RATE	11.2	17.5

ECONOMICS AND LABOR

GDP PER CAPITA US$	$1,130	
LABOR FORCE M/F		
AGRICULTURE	59/74%	
INDUSTRY	14/19%	
SERVICES	26/7%	
UNION DENSITY	4.3%	

TRANSPORT

JOURNEYS (by transport mode)		
RAILROAD PASSENGER TRIPS	3,343/5,348	
(millions of miles/kilometers)		
AIR PASSENGER TRIPS (thousands)	1,216 (94)	
VEHICLES		
PRIVATE CARS	46,600 (93)	45,100
COMMERCIAL	59,500 (93)	36,500

HEALTH AND HEALTH CARE

HEALTH CARE		
RATE OF PHYSICIANS	0.2	0.1
RATE OF HOSPITAL BEDS	0.3	0.2

	1995	1980[1]
ACCESS TO SAFE WATER	79%	
ACCESS TO SANITATION	35%	
MEASLES IMMUNIZATION	96%	
HEALTH INDICATORS		
PREGNANT WOMEN WITH ANEMIA	53%	
LOW-BIRTH-WEIGHT BABIES	34%	
CHILD MALNUTRITION	68%	
SMOKING PREVALENCE M/F	60/15%	
TUBERCULOSIS INCIDENCE RATE	2.2	
AIDS/HIV CASES	7	1 (93)

EDUCATION

	1995	1980[1]
SCHOOL AGE IN SCHOOL		
PRIMARY	n/a	61%
SECONDARY	n/a	18%
HIGHER	n/a	3%
FEMALES IN SCHOOL		
PRIMARY		37%
ADULT ILLITERACY M/F	51/74%	60.3/82% (81)

COMMUNICATIONS

	1995	1980[1]
RATE OF NEWSPAPERS	6	3
RATE OF RADIOS	47	17
RATE OF TELEVISIONS	6	1

FOOTNOTE
1. Part of Pakistan in 1965.

Source: CIA, *The World Factbook, 1997*; ILO, *World Labour Report, 1997*; UN, *Demographic Yearbook, 1997*; UN, *Statistical Yearbook, 1996*; World Bank, *World Development Indicators, 1998*.

BARBADOS

Barbados is a tropical island located in the eastern Caribbean east of the Windward Islands. The island's northeast shores border the Atlantic Ocean. The 166-square-mile (430-square-kilometer) country is located approximately 200 miles northeast of Trinidad. The country received independence from the United Kingdom in November 1966. Barbados's leading economic activities are sugar production and tourism, making the country highly dependent on world market prices for sugar and tourism from North America and Western Europe. In 1995, the national per capita gross domestic product was $9,800. Although Barbados's population has grown slowly at a pace of 0.3 percent in recent years, the country has a relatively high density of 1,590 persons per square mile (614 per square kilometer). Persons of African descent compose nearly 84 percent of the country's population.

	1995	**1980**	**1965**
GEOGRAPHY			
AREA (square miles/kilometers)	166/430		
LAND AREA (square miles/kilometers)	166/430		
COASTLINE (miles/kilometers)	60/97		
CITIES			
CAPITAL	Bridgetown n/a	7,466	n/a
POPULATION			
TOTAL	257,030	248,983	243,810
DENSITY (per square mile/kilometer)	1,590/614	1,520/587	n/a
ANNUAL GROWTH	0.3%	0.3%	n/a
AGE COHORTS			
0–14	24%	n/a	39%
15–64	66%	n/a	54%
65 AND OVER	10%	n/a	7%
URBAN	47%	32.2%	n/a
RURAL	53%	68.8%	n/a
NET MIGRATION RATE	−4.5	n/a	28.6

	1995	1980	1965

IDENTITY

ETHNICITY

AFRICAN	84%		
EUROPEAN	4%		

LANGUAGE

ENGLISH	100%		

RELIGION

ANGLICAN	40%		
PENTECOSTAL	8%		
METHODIST	7%		

VITAL STATISTICS

BIRTHS

BIRTH RATE	15.3	16.7 (84)	29–32
INFANT MORTALITY RATE	13.2	10.9 (84)	49.3
LIFE EXPECTANCY AT BIRTH	74.4	69.8 (84)	65.1

MARRIAGES

MARRIAGE RATE	11.2	5 (84)	3.9
DIVORCE RATE	1.4	1.3 (84)	0.3

DEATHS

DEATH RATE	8.2	7.8 (84)	9

HOUSEHOLDS

	1995	1980	1965
NUMBER	n/a	n/a	57,622 (60)
AVERAGE SIZE	n/a	n/a	4 (60)

ECONOMICS AND LABOR

GDP PER CAPITA US$	$9,800		

LABOR FORCE M/F (thousands)	54.1/46.6 (94)		
AGRICULTURE	3.5/2.4		
MINING	0.0/0.0		
MANUFACTURING	5.2/4.8		
UTILITIES	0.9/0.1		

	1995	**1980**	**1965**
CONSTRUCTION	7.4/0.3		
TRADE/FOOD/TOURISM	6.9/8.4		
TRANSPORT/COMMUNICATIONS	3.1/1.1		
FINANCE/INSURANCE/REAL ESTATE	2.2/4.1		
SOCIAL AND PERSONAL SERVICES	10.8/19.8		
UNEMPLOYMENT (official)	21.9% (94)		

TRANSPORT

JOURNEYS (by transport mode)			
AIR PASSENGER TRIPS (thousands)	46 (80)		
VEHICLES (thousands)			
PRIVATE CARS	42,600	29,400 (79)	10,500
COMMERCIAL	6,800	2,300	3,200

HEALTH AND HEALTH CARE

HEALTH CARE			
RATE OF PHYSICIANS	n/a	n/a	0.3 (60)
RATE OF HOSPITAL BEDS	n/a	n/a	5.9 (60)
HEALTH INDICATORS			
AIDS/HIV CASES	632	418 (93)	
TOTAL DEATHS	2,481		

EDUCATION

SCHOOL AGE IN SCHOOL			
PRIMARY	n/a	100%	89%
SECONDARY	n/a	84%	34%
HIGHER	n/a	14.5%	1.5%
FEMALES IN SCHOOL			
PRIMARY	n/a	100%	93%
SECONDARY	n/a	84%	31%
HIGHER	n/a	15.3	n/a
ADULT ILLITERACY M/F	n/a	n/a	0.3/0.3% (70)

	1995	1980	1965
COMMUNICATIONS			
RATE OF NEWSPAPERS	160	156	112
RATE OF RADIOS	877	542	176
RATE OF TELEVISIONS	279	209	25

Source: CIA, *The World Factbook, 1997;* ILO, *World Labour Report, 1997;* UN, *Demographic Yearbook, 1997;* UN, *Statistical Yearbook, 1996;* World Bank, *World Development Indicators, 1998.*

BELARUS

Belarus is a landlocked country, located in Eastern Europe, west of the Russian Federation. Latvia and Lithuania border the 80,154-square-mile (207,600-square-kilometer) country on the north. Poland borders it on the west and the Ukraine on the south. Although Belarus had nominal independence as a soviet socialistic republic of the Soviet Union, the country gained formal independence in August 1991 amid the breakup of the Soviet Union. Belarus is one of the most economically developed countries of the former Soviet Union. In 1995, Belarus had a per capita gross domestic product of $4,700. In 1993, the official unemployment rate was under 1 percent and only 6.4 percent of the country's population lived on less than $2 a day. Under the leadership of President Aleksandr Lukashenko, the government has resisted market reforms that have been implemented elsewhere in the region. Byelorussians (78 percent) are the country's leading ethnic group, followed by Russians (13 percent) and Poles (4 percent). In 1993, life expectancy at birth was 68.6 percent, and the infant mortality rate was 13.3 per 1,000 live births.

	1995	1980[1]	1965[1]

GEOGRAPHY

AREA (square miles/kilometers)	80,154/207,600		
LAND AREA (square miles/kilometers)	80,154/207,600		
COASTLINE (miles/kilometers)	Landlocked		
CITIES			
CAPITAL	Minsk	1,659,700 (93)	
MAJOR CITIES	Gomel	503,900 (93)	
	Mogilev	364,600 (93)	
	Vitebsk	362,700 (93)	
	Grodno	298,400 (93)	

POPULATION

TOTAL	10,415,973	0,543 (79)	8,054,648 (59)
DENSITY (per square mile/kilometer)	125/49	n/a	109/42
ANNUAL GROWTH	0.2%	n/a	1%
AGE COHORTS			
0–14	21%		
15–64	66%		
65 AND OVER	13%		
MALE	47%		
FEMALE	53%		

	1995	1980[1]	1965[1]
URBAN	71%	56.8%	n/a
RURAL	29%	43.2%	n/a
NET MIGRATION RATE	3.5		

IDENTITY

ETHNICITY

BYELORUSSIAN	78%		
RUSSIAN	13%		
POLISH	4%		

LANGUAGE

BYELORUSSIAN	n/a		
RUSSIAN	n/a		

RELIGION

EASTERN ORTHODOX	60%		
ROMAN CATHOLIC	40%		

VITAL STATISTICS

BIRTHS

BIRTH RATE	12.2	n/a	17.7
URBAN BIRTH RATE	11.6 (93)		
RURAL BIRTH RATE	10.9 (93)		
INFANT MORTALITY RATE	13.3 (93)	n/a	22
ABORTION RATE	732.4		
LIFE EXPECTANCY AT BIRTH	68.6		

MARRIAGES

MARRIAGE RATE	7.3	n/a	8.3
AVERAGE AGE AT MARRIAGE M/F	24.5/21.9		
DIVORCE RATE	3.9	n/a	1

DEATHS

DEATH RATE	13.6	n/a	6.7

HOUSEHOLDS

NUMBER	2,796,121 (89)		
AVERAGE SIZE	3.6 (89)		

	1995	1980[1]	1965[1]

ECONOMICS AND LABOR

GDP PER CAPITA US$	$4,700		
LABOR FORCE (thousands)	4,696,000 (94)		
AGRICULTURE	995.7		
MINING	27.2		
MANUFACTURING	1,245.60		
UTILITIES	38.7		
CONSTRUCTION	328.9		
TRADE/FOOD/TOURISM	422.3		
TRANSPORT/COMMUNICATIONS	318		
FINANCE/INSURANCE/REAL ESTATE	40.9		
SOCIAL AND PERSONAL SERVICES	1,099.70		
UNEMPLOYMENT (official)	0.7% (93)		
UNION DENSITY	96.1%		
POVERTY			
UNDER $2/DAY	6.4% (93)		

TRANSPORT

JOURNEYS (by transport mode)			
RAILROAD PASSENGER TRIPS			
(millions of miles/kilometers)	10,039/16,063 (94)		
AIR PASSENGER TRIPS (thousands)	805.0 (94)		

HEALTH AND HEALTH CARE

HEALTH CARE			
RATE OF PHYSICIANS	4.1	3.4	n/a
RATE OF HOSPITAL BEDS	12.4	12.5	n/a
ACCESS TO SANITATION	100%		
MEASLES IMMUNIZATION	96%		
HEALTH INDICATORS			
LOW-BIRTH-WEIGHT BABIES	5%		
TUBERCULOSIS INCIDENCE RATE	0.5		
AIDS/HIV CASES	15	10 (93)	
TOTAL DEATHS	130,003 (94)		

	1995	1980[1]	1965[1]
EDUCATION			
SCHOOL AGE IN SCHOOL			
PRIMARY	97%	104%	n/a
SECONDARY	n/a	98%	n/a
HIGHER	n/a	39%	12.1%
FEMALES IN SCHOOL			
OF PRIMARY STUDENTS	48%		
OF SECONDARY STUDENTS	50%		
COMMUNICATIONS			
RATE OF NEWSPAPERS	186	243	n/a
RATE OF RADIOS	313	223	n/a
RATE OF TELEVISIONS	272	218	n/a

FOOTNOTE
1. Part of Union of Soviet Socialist Republics.

Source: CIA, *The World Factbook, 1997;* ILO, *World Labour Report, 1997;* UN, *Demographic Yearbook, 1997;* UN, *Statistical Yearbook, 1996;* World Bank, *World Development Indicators, 1998.*

BELGIUM

Belgium is located in Western Europe on the North Sea. The 11,780-square-mile (30,510-square-kilometer) country is bordered by the Netherlands on the north; Germany, and Luxembourg on the east; and France on the south and southwest. Belgium received its independence in October 1830 from the Netherlands. It has few natural resources, and its highly industrialized economy is linked to Western European and global markets. The country has a density of 857 persons per square mile (331 per square kilometer). The leading social division is between the Dutch-speaking Flemish (56 percent) in the industrial north and the French-speaking Walloons (32 percent) in the less economically developed southern region. Although the Flemish are an ethnic majority, about 75 percent of the country's population are Roman Catholic and 25 percent are Protestant. The country is almost entirely urban, with 97 percent of the population living in cities and only 3 percent in rural zones. In 1995, Belgium had a relatively slow annual population growth rate of 0.33 percent. Belgium has a high average life expectancy at birth of 77.1 years and a low infant mortality rate of 7.6 per 1,000 live births.

	1995	1980	1965
GEOGRAPHY			
AREA (square miles/kilometers)	11,780/30,510		
LAND AREA (square miles/kilometers)	11,672/30,230		
COASTLINE (miles/kilometers)	40/64		
CITIES			
CAPITAL	Brussels (91)	136,488	
MAJOR CITIES	Antwerp (90)	470,349	
	Ouvers (91)	467,875	
	Gent	230,466	
	Charleroi	206,928	
POPULATION			
TOTAL	10,170,241	9,848,647 (81)	9,189,741 (61)
DENSITY (per square mile/kilometer)	857/331	842/325	808/312
ANNUAL GROWTH	0.3%		
AGE COHORTS			
0–14	18%	n/a	23.8% (64)
15–64	66%	n/a	64% (64)
65 AND OVER	16%	12.4% (64)	n/a
URBAN	97%	94.6 (76)	n/a
RURAL	3%	5.4% (76)	n/a

	1995	1980	1965
NET MIGRATION RATE	1.6	n/a	0.6 (64)

IDENTITY

ETHNICITY

FLEMING	55%		
WALLOON	33%		

LANGUAGE

DUTCH	56%		
FRENCH	32%		
GERMAN	1%		

RELIGION

ROMAN CATHOLIC	75%		
PROTESTANT	25%		

VITAL STATISTICS

BIRTHS

BIRTH RATE	12	11.5 (85)	15.8
INFANT MORTALITY RATE	7.6	9.4 (85)	24.1
LIFE EXPECTANCY AT BIRTH	77.1	73.4 (85)	70.5

MARRIAGES

MARRIAGE RATE	5.1	5.8 (85)	7.2
AVERAGE AGE AT MARRIAGE M/F	27.5/25.1 (91)		
DIVORCE RATE	2.1	1.9 (85)	0.6

DEATHS

DEATH RATE	10.3	11.2 (85)	12

ECONOMICS AND LABOR

GDP PER CAPITA US$　　$19,500

LABOR FORCE M/F (thousands)　　2,236.0/1,517.1 (92)

AGRICULTURE	68.5/26.4
MINING	6.3/0.3
MANUFACTURING	576.1/175.6
UTILITIES	25.7/3.4
CONSTRUCTION	229.6/15.7
TRADE/FOOD/TOURISM	318.0/316.2
TRANSPORT/COMMUNICATIONS	211.3/45.8

	1995	1980	1965
FINANCE/INSURANCE/REAL ESTATE	196.8/144.8		
SOCIAL AND PERSONAL SERVICES	603.7/788.8		
UNEMPLOYMENT (official)	13.9% (94)		
UNION DENSITY	38.1%		

TRANSPORT

	1995	1980	1965
JOURNEYS (by transport mode)			
RAILROAD PASSENGER TRIPS			
(millions of miles/kilometers)	4,149/6,638 (94)		
AIR PASSENGER TRIPS (thousands)	4,193 (94)		
VEHICLES (thousands)			
PRIVATE CARS	4,281.1	3,315.00	1,340
COMMERCIAL	444.4	318.6	233.5

HEALTH AND HEALTH CARE

	1995	1980	1965
HEALTH CARE			
RATE OF PHYSICIANS	3.7	2.5	1.3 (60)
RATE OF HOSPITAL BEDS	7.6	9.4	8 (60)
ACCESS TO SANITATION	100%		
MEASLES IMMUNIZATION	70%		
HEALTH INDICATORS			
LOW-BIRTH-WEIGHT BABIES	6%		
SMOKING PREVALENCE M/F	31/19%		
TUBERCULOSIS INCIDENCE RATE	0.16		
AIDS/HIV CASES	2,072	1,631 (93)	
TOTAL DEATHS	105,933		

EDUCATION

	1995	1980	1965
SCHOOL AGE IN SCHOOL			
PRIMARY	103%	104%	109%
SECONDARY	144%	91%	75%
HIGHER	4.9%	26%	8.9%
FEMALES IN SCHOOL			
OF PRIMARY STUDENTS	49%	49%	49%
OF SECONDARY STUDENTS	n/a	49%	49%

	1995	1980	1965
COMMUNICATIONS			
RATE OF NEWSPAPERS	310	232	285
RATE OF RADIOS	771	731	329
RATE OF TELEVISIONS	453	387	168

Source: CIA, The World Factbook, 1997; ILO, World Labour Report, 1997; UN, Demographic Yearbook, 1997; UN, Statistical Yearbook, 1996; World Bank, World Development Indicators, 1998.

BELIZE

Belize is located on the Central American isthmus on the Caribbean Sea. Mexico borders the 8,865-square-mile (22,960-square-kilometer) country on the north, and Guatemala borders it on the south. In 1995, the country's population of 219,296 was growing at a relatively rapid 2.4 percent per year. Belize has a low density of 26 persons per square mile (10 persons per square kilometer). Once known as British Honduras, Belize gained independence from the United Kingdom in September 1981. The country's southwestern border with Guatemala is in dispute. Belize is an ethnically and linguistically divided country. The three leading ethnic minorities in the country are Mestizo (44 percent), Creole (30 percent), and Maya (11 percent). The leading languages spoken are English, Spanish, and indigenous Mayan. Average life expectancy at birth has increased dramatically over the last four decades of the twentieth century, from 47 years in 1960 to 68.5 years in 1995. The national economy is highly dependent on the production of sugar for sale in North American and other export markets. The per capita gross domestic product in 1995 was $2,750.

	1995	**1980**	**1965**
GEOGRAPHY			
AREA (square miles/kilometers)	8,865/22,960		
LAND AREA (square miles/kilometers)	8,803/22,800		
COASTLINE (miles/kilometers)	241/386		
CITIES			
CAPITAL	Belmopan 44,087 (91)		
POPULATION			
TOTAL	219,296	142,847	90,505 (60)
DENSITY (per square mile/kilometer)	26/10	18/7	n/a
ANNUAL GROWTH	2.4%	2.7%	n/a
AGE COHORTS			
0–14	43%	n/a	45%
15–64	53%	n/a	51%
65 AND OVER	4%	n/a	4%
MALE	51%		
FEMALE	49%		
URBAN	47%		
RURAL	53%		
NET MIGRATION RATE	−2.9	n/a	3.7

	1995	1980	1965

IDENTITY

ETHNICITY

MESTIZO	44%
CREOLE	30%
MAYA	11%

LANGUAGE

ENGLISH	n/a
SPANISH	n/a
MAYA	n/a

RELIGION

ROMAN CATHOLIC	62%
ANGLICAN	12%
METHODIST	6%

VITAL STATISTICS

BIRTHS

	1995	1980	1965
BIRTH RATE	32.8	40.1 (85)	n/a
INFANT MORTALITY RATE	32.5	18.9 (85)	n/a
LIFE EXPECTANCY AT BIRTH	68.5	n/a	47 (60)

MARRIAGES

	1995	1980	1965
MARRIAGE RATE	6.5	5.2 (85)	n/a
DIVORCE RATE	0.6	0.4 (85)	n/a

DEATHS

	1995	1980	1965
DEATH RATE	n/a	5.7 (85	4 (60)

HOUSEHOLDS

	1995	1980	1965
NUMBER	39,929 (91)	n/a	19,187 (60)
AVERAGE SIZE	4.8(91)	n/a	4.7 (61)

TYPE OF HOUSEHOLD

SINGLE	35.6%
MARRIED	54.3%
WIDOWED	6.4%
DIVORCED/SEPARATED	3.7%

	1995	1980	1965

ECONOMICS AND LABOR

GDP PER CAPITA US$ $2,750

LABOR FORCE M/F (thousands)	43.0/19.0 (94)		
AGRICULTURE	13.3/0.8		
MINING	0.3/0.0		
MANUFACTURING	5.0/1.7		
UTILITIES	1.0/0.2		
CONSTRUCTION	3.5/0.1		
TRADE/FOOD/TOURISM	1.3/1.9		
TRANSPORT/COMMUNICATIONS	3.2/0.5		
FINANCE/INSURANCE/REAL ESTATE	0.5/0.7		
SOCIAL AND PERSONAL SERVICES	1.4/1.4		

UNEMPLOYMENT (official) 11.1% (94)

TRANSPORT

VEHICLES

	1995	1980	1965
PRIVATE CARS	n/a	1,400	1,300
COMMERCIAL	n/a	1,200	700

HEALTH AND HEALTH CARE

HEALTH CARE

	1995	1980	1965
RATE OF PHYSICIANS	n/a	n/a	0.3 (60)
RATE OF HOSPITAL BEDS	n/a	n/a	4.7 (60)

HEALTH INDICATORS

	1995	1980	1965
AIDS/HIV CASE	138	92 (93)	
TOTAL DEATHS	863 (94)		

EDUCATION

SCHOOL AGE IN SCHOOL

	1995	1980	1965
PRIMARY	n/a	n/a	114%
SECONDARY	n/a	n/a	26%
HIGHER	n/a	n/a	0.6%

FEMALES IN SCHOOL

	1995	1980	1965
PRIMARY	n/a	n/a	111%
SECONDARY	n/a	n/a	27%

	1995	1980	1965
ADULT ILLITERACY M/F	n/a	n/a	8.8/8.8 (70)

COMMUNICATIONS

	1995	1980	1965
RATE OF NEWSPAPERS	578	21	58
RATE OF RADIOS	167	486	72

Source: CIA, The World Factbook, 1997; ILO, World Labour Report, 1997; UN, Demographic Yearbook, 1997; UN, Statistical Yearbook, 1996; World Bank, World Development Indicators, 1998.

BENIN

Benin, formerly known as Dahomey, is located in western Africa on the Bight of Benin, an inlet of the North Atlantic Ocean. Nigeria borders the narrow 48,483-square-mile (112,620-square-kilometer) country on the east. Niger and Burkina Faso lie to the north, and Togo to the west. Benin received independence from France in December 1960. Most residents depend on subsistence agriculture for survival. Cotton, the leading crop, is sold to regional West African markets. The national economy is in heavy debt to external lenders, including the International Monetary Fund and Western banks. In 1995, the nation's per cap-

ita gross domestic product was $1,380. Benin's population growth has continued to accelerate in the 1990s from an annual rate of 2.8 percent in 1979 to 3.3 percent in 1995. In 1995, the national population exceeded 5.7 million. French is Benin's official language. The Fon, Adja, and Yoruba are Benin's leading ethnic minorities. Most of the national population practices indigenous African religions (70 percent), followed by Christianity (15 percent) and Muslim (15 percent). Average life expectancy at birth increased from 44 years in 1965 to 52.7 years in 1995.

	1995	**1980**	**1965**
GEOGRAPHY			
AREA (square miles/kilometers)	43,483/112,620		
LAND AREA (square miles/kilometers)	42,710/110,620		
COASTLINE (miles/kilometers)	76/121		
CITIES			
CAPITAL	Porto-Novo	179,138	
MAJOR CITIES	Cotonou	536,827 (90)	
	Djougou	134,099 (90)	
	Parakou	103,577 (90)	
POPULATION			
TOTAL	5,709,529	3,331,210 (79)	2,082,511 (61)
DENSITY (per square mile/kilometer)	49	35	n/a
ANNUAL GROWTH	3.3%	2.8%	n/a
AGE COHORTS			
0–14	48%	n/a	46%
15–64	50%	n/a	50%
65 AND OVER	2%	n/a	4%
MALE	49%		
FEMALE	51%		

	1995	1980	1965
URBAN	31%	39.4	n/a
RURAL	69%	60.60%	n/a
NET MIGRATION RATE	0		

IDENTITY

ETHNICITY
FON	n/a
ADJA	n/a
YORUBA	n/a

LANGUAGE
FRENCH (official)	n/a
FON	n/a
YORUBA	n/a

RELIGION
ANIMIST	70%
CHRISTIAN	15%
MUSLIM	15%

VITAL STATISTICS

BIRTHS
	1995	1980	1965
BIRTH RATE	46.8	50.7	n/a
INFANT MORTALITY RATE	85.8	109.6	n/a
LIFE EXPECTANCY AT BIRTH	52.7	44	n/a

DEATHS
	1995	1980	1965
DEATH RATE	13.5	21.2	n/a

HOUSEHOLDS

NUMBER	832,526 (92)
AVERAGE SIZE	5.9 (92)

TYPE OF HOUSEHOLD
SINGLE	9.7%
MARRIED	75.4%
WIDOWED	9.2%
DIVORCED/SEPARATED	4.3%
FEMALE HEADED	21.4%

	1995	1980	1965

ECONOMICS AND LABOR

GDP PER CAPITA US$ | $1,380

LABOR FORCE M/F
	1995	1980	1965
AGRICULTURE	62/65%		
INDUSTRY	12.0/4.0%		
SERVICES	27/30%		

TRANSPORT

JOURNEYS (by transport mode)
RAILROAD PASSENGER TRIPS

	1995	1980	1965
(millions of miles/kilometers)	n/a	75/120 (87)	n/a
AIR PASSENGER TRIPS (thousands)	69 (94)		

VEHICLES
	1995	1980	1965
PRIVATE CARS	22,000	n/a	5,700
COMMERCIAL	12,300	n/a	3,900

HEALTH AND HEALTH CARE

HEALTH CARE
	1995	1980	1965
RATE OF PHYSICIANS	0.1	0.1	n/a
RATE OF HOSPITAL BEDS	0.2	1.5	1.3 (60)
ACCESS TO SAFE WATER	50%		
ACCESS TO SANITATION	20%		
MEASLES IMMUNIZATION	81%		

HEALTH INDICATORS
	1995	1980	1965
PREGNANT WOMEN WITH ANEMIA	41%		
LOW-BIRTH-WEIGHT BABIES	10%		
CHILD MALNUTRITION	24%		
TUBERCULOSIS INCIDENCE RATE	1.35%		
AIDS/HIV CASES	1,280	742 (93)	

EDUCATION

SCHOOL AGE IN SCHOOL
	1995	1980	1965
PRIMARY	72%	67%	35%
SECONDARY	16%	16%	3%
HIGHER	3%	1%	0.1%

	1995	1980	1965
FEMALES IN SCHOOL			
PRIMARY	n/a	32%	21%
SECONDARY	n/a	26%	2%
ADULT ILLITERACY M/F	51/74%	74.8/90.5%	

COMMUNICATIONS

	1995	1980	1965
RATE OF NEWSPAPERS	2	0.3	1
RATE OF RADIOS	91	66	17
RATE OF TELEVISIONS	6	1	1 (70)

Source: CIA, The World Factbook, 1997; ILO, World Labour Report, 1997; UN, Demographic Yearbook, 1997; UN, Statistical Yearbook, 1996; World Bank, World Development Indicators, 1998.

BHUTAN

Bhutan is a landlocked country located in the Great Himalaya mountain range of southern Asia. China borders the 18,147-square-mile (47,000-square-kilometer) country on the north, and India borders it on the south, east, and west. The nation's annual rate of population growth increased from 1.8 percent in 1969 to 2.3 percent in 1995, with a population increase from about 1.3 million to over 1.8 million. The country received independence from India in August 1949 and became the Kingdom of Bhutan. Since 1907 the country has been ruled by a monarchy. Bhutan is one of the poorest countries in the world, with an economy that is highly dependent on India for technological assistance and skilled labor. In 1995,

the country's per capita gross domestic product was only $730 per year. Subsistence farming and agriculture are the primary economic activity of the country's population. The country's leading ethnic groups are Bhote (50 percent) and Nepalese (35 percent), and the leading religions are Buddhism (75 percent) and Hinduism (25 percent). In 1965, only 7 percent of the school-aged population was enrolled in primary schools, and a mere 0.3 percent was enrolled in institutions of higher education. Between 1980 and 1995, Bhutan's infant mortality rate fell from 139 to 124 per 1,000 live births, as life expectancy at birth increased from 45.8 years to 51.5 years.

	1995	**1980**	**1965**
GEOGRAPHY			
AREA (square miles/kilometers)	18,147/47,000		
LAND AREA (square miles/kilometers)	18,147/47,000		
COASTLINE	Landlocked		
CITIES			
CAPITAL	Thimphu	n/a	8,922 (77)	n/a
POPULATION			
TOTAL	1,822,625	n/a	1,304,774 (69)
DENSITY (per square mile/kilometer)	91/35	78/30	41/16
ANNUAL GROWTH	2.3%	2%	1.8%
AGE COHORTS			
0–14	40%		
15–64	56%		
65 AND OVER	4%		
URBAN	6%		
RURAL	94%		
NET MIGRATION RATE	0		

	1995	1980	1965
## IDENTITY			
ETHNICITY			
BHOTE	50%		
NEPALESE	35%		
TRIBAL	15%		
LANGUAGE			
DZONGKHA (official)	n/a		
TIBETAN	n/a		
NEPALESE	n/a		
RELIGION			
BUDDHIST	75%		
HINDU	25%		
## VITAL STATISTICS			
BIRTHS			
BIRTH RATE	38.5	38.4	n/a
INFANT MORTALITY RATE	124	139	n/a
LIFE EXPECTANCY AT BIRTH	51.5	45.8	n/a
DEATH			
DEATH RATE	15.3	18.1	n/a
## ECONOMICS AND LABOR			
GDP PER CAPITA US$	$730		
## TRANSPORT			
JOURNEYS (by transport mode)			
RAILROAD PASSENGER TRIPS	5.6/9 (94)		
(millions of miles/kilometers)			

	1995	1980	1965

EDUCATION

SCHOOL AGE IN SCHOOL

	1995	1980	1965
PRIMARY	n/a	15%	7%
SECONDARY	n/a	n/a	4%
HIGHER	n/a	0.3%	n/a

FEMALES IN SCHOOL

	1995	1980	1965
PRIMARY	n/a	n/a	3%
SECONDARY	n/a	n/a	2%
HIGHER	n/a	0.1%	n/a

COMMUNICATIONS

	1995	1980	1965
RATE OF NEWSPAPERS	17	n/a	n/a
RATE OF RADIOS	n/a	5	n/a

Source: CIA, *The World Factbook, 1997;* ILO, *World Labour Report, 1997;* UN, *Demographic Yearbook, 1997;* UN, *Statistical Yearbook, 1996;* World Bank, *World Development Indicators, 1998.*

BOLIVIA

Bolivia is a landlocked country located in central South America. Brazil borders the 424,162-square-mile (1,098,580-square-kilometer) country on the north and east. Peru borders it on the north and west, Chile on the southwest, Argentina on the south, and Paraguay on the southeast. Although the country's population increased from 4,613,486 million in 1950 to 7,165,257 in 1995, the annual rate of population growth declined from 2.8 percent to 1.8 percent. Since receiving independence from Spain in August 1825, Bolivia has endured frequent internal political turmoil and unrest. In addition, Bolivia has sought to regain a land corridor to the Pacific Ocean, lost to Chile in 1884.

In recent years the country has made the transition from military rule to nominal democracy. The country's leading ethnic minorities are Quechua (30 percent), Aymara (25 percent), and Mestizo (25 percent). About 95 percent of Bolivia's population are Roman Catholic. In 1995, just over 60 percent of the country's population lived in urban areas. Although infant mortality has declined substantially, from 124 per 1,000 live births in 1975 to 75.1 per 1,000 live births in 1995, infant mortality continues to be higher than in other countries in the region. Over the same period, life expectancy increased from 50.8 years to 59.8 years.

		1995	1980	1965
GEOGRAPHY				
AREA (square miles/kilometers)		424,162/1,098,580		
LAND AREA (square miles/kilometers)		418,683/1,084,390		
COASTLINE (miles/kilometers)		Landlocked		
CITIES				
CAPITAL	La Paz	784,976 (93)		
MAJOR CITIES	Santa Cruz	767,260		
	Cochabamba	448,756		
	El Alto	446,189		
	Oruro	201,831		
POPULATION				
TOTAL		7,165,257	4,613,486 (76)	2,704,165 (50)
DENSITY (per square mile/kilometer)		18/7	16/6	8.0/3.0
ANNUAL GROWTH		1.8%	2.8%	1.4%
AGE COHORTS				
0–14		39%		
15–64		56%		
65 AND OVER		5%		

	1995	**1980**	**1965**
MALE	49%		
FEMALE	51%		
URBAN	61%	44.4	n/a
RURAL	39%	55.60%	n/a
MIGRATION	−3.4		

IDENTITY

ETHNICITY
QUECHUA	30%		
AYMARA	25%		
MESTIZO	25%		

LANGUAGE
SPANISH	n/a		
QUECHUA	n/a		
AYMARA	n/a		

RELIGION
ROMAN CATHOLIC	95%		
PROTESTANT	5%		

VITAL STATISTICS

BIRTHS
BIRTH RATE	32.4	46.6 (75)	45
INFANT MORTALITY RATE	75.1	124 (75)	86
LIFE EXPECTANCY AT BIRTH	59.8	50.8 (75)	49.7

MARRIAGES
MARRIAGE RATE	5	4.8 (75)	5.5
AVERAGE AGE AT MARRIAGE M/F	25.1/22.7 (92)		

DEATHS
DEATH RATE	10.8	18 (75)	22

HOUSEHOLDS

NUMBER	1,444,817 (92)	
AVERAGE SIZE	4.3 (92)	

	1995	1980	1965
TYPE OF HOUSEHOLD			
SINGLE	10.3%		
MARRIED	74.6%		
WIDOWED	10.8%		
DIVORCED/SEPARATE	4%		
FEMALE HEADED	24.5%		

ECONOMICS AND LABOR

	1995	1980	1965
GDP PER CAPITA US$	$2,530		
LABOR FORCE M/F (thousands)	616.3/432 (92)		
AGRICULTURE	16.7/5.4		
MINING	18.8/0.9		
MANUFACTURING	136.5/67.0		
UTILITIES	8.2/1.1		
CONSTRUCTION	95.9/1.3		
TRADE/FOOD/TOURISM	121.8/183.4		
TRANSPORT/COMMUNICATIONS	70.7/4.8		
FINANCE/INSURANCE/REAL ESTATE	26.5/13.9		
SOCIAL AND PERSONAL SERVICES	120.4/154.3		
UNEMPLOYMENT (official)	5.4% (92)		
UNION DENSITY	16.40%		

TRANSPORT

	1995	1980	1965
JOURNEYS (by transport mode)			
RAILROAD PASSENGER TRIPS			
(millions of miles/kilometers)	276.0 (94)		
AIR PASSENGER TRIPS (thousands)	1,175.0 (94)		
VEHICLES			
PRIVATE CARS	261,000	50,200	14,500
COMMERCIAL	66,300	32,500	26,600

HEALTH AND HEALTH CARE

	1995	1980	1965
HEALTH CARE			
RATE OF PHYSICIANS	0.4	0.5	0.2 (60)
RATE OF HOSPITAL BEDS	1.4	n/a	1.6 (60)
ACCESS TO SAFE WATER	60%		
ACCESS TO SANITATION	44%		
MEASLES IMMUNIZATION	83%		

	1995	1980	1965
HEALTH INDICATORS			
PREGNANT WOMEN WITH ANEMIA	51%		
LOW-BIRTH-WEIGHT BABIES	10%		
CHILD MALNUTRITION	16%		
SMOKING PREVALENCE M/F	50/21%		
TUBERCULOSIS INCIDENCE RATE	3.35		
AIDS/HIV CASES	109	88 (93)	

EDUCATION

	1995	1980	1965
SCHOOL AGE IN SCHOOL			
PRIMARY	n/a	87%	76%
SECONDARY	n/a	37%	19%
HIGHER		16%	3.70%
	n/a		
FEMALES IN SCHOOL			
PRIMARY	n/a	47%	63%
SECONDARY	n/a	n/a	14%
ADULT ILLITERACY M/F	10.0/24%		

COMMUNICATIONS

	1995	1980	1965
RATE OF NEWSPAPERS	57	42	26
RATE OF RADIOS	669	523	194
RATE OF TELEVISIONS	113	56	0

Source: CIA, *The World Factbook, 1997;* ILO, *World Labour Report, 1997;* UN, *Demographic Yearbook, 1997;* UN, *Statistical Yearbook, 1996;* World Bank, *World Development Indicators, 1998.*

BOSNIA AND HERZEGOVINA

Bosnia and Herzegovina is located in southeastern Europe in a region that formed part of Yugoslavia before the early 1990s. Although the country declared independence in April 1992, both Yugoslavia (Serbia) and Croatia disputed the country's autonomy. Armed factions loyal to Yugoslavia, Croatia, and the Muslim-led government of Bosnia fought an ongoing regional war from 1992 to March 1994, when a regional settlement was achieved among the warring parties. The March 1994 accords, enforced by North Atlantic Treaty Organization (NATO) forces, created the government of Bosnia and Herzegovina made up of the Muslim/Croat Federation and the Republika Srpska, an autonomous region controlled by Bosnian Serbs. Croatia borders the 19,781-square-mile (51,233-square-kilometer) country on the north and west, and Serbia and Montenegro lie to the east and south. In 1995, the country's population was 2,656,240. In the same year, Bosnia and Herzegovina's population declined by 2.84 percent, primarily as a consequence of out-migration. Serbs (40 percent) are the ethnic majority, followed by Muslims (38 percent) and Croats (22 percent). Despite the ethnic differences, nearly all the population speaks Serbo-Croatian.

1995[1]

GEOGRAPHY

AREA (square miles/kilometers)	19,781/51,233	
LAND AREA (square miles/kilometers)	19,781/51,233	
COASTLINE (miles/kilometers)	13/20	

CITIES		
CAPITAL	Sarajevo	529,021 (91)
MAJOR CITIES	Banja Luka	195,994 (91)
	Zenica	145,837 (91)
	Tuzla	131,866 (91)
	Mostar	127,034 (91)

POPULATION

TOTAL	2,656,240
DENSITY (per square mile/kilometer)	228/88
ANNUAL GROWTH	−2.8%

AGE COHORTS	
0–14	20%
15–64	68%
65 AND OVER	12%

	1995[1]
URBAN	49%
RURAL	51%
NET MIGRATION RATE	−18.9

IDENTITY

ETHNICITY	
SERB	40%
MUSLIM	38%
CROATIAN	22%
LANGUAGE	
SERBO-CROATIAN	99%
RELIGION	
MUSLIM	40%
EASTERN ORTHODOX	31%
ROMAN CATHOLIC	15%

VITAL STATISTICS

BIRTHS	
BIRTH RATE	6.3
INFANT MORTALITY RATE	15.3
LIFE EXPECTANCY AT BIRTH	56.1
DEATHS	
DEATH RATE	15.9

ECONOMICS AND LABOR

GDP PER CAPITA US$	$300
LABOR FORCE M/F	
AGRICULTURE	9/16%
INDUSTRY	54/37%
SERVICES	37/48%

1995[1]

HEALTH AND HEALTH CARE

HEALTH CARE

RATE OF PHYSICIANS   0.6
RATE OF HOSPITAL BEDS   2
MEASLES IMMUNIZATION   57%

HEALTH INDICATORS

TUBERCULOSIS INCIDENCE RATE   0.8
AIDS/HIV CASES   6

COMMUNICATIONS

RATE OF NEWSPAPERS   131

FOOTNOTE
1. Part of Yugoslavia in 1965 and 1980.

Source: CIA, *The World Factbook, 1997;* ILO, *World Labour Report, 1997;* UN, *Demographic Yearbook, 1997;* UN, *Statistical Yearbook, 1996;* World Bank, *World Development Indicators, 1998.*

BOTSWANA

Botswana is a landlocked country located in southern Africa. South Africa borders the 231,803-square-mile (600,370-square-kilometer) country on the south and east. Zimbabwe borders it on the northeast, and Namibia lies to the north and west. The country received independence in September 1966 from the United Kingdom. Subsistence agriculture and animal husbandry are the primary economic activities of the majority of Botswana's population. The country has a small but growing diamond-mining industry. The leading exports are diamonds, copper, nickel, and livestock. Botswana is relatively more affluent than other African countries south of the Sahara, with a 1995 per capita gross domestic product of $3,200. However, a substantial share of the national population remains mired in poverty. In 1986, 61 percent of the population lived on the equivalent of less than $2 a day, and 33 percent subsisted on $1 a day. Botswana has a relatively small population. Still, the population grew rapidly from 543,105 in 1965 to 1,477,630 in 1981. Over the same period, Botswana's annual population growth rate declined from 3.1 percent to 1.6 percent. Life expectancy at birth is 56 years. Botswana's infant mortality rate has declined steadily to 43 infant deaths per 1,000 live births in 1991 from 76 in 1980. Although the urban population is growing at a rapid pace, Botswana is still primarily a rural country, with 28 percent of the population residing in urban areas.

	1995	**1980**	**1965**
GEOGRAPHY			
AREA (square miles/kilometers)	231,803/600,370		
LAND AREA (square miles/kilometers)	226,012/585,370		
COASTLINE (miles/kilometers)	Landlocked		
CITIES			
CAPITAL	Gaborone	133,468 (91)	
POPULATION			
TOTAL	1,477,630 (81)	941,027	543,105
DENSITY (per square mile/kilometer)	8.0/3.0	5.0/2.0	3.0/1.0
ANNUAL GROWTH	1.6%	n/a	3.1%
AGE COHORTS			
0–14	42%	n/a	44%
15–64	54%	n/a	52%
65 AND OVER	4%	n/a	4%
MALE	48%		
FEMALE	52%		

	1995	1980	1965
URBAN	28%	15.9%	n/a
RURAL	72%	84.1%	n/a
NET MIGRATION RATE	0		

IDENTITY

ETHNICITY

BOTSWANA	95%		
OTHER AFRICAN	4%		
WHITE	1%		

LANGUAGE

ENGLISH (official)	n/a		
SETSWANA	n/a		

RELIGION

ANIMIST	50%		
CHRISTIAN	50%		

VITAL STATISTICS

BIRTHS

BIRTH RATE	6,600.00%	49.9	
INFANT MORTALITY RATE	43	76	
LIFE EXPECTANCY AT BIRTH	56	55	

MARRIAGES

MARRIAGE RATE	n/a	1.6 (87)	n/a
AVERAGE AGE AT MARRIAGE M/F	30.9/26.9		

DEATH

DEATH RATE	6.6	12.6	n/a

HOUSEHOLDS

NUMBER	276,209 (91)	
AVERAGE SIZE	4.8 (91)	
FEMALE HEADED	47.1%	

	1995	1980	1965

ECONOMICS AND LABOR

GDP PER CAPITA US$	$3,200		
LABOR FORCE M/F (thousands)	145.6/81.9 (92)		
AGRICULTURE	4.2/1.8		
MINING	7.3/0.4		
MANUFACTURING	16.1/9.5		
UTILITIES	2.3/0.3		
CONSTRUCTION	28.9/4.8		
TRADE/FOOD/TOURISM	18.4/22.5		
TRANSPORT/COMMUNICATIONS	7.5/2.7		
FINANCE/INSURANCE/REAL ESTATE	11.4/6.2		
SOCIAL AND PERSONAL SERVICES	49.4/33.8		
UNION DENSITY	11.50%		
POVERTY			
UNDER $1/DAY	n/a	33% (86)	n/a
UNDER $2/DAY	n/a	61% (86)	n/a

TRANSPORT

JOURNEYS (by transport mode)			
AIR PASSENGER TRIPS (thousands)	101 (94)		
VEHICLES			
PRIVATE CARS	81,900 (94)	16,400	n/a
COMMERCIAL	27,600 (94)	7,800	n/a

HEALTH AND HEALTH CARE

HEALTH CARE			
ACCESS TO SAFE WATER	70%		
ACCESS TO SANITATION	55%		
MEASLES IMMUNIZATION	68%		
RATE OF PHYSICIANS	0.2	0.1	n/a
RATE OF HOSPITAL BEDS	1.6	2.4	2 (60)
HEALTH INDICATORS			
LOW-BIRTH-WEIGHT BABIES	8%		
CHILD MALNUTRITION	27%		
SMOKING PREVALENCE M/F	21/0%		

	1995	1980	1965
TUBERCULOSIS INCIDENCE RATE	0.04		
AIDS/HIV CASES	3,451	1,948 (93)	

EDUCATION

SCHOOL AGE IN SCHOOL

	1995	1980	1965
PRIMARY	115%	91%	69%
SECONDARY	56%	19%	3%
HIGHER	4%	1%	0%

FEMALES IN SCHOOL

	1995	1980	1965
PRIMARY	50%	91%	76%
SECONDARY	53%	19%	n/a
HIGHER	2%	n/a	n/a

| **ADULT ILLITERACY M/F** | n/a | n/a | 63.1/56% (71) |

COMMUNICATIONS

	1995	1980	1965
RATE OF NEWSPAPERS	29	21	23
RATE OF RADIOS	119	83	9
RATE OF TELEVISIONS	17	0	0

Source: CIA, The World Factbook, 1997; ILO, World Labour Report, 1997; UN, Demographic Yearbook, 1997; UN, Statistical Yearbook, 1996; World Bank, World Development Indicators, 1998.

BRAZIL

Brazil is the largest and most populous country in South America. The 3,286,473-square-mile (8,511,965-square-kilometer) country is located in eastern South America. Brazil's boundaries extend north, south, and west, bordering all but two of South America's political units, including French Guyana, Suriname, Guyana, Venezuela, Columbia, Peru, Bolivia, Paraguay, Argentina, and Uruguay. Chile and Ecuador are the only two South American countries that do not have a land boundary with Brazil. The country, which received its independence in 1822, is a study in contrasts. Brazil is one of the most economically advanced nations of South America, with a large service and manufacturing sector. However, due to an inequitable distribution of income, Brazil has one of the most impoverished populations on the continent. In the late 1990s, the government of President Cardoso has reduced Brazil's hyperinflation and increased economic growth, increasing the spending power of the country's working and peasant classes. The government has imposed a strict monetary policy and has sold large segments of the country's public-sector enterprises to private firms. Still, much of the country's population continues to live in poverty. In 1995, 43.5 percent of Brazil's population subsisted on the equivalent of less than $2 a day. Population growth slowed in the 35 years between 1960 and 1995 from 3 percent to 1.16 percent, but the national population more than doubled, from nearly 71 million to 162.7 million. Brazil's poulation is white (55 percent), mulatto (38 percent), and black (6 percent).

Poverty Rate

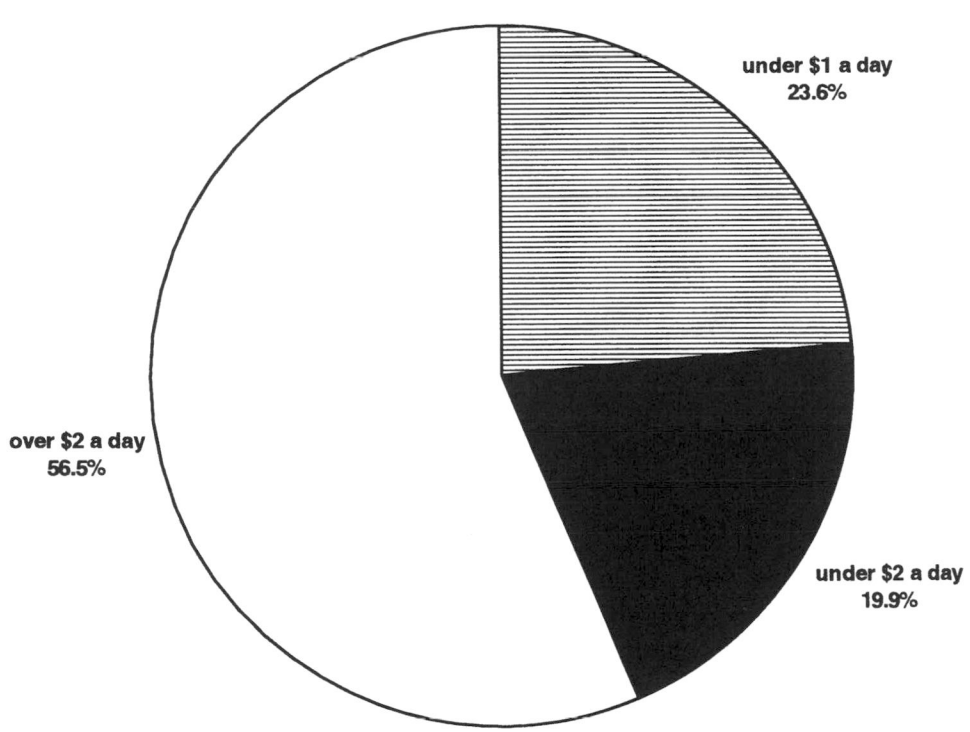

under $1 a day
23.6%

over $2 a day
56.5%

under $2 a day
19.9%

Despite its relatively high gross domestic product of $6,100, Brazil has one of the most unequal distributions of wealth in the world, a fact reflected in its high poverty rates.

Birth Rate per 1,000

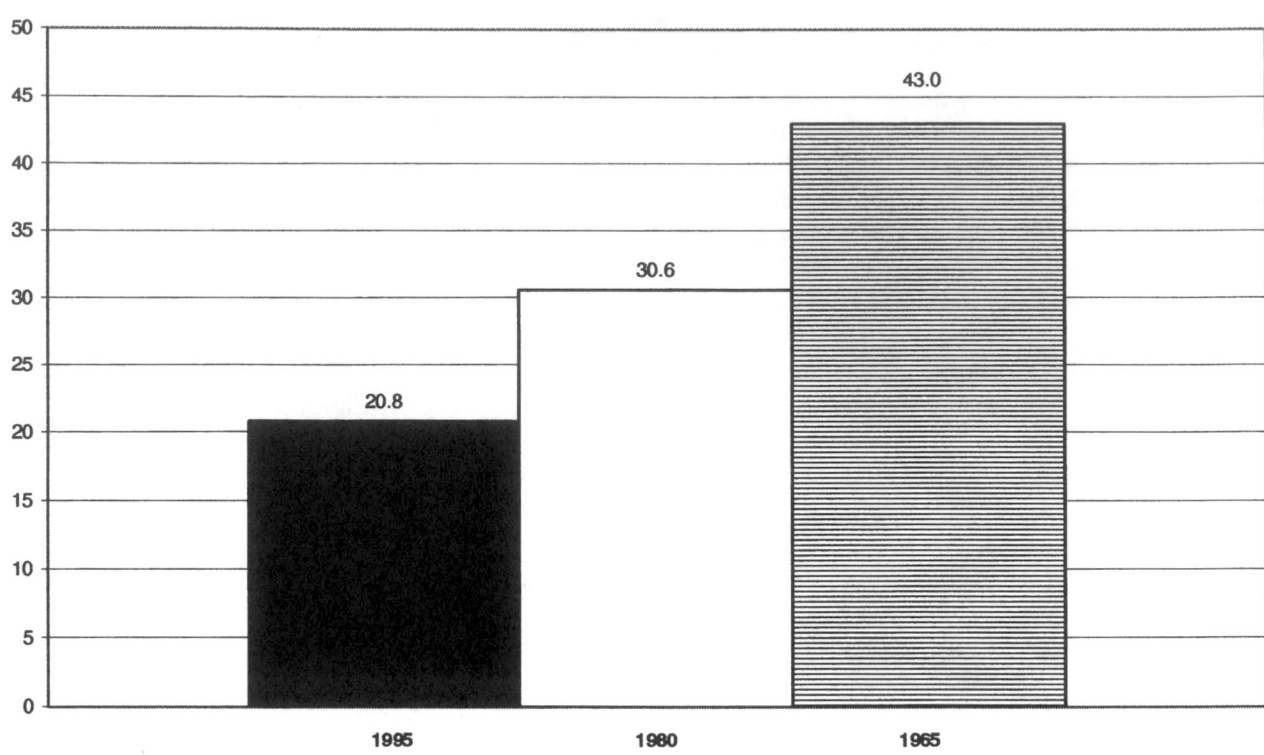

As in much of Latin America, rising educational levels have helped bring down birth rates dramatically over the past 30 years.

CHRONOLOGY

1964   Right-wing military coup ends civilian rule, leads to repressive regime.
1969   Army-approved constitution takes force.
1978   Military begins to prepare country for transfer to civilian rule.
1985   Return to civilian rule.
1990   Conservative Fernando Collor de Mello defeats leftist in national elections.
1992   Collor de Mello is impeached on charges of corruption.

	1995	**1980**	**1965**

GEOGRAPHY

AREA (square miles/kilometers)   3,286,473/8,511,965
LAND AREA (square miles/kilometers)   3,265,062/8,456,510
COASTLINE (miles/kilometers)   4,682/7,491

CITIES
CAPITAL   Brasília   1,601,964 (91)
MAJOR CITIES   São Paulo   9,842,059
                 Rio de Janeiro   5,547,033
                 Salvador   2,174,072
                 Belo Horizonte   2,060,804

POPULATION

	1995	**1980**	**1965**
TOTAL	162,661,214	118,674,604	70,967,185 (60)
DENSITY (per square mile/kilometer)	47/18	41/16	26/10
ANNUAL GROWTH	1.16%	2.30%	3%
AGE COHORTS			
0–14	31%	n/a	43%
15–64	65%	n/a	54%
65 AND OVER	4%	n/a	3%
MALE	49%		
FEMALE	51%		
URBAN	78%	67.60%	n/a
RURAL	22%	32.40%	n/a
NET MIGRATION RATE	0		

IDENTITY

ETHNICITY
WHITE   55%
MULATTO   38%
BLACK   6%

LANGUAGE
PORTUGUESE (official)   n/a
SPANISH   n/a

	1995	1980	1965
RELIGION			
ROMAN CATHOLIC	70%		
SYNCRETIC AFRICAN FAITHS	5%		

VITAL STATISTICS

	1995	1980	1965
BIRTHS			
BIRTH RATE	20.8	30.6	43
INFANT MORTALITY RATE	57.7	71	170
LIFE EXPECTANCY AT BIRTH	61.6	59.4	42.4
MARRIAGES			
MARRIAGE RATE	5	n/a	7.1
DIVORCE RATE	0.6		
DEATHS			
DEATH RATE	9.2	8.4	12

HOUSEHOLDS

	1995	1980	1965
NUMBER	34,734,715 (91)	n/a	13,475,472 (60)
AVERAGE SIZE	4.2 (91)	n/a	5.1 (60)
FEMALE HEADED	18.1%		

ECONOMICS AND LABOR

	1995
GDP PER CAPITA US$	$6,100
LABOR FORCE M/F (thousands)	40,018.0/22,083.0 90
AGRICULTURE	11,235.0/2,945.0
MINING	764.0/96.0
MANUFACTURING	6,774/2,637.0
UTILITIES	
CONSTRUCTION	3,726.0/97.0
TRADE/FOOD/TOURISM	5,060.0/2,916.0
TRANSPORT/COMMUNICATIONS	2,246.0/194.0
FINANCE/INSURANCE/REAL ESTATE	1,151.0/565.0
SOCIAL AND PERSONAL SERVICES	9,062.0/12,633.0
UNEMPLOYMENT (official)	3.7% (90)
UNION DENSITY	32.1%

	1995	1980	1965
POVERTY			
UNDER $1/DAY	23.6%		
UNDER $2/DAY	43.5%		

TRANSPORT

	1995	1980	1965
JOURNEYS (by transport mode)			
RAILROAD PASSENGER TRIPS			
(millions of miles/kilometers)	8,774/14,038 (94)		
AIR PASSENGER TRIPS (thousands)	17,885 (94)		
VEHICLES (thousands)			
PRIVATE CARS	8,098.4	8,004.6	1,140.8
COMMERCIAL	1,839	1,569.8	989.7

HEALTH AND HEALTH CARE

	1995	1980	1965
HEALTH CARE			
RATE OF PHYSICIANS	1.4	0.8	0.4 (60)
RATE OF HOSPITAL BEDS	3	n/a	3.2 (60)
ACCESS TO SAFE WATER	72%		
ACCESS TO SANITATION	41%		
MEASLES IMMUNIZATION	78%		
HEALTH INDICATORS			
PREGNANT WOMEN WITH ANEMIA	33%		
LOW-BIRTH-WEIGHT BABIES	11%		
CHILD MALNUTRITION	7%		
SMOKING PREVALENCE M/F	40/25%		
TUBERCULOSIS INCIDENCE RATE	0.8		
AIDS/HIV CASES	79,908	58,321 (93)	
TOTAL DEATHS	912,110 (94)		

EDUCATION

	1995	1980	1965
SCHOOL AGE IN SCHOOL			
PRIMARY	112%	98%	120%
SECONDARY	45%	33%	19%
HIGHER	11%	11%	1.9%
FEMALES IN SCHOOL			
OF PRIMARY STUDENTS	n/a	49%	49%
OF SECONDARY STUDENTS	n/a	51%	50%
ADULT ILLITERACY M/F	17/17%	23.7/27.2%	n/a

	1995	1980	1965
COMMUNICATIONS			
RATE OF NEWSPAPERS	55	45	32
RATE OF RADIOS	390	313	106
RATE OF TELEVISIONS	209	124	32

Source: CIA, The World Factbook, 1997; ILO, World Labour Report, 1997; UN, Demographic Yearbook, 1997; UN, Statistical Yearbook, 1996; World Bank, World Development Indicators, 1998.

BRUNEI DARUSSALAM

The sultanate of Brunei Darussalam is located on two noncontiguous territories in Southeastern Asia on the northeast coast of the island of Borneo. Brunei shares the island with Indonesia and Malaysia. The two 2,228-square-mile (5,770-square-kilometer) territories that compose Brunei border the South China Sea and Malaysia. Brunei's economy is almost totally dominated by the export of unrefined petroleum products. Due to the presence of abundant oil reserves and the relatively small population, Brunei has one of the wealthiest populations in the world, with a per capita gross domestic product of $15,800 in 1995.

As a result of the abundant oil reserves, the government provides the population with an advanced social safety net, including medical care, subsidized housing, and other social services. Brunei's population, which expanded at a rapid annual rate of about 4 percent from the early 1960s to the 1980s, more than tripled from 83,877 in 1960 to nearly 300,000 in 1995. From 1980 to 1995, net migration has declined from 7.8 per 1,000 to 5.2 per 1,000 residents. Malay is the official language, although English and Chinese are also spoken.

		1995	1980	1965
GEOGRAPHY				
AREA (square miles/kilometers)	2,228/5,770			
LAND AREA (square miles/kilometers)	2,035/5,270			
COASTLINE (miles/kilometers)	100/161			
CITIES				
CAPITAL	Bandar Seri Begawan	n/a	49,902 (81)	n/a
POPULATION				
TOTAL		299,939	192,832 (81)	83,877 (60)
DENSITY (per square mile/kilometer)		127/49	101/39	47/18
ANNUAL GROWTH		2.6%	3.9%	4%
AGE COHORTS				
0–14		33%	47%	n/a
15–64		62%	50%	n/a
65 AND OVER		5%	n/a	3%
MALE		53%		
FEMALE		47%		
URBAN		58%	59.4%	n/a
RURAL		42%	40.1%	n/a

	1995	1980	1965
NET MIGRATION RATE	5.2	n/a	7.8

IDENTITY

ETHNICITY

MALAY	64%		
CHINESE	20%		

LANGUAGE

MALAY (official)	n/a		
ENGLISH	n/a		
CHINESE	n/a		

RELIGION

MUSLIM	64%		
BUDDHIST	14%		
CHRISTIAN	8%		

VITAL STATISTICS

BIRTHS

BIRTH RATE	25.5	29.8 (85)	39.3
URBAN BIRTH RATE	39 (91)		
RURAL BIRTH RATE	4 (91)		
INFANT MORTALITY RATE	11.2	12 (85)	75.8
LIFE EXPECTANCY AT BIRTH	71.4	71.4	n/a

MARRIAGES

MARRIAGE RATE	7.1	4.6	8.5 (85)
AVERAGE AGE OF MARRIAGE M/F	27.3/25.1		
DIVORCE RATE	1.1	0.7 (85)	0.5

DEATHS

DEATH RATE	5.1	3.5 (85)	6.3

HOUSEHOLDS

NUMBER	n/a	n/a	8,091 (60)
AVERAGE SIZE	n/a	n/a	4.5 (60)

ECONOMICS AND LABOR

GDP PER CAPITA US$	$15,800

	1995	1980	1965

TRANSPORT

JOURNEYS (by transport mode)
AIR PASSENGER TRIPS (thousands) — 769.0 94

VEHICLES (thousands)

	1995	1980	1965
PRIVATE CARS	134,000	43,600	5,400
COMMERCIAL	14,500	7,000	1,600

HEALTH AND HEALTH CARE

HEALTH CARE

	1995	1980	1965
RATE OF PHYSICIANS	n/a	n/a	0.1 (60)
RATE OF HOSPITAL BEDS	n/a	n/a	4.8 (60)

HEALTH INDICATORS

	1995	1980	1965
AIDS/HIV CASES	6	2 (93)	
TOTAL DEATHS	1,018 (93)		

EDUCATION

SCHOOL AGE IN SCHOOL

	1995	1980	1965
PRIMARY	n/a	n/a	134%
SECONDARY	n/a	n/a	44%

FEMALES IN SCHOOL

	1995	1980	1965
PRIMARY	n/a	n/a	125%
SECONDARY	n/a	n/a	33%

	1995	1980	1965
ADULT ILLITERACY M/F	n/a	14.8/31.0%	n/a

COMMUNICATIONS

	1995	1980	1965
RATE OF NEWSPAPERS	74	n/a	n/a
RATE OF RADIOS	270	212	107
RATE OF TELEVISIONS	241	135	n/a

Source: CIA, *The World Factbook, 1997*; ILO, *World Labour Report, 1997*; UN, *Demographic Yearbook, 1997*; UN, *Statistical Yearbook, 1996*; World Bank, *World Development Indicators, 1998*.

BULGARIA

Bulgaria is located in Southeastern Europe on the western shores of the Black Sea. The 42,822-square-mile (110,910-square-kilometer) country is bordered by Romania on the north, Serbia and Macedonia on the west, and Greece and Turkey on the south. Bulgaria received its independence from the Ottoman Empire in September 1908. For much of the post–World War II era, Bulgaria was in the orbit of the Soviet Union. Following the breakup of the Soviet Union in 1991, Bulgaria adopted a new constitutional system that allowed for greater party competition. During the 1990s, Bulgaria has moved more slowly than its Eastern European counterparts in implementing structural adjustment policies and other economic market reforms. Overall, the country's population remained relatively static between 1965 and 1995. It grew from 8.2 million to 8.7 million between 1965 and 1975, but declined to 8.6 million over the next 20 years. The decline was caused in part by an excess of deaths over births due to a high abortion rate. The country has a life expectancy at birth of 71 years. The vast majority (85 percent) of the country's residents are Bulgarians, but Turks (9 percent) and Gypsies (3 percent) represent large ethnic minorities.

	1995	1980	1965
GEOGRAPHY			
AREA (square miles/kilometers)	42,822/110,910		
LAND AREA (square miles/kilometers)	42,683/110,550		
COASTLINE (miles/kilometers)	221/354		
CITIES			
CAPITAL	Sofia	1,113,674 (93)	
MAJOR CITIES	Plovdiv	345,205	
	Varna	307,200	
	Bourgas	198.439	
	Ruse	170,209	
POPULATION			
TOTAL	8,612,757	8,729,666 (75)	8,226,564
DENSITY (per square mile/kilometer)	197/76	210/81	192/74
ANNUAL GROWTH	0.5%	0.2%	0.8%
AGE COHORTS			
0–14	17%	n/a	24%
15–64	68%	n/a	67%
65 AND OVER	15%	n/a	9%
URBAN	71%	62.1	n/a
RURAL	29%	27.9%	n/a

	1995	**1980**	**1965**
NET MIGRATION RATE	9.8	n/a	0

IDENTITY

ETHNICITY

BULGARIAN	85%		
TURKISH	9%		
ROMANISM (Gypsy)	3%		

LANGUAGE

BULGARIAN	n/a		
TURKISH	n/a		

RELIGION

BULGARIAN ORTHODOX	85%		
MUSLIM	13%		
JEWISH	1%		

VITAL STATISTICS

BIRTHS

BIRTH RATE	8.3	13.2 (85)	14.9
URBAN BIRTH RATE	10.2 (93)		
RURAL BIRTH RATE	9.5 (93)		
INFANT MORTALITY RATE	15.8	15.8 (85)	32.2
ABORTION RATE	1,278.80		
LIFE EXPECTANCY AT BIRTH	71	70.9 (85)	69.1

MARRIAGES

MARRIAGE RATE	5	7.2 (85)	8.2
AVERAGE AGE AT MARRIAGE M/F	n/a	24.9/21.1	n/a
DIVORCE RATE	1.1	1.7 (85)	1

DEATHS

DEATH RATE	13.6	12	8.3

HOUSEHOLDS

NUMBER

NUMBER	n/a	3,020,335 (85)	1,964,551 (56)
AVERAGE SIZE	n/a	2.9 (85)	3.7 (56)

TYPE OF HOUSEHOLD

SINGLE	n/a	6.7%	n/a
MARRIED	n/a	74.1%	n/a
WIDOWED	n/a	13.4%	n/a

	1995	1980	1965
DIVORCED/SEPARATED	n/a	5.8%	n/a
FEMALE HEADED	n/a	17.6%	n/a

ECONOMICS AND LABOR

GDP PER CAPITA US$ $4,920

LABOR FORCE (thousands)	3,157.9 (94)
AGRICULTURE	698.1
MANUFACTURING	934.9
CONSTRUCTION	177.8
TRADE/FOOD/TOURISM	389.2
TRANSPORT/COMMUNICATIONS	230.8
FINANCE/INSURANCE/REAL ESTATE	68
SOCIAL AND PERSONAL SERVICES	659.1

UNEMPLOYMENT (official)	12.4% (94)
UNION DENSITY	51.4%

POVERTY
UNDER $1/DAY	2.6% (92)
UNDER $2/DAY	23.5% (92)

TRANSPORT

JOURNEYS (by transport mode)
RAILROAD PASSENGER TRIPS
(millions of miles/kilometers)	3,162/5,059 (94)
AIR PASSENGER TRIPS (thousands)	789 (94)

VEHICLES (thousands)
PRIVATE CARS	1,587.9 94
COMMERCIAL	255.4

HEALTH AND HEALTH CARE

HEALTH CARE
	1995	1980	1965
RATE OF PHYSICIANS	3.3	2.5	1.4 (60)
RATE OF HOSPITAL BEDS	10.2	11.1	6.2 (60)
ACCESS TO SAFE WATER	n/a	96	n/a
ACCESS TO SANITATION	99%		
MEASLES IMMUNIZATION	93%		

	1995	1980	1965
HEALTH INDICATORS			
LOW-BIRTH-WEIGHT BABIES	6%		
SMOKING PREVALENCE M/F	49/17%		
TUBERCULOSIS INCIDENCE RATE	0.4		
AIDS/HIV CASES	35	24 (93)	
TOTAL DEATHS	112,632		

EDUCATION

	1995	1980	1965
SCHOOL AGE IN SCHOOL			
PRIMARY	94%	98%	105%
SECONDARY	78%	84%	90%
HIGHER	39.0%	16%	12.2%
FEMALES IN SCHOOL			
OF PRIMARY STUDENTS	48%	49%	49%
OF SECONDARY STUDENTS	45%	44%	48%
HIGHER	n/a	18%	14.8 (70)
ADULT ILLITERACY M/F	n/a	n/a	4.8/14.7%

COMMUNICATIONS

	1995	1980	1965
RATE OF NEWSPAPERS	164	253	172
RATE OF RADIOS	450	395	250
RATE OF TELEVISIONS	260	243	23

Source: CIA, The World Factbook, 1997; ILO, World Labour Report, 1997; UN, Demographic Yearbook, 1997; UN, Statistical Yearbook, 1996; World Bank, World Development Indicators, 1998.

BURKINA FASO

Burkina Faso is a vast, 105,869-square-mile (274,200-square-kilometer) landlocked country in West Africa. It is north of Côte d'Ivoire, Ghana, Togo, and Benin; west of Niger; and south and east of Mali. Formerly known as Upper Volta, Burkina Faso gained independence from France in August 1960. The country's 1995 population of 10.6 million is continuing to grow at a high annual rate of 2.5 percent. Burkina Faso is one of the poorest countries in the world, with an estimated 1995 per capita gross domestic product of only $700. Nearly three-quarters of Burkina Faso's population resides in rural areas. Most of the population is engaged in subsistence farming and agriculture. The country has a very limited and unproductive industrial base with few exports. In 1996, the country's leading exports were cotton, gold, and animal products. The population remains mired in poverty. Life expectancy at birth increased from 31.6 years in 1980 to 43.2 years in 1995, but remains one of the lowest in the world. In 1995, the country had a rate of 129.9 infant deaths per 1,000 live births. The leading causes of illness and premature death in Burkina Faso are communicable diseases, due in part to the lack of access to clean water and sanitation facilities. The three major religions in Burkina Faso are Muslim (50 percent), Animism (40 percent), and Roman Catholicism (10 percent).

	1995	1980	1965
GEOGRAPHY			
AREA (square miles/kilometers)	105,869/274,200		
LAND AREA (square miles/kilometers)	105,714/273,800		
COASTLINE	Landlocked		
CITIES			
CAPITAL	Ouagadougou	634,479 (91)	
MAJOR CITY	Bobo Dioulasso	268,926	
POPULATION			
TOTAL	10,623,323	7,919,895 (85)	4,300,000
DENSITY (per square mile/kilometer)	96/37	62/24	n/a
ANNUAL GROWTH	2.5%		
AGE COHORTS			
0–14	48%	n/a	42%
15–64	49%	n/a	55%
65 AND OVER	3%	n/a	3%
MALE	48%		
FEMALE	52%		

	1995	1980	1965
URBAN	27%		
RURAL	73%		
NET MIGRATION RATE	−1.7		

IDENTITY

ETHNICITY
MOSSI	n/a		
GURUNSI	n/a		
SENUFO	n/a		

LANGUAGE
FRENCH (official)	n/a		
SUDANIC LANGUAGES	n/a		

RELIGION
MUSLIM	50%		
ANIMIST	40%		
ROMAN CATHOLIC	10%		

VITAL STATISTICS

BIRTHS
BIRTH RATE	47	47.8	n/a
INFANT MORTALITY RATE	129.9	182	n/a
LIFE EXPECTANCY AT BIRTH	43.2	31.6	n/a

MARRIAGES
MARRIAGE RATE			
AVERAGE AGE AT MARRIAGE M/F	27.6/19		

DEATHS
DEATH RATE	20	20.1	n/a

ECONOMICS AND LABOR

GDP PER CAPITA US$	$700		

TRANSPORT

JOURNEYS (by transport mode)
AIR PASSENGER TRIPS (thousands)	130 (94)		

	1995	1980	1965
VEHICLES			
PRIVATE CARS	32,000	14,700	4,200
COMMERCIAL	24,000	15,200	4,800

HEALTH AND HEALTH CARE

	1995	1980	1965
HEALTH CARE			
ACCESS TO SAFE WATER	78%		
ACCESS TO SANITATION	18%		
MEASLES IMMUNIZATION	55%		
RATE OF HOSPITAL BEDS	0.3	n/a	0.5 (60)
HEALTH INDICATORS			
PREGNANT WOMEN WITH ANEMIA	24%		
LOW-BIRTH-WEIGHT BABIES	21%		
CHILD MALNUTRITION	33%		
TUBERCULOSIS INCIDENCE RATE	2.89		
AIDS/HIV CASES	3,966	3,722 (93)	

EDUCATION

	1995	1980	1965
SCHOOL AGE IN SCHOOL			
PRIMARY	38%	17%	12%
SECONDARY	8%	3%	1%
HIGHER	1%	negligible	negligible
FEMALES IN SCHOOL			
PRIMARY	39%	37%	8%
SECONDARY	3.4%	3.3%	1.0%
ADULT ILLITERACY M/F	71/91%	79.3/93.9%	n/a

COMMUNICATIONS

	1995	1980	1965
RATE OF NEWSPAPERS	0.3	0.2	0.1
RATE OF RADIOS	27	18	12
RATE OF TELEVISIONS	6	3	0.1

Source: CIA, *The World Factbook, 1997;* ILO, *World Labour Report, 1997;* UN, *Demographic Yearbook, 1997;* UN, *Statistical Yearbook, 1996;* World Bank, *World Development Indicators, 1998.*

BURUNDI

Burundi is a landlocked country located on the eastern shores of Lake Tanganyika in east Central Africa. The 10,733-square-mile (27,830-square-kilometer) country is bordered by the Democratic Republic of the Congo (formerly Zaire) on the northwest, Rwanda on the north, and Tanzania on the east and south. Burundi received independence from a U.N. trusteeship under Belgian administration in July 1962. Since independence, Burundi has been rife with ethnic strife between the Hutu (85 percent of the population) and the Tutsi (14 percent of the population), the country's two leading ethnic groups. The escalation of ethnic unrest in 1993 created mass waves of refugees who fled to Rwanda, Tanzania, and the Democratic Republic of the Congo. The country's economy is dominated by agricultural production, chiefly for subsistence use. The leading export product is coffee, which generates minimal income. At $600 a year, Burundi's per capita gross domestic product is one of the lowest in the world. The country is densely populated, and the population was growing at a pace of 1.5 percent a year in 1995. In the same year, Burundi's life expectancy at birth was 49.3 years, and the country's infant mortality rate was 102 infant deaths per 1,000 live births.

	1995	1980	1965
GEOGRAPHY			
AREA (square miles/kilometers)	10,733/27,830		
LAND AREA (square miles/ kilometers)	9,869/25,650		
COASTLINE (miles/kilometers)	Landlocked		
CITIES			
CAPITAL	Bujumbura	235,440 (90)	
POPULATION			
TOTAL	5,943,057	4,114,135 (79)	3,210,090
DENSITY (per square mile/kilometer)	557/215	438/169	306,118
ANNUAL GROWTH	1.5%	2.7%	2.0%
AGE COHORTS			
0–14	47%	n/a	47%
15–64	50%	n/a	49%
65 AND OVER	3%	n/a	4%
MALE	48%		
FEMALE	52%		

	1995	1980	1965
URBAN	8%	3.90%	n/a
RURAL	92%	96.10%	n/a
NET MIGRATION RATE	−12.5		

IDENTITY

ETHNICITY

HUTU	85%
TUTSI	14%
TWA (PYGMY)	1%

LANGUAGE

KIRUNDI	n/a
FRENCH	n/a

RELIGION

ROMAN CATHOLIC	62%
ANIMIST	32%
PROTESTANT	5%

VITAL STATISTICS

BIRTHS

BIRTH RATE	43	20.4	46.1 (71)
INFANT MORTALITY RATE	102	150	150 (71)
LIFE EXPECTANCY AT BIRTH	49.3	41.5	36.8 (71)

MARRIAGES

MARRIAGE RATE	
AVERAGE AGE AT MARRIAGE M/F	25.7/22.5

DEATH

DEATH RATE	15.2	20.4	25.6 (71)

HOUSEHOLDS

NUMBER	1,145,479 (90)
AVERAGE SIZE	4.5 (90)

ECONOMICS AND LABOR

GDP PER CAPITA US$	$600

	1995	**1980**	**1965**
LABOR FORCE (thousands)	44.7 (91)		
AGRICULTURE	6.6		
MINING	0.3		
MANUFACTURING	6.2		
UTILITIES	0.9		
CONSTRUCTION	2.4		
TRADE/FOOD/TOURISM	3.8		
TRANSPORT/COMMUNICATIONS	2.9		
FINANCE/INSURANCE/REAL ESTATE	1.9		
SOCIAL AND PERSONAL SERVICES	17.7		
UNEMPLOYMENT (official)	7.30%		

TRANSPORT

	1995	**1980**	**1965**
JOURNEYS (by transport mode)			
AIR PASSENGER TRIPS (thousands)	9 (94)		
VEHICLES			
PRIVATE CARS	17,000	5,600	n/a
COMMERCIAL	17,500	2,700	n/a

HEALTH AND HEALTH CARE

	1995	**1980**	**1965**
HEALTH CARE			
MEASLES IMMUNIZATION	44%		
RATE OF PHYSICIANS	0.1	n/a	negligible (60)
RATE OF HOSPITAL BEDS	0.7	n/a	1.1 (60)
HEALTH INDICATORS			
PREGNANT WOMEN WITH ANEMIA	68%		
CHILD MALNUTRITION	38%		
TUBERCULOSIS INCIDENCE RATE	3.67		
AIDS/HIV CASES	7,024	6,880 (93)	

EDUCATION

	1995	**1980**	**1965**
SCHOOL AGE IN SCHOOL			
PRIMARY	70%	26%	26%
SECONDARY	7%	3%	%
HIGHER	1%	1%	negligible
FEMALES IN SCHOOL			
PRIMARY	45%	39%	15%
SECONDARY	38%	25%	0.70%

	1995	1980	1965
ADULT ILLITERACY M/F	51/78%	57.2/74.3% (82)	n/a

COMMUNICATIONS

	1995	1980	1965
RATE OF NEWSPAPERS	3	0.2	0.1 (70)
RATE OF RADIOS	62	39	18 (70)
RATE OF TELEVISIONS	2	0	0

Source: CIA, *The World Factbook, 1997;* ILO, *World Labour Report, 1997;* UN, *Demographic Yearbook, 1997;* UN, *Statistical Yearbook, 1996;* World Bank, *World Development Indicators, 1998.*

CAMBODIA

Cambodia is located in Southeastern Asia on the Gulf of Thailand. The 69,900-square-mile (181,040-square-kilometer) country is bordered by Vietnam on the east, Laos on the north, and Thailand on the north and west. Cambodia's fate was inextricably tied to the war between Vietnam and the United States. The secret bombing of alleged Vietcong bases in Cambodia by U.S. war planes gave rise to animosity toward the United States, and caused an escalation of internal hostilities and rivalries for leadership over the nation. The resulting civil war contributed to mass killings of civilians, foreign invasions, and intrigue that continued into the late 1990s. The conflicts have severely eroded Cambodia's economy, leaving the population in abject poverty. In 1995, the country had an estimated per capita gross domestic product of only $660. Most of the population is engaged in subsistence farming. In 1995, Cambodia's population of 10,861,218 was growing at a rate of 2.8 percent. The vast majority of Cambodians are Khmer (90 percent). Vietnamese (5 percent) and Chinese (1 percent) are Cambodia's leading minorities.

	1995	1980	1965
GEOGRAPHY			
AREA (square miles/kilometers)	69,900/181,040		
LAND AREA (square miles/kilometers)	68,154/176,520		
COASTLINE (miles/kilometers)	277/443		
CITIES			
CAPITAL	Phnom Penh	n/a	n/a	393,995 (62)
POPULATION			
TOTAL	10,861,218	n/a	5,740,115 (62)
DENSITY (per square mile/kilometer)	140/54	n/a	91/35 (59)
ANNUAL GROWTH	2.8%	n/a	2.6% (59)
AGE COHORTS			
0–14	45%	n/a	43.8% (59)
15–64	51%	n/a	53% (59)
65 AND OVER	4%	n/a	3% (59)
MALE	50%		
FEMALE	50%		
URBAN	21%		
RURAL	79%		
NET MIGRATION MIGRATION	0		

	1995	1980	1965

IDENTITY

ETHNICITY
KHMER	90%		
VIETNAMESE	5%		
CHINESE	1%		

LANGUAGE
KHMER (official)	n/a		
FRENCH	n/a		

RELIGION
BUDDHIST	95%		

VITAL STATISTICS

BIRTHS
BIRTH RATE	43.5	n/a	41.4 (59)
INFANT MORTALITY RATE	115.7	n/a	127 (59)
LIFE EXPECTANCY AT BIRTH	49.9	n/a	43.8 (59)

DEATHS
DEATH RATE	15.8	n/a	19.7 (59)

ECONOMICS AND LABOR

GDP PER CAPITA US$
	$660		

LABOR FORCE M/F
AGRICULTURE	69/78%		
INDUSTRY	7/8%		
SERVICES	24/14%		

TRANSPORT

VEHICLES
PRIVATE CARS	n/a	n/a	16,400 (59)
COMMERCIAL	n/a	n/a	9,300 (59)

	1995	1980	1965

HEALTH AND HEALTH CARE

HEALTH CARE

	1995	1980	1965
ACCESS TO SAFE WATER	13%		
MEASLES IMMUNIZATION	75		
RATE OF PHYSICIANS	0.1	0.1	n/a
RATE OF HOSPITAL BEDS	2.1		

HEALTH INDICATORS

	1995	1980	1965
CHILD MALNUTRITION	38		
TUBERCULOSIS INCIDENCE RATE	2.35		
AIDS/HIV CASES	86	1 (93)	

EDUCATION

SCHOOL AGE IN SCHOOL

	1995	1980	1965
PRIMARY	122%	n/a	74% (59)
SECONDARY	27%	32%	9% (59)
HIGHER	2%	1%	1.20%

FEMALES IN SCHOOL

	1995	1980	1965
OF PRIMARY STUDENTS	110%	n/a	54% (59)
SECONDARY	38%	n/a	6% (59)

	1995	1980	1965
ADULT ILLITERACY M/F	20/47%	n/a	30.1/87.3% (62)

COMMUNICATIONS

	1995	1980	1965
RATE OF NEWSPAPERS	n/a	n/a	7 (59)
RATE OF RADIOS	108	92	168 (59)
RATE OF TELEVISIONS	8	5	1 (59)

Source: CIA, *The World Factbook, 1997;* ILO, *World Labour Report, 1997;* UN, *Demographic Yearbook, 1997;* UN, *Statistical Yearbook, 1996;* World Bank, *World Development Indicators, 1998.*

CAMEROON

Cameroon is located in West Africa on the Gulf of Guinea, an inlet of the Atlantic Ocean. The 183,568-square-mile (475,440-square-kilometer) country is bordered by the Central African Republic on the east; Chad on the north; Nigeria on the west; and Equitorial Guinea, Gabon, and Congo (Brazzaville) on the south. Prior to gaining independence in January 1960, Cameroon was a U.N. trusteeship under French administration. Paul Biya has been president since November 1982. The economy is dominated by the export of oil, petroleum, and agricultural products, including lumber, aluminum, cocoa, beans, coffee, and cotton. Due to the revenue generated from offshore oil drilling, the country's per capita gross domestic product of $1,200 is higher than the GDPs of most other African countries south of the Sahara. The country's population grew rapidly from 4.8 million in 1965 to over 14.2 million in 1995. Cameroon's annual population growth, which approached 3 percent in the mid-1990s, continues to be among the highest in the world in the late 1990s. Cameroon tends to have a healthier population than neighboring African countries. In 1995, the country's average life expectancy at birth was 52.6 years, and its infant mortality rate of 63 per 1,000 live births, high by Western standards, was lower than that of other impoverished countries in Africa.

	1995	1980	1965

GEOGRAPHY

AREA (square miles/kilometers)	183,568/475,440		
LAND AREA (square miles/kilometers)	181,236/469,400		
COASTLINE (miles/kilometers)	251/402		

CITIES

CAPITAL	Yaounde	653,670 (86)	
MAJOR CITIES	Douala	1,029,731 (86)	
	Nkongsamba	123,149	
	Maroua	103,653	

POPULATION

	1995	1980	1965
TOTAL	14,261,557	7,090,115 (76)	4,807,000
DENSITY (per square mile/kilometer)	73/28	54/21	28/11
ANNUAL GROWTH	2.9%	3.5%	2.2%

AGE COHORTS

	1995		
0–14	46%		
15–64	51%		
65 AND OVER	3%		

	1995	**1980**	**1965**
URBAN	45%	28% (76)	n/a
RURAL	55%	72% (76)	n/a
NET MIGRATION RATE	0	n/a	n/a

IDENTITY

ETHNICITY

CAMEROON HIGHLANDERS	31%
EQUATORIAL BANTU	19%
KIRDI	11%

LANGUAGE

ENGLISH (official)	n/a
FRENCH (official)	n/a

RELIGION

ANIMIST	51%
CHRISTIAN	33%
MUSLIM	16%

VITAL STATISTICS

BIRTHS

BIRTH RATE	42.5	42.9	49.9
INFANT MORTALITY RATE	63	103	137.2
LIFE EXPECTANCY AT BIRTH	52.6	50.9	35.8

DEATHS

DEATH RATE	13.6	n/a	25.7

ECONOMICS AND LABOR

GDP PER CAPITA US$	$1,200

LABOR FORCE M/F

AGRICULTURE	62/83%
INDUSTRY	12/3%
SERVICES	26/14%
UNION DENSITY	14.7%

	1995	1980	1965
TRANSPORT			
JOURNEYS (by transport mode)			
RAILROAD PASSENGER TRIPS			
(millions of miles/kilometers)	3,162/5,059 (94)		
AIR PASSENGER TRIPS (thousands)	789 (94)		
VEHICLES			
PRIVATE CARS	90,000	n/a	17,300
COMMERCIAL	79,000	n/a	21,900
HEALTH AND HEALTH CARE			
HEALTH INDICATORS			
PREGNANT WOMEN WITH ANEMIA	44%		
LOW-BIRTH-WEIGHT BABIES	13%		
CHILD MALNUTRITION	15%		
TUBERCULOSIS INCIDENCE RATE	1.94		
AIDS/HIV CASES	5,375	3,958 (93)	
HEALTH CARE			
ACCESS TO SAFE WATER	41%		
ACCESS TO SANITATION	40%		
MEASLES IMMUNIZATION	51%		
RATE OF PHYSICIANS	0.1	n/a	negligible (60)
RATE OF HOSPITAL BEDS	2.6	n/a	2.2 (60)
EDUCATION			
SCHOOL AGE IN SCHOOL			
PRIMARY	88%	98%	78%
SECONDARY	27%	18%	5%
HIGHER	n/a	2	0.3
FEMALES IN SCHOOL			
PRIMARY	47	45%	44%
SECONDARY	40%	34%	40%
ADULT ILLITERACY M/F	25/48%	45.4/70.9%	n/a

	1995	1980	1965
COMMUNICATIONS			
RATE OF NEWSPAPERS	4	8	4
RATE OF RADIOS	146	88	n/a
RATE OF TELEVISIONS	25	n/a	n/a

Source: CIA, *The World Factbook, 1997;* ILO, *World Labour Report, 1997;* UN, *Demographic Yearbook, 1997;* UN, *Statistical Yearbook, 1996;* World Bank, *World Development Indicators, 1998.*

CANADA

Canada is located in North America, north of the United States. The 3,851,792-square-mile (9,976,140-square-kilometer) country has coastlines on the Pacific, Atlantic, and Arctic oceans. Although Canada is the world's second largest country in total area, it is one of the most sparsely populated countries in the world. The country received independence from the United Kingdom in July 1867. It is divided primarily along linguistic lines, and much of Quebec's French-speaking population continues to seek autonomy from the rest of the confederation, where English tends to be the dominant language. Although

Canada continues to depend on exports of natural resources, it has a diversified and industrialized national economy. However, the national economy has been mired in a recession through much of the 1990s. In 1995, Canada had a density of only 3 persons per square mile. Canada's 28.8 million people tend to live in the southern tier of the country along the border with the United States. Canada has a higher average life expectancy at birth (79.1 years) and a lower infant mortality rate (6.2 persons per 1,000 live births) than the United States.

Life Expectancy at Birth

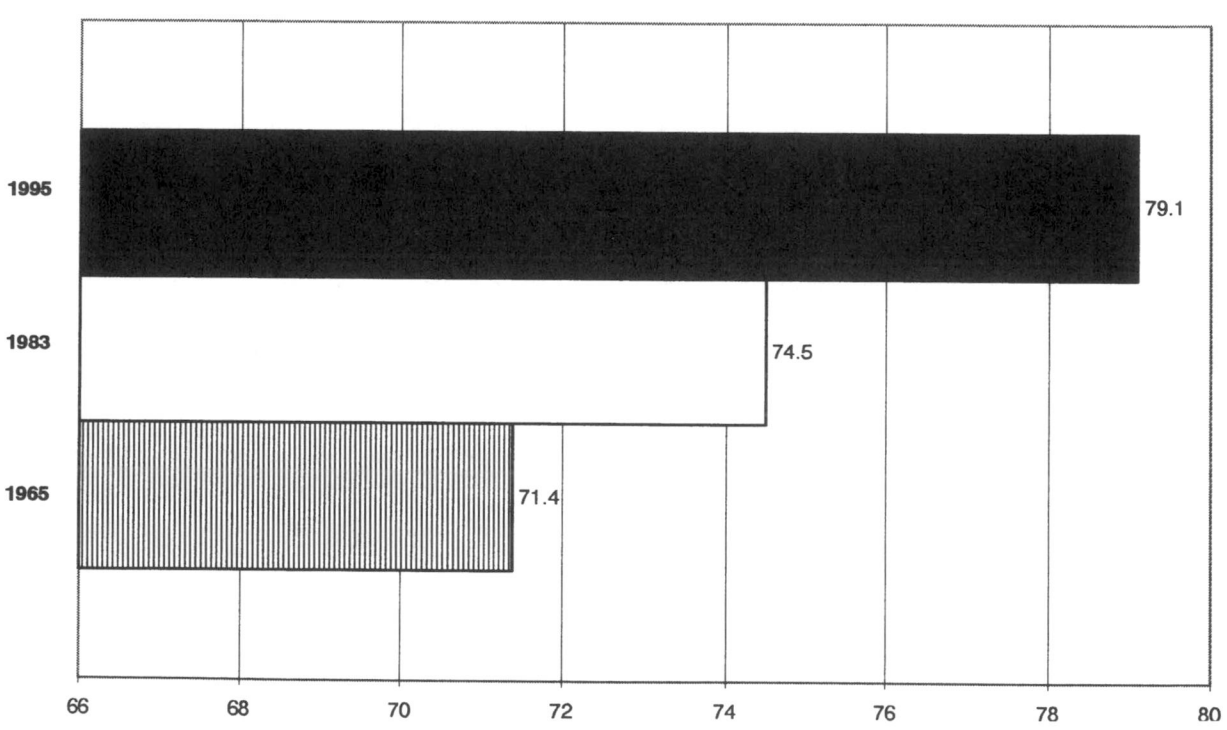

With one of the most admired and successful national health care programs outside of Western Europe, Canada has seen its life expectancy rates climb dramatically in the past three decades.

Divorce Rate

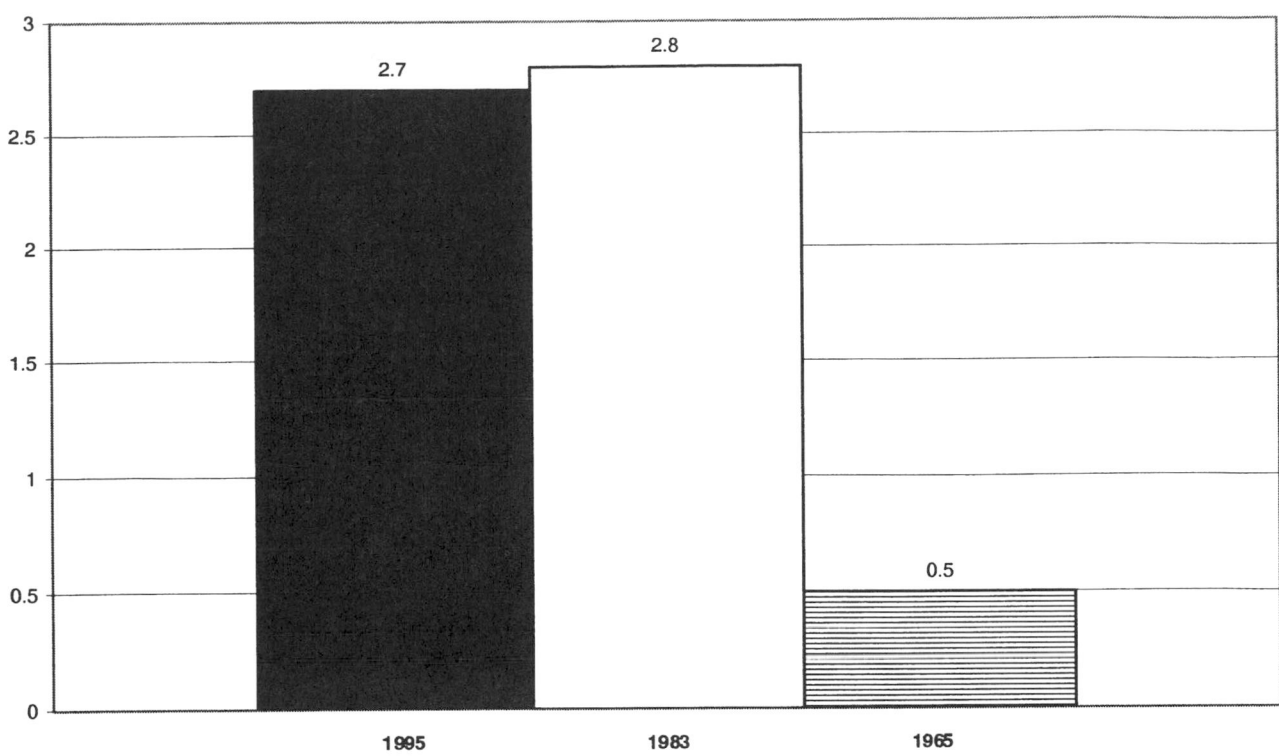

Like its vast neighbor to the south, Canada has seen a significant liberalization of social attitudes in recent decades, including those concerning marriage. Divorce rates have climbed substantially in the past 30 years.

CHRONOLOGY

1966   Canada unveils new maple leaf flag as symbol of break with British heritage.
1967   Nations hosts World's Fair in Montreal, celebrating 100 years of nationhood.
1968   Charismatic Liberal Party candidate Pierre Trudeau wins election and becomes prime minister.
1969   French and English declared official languages of Canada.
1976   Separatist party wins provincial elections in French-speaking Quebec.
1979   Trudeau loses power for last time.
1990   Meech Lake Accords, designed to give Quebec special status, fails to be ratified by provinces.
1997   Separatist referendum in Quebec defeated by narrow majority.

	1995	1980	1965

GEOGRAPHY

AREA (square miles/kilometers)   3,851,792/9,976,140
LAND AREA (square miles/kilometers)   3,569,220/9,220,970
COASTLINE (miles/kilometers)   152,369/243,791

CITIES
CAPITAL   Ottawa   1,010,288 (94)
MAJOR CITIES   Toronto   4,281,906
                 Montreal   3,127,424
                 Vancouver   1,774,672
                 Edmonton   888,465

POPULATION

	1995	1980	1965
TOTAL	28,820,671	24,343,180 (81)	19,919,000 (66)
DENSITY (per square mile/kilometer)	3	3	n/a
ANNUAL GROWTH	1.1%	1.1%	n/a
AGE COHORTS			
0–14	21%	n/a	33%
15–64	67%	n/a	59%
65 AND OVER	12%	n/a	8%
URBAN	77%	75.7	n/a
RURAL	23%	24.3%	n/a
NET MIGRATION RATE	4.5	n/a	n/a

IDENTITY

ETHNICITY
BRITISH   40%
FRENCH   27%
OTHER EUROPEAN   20%

LANGUAGE
ENGLISH (official)   n/a
FRENCH (official)   n/a

RELIGION
ROMAN CATHOLIC   45%
UNITED CHURCH   12%
ANGLICAN   8%

	1995	1980	1965

VITAL STATISTICS

BIRTHS
BIRTH RATE	13.3	15 (83)	19.6
INFANT MORTALITY RATE	6.2	8.5 (83)	23.6
LIFE EXPECTANCY AT BIRTH	79.1	74.5 (83)	71.4

MARRIAGES
MARRIAGE RATE	5.4	7.4 (83)	7.8
AVERAGE AGE AT MARRIAGE M/F	28.9/26.2		
DIVORCE RATE	2.7	2.8 (83)	0.5

DEATHS
DEATH RATE	7.2	n/a	7.5

HOUSEHOLDS

	1995	1980	1965
NUMBER	10,018,265 (91)	n/a	4,554,493 (61)
AVERAGE SIZE	2.7 (91)	n/a	3.9 (61)

TYPE OF HOUSEHOLD
SINGLE	14.9%
MARRIED	56.7%
WIDOWED	10.1%
DIVORCED/SEPARATED	11.3%

ECONOMICS AND LABOR

GDP PER CAPITA US$	$24,400

LABOR FORCE M/F (thousands)	6,753/5,630 (93)
AGRICULTURE	395.0/155.0
MINING	129.0/20.0
MANUFACTURING	1,297.0/503.0
UTILITIES	108.0/34.0
CONSTRUCTION	585.0/75.0
TRADE/FOOD/TOURISM	1,514.0/1,398.0
TRANSPORT/COMMUNICATIONS	559.0/208.0
FINANCE/INSURANCE/REAL ESTATE	699.0/767.0
SOCIAL AND PERSONAL SERVICES	1,468.0/2,469.0

UNEMPLOYMENT (official)	10.4% (94)
UNION DENSITY	31%

	1995	1980	1965

TRANSPORT

JOURNEYS (by transport mode)
RAILROAD PASSENGER TRIPS
  (millions of miles/kilometers)

	1995	1980	1965
RAILROAD PASSENGER TRIPS (millions of miles/kilometers)	900/1,440 (94)		
AIR PASSENGER TRIPS (thousands)	18,105 (94)		
VEHICLES (thousands)			
PRIVATE CARS	13,639.4	10,255.50	5,279.40
COMMERCIAL	3,764.9	2,955.30	1,348.70

HEALTH AND HEALTH CARE

HEALTH CARE

	1995	1980	1965
RATE OF PHYSICIANS	2.2	1.8	1.1 (60)
RATE OF HOSPITAL BEDS	5.4	n/a	11.1 (60)
ACCESS TO SAFE WATER	100%		
ACCESS TO SANITATION	85%		
MEASLES IMMUNIZATION	98%		

HEALTH INDICATORS

	1995	1980	1965
LOW-BIRTH-WEIGHT BABIES	6%		
SMOKING PREVALANCE M/F	31/29%		
TUBERCULOSIS INCIDENCE RATE	0.08		
AIDS/HIV CASES	13,235	10,781 (93)	
TOTAL DEATHS	211,535 (94)		

EDUCATION

SCHOOL AGE IN SCHOOL

	1995	1980	1965
PRIMARY	102%	99%	117%
SECONDARY	106%	88%	52%
HIGHER	n/a	n/a	18.60%

FEMALES IN SCHOOL

	1995	1980	1965
PRIMARY	49%	49%	49%
SECONDARY	49%	49%	51%

	1995	1980	1965
COMMUNICATIONS			
RATE OF NEWSPAPERS	204	221	227
RATE OF RADIOS	992	721	502
RATE OF TELEVISIONS	618	432	267

Source: CIA, *The World Factbook, 1997;* ILO, *World Labour Report, 1997;* UN, *Demographic Yearbook, 1997;* UN, *Statistical Yearbook, 1996;* World Bank, *World Development Indicators, 1998.*

CAPE VERDE

Cape Verde is an island group situated in the Atlantic Ocean about 300 miles (500 kilometers) west of the African country of Senegal. The 1,556-square-mile (4,030-square-kilometer) country received independence from Portugal in July 1975. Cape Verde is lacking in natural resources and produces few agricultural commodities for foreign export. Moreover, the country experiences frequent droughts and water shortages. Much of the country's revenue base is generated through remittances from workers living abroad. In 1995, Cape Verde's out-migration rate was 6.7 percent, owing to the country's limited economic development and lack of job opportunities. The country has a high birth rate of 44.3 live births per 1,000 residents. Creoles (71 percent) and Africans of various nationalities (28 percent) are Cape Verde's two leading ethnic groups. About 54 percent of Cape Verde's national population of nearly 450,000 reside in urban areas.

		1995	1980	1965
GEOGRAPHY				
AREA (square miles/kilometers)		1,556/4,030		
LAND AREA (square miles/kilometers)		1,556/4,030		
COASTLINE (miles/kilometers)		603/965		
CITIES				
CAPITAL	Praia	61,644		
POPULATION				
TOTAL		449,066	295,703	199,661
DENSITY (per square mile/kilometer)		97	81	
ANNUAL GROWTH		2.9%	1.9%	2.0%
AGE COHORTS				
0–14		50%		
15–64		46%		
65 AND OVER		4%		
MALE		47%		
FEMALE		53%		
URBAN		54%		
RURAL		46%		
NET MIGRATION RATE		−6.7	n/a	−0.9

	1995	1980	1965

IDENTITY

ETHNICITY

CREOLE	71%		
AFRICAN	28%		
EUROPEAN	1%		

LANGUAGE

PORTUGUESEA	n/a		
CRIOULO	n/a		

RELIGION

ROMAN CATHOLIC	n/a		

VITAL STATISTICS

BIRTHS

BIRTH RATE	44.3	31	42.9
INFANT MORTALITY RATE	65.1 (92)	71.4	109.7
LIFE EXPECTANCY AT BIRTH	69.4	60	n/a

MARRIAGES

MARRIAGE RATE	3.8 (92)	5.4	3.8
AVERAGE AGE AT MARRIAGE M/F	28.1/25.7		

DEATHS

DEATH RATE	8.3	7.6	10.6

HOUSEHOLDS

NUMBER

NUMBER	67,619 (90)		
URBAN HOUSEHOLDS	30,659		
RURAL HOUSEHOLDS	36,900		

AVERAGE SIZE

AVERAGE SIZE	5 (90)		
URBAN	4.9		
RURAL	5.1		

FEMALE HEADED

FEMALE HEADED	38.4%		

	1995	1980	1965

ECONOMICS AND LABOR

GDP PER CAPITA US$	$1,040		
UNION DENSITY	16.90%		

TRANSPORT

JOURNEYS (by transport mode)			
AIR PASSENGER TRIPS (thousands)	118 (94)		
VEHICLES			
PRIVATE CARS	10,000 (92)	4,000 (81)	
COMMERCIAL	10,000 (92)	1,300 (81)	

HEALTH AND HEALTH CARE

HEALTH CARE			
RATE OF PHYSICIANS	n/a	n/a	0.1 (60)
RATE OF HOSPITAL BEDS	n/a	n/a	2.5 (60)
HEALTH INDICATORS			
AIDS/HIV CASES	117	82 (93)	
TOTAL DEATHS	2,843 (92)		

EDUCATION

SCHOOL AGE IN SCHOOL			
PRIMARY	n/a	66%	71%
SECONDARY	n/a	10%	7%
FEMALES IN SCHOOL			
PRIMARY	n/a	n/a	56%
SECONDARY	n/a	n/a	7%
ADULT ILLITERACY M/F	n/a	38.6/61.4%	60.7/82.6% (60)

	1995	1980	1965
COMMUNICATIONS			
RATE OF RADIOS	176	142	18
RATE OF TELEVISIONS	3	0	0

Source: CIA, The World Factbook, 1997; ILO, World Labour Report, 1997; UN, Demographic Yearbook, 1997; UN, Statistical Yearbook, 1996; World Bank, World Development Indicators, 1998.

CENTRAL AFRICAN REPUBLIC

The Central African Republic (CAR) is a landlocked country located in central Africa. The two Congos (Republic of Congo and Democratic Republic of Congo) border the 240,533-square-mile (622,980-square-kilometer) country on the south, Sudan on the east, Chad on the north, and Cameroon on the west. CAR gained nominal independence from France in December 1958, but the economy remains dependent on French foreign assistance. Between 1975 and 1995, CAR's population expanded from just over 2 million to nearly 3.3 million. But CAR's annual growth rate declined from 2.5 percent in 1975 to 2.1 percent in 1995. In the late 1990s, the majority of the country's population remain subsistence farmers. CAR's principal exports are diamonds, timber products, and agricultural commodities. Throughout the 1970s and 1980s, a military dictatorship plundered the wealth of much of CAR's natural resources for personal use. The country has a low average life expectancy of only 45.9 years and a high infant mortality rate of 101.7 infant deaths per 1,000 live births.

	1995	1980	1965
GEOGRAPHY			
AREA (square miles/kilometers)	240,533/622,980		
LAND AREA (square miles/kilometers)	240,533/622,980		
COASTLINE (miles/kilometers)	landlocked		
CITIES			
CAPITAL	Bangui　　n/a	473,817 (84)	n/a
POPULATION			
TOTAL	3,274,426	2,054,610 (75)	1,202,910
DENSITY (per square mile/kilometer)	13/5	10.0/4.0	5.0/2.0
ANNUAL GROWTH	2.10%	2.50%	2.20%
AGE COHORTS			
0–14	44%	n/a	26%
15–64	52%	n/a	73%
65 AND OVER	4%	n/a	1%
MALE	49%		
FEMALE	51%		
URBAN	39%	35.3%	n/a

	1995	1980	1965
RURAL	61%	64.70%	n/a
NET MIGRATION RATE	−1.5		

IDENTITY

ETHNICITY

BAYA	34%
BANDA	27%
MANDIJA	21%
OTHER	18%

LANGUAGE

FRENCH (official)	n/a
SANGHO	n/a
ARABIC	n/a

RELIGION

PROTESTANT	25%
ROMAN CATHOLIC	25%
ANIMIST	24%
OTHER	26%

VITAL STATISTICS

BIRTHS

	1995	1980	1965
BIRTH RATE	40	44.6	48
INFANT MORTALITY RATE	101.7	190	190
LIFE EXPECTANCY AT BIRTH	45.9	34.5	34.5

MARRIAGES

AVERAGE AGE AT MARRIAGE M/F	24.1/19.1 (88)

DEATHS

	1995	1980	1965
DEATH RATE	17.6	21.8	30 (60)

HOUSEHOLDS

NUMBER

	519,314 (88)
URBAN	170,149 (88)
RURAL	349,165 (88)

AVERAGE SIZE

	4.7 (88)
URBAN	5.3 (88)
RURAL	4.4 (88)

	1995	1980	1965
TYPE OF HOUSEHOLD			
SINGLE	13.1%		
MARRIED	71.4%		
WIDOWED	8.6%		
DIVORCED/SEPARATED	6.5%		
FEMALE HEADED	18.7%		

ECONOMICS AND LABOR

	1995	1980	1965
GDP PER CAPITA US$	$800		
LABOR FORCE (thousands)	13 (90)		
AGRICULTURE	2.3		
MINING	n/a		
MANUFACTURING	n/a		
UTILITIES	0.8		
CONSTRUCTION	1.3		
TRADE/FOOD/TOURISM	4.3		
TRANSPORT/COMMUNICATIONS	1.5		
FINANCE/INSURANCE/REAL ESTATE	0.3		

TRANSPORT

	1995	1980	1965
JOURNEYS (by transport mode)			
AIR PASSENGER TRIPS (thousands)	123 (94)		
VEHICLES			
PRIVATE CARS	11,900	14,500	3,600
COMMERCIAL	2,800	n/a	5,900

HEALTH AND HEALTH CARE

	1995	1980	1965
HEALTH INDICATORS			
PREGNANT WOMEN WITH ANEMIA	67%		
LOW-BIRTH-WEIGHT BABIES	15%		
CHILD MALNUTRITION	23%		
TUBERCULOSIS INCIDENCE RATE	1.39		
AIDS/HIV CASES	4,939	4,240 (93)	
HEALTH CARE			
ACCESS TO SAFE WATER	18%	n/a	n/a
MEASLES IMMUNIZATION	70%		

	1995	1980	1965
RATE OF PHYSICIANS	negligible	negligible	negligible (60)
RATE OF HOSPITAL BEDS	0.9	1.6	1.5 (60)

EDUCATION

SCHOOL AGE IN SCHOOL

	1995	1980	1965
PRIMARY	58%	71%	59%
SECONDARY	10%	14%	2%
HIGHER	1%	1%	n/a

FEMALES IN SCHOOL

	1995	1980	1965
PRIMARY	n/a	37%	26%
SECONDARY	n/a	25%	1%

	1995	1980	1965
ADULT ILLITERACY M/F	32/48%	67/85%	n/a

COMMUNICATIONS

	1995	1980	1965
RATE OF NEWSPAPERS	1	n/a	0.3 (62)
RATE OF RADIOS	72	52	25
RATE OF TELEVISIONS	5	0	0

Source: CIA, *The World Factbook, 1997;* ILO, *World Labour Report, 1997;* UN, *Demographic Yearbook, 1997;* UN, *Statistical Yearbook, 1996;* World Bank, *World Development Indicators, 1998.*

CHAD

Chad, a landlocked country in north central Africa, is bounded by six countries: Libya on the north, Sudan on the east, Central African Republic on the south, Cameroon and Nigeria on the southwest, and Niger on the west. Chad has a land area of 495,753 square miles (1,284,000 square kilometers). Chad gained independence from France in August 1960 and has since been ruled by a series of military governments supported by competing internal and external groups. In the late 1990s, Chad was undergoing an uneasy transition to democracy. Nearly 80 percent of Chad's population resides in rural areas and engages in subsistence farming as a primary economic activity. In 1995, Chad's per capita gross domestic product (GDP) was only $600 per year, among the lowest in the world. Between 1964 and 1995, Chad's population nearly doubled from 3,254,000 to 6,976,845. By 1995, the country's population was continuing to grow at a rapid rate of 2.7 percent per year. French and Arab are Chad's two official languages. Half of the country's people are Muslim, 25 percent are Christian, and 25 percent are adherents of various Animist faiths.

		1995	1980	1965
GEOGRAPHY				
AREA (square miles/kilometers)		495,753/1,284,000		
LAND AREA (square miles/kilometers)		486,178/1,259,200		
COASTLINE (miles/kilometers)		landlocked		
CITIES				
CAPITAL	N'Djamena	613,000	n/a	179,000 (72)
POPULATION				
TOTAL		6,976,845	n/a	3,254,000 (64)
DENSITY		13/5	10.0/4	n/a
CHANGE		2.7%	2.3%	1.5%
AGE COHORTS				
0–14		44%		46%
15–64		53%		50%[1]
65 AND OVER		3%		3.6%[2]
MALE		48%		
FEMALE		52%		
URBAN		21%	18.4% (78)	n/a
RURAL		79%	81.6% (78)	n/a

	1995	**1980**	**1965**
NET MIGRATION RATE	0		

IDENTITY

ETHNICITY

ARAB	n/a		
SARA	n/a		

LANGUAGE

FRENCH (official)	n/a		
ARABIC (official)	n/a		
SARA	n/a		

RELIGION

MUSLIM	50%		
CHRISTIAN	25%		
ANIMIST	25%		

VITAL STATISTICS

BIRTHS

BIRTH RATE	44.3	44.2	45
INFANT MORTALITY RATE	122	160	160
LIFE EXPECTANCY AT BIRTH	47.6	32	31

DEATHS

DEATH RATE	17.4	21.4	31 (64)

ECONOMICS AND LABOR

GDP PER CAPITA US$	$600		

LABOR FORCE M/F (thousands)	11.8/0.7 (91)		
AGRICULTURE	1.3/0.1		
MINING	0.2/0.0		
MANUFACTURING	5.2/0.1		
UTILITIES	0.0/0.0		
CONSTRUCTION	1.0/0.0		
TRADE/FOOD/TOURISM	0.6/0.1		
TRANSPORT/COMMUNICATIONS	0.9/0.1		
FINANCE/INSURANCE/REAL ESTATE	0.3/0.0		
SOCIAL AND PERSONAL SERVICES	2.1/0.3		

	1995	1980	1965

TRANSPORT

JOURNEYS (by transport mode)

	1995	1980	1965
RAILROAD PASSENGER TRIPS (millions of miles/kilometers)	86 (94)		

VEHICLES

	1995	1980	1965
PRIVATE CARS	9,000	n/a	3,300
COMMERCIAL	7,000	n/a	4,800

HEALTH AND HEALTH CARE

HEALTH CARE

	1995	1980	1965
ACCESS TO SAFE WATER	24%		
ACCESS TO SANITATION	21%		
MEASLES IMMUNIZATION	24%		
RATE OF PHYSICIANS	0.7		
RATE OF HOSPITAL BEDS	n/a	n/a	0.7 (60)

HEALTH INDICATORS

	1995	1980	1965
PREGNANT WOMEN WITH ANEMIA	37%		
LOW-BIRTH-WEIGHT BABIES	11%		
TUBERCULOSIS INCIDENCE RATE	1.67		
AIDS/HIV CASES	3,457	1,597 (93)	

EDUCATION

SCHOOL AGE IN SCHOOL

	1995	1980	1965
PRIMARY	55%	38% (84)	30%
SECONDARY	9%	6% (84)	1%
HIGHER	1%	0.3% (84)	negligible

FEMALES IN SCHOOL

	1995	1980	1965
PRIMARY	32%	18% (84)	11%
SECONDARY	1.7%	2% (84)	0.2%

	1995	1980	1965
ADULT ILLITERACY M/F	38/65%	59.5/89.1%	n/a

	1995	1980	1965
COMMUNICATIONS			
RATE OF NEWSPAPERS	0.4	0.2	0.4
RATE OF RADIOS	245	168	7
RATE OF TELEVISIONS	1	0	0

FOOTNOTES
1. Ages 15–59.
2. Age 60 and over.

Source: CIA, The World Factbook, 1997; ILO, World Labour Report, 1997; UN, Demographic Yearbook, 1997; UN, Statistical Yearbook, 1996; World Bank, World Development Indicators, 1998.

CHILE

Chile consists of a long coastal strip of land that extends about 3,750 miles (6,000 kilometers) from the Pacific Coast border with Peru southeast to the Strait of Magellan on the South Atlantic Ocean border with Argentina. Peru and Bolivia border the 292,259-square-mile (756,950-square-kilometer) country on the north and northeast, and Argentina borders it on the east. In 1973, the Chilean military, in a bloody coup backed by the United States, overthrew the democratically elected government of Salvador Allende. In 1989, the military junta was forced to turn power over to a democratically elected government. Though democratic rule was suspended for nearly two decades, the government was credited with accelerating economic growth through market reforms and privatization. Although Chile has a fairly high annual per capita gross domestic product (GDP) of $8,000, income inequality remains extremely high for a modern economy. In 1992, nearly 40 percent of the country's population subsisted on less than the equivalent of $2 a day. The country has almost doubled in population from 1965 to 1995, but annual growth rates have significantly declined from 2.3 percent to 1.2 percent. Chile has a comparatively high average life expectancy and a low infant mortality rate.

	1995	1980	1965
GEOGRAPHY			
AREA (square miles/kilometers)	292,259/756,950		
LAND AREA (square miles/kilometers)	289,252/748,900		
COASTLINE (miles/kilometers)	4,022/6,435		
CITIES			
CAPITAL	Santiago	4,229,970	
MAJOR CITIES	Concepción	350,268	
	Viña del Mar	322,220	
	Puente Alto	318,898	
	Valparaíso	282,168	
POPULATION			
TOTAL	14,333,528	11,275,440 (82)	7,374,115 (60)
DENSITY (per square mile/kilometer)	49/19	41/16	31/12
ANNUAL CHANGE	1.2%	1.7%	2.3%
AGE COHORTS			
0–14	29%	n/a	28%
15–64	65%	n/a	68%
65 AND OVER	6%	n/a	4%

	1995	1980	1965
MALE	49%		
FEMALE	51%		
URBAN	84%	81%	n/a
RURAL	16%	19%	n/a
NET MIGRATION RATE	0	n/a	0.2 (64)

IDENTITY

ETHNICITY	
EUROPEAN/EUROPEAN-INDIAN	95%
INDIAN	3%

LANGUAGE	
SPANISH	100%

RELIGION	
ROMAN CATHOLIC	89%
PROTESTANT	11%

VITAL STATISTICS

BIRTHS	1995	1980	1965
BIRTH RATE	18.1	22.3 (84)	36
URBAN BIRTH RATE	21.2 (94)		
RURAL BIRTH RATE	17.6 (94)		
INFANT MORTALITY RATE	12	19.6	107.1
ABORTION RATE	0.22		
LIFE EXPECTANCY AT BIRTH	74.5	64.4	52.3
MARRIAGES			
MARRIAGE RATE	6.7	7.3 (84)	7.6
AVERAGE AGE AT MARRIAGE M/F	25.8/23.4		
DEATHS			
DEATH RATE	5.7	6.3 (84)	12

HOUSEHOLDS

	1995	1980	1965
NUMBER	3,293,779 (92)	n/a	1,322,896 (60)
AVERAGE SIZE	4 (92)	n/a	5.4 (62)
FEMALE HEADED	25.3%		

	1995	1980	1965

ECONOMICS AND LABOR

GDP PER CAPITA US$ $8,000

LABOR FORCE M/F (thousands)	3,375.0/1,614.8 (94)		
AGRICULTURE	720.1/88.8		
MINING	82.9/3.5		
MANUFACTURING	594.9/223.9		
UTILITIES	30.6/3.0		
CONSTRUCTION	350.7/10.2		
TRADE/FOOD/TOURISM	530.0/410.7		
TRANSPORT/COMMUNICATIONS	328.2/43.1		
FINANCE/INSURANCE/REAL ESTATE	192.5/106.0		
SOCIAL AND PERSONAL SERVICES	542.8/725.6		

UNEMPLOYMENT (official)	5.9% (94)		
UNION DENSITY	15.9%		

POVERTY

UNDER $1/DAY	15% (92)		
UNDER $2/DAY	38.5 (92)		

TRANSPORT

JOURNEYS (by transport mode)			
RAILROAD PASSENGER TRIPS	510/816.0 (94)		
(millions of miles/kilometers)			
AIR PASSENGER TRIPS (thousands)	2,962.0 (94)		

VEHICLES			
PRIVATE CARS	914,000	448,500	97,700
COMMERCIAL	208,300	219,600	105,400

HEALTH AND HEALTH CARE

HEALTH CARE			
ACCESS TO SANITATION	83%		
MEASLES IMMUNIZATION	93%		
RATE OF PHYSICIANS	1.1	n/a	0.6 (60)
RATE OF HOSPITAL BEDS	3.2	3.4	3.6 (60)

	1995	**1980**	**1965**
HEALTH INDICATORS			
PREGNANT WOMEN WITH ANEMIA	13%		
LOW-BIRTH-WEIGHT BABIES	7%		
CHILD MALNUTRITION	1%		
SMOKING PREVALENCE M/F	38/25%		
TUBERCULOSIS INCIDENCE RATE	0.67		
AIDS/HIV CASES	1,429	970 (93)	
TOTAL DEATHS	75,445 (94)		

EDUCATION

	1995	**1980**	**1965**
SCHOOL AGE IN SCHOOL			
PRIMARY	99%	109%	116%
SECONDARY	69%	53%	33%
HIGHER	27%	12%	5.1%
FEMALES IN SCHOOL			
PRIMARY STUDENTS	49%	49%	49%
SECONDARY STUDENTS	54%	55%	51%
ADULT ILLITERACY	5%	5.6%	n/a

COMMUNICATIONS

	1995	**1980**	**1965**
RATE OF NEWSPAPERS	147	115 (82)	118
RATE OF RADIOS	345	292	203
RATE OF TELEVISIONS	211	110	7

Source: CIA, *The World Factbook, 1997;* ILO, *World Labour Report, 1997;* UN, *Demographic Yearbook, 1997;* UN, *Statistical Yearbook, 1996;* World Bank, *World Development Indicators, 1998.*

CHINA

China, the world's most populous country, is located in east central Asia. China is the world's third largest country, following Russia and Canada, with a land area of 3,705,390 square miles (9,596,960 square kilometers). China continues to be governed by the Communist Party that gained power in the 1949 revolution that defeated the Chinese Nationalists. Since the late 1970s, however, the Communist Party has opened the economy to foreign trade and investment, implemented market reforms that have eroded many social protections and, as a result of a lack of reg-ulations, degraded the physical environment. Though the economy has industrialized rapidly, poverty, particularly in rural areas, has increased dramatically. By the mid-1990s, up to 100 million migrant workers roamed the countryside and cities in search of work. China is the world's most populous country with over 1.2 million people in 1995. The country's population growth has declined from 1.5 percent in 1953 to 1.0 percent in 1995, equivalent to growth rates in most industrialized countries. About 70 percent of the national population continues to live in rural areas.

Population Growth

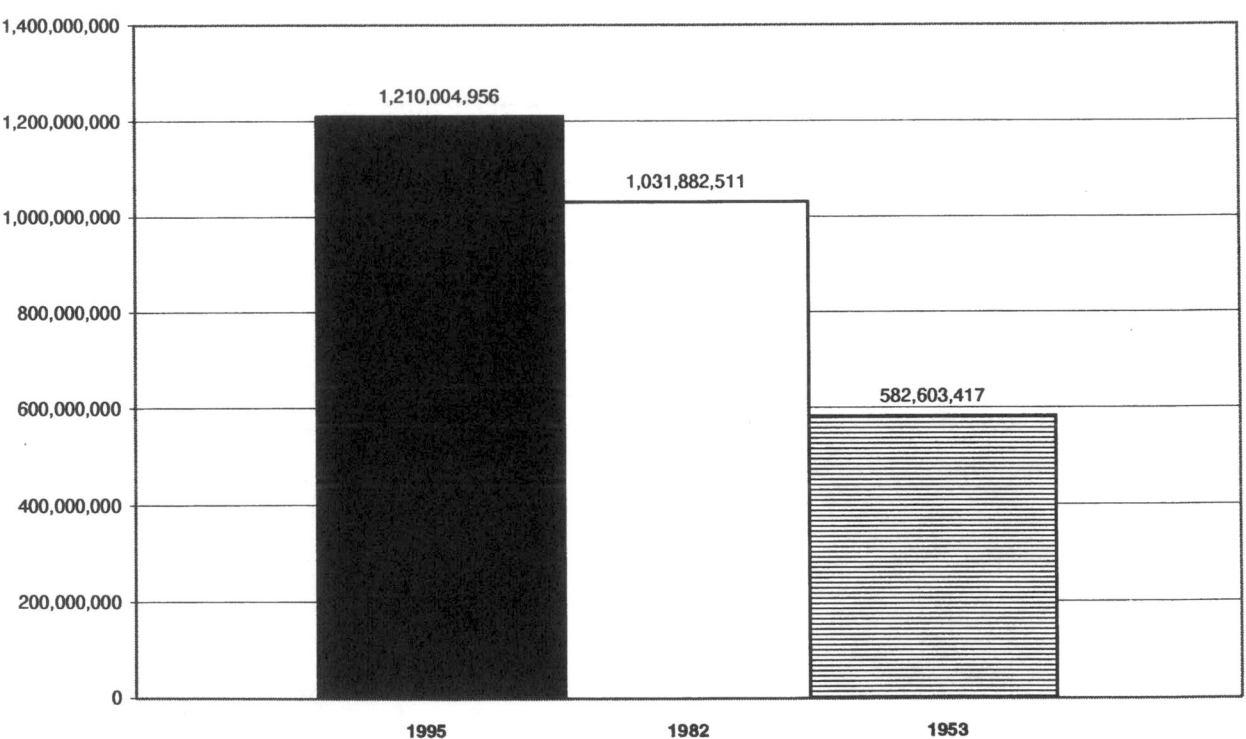

Though it has instituted one of the most draconian birth-control policies in the world, China is still experiencing population growth on an epic scale. This is due to demographic lag, whereby a generally young population means a high fertility rate.

Higher Education

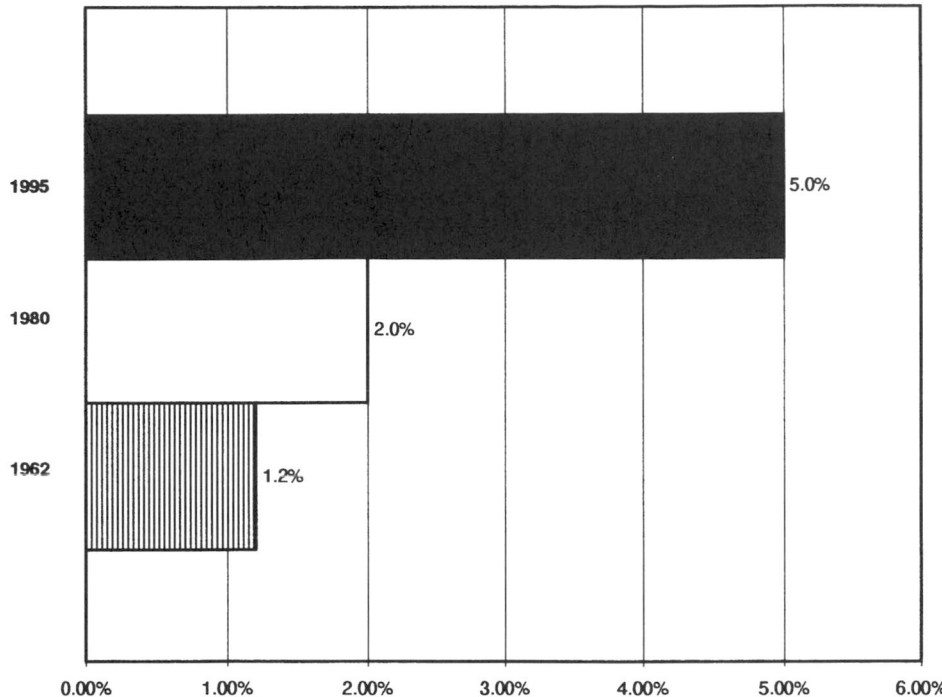

Since the rise of reformist, pro-market governments, China has put a great deal of resources into higher education, partly to help the country progress economically and partly to overcome the anti-intellectualism of the Cultural Revolution of the 1960s.

CHRONOLOGY

1966 Communist Party Chairman Mao Zedong launches radical Cultural Revolution.

1970 Cultural Revolution ends.

1971 Mainland China takes over Taiwan's seat at United Nations.

1972 President Richard Nixon visits China.

1976 Mao and Zhou Enlai, architects of China's communist revolution, die.

1979 Conservative Deng Xiaoping defeats radical Gang of Four to take power in China; he launches economic reforms.

1989 Chinese pro-democracy movement crushed when troops open fire on protesters in Tiananmen Square in Beijing, killing thousands.

1997 Chinese economic progress undermined by economic crisis in Asia.

	1995	1980	1965

GEOGRAPHY

AREA (square miles/kilometers)	3,705,390/9,596,960
LAND AREA (square miles/kilometers)	3,600,931/9,326,410
COASTLINE (miles/kilometers)	9,063/14,500

CITIES

CAPITAL	Beijing	7,362,426 (90)
MAJOR CITIES	Shanghai	8,205,598
	Tianjin	5,804,023
	Qingdao	5,124,668
	Shenyang	4,655,280

POPULATION

	1995	1980	1965
TOTAL	1,210,004,956	1,031,882,511 (82)	582,603,417 (53)
DENSITY (per square mile/kilometer)	329/127	285/110	192/74
ANNUAL GROWTH	1.00%	1.2%	1.5%

AGE COHORTS

0–14	26%
15–64	67%
65 AND OVER	7%

	1995	1980	1965
URBAN	30%	20.6% (82)	n/a
RURAL	70%	79.4% (82)	n/a

NET MIGRATION RATE	−0.3

IDENTITY

ETHNICITY

HAN CHINESE	91.9%
ZHUANG	n/a
UYGUR	n/a

LANGUAGE

MANDARIN	n/a
CANTONESE	n/a
WU	n/a

	1995	1980	1965
RELIGION			
TAOIST	n/a		
BUDDHIST	n/a		
MUSLIM	n/a		

VITAL STATISTICS

	1995	1980	1965
BIRTHS			
BIRTH RATE	17	19	34 (57)
INFANT MORTALITY RATE	44.5	39	n/a
LIFE EXPECTANCY AT BIRTH	69.6	67.8	n/a
MARRIAGES			
AVERAGE AGE AT MARRIAGE M/F	23.8/22.1		
DEATHS			
DEATH RATE	6.9	6.7	11 (57)

HOUSEHOLDS

	1995
NUMBER	276,911,767 (90)
AVERAGE SIZE	4 (90)

ECONOMICS AND LABOR

	1995
GDP PER CAPITA US$	$2,900
LABOR FORCE M/F (thousands)	66,867.0/34,220 (89)
AGRICULTURE	5,076/2867
MINING	6,218/1,589
MANUFACTURING	20,292/13,144
UTILITIES	1,089/395
CONSTRUCTION	4,550/1,233
TRADE/FOOD/TOURISM	5,639/4,167
TRANSPORT/COMMUNICATIONS	4,947/1,453
FINANCE/INSURANCE/REAL ESTATE	864/492
SOCIAL AND PERSONAL SERVICES	17,396/8,637
UNEMPLOYMENT M/F (official)	0.8/1.1 (94)
UNION DENSITY	54.70%

	1995	1980	1965
POVERTY			
UNDER $1/DAY	22.2%		
UNDER $2/DAY	57.8%		

TRANSPORT

JOURNEYS (by transport mode)			
RAILROAD PASSENGER TRIPS	227,253/363,605 (94)		
(millions of miles/kilometers)			
AIR PASSENGER TRIPS (thousands)	37,498 (94)		

HEALTH AND HEALTH CARE

	1995	1980	1965
HEALTH CARE			
ACCESS TO SAFE WATER	90%		
ACCESS TO SANITATION	21%		
MEASLES IMMUNIZATION	89%		
RATE OF PHYSICIANS	1.6	0.9	n/a
RATE OF HOSPITAL BEDS	2.4	2	n/a
HEALTH INDICATORS			
PREGNANT WOMEN WITH ANEMIA	52%		
LOW-BIRTH-WEIGHT BABIES	6%		
CHILD MALNUTRITION	16%		
SMOKING PREVALENCE M/F	61/7%		
TUBERCULOSIS INCIDENCE RATE	0.85		
AIDS/HIV CASES	117	36 (93)	
TOTAL DEATHS	7,800,000 (93)		

EDUCATION

	1995	1980	1965
SCHOOL AGE IN SCHOOL			
PRIMARY	118%	113%	89% (70)
SECONDARY	67%	46%	24%
HIGHER	5%	2	1.2% (62)
FEMALES IN SCHOOL			
PRIMARY STUDENTS	47%	45%	n/a
SECONDARY STUDENTS	44%	40%	n/a
ADULT ILLITERACY M/F	27.0/10.0%	20.8/48.9% (82)	n/a

	1995	1980	1965
COMMUNICATIONS			
RATE OF NEWSPAPERS	43	34	19 (55)
RATE OF RADIOS	184	55	14
RATE OF TELEVISIONS	38	4	0.2

Source: CIA, *The World Factbook, 1997*; ILO, *World Labour Report, 1997*; UN, *Demographic Yearbook, 1997*; UN, *Statistical Yearbook, 1996*; World Bank, *World Development Indicators, 1998*.

COLOMBIA

Colombia, located in northwestern South America, borders the Caribbean Sea on the north and the Pacific Ocean on the west. Venezuela borders the 439,737-square-mile (1,138,920-square-kilometer) country on the northeast, Panama on the northwest, Ecuador on the southwest, Peru on the South, and Brazil on the southeast. Colombia's government has been embroiled in a civil war against rebels who control large regions of the country. In 1995, the country's annual per capita gross national product (GNP) was $5,300. Still, over 21 percent of the population survives on incomes of under $2 a day. Colombia has a comparatively high life expectancy at birth of 72.8 years and an infant mortality rate of 37 infant deaths per 1,000 live births. The three primary ethnic divisions in Colombia are mestizo (58 percent), white (20 percent), and mulatto (14 percent). About 95 percent of the country's population is Roman Catholic.

		1995	1980	1965
GEOGRAPHY				
AREA (square miles/kilometers)	439,737/1,138,920			
LAND AREA (square miles/kilometers)	401,042/1,038,700			
COASTLINE (miles/kilometers)	2,005/3,208			
CITIES				
CAPITAL	Bogotá	n/a	3,974,813 (85)	n/a
MAJOR CITIES	Medellín	n/a	1,452,392 (85)	n/a
	Cali	n/a	1,369,331 (85)	n/a
	Barranquilla	n/a	917,486 (85)	n/a
	Cartagena	n/a	513,986 (85)	n/a
POPULATION				
TOTAL		36,813,161	22,551,811 (73)	17,484,508 (64)
DENSITY (per square mile/kilometer)		80/31	65/25	41/16
ANNUAL GROWTH		1.7%		
AGE COHORTS				
0–14		32%	n/a	47%
15–64		64%	n/a	48%
65 AND OVER		4%	n/a	5%
MALE		49%		
FEMALE		51%		
URBAN		73%	65.4% (83)	n/a
RURAL		27%	34.6% (83)	n/a

	1995	1980	1965
NET MIGRATION RATE	−0.1	n/a	0

IDENTITY

ETHNICITY

MESTIZO	58%		
WHITE	20%		
MULATTO	14%		

LANGUAGE

SPANISH	n/a		

RELIGION

ROMAN CATHOLIC	95%		

VITAL STATISTICS

BIRTHS

BIRTH RATE	21.3	31	44
INFANT MORTALITY RATE	37	50	82.4
LIFE EXPECTANCY AT BIRTH	72.8	63.7	45

MARRIAGES

MARRIAGE RATE	2.3	3.6	4.8

DEATHS

DEATH RATE	4.7	7.7	14

HOUSEHOLDS

NUMBER	n/a	5,251,273 (85)	n/a
AVERAGE SIZE	n/a	5.2	n/a

ECONOMICS AND LABOR

GDP PER CAPITA US$	$5,300		

LABOR FORCE M/F (thousands)   2,819.5/2,021.7 (92)

AGRICULTURE	53.0/15.4		
MINING	15.0/4.3		
MANUFACTURING	660.8/477.9		
UTILITIES	27.1/5.4		
CONSTRUCTION	288.3/16.3		

	1995	1980	1965
TRADE/FOOD/TOURISM	680.0/552.7		
TRANSPORT/COMMUNICATIONS	266.2/32.1		
FINANCE/INSURANCE/REAL ESTATE	216.0/130.0		
SOCIAL AND PERSONAL SERVICES	604.4/781.3		
UNION DENSITY	7%		
POVERTY			
UNDER $1/DAY	7.4% (91)		
UNDER $2/DAY	21.7% (91)		

TRANSPORT

	1995	1980	1965
JOURNEYS (by transport mode)			
RAILROAD PASSENGER TRIPS	10/16 (92)		
(millions of miles/kilometers)			
AIR PASSENGER TRIPS (thousands)	7,686 (94)		
VEHICLES (thousands)			
PRIVATE CARS	761.7	522.7	112.9
COMMERCIAL	672.6	294.9	104.4

HEALTH AND HEALTH CARE

	1995	1980	1965
HEALTH CARE			
ACCESS TO SAFE WATER	76%		
ACCESS TO SANITATION	63%		
MEASLES IMMUNIZATION	77%		
RATE OF PHYSICIANS	0.9	n/a	0.4 (60)
RATE OF HOSPITAL BEDS	1.4	1.6	2.8 (60)
HEALTH INDICATORS			
PREGNANT WOMEN WITH ANEMIA	24		
LOW-BIRTH-WEIGHT BABIES	9		
CHILD MALNUTRITION	8		
SMOKING PREVALENCE M/F	35/19		
TUBERCULOSIS INCIDENCE RATE	167		
AIDS/HIV CASES	6,541	4,453 (93)	
TOTAL DEATHS	163,692 (91)		

	1995	**1980**	**1965**
EDUCATION			
SCHOOL AGE IN SCHOOL			
PRIMARY	114%	124%	88%
SECONDARY	67%	41%	17%
HIGHER	17%	9%	2.40%
FEMALES IN SCHOOL			
PRIMARY	114%	124%	90%
SECONDARY	n/a	41%	16%
ADULT ILLITERACY M/F	9/9%	13.6/16.1% (81)	25.2/28.9%
COMMUNICATIONS			
RATE OF NEWSPAPERS	63	53	52
RATE OF RADIOS	177	124	172
RATE OF TELEVISIONS	118	85	20

Source: CIA, *The World Factbook, 1997;* ILO, *World Labour Report, 1997;* UN, *Demographic Yearbook, 1997;* UN, *Statistical Yearbook, 1996;* World Bank, *World Development Indicators, 1998.*

COMOROS

The Comoros are a group of islands located in the Indian Ocean northeast of southern Africa. The Comoros, with a total area of 839 square miles (2,170 square kilometers) are located on the northern extension of the Mozambique Channel, east of the African coast and northwest of Madagascar. Comoros, which gained independence from France in July 1975, claims sovereignty over Mayotte, an island to the southeast that continues to be administered by France. The Comoros have few natural resources, and most of the population is engaged in subsistence agriculture. In 1995, the annual per capita gross domestic product (GDP) was $700, among the lowest in the world. Between 1966 and 1995, the population of the Comoros increased from 183,133 to 569,237. The country is continuing to grow at a rapid annual rate of 3.6 percent. In 1995, the country's life expectancy at birth was 58.7 years. Although the Comoros education system is limited by global standards, access to education has significantly improved. By 1980, nearly 75 percent of all children were attending primary schools.

	1995	1980	1965
GEOGRAPHY			
AREA (square miles/kilometers)	839/2,170		
LAND AREA (square miles/kilometers)	839/2,170		
COASTLINE (miles/kilometers)	213/340		
CITIES			
CAPITAL	Moroni	n/a	17,267	n/a
POPULATION			
TOTAL	569,237	385,890	183,133 (66)
DENSITY (per square mile/kilometer)	756/292	531/205	n/a
ANNUAL GROWTH	3.6%	3.1%	2.7%
AGE COHORTS			
0–14	48%	n/a	44%
15–64	49%	n/a	49%
65 AND OVER	3%	n/a	5%
MALE	49%		
FEMALE	51%		
URBAN	31%	23.3	n/a
RURAL	69%	77.70%	n/a
NET MIGRATION RATE	0	n/a	0 (63)

	1995	1980	1965

IDENTITY

ETHNICITY
ANTALOTE	n/a		
CAFRE	n/a		
MAKOA	n/a		

LANGUAGE
ARABIC (official)	n/a		
FRENCH (official)	n/a		
COMORAN	n/a		

RELIGION
SUNNI MUSLIM	86%		
ROMAN CATHOLIC	14%		

VITAL STATISTICS

BIRTHS
BIRTH RATE	45.8	46.4	n/a
INFANT MORTALITY RATE	88.9	88	n/a
LIFE EXPECTANCY AT BIRTH	58.7	50	n/a

MARRIAGES
MARRIAGE RATE	n/a	8.3	n/a
AVERAGE AGE AT MARRIAGE M/F	28.6/22.4		
DIVORCE RATE	n/a	1.3	n/a

DEATHS
DEATH RATE	10.3	15.9	n/a

HOUSEHOLDS

NUMBER	71,995 (91)		
AVERAGE SIZE	6.2 (91)		

TYPE OF HOUSEHOLD
SINGLE	2.7%		
MARRIED	82.6%		
WIDOWED	3.3%		
DIVORCED/SEPARATED	11.4%		

FEMALE HEADED	24.5%		

	1995	1980	1965

ECONOMICS AND LABOR

	1995	1980	1965
GDP PER CAPITA US$	$700		

TRANSPORT

	1995	1980	1965
JOURNEYS (by transport mode)			
AIR PASSENGER TRIPS (thousands)	26.0 (94)		
VEHICLES			
PRIVATE CARS	n/a	1,000 (87)	n/a
COMMERCIAL	n/a	4,000 (87)	n/a

HEALTH AND HEALTH CARE

	1995	1980	1965
HEALTH CARE			
RATE OF PHYSICIANS	n/a	n/a	0.1 (60)
RATE OF HOSPITAL BEDS	n/a	n/a	2.1 (60)
HEALTH INDICATORS			
AIDS/HIV CASES	15	10 (93)	

EDUCATION

	1995	1980	1965
SCHOOL AGE IN SCHOOL			
PRIMARY	n/a	91%	27%
SECONDARY	n/a	23%	3%
FEMALES IN SCHOOL			
PRIMARY	n/a	76%	14%
SECONDARY	n/a	36%	1%
ADULT ILLITERACY M/F	n/a	44/60%	33.9/48.3%

COMMUNICATIONS

	1995	1980	1965
RATE OF NEWSPAPERS	n/a	n/a	n/a
RATE OF RADIOS	129	120	n/a
RATE OF TELEVISIONS	0	0	0

Source: CIA, *The World Factbook, 1997;* ILO, *World Labour Report, 1997;* UN, *Demographic Yearbook, 1997;* UN, *Statistical Yearbook, 1996;* World Bank, *World Development Indicators, 1998.*

CONGO, DEMOCRATIC REPUBLIC OF (ZAIRE)

The second largest country in Africa (after Sudan), the Democratic Republic of Congo (formerly Zaire), is located in the heart of the continent, bordered by no less than nine countries. A collection of various kingdoms and ethnic groups in the precolonial era, the Congo was conquered by the Belgians in the late nineteenth century. In 1960, it received its independence from its colonial master and plunged immediately into a civil war between factions and regions. With the rise to power of Joseph Mobutu (later Mobutu Sese Seko), the country, covering some 905,564 square miles, achieved a certain amount of political stability, but at a high price. One of the most repressive and corrupt of African dictators, Mobutu systematically robbed the country of much of its mineral wealth. In the early 1990s, protests among the nation's 46.5 million persons—up from 12.73 million in 1965—spread from the capital to the eastern reaches of the vast Central African realm. In 1997, rebel leader Laurent Kabila, backed by the armed forces of Rwanda, swept across the country, eventually forcing Mobutu into exile. Kabila revived the original independence name of the country—Mobutu had changed the name of the country to Zaire in 1971—and attempted to establish a less corrupt regime. The international community claimed that Kabila's Rwandan forces had massacred tens of thousands of political and ethnic opponents. But an international commission trying to unearth the truth was forced to leave the country in 1998. During the summer of that year, a new rebellion broke out, this time against Kabila by his former Rwandan backers.

	1995	1980	1965
GEOGRAPHY			
AREA (square miles/kilometers)	905,564/2,345,410		
LAND AREA (square miles/kilometers)	875,521/2,267,600		
COASTLINE (miles/kilometers)	23/37		
CITIES			
CAPITAL	Kinshasa	n/a	2,664,309 (84)	
MAJOR CITIES	Lubumbashi	n/a	564,830	
	Luluabourg	n/a	n/a	506,033 (72)
	Mbuji-Mayi	n/a	486,235	
	Kisangani	n/a	317,581	
POPULATION			
TOTAL	46,498,539	29,671,407 (84)	12,733,590 (57)
DENSITY (per square mile/kilometer)	53/21	33/13	15/6
ANNUAL GROWTH	1.67%	2.9	

	1995	1980	1965
AGE COHORTS			
0–14	48%	n/a	39.4%
15–64	49%	n/a	n/a
65 AND OVER	3%	5.6%[1]	n/a
MALE	49%		
FEMALE	51%		
URBAN	n/a	34.2%	n/a
RURAL	n/a	65.8%	n/a
NET MIGRATION RATE	−14.56		

IDENTITY

ETHNICITY

BANTU (Mongo, Luba, Kongo)	55%
HAMITIC (Mangbetu-Azande)	45%

LANGUAGE

FRENCH	n/a
LINGALA	n/a
KINGWANA	n/a
KIKONGO	n/a
TSHILUBA	n/a

RELIGION

ROMAN CATHOLIC	50%
PROTESTANT	20%
KIMBANGUIST	10%
MUSLIM	10%
OTHER INDIGENOUS	10%

VITAL STATISTICS

BIRTH

	1995	1980	1965
BIRTH RATE	48.1	45.1	n/a
INFANT MORTALITY RATE	108	104	n/a
LIFE EXPECTANCY AT BIRTH	46.7	50	n/a

DEATHS

	1995	1980	1965
DEATH RATE	16.9	15.8	n/a

	1995	1980	1965

ECONOMICS AND LABOR

GDP PER CAPITA US$	$400		

TRANSPORT

	1995	1980	1965
JOURNEYS (by transport mode)	469. (90)		
RAILROAD PASSENGER TRIPS	178. (94)		
(millions of miles/kilometers)			
VEHICLES (thousands)			
CARS	145.1	75.4	42.5
COMMERCIAL VEHICLES	92.8	n/a	32.9

HEALTH AND HEALTH CARE

	1995	1980	1965
RATE OF PHYSICIANS	0.1	n/a	0 (60)
RATE OF HOSPITAL BEDS	1.4	n/a	6.1 (60)
AIDS/HIV CASES	29,434	26,161 (93)	

EDUCATION

	1995	1980	1965
SCHOOL AGE IN SCHOOL			
PRIMARY	72%	80%	86%
SECONDARY	26%	24%	6%
HIGHER	2%	1%	24%
FEMALES IN SCHOOL			
PRIMARY	43%	72% (75)	58%
SECONDARY	30%	8% (75)	2%
ADULT ILLITERACY M/F	13/32%	21.4/55.3% (85)	n/a

	1995	1980	1965
COMMUNICATIONS			
RATE OF NEWSPAPERS	3	2	n/a
RATE OF RADIOS	97	56	3
RATE OF TELEVISIONS	2	0	n/a

FOOTNOTE
1. 1957, 55 and over.

Source: CIA, The World Factbook, 1997; ILO, World Labour Report, 1997; UN, Demographic Yearbook, 1997; UN, Statistical Yearbook, 1996; World Bank, World Development Indicators, 1998.

CONGO, REPUBLIC OF

The Republic of Congo is located in West Africa, northwest of the Democratic Republic of Congo (formerly Zaire). The 132,046-square-mile (342,000-square-kilometer) country borders the Atlantic Ocean on the southwest, Gabon on the west, Cameroon on the northwest, and the Central African Republic on the northeast. In 1992, Congo made the transition from military rule to democracy with national elections. In 1997, however, hostilities broke out between two competing parties backed by militias. Elections were suspended after the conflict escalated into armed bat-tles in Brazzaville, Congo's capital, and in major cities. The vast majority of Congo's productive population is engaged in subsistence agricultural activities. The country has a growing oil industry, which generates a significant share of foreign reserves. Congo's per capita gross domestic product (GDP) is $3,100 per year, higher than other countries in Africa, owing to the substantial revenues earned from oil exploration and extraction and the relatively small population. The country has a population of 2.5 million that was growing at an annual rate of 2.2 percent in 1995.

	1995		**1980**	**1965**
GEOGRAPHY				
AREA (square miles/kilometers)	132,046/342,000			
LAND AREA (square miles/kilometers)	131,853/341,500			
COASTLINE (miles/kilometers)	106/169			
CITIES				
CAPITAL	Brazzaville	n/a	596,200 (84)	n/a
MAJOR CITIES	Pointe-Noire	n/a	298,014	n/a
POPULATION				
TOTAL	2,527,841		1,300,120 (74)	581,600 (61)
DENSITY (per square mile/kilometer)	19/7		10/4	4/2
ANNUAL GROWTH	2.2%		2.6%	1.6%
AGE COHORTS				
0–14	43%		n/a	41%
15–64	53%		n/a	57%
65 AND OVER	4%		n/a	2%
URBAN	59%			
RURAL	41%			
NET MIGRATION RATE	0			

	1995	1980	1965

IDENTITY

ETHNICITY
KONGO	48%		
SANGHA	20%		
TEKE	17%		

LANGUAGE
FRENCH (official)	n/a		
LINGALA	n/a		
KIKONGO	n/a		

RELIGION
CHRISTIAN	50%		
ANIMIST	48%		
MUSLIM	2%		

VITAL STATISTICS

BIRTHS
BIRTH RATE	39.2	44.5	43 (58)
INFANT MORTALITY RATE	91.7	180	104 (58)
LIFE EXPECTANCY AT BIRTH	45.8	46.5	38.9 (58)

DEATHS
DEATH RATE	17.4	18.6	20 (58)

HOUSEHOLDS

NUMBER	n/a	n/a	13,428 (58)
AVERAGE SIZE	n/a	n/a	4 (58)

ECONOMICS AND LABOR

GDP PER CAPITA US$	$3,100

LABOR FORCE M/F
AGRICULTURE	58/81%
INDUSTRY	20/5%
SERVICES	23/14%

	1995	1980	1965

TRANSPORT

JOURNEYS (by transport mode)
RAILROAD PASSENGER TRIPS (millions of miles/kilometers)	272/435 (91)		
AIR PASSENGER TRIPS (thousands)	232 (94)		

VEHICLES
PRIVATE CARS	26,000		
COMMERCIAL	20,100		

HEALTH AND HEALTH CARE

HEALTH CARE
MEASLES IMMUNIZATION	41		
RATE OF PHYSICIANS	0.3	n/a	0.1 (60)
RATE OF HOSPITAL BEDS	3.3	n/a	4.9 (60)

HEALTH INDICATORS
PREGNANT WOMEN WITH ANEMIA	76		
LOW-BIRTH-WEIGHT BABIES	15		
CHILD MALNUTRITION	34		
TUBERCULOSIS INCIDENCE RATE	3.33		
AIDS/HIV CASES	7,773		

EDUCATION

SCHOOL AGE IN SCHOOL
PRIMARY	114%	n/a	123%
SECONDARY	53%	n/a	10%
HIGHER	n/a	n/a	1.20%

FEMALES IN SCHOOL
PRIMARY	110%	n/a	100%
SECONDARY	41%	n/a	5%

ADULT ILLITERACY M/F   17/33%

	1995	1980	1965
COMMUNICATIONS			
RATE OF NEWSPAPERS	8	n/a	0.5 (63)
RATE OF RADIOS	115	6,473	n/a
RATE OF TELEVISIONS	7	n/a	0.9

Source: CIA, The World Factbook, 1997; ILO, World Labour Report, 1997; UN, Demographic Yearbook, 1997; UN, Statistical Yearbook, 1996; World Bank, World Development Indicators, 1998.

COSTA RICA

Costa Rica is located in Central America, bordering the Caribbean Sea on the east and the Pacific Ocean on the southwest. Nicaragua borders the 19,730-square-mile (51,100-square-kilometer) country on the north, and Panama borders on the southeast. Under the constitution of 1949, Costa Rica has a democratic government. The country has a national guard and police force but no standard army. Costa Rica has a vibrant economy that produces a significantly higher standard of living than any country in Central America and a social welfare system that has produced higher levels of economic equality than other countries in the region. Still, 43.8 percent of the population remains in poverty. Between 1963 and 1995, Costa Rica's population increased nearly threefold from just over 1.3 million to nearly 3.5 million. Though the population continues to expand at a rapid annual rate of 2.1 percent, growth is almost half the rate of the early 1960s. Due in part to the universal availability of quality health care, Costa Rica has a comparatively high life expectancy at birth of 75.7 years and a low infant mortality rate of 13 deaths per 1,000 live births.

	1995		1980	1965
GEOGRAPHY				
AREA (square miles/kilometers)	19,730/51,100			
LAND AREA (square miles/kilometers)	19,560/50,660			
COASTLINE (miles/kilometers)	806/1,290			
CITIES				
CAPITAL	San Jose	n/a	315,909 (94)	n/a
MAJOR CITIES	Alajuela	n/a	170,080	n/a
	Cartago	n/a	117,004	n/a
POPULATION				
TOTAL	3,463,083 (93)		2,416,809 (84)	1,336,274
DENSITY (per square mile/kilometer)	175/68		122/47	68/26
ANNUAL GROWTH	2.1%		n/a	4.1%
AGE COHORTS				
0–14	35%		n/a	48%
15–64	61%		n/a	49%
65 AND OVER	4%		n/a	3%
MALE	50%			
FEMALE	50%			

	1995	1980	1965
URBAN	50%	43.8%	n/a
RURAL	50%	56.2%	n/a
NET MIGRATION RATE	0.9	n/a	0

IDENTITY

ETHNICITY
WHITE AND MESTIZO	96%		
BLACK	2%		
INDIAN	1%		

LANGUAGE
SPANISH	n/a		
ENGLISH	n/a		

RELIGION
ROMAN CATHOLIC	95%		
PROTESTANT	5%		

VITAL STATISTICS

BIRTHS
BIRTH RATE	23.8	32.7 (84)	n/a
URBAN BIRTH RATE	25.2	32.7 (84)	n/a
RURAL BIRTH RATE	30.7	32.7 (84)	n/a
INFANT MORTALITY RATE	13		
LIFE EXPECTANCY AT BIRTH	75.7	68.4 (84)	63.4 (63)

MARRIAGES
MARRIAGE RATE	6.5	8.5 (84)	6 (63)
DIVORCE RATE	1.1	1 (84)	0.1 (63)

DEATHS
DEATH RATE	4.1	4.5 (84)	9

ECONOMICS AND LABOR

GDP PER CAPITA US$ $5,400

LABOR FORCE M/F (thousands)	801.2/336.4 (94)
AGRICULTURE	226.4/17.2
MINING	2.1/0.0
MANUFACTURING	131.6/71.9
UTILITIES	14.7/2.2

	1995	**1980**	**1965**
CONSTRUCTION	73.1/1.4		
TRADE/FOOD/TOURISM	126.1/83.6		
TRANSPORT/COMMUNICATIONS	51.3/7.1		
FINANCE/INSURANCE/REAL ESTATE	37.7/12.9		
SOCIAL AND PERSONAL SERVICES	130.8/137.2		
UNEMPLOYMENT (official)	4.2% (94)		
UNION DENSITY	13.1%		
POVERTY			
UNDER $1/DAY	18.9% (89)		
UNDER $2/DAY	43.8% (89)		

TRANSPORT

	1995	**1980**	**1965**
JOURNEYS (by transport mode)			
RAILROAD PASSENGER TRIPS	483/773 (94)		
(millions of miles/kilometers)			
VEHICLES			
PRIVATE CARS	238,500	88,100	22,700
COMMERCIAL	127,100	65,900	12,100

HEALTH AND HEALTH CARE

	1995	**1980**	**1965**
HEALTH CARE			
ACCESS TO SANITATION	94%		
RATE OF PHYSICIANS	0.9	n/a	0.4 (60)
RATE OF HOSPITAL BEDS	2.5	3.3	4.5
HEALTH INDICATORS			
PREGNANT WOMEN WITH ANEMIA	28		
LOW-BIRTH-WEIGHT BABIES	7		
CHILD MALNUTRITION	2		
SMOKING PREVALENCE M/F	35/20		
TUBERCULOSIS INCIDENCE RATE	15		
AIDS/HIV CASES	922	586 (93)	
TOTAL DEATHS	12,253		

EDUCATION

	1995	**1980**	**1965**
SCHOOL AGE IN SCHOOL			
PRIMARY	107%	105%	110%
SECONDARY	59%	48%	31%
HIGHER	32%	21%	4.90%

	1995	**1980**	**1965**
FEMALES IN SCHOOL			
PRIMARY	105%	103%	106%
SECONDARY	52%	54%	31%
ADULT ILLITERACY M/F	5/5%	6.0/6.8% (85)	11.4/11.8% (73)

COMMUNICATIONS

RATE OF NEWSPAPERS	101	110	77
RATE OF RADIOS	258	83	97
RATE OF TELEVISIONS	142	68	37

Source: CIA, *The World Factbook, 1997;* ILO, *World Labour Report, 1997;* UN, *Demographic Yearbook, 1997;* UN, *Statistical Yearbook, 1996;* World Bank, *World Development Indicators, 1998.*

CÔTE D'IVOIRE

Côte d'Ivoire is located in West Africa on the Gulf of Guinea, a part of the Atlantic Ocean. Ghana borders the 124,502-square-mile (322,460-square-kilometer) country on the east, Burkino Faso on the northeast and Mali on the northwest, and Guinea and Liberia on the west. The country gained independence from France in August 1960. Felix Houphouet-Boigny served as the country's president from November 1960 to his death in December 1993, a period under which Côte d'Ivoire's economy prospered relative to its neighbors in West Africa. Much of the economic growth is attributed to the export of coffee, cocoa, and other agricultural commodities, primarily to France and other Western European markets.

During the 1990s, however, the country's economy has been subject to downward fluctuations in international market prices for its agricultural exports. Côte d'Ivoire's relative prosperity has not significantly alleviated the poverty among most of the country's population. In 1995, nearly 55 percent of the country's population was subsisting on the equivalent of less than $2 a day. Due to the growth in fertility and the growing access to medicine and clean water between 1965 and 1995, the country's population more than quadrupled to 14,762,445. But by 1995, the country's average life expectancy of 46.7 years continued to remain low.

	1995	1980	1965
GEOGRAPHY			
AREA (square miles/kilometers)	124,502/322,460		
LAND AREA (square miles/kilometers)	122,780/318,000		
COASTLINE (miles/kilometers)	199/515		
CITIES			
CAPITAL	Yamoussoukro	106,786 (88)	
MAJOR CITIES	Abidjan	1,929,079	
	Bouaké	329,850	
	Daloa	121,842	
	Korhogo	109,445	
POPULATION			
TOTAL	14,762,445	6,709,600 (75)	3,300,000
DENSITY (per square mile/kilometer)	114/44	78/30	27/10
ANNUAL GROWTH	2.9%	3.7%	3.0%
AGE COHORTS			
0–14	48%	n/a	43%
15–64[1]	50%	n/a	53%
65 AND OVER[2]	2%	n/a	3.6%

	1995	1980	1965
MALE	51%		
FEMALE	49%		
URBAN	44%	42.5% (83)	n/a
RURAL	56%	57.5% (83)	n/a
NET MIGRATION RATE	2.4		

IDENTITY

ETHNICITY
BAOULE	23%
BETE	18%
SENOUFOU	15%

LANGUAGE
FRENCH (official)	n/a
DIOULA	n/a

RELIGION
MUSLIM	60%
ANIMIST	25%
CHRISTIAN	12%

VITAL STATISTICS

BIRTHS
	1995	1980	1965
BIRTH RATE	42.5	45.6	56.1
INFANT MORTALITY RATE	91.7	138	
LIFE EXPECTANCY AT BIRTH	46.7	50.5	

MARRIAGES
AVERAGE AGE AT MARRIAGE M/F	27.6/19.8

DEATHS
	1995	1980	1965
DEATH RATE	15.7	15.6	33.3

HOUSEHOLDS

NUMBER	1,798,799 (88)
AVERAGE SIZE	66 (88)

	1995	1980	1965

ECONOMICS AND LABOR

GDP PER CAPITA US$	$1,500		
LABOR FORCE (thousands)	385.0 (90)		
AGRICULTURE	53.3		
MANUFACTURING	60		
CONSTRUCTION	17.4		
TRADE/FOOD/TOURISM	25.9		
TRANSPORT/COMMUNICATIONS	53.5		
SOCIAL AND PERSONAL SERVICES	174.9		
UNEMPLOYED	140,300		
UNION DENSITY	13%		
POVERTY			
UNDER $1/DAY	17.7% (88)		
UNDER $2/DAY	54.8% (88)		

TRANSPORT

JOURNEYS (by transport mode)			
RAILROAD PASSENGER TRIPS	n/a	361/578 (87)	n/a
(millions of miles/kilometers)			
AIR PASSENGER TRIPS (thousands)	157 (94)		
VEHICLES			
PRIVATE CARS	155,300	146,100	32,000
COMMERCIAL	90,300	70,600	23,200

HEALTH AND HEALTH CARE

HEALTH CARE			
ACCESS TO SAFE WATER	72%		
ACCESS TO SANITATION	54%		
MEASLES IMMUNIZATION	57%		
RATE OF PHYSICIANS	0.1	n/a	0 (60)
RATE OF HOSPITAL BEDS	0.8	n/a	1.7 (60)
HEALTH INDICATORS			
LOW-BIRTH-WEIGHT BABIES	14%		
CHILD MALNUTRITION	24		
TUBERCULOSIS INCIDENCE RATE	1.96		
AIDS/HIV CASES	25,236	18,670 (93)	

	1995	1980	1965
EDUCATION			
SCHOOL AGE IN SCHOOL			
PRIMARY	69%	75%	60%
SECONDARY	23%	19%	6%
HIGHER	4%	3%	0.40%
FEMALES IN SCHOOL			
PRIMARY	67%	60%	60%
SECONDARY	15%	13%	2%
ADULT ILLITERACY M/F	50/70%	46.9/68.9%	n/a
COMMUNICATIONS			
RATE OF NEWSPAPERS	7	10	3
RATE OF RADIOS	143	122	18
RATE OF TELEVISIONS	60	38	0.5

FOOTNOTES
1. Ages 15–59.
2. Ages 60 and over.

Source: CIA, The World Factbook, 1997; ILO, World Labour Report, 1997; UN, Demographic Yearbook, 1997; UN, Statistical Yearbook, 1996; World Bank, World Development Indicators, 1998.

CROATIA

Croatia is located in southeastern Europe on the Adriatic Sea. The 21,829-square-mile (56,538-square-kilometer) country is located in the southwestern region of the former Yugoslavia on the western border of Bosnia and Herzegovina. Croatia borders Serbia on the northeast and Hungary and Slovenia on the north. The country achieved formal independence in June 1991 amid the breakup of Yugoslavia. Croatia has a developed industrial economy; however, the continued instability in the region has hindered economic stability and renewed growth. In 1995, Croatia's population of 5 million was growing at the slow annual rate of 0.6 percent, due in part to a low birth rate. In the same year, the country had a relatively high life expectancy at birth of 72.8 years and a low infant mortality rate of 10.2 infant deaths per 1,000 residents. Croatians are the country's dominant ethnic majority (78 percent), although there is a sizable Serbian minority (12 percent).

1995[1]

GEOGRAPHY

AREA (square miles/kilometers)	21,829/56,538	
LAND AREA (square miles/kilometers)	21,780/56,410	
COASTLINE (miles/kilometers)	3,619/5,790	
CITIES		
CAPITAL	Zagreb	867,717 (91)
MAJOR CITIES	Split	200,459
	Rijeka	167,964
	Osijek	129,792

POPULATION

TOTAL	5,004,112
DENSITY (per square mile/kilometer)	132/51
ANNUAL GROWTH	0.6%
AGE COHORTS	
0–14	18%
15–64	69%
65 AND OVER	13%
MALE	48%
FEMALE	52%

	1995[1]
URBAN	64%
RURAL	36%
NET MIGRATION RATE	7.3

IDENTITY

ETHNICITY

CROAT	78%
SERB	12%
MUSLIM	1%

LANGUAGE

SERBO-CROATIAN	96%

RELIGION

ROMAN CATHOLIC	77%
EASTERN ORTHODOX	11%
MUSLIM	1%
OTHER	11%

VITAL STATISTICS

BIRTHS

BIRTH RATE	9.8
URBAN BIRTH RATE	12.2 (91)
RURAL BIRTH RATE	9.2 (91)
INFANT MORTALITY RATE	10.2
LIFE EXPECTANCY AT BIRTH	72.8

MARRIAGES

MARRIAGE RATE	4.8
AVERAGE AGE AT MARRIAGE M/F	28/23.8
DIVORCE RATE	1

DEATHS

DEATH RATE	11.3

ECONOMICS AND LABOR

GDP PER CAPITA US$	$4,300
LABOR FORCE M/F (thousands)	601.6/506.8 (93)
AGRICULTURE	42.9/14.6
MINING	5.8/1.1

	1995[1]
MANUFACTURING	214.2/156.4
UTILITIES	21.9/4.9
CONSTRUCTION	58.3/8.7
TRADE/FOOD/TOURISM	73.6/101.2
TRANSPORT/COMMUNICATIONS	74.8/23.7
FINANCE/INSURANCE/REAL ESTATE	16.2/24.7
SOCIAL AND PERSONAL SERVICES	93.9/171.5
UNEMPLOYMENT (official)	17% (93)

TRANSPORT

JOURNEYS (by transport mode)	
RAILROAD PASSENGER TRIPS	601/962 (94)
(millions of miles/kilometers)	
AIR PASSENGER TRIPS (thousands)	624 (94)
VEHICLES	
PRIVATE CARS	698,400 (94)
COMMERCIAL	68,500 (94)

HEALTH AND HEALTH CARE

HEALTH CARE	
ACCESS TO SAFE WATER	96%
ACCESS TO SANITATION	68%
MEASLES IMMUNIZATION	90%
RATE OF PHYSICIANS	2
RATE OF HOSPITAL BEDS	5.9
HEALTH INDICATORS	
LOW-BIRTH-WEIGHT BABIES	8%
SMOKING PREVALENCE M/F	37/38%
TUBERCULOSIS INCIDENCE RATE	0.65
AIDS/HIV CASES	92
TOTAL DEATHS	49,482 (94)

EDUCATION

SCHOOL AGE IN SCHOOL	
PRIMARY	86%
SECONDARY	82%
HIGHER	28%

1995[1]

FEMALES IN SCHOOL

PRIMARY	85%
SECONDARY	65%

COMMUNICATIONS

RATE OF NEWSPAPERS	532
RATE OF RADIOS	301
RATE OF TELEVISIONS	338

FOOTNOTE

1. Part of Yugoslavia; no data available for 1980 and 1965.

Source: CIA, *The World Factbook, 1997;* ILO, *World Labour Report, 1997;* UN, *Demographic Yearbook, 1997;* UN, *Statistical Yearbook, 1996;* World Bank, *World Development Indicators, 1998.*

CUBA

Cuba is located on a large island 90 miles south of the U.S. State of Florida. Cuba borders the Caribbean Sea on the south, the Gulf of Mexico on the northwest, and the Atlantic Ocean on the east. The 42,803-square-mile (110,860-square-kilometer) island country is the largest in the Caribbean. Since the July 1959 Cuban Revolution, the country has nationalized the economy and has instituted programs to foster economic equality, including universal access to health care, education, and housing. The economic programs have contributed to the improvement of the quality of life of the majority of the population. In the early 1990s, however, due to the continuation of a 40-year U.S. embargo and the sudden suspension of Soviet economic assistance, Cuba has endured a period of severe economic retrenchment. The government responded by instituting "special programs" that included some market reforms that did not interfere with the strong system of social protection. By the late 1990s, the country was beginning to emerge from the economic hardships earlier in the decade. The country has a high average life expectancy at birth of 75.1 years and a low infant mortality of 9.4 infant deaths per 1,000 live births. The strong education system trains many Cubans for professional careers. The country's literacy rate is about the same as that of the United States.

Ethnicity

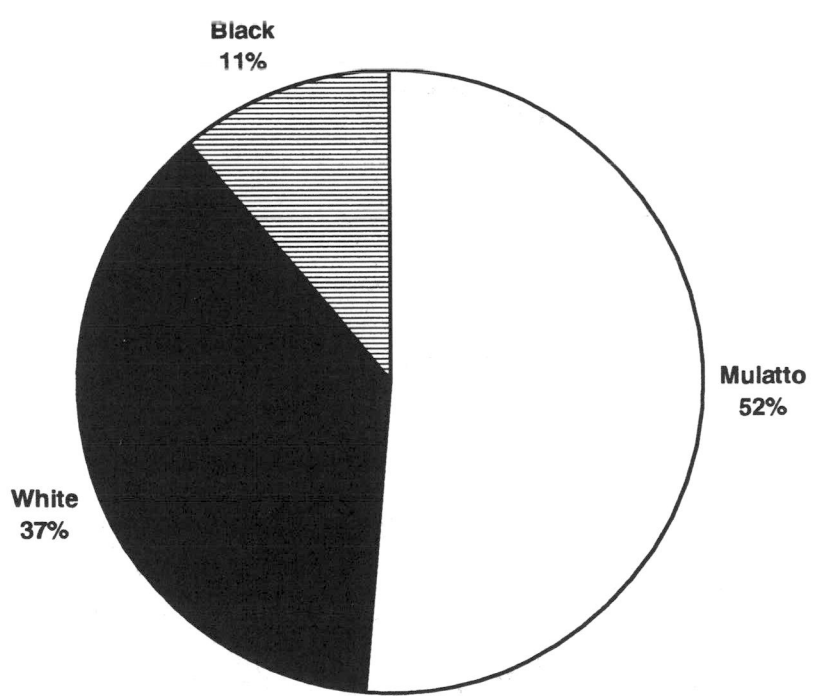

Though whites outnumber blacks in Cuba by a ratio of more than three to one, mulattos, persons of mixed European and African heritage, make up more than 50 percent of the country's population. In the years following the 1959 Cuban Revolution, social reforms significantly improved the socioeconomic status of both blacks and mulattos.

Infant Mortality Rate

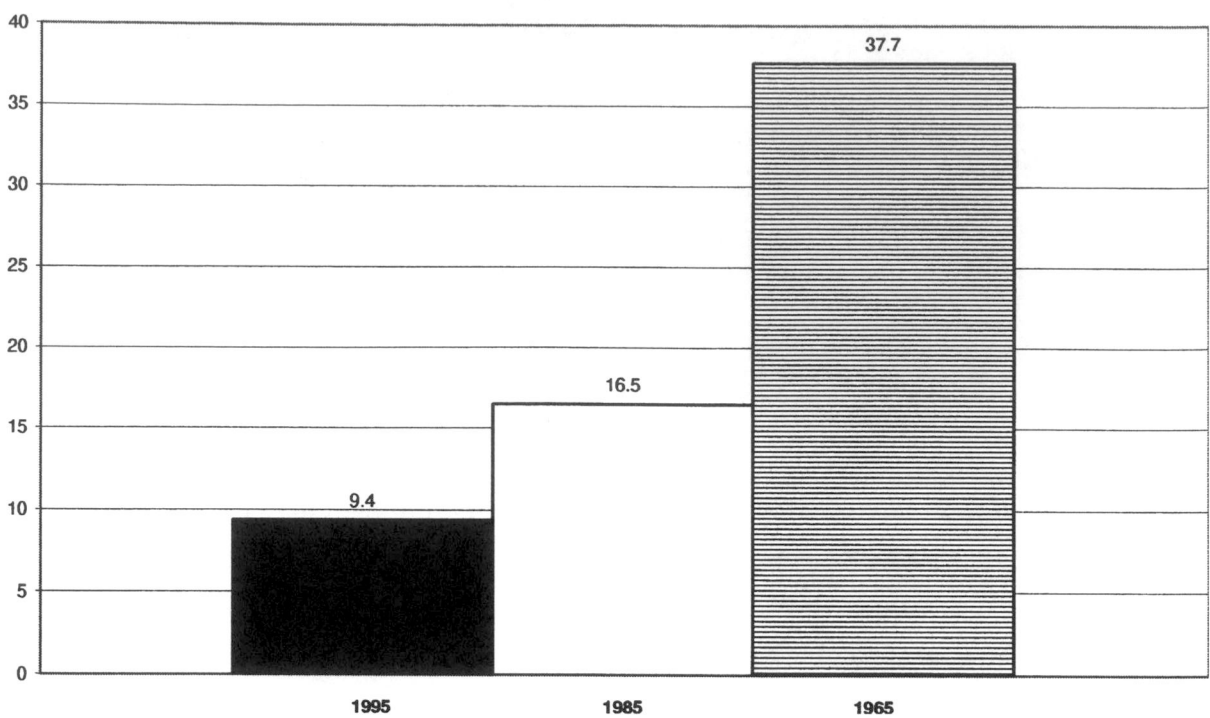

Health care has been another major priority of the Cuban government in recent decades. Its emphasis on rural health care has done much to create dramatically lower rates of infant mortality.

CHRONOLOGY

1959   Revolution. Fidel Castro takes power in Cuba.
1961   The United States severs ties with Cuba; U.S.-sponsored invasion of right-wing exiles at the Bay of Pigs ends in defeat.
1962   The United States announces economic boycott of Cuba; Soviet efforts to place nuclear missiles on island blocked by United States.
1965   Refugees to United States pass 300,000 in number.
1967   Ernesto "Che" Guevara, popular revolutionary leader of Cuba, is killed in Bolivia.
1975   Castro sends troops to defend Angolan government.
1976   Right-wing Cuban exiles blow up Cuban jetliner in Barbados.
1988   Cuba withdraws troops from Africa after signing agreement with United States and South Africa.
1991   Collapse of Soviet Union leads to cutoff in aid and collapse in economy.
1997   Helms-Burton law reenforces economic boycott and angers U.S.'s European trading partners.
1998   Pope John Paul II visits islands and advocates closer ties between United States and Cuba.

	1995	1980	1965

GEOGRAPHY

AREA (square miles/kilometers)   42,803/110,860
LAND AREA (square miles/kilometers)   42,803/110,860
COASTLINE (miles/kilometers)   2,334/3,735

CITIES

CAPITAL	Havana	2,175,888 (93)		
MAJOR CITIES	Santiago de Cuba	430,494		
	Camagüey	294,332		
	Holguín	242,085		
	Guantánamo	207,796		

POPULATION

	1995	1980	1965
TOTAL	10,951,334	9,723,605 (81)	7,630,700
DENSITY (per square mile/kilometer)	259/100	236/91	178/69
ANNUAL GROWTH	n/a	0.7%	n/a

AGE COHORTS

	1995	1980	1965
0–14	22%	n/a	37%
15–64	68%	n/a	59%
65 AND OVER	10%	n/a	4%

	1995
MALE	51%
FEMALE	49%

	1995	1980	1965
URBAN	76%	68.40%	n/a
RURAL	24%	31.60%	n/a

	1995	1980	1965
NET MIGRATION RATE	−1.5	n/a	2.3

IDENTITY

ETHNICITY

	1995
MULATTO	51%
WHITE	37%
BLACK	11%

LANGUAGE

	1995
SPANISH	n/a

	1995	1980	1965
RELIGION			
ROMAN CATHOLIC	85%		
SANTERIA	n/a		
PROTESTANT	n/a		

VITAL STATISTICS

	1995	1980	1965
BIRTHS			
BIRTH RATE	13.4	18 (85)	34–36
URBAN BIRTH RATE	15.5 (91)		
RURAL BIRTH RATE	18.1 (91)		
INFANT MORTALITY RATE	9.4	16.5 (85)	37.7
ABORTION RATE	843.9 (94)		
LIFE EXPECTANCY AT BIRTH	75.1	74 (85)	n/a
MARRIAGES			
MARRIAGE RATE	17.7	7.9 (85)	8.8
DIVORCE RATE	6	2.9 (85)	1.2
DEATHS			
DEATH RATE	7.4	6.4 (85)	9

ECONOMICS AND LABOR

	1995
GDP PER CAPITA US$	$1,300
LABOR FORCE M/F (thousands)	2,135.6/1,309.8 (88)
AGRICULTURE	519.4/142.7
MINING	29.9/5.3
MANUFACTURING	452.2/230.9
UTILITIES	29.2/9.7
CONSTRUCTION	280.1/42.5
TRADE/FOOD/TOURISM	223.3/213.2
TRANSPORT/COMMUNICATIONS	187.4/54.8
FINANCE/INSURANCE/REAL ESTATE	33.5/29.6
SOCIAL AND PERSONAL SERVICES	380.6/581.1
UNION DENSITY	70.2%

TRANSPORT

	1995
JOURNEYS (by transport mode)	
RAILROAD PASSENGER TRIPS	1,807/2,891 (89)
(millions of miles/kilometers)	
AIR PASSENGER TRIPS (thousands)	731.0 (94)

	1995	**1980**	**1965**
VEHICLES			
PRIVATE CARS	241,300	159,400 (88)	162,000
COMMERCIAL	208,400	132,600	103,700

HEALTH AND HEALTH CARE

HEALTH CARE			
ACCESS TO SAFE WATER	93%		
ACCESS TO SANITATION	66%		
MEASLES IMMUNIZATION	100%		
RATE OF PHYSICIANS	3.6	1.4	1 (60)
RATE OF HOSPITAL BEDS	5.4	n/a	4.5 (60)
HEALTH INDICATORS			
PREGNANT WOMEN WITH ANEMIA	47%		
LOW-BIRTH-WEIGHT BABIES	8%		
CHILD MALNUTRITION	8%		
SMOKING PREVALENCE M/F	39/25		
TUBERCULOSIS INCIDENCE RATE	0.2		
AIDS/HIV CASES	440	261 (93)	
TOTAL DEATHS	78,504 (93)		

EDUCATION

SCHOOL AGE IN SCHOOL			
PRIMARY	105%	106%	117%
SECONDARY	80%	81%	23%
HIGHER	14%	17%	3.3%
FEMALES IN SCHOOL			
PRIMARY	103%	102%	116%
SECONDARY	88%	83%	21%
ADULT ILLITERACY M/F	5/4%		

COMMUNICATIONS

RATE OF NEWSPAPERS	122	108	88 (61)
RATE OF RADIOS	346	300	176
RATE OF TELEVISIONS	170	131	72

Source: CIA, *The World Factbook, 1997;* ILO, *World Labour Report, 1997;* UN, *Demographic Yearbook, 1997;* UN, *Statistical Yearbook, 1996;* World Bank, *World Development Indicators, 1998.*

CYPRUS

Cyprus is an island country located in the Mediterranean Sea, south of Turkey. The 3,571-square-mile (9,250-square-kilometer) country gained independence from the United Kingdom in August 1960. Since 1974, however, the country has been divided between the Greek majority (78 percent) and Turkish minority (18 percent). The Greeks control about 59 percent of the island, and the Turks control about 37 percent. Although the country is formally constituted as a republic, in 1975 the Turkish Cypriots, with the support of Turkish troops, established an autonomous political entity in the north nominally known as the "Turkish Republic." The country's diversified economy produces agricultural goods and clothing goods primarily for export to Western European and Middle Eastern markets. In 1995, Cyprus's population of 744,609 was growing at an annual rate of 1.1 percent. The country has a high average life expectancy at birth and a low infant mortality rate.

	1995¹	1980¹	1965
GEOGRAPHY			
AREA (square miles/kilometers)	3,571/9,250		
LAND AREA (square miles/kilometers)	3,568/9,240		
COASTLINE	405/648		
CITIES			
CAPITAL	Nicosia	47,036 (92)	
MAJOR CITIES	Limassol	87,136 (92)	
POPULATION			
TOTAL	744,609	612,851 (76)	577,615 (60)
DENSITY (per square mile/kilometer)	207/80	186/72	168/65
ANNUAL GROWTH	1.1%	1.2%	1.0%
AGE COHORTS			
0–14	25%	n/a	37%
15–64	64%	n/a	57%
65 AND OVER	11%	n/a	6%
MALE	50%		
FEMALE	50%		
URBAN	54%		
RURAL	46%		
NET MIGRATION RATE	3.4	n/a	−0.2

	1995[1]	1980[1]	1965

IDENTITY

ETHNICITY
| GREEK | 78% | | |
| TURKISH | 18% | | |

LANGUAGE
GREEK	n/a		
TURKISH	n/a		
ENGLISH	n/a		

RELIGION
GREEK ORTHODOX	78%		
MUSLIM	18%		
OTHER CHRISTIAN	4%		

VITAL STATISTICS

BIRTHS
BIRTH RATE	15.4	20.7	n/a
INFANT MORTALITY RATE	8.6	17	n/a
LIFE EXPECTANCY AT BIRTH	76.3	74.6	n/a

MARRIAGES
MARRIAGE RATE	8.4	6.3	n/a
AVERAGE AGE AT MARRIAGE M/F	27/23.1	n/a	n/a
DIVORCE RATE	0.7	0.4	n/a

DEATHS
| DEATH RATE | 7.7 | 8.5 | n/a |

HOUSEHOLDS

NUMBER
	185,459 (92)	n/a	145,709 (60)
URBAN	125,484		
RURAL	59,933		

AVERAGE SIZE
	3.2 (95)	n/a	4 (60)
URBAN	3.2		
RURAL	3.2		

TYPE OF HOUSEHOLD
| SINGLE | 4.9% | | |
| MARRIED | 81.2% | | |

	1995[1]	1980[1]	1965
WIDOWED	10.8%		
DIVORCED/SEPARATED	3%		
FEMALE HEADED	14%		

ECONOMICS AND LABOR

GDP PER CAPITA US$	$11,000		
LABOR FORCE M/F (thousands)	163.8/106.6 (93)		
AGRICULTURE	19.3/15.7		
MINING	0.7/0.0		
MANUFACTURING	25.0/20.5		
UTILITIES	1.4/0.1		
CONSTRUCTION	21.9/1.4		
TRADE/FOOD/TOURISM	37.3/30.5		
TRANSPORT/COMMUNICATIONS	12.1/4.1		
FINANCE/INSURANCE/REAL ESTATE	10.3/9.1		
SOCIAL AND PERSONAL SERVICES	33.1/24.5		
UNEMPLOYMENT (official)	2.7% (94)		
UNION DENSITY	53.7%		

TRANSPORT

JOURNEYS (by transport mode)			
AIR PASSENGER TRIPS (thousands)	1,234 (94)		
VEHICLES			
PRIVATE CARS	210,000	92,200	30,500
COMMERCIAL	97,100	25,200	11,200

HEALTH AND HEALTH CARE

HEALTH CARE			
RATE OF PHYSICIANS	n/a	n/a	0.7 (60)
RATE OF HOSPITAL BEDS	n/a	n/a	4.5 (60)
HEALTH INDICATORS			
AIDS/HIV CASES	50	38 (93)	
TOTAL DEATHS	4,924 (94)		

	1995[1]	1980[1]	1965
EDUCATION			
SCHOOL AGE IN SCHOOL			
PRIMARY	n/a	n/a	86%
SECONDARY	n/a	n/a	42%
HIGHER	n/a	n/a	0.50%
FEMALES IN SCHOOL			
PRIMARY	n/a	n/a	84%
SECONDARY	n/a	n/a	37%
ADULT ILLITERACY M/F	n/a	4.0/17.0 (76)	n/a
COMMUNICATIONS			
RATE OF NEWSPAPERS	107	127	217
RATE OF RADIOS	296	258	225
RATE OF TELEVISIONS	152	135	24

FOOTNOTE

1. Since 1974, Cyprus has been divided into Greek and Turkish ethnic sectors; statistics for 1980 and 1995 are for both sectors.

Source: CIA, The World Factbook, 1997; ILO, World Labour Report, 1997; UN, Demographic Yearbook, 1997; UN, Statistical Yearbook, 1996; World Bank, World Development Indicators, 1998.

CZECH REPUBLIC

The Czech Republic is a landlocked country located in east central Europe in the western half of the former Czechoslovakia. In 1993, the country formally seceded from Czechoslovakia to form the Czech Republic. In the same year, Slovakia, occupying the eastern region of the country, also declared independence. Germany borders the 30,426-square-mile (78,703-square-kilometer) country on the northwest, Poland on the northeast, Slovakia on the southeast, and Austria on the south. In the early 1990s, Czechoslo-vakia emerged from the Soviet orbit and embraced a pluralist democratic system and instituted market reforms by privatizing large segments of the economy. Even before independence, Czechoslovakia had developed one of the most advanced industrial economies in the Soviet bloc. In 1995, the Czech Republic's population of more than 10.3 million was contracting by an annual rate of 0.3 percent, due in part to a declining birth rate. The country had a high average life expectancy and a low infant mortality rate.

	1995	1980[1]	1965[1]
GEOGRAPHY			
AREA (square miles/kilometers)	30,426/78,703		
LAND AREA (square miles/kilometers)	30,365/78,645		
COASTLINE (miles/kilometers)	landlocked		
CITIES			
CAPITAL	Prague	1,216,568 (94)	
MAJOR CITIES	Brno	390,073	
	Ostrava	326,049	
	Pilsen	172,055	
	Olomouc	105,998	
POPULATION			
TOTAL	10,321,120		
DENSITY (per square mile/kilometer)	339/131		
ANNUAL GROWTH	−0.3		
AGE COHORTS			
0–14	18%		
15–64	68%		
65 AND OVER	14%		
MALE	49%		
FEMALE	51%		

	1995	**1980**¹	**1965**¹
URBAN	65%		
RURAL	35%		
NET MIGRATION RATE	0.2		

IDENTITY

ETHNICITY
CZECH	94%
SLOVAK	3%
POLISH	1%

LANGUAGE
CZECH	n/a
SLOVAK	n/a

RELIGION
ATHEIST	40%
ROMAN CATHOLIC	39%
PROTESTANT	5%

VITAL STATISTICS

BIRTHS
BIRTH RATE	10.4
URBAN BIRTH RATE	11.6 (93)
RURAL BIRTH RATE	12.2 (93)
INFANT MORTALITY RATE	7.4
ABORTION RATE	512.5 (94)
LIFE EXPECTANCY AT BIRTH	73.8

MARRIAGES
MARRIAGE RATE	5.6
AVERAGE AGE AT MARRIAGE M/F	26/23
DIVORCE RATE	2.9

DEATHS
DEATH RATE	10.9 per 1,000

HOUSEHOLDS

NUMBER	4,051,583 (91)
AVERAGE SIZE	2.5 (91)
FEMALE HEADED	25.60%

	1995	1980[1]	1965[1]

ECONOMICS AND LABOR

GDP PER CAPITA US$	$10,200		
LABOR FORCE M/F			
AGRICULTURE	13/9%		
INDUSTRY	54/36%		
SERVICES	33/55%		
UNEMPLOYMENT (official)	3.2% (94)		
UNION DENSITY	36.30%		

TRANSPORT

JOURNEYS (by transport mode)			
RAILROAD PASSENGER TRIPS	5,301/8,481 (94)		
(millions of miles/kilometers)			
AIR PASSENGER TRIPS (thousands)	1,067 (94)		
VEHICLES (thousands)			
PRIVATE CARS	2,917.3 (94)	2,273.0 (90)	
COMMERCIAL	336.2	340.1	

HEALTH AND HEALTH CARE

HEALTH CARE			
MEASLES IMMUNIZATION	96%		
RATE OF PHYSICIANS	2.9		
RATE OF HOSPITAL BEDS	7.4		
HEALTH INDICATORS			
PREGNANT WOMEN WITH ANEMIA	23%		
LOW-BIRTH-WEIGHT BABIES	6%		
CHILD MALNUTRITION	1%		
SMOKING PREVALENCE M/F	43/31%		
TUBERCULOSIS INCIDENCE RATE	0.25		
AIDS/HIV CASES	72	47 (93)	
TOTAL DEATHS	117,913		

	1995	1980[1]	1965[1]

EDUCATION

SCHOOL AGE IN SCHOOL
PRIMARY	96%	92%	98% (70)
SECONDARY	96%	45%	31%
HIGHER	21%	18%	10.4%

FEMALES IN SCHOOL
PRIMARY	95%	91%	98% (70)
SECONDARY	100%	51%	39%
HIGHER	n/a	14.60%	8%

COMMUNICATIONS

RATE OF NEWSPAPERS	583	313	254 (70)
RATE OF RADIOS	631	509	n/a
RATE OF TELEVISIONS	476	385	216 (70)

FOOTNOTE
1. Statistics for 1980 and 1985 are for Czechoslovakia.

Source: CIA, The World Factbook, 1997; ILO, World Labour Report, 1997; UN, Demographic Yearbook, 1997; UN, Statistical Yearbook, 1996; World Bank, World Development Indicators, 1998.

DENMARK

Denmark is located on the Baltic Sea and North Sea in northern Europe. Germany borders the 16,629-square-mile (43,070-square-kilometer) country on the south. Denmark is a member state of the European Union and has a modern industrial economy with one of the highest per capita gross domestic products (GDP) in the world. The country is a major producer of agricultural and industrial products. Nearly 70 percent of all employed workers are members of trade unions.

Denmark also has a comprehensive system of social protection that includes universal access to health care and education. Denmark's population of 5,249,632 in 1995 was growing at a slow annual rate of 0.4 percent owing to a slow birth rate. In 1995, deaths outnumbered births by a ratio approaching 2 to 1. Due in part to the broad social safety net, Denmark has one of the highest average life expectancies in Europe and among the lowest infant mortality rates in the world.

		1995	1980	1965
GEOGRAPHY				
AREA (square miles/kilometers)		16,629/43,070		
LAND AREA (square miles/kilometers)		16,243/42,070		
COASTLINE (miles/kilometers)		2,109/3,379		
CITIES				
CAPITAL	Copenhagen	1,353,333		
MAJOR CITIES	Odense	182,617		
	Ålborg	159,056		
	Århus	27,477		
POPULATION				
TOTAL		5,249,632	5,123,989 (81)	4,767,597
DENSITY (per square mile/kilometer)		313/121	308/119	287/111
ANNUAL GROWTH		0.4%	0%	0.8%
AGE COHORTS				
0–14		17%	n/a	23.8% (64)
15–64		67%	n/a	65% (64)
65 AND OVER		16%	n/a	11% (64)
MALE		49%		
FEMALE		51%		

	1995	1980	1965
URBAN	85%	83.90%	n/a
RURAL	15%	16.10%	n/a
NET MIGRATION RATE	2	n/a	0 (64)

IDENTITY

ETHNICITY

DANISH	n/a		
INUIT	n/a		
FAEROESE	n/a		

LANGUAGE

DANISH	n/a		
INUIT	n/a		

RELIGION

LUTHERAN	91%		

VITAL STATISTICS

BIRTHS

BIRTH RATE	12.2	10.6 (85)	18.4
INFANT MORTALITY RATE	5.3	7.7 (85)	18.7
LIFE EXPECTANCY AT BIRTH	77.3	74.5 (85)	72.5

MARRIAGES

MARRIAGE RATE	6.8	5.8 (85)	8.8
AVERAGE AGE AT MARRIAGE M/F	27.7/25		
DIVORCE RATE	2.5	2.8 (85)	1.4

DEATHS

DEATH RATE	10.4	11.4 (85)	10.3

HOUSEHOLDS

NUMBER	2,274,265 (91)		1,544,370 (60)
AVERAGE SIZE	2.3 (91)		3 (60)
FEMALE HEADED	41.6%		
SINGLE	14.6%		
MARRIED	55.5%		
WIDOWED	13.2%		
DIVORCED/SEPARATED	7.3%		

	1995	1980	1965

ECONOMICS AND LABOR

GDP PER CAPITA US$ $21,700

LABOR FORCE M/F (thousands)   1,383.1/1,200.9 (93)
AGRICULTURE   100.5/31.3
MINING   1.8/0.7
MANUFACTURING   346.6/155.1
UTILITIES   13.9/2.3
CONSTRUCTION   131.9/15.9
TRADE/FOOD/TOURISM   216.5/185.6
TRANSPORT/COMMUNICATIONS   132.5/51.5
FINANCE/INSURANCE/REAL ESTATE   134.6/122.9
SOCIAL AND PERSONAL SERVICES   300.2/632.0

UNEMPLOYMENT (official)   12.2% (94)
UNION DENSITY   68.2%

TRANSPORT

JOURNEYS (by transport mode)
RAILROAD PASSENGER TRIPS   2,873/4,596 (93)
  (millions of miles/kilometers)
AIR PASSENGER TRIPS (thousands)   5,456 (94)

VEHICLES (thousands)

	1995	1980	1965
PRIVATE CARS	1,622.3	1,397.9	743.8
COMMERCIAL	339.7	267.5	236

HEALTH AND HEALTH CARE

HEALTH CARE

	1995	1980	1965
ACCESS TO SAFE WATER	100%		
ACCESS TO SANITATION	100%		
MEASLES IMMUNIZATION	88%		
RATE OF PHYSICIANS	2.9	2.4	1.2 (60)
RATE OF HOSPITAL BEDS	5	n/a	9.3 (60)

HEALTH INDICATORS
LOW-BIRTH-WEIGHT BABIES   5%
SMOKING PREVALENCE M/F   37/37%
TUBERCULOSIS INCIDENCE RATE   0.12

	1995	1980	1965
AIDS/HIV CASES	1,843	1,399 (93)	
TOTAL DEATHS	63,216		

EDUCATION

SCHOOL AGE IN SCHOOL

	1995	1980	1965
PRIMARY	99%	96%	100%
SECONDARY	118%	105%	66%
HIGHER	45%	28%	10.1%

FEMALES IN SCHOOL

	1995	1980	1965
PRIMARY	100%	100%	100%
SECONDARY	102%	101%	67%
HIGHER	n/a	28.5%	7%

COMMUNICATIONS

	1995	1980	1965
RATE OF NEWSPAPERS	332	366	347
RATE OF RADIOS	1,035	927	333
RATE OF TELEVISIONS	538	498	227

Source: CIA, *The World Factbook, 1997;* ILO, *World Labour Report, 1997;* UN, *Demographic Yearbook, 1997;* UN, *Statistical Yearbook, 1996;* World Bank, *World Development Indicators, 1998.*

DJIBOUTI

Djibouti, formerly known as French Somaliland, is located in East Africa in a region known as the Horn of Africa on the Gulf of Aden and the Red Sea. Ethiopia borders the 8,424-square-mile (22,000-square-kilometer) country on the south and west. The country also maintains a border with Somalia on the south and Eritrea on the north. Yemen is located to the northeast across the Bab el Mandeb Strait. The country formally gained independence from France in June 1977. Located strategically in East Africa and the Middle East, Djibouti is a major trans-shipment and trading point. Djibouti is lacking in arable land and natural resources. The per capita gross domestic product (GDP), dependent on foreign assistance, is about $1,200 a year. Because of substantial out-migration, the population of 427,642 in 1995 was growing at a relatively slow rate by African standards. The Somali (60 percent) and the Afar (35 percent) are Djibouti's two leading ethnic groups. The country has a low average life expectancy and a high infant mortality rate.

	1995	1980[1]	1965[1]
GEOGRAPHY			
AREA (square miles/kilometers)	8,424/22,000		
LAND AREA (square miles/kilometers)	8,486/21,980		
COASTLINE (miles/kilometers)	196/314		
CITIES			
CAPITAL	Djibouti	n/a	n/a	62,000 (70)
POPULATION			
TOTAL	427,642		
DENSITY (per square mile/kilometer)	65/25		
ANNUAL GROWTH	1.5%	6.7%	n/a
AGE COHORTS			
0–14	43%	n/a	37%
15–64	55%	n/a	62%
65 AND OVER	2%	n/a	1%
URBAN	83%		
RURAL	17%		
NET MIGRATION RATE	−12.3		

	1995	1980[1]	1965[1]

IDENTITY

ETHNICITY
SOMALI	60%		
AFAR	35%		

LANGUAGE
FRENCH (official)	n/a		
ARABIC (official)	n/a		
SOMALI	n/a		

RELIGION
MUSLIM	94%		
CHRISTIAN	6%		

VITAL STATISTICS

BIRTHS
BIRTH RATE	42.5	n/a	42 (70)
INFANT MORTALITY RATE	114.9		
LIFE EXPECTANCY AT BIRTH	50.2		

DEATHS
DEATH RATE	15.3	n/a	7.6 (70)

ECONOMICS AND LABOR

GDP PER CAPITA US$	$1,200		

TRANSPORT

VEHICLES
PRIVATE CARS	13,000	14,500	3,700
COMMERCIAL	3,000	4,700	1,100

HEALTH AND HEALTH CARE

HEALTH CARE
RATE OF PHYSICIANS	n/a	n/a	0.2 (60)
RATE OF HOSPITAL BEDS	n/a	n/a	8.1 (60)

	1995	1980[1]	1965[1]
HEALTH INDICATORS			
AIDS/HIV CASES	880	453 (93)	

COMMUNICATIONS

	1995	1980	1965
RATE OF RADIOS	81	75	3
RATE OF TELEVISIONS	45	18	11 (70)

FOOTNOTE

1. Under French rule.

Source: CIA, The World Factbook, 1997; ILO, World Labour Report, 1997; UN, Demographic Yearbook, 1997; UN, Statistical Yearbook, 1996; World Bank, World Development Indicators, 1998.

DOMINICA

Dominica is a small island country located in the Windward Island archipelago of the eastern Caribbean Sea. The island borders the Atlantic Ocean on the east. The 290-square-mile (750-square-kilometer) island is located north of the island of Martinique and south of the island of Guadeloupe. Dominica gained independence from the United Kingdom in November 1978. The two leading sectors of Dominica's economy are agriculture and tourism. In 1995, the country's per capita gross domestic product (GDP) of $2,450 was among the lowest in the West Indies. Dominica's population of 82,926 is growing at a slow rate, due in part to the shortage of economic opportunity on the island that leads to out-migration. The country has a large annual net out-migration rate of 9.3 per 1,000 residents. Dominica has a relatively low infant mortality rate and a high average life expectancy. Roman Catholicism and various Protestant denominations are Dominica's leading religions.

	1995	1980	1965
GEOGRAPHY			
AREA (square miles/kilometers)	290/750		
LAND AREA (square miles/kilometers)	290/750		
COASTLINE (miles/kilometers)	93/148		
CITIES			
CAPITAL	Roseau	16,243 (91)	
POPULATION			
TOTAL	82,926	73,795 (81)	59,916 (60)
DENSITY (per square mile/kilometer)	246/95	262/101	236/91
ANNUAL GROWTH	0.4%	0.8%	2.0%
AGE COHORTS			
0–14	28%	n/a	45%
15–64	64%	n/a	49%
65 AND OVER	8%	n/a	6%
MALE	50%		
FEMALE	50%		
NET MIGRATION RATE	−9.3	n/a	0.2

	1995	1980	1965

IDENTITY

ETHNICITY
BLACK	n/a		
CARIB INDIANS	n/a		

LANGUAGE
ENGLISH	n/a		
FRENCH	n/a		
PATOIS	n/a		

RELIGION
ROMAN CATHOLIC	77%		
METHODIST	5%		
PENTECOSTAL	3%		

VITAL STATISTICS

BIRTHS
BIRTH RATE	18.4	21.4 (78)	42.7 (60)
INFANT MORTALITY RATE	18.4	19.6 (78)	53.6 (60)
LIFE EXPECTANCY AT BIRTH	77.4	58 (78)	58 (60)

MARRIAGES
MARRIAGE RATE	3.1	3.2 (78)	3.7 (60)
DIVORCE RATE	0.4		

DEATHS
DEATH RATE	5.3	5.3 (78)	8.9

HOUSEHOLDS

NUMBER	n/a	n/a	14,218 (60)
AVERAGE SIZE	n/a	n/a	4.2

ECONOMICS AND LABOR

GDP PER CAPITA US$	$2,450	

	1995	1980	1965
TRANSPORT			
VEHICLES			
PRIVATE CARS	2,800 (94)		
COMMERCIAL	2,800 (94)		
HEALTH AND HEALTH CARE			
HEALTH CARE			
RATE OF PHYSICIANS	n/a	n/a	0.1 (60)
RATE OF HOSPITAL BEDS	n/a	n/a	4.6 (60)
HEALTH INDICATORS			
AIDS/HIV CASES	31	26 (93)	
EDUCATION			
SCHOOL AGE IN SCHOOL			
PRIMARY	n/a	n/a	162%
SECONDARY	n/a	n/a	18%
ADULT ILLITERACY M/F	n/a	n/a	6.0/5.8% (70)
COMMUNICATIONS			
RATE OF RADIOS	599	419	n/a
RATE OF TELEVISIONS	75	n/a	n/a

Source: CIA, *The World Factbook, 1997;* ILO, *World Labour Report, 1997;* UN, *Demographic Yearbook, 1997;* UN, *Statistical Yearbook, 1996;* World Bank, *World Development Indicators, 1998.*

DOMINICAN REPUBLIC

The Dominican Republic is located in the Caribbean Sea on the eastern two-thirds of the island of Hispaniola. Haiti occupies the western one-third of the island. The Dominican Republic, which covers an area of 18,815 square miles (48,730 square kilometers), borders the Atlantic Ocean on the north and the Caribbean Sea on the south. National elections held in 1996 produced the first significant shift in government leadership in more than two decades. The Dominican Republic's national economy is dominated by the production of sugar, coffee, and other commodities and a small but growing manufacturing sector. In 1995, the Dominican Republic's population of 8,088,881 was growing at an annual rate of 1.7 percent. Almost three-quarters of the country's population are mulatto (mixed European and African racial heritage). Whites compose about 16 percent of the population, and Africans account for 11 percent of the national population. The country's social service and public health system, though better than Haiti's, is not as advanced as other countries' in the region. Thus, although life expectancy is increasing, it is still lower than Cuba, Jamaica, and the smaller island countries to the southeast.

	1995	1980	1965
GEOGRAPHY			
AREA (square miles/kilometers)	18,815/48,730		
LAND AREA (square miles/ kilometers)	18,680/48,380		
COASTLINE (miles/kilometers)	805/1,288		
CITIES			
CAPITAL	Santo Domingo (93)	2,134,977 (93)	
MAJOR CITIES	Santiago de los		
	Cabelleros	650,548	
	San Cristóbal	409,381	
	La Vega	335,140	
	Duarte	277,270	
POPULATION			
TOTAL	8,088,881	5,647,977 (81)	3,047,070 (60)
DENSITY (per square mile/kilometer)	420/162	332/128 (81)	162/63 (60)
ANNUAL GROWTH	1.7%	2.9%	3.6%
AGE COHORTS			
0–14	34%	n/a	47%
15–64	62%	n/a	50%
65 AND OVER	4%	n/a	3%

	1995	1980	1965
MALE	50%		
FEMALE	50%		
URBAN	65%	51.2%	n/a
RURAL	35%	48.8%	n/a
NET MIGRATION RATE	0.5	n/a	0 (63)

IDENTITY

ETHNICITY

MULATTO	73%		
WHITE	16%		
BLACK	11%		

LANGUAGE

SPANISH	n/a		
CREOLE	n/a		

RELIGION

ROMAN CATHOLIC	95%		
PROTESTANT	5%		

VITAL STATISTICS

BIRTHS

BIRTH RATE	23.5	33.1	45 (60)
INFANT MORTALITY RATE	42	75	72.7 (60)
LIFE EXPECTANCY AT BIRTH	69.1	57.9	57.8 (60)

MARRIAGES

MARRIAGE RATE	3.3	5	3.5 (60)
DIVORCE RATE	1.2	1.7	0.3 (60)

DEATHS

DEATH RATE	5.7	8	14 (60)

HOUSEHOLDS

NUMBER	n/a	n/a	513,779 (55)
AVERAGE SIZE	n/a	n/a	4.9 (55)

	1995	1980	1965

ECONOMICS AND LABOR

GDP PER CAPITA US$ — $3,400

LABOR FORCE

	1995	1980	1965
AGRICULTURE M/F	31/9%		
INDUSTRY M/F	32/23%		
SERVICES M/F	38/68%		

UNION DENSITY — 17.30%

POVERTY

	1995	1980	1965
UNDER $1/DAY	19.9 (89)		
UNDER $2/DAY	47.7 (89)		

TRANSPORT

JOURNEYS (by transport mode)

	1995	1980	1965
AIR PASSENGER TRIPS (thousands)	300 (94)		

VEHICLES

	1995	1980	1965
PRIVATE CARS	174,400	94,400	29,200
COMMERCIAL	111,400	46,900	12,300

HEALTH AND HEALTH CARE

HEALTH CARE

	1995	1980	1965
ACCESS TO SAFE WATER	71%		
ACCESS TO SANITATION	78%		
MEASLES IMMUNIZATION	100%		
RATE OF PHYSICIANS	1.1	n/a	0.2 (60)
RATE OF HOSPITAL BEDS	2	n/a	2.5 (60)

HEALTH INDICATORS

	1995	1980	1965
LOW-BIRTH-WEIGHT BABIES	16%		
CHILD MALNUTRITION	6%		
SMOKING PREVALENCE M/F	66/14%		
TUBERCULOSIS INCIDENCE RATE	1.1		
AIDS/HIV CASES	3,160	2,446 (93)	
TOTAL DEATHS	23,717 (92)		

EDUCATION

SCHOOL AGE IN SCHOOL

PRIMARY	103%	118%	91%
SECONDARY	41%	42%	15%
HIGHER	n/a	n/a	1.8%

FEMALES IN SCHOOL

PRIMARY	103%	90%	92%
SECONDARY	57%	n/a	15%

ADULT ILLITERACY M/F	18/18%	22.3/23.2% (85)	33.3/37.6% (60)

COMMUNICATIONS

RATE OF NEWSPAPERS	36	39	27
RATE OF RADIOS	172	158	46
RATE OF TELEVISIONS	90	70	16

Source: CIA, *The World Factbook, 1997*; ILO, *World Labour Report, 1997*; UN, *Demographic Yearbook, 1997*; UN, *Statistical Yearbook, 1996*; World Bank, *World Development Indicators, 1998*.

ECUADOR

Ecuador is located in northwestern South America on the Pacific Ocean. Colombia borders the 109,483-square-mile (283,560-square-kilometer) country on the north and Peru on the east and south. Throughout much of the 1990s, Ecuador has endured a period of political instability. Recent presidents have been deposed amid charges of corruption, incompetence, and even mental illness. Much of the country's recent political difficulties stem in part from declining prices for the country's major commodities, including petroleum, bananas, coffee, cocoa, and fishing products. These problems have intensified declining wages and eroding living conditions, particularly for the country's urban and rural poor. In 1994, nearly two-thirds of Ecuador's national population was subsisting on the equivalent of less than $2 a day. The country's population of nearly 11.5 million was growing at an average annual rate of 2 percent, down from the 1962 average of 3.3 percent. The country's three leading racial groups are mestizo (55 percent), indigenous Indian (25 percent), and black (10 percent). In 1995, average life expectancy at birth was over 71 years.

		1995	1980	1965
GEOGRAPHY				
AREA (square miles/kilometers)		109,483/283,560		
LAND AREA (square miles/kilometers)		106,888/276,840		
COASTLINE (miles/kilometers)		1,398/2,237		
CITIES				
CAPITAL	Quito	1,100,847 (90)	866,472 (82)	n/a
MAJOR CITIES	Guayaquil	1,508,444	1,199,344	n/a
	Cuenca	194,981	n/a	n/a
	Ambato	124,166	100,454	n/a
	Machala	144,197	105,521	n/a
POPULATION				
TOTAL		11,466,291	8,050,630 (82)	4,476,007 (62)
DENSITY (per square mile/kilometer)		104/40	85/33	49/19
ANNUAL GROWTH		2.0%	2.9%	3.3%
AGE COHORTS				
0–14		35%	n/a	45%
15–64		60%	n/a	52%
65 AND OVER		5%	n/a	3%
MALE		50%		
FEMALE		50%		

	1995	1980	1965
URBAN	58%	47.1	n/a
RURAL	42%	52.9%	n/a
NET MIGRATION RATE	0		

IDENTITY

ETHNICITY

MESTIZO	55%		
INDIAN	25%		
BLACK	10%		

LANGUAGE

SPANISH (official)	n/a		
QUECHUA	n/a		

RELIGION

ROMAN CATHOLIC	95%		
PROTESTANT	5%		

VITAL STATISTICS

BIRTHS

BIRTH RATE	25.1	36.8	50 (62)
URBAN BIRTH RATE	19.8 (93)		
RURAL BIRTH RATE	15.1 (93)		
INFANT MORTALITY RATE	49.7	70	93 (62)
LIFE EXPECTANCY AT BIRTH	71.1	60.6	n/a

MARRIAGES

MARRIAGE RATE	6.2	5.9	5.9 (62)
AVERAGE AGE AT MARRIAGE	25.2/22		
DIVORCE RATE	0.7	0.4	0.3 (62)

DEATHS

DEATH RATE	5.5	8.1	15 (62)

HOUSEHOLDS

NUMBER	n/a	n/a	877,300 (62)
AVERAGE SIZE	n/a	n/a	5.1 (62)

	1995	1980	1965

ECONOMICS AND LABOR

GDP PER CAPITA US$	$4,100		
LABOR FORCE M/F (thousands)	1,665.2/1,032.3 (94)		
AGRICULTURE	164.0/24.7		
MINING	15.0/1.2		
MANUFACTURING	268.6/146.2		
UTILITIES	10.9/1.4		
CONSTRUCTION	165.6/6.1		
TRADE/FOOD/TOURISM	411.9/402.7		
TRANSPORT/COMMUNICATIONS	146.9/9.6		
FINANCE/INSURANCE/REAL ESTATE	75.6/36.4		
SOCIAL AND PERSONAL SERVICES	406.8/404.0		
UNEMPLOYMENT (official)	7.1% (94)		
UNION DENSITY	9.8% (94)		
POVERTY			
UNDER $1/DAY	30.4% (94)		
UNDER $2/DAY	65.8% (94)		

TRANSPORT

JOURNEYS (by transport mode)			
RAILROAD PASSENGER TRIPS	17/27 (94)		
(millions of miles/kilometers)			
AIR PASSENGER TRIPS (thousands)	1,126 (94)		
VEHICLES			
PRIVATE CARS	219,800	65,100	14,400
COMMERCIAL	243,400	112,200	17,600

HEALTH AND HEALTH CARE

HEALTH CARE			
ACCESS TO SAFE WATER	70		
ACCESS TO SANITATION	64		
MEASLES IMMUNIZATION	100		
RATE OF PHYSICIANS	1.5	n/a	0.4 (60)
RATE OF HOSPITAL BEDS	1.6	1.9	2 (60)

	1995	1980	1965
HEALTH INDICATORS			
PREGNANT WOMEN WITH ANEMIA	17%		
LOW-BIRTH-WEIGHT BABIES	13%		
CHILD MALNUTRITION	17%		
TUBERCULOSIS INCIDENCE RATE	1.66		
AIDS/HIV CASES	543	357 (93)	
TOTAL DEATHS	52,453 (93)		

EDUCATION

	1995	1980	1965
SCHOOL AGE IN SCHOOL			
PRIMARY	109%	117%	91%
SECONDARY	50%	53%	17%
HIGHER	n/a	n/a	3%
FEMALES IN SCHOOL			
PRIMARY	107%	115%	88%
SECONDARY	47%	48%	15%
ADULT ILLITERACY	12/8%	15.8/23.8% (82)	27.9/36.9% (62)

COMMUNICATIONS

	1995	1980	1965
RATE OF NEWSPAPERS	64	70	47
RATE OF RADIOS	326	305	114
RATE OF TELEVISIONS	88	63	9

Source: CIA, *The World Factbook, 1997*; ILO, *World Labour Report, 1997*; UN, *Demographic Yearbook, 1997*; UN, *Statistical Yearbook, 1996*; World Bank, *World Development Indicators, 1998*.

EGYPT

Egypt is located in northeast Africa on the Mediterranean Sea. The 386,660-square-mile (1,001,450-square-kilometer) country is bordered by Libya on the west; Sudan on the south; and the Gaza Strip, Israel, Jordan, and Saudi Arabia on the east. The Red Sea also borders Egypt on the east. Since the assassination of President Sadat in 1991, Egypt has been governed by President Mubarak. The government is heavily indebted to the IMF and Western banks, which have imposed austerity programs on the national economy. Over 50 percent of the population survives on the equivalent of less than $2 a day. Although Egypt's major cities are growing rapidly, most of the country's people continue to reside in rural areas. The country's population more than doubled from nearly 26 million in 1960 to nearly 63.6 million in 1995. Despite the continued projected growth in Egypt's population, annual growth rates have declined significantly from the 1970s. Muslims compose the majority (94 percent) of Egypt's population, and Cotpic Christians encompass a substantial minority (6 percent). In 1995, the average life expectancy at birth in Egypt was 61.4 years and the infant mortality rate was 36.3 infant deaths per 1,000 live births.

Major Cities

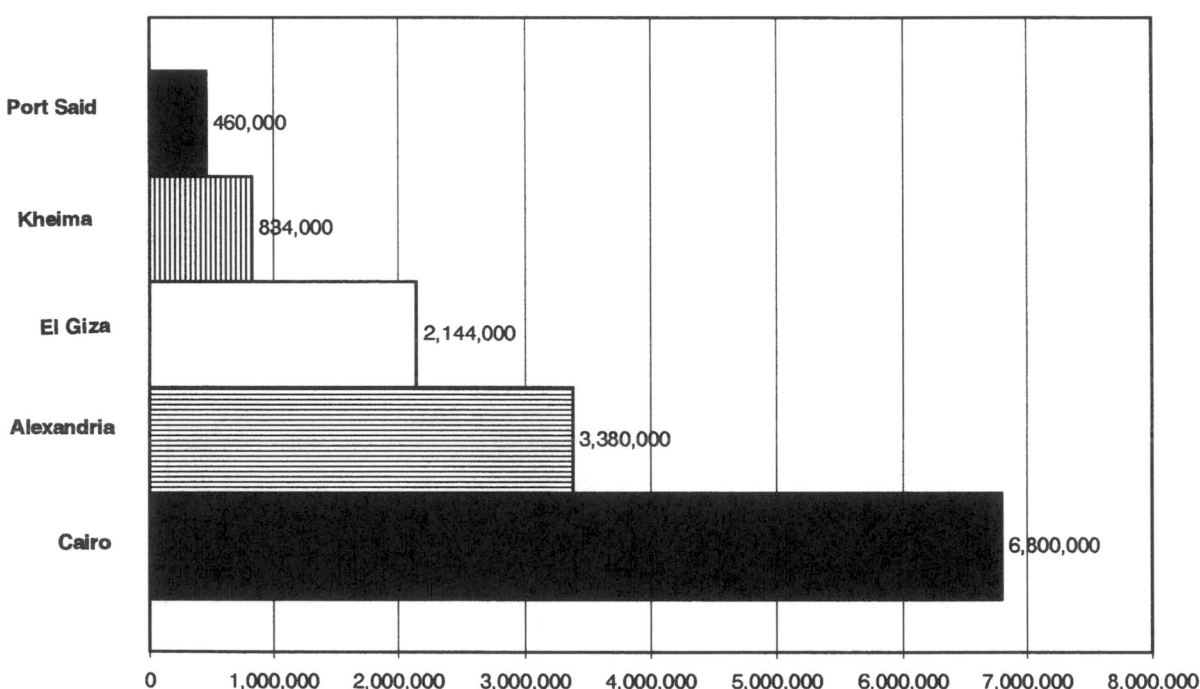

Over 90 percent of Egypt's population lives in the tiny fertile strip of the Nile Valley. Unfortunately, all of Egypt's major cities lie there as well. Thus, as urbanization proceeds, more and more precious farmland is swallowed up. To alleviate the problem, the government has embarked on a major project to irrigate desert lands.

Annual Growth

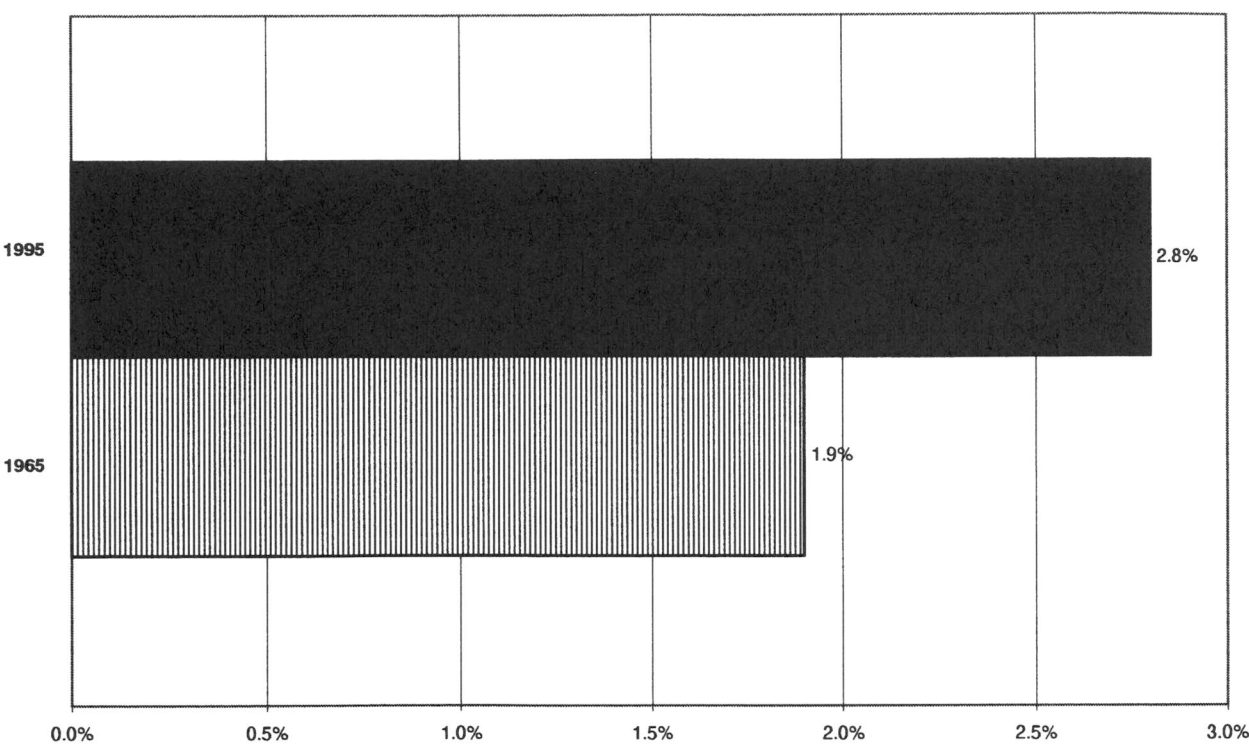

Like many of its fellow Arab countries, Egypt suffers from one of the fastest and, perhaps, most unsustainable rates of population growth in the world. Rising education levels, particularly among women, and birth-control programs have begun to slow this growth in recent years.

CHRONOLOGY

1964   Nationalist Egyptian President Gamel Abdel Nasser sends troops to Yemen.

1967   Egypt defeated in war with Israel; loses Sinai and Gaza.

1970   Nasser dies and is succeeded by lieutenant, Anwar Sadat; Aswan High dam finished with help of Soviets.

1972   Sadat ousts thousands of Soviet advisers from Egypt.

1978   Sadat signs peace treaty with Israel, which leads to Egypt's ostracism from Arab world.

1981   Sadat assassinated by Islamic fundamentalists and succeeded by Vice President Hosni Mubarak.

1982   Sinai returned to Egyptian control.

1990   Egypt allowed to rejoin Arab League.

1997   Islamic fundamentalists launch several terrorist attacks against tourists.

	1995	1980	1965

GEOGRAPHY

AREA (square miles/kilometers)   386,660/1,001,450
LAND AREA (square miles/kilometers)   384,344/995,450
COASTLINE (miles/kilometers)   1,531/2,450

CITIES
CAPITAL   Cairo   6,800,000 (92)
MAJOR CITIES   Alexandria   3,380,000
                       El Gîza   2,144,000
                       Shubra-El-Kheima   834,000
                       Port Said   460,000

POPULATION

	1995	1980	1965
TOTAL	63,575,107	36,626,204 (76)	25,984,101 (60)
DENSITY (per square mile/kilometer)	153/59	124/48	n/a
ANNUAL GROWTH	1.9%	2.8%	n/a
AGE COHORTS			
0–14	37%	n/a	43%
15–64	60%	n/a	53%
65 AND OVER	3%	n/a	4%
MALE	51%		
FEMALE	19%		
URBAN	45%	43.80%	n/a
RURAL	55%	56.20%	n/a
NET MIGRATION RATE	−0.35		

IDENTITY

ETHNICITY
EASTERN HAMITIC   99%

LANGUAGE
ARABIC   n/a

RELIGION
MUSLIM   94%
COPTIC CHRISTIAN   6%

	1995	1980	1965

VITAL STATISTICS

BIRTHS

	1995	1980	1965
BIRTH RATE	28.2	36.9	n/a
URBAN BIRTH RATE	24.1 (92)		
RURAL BIRTH RATE	28.9 (92)		
INFANT MORTALITY RATE	36.3	70.3	n/a
LIFE EXPECTANCY AT BIRTH	61.4	52.7	n/a

MARRIAGES

	1995	1980	1965
MARRIAGE RATE	9.2	9.1	n/a
AVERAGE AGE AT MARRIAGE	26.4/21.6		
DIVORCE RATE	1.6	1.6	n/a

DEATHS

	1995	1980	1965
DEATH RATE	8.7	10.3	n/a

HOUSEHOLDS

	1995	1980	1965
NUMBER	n/a	9,732,735 (86)	1,992,491 (60)
AVERAGE SIZE	n/a	4.9 (86)	4.8 (60)

ECONOMICS AND LABOR

GDP PER CAPITA US$	$2,760
LABOR FORCE M/F (thousands)	11,232.1/3,166.8 (92)
AGRICULTURE	3,876.2/1,658.8
MINING	42.6/2.3
MANUFACTURING	1,718.4/296.2
UTILITIES	136.5/10.8
CONSTRUCTION	863.4/20.8
TRADE/FOOD/TOURISM	1,148.5/183.6
TRANSPORT/COMMUNICATIONS	734.8/42.9
FINANCE/INSURANCE/REAL ESTATE	191.3/45.8
SOCIAL AND PERSONAL SERVICES	2,515.1/905.1
UNEMPLOYMENT (official)	9% (92)
UNION DENSITY	29.6%

POVERTY

UNDER $1/DAY	7.6 (91)
UNDER $2/DAY	51.9 (91)

	1995	1980	1965
TRANSPORT			
JOURNEYS (by transport mode)			
RAILROAD PASSENGER TRIPS	22,903/36,644 (92)		
(millions of miles/kilometers)			
AIR PASSENGER TRIPS (thousands)	3,538 (94)		
VEHICLES (thousands)			
PRIVATE CARS	1,225.0 (94)	432.4	n/a
COMMERCIAL	445	130	n/a
HEALTH AND HEALTH CARE			
HEALTH CARE			
ACCESS TO SAFE WATER	64%		
ACCESS TO SANITATION	11%		
MEASLES IMMUNIZATION	82%		
RATE OF PHYSICIANS	1.8	1.1	0.4 (60)
RATE OF HOSPITAL BEDS	2.1	2	2.1 (60)
HEALTH INDICATORS			
PREGNANT WOMEN WITH ANEMIA	n/a	24%	n/a
LOW-BIRTH-WEIGHT BABIES	n/a	12%	n/a
CHILD MALNUTRITION	n/a	9%	n/a
SMOKING PREVALENCE M/F	n/a	40/1%	n/a
TUBERCULOSIS INCIDENCE RATE	n/a	0.78	n/a
AIDS/HIV CASES	129	91 (93)	
TOTAL DEATHS	414,643 (94)		
EDUCATION			
SCHOOL AGE IN SCHOOL			
PRIMARY	100%	73%	72% (70)
SECONDARY	74%	50%	35%
HIGHER	18%	16%	15.10%
FEMALES IN SCHOOL			
PRIMARY	90%	63%	57% (70)
SECONDARY	44%	36%	23%
ADULT ILLITERACY M/F	36/61%	46.4/77.6% (76)	n/a

	1995	1980	1965
COMMUNICATIONS			
RATE OF NEWSPAPERS	41	39	n/a
RATE OF RADIOS	307	137	n/a
RATE OF TELEVISIONS	113	32	n/a

Source: CIA, The World Factbook, 1997; ILO, World Labour Report, 1997; UN, Demographic Yearbook, 1997; UN, Statistical Yearbook, 1996; World Bank, World Development Indicators, 1998.

EL SALVADOR

El Salvador is located in Central America, facing the Pacific Ocean, southeast of Guatemala and southwest of Honduras. The 8,124-square-mile (21,040-square-kilometer) country is small but is one of the most densely populated in the world. In 1995, El Salvador's population density was 710 persons per square mile (274 per square kilometer). El Salvador has emerged from a civil war between a military-backed government and an insurgent liberation army seeking land reform and greater socioeconomic equality. The civil war has caused widespread death and suffering and has devastated the national economy. In the 1990s, agricultural commodities (coffee and sugar) remain the leading sectors of El Salvador's economy; however, a large and growing share of the country's workers are employed in manufacturing. The country's textile workers earn extremely low wages by the standards of the developed world. In 1995, the country's population of 5.8 million was growing at an annual rate of 1.8 percent, down from 3.4 percent in the early 1960s. Mestizos (persons of mixed indigenous Indian and European ancestry) constitute 94 percent of El Salvador's population.

	1995	1980	1965

GEOGRAPHY

	1995	1980	1965
AREA (square miles/kilometers)	8,124/21,040		
LAND AREA (square miles/kilometers)	8,000/20,720		
COASTLINE (miles/kilometers)	192/307		
CITIES			
CAPITAL	San Salvador	415,346 (92)	
MAJOR CITIES	Soyapango	261,122	
	Santa Ana	139,389	
	Mejicanos	131,972	
	San Miguel	127,696	

POPULATION

	1995	1980	1965
TOTAL	5,828,987	3,554,648 (71)	2,510,984 (61)
DENSITY (per square mile/kilometer)	710/274	593/229	308/119 (61)
ANNUAL GROWTH	1.8%	1.3%	3.4%
AGE COHORTS			
0–14	38%	n/a	45%
15–64	57%	n/a	52%
65 AND OVER	5%	n/a	3%
MALE	48%		
FEMALE	52%		

	1995	**1980**	**1965**
URBAN	45%	41	n/a
RURAL	55%	59%	n/a
NET MIGRATION RATE	4.4	n/a	0

IDENTITY

ETHNICITY
MESTIZO	94%
INDIAN	5%
WHITE	1%

LANGUAGE
SPANISH	n/a
NAHUA	n/a

RELIGION
ROMAN CATHOLIC	75%
PROTESTANT	25%

VITAL STATISTICS

BIRTHS
BIRTH RATE	28.3	29.7 (84)	n/a
URBAN BIRTH RATE	29.1 (92)		
RURAL BIRTH RATE	31 (92)		
INFANT MORTALITY RATE	45.6	35.1 (84)	61.7 (61)
LIFE EXPECTANCY AT BIRTH	68.9	58.5 (84)	58.4 (61)

MARRIAGES
MARRIAGE RATE	4.2	3.5 (84)	3.2 (61)
AVERAGE AGE AT MARRIAGE M/F	25.3/22.3 (92)		
DIVORCE RATE	0.5	0.3 (84)	0.2 (61)

DEATHS
DEATH RATE	5.8	6 (84)	n/a

HOUSEHOLDS

NUMBER	1,236,866 (92)
AVERAGE SIZE	4.1 (92)

	1995	1980	1965

ECONOMICS AND LABOR

GDP PER CAPITA US$	$1,950		
LABOR FORCE M/F (thousands)	1,134.4/647.2 (92)		
AGRICULTURE	542.2/96.1		
MINING	2.3/0.3		
MANUFACTURING	167.4/141.3		
UTILITIES	9.7/1.9		
CONSTRUCTION	79.2/1.8		
TRADE/FOOD/TOURISM	123.6/184.0		
TRANSPORT/COMMUNICATIONS	56.5/4.5		
FINANCE/INSURANCE/REAL ESTATE	12.2/7.8		
SOCIAL AND PERSONAL SERVICES	139.3/209.4		
UNEMPLOYMENT (official)	7.9% (92)		
UNION DENSITY	7.20%		

TRANSPORT

JOURNEYS (by transport mode)			
RAILROAD PASSENGER TRIPS	3.8/6 (94)		
(millions of miles/kilometers)			
AIR PASSENGER TRIPS (thousands)	459/734 (94)		
VEHICLES			
PRIVATE CARS	21,600	n/a	26,200
COMMERCIAL	33,100	n/a	12,000

HEALTH AND HEALTH CARE

HEALTH CARE			
ACCESS TO SAFE WATER	55%		
ACCESS TO SANITATION	68%		
MEASLES IMMUNIZATION	94%		
RATE OF PHYSICIANS	0.7	0.3	0.2 (60)
RATE OF HOSPITAL BEDS	1.5	n/a	2.3 (60)
HEALTH INDICATORS			
PREGNANT WOMEN WITH ANEMIA	14%		
LOW-BIRTH-WEIGHT BABIES	11%		
CHILD MALNUTRITION	11%		
SMOKING PREVALENCE M/F	38/12%		

	1995	**1980**	**1965**
TUBERCULOSIS INCIDENCE RATE	1.1		
AIDS/HIV CASES	1,372	605 (93)	
TOTAL DEATHS	28,694 (94)		

EDUCATION

SCHOOL AGE IN SCHOOL

PRIMARY	88%	74%	84%
SECONDARY	32%	25%	11%
HIGHER	4%	1.2%	1.0%

FEMALES IN SCHOOL

OF PRIMARY STUDENTS	49%	49%	48%
OF SECONDARY STUDENTS	48%	21%	51%

ADULT ILLITERACY M/F	27/30%	25.0/30.7% (85)	46.1/55.5% (61)

COMMUNICATIONS

RATE OF NEWSPAPERS	90	64	47 (63)
RATE OF RADIOS	413	343	158
RATE OF TELEVISIONS	94	66	14

Source: CIA, *The World Factbook, 1997;* ILO, *World Labour Report, 1997;* UN, *Demographic Yearbook, 1997;* UN, *Statistical Yearbook, 1996;* World Bank, *World Development Indicators, 1998.*

EQUATORIAL GUINEA

Equatorial Guinea is a country encompassing a mainland enclave in West Africa and an island in the Gulf of Guinea, an inlet of the Atlantic Ocean. Cameroon borders the mainland region of the 10,830-square-mile (28,050-square-kilometer) country to the north, and Gabon to the west and south. The mainland region is known as Rio Muni, and the island to the northwest is known as Bioko, the site of the capital city of Malabo. In the 1990s, the country, which gained independence in October 1968 from Spain, is making the transition to democratic rule. Though Equatorial Guinea is believed to have abundant minerals and natural resources, the economy is undeveloped by most standards. Much of the population is engaged in various forms of subsistence agricultural and fishing activities. The development of recently discovered oil reserves is expected to increase the country's economic wealth. In 1995, the country's per capita gross domestic product was only $800. In the same year, Equatorial Guinea's population of 431,282 was growing at a relatively high annual rate of 2.6 percent. To help eradicate the high rate of communicable diseases, the country is in need of improved health and sanitation services. Equatorial Guinea has a low life expectancy at birth of 53 years and a high infant mortality rate of 116.6 infant deaths per 1,000 live births.

	1995	1980	1965
GEOGRAPHY			
AREA (square miles/kilometers)	10,830/28,050		
LAND AREA (square miles/kilometers)	10,830/28,050		
COASTLINE (miles/kilometers)	185/296		
CITIES			
CAPITAL	Malabo	n/a	30,418 (83)	n/a
POPULATION			
TOTAL	431,282	n/a	245,989 (60)
DENSITY (per square mile/kilometer)	36/14	n/a	23/9
ANNUAL GROWTH	2.6%	n/a	1.9%
AGE COHORTS			
0–14	43%		
15–64	53%		
65 AND OVER	4%		
MALE	48%		
FEMALE	52%		

	1995	1980	1965
URBAN	42%		
RURAL	52%		
NET MIGRATION RATE	0		

IDENTITY

ETHNICITY
BIOKO	n/a		
FANG	n/a		

LANGUAGE
SPANISH (official)	n/a		
PIDGIN ENGLISH	n/a		
FANG	n/a		

RELIGION
ROMAN CATHOLIC	n/a		
ANIMIST	n/a		

VITAL STATISTICS

BIRTHS
BIRTH RATE	39.8	42.5	n/a
INFANT MORTALITY RATE	116.6	137	n/a
LIFE EXPECTANCY AT BIRTH	53	44	n/a

MARRIAGES
MARRIAGE RATE	n/a	0.8	n/a

DEATHS
DEATH RATE	14	21	n/a

ECONOMICS AND LABOR

GDP PER CAPITA US$	$800		

TRANSPORT

JOURNEYS (by transport mode)
AIR PASSENGER TRIPS (thousands)	14.0 (94)		

	1995	1980	1965

HEALTH AND HEALTH CARE

HEALTH CARE

	1995	1980	1965
RATE OF PHYSICIANS	n/a	n/a	0.2 (60)
RATE OF HOSPITAL BEDS	n/a	n/a	5.2 (60)

HEALTH INDICATORS

	1995	1980	1965
AIDS/HIV CASES	157	43 (93)	

EDUCATION

SCHOOL AGE IN SCHOOL

	1995	1980	1965
PRIMARY	n/a	n/a	85%
SECONDARY	n/a	11% (75)	8%
HIGHER			

FEMALES IN SCHOOL

	1995	1980	1965
PRIMARY	n/a	n/a	69%
SECONDARY	n/a	4% (75)	3%

ADULT ILLITERACY

	1995	1980	1965
ADULT ILLITERACY	n/a	63%	n/a

COMMUNICATIONS

	1995	1980	1965
RATE OF NEWSPAPERS	3	7	4
RATE OF RADIOS	422	401	n/a
RATE OF TELEVISIONS	10	5	0

Source: CIA, *The World Factbook, 1997;* ILO, *World Labour Report, 1997;* UN, *Demographic Yearbook, 1997;* UN, *Statistical Yearbook, 1996;* World Bank, *World Development Indicators, 1998.*

ERITREA

Eritrea is located in East Africa along the coast of the Red Sea. Ethiopia borders the 46,842-square-mile (121,320-square-kilometer) country on the southwest, Sudan on the northwest, and Djibouti on the southeast. Eritrea received its independence from Ethiopia in May 1993, following a two-decade-long armed struggle against the Ethiopian government. Eritrea was granted formal independence following the collapse of a military government in Ethiopia. The two countries maintained friendly relations for five years before a border war broke out in a remote region in June 1998. Eritrea is one of the poorest countries in the Horn of Africa, a region that is also among the poorest in the world. In 1995, the per capita gross domestic product (GDP) was only $570. The vast majority of the country's population resides in rural areas and is engaged in subsistence agriculture. The country has few agricultural exports. The 1995 population of 3.4 million was growing at a high average annual rate of 2.8 percent. Due in part to the scarcity of modern medicine, poor sanitation, and the high rate of communicable diseases, Eritrea has a low life expectancy and a high infant mortality rate. The country has a limited system of education. While a majority of Eritrean school-aged children attend primary school, fewer than 20 percent attend secondary schools.

1995[1]

GEOGRAPHY

AREA (square miles/kilometers)	46,842/121,320
LAND AREA (square miles/kilometers)	46,842/121,320
COASTLINE (miles/kilometers)	719/1,151

CITIES

CAPITAL	Asmara	385,100 (90)

POPULATION

TOTAL	3,427,883
DENSITY (per square mile/kilometer)	7,830
ANNUAL GROWTH	2.8%

AGE COHORTS

0–14	44%
15–64	53%
65 AND OVER	3%

MALE	50%
FEMALE	50%

	1995[1]
URBAN	17%
RURAL	83%
NET MIGRATION RATE	0

IDENTITY

ETHNICITY

TIGRINYA	50%
TIGRE AND KUNAMA	40%
AFAR	4%

LANGUAGE

TIGRINYA	n/a
AMHARIC	n/a
ARABIC	n/a

RELIGION

MUSLIM	n/a
COPTIC CHRISTIAN	n/a
ROMAN CATHOLIC	n/a

VITAL STATISTICS

BIRTHS

BIRTH RATE	43.3
INFANT MORTALITY RATE	105.2
LIFE EXPECTANCY AT BIRTH	50.3

DEATHS

DEATH RATE	15.4

ECONOMICS AND LABOR

GDP PER CAPITA US$	$570

LABOR FORCE M/F

AGRICULTURE	77/85%
INDUSTRY	8/2%
SERVICES	16/13%

UNION DENSITY	7.20%

1995[1]

HEALTH AND HEALTH CARE

HEALTH CARE
MEASLES IMMUNIZATION   29

HEALTH INDICATORS
CHILD MALNUTRITION   41%
TUBERCULOSIS INCIDENCE RATE   1.55
AIDS/HIV CASES   2,021

EDUCATION

SCHOOL AGE IN SCHOOL
PRIMARY   57%
SECONDARY   19%
HIGHER   1%

FEMALES IN SCHOOL
PRIMARY   51%
SECONDARY   15%

FOOTNOTE
1. Part of Ethiopia in 1980 and 1965.

Source: CIA, *The World Factbook, 1997;* ILO, *World Labour Report, 1997;* UN, *Demographic Yearbook, 1997;* UN, *Statistical Yearbook, 1996;* World Bank, *World Development Indicators, 1998.*

ESTONIA

Estonia is located in Eastern Europe on the border of the Baltic Sea and the Gulf of Finland. The Russian Federation borders the 17,413-square-mile country on the east, and Latvia borders on the south. Estonia gained formal independence in September 1991 amid the collapse and breakup of the Soviet Union. Estonia's industrialized modern economy produces fabricated goods for regional and Western European markets. Following independence, the institution of market reforms in the early 1990s reduced inflation rates. But the transition to a market economy produced high levels of unemployment. In 1995, the country's population of 1,459,428 was declining at an annual rate of 1.1 percent, due substantially to a net out-migration of 8 percent. Though Estonians constitute a majority of the country's population (62 percent), Russians, who migrated to the region in the post–World War II era, constitute a large (30 percent) minority. The country has a life expectancy at birth of 68.1 years and an infant mortality rate of 14.5 per 1,000 live births.

1995[1]

GEOGRAPHY

AREA (square miles/kilomters)	17,413/45,100	
LAND AREA (square miles/kilometers)	16,680/43,200	
COASTLINE (miles/kilometers)	871/1,393	
CITIES		
CAPITAL	Tallinn	447,672 (93)
MAJOR CITY	Tartu	107,303

POPULATION

TOTAL	1,459,428
DENSITY	34
ANNUAL GROWTH	−1.1%
AGE COHORTS	
0–14	20%
15–64	66%
65 AND OVER	14%
MALE	47%
FEMALE	53%
URBAN	73%
RURAL	27%
NET MIGRATION RATE	−8

1995[1]

IDENTITY

ETHNICITY

ESTONIAN	62%
RUSSIAN	30%
UKRAINIAN	3%

LANGUAGE

ESTONIAN (official)	n/a
RUSSIAN	n/a

RELIGION

LUTHERAN	n/a
EASTERN ORTHODOX	n/a

VITAL STATISTICS

BIRTHS

BIRTH RATE	10.7
URBAN BIRTH RATE	8.9 (93)
RURAL BIRTH RATE	12.4 (93)
INFANT MORTALITY RATE	14.5
ABORTION RATE	1577.9 (92)
LIFE EXPECTANCY AT BIRTH	68.1

MARRIAGES

MARRIAGE RATE	4.5
DIVORCE RATE	3.7

DEATHS

DEATH RATE	14.1

ECONOMICS AND LABOR

GDP PER CAPITA US$	$7,600
LABOR FORCE (thousands)	461.7 (94)
AGRICULTURE	40.2
MINING	11.6
MANUFACTURING	109.4
UTILITIES	14.3
CONSTRUCTION	29.4
TRADE/FOOD/TOURISM	56.7
TRANSPORT/COMMUNICATIONS	43.2

	1995[1]
FINANCE/INSURANCE/REAL ESTATE	27.1
SOCIAL AND PERSONAL SERVICES	129.7
UNEMPLOYMENT (official)	1.9% (93)
UNION DENSITY	26.4%
POVERTY	
UNDER $1/DAY	6% (93)
UNDER $2/DAY	32.5% (93)

TRANSPORT

JOURNEYS (by transport mode)	
RAILROAD PASSENGER TRIPS	336/537 (94)
(millions of miles/kilometers)	
AIR PASSENGER TRIPS (thousands)	157 (94)
PRIVATE CARS	337,800 (94)

HEALTH AND HEALTH CARE

HEALTH CARE	
MEASLES IMMUNIZATION	81%
RATE OF PHYSICIANS	3.1
RATE OF HOSPITAL BEDS	8.4
HEALTH INDICATORS	
SMOKING PREVALENCE M/F	52/24%
TUBERCULOSIS INCIDENCE RATE	0.6
AIDS/HIV CASES	7
TOTAL DEATHS	21,071

EDUCATION

SCHOOL AGE IN SCHOOL	
PRIMARY	91%
SECONDARY	86%
HIGHER	38%
FEMALES IN SCHOOL	
PRIMARY	88%
SECONDARY	86%

1995[1]

COMMUNICATIONS

RATE OF TELEVISIONS   361

FOOTNOTE
1. Part of Soviet Union in 1980 and 1965.

Source: CIA, *The World Factbook, 1997;* ILO, *World Labour Report, 1997;* UN, *Demographic Yearbook, 1997;* UN, *Statistical Yearbook, 1996;* World Bank, *World Development Indicators, 1998.*

ETHIOPIA

Ethiopia is a landlocked country located in the Horn of Africa in East Africa. Sudan borders the 435,184-square-mile (1,127,127-square-kilometer) country on the west, Eritrea on the north, Somalia on the southeast, and Kenya on the south. In 1991, the military government of Mengistu Haile-Mariam was overthrown by the Ethiopian People's Revolutionary Democratic Front and began a process of the transition to democratic rule. National elections were held following the promulgation of a new constitution in 1994. In April 1993, the new government ended a long war in Eritrea by granting that country formal indepen-dence. As a result, Ethiopia lost its access to the Red Sea and became landlocked. A border skirmish with Eritrean government troops in June 1998 exposed Ethiopia's dependence on regional states for access to the coast. The national economy remains relatively undeveloped with limited industrial development. Most of Ethiopia's population is engaged in agriculture, primarily for subsistence. In 1995, the population of nearly 57.2 million was growing at a rapid 2.7 annual pace. Due in part to the limited resources available for social and human development, life expectancy is low and infant mortality is high.

Poverty

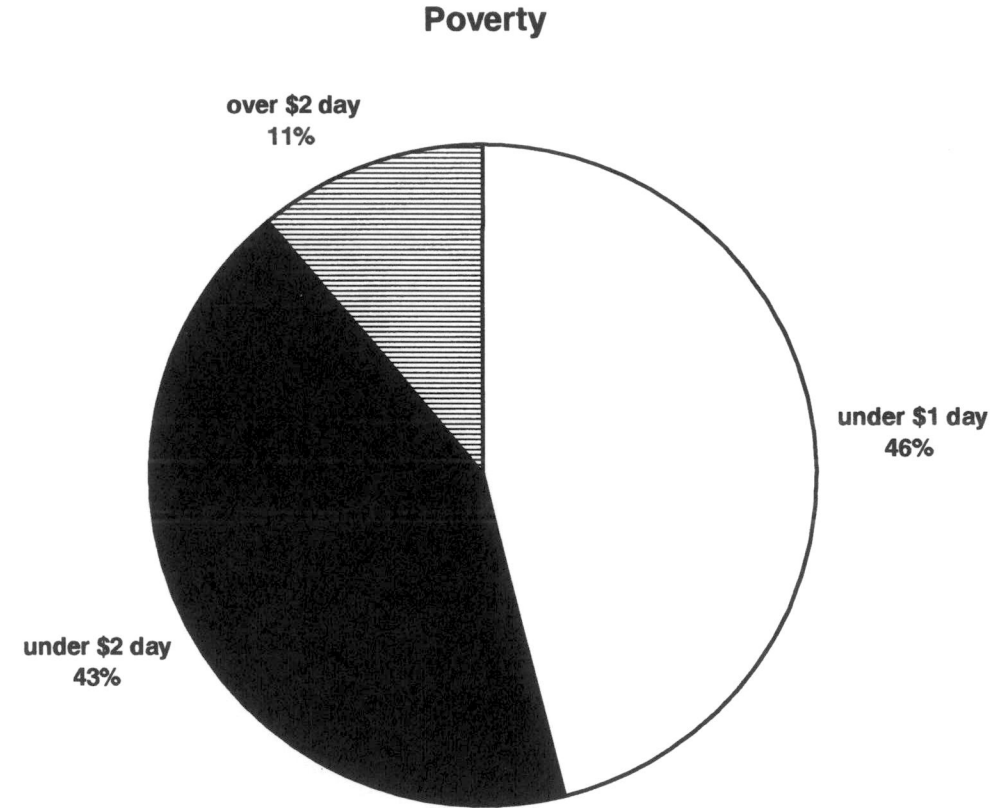

Due to the country's long feudal legacy that only came to an end in 1974, Ethiopia remains one of the most economically destitute countries in the world. Since the mid-1970s, economic modernization and development has been stifled by continuous military conflicts in the region. Nearly 90 percent of the country's population subsists on less than $2 a day.

Religion

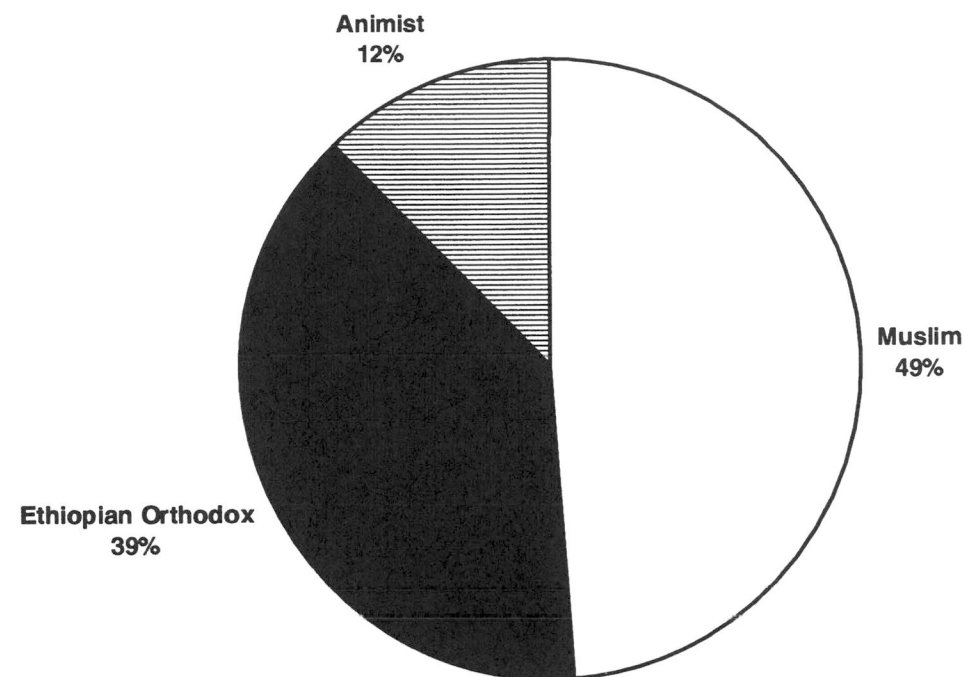

Animist
12%

Muslim
49%

Ethiopian Orthodox
39%

Religious disputes between Christians and Muslims are a major source of conflict in Ethiopia. From the 1970s to the 1990s, Muslim minorities have sought independence from the Ethiopian Orthodox Christian–dominated government. Although Eritrea successfully gained independence, other movements in the north and southwest were quelled militarily. In the early 1990s, most of the Falasha, a small Jewish minority, emigrated to Israel.

CHRONOLOGY

1962 Eritreans launch separatist war against Ethiopian government.
1974 Aging Emperor Haile Selassie overthrown in Marxist military coup.
1977 War breaks out with Somalia over disputed Ogaden region.
1980 War with Tigrean and Eritrean separatists intensifies.
1984 Famine breaks out in much of the country.
1991 Facing defeat in war, Marxist government overthrown.
1993 Eritrea wins independence.

	1995	1980[1]	1965[1]

GEOGRAPHY

AREA (square miles/kilometers) 435,184/1,127,127
LAND AREA (square miles/kilometers) 432,310/1,119,683
COASTLINE (miles/kilometers) landlocked

CITIES
CAPITAL Addis Ababa 2,316,400 (94)
MAJOR CITIES Dire Dawa 194,587
  Gondar 166,593
  Nazeret 147,088
  Harar 122,932

POPULATION

	1995	1980[1]	1965[1]
TOTAL	57,171,662	42,169,203 (84)	n/a
DENSITY (per square mile/kilometer)	132/51	91/35	n/a
CHANGE	2.7%	2.4%	1.7%

AGE COHORTS
0–14	46%		
15–64	51%		
65 AND OVER	3%		

MALE	46%		
FEMALE	54%		

	1995	1980[1]	1965[1]
URBAN	13%	13.6	n/a
RURAL	87%	86.4	n/a

NET MIGRATION RATE	−1.4		

IDENTITY

ETHNICITY
OROMO	40%		
MHARA AND TIGREAN	32%		
SIDAMO	9%		

LANGUAGE
AMHARIC (official)	n/a		
TIGRINYA	n/a		
OROMINGA	n/a		

	1995	**1980**[1]	**1965**[1]
RELIGION			
MUSLIM	49%		
ETHIOPIAN ORTHODOX	39%		
ANIMIST	12%		

VITAL STATISTICS

BIRTHS			
BIRTH RATE	46.1	49.7	n/a
INFANT MORTALITY RATE	119.2	84.2	n/a
LIFE EXPECTANCY AT BIRTH	46.9	40.9	n/a
DEATHS			
DEATH RATE	17.5	23.2	n/a

HOUSEHOLDS

NUMBER	n/a	n/a	123,755
AVERAGE SIZE	n/a	n/a	3.5

ECONOMICS AND LABOR

GDP PER CAPITA US$	$400		
LABOR FORCE M/F (thousands)	504.6/178.3 (93)		
AGRICULTURE	82.7/17.2		
MINING	0.4/0.1		
MANUFACTURING	96.3/39.0		
UTILITIES	18.2/3.6		
CONSTRUCTION	23.3/4.3		
TRADE/FOOD/TOURISM	18.9/11.4		
TRANSPORT/COMMUNICATIONS	21.2/6.9		
FINANCE/INSURANCE/REAL ESTATE	15.2/6.4		
SOCIAL AND PERSONAL SERVICES	228.6/89.5		
UNEMPLOYMENT (official)	62.9% (93)		
UNION DENSITY	4.10%		
POVERTY			
UNDER $1/DAY	n/a	46% (82)	n/a
UNDER $2/DAY	n/a	89% (82)	n/a

	1995	1980[1]	1965[1]

TRANSPORT

JOURNEYS (by transport mode)
RAILROAD PASSENGER TRIPS	144/230 (93)		
(millions of miles/kilometers)			
AIR PASSENGER TRIPS (thousands)	716 (94)		

VEHICLES
PRIVATE CARS	41,000	41,600	23,900
COMMERCIAL	20,300	13,500	8,900

HEALTH AND HEALTH CARE

HEALTH CARE
ACCESS TO SAFE WATER	10%		
RATE OF PHYSICIANS	38%		
RATE OF PHYSICIANS	negligible	negligible	negligible (60)
RATE OF HOSPITAL BEDS	0.2	0.3	0.3 (60)

HEALTH INDICATORS
PREGNANT WOMEN WITH ANEMIA	42%		
LOW-BIRTH-WEIGHT BABIES	16%		
CHILD MALNUTRITION	48%		
TUBERCULOSIS INCIDENCE RATE	1.55		
AIDS/HIV CASES	19,433	10,008 (93)	

EDUCATION

SCHOOL AGE IN SCHOOL
PRIMARY	31%	36%	12%
SECONDARY	11%	9%	2%
HIGHER	1%	negligible	0.1%

FEMALES IN SCHOOL
PRIMARY	38%	35%	6%
SECONDARY	9%	6%	1%

ADULT ILLITERACY
	65%	44.8%	n/a

	1995	1980[1]	1965[1]
COMMUNICATIONS			
RATE OF NEWSPAPERS	1	1	2
RATE OF RADIOS	197	82	6 (70)
RATE OF TELEVISIONS	3	1	1 (70)

FOOTNOTE
1. Includes Eritrea.

Source: CIA, The World Factbook, 1997; ILO, World Labour Report, 1997; UN, Demographic Yearbook, 1997; UN, Statistical Yearbook, 1996; World Bank, World Development Indicators, 1998.

FIJI

Fiji is an island group located in Oceania, about 1,500 miles (2,400 kilometers) east of Australia. The 7,054-square-mile (18,270-square-kilometer) country is located in the South Pacific Ocean, west of Tonga, south of Tuvalu, east of Vanuatu, and north of New Zealand. The country received independence from the United Kingdom in October 1970. Fiji is rich in agriculture (sugar, coconuts) and minerals (gold), much of which is produced for foreign export primarily to regional countries in Oceania, Japan, Europe, and North America. Tourism remains a large and growing sector of the economy. The country has a relatively high annual per capita gross domestic product (GDP) of $6,100. In 1995, Fiji's population of 782,381 was growing at an annual rate of 1.3 percent, significantly lower than the 3.3 percent annual rate of growth four decades earlier. Fiji has a net out-migration rate of 4.2 per 1,000 residents. In 1995, the country had an average life expectancy at birth of 65.7 years and an infant mortality rate of 13.8 per 1,000 live births.

	1995	1980	1965
GEOGRAPHY			
AREA (square miles/kilometers)	7,054/18,270		
LAND AREA (square miles/kilometers)	7,054/18,270		
COASTLINE (miles/kilometers)	706/1,129		
CITIES			
CAPITAL	Suva	n/a	69,665 (86)	n/a
POPULATION			
TOTAL	782,381	588,068 (76)	345,737 (56)
DENSITY (per square mile/kilometer)	114/44	98/38	67/26
ANNUAL GROWTH	1.3%	1.9%	3.3%
AGE COHORTS			
0–14	35%	n/a	44% (66)
15–64	62%	n/a	53% (66)
65 AND OVER	3%	n/a	3% (66)
MALE	51%		
FEMALE	49%		
URBAN	41%	37.2% (76)	n/a
RURAL	59%	62.8% (76)	n/a
NET MIGRATION RATE	−4.2	n/a	0

	1995	1980	1965

IDENTITY

ETHNICITY

FIJIAN	49%		
INDIAN	46%		

LANGUAGE

ENGLISH (official)	n/a		
FIJIAN	n/a		
HINDI	n/a		

RELIGION

HINDU	38%		
METHODIST	37%		
ROMAN CATHOLIC	9%		

VITAL STATISTICS

BIRTHS

	1995	1980	1965
BIRTH RATE	23.4	28.4 (84)	n/a
INFANT MORTALITY RATE	13.8	16.4 (84)	n/a
LIFE EXPECTANCY AT BIRTH	65.7	69 (84)	n/a

MARRIAGES

	1995	1980	1965
MARRIAGE RATE	8.7	9.6 (84)	n/a
AVERAGE AGE AT MARRIAGE M/F	n/a	25.3/22.5	n/a
DIVORCE RATE	0.7	0.7 (84)	n/a

DEATHS

	1995	1980	1965
DEATH RATE	6.4	4.6 (84)	n/a

ECONOMICS AND LABOR

	1995	1980	1965
GDP PER CAPITA US$	$6,100		

	1995	1980	1965
LABOR FORCE M/F (thousands)	65.0/27.1 (90)		
AGRICULTURE	2.0/0.3		
MINING	1.6/0.1		
MANUFACTURING	12.4/8.6		
UTILITIES	2.0/0.1		
CONSTRUCTION	5.6/0.1		

	1995	1980	1965
TRADE/FOOD/TOURISM	10.1/4.8		
TRANSPORT/COMMUNICATIONS	8.2/1.3		
FINANCE/INSURANCE/REAL ESTATE	3.6/2.1		
SOCIAL AND PERSONAL SERVICES	19.6/9.7		
UNEMPLOYMENT (official)	6% (94)		

TRANSPORT

	1995	1980	1965
JOURNEYS (by transport mode)			
AIR PASSENGER TRIPS (thousands)	465.0 (94)		
VEHICLES			
PRIVATE CARS	47,700	23,400	7,300
COMMERCIAL	36,800	15,500	3,900

HEALTH AND HEALTH CARE

	1995	1980	1965
HEALTH CARE			
RATE OF PHYSICIANS	n/a	n/a	0.5 (60)
RATE OF HOSPITAL BEDS	n/a	n/a	4 (60)
HEALTH INDICATORS			
AIDS/HIV CASES	7	5 (93)	
TOTAL DEATHS	4,959		

EDUCATION

	1995	1980	1965
SCHOOL AGE IN SCHOOL			
PRIMARY	n/a	110%	92% (63)
SECONDARY	n/a	74%	19% (63)
HIGHER	n/a	2.7%	0.9%
FEMALES IN SCHOOL			
PRIMARY	n/a	109%	78% (63)
SECONDARY	n/a	76%	13% (63)
HIGHER	n/a	2% (81)	1.1%
ADULT ILLITERACY M/F	n/a	16.0/26.0% (76)	n/a

	1995	1980	1965
COMMUNICATIONS			
RATE OF NEWSPAPERS	36	102	17
RATE OF RADIOS	607	473	101
RATE OF TELEVISIONS	17	5.2	0

Source: CIA, The World Factbook, 1997; ILO, World Labour Report, 1997; UN, Demographic Yearbook, 1997; UN, Statistical Yearbook, 1996; World Bank, World Development Indicators, 1998.

FINLAND

Finland is located on the Gulf of Bothnia and the Gulf of Finland, inlets of the Baltic Sea, in the Scandinavian region of northern Europe. The Russian Federation bounds the 130,127-square-mile (337,030-square-kilometer) country on the east, Norway on the north, and Sweden on the west. The country achieved independence from the Soviet Union in December 1917. The country has a democratic government and a mixed modern and industrialized economy. Finland's key exports are fabricated wood products such as furniture, food products, machinery, and large ships.

The country has one of the highest standards of living in the world. In October 1994, Finns voted in a referendum to join the European Union. In 1995, Finland's population of 5.1 million was growing at a slow rate of 0.1 percent, due in part to a slow birth rate. Finns constitute the ethnic majority. The two leading ethnic minorities in Finland are Swedes and Lapps. In 1995, the country had a high life expectancy at birth of 75.5, and 4.7 infant deaths per 1,000 live births, one of the lowest infant mortality rates in the world.

		1995	1980	1965
GEOGRAPHY				
AREA (square miles/kilometers)		130,127/337,030		
LAND AREA (square miles/kilometers)		117,942/305,470		
COASTLINE (miles/kilometers)		704/1,126		
CITIES				
CAPITAL	Helsinki	512,176 (94)		
MAJOR CITIES	Tampere	175,504		
	Vantaa	162,739		
	Turku	161,380		
	Oulu	105,382		
POPULATION				
TOTAL		5,105,230	4,784,710	4,446,222 (60)
DENSITY (per square mile/kilometer)		39/15	39/15	36/14
CHANGE		0.1%	0.5%	0.8%
AGE COHORTS				
0–14		19%	n/a	27%
15–64		67%	n/a	65%
65 AND OVER		14%	n/a	8%
MALE		49%		
FEMALE		51%		

	1995	1980	1965
URBAN	63%	59.8	n/a
RURAL	37%	40.20%	n/a
NET MIGRATION RATE	0.6	n/a	0 (61)

IDENTITY

ETHNICITY			
FINN	n/a		
SWEDE	n/a		
LAPP	n/a		
LANGUAGE			
FINNISH	94%		
SWEDISH	6%		
RELIGION			
LUTHERAN	89%		

VITAL STATISTICS

BIRTHS			
BIRTH RATE	11.3	13.3 (84)	16.7
URBAN BIRTH RATE	13.2 (94)		
RURAL BIRTH RATE	12.1 (94)		
INFANT MORTALITY RATE	4.7	6.5 (84)	17.6
ABORTION RATE	154 (94)		
LIFE EXPECTANCY AT BIRTH	75.5	74.5 (84)	67.7
MARRIAGES			
MARRIAGE RATE	4.7	5.8 (84)	8.2
AVERAGE AGE AT MARRIAGE	31.5/29		
DIVORCE RATE	2.4	2 (84)	1
DEATHS			
DEATH RATE	10.9	9.2 (84)	9.4

HOUSEHOLDS

NUMBER	2,036,732 (90)	n/a	1,315,434 (60)
AVERAGE SIZE	2.5 (90)	n/a	3.3
FEMALE HEADED	37.3%		
SINGLE	20.2%		
MARRIED	4.7%		

	1995	1980	1965
WIDOWED	9.6%		
DIVORCED/SEPARATED	14.2%		

ECONOMICS AND LABOR

| **GDP PER CAPITA US$** | $18,200 | | |

LABOR FORCE M/F (thousands)	1,065.0981 (94)		
AGRICULTURE	110/57		
MINING	5/0		
MANUFACTURING	271/127		
UTILITIES	19/4		
CONSTRUCTION	103/10		
TRADE/FOOD/TOURISM	133/161		
TRANSPORT/COMMUNICATIONS	120/41		
FINANCE/INSURANCE/REAL ESTATE	84/91		
SOCIAL AND PERSONAL SERVICES	216/487		

| **UNEMPLOYMENT** (official) | 18.2% (94) | | |
| **UNION DENSITY** | 59.70% | | |

TRANSPORT

JOURNEYS (by transport mode)			
RAILROAD PASSENGER TRIPS (millions of miles/kilometers)	1,898/3,037 (94)		
AIR PASSENGER TRIPS (thousands)	4,492 (94)		

VEHICLES (thousands)			
PRIVATE CARS	1,872.6	1,225.9	n/a
COMMERCIAL	257.5	158.1	n/a

HEALTH AND HEALTH CARE

HEALTH CARE			
ACCESS TO SAFE WATER	100%		
ACCESS TO SANITATION	100%		
MEASLES IMMUNIZATION	98%		
RATE OF PHYSICIANS	2.7	1.9	0.6 (60)
RATE OF HOSPITAL BEDS	10.1	15.5	10 (60)

HEALTH INDICATORS			
LOW-BIRTH-WEIGHT BABIES	5%		
SMOKING PREVALENCE M/F	27/19%		

	1995	**1980**	**1965**
TUBERCULOSIS INCIDENCE RATE	0.15		
AIDS/HIV CASES	230	147	
TOTAL DEATHS	49,352		

EDUCATION

SCHOOL AGE IN SCHOOL

	1995	**1980**	**1965**
PRIMARY	100%	96%	109%
SECONDARY	116%	100%	57%
HIGHER	67%	32%	8.4%

FEMALES IN SCHOOL

	1995	**1980**	**1965**
PRIMARY	98%	104%	106%
SECONDARY	122%	106%	79%
HIGHER	n/a	31.5%	13.3% (70)

COMMUNICATIONS

	1995	**1980**	**1965**
RATE OF NEWSPAPERS	512	505	n/a
RATE OF RADIOS	996	837	347
RATE OF TELEVISIONS	504	414	165

Source: CIA, *The World Factbook, 1997*; ILO, *World Labour Report, 1997*; UN, *Demographic Yearbook, 1997*; UN, *Statistical Yearbook, 1996*; World Bank, *World Development Indicators, 1998*.

FRANCE

France is located in the heart of Western Europe, between the Mediterranean Sea and the Bay of Biscay, an inlet of the Atlantic Ocean. Spain borders the 211,208-square-mile (547,030-square-kilometer) country on the south; Italy and Switzerland on the southeast; and Belgium, Germany, and Luxembourg on the northeast. The United Kingdom lies to France's north, across the English Channel. A new constitution was established in September 1958. The country has a diversified and highly industrialized economy that produces a high standard of living. In 1995, France's annual per capita gross domestic product (GDP) was $20,200. The country is one of the original members of the European Union.

France's 1995 population of more than 58.3 million was growing at an annual rate of less than 0.3 percent, due in part to a steady decline in the birth rate. The French constitute an ethnic majority, although since the 1950s a large and growing number of Africans from the former colonies have migrated to the country. The country has a strong system of social protection that includes universal access to health care and education, although, during the 1990s, the government has sought to curb some of the social benefits as a means to conform to the standards for entry into the European Monetary System. France has a relatively high life expectancy and a low infant mortality rate.

AIDS/HIV

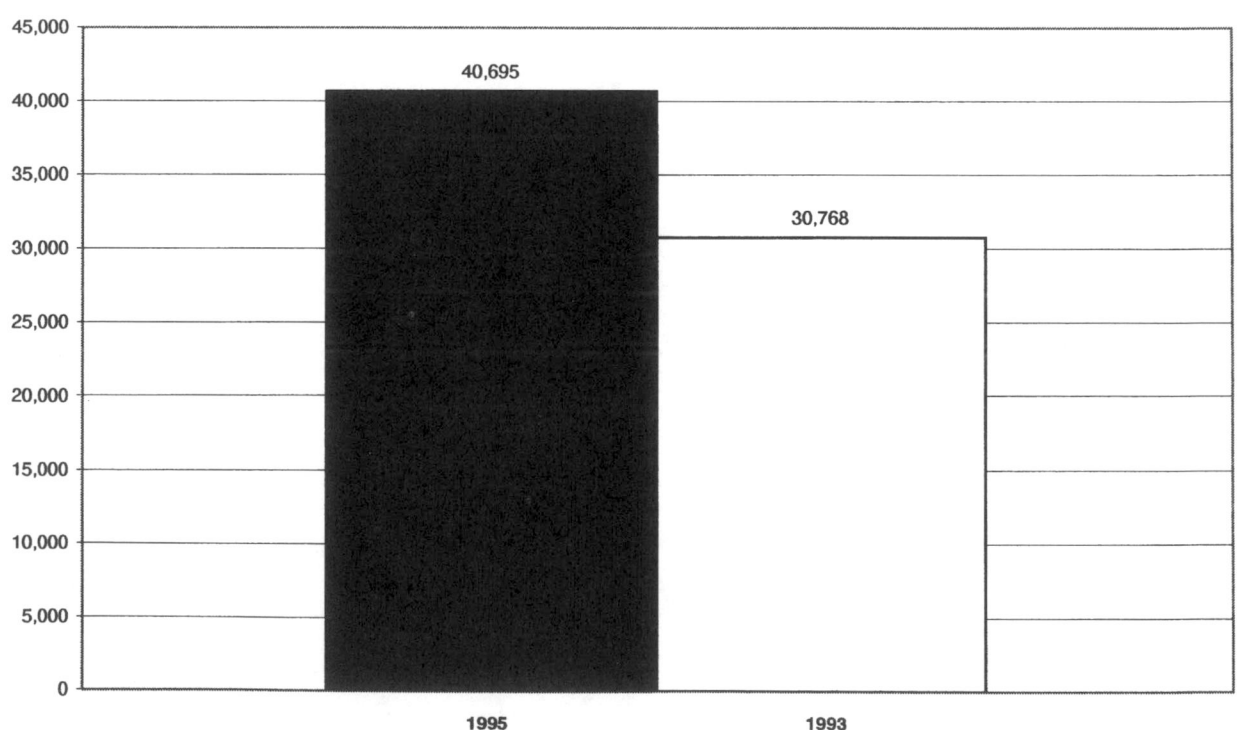

With the highest AIDS/HIV rates in Europe, France has been a leader in AIDS research.

Net Migration Rate

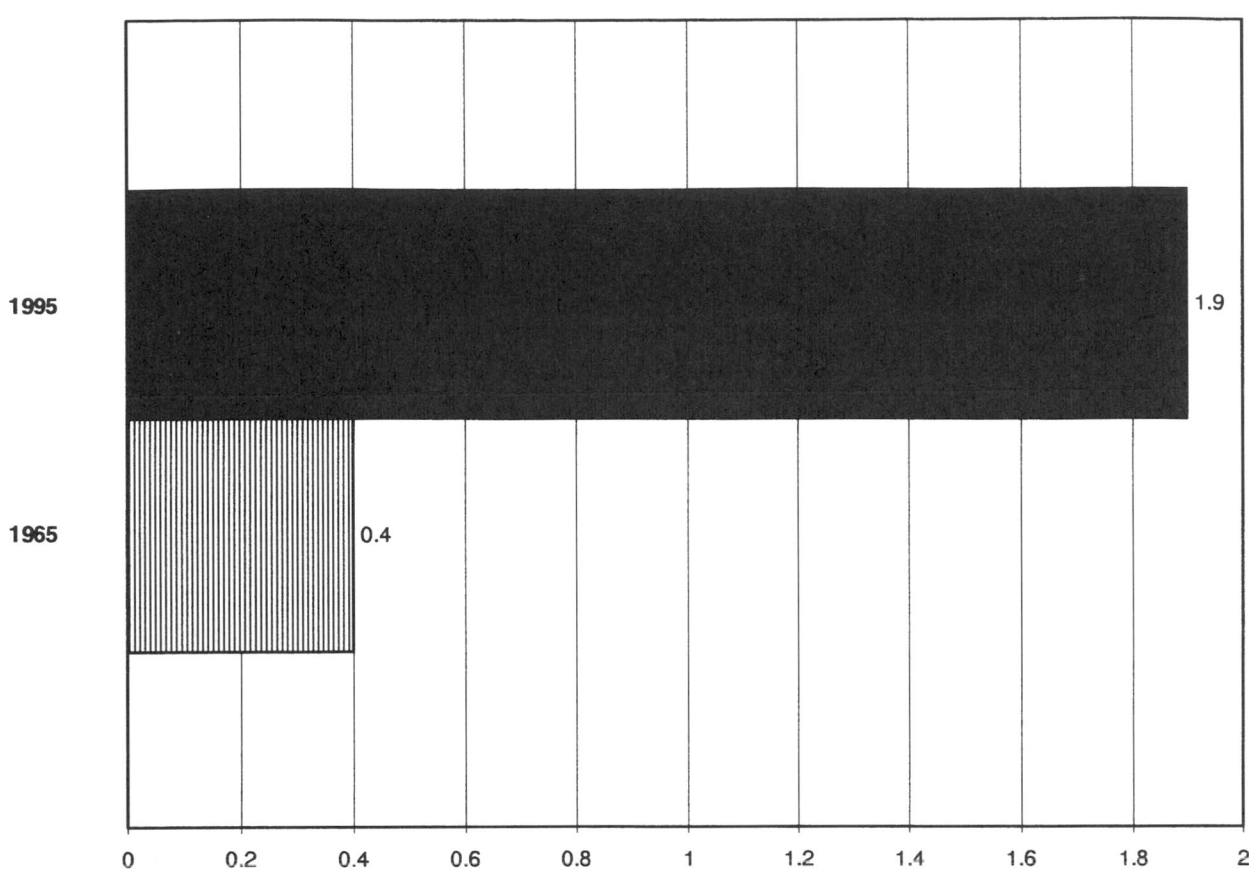

Rising levels of immigration to France from former colonies in the Arab world and sub-Saharan Africa have produced a major anti-immigrant backlash in French politics.

CHRONOLOGY

1962   France defeated in colonial war in Algeria; 1 million Europeans flee Algeria for France.
1966   French President Charles de Gaulle pulls France out of NATO military command.
1968   Radical leftist protests engulf students and workers across France.
1969   De Gaulle forced to resign.
1981   Socialist François Mitterand wins elections as president.
1982   Dozens of French troops killed in terrorist attack in Lebanon.
1989   France celebrates bicentennial of its revolution.
1995   Conservative Jacques Chirac wins presidency.

	1995	1980	1965

GEOGRAPHY

AREA (square miles/kilometers)   211,208/547,030
LAND AREA (square miles/kilometers)   210,668/545,630
COASTLINE (miles/kilometers)   2,142/3,427

CITIES

		1995		
CAPITAL	Paris	2,152,329 (90)		
MAJOR CITIES	Marseille	800,309		
	Lyon	415,479		
	Toulouse	358,598		
	Nice	342,903		

POPULATION

	1995	1980	1965
TOTAL	58,317,450	54,334,871 (82)	46,520,271 (62)
DENSITY (per square mile/kilometer)	272/105	259/100	233/90
ANNUAL GROWTH	0.3%	0.3%	1.2%
AGE COHORTS			
0–14	19%	n/a	25%
15–64	66%	n/a	62%
65 AND OVER	15%	n/a	13%
MALE	49%		
FEMALE	51%		
URBAN	73%	73.3% (82)	n/a
RURAL	27%	26.7%	n/a
NET MIGRATION RATE	1.9	n/a	0.4

IDENTITY

ETHNICITY

	1995
EUROPEAN	n/a
ARAB	n/a
AFRICAN	n/a

LANGUAGE

	1995
FRENCH	n/a
ARABIC	n/a

RELIGION

	1995
ROMAN CATHOLIC	90%

	1995	**1980**	**1965**
MUSLIM	n/a		
PROTESTANT	n/a		

VITAL STATISTICS

BIRTHS

	1995	**1980**	**1965**
BIRTH RATE	10.8	17.5	14.1 (85)
URBAN BIRTH RATE	13.8 (92)		
RURAL BIRTH RATE	10.5 (92)		
INFANT MORTALITY RATE	4.9	21.7	8 (85)
ABORTION RATE	215.2 (91)		
LIFE EXPECTANCY AT BIRTH	77.9	71.5	74.5

MARRIAGES

MARRIAGE RATE	4.7	6.9	4.9 (85)
AVERAGE AGE AT MARRIAGE	29.2/27.2		
DIVORCE RATE	1.9	0.7	1.9 (85)

DEATHS

DEATH RATE	9.3	10.7	10.1 (85)

HOUSEHOLDS

	1995	**1980**	**1965**
NUMBER	21,520,700 (92)	n/a	14,561,620 (62)
AVERAGE SIZE	2.6 (90)	n/a	3.1

FEMALE HEADED

SINGLE	19.2%
MARRIED	59.3%
WIDOWED	14.1%
DIVORCED/SEPARATED	7.4%

ECONOMICS AND LABOR

GDP PER CAPITA US$	$20,200
LABOR FORCE M/F (thousands)	12,446.3/9,629.9 (93)
AGRICULTURE	748.7/352.1
MANUFACTURING	4,551.8/1,479.8
TRADE/FOOD/TOURISM	7,145.8/7,798.0
UNEMPLOYMENT (official)	12.5% (94)
UNION DENSITY	6.1%

	1995	1980	1965
TRANSPORT			
JOURNEYS (by transport mode)			
RAILROAD PASSENGER TRIPS	36,831/58,930 (94)		
(millions of miles/kilometers)			
AIR PASSENGER TRIPS (thousands)	38,060 (94)		
VEHICLES (thousands)			
PRIVATE CARS	24,900	18,400.00	9,600
COMMERCIAL	4,027	2,710.00	2,181.5
HEALTH AND HEALTH CARE			
HEALTH CARE			
ACCESS TO SAFE WATER	100%		
ACCESS TO SANITATION	96%		
MEASLES IMMUNIZATION	78%		
RATE OF PHYSICIANS	2.8	2.2	1.1 (60)
RATE OF HOSPITAL BEDS	9	n/a	8.4 (60)
HEALTH INDICATORS			
LOW-BIRTH-WEIGHT BABIES	5%		
SMOKING PREVALENCE M/F	40/27%		
TUBERCULOSIS INCIDENCE RATE	0.2		
AIDS/HIV CASES	40,695	30,768 (93)	
TOTAL DEATHS	529,000		
EDUCATION			
SCHOOL AGE IN SCHOOL			
PRIMARY	106%	111%	135%
SECONDARY	111%	85%	56%
HIGHER	50%	25%	10.5%
FEMALES IN SCHOOL			
PRIMARY	102%	109%	134%
SECONDARY	113%	83%	59%

	1995	1980	1965
COMMUNICATIONS			
RATE OF NEWSPAPERS	205	192	245
RATE OF RADIOS	890	741	330
RATE OF TELEVISIONS	412	353	138

Source: CIA, *The World Factbook, 1997;* ILO, *World Labour Report, 1997;* UN, *Demographic Yearbook, 1997;* UN, *Statistical Yearbook, 1996;* World Bank, *World Development Indicators, 1998.*

GABON

Gabon is located in west central Africa on the Gulf of Guinea, an inlet of the Atlantic Ocean. The Republic of Congo borders the 103,347-square-mile (267,670-square-kilometer) country on the east, and Cameroon and Equatorial Guinea border on the north. In August 1960, the country gained independence from France. Since December 1967, the country has been led by the government of President Omar Bongo. Owing to the presence of rich oil fields in the Gulf of Guinea, Gabon is one of the most economically prosperous countries in Africa. In 1995, the country had an annual per capita gross domestic product (GDP) of $5,200. The petroleum fields are complemented by significant other natural resources, including timber, manganese, uranium, and gold. Despite the country's abundant wealth, a large share of the population continues to live in rural areas under subsistence conditions. In 1995, the country had a relatively small population of 1,172,798 growing at an annual rate of 1.5 percent, of which about 50 percent resided in urban areas. The average life expectancy at birth is 55.6 years, and the infant mortality rate is 50 per 1,000 live births.

	1995	1980	1965
GEOGRAPHY			
AREA (square miles/kilometers)	103,347/267,670		
LAND AREA (square miles/kilometers)	99,486/257,670		
COASTLINE (miles/kilometers)	553/885		
CITIES			
CAPITAL	Libreville	n/a	n/a	57,000 (67)
POPULATION			
TOTAL	1,172,798	n/a	448,564 (61)
DENSITY (per square mile/kilometer)	13/5	10.0/4.0	n/a
ANNUAL GROWTH	1.5%	1.6%	1.5%
AGE COHORTS			
0–14	34%	n/a	36%
15–64	61%	n/a	57%
65 AND OVER	5%	n/a	7%
MALE	49%		
FEMALE	51%		

	1995	1980	1965
URBAN	50%		
RURAL	50%		
NET MIGRATION RATE	0		

IDENTITY

ETHNICITY
FANG	n/a		
ESHIRU	n/a		
BAPOUNOU	n/a		

LANGUAGE
FRENCH (official)	n/a		
FANG	n/a		
MYENE	n/a		

RELIGION
CHRISTIAN	65%		
ANIMIST	34%		
MUSLIM	1%		

VITAL STATISTICS

BIRTHS
	1995	1980	1965
BIRTH RATE	28.2	33.8	35
INFANT MORTALITY RATE	94	229	229
LIFE EXPECTANCY AT BIRTH	55.6	35	35

DEATHS
	1995	1980	1965
DEATH RATE	13.6	18.1	30

ECONOMICS AND LABOR

GDP PER CAPITA US$	$5,200		

LABOR FORCE M/F
AGRICULTURE	46/59%		
INDUSTRY	21/10%		
SERVICES	33/32%		

UNION DENSITY	2%		

	1995	1980	1965

TRANSPORT

JOURNEYS (by transport mode)
	1995	1980	1965
AIR PASSENGER TRIPS (thousands)	481.0 (94)		

VEHICLES
	1995	1980	1965
PRIVATE CARS	23,000	n/a	3,200
COMMERCIAL	17,000	n/a	5,800

HEALTH AND HEALTH CARE

HEALTH CARE
	1995	1980	1965
ACCESS TO SAFE WATER	67%		
ACCESS TO SANITATION	76%		
MEASLES IMMUNIZATION	50%		
RATE OF PHYSICIANS	0.5	0.5	0.1 (60)
RATE OF HOSPITAL BEDS	3.2	n/a	6.2 (60)

HEALTH INDICATORS
	1995	1980	1965
LOW-BIRTH-WEIGHT BABIES	10%		
CHILD MALNUTRITION	15%		
TUBERCULOSIS INCIDENCE RATE	1		
AIDS/HIV CASES	890	521 (93)	

EDUCATION

SCHOOL AGE IN SCHOOL
	1995	1980	1965
PRIMARY	142%	115%	136%
SECONDARY	n/a	21%	11%

FEMALES IN SCHOOL
	1995	1980	1965
PRIMARY	142%	113%	120%
SECONDARY	n/a	17%	4%

	1995	1980	1965
ADULT ILLITERACY M/F	26/47	29.8/46.6 (85)	n/a

COMMUNICATIONS

	1995	1980	1965
RATE OF NEWSPAPERS	16	19	n/a
RATE OF RADIOS	147	130	80
RATE OF TELEVISIONS	38	12	3

Source: CIA, *The World Factbook, 1997;* ILO, *World Labour Report, 1997;* UN, *Demographic Yearbook, 1997;* UN, *Statistical Yearbook, 1996;* World Bank, *World Development Indicators, 1998.*

THE GAMBIA

The Gambia is a narrow strip of land lying inside Senegal on both sides of the Gambia River in western Africa. Senegal envelops the 4,363-square-mile (11,300-square-kilometer) country on the north, east, and south, and on the narrow west coast is the Atlantic Ocean. In 1965, The Gambia received independence from the United Kingdom. A 1981 agreement calling for confederation with Senegal was abandoned in 1989. The majority of the country's population is engaged in subsistence agriculture, though some commodities (e.g., peanuts, cotton) are sold to export markets. In 1995, the densely populated country of 1.2 million was growing at a very high rate of 3.6 percent, owing to a birth rate of 44.4 and a death rate of 13.7 per 1,000 residents. In the same year, The Gambia's life expectancy at birth was 53 years and the infant mortality rate was 132 per 1,000 live births.

	1995	1980	1965
GEOGRAPHY			
AREA (square miles/kilometers)	4,363/11,300		
LAND AREA (square miles/kilometers)	3,861/10,000		
COASTLINE (miles/kilometers)	50/80		
CITIES			
CAPITAL	Banjul	n/a	49,181	n/a
POPULATION			
TOTAL	1,204,984	695,886 (83)	315,486 (63)
DENSITY (per square mile/kilometer)	256/99	145/56	n/a
ANNUAL GROWTH	3.6%	1.4%	1.9%
AGE COHORTS			
0–14	46%		
15–64	51%		
65 AND OVER	3%		
MALE	50%		
FEMALE	50%		
URBAN	26%	18.20%	n/a
RURAL	74%	81.80%	n/a
NET MIGRATION RATE	4.7		

	1995	1980	1965

IDENTITY

ETHNICITY

MADINKA	42%
FULA	18%
WOLOF	16%

LANGUAGE

ENGLISH (official)	n/a
MANDINKA	n/a
WOLOF	n/a

RELIGION

MUSLIM	90%
CHRISTIAN	9%
ANIMIST	1%

VITAL STATISTICS

BIRTHS

	1995	1980	1965
BIRTH RATE	44.4	48.4	38.7
INFANT MORTALITY RATE	132	174	n/a
LIFE EXPECTANCY AT BIRTH	53	35	43

DEATHS

	1995	1980	1965
DEATH RATE	13.7	29	21

ECONOMICS AND LABOR

GDP PER CAPITA US$ $1,100

LABOR FORCE M/F (thousands)	21.1/5.0 (87)
AGRICULTURE	1.4/0.6
MINING	0.0/0.0
MANUFACTURING	1.9/0.5
UTILITIES	0.8/0.1
CONSTRUCTION	2.9/0.0
TRADE/FOOD/TOURISM	3.7/0.8
TRANSPORT/COMMUNICATIONS	2.7/0.4
FINANCE/INSURANCE/REAL ESTATE	0.8/0.3
SOCIAL AND PERSONAL SERVICES	7.0/2.3

	1995	1980	1965

TRANSPORT

JOURNEYS (by transport mode)

	1995	1980	1965
AIR PASSENGER TRIPS (thousands)	19.0 (94)		

VEHICLES

	1995	1980	1965
PRIVATE CARS	7,000	6,000	2,000
COMMERCIAL	3,000	1,600	1,800

HEALTH AND HEALTH CARE

HEALTH CARE

	1995	1980	1965
ACCESS TO SAFE WATER	76%		
ACCESS TO SANITATION	37%		
MEASLES IMMUNIZATION	68%		
RATE OF PHYSICIANS	n/a	n/a	0.1
RATE OF HOSPITAL BEDS	0.6	n/a	1.4

HEALTH INDICATORS

	1995	1980	1965
PREGNANT WOMEN WITH ANEMIA	80%		
LOW-BIRTH-WEIGHT BABIES	10%		
CHILD MALNUTRITION	17%		
TUBERCULOSIS INCIDENCE RATE	1.66		
AIDS/HIV CASES	410	295 (93)	

EDUCATION

SCHOOL AGE IN SCHOOL

	1995	1980	1965
PRIMARY	73%	53%	26%
SECONDARY	22%	11%	6%
HIGHER	2%	n/a	n/a

FEMALES IN SCHOOL

	1995	1980	1965
PRIMARY	41%	35%	15%
SECONDARY	n/a	7%	4%

	1995	1980	1965
ADULT ILLITERACY M/F	47/75%	64.4/84.9% (85)	n/a

	1995	1980	1965
COMMUNICATIONS			
RATE OF NEWSPAPERS	2	n/a	5 (59)
RATE OF RADIOS	162	114	95

Source: CIA, The World Factbook, 1997; ILO, World Labour Report, 1997; UN, Demographic Yearbook, 1997; UN, Statistical Yearbook, 1996; World Bank, World Development Indicators, 1998.

GEORGIA

Georgia is located south of the Russian Federation on the Black Sea. Turkey, Armenia, and Azerbaijan border the 26,911-square-mile (69,700-square-kilometer) country on the south. In 1991, Georgia gained independence amid the breakup and collapse of the Soviet Union. Subsequently, civil conflicts between rival ethnic groups and Georgia have destabilized the political and economic transition to independence. Between 1991 and 1994, the Abkhazian and South Osssetian autonomy movements were the two most significant challenges to the new Georgian state. In the mid-1990s, the conflicts subsided. Under Soviet rule, Georgia's economy industrialized and modernized rapidly. The leading exports are citrus and food products and manufactured goods. The country's population of 5,219,810 in 1995 was declining at an annual rate of 1 percent, due in part to a high out-migration rate. Although Georgians are the country's ethnic majority with about 70 percent of the population, Russians (6 percent) and Armenians (8 percent) remain significant ethnic minorities. The country has a fairly high life expectancy of 68.1 and an infant mortality rate of 19.6 deaths per 1,000 live births.

1995[1]

GEOGRAPHY

AREA (square miles/kilometers)	26,911/69,700	
LAND AREA (square miles/kilometers)	26,911/69,700	
COASTLINE (miles/kilometers)	194/310	
CITIES		
CAPITAL	Tbilisi	1,268,000 (90)
MAJOR CITIES	Kutaisi	236,000
	Rustavi	160,000
	Batumi	137,000
	Sukhumi	122,000

POPULATION

TOTAL	5,219,810
DENSITY (per square mile/kilometer)	202/78
ANNUAL GROWTH	−1%
AGE COHORTS	
0–14	22%
15–64	66%
65 AND OVER	12%
MALE	47%
FEMALE	53%

	1995[1]
URBAN	58%
RURAL	42%
NET MIGRATION RATE	−10.8

IDENTITY

ETHNICITY
GEORGIAN	70%
ARMENIAN	8%
RUSSIAN	6%

LANGUAGE
GEORGIAN	71%
RUSSIAN	9%
ARMENIAN	7%

RELIGION
EASTERN ORTHODOX	75%
MUSLIM	11%
ARMENIAN ORTHODOX	8%

VITAL STATISTICS

BIRTHS
BIRTH RATE	12.8
INFANT MORTALITY RATE	19.6
LIFE EXPECTANCY AT BIRTH	68.1

MARRIAGES
MARRIAGE RATE	7
DIVORCE RATE	1.4

DEATHS
DEATH RATE	12.2

ECONOMICS AND LABOR

GDP PER CAPITA US$ $1,080

LABOR FORCE M/F
AGRICULTURE	27/24%
INDUSTRY	38/23%
SERVICES	34/52%

1995[1]

TRANSPORT

JOURNEYS (by transport mode)
RAILROAD PASSENGER TRIPS   627/1,003 (93)
   (millions of miles/kilometers)
AIR PASSENGER TRIPS (thousands)   224.0 (94)

VEHICLES
PRIVATE CARS   468,800 (93)
COMMERCIAL   56,000

HEALTH AND HEALTH CARE

HEALTH CARE
MEASLES IMMUNIZATION   63%
RATE OF PHYSICIANS   4.2
RATE OF HOSPITAL BEDS   8.2

HEALTH INDICATORS
TUBERCULOSIS INCIDENCE RATE   0.7
AIDS/HIV CASES   2

EDUCATION

SCHOOL AGE IN SCHOOL
PRIMARY   82%
SECONDARY   73%
HIGHER   38%

FOOTNOTE
1. Part of Soviet Union in 1950 and 1965.

Source: CIA, The World Factbook, 1997; ILO, World Labour Report, 1997; UN, Demographic Yearbook, 1997; UN, Statistical Yearbook, 1996; World Bank, World Development Indicators, 1998.

GERMANY

Gemany, the most populous country in Western Europe, is located on the North Sea and the Baltic Sea. Poland and the Czech Republic border the 137,803-square-mile (356,910-square-kilometer) country on the east; Switzerland and Austria on the south; France, Luxembourg, Belgium, and Netherlands on the west; and Denmark on the north. Germany remained divided between east and west from the end of World War II until October 1990. East Germany, known as the German Democratic Republic, was in the Soviet military and economic alliance and developed a state-controlled economy with a strong system of social protection. West Germany, the German Federal Republic, became part of the Western alliance and developed a mixed economy with private enter-prise and a strong social welfare system. Following unification of the two Germanys in 1990, much of the East German economy was privatized. The Federal Republic financed much of the cost of modernizing East German infrastructure and industry. East Germans have had to bear the cost of foreign speculation and steeply higher unemployment. In 1995, Germany's population of over 83.5 million was growing at a rate of 0.7 percent. Much of this new population growth is due to rising migration. The country has a relatively high life expectancy and a low infant mortality rate. Germans account for 95 percent of the population. A Turkish minority that immigrated in the post–World War II years constitutes 2 percent of the national population.

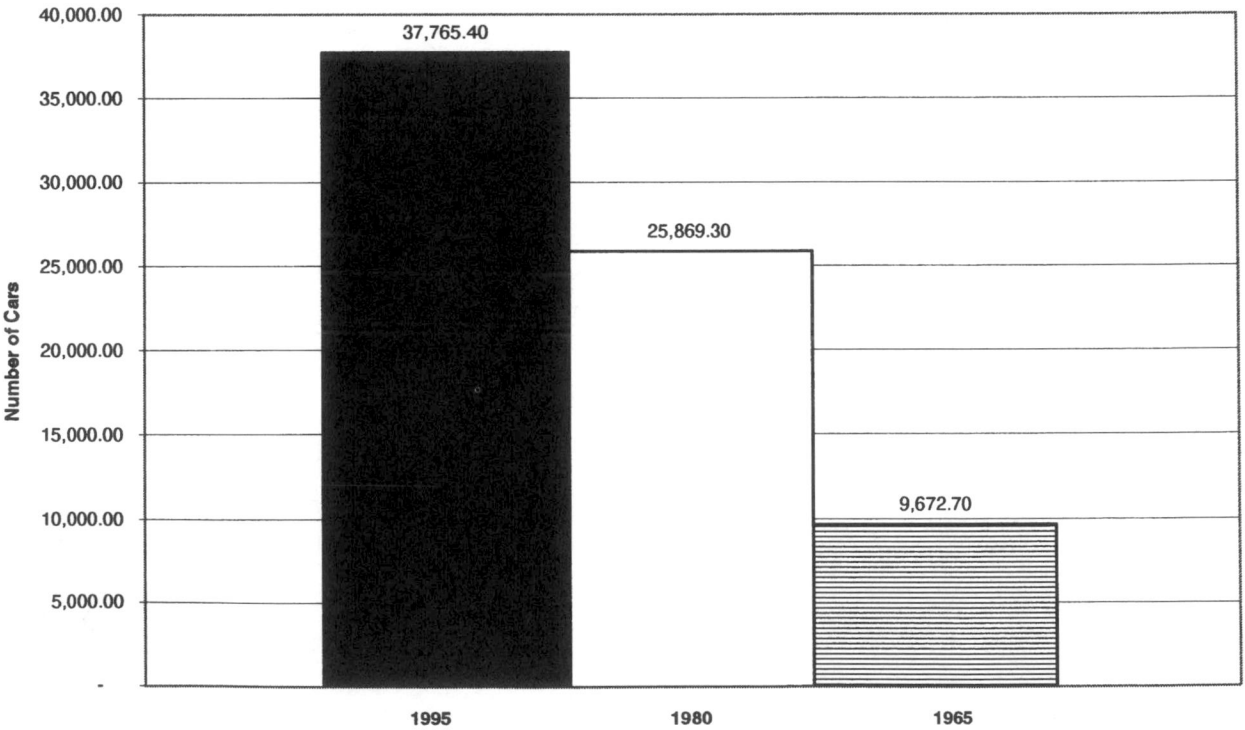

Private Cars

Germany's phenomenal economic rise out of the ashes of World War II has been likened to a "miracle." That miraculous rise can be seen in the explosive growth of private car ownership.

Labor Market

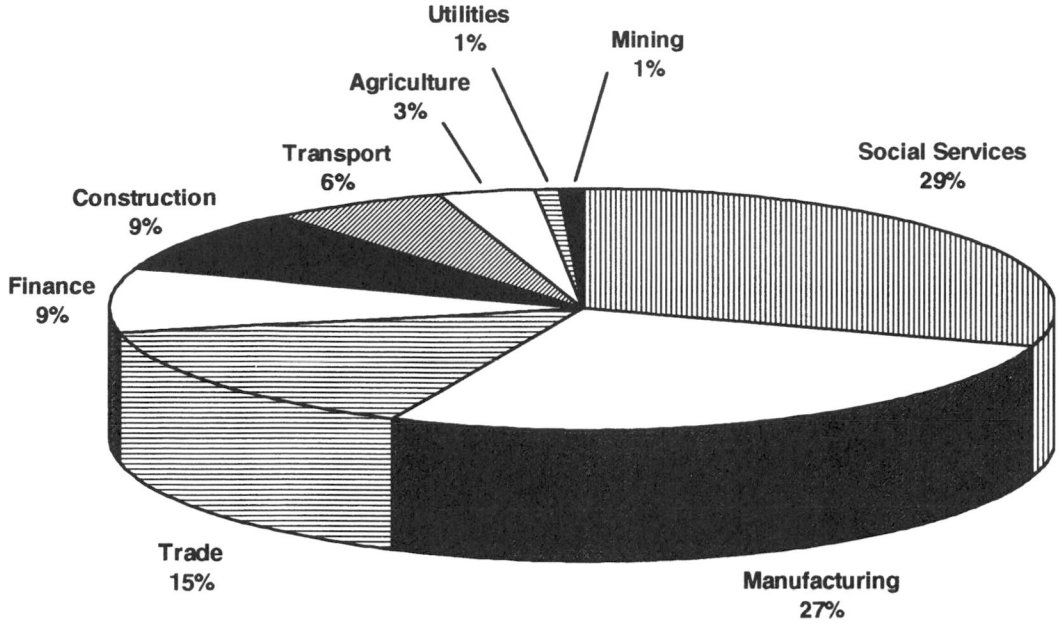

Note: Finance includes insurance and real estate;
Transport includes communications;
Trade includes food and tourist industries.

Like many other advanced economies, Germany's has seen a shift from a labor-force profile, in which manufacturing dominates, to one in which service-sector jobs predominate. Germany's current labor-force divisions reflect that transformation.

CHRONOLOGY

1961   Berlin Wall constructed, physically separating West Germany and East Germany.
1966   Long-time conservative Chancellor Konrad Adenauer loses office.
1969   Social Democrats under Willy Brandt win control of government.
1970   Brandt launches *ostpolitik*, calling for closer relations between Germany and socialist bloc.
1973   West Germany and East Germany join United Nations.
1975   Left-wing terrorism increases.
1982   Conservative Christian Democrat Helmut Kohl wins national elections in Germany, ending 13 years of Social Democrat rule.
1989   Berlin Wall comes down; communist government in East Germany falls.
1990   West Germany and East Germany formally united.
1998   Kohl government loses elections, ending 16 years of conservative rule.

	1995	1980[1]	1965[1]

GEOGRAPHY

AREA (square miles/kilometers)	137,803/356,910		
LAND AREA (square miles/kilometers)	134,950/349,520		
COASTLINE (miles/kilometers)	1,493/2,389		

CITIES

CAPITAL	Berlin	3,472,009 (94)
MAJOR CITIES	Hamburg	1,705,872
	Munich	1,244,676
	Cologne	963,817
	Frankfurt am Main	652,412

POPULATION

	1995	1980[1]	1965[1]
TOTAL	83,536,115	n/a	75,278,231
DENSITY (per square mile/kilometer)	593/229		
ANNUAL GROWTH	0.7%		

AGE COHORTS

	1995	1980[1]	1965[1]
0–14	16%	n/a	23%
15–64	69%	n/a	65%
65 AND OVER	15%	n/a	12%

	1995
MALE	48%
FEMALE	52%

	1995	1980[1]	1965[1]
URBAN	87%	76.2%	n/a
RURAL	13%	23.8%	n/a

	1995
NET MIGRATION RATE	8.3

IDENTITY

ETHNICITY

	1995
GERMAN	95%
TURKISH	2%
ITALIAN	1%

LANGUAGE

	1995
GERMAN	n/a

	1995	1980[1]	1965[1]
RELIGION			
PROTESTANT	45%		
ROMAN CATHOLIC	37%		
MUSLIM	2%		

VITAL STATISTICS

BIRTHS

BIRTH RATE	9.7		
INFANT MORTALITY RATE	5.6		
LIFE EXPECTANCY AT BIRTH	76		

MARRIAGES

MARRIAGE RATE	5.4		
AVERAGE AGE AT MARRIAGE M/F	30.3/27.5		
DIVORCE RATE	1.9		

DEATHS

DEATH RATE	12.2		

HOUSEHOLDS

	1995	1980	1965
NUMBER	n/a	6,218,438 (87)[2]	n/a
AVERAGE SIZE	n/a	2.3 (87)[2]	n/a

TYPE OF HOUSEHOLD

SINGLE	19.6%		
MARRIED	57.9%		
WIDOWED	15.1%		
DIVORCED/SEPARATED	7.4%		
FEMALE HEADED	27.1%		

ECONOMICS AND LABOR

GDP PER CAPITA US$	$17,900		

LABOR FORCE M/F (thousands)	20,987.0/14,088.0 (94)		
AGRICULTURE	714.0/477		
MINING	234.0/32		
MANUFACTURING	6,877.0/2,765		
UTILITIES	295.0/79		
CONSTRUCTION	2,753.0/355		
TRADE/FOOD/TOURISM	2,273.6/3,111		

	1995	1980[1]	1965[1]
TRANSPORT/COMMUNICATIONS	1,555.0/614		
FINANCE/INSURANCE/REAL ESTATE	1,636.0/1,523		
SOCIAL AND PERSONAL SERVICES	4,651.0/6,133		
UNEMPLOYMENT M/F (official)	8.4/19.2%[3] (94)		
UNION DENSITY	29.6%		

TRANSPORT

	1995	1980[1]	1965[1]
JOURNEYS (by transport mode)			
RAILROAD PASSENGER TRIPS	38,329/61,327 (94)		
(millions of miles/kilometers)			
AIR PASSENGER TRIPS (thousands)	30,964.0 (94)		
VEHICLES (thousands)			
PRIVATE CARS	37,765.4	25,869.30	9,672.70
COMMERCIAL	3,150.7	2,200.60	1023.5

HEALTH AND HEALTH CARE

	1995	1980[1]	1965[1]
HEALTH CARE			
ACCESS TO SANITATION	100%		
MEASLES IMMUNIZATION	75%		
RATE OF PHYSICIANS	3.3	2.2	n/a
RATE OF HOSPITAL BEDS	9.7		
HEALTH INDICATORS			
SMOKING PREVALENCE M/F	37/22%		
TUBERCULOSIS INCIDENCE RATE	0.18		
AIDS/HIV CASES	14,423	11,552 (93)	
TOTAL DEATHS	875,071		

EDUCATION

	1995	1980[1]	1965[1]
SCHOOL AGE IN SCHOOL			
PRIMARY	102%	n/a	n/a
SECONDARY	103%	98%	n/a
HIGHER	43%	34%	n/a
FEMALES IN SCHOOL			
PRIMARY	100%	n/a	n/a
SECONDARY	103%	n/a	n/a
HIGHER	n/a	36.4% (70)	28.8% (70)

	1995	1980[1]	1965[1]
COMMUNICATIONS			
RATE OF NEWSPAPERS	323	335/524[3]	n/a
RATE OF RADIOS	890	893/536[3]	351/323 (70)[3]
RATE OF TELEVISIONS	559	439/514[3]	275/264[3]

FOOTNOTES

1. Statistics for both West and East Germany unless otherwise noted.
2. West Germany only.
3. First statistic for the former West Germany; second statistic for former East Germany.

Source: CIA, The World Factbook, 1997; ILO, World Labour Report, 1997; UN, Demographic Yearbook, 1997; UN, Statistical Yearbook, 1996; World Bank, World Development Indicators, 1998.

GHANA

Ghana is located in West Africa on the Gulf of Guinea, an inlet of the Atlantic Ocean. Côte d'Ivoire borders the 92,100-square-mile (238,540-square-kilometer) country on the west, Burkina Faso on the north, and Togo on the east. Ghana gained independence from the United Kingdom in March 1957. Much of the formative years of Ghana's independence were marked by military intervention and economic and political instability. Jerry Rawlings, the current president, himself gained power in a military putsch. In recent years, however, the government has had relative political stability and economic growth. The

country emerged from a painful privatization and market-reform process and is now expanding exports dramatically. Nevertheless, the majority of Ghana's exports are raw materials and agricultural commodities. In 1995 the country had a per capita gross domestic product (GDP) of $1,400. The population of 17.7 million in 1995 was growing at an annual rate of 2.3 percent, lower than preceding years, but still fairly high by international standards. Ghana has a life expectancy at birth of 56.2 years and an infant mortality rate of 81.1 infant deaths per 1,000 live births. The country has an ethnically diverse population.

	1995	1980	1965
GEOGRAPHY			
AREA (square miles/kilometers)	92,100/238,540		
LAND AREA (square miles/kilometers)	88,811/230,020		
COASTLINE (miles/kilometers)	337/539		
CITIES			
CAPITAL	Accra	n/a	n/a	564,194 (70)
MAJOR CITIES	Kumasi	n/a	n/a	260,286
	Sekondi-Takoradi	n/a	n/a	91,874
POPULATION			
TOTAL	17,698,271	12,205,574 (84)	6,726,815 (60)
DENSITY (per square mile/kilometer)	189/73	148/57	n/a
ANNUAL GROWTH	2.3%	3.3%	2.7%
AGE COHORTS			
0–14	43%		45%
15–64	54%		52%
65 AND OVER	3%		3%
MALE	49%		
FEMALE	51%		

	1995	**1980**	**1965**
URBAN	36%	31.3% (84)	n/a
RURAL	64%	68.7% (84)	n/a
NET MIGRATION	−0.9	n/a	0 (64)

IDENTITY

ETHNICITY
AKAN	44%
MOSHI-DAGOMBA	16%
EWE	13%

LANGUAGE
ENGLISH (official)	n/a
AKAN	n/a
MOSHI-DAGOMBA	n/a

RELIGION
ANIMIST	38%
MUSLIM	30%
CHRISTIAN	24%

VITAL STATISTICS

BIRTHS
	1995	1980	1965
BIRTH RATE	35	46.9	47.5
INFANT MORTALITY RATE	81.1	156	156
LIFE EXPECTANCY AT BIRTH	56.2	52	38.7

DEATHS
	1995	1980	1965
DEATH RATE	11.2	14.6	24

ECONOMICS AND LABOR

GDP PER CAPITA US$	$1,400

LABOR FORCE (thousands) | 186.3 (91)
AGRICULTURE	14.7
MINING	17.1
MANUFACTURING	20.6
UTILITIES	1.7
CONSTRUCTION	7.8
TRADE/FOOD/TOURISM	7.5
TRANSPORT/COMMUNICATIONS	10.4

	1995	1980	1965
FINANCE/INSURANCE/REAL ESTATE	8.4		
SOCIAL AND PERSONAL SERVICES	98.1		
UNION DENSITY	25.9%		

TRANSPORT

	1995	1980	1965
JOURNEYS (by transport mode)			
RAILROAD PASSENGER TRIPS	199/318 (87)		
(millions of miles/kilometers)			
AIR PASSENGER TRIPS (thousands)	182 (94)		
VEHICLES			
PRIVATE CARS	90,000	75,200	30,000
COMMERCIAL	44,700	33,200	19,500

HEALTH AND HEALTH CARE

	1995	1980	1965
HEALTH CARE			
ACCESS TO SAFE WATER	56%		
ACCESS TO SANITATION	27%		
MEASLES IMMUNIZATION	54%		
RATE OF PHYSICIANS	n/a	n/a	0.1 (60)
RATE OF HOSPITAL BEDS	1.5	n/a	0.8 (60)
HEALTH INDICATORS			
LOW-BIRTH-WEIGHT BABIES	17%		
CHILD MALNUTRITION	27%		
TUBERCULOSIS INCIDENCE RATE	2.22		
AIDS/HIV CASES	17,564	12,656 (93)	

EDUCATION

	1995	1980	1965
SCHOOL AGE IN SCHOOL			
PRIMARY	76%	79%	97%
SECONDARY	37%	41%	15%
HIGHER	n/a	2%	0.60%
FEMALES IN SCHOOL			
PRIMARY	74%	76%	81%
SECONDARY	n/a	38%	9%
ADULT ILLITERACY M/F	24/47%	35.9/57.2% (85)	56.9/89.6% (70)

	1995	1980	1965
COMMUNICATIONS			
RATE OF NEWSPAPERS	18	47	29
RATE OF RADIOS	269	158	83
RATE OF TELEVISIONS	16	5	0.1

Source: CIA, The World Factbook, 1997; ILO, World Labour Report, 1997; UN, Demographic Yearbook, 1997; UN, Statistical Yearbook, 1996; World Bank, World Development Indicators, 1998.

GREECE

Greece is located in southeastern Europe on the Aegean Sea, Ionian Sea, and Mediterranean Sea. Turkey borders the 50,942-square-mile (131,940-square-kilometer) country on the east; Albania, the former Yugoslav Republic of Macedonia, and Bulgaria on the north. Greece, a member state of the European Union, has a diversified economy consisting of industry, agriculture, and services, including tourism. The Greek economy has a large and growing state-owned public sector. The Greek government's effort to conform to the spending restrictions for entry into the European Monetary Union by curbing spending has in-

creased unemployment. In 1995, the country's per capita gross domestic product (GDP) was $9,500. In the same year, due to a slowing of Greece's birth rate, the country's population of more than 10.5 million was growing at the fairly slow annual pace of 0.4 percent. The country has comprehensive social and economic protection, including universal health insurance and compulsory education. In 1995, Greece had a very high average life expectancy of 78.1 years and a low infant mortality rate of 7.9 infant deaths per 1,000 live births.

	1995	1980	1965
GEOGRAPHY			
AREA (square miles/kilometers)	50,942/131,940		
LAND AREA (square miles/kilometers)	50,502/130,800		
COASTLINE (miles/kilometers)	8,548/13,676		
CITIES			
CAPITAL	Athens	772,072 (91)	
MAJOR CITIES	Thessaloniki	383,967	
	Piraeus	182,671	
	Patras	153,344	
	Peristeri	137,288	
POPULATION			
TOTAL	10,538,594	9,740,151 (81)	8,387,201 (61)
DENSITY (per square mile/kilometer)	205/79	194/75	168/65
ANNUAL GROWTH	0.4%	0.6%	0.7%
AGE COHORTS			
0–14	16%	n/a	26%
15–64	68%	n/a	65%
65 AND OVER	16%	n/a	9%
MALE	49%		
FEMALE	51%		

	1995	1980	1965
URBAN	65%	58.1%	n/a
RURAL	35%	41.9%	n/a
NET MIGRATION RATE	4.0		

IDENTITY

ETHNICITY
GREEK	98%		

LANGUAGE
GREEK	n/a		

RELIGION
GREEK ORTHODOX	98%		
MUSLIM	1%		

VITAL STATISTICS

BIRTHS
BIRTH RATE	9.8	11.7 (85)	18.1
URBAN BIRTH RATE	11.2 (91)		
RURAL BIRTH RATE	8.2 (91)		
INFANT MORTALITY RATE	7.9	14 (85)	33.7
ABORTION RATE	115. 2 (92)		
LIFE EXPECTANCY AT BIRTH	78.1	72.4 (85)	69.1

MARRIAGES
MARRIAGE RATE	5.7	6.3 (85)	8.8
AVERAGE AGE AT MARRIAGE M/F	29.4/24.5		
DIVORCE RATE	0.7	0.6 (85)	0.4

DEATHS
DEATH RATE	9.5	9.3 (85)	7.9

HOUSEHOLDS

NUMBER	3,203,834 (91)	n/a	2,142,968 (61)
URBAN	1,945,097		
RURAL	1,258,737		

	1995	1980	1965
AVERAGE SIZE	3 (91)		
URBAN	2.9		
RURAL	3.1		
TYPE OF HOUSEHOLD			
SINGLE	8.9%		
MARRIED	76.4%		
WIDOWED	12.0%		
DIVORCED/SEPARATED	2.8%		
FEMALE HEADED	20.2%		

ECONOMICS AND LABOR

	1995	1980	1965
GDP PER CAPITA US$	$9,500		
LABOR FORCE M/F (thousands)	2,403.2/1,281.3 (92)		
AGRICULTURE	468.7/338.0		
MINING	17.6/0.7		
MANUFACTURING	487.3/211.4		
UTILITIES	30.9/5.8		
CONSTRUCTION	242.5/3.7		
TRADE/FOOD/TOURISM	423.9/263.4		
TRANSPORT/COMMUNICATIONS	220.7/29.5		
FINANCE/INSURANCE/REAL ESTATE	120.1/80.5		
SOCIAL AND PERSONAL SERVICES	391.5/348.1		
UNEMPLOYMENT (official)	9.7% (93)		
UNION DENSITY	15.4%		

TRANSPORT

	1995	1980	1965
JOURNEYS (by transport mode)			
RAILROAD PASSENGER TRIPS	874/1,399 (94)		
(millions of miles/kilometers)			
AIR PASSENGER TRIPS (thousands)	5,813 (94)		
VEHICLES (thousands)			
PRIVATE CARS	2,074.10	862.6	104.3
COMMERCIAL	849.1	425	73.4

	1995	1980	1965

HEALTH AND HEALTH CARE

HEALTH CARE

	1995	1980	1965
ACCESS TO SANITATION	96%		
MEASLES IMMUNIZATION	70%		
RATE OF PHYSICIANS	4	2.4	1.3 (60)
RATE OF HOSPITAL BEDS	5	6.2	5.8 (60)

HEALTH INDICATORS

	1995	1980	1965
LOW-BIRTH-WEIGHT BABIES	9%		
SMOKING PREVALENCE M/F	46/28%		
TUBERCULOSIS INCIDENCE RATE	12%		
AIDS/HIV CASES	1,314	953 (93)	
TOTAL DEATHS	98,000		

EDUCATION

SCHOOL AGE IN SCHOOL

	1995	1980	1965
PRIMARY	n/a	103%	111%
SECONDARY	95%	81%	54%
HIGHER	38%	17%	6.8%

FEMALES IN SCHOOL

	1995	1980	1965
PRIMARY	91%	99%	109%
SECONDARY	38%	81%	44%
HIGHER	n/a	14.2%	8.8% (70)

	1995	1980	1965
ADULT ILLITERACY M/F	n/a	3.9/15.7 (81)	n/a

COMMUNICATIONS

	1995	1980	1965
RATE OF NEWSPAPERS	135	120	80 (70)
RATE OF RADIOS	416	343	108
RATE OF TELEVISIONS	202	171	19 (70)

Source: CIA, The World Factbook, 1997; ILO, World Labour Report, 1997; UN, Demographic Yearbook, 1997; UN, Statistical Yearbook, 1996; World Bank, World Development Indicators, 1998.

GRENADA

Grenada is an island located in the Windward Islands Archipelago of the southeastern Caribbean Sea. The 340-square-mile (131-square-kilometer) island is located south of The Grenadines and north of Trinidad and Tobago, and the Venezuelan coast. Grenada gained independence from the United Kingdom in February 1974. In 1983, American armed forces and allies in the region invaded the country, ousted the government, and expelled Cuban nationals assisting with the country's economic development. The country had previously relied almost exclusively on the export of spices and plants to North American and Western European markets. Cuban assistance in constructing the airport greatly contributed to the development of a rapidly growing tourist industry. The country's population of 94,961 in 1995 was growing at the slow pace of 0.6 percent, primarily due to a net out-migration rate of 17.9 per 1,000 residents. Grenadans have an average life expectancy at birth of 70.9 years and an infant mortality rate of 15.4 deaths per 1,000 live births.

	1995	1965	1980
GEOGRAPHY			
AREA (square miles/kilometers)	340/131		
LAND AREA (square miles/kilometers)	340/131		
COASTLINE (miles/kilometers)	76/121		
CITIES			
CAPITAL	Saint George's n/a	4,788 (81)	n/a
POPULATION			
TOTAL	94,961	89,068 (81)	88,677 (60)
DENSITY (per square mile/kilometer)	692/267	844/326	733/283
CHANGE	0.6%	0.9%	1.2%
AGE COHORTS			
0–14	43%	n/a	36%
15–64	52%	n/a	59%
65 AND OVER	5%	n/a	5%
NET MIGRATION RATE	−17.9	n/a	−1.8
IDENTITY			
ETHNICITY			
BLACK	n/a		

	1995	**1980**	**1965**
LANGUAGE			
ENGLISH	n/a		
FRENCH PATOIS	n/a		
RELIGION			
ROMAN CATHOLIC	n/a		
ANGLICAN	n/a		

VITAL STATISTICS

BIRTHS			
BIRTH RATE	29.1	25.1	29
INFANT MORTALITY RATE	15.4	15.4	42.9
LIFE EXPECTANCY AT BIRTH	70.9	62.9	62.7
MARRIAGES			
MARRIAGE RATE	3.3	3.3	3.4
DIVORCE RATE	0.2	0.4	0.1
DEATHS			
DEATH RATE	5.7	7	8.8

HOUSEHOLDS

NUMBER	n/a	n/a	19,564 (60)
AVERAGE SIZE	n/a	n/a	4.5 (60)

ECONOMICS AND LABOR

GDP PER CAPITA US$	$3,000		

TRANSPORT

VEHICLES			
PRIVATE CARS	n/a	n/a	2,400
COMMERCIAL	n/a	n/a	600

HEALTH AND HEALTH CARE

HEALTH CARE			
RATE OF PHYSICIANS	n/a	n/a	0.2 (60)
RATE OF HOSPITAL BEDS	n/a	n/a	6.1 (60)

	1995	1980	1965
HEALTH INDICATORS			
AIDS/HIV CASES	76	56 (93)	

EDUCATION

	1995	1980	1965
SCHOOL AGE IN SCHOOL			
PRIMARY	n/a	n/a	156%
SECONDARY	n/a	n/a	21%
FEMALES IN SCHOOL			
PRIMARY	n/a	n/a	155%
SECONDARY	n/a	n/a	24%
ADULT ILLITERACY M/F	n/a	n/a	2.0/2.4% (70)

COMMUNICATIONS

	1995	1980	1965
RATE OF NEWSPAPERS	n/a	45	13
RATE OF RADIOS	594	393	79
RATE OF TELEVISIONS	332	n/a	0

Source: CIA, *The World Factbook, 1997;* ILO, *World Labour Report, 1997;* UN, *Demographic Yearbook, 1997;* UN, *Statistical Yearbook, 1996;* World Bank, *World Development Indicators, 1998.*

GUATEMALA

Guatemala is located in Central America, bordered by the Caribbean Sea on the northeast and the Pacific Ocean on the southwest. Mexico borders the 42,042-square-mile (108,890-square-kilometer) country on the northwest, Belize on the northeast, Honduras on the east, and El Salvador on the southeast. In 1954, the Guatemalan military overthrew a democratically elected government. The military was supported by the U.S. government, which subsequently supplied the country with arms to fight an internal guerrilla insurgency that continued through the mid-1990s. The Guatemalan economy is dominated by the production of coffee, bananas, and other agricultural commodities. Guatemala is one of the poorest countries in the Western Hemisphere. Though

the country has a per capita gross domestic product (GDP) of $3,300, over 75 percent of the population survives on the equivalent of under $2 a day and over 53 percent survives on less than $1 a day. Guatemala's population of 11,277,614 in 1995 was growing at a rapid annual rate of 2.5 percent, even though the country had a net out-migration rate of 2 percent. Guatemala has a larger proportion of indigenous people than any other country in the Western Hemisphere (aside Bolivia). About 56 percent of the Guatemala's population is mestizo (mixture of indigenous Indian and white), and 44 percent is Indian. Though Spanish is the country's official language, 40 percent of the population speak indigenous Indian languages.

Poverty, 1989

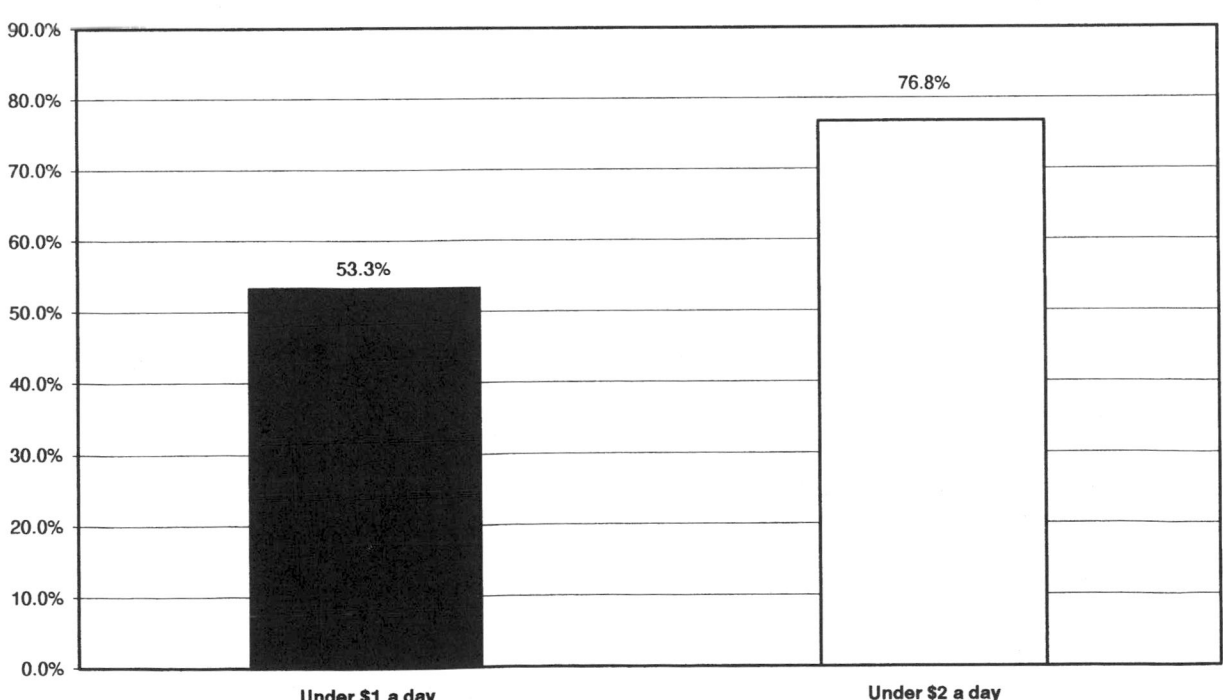

For most of the post–World War era, the Guatemalan economy has been dominated by outside financial interests, especially the North American firm United Fruit. This domination, say many experts, is reflected in the high levels of poverty that have persisted throughout the era.

Urbanization

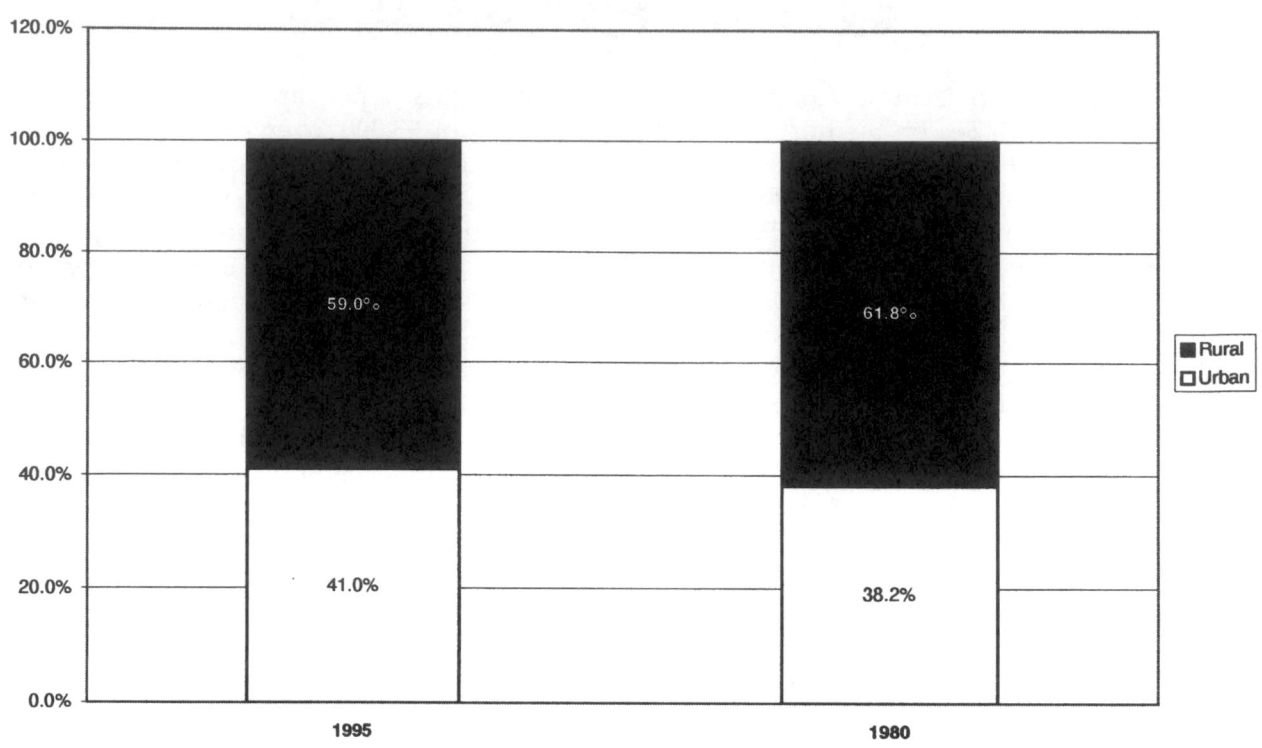

The need of United Fruit and other agricultural giants for a readily available labor force is one of the reasons Guatemala's population, which is dominated by Indians to an extent not seen in any other Latin American nation (with the exception of Bolivia), remains predominantly rural.

CHRONOLOGY

1966   Julio César Méndez Montenegro, a moderate, wins presidential elections over military candidate.

1970   Conservative Arana Osorio wins presidential elections, launches massive antiguerrilla campaign.

1974   Right-wing candidate wins suspicious election.

1981   Guatemala signs agreement with Britain, leading to independence of British Honduras (Belize), a territory claimed by Guatemala.

1982   Military officers, led by Efrem Rios Montt, seize power in coup.

1983   Montt overthrown.

1985   Election of centrist candidate sparks hope of end to vicious war against leftist guerrillas and massacre of civilians.

1991   Government begins negotiations with leftist guerrillas.

	1995	**1980**	**1965**

GEOGRAPHY

AREA (square miles/kilometers)	42,042/108,890
LAND AREA (square miles/kilometers)	41,865/108,430
COASTLINE (miles/kilometers)	250/400

CITIES

CAPITAL	Guatemala City	1,675,589 (90)
MAJOR CITY	Quetzaltenango	101,168

POPULATION

	1995	**1980**	**1965**
TOTAL	11,227,614	6,054,227 (81)	4,284,473 (64)
DENSITY (per square mile/kilometer)	254/98	189/73	n/a
ANNUAL GROWTH	2.5%	2.9%	3.1%
AGE COHORTS			
0–14	43%	n/a	46%
15–64	54%	n/a	51%
65 AND OVER	3%	n/a	3%
MALE	50%		
FEMALE	50%		
URBAN	41%	38.20%	n/a
RURAL	59%	61.80%	n/a
NET MIGRATION RATE	−2	n/a	−1.9

IDENTITY

ETHNICITY	
MESTIZO	56%
INDIAN	44%
LANGUAGE	
SPANISH	60%
INDIAN LANGUAGES	40%
RELIGION	
ROMAN CATHOLIC	n/a
PROTESTANT	n/a
MAYAN	n/a

	1995	1980	1965

VITAL STATISTICS

BIRTHS

BIRTH RATE	34	38.3 (83)	46.5
URBAN BIRTH RATE	35.5 (92)		
RURAL BIRTH RATE	38.5 (92)		
INFANT MORTALITY RATE	46.2	71.2 (83)	91.5
LIFE EXPECTANCY AT BIRTH	65.2	54.6 (83)	43.6

MARRIAGES

MARRIAGE RATE	4.7	4 (83)	3.5
AVERAGE AGE AT MARRIAGE M/F	23.8/21.3		
DIVORCE RATE	0.2	0.2 (83)	0.1

DEATHS

DEATH RATE	7.2	7.2 (83)	n/a

HOUSEHOLDS

NUMBER	n/a	n/a	804,940 (64)
AVERAGE SIZE	n/a	n/a	5.2 (64)

ECONOMICS AND LABOR

GDP PER CAPITA US$	$3,300

LABOR FORCE (thousands)	823.2 (93)
AGRICULTURE	214.6
MINING	2.4
MANUFACTURING	136.7
UTILITIES	11.1
CONSTRUCTION	26.4
TRADE/FOOD/TOURISM	102.6
TRANSPORT/COMMUNICATIONS	25.2
SOCIAL AND PERSONAL SERVICES	304.2

UNEMPLOYMENT (official)	1% (93)
UNION DENSITY	4.40%

POVERTY

UNDER $1/DAY	53.3% (89)
UNDER $2/DAY	76.8% (89)

	1995	1980	1965

TRANSPORT

JOURNEYS (by transport mode)

	1995	1980	1965
RAILROAD PASSENGER TRIPS (millions of miles/kilometers)	12,531.0 (91)		
AIR PASSENGER TRIPS (thousands)	252.0 (94)		

VEHICLES

	1995	1980	1965
PRIVATE CARS	102,000	n/a	29,000
COMMERCIAL	96,800	n/a	17,200

HEALTH AND HEALTH CARE

HEALTH CARE

	1995	1980	1965
ACCESS TO SAFE WATER	60%		
ACCESS TO SANITATION	66%		
MEASLES IMMUNIZATION	84%		
RATE OF PHYSICIANS	0.3	n/a	0.2 (60)
RATE OF HOSPITAL BEDS	1.1	n/a	2.7 (60)

HEALTH INDICATORS

	1995	1980	1965
PREGNANT WOMEN W/ANEMIA	39%		
LOW-BIRTH-WEIGHT BABIES	14%		
CHILD MALNUTRITION	33%		
SMOKING PREVALENCE M/F	38/25%		
TUBERCULOSIS INCIDENCE RATE	1.1		
AIDS/HIV CASES	711	497 (93)	
TOTAL DEATHS	73,870 (93)		

EDUCATION

SCHOOL AGE IN SCHOOL

	1995	1980	1965
PRIMARY	84%	71%	55%
SECONDARY	25%	18%	9%
HIGHER	8%	8%	1.7%

FEMALES IN SCHOOL

	1995	1980	1965
PRIMARY	76%	61%	55%
SECONDARY	n/a	11%	7%

	1995	1980	1965
ADULT ILLITERACY M/F	38/51%	37.4/52.% (85)	55.9/68.2%

	1995	1980	1965
COMMUNICATIONS			
RATE OF NEWSPAPERS	18	29	31
RATE OF RADIOS	68	51	n/a
RATE OF TELEVISIONS	53	25	13

Source: CIA, *The World Factbook, 1997;* ILO, *World Labour Report, 1997;* UN, *Demographic Yearbook, 1997;* UN, *Statistical Yearbook, 1996;* World Bank, *World Development Indicators, 1998.*

GUINEA

Guinea is located in West Africa, facing the Atlantic Ocean. Guinea-Bissau borders the 94,927-square-mile (245,860-square-kilometer) country on the northwest, Senegal and Mali on the north, Côte D'Ivoire on the southeast, and Liberia and Sierra Leone on the south. In October 1958 Guinea gained independence from France. For much of its formative years of independence, Guinea was ruled by a one-party state. In the early 1990s, the country adopted a multiparty democracy-style political system and held elections in June 1995. Though Guinea is endowed with abundant natural resources, the country is one of the least-developed countries in the world with a 1995 annual per capita gross domestic product (GDP) of only $1,020. In 1995, the country's population of over 7.4 million was growing at an annual rate of 1.9 percent, lower than other countries in the region, but still high by international standards. In part because of the lack of economic opportunity, a growing number of residents are migrating out of the country to Western Europe. The three leading ethnic groups in the country are the Peuhl (40 percent), Malinke (30 percent), and Soussou (20 percent). Although the country has one of the lowest life expectancies at birth (45.1 percent) and highest infant mortality rates (134.2 per 1,000 live births), life expectancy and infant mortality have both shown improvement over the past three decades.

	1995	**1980**	**1965**
GEOGRAPHY			
AREA (square miles/kilometers)	94,927/245,860		
LAND AREA (square miles/kilometers)	94,927/245,860		
COASTLINE (miles/kilometers)	200/320		
CITIES			
CAPITAL	Conakry	n/a	n/a	197,267 (67)
POPULATION			
TOTAL	7,411,981	5,781,014 (83)	2,570,219 (64)
DENSITY (per square mile/kilometer)	70/27	65/25	70/27
ANNUAL GROWTH	1.9%	2.4%	2.8%
AGE COHORTS			
0–14	44%	n/a	42%
15–64	53%	n/a	53% (64)[1]
65 AND OVER	3%	n/a	5.1% (64)[2]
URBAN	30%		
RURAL	70%		
NET MIGRATION RATE	−5.4		

	1995	1980	1965

IDENTITY

ETHNICITY
PEUHL	40%		
MALINKE	30%		
SOUSSOU	20%		

LANGUAGE
FRENCH (official)	n/a		

RELIGION
MUSLIM	85%		
CHRISTIAN	8%		
ANIMIST	7%		

VITAL STATISTICS

BIRTHS
BIRTH RATE	42.6	46.8	62
INFANT MORTALITY RATE	134.2	216	216
LIFE EXPECTANCY AT BIRTH	45.1	40.2	27

DEATHS
DEATH RATE	18.7	23.5	40

ECONOMICS AND LABOR

GDP PER CAPITA US$
	$1,020		

LABOR FORCE M/F
AGRICULTURE M/F	83/92%		
INDUSTRY M/F	2/1%		
SERVICES M/F	15/7%		

UNION DENSITY
	2.5%		

POVERTY
UNDER $1/DAY	26.3% (91)		
UNDER $2/DAY	50.2% (91)		

	1995	1980	1965

TRANSPORT

JOURNEYS (by transport mode)
AIR PASSENGER TRIPS (thousands)   45 (94)

VEHICLES

	1995	1980	1965
PRIVATE CARS	23,100	23,000 (83)	9,300
COMMERCIAL	13,000	9,900	13,500

HEALTH AND HEALTH CARE

HEALTH CARE

	1995	1980	1965
ACCESS TO SAFE WATER	62%		
ACCESS TO SANITATION	70%		
MEASLES IMMUNIZATION (under 12)	69%		
RATE OF PHYSICIANS	0.2	negligible	negligible (60)
RATE OF HOSPITAL BEDS	0.6		0.8 (60)

HEALTH INDICATORS

	1995	1980
PREGNANT WOMEN WITH ANEMIA		
LOW-BIRTH-WEIGHT BABIES	21%	
CHILD MALNUTRITION	24%	
SMOKING PREVALENCE M/F	40/2%	
TUBERCULOSIS INCIDENCE RATE	1.66	
AIDS/HIV CASES	2,158	1,005 (93)

EDUCATION

SCHOOL AGE IN SCHOOL

	1995	1980	1965
PRIMARY	48%	36%	31%
SECONDARY	12%	17%	5%
HIGHER	n/a	5%	0.1%

FEMALES IN SCHOOL

	1995	1980	1965
PRIMARY	33%	33%	19%
SECONDARY	24%	28%	1%

ADULT ILLITERACY M/F   50/78%   60.3/82.8% (85)   n/a

	1995	1980	1965
COMMUNICATIONS			
RATE OF NEWSPAPERS	n/a	4 (79)	1 (70)
RATE OF RADIOS	43	30	29
RATE OF TELEVISIONS	8	1	0

FOOTNOTES
1. Ages 15–19.
2. Ages 60 and over.

Source: CIA, *The World Factbook, 1997;* ILO, *World Labour Report, 1997;* UN, *Demographic Yearbook, 1997;* UN, *Statistical Yearbook, 1996;* World Bank, *World Development Indicators, 1998.*

GUINEA-BISSAU

Guinea-Bissau is located in West Africa, facing the Atlantic Ocean. Senegal borders the 13,946-square-mile (36,120-square-kilometer) country on the north, and Guinea on the east and south. Formerly known as Portuguese Guinea, the country gained independence from Portugal in September 1974. In early 1991, Guinea-Bissau made the transition to multiparty democracy. Though the country exports agricultural commodities, the vast majority of the country's population resides in rural areas and engages in subsistence farming.

Guinea-Bissau has one of the world's highest poverty rates. In 1991, 96.7 percent of the population was subsisting on the equivalent of under $2 a day, and 88.2 percent were surviving on less than $1 a day. The country's population of 1,151,330 in 1995 was growing at 2.4 percent per year. Average life expectancy at birth in Guinea-Bissau is only 48.3 years, and the country has one of the highest infant mortality rates in the world. Portuguese is the official language, though much of the population speaks local languages.

	1995	1980	1965
GEOGRAPHY			
AREA (square miles/kilometers)	13,946/36,120		
LAND AREA (square miles/kilometers)	10,811/28,000		
COASTLINE (miles/kilometers)	219/350		
CITIES			
CAPITAL	Bissau	n/a	109,214 (79)	n/a
POPULATION			
TOTAL	1,151,330	767,739 (79)	n/a
DENSITY (per square mile/kilometer)	78/30	65/25	n/a
ANNUAL GROWTH	2.4%	1.9%	n/a
AGE COHORTS			
0–14	43%		
15–64	54%		
65 AND OVER	3%		
MALE	48%		
FEMALE	52%		
URBAN	22%		
RURAL	78%		
NET MIGRATION RATE	0	n/a	0

	1995	1980	1965

IDENTITY

ETHNICITY

BALANTA	30%		
FULA	20%		
MANJACA	14%		

LANGUAGE

PORTUGUESE (official)	n/a		
CRIOLO	n/a		

RELIGION

ANIMIST	65%		
MUSLIM	30%		
CHRISTIAN	5%		

VITAL STATISTICS

BIRTHS

BIRTH RATE	39.7	40.7	n/a
INFANT MORTALITY RATE	140	143	n/a
LIFE EXPECTANCY AT BIRTH	48.3	43	n/a

MARRIAGES

MARRIAGE RATE	n/a	0.2	n/a

DEATHS

DEATH RATE	16.2	21.7	n/a

ECONOMICS AND LABOR

GDP PER CAPITA US$	$900		

LABOR FORCE M/F

AGRICULTURE	78/96%		
INDUSTRY	3/1%		
SERVICES	19/3%		

POVERTY

UNDER $1/DAY	88.2% (91)		
UNDER $2/DAY	96.7% (91)		

	1995	1980	1965

TRANSPORT

JOURNEYS (by transport mode)
AIR PASSENGER TRIPS (thousands) 21.0 (94)

VEHICLES
PRIVATE CARS 3,500 (92)
COMMERCIAL 2,500

HEALTH AND HEALTH CARE

HEALTH CARE

	1995	1980	1965
ACCESS TO SAFE WATER	23%		
ACCESS TO SANITATION	20%		
MEASLES IMMUNIZATION	68%		
RATE OF PHYSICIANS	n/a	0.1	0.1 (60)
RATE OF HOSPITAL BEDS	1.5	1.8	1.7 (60)

HEALTH INDICATORS

	1995	1980	1965
PREGNANT WOMEN WITH ANEMIA	74%		
LOW-BIRTH-WEIGHT BABIES	20%		
CHILD MALNUTRITION	23%		
TUBERCULOSIS INCIDENCE RATE	2.2		
AIDS/HIV CASES	786	453 (93)	

EDUCATION

SCHOOL AGE IN SCHOOL

	1995	1980	1965
PRIMARY	64%	68%	39% (70)
SECONDARY	n/a	6%	8% (70)

Source: CIA, *The World Factbook, 1997;* ILO, *World Labour Report, 1997;* UN, *Demographic Yearbook, 1997;* UN, *Statistical Yearbook, 1996;* World Bank, *World Development Indicators, 1998.*

GUYANA

Guyana is located in north central South America, facing the Atlantic Ocean. Brazil borders the 83,000-square-mile (214,970-square-kilometers) country on the south, Suriname on the east, and Venezuela on the west. Guyana received its independence from the United Kingdom in May 1966. The country has a multiparty democracy. The primary industries in Guyana, one of the poorest countries in the Western Hemisphere, are mining, agriculture, and forestry. In the 1990s, to conform to structural adjustment demands made by Western lenders, Guyana implemented severe national austerity programs that reduced the value of the currency and led to rising unemployment. The country has a union density in excess of 25 percent, primarily due to the unionization of large segments of the mining industry. Guyana's small population of 712,091 was declining at a rate of nearly 1 percent in 1995, due mainly to the out-migration of residents seeking gainful employment. Guyana's population is divided racially between East Indians (constituting 51 percent of the country's population) and Africans (accounting for 43 percent of the population). Amer-Indians make up about 4 percent of the nation's residents. The ethnic divisions have frequently flared into conflict between the two major groups. The national life expectancy at birth in 1995 is 60.1 years, lower than the life expectancy in 1960. The infant mortality rate is 52.3 deaths per 1,000 live births.

	1995	1980	1965
GEOGRAPHY			
AREA (square miles/kilometers)	83,000/214,970		
LAND AREA (square miles/kilometers)	76,004/196,850		
COASTLINE (miles/kilometers)	287/459		
CITIES			
CAPITAL	Georgetown	n/a	72,049 (76)	n/a
POPULATION			
TOTAL	712,091	758,619	560,330 (60)
DENSITY (per square mile/kilometer)	10.4/4	10.4/4	7.8/3
ANNUAL GROWTH	−0.9%	n/a	2.8%
AGE COHORTS			
0–14	33%	n/a	46%
15–64	63%	n/a	51%
65 AND OVER	4%	n/a	3%
MALE	50%		
FEMALE	50%		

	1995	1980	1965
URBAN	36%		
RURAL	64%		
NET MIGRATION RATE	−18.5	n/a	−0.6

IDENTITY

ETHNICITY
EAST INDIAN	51%		
AFRICAN	43%		
AMER-INDIAN	4%		

LANGUAGE
ENGLISH	n/a		

RELIGION
CHRISTIAN	57%		
HINDU	33%		
MUSLIM	9%		

VITAL STATISTICS

BIRTHS
BIRTH RATE	19	28.3 (78)	41 (60)
INFANT MORTALITY RATE	52.3	45.9 (78)	39.8 (60)
LIFE EXPECTANCY AT BIRTH	60.1	61 (78)	61 (60)

MARRIAGES
MARRIAGE RATE	n/a	4 (78)	3.5 (60)
DIVORCE RATE	n/a	0.6 (78)	0.6 (60)

DEATHS
DEATH RATE	9.6	7.3 (78)	10 (60)

HOUSEHOLDS

NUMBER	n/a	n/a	110,057 (61)

ECONOMICS AND LABOR

GDP PER CAPITA US$	$2,200		
UNION DENSITY	25.2%		

	1995	1980	1965
TRANSPORT			
JOURNEYS (by transport mode)			
AIR PASSENGER TRIPS (thousands)	115 (94)		
VEHICLES			
PRIVATE CARS	24,000	n/a	10,400
COMMERCIAL	9,000	n/a	3,600
HEALTH AND HEALTH CARE			
HEALTH CARE			
RATE OF PHYSICIANS	n/a	n/a	0.3 (60)
HEALTH INDICATORS			
AIDS/HIV CASES	698	497 (93)	
EDUCATION			
SCHOOL AGE IN SCHOOL			
PRIMARY	n/a	100%	117%
SECONDARY	n/a	60%	44%
HIGHER	n/a	2.6%	0.5%
FEMALES IN SCHOOL			
PRIMARY		99%	116%
SECONDARY	n/a	62%	43%
HIGHER	n/a	2.3%	0.8% (70)
ADULT ILLITERACY M/F	n/a	3.0/5.2% (85)	5.7/11.0% (70)
COMMUNICATIONS			
RATE OF NEWSPAPERS	99	76	93
RATE OF RADIOS	490	408	125
RATE OF TELEVISIONS	39	n/a	0

Source: CIA, *The World Factbook, 1997*; ILO, *World Labour Report, 1997*; UN, *Demographic Yearbook, 1997*; UN, *Statistical Yearbook, 1996*; World Bank, *World Development Indicators, 1998*.

HAITI

Haiti is located in the Caribbean Sea on the western one-third of the island of Hispaniola. Haiti shares the island with the Dominican Republic, which occupies the eastern two-thirds of the island. The Caribbean borders the 10,714-square-mile (27,750-square-kilometer) country on the south and the Atlantic Ocean on the north. The country is located about 50 miles east of Cuba. Under authoritarian rule for much of the post–World War II era, Haiti has endured a long history of political turmoil and economic despair. Even with the emergence of democratic rule in the early 1990s, the vast majority of Haiti's pop-ulation continues to suffer economic hardship. In exchange for international aid, the country has had to conform to rigid economic conditions imposed by Western banks and lending agencies. In 1995, the country's per capita gross domestic product (GDP) was only $1,000. Even this low figure does not account for the country's unequal distribution of resources between an affluent minority and the poor majority. In 1995, the estimated unemployment rate was 60 percent. The country has a low life expectancy (under 50 years of age) and a high infant mortality rate of 86.2 deaths per 1,000 live births.

		1995	1980	1965
GEOGRAPHY				
AREA (square miles/kilometers)	10,714/27,750			
LAND AREA (square miles/kilometers)	10,641/27,560			
COASTLINE (miles/kilometers)	1,107/1,771			
CITIES				
CAPITAL	Port-au-Prince	690,168 (90)		
MAJOR CITIES	Carrefour	216,930		
	Delmas	178,990		
POPULATION				
TOTAL		6,731,539	5,053,792 (82)	4,450,900 (66)
DENSITY (per square mile/kilometer)		671/259	614/237 (82)	415/160
AGE COHORTS				
0–14		46%	n/a	38%
15–64		50%	n/a	59%
65 AND OVER		4%	n/a	3%
MALE		48%		
FEMALE		52%		

	1995	**1980**	**1965**
URBAN	32%	23.9%	n/a
RURAL	68%	76.1%	n/a
NET MIGRATION RATE	−4.5		

IDENTITY

ETHNICITY
BLACK	95%
MULATTO	5%

LANGUAGE
FRENCH (official)	10%
CREOLE	90%

RELIGION
ROMAN CATHOLIC AND VOODOO	80%
PROTESTANT	16%

VITAL STATISTICS

BIRTHS
BIRTH RATE	38.2	41.3	45.5
INFANT MORTALITY RATE	86.2	128	n/a
LIFE EXPECTANCY AT BIRTH	49.3	53	32.6

MARRIAGES
AVERAGE AGE AT MARRIAGE M/F	27.3/23.8

DEATHS
DEATH RATE	16	14.2	20.2

ECONOMICS AND LABOR

GDP PER CAPITA US$ $1,000

LABOR FORCE M/F
AGRICULTURE	76/57%
INDUSTRY	9/8%
SERVICES	15/35%

	1995	1980	1965

TRANSPORT

VEHICLES

	1995	1980	1965
PRIVATE CARS	32,000	21,800	4,800
COMMERCIAL	21,000	11,200	1,500

HEALTH AND HEALTH CARE

HEALTH CARE

	1995	1980	1965
ACCESS TO SAFE WATER	28%		
ACCESS TO SANITATION	24%		
MEASLES IMMUNIZATION	24%		
RATE OF PHYSICIANS	0.1	0.1	0.1 (60)
RATE OF HOSPITAL BEDS	0.8	0.7	0.6 (60)

HEALTH INDICATORS

	1995	1980	1965
PREGNANT WOMEN WITH ANEMIA	38%		
LOW-BIRTH-WEIGHT BABIES	15%		
CHILD MALNUTRITION	28%		
TUBERCULOSIS INCIDENCE RATE	3.33		
AIDS/HIV CASES	4,967	4,967 (93)	

EDUCATION

SCHOOL AGE IN SCHOOL

	1995	1980	1965
PRIMARY	n/a	76%	40%
SECONDARY	n/a	14%	4%
HIGHER	n/a	1%	0.4%

FEMALES IN SCHOOL

	1995	1980	1965
PRIMARY	n/a	46%	26%
SECONDARY	n/a	11%	3%

	1995	1980	1965
ADULT ILLITERACY M/F	n/a	52/58%	n/a

COMMUNICATIONS

	1995	1980	1965
RATE OF NEWSPAPERS	7	7	5
RATE OF RADIOS	48	20	1
RATE OF TELEVISIONS	5	3	0.1

Source: CIA, *The World Factbook, 1997*; ILO, *World Labour Report, 1997*; UN, *Demographic Yearbook, 1997*; UN, *Statistical Yearbook, 1996*; World Bank, *World Development Indicators, 1998*.

HONDURAS

Honduras, the largest country in Central America, is located between the Caribbean Sea and the Gulf of Fonseca, an inlet of the Pacific Ocean. Nicaragua borders the 43,278-square-mile (112,090-square-kilometer) country on the south, Guatemala on the west, and El Salvador on the southwest. Honduras has a democratic multiparty form of government. The economy is dominated by the production of cash crops and primary products for export, primarily to Western markets. The country's per capita gross domestic product (GDP) in 1995 was $1,980 per year. Because of the unequal distribution of land and resources, much of the country lives in poverty. In 1992, 75.7 percent of the population survived on the equivalent of less than $2 a day, and 46.9 percent lived on less than $1 a day. Mestizos make up the vast majority (90 percent) of the nation's population. Indigenous Indians (7 percent) and persons of African descent (2 percent) are the two leading minorities. Honduras's life expectancy at birth in 1995 was 68.4 years, and the infant mortality rate was 43 deaths per 1,000 live births.

	1995	1965	1980
GEOGRAPHY			
AREA (square miles/kilometers)	43,278/112,090		
LAND AREA (square miles/kilometers)	43,201/111,890		
COASTLINE (miles/kilometers)	513/820		
CITIES			
CAPITAL	Tegucigalpa	n/a	597,512 (86)	n/a
MAJOR CITIES	San Pedro Sula	n/a	397,201 (85)	n/a
	La Ceiba	n/a	103,600 (85)	n/a
POPULATION			
TOTAL	5,605,193	2,656,948 (74)	2,362,817 (66)
DENSITY (per square mile/kilometer)	137/53	61/24	55/21
ANNUAL GROWTH	n/a	3.4%	n/a
AGE COHORTS			
0–14	43%	n/a	40%
15–64	54%	n/a	58%
65 AND OVER	3%	n/a	2%
MALE	50%		
FEMALE	50%		

	1995	1980	1965
URBAN	44%	35.9%	n/a
RURAL	56%	64.1%	n/a
NET MIGRATION RATE	1.5	n/a	0.2 (63)

IDENTITY

ETHNICITY
MESTIZO	90%		
INDIAN	7%		
BLACK	2%		

LANGUAGE
SPANISH	n/a		

RELIGION
ROMAN CATHOLIC	97%		
PROTESTANT	3%		

VITAL STATISTICS

BIRTHS
	1995	1980	1965
BIRTH RATE	33.4	43.9	47.5
INFANT MORTALITY RATE	43	82	45.4
LIFE EXPECTANCY AT BIRTH	68.4	55.2	n/a

MARRIAGES
MARRIAGE RATE	4.9	4.9	3.3
DIVORCE RATE	0.4	0.4	0.2

DEATHS
DEATH RATE	5.8	10.1	n/a

HOUSEHOLDS

NUMBER	n/a	n/a	325,492 (61)
AVERAGE SIZE	n/a	n/a	5.7 (61)

ECONOMICS AND LABOR

GDP PER CAPITA US$	$1,980		

	1995	1980	1965
LABOR FORCE M/F (thousands)	1,152.0/522.7 (92)		
AGRICULTURE	607.6/32.3		
MINING	5.4/358.0		
MANUFACTURING	125.4/125.0		
UTILITIES	6.8/1.1		
CONSTRUCTION	70.0/2.6		
TRADE/FOOD/TOURISM	130.8/151.1		
TRANSPORT/COMMUNICATIONS	45.7/6.3		
FINANCE/INSURANCE/REAL ESTATE	19.6/10.4		
SOCIAL AND PERSONAL SERVICES	140.1/193.5		
UNION DENSITY	4.5%		
POVERTY			
UNDER $1/DAY	46.9 (92)		
UNDER $2/DAY	75.7% (92)		

TRANSPORT

	1995	1980	1965
JOURNEYS (by transport mode)			
AIR PASSENGER TRIPS (thousands)	449 (94)		
VEHICLES			
PRIVATE CARS	68,500	25,600	9,000
COMMERCIAL	102,000	45,400	7,500

HEALTH AND HEALTH CARE

	1995	1980	1965
HEALTH CARE			
ACCESS TO SAFE WATER	65%		
ACCESS TO SANITATION	62%		
MEASLES IMMUNIZATION	90%		
RATE OF PHYSICIANS	0.4	0.3	0.1 (60)
RATE OF HOSPITAL BEDS	1	1.3	1.7 (60)
HEALTH INDICATORS			
PREGNANT WOMEN WITH ANEMIA	14%		
LOW-BIRTH-WEIGHT BABIES	9%		
CHILD MALNUTRITION	18%		
SMOKING PREVALENCE M/F	36/11%		
TUBERCULOSIS INCIDENCE RATE	1.33		
AIDS/HIV CASES	5,084	3,416 (93)	

	1995	**1980**	**1965**

EDUCATION

SCHOOL AGE IN SCHOOL

	1995	1980	1965
PRIMARY	111%	98%	73%
SECONDARY	30%	30%	8%
HIGHER	10%	8%	1.10%

FEMALES IN SCHOOL

	1995	1980	1965
PRIMARY	111%	98%	73%
SECONDARY	n/a	30%	6%

	1995	1980	1965
ADULT ILLITERACY M/F	27/27%	39.3/41.6% (85)	n/a

COMMUNICATIONS

	1995	1980	1965
RATE OF NEWSPAPERS	31	59	19
RATE OF RADIOS	408	140	57
RATE OF TELEVISIONS	78	18	3

Source: CIA, *The World Factbook, 1997;* ILO, *World Labour Report, 1997;* UN, *Demographic Yearbook, 1997;* UN, *Statistical Yearbook, 1996;* World Bank, *World Development Indicators, 1998.*

HUNGARY

Hungary is a landlocked country located in east central Europe. The 35,919-square-mile (93,030-square-kilometer) country is bordered by Romania on the east, Serbia and Croatia on the south, Slovenia on the southwest, Austria on the west, Slovakia on the north, and Ukraine on the northeast. After World War II, Hungary became part of the Soviet political and economic system, as a member state of the Warsaw Pact and the COMECON economic alliance. Following the collapse and breakup of the Soviet Union, Hungary sought to gain closer linkages with the West. In 1997, the country was admitted into the NATO military alliance and sought to gain entry into the European Union. Even before the breakup of the Soviet Union, Hungary had initiated market reforms. In the 1990s, the country implemented mass privatization of state-owned industry, and austerity programs were aimed at attracting foreign investors. Indeed, since the early 1990s, foreign investors have purchased large segments of Hungary's industry. By the late 1990s, however, many of the programs became politically unpopular. In 1995, the country's population of more than 10 million was declining at an annual rate of 0.7 percent, the result of a low birth rate and out-migration. In the 1990s, though infant mortality rates continued to decline, average life expectancy declined marginally from the levels in previous decades. Hungarians compose about 90 percent of the population; Gypsies and Germans are Hungary's two leading ethnic minorities.

	1995	**1980**	**1965**
GEOGRAPHY			
AREA (square miles/kilometers)	35,919/93,030		
LAND AREA (square miles/kilometers)	35,653/92,340		
COASTLINE	landlocked		
CITIES			
CAPITAL	Budapest	1,962,855 (94)	
MAJOR CITIES	Debrecen	214,245	
	Miskolc	185,877	
	Szeged	173,860	
	Pecs	167,772	
POPULATION			
TOTAL	10,002,541	10,709,463	9,961,044 (60)
DENSITY (per square mile/kilometer)	285/110	295/114	282/109
ANNUAL GROWTH	−0.7%	−0.1%	0.4%
AGE COHORTS			
0–14	18%	n/a	22%
15–64	68%	n/a	68%
65 AND OVER	14%	n/a	10%

	1995	1980	1965
MALE	48%		
FEMALE	52%		
URBAN	65%	53.2%	n/a
RURAL	35%	46.8%	n/a
NET MIGRATION RATE	−2.5	n/a	0

IDENTITY

ETHNICITY			
HUNGARIAN	90%		
ROMANISH (Gypsy)	4%		
GERMAN	3%		
LANGUAGE			
HUNGARIAN	98%		
RELIGION			
ROMAN CATHOLIC	68%		
CALVINIST	20%		
LUTHERAN	5%		

VITAL STATISTICS

	1995	1980	1965
BIRTHS			
BIRTH RATE	10.7	12.2 (85)	13.6
URBAN BIRTH RATE	10.6 (94)		
RURAL BIRTH RATE	12.2 (94)		
INFANT MORTALITY RATE	12.3	20.4 (85)	38.8
ABORTION RATE	647.7 (94)		
LIFE EXPECTANCY AT BIRTH	69	69.6	69.5
MARRIAGES			
MARRIAGE RATE	5.3	6.9 (85)	9.1
AVERAGE AGE AT MARRIAGE M/F	27.1/23.8		
DIVORCE RATE	2.3	2.7 (85)	2
DEATHS			
DEATH RATE	15.1	13.8 (85)	10

HOUSEHOLDS

	1995	1980	1965
NUMBER	3,889,532 (90)	n/a	3,309,900 (63)
AVERAGE SIZE	2.6 (90)	n/a	2.9 (63)

	1995	1980	1965
TYPE OF HOUSEHOLD			
SINGLE	8.5%		
MARRIED	64.3%		
WIDOWED	16.1%		
DIVORCED/SEPARATED	11.1%		
FEMALE HEADED	26.5%		

ECONOMICS AND LABOR

	1995	1980	1965
GDP PER CAPITA US$	$7,000		
LABOR FORCE M/F (thousands)	2,185.2/2,131.3 (92)		
AGRICULTURE	364.8/204.7		
MANUFACTURING	718.2/599.6		
CONSTRUCTION	211.2/60.1		
TRADE/FOOD/TOURISM	205.4/412.3		
TRANSPORT/COMMUNICATIONS	250.4/123.6		
SOCIAL AND PERSONAL SERVICES	435.2/791.0		
UNEMPLOYMENT (official)	10.9% (94)		
UNION DENSITY	52.5%		
POVERTY			
UNDER $1/DAY	1%		
UNDER $2/DAY	10.7%		

TRANSPORT

	1995	1980	1965
JOURNEYS (by transport mode)			
RAILROAD PASSENGER TRIPS	8,508.0 (94)		
(millions of miles/kilometers)			
AIR PASSENGER TRIPS (thousands)	1,325.0 (94)		
VEHICLES (thousands)			
PRIVATE CARS	2,176.9	1,013.4	99.4
COMMERCIAL	297.1	162.8	n/a

HEALTH AND HEALTH CARE

	1995	1980	1965
HEALTH CARE			
ACCESS TO SANITATION	94%		
MEASLES IMMUNIZATION	100%		

	1995	1980	1965
RATE OF PHYSICIANS	3.6	2.5	1.4 (60)
RATE OF HOSPITAL BEDS	9.6	9.1	6.9 (60)

HEALTH INDICATORS

	1995	1980	1965
LOW-BIRTH-WEIGHT BABIES	9%		
SMOKING PREVALENCE M/F	40/27%		
TUBERCULOSIS INCIDENCE RATE	0.5		
AIDS/HIV CASES	202	148 (93)	
TOTAL DEATHS	144,000		

EDUCATION

SCHOOL AGE IN SCHOOL

	1995	1980	1965
PRIMARY	97%	96%	101%
SECONDARY	81%	70%	35%
HIGHER	19%	14%	5%

FEMALES IN SCHOOL

	1995	1980	1965
PRIMARY	96%	94%	100%
SECONDARY	63%	65%	41%
HIGHER	n/a	13.1%	8.8% (70)

	1995	1980	1965
ADULT ILLITERACY	n/a	0.7/1.5%	2.1/3.1% (63)

COMMUNICATIONS

	1995	1980	1965
RATE OF NEWSPAPERS	282	178	247
RATE OF RADIOS	617	249	499
RATE OF TELEVISIONS	427	83	310

Source: CIA, The World Factbook, 1997; ILO, World Labour Report, 1997; UN, Demographic Yearbook, 1997; UN, Statistical Yearbook, 1996; World Bank, World Development Indicators, 1998.

ICELAND

Iceland is an island located in Northern Europe in the Atlantic Ocean, northwest of the British Isles. The mountainous 39,768-square-mile (103,000-square-kilometer) island is located southeast of Greenland. In June 1944, Iceland gained independence from Denmark. The country has a democratic multiparty political system. The country has an advanced economy dominated by the commercial fishing industry. In 1995, Iceland had an average annual per capita gross domestic product of $18,800. The country has a high standard of living, due in part to the result of an extensive system of social protection provided by the Icelandic government. The country's 1995 population of 270,292 was declining by 0.8 percent. The country's decline in population reflects a net out-migration trend. Iceland has among the world's highest life expectancies that reached over 80 years in 1995. The country's infant mortality rate of 4.3 deaths per 1,000 live births is also among the lowest in the world. Nearly all of the country's population are descendants of Norwegians and Celtics, and Icelandic is the country's official language.

		1995	1980	1965
GEOGRAPHY				
AREA (square miles/kilometers)	39,768/103,000			
LAND AREA (square miles/kilometers)	38,707/100,250			
COASTLINE (miles/kilometers)	3,118/4,988			
CITIES				
CAPITAL	Reykjavik	101,418 (93)		
POPULATION				
TOTAL		270,292	204,930 (70)	175,680 (60)
DENSITY (per square mile/kilometer)		7.8/3	5.2/2	5.2/2
ANNUAL GROWTH		−0.8%	1.1%	1.8%
AGE COHORTS				
0–14		24%	n/a	35%
15–64		64%	n/a	57%
65 AND OVER		12%	n/a	8%
MALE		51%		
FEMALE		49%		
URBAN		92%	88.2	n/a
RURAL		8%	10.8%	n/a
NET MIGRATION RATE		−2.5	n/a	0

	1995	1980	1965

IDENTITY

ETHNICITY
NORWEGIAN AND CELT   100%

LANGUAGE
ICELANDIC   100%

RELIGION
EVANGELICAL LUTHERAN   96%
OTHER PROTESTANT AND ROMAN   3%
  CATHOLIC
NO RELIGION   1%

VITAL STATISTICS

BIRTHS

	1995	1980	1965
BIRTH RATE	16.9	n/a	24.7
URBAN BIRTH RATE	17.7 (93)		
RURAL BIRTH RATE	15.2 (93)		
INFANT MORTALITY RATE	4.3	n/a	15
ABORTION RATE	161.5 (92)		
LIFE EXPECTANCY AT BIRTH	80.8	n/a	72.9

MARRIAGES

	1995	1980	1965
MARRIAGE RATE	4.6	n/a	8.1
AVERAGE AGE AT MARRIAGE M/F	31.7/30.2		
DIVORCE RATE	1.8	n/a	1

DEATHS

	1995	1980	1965
DEATH RATE	9.6	n/a	6.7

HOUSEHOLDS

	1995	1980	1965
NUMBER			35,869 (50)
AVERAGE SIZE			3.9 (50)

ECONOMICS AND LABOR

	1995	1980	1965
GDP PER CAPITA US$	$18,800		
LABOR FORCE (thousands)	124.6 (90)		
AGRICULTURE	13.1		

	1995	1980	1965
MANUFACTURING	23.3		
UTILITIES	1.1		
CONSTRUCTION	12.4		
TRADE/FOOD/TOURISM	18.1		
TRANSPORT/COMMUNICATIONS	8.4		
FINANCE/INSURANCE/REAL ESTATE	10		
SOCIAL AND PERSONAL SERVICES	38.2		
UNEMPLOYMENT (official)	5.3% (94)		
UNION DENSITY	70.7%		

TRANSPORT

JOURNEYS (by transport mode)

AIR PASSENGER TRIPS (thousands)	1,031.0 (94)		

VEHICLES

	1995	1980	1965
PRIVATE CARS	116,200	86,000	28,300
COMMERCIAL	15,600	9,700	6,600

HEALTH AND HEALTH CARE

HEALTH CARE

	1995	1980	1965
RATE OF PHYSICIANS	n/a	n/a	1.3 (60)
RATE OF HOSPITAL BEDS	n/a	n/a	10.6 (60)

HEALTH INDICATORS

	1995	1980	1965
AIDS/HIV CASES	38	32 (93)	
TOTAL DEATHS	1,720 (94)		

EDUCATION

SCHOOL AGE IN SCHOOL

	1995	1980	1965
PRIMARY	n/a	97.0%	101.0%
SECONDARY	n/a	70.0%	68.0%
HIGHER	n/a	12.8%	5.8%

FEMALES IN SCHOOL

	1995	1980	1965
PRIMARY	n/a	n/a	100% (70)
SECONDARY	n/a	83.0%	71.0%
HIGHER	n/a	18.7%	5.3%

	1995	1980	1965
COMMUNICATIONS			
RATE OF NEWSPAPERS	519	548	435
RATE OF RADIOS	791	711	330
RATE OF TELEVISIONS	335	285	201 (70)

Source: CIA, *The World Factbook, 1997*; ILO, *World Labour Report, 1997*; UN, *Demographic Yearbook, 1997*; UN, *Statistical Yearbook, 1996*; World Bank, *World Development Indicators, 1998*.

INDIA

India is located in southern Asia on the Arabian Sea, Bay of Bengal, and Indian Ocean. Pakistan borders the 1,269,397-square-mile (3,287,590-square-kilometer) country on the west; Bhutan, China, and Nepal on the north; and Bangladesh and Myanmar (Burma) on the east. India gained independence from the United Kingdom in 1947. Until the 1990s, India had a multiparty democracy dominated by the Congress Party. In 1997, the Bharatiya Janata Party, a Hindu-dominated group, gained enough votes to lead the government. Though India is undergoing industrial development and modernization, nearly 75 percent of the population continues to live in rural areas, and poverty remains a significant problem. Nearly 90 percent of the country's population subsists on less than the equivalent of $2 a day,

and over 50 percent survives on less than $1 a day. The country's population of more than 950 million is the second largest in the world. Though growth rates have declined from 2.4 percent in 1961 to 1.6 percent in 1995, India's population is still increasing faster than the country can accommodate. Religious differences are the country's major source of internal political conflict. Hindus are the religious majority (80 percent), followed by Muslims (14 percent), Christians (2.4 percent), Sikhs (2 percent), and Buddhists (1 percent). In the 1990s, conflicts between Hindus and Muslims have been accompanied by violence. In recent decades, as a result of improvements in health care and sanitation, life expectancy has increased and infant mortality has declined.

Annual Growth

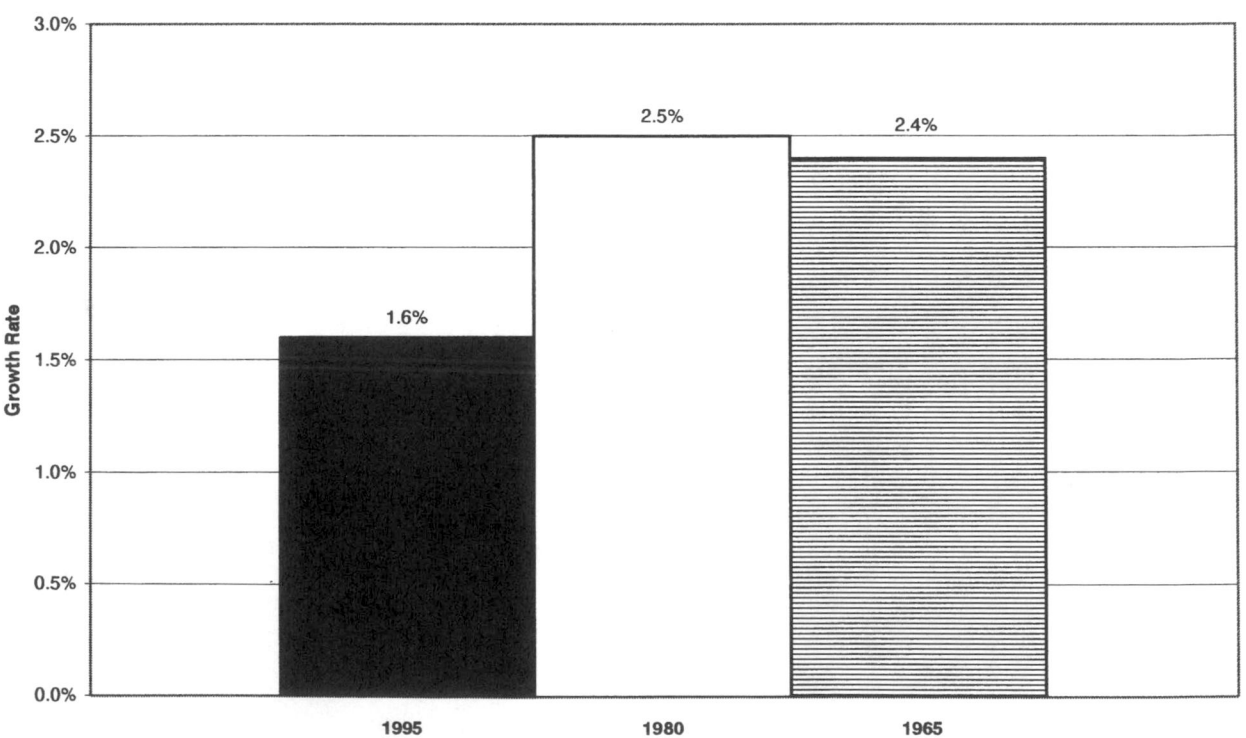

Unlike China, its giant neighbor to the north, India never imposed draconian birth-control programs. Not surprisingly, its annual growth rate has fallen, but not to the degree necessary to stop the huge growth in population.

Population

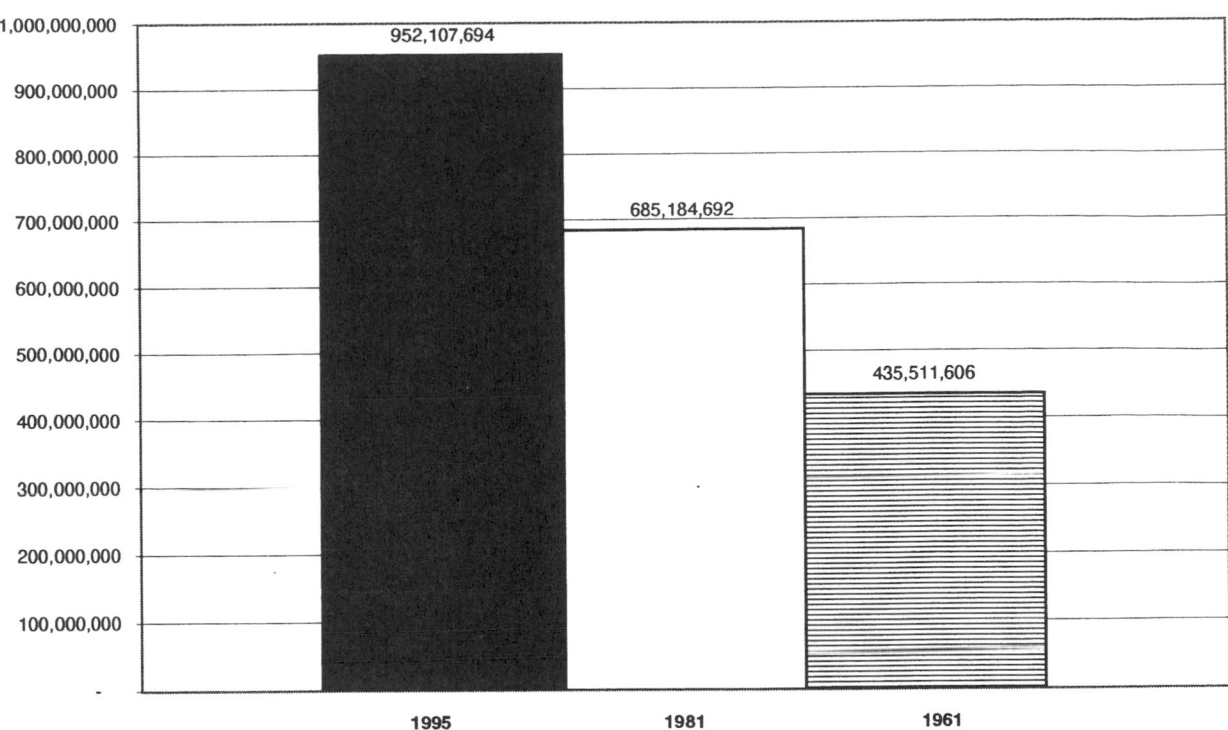

The country's continuing high birth rates, versus China's falling ones, make it almost inevitable that India will replace its East Asian counterpart as the most populous nation on earth sometime in the first half of the twenty-first century.

CHRONOLOGY

1965 India and Pakistan go to war for second time, over disputed territory in Kashmir.

1966 Indira Gandhi, daughter of Indian founding father Jawaharlal Nehru, becomes prime minister.

1971 India defeats Pakistan in third war, leading to independence of Bangladesh.

1974 India tests first nuclear bomb.

1977 Harsh policies lead to Gandhi's ouster from power and expulsion from parliament.

1980 Gandhi returns to power.

1984 Gandhi sends troops into Punjab to end Sikh separatist uprising there, and thousands are killed; Gandhi assassinated by Sikh bodyguards and succeeded by son, Rajiv.

1989 Congress Party loses power for first time since independence.

1991 Rajiv Gandhi assassinated by Tamil terrorists.

1998 Right-wing Hindu Nationalist Party wins power in parliament and launches renewed nuclear testing.

	1995	1980	1965

GEOGRAPHY

AREA (square miles/kilometers)   1,269,397/3,287,590
LAND AREA (square miles/kilometers)   1,147,950/2,973,190
COASTLINE (miles/kilometers)   4,375/7,000

CITIES

		1995
CAPITAL	New Delhi	301,297 (91)
MAJOR CITIES	Bombay	9,925,891
	Delhi	7,206,704
	Calcutta	4,399,819
	Madras	3,841,396

POPULATION

	1995	1980	1965
TOTAL	952,107,694	685,184,692 (81)	435,511,606 (61)
DENSITY (per square mile/kilometer)	738/285	591/228	422/163
ANNUAL GROWTH	1.6%	2.5%	2.4%
AGE COHORTS			
0–14	34%	n/a	41%
15–64	62%	n/a	56%
65 AND OVER	4%	n/a	3%
MALE	52%		
FEMALE	48%		
URBAN	27%	21.9%	n/a
RURAL	73%	78.1%	n/a
NET MIGRATION RATE	0.04		

IDENTITY

ETHNICITY

	1995
INDO-ARYAN	72%
DRAVIDIAN	25%
MONGOLOID/OTHER	3%

LANGUAGE

	1995
ENGLISH	n/a
HINDI	30%
BENGALI	n/a

	1995	1980	1965
RELIGION			
HINDU	80%		
MUSLIM	14%		
CHRISTIAN	2.4%		
SIKH	2%		
BUDDHIST	1%		

VITAL STATISTICS

	1995	1980	1965
BIRTHS			
BIRTH RATE	25.9	33.7 (83)	38.4 (61)
URBAN BIRTH RATE	24.3 (91)		
RURAL BIRTH RATE	30.9 (91)		
INFANT MORTALITY RATE	71.1	110.4 (83)	139 (61)
LIFE EXPECTANCY AT BIRTH	59.7	45.1 (83)	41.2 (61)
DEATHS			
DEATH RATE	9.6	11.9 (83)	12.9 (61)

HOUSEHOLDS

	1995	1980	1965
NUMBER	152,009,467 (91)	n/a	83,523,895 (60)
URBAN	40,418,141		
RURAL	111,591,326		
AVERAGE SIZE	5.5 (91)	n/a	5.2 (60)
URBAN	5.3		
RURAL	5.6		

ECONOMICS AND LABOR

	1995	1980	1965
GDP PER CAPITA US$	$1,500		
LABOR FORCE M/F (thousands)	22,417.0/3,545 (89)		
AGRICULTURE	953/467		
MINING	975/78		
MANUFACTURING	5,670/575		
UTILITIES	880/28		
CONSTRUCTION	1,157/58		
TRADE/FOOD/TOURISM	404/31		
TRANSPORT/COMMUNICATIONS	2,895/130		
FINANCE/INSURANCE/REAL ESTATE	1,204/152		
SOCIAL AND PERSONAL SERVICES	8,280/2,025		

	1995	1980	1965
UNION DENSITY	5.4%		
POVERTY			
UNDER $1/DAY	52.5%		
UNDER $2/DAY	88.8%		

TRANSPORT

	1995	1980	1965
JOURNEYS (by transport mode)			
RAILROAD PASSENGER TRIPS	314,564.0 (91)		
(millions of miles/kilometers)			
AIR PASSENGER TRIPS (thousands)	11,518.0 (94)		
VEHICLES (thousands)			
PRIVATE CARS	3,205	1,054.4	415.7
COMMERCIAL	2,396.7	1,002.7	314.5

HEALTH AND HEALTH CARE

	1995	1980	1965
HEALTH CARE			
ACCESS TO SAFE WATER	81%		
ACCESS TO SANITATION	29%		
MEASLES IMMUNIZATION	84%		
RATE OF PHYSICIANS	0.4	0.4	0.2 (60)
RATE OF HOSPITAL BEDS	0.8	0.8	0.5 (60)
HEALTH INDICATORS			
PREGNANT WOMEN WITH ANEMIA	88%		
LOW-BIRTH-WEIGHT BABIES	33%		
CHILD MALNUTRITION	66%		
SMOKING PREVALENCE M/F	40/3%		
TUBERCULOSIS INCIDENCE RATE	2.2		
AIDS/HIV CASES	2,095	494 (93)	

EDUCATION

	1995	1980	1965
SCHOOL AGE IN SCHOOL			
PRIMARY	100%	83%	56%
SECONDARY	49%	30%	15%
HIGHER	6%	5%	2.2%
FEMALES IN SCHOOL			
PRIMARY	93%	72%	46%
SECONDARY	38%	32%	7%

	1995	1980	1965
ADULT ILLITERACY M/F	35/62%	45.2/74.3% (81)	n/a

COMMUNICATIONS

	1995	1980	1965
RATE OF NEWSPAPERS	31	21	12
RATE OF RADIOS	80	38	10
RATE OF TELEVISIONS	40	4	0

Source: CIA, The World Factbook, 1997; ILO, World Labour Report, 1997; UN, Demographic Yearbook, 1997; UN, Statistical Yearbook, 1996; World Bank, World Development Indicators, 1998.

INDONESIA

Indonesia is an island archipelago located in Southeast Asia between the Indian Ocean and the Pacific Ocean. Australia is southeast of the 741,097-square-mile (1,919,440-square-kilometer) country, Papua New Guinea is east, and Malaysia and the Philippines are to the country's north. Indonesia gained independence from the Netherlands in August 1945. Following the collapse of Indonesia's economy in May 1998, President Suharto, who came to power in a military coup in March 1968, was forced to resign by a mass opposition movement. Although Indonesia was considered a model for economic development by Western economists in the mid-1990s, nearly 60 percent of the population was subsisting on under $2 a day. In the late 1990s, the Indonesian government was forced by Western lending agencies and banks to conform to severe austerity measures. The government collapsed under popular pressure following the plummeting of the currency and spiraling unemployment. In 1995, Indonesia's population of nearly 207 million was growing at an annual rate of 1.5 percent. The Javanese are the most populous ethnic group in Indonesia (45 percent), followed by the Sundanese (14 percent), Madurese (7.5 percent), and Malays (7.5 percent). Muslims constitute about 87 percent of the country's population. Indonesia's average life expectancy at birth in 1995 was 61.6 years, and the country had an infant mortality rate of 63.1 deaths per 1,000 live births.

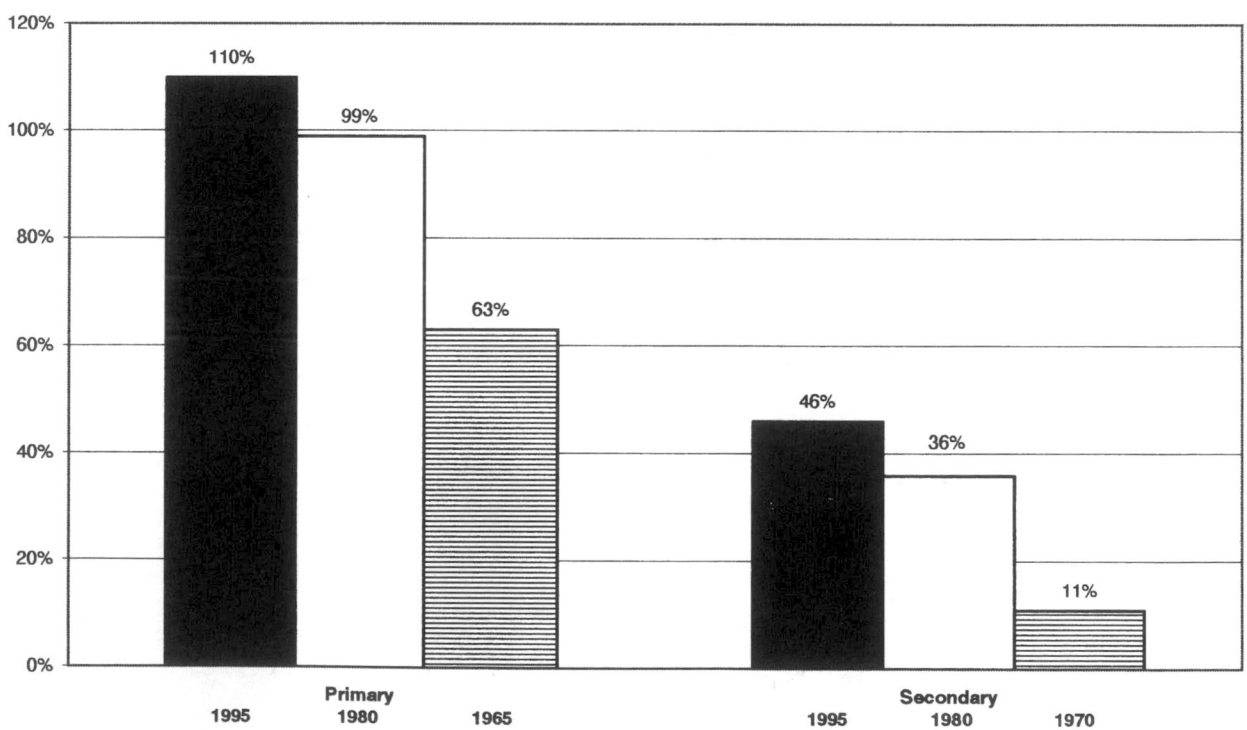

Females in School

Unlike the more orthodox Muslim nations of the Persian Gulf, Indonesia has always emphasized equal educational opportunities for its girls, a fact reflected in the number of male and female students attending secondary school.

Rate of Televisions per 1,000 Persons

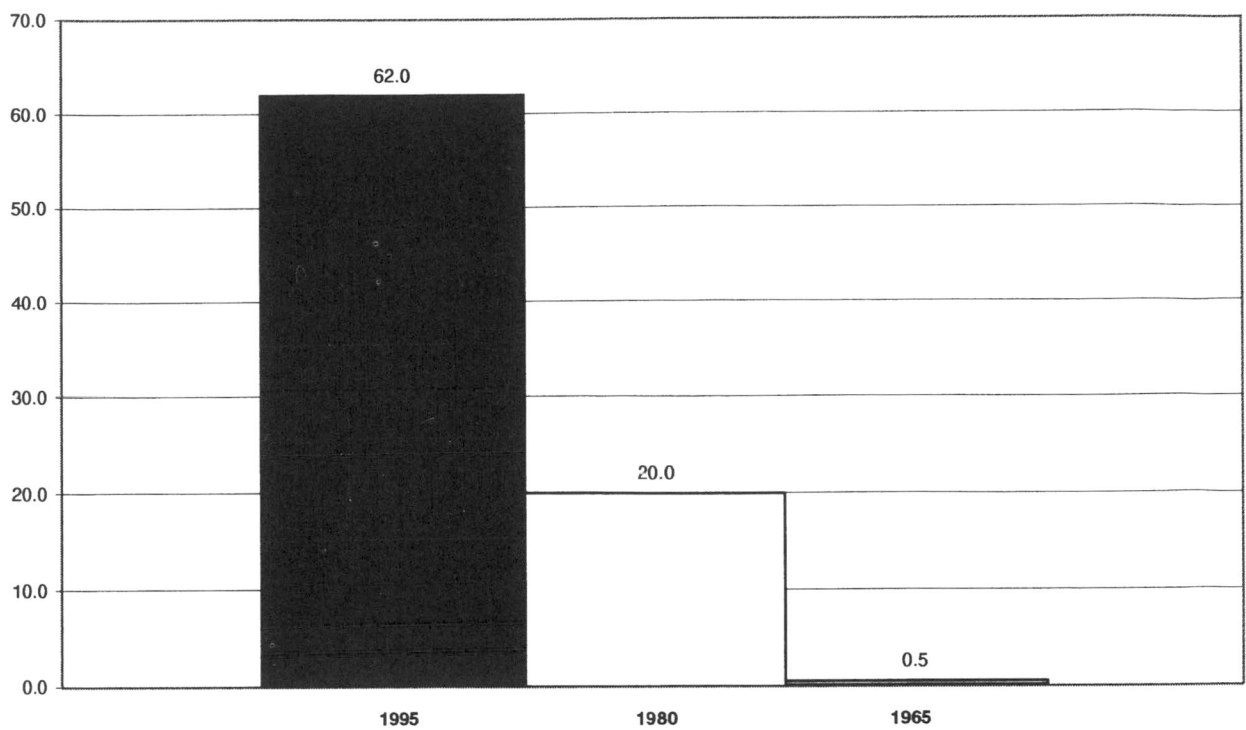

With its population of more than 200 million spread out over hundreds of islands across thousands of miles of ocean, Indonesia has found that television offers one of the best media for promoting a common nationalism.

CHRONOLOGY

1965   Leftist prime minister Sukarno overthrown in military coup by Suharto; 200,000 leftists massacred.
1968   Suharto declared Indonesian president.
1974   Portugal vacates East Timor; Indonesia invades.
1975   Economic boom in country begins.
1997   Economic crisis hits Indonesia; forest fires burn out of control.
1998   Popular uprising leads to overthrow of Suharto.

	1995	1980	1965

GEOGRAPHY

AREA (square miles/kilometers) 741,097/1,919,440
LAND AREA (square miles/kilometers) 705,189/1,826,440
COASTLINE (miles/kilometers) 34,198/54,716

CITIES

		1995
CAPITAL	Jakarta	9,160,500
MAJOR CITIES	Surabaya	2,701,300
	Bandung	2,368,200
	Medan	1,909,700
	Semarang	1,366,500

POPULATION

	1995	1980	1965
TOTAL	206,611,600	147,490,298	96,318,829 (61)
DENSITY (per square mile/kilometer)	264/102	223/86	186/72
ANNUAL GROWTH	1.5%	2.2%	2.3%

AGE COHORTS

	1995	1980	1965
0–14	32%	n/a	42%
15–64	64%	n/a	55%
65 AND OVER	4%	n/a	3%

	1995	1980	1965
URBAN	35%	22.4%	n/a
RURAL	65%	77.6%	n/a

	1995	1980	1965
NET MIGRATION RATE	0	n/a	0 (62)

IDENTITY

ETHNICITY

	1995
JAVANESE	45%
SUNDANESE	14%
MADURESE	7.5%
MALAYS	7.5%

LANGUAGE

	1995
BAHASA INDONESIA	n/a
ENGLISH	n/a
DUTCH	n/a

	1995	1980	1965
RELIGION			
MUSLIM	87%		
PROTESTANT	6%		
ROMAN CATHOLIC	3%		
HINDU	2%		
BUDDHIST	1%		

VITAL STATISTICS

	1995	1980	1965
BIRTHS			
BIRTH RATE	23.7	32.1	43 (61)
INFANT MORTALITY RATE	63.1	125	125 (61)
LIFE EXPECTANCY AT BIRTH	61.6	47.5	n/a
MARRIAGES			
MARRIAGE RATE	7.4	10.6	10.6 (61)
AVERAGE AGE AT MARRIAGE M/F	25.2/21.6		
DIVORCE RATE	0.8		
DEATHS			
DEATH RATE	8.4	12.6	21.4 (61)

HOUSEHOLDS

NUMBER	39,695,158 (90)
URBAN	11,692,856
RURAL	28,002,302
AVERAGE SIZE	4.5 (90)
URBAN	4.7
RURAL	4.4

ECONOMICS AND LABOR

GDP PER CAPITA US$	$3,500
LABOR FORCE M/F (thousands)	47,644.6/30,459.5 (92)
AGRICULTURE	25,629.5/17,224.0
MINING	489.9/104.9
MANUFACTURING	4,187.1/3,660.5
UTILITIES	157.5/15.8
CONSTRUCTION	2,259.4/104.0
TRADE/FOOD/TOURISM	5,604.6/5,495.7
TRANSPORT/COMMUNICATIONS	2,439.7/72.5

	1995	1980	1965
FINANCE/INSURANCE/REAL ESTATE	376.9/184.9		
SOCIAL AND PERSONAL SERVICES	6,447.5/3,525.5		
UNEMPLOYMENT (official)	2.8% (92)		
UNION DENSITY	2.6%		
POVERTY			
UNDER $1/DAY	11.8% (92)		
UNDER $2/DAY	58.7% (92)		

TRANSPORT

	1995	1980	1965
JOURNEYS (by transport mode)			
RAILROAD PASSENGER TRIPS	13,610.0 (94)		
(millions of miles/kilometers)			
AIR PASSENGER TRIPS (thousands)	12,290 (94)		
VEHICLES (thousands)			
PRIVATE CARS	1,890.3	639.5	151
COMMERCIAL	1,903.6	560.1	108.4

HEALTH AND HEALTH CARE

	1995	1980	1965
HEALTH CARE			
ACCESS TO SAFE WATER	62%		
ACCESS TO SANITATION	51%		
MEASLES IMMUNIZATION	89%		
RATE OF PHYSICIANS	0.2	0.1	negligible (60)
RATE OF HOSPITAL BEDS	0.7	n/a	0.7 (60)
HEALTH INDICATORS			
PREGNANT WOMEN WITH ANEMIA	64%		
LOW-BIRTH-WEIGHT BABIES	14%		
CHILD MALNUTRITION	40%		
SMOKING PREVALENCE M/F	53/4%		
TUBERCULOSIS INCIDENCE RATE	2.2		
AIDS/HIV CASES	87	51 (93)	

EDUCATION

	1995	1980	1965
SCHOOL AGE IN SCHOOL			
PRIMARY	114%	107%	69%
SECONDARY	48%	29%	11%
HIGHER	11%	4%	1.8%

	1995	1980	1965
FEMALES IN SCHOOL			
PRIMARY	110%	99%	63%
SECONDARY	46%	36%	11% (70)
ADULT ILLITERACY M/F	22/10%	22.5/42.3%	47.2/73.9% (61)

COMMUNICATIONS

	1995	1980	1965
RATE OF NEWSPAPERS	24	15	7
RATE OF RADIOS	148	99	2 (48)
RATE OF TELEVISIONS	62	20	0.5

Source: CIA, *The World Factbook, 1997;* ILO, *World Labour Report, 1997;* UN, *Demographic Yearbook, 1997;* UN, *Statistical Yearbook, 1996;* World Bank, *World Development Indicators, 1998.*

IRAN

Iran is located in Southwest Asia on the Persian Gulf. Pakistan and Afghanistan border the 636,293-square-mile (1,648,000-square-kilometer) country on the east, the former Soviet Republic of Turkmenistan on the northeast, Armenia and Azerbaijan on the northwest, and Iraq on the west. Across the Persian Gulf lie Saudi Arabia and the Gulf States of Bahrain, Kuwait, Oman, and the United Arab Emirates. In 1979, amid the the Iranian Revolution, the autocratic government of Shah Pahlevi was ousted and replaced by an Islamic government. During much of the 1980s, Iran was embroiled in a major border war with Iraq. Though Iran had tremendous wealth, the shah had squandered most of the earnings and had failed to modernize the economy equitably. Following the revolution, as a result of relative international isolation, the Iranian economy continued to contract. In 1997, after nearly two decades of strict Islamic rule, a moderate government was elected to office. In 1995, Iran's population of more than 66 million was growing at a rapid annual rate of 2.2 percent. The country has a life expectancy at birth of 67.4 years, and an infant mortality rate of 52.7 deaths per 1,000 live births. The leading ethnic groups in Iran are Persian (51 percent) and Azerbaijani (24 percent).

Age Distribution

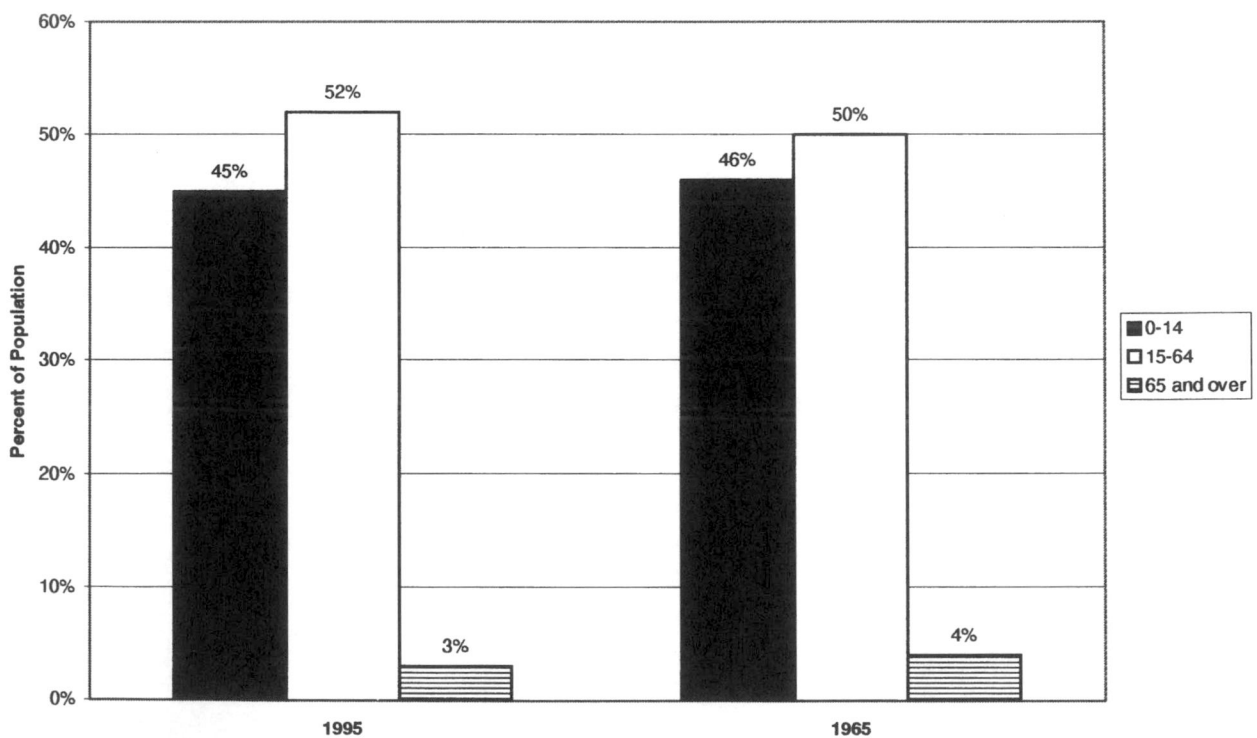

Like many Islamic countries, Iran has an extremely young population, a factor, many observers say, in the volatile politics of the country.

Divorce Rate per 1,000 Residents

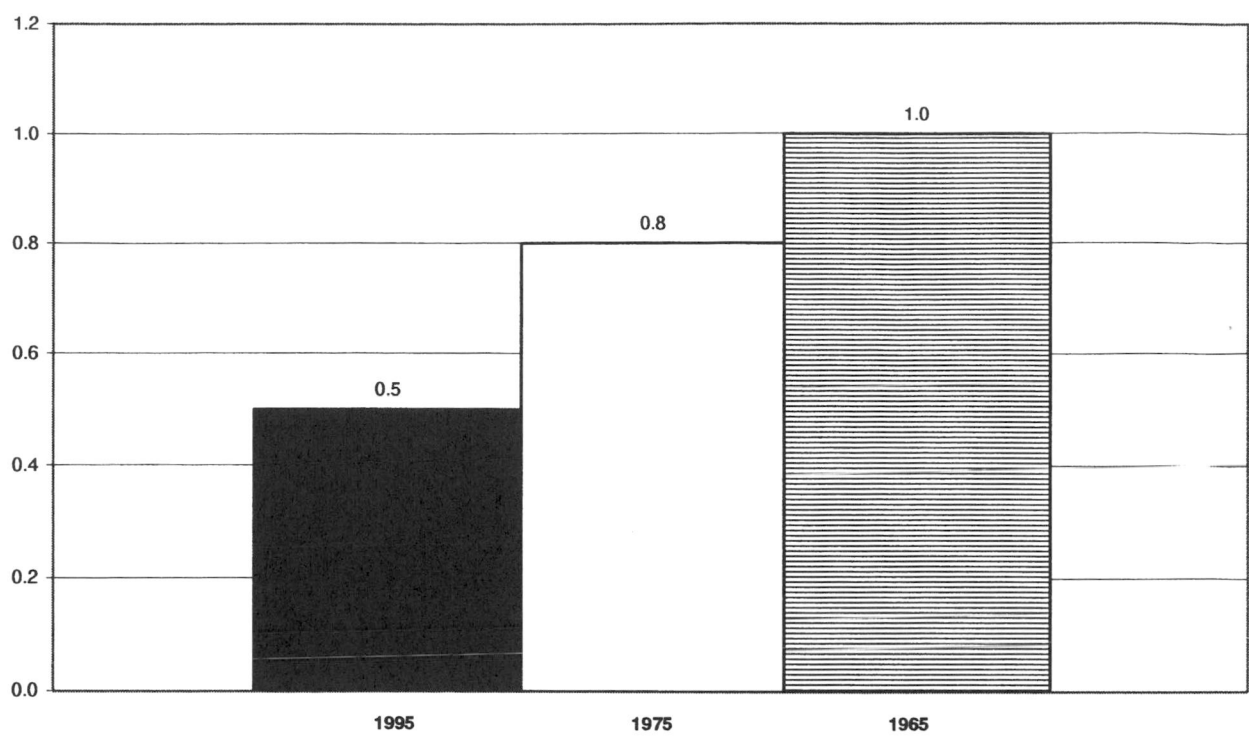

The impact of the socially conservative Islamic revolution is reflected in the country's falling divorce rate since 1979; it contrasts with most other countries in the region and world, where the divorce rates have climbed.

CHRONOLOGY

1962   Shah Reza Pahlevi launches economic "White Revolution."

1974   Quadrupling of oil prices leads to vast increase in government revenues.

1978   Unrest against Shah's regime increases.

1979   Shah overthrown and exiled from country as Ayatollah Khomeini takes power; national referendum approves Islamic government.

1980   Iraq invades Iran, leading to eight-year civil war.

1981   American embassy hostages freed after 444-day captivity.

1988   Iran-Iraq War ends largely in a draw.

1989   Khomeini dies.

1996   Liberal reformist prime minister wins power, leading to struggle with hard-liners.

	1995	1980	1966

GEOGRAPHY

AREA (square miles/kilometers)	636,293/1,648,000			
LAND AREA (square miles/kilometers)	631,660/1,636,000			
COASTLINE (miles/kilometers)	1,525/2,440			

CITIES

CAPITAL	Teheran	6,750,043 (94)	
MAJOR CITIES	Mashhad	1,964,489	
	Esfahan	1,220,595	
	Tabriz	1,166,203	
	Shiraz	1,042,801	

POPULATION

	1995	1980	1966
TOTAL	66,094,264	33,708,744 (76)	25,781,090
DENSITY (per square mile/kilometer)	106/41	70/27	39/15
ANNUAL GROWTH	2.2%	2.9%	2.8%

AGE COHORTS

	1995	1980	1966
0–14	45%	n/a	46%
15–64	52%	n/a	50%
65 AND OVER	3%	n/a	4%

MALE	52%	
FEMALE	48%	

	1995	1980	1966
URBAN	59%	49%	n/a
RURAL	41%	51%	n/a

NET MIGRATION RATE	−0.5

IDENTITY

ETHNICITY

PERSIAN	51%
AZERBAIJANI	24%
GILAKI AND MAZANDURANI	8%
KURD	7%
ARAB	3%

	1995	**1980**	**1965**
LANGUAGE			
PERSIAN	58%		
TURKIC	26%		
KURDISH	9%		
LURI	2%		
RELIGION			
SHI'A MUSLIM	89%		
SUNNI MUSLIM	10%		
ZOROASTRIAN, JEWISH, CHRISTIAN, BAHA'I	1%		

VITAL STATISTICS

	1995	**1980**	**1965**
BIRTHS			
BIRTH RATE	33.7	42.5 (75)	48
INFANT MORTALITY RATE	52.7	108.1 (75)	n/a
LIFE EXPECTANCY AT BIRTH	67.4	55.4 (75)	n/a
MARRIAGES			
MARRIAGE RATE	7.9	8.9 (75)	6
AVERAGE AGE AT MARRIAGE M/F	24.5/21.1		
DIVORCE RATE	0.5	0.8 (75)	1
DEATHS			
DEATH RATE	6.6	11.5 (75)	24.5

HOUSEHOLDS

NUMBER	10,785,221 (91)
AVERAGE SIZE	5.2 (91)
FEMALE HEADED	5.9%

ECONOMICS AND LABOR

GDP PER CAPITA US$	$4,700

LABOR FORCE M/F (thousands)	
AGRICULTURE	30/73
INDUSTRY	26/9
SERVICES	44/18

	1995	1980	1965

TRANSPORT

JOURNEYS (by transport mode)

	1995	1980	1965
RAILROAD PASSENGER TRIPS (millions of miles/kilometers)	6,422.0 (93)		
AIR PASSENGER TRIPS (thousands)	5,803.0 (94)		

VEHICLES (thousands)

	1995	1980	1965
PRIVATE CARS	1,557	958	105.9
COMMERCIAL	588.9	132	44.1

HEALTH AND HEALTH CARE

HEALTH CARE

	1995	1980	1965
ACCESS TO SAFE WATER	n/a	50%	n/a
ACCESS TO SANITATION	n/a	60%	n/a
MEASLES IMMUNIZATION	88%		
RATE OF PHYSICIANS	0.3		0.3 (60)
RATE OF HOSPITAL BEDS	1.4	1.5 (70)	0.9 (60)

HEALTH INDICATORS

	1995	1980	1965
LOW-BIRTH-WEIGHT BABIES	12%		
CHILD MALNUTRITION	16%		
TUBERCULOSIS INCIDENCE RATE	0.5		
AIDS/HIV CASES	118	92 (93)	
TOTAL DEATHS	461,443 (91)		

EDUCATION

SCHOOL AGE IN SCHOOL

	1995	1980	1965
PRIMARY	99%	87%	53%
SECONDARY	69%	42%	17%
HIGHER	15%	n/a	1.2%

FEMALES IN SCHOOL

	1995	1980	1965
PRIMARY	47%	40%	36%
SECONDARY	46%	36%	11%

	1995	1980	1965
ADULT ILLITERACY M/F	22/34%	51.8/75.6% (76)	67.2/87.8%

	1995	1980	1965
COMMUNICATIONS			
RATE OF NEWSPAPERS	20	25	15 (61)
RATE OF RADIOS	230	163	62
RATE OF TELEVISIONS	63	51	4

Source: CIA, *The World Factbook, 1997;* ILO, *World Labour Report, 1997;* UN, *Demographic Yearbook, 1997;* UN, *Statistical Yearbook, 1996;* World Bank, *World Development Indicators, 1998.*

IRAQ

Iraq is located in Southwest Asia, northwest of the Persian Gulf. The 168,754-square-mile (437,072-square-kilometer) country is bordered by Iran on the east, Turkey on the north, Jordan and Syria on the west, and Kuwait and Saudi Arabia on the south. In the early 1970s, the Iraqi Ba'th Party came to power and dramatically expanded central planning. Since 1975, under the leadership of President Saddam Hussein, Iraq has come into conflict with neighboring countries. In the 1980s, the government was embroiled in a costly eight-year border war with Iran. After invading Kuwait in 1990, Iraqi troops were expelled by an alliance of international forces. The border hostilities have severely interfered with industrial growth and economic development. An international embargo against Iraqi oil exports has further limited the country's ability to earn foreign exchange for essential goods and has impoverished the population. Iraq's 1995 population of 21.4 million was growing at a rapid annual rate of 3.7 percent, due in part to a high birth rate. In the same year, Iraq had a life expectancy at birth of 67 years and an infant mortality rate of 60 deaths per 1,000 live births. Iraq is an ethnically and religiously divided nation. Just over 75 percent of the country's population is Arab and 18 percent is Kurdish. The three leading religious denominations are Shi'a Muslim (62 percent), Sunni Muslim (35 percent) and Christian (3 percent).

Rate of Physicians per 1,000 Persons

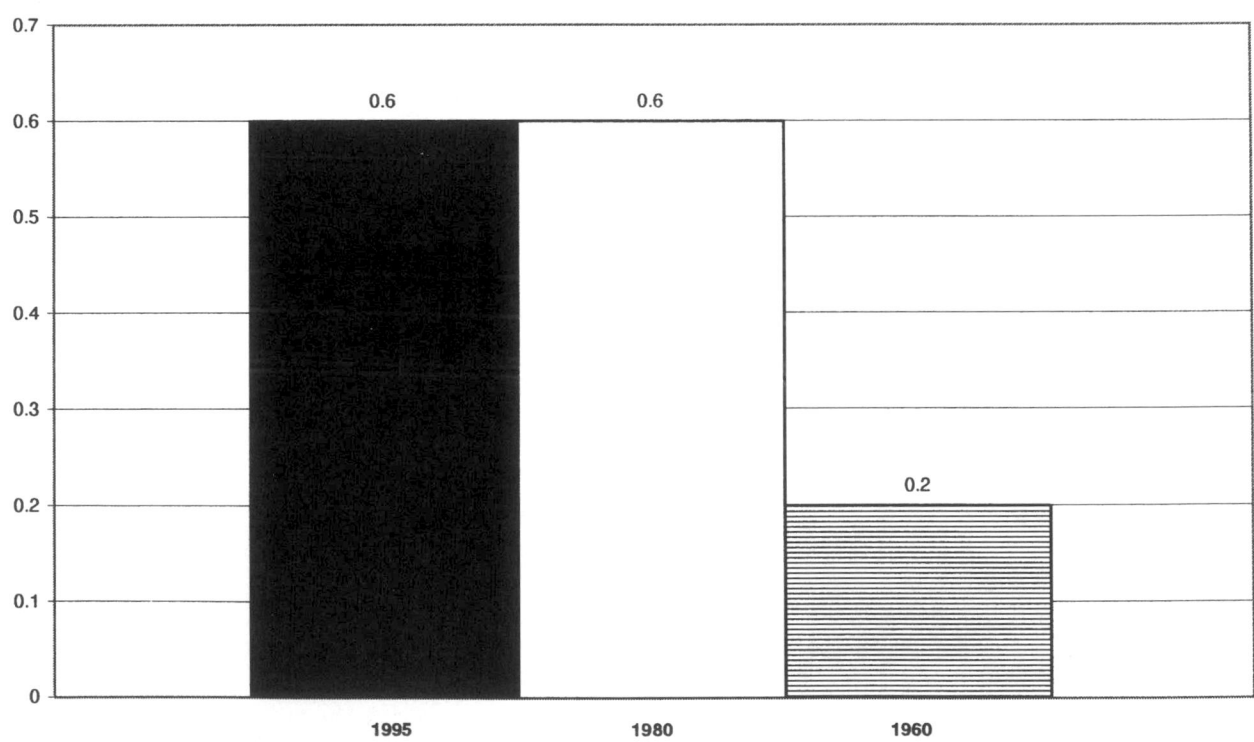

The impact of eight years of war with Iran (from 1980 to 1988), the Gulf War (1991), and international sanctions (1991–present) can be seen in stagnant or falling social indices, like the number of physicians per resident.

Secondary School Students

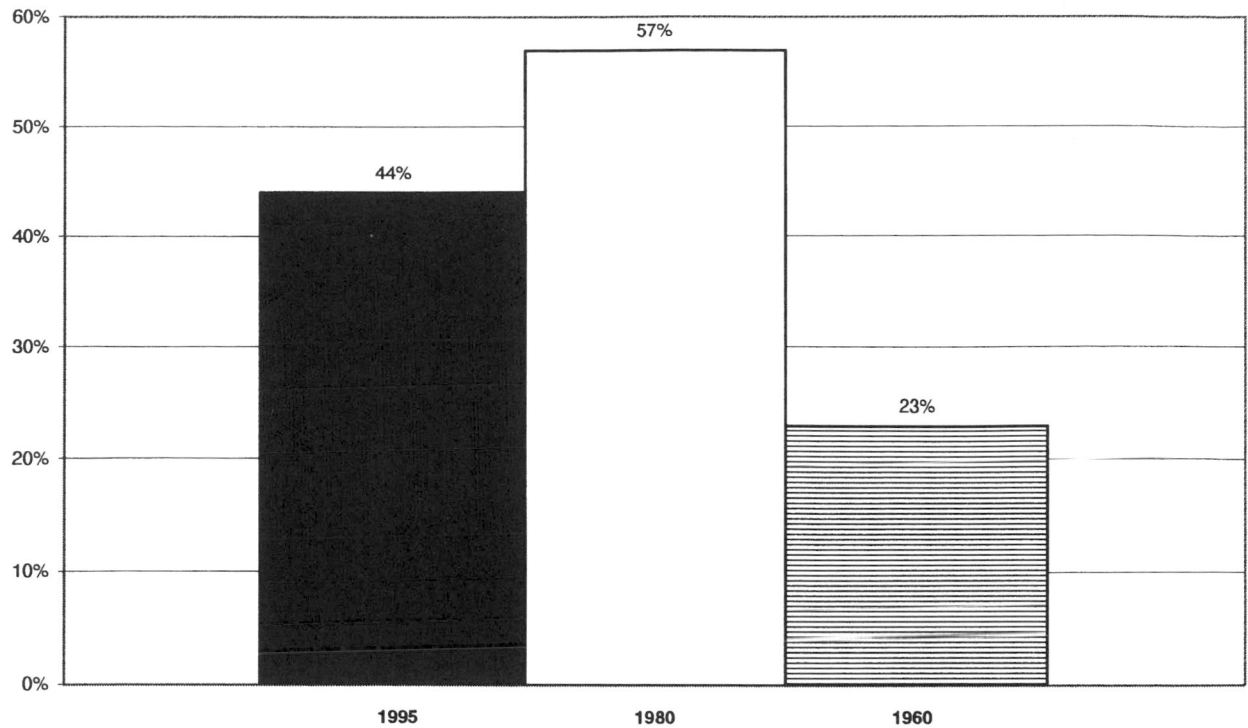

Another measure of the internationally perilous position of Iraq—and its impact on domestic social measures—can be seen in the continuing lack of educational opportunities.

CHRONOLOGY

1963   Baathist Party takes and loses power in a series of coups.

1968   Baathist Party, led by Saddam Hussein, retakes power.

1975   Government signs treaty with Iran, ceding territory in exchange for a halt in Iranian aid to Iraqi Kurd separatists.

1980   Iraq launches invasion of Iran, beginning eight-year war.

1987   Hussein government uses chemical weapons against Iranian troops and Kurdish civilians.

1988   Government signs truce with Iran, ending war with no discernible gains by either side.

1990   Hussein invades Kuwait.

1991   Allied coalition, led by United States, defeats Hussein, ousting Iraq from Kuwait; Kurds lead failed uprising; Allies establish economic sanctions againt Iraq and safe haven for Kurds.

1998   Obstruction of UN weapons inspectors leads to confrontation with United States; UN secretary-general defuses crisis.

	1995	1980	1965

GEOGRAPHY

AREA (square miles/kilometers)	168,754/437,072			
LAND AREA (square miles/kilometers)	166,858/432,162			
COASTLINE (miles/kilometers)	36/58			

CITIES				
CAPITAL	Baghdad	n/a	3,841,268 (87)	n/a
MAJOR CITIES	Diyala	n/a	961,073	n/a
	Al-Sulaimaniya	n/a	951,723	n/a
	Arbil	n/a	770,439	n/a
	Mosul	n/a	664,221	n/a

POPULATION

	1995	1980	1965
TOTAL	21,422,292	12,000,497 (77)	8,261,527
DENSITY (per square mile/kilometer)	122/47	96/37	49/19
ANNUAL GROWTH	3.7%	3.7%	3.1%

AGE COHORTS			
0–14	48%	n/a	45.5% (57)
15–64	49%	n/a	49% (57)
65 AND OVER	3%	n/a	5.1% (57)

MALE	51%		
FEMALE	49%		

URBAN	75%	68%	n/a
RURAL	25%	32%	n/a

NET MIGRATION RATE	0.4	n/a	0.3 (64)

IDENTITY

ETHNICITY	
ARAB	77%
KURDISH	18%
TURKOMAN, ASSYRIAN, OTHER	5%

LANGUAGE	
ARABIC	n/a
KURDISH	n/a
ASSYRIAN	n/a
ARMENIAN	n/a

	1995	1980	1965
RELIGION			
SHI'A MUSLIM	62%		
SUNNI MUSLIM	35%		
CHRISTIAN, OTHER	3%		

VITAL STATISTICS

	1995	1980	1965
BIRTHS			
BIRTH RATE	43.1	44.4	n/a
INFANT MORTALITY RATE	60	77	n/a
LIFE EXPECTANCY AT BIRTH	67	62.4	n/a
MARRIAGES			
MARRIAGE RATE	8.6	8.5	n/a
AVERAGE AGE AT MARRIAGE M/F	n/a	26.3/22.3	n/a
DIVORCE RATE	0.1	0.1	n/a
DEATHS			
DEATH RATE	6.6	8.7	n/a

ECONOMICS AND LABOR

	1995	1980	1965
GDP PER CAPITA US$	2,000		
LABOR FORCE M/F			
AGRICULTURE	12/1%		
INDUSTRY	19/9%		
SERVICES	69/52%		

TRANSPORT

	1995	1980	1965
JOURNEYS (by transport mode)			
RAILROAD PASSENGER TRIPS	1,570 (88)		
(millions of miles/kilometers)			
AIR PASSENGER TRIPS (thousands)	53 (92)		
VEHICLES (thousands)			
PRIVATE CARS	672.4	237.1	62.9
COMMERCIAL	309.3	145.2	26

	1995	1980	1965

HEALTH AND HEALTH CARE

HEALTH CARE

	1995	1980	1965
ACCESS TO SAFE WATER	44%		
ACCESS TO SANITATION	87%		
MEASLES IMMUNIZATION	88%		
RATE OF PHYSICIANS	0.6	0.6	0.2 (60)
RATE OF HOSPITAL BEDS	1.7	1.9	1.8 (60)

HEALTH INDICATORS

	1995	1980	1965
PREGNANT WOMEN WITH ANEMIA	18%		
LOW-BIRTH-WEIGHT BABIES	15%		
CHILD MALNUTRITION	12%		
SMOKING PREVALENCE M/F	40/5%		
TUBERCULOSIS INCIDENCE RATE	1.5		
AIDS/HIV CASES	42	24 (93)	

EDUCATION

SCHOOL AGE IN SCHOOL

	1995	1980	1965
PRIMARY	90%	113%	72%
SECONDARY	44%	57%	23%
HIGHER	n/a	9%	3.5%

FEMALES IN SCHOOL

	1995	1980	1965
PRIMARY	85%	109%	65%
SECONDARY	39%	32%	11%
HIGHER	n/a	6.1%	2.4% (70)

	1995	1980	1965
ADULT ILLITERACY M/F	n/a	9.8/12.5% (85)	n/a

COMMUNICATIONS

	1995	1980	1965
RATE OF NEWSPAPERS	35	26	12 (63)
RATE OF RADIOS	217	161	85
RATE OF TELEVISIONS	75	50	18

Source: CIA, *The World Factbook, 1997;* ILO, *World Labour Report, 1997;* UN, *Demographic Yearbook, 1997;* UN, *Statistical Yearbook, 1996;* World Bank, *World Development Indicators, 1998.*

IRELAND

Ireland occupies about 85 percent of the island of Ireland between the Atlantic Ocean and the Irish Sea. Northern Ireland is located to the northeast of the 27,135-square-mile (70,280-square-kilometer) country. The United Kingdom is located to Ireland's east, across the Irish Sea. Ireland gained independence from the United Kingdom in December 1921. The country is a competitive multiparty democracy with a wide range of parties competing in a bicameral parliamentary system. Ireland has a modern, diversified, export-oriented economy dominated by manufacturing and agriculture. Though Ireland has one of the fastest-growing economies in the world, the country suffers from persistent unemployment. In 1995, the country's per capita gross domestic product (GDP) was $15,400. Because of a rapidly declining birth rate and a high rate of out-migration, the country's population of nearly 3.6 million is growing at a slow rate of 0.4 percent. Ireland has a life expectancy at birth of 75.6 years and an infant mortality rate of 6.4 deaths per 1,000 live births.

	1995	**1980**	**1965**
GEOGRAPHY			
AREA (square miles/kilometers)	27,135/70,280		
LAND AREA (square miles/kilometers)	26,598/68,890		
COASTLINE (miles/kilometers)	905/1,448		
CITIES			
CAPITAL	Dublin	533,929 (91)	
MAJOR CITY	Cork	127,253	
POPULATION			
TOTAL	3,566,833	3,443,405 (81)	2,880,752 (66)
DENSITY (per square mile/kilometer)	132/51	127/49	106/41
ANNUAL GROWTH	0.4%	0.9%	0.1%
AGE COHORTS			
0–14	23%	n/a	31.1% (61)
15–64	65%	n/a	61% (61)
65 AND OVER	12%	n/a	8.2% (61)
MALE	50%		
FEMALE	50%		

	1995	1980	1965
URBAN	58%	55.6%	
RURAL	42%	44.4%	
NET MIGRATION RATE	−6.5		

IDENTITY

ETHNICITY
CELTIC	n/a		
ENGLISH	n/a		

LANGUAGE
ENGLISH	n/a		
IRISH (Gaelic)	n/a		

RELIGION
ROMAN CATHOLIC	93%		
ANGLICAN	3%		
NONE	1%		

VITAL STATISTICS

BIRTHS
BIRTH RATE	13.2	18.2 (84)	21.6
URBAN BIRTH RATE	12.2 (91)		
RURAL BIRTH RATE	18.6 (91)		
INFANT MORTALITY RATE	6.4	10.1 (84)	24.9
LIFE EXPECTANCY AT BIRTH	75.6	72.7 (84)	70

MARRIAGES
MARRIAGE RATE	4.4	5.2 (84)	5.8
AVERAGE AGE AT MARRIAGE M/F	29.2/28		

DEATHS
DEATH RATE	8.9 (94)	9.1	12.1

HOUSEHOLDS

NUMBER	1,029,080 (91)	n/a	676,402 (61)
AVERAGE SIZE	3.3 (91)	n/a	4 (61)

TYPE OF HOUSEHOLD
SINGLE	19.2%		
MARRIED	63.0%		

	1995	1980	1965
WIDOWED	13.7%		
DIVORCED/SEPARATED	4.1%		
FEMALE HEADED	26.3%		

ECONOMICS AND LABOR

GDP PER CAPITA US$	$15,400		
LABOR FORCE M/F (thousands)	748.1/377.0 (91)		
AGRICULTURE	141.9/12.3		
MINING	6.1/0.5		
MANUFACTURING	157.8/63.4		
UTILITIES	12.5/1.5		
CONSTRUCTION	76.3/3.5		
TRADE/FOOD/TOURISM	113.9/85.7		
TRANSPORT/COMMUNICATIONS	52.3/12.9		
FINANCE/INSURANCE/REAL ESTATE	51.0/43.5		
SOCIAL AND PERSONAL SERVICES	133.7/151.3		
UNEMPLOYMENT (official)	19% (91)		
UNION DENSITY	36%		

TRANSPORT

	1995	1980	1965
JOURNEYS (by transport mode)			
RAILROAD PASSENGER TRIPS	1,102 (94)		
(millions of miles/kilometers)			
AIR PASSENGER TRIPS (thousands)	4,826 (94)		
VEHICLES (thousands)			
PRIVATE CARS	947.2	738.1	284.9
COMMERCIAL	143.9	70.1	51.1

HEALTH AND HEALTH CARE

	1995	1980	1965
HEALTH CARE			
ACCESS TO SANITATION	100%		
RATE OF PHYSICIANS	2	1.3	1 (60)
RATE OF HOSPITAL BEDS	5	9.7	15.2 (60)
HEALTH INDICATORS			
LOW-BIRTH-WEIGHT BABIES	4%		
SMOKING PREVALENCE M/F	29/28%		

	1995	1980	1965
TUBERCULOSIS INCIDENCE RATE	0.18		
AIDS/HIV CASES	511	418 (43)	
TOTAL DEATHS	31,494		

EDUCATION

SCHOOL AGE IN SCHOOL

	1995	1980	1965
PRIMARY	104%	100%	105%
SECONDARY	114%	90%	40%
HIGHER	37%	18%	7.6%

FEMALES IN SCHOOL

	1995	1980	1965
PRIMARY	103%	99%	106%
SECONDARY	114%	91%	44%
HIGHER	n/a	17.20%	9.4% (70)

COMMUNICATIONS

	1995	1980	1965
RATE OF NEWSPAPERS	186	229	246
RATE OF RADIOS	636	375	212
RATE OF TELEVISIONS	301	231	114

Source: CIA, *The World Factbook, 1997*; ILO, *World Labour Report, 1997*; UN, *Demographic Yearbook, 1997*; UN, *Statistical Yearbook, 1996*; World Bank, *World Development Indicators, 1998*.

ISRAEL

Israel is located in Southwest Asia on the Mediterranean Sea within borders disputed by regional states and the international community. In 1948, the country gained independence from the United Kingdom. Israel has occupied the territory of bordering states following the 1967 Arab-Israeli war, including most of the West Bank and part of the Gaza Strip (claimed by the Palestine Authority) and the Golan Heights (claimed by Syria). In 1979, Israel withdrew from the Sinai Peninsula, captured from Egypt in 1967. The country's internationally recognized boundaries encompass a 8,019-square-mile (20,770-square kilometer) area that extends from Lebanon on the north to the Gulf of Aqaba on the south. Although the status of the West Bank is under negotiation with the Palestine Authority, the Israeli government continues to sanction the expansion of Jewish settlement of the territory. The country is the most economically and technologically advanced in the region, with a 1995 per capita gross domestic product (GDP) of $15,500. Despite Israel's modernity (which tends to produce population stabilization) the country's population of more than 5.4 million is growing faster than Egypt, in part due to a high rate of in-migration and a high birth rate by Western standards. Jews represent a population majority of 82 percent, but only but 50 percent of the Jewish population is native born. Arabs account for 18 percent of the population. Millions of Palestinian refugees from within Israel's 1948 boundaries and the Occupied Territories are scattered throughout the region. The country has an average life expectancy at birth of 78 years and an infant mortality rate of 8.5 deaths per 1,000 live births.

Urban Population

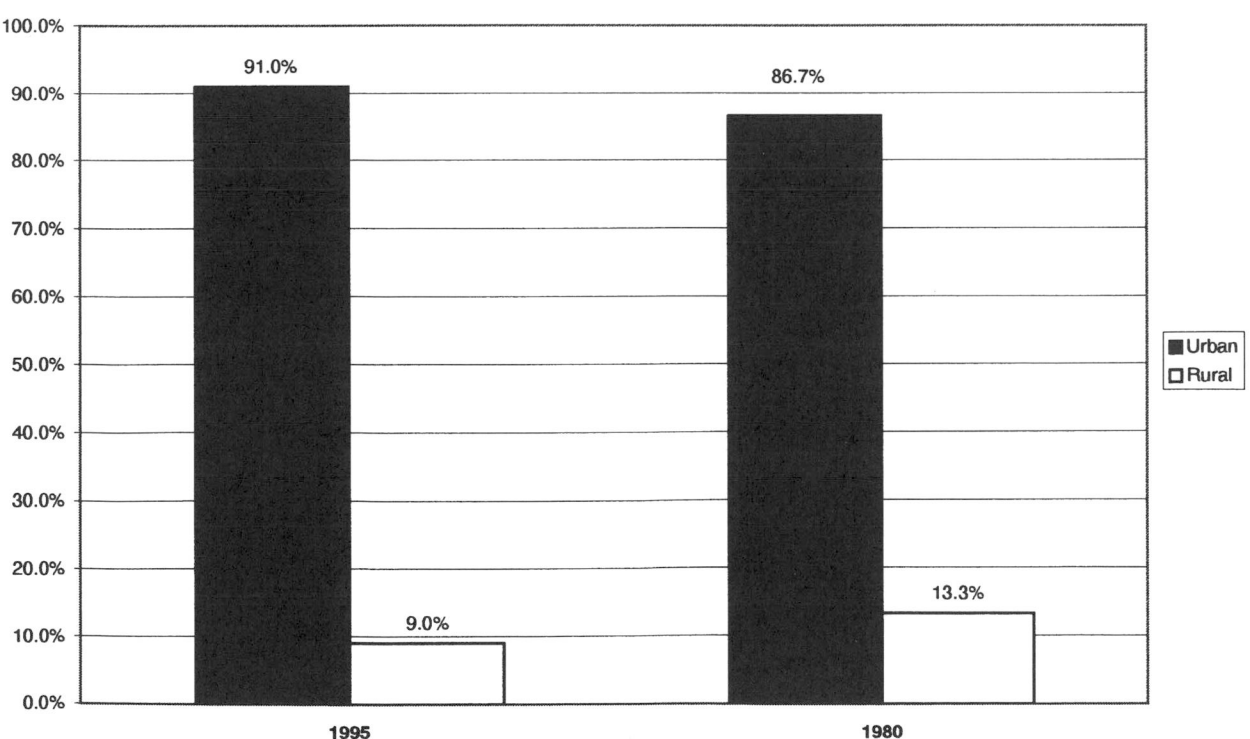

Although many of Israel's Zionist founders hoped that the new society would be rooted in the land, through farming and rural living, most citizens have always lived in urban areas.

Percentage of Students in Higher Education

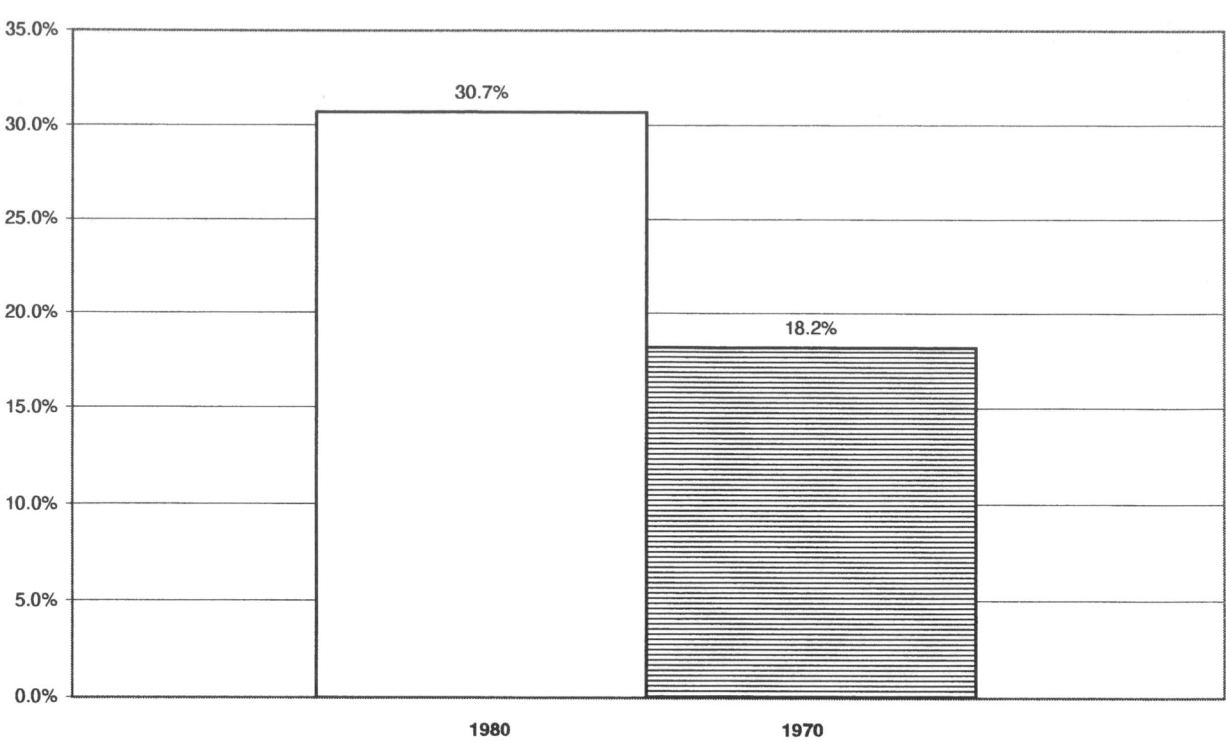

Israel has increasingly become one of the high-tech hubs of the world, a development that has much to do with the country's extensive system of higher education and large number of university students and graduates.

CHRONOLOGY

1967   Israel decisively defeats Arab countries in war; occupies Sinai, West Bank, East Jerusalem, and Gaza.

1973   Israel fights Arab countries to draw.

1977   Conservative Likud Party takes power for first time.

1978   Prime Minister Menachem Begin signs peace treaty with Egypt.

1982   Israel launches second invasion of Lebanon in effort to destroy Palestine Liberation Organization.

1987   Palestinian uprising, known as *intifada,* begins.

1992   Labor Party returns to power.

1993   Labor government signs accords with PLO, recognizing it for first time.

1996   Likud Party returns to power under Binyamin Netanyahu, vowing to go slower on peace process.

	1995[1]	1980[1]	1965

GEOGRAPHY

AREA (square miles/kilometers)	8,019/20,770		
LAND AREA (square miles/kilometers)	7,849/20,330		
COASTLINE (miles/kilometers)	171/273		

CITIES

CAPITAL	Jerusalem	573,000 (94)		
MAJOR CITIES	Tel Aviv-Yafo	356,300		
	Haifa	246,600		
	Holon	163,300		
	Rishon Leziyyon	157,200		

POPULATION

	1995	1980	1965
TOTAL	5,421,995	4,037,620 (83)	2,183,332 (61)
DENSITY (per square mile/kilometer)	681/263	528/204	329/127
ANNUAL GROWTH	2.1%	1.8%	3.5%

AGE COHORTS

0–14	29%	n/a	35%
15–64	62%	n/a	59%
65 AND OVER	9%	n/a	6%

MALE	50%		
FEMALE	50%		

URBAN	91%	86.7%	n/a
RURAL	9%	13.3%	n/a

NET MIGRATION RATE	7.0	n/a	8.4 (64)

IDENTITY

ETHNICITY

JEWISH	82%	
ARAB	18%	

LANGUAGE

HEBREW	n/a	
ARAB	n/a	
ENGLISH	n/a	

	1995[1]	1980[1]	1965
RELIGION			
JUDAISM	82%		
ISLAM	14%		
CHRISTIAN	2%		
DRUZE, OTHER	2%		

VITAL STATISTICS

	1995[1]	1980[1]	1965
BIRTHS			
BIRTH RATE	20.3	23.7 (84)	22.6
URBAN BIRTH RATE	20.9 (94)		
RURAL BIRTH RATE	23.9 (94)		
INFANT MORTALITY RATE	8.5	12.8 (84)	22.7
ABORTION RATE	153.3 (93)		
LIFE EXPECTANCY AT BIRTH	78	74.8 (84)	71.3
MARRIAGES			
MARRIAGE RATE	6.5	7.2 (84)	8
AVERAGE AGE AT MARRIAGE M/F	27.5/24.3		
DIVORCE RATE	1.4	1.2 (84)	1
DEATHS			
DEATH RATE	6.3	6.7 (84)	6.4

HOUSEHOLDS

	1995[1]	1980[1]	1965
NUMBER	n/a	n/a	594,800 (63)
AVERAGE SIZE	n/a	n/a	3.8 (63)

ECONOMICS AND LABOR

	1995[1]
GDP PER CAPITA US$	15,500
LABOR FORCE (M/F) (thousands)	1,090.3/781.1 (94)
AGRICULTURE	48.3/14.0
MINING	
MANUFACTURING	285.4/110.7
UTILITIES	17.1/3.2
CONSTRUCTION	111.5/6.5
TRADE/FOOD/TOURISM	162.2/118.6
TRANSPORT/COMMUNICATIONS	83.8/25.2
FINANCE/INSURANCE/REAL ESTATE	111.2/95.2
SOCIAL AND PERSONAL SERVICES	262.3/405.0

	1995[1]	1980[1]	1965
UNEMPLOYMENT (official)	7.8% (94)		
UNION DENSITY	23.1%		

TRANSPORT

JOURNEYS (by transport mode)

RAILROAD PASSENGER TRIPS	238.0 (94)		
(millions of miles/kilometers)			
AIR PASSENGER TRIPS (thousands)	2,980.0 (94)		

VEHICLES (thousands)

PRIVATE CARS	1,057	409.5	75.7
COMMERCIAL	251.7	89	40

HEALTH AND HEALTH CARE

HEALTH CARE

ACCESS TO SAFE WATER	99%		
ACCESS TO SANITATION	70%		
MEASLES IMMUNIZATION	94%		
RATE OF PHYSICIANS	n/a	2.5	2.5 (60)
RATE OF HOSPITAL BEDS	6	5.1	6.8 (60)

HEALTH INDICATORS

SMOKING PREVALENCE M/F	45/30%		
TUBERCULOSIS INCIDENCE RATE	0.12		
AIDS/HIV CASES	372	293 (93)	
TOTAL DEATHS	35,117		

EDUCATION

SCHOOL AGE IN SCHOOL

PRIMARY	99%	95%	96%
SECONDARY	89%	73%	48%
HIGHER	41%	29%	14%

FEMALES IN SCHOOL

PRIMARY	98%	94%	95%
SECONDARY	53%	56%	51%
HIGHER	n/a	30.70%	18.2% (70)

ADULT ILLITERACY M/F	n/a	5.0/11.3% (83)	n/a

	1995[1]	1980[1]	1965
COMMUNICATIONS			
RATE OF NEWSPAPERS	246	260	202 (70)
RATE OF RADIOS	478	245	273
RATE OF TELEVISIONS	272	232	7

FOOTNOTE

1. Statistics are for Israel proper only; they do not include the Occupied Territories.

Source: CIA, *The World Factbook, 1997*; ILO, *World Labour Report, 1997*; UN, *Demographic Yearbook, 1997*; UN, *Statistical Yearbook, 1996*; World Bank, *World Development Indicators, 1998*.

ITALY

Italy is located in southern Europe on a peninsula bordering the Adriatic Sea, Ionian Sea, Mediterranean Sea, and Tyrrhenian Sea. The country also includes Sicily and Sardinia, two large adjacent islands. Austria and Slovenia border the 116,305-square-mile (301,230-square-kilometer) country on the northeast, and France and Switzerland on the northwest. Tunisia, on the North African coast, lies across the Mediterranean from Sicily. The country is a multiparty democracy that, since World War II, has endured extensive political instability. In 1996, Italians elected the first left-leaning government under a coalition known as the Olive Tree. Since taking office, however, the new government has imposed an economic austerity program and reduced social benefits to conform to the demands for integration in the European Monetary Union. Though Italy as a whole has a high standard of living, the country is divided between a highly industrial north and a less-developed south. The country's 1995 population of nearly 57.5 million was growing at a very slow pace of 0.1 percent, owing to a declining birth rate. The country has a life expectancy at birth of 78.1 years and an infant mortality rate of 6.9 deaths per 1,000 live births.

Annual Population Growth Rate

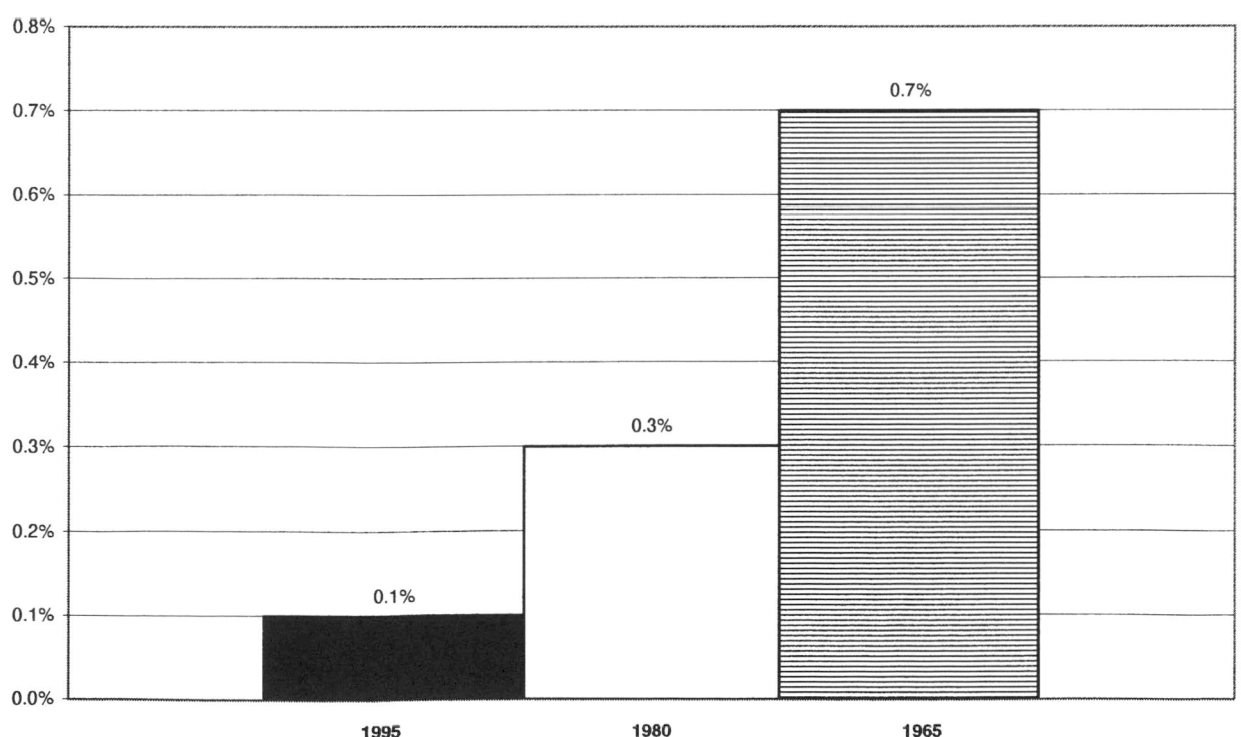

Like many Western European countries, Italy has seen its annual growth rate drop to near zero. Indeed, deaths now outnumber births, and the population's slight growth is due entirely to immigration.

Age Distribution

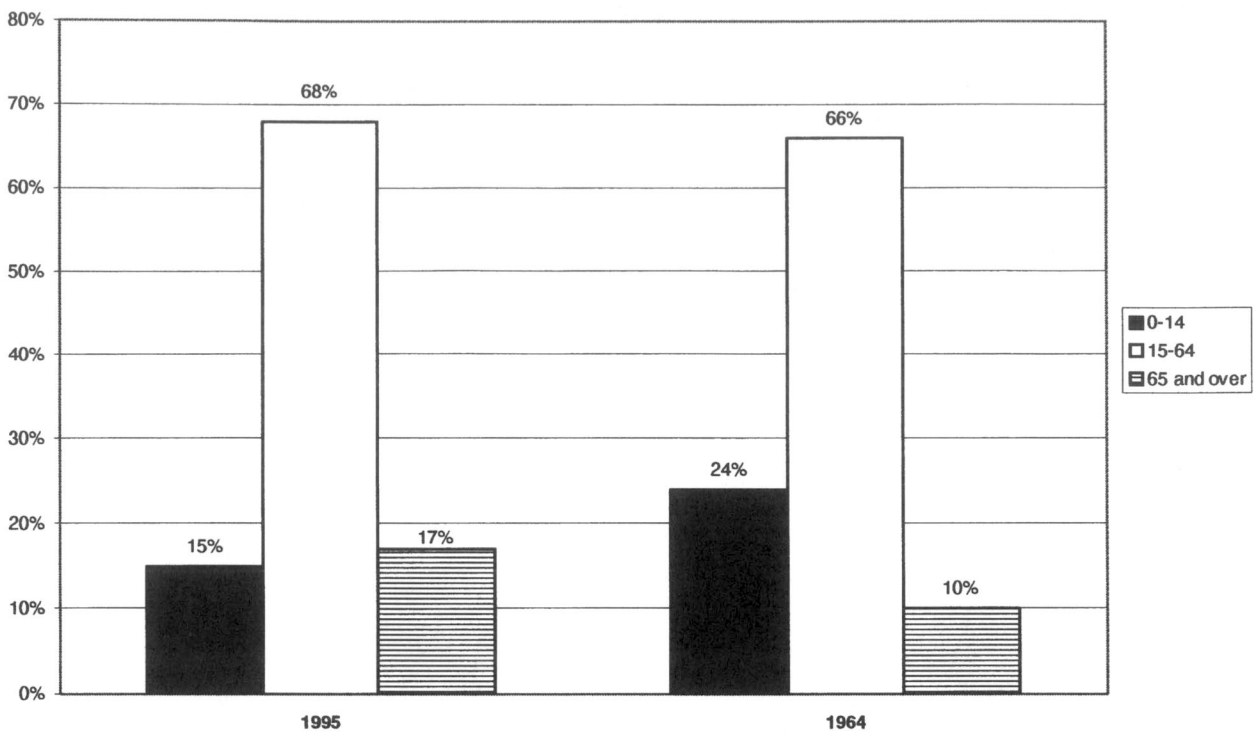

The falling birth rate in Italy can be reflected in the population's age profile. Like most other industrialized countries, Italy is becoming increasingly elderly, a trend that concerns many economists, who wonder how a large population of retired persons will be supported by a shrinking number of working-age people.

CHRONOLOGY

1966   Italy hurt by worst floods in centuries; hundreds die; precious artworks destroyed.

1971   Worst recession since World War II sets off nationwide strikes.

1978   Former prime minister Aldo Moro kidnapped and assassinated by left-wing terrorists.

1981   Corruption scandal leads to overthrow of Christian Democrats; Benito Craxi becomes first Socialist prime minister in Italy's postwar history.

1986   Major government campaign against Mafia in southern Italy begins.

1989   Major banking scandal rocks Italian government and business community.

1994   Silvio Berlusconi, a media mogul, leads his Forza Italia Party to victory in elections, as voters grow disgusted with corruption in government; personal corruption leads to his fall at end of year.

	1995	1980	1965

GEOGRAPHY

AREA (square miles/kilometers)   116,305/301,230
LAND AREA (square miles/kilometers)   113,521/294,020
COASTLINE (miles/kilometers)   4,750/7,600

CITIES

		1995	1980	1965
CAPITAL	Rome	2,693,383 (91)		
MAJOR CITIES	Milan	1,371,008		
	Naples	1,054,601		
	Turin	961,916		
	Palermo	697,162		

POPULATION

	1995	1980	1965
TOTAL	57,460,274	56,556,911 (81)	49,903,878 (61)
DENSITY (per square mile/kilometer)	492/190	483/186	445/172
ANNUAL GROWTH	0.1%	0.3%	0.7%
AGE COHORTS			
0–14	15%	n/a	23.8% (64)
15–64	68%	n/a	66% (64)
65 AND OVER	17%	n/a	9.7% (64)
URBAN	67%		
RURAL	33%		
NET MIGRATION RATE	1.25	n/a	−0.1

IDENTITY

	1995	1980	1965
ETHNICITY			
ITALIAN	n/a		
SICILIAN	n/a		
SARDINIAN	n/a		
LANGUAGE			
ITALIAN	n/a		
GERMAN	n/a		
FRENCH	n/a		
SLOVENE	n/a		

	1995	1980	1965
RELIGION			
ROMAN CATHOLIC	98%		
OTHER	2%		

VITAL STATISTICS

	1995	1980	1965
BIRTHS			
BIRTH RATE	9.9	10.1 (85)	18.9
INFANT MORTALITY RATE	6.9	10.9 (85)	35.6
LIFE EXPECTANCY AT BIRTH	78.1	73.9 (85)	69.7
MARRIAGES			
MARRIAGE RATE	5	5.2	7.4
DIVORCE RATE	0.4	0.3	n/a
DEATHS			
DEATH RATE	9.8	9.5	9.5

HOUSEHOLDS

NUMBER	13,681,568 (61)
AVERAGE SIZE	3.6 (61)

ECONOMICS AND LABOR

GDP PER CAPITA US$	$18,700
LABOR FORCE M/F (thousands)	12,972.0/7,030 (94)
AGRICULTURE	998/574
MINING	267/27
MANUFACTURING	3,120/1,421
UTILITIES	
CONSTRUCTION	1,554/88
TRADE/FOOD/TOURISM	2,663/1,557
TRANSPORT/COMMUNICATIONS	914/168
FINANCE/INSURANCE/REAL ESTATE	959/557
SOCIAL AND PERSONAL SERVICES	2,496/2,638
UNEMPLOYMENT (official)	11.3% (94)
UNION DENSITY	30.6%

	1995	1980	1965

TRANSPORT

JOURNEYS (by transport mode)

RAILROAD PASSENGER TRIPS (millions of miles/kilometers)	47,101.0 (93)		
AIR PASSENGER TRIPS (thousands)	22,933.0 (94)		

VEHICLES (thousands)

PRIVATE CARS	29,600	17,686.2	5,469
COMMERCIAL	2,745.5	1,691.2	665.8

HEALTH AND HEALTH CARE

HEALTH CARE

ACCESS TO SAFE WATER	n/a	99%	n/a
ACCESS TO SANITATION	100%		
MEASLES IMMUNIZATION	50%		
RATE OF PHYSICIANS	1.7	1.3	1.6 (60)
RATE OF HOSPITAL BEDS	6.5	n/a	9.1 (60)

HEALTH INDICATORS

LOW-BIRTH-WEIGHT BABIES	7%		
SMOKING PREVALENCE M/F	38/26%		
TUBERCULOSIS INCIDENCE RATE	0.25		
AIDS/HIV CASES	32,624	21,928 (93)	
TOTAL DEATHS	548,081 (94)		

EDUCATION

SCHOOL AGE IN SCHOOL

PRIMARY	98%	100%	109%
SECONDARY	74%	72%	47%
HIGHER	41%	27%	5.8%

FEMALES IN SCHOOL

PRIMARY	97%	99%	107%
SECONDARY	74%	70%	42%

ADULT ILLITERACY M/F	n/a	n/a	7.3/11.2% (61)

	1995	1980	1965
COMMUNICATIONS			
RATE OF NEWSPAPERS	106	85	113
RATE OF RADIOS	802	602	215
RATE OF TELEVISIONS	429	390	121

Source: CIA, *The World Factbook, 1997;* ILO, *World Labour Report, 1997;* UN, *Demographic Yearbook, 1997;* UN, *Statistical Yearbook, 1996;* World Bank, *World Development Indicators, 1998.*

JAMAICA

Jamaica is located on an island in the Caribbean Sea, west of Haiti on Hispaniola Island, across the Jamaica Channel. The island of Cuba is located north of the 4,243-square-mile (10,990-square-kilometer) country. In August 1962, Jamaica received independence from the United Kingdom. Since independence, the country has maintained a democratic form of government dominated by two leading parties that formed in the colonial period. The country has endured severe economic difficulties stemming from the enormous debt owed to Western banks and lending agencies. The country's major industries are tourism and bauxite mining. In the 1980s, Jamaica' economy began to expand into textile and garment manu-

facturing. The country has a high and growing unemployment rate that contributes to a high poverty rate. The country's 1995 population of nearly 2.6 million was growing at a relatively slow pace of 0.9 percent, mainly resulting from a high and growing rate of out-migration. Persons of African descent make up Jamaica's population majority (76.3 percent), followed by Afro-Europeans (15.1 percent), East Indians (3 percent), whites (3 percent), and Chinese and Afro Chinese (1 percent). Jamaica has a high life expectancy for a developing country 74.9 years—and an infant mortality rate of 15.6 infant deaths per 1,000 live births.

Net Migration Rate

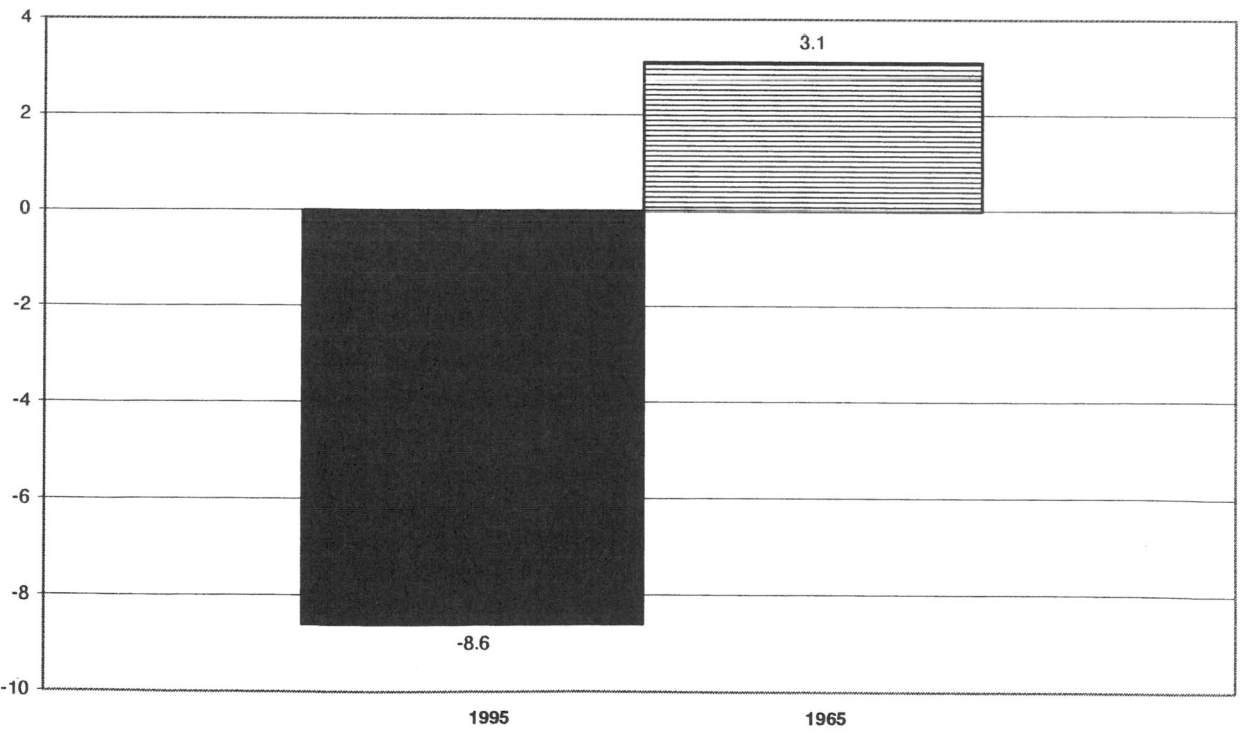

Like many other Caribbean nations, Jamaica has seen a steady drain of people to the United Kingdom and, increasingly, the United States in recent years. Especially troubling has been the loss of well-educated persons looking for better occupational opportunities in the industrialized world.

Infant Mortality Rate

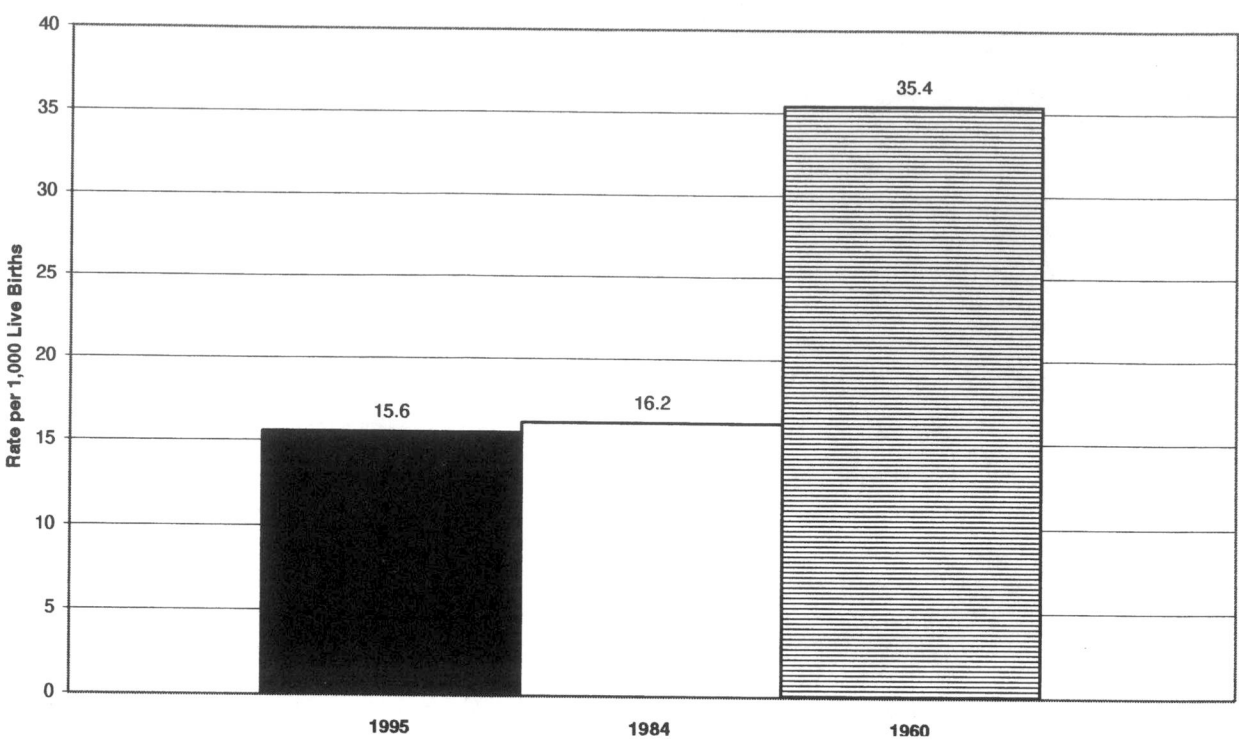

During its first two decades of independence, Jamaica enjoyed steady economic growth. Since 1980, however, the nation's economy, like that of many in the Third World, has been somewhat stagnant. These changing economic fortunes are reflected in the drop in infant mortality rates, in the first period, and their stagnation in the second.

CHRONOLOGY

1962   Jamaica gains independence from Great Britain.

1972   Leftist Michael Manley wins election, becomes prime minister.

1977   Manley government assumes majority ownership of bauxite mines, source of Jamaica's main export.

1980   Conservative Edward Seaga defeats Manley amid election violence.

1988   Hurricane Gilbert wreaks extensive damage throughout island.

1989   Manley returned to power.

	1995	1980	1965

GEOGRAPHY

AREA (square miles/kilometers)   4,243/10,990
LAND AREA (square miles/kilometers)   4,181/10,830
COASTLINE (miles/kilometers)   639/1,022

CITIES

		1995	1980	1965
CAPITAL	Kingston	103,962 (91)	104,041 (82)	n/a

POPULATION

	1995	1980	1965
TOTAL	2,595,275	2,095,878 (82)	1,609,814 (60)
DENSITY (per square mile/kilometer)	596/230	552/213	379/146
ANNUAL GROWTH	0.9%	1.5%	2.0%

AGE COHORTS

	1995	1980	1965
0–14	32%	n/a	41%
15–64	61%	n/a	55%
65 AND OVER	7%	n/a	4%

	1995
URBAN	54%
RURAL	46%

	1995	1980	1965
NET MIGRATION RATE	−8.6	n/a	3.1

IDENTITY

ETHNICITY

	1995
AFRICAN	76.3%
AFRO-EUROPEAN	15.1%
EAST INDIAN AND AFRO-EAST INDIAN	3%
WHITE	3%
CHINESE AND AFRO-CHINESE	1%

LANGUAGE

	1995
ENGLISH	n/a
CREOLE	n/a

RELIGION

	1995
PROTESTANT	55.9%
ROMAN CATHOLIC	5%
OTHERS	39%

	1995	1980	1965

VITAL STATISTICS

BIRTHS

BIRTH RATE	22.2	23.5 (84)	39.4 (60)
INFANT MORTALITY RATE	15.6	16.2 (84)	35.4 (60)
LIFE EXPECTANCY AT BIRTH	74.9	64.6 (84)	64.7 (60)

MARRIAGES

MARRIAGE RATE	6.1	4.6 (84)	4.1 (60)
DIVORCE RATE	0.5	0.4 (84)	0.4 (60)

DEATHS

DEATH RATE	5.6	5.4 (84)	9 (60)

HOUSEHOLDS

NUMBER	n/a	n/a	401,743 (60)
AVERAGE SIZE	n/a	n/a	4 (60)

ECONOMICS AND LABOR

GDP PER CAPITA US$	$3,200

LABOR FORCE M/F (thousands)	517.5/389.9 (92)
AGRICULTURE	185.0/60.5
MINING	4.2/0.4
MANUFACTURING	57.6/41.6
CONSTRUCTION	62.4/0.6
TRANSPORT/COMMUNICATIONS	28.5/8.7
FINANCE/INSURANCE/REAL ESTATE	84.6/134.1
SOCIAL AND PERSONAL SERVICES	91.8/139.3

UNEMPLOYMENT (official)	15.9% (92)
UNION DENSITY	9.7/22.9

POVERTY

UNDER $1/DAY	4.3%
UNDER $2/DAY	24.9%

	1995	1980	1965

TRANSPORT

JOURNEYS (by transport mode)

RAILROAD PASSENGER TRIPS	24.0 (89)		
(millions of miles/kilometers)			
AIR PASSENGER TRIPS (thousands)	1,011.0 (94)		

VEHICLES

PRIVATE CARS	86,800	n/a	46,000
COMMERCIAL	41,300	n/a	19,300

HEALTH AND HEALTH CARE

HEALTH AND HEALTH CARE

ACCESS TO SAFE WATER	70%		
ACCESS TO SANITATION	74%		
MEASLES IMMUNIZATION	82%		
RATE OF PHYSICIANS	0.5	0.4	0.4 (60)
RATE OF HOSPITAL BEDS	2.1	n/a	4.1 (60)

HEALTH INDICATORS

PREGNANT WOMEN WITH ANEMIA	40%		
LOW-BIRTH-WEIGHT BABIES	11%		
CHILD MALNUTRITION	10%		
SMOKING PREVALENCE M/F	43/13%		
TUBERCULOSIS INCIDENCE RATE	10%		
AIDS/HIV CASES	1,533	669 (93)	
TOTAL DEATHS	13,503 (94)		

EDUCATION

SCHOOL AGE IN SCHOOL

PRIMARY	109%	103%	102%
SECONDARY	66%	67%	16%
HIGHER	6%	7%	1.1%

FEMALES IN SCHOOL

PRIMARY	107%	103%	105%
SECONDARY	n/a	69%	16%

ADULT ILLITERACY M/F	19/11%	n/a	4.4/3.5% (70)

	1995	1980	1965
COMMUNICATIONS			
RATE OF NEWSPAPERS	67	51	69
RATE OF RADIOS	433	375	217
RATE OF TELEVISIONS	141	80	16

Source: CIA, *The World Factbook, 1997;* ILO, *World Labour Report, 1997;* UN, *Demographic Yearbook, 1997;* UN, *Statistical Yearbook, 1996;* World Bank, *World Development Indicators, 1998.*

JAPAN

Japan is an island country located in East Asia on the East China Sea, Pacific Ocean, and Sea of Japan. The Korean Peninsula lies west of the 145,882-square-mile (377,835-square-kilometer) country, and the Russian Federation is to the northwest. Japan has a democratic system of government dominated by the Liberal Democratic Party. The country is among the world's leading economic powers, with a modern and highly efficient industrial sector. The Japanese government plays an important role in assisting industrial growth. In the late 1990s, Japan was enduring a long economic recession caused in part by a financial crisis brought on in part by high levels of speculation on real estate and equities. Japan's leading industries have provided workers with a cradle-to-grave safety net. The Japanese are among the healthiest people in the world with a comprehensive and accessible medical care system. In 1995, Japan's population of nearly 125.5 million was growing at a slow rate of 0.2 percent, due to a declining birth rate. The country has a high life expectancy at birth of nearly 80 years and the lowest infant mortality rate in the world of 4.4 deaths per 1,000 live births.

Private Cars

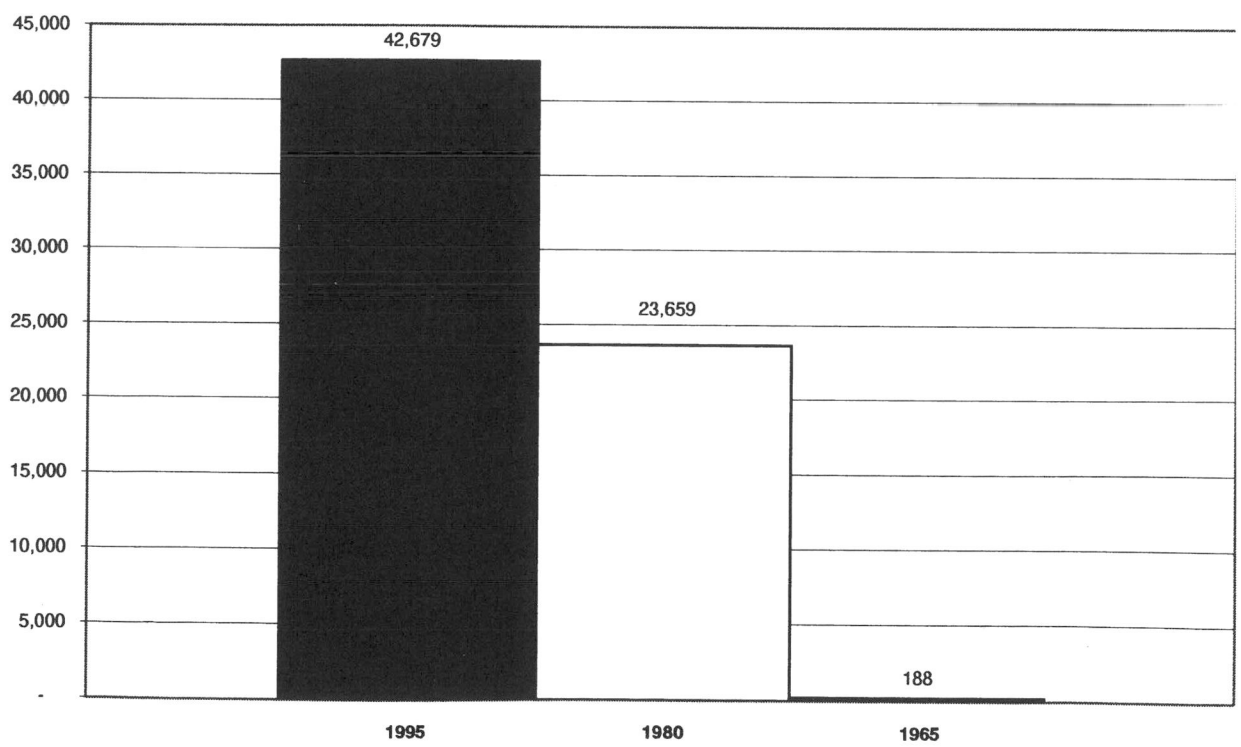

Like Germany, Japan underwent a miraculous economic transformation in the postwar era. Its manufacturing capacity, which was almost entirely destroyed by American bombing in World War II, revived to such an extent that it seriously threatened U.S. economic hegemony by the 1980s. This economic growth can be measured in the rapid rise in automobile ownership, nearly all of it in Japanese-produced cars.

Life Expectancy at Birth

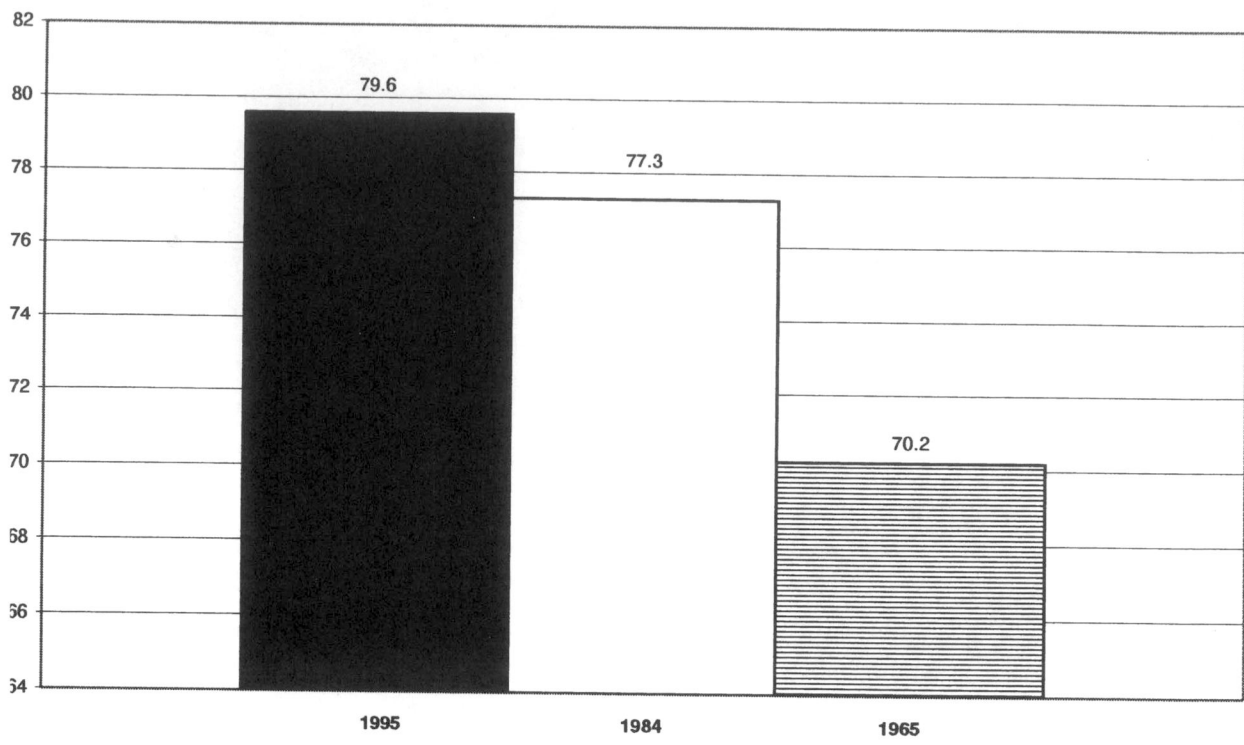

Always a country with a healthy population, most demographers believe that Japan has the highest average life expectancy rate of any major nation in the world, a factor attributed, in part, to the country's high-protein, low-fat diet. The introduction of high-fat Western diets in recent years, however, may change that.

CHRONOLOGY

1964   Japan hosts Olympic Games, marking return to international sports.

1972   United States returns Okinawa, captured in World War II, to Japan.

1974   Japan hit hard by oil boycott of Arab nations.

1989   Liberal Democrats lose control of Upper House of parliament for first time since end of World War II; Emperor Hirohito dies, replaced by son Akihito.

1994   Socialist Party head becomes prime minister for first time; massive earthquake destroys Kobe, killing more than 5,000.

1997   Weakening Japanese economy faces further blows from collapsing East Asian economies.

	1995	1980	1965

GEOGRAPHY

AREA (square miles/kilometers)	145,882/377,835		
LAND AREA (square miles/kilometers)	144,689/374,744		
COASTLINE (miles/kilometers)	18,594/29,751		

CITIES				
CAPITAL	Tokyo	8,021,943 (94)		
MAJOR CITIES	Osaka	2,575,042		
	Nagoya	2,153,293		
	Sapporo	1,744,806		
	Kobe	1,518,982		

POPULATION

	1995	1980	1965
TOTAL	125,449,703	117,060,396	98,274,961 (66)
DENSITY (per square mile/kilometer)	857/331	829/320	692/267
ANNUAL GROWTH	0.2%	0.7%	1.0%

AGE COHORTS			
0–14	16%	n/a	25%
15–64	69%	n/a	68%
65 AND OVER	15%	n/a	7%

MALE	49%		
FEMALE	51%		

URBAN	77.4% (90)	76.2%	n/a
RURAL	22.6% (90)	23.8%	n/a

NET MIGRATION RATE	−0.4	n/a	0

IDENTITY

ETHNICITY			
JAPANESE	99.4%		
KOREAN	0.6%		

	1995	1980	1965
LANGUAGE			
JAPANESE	100%		
RELIGION			
SHINTO AND BUDDHIST	84.0%		
OTHER	16.0%		
CHRISTIAN	0.7%		

VITAL STATISTICS

	1995	1980	1965
BIRTHS			
BIRTH RATE	10.2	12.5 (84)	13.7
INFANT MORTALITY RATE	4.4	6 (84)	18.5
ABORTION RATE	294.3 (94)		
LIFE EXPECTANCY AT BIRTH	79.6	77.3 (84)	70.2
MARRIAGES			
MARRIAGE RATE	6.3	6.2 (84)	9.5
AVERAGE AGE AT MARRIAGE M/F	30.3/26.9 (90)		
DIVORCE RATE	1.5	1.5 (84)	0.8
DEATHS			
DEATH RATE	7.7	6.2 (84)	6.8

HOUSEHOLDS

	1995	1980	1965
NUMBER	40,670,475 (90)	n/a	21,110,500 (63)
URBAN	32,682,533		
RURAL	7,987,942		
AVERAGE SIZE	3 (90)		4.2
URBAN	2.9		
RURAL	3.5		
TYPE OF HOUSEHOLD			
SINGLE	16.2%		
MARRIED	68.9%		
WIDOWED	8.6%		
DIVORCED/SEPARATED	4.7%		
FEMALE HEADED	17.%		

	1995	1980	1965

ECONOMICS AND LABOR

GDP PER CAPITA US$	$21,300		
LABOR FORCE M/F (thousands)	38,400.0/26,100.0 (93)		
AGRICULTURE	2,070/1,760		
MINING	50/10		
MANUFACTURING	9,450/5,850		
UTILITIES	300/50		
CONSTRUCTION	5,370/1,030		
TRADE/FOOD/TOURISM	7,300/7,180		
TRANSPORT/COMMUNICATIONS	3,300/640		
FINANCE/INSURANCE/REAL ESTATE	3,020/2,450		
SOCIAL AND PERSONAL SERVICES	7,360/7,020		
UNEMPLOYMENT (official)	2.5% (93)		
UNION DENSITY	18.6%		

TRANSPORT

JOURNEYS (by transport mode)			
RAILROAD PASSENGER TRIPS	402,513.0 (94)		
(millions of miles/kilometers)			
AIR PASSENGER TRIPS (thousands)	83,913.0 (94)		
VEHICLES (thousands)			
PRIVATE CARS	42,679	23,659.00	188
COMMERCIAL	20,610	13,423.00	283

HEALTH AND HEALTH CARE

HEALTH CARE			
ACCESS TO SANITATION	85%		
MEASLES IMMUNIZATION	68%		
RATE OF PHYSICIANS	1.8	1.4	1.1 (60)
RATE OF HOSPITAL BEDS	16.2	11.3	9 (60)
TOTAL DEATHS	922,062		
HEALTH INDICATORS			
LOW-BIRTH-WEIGHT BABIES	6%		
CHILD MALNUTRITION	3%		
SMOKING PREVALENCE M/F	59/15%		
TUBERCULOSIS INCIDENCE RATE	0.42		
AIDS/HIV CASES	1,154	685 (93)	

	1995	1980	1965
EDUCATION			
SCHOOL AGE IN SCHOOL			
PRIMARY	102%	101%	101%
SECONDARY	99%	93%	85%
HIGHER	40%	31%	11.10%
FEMALES IN SCHOOL			
PRIMARY	101%	100%	100%
SECONDARY	99%	93%	83%
HIGHER	n/a	20.40%	9.6%(70)
COMMUNICATIONS			
RATE OF NEWSPAPERS	577	567	451
RATE OF RADIOS	911	678	208
RATE OF TELEVISIONS	618	539	183

Source: CIA, *The World Factbook, 1997;* ILO, *World Labour Report, 1997;* UN, *Demographic Yearbook, 1997;* UN, *Statistical Yearbook, 1996;* World Bank, *World Development Indicators, 1998.*

JORDAN

Jordan is located in Southwest Asia, northwest of Saudi Arabia. The 34,445-square-mile (89,213-square-kilometer) country is bordered by Iraq on the northeast, Syria on the north, and Israel and the disputed West Bank on the west. In 1946, Jordan, then part of a League of Nations mandate, gained independence from the United Kingdom. King Hussein Bin Talal Al Hashimi is the country's chief of state. A prime minister, appointed by the king, heads a national assembly. Jordan's leading industries are raw materials and agricultural products. The country's economy also depends on remittances from workers employed abroad. Jordan has a per capita gross domestic product (GDP) of only $4,700 per year. About 23.5 percent of the country's residents subsist on the equivalent of less than $2 a day, and 2.5 percent survive on $1 a day or less. Between 1961 and 1995, Jordan's population grew from just over 1.7 million to 5,654,000. Despite a net out-migration rate of 6.2 per 1,000 residents in 1995, the country's population was continuing to grow at the rapid annual rate of 3 percent, due to a high birth rate. Jordan's life expectancy at birth is 72.5 years and the infant mortality rate is 31.5 deaths per 1,000 live births.

		1995	1980	1965[1]

GEOGRAPHY

		1995	1980	1965[1]
AREA (square miles/kilometers)		34,445/89,213		
LAND AREA (square miles/kilometers)		34,318/88,884		
COASTLINE (miles/kilometers)		16/26		
CITIES				
CAPITAL	Amman	965,000 (91)		
MAJOR CITIES	Zarqa	359,000		
	Irbid	216,000		
	Russiefa	115,500		

POPULATION

	1995	1980	1965[1]
TOTAL	5,654,000	2,132,997 (79)	1,706,226 (61)
DENSITY (per square mile/kilometer)	145/56	93/36	54/21
ANNUAL GROWTH	3.0%	3.8%	3.2%
AGE COHORTS			
0–14	44%	n/a	46%
15–64	53%	n/a	50%
65 AND OVER	3%	n/a	4%
MALE	52%		
FEMALE	48%		

	1995	**1980**	**1965**[1]
URBAN	71%	59.4%	n/a
RURAL	29%	40.6%	n/a
NET MIGRATION RATE	−6.2	n/a	1.4

IDENTITY

ETHNICITY
ARAB	98%
CIRCASSIAN	1%
ARMENIAN	1%

LANGUAGE
ARABIC	n/a
ENGLISH	n/a

RELIGION
SUNNI MUSLIM	92%
CHRISTIAN	8%

VITAL STATISTICS

BIRTHS
	1995	1980	1965
BIRTH RATE	36.7	n/a	47 (63)
INFANT MORTALITY RATE	31.5	n/a	42 (63)
LIFE EXPECTANCY AT BIRTH	72.5	n/a	52.3 (63)

MARRIAGES
MARRIAGE RATE	8	n/a	7.8 (63)
AVERAGE AGE AT MARRIAGE M/F	28/24.5		
DIVORCE RATE	1.2	n/a	1 (63)

DEATHS
DEATH RATE	3.9	n/a	16 (63)

HOUSEHOLDS

NUMBER	n/a	n/a	313,613 (63)
AVERAGE SIZE	n/a	n/a	5.3 (61)

	1995	1980	1965[1]

ECONOMICS AND LABOR

GDP PER CAPITA US$	$4,700		
LABOR FORCE M/F (thousands)	240.4/70.7 (93)		
MINING	7.4/0.2		
MANUFACTURING	48.4/5.7		
UTILITIES	11.9/0.4		
CONSTRUCTION	7.5/0.2		
TRADE/FOOD/TOURISM	22.2/1.7		
TRANSPORT/COMMUNICATIONS	22.7/2.2		
FINANCE/INSURANCE/REAL ESTATE	10.5/3.5		
SOCIAL AND PERSONAL SERVICES	109.0/56.8		
POVERTY			
UNDER $1/DAY	2.5% (92)		
UNDER $2/DAY	23.5% (92)		

TRANSPORT

JOURNEYS (by transport mode)			
RAILROAD PASSENGER TRIPS	2.0 (94)		
(millions of miles/kilometers)			
AIR PASSENGER TRIPS (thousands)	1,220.0 (94)		
VEHICLES			
PRIVATE CARS	164,000	11,200	95,100
COMMERCIAL	75,300	7,800	48,200

HEALTH AND HEALTH CARE

HEALTH AND HEALTH CARE			
ACCESS TO SAFE WATER	89%		
ACCESS TO SANITATION	100%		
MEASLES IMMUNIZATION	92%		
RATE OF PHYSICIANS	1.6	0.8	0.2 (60)
RATE OF HOSPITAL BEDS	1.6	1.3	1.8 (60)
HEALTH INDICATORS			
LOW-BIRTH-WEIGHT BABIES	7%		
CHILD MALNUTRITION	10%		
SMOKING PREVALENCE M/F	43/5%		
TUBERCULOSIS INCIDENCE RATE	0.14		

	1995	1980	1965[1]
AIDS/HIV CASES	40	31 (93)	
TOTAL DEATHS	12,290 (94)		

EDUCATION

SCHOOL AGE IN SCHOOL

	1995	1980	1965[1]
PRIMARY	94%	104%	94%
SECONDARY	n/a	75%	38%
HIGHER	n/a	27%	1.6%

FEMALES IN SCHOOL

	1995	1980	1965[1]
PRIMARY	92%	100%	82%
SECONDARY	55%	46%	22%

ADULT ILLITERACY M/F	21/7%	19.9/49.5% (79)	n/a

COMMUNICATIONS

	1995	1980	1965[1]
RATE OF NEWSPAPERS	53	23	8
RATE OF RADIOS	243	188	158
RATE OF TELEVISIONS	76	59	20 (70)

FOOTNOTE
1. Includes what is now the Israeli-occupied West Bank.

Source: CIA, The World Factbook, 1997; ILO, World Labour Report, 1997; UN, Demographic Yearbook, 1997; UN, Statistical Yearbook, 1996; World Bank, World Development Indicators, 1998.

KAZAKSTAN

Formerly known as Kazakh Soviet Socialist Republic, Kazakstan is the second largest former Soviet Republic in geographic area. The country is located in Central Asia, south of the Russian Federation. China borders the 1,049,151-square-mile (2,717,300-square-kilometer) country on the southeast; and Kyrgyzstan, Uzbekistan, and Turkmenistan border on the south. Kazakstan gained independence in December 1991 following the collapse and breakup of the Soviet Union. President Nursultan A. Nazarbayev, who took office in February 1990, has consolidated power throughout the period of independence. Kazakstan is both resource rich and industrialized, owing to the modernization of the country under Soviet rule. Though other former Soviet states have embraced market reforms, the Kazakstan government continues to maintain control over the leading sectors of the economy. A smaller share of Kazakstan's population lives in poverty than in other developing countries with a comparable gross domestic product. In 1995, Kazakstan's population of 16,916,463 was contracting at an annual rate of 0.1 percent, primarily due to out-migration of Russian nationals in the post-Soviet era. Kazakstan is an ethnically heterogeneous country. Although Kazaks are the ethnic majority, encompassing 41.9 percent of the population, Russians still maintain a sizable 37 percent share of the country's population. Other ethnic minorities include Ukrainians, Germans, Uzbeks, and Tatars.

Languages

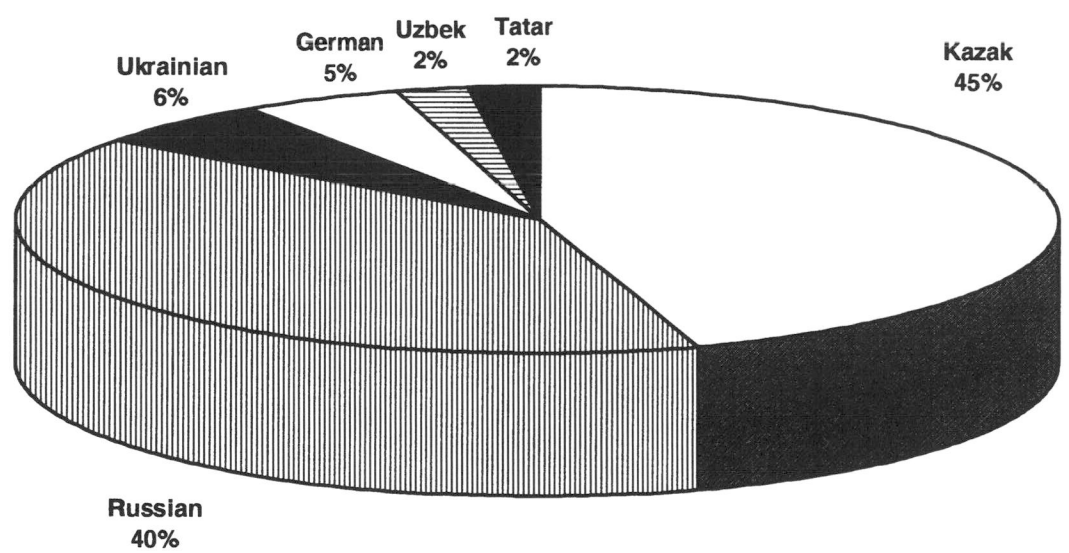

Like many republics within the former Soviet Union, Kazakstan's culture was heavily Russified during 70 years of communist rule. Since independence, the new government of Kazakstan has emphasized a return to Kazak teaching in schools, a move that has alienated many Russian speakers in the country.

Average Size of Urban and Rural Households, 1989

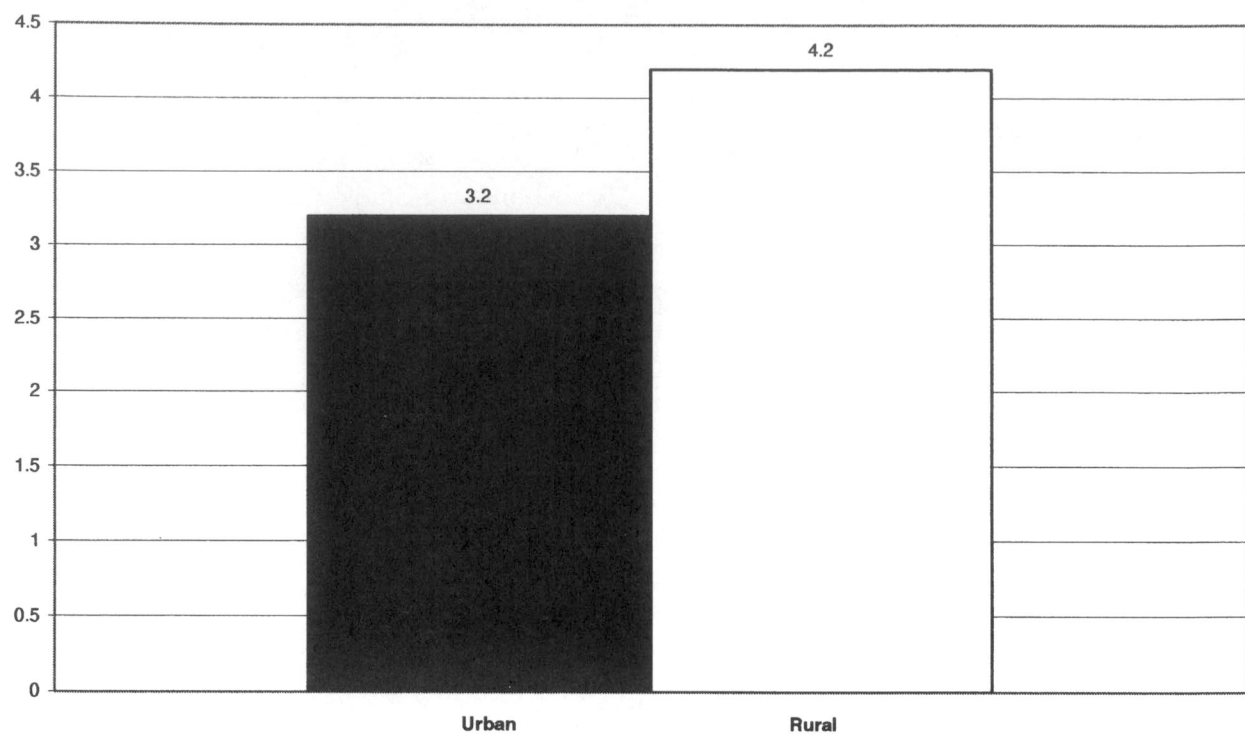

The two distinct cultures within Kazakstan, the more modern Russified cities and the traditional Kazak-dominated countryside, are reflected in the relative size of households. Urban households are fully one-third larger than their rural counterparts.

1995[1]

GEOGRAPHY

AREA (square miles/kilometers)	1,049,151/2,717,300
LAND AREA (square miles/kilometers)	1,030,811/2,669,800
COASTLINE (miles/kilometers)	1,184/1,894

CITIES

CAPITAL	Almaty	1,176,000 (93)
MAJOR CITIES	Karaganda	596,000
	Shimkent	404,000
	Pavlograd	349,000
	Semipalatinsk	342,000

POPULATION

TOTAL	16,916,463
DENSITY (per square mile/kilometer)	16/6
ANNUAL GROWTH	−0.1%

	1995[1]
AGE COHORTS	
0–14	30%
15–64	63%
65 AND OVER	7%
MALE	48%
FEMALE	52%
URBAN	60%
RURAL	40%
NET MIGRATION RATE	−10.88

IDENTITY

LANGUAGE

KAZAK	41.9%
RUSSIAN	37%
UKRAINIAN	5.20%
GERMAN	4.7%
UZBEK	2.1%
TATAR	2.0%

RELIGION

MUSLIM	47%
RUSSIAN ORTHODOX	44%
PROTESTANT	2%

VITAL STATISTICS

BIRTHS

BIRTH RATE	19
URBAN BIRTH RATE	15.2 (93)
RURAL BIRTH RATE	23.3 (93)
INFANT MORTALITY RATE	63.2
ABORTION RATE	654.7 (93)
LIFE EXPECTANCY AT BIRTH	64.1

MARRIAGES

MARRIAGE RATE	8.7
AVERAGE AGE AT MARRIAGE M/F	24.6/22.4
DIVORCE RATE	2.7

DEATHS

DEATH RATE	9.6

1995[1]

HOUSEHOLDS

NUMBER	4,397,043 (89)
URBAN	2,771,234
RURAL	1,625,809
AVERAGE SIZE	3.6 (89)
URBAN	3.2
RURAL	4.2

ECONOMICS AND LABOR

GDP PER CAPITA US$	$2,700
LABOR FORCE (thousands)	7,356 (92)
AGRICULTURE	1,762
MINING	257
MANUFACTURING	1,160
UTILITIES	83
CONSTRUCTION	681
TRADE/FOOD/TOURISM	437
TRANSPORT/COMMUNICATIONS	665
FINANCE/INSURANCE/REAL ESTATE	46
SOCIAL AND PERSONAL SERVICES	1,906
UNEMPLOYMENT (official)	1% (93)
POVERTY	
UNDER $1/DAY	1%
UNDER $2/DAY	12.1%

TRANSPORT

JOURNEYS (by transport mode)	
RAILROAD PASSENGER TRIPS	17,632 (94)
(millions of miles/kilometers)	
AIR PASSENGER TRIPS (thousands)	702 (94)

HEALTH AND HEALTH CARE

HEALTH CARE	
MEASLES IMMUNIZATION	72%

	1995[1]
RATE OF PHYSICIANS	3.8
RATE OF HOSPITAL BEDS	12.2

HEALTH INDICATORS

PREGNANT WOMEN WITH ANEMIA	11%
CHILD MALNUTRITION	1%
TUBERCULOSIS INCIDENCE RATE	77
AIDS/HIV CASES	5
TOTAL DEATHS	160,591 (94)

EDUCATION

SCHOOL AGE IN SCHOOL

PRIMARY	96%
SECONDARY	83%
HIGHER	33%

FEMALES IN SCHOOL

PRIMARY	94%
SECONDARY	87%

FOOTNOTE

1. Part of the Soviet Union in 1965 and 1980.

Source: CIA, *The World Factbook, 1997*; ILO, *World Labour Report, 1997*; UN, *Demographic Yearbook, 1997*; UN, *Statistical Yearbook, 1996*; World Bank, *World Development Indicators, 1998*.

KENYA

Kenya is located in East Africa on the western shores of the Indian Ocean. Somalia borders the 224,961-square-mile (582,650-square-kilometer) country on the northeast, Ethiopia on the north, Sudan on the northwest, Uganda on the west, and Tanzania on the south. Kenya gained independence from the United Kingdom in December 1963. President Daniel Arap Moi, who has limited political opposition, has dominated the country since taking office in October 1978. In 1998, President Moi was reelected for yet another five-year term, in part the result of division among his opponents. The country's principal industries are tea, coffee, and petroleum. Nearly 80 percent of

Kenya's population is mired in poverty, subsisting on the equivalent of less than $2 a day. The country is growing at one of the fastest paces in the world, increasing from more than 8.6 million in 1962 to nearly 28.2 million in 1995. The country's high population growth is placing severe pressure on the economy and environment. In 1995, Kenya's life expectancy at birth was 55.6 years, and the country had an infant mortality rate of 33.4 deaths per 1,000 live births. The country is divided among eight leading ethnic groups, including the Kikuyu, Luhya, Luo, Kanejin, Kamba, Kisii, Meru, and Asians, Europeans, and Arabs.

Population

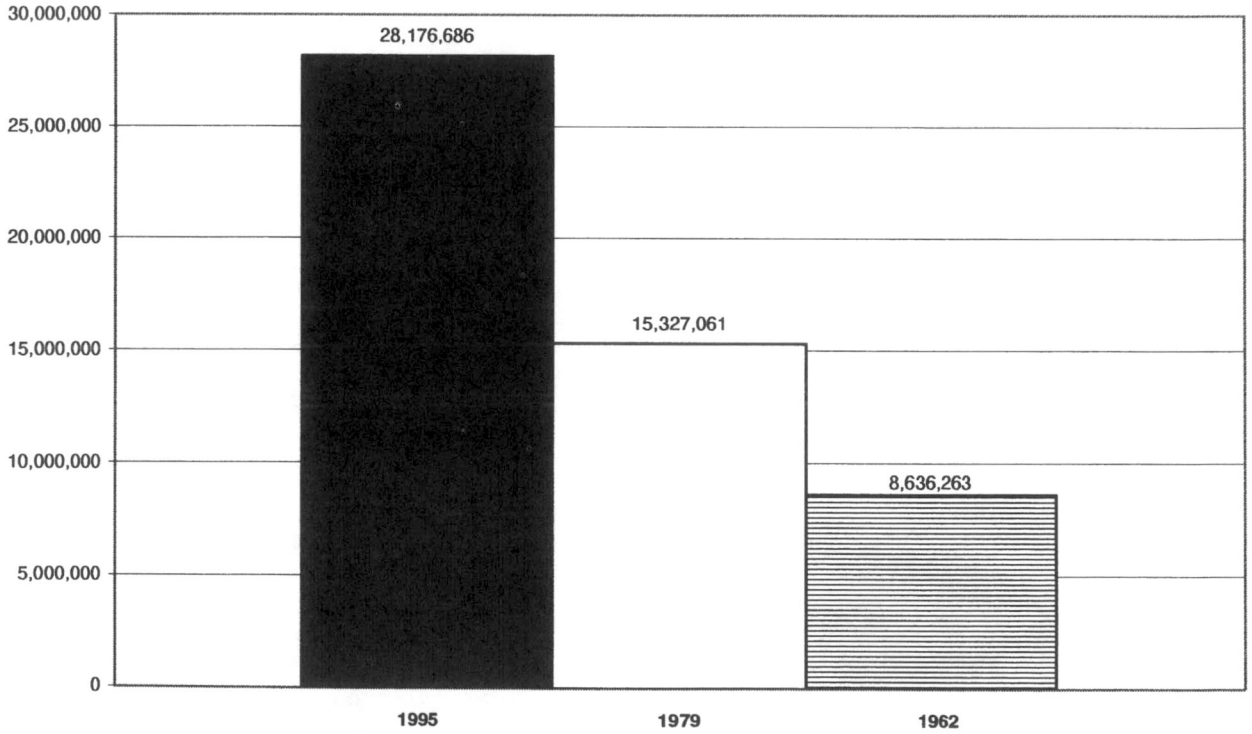

With its relative success in bringing down death rates and its near-total lack of effort in bringing down birth rates, Kenya has seen one of the most rapid population growths of any country in the developing world, a factor that worries many observers of the Kenyan situation.

Density per Square Mile

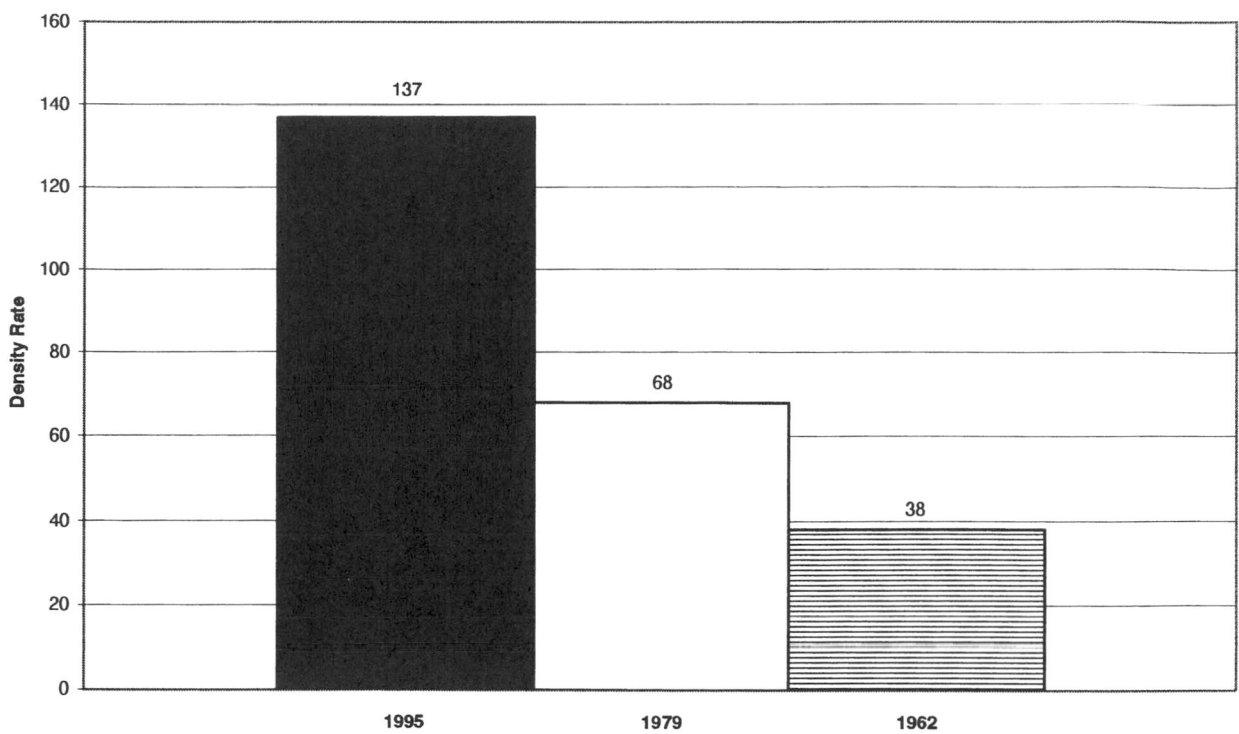

Despite its rapid population growth, Kenya remains a country with a low density of population. For many African scholars, this indicates that Kenya, like many other countries on the continent, has plenty of room for its growing population. The dire warning of developing-world population experts, they say, hides racial fears that the non-white population of the world is outgrowing the white population.

CHRONOLOGY

1963   Kenya wins independence from Great Britain; major land reform launched.
1964   Nation declares itself a republic within British Commonwealth.
1978   Kenyan independence leader and president Jomo Kenyatta dies; succeeded by Vice-President Daniel Arap Moi.
1982   Kenya African National Union is declared only legal party in country.
1991   Under pressure from domestic critics and international lenders and aid givers, Moi agrees to multiparty elections.
1997   Moi reelected in poll viewed as corrupt; protests break out in capital; ethnic violence breaks out along coast.

	1995	1980	1965

GEOGRAPHY

AREA (square miles/kilometers)	224,961/582,650		
LAND AREA (square miles/kilometers)	219,788/569,250		
COASTLINE (miles/kilometers)	335/536		

CITIES

		1995	1980	1965
CAPITAL	Nairobi	n/a	1,162,189 (85)	n/a
MAJOR CITIES	Mombasa	n/a	442,369	n/a
	Kisumu	n/a	152,643 (79)	n/a

POPULATION

	1995	1980	1965
TOTAL	28,176,686	15,327,061 (79)	8,636,263 (62)
DENSITY (per square mile/kilometer)	137/53	68/35	38/15
ANNUAL GROWTH	n/a	4.1%	2.9%

AGE COHORTS

	1995	1980	1965
0–14	45%	n/a	46% (62)
15–64	53%	n/a	49% (62)[1]
65 AND OVER	2%	n/a	4.8% (62)[2]

	1995	1980	1965
MALE	50%		
FEMALE	50%		
URBAN	28%	15.5%	n/a
RURAL	72%	84.5%	n/a
NET MIGRATION RATE	−0.35	n/a	0

IDENTITY

ETHNICITY

	1995
KIKUYU	22%
LUHYA	14%
LUO	13%
KALENJIN	12%
KAMBA	11%
KISII	6%
MERU	6%
ASIAN, EUROPEAN, AND ARAB	1%

	1995	1980	1965
LANGUAGE			
SWAHILI	n/a		
ENGLISH	n/a		
INDIGENOUS	n/a		
RELIGION			
PROTESTANT	38%		
ROMAN CATHOLIC	28%		
INDIGENOUS	26%		

VITAL STATISTICS

	1995	1980	1965
BIRTHS			
BIRTH RATE	33.4	55.1	50
INFANT MORTALITY RATE	55.3	80	n/a
LIFE EXPECTANCY AT BIRTH	55.6	49.1	40.5
DEATHS			
DEATH RATE	10.3	14	20

ECONOMICS AND LABOR

	1995
GDP PER CAPITA US$	$1,300
LABOR FORCE M/F (thousands)	1,117.1/324.6 (91)
AGRICULTURE	207.6/64.4
MINING	3.5/0.9
MANUFACTURING	167.0/21.9
UTILITIES	19.2/3.2
CONSTRUCTION	68.3/4.2
TRADE/FOOD/TOURISM	97.1/19.6
TRANSPORT/COMMUNICATIONS	65.6/10.6
FINANCE/INSURANCE/REAL ESTATE	51.4/14.9
SOCIAL AND PERSONAL SERVICES	437.4/185.0
UNION DENSITY	16.90%
POVERTY	
UNDER $1/DAY	50.2 (92)
UNDER $2/DAY	78.1 (92)

	1995	1980	1965

TRANSPORT

JOURNEYS (by transport mode)

	1995	1980	1965
RAILROAD PASSENGER TRIPS	464.0 (93)		
(millions of miles/kilometers)			
AIR PASSENGER TRIPS (thousands)	754.0 (94)		

VEHICLES

	1995	1980	1965
PRIVATE CARS	171,500	114,200	73,000
COMMERCIAL	172,800	87,400	11,000

HEALTH AND HEALTH CARE

HEALTH CARE

	1995	1980	1965
ACCESS TO SAFE WATER	53%		
ACCESS TO SANITATION	77%		
MEASLES IMMUNIZATION	35%		
RATE OF PHYSICIANS	negligible	0.1	0.1 (60)
RATE OF HOSPITAL BEDS	1.7	n/a	1.3 (60)

HEALTH INDICATORS

	1995	1980	1965
PREGNANT WOMEN WITH ANEMIA	35%		
LOW-BIRTH-WEIGHT BABIES	16%		
CHILD MALNUTRITION	23%		
SMOKING PREVALENCE M/F	52/7%		
TUBERCULOSIS INCIDENCE RATE	1.4		
AIDS/HIV CASES	63,813	49,251 (93)	
TOTAL DEATHS	111,728 (92)		

EDUCATION

SCHOOL AGE IN SCHOOL

	1995	1980	1965
PRIMARY	85%	115%	55%
SECONDARY	24%	20%	4%
HIGHER	n/a	1%	0.3%

FEMALES IN SCHOOL

	1995	1980	1965
PRIMARY	83%	109%	40%
SECONDARY	18%	16%	3%

ADULT ILLITERACY M/F

	1995	1980	1965
ADULT ILLITERACY M/F	14/30%	30.4/50.8% (85)	n/a

	1995	1980	1965
COMMUNICATIONS			
RATE OF NEWSPAPERS	14	13	7
RATE OF RADIOS	87	39	41
RATE OF TELEVISIONS	11	4	1

FOOTNOTES
1. Ages 15–59.
2. Age 60 and over.

Source: CIA, The World Factbook, 1997; ILO, World Labour Report, 1997; UN, Demographic Yearbook, 1997; UN, Statistical Yearbook, 1996; World Bank, World Development Indicators, 1998.

KIRIBATI

Kiribati, formerly known as the Gilbert Islands, is an island archipelago in Micronesia made up of 33 coral atolls, extending above and below the Equator in the Pacific Ocean. The Marshall Islands lie to the north of the 277-square-mile (717-square-kilometer) country, Nauru to the west, and Howard Island and Baker Island to the east. In July 1979, the country received independence from the United Kingdom; however, the country continues to remain dependent on foreign aid. Kiribati has a negligible economic base consisting of fishing and handicrafts. The country's per capita gross domestic product (GDP) in 1995 was $860, reflecting the country's limited resources and economic development. In 1995, Kiribati's population of 89,919 was growing at a pace of 1.9 percent. In the same year, the country's life expectancy at birth was 62 years, and the infant mortality rate was 52.9 deaths per 1,000 live births.

	1995	1980	1965
GEOGRAPHY			
AREA (square miles/kilometers)	277/717		
LAND AREA (square miles/kilometers)	277/717		
COASTLINE (miles/kilometers)	714/1,143		
CITIES			
CAPITAL	Tarawa	n/a	17,921 (78)	n/a
POPULATION			
TOTAL	89,919	56,213 (78)	n/a
DENSITY (per square mile/kilometer)	282/109	228/88	n/a
ANNUAL GROWTH	1.9%	2%	n/a
URBAN	36%		
RURAL	64%		
NET MIGRATION RATE	−0.3		
IDENTITY			
ETHNICITY			
MICRONESIAN	n/a		
LANGUAGE			
ENGLISH	n/a		
GILBERTESE	n/a		

	1995	1980	1965
RELIGION			
ROMAN CATHOLIC	52.6%		
PROTESTANT (traditional)	40.9%		
SEVENTH-DAY ADVENT	n/a		
BAHAI	n/a		
CHURCH OF GOD	n/a		
MORMON	n/a		

VITAL STATISTICS

	1995	1980	1965
BIRTHS			
BIRTH RATE	27.1	21.9 (71)	n/a
INFANT MORTALITY RATE	52.9	48.9 (71)	n/a
LIFE EXPECTANCY AT BIRTH	62	58 (71)	n/a
MARRIAGES			
MARRIAGE RATE	n/a	5 (71)	n/a
DIVORCE RATE	n/a	5 (71)	n/a
DEATHS			
DEATH RATE	7.9	6.5 (71)	n/a

ECONOMICS AND LABOR

	1995	1980	1965
GDP PER CAPITA US$	$860		

TRANSPORT

	1995	1980	1965
JOURNEYS (by transport mode)			
AIR PASSENGER TRIPS (thousands)	26 (94)		

HEALTH AND HEALTH CARE

	1995	1980	1965
RATE OF PHYSICIANS	n/a	n/a	0.5 (60)
RATE OF HOSPITAL BEDS	n/a	n/a	5.6 (60)

COMMUNICATIONS

	1995	1980	1965
RATE OF RADIOS	208	193	n/a

Source: CIA, The World Factbook, 1997; ILO, World Labour Report, 1997; UN, Demographic Yearbook, 1997; UN, Statistical Yearbook, 1996; World Bank, World Development Indicators, 1998.

KOREA, NORTH

North Korea, also known as the Democratic People's Republic of Korea, is located in East Asia, on the northern extremity of the Korean Peninsula, between the Sea of Japan and Korea Bay. China and Russia border the 46,541-square-mile (120,540-square-kilometer) country on the north, and South Korea borders on the south. North Korea continues to maintain hostile relations with South Korea; a militarized demarcation line separates the two nation-states. North Korea declared independence from Japan in September 1948. Since that time, North Korea has been governed by Kim Il Sung and his son Kim Jong Il. North Korea has maintained a socialist economy under state and collective control. Since the early

1990s, North Korea's economy has declined as a result of the erosion of support from China and the collapse of the Soviet Union, which was a major trading partner. Moreover, extensive flooding and poor harvests have contributed to severe food shortages and reports of mass starvation by foreign observers. Though North Korea has a low per capita gross domestic product, the socialized economy has produced high levels of income equality. The country's 1995 population of over 29.2 million was growing at an annual rate of 1.7 percent, significantly lower than in preceding decades. North Korea has a life expectancy at birth of 70.3 years and an infant mortality rate of 25.9 deaths per 1,000 live births.

	1995	1980	1960
GEOGRAPHY			
AREA (square miles/kilometers)	46,541/120,540		
LAND AREA (square miles/kilometers)	46,490/120,410		
COASTLINE (miles/kilometers)	1,559/2,495		
CITIES			
CAPITAL	Pyongyang	2,470,000	
POPULATION			
TOTAL	29,207,856	n/a	23,904,124
DENSITY (per square mile/kilometer)	764/295	n/a	513/198
CHANGE	1.7%	n/a	2.8%
AGE COHORTS			
0–14	30%		
15–64	66%		
65 AND OVER	4%		
URBAN	61%		
RURAL	39%		
NET MIGRATION RATE	0		

	1995	1980	1965

IDENTITY

ETHNICITY
KOREAN | 100%

LANGUAGE
KOREAN | 100%

RELIGION
ATHEIST | n/a
BUDDHIST | n/a
CONFUCIANIST | n/a
CHRISTIAN | n/a

VITAL STATISTICS

BIRTHS

	1995	1980	1965
BIRTH RATE	22.9	30.5	44.7
INFANT MORTALITY RATE	25.9	30	n/a
LIFE EXPECTANCY AT BIRTH	70.3	67.8	52.4

DEATHS

	1995	1980	1965
DEATH RATE	5.5	6	16

ECONOMICS AND LABOR

GDP PER CAPITA US$ | $920

LABOR FORCE M/F
AGRICULTURE | 13/17%
INDUSTRY | 37/25%
SERVICES | 47/56%

TRANSPORT

JOURNEYS (by transport mode)
AIR PASSENGER TRIPS (thousands) | 242.0 (94)

	1995	1980	1965
HEALTH AND HEALTH CARE			
HEALTH CARE			
ACCESS TO SAFE WATER	89%		
ACCESS TO SANITATION	100%		
MEASLES IMMUNIZATION	92%		
RATE OF PHYSICIANS	n/a	2.5	n/a
TOTAL DEATHS	239,523 (94)		
HEALTH INDICATORS			
LOW-BIRTH-WEIGHT BABIES	4%		
SMOKING PREVALENCE M/F	68/7%		
TUBERCULOSIS INCIDENCE RATE	1.62		
EDUCATION			
ADULT ILLITERACY M/F	1/3%		
COMMUNICATIONS			
RATE OF NEWSPAPERS	221	219	n/a
RATE OF RADIOS	124	82	n/a
RATE OF TELEVISIONS	19	7	n/a

Source: CIA, The World Factbook, 1997; ILO, World Labour Report, 1997; UN, Demographic Yearbook, 1997; UN, Statistical Yearbook, 1996; World Bank, World Development Indicators, 1998.

KOREA, SOUTH (REPUBLIC OF KOREA)

South Korea is located in East Asia on the southern half of the Korean Peninsula on the Sea of Japan and the Yellow Sea. North Korea borders the 38,023-square-mile (98,480-square-kilometer) country on the north, and Japan lies to the southeast, across the Korea Strait. South Korea gained independence in August 1948. The country has a modern industrial economy with a highly skilled and trained labor force. South Korea's dramatic economic progress between the 1960s and 1990s has been achieved with the key support of government planning and investment. The country's startling industrial advance has been accompanied by the development of an autonomous workers' movement demanding higher wages and improved working conditions. Economic growth has slowed following the Asian financial crisis that has brought many of the country's industries into financial collapse. During the 30-year period between 1965 and 1995, South Korea's population increased from more than 16.2 million to 45.5 million. As the South Korean economy modernized and urbanization increased, population growth stabilized and gradually declined to less than half the growth rate in North Korea. The country has a high life expectancy and a low infant mortality rate.

Average Household Size, 1990

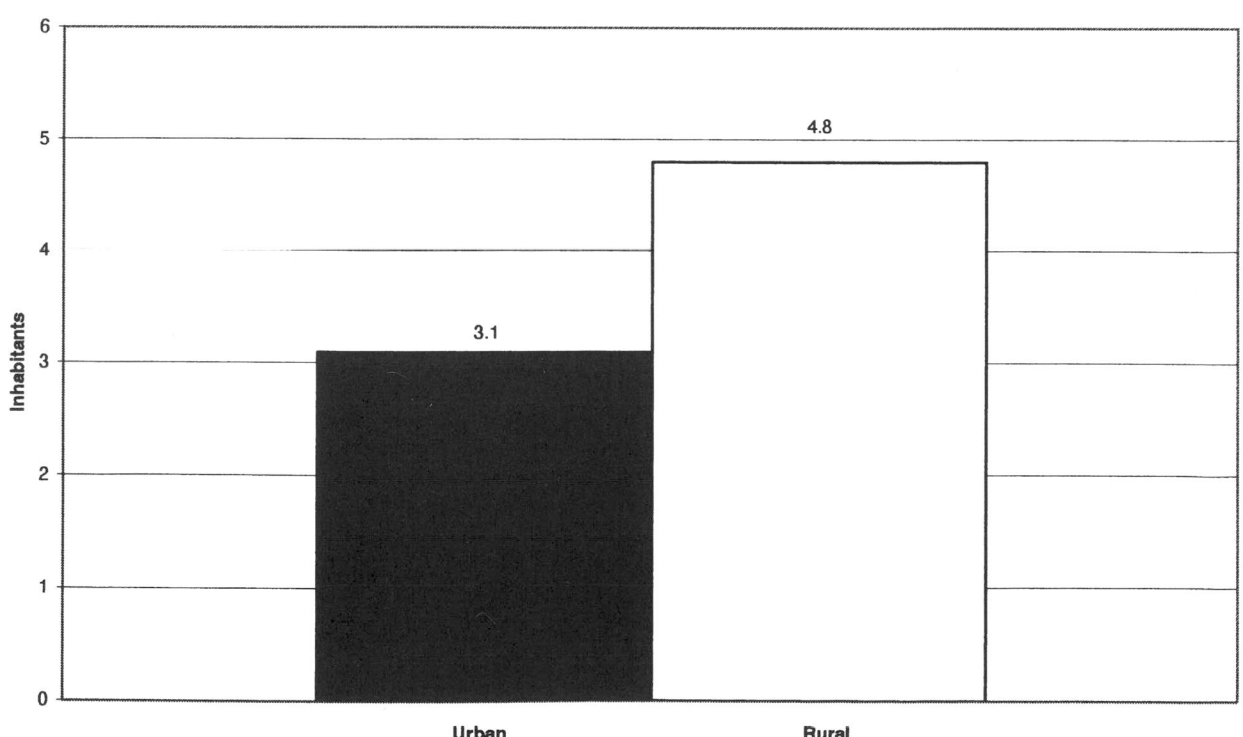

From the 1960s to the 1980s, South Korea underwent one of the most dramatic social, economic, and political transformations of any country on the face of the earth. Among other things, it went from a primarily rural and agricultural society to a largely industrialized and urban one, a fact reflected in dramatically smaller households.

Secondary Schooling

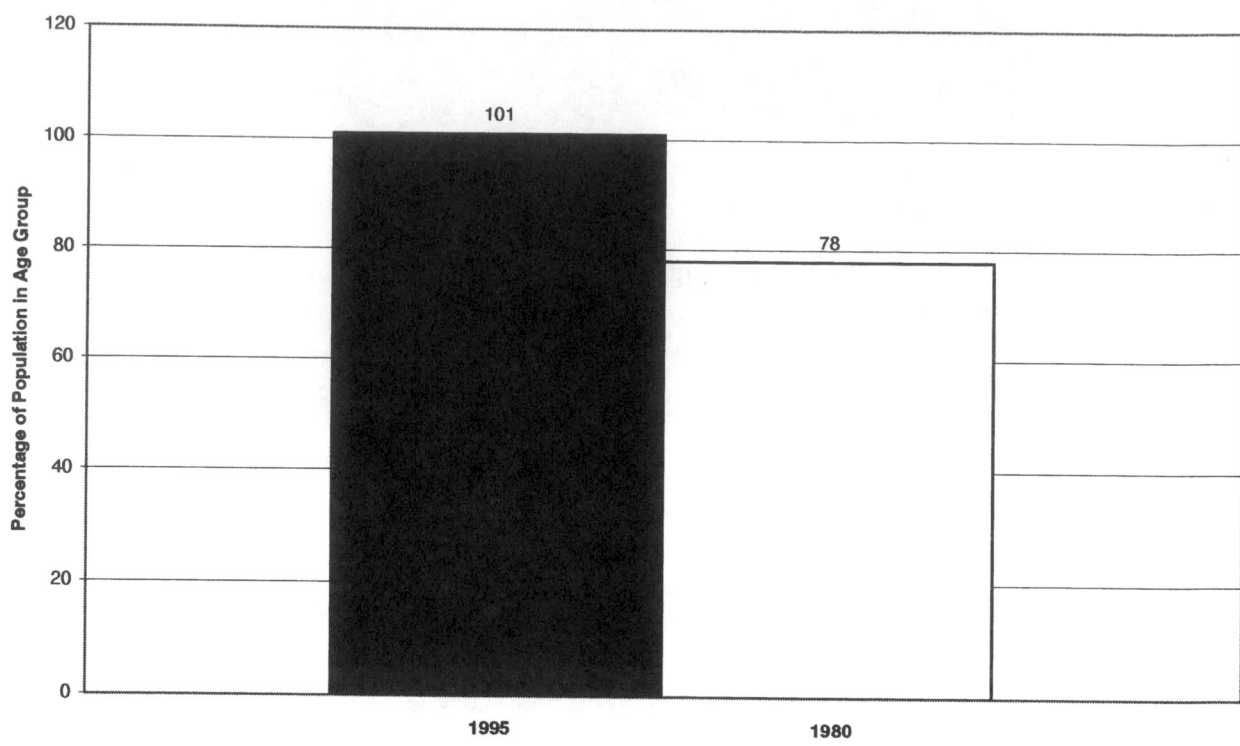

One of the main factors in South Korea's impressive economic prowess has been the rising numbers of skilled workers. In addition, dramatically higher levels of secondary education have brought a greater political sophistication among the populace, which eventually helped turn the country from a military dictatorship to a thriving democracy.

CHRONOLOGY

1961   Military takes power in coup.
1963   Coup leader General Park Chung Hee elected president.
1972   Facing rising protests, Park outlaws all political associations and dissolves national assembly.
1979   Park assassinated.
1980   Chun Doo Hwan, Park's lieutenant, elected president.
1987   Increasing protests by students and workers leads to reforms and election of civilian prime minister Roh Tae Woo.
1988   Korea hosts Summer Olympics.
1991   South Korea and North Korea win membership in United Nations.
1997   Former dissident wins presidency of Korea; economic crisis in Asia hits Korean economy hard.

	1995	1980	1965

GEOGRAPHY

AREA (square miles/kilometers) 38,023/98,480
LAND AREA (square miles/kilometers) 37,912/98,190
COASTLINE (miles/kilometers) 1,508/2,413

CITIES
CAPITAL Seoul 10,776,201
MAJOR CITIES Pusan 3,802,319
Taegu 2,255,805
Inchon 2,203,102
Kwangju 1,236,312

POPULATION

	1995	1980	1965
TOTAL	45,482,291	37,436,315	29,086,000 (66)
DENSITY (per square mile/kilometer)	1,171/452	1,083/418	765/295
ANNUAL GROWTH	n/a	1.6%	n/a
AGE COHORTS			
0–14	23%	n/a	42%
15–64	71%	n/a	54%
65 AND OVER	6%	n/a	4%
MALE	50%		
FEMALE	50%		
URBAN	81%	57.3%	n/a
RURAL	19%	42.7%	n/a
NET MIGRATION RATE	−0.4	n/a	0

IDENTITY

ETHNICITY
KOREAN n/a

LANGUAGE
KOREAN n/a
ENGLISH n/a

	1995	1980	1965
RELIGION			
CHRISTIAN	n/a		
BUDDHIST	n/a		
CONFUCIANIST	n/a		

VITAL STATISTICS

	1995	1980	1965
BIRTHS			
BIRTH RATE	16.24	23 (84)	n/a
URBAN BIRTH RATE	18.4 (93)		
RURAL BIRTH RATE	23.7 (93)		
INFANT MORTALITY RATE	8.2	30 (84)	n/a
LIFE EXPECTANCY AT BIRTH	73.3	65.9 (84)	n/a
MARRIAGES			
MARRIAGE RATE	7	8.3 (84)	n/a
AVERAGE AGE AT MARRIAGE M/F	28.5/25.4		
DIVORCE RATE	1%	0.6% (84)	n/a
DEATHS			
DEATH RATE	5.7	6.2	n/a

HOUSEHOLDS

	1995	1980	1965
NUMBER	11,354,540 (90)	n/a	4,357,600 (60)
AVERAGE SIZE	3.7 (90)	n/a	5.6 (60)
TYPE OF HOUSEHOLD			
SINGLE	8.3%		
MARRIED	79.6%		
WIDOWED	10.5%		
DIVORCED/SEPARATED	1.5%		
FEMALE HEADED	15.7%		

ECONOMICS AND LABOR

	1995
GDP PER CAPITA US$	$13,000
LABOR FORCE M/F (thousands)	11,832/8,005 (94)
AGRICULTURE	1,427/1,272
MINING	37/3
MANUFACTURING	2,930/1,765
UTILITIES	59/12

	1995	**1980**	**1965**
CONSTRUCTION	1,616/161		
TRADE/FOOD/TOURISM	2,554/2,645		
TRANSPORT/COMMUNICATIONS	901/106		
FINANCE/INSURANCE/REAL ESTATE	850/645		
SOCIAL AND PERSONAL SERVICES	1,458/1,398		
UNEMPLOYMENT (official)	2.4 (94)		
UNION DENSITY	9%		

TRANSPORT

	1995	**1980**	**1965**
JOURNEYS (by transport mode)			
RAILROAD PASSENGER TRIPS	31,912 (94)		
(millions of miles/kilometers)			
AIR PASSENGER TRIPS (thousands)	24,932 (94)		
VEHICLES (thousands)			
PRIVATE CARS	5,148.7	249.1	16.3
COMMERCIAL	2,226.7	269.4	25.2

HEALTH AND HEALTH CARE

	1995	**1980**	**1965**
HEALTH CARE			
ACCESS TO SAFE WATER	100%		
ACCESS TO SANITATION	100%		
MEASLES IMMUNIZATION	98%		
RATE OF PHYSICIANS	1.2	0.6	0.3 (60)
RATE OF HOSPITAL BEDS	4.1	1.7	0.4 (60)
HEALTH INDICATORS			
TUBERCULOSIS INCIDENCE RATE	1.62		
AIDS/HIV CASES	41	16 (93)	
TOTAL DEATHS	115,609 (93)		

EDUCATION

	1995	**1980**	**1965**
SCHOOL AGE IN SCHOOL			
PRIMARY	101%	110%	100%
SECONDARY	101%	78%	34%
HIGHER	52%	15%	5%
FEMALES IN SCHOOL			
PRIMARY	97%	108%	97%
SECONDARY	97%	74%	25%

	1995	1980	1965
ADULT ILLITERACY M/F	1/3%	n/a	5.6/19.0% (70)

COMMUNICATIONS

RATE OF NEWSPAPERS	412	210	64
RATE OF RADIOS	1,013	525	67
RATE OF TELEVISIONS	215	165	2

Source: CIA, *The World Factbook, 1997;* ILO, *World Labour Report, 1997;* UN, *Demographic Yearbook, 1997;* UN, *Statistical Yearbook, 1996;* World Bank, *World Development Indicators, 1998.*

KUWAIT

Kuwait is located in southwest Asia on the Persian Gulf. Iraq borders the 6,880-square-mile (17,820-square-kilometer) country on the north and west, and Saudi Arabia borders on the south. In June 1961, Kuwait gained independence from the United Kingdom. The country is led by a hereditary monarchy. Only adult males who have been naturalized for 30 years or more or have resided in Kuwait since before 1920 may vote in the government's elections. In 1990, Iraq invaded and plundered Kuwait and declared the country an integral part of its national territory. In January 1991, Iraqi forces were forcibly removed from Kuwait by an international military alliance led by the United States. The national economy depends on the extraction of crude petroleum reserves, giving the country a high per capita gross domestic product (GDP) of $17,000. Kuwait's 1995 population of 1,950,047 was growing at an annual rate of 6.6 percent, due mainly to a high rate of in-migration. Kuwaitis (Arabs from the local region) are the largest ethnic minority, constituting 45 percent of the population, followed by Arabs from other regions, who make up 35 percent of the population. The country has a high average life expectancy and a low infant mortality rate.

	1995		**1980**	**1965**
GEOGRAPHY				
AREA (square miles/kilometers)	6,880/17,820			
LAND AREA (square miles/kilometers)	6,880/17,820			
COASTLINE (miles/kilometers)	312/499			
CITIES				
CAPITAL	Kuwait City	n/a	78,116 (75)	n/a
MAJOR CITIES	Hawalli	n/a	130,565	n/a
	Salmiya	n/a	113,943	n/a
POPULATION				
TOTAL	1,950,047		1,695,128 (85)	467,339
DENSITY (per square mile/kilometer)	283/110		246/95	80/31
ANNUAL GROWTH	6.6%		4.5%	10.5%
AGE COHORTS				
0–14	33%		n/a	38%
15–64	65%		n/a	60%
65 AND OVER	2%		n/a	2%
MALE	57%			
FEMALE	43%			

	1995	1980	1965
URBAN	97%		
RURAL	3%		
NET MIGRATION RATE	48.5		

IDENTITY

ETHNICITY
KUWAITI	45%		
OTHER ARAB	35%		
SOUTH ASIAN	9%		
IRANIAN	4%		

LANGUAGE
ARABIC	n/a		
ENGLISH	n/a		

RELIGION
SUNNI MUSLIM	45%		
SHI'A MUSLIM	30%		
CHRISTIAN	n/a		
HINDU	n/a		
PARSI	n/a		

VITAL STATISTICS

BIRTHS
BIRTH RATE	20.3	34.4 (84)	n/a
INFANT MORTALITY RATE	11.1	19 (84)	n/a
LIFE EXPECTANCY AT BIRTH	75.9	70 (84)	n/a

MARRIAGES
MARRIAGE RATE	7.6	4.4 (84)	n/a
AVERAGE AGE AT MARRIAGE M/F	29.6/25		
DIVORCE RATE	1.9	1.5	n/a

DEATHS
DEATH RATE	2.2	2.8 (84)	n/a

HOUSEHOLDS

NUMBER	n/a	227,288 (85)	52,851 (61)
AVERAGE SIZE	n/a	6.5 (85)	6.1 (61)
FEMALE HEADED	n/a	4.8	n/a

	1995	1980	1965

ECONOMICS AND LABOR

GDP PER CAPITA US$	$17,000		
LABOR FORCE M/F			
INDUSTRY	n/a		
AGRICULTURE	2/1%		
INDUSTRY	32/2%		
SERVICES	67/98%		

TRANSPORT

JOURNEYS (by transport mode)			
AIR PASSENGER TRIPS (thousands)	1,756 (94)		
VEHICLES (thousands)			
PRIVATE CARS	629.7	398.9	58
COMMERCIAL	148.7	144	22.1

HEALTH AND HEALTH CARE

HEALTH CARE			
ACCESS TO SANITATION	100%		
MEASLES IMMUNIZATION	93%		
RATE OF PHYSICIANS	0.2	1.7	0.9 (60)
RATE OF HOSPITAL BEDS	n/a	4.1	6.8 (60)
HEALTH INDICATORS			
PREGNANT WOMEN WITH ANEMIA	40%		
LOW-BIRTH-WEIGHT BABIES	7%		
CHILD MALNUTRITION	6%		
SMOKING PREVALENCE M/F	52/12%		
TUBERCULOSIS INCIDENCE RATE	0.4		
AIDS/HIV CASES	19	10 (93)	
TOTAL DEATHS	3,464		

EDUCATION

SCHOOL AGE IN SCHOOL			
PRIMARY	73%	102%	113%
SECONDARY	64%	80%	52%
HIGHER	25%	11%	1.70%

	1995	1980	1965
FEMALES IN SCHOOL			
PRIMARY	71%	98%	97%
SECONDARY	62%	72%	44%
ADULT ILLITERACY M/F	18/25%	27.2/40.9%	41/59.9%

COMMUNICATIONS

	1995	1980	1965
RATE OF NEWSPAPERS	248	222	28
RATE OF RADIOS	408	284	375
RATE OF TELEVISIONS	346	257	128

Source: CIA, *The World Factbook, 1997;* ILO, *World Labour Report, 1997;* UN, *Demographic Yearbook, 1997;* UN, *Statistical Yearbook, 1996;* World Bank, *World Development Indicators, 1998.*

KYRGYZSTAN

Kyrgystan, a former Soviet Socialist Republic, is a landlocked country located in central Asia. Kazakstan borders the 76,641-square-mile (198,500-square-kilometer) country on the north, China on the southeast, Tajikistan on the southwest, and Uzbekistan on the west. Kyrgyzstan gained independence in August 1991, following the collapse and breakup of the Soviet Union. Although Kyrgyzstan subsequently adopted a multiparty democratic system, in the formative years of independence President Askar Akayev has dominated the government. The country's leading industries are agriculture, natural-resource extraction, and primary manufacturing. In the post-Soviet era, much of the population's standard of living has declined dramatically, due to non-payment of wages, high unemployment, and the erosion of pensions. Over 55 percent of the population survives on the equivalent of less than $2 a day. The country's 1995 population of 4,529,648 was growing at the slow annual rate of .07 percent. Moreover, Kyrgystan has a high out-migration rate because of the departure of Russians. Kirghizis are the ethnic majority, accounting for 52.4 percent of the population. The country's leading ethnic minorities are Russians (21.5 percent), Uzbekis (12.9 percent), Ukrainians (2.5 percent), and Germans (2.4 percent). Kyrgystan has a life expectancy of 63.9 years and an infant mortality rate of 77.8 deaths per 1,000 live births.

1995[1]

GEOGRAPHY

AREA (square miles/kilometers)	76,641/198,500	
LAND AREA (square miles/kilometers)	73,861/191,300	
COASTLINE	landlocked	
CITIES		
CAPITAL	Bishkek	583,900
MAJOR CITY	Osh	218,300

POPULATION

TOTAL	4,529,648
DENSITY (per square mile/kilometer)	62/24
ANNUAL GROWTH	.07%
AGE COHORTS	
0–14	37%
15–64	57%
65 AND OVER	6%
MALE	49%
FEMALE	51%

	1995	1980	1965
URBAN	39%		
RURAL	61%		
NET MIGRATION RATE	−16.5		

IDENTITY

ETHNICITY

KIRGHIZ	52.4%		
RUSSIAN	21.5%		
UZBEK	12.9%		
UKRAINIAN	2.5%		
GERMAN	2.4%		

LANGUAGE

KIRGHIZ	n/a		
RUSSIAN	n/a		

RELIGION

NONE	n/a		
MUSLIM	n/a		
RUSSIAN ORTHODOX	n/a		

VITAL STATISTICS

BIRTHS

BIRTH RATE	26		
URBAN BIRTH RATE	18.5 (94)		
RURAL BIRTH RATE	27.9 (94)		
INFANT MORTALITY RATE	77.8		
ABORTION RATE	285.4 (94)		
LIFE EXPECTANCY AT BIRTH	63.9		

MARRIAGES

MARRIAGE RATE	9.1		
AVERAGE AGE AT MARRIAGE M/F	24/21.6		
DIVORCE RATE	1.8		

DEATHS

DEATH RATE	8.8		

	1995	1980	1965

HOUSEHOLDS

NUMBER	856,148 (89)		
URBAN	369,620		
RURAL	486,528		
AVERAGE SIZE	4.7 (89)		
URBAN	3.9		
RURAL	5.2		

ECONOMICS AND LABOR

GDP PER CAPITA US$	$1,140		
LABOR FORCE M/F			
AGRICULTURE	36/28%		
INDUSTRY	30/23%		
SERVICES	34/50%		
POVERTY			
UNDER $1/DAY	18.9%		
UNDER $2/DAY	55.3%		

TRANSPORT

JOURNEYS (by transport mode)			
AIR PASSENGER TRIPS (thousands)	464.0 (94)		

HEALTH AND HEALTH CARE

HEALTH AND HEALTH CARE			
ACCESS TO SAFE WATER	75%		
ACCESS TO SANITATION	53%		
MEASLES IMMUNIZATION	89%		
RATE OF PHYSICIANS	3.1		
RATE OF HOSPITAL BEDS	9.9		
HEALTH INDICATORS			
TUBERCULOSIS INCIDENCE RATE	0.68		
TOTAL DEATHS	37,109 (94)		

	1995	1980	1965
EDUCATION			
SCHOOL AGE IN SCHOOL			
PRIMARY	107%		
SECONDARY	81%		
HIGHER	14%		
FEMALES IN SCHOOL			
PRIMARY	107%		
SECONDARY	83%		

FOOTNOTE
1. Part of the Soviet Union in 1980 and 1965.

Source: CIA, The World Factbook, 1997; ILO, World Labour Report, 1997; UN, Demographic Yearbook, 1997; UN, Statistical Yearbook, 1996; World Bank, World Development Indicators, 1998.

LAOS

Laos is a landlocked country located in Southeast Asia. Vietnam borders the 91,429-square-mile (236,800-square-kilometer) country on the east and northeast, China on the north, Myanmar on the northwest, and Thailand and Cambodia on the southwest. Laos gained independence from France in July 1949. The country, officially known as the Lao People's Democratic Republic, is governed by a socialist leadership that gained power in December 1975. Although the government maintains control over the leading sectors of the economy, it has allowed a small market sector to grow and flourish. Following the collapse of the Soviet Union, foreign economic assistance has been reduced substantially. Laos has a largely undeveloped infrastructure that is in great need of expansion. Most of the population engages in subsistence agriculture. Laos's per capita gross domestic product (GDP) was only $1,100 in 1995. In the same year, the country's population of nearly 5 million was growing at an annual rate of 2.8 percent, primarily due to a high birth rate. The country's 1995 infant mortality rate approached 96.8 deaths per 1,000 live births. Laos make up the vast majority of the country's population.

	1995	1980	1965
GEOGRAPHY			
AREA (square miles/kilometers)	91,429/236,800		
LAND AREA (square miles/kilometers)	89,112/230,800		
COASTLINE	landlocked		
CITIES			
CAPITAL	Vientiane	415,000	132,233 (66)
POPULATION			
TOTAL	4,975,772	3,584,803 (85)	n/a
DENSITY (per square mile/kilometer)	54/21	44/17	28/11
CHANGE	2.8%	2.3%	2.5%
AGE COHORTS			
0–14	45%		
15–64	51%		
65 AND OVER	4%		
MALE	49%		
FEMALE	51%		
URBAN	22%		
RURAL	78%		

	1995	1980	1965
NET MIGRATION RATE	0		

IDENTITY

ETHNICITY

LAO LOUM (lowland)	68%		
LAO THEUNG (upland)	22%		
LAO SOUNG (highland)	9%		
VIETNAMESE/CHINESE	1%		

LANGUAGE

LAO	n/a		
FRENCH	n/a		
ENGLISH	n/a		

RELIGION

BUDDHIST	n/a		
ANIMIST	n/a		
NONE	n/a		

VITAL STATISTICS

BIRTHS

	1995	1980	1965
BIRTH RATE	42	40.8	47
INFANT MORTALITY RATE	96.8	122	n/a
LIFE EXPECTANCY AT BIRTH	52.7	49.7	n/a

DEATHS

	1995	1980	1965
DEATH RATE	13.8	15.7	23

ECONOMICS AND LABOR

GDP PER CAPITA US$	$1,100		

LABOR FORCE M/F

AGRICULTURE	76/81%		
INDUSTRY	7/5%		
SERVICES	17/14%		

TRANSPORT

JOURNEYS (by transport mode)

AIR PASSENGER TRIPS (thousands)	119.0 (94)		

	1995	**1980**	**1965**
VEHICLES (thousands)			
PRIVATE CARS	n/a	n/a	6,000
COMMERCIAL	n/a	n/a	1,900

HEALTH AND HEALTH CARE

HEALTH CARE

ACCESS TO SAFE WATER	39%		
ACCESS TO SANITATION	19%		
MEASLES IMMUNIZATION	65%		
RATE OF PHYSICIANS	0.2	n/a	negligible (60)
RATE OF HOSPITAL BEDS	2.6	n/a	0.4 (60)

HEALTH INDICATORS

LOW-BIRTH-WEIGHT BABIES	18%		
CHILD MALNUTRITION	40%		
TUBERCULOSIS INCIDENCE RATE	2.35		
AIDS/HIV CASES	14	6	

EDUCATION

SCHOOL AGE IN SCHOOL

PRIMARY	107%	113%	39%
SECONDARY	25%	21%	2%
HIGHER	2%	0.40%	0.2% (70)

FEMALES IN SCHOOL

PRIMARY	93%	103%	29%
SECONDARY	18%	15%	0.30%

ADULT ILLITERACY M/F	31/56%	8.0/24.2% (85)	n/a

COMMUNICATIONS

RATE OF NEWSPAPERS	3	4	5
RATE OF RADIOS	126	109	17 (70)
RATE OF TELEVISIONS	7	0	0

Source: CIA, *The World Factbook, 1997*; ILO, *World Labour Report, 1997*; UN, *Demographic Yearbook, 1997*; UN, *Statistical Yearbook, 1996*; World Bank, *World Development Indicators, 1998.*

LATVIA

A former member of the Union of Soviet Socialist Republics, Latvia became independent on September 6, 1991. The country, about the size of West Virginia, is located on the eastern shores of the Baltic Sea. Under Soviet rule, hundreds of thousands of ethnic Russians migrated to the republic. Today they constitute 33.8 percent of the population. Ethnic Latvians compose 51.8 percent, and the rest is made up of minor ethnic groups. Since independence, Latvia has experienced significant population loss. In 1995, Latvia lost 9.7 percent of its population to out-migration.

One of the main reasons for this is economic chaos. Though the country's economy grew at a moderate pace in the early 1990s, major banking and budget crises hit the GDP hard, and it fell to $5,300 in 1995. Despite the economic troubles, education level in the country remains fairly high. Nearly 90 percent of all young people attend primary and secondary schools, while 26 percent attend universities. Health indexes are not as good, however. The infant mortality rate is high for Europe, at 21.2 per 1,000 live births.

1995[1]

GEOGRAPHY

AREA (square miles/kilometers)	24,749/64,100	
LAND AREA (square miles/kilometers)	24,749/64,100	
COASTLINE (miles/kilometers)	332/531	
CITIES		
CAPITAL	Riga	7,976 (94)
MAJOR CITIES	Daugavpils	121,063
	Liepaja	102,450

POPULATION

TOTAL	2,468,982
DENSITY (per square mile/kilometer)	101/39
ANNUAL GROWTH	−1.4%
AGE COHORTS	
0–14	20%
15–64	66%
65 AND OVER	14%
MALE	46%
FEMALE	54%
URBAN	73%
RURAL	27%
NET MIGRATION RATE	−9.7

	1995[1]
IDENTITY	

ETHNICITY
LATVIAN	51.8%
RUSSIAN	33.8%
BYELORUSSIAN	4.5%
UKRAINIAN	3.4%
POLISH	2.3%

LANGUAGE
LETTISH	n/a
LITHUANIAN	n/a
RUSSIAN	n/a

RELIGION
LUTHERAN	n/a
ROMAN CATHOLIC	n/a
RUSSIAN ORTHODOX	n/a
ATHEIST	n/a

VITAL STATISTICS

BIRTHS
BIRTH RATE	10.9
URBAN BIRTH RATE	8.4 (94)
RURAL BIRTH RATE	12.1 (94)
INFANT MORTALITY RATE	21.2
ABORTION RATE	1107.2 (94)
LIFE EXPECTANCY AT BIRTH	66.9

MARRIAGES
MARRIAGE RATE	4.5
AVERAGE AGE AT MARRIAGE	24.3/22.2
DIVORCE RATE	3.4

DEATHS
DEATH RATE	15.2

HOUSEHOLDS

NUMBER	731,855 (89)
URBAN	523,370
RURAL	208,485

	1995[1]
AVERAGE SIZE	3.1 (89)
URBAN	3.1
RURAL	3.2

ECONOMICS AND LABOR

GDP PER CAPITA US$	$5,300
LABOR FORCE M/F (thousands)	703/642 (92)
AGRICULTURE	177/92
MINING	2/1
MANUFACTURING	169/152
UTILITIES	11/5
CONSTRUCTION	78/11
TRADE/FOOD/TOURISM	62/125
TRANSPORT/COMMUNICATIONS	70/35
FINANCE/INSURANCE/REAL ESTATE	34/41
SOCIAL AND PERSONAL SERVICES	41/31
UNEMPLOYMENT (official)	6.5% (94)

TRANSPORT

JOURNEYS (by transport mode)	
RAILROAD PASSENGER TRIPS	1,794 (94)
(millions of miles/kilometers)	
AIR PASSENGER TRIPS (thousands)	133 (94)
VEHICLES (thousands)	
PRIVATE CARS	251.6 (94)
COMMERCIAL	73.5 (94)

HEALTH AND HEALTH CARE

HEALTH CARE	
MEASLES IMMUNIZATION	85%
RATE OF PHYSICIANS	3
RATE OF HOSPITAL BEDS	11.9
TOTAL DEATHS	40,080
HEALTH INDICATORS	
SMOKING PREVALENCE M/F	67/12%
TUBERCULOSIS INCIDENCE RATE	0.7
AIDS/HIV CASES	12

	1995[1]

EDUCATION

SCHOOL AGE IN SCHOOL
PRIMARY 89%
SECONDARY 85%
HIGHER 26%

FEMALES IN SCHOOL
PRIMARY 85%
SECONDARY 89%

COMMUNICATIONS

RATE OF NEWSPAPERS 98
RATE OF RADIOS 651
RATE OF TELEVISIONS 460

FOOTNOTE
1. Part of the Soviet Union in 1965 and 1980.

Source: CIA, *The World Factbook, 1997;* ILO, *World Labour Report, 1997;* UN, *Demographic Yearbook, 1997;* UN, *Statistical Yearbook, 1996;* World Bank, *World Development Indicators, 1998.*

LEBANON

Lebanon is a country under reconstruction. From 1975 through 1990, the country was ravaged by a multisided civil war that left tens of thousands dead and millions homeless. The origins of the war lay in Lebanon's complicated ethnic melange. After independence was gained in the 1930s, the country was ruled by Christians, because they represented a slight majority at the time. By the 1970s, however, they were widely outnumbered by Muslims. Despite this demographic change, the Christians refused to cede power, setting off the civil war. Since 1990, the country has utilized its deep well of entrepreneu-rial energy and skilled labor to refashion itself as the financial, tourist, and skilled craft center of the Arab world. Surrounded by Israel on the south—which continues to occupy a swath of territory along the border—and politically dominant Syria to the east and north, Lebanon's 3.78 million are still not entirely in control of their own political destiny. Economically, however, the country ranks near the top of the Middle East. Its per capita income is nearly $5,000 annually. Other economic indexes are high as well. Car ownership is roughly one vehicle for every four citizens.

	1995	1980	1965
GEOGRAPHY			
AREA (square miles/kilometers)	4,015/10,400		
LAND AREA (square miles/kilometers)	3,950/10,230		
COASTLINE (miles/kilometers)	141/225		
CITIES			
CAPITAL	Beirut	n/a	n/a	474,870 (70)
MAJOR CITY	Tripoli	n/a	n/a	127,611
POPULATION			
TOTAL	3,776,317	n/a	2,126,325 (70)
DENSITY (per square mile/kilometer)	749/289	n/a	666/257
ANNUAL GROWTH	2.2%	n/a	0%
AGE COHORTS			
0–14	36%		
15–64	59%		
65 AND OVER	5%		
MALE	51%		
FEMALE	49%		
URBAN	87%		
RURAL	13%		
NET MIGRATION RATE	0		

	1995	1980	1965

IDENTITY

ETHNICITY

ARAB	95%		
ARMENIAN	4%		

LANGUAGE

ARABIC	n/a		
FRENCH	n/a		
ARMENIAN	n/a		
ENGLISH	n/a		

RELIGION

ISLAM (Alawite, Druze, Isma'ilite, Shi'a, Sunni)	70%		
CHRISTIAN (Orthodox Christian, Catholic, Protestant)	30%		

VITAL STATISTICS

BIRTHS

BIRTH RATE	27.9	29.3	n/a
INFANT MORTALITY RATE	36.7	48	n/a
LIFE EXPECTANCY AT BIRTH	70	65	n/a

MARRIAGES

MARRIAGE RATE	n/a	6.9	n/a
DIVORCE RATE	n/a	0.6	n/a

DEATHS

DEATH RATE	6.4	8.8	n/a

HOUSEHOLDS

NUMBER	n/a	n/a	51,394 (53)

ECONOMICS AND LABOR

GDP PER CAPITA US$	$4,900		

	1995	1980	1965
LABOR FORCE M/F			
AGRICULTURE	6/10%		
INDUSTRY	34/22%		
SERVICES	59/68%		

TRANSPORT

	1995	1980	1965
JOURNEYS (by transport mode)			
AIR PASSENGER TRIPS (thousands)	706.0 (94)		
VEHICLES (thousands)			
PRIVATE CARS	1,035.1	99	n/a
COMMERCIAL	808	14	n/a

HEALTH AND HEALTH CARE

	1995	1980	1965
HEALTH CARE			
ACCESS TO SAFE WATER	n/a	92%	n/a
ACCESS TO SANITATION	n/a	59%	n/a
MEASLES IMMUNIZATION	65%		
RATE OF PHYSICIANS	1.9	1.7	0.7 (60)
RATE OF HOSPITAL BEDS	3.1	n/a	4.2 (60)
HEALTH INDICATORS			
CHILD MALNUTRITION	9		
TUBERCULOSIS INCIDENCE RATE	0.35		
AIDS/HIV CASES	91	69 (93)	

EDUCATION

	1995	1980	1965
SCHOOL AGE IN SCHOOL			
PRIMARY	109%	111%	104%
SECONDARY	81%	59%	25%
HIGHER	27%	30%	8.40%
FEMALES IN SCHOOL			
PRIMARY	105%	107%	95%
SECONDARY	87%	51%	19%
ADULT ILLITERACY M/F	20/10%	n/a	14.3/31.1% (85)

	1995	**1980**	**1965**
COMMUNICATIONS			
RATE OF NEWSPAPERS	185	109	n/a
RATE OF RADIOS	887	749	243 (70)
RATE OF TELEVISIONS	346	281	105 (70)

Source: CIA, The World Factbook, 1997; ILO, World Labour Report, 1997; UN, Demographic Yearbook, 1997; UN, Statistical Yearbook, 1996; World Bank, World Development Indicators, 1998.

LESOTHO

Entirely surrounded by South Africa, the mountainous kingdom of Lesotho has long served as a source of mining and industrial labor for the African giant's economy, as the labor profile of the country reveals. Of the female population, which largely remains behind in Lesotho, some 59 percent work in agriculture. The majority of men, some 41 percent, migrate to South Africa to work in industry, while just 29 percent farm. Recent setbacks in the South African economy, due to international sanctions under apartheid and the current drop in world gold prices, have hit the Lesotho economy hard. Per capita income is now just $1,430 a year, high for Africa but lower than in previous years. This economic downturn is reflected in vital statistics. The death rate, for example, which dropped from 23 to 14.5 per 1,000 persons between 1965 and 1980, has remained relatively stable since. Similarly, life expectancy climbed 19 percent between 1965 and 1980, and just 6.6 percent since.

	1995	1980	1965
GEOGRAPHY			
AREA (square miles/kilometers)	11,718/30,350		
LAND AREA (square miles/kilometers)	11,718/30,350		
COASTLINE	Landlocked		
CITIES			
CAPITAL	Maseru	n/a	n/a	13,312 (72)
POPULATION			
TOTAL	1,970,781	1,216,815 (76)	859,058 (66)
DENSITY (per square mile/kilometer)	176/68	130/50	96/37
ANNUAL GROWTH	1.9%	2.7%	3.0%
AGE COHORTS			
0–14	41%		
15–64	54%		
65 AND OVER	5%		
URBAN	23%		
RURAL	73%		
NET MIGRATION RATE	0		

	1995	1980	1965

IDENTITY

ETHNICITY
SOTHO	99.7%		

LANGUAGE
LESOTHO	n/a		
ENGLISH	n/a		
ZULU	n/a		
XHOSA	n/a		

RELIGION
CHRISTIAN	n/a		
INDIGENOUS	n/a		

VITAL STATISTICS

BIRTHS
BIRTH RATE	32.7	36.7	40
INFANT MORTALITY RATE	81.6	114.4	181
LIFE EXPECTANCY AT BIRTH	52	48.8	41

DEATHS
DEATH RATE	13.7	14.5	23

ECONOMICS AND LABOR

GDP PER CAPITA US$
	$1,430		

LABOR FORCE M/F
AGRICULTURE	29/59%		
INDUSTRY	41/5%		
SERVICES	30/36%		

POVERTY
UNDER $1/DAY	48.8% (87)		
UNDER $2/DAY	74.1% (87)		

TRANSPORT

JOURNEYS (by transport mode)
AIR PASSENGER TRIPS (thousands)	27 (94)		

	1995	1980	1965
VEHICLES			
PRIVATE CARS	n/a	5,500 (87)	n/a

HEALTH AND HEALTH CARE

HEALTH CARE			
ACCESS TO SAFE WATER	52%		
ACCESS TO SANITATION	6%		
MEASLES IMMUNIZATION	82%		
RATE OF PHYSICIANS	negligible	n/a	0.1 (60)
RATE OF HOSPITAL BEDS	n/a	n/a	1.4 (60)
HEALTH INDICATORS			
PREGNANT WOMEN WITH ANEMIA	7%		
LOW-BIRTH-WEIGHT BABIES	11%		
CHILD MALNUTRITION	21%		
SMOKING PREVALENCE M/F	38/1%		
TUBERCULOSIS INCIDENCE RATE	2.5		
AIDS/HIV CASES	936	357 (93)	

EDUCATION

SCHOOL AGE IN SCHOOL			
PRIMARY	99%	102%	106%
SECONDARY	28%	18%	4%
HIGHER	2%	1%	0.30%
FEMALES IN SCHOOL			
PRIMARY	105%	120%	129%
SECONDARY	37%	28%	4%
ADULT ILLITERACY M/F	19/38%	n/a	41.4/56%

COMMUNICATIONS

RATE OF NEWSPAPERS	n/a	33 (82)	n/a
RATE OF RADIOS	32	25	29
RATE OF TELEVISIONS	7	0	0

Source: CIA, *The World Factbook, 1997;* ILO, *World Labour Report, 1997;* UN, *Demographic Yearbook, 1997;* UN, *Statistical Yearbook, 1996;* World Bank, *World Development Indicators, 1998.*

LIBERIA

Africa's oldest republic, founded in 1847, by former slaves and free blacks from North America, has had a tumultuous recent history. In 1980, the long reign of Americo-Liberians—as the descendants of the founders were called—ended in a military coup, which led to the military dictatorship of Samuel Doe. A rebellion against the dictator in late 1989 soon descended into a multilateral civil war that left nearly 10 percent of the country's 2 million citizens dead. The countryside was emptied, as refugees flooded into Liberia's West African neighbors—Guinea, Cote d'Ivoire, and Sierra Leone—or became internally displaced within the capital, Monrovia, which saw its population swell from 250,000 to over 1 million. This is reflected in the negative migration rate in 1995 of 9.5 percent. Since a general ceasefire in early 1997, the country has largely been at peace, with order enforced by a coalition of West African peacekeepers. In July 1997, the people of Liberia overwhelmingly elected Charles Taylor—the man who launched the initial rebellion against Doe. Once a relatively prosperous country, by West African standards, Liberia is now near the bottom in most economic and social indexes.

	1995	1980	1965
GEOGRAPHY			
AREA (square miles/kilometers)	43,000/111,370		
LAND AREA (square miles/kilometers)	37,189/96,320		
COASTLINE (miles/coastline)	362/579		
CITIES			
CAPITAL	Monrovia	n/a	421,053 (84)	n/a
POPULATION			
TOTAL	2,109,789	1,503,368 (74)	1,016,443
DENSITY (per square mile/kilometer)	49/19	35/14	24/9
ANNUAL GROWTH	2.1%	2.7%	1.6%
AGE COHORTS			
0–14	45%	n/a	37%
15–64	52%	n/a	59%
65 AND OVER	3%	n/a	4%
URBAN	45%	35	n/a
RURAL	55%	65%	n/a
NET MIGRATION RATE	−9.5		

	1995	1980	1965

IDENTITY

ETHNICITY

KPELLE, BASSA, BIO, KRU, GREBO	n/a		
MANO, KRAHN, GOLA, GBANDI, LOMA	n/a		
KISSI, VAI, BELLA, AMERICO-LIBERIAN	n/a		

LANGUAGE

ENGLISH	n/a		
NIGER-CONGO	n/a		

RELIGION

TRADITIONAL	70%		
MUSLIM	20%		
CHRISTIAN	10%		

VITAL STATISTICS

BIRTHS

BIRTH RATE	42.7	49.8	n/a
INFANT MORTALITY RATE	108.1	159.2	n/a
LIFE EXPECTANCY AT BIRTH	58.6	44.9	n/a

DEATHS

DEATH RATE	12	20.9	n/a

ECONOMICS AND LABOR

GDP PER CAPITA US$	$770		

TRANSPORT

JOURNEYS (by transport mode)

AIR PASSENGER TRIPS (thousands)	32 (92)		

VEHICLES

PRIVATE CARS	18,000 (87)	10,900	n/a
COMMERCIAL	15,000 (87)	6,100	n/a

	1995	1980	1965

HEALTH AND HEALTH CARE

HEALTH CARE

	1995	1980	1965
RATE OF PHYSICIANS	n/a	n/a	0.1 (60)
RATE OF HOSPITAL BEDS	n/a	n/a	1.4 (60)

HEALTH INDICATORS

	1995	1980	1965
AIDS/HIV CASES	191	191 (93)	

EDUCATION

SCHOOL AGE IN SCHOOL

	1995	1980	1965
PRIMARY	n/a	76%	48%
SECONDARY	n/a	23%	7%
HIGHER	n/a	2.5% (79)	0.9% (70)

FEMALES IN SCHOOL

	1995	1980	1965
PRIMARY	n/a	57%	26%
SECONDARY	n/a	13%	3%
HIGHER	n/a	n/a	0.6%

	1995	1980	1965
ADULT ILLITERACY M/F	n/a	52.7/77.2 (85)	71.0/89.7 (74)

COMMUNICATIONS

	1995	1980	1965
RATE OF NEWSPAPERS	13	6	4
RATE OF RADIOS	227	179	128
RATE OF TELEVISIONS	19	11	3

Source: CIA, The World Factbook, 1997; ILO, World Labour Report, 1997; UN, Demographic Yearbook, 1997; UN, Statistical Yearbook, 1996; World Bank, World Development Indicators, 1998.

LIBYA

Located along the Mediterranean coast of North Africa, between Egypt on the east and Tunisia and Algeria on the west, Libya is an oil-rich, sparsely populated desert nation. With some 5.45 million people in 679 thousand square miles—an area slightly larger than Alaska—it has a population density of just 7.8 persons per square mile, one of the lowest in the world. Still, it has seen explosive population growth in recent times, roughly 3.7 percent annually for the past three decades. This is a reflection of the dramatically falling infant mortality rate, which dropped from 97 to 59.5 per 1,000 live births. Indeed, the government of Muammar Khadafi, who took power in a nationalist coup in 1969, has used the vast oil earnings to provide a significant public health structure. Some 90 percent of the country has access to safe water, and the child malnutrition rate is just 5 percent. Educational levels have shown significant increases as well. Where just 14 percent of the school-age population were receiving a secondary education in 1965, that figure had climbed to 97 percent by 1995. Still, Khadafi's regime remains under siege from outside. Accused of supporting terrorism, the country has been hit by severe travel restrictions by the international community. For a moderately wealthy country—$6,510 per capita income annually—its citizens went on just 641,000 air passenger trips in 1995.

	1995	1980	1965
GEOGRAPHY			
AREA (square miles/kilometers)	679,359/1,759,540		
LAND AREA (square miles/kilometers)	679,3591,759,540		
COASTLINE (miles/kilometers)	1,106/,770		
CITIES			
CAPITAL	Tripoli	n/a	551,477 (73)	n/a
MAJOR CITIES	Benghazi	n/a	282,192 (73)	n/a
	Misrata	n/a	103,302	n/a
POPULATION			
TOTAL	5,445,436	3,637,488 (84)	1,564,369 (64)
DENSITY (per square mile/kilometer)	7.8/3	5.2/2	2.3/0.9
ANNUAL GROWTH	3.7%	n/a	3.7%
AGE COHORTS			
0–14	48%	n/a	44%
15–64	49%	n/a	51%
65 AND OVER	3%	n/a	5%
MALE	54%		
FEMALE	46%		

	1995	1980	1965
URBAN	86%	75.9% (84)	n/a
RURAL	14%	24.1% (84)	n/a
NET MIGRATION RATE	0	n/a	1.4

IDENTITY

ETHNICITY
BERBER AND ARAB	97%		
GREEK, MALTESE, ITALIAN, EGYPTIAN,	n/a		
PAKISTANI, TURK, INDIAN, TUNISIAN	n/a		

LANGUAGE
ARABIC	n/a		
ITALIAN	n/a		
ENGLISH	n/a		

RELIGION
SUNNI MUSLIM	n/a		

VITAL STATISTICS

BIRTHS
BIRTH RATE	44.4	45.6	n/a
INFANT MORTALITY RATE	59.5	97	n/a
LIFE EXPECTANCY AT BIRTH	64.7	58.3	n/a

MARRIAGES
MARRIAGE RATE	5.1	4.4	n/a
DIVORCE RATE	0.5	1.1	n/a

DEATHS
DEATH RATE	7.7	10.9	n/a

ECONOMICS AND LABOR

GDP PER CAPITA US$	$6,510

LABOR FORCE M/F
AGRICULTURE	7/28%
INDUSTRY	27/5%
SERVICES	66/68%

	1995	1980	1965

TRANSPORT

JOURNEYS (by transport mode)

	1995	1980	1965
AIR PASSENGER TRIPS (thousands)	641.0 (92)		

VEHICLES

	1995	1980	1965
PRIVATE CARS	448,000	427,400	42,300
COMMERCIAL	322,000	211,100	20,700

HEALTH AND HEALTH CARE

HEALTH CARE

	1995	1980	1965
ACCESS TO SAFE WATER	90%		
ACCESS TO SANITATION	n/a	70%	n/a
MEASLES IMMUNIZATION	n/a	65%	n/a
RATE OF PHYSICIANS	1.1	1.3	0.1 (60)
RATE OF HOSPITAL BEDS	4.2	4.8	2.8 (60)

HEALTH INDICATORS

	1995	1980	1965
LOW-BIRTH-WEIGHT BABIES	5%		
CHILD MALNUTRITION	5%		
TUBERCULOSIS INCIDENCE RATE	0.12		

	1995	1980	1965
AIDS/HIV CASES	17	12 (93)	
TOTAL DEATHS	29,720 (91)		

EDUCATION

SCHOOL AGE IN SCHOOL

	1995	1980	1965
PRIMARY	110%	125%	75%
SECONDARY	97%	76%	14%
HIGHER	16%	8%	1.20%

FEMALES IN SCHOOL

	1995	1980	1965
PRIMARY	108%	119%	43%
SECONDARY	n/a	39%	4%

	1995	1980	1965
ADULT ILLITERACY M/F	12/37%	38.7/85.2%	62.5/95.8%

	1995	1980	1965
COMMUNICATIONS			
RATE OF NEWSPAPERS	15	18	5
RATE OF RADIOS	226	66	32
RATE OF TELEVISIONS	100	61	1 (70)

Source: CIA, *The World Factbook, 1997*; ILO, *World Labour Report, 1997*; UN, *Demographic Yearbook, 1997*; UN, *Statistical Yearbook, 1996*; World Bank, *World Development Indicators, 1998*.

LIECHTENSTEIN

One of the world's tiniest countries by area and population, Liechtenstein is located in a mountainous region between Switzerland and Austria. With just 31,000 people in 62 square miles of territory, Liechtenstein is largely subsumed within the economic framework of Switzerland. It enjoys a customs union with Switzerland and uses the Swiss franc as its national currency. Like its neighbors, Liechtenstein is prosperous—with a per capital income of $22,300 annually—and healthy. Its death rate is just 6.8 per 1,000 persons and life expectancy averages some 76 years for men and 82 years for women. Liechtenstein, though governed by a prince, is in fact a constitutional monarchy.

	1995	1980	1965
GEOGRAPHY			
AREA (square miles/kilometers)	62/160		
LAND AREA (square miles/kilometers)	62/160		
COASTLINE	Landlocked		
CITIES			
CAPITAL	Vaduz	n/a	4,904 (82)	n/a
POPULATION			
TOTAL	31,122	26,130 (81)	16,628 (60)
DENSITY (per square mile/kilometer)	194	178	121
ANNUAL GROWTH	1.1%	1.9%	2.6%
AGE COHORTS			
0–14	19%	n/a	29%
15–64	70%	n/a	63%
65 AND OVER	11%	n/a	8%
URBAN	21%		
RURAL	79%		
NET MIGRATION RATE	6.1		

	1995	**1980**	**1965**

IDENTITY

ETHNICITY

ALEMANNIC	95%		
ITALIAN AND OTHER	5%		

LANGUAGE

GERMAN	n/a		
ALEMANNIC DIALECT	n/a		

RELIGION

ROMAN CATHOLIC	87.3%		
PROTESTANT	8.3%		

VITAL STATISTICS

BIRTHS

BIRTH RATE	11.5	13.2 (84)	n/a
INFANT MORTALITY RATE	5.3		
LIFE EXPECTANCY AT BIRTH	78.8		

MARRIAGES

MARRIAGE RATE	12.9	13.7	n/a
AVERAGE AGE AT MARRIAGE M/F	n/a	28.8/26.1	n/a
DIVORCE RATE	1	0.6 (83)	n/a

DEATHS

DEATH RATE	6.8	5.7	n/a

ECONOMICS AND LABOR

GDP PER CAPITA US$	$22,300		

EDUCATION

SCHOOL AGE IN SCHOOL

PRIMARY	n/a	n/a	122%
SECONDARY	n/a	n/a	22%

FEMALES IN SCHOOL

PRIMARY	n/a	n/a	123%
SECONDARY	n/a	n/a	24%

	1995	1980	1965
COMMUNICATIONS			
RATE OF NEWSPAPERS	653	540	248 (70)
RATE OF RADIOS	661	520	n/a
RATE OF TELEVISIONS	337	280	84

Source: CIA, The World Factbook, 1997; ILO, World Labour Report, 1997; UN, Demographic Yearbook, 1997; UN, Statistical Yearbook, 1996; World Bank, World Development Indicators, 1998.

LITHUANIA

Of the three Baltic republics of the former Soviet Union, Lithuania, with a population of 3.6 million, is by far the largest. Situated on the Baltic Sea, with the Latvia to the north, and Poland, Belarus, and the Kaliningrad enclave of the Russian federation to the east and south, the country is far more ethnically homogenous than its Baltic neighbors, with approximately 80 percent of the people of Lithuanian extraction. Most of the rest are Russians who settled in the country during its occupation by the Soviet Union from just before World War II until 1991. Like other parts of the Soviet Union, Lithuania has a relatively aged population, with just 22 percent under the age of 15. Indeed, its population actually sank slightly in 1995, declining by 0.4 percent, largely a result of an out-migration rate of 3.1 percent. Highly educated—some 28 percent of the youths attend university—the country has been trying to rebuild itself as a capitalist economy in the 1990s, with mixed success. Its per capita income is still quite low by European standards, at just $3,400 per person. At the same time, poverty rates remain high for Europe, with some 18.9 percent of the population subsisting on incomes of under $2 per day.

Birth and Death Rates, 1995

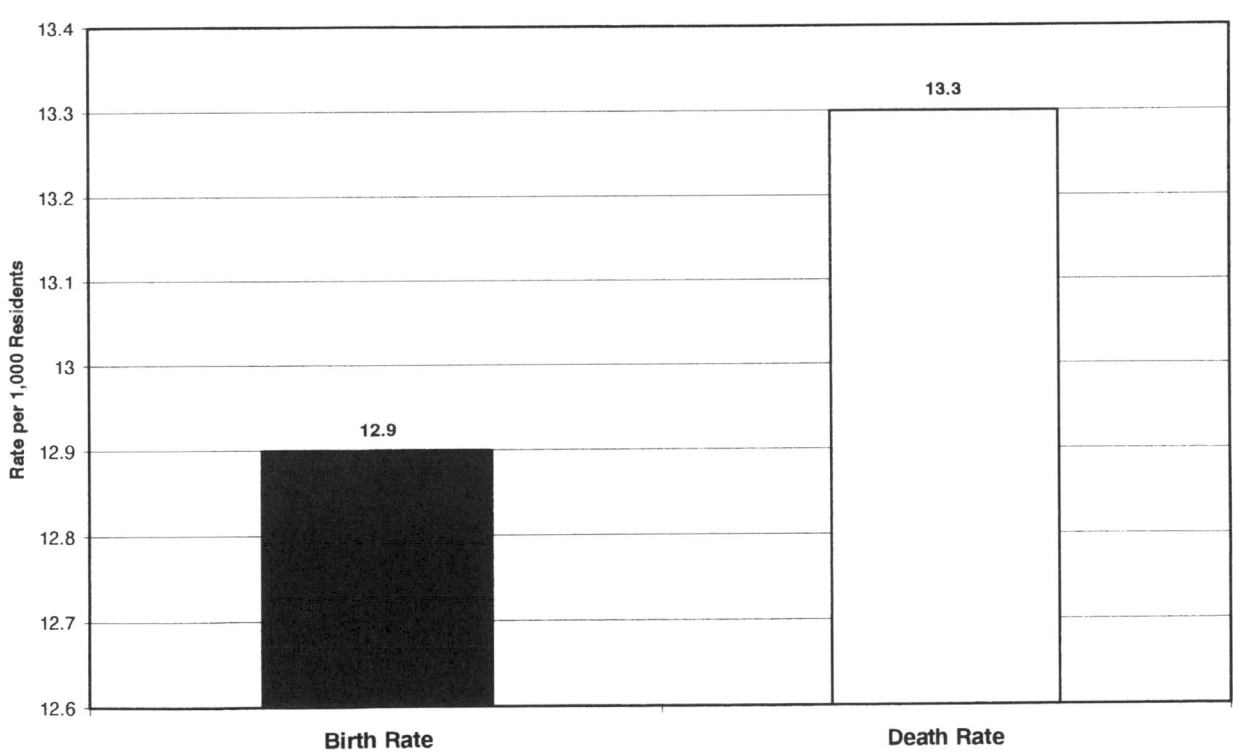

Like many other Eastern European countries, Lithuania has experienced negative growth rates, a factor caused by falling birth rates and an increasingly aged population, which results in higher death rates.

Age Distribution

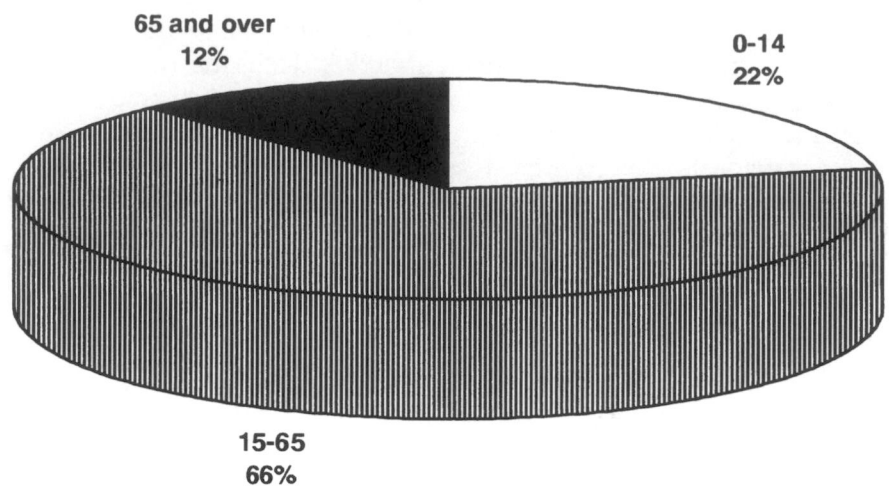

65 and over
12%

0-14
22%

15-65
66%

Falling birth rates and the increasing departure of younger persons for Western Europe and North America—
a trend made possible by the collapse of the Soviet Union and its restrictions on emigration—has resulted in an
increasingly aged population.

1995[1]

GEOGRAPHY

AREA (square miles/kilometers)	25,174/65,200
LAND AREA (square miles/kilometers)	25,174/65,200
COASTLINE (miles/kilometers)	68/108

CITIES

CAPITAL	Vilnius	581,500 (93)
MAJOR CITIES	Kaunas	421,600
	Klaipeda	204,300
	Siauliai	147,900
	Panevezys	131,800

POPULATION

TOTAL	3,646,041
DENSITY (per square mile/kilometer)	57
ANNUAL GROWTH	−0.4%

	1995[1]
AGE COHORTS	
0–14	22%
15–64	66%
65 AND OVER	12%
MALE	47%
FEMALE	53%
URBAN	72%
RURAL	28%
NET MIGRATION RATE	−3.1

IDENTITY

ETHNICITY	
LITHUANIAN	80.1%
RUSSIAN	8.6%
POLISH	7.7%
BYELORUSSIAN	1.5%
LANGUAGE	
LITHUANIAN	n/a
POLISH	n/a
RUSSIAN	n/a
RELIGION	
ROMAN CATHOLIC	n/a
LUTHERAN	n/a

VITAL STATISTICS

BIRTHS	
BIRTH RATE	12.9
URBAN BIRTH RATE	10.5
RURAL BIRTH RATE	12.2
INFANT MORTALITY RATE	17
ABORTION RATE	708.6
LIFE EXPECTANCY AT BIRTH	68
MARRIAGES	
MARRIAGE RATE	6.3
AVERAGE AGE AT MARRIAGE M/F	24.7/22.3
DIVORCE RATE	3

	1995[1]
DEATHS	
DEATH RATE	13.3

ECONOMICS AND LABOR

GDP PER CAPITA US$	$3,400
LABOR FORCE M/F (thousands)	846.4/931.8 (93)
AGRICULTURE	263.3/164.5
MINING	2.6/1.4
MANUFACTURING	198.5/221.1
UTILITIES	24.2/9.2
CONSTRUCTION	107.7/19.1
TRADE/FOOD/TOURISM	35.1/155.8
TRANSPORT/COMMUNICATIONS	66.3/33.6
FINANCE/INSURANCE/REAL ESTATE	19.0/31.1
SOCIAL AND PERSONAL SERVICES	152.3/289.7
UNEMPLOYMENT (official)	3.5% (93)
POVERTY	
UNDER $1/DAY	1%
UNDER $2/DAY	18.9%

TRANSPORT

JOURNEYS (by transport mode)	
RAILROAD PASSENGER TRIPS	1,574 (94)
(millions of miles/kilometers)	
AIR PASSENGER TRIPS (thousands)	195 (94)
VEHICLES (thousands)	
PRIVATE CARS	652.8 (94)
COMMERCIAL	118.2 (94)

HEALTH AND HEALTH CARE

HEALTH CARE	
MEASLES IMMUNIZATION	94%
RATE OF PHYSICIANS	4
RATE OF HOSPITAL BEDS	11.1
HEALTH INDICATORS	
SMOKING PREVALENCE M/F	52/10%
TUBERCULOSIS INCIDENCE RATE	0.82

	1995[1]
AIDS/HIV CASES	8
TOTAL DEATHS	45,306

EDUCATION

SCHOOL AGE IN SCHOOL

PRIMARY	96%
SECONDARY	84%
HIGHER	28%

FEMALES IN SCHOOL

PRIMARY	92%
SECONDARY	88%

COMMUNICATIONS

RATE OF NEWSPAPERS	225
RATE OF RADIOS	385
RATE OF TELEVISIONS	383

FOOTNOTE
1. Part of the Soviet Union in 1965 and 1980.

Source: CIA, *The World Factbook, 1997;* ILO, *World Labour Report, 1997;* UN, *Demographic Yearbook, 1997;* UN, *Statistical Yearbook, 1996;* World Bank, *World Development Indicators, 1998.*

LUXEMBOURG

A tiny country tucked between Belgium, France, and Germany, Luxembourg has slightly less than 1,000 square miles in territory, slightly smaller than Rhode Island. Its 415,000 citizens are heavily influenced by their giant neighbors. Most speak a dialect of German, though many speak French as well. The vast majority are Roman Catholic. Governed as a duchy, Luxembourg is a constitutional monarchy, and was one of the founding member-states of the European Union. It is an extremely prosperous country, with a per capita income in 1995 of $24,800, and its union membership is a high 39.5 percent of all working people. Its citizenry are also highly literate, consuming 372 newspapers per 1,000 persons daily in 1995.

	1995	1980	1965
GEOGRAPHY			
AREA (square miles/kilometers)	998/2,586		
LAND AREA (square miles/kilometers)	998/2,586		
COASTLINE	Landlocked		
CITIES			
CAPITAL	Luxembourg 76,446 (94)		
POPULATION			
TOTAL	415,870	364,602 (81)	314,889 (60)
DENSITY (per square mile/kilometer)	407/157	365/141	337/130
ANNUAL GROWTH	1.6%	0.1%	1%
AGE COHORTS			
0–14	18%	n/a	22%
15–64	68%	n/a	67%
65 AND OVER	14%	n/a	11%
MALE	49%		
FEMALE	51%		
URBAN	89%	77.80%	n/a
RURAL	11%	22.20%	n/a
NET MIGRATION RATE	10.9	n/a	1.3 (64)

	1995	1980	1965

IDENTITY

ETHNICITY

CELTIC (French/German)	n/a		
PORTUGUESE	n/a		
ITALIAN	n/a		

LANGUAGE

LUXEMBOURGISCH	n/a		
GERMAN	n/a		
FRENCH	n/a		
ENGLISH	n/a		

RELIGION

ROMAN CATHOLIC	97%		
PROTESTANT	n/a		
JEWISH	n/a		

VITAL STATISTICS

BIRTHS

BIRTH RATE	13.1	11.1	15.5
INFANT MORTALITY RATE	4.7	11.7 (85)	26.8
LIFE EXPECTANCY AT BIRTH	78.3	73.3 (85)	64

MARRIAGES

MARRIAGE RATE	6	5.4 (85)	6.6
AVERAGE AGE AT MARRIAGE M/F	28.5/26		
DIVORCE RATE	1.9	1.8 (85)	0.6

DEATHS

DEATH RATE	8.3	10.8 (85)	12.1

HOUSEHOLDS

NUMBER	144,684 (91)	n/a	94,839 (60)
AVERAGE SIZE	2.7 (91)	n/a	3.3 (60)

TYPE OF HOUSEHOLD

SINGLE	15.2%		
MARRIED	62.7%		
WIDOWED	14.7%		
DIVORCED/SEPARATED	7.4%		
FEMALE HEADED	25.8%		

	1995	1980	1965

ECONOMICS AND LABOR

GDP PER CAPITA US$ | $24,800

LABOR FORCE M/F (thousands) | 125.0/64.6 (90)
AGRICULTURE | 4.3/1.9
MINING | 0.2/0.0
MANUFACTURING | 33.1/4.1
UTILITIES | 1.2/0.2
CONSTRUCTION | 17.7/1.1
TRADE/FOOD/TOURISM | 20.9/19.3
TRANSPORT/COMMUNICATIONS | 10.6/2.3
FINANCE/INSURANCE/REAL ESTATE | 9.1/7.7
SOCIAL AND PERSONAL SERVICES | 27.9/28.0

UNEMPLOYMENT (official) | 1.6% (92)
UNION DENSITY | 39.5%

TRANSPORT

JOURNEYS (by transport mode)
RAILROAD PASSENGER TRIPS | 261.0 (90)
　(millions of miles/kilometers)
AIR PASSENGER TRIPS (thousands) | 533.0 (94)

VEHICLES (thousands)

	1995	1980	1965
PRIVATE CARS	217.8	128.6	61.7
COMMERCIAL	45.6	25.5	10.8

HEALTH AND HEALTH CARE

HEALTH CARE

	1995	1980	1965
RATE OF PHYSICIANS	n/a	n/a	1 (60)
RATE OF HOSPITAL BEDS	n/a	n/a	10.9 (60)

	1995	1980	1965
AIDS/HIV CASES	105	77 (93)	

TOTAL DEATHS | 3,797

	1995	1980	1965

EDUCATION

SCHOOL AGE IN SCHOOL

	1995	1980	1965
PRIMARY	n/a	99%	81%
SECONDARY	n/a	62%	48%
HIGHER	n/a	2.8%	1.9%

FEMALES IN SCHOOL

	1995	1980	1965
PRIMARY	n/a	97%	78%
SECONDARY	n/a	63%	32%
HIGHER	n/a	2%	1.4% (70)

COMMUNICATIONS

	1995	1980	1965
RATE OF NEWSPAPERS	372	371	425
RATE OF RADIOS	633	549	378
RATE OF TELEVISIONS	261	247	98

Source: CIA, *The World Factbook, 1997;* ILO, *World Labour Report, 1997;* UN, *Demographic Yearbook, 1997;* UN, *Statistical Yearbook, 1996;* World Bank, *World Development Indicators, 1998.*

MACEDONIA, FORMER YUGOSLAV REPUBLIC OF

Macedonia, part of the Yugoslav federation until its independence in 1991, is a landlocked country surrounded by Serbia to the north, Bulgaria to the east, Greece to the south, and Albania to the west. Roughly 9,800 square miles in area—or the size of Vermont—Macedonia has a population of 2.1 million. Ethnically, the country is quite diverse, though at 65 percent, ethnic Macedonians predominate. The largest minority is Albanian, at 22 percent of the population. Since its independence, Macedonia has been involved in several international incidents. A U.N. peacekeeping force patrols the border with Serbia, where there have been ethnic tensions among the Albanian minority, and there is a long-standing dispute with Greece over the official name of the country. (Greece fears that Macedonia has ambitions on its northern province of the same name, home to many ethnic Macedonians.) Because of the many political disputes and the sharp break with Yugoslavia, Macedonia suffers from a severe economic crisis. Its per capita income of just $880 annually is among the lowest in the Balkans. Health indexes present a mixed picture. The infant mortality rate is a high 29.7 per 1,000 live births, though life expectancy is 71.9 years.

	1995[1]	1980
GEOGRAPHY		
AREA (square miles/kilometers)	9,781/25,333	
LAND AREA (square miles/kilometers)	9,597/24,856	
COASTLINE (miles/kilometers)	Landlocked	
CITIES		
CAPITAL	Skopje	448,229 (92)
POPULATION		
TOTAL		2,104,035
DENSITY		84
ANNUAL GROWTH		0.46%
AGE COHORTS		
0–14		22%
15–64		68%
65 AND OVER		10%
MALE		51%
FEMALE		49%

	1995[1]	1980
URBAN	58%	
RURAL		
NET MIGRATION RATE	−0.2	

IDENTITY

ETHNICITY
MACEDONIAN	65%
ALBANIAN	22%
TURKISH	4%
GYPSY	3%
SERB	2%

LANGUAGE
MACEDONIAN	70%
ALBANIAN	21%
TURKISH	3%
SERBO-CROATIAN	3%

RELIGION
EASTERN ORTHODOX	67%
MUSLIM	30%

VITAL STATISTICS

BIRTHS
BIRTH RATE	13.3
URBAN BIRTH RATE	16 (91)
RURAL BIRTH RATE	18.7
INFANT MORTALITY RATE	29.7
ABORTION RATE	n/a
LIFE EXPECTANCY AT BIRTH	71.9

MARRIAGES
MARRIAGE RATE	7.1
DIVORCE RATE	0.3

DEATHS
DEATH RATE	8.5

	1995[1]	1980

HOUSEHOLDS

NUMBER	503,546 (94)	
AVERAGE SIZE	3.8 (94)	

ECONOMICS AND LABOR

GDP PER CAPITA US$	$880	
LABOR FORCE M/F (thousands)	248/148 (94)	
AGRICULTURE	25/9	
MINING	9/1	
MANUFACTURING	83/56	
UTILITIES	10/1	
CONSTRUCTION	30/3	
TRADE/FOOD/TOURISM	20/18	
TRANSPORT/COMMUNICATIONS	18/3	
FINANCE/INSURANCE/REAL ESTATE	6/6	
SOCIAL AND PERSONAL SERVICES	36/49	
UNEMPLOYMENT		
TOTAL	32% (94)	

TRANSPORT

JOURNEYS (by transport mode)		
RAILROAD PASSENGER TRIPS	203.0 (94)	
(millions of miles/kilometers)		

HEALTH AND HEALTH CARE

RATE OF PHYSICIANS	2.3	
RATE OF HOSPITAL BEDS	5.5	
TOTAL DEATHS	15,591 (93)	
HEALTH INDICATORS		
TUBERCULOSIS INCIDENCE RATE	.60	

	1995[1]	1980
HEALTH CARE		
MEASLES IMMUNIZATION	85%	
AIDS/HIV CASES	18	

EDUCATION

	1995[1]	1980
SCHOOL AGE IN SCHOOL		
PRIMARY	89	100
SECONDARY	57	61
HIGHER	18	28
FEMALES IN SCHOOL		
PRIMARY	48	49
SECONDARY	52	n/a

COMMUNICATIONS

	1995[1]	1980
RATE OF NEWSPAPERS	27	n/a
RATE OF RADIOS	180	n/a
RATE OF TELEVISIONS	165	146

FOOTNOTE
1. Part of Yugoslavia in 1965 and 1980.

Source: CIA, *The World Factbook, 1997*; ILO, *World Labour Report, 1997*; UN, *Demographic Yearbook, 1997*; UN, *Statistical Yearbook, 1996*; World Bank, *World Development Indicators, 1998*.

MADAGASCAR

Occupying one of the world's largest islands, Madagascar is situated in the Indian Ocean, some 200–400 miles off the southeast coast of Mozambique. Once heavily forested, the country has experienced serious overgrazing and foresting in recent decades, resulting in severe environmental problems, including erosion and loss of habitat for the many unique animal species that inhabit the island. The source of much of this environmental problem is a rapidly growing population. Between 1965 and 1995, the population more than doubled, from 6.2 million to 13.7 million. Population growth has eased somewhat. While the an-

nual growth rate was 3.6 percent in 1965, it had fallen to 2.8 percent by 1980. Still, some 45 percent of the population is aged 14 or under, and life expectancy climbed from 37.9 years in the 1960s to 52.2 years in 1995. Meanwhile, poverty remains endemic among the mostly rural (73 percent) population. In 1995, some 93.2 percent of the population survived on less than $2 per person daily, and 72.3 percent lived on less than $1 in 1993. This poverty is reflected in the health care profile of the country. There is just 1 physician per 10,000 persons in Madagascar and not even 1 hospital bed per 1,000 people.

	1995	1980	1965
GEOGRAPHY			
AREA (square miles/kilometers)	226,656/587,040		
LAND AREA (square miles/kilometers)	224,533/581,540		
COASTLINE (miles/kilometers)	3017.5/4828		
CITIES			
CAPITAL	Antananarivo	n/a	n/a	347,466 (71)
POPULATION			
TOTAL	13,670,507	7,603,790 (75)	6,219,912 (64)
DENSITY	25	17	12
ANNUAL GROWTH	2.83%	2.8	3.6
AGE COHORTS			
0–14	45%		38%
15–64	52%		
65 AND OVER	3%		
MALE	50%		
FEMALE	50%		

	1995	1980	1965
URBAN	27%		
RURAL	73%		
NET MIGRATION RATE	0	n/a	0

IDENTITY

ETHNICITY

MALAYO-INDONESIAN	n/a
COTIERS	n/a
FRENCH	n/a
INDIAN	n/a
CREOLE	n/a
COMORAN	n/a

LANGUAGE

FRENCH	n/a
MALAGASY	n/a

RELIGION

INDIGENOUS	52%
CHRISTIAN	41%
MUSLIM	7%

VITAL STATISTICS

BIRTHS

BIRTH RATE	42.6	46
INFANT MORTALITY RATE	93.5	102
LIFE EXPECTANCY AT BIRTH	52.2	37.9

DEATHS

DEATH RATE	14.4	25

ECONOMICS AND LABOR

GDP PER CAPITA US$	$820

LABOR FORCE | 285.9 (91)

AGRICULTURE	76.3
MINING	4.5
MANUFACTURING	93.1
UTILITIES	11.5

	1995	1980	1965
CONSTRUCTION	28.4		
TRADE/FOOD/TOURISM			
TRANSPORT/COMMUNICATIONS	26.1		
FINANCE/INSURANCE/REAL ESTATE	37.6		
SOCIAL AND PERSONAL SERVICES	169.2		

POVERTY

	1995	1980	1965
UNDER $1/DAY	72.3% (93)		
UNDER $2/DAY	93.2%		

TRANSPORT

JOURNEYS (by transport mode)

	1995	1980	1965
RAILROAD PASSENGER TRIPS	198 (90)		
(millions of miles/kilometers)			
AIR PASSENGER TRIPS (thousands)	451 (94)		

VEHICLES (thousands)

	1995	1980	1965
CARS	47	48.5	32.1
COMMERCIAL VEHICLES	33.3	47.6	27.1

HEALTH AND HEALTH CARE

	1995	1980	1965
RATE OF PHYSICIANS	0.1	0.1	0.1 (60)
RATE OF HOSPITAL BEDS	0.9		2.3 (60)

HEALTH INDICATORS

	1995	1980	1965
LOW-BIRTH-WEIGHT BABIES	10%		
CHILD MALNUTRITION	32%		
SMOKING PREVALENCE M/F	29/28%		
TUBERCULOSIS INCIDENCE RATE	3.1		

HEALTH AND HEALTH CARE

HEALTH CARE

	1995	1980	1965
ACCESS TO SAFE WATER	29%		
ACCESS TO SANITATION	3%		
MEASLES IMMUNIZATION	59%		

	1995	1980	1965
AIDS/HIV CASES	24	11 (93)	

	1995	1980	1965
EDUCATION			
SCHOOL AGE IN SCHOOL			
PRIMARY	72%	133%	70%
SECONDARY	14%	12% (75)	7%
HIGHER	3%	3%	0.50%
FEMALES IN SCHOOL			
PRIMARY	49	49	n/a
SECONDARY	50	10 (75)	5
ADULT ILLITERACY M/F	n/a	26.3/38.4	n/a
COMMUNICATIONS			
RATE OF NEWSPAPERS	4	6	9 (62)
RATE OF RADIOS	192	177	46
RATE OF TELEVISIONS	20	5	1 (70)

Source: CIA, The World Factbook, 1997; ILO, World Labour Report, 1997; UN, Demographic Yearbook, 1997; UN, Statistical Yearbook, 1996; World Bank, World Development Indicators, 1998.

MALAWI

Malawi is a long, thin, landlocked country in southern Africa. It is surrounded by Tanzania to the north, Zambia to the west, and Mozambique to the south. Its long eastern side is flanked by Lake Malawi, the southernmost of East Africa's great lakes. Hilly and lushly fertile, the relatively small country—just 36,324 square miles, or an area the size of Pennsylvania—is quite crowded. With some 9.5 million persons in 1995, it had a population density of 215 persons per square mile, one of the highest rates in Africa. Ruled by president-for-life Hastings Banda from independence in 1964 until the early 1990s, it is now nominally democratic. Banda, one of the few black

African leaders who maintained relations with the apartheid regime in South Africa, helped sponsor Pretoria-supported rebels fighting the leftist regime in neighboring Mozambique in the 1980s, earning the country tense relations with its black-ruled neighbors. In recent years, the country has opened up to the rest of southern Africa, joining the regional economic bloc, the Southern African Development Community. Still, it remains extremely poor. Per capita income is just $700 annually, and well over half the country's working people are farmers, largely subsistence ones.

		1995	**1980**	**1965**
GEOGRAPHY				
AREA (square miles/kilometers)	45,745/118,480			
LAND AREA (square miles/kilometers)	36,324/94,080			
COASTLINE (miles/kilometers)	Landlocked			
CITIES				
CAPITAL	Lilongwe	n/a	233,973 (87)	n/a
MAJOR CITIES	Blantyre-Limbe	n/a	331,588	n/a
POPULATION				
TOTAL[1]		9,452,844	5,547,460 (77)	4,042,412 (66)
DENSITY		207	121	88
ANNUAL GROWTH		1.71%	3.1%	2.4%
AGE COHORTS				
0–14		46%	n/a	45%
15–64		51%	n/a	48%
65 AND OVER		3%	n/a	7.2% (66)
MALE		48%		
FEMALE		52%		

	1995	**1980**	**1965**
URBAN	14%	9.8%	n/a
RURAL	86%	90.2%	n/a
NET MIGRATION RATE	0		

IDENTITY

ETHNICITY

CHEWA, NYANJA, TUMBUKO, YAO	n/a		
LOMWE, SENA, TONGA, NGONI	n/a		
NGONDE, ASIAN, EUROPEAN	n/a		

LANGUAGE

ENGLISH	n/a		
CHICHEWA	n/a		

RELIGION

PROTESTANT	55%		
ROMAN CATHOLIC	20%		
MUSLIM	20%		
INDIGENOUS			

VITAL STATISTICS

BIRTHS

BIRTH RATE	41.6	48.5 (77)	n/a
LIFE EXPECTANCY AT BIRTH	36.2	39.7	n/a

MARRIAGES

MARRIAGE RATE	n/a	7.8	n/a
AVERAGE AGE AT MARRIAGE M/F	n/a	23.6/18.6	n/a

DEATHS

DEATH RATE	24.5	25.1	n/a

HOUSEHOLDS

NUMBER	n/a	1,859,572 (87)	n/a
AVERAGE SIZE	n/a	4.3	n/a

TYPE OF HOUSEHOLD

FEMALE HEADED	n/a	33.5%	n/a

	1995	1980	1965

ECONOMICS AND LABOR

GDP PER CAPITA US$	$700		
LABOR FORCE M/F (thousands)	487.9/106.5 (91)		
AGRICULTURE	243.4/77.6		
MINING	0.8/0.0		
MANUFACTURING	70.3/6.5		
UTILITIES	6.3/0.6		
CONSTRUCTION	44.1/0.5		
TRADE/FOOD/TOURISM	26.3/3.1		
TRANSPORT/COMMUNICATIONS	20.9/1.4		
FINANCE/INSURANCE/REAL ESTATE	15.2/1.8		
SOCIAL AND PERSONAL SERVICES	60.6/15.1		

TRANSPORT

JOURNEYS (by transport mode)			
RAILROAD PASSENGER TRIPS	72 (92)		
(millions of miles/kilometers)			
AIR PASSENGER TRIPS (thousands)	142 (94)		
VEHICLES (thousands)			
CARS	5.3	11.8	8
COMMERCIAL VEHICLES	2.7	13.5	7.6

HEALTH AND HEALTH CARE

RATE OF PHYSICIANS	0	0	0 (60)
RATE OF HOSPITAL BEDS	1.6	n/a	1.1 (60)
HEALTH INDICATORS			
PREGNANT WOMEN WITH ANEMIA	55%		
LOW-BIRTH-WEIGHT BABIES	20%		
CHILD MALNUTRITION	28%		
TUBERCULOSIS INCIDENCE RATE	1.7		
HEALTH CARE			
ACCESS TO SAFE WATER	45%		
ACCESS TO SANITATION	53%		
MEASLES IMMUNIZATION	99%		
AIDS/HIV CASES	41,864	31,871 (93)	

	1995	1980	1965

EDUCATION

SCHOOL AGE IN SCHOOL

PRIMARY	135%	60%	38%
SECONDARY	98%	30%	20%
HIGHER	2%	1%	0%

FEMALES IN SCHOOL

PRIMARY	47%	41%	30%
SECONDARY	39%	29%	1%

ADULT ILLITERACY M/F	28%/58%	47.8%/69.2% (85)	66.3%/87.7%

COMMUNICATIONS

RATE OF NEWSPAPERS	2	3	n/a
RATE OF RADIOS	226	42	24 (70)

FOOTNOTE
1. For 1966, age 60 and over.

Source: CIA, The World Factbook, 1997; ILO, World Labour Report, 1997; UN, Demographic Yearbook, 1997; UN, Statistical Yearbook, 1996; World Bank, World Development Indicators, 1998.

MALAYSIA

Located on the southern tip of the Malay peninsula and the northern third of the island of Borneo, Malaysia has a population of 20 million. Ethnically, the country is divided into three main groups. The Muslim Malay population constitutes about 60 percent of the population, ethnic Chinese another roughly 30 percent, and Indians some 10 percent. This ethnic and religious division produced tensions in the 1960s and 1970s, though they have died down in recent years, partly as a result of economic change. Until the economic meltdown in East Asia in 1997, Malaysia enjoyed one of the fastest-growing economies in the world. By 1995, its per capita income had risen to $9,800 and the number of manufacturing workers had outgrown those involved in farming. Interestingly, the changes in the labor profile have been more apparent among the female cohort, where some 766,000 worked in manufacturing in 1993, while just 481,000 continued to labor on the land. At the same time, while male illiteracy has remained roughly the same between 1980 and 1995, it had fallen among women from 34 to 11 percent. The effect of the new wealth in Malaysia can be measured by private car ownership which rose from just 13,400 in 1965 to fully 2.3 million thirty years later.

	1995	1980	1965
GEOGRAPHY			
AREA (square miles/kilometers)	127,317/329,750		
LAND AREA (square miles/kilometers)	126,853/328,550		
COASTLINE (miles/kilometers)	2,922/4,675		
CITIES			
CAPITAL	Kuala Lumpur (91)	1,145,075	
MAJOR CITIES	Ipoh	382,633	
	Johore Bahru	328,646	
	Petaling Jaya	254,849	
	Klang	243,698	
POPULATION			
TOTAL	19,962,893	13,183,005	7,477,708
DENSITY	61	47	n/a
ANNUAL GROWTH	2.07%	2.6%	n/a
AGE COHORTS			
0–14	36%	n/a	44%
15–64	60%	n/a	53%
65 AND OVER	4%	n/a	3%

	1995	**1980**	**1965**
MALE	50%		
FEMALE	50%		
URBAN	54%	37.2	n/a
RURAL			
NET MIGRATION	0	n/a	0.3

IDENTITY

ETHNICITY			
MALAY	59%		
CHINESE	32%		
INDIAN	9%		
LANGUAGE			
MALAY	n/a		
CHINESE	n/a		
ENGLISH	n/a		
TAMIL	n/a		
RELIGION			
MUSLIM	n/a		
BUDDHIST	n/a		
CONFUCIANIST	n/a		
HINDU	n/a		
CHRISTIAN	n/a		

VITAL STATISTICS

BIRTHS			
BIRTH RATE	26.2	31.2	36.7
INFANT MORTALITY RATE	24	24.9	50
ABORTION RATE			
LIFE EXPECTANCY AT BIRTH	69.8	70.1	57
MARRIAGES			
MARRIAGE RATE	n/a	1.7	1.1
DIVORCE RATE	n/a	0	n/a
DEATHS			
DEATH RATE	5.5	5.8	7.9

	1995	1980	1965

HOUSEHOLDS

NUMBER	3,580,016 (91)	n/a	30,238 (60)
URBAN	1,826,256		
RURAL	1,753,760		
AVERAGE SIZE	4.9 (91)	n/a	5.7
URBAN	4.9		
RURAL	4.9		

ECONOMICS AND LABOR

GDP PER CAPITA US$	$9,800		
LABOR FORCE M/F (thousands)	4,853.8/2,529.6 93		
AGRICULTURE	1,077.0/481.6		
MINING	34.0/3.6		
MANUFACTURING	960.7/766.3		
UTILITIES	54.6/5.7		
CONSTRUCTION	508.1/30.7		
TRADE/FOOD/TOURISM	770.5/495.7		
TRANSPORT/COMMUNICATIONS	309.5/34.4		
FINANCE/INSURANCE/REAL ESTATE	208.1/121.9		
SOCIAL AND PERSONAL SERVICES	931.2/589.7		
UNEMPLOYMENT			
TOTAL	35.6% (93)		
UNION DENSITY	11.70%		
POVERTY			
UNDER $1/DAY	5.6% (89)		
UNDER $2/DAY	26.6%		

TRANSPORT

JOURNEYS (by transport mode)			
RAILROAD PASSENGER TRIPS	1,367 (94)		
(millions of miles/kilometers)			
AIR PASSENGER TRIPS (thousands)	14,250 (94)		
VEHICLES (thousands)			
CARS	2,333	862	13.4
COMMERCIAL VEHICLES	422	284.4	4.9

	1995	**1980**	**1965**

HEALTH AND HEALTH CARE

	1995	1980	1965
RATE OF PHYSICIANS	0.4	0.3	n/a
RATE OF HOSPITAL BEDS	2	2.3	n/a
TOTAL DEATHS	91,700		

HEALTH INDICATORS			
PREGNANT WOMEN WITH ANEMIA	56%		
LOW-BIRTH-WEIGHT BABIES	8%		
CHILD MALNUTRITION	23%		
SMOKING PREVALENCE M/F	41/4		
TB INCIDENCE/100,000	67		

HEALTH CARE			
ACCESS TO SAFE WATER	88%		
ACCESS TO SANITATION	91%		
MEASLES IMMUNIZATION	81%		

AIDS/HIV CASES	331	117 (93)	

EDUCATION

SCHOOL AGE IN SCHOOL	1995	1980	1965
PRIMARY	91%	93%	87% (70)
SECONDARY	61%	48%	41%
HIGHER	11.0%	4%	1.60%

FEMALES IN SCHOOL			
PRIMARY	49%	49%	84%
SECONDARY	51%	48%	28%

ADULT ILLITERACY M/F	22%/11%	19.1%/34% (85)	n/a

COMMUNICATIONS

	1995	1980	1965
RATE OF NEWSPAPERS	117	59	57
RATE OF RADIOS	430	411	49
RATE OF TELEVISIONS	151	87	7

Source: CIA, *The World Factbook, 1997;* ILO, *World Labour Report, 1997;* UN, *Demographic Yearbook, 1997;* UN, *Statistical Yearbook, 1996;* World Bank, *World Development Indicators, 1998.*

MALDIVES

The Republic of the Maldives consists of a set of low, coral-ringed islands in the Indian Ocean, off the southwest coast of India and just north of the equator. Just 115.8 square miles in area, the entire country could fit into an area twice the size of Washington, D.C. Its population represents a mix of ethnic groups from around the Indian Ocean basin, including Indians, Sinhalese, Arabs, and Africans. With a per capita income of some $1,560 per person annually, the people of the islands largely depend on tourism and fishing for their livelihood. The population is growing extremely rapidly, at some 3.5 percent annually. Between 1965 and 1995, the population grew from 100,000 to its current 270,000, while the density grew from 871 to 2,338 per square mile. This growth can be expected to continue in coming years, since fully 47 percent of the population is under 15 years of age.

		1995	1980	1965
GEOGRAPHY				
AREA (square miles/kilometers)		115.8/300		
LAND AREA (square miles/kilometers)		115.8/300		
COASTLINE (miles/kilometers)		245/644		
CITIES				
CAPITAL	Male	n/a	29,522 (77)	n/a
POPULATION				
TOTAL		270,758	181,453 (85)	100,883 (66)
DENSITY (per square mile/square kilometer)		2,338/902	1,567/605	871/336
ANNUAL GROWTH		3.52%	3%	1.7%
AGE COHORTS				
0–14		47%		
15–64		50%		
65 AND OVER		3%		
MALE		51%		
FEMALE		49%		
URBAN		27%	21.3%	n/a
RURAL		73%	78.7%	n/a
NET MIGRATION		0		

	1995	1980	1965

IDENTITY

ETHNICITY

SINHALESE	n/a		
DRAVIDIAN	n/a		
ARAB	n/a		
AFRICAN	n/a		

LANGUAGE

MALDIVIAN DIVEHI	n/a		
ENGLISH	n/a		

RELIGION

SUNNI MUSLIM	n/a		

VITAL STATISTICS

BIRTHS

BIRTH RATE	41.9	47.8 (84)	n/a
INFANT MORTALITY RATE	47	67.9	n/a
LIFE EXPECTANCY AT BIRTH	66.2	51.5	n/a

MARRIAGES

MARRIAGE RATE	19.7	34.4 (84)	n/a
AVERAGE AGE AT MARRIAGE M/F	23.2/10.8 (90)	n/a	n/a
DIVORCE RATE	10.8	25.4	n/a

DEATHS

DEATH RATE	6.6	9.5 (84)	n/a

ECONOMICS AND LABOR

GDP PER CAPITA US$ $1,560

TRANSPORT

JOURNEYS (by transport mode)

AIR PASSENGER TRIPS (thousands)	38.0 (94)		

	1995	1980	1965

HEALTH AND HEALTH CARE

TOTAL DEATHS	1,319 (93)		
AIDS/HIV CASES	5	0 (93)	

EDUCATION

ADULT ILLITERACY M/F	n/a	17.5%17.7% (77)	n/a

COMMUNICATIONS

RATE OF NEWSPAPERS	13	6	n/a
RATE OF RADIOS	118	44	11 (70)
RATE OF TELEVISIONS	25	7	n/a

Source: CIA, The World Factbook, 1997; ILO, World Labour Report, 1997; UN, Demographic Yearbook, 1997; UN, Statistical Yearbook, 1996; World Bank, World Development Indicators, 1998.

MALI

Mali is a vast, sparsely populated country located in the Sahara Desert and the Sahel region of northwestern Africa. With a population of some 9.7 million scattered across nearly 479,000 square miles of territory, Mali has a population density of just 21 persons per square mile. Since most of these people live in the southwestern panhandle of the country, much of Mali is nearly uninhabited, the population confined to isolated oases in the desert. Mali's population growth rate, unlike that in many other developing countries, continues to rise, from 2.2 percent annually in 1965 to nearly 3 percent in 1980. This has more than doubled the population in 30 years. This rapid growth should continue, since just under half the population is under the age of 15. While the urban population has climbed from 17 percent to 27 percent of the total since 1980, most of the population is still involved in agricultural labor or pasturage. Indeed, the 10 percent of the country that is ethnically Tuareg or Moor is largely nomadic. Virtually all Muslim, the population of Mali speaks numerous African languages, though the country's official tongue is French, a legacy of colonial days before 1960. Subject to political turmoil in its past, Mali has had one of the more successful democratic experiments in the 1990s, having elected and reelected its government twice in the past decade.

	1995	1980	1965
GEOGRAPHY			
AREA (square miles/kilometers)	478,764/1,240,000		
LAND AREA (square miles/kilometers)	471,042/1,220,000		
COASTLINE (miles/kilometers)	Landlocked		
CAPITAL	Bamako	n/a 658,275 (87)	n/a
POPULATION			
TOTAL	9,653,261	6,394,918 (76)	4,654,100 (66)
DENSITY (per square mile/square kilometer)	21/8	14/5	10/4
ANNUAL GROWTH	2.95%	2.9%	2.2%
AGE COHORTS			
0–14	48%	n/a	49%
15–64	49%	n/a	49%
65 AND OVER	3%	n/a	2%
MALE	49%		
FEMALE	51%		
URBAN	27%	17.2%	n/a
RURAL	73%	82.8%	n/a

	1995	1980	1965
NET MIGRATION RATE	−2.37		

IDENTITY

ETHNICITY

MANDE	50%		
PEUL	17%		
VOLTAIC	12%		
TUAREG AND MOOR	10%		
SONGHAI	6%		

LANGUAGES

BAMBARA	80%		
FRENCH	n/a		
INDIGENOUS AFRICAN	n/a		

RELIGION

MUSLIM	90%		
INDIGENOUS	9%		
CHRISTIAN	1%		

VITAL STATISTICS

BIRTHS

BIRTH RATE	51.4	43.2 (76)	61
INFANT MORTALITY RATE	102.7	120.9	123
ABORTION RATE			
LIFE EXPECTANCY AT BIRTH	46.8	48.3	n/a

MARRIAGES

MARRIAGE RATE	4.4		
AVERAGE AGE AT MARRIAGE M/F	n/a	28.1/18.9 (87)	n/a

DEATHS

DEATH RATE	19.5	18.1 (76)	30

HOUSEHOLDS

NUMBER	n/a	1,364,079 (87)	n/a

	1995	1980	1965

ECONOMICS AND LABOR

	1995	1980	1965
GDP PER CAPITA US$	$600		
LABOR FORCE M/F			
AGRICULTURE	83/89%		
INDUSTRY	2/2%		
SERVICES	15/9%		
UNION DENSITY	13.7%		

TRANSPORT

	1995	1980	1965
JOURNEYS (by transport mode)			
RAILROAD PASSENGER TRIPS	184.0 (90)		
(millions of miles/kilometers)			
AIR PASSENGER TRIPS (thousands)	69.0 (94)		
VEHICLES (thousands)			
CARS	21	n/a	4.5
COMMERCIAL VEHICLES	8.6	n/a	4.9

HEALTH AND HEALTH CARE

	1995	1980	1965
RATE OF PHYSICIANS	0.1	0	0.2 (60)
RATE OF HOSPITAL BEDS	n/a	n/a	0.7 (60)
HEALTH INDICATORS			
PREGNANT WOMEN WITH ANEMIA	58%		
LOW-BIRTH-WEIGHT BABIES	17%		
CHILD MALNUTRITION	31%		
TUBERCULOSIS INCIDENCE RATE	2.89		
HEALTH CARE			
ACCESS TO SAFE WATER	37%		
ACCESS TO SANITATION	31%		
MEASLES IMMUNIZATION	49%		
AIDS/HIV CASES	3,048	1,985 (93)	

	1995	1980	1965

EDUCATION

SCHOOL AGE IN SCHOOL

	1995	1980	1965
PRIMARY	34%	26%	16%
SECONDARY	9%	8%	1%
HIGHER	n/a	1%	0

FEMALES IN SCHOOL

	1995	1980	1965
PRIMARY	39%	36%	10%
SECONDARY	34%	29%	0.5%

	1995	1980	1965
ADULT ILLITERACY M/F	61/77%	77.1/89.0% (85)	96/99.5%

COMMUNICATIONS

	1995	1980	1965
RATE OF NEWSPAPERS	4	1	0.5 (62)
RATE OF RADIOS	44	15	10
RATE OF TELEVISIONS	1	0	n/a

Source: CIA, The World Factbook, 1997; ILO, World Labour Report, 1997; UN, Demographic Yearbook, 1997; UN, Statistical Yearbook, 1996; World Bank, World Development Indicators, 1998.

MALTA

A small island nation situated in the Mediterranean less than 100 miles south of Sicily, Malta won its independence from Britain in 1964. With just 376,000 people, Malta has one of the longest recorded histories of any country in the world, having been an outpost of the Greeks, Romans, Arabs, Turks, and British over the past 2,500 years. During World War II, it served as a major German naval base and was bombed repeatedly by the Allies. Since the war, the country has survived economically on businesses like trade, light manufacturing, and tourism, and on illegal smuggling. The population is an ethnic and religious mix of Muslim Arabs and southern European Catholics. The dominant language is Maltese, a language related to Italian, but English is widely spoken. The country's health and educational profiles reflect its geographic position between southern Europe and North Africa. At 6.9 deaths per 1,000 live births, it has a low infant mortality rate, but less than two-thirds of the school-age population attends secondary institutions. Television and radio ownership is high at 745 and 526 units per 1,000 persons respectively, reflecting its moderately wealthy per capita income of $12,000 annually.

	1995	1980	1965
GEOGRAPHY			
AREA (square miles/kilometers)	124/320		
LAND AREA (square miles/kilometers)	124/320		
COASTLINE (miles/kilometers)	87.5/140		
CITIES			
CAPITAL	Valletta	9,144 (93)	
POPULATION			
TOTAL	375,576	n/a	319,620 (57)
DENSITY (per square mile/per square kilometer)	3,029/1,174	n/a	2,578/999
ANNUAL GROWTH	1.01%	1.0%	−0.2%
AGE COHORTS			
0–14	22%	n/a	33%
15–64	67%	n/a	58%
65 AND OVER	11%	n/a	9%
MALE	49%		
FEMALE	51%		
URBAN	89%		
RURAL	11%		

	1995	1980	1965
NET MIGRATION RATE	2.1	n/a	2.4

IDENTITY

ETHNICITY

ARAB	n/a		
SICILIAN	n/a		
NORMAN	n/a		
SPANISH	n/a		
ITALIAN	n/a		
ENGLISH	n/a		

LANGUAGE

MALTESE	n/a		
ENGLISH	n/a		

RELIGION

ROMAN CATHOLIC	98%		

VITAL STATISTICS

BIRTHS

BIRTH RATE	14.8	14.2 (85)	16.8
INFANT MORTALITY RATE	6.9	15.6	30.3
LIFE EXPECTANCY AT BIRTH	78.1	72.9	69

MARRIAGES

MARRIAGE RATE	7	7.1 (85)	6.7
AVERAGE AGE AT MARRIAGE M/F	n/a	26.2/22.1	n/a

DEATHS

DEATH RATE	6.8	7.4 (85)	9

HOUSEHOLDS

NUMBER	n/a	104,742 (85)	76,620 (57)
AVERAGE SIZE	n/a	3.3	4.1

ECONOMICS AND LABOR

GDP PER CAPITA US$	$12,000		

	1995	1980	1965
LABOR FORCE M/F (thousands)	96.0/34.3 (91)		
AGRICULTURE	2.9/0.4		
MINING	0.6/0.0		
MANUFACTURING	25.0/10.9		
UTILITIES	1.8/0.1		
CONSTRUCTION	5.8/0.1		
TRADE/FOOD/TOURISM	9.9/3.7		
TRANSPORT/COMMUNICATIONS	8.4/1.1		
FINANCE/INSURANCE/REAL ESTATE	2.9/2.1		
SOCIAL AND PERSONAL SERVICES	38.9/15.9		
UNEMPLOYMENT			
TOTAL	4.5% (93)		
UNION DENSITY	57.90%		

TRANSPORT

	1995	1980	1965
JOURNEYS (by transport mode)			
AIR PASSENGER TRIPS (thousands)	1,010.0 (94)		
VEHICLES (thousands)			
CARS	170.6	66.2	22.1
COMMERCIAL VEHICLES	55.7	14.3	7.2

HEALTH AND HEALTH CARE

	1995	1980	1965
RATE OF PHYSICIANS	n/a	n/a	0.9 (60)
RATE OF HOSPITAL BEDS	n/a	n/a	9.3
TOTAL DEATHS	2,711		
AIDS/HIV CASES	37	29 (93)	

EDUCATION

	1995	1980	1965
SCHOOL AGE IN SCHOOL			
PRIMARY	n/a	100%	88%
SECONDARY	n/a	66%	27%
HIGHER	n/a	2.70%	3.1%
FEMALES IN SCHOOL			
PRIMARY	n/a	96%	91%
SECONDARY	n/a	60%	23%
HIGHER	n/a	1.3%	3.7% (70)

	1995	1980	1965
COMMUNICATIONS			
RATE OF NEWSPAPERS	150	185	n/a
RATE OF RADIOS	526	509	235
RATE OF TELEVISIONS	745	623	81

Source: CIA, *The World Factbook, 1997;* ILO, *World Labour Report, 1997;* UN, *Demographic Yearbook, 1997;* UN, *Statistical Yearbook, 1996;* World Bank, *World Development Indicators, 1998.*

MARSHALL ISLANDS

One of the newest nations in the world, the Marshall Islands became independent from its status as a U.S.-administered U.N. trusteeship in 1986. It is also one of the most dispersed nations. Scattered across over half a million miles of the western Pacific Ocean, just north of the equator, the roughly 70 square miles of territory, consisting of dozens of small coral-ringed islands, has a population of 58,000. Ethnically, the population is Micronesian, most of whom practice various forms of Protestant Christianity. The growth rate on the islands is high, at about 3.9 percent annually, and just over half the population is under the age of 15. A democratic republic, based on a federal system, the Marshall Islands economy depends almost entirely on tourism and fishing. An unbalanced diet and lack of available health care services on the isolated islands result in a high infant mortality rate of 46.9 per 1,000 live births and a relatively short life expectancy of 63.8 years.

	1995	1980
GEOGRAPHY		
AREA (square miles/kilometers)	70/181	
LAND AREA (square miles/kilometers)	70/181	
COASTLINE (miles/kilometers)	231/370	
CITIES		
CAPITAL	Majuro	
POPULATION		
TOTAL	58,363	
DENSITY (per square mile/square kilometer)	834/322	
CHANGE	3.85%	
GROWTH/SHRINKAGE		
AGE COHORTS		
0–14	51%	
15–64	47%	
65 AND OVER	2%	
URBAN	69%	
RURAL	31%	
NET MIGRATION RATE	0	

	1995	1980

IDENTITY

ETHNICITY
MICRONESIAN   n/a

LANGUAGE
ENGLISH   n/a
MARSHALLESE DIALECTS   n/a
JAPANESE   n/a

RELIGION
CHRISTIAN (mostly Protestant)   n/a

VITAL STATISTICS

BIRTHS
BIRTH RATE   n/a   45.8
INFANT MORTALITY RATE   n/a   46.9
LIFE EXPECTANCY AT BIRTH   n/a   63.8

MARRIAGES
MARRIAGE RATE   n/a   3.1
DIVORCE RATE   n/a   0.3

DEATHS
DEATH RATE   n/a   7.3

ECONOMICS AND LABOR

GDP PER CAPITA US$ $1,680

TRANSPORT

JOURNEYS (by transport mode)
AIR PASSENGER TRIPS (thousands)   42 (94)

	1995	1980
HEALTH AND HEALTH CARE		
TOTAL DEATHS	213 (94)	n/a
AIDS/HIV CASES	2	2 (93)

Source: CIA, *The World Factbook, 1997;* ILO, *World Labour Report, 1997;* UN, *Demographic Yearbook, 1997;* UN, *Statistical Yearbook, 1996;* World Bank, *World Development Indicators, 1998.*

MAURITANIA

A vast, sparsely populated country on the Atlantic coast of northwestern Africa, Mauritania is surrounded by Moroccan-occupied Western Sahara and Algeria to the north, Mali to the east and south, and Senegal on the southwest. The country covers some 398,000 square miles and, with a population of 2.34 million, has a density of just 6 persons per square mile, one of the lowest rates in Africa and the world. Much of the country is covered by the Sahara Desert, though the south is part of the semidesert Sahel region. Repeated droughts in recent years have caused the Sahara to spread south into the Sahel, resulting in diminished cropland and pasturage, which has forced hundreds of thousands of rural residents to seek shelter in the rapidly expanding capital of Nouakchott. Mauritania suffers from some of the lowest social indexes in the developing world. Though its infant mortality rate has fallen sharply from 187 in 1980 to 81.7 in 1995, it remains high. Similarly, life expectancy has climbed from 40 to 49 since 1965, but is still low even by developing world standards. There was about one physician for every 10,000 persons in 1995, and most of these were in the capital. Just 15 percent of the school-age population attends secondary institutions, though the primary school rate has climbed from just 8 percent at independence from France in 1960 to 78 percent in 1995.

	1995	1980	1965
GEOGRAPHY			
AREA (square miles/kilometers)	397,954/1,030,700		
LAND AREA (square miles/kilometers)	397,838/1,030,400		
COASTLINE (miles/kilometers)	471/754		
CITIES			
CAPITAL	Nouakchott	n/a	134,986 (76)	n/a
POPULATION			
TOTAL	2,336,048	1,419,939 (76)	1,050,000
DENSITY (per square mile/square kilometer)	6/2	4/1	3/1
ANNUAL GROWTH	3.17%	3%	1.6%
AGE COHORTS			
0–14	48%		
15–64	49%		
65 AND OVER	3%		
MALE	50%		
FEMALE	50%		

	1995	**1980**	**1965**
URBAN	n/a	22.8% (77)	n/a
RURAL	n/a	77.20%	n/a
NET MIGRATION RATE	0		

IDENTITY

ETHNICITY
MAUR/BLACK	40%
MAUR	30%
BLACK	30%

LANGUAGE
HASANIYA (Arabic)	n/a
PULAR	n/a
SONINKE	n/a
WOLOF	n/a

RELIGION
MUSLIM	100%

VITAL STATISTICS

	1995	**1980**	**1965**
BIRTHS			
BIRTH RATE	46.9	50.1	45
INFANT MORTALITY RATE	81.7	187	191
LIFE EXPECTANCY AT BIRTH	49	44	40
DEATHS			
DEATH RATE	15.2	20.9	29

ECONOMICS AND LABOR

GDP PER CAPITA US$ $1,200

LABOR FORCE M/F (thousands)
AGRICULTURE	49/63
INDUSTRY	16/4
SERVICES	35/34

UNION DENSITY 2.7%

POVERTY
UNDER $1/DAY	31.4% (88)
UNDER $2/DAY	68.4%

	1995	1980	1965

TRANSPORT

JOURNEYS (by transport mode)

AIR PASSENGER TRIPS (thousands)	216 (94)		

VEHICLES (thousands)

CARS	8	n/a	0.1
COMMERCIAL VEHICLES	5.7	n/a	0.2

HEALTH AND HEALTH CARE

RATE OF PHYSICIANS	0.1	n/a	0 (60)
RATE OF HOSPITAL BEDS	0.7	n/a	0.2 (60)
TOTAL DEATHS	35,509		

HEALTH INDICATORS

LOW-BIRTH-WEIGHT BABIES	11%		
CHILD MALNUTRITION	48%		
TUBERCULOSIS INCIDENCE RATE	2.2		

HEALTH CARE

MEASLES IMMUNIZATION	53%		

AIDS/HIV CASES	130	90 (93)	

EDUCATION

SCHOOL AGE IN SCHOOL

PRIMARY	78%	37%	8% (60)
SECONDARY	15%	11%	0.4% (60)
HIGHER	4%	n/a	n/a

FEMALES IN SCHOOL

PRIMARY	45%	35%	3% (60)
SECONDARY	36%	21%	0% (60)

ADULT ILLITERACY M/F	50/74%		

	1995	1980	1965
COMMUNICATIONS			
RATE OF NEWSPAPERS	0.5	n/a	n/a
RATE OF RADIOS	147	97	30
RATE OF TELEVISIONS	23	0	0

Source: CIA, *The World Factbook, 1997;* ILO, *World Labour Report, 1997;* UN, *Demographic Yearbook, 1997;* UN, *Statistical Yearbook, 1996;* World Bank, *World Development Indicators, 1998.*

MAURITIUS

Mauritius is a medium-sized island of 718 square miles—roughly 11 times the size of Washington, D.C.—located in the southern Indian Ocean, about 1,000 miles east of Madagascar. Until its independence from Britain in 1968, Mauritius was largely an agricultural island, with large commercial plantations producing tropical products for the European and Asian markets. But a concerted government effort to develop the island industrially has resulted both in a dramatic shift in the economic base of the island and in the per capita income, which in 1995 was $9,600 annually, the highest in all of Africa, of which the island is considered a part politically. In 1994, more than 100,000 of the 300,000-person workforce—out of a total population of 1.14 million—was involved in manufacturing, mostly textiles and light electronics. This new-found prosperity is reflected in dramatically improved social indexes. Between 1965 and 1995, the infant mortality rate fell from 64.2 to 17.2 per 1,000 live births. Meanwhile the number of physicians quadrupled. And while just 28 percent of the school-age population attended secondary institutions in 1965, that rate had grown to 62 percent thirty years later.

	1995	1980	1965
GEOGRAPHY			
AREA (square miles/kilometers)	718/1,860		
LAND AREA (square miles/kilometers)	718/1,860		
COASTLINE (miles/kilometers)	111/177		
CITIES			
CAPITAL	Port Louis 144,766 (94)		
POPULATION			
TOTAL	1,140,256	851,334 (72)	681,619 (62)
DENSITY (per square mile/square kilometer)	1,588/613	1,186/458	949/366
ANNUAL GROWTH	1.23%	1.3%	2.8%
AGE COHORTS			
0–14	27%	n/a	45%
15–64	67%	n/a	52%
65 AND OVER	6%	n/a	3%
MALE	50%		
FEMALE	50%		
URBAN	43.6%	42.8%	n/a
RURAL	56.4%	57.2%	n/a

	1995	**1980**	**1965**
NET MIGRATION RATE	0	n/a	0

IDENTITY

ETHNICITY
INDO-MAURITIAN	68%
CREOLE	27%
SINO-MAURITIAN	3%
FRANCO-MAURITIAN	2%

LANGUAGE
ENGLISH	n/a
CREOLE	n/a
FRENCH	n/a
HINDIN	n/a
URDU	n/a
HAKKA	n/a
BOJPOORI	n/a

RELIGION
HINDU	52%
ROMAN CATHOLIC	26%
MUSLIM	16.6%
PROTESTANT	2.3%

VITAL STATISTICS

BIRTHS
	1995	1980	1965
BIRTH RATE	19 (94)	18.8	35.3
URBAN BIRTH RATE	18.9		
RURAL BIRTH RATE	20.1		
INFANT MORTALITY RATE	17.2	23.8	64.2
LIFE EXPECTANCY AT BIRTH	70.5	67.8	60.1

MARRIAGES
	1995	1980	1965
MARRIAGE RATE	10.5	11.3	5.5
AVERAGE AGE AT MARRIAGE M/F	23.8/28.2 (90)		
DIVORCE RATE	0.7	0.5	0.2

DEATHS
	1995	1980	1965
DEATH RATE	6.7	6.8	8.8

	1995	1980	1965

HOUSEHOLDS

	1995	1980	1965
NUMBER	236,100 (90)	n/a	138,368 (62)
AVERAGE SIZE	4.5	n/a	4.9
TYPE OF HOUSEHOLD			
FEMALE HEADED	17.6%		
SINGLE	3.4%		
MARRIED	75.5%		
WIDOWED	14.0%		
DIVORCED/SEPARATED	4.0%		

ECONOMICS AND LABOR

	1995	1980	1965
GDP PER CAPITA US$	$9,600		
LABOR FORCE M/F (thousands)	188.6/103.8 (94)		
AGRICULTURE	30.0/11.7		
MINING	0.1/0.1		
MANUFACTURING	41.9/62.8		
UTILITIES	3.4/0.2		
CONSTRUCTION	13.2/0.2		
TRADE/FOOD/TOURISM	17.7/5.7		
TRANSPORT/COMMUNICATIONS	12.5/1.7		
FINANCE/INSURANCE/REAL ESTATE	8.1/3.4		
SOCIAL AND PERSONAL SERVICES	58.7/18.1		
UNION DENSITY	25.9%		

TRANSPORT

	1995	1980	1965
JOURNEYS (mode of transport)			
RAILROAD PASSENGER TRIPS	636 (94)		
(millions of miles/kilometers)			
VEHICLES (thousands)			
CARS	53.8	31.2	13.7
COMMERCIAL VEHICLES	11.1	10.1	5.3

HEALTH AND HEALTH CARE

	1995	1980	1965
RATE OF PHYSICIANS	0.8	0.5	0.2 (60)
RATE OF HOSPITAL BEDS	3.1	3.1	4.7 (60)
TOTAL DEATHS	7,465		

	1995	1980	1965
HEALTH INDICATORS			
PREGNANT WOMEN WITH ANEMIA	29%		
LOW-BIRTH-WEIGHT BABIES	8%		
CHILD MALNUTRITION	15%		
SMOKING PREVALENCE M/F	47/4%		
TUBERCULOSIS INCIDENCE RATE	.50		
HEALTH CARE			
ACCESS TO SAFE WATER	98%		
ACCESS TO SANITATION	100%		
MEASLES IMMUNIZATION	85%		
AIDS/HIV CASES	27	18 (93)	

EDUCATION

	1995	1980	1965
SCHOOL AGE IN SCHOOL			
PRIMARY	107%	93%	102%
SECONDARY	62%	50%	28%
HIGHER	6%	1%	0.1%
FEMALES IN SCHOOL			
PRIMARY	49%	49%	97%
SECONDARY	51%	48%	19%
ADULT ILLITERACY M/F	13/21%	11.3/22.9% (85)	

COMMUNICATIONS

	1995	1980	1965
RATE OF NEWSPAPERS	74	83	113
RATE OF RADIOS	366	269	176
RATE OF TELEVISIONS	222	95	7

Source: CIA, *The World Factbook, 1997;* ILO, *World Labour Report, 1997;* UN, *Demographic Yearbook, 1997;* UN, *Statistical Yearbook, 1996;* World Bank, *World Development Indicators, 1998.*

MEXICO

The largest Spanish-speaking country in the world—and the second largest country by population in Latin America, after Brazil—Mexico is situated in southern North America. It is bordered on the north by the United States and the south by Guatemala and Belize. Its roughly 16,000 miles of coastline border on the Pacific to the west and on the Gulf of Mexico and the Caribbean to the east. Politically, Mexico has largely been a one-party state under the rule of the Institutional Revolutionary Party since 1929, though recent advances by left- and right-wing parties have challenged the dominant party's rule. During much of this century, the economy was heavily regulated by the government. But in the past decade or so, a liberalization has occurred, cre-

ating enormous discrepancies in wealth and large fluctuations in the business cycle. This economic change has produced numerous rebellions among the largely Indian population of certain areas, the largest of which is the Zapatista revolt in the southern state of Chiapas. Despite its corruption, the government has made significant advances in education and health in recent decades, funded in part by revenues from the vast state-owned oil industry. The number of physicians, for example, has climbed from just 1 for every 1,800 residents to 1 for every 700, though most of these are in urban areas. Indeed, massive migration to the country's capital—Mexico City—is expected to turn that urban agglomeration into the largest in the world in a few years.

Migration

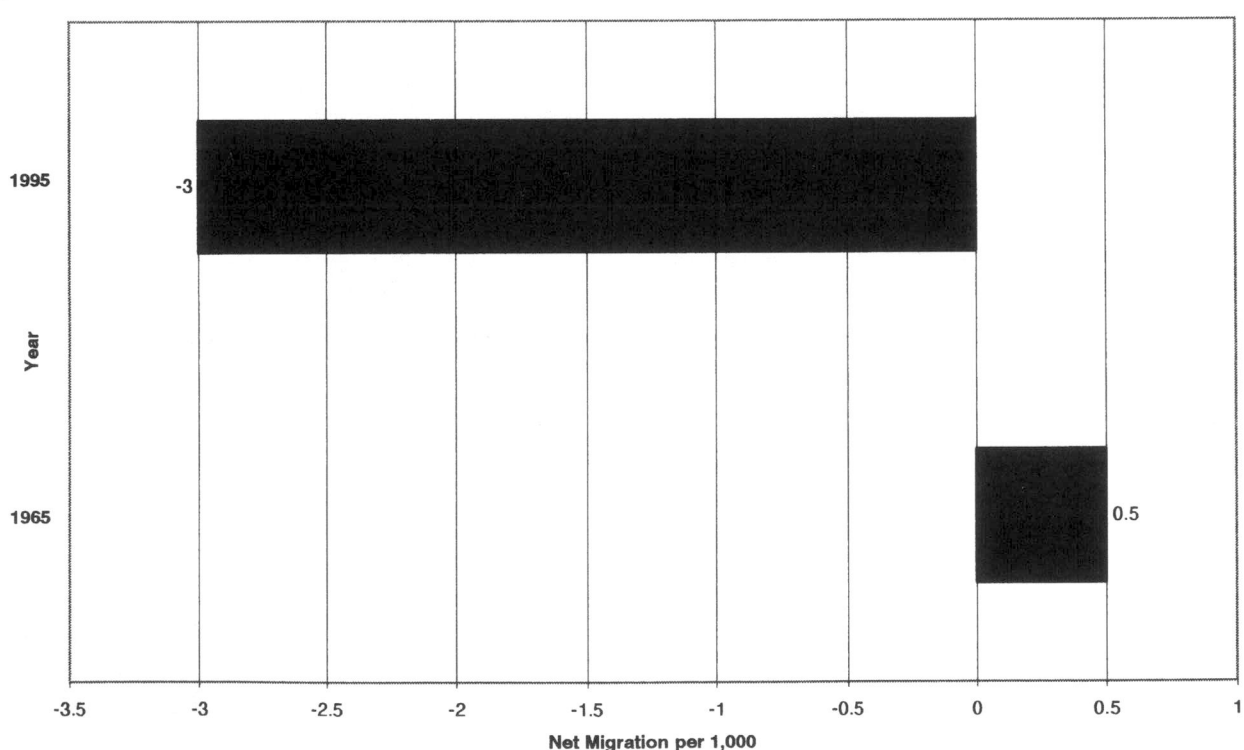

By North American standards, Mexico has always been a poor country. But, as demographers understand, out-migration has less to do with poverty than with economic change. Relatively stable economically until the reforms of the 1970s, Mexico's net migration rate was near zero in 1965. By 1995, it had risen to 3 persons out of every 1,000, the vast majority of these were headed for the United States.

Industry

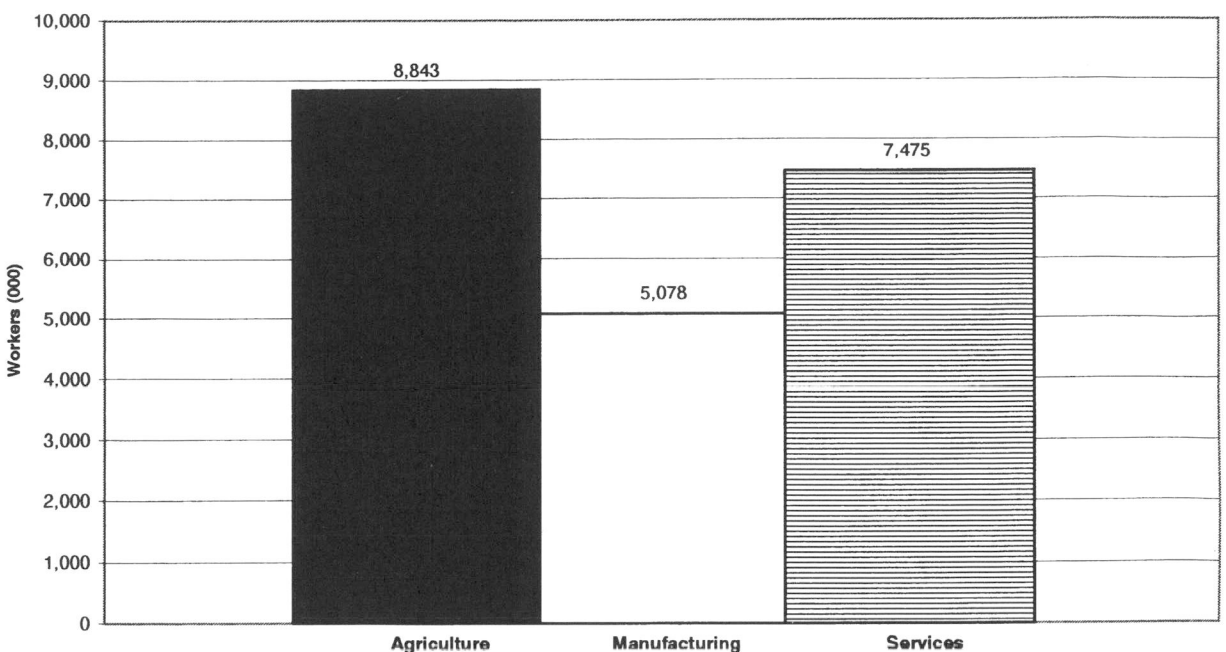

Once a predominantly agricultural country, Mexico has undergone rapid industrialization in the post-war era, and especially since the opening up of its markets under the North American Free Trade Agreement in the past decade. These changes are reflected in the increased number of workers involved in the service and manufacturing sectors.

CHRONOLOGY

1968   Mexico hosts Summer Olympics; hundreds of pro-democracy protesters killed by police and military.

1976   Vast new oil discoveries made in states of Chiapas and Tabasco.

1983   Debt crisis escalates; Mexico renegotiates loans with international lending institutions.

1985   Massive earthquake kills over 7,000 in Mexico City.

1988   President Carlos Salinas de Gortari wins presidency in disputed election.

1992   Mexico joins Canada and the United States in North American Free Trade Agreement (NAFTA).

1994   NAFTA goes into effect; Zapatista guerrilla movement seizes towns in southern state of Chiapas; Ernesto Zedillo elected president.

1996   Cuautemoc Cardenas, leftist opposition politician, wins election as mayor of Mexico City.

	1995	1980	1965

GEOGRAPHY

AREA (square miles/kilometers)   761,602/1,972,550
LAND AREA (square miles/kilometers)   742,486/1,923,040
COASTLINE (miles/kilometers)   5,831/9,330

CITIES

		1995	1980	1965
CAPITAL	Mexico City	8,235,744 (90)		
MAJOR CITIES	Guadalajara	2,870,417	1,626,152	
	Nezahualcoyotl	1,255,456		
	Ecatepec de Morelos	1,218,315		
	Monterrey	1,069,238	1,084,696	

POPULATION

	1995	1980	1965
TOTAL	95,772,462	66,846,833	44,145,000 (66)
DENSITY (per square mile/square kilometer)	129/50	90/35	59/23
ANNUAL GROWTH	n/a	2.5%	n/a
AGE COHORTS			
0–14	36%	n/a	46%
15–64	59%	n/a	51%
65 AND OVER	5%	n/a	3%
MALE	49%		
FEMALE	51%		
URBAN	n/a	66.3%	n/a
RURAL	n/a	33.7%	n/a
NET MIGRATION RATE	−3	n/a	0.5

IDENTITY

ETHNICITY

	1995
MESTIZO	60%
AMERINDIAN	30%
CAUCASIAN	9%

LANGUAGE

	1995
SPANISH	n/a
MAYAN DIALECTS	n/a

	1995	1980	1965
RELIGION			
ROMAN CATHOLIC	89%		
PROTESTANT	6%		

VITAL STATISTICS

	1995	1980	1965
BIRTHS			
BIRTH RATE	26.2	33.9	45
URBAN BIRTH RATE	20.5 (91)		
RURAL BIRTH RATE	11.7		
INFANT MORTALITY RATE	25	53	60.7
ABORTION RATE	10.5 (94)		
LIFE EXPECTANCY AT BIRTH	73.7	64	56.6
MARRIAGES			
MARRIAGE RATE	7.2	7.2	6.8
DIVORCE RATE	0.4	0.4	0.6
DEATHS			
DEATH RATE	4.6	7.1	11

HOUSEHOLDS

	1995	1980	1965
NUMBER	16,202,846 (90)	n/a	6,738,605 (60)
AVERAGE SIZE	5	n/a	5.5
TYPE OF HOUSEHOLD			
FEMALE HEADED	17.3%		

ECONOMICS AND LABOR

	1995
GDP PER CAPITA US$	$7,700
LABOR FORCE M/F (thousands)	22,748.0/10,085.0 (93)
AGRICULTURE	7,721/1,122
MINING	165/6
MANUFACTURING	3,372/1,706
UTILITIES	87/12
CONSTRUCTION	1,816/63
TRADE/FOOD/TOURISM	3,646/3,246
TRANSPORT/COMMUNICATIONS	1,243/119
FINANCE/INSURANCE/REAL ESTATE	657/423
SOCIAL AND PERSONAL SERVICES	3,837/3,368

	1995	1980	1965
UNEMPLOYMENT			
TOTAL	3.8% (94)		
UNION DENSITY	31%		
POVERTY			
UNDER $1/DAY	14.9% (92)		
UNDER $2/DAY	40%		

TRANSPORT

	1995	1980	1965
JOURNEYS (by transport mode)			
AIR PASSENGER TRIPS (thousands)	18,791 (94)		
VEHICLES (thousands)			
CARS	8,451.1	4,241.40	771.1
COMMERCIAL VEHICLES	3,839.4	1,574.80	419.4

HEALTH AND HEALTH CARE

	1995	1980	1965
RATE OF PHYSICIANS	1.3	0.9	0.6 (60)
RATE OF HOSPITAL BEDS	1.2		
TOTAL DEATHS	419,074 (94)		
HEALTH INDICATORS			
PREGNANT WOMEN WITH ANEMIA	14%		
LOW-BIRTH-WEIGHT BABIES	12%		
CHILD MALNUTRITION	14%		
SMOKING PREVALENCE M/F	38/14%		
TUBERCULOSIS INCIDENCE RATE	.60		
HEALTH CARE	83%		
ACCESS TO SAFE WATER	66%		
ACCESS TO SANITATION	90%		
MEASLES IMMUNIZATION			
AIDS/HIV CASES	27,639	19,281 (93)	

EDUCATION

	1995	1980	1965
SCHOOL AGE IN SCHOOL			
PRIMARY	115%	120.0%	104% (70)
SECONDARY	n/a	4.7%	22.0%
HIGHER	n/a	14.1%	5.9%

	1995	**1980**	**1965**
FEMALES IN SCHOOL			
PRIMARY	n/a	119%	92%
SECONDARY	n/a	45%	17%
ADULT ILLITERACY M/F	n/a	13.8/20.1%	n/a

COMMUNICATIONS

	116	124	116
RATE OF NEWSPAPERS	255	134	187
RATE OF RADIOS	150	57	41
RATE OF TELEVISIONS			

Source: CIA, The World Factbook, 1997; ILO, World Labour Report, 1997; UN, Demographic Yearbook, 1997; UN, Statistical Yearbook, 1996; World Bank, World Development Indicators, 1998.

MICRONESIA, FEDERATED STATES OF

Scattered across about 1 million square miles of the western Pacific, just north of the equator, the four Federated States of Micronesia are among the most isolated points of land in the world. Largely of Micronesian and Polynesian descent, the 135,000 persons of Micronesia live on islands at distances of hundreds of miles from the each other. Freed from a U.S.-administered, U.N. trusteeship in 1986, the country remains in free association with the United States, using the latter country's postal service and money. The economy is almost entirely dependent on tourism and fishing, and has a per capita income of $1,700 annually, though many of the residents in outlying islands exist largely outside the money economy. While a high birth rate of 27.9 per 1,000 persons contributes heavily to the 3.3 percent annual rate of population growth, so too does the net migration rate of 11 per 1,000 persons.

	1995	1980
GEOGRAPHY		
AREA (square miles/kilometers)	271/702	
LAND AREA (square miles/kilometers)	271/702	
COASTLINE (miles/kilometers)	3,820/6,112	
CITIES		
CAPITAL	Palikir	
POPULATION		
TOTAL	135,377	
DENSITY (per square mile/square kilometer)	499/193	
ANNUAL GROWTH	3.34%	
AGE COHORTS		
0–14	n/a	
15–64	35%	
65 AND OVER	n/a	
MALE	51%	
FEMALE	49%	
NET MIGRATION	11.6	

	1995	1980

IDENTITY

ETHNICITY
MICRONESIAN   n/a
POLYNESIAN   n/a

LANGUAGE   n/a
ENGLISH   n/a
TRUKESE   n/a
POHNPEIAN   n/a
YAPESE   n/a
KOSREAN   n/a

RELIGION   n/a
ROMAN CATHOLIC   50%
PROTESTANT   47%

VITAL STATISTICS

BIRTH
BIRTH RATE   27.9
INFANT MORTALITY RATE   35.8
LIFE EXPECTANCY AT BIRTH   68

DEATH
DEATH RATE   6.2

ECONOMICS AND LABOR

GDP PER CAPITA US$ $1,700

HEALTH AND HEALTH CARE

AIDS/HIV CASES   2   2 (93)

Source: CIA, *The World Factbook, 1997;* ILO, *World Labour Report, 1997;* UN, *Demographic Yearbook, 1997;* UN, *Statistical Yearbook, 1996;* World Bank, *World Development Indicators, 1998.*

MOLDOVA

A constituent republic of the former Soviet Union, Moldova has been an independent country since 1991.[1] Tucked between Romania on the west and the Ukraine on the other three sides, Moldova covers 13,000 square miles and has a population of 4.46 million persons. Largely Moldovan/Romanian and Ukrainian, the vast majority of the country's citizens are Eastern Orthodox. Like many other republics in the former Soviet Union, Moldova has a slow rate of population growth. In 1995, the rate was just 0.2 percent annually. The net migration rate was −2.8 persons per 1,000 annually. With nearly one-third of the population living on less than $2 per day, the per capita income is just $2,300, quite low by European standards. Still, the country enjoys relatively high social indexes. Approximately 25 percent of the school-age population attends university and there are approximately 1 physician for every 300 citizens and 1 hospital for every 80 citizens, although many hospitals and clinics have suffered from a shortage of supplies since the country achieved its independence from the Soviet Union.

	1995	1980
GEOGRAPHY		
AREA (square miles/kilometers)	13,012/33,700	
LAND AREA (square miles/kilometers)	13,012/33,700	
COASTLINE (miles/kilometers)	Landlocked	
CITIES		
CAPITAL	Chişinău	667,100 (92)
MAJOR CITIES	Tiraspol	186,200
	Beltsy	159,000
	Bendery	132,700
POPULATION		
TOTAL	4,463,847	
DENSITY (per square mile/square kilometer)	343/132	
CHANGE	0.18%	
GROWTH/SHRINKAGE	0.2%	
AGE COHORTS		
0–14	26%	
15–64	64%	
65 AND OVER	10%	
MALE	47%	
FEMALE	53%	

	1995	**1980**
URBAN	46.9% (92)	
RURAL	53.1% (92)	
NET MIGRATION RATE	−2.8	

IDENTITY

ETHNICITY

MOLDOVIAN/ROMANIAN	64.5%
UKRAINIAN	13.8%
RUSSIAN	13.0%
GAGAUZ	3.5%
BULGARIAN	2.0%
JEWISH	1.5%

LANGUAGE

MOLDOVAN	n/a
RUSSIAN	n/a
GAGAUZ	n/a

RELIGION

EASTERN ORTHODOX	98.5%
JEWISH	1.5%

VITAL STATISTICS

BIRTHS

BIRTH RATE	16.3
URBAN BIRTH RATE	14.2 (92)
RURAL BIRTH RATE	17.6
INFANT MORTALITY RATE	47.6
ABORTION RATE	746.1 (92)
LIFE EXPECTANCY AT BIRTH	65.1

MARRIAGES

MARRIAGE RATE	9
AVERAGE AGE AT MARRIAGE M/F	23.8/21.1 (89)
DIVORCE RATE	3.2

DEATHS

DEATH RATE	11.8

	1995	**1980**

HOUSEHOLDS

NUMBER	1,143,423 (89)	
URBAN	520,712	
RURAL	622,711	

AVERAGE SIZE	3.4	
URBAN	3.3	
RURAL	3.5	

ECONOMICS AND LABOR

GDP PER CAPITA US$	$2,300	

LABOR FORCE (thousands)	2,050 (92)	
AGRICULTURE	820	
MANUFACTURING	394	
UTILITIES	14	
CONSTRUCTION	120	
TRADE/FOOD/TOURISM	111	
TRANSPORT/COMMUNICATIONS	102	
FINANCE/INSURANCE/REAL ESTATE	9	
SOCIAL AND PERSONAL SERVICES	422	

UNEMPLOYMENT		
TOTAL	1.1 (94)	

POVERTY		
UNDER $1/DAY	6.8 (92)	
UNDER $2/DAY	30.6	

TRANSPORT

JOURNEYS (by transport mode)		
RAILROAD PASSENGER TRIPS	1,661 (93)	
(millions of miles/kilometers)		
AIR PASSENGER TRIPS (thousands)	312 (94)	

VEHICLES		
PRIVATE CARS	169.4 (94)	
COMMERCIAL VEHICLES	7.8	

	1995	**1980**

HEALTH AND HEALTH CARE

RATE OF PHYSICIANS	3.6	3.1
RATE OF HOSPITAL BEDS	12.2	12
TOTAL DEATHS	52,153 (94)	
HEALTH INDICATORS		
PREGNANT WOMEN WITH ANEMIA	50%	
TUBERCULOSIS INCIDENCE RATE	.70	
HEALTH CARE		
ACCESS TO SANITATION	50%	
MEASLES IMMUNIZATION	98%	
AIDS/HIV CASES	6	4 (93)

EDUCATION

SCHOOL AGE IN SCHOOL		
PRIMARY	94%	83%
SECONDARY	80%	78%
HIGHER	25%	30%
FEMALES IN SCHOOL		
PRIMARY	49%	49%
SECONDARY	51%	51%

COMMUNICATIONS

RATE OF NEWSPAPERS	47	

FOOTNOTE
1. Part of Soviet Union until 1991.

Source: CIA, *The World Factbook, 1997*; ILO, *World Labour Report, 1997*; UN, *Demographic Yearbook, 1997*; UN, *Statistical Yearbook, 1996*; World Bank, *World Development Indicators, 1998*.

MONACO

Situated on the French Mediterranean coast, Monaco is a tiny principality just over 1 square mile in territory, part of it dredged out as landfill. Largely urban, Monaco has over 31,000 citizens for a density of 21,000 persons per square mile, among the highest of any country in the world. Utilizing France for its money supply and other services, Monaco relies primarily on earnings from its casino and tourism. Most of the population speaks French, in the local Monaco dialect.

The country enjoys relatively high indexes for health and education, much like its neighbor France. The infant mortality rate is 6.9 per 1,000 live births, which climbed from 3.7 in 1980. Because of the small cohort upon which this rate is based, the fluctuation may not be statistically significant. The prosperity of the country—it has a per capita income of $25,000 annually—is reflected in the high rate of television ownership, at nearly one set per person in 1995.

	1995	**1980**	**1965**
GEOGRAPHY			
AREA (square miles/kilometers)	0.7/1.9		
LAND AREA (square miles/kilometers)	0.7/1.9		
COASTLINE (miles/kilometers)	2.6/4.1		
CITIES			
CAPITAL	Monaco-Ville	n/a	27,063 (82)
POPULATION			
TOTAL	31,719	27,063 (82)	21,783 (62)
DENSITY (per square mile/square kilometer)	45,313/16,694	38,661/14,244	31,119/11,465
ANNUAL GROWTH	0.59%	0.8%	1.1%
AGE COHORTS			
0–14	17%		12.6% (62)
15–64	63%		67.0%
65 AND OVER	20%		19.9%
MALE	47%		
FEMALE	53%		
NET MIGRATION RATE	7.38		

	1995	1980	1965

IDENTITY

ETHNICITY
FRENCH	47%		
MONEGASQUE	16%		
ITALIAN	16%		

LANGUAGE
FRENCH	n/a		
ENGLISH	n/a		
ITALIAN	n/a		
MONEGASQUE	n/a		

RELIGION
ROMAN CATHOLIC	95%		

VITAL STATISTICS

BIRTHS
BIRTH RATE	10.7	19.6 (83)	
INFANT MORTALITY RATE	6.9	3.7	
LIFE EXPECTANCY AT BIRTH	78.1		

MARRIAGES
MARRIAGE RATE	7.3	7.3 (83)	
DIVORCE RATE	1.4	1.4	

DEATHS
DEATH RATE	12.11	16.3 (83)	

ECONOMICS AND LABOR

GDP PER CAPITA US$ $25,000

TRANSPORT

JOURNEYS (by transport mode)
RAILROAD PASSENGER TRIPS	44.0 (94)		
(millions of miles/kilometers)			

	1995	1980	1965

HEALTH AND HEALTH CARE

	1995	1980	1965
AIDS/HIV CASES	37	30 (93)	

COMMUNICATIONS

	1995	1980	1965
RATE OF NEWSPAPERS	258	381	
RATE OF RADIOS	1,013	967	289
RATE OF TELEVISIONS	739	630	596

Source: CIA, The World Factbook, 1997; ILO, World Labour Report, 1997; UN, Demographic Yearbook, 1997; UN, Statistical Yearbook, 1996; World Bank, World Development Indicators, 1998.

MONGOLIA

A vast, sparsely populated country in northeastern Asia, Mongolia is situated between China to the south and the Siberian expanses of the Russian Federation to the north. Dominated topographically by the Gobi Desert, Mongolia covers some 604,000 square miles and has a population of 2.5 million, for a density of 4 persons per square mile, one of the lowest rates in the world. A communist state during most of the post–World War II era, Mongolia became a democracy in the early 1990s, following the lead of its former patron, the Soviet Union. Once a largely nomadic society, depending on pasturage for sustenance, less than one-third of the population in 1995 made its living off the land. In 1989, fully 57 percent of the population lived in urban areas. The economic chaos following the end of communism can be witnessed in declining educational rates. While 91 percent of the school-age population attended secondary institutions in 1980, that rate had dropped to just 59 percent in 1995. At the same time, the infant mortality rate climbed from 53 to 69.7 per 1,000 live births.

	1995	1980	1965
GEOGRAPHY			
AREA (square miles/kilometers)	604,247/1,565,000		
LAND AREA (square miles/kilometers)	604,247/1,565,000		
COASTLINE (miles/kilometers)	Landlocked		
CITIES			
CAPITAL	Ulaanbaatar	n/a	515,100 (87)
POPULATION			
TOTAL	2,496,617	1,594,800 (79)	1,017,100 (63)
DENSITY (per square mile/square kilometer)	4/2	3/1	2/0.6
ANNUAL GROWTH	1.69%	2.6%	3% (56)
AGE COHORTS			
0–14	38%	n/a	30%
15–64	58%	n/a	61%
65 AND OVER	4%	n/a	9%
URBAN	57.1% (89)	51.2	
RURAL	42.9	48.8	
NET MIGRATION RATE	0		

	1995	1980	1965

IDENTITY

ETHNICITY

MONGOL	90%		
KAZAK	4%		
CHINESE	2%		
RUSSIAN	2%		

LANGUAGE

KHALKHA MONGOL	90%		
TURKIC	n/a		
RUSSIAN	n/a		
CHINESE	n/a		

RELIGION

TIBETAN BUDDHIST	n/a		
MUSLIM	n/a		
NONE	n/a		

VITAL STATISTICS

BIRTHS

BIRTH RATE	25.6	35.9	
INFANT MORTALITY RATE	69.7	53	
LIFE EXPECTANCY AT BIRTH	60.8	62	

MARRIAGES

MARRIAGE RATE	7.5	6.1	
DIVORCE RATE	0.5	3.2	

DEATHS

DEATH RATE	8.6	8.5	

ECONOMICS AND LABOR

GDP PER CAPITA US$

	$1,970		

LABOR FORCE M/F

AGRICULTURE	34/30%		
INDUSTRY	23/22%		
SERVICES	44/48%		

	1995	1980	1965

TRANSPORT

JOURNEYS (by transport mode)

RAILROAD PASSENGER TRIPS	579.0 (89)		
(millions of miles/kilometers)			
AIR PASSENGER TRIPS (thousands)	630.0 (94)		

HEALTH AND HEALTH CARE

RATE OF PHYSICIANS	2.7	9.9	0.9 (60)
RATE OF HOSPITAL BEDS	11.5	11.2	8.8
TOTAL DEATHS			

HEALTH INDICATORS

PREGNANT WOMEN WITH ANEMIA	45%		
LOW-BIRTH-WEIGHT BABIES	10%		
CHILD MALNUTRITION	12%		
SMOKING PREVALENCE M/F	40/7%		
TUBERCULOSIS INCIDENCE RATE	1		

HEALTH CARE

MEASLES IMMUNIZATION	85		

EDUCATION

SCHOOL AGE IN SCHOOL

PRIMARY	88%	107%	113% (70)
SECONDARY	59%	91%	87%
HIGHER	15%	n/a	7.6%

FEMALES IN SCHOOL

PRIMARY	51%	49%	
SECONDARY	58%	52%	

COMMUNICATIONS

RATE OF NEWSPAPERS	92	106	88 (63)
RATE OF RADIOS	136	96	n/a
RATE OF TELEVISIONS	41	3	1 (70)

Source: CIA, *The World Factbook, 1997;* ILO, *World Labour Report, 1997;* UN, *Demographic Yearbook, 1997;* UN, *Statistical Yearbook, 1996;* World Bank, *World Development Indicators, 1998.*

MOROCCO

Situated in the northwest corner of Africa, Morocco has coastlines on the Mediterranean to the north and on the Atlantic Ocean to the west. Its land borders include Algeria to the east and Western Sahara to the south. (Since the departure of Spanish colonialists from Western Sahara in 1975, the territory has been illegally occupied by Morocco.) Ethnically, the country is divided between Berbers and Arabs, both of whom are Muslim. The country saw dramatic population growth in the 30 years from 1965 to 1995, climbing from 11.6 million in 1965 to 29.8 million in 1995. Over the same time period, the growth rate dropped from 2.6 percent to 2.1 percent annually

and the percentage of residents under the age of 15 dropped from 46 to 38 percent. Morocco has a migration rate of −1.1 per 1,000 persons, reflecting out-migration to Europe. Morocco has a modernizing economy. Just 120,000 workers out of a labor force of 3.5 million labor in agriculture, while nearly 900,000 are in the manufacturing sector. The number of persons living on incomes of less than $2 daily is just under 20 percent, a relatively low rate for Africa. The growing prosperity of Morocco is reflected in car ownership, which rose from 164,400 in 1965 to 846,600 in 1995.

Population Change

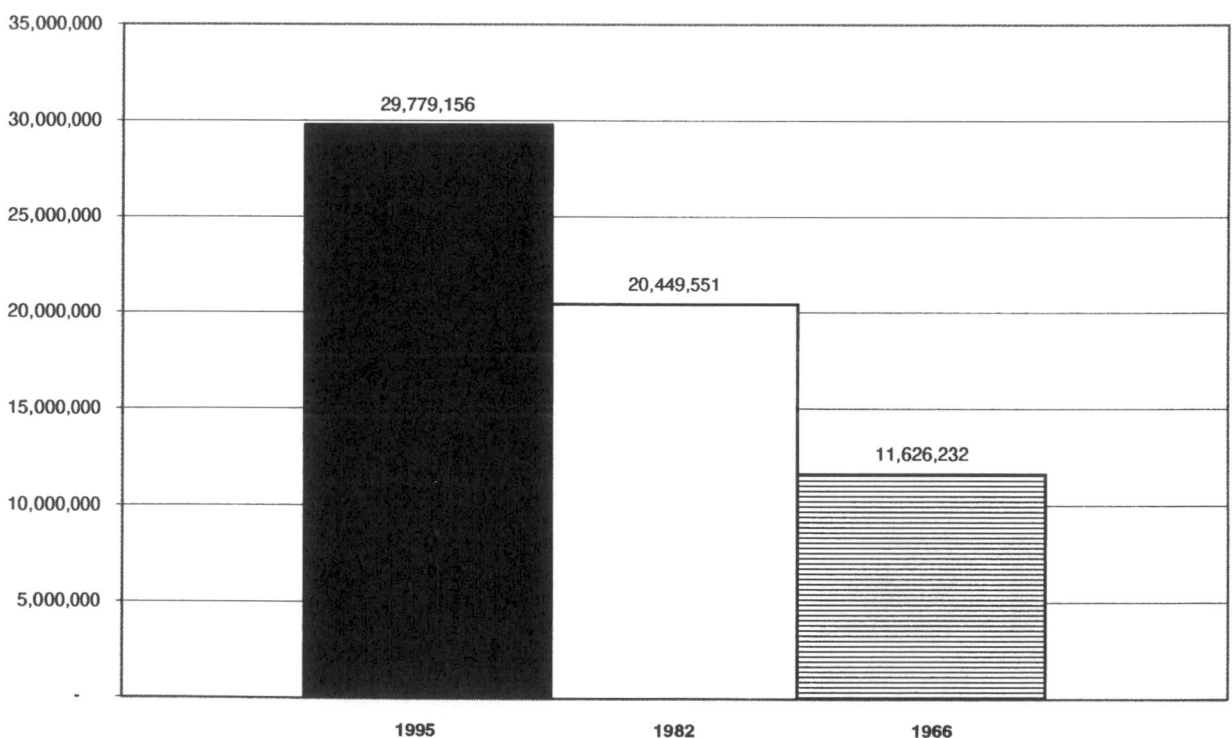

The two charts in this entry display a phenomenon population experts refer to as "demographic lag." That is to say, changes in birth rate often take some time to be reflected in population change. In Morocco's case, the population grew rapidly from about 11.6 million in 1965 to 29.78 million in 1995. Yet age cohorts reflect an aging population as shown in the second chart.

Age Distribution

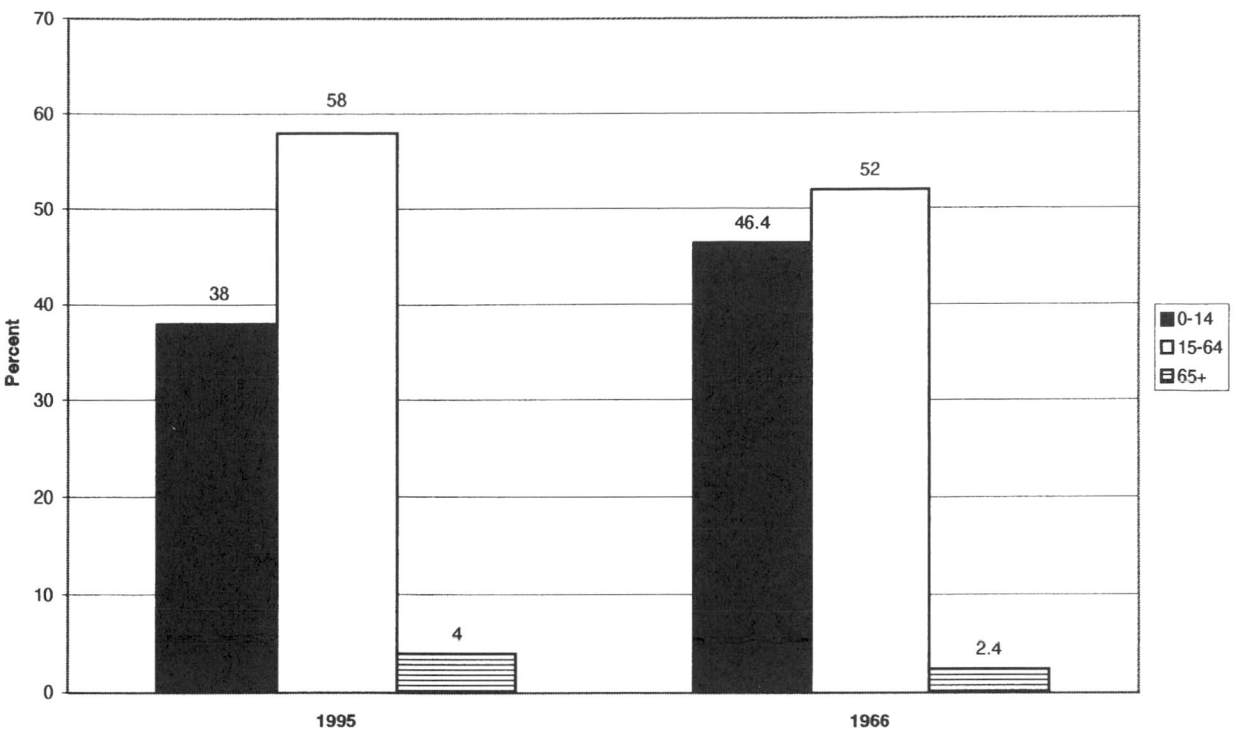

The number of Moroccans under the age of 15 declined from 46 percent to 38 percent between 1966 and 1995, promising slower population growth in the future. But with more young persons in absolute numbers, the population will continue to grow rapidly for some time.

CHRONOLOGY

1961   King Hassan ascends to throne on death of his father.

1975   Tens of thousands of Moroccans cross border to seize northern part of Western Sahara, a colony being abandoned by Spain.

1979   Morocco militarily occupies all of Western Sahara, in face of Polisario independence war.

1986   Hassan becomes second Arab head of state—after Egypt's Anwar Sadat—to welcome Israeli head of state to country.

1990   Morocco becomes first Arab state to condemn Iraqi invasion of Kuwait; joins allied coalition against Baghdad.

1997   U.N. mediators get Morocco to agree to referendum on independence of Western Sahara.

	1995	1980	1965

GEOGRAPHY

AREA (square miles/kilometers)   172,413/446,550
LAND AREA (square miles/kilometers)   172,317/446,300
COASTLINE (miles/kilometers)   1,147/1,835

CITIES
CAPITAL   Rabat   1,220,000 (93)
MAJOR CITIES   Casablanca   2,943,000
                   Marrakech   602,000
                   Fez   564,000
                   Sale   521,000

POPULATION

	1995	1980	1965
TOTAL	29,779,156	20,449,551 (82)	11,626,232 (66)
DENSITY (per square mile/square kilometer)	173/67	119/46	67/26
ANNUAL GROWTH	2.05%	n/a	2.6%
AGE COHORTS			
0–14	38%	n/a	46.4% (66)
15–64	58%	n/a	52.0%
65 AND OVER	4%	n/a	2.4%
URBAN	51.6%	42.1%	
RURAL	48.4%	57.9%	
NET MIGRATION RATE	−1.08	n/a	0

IDENTITY

ETHNICITY
ARAB-BERBER   99.1%
JEWISH   0.2%

LANGUAGE
ARABIC   n/a
FRENCH   n/a

RELIGION
MUSLIM   98.70%
CHRISTIAN   1.10%
JEWISH   0.20%

	1995	**1980**	**1965**

VITAL STATISTICS

BIRTHS

BIRTH RATE	27.4	36.4	46.1
URBAN BIRTH RATE	16.4 (91)		
RURAL BIRTH RATE	16.4		
INFANT MORTALITY RATE	16.4	149	149
LIFE EXPECTANCY AT BIRTH	69.5	58.3	49.6

DEATHS

DEATH RATE	5.8	11.3	18.7

HOUSEHOLDS

NUMBER	n/a	n/a	2,409,750 (60)
AVERAGE SIZE	n/a	n/a	4.8 (60)

ECONOMICS AND LABOR

GDP PER CAPITA US$	$3,000

LABOR FORCE M/F (thousands)	2,733.5/760.8 (92)
AGRICULTURE	104.0/21.1
MINING	43.9/1.5
MANUFACTURING	548.4/340.9
UTILITIES	30.5/2.5
CONSTRUCTION	278.1/3.8
TRADE/FOOD/TOURISM	698.6/62.8
TRANSPORT/COMMUNICATIONS	189.8/10.3
FINANCE/INSURANCE/REAL ESTATE	52.8/23.3
SOCIAL AND PERSONAL SERVICES	779.8/293.0

UNEMPLOYMENT	
TOTAL	16.0% (92)

UNION DENSITY	4.8%

POVERTY	
UNDER $1/DAY	<2% (91)
UNDER $2/DAY	19.6%

	1995	1980	1965

TRANSPORT

	1995	1980	1965
JOURNEYS (by transport mode)			
RAILROAD PASSENGER TRIPS	1,881.0 (94)		
(millions of miles/kilometers)			
AIR PASSENGER TRIPS (thousands)	2,184		
VEHICLES (thousands)			
CARS	846.6	429.6	164.4
COMMERCIAL VEHICLES	317	200.6	65/1

HEALTH AND HEALTH CARE

	1995	1980	1965
RATE OF PHYSICIANS	0.4	0.1	0.1 (60)
RATE OF HOSPITAL BEDS	1.1	1.2	1.6
TOTAL DEATHS	82,729 (92)		
HEALTH INDICATORS			
PREGNANT WOMEN WITH ANEMIA	45%		
LOW-BIRTH-WEIGHT BABIES	9%		
CHILD MALNUTRITION	10%		
SMOKING PREVALENCE M/F	40/9%		
TUBERCULOSIS INCIDENCE RATE	1.25		
HEALTH CARE			
ACCESS TO SAFE WATER	52%		
ACCESS TO SANITATION	40%		
MEASLES IMMUNIZATION	87%		
AIDS/HIV CASES	306	172 (93)	

EDUCATION

	1995	1980	1965
SCHOOL AGE IN SCHOOL			
PRIMARY	83%	83%	60%
SECONDARY	39%	26%	10%
HIGHER	11%	6%	0.7%
FEMALES IN SCHOOL			
PRIMARY	42%	37%	36%
SECONDARY	42%	38%	5%
ADULT ILLITERACY M/F	43/69%	55.2/78.3% (85)	66.4/90.2% (71)

	1995	1980	1965
COMMUNICATIONS			
RATE OF NEWSPAPERS	13	14	17 (63)
RATE OF RADIOS	219	155	60
RATE OF TELEVISIONS	79	46	3

Source: CIA, *The World Factbook, 1997;* ILO, *World Labour Report, 1997;* UN, *Demographic Yearbook, 1997;* UN, *Statistical Yearbook, 1996;* World Bank, *World Development Indicators, 1998.*

MOZAMBIQUE

Nearly twice the size of California, Mozambique is a vast country located along the southeastern coast of Africa. A Portuguese colony until 1975, Mozambique was enveloped almost continuously by war from 1964 until 1992. During the first 11 years, the country was caught up in an anticolonial struggle; from the late 1970s until 1992, it was under attack from rebels supported first by the white minority regime in Rhodesia (now Zimbabwe) and later by South Africa, under the apartheid regime. The nearly constant warfare reduced Mozambique to the poorest country in the world, and the most dependent on international aid: Over half the economy came in the form of aid from outside by the early 1990s. While the revolutionary government after independence was able to lift various social indexes, the war set back progress significantly. For example, though the percentage of young persons in primary school went from 55 percent in 1965 (including Portuguese settlers) to 99 percent in 1980, it had fallen to just 60 percent in 1995. Similarly, though the rate of hospital beds climbed by nearly 20 percent from 1965 to 1980, it fell by 20 percent over the next 15 years.

	1995	1980	1965
GEOGRAPHY			
AREA (square miles/kilometers)	309,494/801,590		
LAND AREA (square miles/kilometers)	302,737/784,090		
COASTLINE (miles/kilometers)	1,544/2,470		
CITIES			
CAPITAL	Maputo	n/a	882,601 (88)
MAJOR CITIES	Beira	n/a	264,202
	Nampula	n/a	182,505
POPULATION			
TOTAL	17,877,927	11,673,725	6,578,604 (60)
DENSITY (per square mile/square kilometer)	59/22	39/15	22/8
ANNUAL GROWTH	2.65%	2.9%	1.3%
AGE COHORTS			
0–14	46%		
15–64	51%		
65 AND OVER	3%		
MALE	49%		
FEMALE	51%		

	1995	**1980**	**1965**
URBAN	n/a	13.2%	
RURAL	n/a	86.8%	
NET MIGRATION RATE	0	n/a	0

IDENTITY

ETHNICITY

SHANGAAN, CHOKWE, MANYIKA, SENA, MAKUA	99.66%		
EUROPEANS	n/a		
EURO-AFRICANS	n/a		
INDIANS	n/a		

LANGUAGE

PORTUGUESE	n/a		
INDIGENOUS DIALECTS	n/a		

RELIGION

INDIGENOUS	50%		
CHRISTIAN	30%		
MUSLIM	20%		

VITAL STATISTICS

BIRTHS

BIRTH RATE	45.5	45.1	
INFANT MORTALITY RATE	125.6	153	
LIFE EXPECTANCY AT BIRTH	44.3	45.3	

MARRIAGES

MARRIAGE RATE	n/a	0.7	
DIVORCE RATE	n/a	0	

DEATHS

DEATH RATE	19	19.7	

ECONOMICS AND LABOR

GDP PER CAPITA US$	$700		
LABOR FORCE (thousands)	201.6 (88)		
AGRICULTURE	16.9		
MINING	4.9		
MANUFACTURING	117		

	1995	1980	1965
UTILITIES	2.9		
CONSTRUCTION	21.5		
TRADE/FOOD/TOURISM	6.4		
TRANSPORT/COMMUNICATIONS	29.3		
FINANCE/INSURANCE/REAL ESTATE			
SOCIAL AND PERSONAL SERVICES	2.7		

TRANSPORT

	1995	1980	1965
JOURNEYS (by transport mode)			
RAILROAD PASSENGER TRIPS	74 (89)		
(millions of miles/kilometers)			
AIR PASSENGER TRIPS (thousands)	221 (94)		
VEHICLES (thousands)			
CARS	84	30.7 (83)	47.3
COMMERCIAL VEHICLES	26.8	8.3	8.5

HEALTH AND HEALTH CARE

	1995	1980	1965
RATE OF PHYSICIANS	n/a	0 (60)	0.1
RATE OF HOSPITAL BEDS	0.9	1.1	0.9
HEALTH INDICATORS			
PREGNANT WOMEN WITH ANEMIA	58%		
LOW-BIRTH-WEIGHT BABIES	20%		
CHILD MALNUTRITION	47%		
SMOKING PREVALENCE M/F			
TUBERCULOSIS INCIDENCE RATE	1.89		
HEALTH CARE			
ACCESS TO SAFE WATER	32%		
ACCESS TO SANITATION	21%		
MEASLES IMMUNIZATION	71%		
AIDS/HIV CASES	2,540	826 (93)	

EDUCATION

	1995	1980	1965
SCHOOL AGE IN SCHOOL			
PRIMARY	60%	99%	55%
SECONDARY	7%	5%	3%
HIGHER	1%	0%	0%

	1995	**1980**	**1965**
FEMALES IN SCHOOL			
PRIMARY	48%	48%	38%
SECONDARY		45%	2%
ADULT ILLITERACY M/F	42/77%	56.0/87.8%	

COMMUNICATIONS

	1995	**1980**	**1965**
RATE OF NEWSPAPERS	5	4	6
RATE OF RADIOS	48	21	15
RATE OF TELEVISIONS	4	0	

Source: CIA, *The World Factbook, 1997;* ILO, *World Labour Report, 1997;* UN, *Demographic Yearbook, 1997;* UN, *Statistical Yearbook, 1996;*
World Bank, *World Development Indicators, 1998.*

MYANMAR

Known as Burma through most of its independent period—it won its freedom from Britain in 1948—Myanmar had its name changed under the current military government, which came to power in a coup in 1988. Under various sets of international sanctions, Myanmar remained relatively isolated over the past decade, thereby lagging economically behind its booming southeast Asian neighbors. Its per capita income of $1,000 annually is extremely low by regional standards. Moreover, its population, unlike the populations of its neighbors, has largely remained on the land. Of the workforce of some 16 million persons, over

11.5 million labor in agriculture or forestry. Social indexes reflect the stagnant economy. Between 1965 and 1995, there was virtually no growth in the rate of physicians or hospital beds. While the percentage of students in secondary institutions climbed by about half between 1965 and 1995, it remains low for the region, at just 32 percent. In addition, reflecting the country's poverty and its closed-off situation, radio and television ownership is extremely low by developing world standards. In 1995 there were just 3 televisions and 82 radios per 1,000 residents.

	1995	1980	1965
GEOGRAPHY			
AREA (square miles/kilometers)	261,969/678,500		
LAND AREA (square miles/kilometers)	253,954/657,740		
COASTLINE (miles/kilometers)	1,206/1,930		
CITIES			
CAPITAL	Yangon	n/a	2,513,023 (83)
MAJOR CITIES	Mandalay	n/a	532,949
	Moulmein	n/a	219,961
	Pegu	n/a	150,528
	Bassein	n/a	144,096
POPULATION			
TOTAL	45,975,625	35,313,905 (83)	25,246,000 (66)
DENSITY (per square mile/square kilometer)	181/70	139/54	99/38
ANNUAL GROWTH	1.74%		
AGE COHORTS			
0–14	37%	n/a	40%
15–64	59%	n/a	57%
65 AND OVER	4%	n/a	3%
MALE	50%		
FEMALE	50%		

	1995	**1980**	**1965**
URBAN	n/a	23.9%	
RURAL	n/a	76.1%	
NET MIGRATION RATE	0	n/a	−0.3

IDENTITY

ETHNICITY
MYANMARN	68%
SHAN	9%
KAREN	7%

LANGUAGE
BURMESE	n/a

RELIGION
BUDDHIST	89%
CHRISTIAN	4%
MUSLIM	4%

VITAL STATISTICS

BIRTHS
BIRTH RATE	30	30.5
INFANT MORTALITY RATE	84	195–300
LIFE EXPECTANCY AT BIRTH	56.1	57.5

DEATHS
DEATH RATE	11.7	11

ECONOMICS AND LABOR

GDP PER CAPITA US$	$1,000

LABOR FORCE (thousands)	16,817.0 (94)
AGRICULTURE	11,551.00
MINING	87
MANUFACTURING	1,250.00
UTILITIES	17
CONSTRUCTION	292
TRADE/FOOD/TOURISM	1,450.00
TRANSPORT/COMMUNICATIONS	420
FINANCE/INSURANCE/REAL ESTATE	1,264.00
SOCIAL AND PERSONAL SERVICES	486

	1995	1980	1965
UNEMPLOYMENT			
TOTAL	541.5% (94)		

TRANSPORT

JOURNEYS (by transport mode)			
RAILROAD PASSENGER TRIPS	4,390 (94)		
(millions of miles/kilometers)			
AIR PASSENGER TRIPS (thousands)	319 (94)		
VEHICLES (thousands)			
CARS	125.4	43.3	25.2
COMMERCIAL VEHICLES	58.2	44.7	24.8

HEALTH AND HEALTH CARE

RATE OF PHYSICIANS	0.1	0.2	0 (60)
RATE OF HOSPITAL BEDS	0.6	0.9	0.6
HEALTH INDICATORS			
PREGNANT WOMEN WITH ANEMIA	58%		
LOW-BIRTH-WEIGHT BABIES	16%		
CHILD MALNUTRITION	31%		
TUBERCULOSIS INCIDENCE RATE	1.89		
HEALTH CARE			
ACCESS TO SAFE WATER	38%		
ACCESS TO SANITATION	41%		
MEASLES IMMUNIZATION	66%		
AIDS/HIV CASES	1,093	189 (93)	

EDUCATION

SCHOOL AGE IN SCHOOL			
PRIMARY	100%	91%	80%
SECONDARY	32%	22%	21% (70)
HIGHER	5%	5%	1.10%
FEMALES IN SCHOOL			
PRIMARY	48%	48%	77% (77)
SECONDARY	n/a	45%	16%
ADULT ILLITERACY M/F	11/22%	n/a	15.9/41.7% (73)

	1995	1980	1965
COMMUNICATIONS			
RATE OF NEWSPAPERS	7	10	10
RATE OF RADIOS	82	23	10
RATE OF TELEVISIONS	3	0	

Source: CIA, *The World Factbook, 1997;* ILO, *World Labour Report, 1997;* UN, *Demographic Yearbook, 1997;* UN, *Statistical Yearbook, 1996;* World Bank, *World Development Indicators, 1998.*

NAMIBIA

A vast and sparsely populated country on the southwestern coast of Africa, Namibia is located between Angola on the north, Botswana and Zambia on the east, and South Africa on the west. Its long coastline—almost entirely devoid of natural harbors—faces the southern Atlantic Ocean. Covering 318,694 square miles, Namibia has a population of just 1.67 million, for a density rate of 5.2 persons per square mile. From the end of World War I until 1990, Namibia—then known as Southwest Africa—was ruled as a mandate by South Africa, an illegal state of affairs since the 1960s. From the 1960s until the late 1980s, the country was involved in a conflict between anti–South Africa rebels and the apartheid government. A peace treaty, signed in 1988, led to independence in 1990. By African standards, Namibia is relatively prosperous, with a per capita income of $3,600 annually, reflecting its great wealth of diamonds. Educational levels are relatively high, with virtually all young persons receiving a primary education and almost two-thirds going on to secondary institutions. Its health indexes are not as positive. Just over one quarter of children under the age of 5 suffer from malnutrition, and the prevalence of AIDS is quite high, with some 5,000 infected persons in 1995.

	1995	1980	1965
GEOGRAPHY			
AREA (square miles/kilometers)	318,694/825,418		
LAND AREA (square miles/kilometers)	318,694/825,418		
COASTLINE (miles/kilometers)	982/1,572		
CITIES			
CAPITAL	Windhoek	147,056 (91)	
POPULATION			
TOTAL	1,677,243	762,184 (70)	526,004 (60)
DENSITY (per square mile/square kilometer)	5/2	2/0.7	2/0.6
ANNUAL GROWTH	2.93%	2.8%	
AGE COHORTS			
0–14	44%	n/a	40%
15–64	52%	n/a	55%
65 AND OVER	4%	n/a	5%
MALE	49%		
FEMALE	51%		

	1995	**1980**	**1965**
URBAN	27.1% (91)		
RURAL	72.9%		
NET MIGRATION RATE	0	n/a	0 (62)

IDENTITY

ETHNICITY

OVAMBO	50%
KAVANGOS	9%
MIXED	7%
HERERO	7%
DAMARA	7%
WHITE	6.6%
NAMA	5%
CAPRIVIAN	4%
BUSHMEN (San)	3%
BASTER	2%
TSWANA	.50%

LANGUAGE

GERMAN	n/a
INDIGENOUS	n/a
ENGLISH	n/a

RELIGION

LUTHERAN	50%
OTHER CHRISTIAN DENOMINATIONS	30%
INDIGENOUS	10%–20%

VITAL STATISTICS

BIRTHS

BIRTH RATE	37.3	45.1
INFANT MORTALITY RATE	47.2	116
LIFE EXPECTANCY AT BIRTH	64.5	48.2

DEATHS

DEATH RATE	8

	1995	1980	1965

HOUSEHOLDS

NUMBER	1,003,553 (91)		
URBAN	84,539		
RURAL	919,014		
AVERAGE SIZE	5.2		
URBAN	4.7		
RURAL	5.4		
FEMALE HEADED	39.3%		
SINGLE	19.6%		
MARRIED	46.0%		
WIDOWED	10.0%		
DIVORCED/SEPARATED	6.3%		

ECONOMICS AND LABOR

GDP PER CAPITA US$	$3,600		
LABOR FORCE M/F (thousands)			
AGRICULTURE	46/54%		
INDUSTRY	21/8%		
SERVICES	33/39%		
UNION DENSITY	22%		

TRANSPORT

JOURNEYS (by transport mode)			
RAILROAD PASSENGER TRIPS	199 (94)		
(millions of miles/kilometers)			

HEALTH AND HEALTH CARE

RATE OF PHYSICIANS	0.2		
HEALTH INDICATORS			
PREGNANT WOMEN WITH ANEMIA	16%		
LOW-BIRTH-WEIGHT BABIES	12%		
CHILD MALNUTRITION	26%		
TUBERCULOSIS INCIDENCE RATE	4		

	1995	1980	1965
HEALTH CARE			
ACCESS TO SANITATION	34%		
MEASLES IMMUNIZATION	57%		
AIDS/HIV CASES	5,101	5,101 (93)	

EDUCATION

	1995	1980	1965
SCHOOL AGE IN SCHOOL			
PRIMARY	133%		
SECONDARY	62%		
HIGHER	8%		
FEMALES IN SCHOOL			
PRIMARY	50%		
SECONDARY	55%		
ADULT ILLITERACY M/F	n/a	25.8/29.2% (85)	

COMMUNICATIONS

	1995	1980	1965
RATE OF NEWSPAPERS	147	26	12
RATE OF RADIOS	140	127 (85)	n/a
RATE OF TELEVISIONS	23	5	0

Source: CIA, *The World Factbook, 1997;* ILO, *World Labour Report, 1997;* UN, *Demographic Yearbook, 1997;* UN, *Statistical Yearbook, 1996;* World Bank, *World Development Indicators, 1998.*

NAURU

A tiny island-state situated almost directly on the equator in the central Pacific, Nauru is one of the smallest and most isolated independent states in the world. Just 8 square miles in area, the coral-ringed island has a population of 10,273 persons. Of all the microstates of the vast Pacific basin, Nauru is by far the wealthiest, with a per capita income of roughly $10,000 annually. This wealth is largely a by-product of phosphate mining. Over the millennia, the droppings of sea birds have coated the island with the mineral essential to fertilizer manufacturing. The extensive mining of the island, however, has left much of the tiny territory an uninhabitable environmental wasteland. There are ongoing plans to use the country's large financial reserves to import topsoil to repair the damage. The limited inhabited area of the island and the rising income rates have led to a dramatic drop in population growth rates, from 4.3 percent in 1965 to just 1.3 in 1995.

	1995	1980	1965
GEOGRAPHY			
AREA (square miles/kilometers)	8.1/21		
LAND AREA (square miles/kilometers)	8.1/21		
COASTLINE (miles/kilometers)	18.8/30		
CITIES			
CAPITAL	Nauru		
POPULATION			
TOTAL	10,273	7,254 (77)	6,056 (66)
DENSITY (per square mile/square kilometer)	1,268/489	896/345	748/288
ANNUAL GROWTH	1.33%	n/a	4.3%
AGE COHORTS			
0–14	n/a	n/a	36.6% (61)
15–64	n/a	n/a	62%
65 AND OVER	n/a	n/a	1%
NET MIGRATION RATE	0.4		
IDENTITY			
ETHNICITY			
NAURUAN	58%		
PACIFIC ISLANDER	26%		

	1995	1980	1965
CHINESE	8%		
EUROPEAN	8%		
LANGUAGE			
NAURUAN	n/a		
ENGLISH	n/a		
RELIGION			
PROTESTANT	n/a		
ROMAN CATHOLIC	n/a		

VITAL STATISTICS

	1995	1980	1965
BIRTHS			
BIRTH RATE	18	22.6	41.9
INFANT MORTALITY RATE	40.6	19	34.3
LIFE EXPECTANCY AT BIRTH	67		
MARRIAGES			
MARRIAGE RATE	5.3	5.4	5.7
DEATHS			
DEATH RATE	5.1	5.1	7.6

ECONOMICS AND LABOR

	1995	1980	1965
GDP PER CAPITA US$	$10,000		

TRANSPORT

	1995	1980	1965
JOURNEYS (by transport mode)			
RAILROAD PASSENGER TRIPS	117.0 (94)		
(millions of miles/kilometers)			

HEALTH CARE

	1995	1980	1965
RATE OF PHYSICIANS	n/a	n/a	1.8 (60)
RATE OF HOSPITAL BEDS	n/a	n/a	50
TOTAL DEATHS	49		

	1995	1980	1965
EDUCATION			
SCHOOL AGE IN SCHOOL			
PRIMARY	n/a	n/a	123%
SECONDARY	n/a	n/a	41%
FEMALES IN SCHOOL			
PRIMARY	n/a	n/a	132%
SECONDARY	n/a	n/a	42%
COMMUNICATIONS			
RATE OF RADIOS	575	557	

Source: CIA, *The World Factbook, 1997;* ILO, *World Labour Report, 1997;* UN, *Demographic Yearbook, 1997;* UN, *Statistical Yearbook, 1996;* World Bank, *World Development Indicators, 1998.*

NEPAL

Situated between China to the north and India to the south, Nepal is a medium-sized, landlocked country in southern Asia. Topographically, the country is dominated by the Himalayas, including Mount Everest, at 29,000 feet the highest peak in the world. These mountains cover roughly one-third of the country and are virtually uninhabited. South of the high peaks are the foothills and valleys where the vast majority of the population lives. Though ethnically diverse, the Nepali society is dominated by the Hinduism and cultural forms of its giant neighbor to the south. Among the poorest countries in Asia, Nepal has a per capita income of $1,200 annually. The nation also

has one of the highest growth rates in the world, with its population more than doubling from 9.4 million in 1965 to 22.1 million in 1995. This growth, and the fact that well over 90 percent of the nation's workers labor on the land, has resulted in enormous deforestation of the country's landscape, creating serious erosion and other environmental problems. The country also has one of the widest educational discrepancies between girls and boys. While virtually all boys receive a primary education, the rate for girls is just 38 percent. Similarly, the illiteracy rate for men is 59 percent, while that for women is fully 86 percent.

	1995	1980	1965
GEOGRAPHY			
AREA (square miles/kilometers)	54,363/140,800		
LAND AREA (square miles/kilometers)	52,819/136,800		
COASTLINE (miles/kilometers)	Landlocked		
CITIES			
CAPITAL	Kathmandu	n/a	235,160 (81)
POPULATION			
TOTAL	22,094,033	15,022,839 (81)	9,387,661 (61)
DENSITY (per square mile/square kilometer)	418/162	284/110	178/69
ANNUAL GROWTH	2.45%	3.5%	1.8%
AGE COHORTS			
0–14	42%		
15–64	55%		
65 AND OVER	3%		
MALE	50%		
FEMALE	50%		

	1995	1980	1965
URBAN	n/a	6.4%	
RURAL	n/a	93.6%	
NET MIGRATION	0		

IDENTITY

ETHNICITY

NEWARS, INDIANS, TIBETANS, GURUNGS,	n/a
MAGARS, TAMANGS, BHOTIAS, RAIS,	n/a
LIMBUS, SHERPAS	n/a

LANGUAGE

| NEPALI | n/a |

RELIGION

HINDU	90%
BUDDHIST	5%
MUSLIM	4%

VITAL STATISTICS

BIRTHS

	1995	1980	1965
BIRTH RATE	37	41.7	41.1 (61)
INFANT MORTALITY RATE	79	139	
LIFE EXPECTANCY AT BIRTH	53.6	49.4	

DEATHS

	1995	1980	1965
DEATH RATE	12.6	18.4	20.8 (61)

HOUSEHOLDS

| **NUMBER** | 3,345,052 (91) |
| **AVERAGE SIZE** | 5.5 |

ECONOMICS AND LABOR

| **GDP PER CAPITA US$** | $1,200 |

	1995	**1980**	**1965**
LABOR FORCE M/F			
AGRICULTURE	91/98%		
INDUSTRY	0/0%		
SERVICES	9/2%		
POVERTY			
UNDER $1/DAY	50.3%		
UNDER $2/DAY	86.7%		

TRANSPORT

JOURNEYS (by transport mode)	
RAILROAD PASSENGER TRIPS	683.0 (94)
(millions of miles/kilometers)	

HEALTH AND HEALTH CARE

	1995	**1980**	**1965**
RATE OF PHYSICIANS	0.1	0	0 (60)
RATE OF HOSPITAL BEDS	0.2	0.2	0.1
HEALTH INDICATORS			
PREGNANT WOMEN WITH ANEMIA	65%		
LOW-BIRTH-WEIGHT BABIES	26%		
CHILD MALNUTRITION	49%		
TUBERCULOSIS INCIDENCE RATE	1.67		
HEALTH CARE			
ACCESS TO SAFE WATER	48%		
ACCESS TO SANITATION	20%		
MEASLES IMMUNIZATION	78%		
AIDS/HIV CASES	48	24 (93)	

EDUCATION

	1995	**1980**	**1965**
SCHOOL AGE IN SCHOOL			
PRIMARY	110%	86%	24%
SECONDARY	38%	22%	7%
HIGHER	5%	3%	0.8%
FEMALES IN SCHOOL			
PRIMARY	39%	28%	7%
SECONDARY	n/a	9%	2%
ADULT ILLITERACY M/F	59/86%	68.3/90.8% (81)	83.3/98.5% (61)

	1995	1980	1965
COMMUNICATIONS			
RATE OF NEWSPAPERS	7	8	3
RATE OF RADIOS	35	20	5 (70)
RATE OF TELEVISIONS	3	0	0

Source: CIA, *The World Factbook, 1997;* ILO, *World Labour Report, 1997;* UN, *Demographic Yearbook, 1997;* UN, *Statistical Yearbook, 1996;* World Bank, *World Development Indicators, 1998.*

NETHERLANDS

The Netherlands is one of the wealthiest and most socially equitable countries in the world, with narrow discrepancies in income and a well-funded and inclusive social welfare system. This wealth and equity is reflected in some of the highest social indexes in Europe and the world. There are roughly 1 physician and 1 hospital bed for every 400 and 100 residents, respectively. Given the large health care system, the infant mortality rate is just 4.9 per 1,000 live births annually, down from 14.4 in 1965. The only blot in this picture is the high rate of HIV infection—some 3,954 people were infected as of 1995. Education is also widespread. At least one-half of all young persons of both sexes attend institutions of higher learning. Netherlands has a diversified economy. It has a major agricultural sector, much of it based on below-sea-level lands, focused on truck farming and flowers. It also is a major manufacturing country. Of the roughly 6.7 million workers, some 1.2 million labor in industry. Still, as in other modern economies, the largest sector of the laboring population—roughly one-third—is involved in the provision of services. The rate of TV and car ownership is widespread with roughly one unit for every two and three persons respectively.

Density

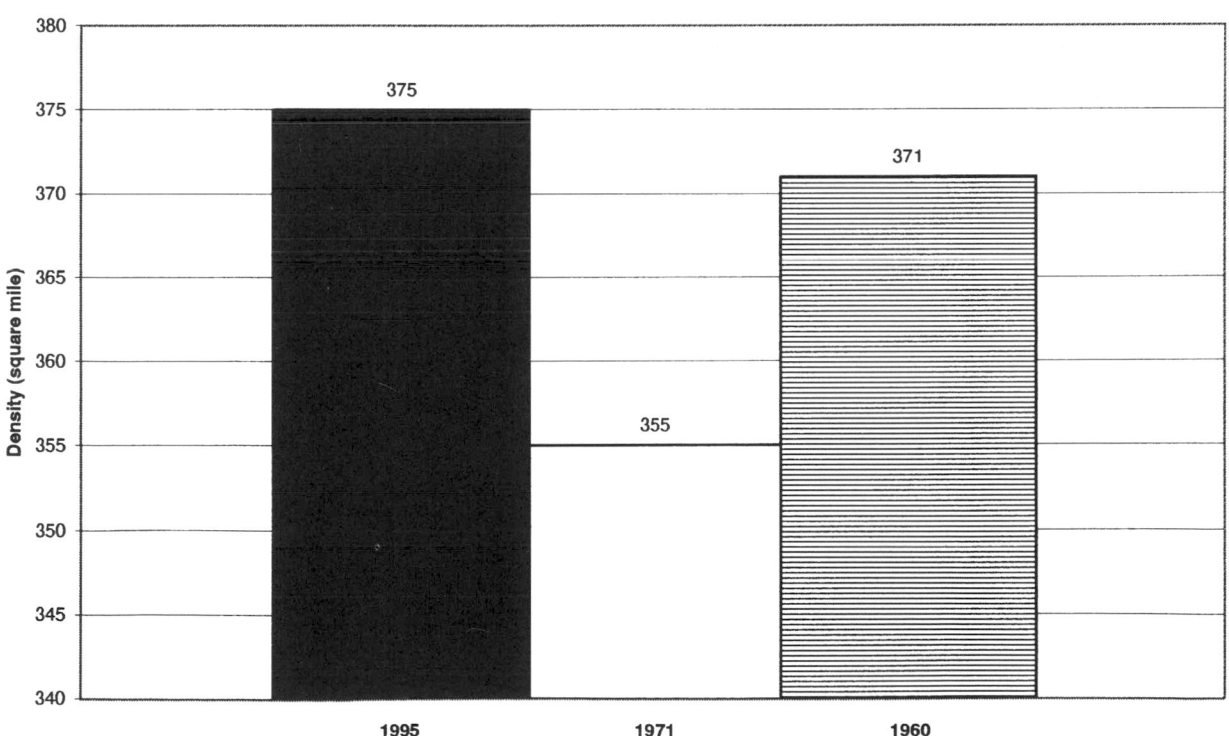

Anti-Malthusian population experts—that is, those who believe that continuing population increases can be handled by new technologies—often point to the Netherlands as an increasingly densely populated country that provides its citizens with a constantly rising standard of living. But, as their opponents point out, the Netherlands uses its wealth to import many of the foods and goods it has no room to produce in its own limited territory.

Urbanization

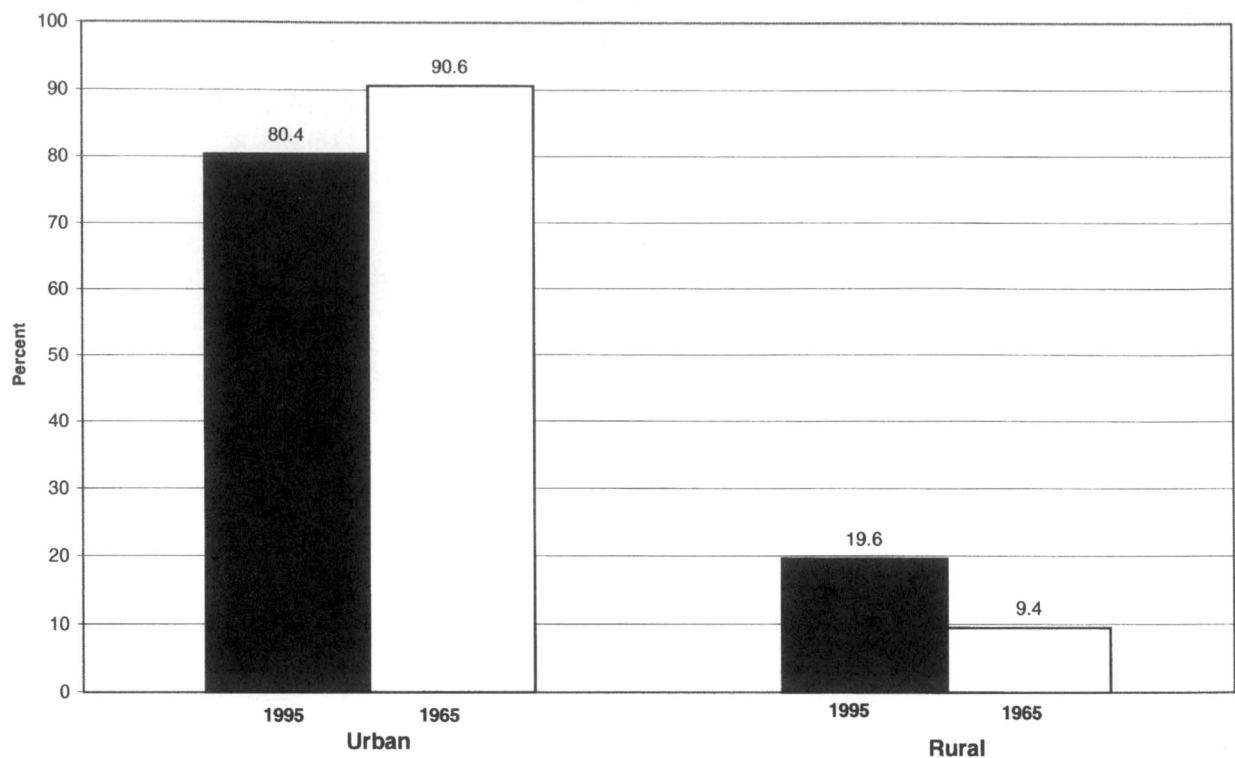

While most of the developing world is rapidly urbanizing, many countries in the developed world are beginning to see an opposite trend towards more rural living. Advances in communications make it possible for many to work at home, eliminating the necessity of commuting to offices in the city. Others are drawn to the countryside by the desire for a more relaxed life-style. Nowhere are these trends toward rural living more apparent than in the Netherlands.

CHRONOLOGY

1963   Netherlands hands over western half of New Guinea to Indonesia, ending 300-year Dutch presence in Asia.
1975   Netherlands grants Suriname its independence.
1981   Centrist prime minister Van Agt loses elections after supporting the placement of United States cruise missiles on Dutch soil.
1994   Leftist Labor Party becomes dominant party in parliament.
1997   Government legalizes prostitution in brothels.

	1995	**1980**	**1965**

GEOGRAPHY

AREA (square miles/kilometers)   14,402/37,300
LAND AREA (square miles/kilometers)   13,097/33,920
COASTLINE (miles/kilometers)   282/451

CITIES
CAPITAL   Amsterdam (94)   723,163
MAJOR CITIES   Rotterdam   598,236
                                  Gravenhage   444,108
                                  Utrecht   234,352
                                  Eindhoven   196,547

POPULATION

	1995	**1980**	**1965**
TOTAL	15,568,034	13,061,115 (71)	11,461,964 (60)
DENSITY (per square mile/square kilometer)	1,189/459	997/385	875/338
ANNUAL GROWTH	0.56%	0.5%	1.4%
AGE COHORTS			
0–14	18%	n/a	28% (65)
15–64	68%	n/a	62%
65 AND OVER	14%	n/a	10%
URBAN	90.6% (94)	88.4%	
RURAL	9.4%	11.6%	
NET MIGRATION RATE	2.3	n/a	0.2

IDENTITY

ETHNICITY
DUTCH   96%
MOROCCANS, TURKS AND OTHER   4%

LANGUAGE
DUTCH   n/a

RELIGION
UNAFFILIATED   36%
ROMAN CATHOLIC   34%
PROTESTANT   25%
MUSLIM   3%

	1995	1980	1965

VITAL STATISTICS

BIRTHS

	1995	1980	1965
BIRTH RATE	12.08	12.3 (85)	19.2
URBAN BIRTH RATE	12.6 (94)		
RURAL BIRTH RATE	12.9 (94)		
INFANT MORTALITY RATE	4.9	7.9 (85)	14.4
ABORTION RATE	106.4 (94)		
LIFE EXPECTANCY AT BIRTH	77.7	74.3 (85)	73.5

MARRIAGES

	1995	1980	1965
MARRIAGE RATE	5.3	5.7 (85)	9
AVERAGE AGE AT MARRIAGE M/F	30.8/28.2		
DIVORCE RATE	2.4	2.3 (85)	0.5

DEATHS

	1995	1980	1965
DEATH RATE	8.7	8.5 (85)	8.1

HOUSEHOLDS

	1995	1980	1965
NUMBER	n/a	n/a	2.940,005 (56)
AVERAGE SIZE	3.3 (93)	n/a	3.7

ECONOMICS AND LABOR

GDP PER CAPITA US$ $19,500

LABOR FORCE M/F (thousands)	3,979.0/2,713 (94)
AGRICULTURE	193/71
MINING	9/0
MANUFACTURING	855/220
UTILITIES	40/7
CONSTRUCTION	364/29
TRADE/FOOD/TOURISM	654/573
TRANSPORT/COMMUNICATIONS	323/96
FINANCE/INSURANCE/REAL ESTATE	425/279
SOCIAL AND PERSONAL SERVICES	1,032/1,339

UNEMPLOYMENT

TOTAL   6.8% (98)

UNION DENSITY   21.8%

	1995	1980	1965

TRANSPORT

JOURNEYS (by transport mode)

	1995	1980	1965
RAILROAD PASSENGER TRIPS	14,439 (94)		
(millions of miles/kilometers)			
AIR PASSENGER TRIPS (thousands)	12,895		
VEHICLES (thousands)			
CARS	5,883.9	4,552.00	1,272.9
COMMERCIAL VEHICLES	687.3	347	234.8

HEALTH AND HEALTH CARE

	1995	1980	1965
RATE OF PHYSICIANS	2.5	2.1	1.1 (60)
RATE OF HOSPITAL BEDS	11.3	12.5	7.8
TOTAL DEATHS	136,154		
HEALTH INDICATORS			
PREGNANT WOMEN WITH ANEMIA			
LOW-BIRTH-WEIGHT BABIES	4%		
SMOKING PREVALENCE M/F	36/29%		
TUBERCULOSIS INCIDENCE RATE	.13		
HEALTH CARE			
ACCESS TO SAFE WATER	100%		
ACCESS TO SANITATION	100%		
MEASLES IMMUNIZATION	95%		
AIDS/HIV CASES	3,954	3,045 (93)	

EDUCATION

	1995	1980	1965
SCHOOL AGE IN SCHOOL			
PRIMARY	107%	100%	104%
SECONDARY	139%	93%	59%
HIGHER	49%	29%	12.1%
FEMALES IN SCHOOL			
PRIMARY	50%	49%	103%
SECONDARY	52%	52%	55%
HIGHER	n/a	24.5%	11.1 (70)

	1995	1980	1965
COMMUNICATIONS			
RATE OF NEWSPAPERS	303	326	293
RATE OF RADIOS	907	650	270
RATE OF TELEVISIONS	491	399	184

Source: CIA, *The World Factbook, 1997*; ILO, *World Labour Report, 1997*; UN, *Demographic Yearbook, 1997*; UN, *Statistical Yearbook, 1996*; World Bank, *World Development Indicators, 1998*.

NEW ZEALAND

Situated on two large islands and several minor ones, New Zealand lies in the southwest Pacific roughly 1,500 miles off the southeast coast of Australia. It enjoys a temperate climate and possesses some of the highest mountains in the South Pacific. Settled by the English in the early nineteenth century, New Zealand is dominated by the descendants of those settlers, as well as later immigrants. The native Maoris—a Polynesian people—represent about 9 percent of the population, and suffer from lower income levels and social indexes. Overall, the country is among the wealthiest in the world, outside Europe, with a per capita income of $18,300. In addition, the economy of New Zealand is quite modern, with an advanced, export-oriented agricultural sector centered on sheep production. Of the 1.5 million–strong labor force, roughly 255,000 work in manufacturing and 430,000 are involved in the provision of services. Most social indexes are at developed-world levels as well. Over half of all young persons attend university, while just 6 percent of all babies are born underweight. At 37.2 percent, New Zealand has a relatively high rate of female-headed households, while just over half of all households include both parents.

	1995	**1980**	**1965**
## GEOGRAPHY			
AREA (square miles/kilometers)	103,737/268,680		
LAND AREA (square miles/kilometers)	103,579/268,670		
COASTLINE (miles/kilometers)	9,459/15,134		
CITIES			
CAPITAL	Wellington	150,800 (93)	
MAJOR CITIES	Auckland	321,100	
	Christchurch	297,600	
	Manukau	233,600	
	Northshore	155,500	
## POPULATION			
TOTAL	3,547,983	3,175,737 (81)	2,676,919
DENSITY (per square mile/square kilometer)	34/13	31/12	26/10
ANNUAL GROWTH	1.12%	0.9%	2%
AGE COHORTS			
0–14	23%		33%
15–64	65%		59%
65 AND OVER	12%		8%

	1995	1980	1965
URBAN	84.9% (91)	83.5%	
RURAL	15.1%	16.5%	
NET MIGRATION RATE	3.17		

IDENTITY

ETHNICITY
EUROPEAN	88%		
MAORI	8.9%		
PACIFIC ISLANDER	2.9%		

LANGUAGE
ENGLISH	n/a		
MAORI	n/a		

RELIGION
ANGLICAN	24%		
PRESBYTERIAN	18%		
ROMAN CATHOLIC	15%		
METHODIST	5%		
BAPTIST	2%		

VITAL STATISTICS

BIRTHS
BIRTH RATE	15.8	15.6 (85)	22.5
INFANT MORTALITY RATE	6.7	10.8	17.7
ABORTION RATE	193.6 (92)		
LIFE EXPECTANCY AT BIRTH	77	74.1	71.3

MARRIAGES
MARRIAGE RATE	4.9	7.8 (85)	8.6
AVERAGE AGE AT MARRIAGE M/F	28.8/26.7		
DIVORCE RATE	1.2	2.8	0.7

DEATHS
DEATH RATE	7.7	8.4	8.9

HOUSEHOLDS

NUMBER	1,175,634 (91)		633,707 (61)
URBAN	1,011,330		
RURAL	164,301		

	1995	**1980**	**1965**
AVERAGE SIZE	2.8 (91)	n/a	3.6
URBAN	2.7		
RURAL	2.9		

TYPE OF HOUSEHOLD	
FEMALE HEADED	37.2%
SINGLE	17.9%
MARRIED	55.5%
WIDOWED	11.5%
DIVORCED/SEPARATED	14.0%

ECONOMICS AND LABOR

GDP PER CAPITA US$	$18,300

LABOR FORCE M/F (thousands)	838.0/657 (93)
AGRICULTURE	108/49
MINING	4/0
MANUFACTURING	175/80
UTILITIES	9/2
CONSTRUCTION	72/9
TRADE/FOOD/TOURISM	162/155
TRANSPORT/COMMUNICATIONS	66/25
FINANCE/INSURANCE/REAL ESTATE	77/72
SOCIAL AND PERSONAL SERVICES	164/265

UNEMPLOYMENT	
TOTAL	8.2% (94)

UNION DENSITY	23.2%

TRANSPORT

JOURNEYS (by transport mode)	
RAILROAD PASSENGER TRIPS (millions of miles/kilometers)	7,716 (94)

VEHICLES (thousands)	**1995**	**1980**	**1965**
CARS	1,611.8	1,303.4	715.6
COMMERCIAL VEHICLES	353	260.3	162.2

	1995	1980	1965

HEALTH AND HEALTH CARE

	1995	1980	1965
RATE OF PHYSICIANS	2.1	1.6	1.2 (60)
RATE OF HOSPITAL BEDS	7.3	n/a	10.8
TOTAL DEATHS	27960		
HEALTH INDICATORS			
LOW-BIRTH-WEIGHT BABIES	6%		
SMOKING PREVALENCE M/F	24/22%		
TUBERCULOSIS INCIDENCE RATE	.10		
HEALTH CARE			
ACCESS TO SAFE WATER	n/a	87%	
MEASLES IMMUNIZATION	87%	n/a	
AIDS/HIV CASES	523	441 (93)	

EDUCATION

	1995	1980	1965
SCHOOL AGE IN SCHOOL			
PRIMARY	104%	111%	104%
SECONDARY	117%	83%	54%
HIGHER	58%	27%	9.6%
FEMALES IN SCHOOL			
PRIMARY	49%	49%	103%
SECONDARY	50%	49%	53%
HIGHER	n/a	21.8%	13.9% (70)

COMMUNICATIONS

	1995	1980	1965
RATE OF NEWSPAPERS	305	340	399
RATE OF RADIOS	935	885	241
RATE OF TELEVISIONS	451	332	154

Source: CIA, *The World Factbook, 1997*; ILO, *World Labour Report, 1997*; UN, *Demographic Yearbook, 1997*; UN, *Statistical Yearbook, 1996*; World Bank, *World Development Indicators, 1998*.

NICARAGUA

Nicaragua is a medium-sized country, of some 50,000 square miles. It is located on the Central American isthmus, with Honduras to the north and Costa Rica to the south. Of Nicaragua's 4.27 million people, the vast majority live in the western third of the country, around two large lakes or on the Pacific Coast. This part of Nicaragua is Spanish-speaking and is largely white or mestizo—that is, mixed white-Indian. The marshy, isolated Caribbean coast on the east has a large proportion of people of African descent, many of whom speak English, and Indians. Dominated by a dictatorship from the 1930s until 1979, Nicaragua underwent a social and political revolution led by Sandinista guerrillas, who fought against the dictatorship of Anastazio Somoza for most of the 1970s. While progress in health care and education came out of the revolution, many of these gains were undermined by a war against U.S.-sponsored rebels, known as "contras." Like many other Latin American countries, Nicaragua has been slow in containing its explosive population growth. Between 1965 and 1995, the population grew from 1.54 million to roughly 4.27 million, at an annual rate of 3.2 percent in the former year and 2.7 in the latter.

	1995	**1980**	**1965**
GEOGRAPHY			
AREA (square miles/kilometers)	49,998/129,494		
LAND AREA (square miles/kilometers)	46,430/120,254		
COASTLINE (miles/kilometers)	569/910		
CITIES			
CAPITAL	Managua	n/a	608,020 (79)
POPULATION			
TOTAL	4,272,352	1,887,952 (71)	1,535,588 (63)
DENSITY (per square mile/square kilometer)	92/36	40/16	33/13
ANNUAL GROWTH	2.7%	3.7%	3.2%
AGE COHORTS			
0–14	44%	n/a	48%
15–64	53%	n/a	49%
65 AND OVER	3%	n/a	3%
MALE	49%		
FEMALE	51%		
URBAN	63.3%	53.4%	
RURAL			

	1995	1980	1965
NET MIGRATION RATE	−1.17		

IDENTITY

ETHNICITY

MESTIZO	69%		
WHITE	17%		
BLACK	9%		
INDIAN	5%		

LANGUAGE

SPANISH	n/a		

RELIGION

ROMAN CATHOLIC	95%		
PROTESTANT	5%		

VITAL STATISTICS

BIRTHS

BIRTH RATE	33.8	44.2	47–50
INFANT MORTALITY RATE	45.8	76	51.6
LIFE EXPECTANCY AT BIRTH	65.7	59.9	n/a

MARRIAGES

MARRIAGE RATE	3.3	6.3	3.8
DIVORCE RATE	0.2	0.3	0.2

DEATHS

DEATH RATE	6.01	9.7	14–16

HOUSEHOLDS

NUMBER	n/a	n/a	247,253 (63)
AVERAGE SIZE	n/a	n/a	6.1

ECONOMICS AND LABOR

GDP PER CAPITA US$	$1,700	

LABOR FORCE	214.7 (92)	
AGRICULTURE	28	
MINING	1.3	

	1995	**1980**	**1965**
MANUFACTURING	33.4		
UTILITIES	6.1		
CONSTRUCTION	6.6		
TRADE/FOOD/TOURISM	21.5		
TRANSPORT/COMMUNICATIONS	8.8		
FINANCE/INSURANCE/REAL ESTATE	11.2		
SOCIAL AND PERSONAL SERVICES	96.3		
UNEMPLOYMENT			
TOTAL	14.0% (91)		
UNION DENSITY	23.4%		
POVERTY			
UNDER $1/DAY	43.8% (93)		
UNDER $2/DAY	74.5% (93)		

TRANSPORT

JOURNEYS (by transport mode)			
RAILROAD PASSENGER TRIPS	6 (92)		
(millions of miles/kilometers)			
AIR PASSENGER TRIPS (thousands)	44 (94)		
VEHICLES (thousands)			
CARS	31.3	n/a	13
COMMERCIAL VEHICLES	43.6	n/a	5

HEALTH AND HEALTH CARE

RATE OF PHYSICIANS	0.7	0.4	0.4 (60)
RATE OF HOSPITAL BEDS	1.8	n/a	2.3
TOTAL DEATHS	12,515 (91)		
HEALTH INDICATORS			
PREGNANT WOMEN WITH ANEMIA	36%		
LOW-BIRTH-WEIGHT BABIES	15%		
CHILD MALNUTRITION	24%		
TUBERCULOSIS INCIDENCE RATE	1.1		
HEALTH CARE			
ACCESS TO SAFE WATER	61%		
ACCESS TO SANITATION	31%		
MEASLES IMMUNIZATION	81%		
AIDS/HIV CASES	117	71 (93)	

	1995	1980	1965
EDUCATION			
SCHOOL AGE IN SCHOOL			
PRIMARY	110%	98%	69%
SECONDARY	47%	43%	14%
HIGHER	9%	13%	2%
FEMALES IN SCHOOL			
PRIMARY	50%	51%	69%
SECONDARY	50%	52%	13%
ADULT ILLITERACY M/F	35/33%	13%	42.0/42.9% (71)
COMMUNICATIONS			
RATE OF NEWSPAPERS	23	49	49
RATE OF RADIOS	261	239	65
RATE OF TELEVISIONS	67	57	10

Source: CIA, *The World Factbook, 1997;* ILO, *World Labour Report, 1997;* UN, *Demographic Yearbook, 1997;* UN, *Statistical Yearbook, 1996;* World Bank, *World Development Indicators, 1998.*

NIGER

Niger is a vast, arid country whose northern two-thirds consists of the Sahara Desert. The southern third, part of the semi-desert Sahel region, is where most of the country's 9.1 million people live. At slightly smaller than twice Texas in size, Niger covers 489,189 square miles in territory. Though it has a low density rate of just 19 persons per square mile, it has seen dramatic population growth since winning its independence from France in 1960. Growing at a rate of roughly 3 percent annually, the population has grown to its present size from just 2.5 million in 1965 and fully 48 percent of population is under the age of 15. Divided deeply between the Arab-influenced Tuareg of the north and the African population of various ethnicities to the south, the country has suffered from numerous periods of interethnic fighting in its nearly 40 years of sovereignty. One of the world's poorest states, with a per capita income of $600, partly reflecting the fact that many of its citizens sustain themselves outside the commercial economy, Niger has low social indexes. Though infant mortality rates have declined by some 40 percent in the last 30 years, they remain high at 117 per 1,000 live births. Life expectancy has actually dropped in the past two decades from 42.5 in the early 1980s to 40.7 in the late 1990s. Only 29 percent of all children attend primary school.

	1995	1980	1965
GEOGRAPHY			
AREA (square miles/kilometers)	489,189/1,267,000		
LAND AREA (square miles/kilometers)	489,073/1,266,700		
COASTLINE (miles/kilometers)	Landlocked		
CITIES			
CAPITAL	Niamey	n/a	225,314 (77)
POPULATION			
TOTAL	9,113,001	5,098,427 (77)	2,501,800 (60)
DENSITY (per square mile/square kilometer)	19/7	10/4	5/2
ANNUAL GROWTH	3.4%	2.9%	3.2%
AGE COHORTS			
0–14	48%		45.5% (62)
15–64	50%		51.0%
65 AND OVER	2%		2.7%
MALE	37%		
FEMALE	63%		

	1995	1980	1965
URBAN	15.3% (88)		
RURAL	84.7%		
NET MIGRATION RATE	0		

IDENTITY

ETHNICITY

HAUSA	56%		
DJERMA	22%		
FULA	8.50%		
TUAREG	8%		
BERI BERI (Kanouri)	4.30%		
ARAB, TOUBOU, AND GOURMANTCHE	1.20%		

LANGUAGE

FRENCH	n/a		
HAUSA	n/a		
DJERMA	n/a		

RELIGION

MUSLIM	80%		
INDIGENOUS	n/a		
CHRISTIAN	n/a		

VITAL STATISTICS

BIRTHS

	1995	1980	1965
BIRTH RATE	54.5	51	52
INFANT MORTALITY RATE	117.6	200	200
LIFE EXPECTANCY AT BIRTH	40.7	42.5	37

MARRIAGES

AVERAGE AGE AT MARRIAGE M/F	23.4/16.6		

DEATHS

DEATH RATE	24.6	22.9	27

HOUSEHOLDS

NUMBER	1,134,230 (88)		
AVERAGE SIZE	6.4		

	1995	1980	1965
TYPE OF HOUSEHOLD			
SINGLE	3.1%		
MARRIED	88.0%		
WIDOWED	4.9%		
DIVORCED/SEPARATED	3.9%		

ECONOMICS AND LABOR

	1995	1980	1965
GDP PER CAPITA US$	$600		
LABOR FORCE M/F (thousands)	22.1/2.0 (91)		
AGRICULTURE	1.8/0.1		
MINING	3.0/0.1		
MANUFACTURING	1.7/0.1		
UTILITIES	4.2/0.3		
CONSTRUCTION	2.3/0.0		
TRADE/FOOD/TOURISM	2.1/0.3		
TRANSPORT/COMMUNICATIONS	2.9/0.5		
FINANCE/INSURANCE/REAL ESTATE	0.6/0.2		
SOCIAL AND PERSONAL SERVICES	3.5/0.5		
UNEMPLOYMENT			
TOTAL	20.9 (91)		
POVERTY			
UNDER $1/DAY	61.5% (92)		
UNDER $2/DAY	92% (92)		

TRANSPORT

	1995	1980	1965
JOURNEYS (by transport mode)			
RAILROAD PASSENGER TRIPS	69.0 (94)		
(millions of miles/kilometers)			
VEHICLES (thousands)			
CARS	16	16	2.6
COMMERCIAL VEHICLES	18	16.9	4.5

HEALTH AND HEALTH CARE

	1995	1980	1965
RATE OF PHYSICIANS	0	n/a	0 (60)
RATE OF HOSPITAL BEDS	n/a	n/a	0.4 (60)

	1995	**1980**	**1965**
HEALTH INDICATORS			
PREGNANT WOMEN WITH ANEMIA	41%		
LOW-BIRTH-WEIGHT BABIES	15%		
CHILD MALNUTRITION	43%		
TUBERCULOSIS INCIDENCE RATE	1.14%		
HEALTH CARE			
ACCESS TO SAFE WATER	39%		
ACCESS TO SANITATION	36%		
MEASLES IMMUNIZATION	50%		
AIDS/HIV CASES	1,729	1,262 (93)	

EDUCATION

SCHOOL AGE IN SCHOOL			
PRIMARY	29%	25%	12%
SECONDARY	7%	5%	0.6%
HIGHER	0%	0%	
FEMALES IN SCHOOL			
PRIMARY	38%	35%	7%
SECONDARY	33%	29%	0.2%
ADULT ILLITERACY M/F	79/93%	80.6/91.4% (85)	

COMMUNICATIONS

RATE OF NEWSPAPERS	1	1	0.4
RATE OF RADIOS	61	45	18
RATE OF TELEVISIONS	5	1	

Source: CIA, *The World Factbook, 1997;* ILO, *World Labour Report, 1997;* UN, *Demographic Yearbook, 1997;* UN, *Statistical Yearbook, 1996;* World Bank, *World Development Indicators, 1998.*

NIGERIA

Approximately one out of every four people on the continent of Africa lives in Nigeria, located on the Gulf of Guinea in West Africa. With a total population of 103.9 million, Nigeria dominates the politics and economy of West Africa. As the key member of the Economic Community of West African States—an economic and military organization—Nigeria has sent peacekeepers to resolve conflicts in Liberia and Sierra Leone. The largest producer of oil in Africa, Nigeria has the potential to be an economic giant, but much of this wealth has been wasted by a series of corrupt and incompetent military dictatorships. With a per capita income of $1,300, distorted upward by oil wealth, which is very unevenly divided, Nigeria suffers from a high poverty rate. Approxi-mately 60 percent of the populace lives on less than $2 per person daily. Ethnically divided between the Christian south and the Muslim north, the country was devastated by a three-year civil war in the late 1960s. Currently, the country is undergoing one of its periodic transitions to democracy. After the death of the unpopular Sani Abacha in 1998, a new military leader promised elections within the year, but these promises have been made and broken before. Social indexes reflect the economic inequalities and history of political turmoil in the country. The infant mortality rate is over 72 per 1,000 live births. Fewer than one-third of all young persons attend secondary schools.

Poverty

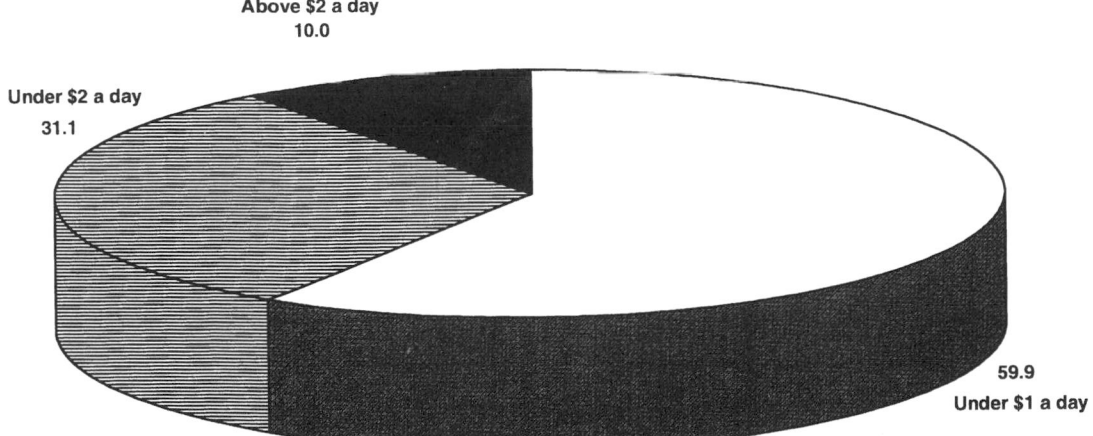

Above $2 a day
10.0

Under $2 a day
31.1

59.9
Under $1 a day

Despite its great natural and human wealth, Nigeria has remained a country with an extremely large and impoverished population. This has largely been attributed to the country's corrupt government. Since independence, it has been almost continuously ruled by unpopular military regimes. Thus, while it is among the largest exporters of oil in the world, nearly 60 percent of its citizens live on less than $2 a day.

Religion

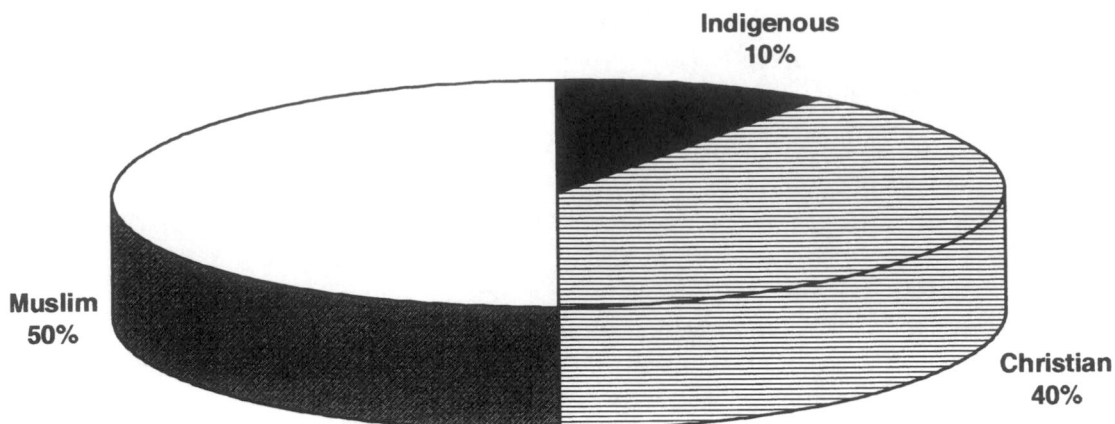

One of the main reasons for Nigeria's continuing instability are the ethnic and religious divides permeating its society. While most of the country's oil wealth is situated in the Christian south, the country has largely been led by military men from the Muslim north, producing great tensions between the two regions.

CHRONOLOGY

1960	Nigeria wins its independence from Great Britain.
1967	Following ethnic clashes, the southeast part of the country secedes to form new nation of Biafra; civil war ensues.
1970	After deaths of hundreds of thousands, civil war comes to an end with defeat of secession movement.
1975	Bloodless military coup ends nine-year reign of Colonel Yakubu Gowon.
1979	Nigeria returns to civilian rule with election of Alhaji Shehu Shagari as president.
1983	Military coup ends civilian government.
1985	Major General Ibrahim Babangida comes to power in coup.
1993	Military government voids election victory of Moshood Abiola; Sani Abacha takes power.
1996	Despite international protests, government executes Ken Saro-Wiwa and other Ogoni rights activists.
1998	Abacha dies of heart attack; Abiola, in jail since 1994, dies of heart attack one month later.

	1995	1980	1965

GEOGRAPHY

	1995	1980	1965
AREA (square miles/kilometers)	356,668/923,770		
LAND AREA (square miles/kilometers)	356,668/923,770		
COASTLINE (miles/kilometers)	329/853		

CITIES

	1995	1980	1965
CAPITAL	Abuja		
MAJOR CITIES	Lagos	1,060,848 (75)	
	Ibadan	847,000	
	Ogbomosho	432,000	
	Kano	399,000	
	Oshogbo	282,000	

POPULATION

	1995	1980	1965
TOTAL	103,912,489	n/a	55,670,052 (63)
DENSITY (per square mile/square kilometer)	291/113	103	156/60
ANNUAL GROWTH	3.05%	3.4%	2%

AGE COHORTS

	1995	1980	1965
0–14	45%		
15–64	52%		
65 AND OVER	3%		

	1995	1980	1965
MALE	50%		
FEMALE	50%		

	1995	1980	1965
URBAN	16.1% (88)		
RURAL			

	1995	1980	1965
NET MIGRATION RATE	0.34	n/a	0

IDENTITY

ETHNICITY

	1995	1980	1965
HAUSA	n/a		
FULANI	n/a		
YORUBA	n/a		
IBO	n/a		

LANGUAGE

	1995	1980	1965
ENGLISH	n/a		
HAUSA	n/a		

	1995	1980	1965
YORUBA	n/a		
IBO	n/a		
FULANI	n/a		
RELIGION			
MUSLIM	50%		
CHRISTIAN	40%		
INDIGENOUS	10%		

VITAL STATISTICS

	1995	1980	1965
BIRTHS			
BIRTH RATE	42.9	50.4	
INFANT MORTALITY RATE	72.4	114	
LIFE EXPECTANCY AT BIRTH	54.3	37	
DEATHS			
DEATH RATE	12.7	17.1	

ECONOMICS AND LABOR

	1995	1980	1965
GDP PER CAPITA US$	$1,300		
LABOR FORCE M/F			
AGRICULTURE	42/44%		
INDUSTRY	9/3%		
SERVICES	49/53%		
UNION DENSITY	17.2%		
POVERTY			
UNDER $1/DAY	31.1% (93)		
UNDER $2/DAY	59.9%		

TRANSPORT

	1995	1980	1965
JOURNEYS (by transport mode)			
RAILROAD PASSENGER TRIPS	555 (93)		
(millions of miles/kilometers)			
AIR PASSENGER TRIPS (thousands)	650 (94)		
VEHICLES (thousands)			
CARS	227	n/a	46
COMMERCIAL VEHICLES	22.3	n/a	24

	1995	1980	1965

HEALTH AND HEALTH CARE

	1995	1980	1965
RATE OF PHYSICIANS	0.2	0.1	0 (60)
RATE OF HOSPITAL BEDS	1.7	0.9	0.4
HEALTH INDICATORS			
PREGNANT WOMEN WITH ANEMIA	55%		
LOW-BIRTH-WEIGHT BABIES	16%		
CHILD MALNUTRITION	35%		
SMOKING PREVALENCE M/F	24/7%		
TUBERCULOSIS INCIDENCE RATE	2.2		
HEALTH CARE			
ACCESS TO SAFE WATER	39%		
ACCESS TO SANITATION	36%		
MEASLES IMMUNIZATION	50%		
AIDS/HIV CASES	1,591	961 (93)	

EDUCATION

	1995	1980	1965
SCHOOL AGE IN SCHOOL			
PRIMARY	89%	105%	36%
SECONDARY	30%	16%	3%
HIGHER	4%	2%	0.2%
FEMALES IN SCHOOL			
PRIMARY	44%	43%	27%
SECONDARY		36%	2%
ADULT ILLITERACY M/F	33/53%	46.2/68.5% (85)	

COMMUNICATIONS

	1995	1980	1965
RATE OF NEWSPAPERS	18	15	7
RATE OF RADIOS	196	97	11
RATE OF TELEVISIONS	38	8	0.5

Source: CIA, *The World Factbook, 1997*; ILO, *World Labour Report, 1997*; UN, *Demographic Yearbook, 1997*; UN, *Statistical Yearbook, 1996*; World Bank, *World Development Indicators, 1998*.

NORWAY

Norway is a Scandinavian country located on the North Atlantic Ocean, bordered by Sweden, Finland, and the Russian Federation to the east. Its long coastline, punctuated by deepwater fjords, or inlets, has led the Norwegian people to look to the sea for much of their history, going back at least 1,000 years to the time of the Vikings. Ethnically homogenous, virtually the entire population of 4.39 million is of Nordic stock. There is also a small minority of native Lapps in the north, and various immigrants from southern Europe and the Middle East live and work in the major cities. Having been one of the more prosperous countries in the Europe and the world during most of this century, Norway was bolstered by the discovery and exploitation of vast reserves of oil under the nearby North Sea in the 1970s and 1980s. The revenues are shared with Britain. Norway has a complete and inclusive health care system. There is roughly 1 physician for every 333 persons, up from 1 for every 900 in 1965. Educational opportunities are widespread as well. Over half of all young persons attend institutions of higher education. Literacy is high, with some 600 newspapers sold daily for every 1,000 persons, one of the highest rates in the world. The relative wealth of the country is reflected in the high level of private car ownership, which has risen from 465,000 vehicles in 1965 to 1.66 million in 1995.

	1995	1980	1965
GEOGRAPHY			
AREA (square miles/kilometers)	125,181/324/220		
LAND AREA (square miles/kilometers)	118,865/307,860		
COASTLINE (miles/kilometers)	13,703/21,925		
CITIES			
CAPITAL	Oslo	473,454 (93)	
MAJOR CITIES	Bergen	218,144	
	Trondheim	140,656	
	Stavanger	101,403	
POPULATION			
TOTAL	4,383,807	4,091,132	3,591,234 (60)
DENSITY (per square mile/square kilometer)	37/14	34/13	30/12
ANNUAL GROWTH	0.48%	0.3%	0.8%
AGE COHORTS			
0–14	19%		24.8% (64)
15–64	65%		63%
65 AND OVER	16%		11.8%

	1995	1980	1965
MALE	49%		
FEMALE	51%		
URBAN	72% (90)	71%	
RURAL	28%	29%	
NET MIGRATION RATE	3.6	n/a	0

IDENTITY

ETHNICITY

GERMANIC (Nordic, Alpine, Baltic)	n/a		
LAPPS (Sami)	n/a		

LANGUAGE

NORWEGIAN	n/a		
LAPP	n/a		
FINNISH	n/a		

RELIGION

EVANGELICAL LUTHERAN	87.8		
PROTESTANT	n/a		
ROMAN CATHOLIC	n/a		

VITAL STATISTICS

BIRTHS

BIRTH RATE	12	12.1 (85)	17.5
INFANT MORTALITY RATE	4.9	8.3	16.4
LIFE EXPECTANCY AT BIRTH	77.5	75.6	73.4

MARRIAGES

MARRIAGE RATE	4.6	5 (85)	6.8
AVERAGE AGE AT MARRIAGE M/F	31.1/28.6		
DIVORCE RATE	2.5	1.9 (85)	0.7

DEATHS

DEATH RATE	10.7	10.3 (85)	9.1

HOUSEHOLDS

NUMBER	1,751,363 (90)	n/a	1,138,987 (60)
URBAN	1,300,372		
RURAL	439,216		

	1995	1980	1965
AVERAGE SIZE	2.4	n/a	3.1
URBAN	2.3		
RURAL	2.6		

TYPE OF HOUSEHOLD	
FEMALE HEADED	34.3%
SINGLE	26.3%
MARRIED	49.2%
WIDOWED	12.7%
DIVORCED/SEPARATED	11.8%

ECONOMICS AND LABOR

GDP PER CAPITA US$	$24,500

LABOR FORCE M/F (thousands)	1,102.0/932 (94)
AGRICULTURE	80/27
MINING	19/6
MANUFACTURING	224/79
UTILITIES	18/4
CONSTRUCTION	111/8
TRADE/FOOD/TOURISM	163/185
TRANSPORT/COMMUNICATIONS	116/48
FINANCE/INSURANCE/REAL ESTATE	92/68
SOCIAL AND PERSONAL SERVICES	276/508

UNEMPLOYMENT	
TOTAL	5.4% (94)

UNION DENSITY	51.7%

TRANSPORT

JOURNEYS (by transport mode)	
RAILROAD PASSENGER TRIPS (millions of miles/kilometers)	2,341 (94)
AIR PASSENGER TRIPS (thousands)	11,133 (94)

VEHICLES (thousands)	1995	1980	1965
CARS	1,653.7	1,232.60	465.2
COMMERCIAL VEHICLES	366.3	164.1	131.5

	1995	1980	1965

HEALTH AND HEALTH CARE

RATE OF PHYSICIANS	3.3	1.9	1.1 (60)
RATE OF HOSPITAL BEDS	13.5	15	9.7
TOTAL DEATHS	45117		
HEALTH INDICATORS			
LOW-BIRTH-WEIGHT BABIES	5%		
SMOKING PREVALENCE M/F	36/36%		
TUBERCULOSIS INCIDENCE RATE	.08%		
HEALTH CARE			
ACCESS TO SANITATION	100%		
MEASLES IMMUNIZATION	93%		
AIDS/HIV CASES	511	374 (93)	

EDUCATION

SCHOOL AGE IN SCHOOL			
PRIMARY	99%	100%	97%
SECONDARY	92%	94%	70%
HIGHER	55%	26%	5.3%
FEMALES IN SCHOOL			
PRIMARY	49%	49%	96%
SECONDARY	51%	51%	66%
HIGHER	n/a	24.9%	10% (70)

COMMUNICATIONS

RATE OF NEWSPAPERS	607	463	384
RATE OF RADIOS	798	661	303
RATE OF TELEVISIONS	427	350	136

Source: CIA, The World Factbook, 1997; ILO, World Labour Report, 1997; UN, Demographic Yearbook, 1997; UN, Statistical Yearbook, 1996; World Bank, World Development Indicators, 1998.

OMAN

Situated in the southeastern corner of the Arabian peninsula, Oman borders on Yemen to the west, Saudi Arabia to the west, and the United Arab Emirates to the northwest. The country has a coastline of some 1,308 miles on the Arabian Sea and the Gulf of Oman. Covering some 82,000 square miles, Oman has a population of 2.19 million, with a density of 27 persons per square mile. Until the 1970s, Oman was a largely closed kingdom under an aged sultan, but the transition to the sultan's son saw the country open up to the outside world. Around the same time, discoveries of modest oil reserves helped raise the per capita income to $10,800 by 1995 and expanded the country's relatively primitive health and educational facilities. While Oman had almost no doctors in 1965, it had 1 per every 1,100 persons by 1995. During the same period, the number of hospital beds increased from 1 for every 3,300 to 1 for every 500. The percentage of low-birth-weight babies stood at just 10 percent in 1995. Educational indexes have risen dramatically as well. While just 3 percent of all children attended primary schools in 1970, fully 80 percent were doing so three decades later.

	1995	1980	1965
GEOGRAPHY			
AREA (square miles/kilometers)	82,031/212,460		
LAND AREA (square miles/kilometers)	82,031/212,460		
COASTLINE (miles/kilometers)	1,308/2,092		
CITIES			
CAPITAL	Muscat	n/a	n/a	5,080 (60)
POPULATION			
TOTAL	2,186,548		
DENSITY (per square mile/square kilometer)	27/10	6	
ANNUAL GROWTH	3.53%	4.8%	0.3%
AGE COHORTS			
0–14	46%		
15–64	51%		
65 AND OVER	3%		
NET MIGRATION RATE	1.84		

	1995	1980	1965

IDENTITY

ETHNICITY

ARAB	n/a		
BALUCHI	n/a		
SOUTH ASIAN	n/a		
AFRICAN	n/a		

LANGUAGE

ARABIC	n/a		
ENGLISH	n/a		
URDU	n/a		
INDIAN DIALECTS	n/a		

RELIGION

IBADHI MUSLIM	75%		
SUNNI MUSLIM	n/a		
SHI'A MUSLIM	n/a		
HINDU	n/a		

VITAL STATISTICS

BIRTHS

BIRTH RATE	37.9	47	
INFANT MORTALITY RATE	27.3	117	
LIFE EXPECTANCY AT BIRTH	70.5	52.3	

DEATHS

DEATH RATE	4.4	14.3	

HOUSEHOLDS

NUMBER	n/a	49,783 (86)	
AVERAGE SIZE	n/a	5.6	

ECONOMICS AND LABOR

GDP PER CAPITA US$	$10,800		

LABOR FORCE M/F

AGRICULTURE	48/20%		
INDUSTRY	22/35%		
SERVICES	30/45%		

	1995	1980	1965

TRANSPORT

JOURNEYS (by transport mode)
AIR PASSENGER TRIPS (thousands)　　　　1,512.0 (94)

VEHICLES
PRIVATE CARS　　　　180.0 (93)
COMMERCIAL VEHICLES　　　　85.5

HEALTH AND HEALTH CARE

	1995	1980	1965
RATE OF PHYSICIANS	0.9	0.5	0 (60)
RATE OF HOSPITAL BEDS	2.1	1.6	0.3
TOTAL DEATHS			

HEALTH INDICATORS
PREGNANT WOMEN WITH ANEMIA	54%		
LOW-BIRTH-WEIGHT BABIES	10%		
CHILD MALNUTRITION	14%		
TUBERCULOSIS INCIDENCE RATE	.20%		

HEALTH CARE
ACCESS TO SAFE WATER	15%		
ACCESS TO SANITATION	79%		
MEASLES IMMUNIZATION	98%		

AIDS/HIV CASES	55	34 (93)	

EDUCATION

SCHOOL AGE IN SCHOOL
	1995	1980	1965
PRIMARY	80%	51%	3 (70)
SECONDARY	66%	12%	n/a
HIGHER	5%	n/a	n/a

FEMALES IN SCHOOL
	1995	1980	1965
PRIMARY	48%	34%	1%
SECONDARY	48%	25%	n/a

	1995	1980	1965
COMMUNICATIONS			
RATE OF NEWSPAPERS	41	37 (85)	n/a
RATE OF RADIOS	580	272	n/a
RATE OF TELEVISIONS	653	32	n/a

Source: CIA, *The World Factbook, 1997*; ILO, *World Labour Report, 1997*; UN, *Demographic Yearbook, 1997*; UN, *Statistical Yearbook, 1996*; World Bank, *World Development Indicators, 1998*.

PAKISTAN

With a population of 129.3 million, Pakistan is the second largest Muslim country in the world, after Indonesia. Located in the northwest corner of the Indian subcontinent, Pakistan is bordered by Afghanistan and China on the west and north, India on the east, and Iran on the west. It has a 654-mile coastline on the Arabian Sea. Established in 1947—as a homeland for the subcontinent's Muslim population—Pakistan was born in war with India and continues to have tense relations with its giant Hindu neighbor. In 1971, the eastern half of the country, now called Bangladesh, won its independence in a war with India as its ally. Since a 1965 conflict, India and Pakistan have battled off and on over the disputed Kashmir region, a predominantly Muslim area occupied by India but claimed by Pakistan. With the testing of nuclear devices by both countries in 1998, tensions in Kashmir have the possibility of escalating dramatically. Pakistan has been torn by internal political conflict since independence, with several military coups in its history. The political and military problems have contributed to a stagnant economy. With a $2,100 per capita income, the country is among the poorest in Asia. At the same time, approximately one-half of the 33-million–person workforce continues to labor in agriculture. Social indexes have done better. The infant mortality rate, for example, has fallen from 145 per 1,000 live births to just 11 between 1965 and 1995.

Change in Land Area

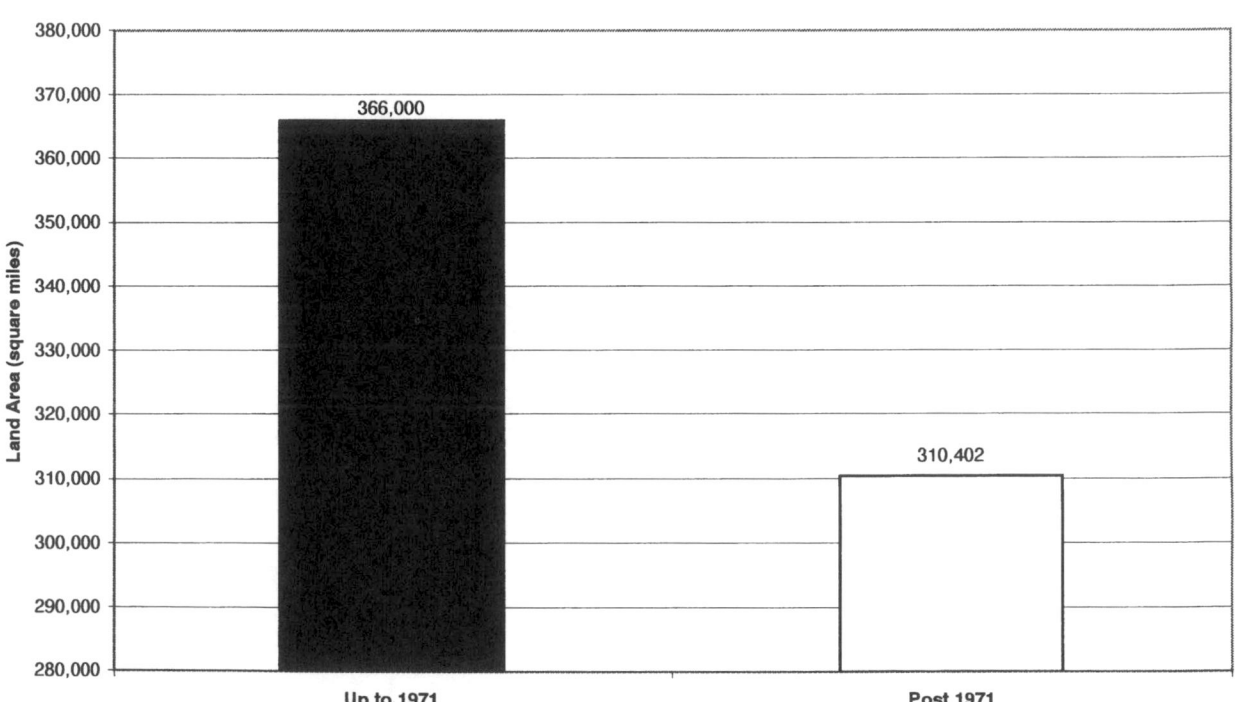

Since the end of the colonial era, the territorial and political integrity of nation-states has been one of the pillars of the international order. The irony of this situation has been noted by many experts, since many of the boundaries were established by colonial powers with little regard to existing patterns of population settlement. Occasionally, however, there are dramatic changes in the political order. One of the most significant came when East Pakistan broke from West Pakistan to form Bangladesh.

Health Indicators

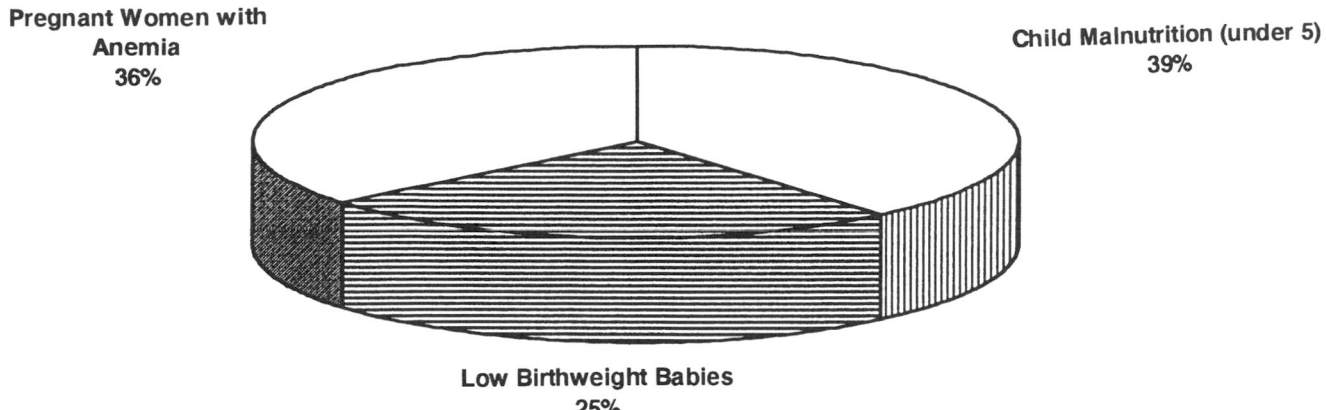

Pregnant Women with Anemia 36%

Child Malnutrition (under 5) 39%

Low Birthweight Babies 25%

Plagued by poverty and political instability, Pakistan has lagged behind many of its Asian neighbors in the provision of health care to its citizens. This poor performance is especially notable in key statistics about child health and nutrition.

CHRONOLOGY

1965   Pakistan and India fight war over disputed territory in Kashmir.
1971   A civil war between East Pakistan (supported by India) and West Pakistan leads to independence of former as new state of Bangladesh.
1976   India and Pakistan resume diplomatic ties broken by 1971 war.
1977   Zulkifar Ali Bhutto wins disputed election; violence erupts; military seizes power.
1979   Bhutto executed after being found guilty of murder.
1985   Military leader Mohammed Zia ul-Haq ends martial law.
1988   Zia dies in airplane crash; Bhutto's daughter, Benazir, elected prime minister.
1990   President dismisses Benazir Bhutto as prime minister.
1993   Benazir Bhutto returns to power after election victory.
1996   President dismisses Bhutto government for second time.
1998   Following nuclear bomb tests by India, Pakistan sets off tests of its own.

	1995	1980	1965
GEOGRAPHY			
AREA (square miles/kilometers)	310,402/803,940		
LAND AREA (square miles/kilometers)	300,664/778,720		
COASTLINE (miles/kilometers)	654/1,046		
CITIES			
CAPITAL	Islamabad	n/a	204364 (81)
MAJOR CITIES	Karachi	n/a	5,180,562
	Lahore	n/a	2,952,689
	Faisalabad	n/a	1,104,209
	Rawalpindi	n/a	794,843
POPULATION			
TOTAL	129,275,660	93,831,982 (81)	84,253,644 (61)
DENSITY (per square mile/square kilometer)	430/166	312/120	280/108
ANNUAL GROWTH	2.24%	3.1%	2.1%
AGE COHORTS			
0–14	42%	n/a	45% (61)
15–64	53%	n/a	n/a
65 AND OVER[1]	5%	n/a	6% (61)
MALE	52%		
FEMALE	48%		
URBAN	n/a	28.1%	
RURAL	n/a	71.9%	
NET MIGRATION RATE	−2.6		
IDENTITY			
ETHNICITY			
PUNJABI, SINDI, PASHTUN,	n/a		
BALOCH, MUHAJIR	n/a		
INDIAN IMMIGRANTS	n/a		
LANGUAGE			
PUNJABI	48%		
SINDHI	12%		
SIRAIKI	10%		
PASHTU	8%		

	1995	**1980**	**1965**
URDU (official)	8%		
BALOCHI	3%		
HINDKO	2%		
BRAHUI	1%		
RELIGION			
SUNNI MUSLIM	77%		
SHI'A	20%		
CHRISTIAN	n/a		
HINDU	n/a		

VITAL STATISTICS

	1995	**1980**	**1965**
BIRTHS			
BIRTH RATE	36.2	41.7	43.4 (63)
INFANT MORTALITY RATE	11.2	94.5	145.6
LIFE EXPECTANCY AT BIRTH	58.5	59.1	50.8
DEATHS			
DEATH RATE	11.2	9.6	15.4 (63)

HOUSEHOLDS

	1995	**1980**	**1965**
NUMBER	n/a	n/a	16,762,486 (60)
AVERAGE SIZE	n/a	n/a	5.4

ECONOMICS AND LABOR

	1995	**1980**	**1965**
GDP PER CAPITA US$	$2,100		
LABOR FORCE M/F (thousands)	28,465.0/4,638.0 (94)		
AGRICULTURE	12,516.0/3,225.0		
MINING	33.0/0.0		
MANUFACTURING	3,105.0/504.0		
UTILITIES	275.0/4.0		
CONSTRUCTION	2,251.0/44.0		
TRADE/FOOD/TOURISM	4,273.0/136.0		
TRANSPORT/COMMUNICATIONS	1,808.0/19.0		
FINANCE/INSURANCE/REAL ESTATE	265.0/5.0		
SOCIAL AND PERSONAL SERVICES	3,882.0/696.0		
UNEMPLOYMENT			
TOTAL	4.7% (94)		

	1995	1980	1965
UNION DENSITY	5.5%		
POVERTY			
UNDER $1/DAY	11.6% (91)		
UNDER $2/DAY	57%		

TRANSPORT

	1995	1980	1965
JOURNEYS (by transport mode)			
RAILROAD PASSENGER TRIPS	18,044 (94)		
(millions of miles/kilometers)			
AIR PASSENGER TRIPS (thousands)	5,664		
VEHICLES (thousands)			
CARS	955.1	283	122.8
COMMERCIAL VEHICLES	359.5	108.9	55.2

HEALTH AND HEALTH CARE

	1995	1980	1965
RATE OF PHYSICIANS	0.5	0.3	0.1 (60)
RATE OF HOSPITAL BEDS	0.7	0.6	0.2
TOTAL DEATHS	932,678 (92)		
HEALTH INDICATORS			
PREGNANT WOMEN WITH ANEMIA	37%		
LOW-BIRTH-WEIGHT BABIES	25%		
CHILD MALNUTRITION	40%		
SMOKING PREVALENCE M/F	27/4%		
TUBERCULOSIS INCIDENCE RATE	1.5		
HEALTH CARE			
ACCESS TO SAFE WATER	60%		
ACCESS TO SANITATION	30%		
MEASLES IMMUNIZATION	53%		
AIDS/HIV CASES	55	38 (93)	

EDUCATION

	1995	1980	1965
SCHOOL AGE IN SCHOOL			
PRIMARY	74%	39%	40%
SECONDARY	26%	14%	17%
HIGHER	3%	n/a	2.6%

	1995	**1980**	**1965**
FEMALES IN SCHOOL			
PRIMARY	31%	33%	22%
SECONDARY		26%	7%
ADULT ILLITERACY M/F	50/76%	64/84.8% (81)	

COMMUNICATIONS

	1995	**1980**	**1965**
RATE OF NEWSPAPERS	6	12	n/a
RATE OF RADIOS	88	64	6
RATE OF TELEVISIONS	18	11	0.1

FOOTNOTE
1. Age 60 and over in 1961.

Source: CIA, *The World Factbook, 1997;* ILO, *World Labour Report, 1997;* UN, *Demographic Yearbook, 1997;* UN, *Statistical Yearbook, 1996;* World Bank, *World Development Indicators, 1998.*

PALAU

The newest sovereign state on Earth, Palau is a tiny island republic situated in the western Pacific, about 600 miles east of the Philippines and some 1,000 miles north of Indonesia. Under a U.S.-administered U.N. trusteeship, Palau won its independence in 1994. The country is situated on some 200 islands in an archipelago, and most of the residents live in Koror, the capital. Of the nearly 17,000 people in Palau, approximately 12,000 are citizens of Micronesian extraction, and the remaining 4,000 consist of alien workers, largely Filipino. Palau still maintains a free association with the United States and uses U.S. money and the U.S. postal system, among other things. The country's economy largely subsists on fishing and tourism and has a per capita income of roughly $5,000. The population in the 177-square-mile territory grew at a rate of 1.7 percent in 1995. A major new highway project on the archipelago's largest island is expected to open new territories for settlement.

	1995	1980
GEOGRAPHY		
AREA (square miles/kilometers)	177/458	
LAND AREA (square miles/kilometers)	177/458	
COASTLINE (miles/kilometers)	949/1,519	
CITIES		
CAPITAL	Koror	8,000
POPULATION		
TOTAL	16,952	
DENSITY (per square mile/square kilometer)	96/37	
CHANGE		
GROWTH/SHRINKAGE	1.7%	
AGE COHORTS		
0–14	n/a	
15–64	n/a	
65 AND OVER	n/a	
NET MIGRATION RATE	2.12	
IDENTITY		
ETHNICITY		
PALAUAN (Polynesian, Malayan, Melanesian)	n/a	

	1995	1980
LANGUAGE		
ENGLISH	n/a	
SONSOROLESE	n/a	
ANGAUR	n/a	
JAPANESE	n/a	
TOBI	n/a	
PALAUAN	n/a	
RELIGION		
CHRISTIAN (various denominations)	n/a	
MODEKNGEI	n/a	

VITAL STATISTICS

BIRTHS		
BIRTH RATE	21.6	
INFANT MORTALITY RATE	25.1	
LIFE EXPECTANCY AT BIRTH	71	
DEATHS		
DEATH RATE	6.6	

ECONOMICS AND LABOR

GDP PER CAPITA US$	$5,000	

HEALTH AND HEALTH CARE

AIDS/HIV CASES	1	1 (93)

COMMUNICATIONS

RATE OF RADIOS	8,438	7,083
RATE OF TELEVISIONS	606	500

Source: CIA, *The World Factbook, 1997;* ILO, *World Labour Report, 1997;* UN, *Demographic Yearbook, 1997;* UN, *Statistical Yearbook, 1996;* World Bank, *World Development Indicators, 1998.*

PANAMA

Panama's geographic location, astride the narrowest point in the Central American isthmus, has determined its history and plays a major role in its economy. Under U.S. aegis, the country was carved out of Colombia in the early 1900s when the government in Bogota refused to accede to U.S. demands for building a canal between the Atlantic and Pacific. The canal—completed in 1914—remains under U.S. jurisdiction until 1999, when it reverts fully to Panamanian control. Today, the economy of this country of 2.66 million depends heavily on the tax revenues and trade the canal produces. Unlike other Central American countries, Panama's ethnic mix is equally dominated by whites, Africans, and Indians, with mestizos and blacks predominating. In the past 30 years, the country's population has more than doubled, from 1.22 million in 1965. Today, some 33 percent of the population is under 15. The country has made significant strides in health and education over the past three decades. In 1965, there was just 1 physician for every 2,500 persons. In 1995, that rate was one for 555. At the same time, life expectancy rose from 59.2 to 73.9. Meanwhile, the number of young persons attending secondary education rose from 36 percent to 68 percent. Most of the health and education gains were made before 1980, signifying a slowdown in the expansion of social services in recent years.

		1995	1980	1965
GEOGRAPHY				
AREA (square miles/kilometers)	30,193/78,200			
LAND AREA (square miles/kilometers)	29,340/75,990			
COASTLINE (miles/kilometers)	1,556/2,490			
CITIES				
CAPITAL	Panama City	452,041		
MAJOR CITIES	San Miguelito	290,919		
POPULATION				
TOTAL		2,655,094	1,824,796	1,221,400 (66)
DENSITY (per square mile/square kilometer)		90/35	62/24	42/16
ANNUAL GROWTH		n/a	2.2%	n/a
AGE COHORTS				
0–14		33%	n/a	44%
15–64		62%	n/a	53%
65 AND OVER		5%	n/a	4%
MALE		51%		
FEMALE		49%		

	1995	**1980**	**1965**
URBAN	54.9%	49.3%	
RURAL	45.1%	50.7%	
NET MIGRATION RATE	−1.4	n/a	−0.4

IDENTITY

ETHNICITY

MESTIZO	70%
WEST INDIAN	14%
WHITE	10%
INDIAN	6%

LANGUAGE

SPANISH	n/a
ENGLISH	n/a

RELIGION

ROMAN CATHOLIC	85%
PROTESTANT	15%

VITAL STATISTICS

BIRTHS

BIRTH RATE	23.2	28	42
URBAN BIRTH RATE	21 (93)		
RURAL BIRTH RATE	26.1		
INFANT MORTALITY RATE	29.7	26	44.7
LIFE EXPECTANCY AT BIRTH	73.9	70.8	59.2

MARRIAGES

MARRIAGE RATE	5.2	5.7	3.7
AVERAGE AGE AT MARRIAGE M/F	25.4/21.9 (90)		
DIVORCE RATE	0.8	0.6	0.5

DEATHS

DEATH RATE	5.4	5.4	11

HOUSEHOLDS

NUMBER	526,456 (90)		222,227 (60)
AVERAGE SIZE	4.4		4.8

	1995	1980	1965

ECONOMICS AND LABOR

GDP PER CAPITA US$	$5,100		
LABOR FORCE M/F (thousands)	560.5/234.6 (92)		
AGRICULTURE	202.0/7.2		
MINING	1.7/0.4		
MANUFACTURING	53.7/21.8		
UTILITIES	7.8/2.0		
CONSTRUCTION	42.1/0.9		
TRADE/FOOD/TOURISM	104.4/52.9		
TRANSPORT/COMMUNICATIONS	40.8/6.5		
FINANCE/INSURANCE/REAL ESTATE	21.7/13.9		
SOCIAL AND PERSONAL SERVICES	85.4/128.9		
UNEMPLOYMENT			
TOTAL	13.8% (94)		
UNION DENSITY	14.2%		
POVERTY			
UNDER $1/DAY	25.6% (89)		
UNDER $2/DAY	46.2%		

TRANSPORT

JOURNEYS (by transport mode)			
RAILROAD PASSENGER TRIPS	51,250 (94)		
(millions of miles/kilometers)			
AIR PASSENGER TRIPS (thousands)	368		
VEHICLES (thousands)			
CARS	161.2	98	24.7
COMMERCIAL VEHICLES	55	32.5	12.1

HEALTH AND HEALTH CARE

RATE OF PHYSICIANS	1.8	1	0.4 (60)
RATE OF HOSPITAL BEDS	2.5		4
TOTAL DEATHS	9,959 (94)	n/a	
HEALTH INDICATORS			
LOW-BIRTH-WEIGHT BABIES	10%		
CHILD MALNUTRITION	7%		

	1995	**1980**	**1965**
SMOKING PREVALENCE M/F	56/20%		
TUBERCULOSIS INCIDENCE RATE	.90		
HEALTH CARE			
ACCESS TO SAFE WATER	83%		
ACCESS TO SANITATION	87%		
MEASLES IMMUNIZATION	84%		
AIDS/HIV CASES	1,045	655 (93)	

EDUCATION

	1995	**1980**	**1965**
SCHOOL AGE IN SCHOOL			
PRIMARY	106%	106%	105%
SECONDARY	68%	61%	36%
HIGHER	30%	21%	6.8%
FEMALES IN SCHOOL			
PRIMARY	n/a	48%	102%
SECONDARY	n/a	51%	38%
ADULT ILLITERACY M/F	9/10%	13.7/15.1%	

COMMUNICATIONS

	1995	**1980**	**1965**
RATE OF NEWSPAPERS	90	56	81
RATE OF RADIOS	227	154	409
RATE OF TELEVISIONS	169	115	57

Source: CIA, *The World Factbook, 1997;* ILO, *World Labour Report, 1997;* UN, *Demographic Yearbook, 1997;* UN, *Statistical Yearbook, 1996;* World Bank, *World Development Indicators, 1998.*

PAPUA NEW GUINEA

Located on the eastern half of the island of New Guinea—which it shares with the Indonesian state of Irian Jaya—and surrounding islands, Papua New Guinea covers 178,259 square miles of territory. The geography of the country is extremely diverse, with low-lying jungle and savannah around the periphery. A cordillera of mountains lies in the interior, and some valleys are inhabited by ethnic groups largely isolated from the outside world. An Australian-administered, U.N. trustee territory through most of the postwar period, Papua New Guinea won its independence in 1975. Between 1965 and 1995, its population grew rapidly from 2.12 million to 4.39 million. Most of the population is rural. In

1980, fully 87 percent lived in the countryside, but this number has certainly declined somewhat since. In 1995, approximately 72 percent of the male workforce and 89 percent of the female workforce labored in agriculture. Ethnically, the country is a melange of peoples, including Melanesians, Papuans, Negritos, Micronesians, and Polynesians. Nearly two-thirds of the country practices some form of Christianity, while the rest observe indigenous faiths. Social indexes have not changed much in 30 years. The school-age population involved in primary education has risen from 71 percent to 80 percent since 1965, while the infant mortality rate fell from 74 per 1,000 live births in 1980 to 68.3 in 1995.

	1995	**1980**	**1965**
GEOGRAPHY			
AREA (square miles/kilometers)	178,370/461,690		
LAND AREA (square miles/kilometers)	174,405/451710		
COASTLINE (miles/kilometers)	3,220/5,152		
CITIES			
CAPITAL	Port Moresby	173,500 (90)	118,424 (80)
POPULATION			
TOTAL	4,394,537	3,010,727	2,117,917
DENSITY (per square mile/square kilometer)	25/10	17/7	12/5
ANNUAL GROWTH	2.29%	2.1%	
AGE COHORTS			
0–14	40%		
15–64	57%		
65 AND OVER	3%		

	1995	1980	1965
URBAN	n/a	13%	
RURAL	n/a	87%	
NET MIGRATION RATE	0		

IDENTITY

ETHNICITY

MELANESIAN	n/a		
PAPUAN	n/a		
NEGRITO	n/a		
MICRONESIAN	n/a		
POLYNESIAN	n/a		

LANGUAGE

PIDGIN ENGLISH	n/a		
MOTU	n/a		
ENGLISH	n/a		

RELIGION

ROMAN CATHOLIC	22%		
LUTHERAN	16%		
PRESBYTERIAN, METHODIST, LONDON MISSIONARY SOCIETY	8%		
ANGLICAN	5%		
EVANGELICAL ALLIANCE	4%		
SEVENTH DAY ADVENT	1%		
PROTESTANT SECTS	10%		
INDIGENOUS	34%		

VITAL STATISTICS

BIRTHS

BIRTH RATE	32.9	38.8	
INFANT MORTALITY RATE	68.3	74	
LIFE EXPECTANCY AT BIRTH	57.2	51.9	

DEATHS

DEATH RATE	10	13.1	

ECONOMICS AND LABOR

GDP PER CAPITA US$	$2,400		

	1995	1980	1965
LABOR FORCE M/F			
AGRICULTURE	72/89%		
INDUSTRY	9/3%		
SERVICES	18/8%		

TRANSPORT

	1995	1980	1965
JOURNEYS (by transport mode)			
RAILROAD PASSENGER TRIPS	1,113.0 (94)		
(millions of miles/kilometers)			
VEHICLES (thousands)			
CARS	11.5	18.5	7.5
COMMERCIAL VEHICLES	29.8	27.1	6.2

HEALTH AND HEALTH CARE

	1995	1980	1965
RATE OF PHYSICIANS	0.1	0.1	
RATE OF HOSPITAL BEDS	4	5.5	
HEALTH INDICATORS			
PREGNANT WOMEN WITH ANEMIA	13%		
LOW-BIRTH-WEIGHT BABIES	23%		
CHILD MALNUTRITION	30%		
SMOKING PREVALENCE M/F	46/28%		
TUBERCULOSIS INCIDENCE RATE	2.75		
HEALTH CARE			
ACCESS TO SAFE WATER	28%		
ACCESS TO SANITATION	22%		
MEASLES IMMUNIZATION	55%		
AIDS/HIV CASES	152	83 (93)	

EDUCATION

	1995	1980	1965
SCHOOL AGE IN SCHOOL			
PRIMARY	80%	59%	71%
SECONDARY	14%	12%	5%
HIGHER	3%	2%	0.1%
FEMALES IN SCHOOL			
PRIMARY	45%	41%	59%
SECONDARY	41%	32%	3%

	1995	**1980**	**1965**
ADULT ILLITERACY M/F	19/37%	45.2/62.7% (85)	65.6/76%

COMMUNICATIONS

RATE OF NEWSPAPERS	16	9
RATE OF RADIOS	75	58
RATE OF TELEVISIONS	3	

Source: CIA, *The World Factbook, 1997;* ILO, *World Labour Report, 1997;* UN, *Demographic Yearbook, 1997;* UN, *Statistical Yearbook, 1996;* World Bank, *World Development Indicators, 1998.*

PARAGUAY

Paraguay is a landlocked country in central South America, bordered by Bolivia and Brazil on the north and Argentina to the east and south. Its roughly 157,000 square miles of territory largely consists of prairie and jungle. Paraguay has seen some of the most rapid population growth in Latin America in the past 30 years. Just 1.82 million in number in 1965, Paraguayans have tripled in number to over 5.5 million by 1995. Most of that growth was in urban areas, which had only 38.6 percent of the population in 1980 but just over half by 1995. This change is reflected in the country's labor profile. Of the roughly 1.05 million workers in 1995, just 40,000 labored in agriculture. Paraguay is a medium-income country within Latin America, with a per capita income of $3,200 annually. Ethnically the country is dominated by mestizos—mixed Indian and white—and is overwhelmingly Roman Catholic and Spanish speaking. Like its neighbors, the country has emerged from dictatorship only in recent years. Despite its political problems, it has made great strides in education and health, though it still lags behind its neighbors. While only 12 percent of young persons attended secondary institutions in 1965, that figure had climbed to 38 percent 30 years later. Infant mortality dropped from 102 per 1,000 live births to just 23.2 during those same years, a major factor in the country's explosive rate of population growth.

	1995	**1980**	**1965**
GEOGRAPHY			
AREA (square miles/kilometers)	157,046/406,750		
LAND AREA (square miles/kilometers)	153,398/397,300		
COASTLINE (miles/kilometers)	Landlocked		
CITIES			
CAPITAL	Asunción	546,637	454,881 (82)
MAJOR CITIES	Ciudad del Este	133,881	
	San Lorenzo	133,395	
POPULATION			
TOTAL	5,504,146	3,029,830 (82)	1,816,890 (62)
DENSITY (per square mile/square kilometer)	36/14	20/8	12/5
ANNUAL GROWTH	2.67%	n/a	2.7%
AGE COHORTS			
0–14	41%	n/a	45%
15–64	55%	n/a	51%
65 AND OVER	4%	n/a	4%
MALE	50%		
FEMALE	50%		

	1995	1980	1965
URBAN	50.3% (92)	38.6%	
RURAL	49.7%	61.4%	
NET MIGRATION RATE	0		

IDENTITY

ETHNICITY			
MESTIZO	95%		
WHITE	n/a		
AMERINDIAN	n/a		
LANGUAGE			
SPANISH	n/a		
GUARANI	n/a		
RELIGION			
ROMAN CATHOLIC	90%		
MENNONITE	n/a		
OTHER PROTESTANT	n/a		

VITAL STATISTICS

BIRTHS			
BIRTH RATE	30.1	36	42–45 (62)
INFANT MORTALITY RATE	23.2	45	102
LIFE EXPECTANCY AT BIRTH	73.8	65.2	
MARRIAGES			
MARRIAGE RATE	3.8	3.9	4.4 (62)
AVERAGE AGE AT MARRIAGE M/F	25.8/21.5 (92)		
DEATHS			
DEATH RATE	4.3	7.2	13 (62)

HOUSEHOLDS

NUMBER	863,990 (92)		
AVERAGE SIZE	4.8		

ECONOMICS AND LABOR

GDP PER CAPITA US$	$3,200		

	1995	1980	1965
LABOR FORCE M/F (thousands)	616.0/433.6 (94)		
AGRICULTURE	36.9/3.5		
MINING	1.8/0.0		
MANUFACTURING	126.7/53.1		
UTILITIES	10.1/1.7		
CONSTRUCTION	89.2/0.0		
TRADE/FOOD/TOURISM	151.1/159.0		
TRANSPORT/COMMUNICATIONS	48.7/6.2		
FINANCE/INSURANCE/REAL ESTATE	30.5/16.8		
SOCIAL AND PERSONAL SERVICES	121.0/193.4		
UNEMPLOYMENT			
TOTAL	4.4% (94)		
UNION DENSITY	9.3%		

TRANSPORT

	1995	1980	1965
JOURNEYS (by transport mode)			
RAILROAD PASSENGER TRIPS	1 (93)		
(millions of miles/kilometers)			
AIR PASSENGER TRIPS (thousands)	324 (94)		
VEHICLES (thousands)			
CARS	250.7	58.5	4.8
COMMERCIAL VEHICLES	37.7	17.7	4.9

HEALTH AND HEALTH CARE

	1995	1980	1965
RATE OF PHYSICIANS	0.3	0.6	0.6 (60)
RATE OF HOSPITAL BEDS	0.6	n/a	2.5
TOTAL DEATHS	9,642 (92)		
HEALTH INDICATORS			
PREGNANT WOMEN WITH ANEMIA	29%		
LOW-BIRTH-WEIGHT BABIES	8%		
CHILD MALNUTRITION	4%		
SMOKING PREVALENCE M/F	24/6%		
TUBERCULOSIS INCIDENCE RATE	1.66		
HEALTH CARE			
ACCESS TO SANITATION	30%		
MEASLES IMMUNIZATION	76%		
AIDS/HIV CASES	190	143 (93)	

	1995	1980	1965

EDUCATION

SCHOOL AGE IN SCHOOL

PRIMARY	109%	106%	103%
SECONDARY	38%	27%	12%
HIGHER	10%	9%	2.9%

FEMALES IN SCHOOL

PRIMARY	48%	48%	98%
SECONDARY	51%	49%	13%

ADULT ILLITERACY M/F	7/9%	9.7/15.2% (82)	19/31.3%

COMMUNICATIONS

RATE OF NEWSPAPERS	37	51	n/a
RATE OF RADIOS	170	112	88
RATE OF TELEVISIONS	83	22	n/a

Source: CIA, *The World Factbook, 1997;* ILO, *World Labour Report, 1997;* UN, *Demographic Yearbook, 1997;* UN, *Statistical Yearbook, 1996;* World Bank, *World Development Indicators, 1998.*

PERU

Located on the Pacific coast of South America, Peru is surrounded by Ecuador and Colombia to the north, Brazil and Bolivia to the east, and Chile to the south. The nation of 24.52 million has an extremely diverse geography. A narrow, arid coastal plain is flanked by the Andean Mountains, with several peaks above 18,000 feet. To the east lie the headwaters of the Amazon River and the westernmost section of the vast Amazon basin. Much of the population lives along the coastal plain, especially in the Lima-Callao metropolitan area. A significant minority lives in the high valleys of the Andes, the heartland of the ancient Incas, where the greatest empire of pre-Columbian America flourished. A small portion of the population lives in the Amazon basin, but that percentage is growing, especially with the discovery of oil and other minerals there. All regions of Peru have experienced rapid population increases since 1965, though the annual growth rate for the country as a whole declined from 3 percent in 1965 to 1.7 percent in 1995. Accounting for some 45 percent of the population, Indians are the largest ethnic group in Peru, and Peru has the second highest percentage of Indians in all South America, after Bolivia. Thus, while Spanish is the dominant and official language, Quecha and Aymara, two native tongues, are widely spoken.

Primate City Population 1995

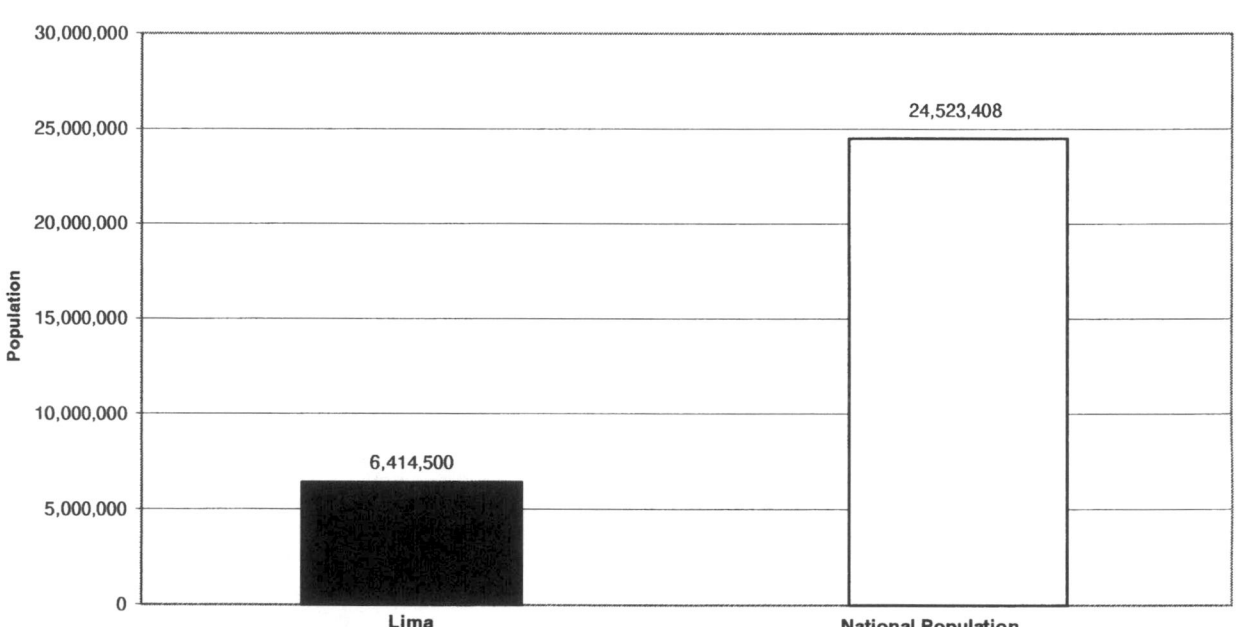

Rapid urbanization is a phenomenon in much of the developing world. In many countries the movement of people from the countryside to urban areas is especially acute, since the majority head for a single metropolis. In the case of Peru, that city is the capital, Lima.

Ethnicity

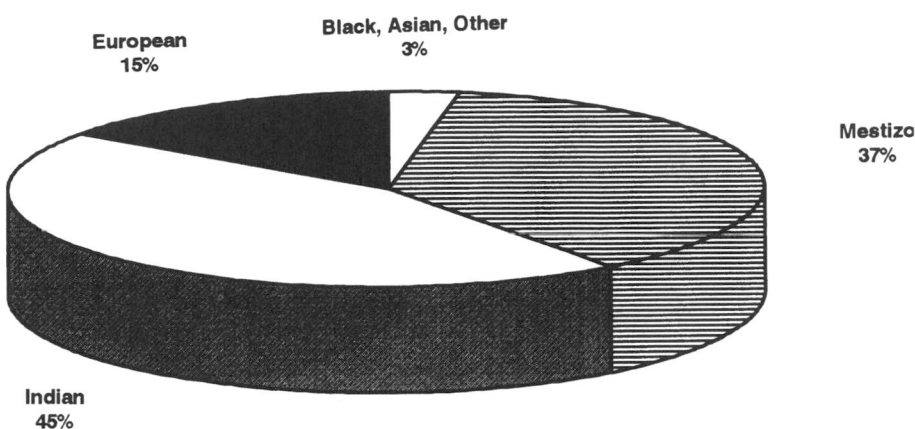

European 15%

Black, Asian, Other 3%

Mestizo 37%

Indian 45%

The population of Peru, the heartland of the ancient Inca Empire of pre-Columbian times, continues to be dominated by Indians almost 500 years after the empire's conquest by the Spanish. Indeed, aside from Bolivia, Peru has the highest Indian population in South America.

CHRONOLOGY

1968	Democratic government of Fernando Belaunde Terry overthrown in leftist military coup.
1970	Military government of General Juan Velasco Alvarado nationalizes banks.
1975	Velasco overthrown in bloodless coup by General Francisco Morales Bermudez; vows to return country to civilian rule.
1980	Terry wins first democratic election since 1968 coup.
1985	First transfer of power from one civilian government to another since the end of World War II.
1990	Alberto Fujimori, son of Japanese immigrants, elected president.
1992	Citing economic crisis and rural guerrilla war against Shining Path Marxist revolutionaries, Fujimori suspends constitution and dissolves congress.
1995	Border fighting breaks out between Ecuador and Peru over disputed land.
1996–97	Tupac Amaru urban guerrillas seize Japanese ambassador's residence in December 1996; army raids house in April 1997, freeing 72 hostages.

		1995	1980	1965
GEOGRAPHY				
AREA (square miles/kilometers)		496,224/1,285,220		
LAND AREA (square miles/kilometers)		496,139/1,285,000		
COASTLINE (miles/kilometers)		1,509/2,414		
CITIES				
CAPITAL	Lima	6,414,500 (90)		
MAJOR CITIES	Arequipa	624,500		
	Trujillo	521,200		
	Callao	515,200		
	Chiclayo	448,400		
POPULATION				
TOTAL		24,523,408	17,005,210 (81)	9,906,746 (61)
DENSITY (per square mile/square kilometer)		49/19	34/13	20/8
ANNUAL GROWTH		1.74%	2.6%	3%
AGE COHORTS				
0–14		35%	n/a	43%
15–64		61%	n/a	53%
65 AND OVER		4%	n/a	4%
MALE		50%		
FEMALE		50%		
URBAN		71.2%	64.2%	
RURAL		28.8%	35.8%	
NET MIGRATION		0.8	n/a	0 (64)
IDENTITY				
ETHNICITY				
INDIAN		45%		
MESTIZO		37%		
WHITE		15%		
BLACK, JAPANESE, CHINESE AND OTHER		3%		

	1995	1980	1965
LANGUAGE			
SPANISH	n/a		
QUECHUA	n/a		
AYMARA	n/a		
RELIGION			
ROMAN CATHOLIC	n/a		

VITAL STATISTICS

	1995	1980	1965
BIRTHS			
BIRTH RATE	24.3	36.7	45 (61)
URBAN BIRTH RATE	26.9 (93)		
RURAL BIRTH RATE	37.2		
INFANT MORTALITY RATE	52.2	99	90.7 (61)
LIFE EXPECTANCY AT BIRTH	69.1	54	52.7
MARRIAGES			
MARRIAGE RATE	4	5.9	4.1 (61)
DIVORCE RATE	n/a	0.1	0.2
DEATHS			
DEATH RATE	6.1	10.7	13 (61)

HOUSEHOLDS

	1995	1980	1965
NUMBER	4,762,779 (93)	n/a	1,969,351 (61)
AVERAGE SIZE	4.6	n/a	5.0

ECONOMICS AND LABOR

	1995
GDP PER CAPITA US$	$3,600.00
LABOR FORCE M/F (thousands)	1,643.6/1,038.6 (94)
AGRICULTURE	8.0/3.4
MINING	6.4/0.9
MANUFACTURING	376.6/138.5
UTILITIES	12.8/4.2
CONSTRUCTION	158.6/5.5
TRADE/FOOD/TOURISM	419.6/462.5
TRANSPORT/COMMUNICATIONS	183.2/16.3
FINANCE/INSURANCE/REAL ESTATE	140.4/66.4
SOCIAL AND PERSONAL SERVICES	338.2/340.8

	1995	1980	1965
UNEMPLOYMENT			
TOTAL	8.9% (94)		
UNION DENSITY	7.5%		

TRANSPORT

	1995	1980	1965
JOURNEYS (by transport mode)			
RAILROAD PASSENGER TRIPS	241.0 (94)		
(millions of miles/kilometers)			
AIR PASSENGER TRIPS (thousands)	1,895.0 (94)		
VEHICLES (thousands)			
CARS	444.2	309.5	155
COMMERCIAL VEHICLES	316.6	176.6	98.7

HEALTH AND HEALTH CARE

	1995	1980	1965
RATE OF PHYSICIANS	1	0.7	0.5 (60)
RATE OF HOSPITAL BEDS	1.4	n/a	2.3
TOTAL DEATHS	171,476 (94)		
HEALTH INDICATORS			
PREGNANT WOMEN WITH ANEMIA	53%		
LOW-BIRTH-WEIGHT BABIES	11%		
CHILD MALNUTRITION	11%		
SMOKING PREVALENCE M/F	41/13%		
TUBERCULOSIS INCIDENCE RATE	2.5		
HEALTH CARE			
ACCESS TO SAFE WATER	60%		
ACCESS TO SANITATION	44%		
MEASLES IMMUNIZATION	97%		
AIDS/HIV CASES	4,084	2,523 (93)	

EDUCATION

	1995	1980	1965
SCHOOL AGE IN SCHOOL			
PRIMARY	123%	114%	102%
SECONDARY	70%	59%	29%
HIGHER	31%	17%	5.5%

	1995	1980	1965
FEMALES IN SCHOOL			
PRIMARY	n/a	48%	93%
SECONDARY	n/a	46%	24%
ADULT ILLITERACY M/F	6/17%	9.9/26.1% (81)	

COMMUNICATIONS

RATE OF NEWSPAPERS	71	81	47 (59)
RATE OF RADIOS	253	159	212
RATE OF TELEVISIONS	99	52	21

Source: CIA, *The World Factbook, 1997;* ILO, *World Labour Report, 1997;* UN, *Demographic Yearbook, 1997;* UN, *Statistical Yearbook, 1996;* World Bank, *World Development Indicators, 1998.*

PHILIPPINES

The largest U.S. colony until the end of World War II, the Philippines won its independence in 1946. Situated on hundreds of large and small islands that separate the South China and Philippine seas, the country lies some 500 miles off the southeastern coast of China. Though the country was under the dictatorship of Ferdinand Marcos until the mid-1980s, its 74.48 million citizens have enjoyed some of the freest democratic elections in Asia in the years since. While the Philippines has lagged behind some of its Southeast Asian neighbors in economic growth in recent decades, it has weathered the current economic crisis in that region quite well. As of 1995, its per capita income stood at $2,530, a low figure but one that has been rising steadily in recent years. Still, of the coun-try's 26-million–strong labor force, nearly half continued to work in agriculture as of 1995. At the same time, fully 64.5 percent of the population lived in poverty, defined as living on less than $2 per day. One of the main economic outlets for the Filipino people remains working abroad, a trend reflected in its −1.1 percent net migration rate. Though largely Roman Catholic, the country has a significantly large Muslim minority, which was a source of armed conflict with the government through much of the 1970s and 1980s. Despite its poverty, Filipinos have made dramatic gains in education. While just 39 percent of youth attended secondary school in 1965, that figure had more than doubled to 79 percent by 1995.

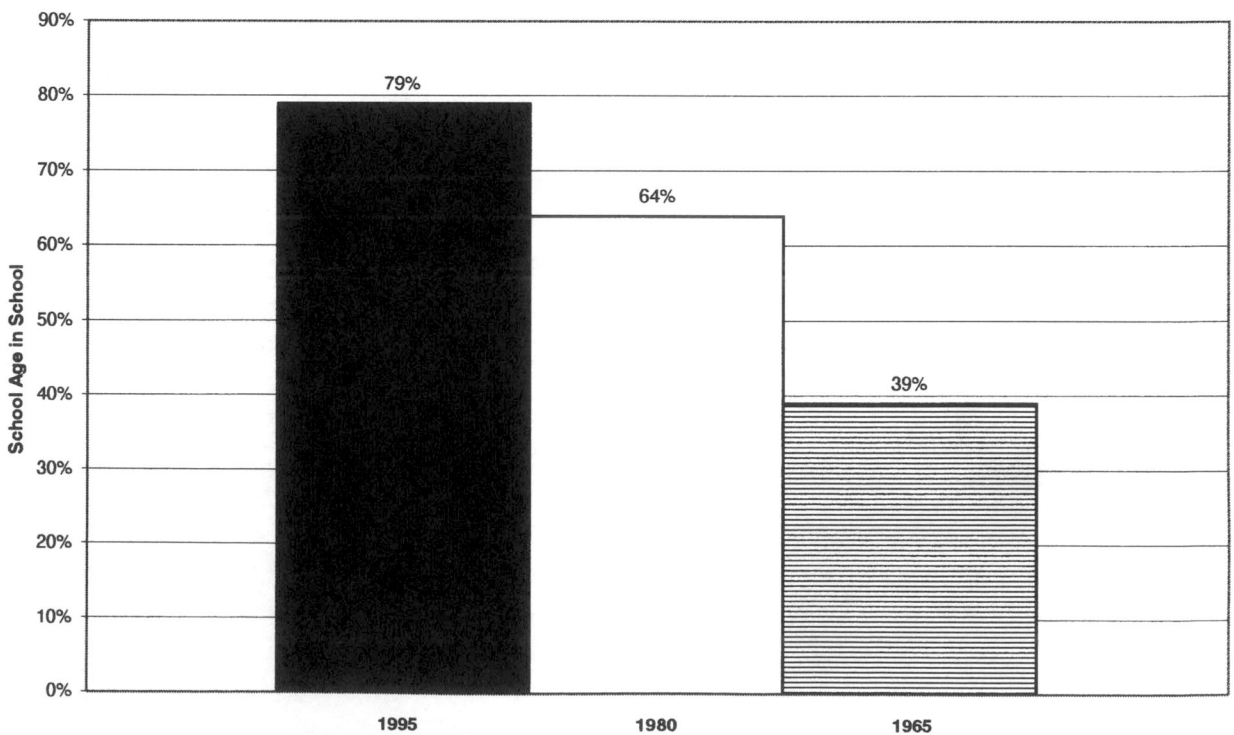

Secondary Education

Although relatively poverty-stricken by East Asian standards, the Philippines has had one of the most vigorous democracies in the region since the fall of the Ferdinand Marcos dictatorship in the mid-1980s. One of the reasons for this, say Filipino political scientists, is the rise in educational rates.

Smoking 1995

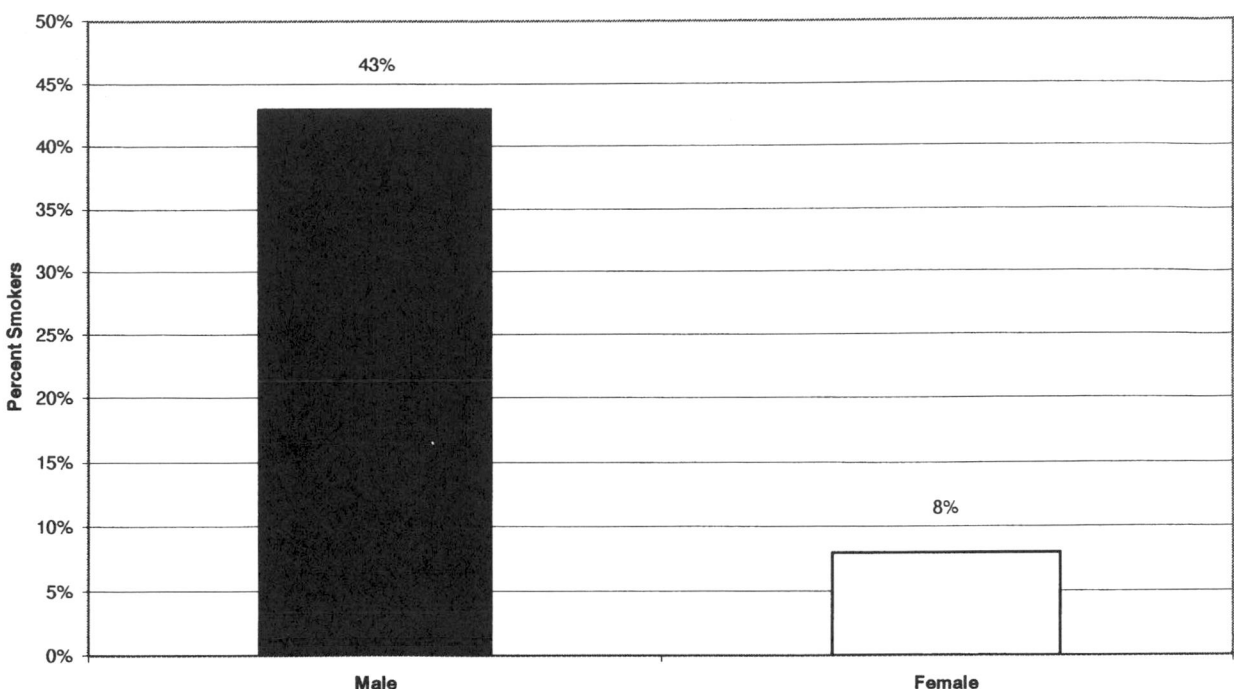

Smoking is becoming an increasingly significant health problem in East Asian countries, as the rising per capita income puts the cost of cigarettes within the reach of more and more people. For cultural reasons, however, the problem is more prevalent among men.

CHRONOLOGY

1965   Ferdinand Marcos elected president of the Philippines.

1973   Marcos declares martial law; jails opposition leaders.

1980   Benigno Aquino, major opposition figure, released from jail and leaves for the United States.

1981   Marcos lifts martial law.

1983   Aquino killed by military police at Manila airport upon his return from the United States.

1986   Popular protests lead to overthrow of Marcos regime; Marcos flees to United States; Corazon Aquino, Benigno's widow, becomes president.

1991   Following eruption of Mount Pinatubo, United States abandons bases in the Philippines.

1992   Fidel Ramos, former defense minister, elected president.

	1995	1980	1965

GEOGRAPHY

AREA (square miles/kilometers)   115,830/300,000
LAND AREA (square miles/kilometers)   115,104/298,120
COASTLINE (miles/kilometers)   22,686/36,298

CITIES

CAPITAL	Manila	8,594,150 (94)	6,720,050 (84)
MAJOR CITIES	Quezon City	1,676,644	
	Davao	960.91	
	Cebu	688,196	
	Caloocan	642,670	

POPULATION

	1995	1980	1965
TOTAL	74,480,848	48,098,460	27,087,685 (60)
DENSITY (per square mile/square kilometer)	647,250	418/161	235/91
ANNUAL GROWTH	2.18%	2.4%	3.3%

AGE COHORTS

	1995	1980	1965
0–14	38%	n/a	47% (66)
15–64	58%	n/a	50%
65 AND OVER	4%	n/a	3%

MALE	50%
FEMALE	50%

	1995	1980
URBAN	42.7% (90)	37.3%
RURAL	57.3%	62.7%

NET MIGRATION RATE	−1.1	n/a	0

IDENTITY

ETHNICITY

CHRISTIAN MALAY	91.50%
MUSLIM MALAY	4%
CHINESE	1.5%

LANGUAGE

PILIPINO (based on Tagalog)	n/a
ENGLISH	n/a

	1995	1980	1965
RELIGION			
ROMAN CATHOLIC	83%		
PROTESTANT	9%		
MUSLIM	5%		
BUDDHIST AND OTHER	3%		

VITAL STATISTICS

	1995	1980	1965
BIRTHS			
BIRTH RATE	29.5	33.3	
INFANT MORTALITY RATE	35.9	51	
LIFE EXPECTANCY AT BIRTH	65.9	61.4	
MARRIAGES			
MARRIAGE RATE	7	6.8	
AVERAGE AGE AT MARRIAGE M/F	26.3/23.8		
DEATHS			
DEATH RATE	6.7	8.4	

HOUSEHOLDS

	1995	1980	1965
NUMBER	n/a	n/a	3,812,000 (56)
AVERAGE SIZE	5.3 (90)	n/a	5.7
FEMALE HEADED	11.3%		

ECONOMICS AND LABOR

	1995	1980	1965
GDP PER CAPITA US$	$2,530		
LABOR FORCE M/F (thousands)	15,985/9,181 (94)		
AGRICULTURE	8,446/2,803		
MINING	95/6		
MANUFACTURING	1,391/1,191		
UTILITIES	83/18		
CONSTRUCTION	1,166/21		
TRADE/FOOD/TOURISM	1,201/2,362		
TRANSPORT/COMMUNICATIONS	1,343/58		
FINANCE/INSURANCE/REAL ESTATE	296/198		
SOCIAL AND PERSONAL SERVICES	1,959/2,521		
UNEMPLOYMENT			
TOTAL	8.4% (94)		

	1995	1980	1965
UNION DENSITY	22.8%		
POVERTY			
UNDER $1/DAY	28.6% (91)		
UNDER $2/DAY	64.5%		

TRANSPORT

	1995	1980	1965
JOURNEYS (by transport mode)			
RAILROAD PASSENGER TRIPS	102 (93)		
(millions of miles/kilometers)			
AIR PASSENGER TRIPS (thousands)	6,851 (94)		
VEHICLES (thousands)			
CARS	531.2	466.4	
COMMERCIAL VEHICLES	1,024	392.9	

HEALTH AND HEALTH CARE

	1995	1980	1965
RATE OF PHYSICIANS	0.1	0.1	0.1 (60)
RATE OF HOSPITAL BEDS	1.1	1.7	0.8
TOTAL DEATHS	319,579 (92)		
HEALTH INDICATORS			
PREGNANT WOMEN WITH ANEMIA	48%		
CHILD MALNUTRITION	30%		
SMOKING PREVALENCE M/F	43/8%		
TUBERCULOSIS INCIDENCE RATE	4		
HEALTH CARE			
MEASLES IMMUNIZATION	86%		
AIDS/HIV CASES	235	129 (93)	

EDUCATION

	1995	1980	1965
SCHOOL AGE IN SCHOOL			
PRIMARY	116%	112%	109%
SECONDARY	79%	64%	39%
HIGHER	27%	24%	16.10%
FEMALES IN SCHOOL			
PRIMARY	n/a	50%	108%
SECONDARY	n/a	53%	38%

	1995	1980	1965
ADULT ILLITERACY M/F	5/7%	16.1/17.2%	

COMMUNICATIONS

RATE OF NEWSPAPERS	50	41	17
RATE OF RADIOS	143	43	45
RATE OF TELEVISIONS	47	22	4

Source: CIA, *The World Factbook, 1997*; ILO, *World Labour Report, 1997*; UN, *Demographic Yearbook, 1997*; UN, *Statistical Yearbook, 1996*; World Bank, *World Development Indicators, 1998*.

POLAND

The largest country in eastern Europe, Poland covers 120,727 miles of territory—roughly the size of New Mexico—and had a population of 38.64 million in 1995. It is a predominantly Roman Catholic country, and religion has played a major role in its recent history. Religion was a rallying point for the struggle against the communist government in the 1980s, helping to pave the way for the overthrow of the Soviet-backed regime and the institution of democracy. Indeed, Poland was the first country in the region to break away from Soviet domination in the late 1980s. The church's impact is also reflected in the fact that of all the former Soviet-bloc countries, Poland continues to see population growth, though the rate of growth has fallen in recent years. Unions too are important in Poland. The country has one of the highest union membership rates in the world, at over one-quarter of the workforce. The union is even more important than the church, in that it was the Solidarity labor union struggle of the 1980s that paved the way to democracy in Poland. Today, Poland is struggling with the economic transition to capitalism. Its per capita income remains low for Europe, at just $5,800 annually. Some, it seems, are doing better than others, as reflected in the fact that, while the number of private cars has grown dramatically from 245,500 in 1965 to 7.15 million in 1995, a car is still a luxury, with just one vehicle for every five persons.

Divorce Rates

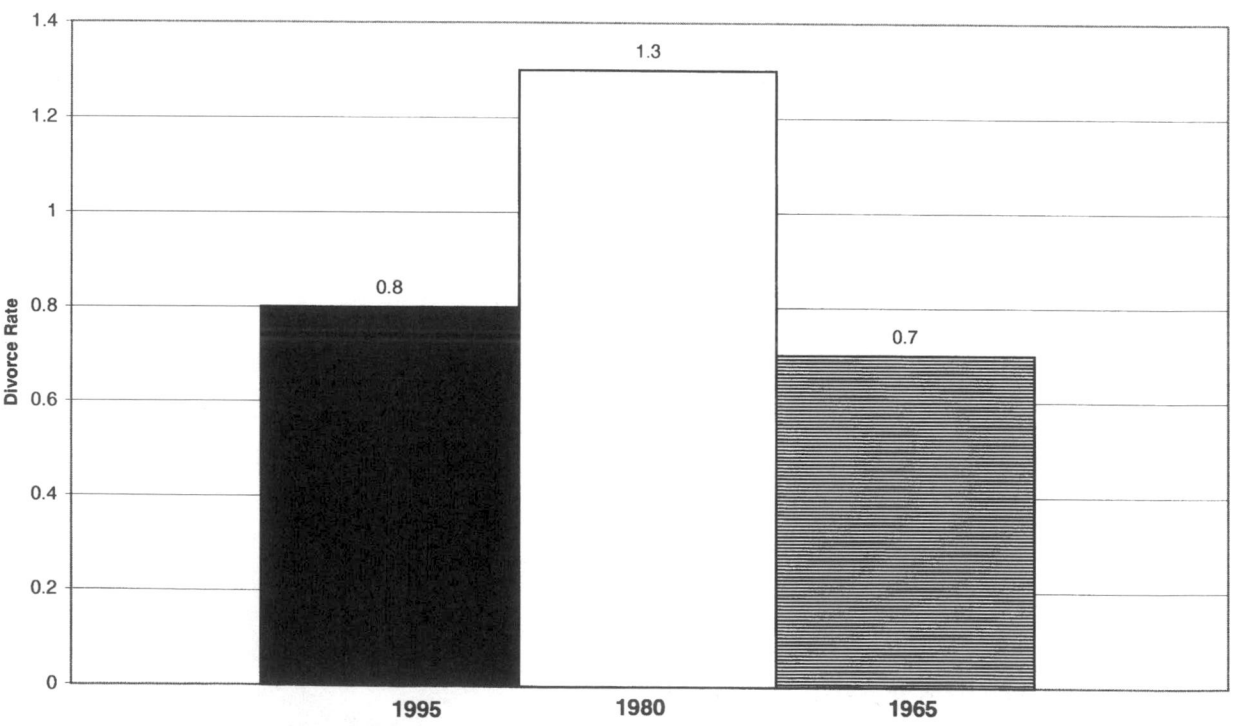

While divorce rates in much of Western and Eastern Europe have been rising in recent decades, they have not in Poland. Most commentators believe this is due to the influence of the Roman Catholic Church. The temporary increase in divorces around 1980 reflects a bulge in the population in their 30s, a prime age for divorce.

Marriage Rates

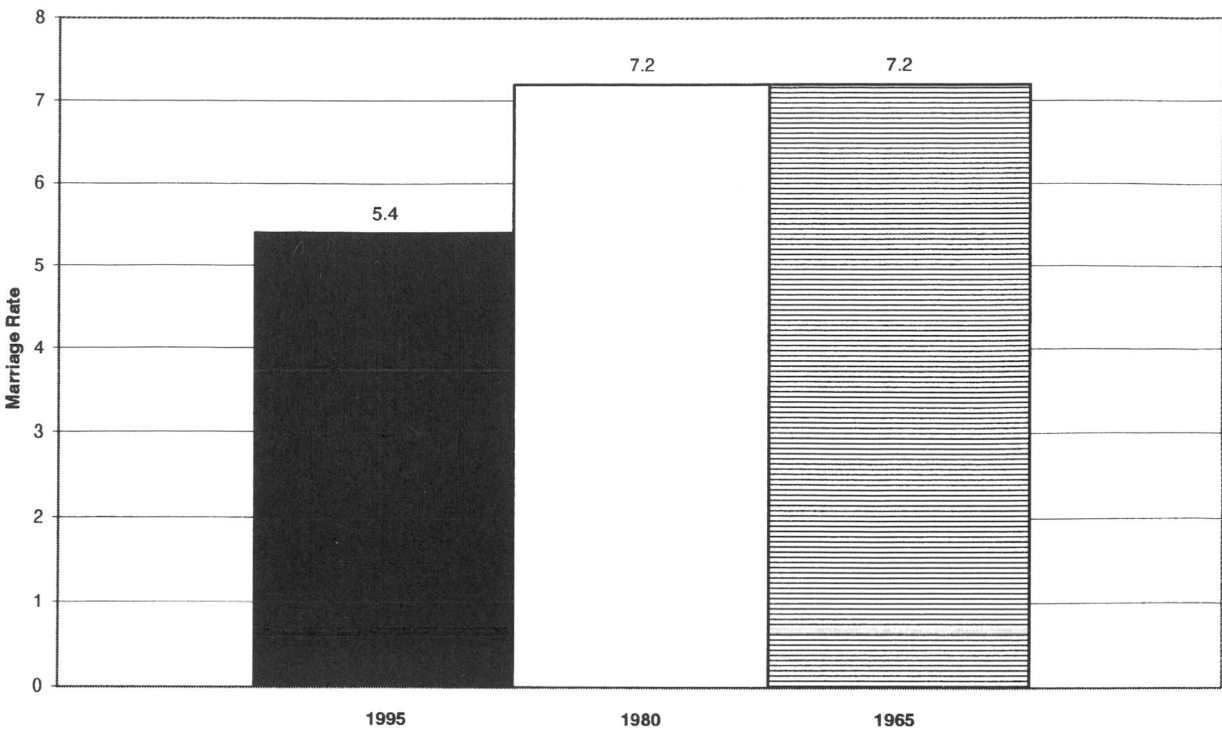

Political and economic turmoil are a major factor in people's decision to get married and have a family. This tendency is clear in Poland, where the rates remained relatively stable until 1980, when the country began its troubled transition from communism.

CHRONOLOGY

1978   Polish cardinal becomes Pope John Paul II.

1980   Nationwide strike that begins in shipyards of Gdansk leads government to recognize workers' rights to form independent union federation, Solidarity.

1981   A national strike leads to military government of General Wojciech Jaruzelski; martial law declared and Solidarity leaders jailed.

1984   Government lifts martial law, but Solidarity remains outlawed.

1988   Nationwide strikes force government to re-legalize Solidarity and call for elections.

1989   Solidarity-backed candidates sweep legislative elections.

1990   Former Solidarity leader Lech Walesa elected president.

1993   Angry at economic downturn, Polish voters elect former communists to power.

	1995	**1980**	**1965**

GEOGRAPHY

AREA (square miles/kilometers)   120,727/312,683
LAND AREA (square miles/kilometers)   117,571/304,510
COASTLINE (miles/kilometers)   307/491

CITIES
CAPITAL   Warsaw   1,643,203 (93)
MAJOR CITIES   Lodz   835,807
                         Cracow   744,203
                         Wroclaw   641,386
                         Poznan   582,839

POPULATION

	1995	**1980**	**1965**
TOTAL	38,642,565	35,061,450 (78)	29,775,508 (60)
DENSITY (per square mile/square kilometer)	329/127	298/115	253/98
ANNUAL GROWTH	0.14%	0.9%	1.2%

AGE COHORTS

	1995	**1980**	**1965**
0–14	22%	n/a	31%
15–64	66%	n/a	62%
65 AND OVER	12%	n/a	7%

	1995	**1980**	**1965**
MALE	49%		
FEMALE	51%		

	1995	**1980**	**1965**
URBAN	61.9%	58.4%	
RURAL	38.1%	41.6%	

	1995	**1980**	**1965**
NET MIGRATION RATE	−0.4	n/a	2.7

IDENTITY

ETHNICITY

	1995
POLISH	97.60%
GERMAN	1.3%
UKRAINIAN	0.6%
BYELORUSSIAN	0.5%

LANGUAGE

	1995
POLISH	n/a

	1995	1980	1965
RELIGION			
ROMAN CATHOLIC	95%		
EASTERN ORTHODOX	n/a		
PROTESTANT	n/a		

VITAL STATISTICS

	1995	1980	1965
BIRTHS			
BIRTH RATE	11.9	18.2	16.7
URBAN BIRTH RATE	10.9 (94)		
RURAL BIRTH RATE	15		
INFANT MORTALITY RATE	12.4	18.5	38.8
ABORTION RATE	1.8		
LIFE EXPECTANCY AT BIRTH	72.1	70	67.6
MARRIAGES			
MARRIAGE RATE	5.4	7.2	7.2
AVERAGE AGE AT MARRIAGE M/F	26.3/23.1		
DIVORCE RATE	0.8	1.3	0.7
DEATHS			
DEATH RATE	10	10.3	7.3

HOUSEHOLDS

	1995	1980	1965
NUMBER	11,970,440 (88)	n/a	8,272,972 (60)
URBAN	7,864,162		
RURAL	4,106,278		
AVERAGE SIZE	3.1	n/a	3.5
URBAN	2.9		
RURAL	3.6		
TYPE OF HOUSEHOLD			
FEMALE HEADED	30.8%		
SINGLE	8.5%		
MARRIED	71.3%		
WIDOWED	20.2%		

ECONOMIC AND LABOR

GDP PER CAPITA US$	$5,800	

	1995	1980	1965
LABOR FORCE (thousands)	15,642.3 (92)		
AGRICULTURE	3,860.00		
MINING	477.9		
MANUFACTURING	3,589.70		
UTILITIES	149.6		
CONSTRUCTION	1,131.80		
TRADE/FOOD/TOURISM	1,827.30		
TRANSPORT/COMMUNICATIONS	1,023.50		
FINANCE/INSURANCE/REAL ESTATE	405		
SOCIAL AND PERSONAL SERVICES	2,895.80		
UNEMPLOYMENT			
TOTAL	16.0% (94)		
UNION DENSITY	27%		
POVERTY			
UNDER $1/DAY	6.8% (93)		
UNDER $2/DAY	15.1%		

TRANSPORT

	1995	1980	1965
JOURNEYS (by transport mode)			
RAILROAD PASSENGER TRIPS	27,610 (94)		
(millions of miles/kilometers)			
AIR PASSENGER TRIPS (thousands)	1,452		
VEHICLES (thousands)			
CARS	7,153.1	2,383.00	245.5
COMMERCIAL VEHICLES	1,395.1	684.2	183.3

HEALTH AND HEALTH CARE

	1995	1980	1965
RATE OF PHYSICIANS	2.3	1.8	0.9 (60)
RATE OF HOSPITAL BEDS	6.3	5.6	7 (60)
TOTAL DEATHS	384,000		
HEALTH INDICATORS			
PREGNANT WOMEN WITH ANEMIA	16%		
LOW-BIRTH-WEIGHT BABIES	8%		
SMOKING PREVALENCE M/F	51/29%		
TUBERCULOSIS INCIDENCE RATE	.50		

	1995	1980	1965
HEALTH CARE			
ACCESS TO SAFE WATER	67%		
ACCESS TO SANITATION	100%		
MEASLES IMMUNIZATION	96%		
AIDS/HIV CASES	422 (95)	222 (93)	

EDUCATION

	1995	1980	1965
SCHOOL AGE IN SCHOOL			
PRIMARY	98%	100%	105%
SECONDARY	96%	77%	58%
HIGHER	27%	18%	8%
FEMALES IN SCHOOL			
PRIMARY	48%	49%	103%
SECONDARY	68%	71%	65%
HIGHER	n/a	19.6%	13.5% (70)
ADULT ILLITERACY M/F	n/a	0.7/1.7% (78)	n/a

COMMUNICATIONS

	1995	1980	1965
RATE OF NEWSPAPERS	159	236	167
RATE OF RADIOS	439	298	190
RATE OF TELEVISIONS	298	246	70

Source: CIA, *The World Factbook, 1997;* ILO, *World Labour Report, 1997;* UN, *Demographic Yearbook, 1997;* UN, *Statistical Yearbook, 1996;* World Bank, *World Development Indicators, 1998.*

PORTUGAL

Situated in the western part of the Iberian peninsula, Portugal is surrounded to the north and east by Spain, and to the west and south by the Atlantic Ocean. From the 1920s until 1974, the country was governed by a fascist dictatorship, which fell to leftist officers in the Carnation Revolution of 1974. One of the first things the new government did was rid Portugal of its far-flung colonial empire. At the same time, the government—which was quickly transformed into a democracy—focused its attention on joining the European Community, which it did in 1982. Since then, the 9.87 million Portuguese have made significant progress in the economic and social spheres. Per capita income has risen to $11,000 annually, still near the bottom as compared to other European Union countries, but rising. The number of privately owned cars has climbed from 195,000 in 1965 to over 3.5 million in 1995, or roughly 1 car for every three persons. At the same time, the number of physicians has climbed from 1 for every 1,200 persons to 1 for every 345. This improvement in health care is reflected in an infant mortality rate that has dropped from 65 to 7.6 per 1,000 live births and a life expectancy that has climbed from 63.5 years to 75.3 Even more dramatic gains have been made in the realm of education. While just 28 percent of young people attended secondary institutions in 1965, virtually all did so by 1995.

	1995	1980	1965
GEOGRAPHY			
AREA (square miles/kilometers)	35,552/92,080		
LAND AREA (square miles/kilometers)	35,382/91,640		
COASTLINE (miles/kilometers)	1,121/1,793		
CITIES			
CAPITAL	Lisbon	663,694 (91)	
MAJOR CITIES	Porto	302,467	
	Amadora	181,774	
	Funchal	115,403	
	Setúbal	103,634	
POPULATION			
TOTAL	9,865,114	9,833,014 (81)	8,851,289 (60)
DENSITY (per square mile/square kilometer)	279/108	278/107	250/97
ANNUAL GROWTH	0.02%	0.7%	0.7%
AGE COHORTS			
0–14	18%	n/a	29% (65)
15–64	68%	n/a	63%
65 AND OVER	14%	n/a	8%

	1995	**1980**	**1965**
MALE	48%		
FEMALE	52%		
URBAN	48.2% (91)	29.7%	
RURAL	51.8%	70.3%	
NET MIGRATION RATE	−0.2	n/a	−1.0

IDENTITY

ETHNICITY			
PORTUGUESE	n/a		
AFRICAN	n/a		
LANGUAGE			
PORTUGUESE	n/a		
RELIGION			
ROMAN CATHOLIC	97%		
PROTESTANT	n/a		

VITAL STATISTICS

BIRTHS			
BIRTH RATE	10.5	14.4 (83)	22.3
INFANT MORTALITY RATE	7.6	19.3	65
LIFE EXPECTANCY AT BIRTH	75.3	69 (83)	63.5
MARRIAGES			
MARRIAGE RATE	6.9	7.5 (83)	8.4
AVERAGE AGE AT MARRIAGE M/F	26.7/23.9 (91)		
DIVORCE RATE	1.2 (93)	0.8	0.1
DEATHS			
DEATH RATE	10.2	9.6 (83)	10.9

HOUSEHOLDS

NUMBER	3,145,734 (91)		2,232.818 (60)
AVERAGE SIZE	3.1		3.9
TYPE OF HOUSEHOLD			
FEMALE HEADED	19.9%		
SINGLE	6.5%		
MARRIED	72.4%		

	1995	1980	1965
WIDOWED	13.7%		
DIVORCED/SEPARATED	4.6%		

ECONOMICS AND LABOR

GDP PER CAPITA US$	$11,000		
LABOR FORCE M/F (thousands)	2,486.0/1,971.6 (93)		
AGRICULTURE	262.7/252.9		
MINING	19.0/0.7		
MANUFACTURING	598.2/444.4		
UTILITIES	25.8/6.3		
CONSTRUCTION	349.5/15.8		
TRADE/FOOD/TOURISM	498.1/369.1		
TRANSPORT/COMMUNICATIONS	160.9/47.0		
FINANCE/INSURANCE/REAL ESTATE	182.1/117.9		
SOCIAL AND PERSONAL SERVICES	389.7/717.6		
UNEMPLOYMENT			
TOTAL	5.5% (93)		
UNION DENSITY	18.8%		

TRANSPORT

JOURNEYS (by transport mode)			
RAILROAD PASSENGER TRIPS	5,149 (94)		
(millions of miles/kilometers)			
AIR PASSENGER TRIPS (thousands)	4,360 (94)		
VEHICLES (thousands)			
CARS	3,532	1,269.00	195
COMMERCIAL VEHICLES	1,158.6	465.1	68.5

HEALTH AND HEALTH CARE

RATE OF PHYSICIANS	2.9	2	0.8 (60)
RATE OF HOSPITAL BEDS	4.3	n/a	5.5 (60)
TOTAL DEATHS	103,939		
HEALTH INDICATORS			
LOW-BIRTH-WEIGHT BABIES	5%		
SMOKING PREVALENCE M/F	38/15%		
TUBERCULOSIS INCIDENCE RATE	.60		

	1995	**1980**	**1965**
HEALTH CARE			
ACCESS TO SAFE WATER	57%		
ACCESS TO SANITATION	100%		
MEASLES IMMUNIZATION	94%		
AIDS/HIV CASES	3,106 (95)	1,972 (93)	

EDUCATION

	1995	**1980**	**1965**
SCHOOL AGE IN SCHOOL			
PRIMARY	128%	123%	83%
SECONDARY	102%	37%	28%
HIGHER	34%	11%	3.80%
FEMALES IN SCHOOL			
PRIMARY	n/a	48%	83%
SECONDARY	n/a	48%	23%
HIGHER	n/a	11%	6.8% (70)
ADULT ILLITERACY M/F	n/a	15.2/25.4% (81)	n/a

COMMUNICATIONS

	1995	**1980**	**1965**
RATE OF NEWSPAPERS	47	49	68
RATE OF RADIOS	232	170	133
RATE OF TELEVISIONS	190	158	20

Source: CIA, The World Factbook, 1997; ILO, World Labour Report, 1997; UN, Demographic Yearbook, 1997; UN, Statistical Yearbook, 1996; World Bank, World Development Indicators, 1998.

PUERTO RICO

Since the return of Hong Kong to China in 1997, Puerto Rico has become the largest nonindependent territory in the world by population. The 3.82 million people of Puerto Rico exist in what is called a Commonwealth within the United States, enjoying some but not all the rights of U.S. citizenship. Located between the Caribbean and the Atlantic, Puerto Rico covers some 3,515 square miles, making it the fourth largest island in the West Indies. As part of the United States, Puerto Rico enjoys the highest per capita income in the Caribbean region, at some $7,800 annually. The economy of Puerto Rico is relatively modern as well. While just 3 percent of the island's 1-million–strong workforce labored in agriculture in 1995, nearly half were involved in the service sector. In addition, many Puerto Ricans take advan-

tage of their legal connection to the United States by migrating to the mainland for jobs, since unemployment, at 14.6 percent in 1994, remains high. Similarly, the island's social indexes reflect its connection to the United States as well. As early as 1965, virtually all Puerto Rican children attended primary school and 70 percent went on to secondary institutions. Health indexes are relatively high as well. The infant mortality rate was just 12.4 in 1995 and life expectancy was 75.4, both comparable though somewhat inferior to those on the U.S. mainland. The future status of Puerto Rico remains unclear. Recent polls indicate that the populace remains deeply divided between maintaining the status quo and opting for statehood, with a small minority advocating full independence.

	1995	1980	1965
GEOGRAPHY			
AREA (square miles/kilometers)	3,515/9,104		
LAND AREA (square miles/kilometers)	3,459/8,959		
COASTLINE (miles/kilometers)	313/501		
CITIES			
CAPITAL	San Juan	451,168 (94)	
MAJOR CITIES	Bayamón	229,299	
	Ponce	193,069	
	Carolina	188,997	
	Caguas	141,675	
POPULATION			
TOTAL	3,819,023	3,196,520	2,349,544 (60)
DENSITY (per square mile/square kilometer)	1104/426	924/357	679/262
ANNUAL GROWTH	0.18%	n/a	1.9%

	1995	**1980**	**1965**
AGE COHORTS			
0–14	25%		
15–64	65%		
65 AND OVER	10%		
URBAN	71.2% (90)	66.8%	
RURAL	29.8%	33.2%	
NET MIGRATION RATE	−6.35		

IDENTITY

ETHNICITY
HISPANIC   n/a

LANGUAGE
SPANISH   n/a
ENGLISH   n/a

RELIGION
ROMAN CATHOLIC   85%
PROTESTANT AND OTHER   15%

VITAL STATISTICS

	1995	**1980**	**1965**
BIRTHS			
BIRTH RATE	15.6	20.1	30.2 (83)
URBAN BIRTH RATE	8.7 (91)		
RURAL BIRTH RATE	9.3		
INFANT MORTALITY RATE	12.4	16	42.8 (83)
LIFE EXPECTANCY AT BIRTH	75.4	73.9 (83)	69.5
MARRIAGES			
MARRIAGE RATE	9.6	9.1	10.2 (83)
AVERAGE AGE AT MARRIAGE M/F	25.8/23.8		
DIVORCE RATE	4	4	3 (83)
DEATHS			
DEATH RATE	7.5	5.5	6.7 (83)

HOUSEHOLDS

NUMBER   886,339 (90)
AVERAGE SIZE   3.9

	1995	1980	1965
TYPE OF HOUSEHOLD			
FEMALE HEADED	31.9%		

ECONOMICS AND LABOR

	1995	1980	1965
GDP PER CAPITA US$	$7,800		
LABOR FORCE M/F (thousands)	612/414 (94)		
AGRICULTURE	34/1		
MINING	1/0		
MANUFACTURING	95/70		
UTILITIES	15/3		
CONSTRUCTION	52/1		
TRADE/FOOD/TOURISM	130/77		
TRANSPORT/COMMUNICATIONS	34/7		
FINANCE/INSURANCE/REAL ESTATE	17/18		
SOCIAL AND PERSONAL SERVICES	237/235		
UNEMPLOYMENT			
TOTAL	14.6 (94)		

TRANSPORT

	1995	1980	1965
VEHICLES (thousands)			
CARS	1,393.3	n/a	255.2
COMMERCIAL VEHICLES	239.6	n/a	51.3

HEALTH AND HEALTH CARE

	1995	1980	1965
RATE OF PHYSICIANS	n/a	n/a	0.5 (60)
RATE OF HOSPITAL BEDS	n/a	n/a	5.2 (60)
TOTAL DEATHS	28,444 (94)		
HEALTH INDICATORS			
TUBERCULOSIS INCIDENCE RATE	.08		

EDUCATION

	1995	1980	1965
SCHOOL AGE IN SCHOOL			
PRIMARY			114%
SECONDARY			70%
HIGHER			15.3%

	1995	1980	1965
FEMALES IN SCHOOL			
HIGHER	n/a	48%	n/a

COMMUNICATIONS

	1995	1980	1965
RATE OF NEWSPAPERS	141	160	64
RATE OF RADIOS	712	624	
RATE OF TELEVISIONS	267	226	

Source: CIA, *The World Factbook, 1997;* ILO, *World Labour Report, 1997;* UN, *Demographic Yearbook, 1997;* UN, *Statistical Yearbook, 1996;* World Bank, *World Development Indicators, 1998.*

QATAR

Qatar is a peninsular country of some 4,250 square miles, located in the southern Persian Gulf. Its only land border, renegotiated in 1995 but still not official, is with Saudi Arabia to the south. A colony of Britain since the nineteenth century, Qatar won its independence in 1971. Qatar and its 547,761 people have a per capita income of $20,820 annually, reflecting its vast reserves of oil. While the citizenry of the country remains predominantly Arab and Arabic speaking, the majority of residents are alien workers, including some 18 percent from Pakistan and India, respectively, and another 10 percent from Iran. Since the dramatic rise in oil prices in the early 1970s, Qatar has used its revenues to expand its health care and educational infrastructures. These expenditures are reflected in the fact that the percentage of school-age children attending secondary institutions rose from just 15 percent in 1965 to fully 63 percent in 1980, with over 9 percent attending university. The country's newfound wealth is also reflected in the number of private vehicles, which doubled between 1980 and 1994, to 137,600.

	1995	1980	1965
GEOGRAPHY			
AREA (square miles/kilometers)	4,247/11,000		
LAND AREA (square miles/kilometers)	4,247/11,000		
COASTLINE (miles/kilometers)	352/563		
CITIES			
CAPITAL	Doha	n/a	217,294 (86)
POPULATION			
TOTAL	547,761	319,000	
DENSITY (per square mile/square kilometer)	129/50	7529	
ANNUAL GROWTH	2.39%	6.9%	3.7%
AGE COHORTS			
0–14	30%		
15–64	68%		
65 AND OVER	2%		
MALE	67%		
FEMALE	33%		

	1995	1980	1965

IDENTITY

ETHNICITY
ARAB	40%		
PAKISTANI	18%		
INDIAN	18%		
IRANIAN	10%		

LANGUAGE
ARABIC	n/a		
ENGLISH	n/a		

RELIGION
MUSLIM	95%		

VITAL STATISTICS

BIRTHS
BIRTH RATE	21	38.3	
INFANT MORTALITY RATE	19.6	38	
LIFE EXPECTANCY AT BIRTH	73.4	67.6	

MARRIAGES
MARRIAGE RATE	2.8	4.7	
AVERAGE AGE AT MARRIAGE M/F	n/a	26.6/22.7	
DIVORCE RATE	0.8	1	

DEATHS
DEATH RATE	3.6	4.6	

HOUSEHOLDS

AVERAGE SIZE	n/a	5.6	

ECONOMICS AND LABOR

GDP PER CAPITA US$	$20,820		

	1995	1980	1965
TRANSPORT			
VEHICLES (thousands)			
CARS	137.6 (94)	64.1	
COMMERCIAL VEHICLES	65.8	37.9	
HEALTH AND HEALTH CARE			
DEATHS			
TOTAL DEATHS	964 (94)		
AIDS/HIV CASES	80 (95)	69 (93)	
EDUCATION			
SCHOOL AGE IN SCHOOL			
PRIMARY	n/a	102%	97%
SECONDARY	n/a	63%	15%
HIGHER	n/a	9.1%	
FEMALES IN SCHOOL			
PRIMARY	n/a	102%	80%
SECONDARY	n/a	70%	6%
HIGHER	n/a	20.6%	
COMMUNICATIONS			
RATE OF NEWSPAPERS	135	131	n/a
RATE OF RADIOS	389	393	225 (70)
RATE OF TELEVISIONS	397	331	n/a

Source: CIA, The World Factbook, 1997; ILO, World Labour Report, 1997; UN, Demographic Yearbook, 1997; UN, Statistical Yearbook, 1996; World Bank, World Development Indicators, 1998.

ROMANIA

Situated in the eastern part of the Balkans, Romania is surrounded by the Ukraine and Moldova to the north and east, Bulgaria to the south, and Serbia and Hungary to the west. It also has a 140-mile coastline along the Black Sea to the east. In Romania, as in many Eastern European countries, the population has seen declines in recent years. Between 1980 and 1995, the population shrank by some 1.2 percent, falling to 21.66 million. This was largely due to two factors. The post-communist collapse in the social welfare net has caused the death rate to climb from 10.3 per 1,000 persons in 1980 to 12.3 in 1995, and the birth rate fell from 15.5 to 9.8 over the same period. In addition, the country has seen a dramatic increase in out-migration. In 1995, the net migration rate was −9.6 per 1,000 persons, one of the highest in the former communist world. The near total collapse of the Romanian economy is largely to blame, though this had begun under the communist dictator Nicolai Ceausescu, who was overthrown in a violent revolution in 1989. According to Romania's own national standards, some 70.9 percent of the Romanian people were living in poverty in 1995, while the per capita income was just $4,600 annually. The economic decline is reflected in stagnant social indexes. Both the infant mortality rate and life expectancy have remained virtually unchanged between 1980 and 1995, while they improved in most other countries of Europe and the world.

Population Growth

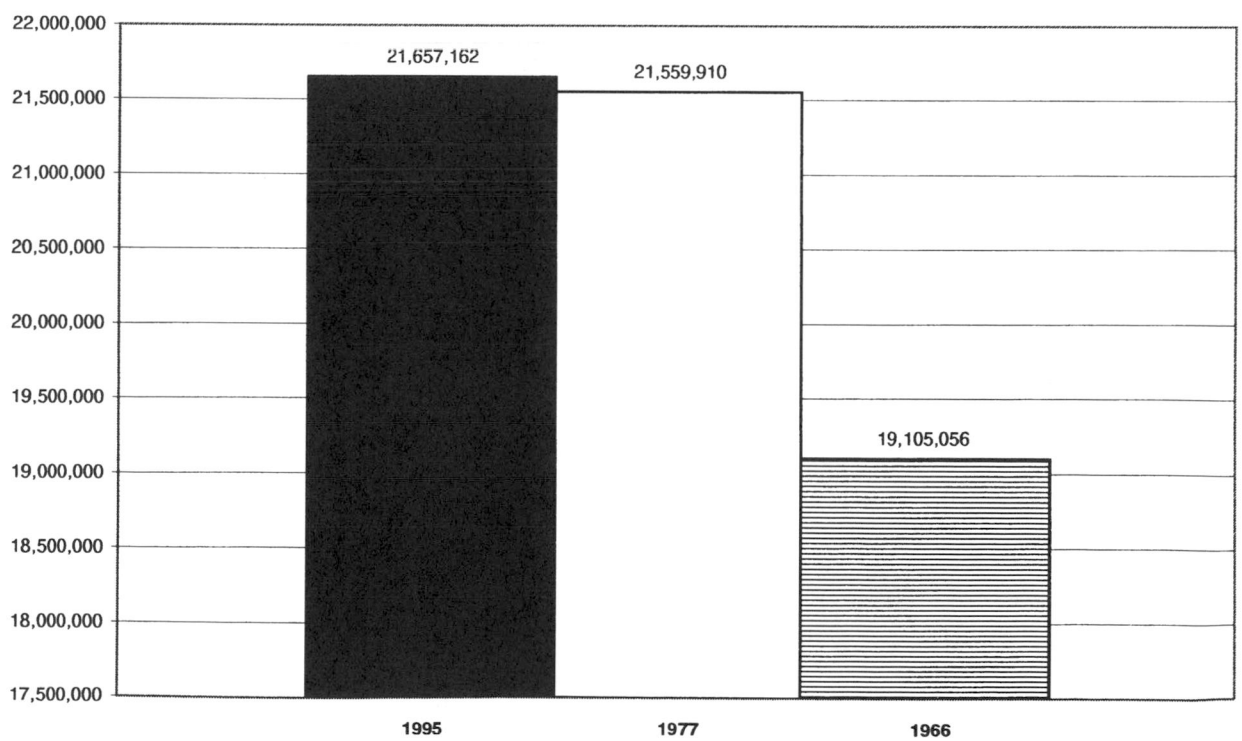

Like other Eastern European countries, Romania witnessed extremely low growth rates from the 1960s through the 1980s. With the economic and political instability in the country since the fall of the Nicolai Ceausescu dictatorship in 1989, the population has even begun to shrink.

Death Rates

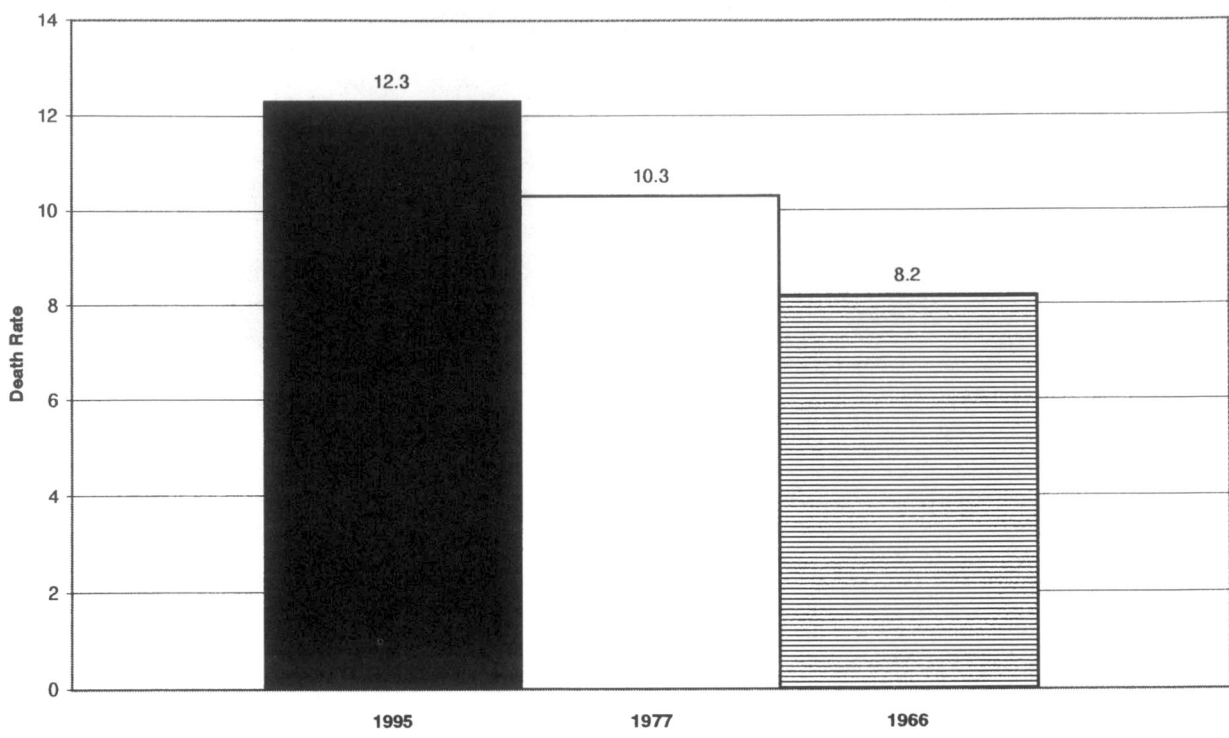

Part of the reason for Romania's declining population can be found in the aging population of the country, as reflected in the rising death rates.

CHRONOLOGY

1965   Nicolai Ceausescu becomes premier of Romania.

1968   Refusing to send troops to Czechoslovakia, Romania asserts independence from Moscow on foreign policy.

1971   Period of relaxed political control ends with declaration of hardline "theses."

1984   Romania attends Summer Olympics in Los Angeles, refusing to go along with Soviet-led boycott.

1989   Ceausescu regime overthrown by popular protest; the premier and his wife are executed.

1990   Ion Iliescu elected to presidency of interim government.

1995   Romania makes application for membership in European Union.

1996   Iliescu elected to third term as president.

		1995	1980	1965

GEOGRAPHY

AREA (square miles/kilometers)	91,699/237,500		
LAND AREA (square miles/kilometers)	88,934/230,340		
COASTLINE (miles/kilometers)	141/225		

CITIES			
CAPITAL	Bucharest	2,060,551 (94)	
MAJOR CITIES	Constanta	348,575	
	Iasi	339,889	
	Timisoara	327,830	
	Galati	326,728	

POPULATION

	1995	1980	1965
TOTAL	21,657,162	21,559,910 (77)	19,105,056 (66)
DENSITY (per square mile/square kilometer)	244/94	242/94	215/83
ANNUAL GROWTH	−1.21%	0.7%	0.7%

	1995	1980	1965
AGE COHORTS			
0–14	20%	n/a	26%
15–64	68%	n/a	66%
65 AND OVER	12%	n/a	8%

MALE	49%
FEMALE	51%

	1995	1980
URBAN	54.7% (94)	49.6%
RURAL	45.3%	50.4%

NET MIGRATION RATE	−9.6

IDENTITY

ETHNICITY	
ROMANIAN	89.1%
HUNGARIAN	8.9%
GERMAN	0.4%
UKRAINIAN, SERB, CROAT, RUSSIAN, TURK, AND GYPSY	n/a

	1995	1980	1965
LANGUAGE			
ROMANIAN	n/a		
HUNGARIAN	n/a		
GERMAN	n/a		
RELIGION			
ROMANIAN ORTHODOX	70%		
ROMAN CATHOLIC	6%		
PROTESTANT	6%		

VITAL STATISTICS

	1995	1980	1965
BIRTHS			
BIRTH RATE	9.77	15.5 (84)	14.3
URBAN BIRTH RATE	9.2 (94)		
RURAL BIRTH RATE	12.8		
INFANT MORTALITY RATE	23.2	23.4	46.5
ABORTION RATE	2,149.1		
LIFE EXPECTANCY AT BIRTH	69.4	68.9 (84)	67.8
MARRIAGES			
MARRIAGE RATE	6.8	7.3 (84)	8.9
AVERAGE AGE AT MARRIAGE M/F	26/22.4 (94)		
DIVORCE RATE	1.7 (94)	1.5	1.9
DEATHS			
DEATH RATE	12.3	10.3	8.2

HOUSEHOLDS

	1995
NUMBER	7,288,676 (92)
URBAN	3,970,435
RURAL	3,318,241
AVERAGE SIZE	3.1
URBAN	3
RURAL	3.1
TYPE OF HOUSEHOLD	
FEMALE HEADED	22.1%
SINGLE	5.7%
MARRIED	71.7%
WIDOWED	17.5%
DIVORCED/SEPARATED	5%

	1995	1980	1965

ECONOMICS AND LABOR

GDP PER CAPITA US$	$4,600		
LABOR FORCE M/F (thousands)	5,415.3/4,646.7 (93)		
AGRICULTURE	1,743.2/1,878.8		
MINING	216.8/42.4		
MANUFACTURING	1,430.8/1,175.5		
UTILITIES	128.8/36.3		
CONSTRUCTION	500.7/73.3		
TRADE/FOOD/TOURISM	332.5/383.2		
TRANSPORT/COMMUNICATIONS	451.5/140.4		
FINANCE/INSURANCE/REAL ESTATE	235.3/246.9		
SOCIAL AND PERSONAL SERVICES	376.6/669.9		
UNEMPLOYMENT			
TOTAL	10.2% (93)		
UNION DENSITY	40.7%		
POVERTY			
UNDER $1/DAY	17.7% (92)		
UNDER $2/DAY	70.9%		

TRANSPORT

JOURNEYS (by transport mode)			
RAILROAD PASSENGER TRIPS	18,313 (94)		
(millions of miles/kilometers)			
AIR PASSENGER TRIPS (thousands)	1,243 (94)		

HEALTH AND HEALTH CARE

RATE OF PHYSICIANS	1.8	1.5	1.3 (60)
RATE OF HOSPITAL BEDS	7.7	8.8	7.3 (60)
TOTAL DEATHS	271,674		
HEALTH INDICATORS			
PREGNANT WOMEN WITH ANEMIA	31%		
CHILD MALNUTRITION	6%		
TUBERCULOSIS INCIDENCE RATE	1.2		

	1995	1980	1965
HEALTH CARE			
ACCESS TO SAFE WATER		77%	
ACCESS TO SANITATION	49%		
MEASLES IMMUNIZATION	93%		
AIDS/HIV CASES	3,852 (95)	2,756 (93)	

EDUCATION

	1995	1980	1965
SCHOOL AGE IN SCHOOL			
PRIMARY	100%	102%	103%
SECONDARY	66%	71%	38%
HIGHER	18%	12%	6.9%
FEMALES IN SCHOOL			
PRIMARY	49%	49%	101%
SECONDARY	53%	65%	32%
HIGHER	n/a	9.4%	8.8% (70)

COMMUNICATIONS

	1995	1980	1965
RATE OF NEWSPAPERS	324	181	157
RATE OF RADIOS	202	177	146
RATE OF TELEVISIONS	200	184	26

Source: CIA, The World Factbook, 1997; ILO, World Labour Report, 1997; UN, Demographic Yearbook, 1997; UN, Statistical Yearbook, 1996; World Bank, World Development Indicators, 1998.

RUSSIAN FEDERATION[1]

With some 6,854,000 square miles of territory, Russia remains the largest country on earth. Though shrunk from Soviet days, the country still encompasses eleven time zones and covers the northern half of the vast Eurasian landmass from the Baltic Sea to the Pacific Ocean. The vast heart of the former Soviet Union, Russia has a population of 148.18 million, which remains diverse ethnically and linguistically. While over 80 percent of the population is Russian, there are about a dozen minorities. Russia's population—now largely shed of its fast-growing Muslim population since the collapse of the Soviet Union in 1991—has been shrinking slightly in recent years. Meanwhile, though it has entered a period of vi-brant democracy, its economy remains a sham-bles. Inflation has destroyed savings and left pensioners broke. Millions of workers in former and current state-owned industries remain un-paid. The government has been having a difficult time maintaining even basic services, in the face of financial woes and worker protests. The coun-try's once-vaunted health care and educational systems, while still operating, are often forced to do without basic materials. The overall life ex-pectancy of Russian citizens has fallen from about 70 years to just 63.2 years, with male rates under 60. In addition, between 1980 and 1995, the num-ber of young persons attending secondary insti-tutions fell from 96 percent to 87 percent.

Gender

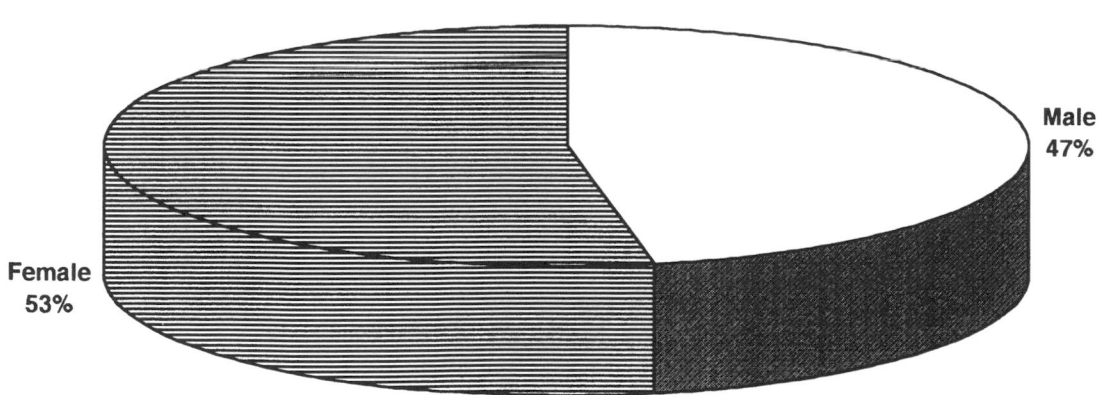

Increasing number of old persons and rising death rates have marked Russian demography in recent years. Since men tend to die younger than women, this distorts the gender profile of the population.

Urban-Rural Birth Rates

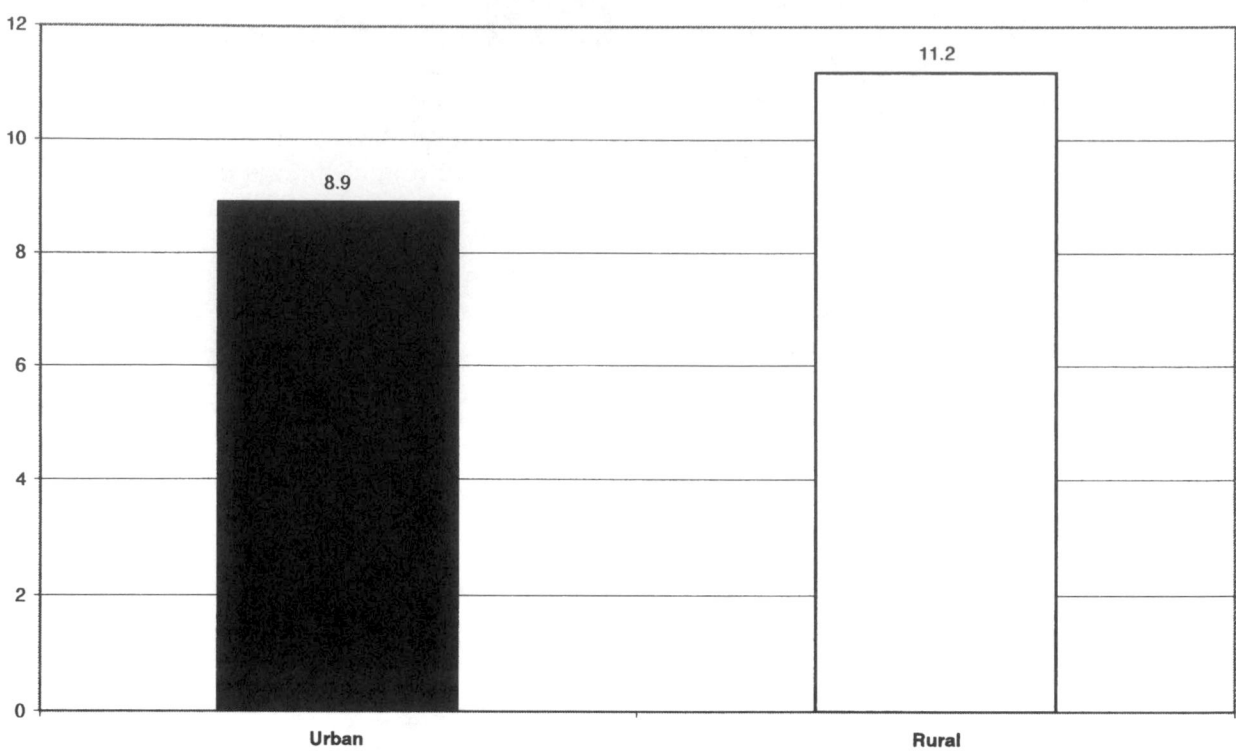

During the communist era, Russian cities suffered from a lack of housing, a problem which continues today. This partially explains the significantly higher birth rates in rural areas—where housing shortages are less of a problem—over urban areas.

CHRONOLOGY

1964   Soviet Premier Nikita Khrushchev forced to retire; Leonid Brezhnev becomes Soviet leader.

1968   Soviet Union leads invasion of Czechoslovakia.

1979   Soviet Union and United States sign SALT II nuclear limitation treaty; Soviets invade Afghanistan.

1980   United States leads boycott of Summer Olympics in Moscow.

1983   Soviet military jet shoots down Korean Air Lines passenger jet, killing hundreds.

1985   Mikhail Gorbachev becomes Soviet leader; announces plans for new political freedoms and economic restructuring.

1986   Accident at Chernobyl nuclear power station leads to widespread fallout.

1991   Attempted military coup leads to dissolution of Soviet Union; Boris Yeltsin becomes president of new Russian Federation; Russia and ten other former Soviet republics form Commonwealth of Independent States.

1994   Russian military attempts to put down Chechnya liberation struggle.

1996   Chechnya ceasefire announced; Yeltsin reelected president.

	1995	1980	1965

GEOGRAPHY

AREA (square miles/kilometers)   6,854,131/17,075,200
LAND AREA (square miles/kilometers)   6,562,085/16,995,800
COASTLINE (miles/kilometers)   23,533/37,653

CITIES

CAPITAL	Moscow	8,436,447 (94)
MAJOR CITIES	St. Petersburg	4,273,001
	Nizhny Novgorod	1,382,115
	Novosirbirsk	1,370,544
	Ekaterinburg	1,277,963

POPULATION

TOTAL	148,178,487
DENSITY (per square mile/square kilometer)	23/9
ANNUAL GROWTH	−0.07

AGE COHORTS

0–14	21%
15–64	67%
65 AND OVER	12%

MALE	47%
FEMALE	53%

URBAN	72.9%
RURAL	27.1%

NET MIGRATION RATE	5.47

IDENTITY

ETHNICITY

RUSSIAN	81.5%
TATAR	3.8%
UKRAINIAN	3%
CHUVASH	1.2%
BASHKIR	0.9%
BYELORUSSIAN	0.8%
MOLDAVIAN	0.7%

	1995	1980	1965
LANGUAGE			
RUSSIAN	n/a		
RELIGION			
RUSSIAN ORTHODOX	n/a		
MUSLIM	n/a		

VITAL STATISTICS

BIRTHS			
BIRTH RATE	10.2		
URBAN BIRTH RATE	8.9 (94)		
RURAL BIRTH RATE	11.2 (94)		
INFANT MORTALITY RATE	24.7		
ABORTION RATE	1,762.3 (94)		
LIFE EXPECTANCY AT BIRTH	63.2		
MARRIAGES			
MARRIAGE RATE	7.5		
AVERAGE AGE AT MARRIAGE M/F	24.4/21.8 (89)		
DIVORCE RATE	4.5		
DEATHS			
DEATH RATE	16.3		

HOUSEHOLDS

NUMBER	57,297,047 (89)		
AVERAGE SIZE	2.6		

ECONOMICS AND LABOR

GDP PER CAPITA US$	$5,300		
LABOR FORCE (thousands)	72,071.1 (92)		
AGRICULTURE	11,078.9		
MINING	1,252.8		
MANUFACTURING	18,682.8		
UTILITIES	669.3		
CONSTRUCTION	7,246.6		
TRADE/FOOD/TOURISM	4,914.2		
TRANSPORT/COMMUNICATIONS	5,631.8		
FINANCE/INSURANCE/REAL ESTATE	493.6		
SOCIAL AND PERSONAL SERVICES	18,641.8		

	1995	1980	1965
UNEMPLOYMENT			
TOTAL	0.8 (92)		
UNION DENSITY	74.8%		
POVERTY			
UNDER $1/DAY	<2%		
UNDER $2/DAY	10.9%		

TRANSPORT

	1995	1980	1965
JOURNEYS (by transport mode)			
RAILROAD PASSENGER TRIPS	227,100.0 (94)		
(millions of miles/kilometers)			
AIR PASSENGER TRIPS (thousands)	29,333.0		

HEALTH AND HEALTH CARE

	1995	1980	1965
RATE OF PHYSICIANS	3.8	4	
RATE OF HOSPITAL BEDS	11.8	13	
TOTAL DEATHS	2,176,400		
HEALTH INDICATORS			
PREGNANT WOMEN WITH ANEMIA	30%		
CHILD MALNUTRITION	3%		
SMOKING PREVALENCE M/F	67/30%		
TUBERCULOSIS INCIDENCE RATE	.99		
HEALTH CARE			
MEASLES IMMUNIZATION	91		
AIDS/HIV CASES	198 (95)	143 (93)	

EDUCATION

	1995	1980	1965
SCHOOL AGE IN SCHOOL			
PRIMARY	108%	102%	
SECONDARY	87%	96%	
HIGHER	43%	46%	
FEMALES IN SCHOOL			
PRIMARY	49%	49%	
SECONDARY	52%	51%	

	1995	1980	1965
COMMUNICATIONS			
RATE OF NEWSPAPERS	387	423[2]	336 (70)[2]
RATE OF RADIOS	338	504	390[2]
RATE OF TELEVISIONS	372	296	143[2]

FOOTNOTES
1. Russia was part of the Soviet Union before 1991.
2. Soviet Union total.

Source: CIA, The World Factbook, 1997; ILO, World Labour Report, 1997; UN, Demographic Yearbook, 1997; UN, Statistical Yearbook, 1996; World Bank, World Development Indicators, 1998.

RWANDA

One of the smallest and most densely populated countries in Africa, Rwanda has a density of 711 persons for each of its 10,170 square miles of territory. A lush, hilly country in East Africa's Great Lakes region, Rwanda borders on Uganda to the north, Tanzania to the east, Burundi to the south, and Lake Kivu and the Democratic Republic of the Congo to the west. Since its independence from Belgian colonial rule in 1962, Rwanda has been torn by some of the worst ethnic strife in Africa. Since the early 1960s, the animosities between the majority, ruling Hutu people and the minority Tutsi have burst out into violence on several occasions. The most recent was in 1994, when a carefully orchestrated genocidal campaign was launched by Hutu extremists against the Tutsi, resulting in the deaths of between 500,000 and 1 million Tutsi in a matter of weeks. Ended by a Tutsi-led rebel invasion, the genocide led to a mass exodus of Hutu people to refugee camps in the Congo and Tanzania. Two years later, most of the Hutu returned from the camps to Rwanda. While the government maintains that it is trying to rebuild a Rwanda for all its citizens, most Hutus remain wary and the remaining Tutsis are scared. Trials of Hutu militia leaders for their acts of genocide continue in Tanzania, but few expect most of the perpetrators to be brought to justice, since the backlog of cases is far more than the limited number of judges and lawyers in the country can handle.

	1995	1980	1965
GEOGRAPHY			
AREA (square miles/kilometers)	10,170/26,340		
LAND AREA (square miles/kilometers)	9,633/24,950		
COASTLINE (miles/kilometers)	Landlocked		
CITIES			
CAPITAL	Kigali	n/a	116,227 (78)
POPULATION			
TOTAL	6,853,359	4,800,433 (78)	2,143,978 (52)
DENSITY (per square mile/square kilometer)	711/275	498/192	223/86
ANNUAL GROWTH	16.49%[1] (96)	3.3%	3.1%
AGE COHORTS			
0–14	46%		
15–64	51%		
65 AND OVER	3%		
URBAN	5.4% (91)	4.7% (78)	
RURAL	94.6%	95.3%	

	1995	1980	1965
NET MIGRATION RATE	146.4		

IDENTITY

ETHNICITY

HUTU	80%		
TUTSI	19%		

LANGUAGE

KINYARWANDA (official)	n/a		
FRENCH (official)	n/a		
KISWAHILI	n/a		

RELIGION

ROMAN CATHOLIC	65%		
PROTESTANT	9%		
MUSLIM	1%		
INDIGENOUS AND OTHER	25%		

VITAL STATISTICS

BIRTHS

BIRTH RATE	38.8	51 (70)	52 (57)
INFANT MORTALITY RATE	118.8	127	137
LIFE EXPECTANCY AT BIRTH	40.1	46.4	n/a

MARRIAGES

MARRIAGE RATE	2.6	2.6 (70)	
DIVORCE RATE	n/a	0	

DEATHS

DEATH RATE	20.3	22 (70)	13.7 (57)

HOUSEHOLDS

NUMBER	1,508,774 (91)		
AVERAGE SIZE	4.7		
FEMALE HEADED	25%		

ECONOMICS AND LABOR

GDP PER CAPITA US$	$400		

	1995	**1980**	**1965**
LABOR FORCE M/F			
AGRICULTURE	86/98%		
INDUSTRY	6/1%		
SERVICES	8/2%		
POVERTY			
UNDER $1/DAY	45.7%		
UNDER $2/DAY	88.7%		

TRANSPORT

	1995	**1980**	**1965**
JOURNEYS (by transport mode)			
RAILROAD PASSENGER TRIPS	9.0 (94)		
(millions of miles/kilometers)			
VEHICLES			
PRIVATE CARS	7.9 (92)	5.3	
COMMERCIAL VEHICLES	2	8.1	

HEALTH CARE

	1995	**1980**	**1965**
RATE OF PHYSICIANS	0	0	0 (60)
RATE OF HOSPITAL BEDS	1.7	1.5	n/a
HEALTH INDICATORS			
LOW-BIRTH-WEIGHT BABIES	17%		
CHILD MALNUTRITION	29%		
TUBERCULOSIS INCIDENCE RATE	2.6		
HEALTH CARE			
MEASLES IMMUNIZATION	74%		
AIDS/HIV CASES	10,706 (95)	10,706 (93)	

EDUCATION

	1995	**1980**	**1965**
SCHOOL AGE IN SCHOOL			
PRIMARY	82%	63%	67%
SECONDARY	11%	3%	2%
HIGHER	0%	0%	0%
FEMALES IN SCHOOL			
PRIMARY	50%	48%	54%
SECONDARY	n/a	28%	1%

	1995	1980	1965
ADULT ILLITERACY M/F	30/48%	49.2/73.4% (78)	n/a

COMMUNICATIONS

RATE OF NEWSPAPERS	0.1	0.1	
RATE OF RADIOS	66	34	

FOOTNOTE

1. Reflects refugees returning from Congo and Tanzania.

Source: CIA, *The World Factbook, 1997;* ILO, *World Labour Report, 1997;* UN, *Demographic Yearbook, 1997;* UN, *Statistical Yearbook, 1996;* World Bank, *World Development Indicators, 1998.*

SAINT KITTS AND NEVIS

Consisting of two small islands at the northern end of the Lesser Antilles of the eastern Caribbean, Saint Kitts and Nevis cover just 104 square miles of territory and have a total population of 41,000 persons, about three-quarters of whom live on the larger Saint Kitts, where the capital of Basseterre is located. Ethnically, most of the inhabitants of the two islands are descendants of Africans brought as slaves. Formerly a British territory, Saint Kitts and Nevis now largely thrives on the tourist trade, though there is a declining sugar cane industry. In recent years, a secession movement has begun among the people of Nevis, who feel that most government revenues are directed to Saint Kitts.

	1995	1980	1960
GEOGRAPHY			
AREA (square miles/kilometers)	104/269		
LAND AREA (square miles/kilometers)	104/269		
COASTLINE (miles/kilometers)	84/135		
CITIES			
CAPITAL	Basseterre	n/a	14,161
POPULATION			
TOTAL	41,000	n/a/	56,591
DENSITY (per square mile/square kilometer)	394/152	n/a	544/210
ANNUAL GROWTH	0.98%	n/a	1.3%
AGE COHORTS			
0–14	36%		46%
15–64	58%		49%
65 AND OVER	7%		5%
NET MIGRATION RATE	−4.3		1.5 (64)
IDENTITY			
ETHNICITY			
AFRICAN	n/a		
LANGUAGE			
ENGLISH	n/a		

	1995	1980	1960
RELIGION			
ANGLICAN	n/a		
PROTESTANT	n/a		
ROMAN CATHOLIC	n/a		

VITAL STATISTICS

	1995	1980	1960
BIRTHS			
BIRTH RATE	23.3		31
INFANT MORTALITY RATE	18.9		59.1
LIFE EXPECTANCY AT BIRTH	66.9		60
MARRIAGES			
MARRIAGE RATE	3.9		3.2
DIVORCE RATE	0.2		0.4
DEATHS			
DEATH RATE	9.2		9.3

HOUSEHOLDS

	1995	1980	1960
NUMBER	n/a	n/a	14,329
AVERAGE SIZE	n/a	n/a	3.9

ECONOMICS AND LABOR

	1995	1980	1960
GDP PER CAPITA US$	$5,380		

TRANSPORT

	1995	1980	1960
VEHICLES			
PRIVATE CARS	3.7 (91)	3	
COMMERCIAL VEHICLES	2.2	0.6	

HEALTH AND HEALTH CARE

	1995	1980	1960
RATE OF PHYSICIANS	n/a	n/a	0.2
RATE OF HOSPITAL BEDS	n/a	n/a	3.5
TOTAL DEATHS	400 (94)		
AIDS/HIV CASES	50	40 (93)	

	1995	**1980**	**1960**
EDUCATION			
SCHOOL AGE IN SCHOOL			
PRIMARY	n/a	n/a	89%
SECONDARY	n/a	n/a	54%
FEMALES IN SCHOOL			
PRIMARY	n/a	n/a	89%
SECONDARY	n/a	n/a	59%
ADULT ILLITERACY M/F	n/a	n/a	2.4/2.3% (70)
COMMUNICATIONS			
RATE OF NEWSPAPERS	n/a	n/a	16
RATE OF RADIOS	650	488 (85)	
RATE OF TELEVISIONS	208	91	

Source: CIA, *The World Factbook, 1997;* ILO, *World Labour Report, 1997;* UN, *Demographic Yearbook, 1997;* UN, *Statistical Yearbook, 1996;* World Bank, *World Development Indicators, 1998.*

SAINT LUCIA

Located on a single mountainous island in the southern part of the Lesser Antilles of the eastern Caribbean, Saint Lucia is a former British territory with an economy largely dependent on tourism. It also has a banana industry, but this has been in decline for several years and is under threat of an end to preferential treatment by the European Union. The per capita income on the island is $4,080 annually. Covering 239 square miles of ter-

ritory, Saint Lucia has a population of 157,900 persons, with a density of 669 persons per square mile. Most of the population is of African descent and practices the Roman Catholic faith. The island is also experiencing an outward drain of people, as citizens seek better educational and job opportunities in Britain, Canada, and the United States. In 1995, the net migration rate was −4.6 per 1,000 persons.

		1995	1980	1965
GEOGRAPHY				
AREA (square miles/kilometers)		239/620		
LAND AREA (square miles/kilometers)		236/610		
COASTLINE (miles/kilometers)		99/158		
CITIES				
CAPITAL	Castries	51,994 (91)		
POPULATION				
TOTAL		157,862	113,409	93,970
DENSITY (per square mile/square kilometer)		669/259	481/186	398/154
ANNUAL GROWTH		n/a	1.6%	n/a
AGE COHORTS				
0–14		34%		
15–64		61%		
65 AND OVER		5%		
MALE		49%		
FEMALE		51%		
NET MIGRATION RATE		−4.6	n/a	1.2

	1995	1980	1965

IDENTITY

ETHNICITY

AFRICAN	90.30%		
MIXED	5.50%		
EAST INDIAN	3.20%		
WHITE	0.80%		

LANGUAGE

ENGLISH (official)	n/a		
FRENCH PATOIS	n/a		

RELIGION

ROMAN CATHOLIC	90%		
PROTESTANT	7%		
ANGLICAN	3%		

VITAL STATISTICS

BIRTHS

BIRTH RATE	22	30.1 (84)	42.4 (63)
INFANT MORTALITY RATE	20	17.6	47.8
LIFE EXPECTANCY AT BIRTH	70.1	70	56.9

MARRIAGES

MARRIAGE RATE	3.4	3.3	3.3
DIVORCE RATE	0.2		

DEATHS

DEATH RATE	6	5.5 (84)	8.1

HOUSEHOLDS

NUMBER	33,105 (91)		20,209 (60)
AVERAGE SIZE	4.0		4.2

ECONOMICS AND LABOR

GDP PER CAPITA US$	$4,080		

	1995	1980	1965
TRANSPORTATION			
VEHICLES			
PRIVATE CARS	9.9 (92)	5.7	
COMMERCIAL VEHICLES	9.1	2.7	
HEALTH AND HEALTH CARE			
RATE OF PHYSICIANS	n/a	n/a	0.1 (60)
RATE OF HOSPITAL BEDS	n/a	n/a	4.3
DEATHS			
TOTAL DEATHS	860		
AIDS/HIV CASES	76	53 (93)	
EDUCATION			
SCHOOL AGE IN SCHOOL			
PRIMARY	n/a	n/a	103%
SECONDARY	n/a	n/a	28%
FEMALES IN SCHOOL			
PRIMARY	n/a	n/a	87%
SECONDARY	n/a	n/a	22%
ADULT ILLITERACY M/F	n/a	n/a	19.2/17.6% (70)
COMMUNICATIONS			
RATE OF NEWSPAPERS	n/a	33 (79)	n/a
RATE OF RADIOS	761	704	n/a
RATE OF TELEVISIONS	189	80	15 (70)

Source: CIA, The World Factbook, 1997; ILO, World Labour Report, 1997; UN, Demographic Yearbook, 1997; UN, Statistical Yearbook, 1996; World Bank, World Development Indicators, 1998.

SAINT VINCENT AND THE GRENADINES

Saint Vincent and the Grenadines are located on one large island and a chain of small ones at the southern end of the Lesser Antilles in the eastern Caribbean, though most people live on the large island of Saint Vincent. With a population of 188,344 in a territory of 131 square miles, the country has a density of 903 persons per square mile. The economy of Saint Vincent and the Grenadines, like those of most of its neighbors in the Lesser Antilles, relies on a mix of a declining banana industry and a rising tourist trade. Indeed, some of the Grenadines islands have become among the most exclusive destinations for the high-end North American and European traveler to the Caribbean. Despite the wealth of the visitors, the lack of educational and job opportunities has produced a net migration rate of −7.6 per 1,000 persons in 1995.

	1995	**1980**	**1965**
GEOGRAPHY			
AREA (square miles/kilometers)	131/340		
LAND AREA (square miles/kilometers)	131/340		
COASTLINE (miles/kilometers)	52/84		
CITIES			
CAPITAL	Kingstown	15,466 (91)	
POPULATION			
TOTAL	118,344	97,845	79,948 (60)
DENSITY (per square mile/square kilometer)	903/348	747/288	610/235
ANNUAL GROWTH	0.64%	n/a	2%
AGE COHORTS			
0–14	33%	n/a	49%
15–64	62%	n/a	47%
65 AND OVER	5%	n/a	4%
MALE	50%		
FEMALE	50%		
NET MIGRATION RATE	−7.6	n/a	−1.6

	1995	1980	1965

IDENTITY

ETHNICITY

AFRICAN	n/a		
WHITE	n/a		
EAST INDIAN	n/a		
CARIB INDIAN	n/a		

LANGUAGE

ENGLISH	n/a		
FRENCH PATOIS	n/a		

RELIGION

ANGLICAN	n/a		
METHODIST	n/a		
ROMAN CATHOLIC	n/a		
SEVENTH-DAY ADVENT	n/a		

VITAL STATISTICS

BIRTHS

BIRTH RATE	19.4	32.2 (83)	39.8 (60)
INFANT MORTALITY RATE	16.8	37	73.4
LIFE EXPECTANCY AT BIRTH	72.9	59.1	59.1

MARRIAGES

MARRIAGE RATE	4.8	4.2	2.9
AVERAGE AGE AT MARRIAGE M/F	30.9/34.5		
DIVORCE RATE	0.8	0.2	0

DEATHS

DEATH RATE	5.4	7.6 (83)	8.7 (60)

HOUSEHOLDS

NUMBER	n/a	n/a	12,967 (46)
AVERAGE SIZE	n/a	n/a	4.8

ECONOMICS AND LABOR

GDP PER CAPITA US$	$2,060		

	1995	1980	1965
TRANSPORT			
VEHICLES			
PRIVATE CARS	5.7 (94)	4.2	
COMMERCIAL VEHICLES	3.2	1.2	
HEALTH AND HEALTH CARE			
RATE OF PHYSICIANS	n/a	n/a	0.1 (60)
RATE OF HOSPITAL BEDS	n/a	n/a	4.7
TOTAL DEATHS	732		
AIDS/HIV CASES	68	54 (93)	
EDUCATION			
SCHOOL AGE IN SCHOOL			
PRIMARY	n/a	n/a	133%
SECONDARY	n/a	n/a	21%
FEMALES IN SCHOOL			
PRIMARY	n/a	n/a	131%
SECONDARY	n/a	n/a	23%
ADULT ILLITERACY M/F	n/a	n/a	4.2/4.3 (70)
COMMUNICATIONS			
RATE OF RADIOS	664	429	
RATE OF TELEVISIONS	145	53	

Source: CIA, *The World Factbook, 1997;* ILO, *World Labour Report, 1997;* UN, *Demographic Yearbook, 1997;* UN, *Statistical Yearbook, 1996;* World Bank, *World Development Indicators, 1998.*

SAN MARINO

One of the tiniest countries in the world—with a territory of 23 square miles, about one-third the size of Washington, D.C.—San Marino is also one of the oldest, dating back, according to tradition, to the late Roman era. The San Marino constitution was written in 1600, making it one of the oldest governing documents in the world. Entirely surrounded by Italy, San Marino is a republic, with a population of 24,500. The country has an aging population, as many young persons leave for opportunities in Italian cities. In 1965, just 9 percent of the population was 65 and over; by 1995, that figure had nearly doubled, to 16 percent. For such a tiny country, hilly San Marino has a remarkably diverse economy, relying on agriculture, light manufacturing, and tourism for a per capita income of $15,800 annually.

	1995	1980	1965
GEOGRAPHY			
AREA (square miles/kilometers)	23/60		
LAND AREA (square miles/kilometers)	23/60		
COASTLINE (miles/kilometers)	Landlocked		
CITIES			
CAPITAL	San Marino	2,768 (94)	
POPULATION			
TOTAL	24,521	19,149 (76)	12,100 (47)
DENSITY (per square mile/square kilometer)	1,066/409	833/319	526/202
ANNUAL GROWTH	0.82%	0.50%	2.5%
AGE COHORTS			
0–14	16%	n/a	24%
15–64	68%	n/a	67%
65 AND OVER	16%	n/a	9%
MALE	50%		
FEMALE	50%		
URBAN	90.4% (94)	74.4% (76)	
RURAL	9.6%	25.6%	
NET MIGRATION RATE	5.1	n/a	0.6

	1995	1980	1965

IDENTITY

ETHNICITY
SAMMARINESE	n/a		
ITALIAN	n/a		

LANGUAGE
ITALIAN	n/a		

RELIGION
ROMAN CATHOLIC	n/a		

VITAL STATISTICS

BIRTHS
BIRTH RATE	10.9 (94)	10 (84)	
URBAN BIRTH RATE	10.8		
RURAL BIRTH RATE	10.5		
INFANT MORTALITY RATE	5.5	4.5	
LIFE EXPECTANCY AT BIRTH	81.3		

MARRIAGES
MARRIAGE RATE	8.6	8.5	
AVERAGE AGE AT MARRIAGE M/F	29.2/26.6		
DIVORCE RATE	0.7		

DEATHS
DEATH RATE	7.8	7	

HOUSEHOLDS

NUMBER	n/a	7,465 (85)	4,983
AVERAGE SIZE	n/a	2.9	3.5

TYPE OF HOUSEHOLD
FEMALE HEADED	18.8%		
SINGLE	8.7%		
MARRIED	77.7%		
WIDOWED	13.4%		
DIVORCED/SEPARATED	0.2%		

	1995	1980	1965

ECONOMICS AND LABOR

GDP PER CAPITA US$ $15,800

LABOR FORCE M/F (thousands)   8.6/5.6 (93)
AGRICULTURE   0.2/0.1
MINING   0.0/0.0
MANUFACTURING   3.2/1.5
CONSTRUCTION   1.2/0.0
TRADE/FOOD/TOURISM   1.2/1.3
TRANSPORT/COMMUNICATIONS   0.2/0.1
FINANCE/INSURANCE/REAL ESTATE   0.2/0.2
SOCIAL AND PERSONAL SERVICES   2.4/2.4

UNEMPLOYMENT
TOTAL   5.1% (93)

HEALTH AND HEALTH CARE

TOTAL DEATHS   186

AIDS/HIV CASES   1   1 (93)

EDUCATION

	1995	1980	1965
SCHOOL AGE IN SCHOOL			
PRIMARY	n/a	n/a	100%
SECONDARY	n/a	n/a	32%
FEMALES IN SCHOOL			
PRIMARY	n/a	n/a	105%
SECONDARY	n/a	n/a	31%

COMMUNICATIONS

	1995	1980	1965
RATE OF NEWSPAPERS	n/a	48	n/a
RATE OF RADIOS	590	476	248
RATE OF TELEVISIONS	352	300	124

Source: CIA, *The World Factbook, 1997*; ILO, *World Labour Report, 1997*; UN, *Demographic Yearbook, 1997*; UN, *Statistical Yearbook, 1996*; World Bank, *World Development Indicators, 1998*.

SAO TOME AND PRINCIPE

Sao Tome and Principe consists of two islands off the coast of West Africa in the Gulf of Guinea, roughly on the equator. A Portuguese colony, Sao Tome and Principe won their independence in 1975. The island country is extremely poor, with a per capita income of just $1,000 annually, largely derived from the export of raw and processed cocoa. Like other West African countries, Sao Tome and Principe has seen extremely rapid population growth over the past 30 years, more than doubling from 64,149 in 1965 to 144,128 in 1995. Its growth rate, however, has shown some signs of slowing in recent years. While it stood at 4.9 percent in 1980, it had fallen to 2.6 percent by 1995. Declining prices for its principal export have dried up revenues, a trend reflected in the social indexes. The infant mortality rate, for example, has fallen only from 76.6 to 61.1 per 1,000 live births between 1965 and 1995. Even as late as 1981, the illiteracy rate for women stood well above 50 percent. The poverty and lack of services is partly a legacy of colonialism, when Portugal, a poor country in itself, did little to develop the islands.

	1995	1980	1965
GEOGRAPHY			
AREA (square miles/kilometers)	371/960		
LAND AREA (square miles/kilometers)	371/960		
COASTLINE (miles/kilometers)	131/209		
CITIES			
CAPITAL	Sao Tome	n/a	n/a	5,714 (60)
POPULATION			
TOTAL	144,128	73,811 (70)	64,149 (60)
DENSITY (per square mile/square kilometer)	399/150	199/77	173/67
ANNUAL GROWTH	2.58%	4.9%	−0.4%
AGE COHORTS			
0–14	40%		
15–64	55%		
65 AND OVER	5%		
MALE	49%		
FEMALE	51%		
NET MIGRATION RATE	0	n/a	−3.5

	1995	1980	1965

IDENTITY

ETHNICITY
MESTICO, ANGOLARES	n/a		
FORROS	n/a		
SERVICAIS	n/a		
TONGAS	n/a		
EUROPEANS (Portuguese)	n/a		

LANGUAGE
PORTUGUESE (official)	n/a		

RELIGION
ROMAN CATHOLIC	n/a		
EVANGELICAL PROTESTANT	n/a		
SEVENTH-DAY ADVENT	n/a		

VITAL STATISTICS

BIRTHS
BIRTH RATE	34.4	36.3	53.1
INFANT MORTALITY RATE	61.1	61.7	76.6
LIFE EXPECTANCY AT BIRTH	63.9		

MARRIAGES
MARRIAGE RATE	0.4	0.8	1.3
AVERAGE AGE AT MARRIAGE M/F	23.1/17.8 (91)		

DEATHS
DEATH RATE	8.6	8.8	15.8

HOUSEHOLDS

NUMBER
	27,449 (91)		
AVERAGE SIZE	4.3		

TYPE OF HOUSEHOLD
FEMALE HEADED	32.6		

ECONOMICS AND LABOR

GDP PER CAPITA US$
	$1,000		

	1995	1980	1965

TRANSPORT

JOURNEYS (by transport mode)
RAILROAD PASSENGER TRIPS | 22.0 (94) | | |
  (millions of miles/kilometers)

VEHICLES (thousands)

	1995	1980	1965
CARS	2.6 (87)	1.8 (81)	0.8
COMMERCIAL VEHICLES	0.4	0.3	0.3

HEALTH AND HEALTH CARE

	1995	1980	1965
RATE OF PHYSICIANS	n/a	n/a	0.3 (60)
RATE OF HOSPITAL BEDS	n/a	n/a	40
TOTAL DEATHS	1,102 (93)		
AIDS/HIV CASES	18	13 (93)	

EDUCATION

SCHOOL AGE IN SCHOOL

	1995	1980	1965
PRIMARY	n/a	n/a	114%
SECONDARY	n/a	n/a	6%

FEMALES IN SCHOOL

	1995	1980	1965
PRIMARY	n/a	n/a	92%
SECONDARY	n/a	n/a	5%
ADULT ILLITERACY M/F	n/a	26.8/57.6% (81)	n/a

COMMUNICATIONS

	1995	1980	1965
RATE OF RADIOS	270	245	30

Source: CIA, *The World Factbook, 1997;* ILO, *World Labour Report, 1997;* UN, *Demographic Yearbook, 1997;* UN, *Statistical Yearbook, 1996;* World Bank, *World Development Indicators, 1998.*

SAUDI ARABIA

A vast desert country encompassing most of the Arabian peninsula, Saudi Arabia covers 756,981 square miles, making it roughly one-fourth the size of the United States. It is a sparsely populated land. Its 19.4 million people represent a density of 25.6 person per square mile, though this figure is exaggerated because most of the people live in scattered urban areas or oases. Sitting atop the largest known oil reserves on the planet, the Saudi people enjoy a relatively high per capita income of $10,100 annually, though this has been in decline in recent years because of the drop in world oil prices. Overall, the economy is relatively modern, with about 20 percent of the men involved in agriculture and manufacturing/mining, and some 60 percent in services. The ex-

tremely conservative nature of the Saudi kingdom—the country is home to Mecca, the holiest city in Islam and the site of massive yearly pilgrimages—means that few women work. The enormous wealth that has flowed into the country over the past 30 years has been used both to improve social services and to lay the foundation for a vast middle class. While the number of hospital beds has quintupled since 1965, the number of private automobiles has grown by a factor of 16, from just 168,700 in 1965 to over 2.66 million in 1995. During these same years, the percentage of young boys and girls attending primary school has risen from 24 percent to 78 percent and 11 percent to 47 percent, respectively.

Motor Vehicles

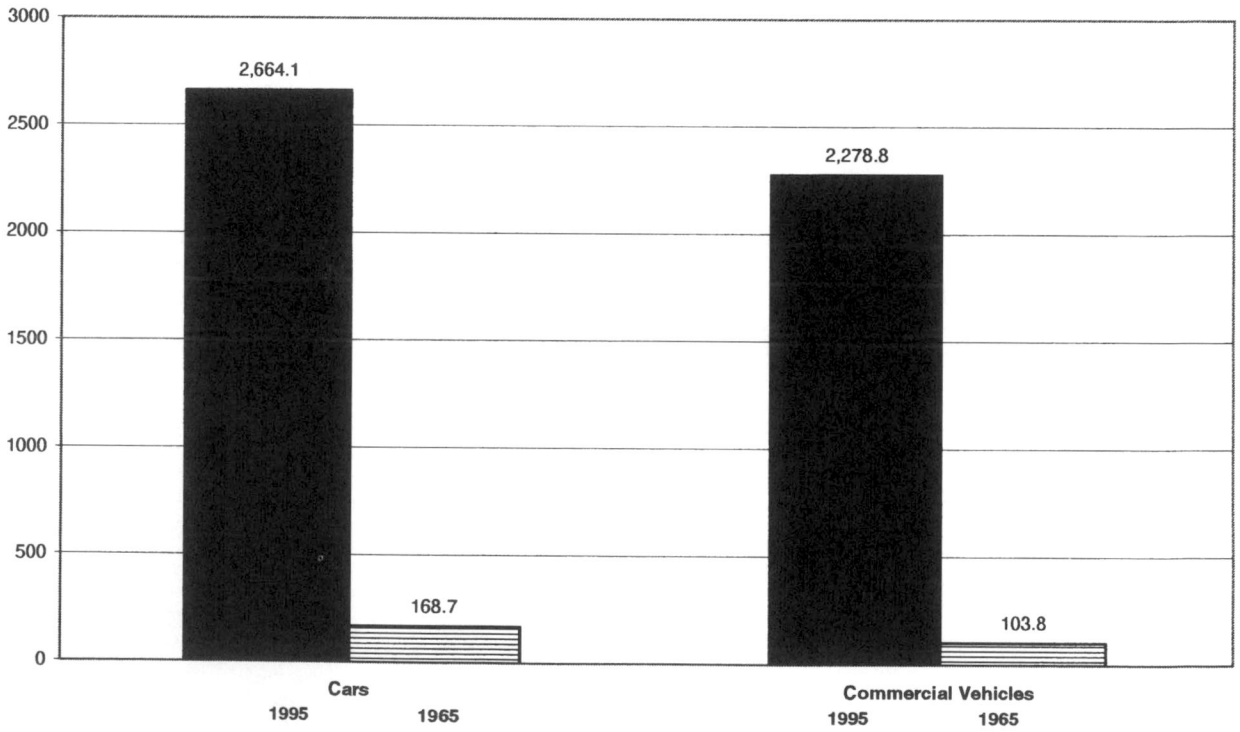

Sitting atop the largest known oil reserves in the world, Saudi Arabia has seen its per capita income rise dramatically in the two decades since the first big hike in oil prices in the early part of the 1970s. The increasing wealth of the country is reflected in the rise in the number of vehicles.

Population Growth

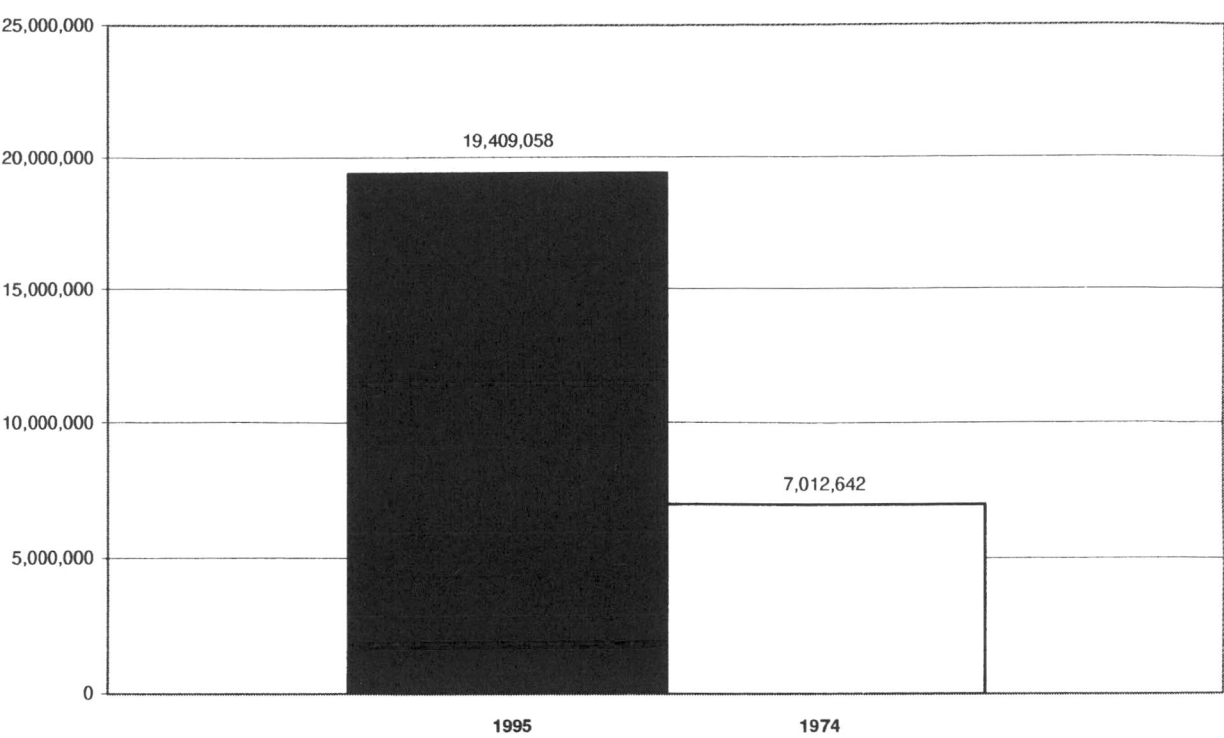

Unlike most countries where increased wealth goes hand in hand with a lower rate of population growth, Saudi Arabia has seen its rate of growth increase rapidly over the past 30 years, even as its per capita income has skyrocketed. This may be because the country's wealth did not come through industrialization, in which smaller families are better able to give their children the educational opportunities necessary to succeed, but from a windfall of petrodollars.

CHRONOLOGY

1964   Crown Prince Faisal becomes king.

1967   Saudi Arabia refuses to join Arab allies in war against Israel.

1973   During Arab-Israeli War, Organization of Petroleum Exporting Countries (OPEC) announces oil boycott against the west; oil prices quadruple.

1975   Faisal assassinated; brother Prince Khalid becomes king.

1980   War breaks out in Persian Gulf between Iran and Iraq; Saudis back Baghdad.

1982   Khalid dies, is replaced by half-brother Prince Fahd.

1984   Iran begins attacks on Saudi oil ships.

1985   Oil revenues fall to one-fifth of late 1970s levels.

1996   An aging Fahd turns over most powers to half-brother Abdullah.

1997   Three hundred killed in stampede during annual pilgrimage to Mecca.

		1995	1980	1965

GEOGRAPHY

AREA (square miles/kilometers) 756,981/1,960,582
LAND AREA (square miles/kilometers) 756,981/1,960,582
COASTLINE (miles/kilometers) 1,650/2,640

CITIES

		1995	1980	1965
CAPITAL	Riyadh	n/a	666,840 (74)	
MAJOR CITIES	Jeddah	n/a	561,104	
	Mecca	n/a	366,801	
	Ta'if	n/a	204,857	
	Medina	n/a	198,186	

POPULATION

	1995	1980	1965
TOTAL	19,409,058	7,012,642 (74)	
DENSITY (per square mile/square kilometer)	26/10	9/4	
ANNUAL GROWTH	3.45%	4.3%	1.7%

AGE COHORTS

	1995
0–14	43%
15–64	55%
65 AND OVER	2%

	1995
MALE	56%
FEMALE	44%

NET MIGRATION RATE 1.55

IDENTITY

ETHNICITY

	1995
ARAB	90%
AFRO-ASIAN	10%

LANGUAGE

	1995
ARABIC	n/a

RELIGION

	1995
MUSLIM	100%

	1995	**1980**	**1965**

VITAL STATISTICS

BIRTHS

BIRTH RATE	38.3	42.1	
INFANT MORTALITY RATE	46.4	66	
LIFE EXPECTANCY AT BIRTH	69	60.9	

DEATHS

DEATH RATE	5.4	8.9	

ECONOMICS AND LABOR

GDP PER CAPITA US$	$10,100		

LABOR FORCE M/F

AGRICULTURE	20/12%		
INDUSTRY	21/6%		
SERVICES	59/82%		

TRANSPORT

JOURNEYS (by transport mode)

RAILROAD PASSENGER TRIPS	139		
(millions of miles/kilometers)			
AIR PASSENGER TRIPS (thousands)	11,922		

VEHICLES (thousands)

CARS	2,664.1	n/a	168.7
COMMERCIAL VEHICLES	2,272.8	n/a	103.8

HEALTH AND HEALTH CARE

RATE OF PHYSICIANS	1.3	0.5 (60)	0
RATE OF HOSPITAL BEDS	2.5	1.5	0.5

HEALTH INDICATORS

SMOKING PREVALENCE M/F	53		
TUBERCULOSIS INCIDENCE RATE	0.22		

	1995	1980	1965
HEALTH CARE			
ACCESS TO SAFE WATER	93%		
ACCESS TO SANITATION	86%		
MEASLES IMMUNIZATION	94%		
AIDS/HIV CASES	137	62 (93)	

EDUCATION

	1995	1980	1965
SCHOOL AGE IN SCHOOL			
PRIMARY	78%	61%	24%
SECONDARY	58%	29%	4%
HIGHER	15%	7%	0.5%
FEMALES IN SCHOOL			
PRIMARY	47%	39%	11%
SECONDARY	49%	33%	1%
ADULT ILLITERACY M/F	29/50%		

COMMUNICATIONS

	1995	1980	1965
RATE OF NEWSPAPERS	43	36	5
RATE OF RADIOS	293	260	n/a
RATE OF TELEVISIONS	255	219	n/a

Source: CIA, *The World Factbook, 1997;* ILO, *World Labour Report, 1997;* UN, *Demographic Yearbook, 1997;* UN, *Statistical Yearbook, 1996;* World Bank, *World Development Indicators, 1998.*

SENEGAL

Situated on the far western tip of Africa, Senegal includes 75,749 square miles consisting of semi-arid territory, along with several well-watered river valleys. The country is surrounded by Mauritania to the north, Mali to the east, and Guinea and Guinea-Bissau to the south. Running through the middle of Senegal is the narrow nation of The Gambia, a former British colony. Once the heart of the French empire in West Africa, Senegal is dominated politically, culturally, and economically by its capital, Dakar, where approximately one-fifth of the country's 9.09 million people live. Like other West African nations, Senegal has seen rapid population growth since winning its independence from France in 1960. Senegal remains heavily dependent on its agricultural output. Some 70 percent of working men and 86 percent of working women labor to produce food crops, including commercial ones, the most important of which is peanuts. The country has a growing light manufacturing sector which employs roughly 10 percent of the male workforce and 4 percent of the female workforce. Despite its extremely stable political history, Senegal remains poor, though it stands above most West African countries, with a per capita income of $1,600. It has made slow but steady progress in health and education. The infant mortality rate fell from 92.9 to 64 per 1,000 live births between 1965 and 1995. The number of children attending primary school rose from 40 to 65 percent over the same period, though rates for girls lag significantly behind those for boys.

Ethnicity

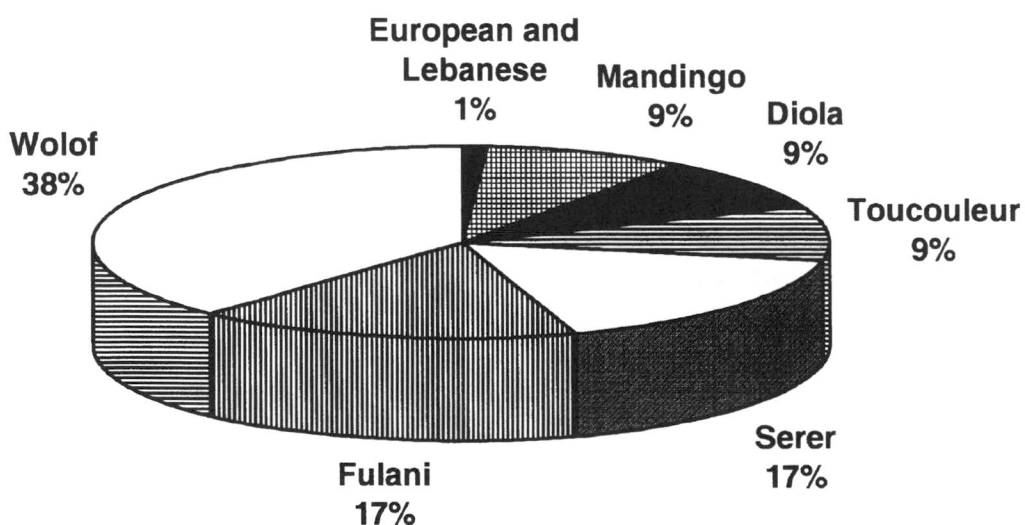

Like the boundaries of many other African countries, Senegal's boundaries were drawn by colonial regimes, with little attention paid to existing ethnic settlement patterns. While this has contributed to civil strife in many countries, it is not a given that ethnic diversity brings political instability. Senegal, one of the most diverse countries in Africa, has also been one of the most stable.

Life Expectancy at Birth

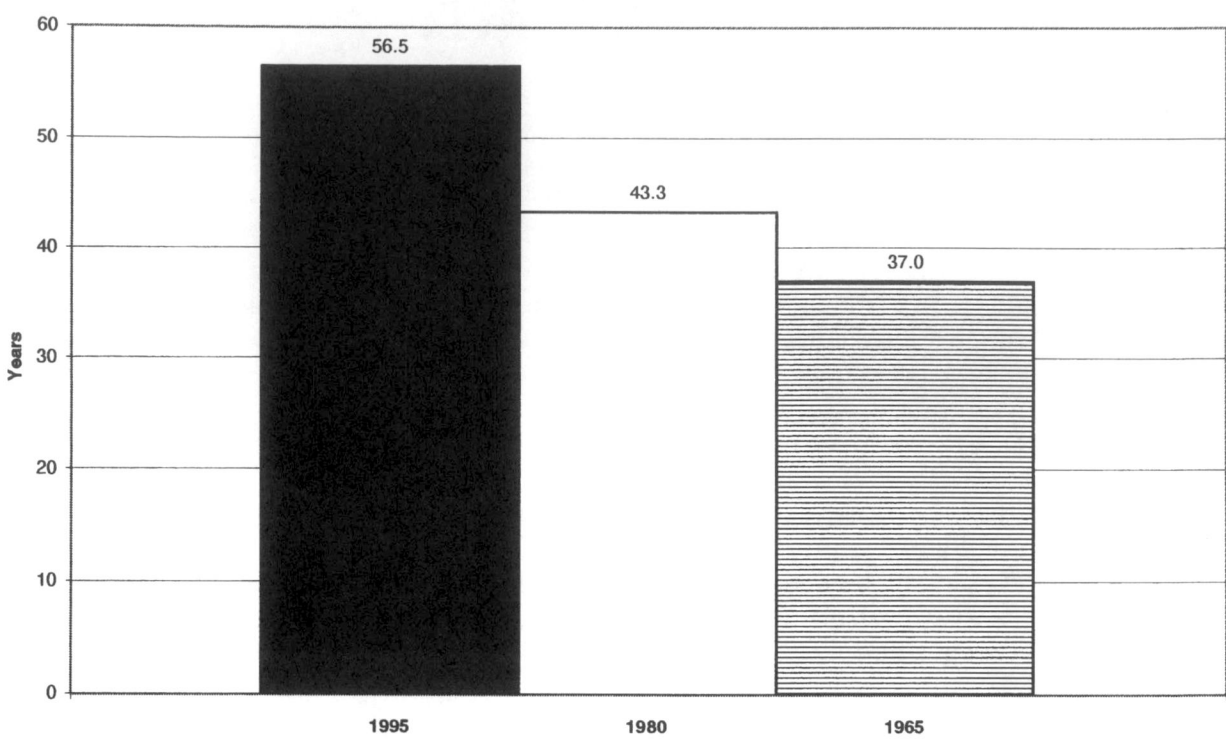

Though lacking in natural resources and relatively poverty stricken, Senegal has proved that a stable political order can bring gradual but steady improvements in social indicators, such as life expectancy. Senegal has been able to lift the figure dramatically from the days in which the French colonial regime did little to provide health services for indigenous Africans.

CHRONOLOGY

1960   Senegal wins its independence from France; independence leader Leopold Senghor becomes president.

1975   Senegal becomes one of founding members of the Economic Community of West African States (ECOWAS).

1976   Senghor permits formation of two opposition parties.

1981   Senghor turns over presidential power to Abdou Diouf, head of one of the two opposition parties; Senegal sends troops into The Gambia to defeat coup; forms confederation with The Gambia.

1983   Diouf's Socialist Party wins 80 percent of vote in disputed elections.

1989   Confederation with The Gambia is dissolved; border dispute with Guinea-Bissau creates tensions in region.

1993   Diouf reelected president.

1995   Major opposition candidate joins coalition government.

1997   Government moves to privatize state-owned electric company.

	1995	1980	1965

GEOGRAPHY

AREA (square miles/kilometers)	75,749/196,190			
LAND AREA (square miles/kilometers)	74,131/192,000			
COASTLINE (miles/kilometers)	332/531			

CITIES			
CAPITAL	Dakar	1,641,258 (94)	
MAJOR CITIES	Thies	216,381	
	Kaolack	193,115	
	Ziguinchor	161,680	
	Saint-Louis	132,499	

POPULATION

	1995	1980	1965
TOTAL	9,092,749	4,907,507 (76)	3,109,840 (61)
DENSITY (per square mile/square kilometer)	123/47	66/26	42/16
ANNUAL GROWTH	3.37%	n/a	2.4%
AGE COHORTS			
0–14	48%	n/a	43%
15–64	49%	n/a	53%
65 AND OVER	3%	n/a	4%
MALE	49%		
FEMALE	51%		
URBAN	42.9% (93)	34.3% (76)	
RURAL	57.1%	65.7%	
NET MIGRATION RATE	0		

IDENTITY

ETHNICITY	
WOLOF	36%
FULANI	17%
SERER	17%
TOUCOULEUR	9%
DIOLA	9%
MANDINGO	9%
EUROPEAN AND LEBANESE	1%

	1995	1980	1965
LANGUAGE			
FRENCH	n/a		
WOLOF	n/a		
PULAAR	n/a		
DIOLA	n/a		
MANDINGO	n/a		
RELIGION			
MUSLIM	92%		
INDIGENOUS	6%		
CHRISTIAN	2%		

VITAL STATISTICS

	1995	1980	1965
BIRTHS			
BIRTH RATE	45.5	46.4	43.3
INFANT MORTALITY RATE	64	92.9	92.9
LIFE EXPECTANCY AT BIRTH	56.5	43.3	37
MARRIAGES			
MARRIAGE RATE M/F	28.5/20.1 (88)		
DEATHS			
DEATH RATE	11.8	20.9	16.7

ECONOMICS AND LABOR

	1995		
GDP PER CAPITA US$	$1,600		
LABOR FORCE M/F			
AGRICULTURE	70/86%		
INDUSTRY	10/4%		
SERVICES	20/11%		
UNION DENSITY	21.90%		
POVERTY			
UNDER $1/DAY	54% (92)		
UNDER $2/DAY	79.6%		

	1995	1980	1965

TRANSPORT

JOURNEYS (by transport mode)

	1995	1980	1965
RAILROAD PASSENGER TRIPS	173 (91)		
(millions of miles/kilometers)			
AIR PASSENGER TRIPS (thousands)	141 (94)		

VEHICLES (thousands)

	1995	1980	1965
CARS	65.4	n/a	28.1
COMMERCIAL VEHICLES	24	n/a	18.1

HEALTH AND HEALTH CARE

	1995	1980	1965
RATE OF PHYSICIANS	0.1	0.1	0.1 (60)
RATE OF HOSPITAL BEDS	0.7	n/a	1.3

HEALTH INDICATORS

	1995	1980	1965
PREGNANT WOMEN WITH ANEMIA	26%		
LOW-BIRTH-WEIGHT BABIES	11%		
CHILD MALNUTRITION	22%		
SMOKING PREVALENCE M/F	48/35%		
TUBERCULOSIS INCIDENCE RATE	1.6		

HEALTH CARE

	1995	1980	1965
ACCESS TO SAFE WATER	50%		
ACCESS TO SANITATION	58%		
MEASLES IMMUNIZATION	80%		
AIDS/HIV CASES	1,573	911 (93)	

EDUCATION

SCHOOL AGE IN SCHOOL

	1995	1980	1965
PRIMARY	65%	46%	40%
SECONDARY	16%	11%	7%
HIGHER	3%	3%	0.8%

FEMALES IN SCHOOL

	1995	1980	1965
PRIMARY	43%	40%	29%
SECONDARY	35%	34%	3%
ADULT ILLITERACY M/F	57/77%	62.6/80.9% (85)	

	1995	1980	1965
COMMUNICATIONS			
RATE OF NEWSPAPERS	6	6	6
RATE OF RADIOS	116	65	64
RATE OF TELEVISIONS	37	1	n/a

Source: CIA, *The World Factbook, 1997;* ILO, *World Labour Report, 1997;* UN, *Demographic Yearbook, 1997;* UN, *Statistical Yearbook, 1996;* World Bank, *World Development Indicators, 1998.*

SERBIA AND MONTENEGRO¹ (YUGOSLAVIA)

Making up the heartland of the former Yugoslav confederation, Serbia and Montenegro cover 39,517 square miles of territory, with Serbia representing about seven-eighths of this area. The total population of the country was 10.61 million in 1995. Of this, approximately 9.98 million live in Serbia. The country is very mountainous and enjoys a temperate climate, with severely cold winters in the interior. With the breakup of the Yugoslav Federation, created out of a number of Balkan lands at the end of World War I, Serbia and Montenegro went to war against separatists first in Croatia and then in Bosnia. Large sections of these latter countries were carved out into Serbian-dominated enclaves that remain unrecognized by the international community. At the same time, the aggressive actions of the Serbian government—which is now currently also fighting separatist guerrillas in the Albanian-dominated province of Kosovo—have resulted in imposition of international economic sanctions against the country. U.N. and NATO peacekeepers are present in several of the former constituent republics of the Yugoslav Federations. The nearly constant state of war and international sanctions has reduced the economy of Serbia and Montenegro, once among the most prosperous areas in the Balkans. The per capita income has fallen to just $2,000 annually, as industries and agricultural enterprises must deal with a lack of funding and spare parts even while they attempt to adjust to a market economy. This economic decline is reflected in social indexes, such as the percentage of children attending primary school, which fell from about 100 percent in 1965 (the figure is for all of Yugoslavia) to just 72 percent in 1995.

Industry

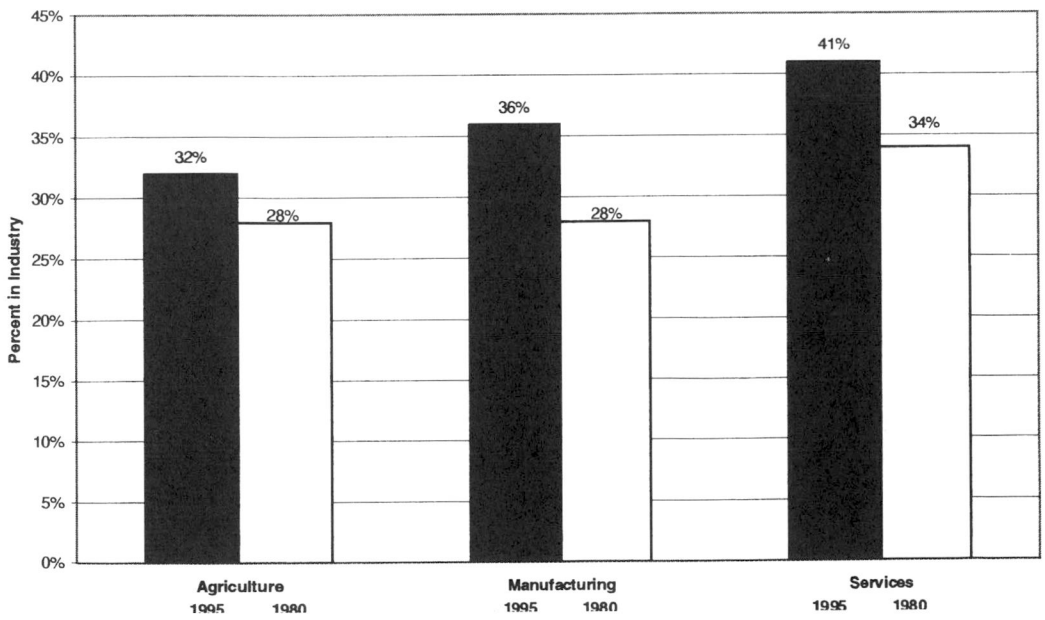

Though it succeeded in industrializing Yugoslavia, the communist government of Marshal Tito was unable to fully modernize the economy of its heartland, Serbia. Today, about one-third of the population remains involved in the agricultural sector, much higher than in other European countries. At the same time, the country has not experienced the shift from a manufacturing economy to a service one, a hallmark of a postindustrial order.

Religion

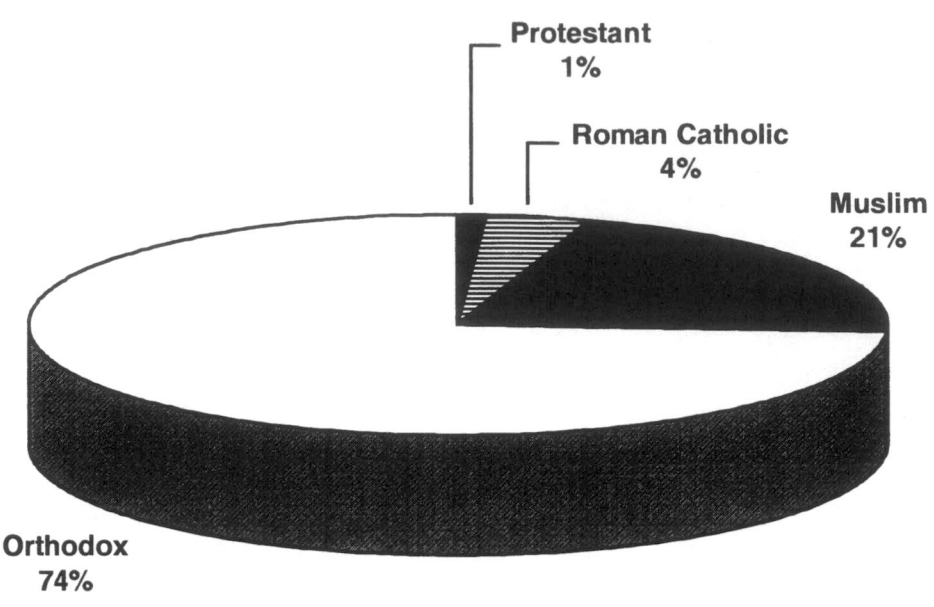

Protestant
1%

Roman Catholic
4%

Muslim
21%

Orthodox
74%

Since the Middle Ages, Serbia has been deeply divided religiously. Since the breakup of Yugoslavia in the early 1990s, religion has also represented the lines of strife within the country, particularly with the rise of Muslim separatism in the Kosovo province in 1997.

CHRONOLOGY

1963   Marshal Tito made president-for-life of Yugoslavia, of which Serbia is the main component republic.

1980   Tito dies.

1984   Bosnian capital of Sarajevo hosts Winter Olympics.

1991   Croatia, Slovenia, and Bosnia declare independence; Serbian-supported irregulars launch civil war in Croatia and Bosnia.

1992   United Nations imposes economic sanctions against Serbia.

1993   Hard-line Serbian nationalist president Slobodan Milosevic wins re-elections by overwhelming margin.

1995   Following signing of Dayton Accords, ending Bosnian War, sanctions against Serbia are partially lifted.

1997   Rebellion by ethnic Albanians breaks out in Serbian province of Kosovo.

	1995	**1980**	**1965**

GEOGRAPHY

AREA (square miles/kilometers)   39,517/102,350
LAND AREA (square miles/kilometers)   39,435/102,131
COASTLINE (miles/kilometers)   124/199

CITIES
CAPITAL   Belgrade   1,136,786 (91)
MAJOR CITIES   Novi Sad   178,896
                              Nis   175,555
                              Kragujevac   146,607
                              Podgorica   118,059

POPULATION

TOTAL   10,614,558
DENSITY (per square mile/square kilometer)   269/104
ANNUAL GROWTH   0.39%

MONTENEGRO
AGE COHORTS
0–14   22%
15–64   67%
65 AND OVER   11%

SERBIA
AGE COHORTS
0–14   21%
15–64   66%
65 AND OVER   13%

NET MIGRATION RATE
MONTENEGRO   −0.2
SERBIA   −0.1

IDENTITY

ETHNICITY
SERBS   63%
ALBANIANS   14%
MONTENEGRANS   6%
HUNGARIANS   4%

	1995	1980	1965
LANGUAGE			
SERBO-CROATIAN	95%		
ALBANIAN	5%		
RELIGION			
ORTHODOX	65%		
MUSLIM	19%		
ROMAN CATHOLIC	4%		
PROTESTANT	1%		

VITAL STATISTICS

	1995	1980	1965
BIRTHS			
BIRTH RATE, MONTENEGRO	11.9		
BIRTH RATE, SERBIA	14		
INFANT MORTALITY RATE, MONTENEGRO	27.5		
INFANT MORTALITY RATE, SERBIA	22.9		
LIFE EXPECTANCY, MONTENEGRO	74.9		
LIFE EXPECTANCY, SERBIA	72		
MARRIAGES			
MARRIAGE RATE	5.7		
DIVORCE RATE	0.7		
DEATHS			
DEATH RATE, MONTENEGRO	7.8		
DEATH RATE, SERBIA	10.2		

HOUSEHOLDS

	1995	1980	1965
NUMBER	2,870,670 (91)		
AVERAGE SIZE	3.6		

ECONOMICS AND LABOR

	1995	1980	1965
GDP PER CAPITA US$	$2,000		
LABOR FORCE M/F			
AGRICULTURE	28/32%		
INDUSTRY	38/26%		
SERVICES	34/41%		

	1995	1980	1965

TRANSPORT

	1995	1980	1965
JOURNEYS (by transport mode)			
RAILROAD PASSENGER TRIPS	2,525 (94)		
(millions of miles/kilometers)			
VEHICLES			
CARS	1,405.5 (90)	2,433.9 1	
COMMERCIAL VEHICLES	132.5	242.9	

HEALTH AND HEALTH CARE

	1995	1980	1965
RATE OF PHYSICIANS	2	n/a	
RATE OF HOSPITAL BEDS	5.4	3.4	
TOTAL DEATHS	n/a	13.6	
HEALTH INDICATORS			
SMOKING PREVALENCE M/F	52/31%		
TUBERCULOSIS INCIDENCE RATE	0.5		
HEALTH CARE			
ACCESS TO SANITATION	100		
MEASLES IMMUNIZATION	81		
AIDS/HIV CASES	530	350 (93)	

EDUCATION

	1995	1980	1965
SCHOOL AGE IN SCHOOL			
PRIMARY	72%	99%	106% (70)
SECONDARY	65%	83%	63%
HIGHER	21%	21.7%	15.9%
FEMALES IN SCHOOL			
PRIMARY	49%	99%	103% (70)
SECONDARY	51%	83%	58%
HIGHER	n/a	20.1%	12.9%
ADULT ILLITERACY M/F	n/a	3.4/13.9% (85)[1]	

	1995	1980	1965
COMMUNICATIONS			
RATE OF NEWSPAPERS	52	56	85 (70)[1]
RATE OF RADIOS	207	224	166
RATE OF TELEVISIONS	179	190	88

FOOTNOTE
1. Federation of Yugoslavia in 1960 and 1985.

Source: CIA, *The World Factbook, 1997;* ILO, *World Labour Report, 1997;* UN, *Demographic Yearbook, 1997;* UN, *Statistical Yearbook, 1996;* World Bank, *World Development Indicators, 1998.*

SEYCHELLES

Situated in the western Indian Ocean 300 miles north of Madagascar, the Seychelles consist of a large number of tiny, coral-ringed islands with a total territorial expanse of 176 square miles. The idyllic tropical islands have a total population of 77,575 persons, for a density rate of 253 persons per square mile, though many of the tinier islands remain uninhabited. Unlike most other territories, the Seychelles were not settled until the eighteenth century, when exiles from the French revolution were sent there. Later, laborers and traders from Africa and Asia were imported, resulting in an ethnic mix of three races. Many of these residents intermarried and produced children. With a per capita income of $6,000 annually, the Seychelles are relatively prosperous. The economy is largely reliant on tourism and cocoanut farming. A lack of educational and job opportunities means that the country sees many of its young persons leaving. In 1995, the net migration rate was −6.1, with many people leaving for France and England. Though first settled by the French, the Seychelles became a British colony and remained so until 1976. Thus, both French and English are official languages

	1995	1980	1965
GEOGRAPHY			
AREA (square miles/kilometers)	176/455		
LAND AREA (square miles/kilometers)	176/455		
COASTLINE (miles/kilometers)	307/491		
CITIES			
CAPITAL	Victoria	n/a	24,324 (87)
POPULATION			
TOTAL	77,575	61,898 (77)	41,425 (60)
DENSITY (per square mile/square kilometer)	253/170	352/136	545/91
ANNUAL GROWTH	0.76%	0.6%	2.9%
AGE COHORTS			
0–14	31%	n/a	38%
15–64	63%	n/a	56%
65 AND OVER	6%	n/a	6%
MALE	50%		
FEMALE	50%		

	1995	1980	1965
URBAN	n/a	37.1% (77)	
RURAL	n/a	62.9%	
NET MIGRATION RATE	−6.14	n/a	−1.1

IDENTITY

ETHNICITY
SEYCHELLOIS (Asian, African, European)   n/a

LANGUAGE
ENGLISH (official)   n/a
FRENCH (official)   n/a
CREOLE   n/a

RELIGION
ROMAN CATHOLIC   90%
ANGLICAN   8%

VITAL STATISTICS

	1995	1980
BIRTHS		
BIRTH RATE	21	26.9
INFANT MORTALITY RATE	12.5	13.8
LIFE EXPECTANCY AT BIRTH	69.2	69.8
MARRIAGES		
MARRIAGE RATE	11.9	6
AVERAGE AGE AT MARRIAGE M/F	n/a	26.4/23.8 (87)
DIVORCE RATE	1.2	0.8
DEATHS		
DEATH RATE	7.3	7.5

HOUSEHOLDS

	1995	1980
NUMBER	n/a	15,118 (87)
AVERAGE SIZE	n/a	4.5

ECONOMICS AND LABOR

GDP PER CAPITA US$ $6,000

	1995	1980	1965
LABOR FORCE (thousands)	22.3 (89)		
AGRICULTURE	2.2		
MANUFACTURING	2.5		
CONSTRUCTION	1.7		
TRADE/FOOD/TOURISM	4.4		
TRANSPORT/COMMUNICATIONS	3.1		
FINANCE/INSURANCE/REAL ESTATE	0.7		
SOCIAL AND PERSONAL SERVICES	4.6		

TRANSPORT

	1995	1980	1965
JOURNEYS (by transport mode)			
RAILROAD PASSENGER TRIPS	112.0 (94)		
(millions of miles/kilometers)			
VEHICLES			
CARS	6.6 (94)	3.9	
COMMERCIAL VEHICLES	2	0.9	

HEALTH AND HEALTH CARE

	1995	1980	1965
RATE OF PHYSICIANS	n/a	n/a	0.3 (60)
RATE OF HOSPITAL BEDS	n/a	n/a	6.9
TOTAL DEATHS	597 (93)		
AIDS/HIV CASES	16	1 (93)	

EDUCATION

	1995	1980	1965
SCHOOL AGE IN SCHOOL			
PRIMARY	n/a	n/a	112%
SECONDARY	n/a	n/a	25%
HIGHER	n/a	n/a	1%
FEMALES IN SCHOOL			
PRIMARY	n/a	n/a	111%
SECONDARY	n/a	n/a	26%
ADULT ILLITERACY M/F	n/a	n/a	44.4/40.2 (76)

	1995	1980	1965
COMMUNICATIONS			
RATE OF NEWSPAPERS	45	48	43
RATE OF RADIOS	486	333	36
RATE OF TELEVISIONS	88	31 (85)	

Source: CIA, The World Factbook, 1997; ILO, World Labour Report, 1997; UN, Demographic Yearbook, 1997; UN, Statistical Yearbook, 1996; World Bank, World Development Indicators, 1998.

SIERRA LEONE

Along with neighboring Liberia, Sierra Leone has the highest rainfall of any country in the world. This has much to do with the country's geography. Situated on the southwest corner of West Africa, Sierra Leone is at the heart of the monsoon trail that produces many of the hurricanes that eventually reach the Western Hemisphere. A country of dense rainforests, Sierra Leone covers 27,699 square miles of territory and has a population of 4.79 million. Extremely poor, Sierra Leone has a per capita income of just $960 annually. This poverty is reflected in the low social indexes. As of 1995, fully 55 percent of men and 82 percent of women could not read or write, while infant mortality remained at an extremely high 135.6 per 1,000 live births. Much of the poverty and human misery in the country is due to Sierra Leone's troubled political history. Originally founded as a haven for freed slaves—or slaves captured by British ships after the outlawing of the international slave trade—Sierra Leone remained a British colony until 1961. Since then, it has suffered numerous coups and has been ravaged by a major civil war through much of the 1990s, a byproduct of the conflict in neighboring Liberia. But while Liberia has achieved peace in recent years, Sierra Leone continues to be plagued by armed banditry and brutal rebel raids, led by members of the military regime toppled in early 1998. The country is currently occupied by a West African peacekeeping force headed by Nigeria.

	1995	1980	1965
GEOGRAPHY			
AREA (square miles/kilometers)	27,699/71,740		
LAND AREA (square miles/kilometers)	27,653/71,620		
COASTLINE (miles/kilometers)	251/402		
CITIES			
CAPITAL	Freetown	n/a	469,766 (85)
POPULATION			
TOTAL	4,793,121	3,517,530 (85)	2,180,355 (63)
DENSITY (per square mile/square kilometer)	173/67	127/49	79/30
ANNUAL GROWTH	4.14%	1.8%	1.2%
AGE COHORTS			
0–14	45%	n/a	37%
15–64	52%	n/a	58%
65 AND OVER	3%	n/a	5%
MALE	50%		
FEMALE	50%		

	1995	1980	1965
NET MIGRATION RATE	12.5		0

IDENTITY

ETHNICITY

TEMNE	30%
MENDE	30%
OTHER AFRICAN	39%
CREOLE, EUROPEAN, LEBANESE, ASIAN	1%

LANGUAGE

ENGLISH	n/a
MENDE	n/a
TEMNE	n/a
KRIO	n/a

RELIGION

MUSLIM	60%
INDIGENOUS	30%
CHRISTIAN	10%

VITAL STATISTICS

BIRTHS

	1995	1980
BIRTH RATE	47.1	47.4
INFANT MORTALITY RATE	135.6	180
LIFE EXPECTANCY AT BIRTH	47.5	34

DEATHS

	1995	1980
DEATH RATE	18.2	29.7

ECONOMICS AND LABOR

GDP PER CAPITA US$ $960

LABOR FORCE (thousands)	70.2 (88)
AGRICULTURE	7.3
MINING	5.8
MANUFACTURING	8.6
UTILITIES	2.7
CONSTRUCTION	7.3
TRADE/FOOD/TOURISM	3.3
TRANSPORT/COMMUNICATIONS	7.7

	1995	1980	1965
FINANCE/INSURANCE/REAL ESTATE	1.8		
SOCIAL AND PERSONAL SERVICES	25.7		

TRANSPORT

JOURNEYS

RAILROAD PASSENGER TRIPS	14.0 (94)		
(millions of miles/kilometers)			

VEHICLES (thousands)

CARS	36	28.4	8.8
COMMERCIAL VEHICLES	12	n/a	4.3

HEALTH AND HEALTH CARE

RATE OF PHYSICIANS	n/a	0.1	0.1 (60)
RATE OF HOSPITAL BEDS	n/a	1.2	0.8

HEALTH INDICATORS

LOW-BIRTH-WEIGHT BABIES	17%		
CHILD MALNUTRITION	29%		
TUBERCULOSIS INCIDENCE RATE	1.6		

HEALTH CARE

ACCESS TO SAFE WATER	34%		
ACCESS TO SANITATION	11%		
MEASLES IMMUNIZATION	44%		

AIDS/HIV CASES	168	111 (93)	

EDUCATION

SCHOOL AGE IN SCHOOL

PRIMARY	n/a	52%	29%
SECONDARY	n/a	14%	4%
HIGHER	n/a	1%	0.3%

FEMALES IN SCHOOL

PRIMARY	n/a	42%	21%
SECONDARY	n/a	21%	

ADULT ILLITERACY M/F	55/82%	62.2/78.7% (85)	90.4/96.1%

	1995	1980	1965
COMMUNICATIONS			
RATE OF NEWSPAPERS	2	3	7
RATE OF RADIOS	233	139	48
RATE OF TELEVISIONS	11	6	0.5

Source: CIA, The World Factbook, 1997; ILO, World Labour Report, 1997; UN, Demographic Yearbook, 1997; UN, Statistical Yearbook, 1996; World Bank, World Development Indicators, 1998.

SINGAPORE

One of the four so-called tiger economies of East Asia—along with Hong Kong, South Korea, and Taiwan—Singapore is a tiny city-state, situated on one large and several small islands at the end of the Malay peninsula in Southeast Asia. Originally a part of Malaysia—after that country won its independence from Britain in 1957—the largely Chinese-populated Singapore broke away to form its own country in 1965. Singapore covers 244 square miles and has a population of nearly 3.4 million persons. With a per capita income of $22,900, Singapore is one of the richest countries in the world. It also has one of the fastest-growing economies, based largely on trade and manufacturing. Of the roughly 1.6 million–strong workforce, approximately one-fourth are in-volved in manufacturing and another one-fifth in trade. The nation's extraordinary economic growth is reflected in the rapidly rising social indexes over the past three decades. The rate of physicians has grown by a factor of almost 4 since 1960 and the infant mortality rate fell from 24.6 per 1,000 live in births in 1965 to just 4.7 in 1995, which is one of the lowest rates in the world. Education has been a major factor in the country's economic success. Between 1965 and 1995, the percentage of young persons attending university rose from 7.4 to 34 percent. But this progress has come with a price. Singapore has one of the most repressive bureaucracies in the world, regulating virtually every facet of life.

Net Migration Rate

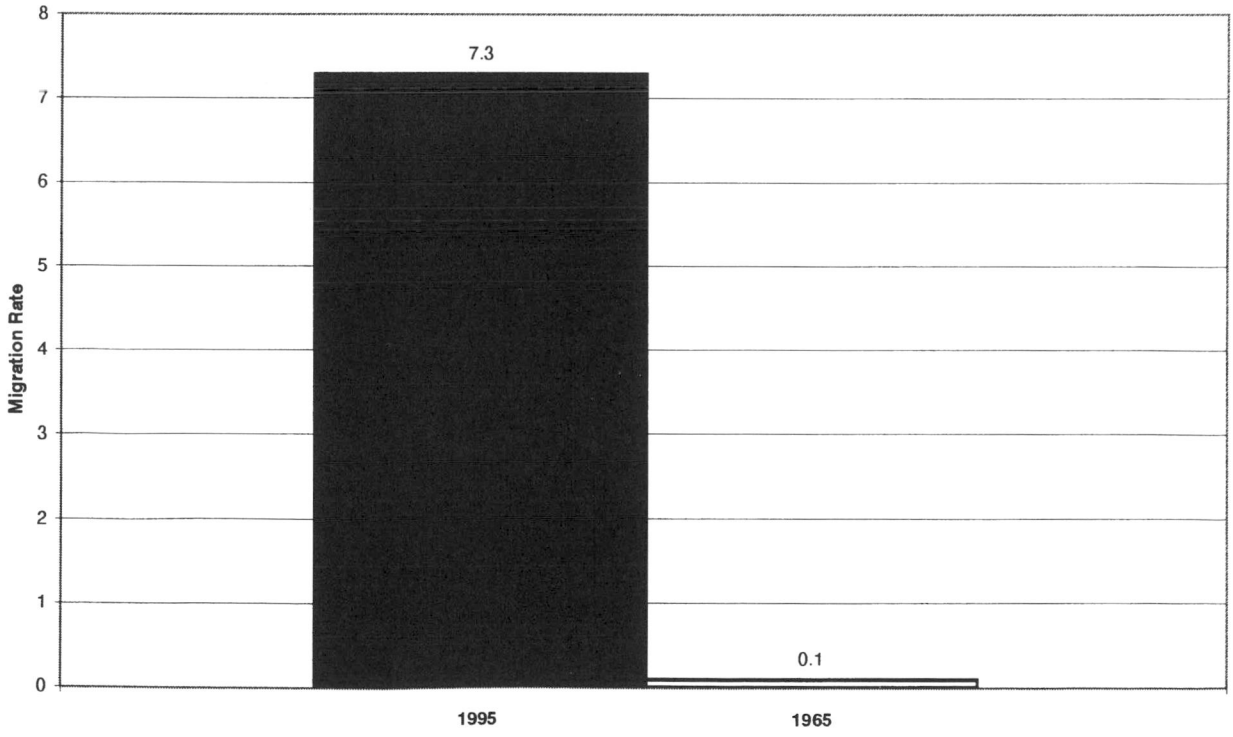

Prosperity often brings immigrants in its wake, especially when the destination country has a per capita income far higher than its neighbors. This is evidenced in Singapore. As the city-state became much wealthier than its surrounding countries, its in-migration rate soared.

Marriage Rate

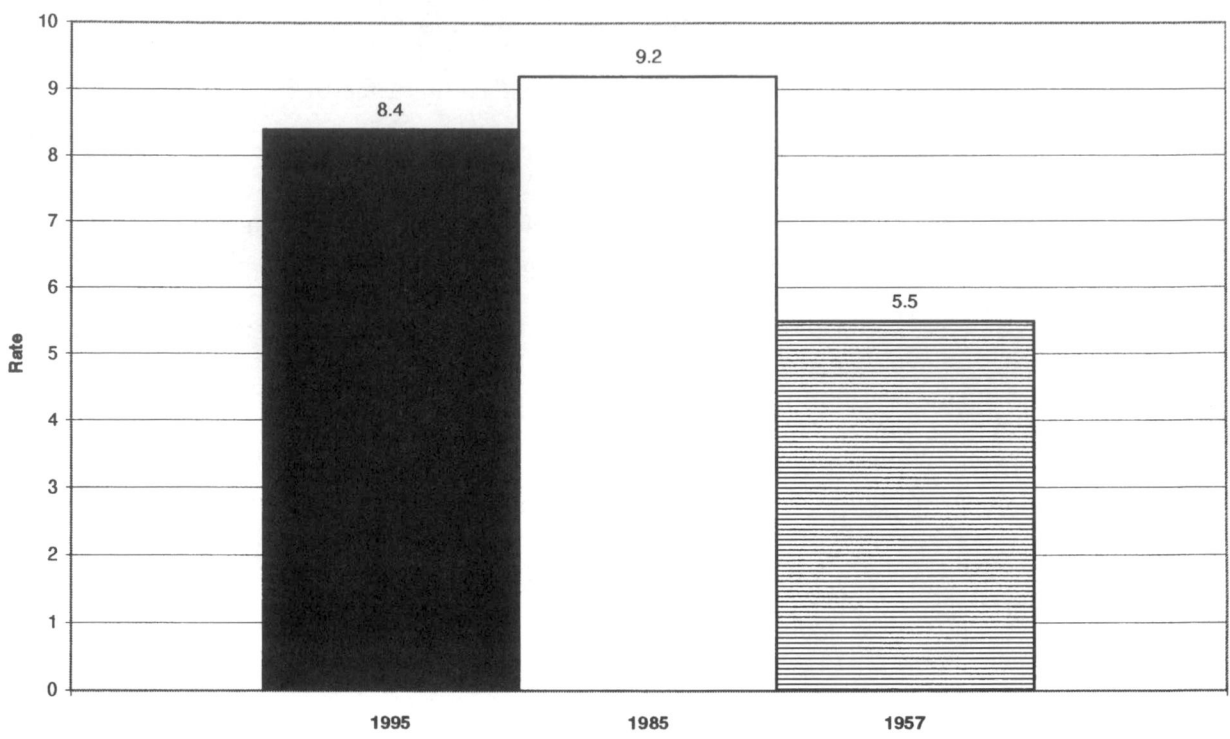

Marriage rates are a tricky indicator. Rising marriage rates often reflect increasing bureaucracy, as the state becomes better able to keep track of its citizens, rather than any social change. The dramatically increased marriage rates in Singapore are probably best explained by the government's growing efficiency.

CHRONOLOGY

1963   Singapore becomes part of Malaysia.
1965   Singapore declares independence from Malaysia, under leadership of president Lee Kuan Yew.
1971   Last British troops leave Singapore.
1991   New law extends power of presidency.
1993   Yew resigns from presidency but retains behind-scenes power; Ong Teng Cheong, Yew follower, becomes president in first direct election.
1997   Massive fires in nearby Indonesia blanket Singapore in smoke for weeks.

	1995	1980	1965

GEOGRAPHY

AREA (square miles/kilometers)	244/633		
LAND AREA (square miles/kilometers)	241/623		
COASTLINE (miles/kilometers)	121/193		

CITIES
CAPITAL	Singapore	2,987,000	

POPULATION

	1995	1980	1965
TOTAL	3,396,924	2,413,945	1,445,929 (57)
DENSITY (per square mile/square kilometer)	14,095/5,453	10,016/3,875	6,000/2,321
ANNUAL GROWTH	1.9%	1.2%	3%

AGE COHORTS
0–14	22%		43%
15–64	72%		55%
65 AND OVER	6%		2%

MALE	51%		
FEMALE	49%		

NET MIGRATION RATE	7.3	n/a	0.1

IDENTITY

ETHNICITY
CHINESE	76.4%		
MALAY	14.9%		
INDIAN	6.4%		

LANGUAGE
CHINESE	n/a		
MALAY	n/a		
TAMIL	n/a		
ENGLISH	n/a		

RELIGION
BUDDHIST	n/a		
MUSLIM	n/a		
CHRISTIAN	n/a		
HINDU	n/a		
SIKH	n/a		

	1995	1980	1965
TAOIST	n/a		
CONFUCIANIST	n/a		

VITAL STATISTICS

BIRTHS

BIRTH RATE	16.3	16.6 (85)	29.9 (57)
INFANT MORTALITY RATE	4.7	9.3	24.6
LIFE EXPECTANCY AT BIRTH	78.1	71.3	

MARRIAGES

MARRIAGE RATE	8.4	9.2 (85)	5.5 (57)
AVERAGE AGE AT MARRIAGE M/F	30/27 (90)		
DIVORCE RATE	1.3	0.9 (85)	

DEATHS

DEATH RATE	4.6	5.2 (85)	5.5 (57)

HOUSEHOLDS

NUMBER	649,100 (90)
AVERAGE SIZE	4.2

ECONOMICS AND LABOR

GDP PER CAPITA US$	$22,900

LABOR FORCE M/F (thousands)	952.3/639.7 (93)
AGRICULTURE	3.6/0.3
MINING	0.3/0.0
MANUFACTURING	247.8/181.7
UTILITIES	5.9/1.6
CONSTRUCTION	91.1/11.0
TRADE/FOOD/TOURISM	216.2/147.4
TRANSPORT/COMMUNICATIONS	131.0/35.8
FINANCE/INSURANCE/REAL ESTATE	88.1/85.3
SOCIAL AND PERSONAL SERVICES	167.6/176.5

UNEMPLOYMENT

TOTAL	2.6 (94)

UNION DENSITY	13.5%

	1995	1980	1965

TRANSPORT

JOURNEYS
RAILROAD PASSENGER TRIPS	9,929.0 94		
(millions of miles/kilometers)			

VEHICLES (thousands)
CARS	340.6	164.5	108.4
COMMERCIAL VEHICLES	136.8	84.5	23

HEALTH AND HEALTH CARE

RATE OF PHYSICIANS	1.4	0.9	0.4 (60)
RATE OF HOSPITAL BEDS	3.6	4.2	4.4
TOTAL DEATHS	15,569		

HEALTH INDICATORS
LOW-BIRTH-WEIGHT BABIES	7%		
CHILD MALNUTRITION	14%		
SMOKING PREVALENCE M/F	32/3%		
TUBERCULOSIS INCIDENCE RATE	0.8		

HEALTH CARE
ACCESS TO SAFE WATER	100%		
ACCESS TO SANITATION	97%		
MEASLES IMMUNIZATION	88%		

AIDS/HIV CASES	179	75 (93)	

EDUCATION

SCHOOL AGE IN SCHOOL
PRIMARY	104%	108%	107%
SECONDARY	62%	58%	49%
HIGHER	34%	8%	7.4%

FEMALES IN SCHOOL
PRIMARY	n/a	48%	101%
SECONDARY	n/a	51%	45%

ADULT ILLITERACY M/F	14/4%	8.4/26%	n/a

	1995	1980	1965
COMMUNICATIONS			
RATE OF NEWSPAPERS	336	286	268
RATE OF RADIOS	644	373	269
RATE OF TELEVISIONS	381	311	44

Source: CIA, The World Factbook, 1997; ILO, World Labour Report, 1997; UN, Demographic Yearbook, 1997; UN, Statistical Yearbook, 1996; World Bank, World Development Indicators, 1998.

SLOVAKIA[1]

Located in the heart of Eastern Europe, Slovakia was a constituent part of Czechoslovakia from the creation of that state after World War I until its peaceful break with the Czech Republic in 1993. The country—bordered by the Czech Republic and Poland to the north, Ukraine to the east, Hungary to the south, and Austria to the west— has a land area of 18,859 square miles and a population of 5.37 million. The poorer and less industrially developed half of the former Czechoslovakia, Slovakia today has a per capita income of $7,200 annually, with fully 85 percent of the country living on $2 a day or less, though this figure says more about the collapse of the Slovakian currency than about the utter poverty it would seem to indicate. Largely Slovakian in ethnicity, the country has a significant Hungarian minority of about 10 percent. Like many of its East European neighbors, Slovakia has seen slow growth in recent years. In 1995, its population grew by just 0.3 percent, and only 22 percent of the population was under 15 years of age. While Slovakia has an expansive health care system, it suffers from significant public health problems. Just half of the population lives in residences with adequate sanitation.

	1995	1980
GEOGRAPHY		
AREA (square miles/kilometers)	17,701/48,845	
LAND AREA (square miles/kilometers)	18,842/48,800	
COASTLINE (miles/kilometers)	Landlocked	
CITIES		
CAPITALS	Bratislava	451,272
MAJOR CITIES	Kosice	240,139
POPULATION		
TOTAL	5,374,362	
DENSITY (per square mile/square kilometer)	285/110	
ANNUAL GROWTH	0.34%	
AGE COHORTS		
0–14	22%	
15–64	67%	
65 AND OVER	11%	
MALE	49%	
FEMALE	51%	

	1995	1980
URBAN	57%	
RURAL	43%	
NET MIGRATION RATE	0.12	

IDENTITY

ETHNICITY

SLOVAK	85.7%
HUNGARIAN	10.7%
GYPSY	1.5%
CZECH	1%
UKRAINIAN	0%
GERMAN	0%
POLISH	0%

LANGUAGE

SLOVAK (official)	n/a
HUNGARIAN	n/a

RELIGION

ROMAN CATHOLIC	60.3%
ATHEIST	9.7%
PROTESTANT	8.4%
ORTHODOX	4.1%

VITAL STATISTICS

BIRTHS

BIRTH RATE	12.6 (94)
URBAN BIRTH RATE	11.7
RURAL BIRTH RATE	13.4
INFANT MORTALITY RATE	10.7
ABORTION RATE	525.3
LIFE EXPECTANCY AT BIRTH	73

MARRIAGES

MARRIAGE RATE	5.3
AVERAGE AGE AT MARRIAGE M/F	25.5/22.6 (91)
DIVORCE RATE	1.6

DEATHS

DEATH RATE	9.4

	1995	1980

HOUSEHOLDS

NUMBER — 1,832,484 (91)
AVERAGE SIZE — 2.9

TYPE OF HOUSEHOLD
FEMALE HEADED — 23.1%

ECONOMICS AND LABOR

GDP PER CAPITA US$ — $7,200

LABOR FORCE M/F (thousands) — 1,264/911 (92)
AGRICULTURE — 169/87
MINING — 24/4
MANUFACTURING — 353/236
UTILITIES — 32/9
CONSTRUCTION — 161/37
TRADE/FOOD/TOURISM — 143/113
TRANSPORT/COMMUNICATIONS — 109/52
FINANCE/INSURANCE/REAL ESTATE — 105/65
SOCIAL AND PERSONAL SERVICES — 168/308

UNEMPLOYMENT
TOTAL — 13.3 (94)

UNION DENSITY — 52.3%

POVERTY
UNDER $1/DAY — 12.8% (92)
UNDER $2/DAY — 85.1%

TRANSPORT

JOURNEYS
RAILROAD PASSENGER TRIPS — 23.0 (94)
  (millions of miles/kilometers)

	1995	1980

HEALTH AND HEALTH CARE

	1995	1980
RATE OF PHYSICIANS	2.8	
RATE OF HOSPITAL BEDS	7.1	
TOTAL DEATHS	52,686	
HEALTH INDICATORS		
LOW-BIRTH-WEIGHT BABIES	6%	
SMOKING PREVALENCE M/F	43/26%	
TUBERCULOSIS INCIDENCE RATE	0.4	
HEALTH CARE		
ACCESS TO SANITATION	51%	
MEASLES IMMUNIZATION	99%	
AIDS/HIV CASES	13	8 (93)

EDUCATION

	1995	1980
SCHOOL AGE IN SCHOOL		
PRIMARY	97%	
SECONDARY	91%	
HIGHER	20%	
FEMALES IN SCHOOL		
PRIMARY	49%	
SECONDARY	51%	

COMMUNICATIONS

	1995	1980
RATE OF NEWSPAPERS	317	313
RATE OF RADIOS	567	509
RATE OF TELEVISIONS	474	395

FOOTNOTE
1. Part of Czechoslovakia in 1965 and 1980.

Source: CIA, *The World Factbook, 1997*; ILO, *World Labour Report, 1997*; UN, *Demographic Yearbook, 1997*; UN, *Statistical Yearbook, 1996*; World Bank, *World Development Indicators, 1998*.

SLOVENIA[1]

By far the most prosperous republic emerging out of the former Yugoslav federation, Slovenia is one of the first former communist states to be earmarked for membership in the European Union. Slovenia's 1.95 million people have a per capita income of $11,000, comparable to incomes in the lower tier of EU countries. Covering some 7,821 square miles of territory, Slovenia is surrounded by Austria to the north, Hungary to the east, Croatia to the east and south, and Italy to the west. It also has a short, 29-mile coastline along the Gulf of Venice, at the north end of the Adriatic Sea. Of Slovenia's 800,000 workers, approximately 300,000 labor in manufacturing—mostly metal production—and mining. While the country is roughly half rural, just 70,000 workers make their living from the land. Slovenia has also been blessed politically, having avoided virtually all the strife endemic to other post-Yugoslav republics. Slovenia also enjoys Western European levels of social welfare. Over 90 percent of the teenage population attends secondary schools and similar percentages of the total population live in residences with healthy sanitation.

	1995	1980	1965
GEOGRAPHY			
AREA (square miles/kilometers)	7,821/20,256		
LAND AREA (square miles/kilometers)	7,821/20,256		
COASTLINE (miles/kilometers)	29/47		
CITIES			
CAPITAL	Ljubljana	280,146 (94)	
MAJOR CITIES	Marebor	130,398	
POPULATION			
TOTAL	1,951,443		
DENSITY (per square mile/square kilometer)	250/96		
ANNUAL GROWTH	−0.27%		
AGE COHORTS			
0–14	17%		
15–64	70%		
65 AND OVER	13%		
MALE	48%		
FEMALE	52%		
URBAN	50%		
RURAL	50%		

	1995	1980	1965
NET MIGRATION RATE	−1.57		

IDENTITY

ETHNICITY

SLOVENE	91%		
CROAT	3%		
SERB	2%		
MUSLIM	1%		

LANGUAGE

SLOVENIAN	91%		
SERBO-CROATIAN	7%		

RELIGION

ROMAN CATHOLIC	96%		
MUSLIM	1%		

VITAL STATISTICS

BIRTHS

BIRTH RATE	8.3		
URBAN BIRTH RATE	9.0 (94)		
RURAL BIRTH RATE	10.5 (94)		
INFANT MORTALITY RATE	7.3		
ABORTION RATE	583.7 (94)		
LIFE EXPECTANCY AT BIRTH	75.1		

MARRIAGES

MARRIAGE RATE	3.8		
AVERAGE AGE AT MARRIAGE M/F	28.5/24.8 (91)		
DIVORCE RATE	1		

DEATHS

DEATH RATE	9.4		

HOUSEHOLDS

NUMBER	640,198 (91)		
URBAN	350,201		
RURAL	289,997		

	1995	**1980**	**1965**
AVERAGE SIZE	3.1		
URBAN	2.8		
RURAL	3.4		
TYPE OF HOUSEHOLD			
FEMALE HEADED	44.1%		
SINGLE	13.0%		
MARRIED	65.4%		
WIDOWED	15.3%		
DIVORCED/SEPARATED	6.0%		

ECONOMICS AND LABOR

	1995	**1980**	**1965**
GDP PER CAPITA US$	$11,000		
LABOR FORCE M/F (thousands)	402.7/363.5 (93)		
AGRICULTURE	32.7/38.5		
MINING	8.7/0.7		
MANUFACTURING	173.9/127.3		
UTILITIES	9.3/2.4		
CONSTRUCTION	29.8/4.5		
TRADE/FOOD/TOURISM	29.7/55.2		
TRANSPORT/COMMUNICATIONS	32.5/10.4		
FINANCE/INSURANCE/REAL ESTATE	14.3/19.3		
SOCIAL AND PERSONAL SERVICES	71.8/105.2		
UNEMPLOYMENT			
TOTAL	14.4% (94)		

TRANSPORT

	1995	**1980**	**1965**
JOURNEYS (by transport mode)			
RAILROAD PASSENGER TRIPS	340 (94)		
(millions of miles/kilometers)			

HEALTH AND HEALTH CARE

	1995	**1980**	**1965**
RATE OF PHYSICIANS	2.2	n/a	
RATE OF HOSPITAL BEDS	5.8	7	
TOTAL DEATHS	18,968	n/a	

	1995	1980	1965
HEALTH INDICATORS			
LOW-BIRTH-WEIGHT BABIES	6%		
SMOKING PREVALENCE M/F	35/23%		
TUBERCULOSIS INCIDENCE RATE	0.3		
HEALTH CARE			
ACCESS TO SANITATION	90%		
MEASLES IMMUNIZATION	91%		
AIDS/HIV CASES	52	31 (93)	

EDUCATION

	1995	1980	1965
SCHOOL AGE IN SCHOOL			
PRIMARY	98%		
SECONDARY	91%		
HIGHER	32%		
FEMALES IN SCHOOL			
PRIMARY	49%		
SECONDARY	52%		

COMMUNICATIONS

	1995	1980	1965
RATE OF NEWSPAPERS	160	108	
RATE OF RADIOS	377	273	
RATE OF TELEVISIONS	297	251	

FOOTNOTE
1. Part of Federation of Yugoslavia in 1980 and 1965.

Source: CIA, *The World Factbook, 1997;* ILO, *World Labour Report, 1997;* UN, *Demographic Yearbook, 1997;* UN, *Statistical Yearbook, 1996;* World Bank, *World Development Indicators, 1998.*

SOLOMON ISLANDS

Situated on a chain of large and small islands off the southwestern tip of New Guinea, the Solomon Islands include a territory of 10,985 square miles scattered across 75,000 square miles of the South Pacific Ocean. Largely Melanesian, with a significant minority of Polynesians, the population of the islands was 412,902 in 1995, up from 124,706 in 1965. Though the population is rapidly growing—at a rate of 3.4 percent in 1995—the islands are still relatively underinhabited, with a density rate of just 39 persons per square mile. The islands are largely rural, and just 9 percent of their inhabitants live in cities, largely in the capital of Honiara. Though the per capita income of the islands is just $2,590 annually, what this figure partly reflects is that many citizens of the republic exist largely outside the commercial economy, making a living by farming and fishing for subsistence. Indeed, the official labor force of the country is just 26,800, of whom 6,400 are involved in commercial agriculture. The island environment and the low density result in relatively high health indexes. The infant mortality rate is 25.8 per 1,000 live births, low for the developing world, and down from 52.4 in 1965. Life expectancy in 1995 was 71.1 years.

	1995	1980	1965
GEOGRAPHY			
AREA (square miles/kilometers)	10,985/28,450		
LAND AREA (square miles/kilometers)	10,633/27,540		
COASTLINE (miles/kilometers)	3,321/5,313		
CITIES			
CAPITAL	Honiara	n/a	30,413 (86)	n/a
POPULATION			
TOTAL	412,902	196,823 (76)	124,076 (59)
DENSITY (per square mile/square kilometer)	39/15	19/7	12/5
ANNUAL GROWTH	3.35%	3.7%	2.1%
AGE COHORTS			
0–14	46%	n/a	44.3%
15–64	51%	n/a	51%
65 AND OVER	3%	n/a	4.6%
MALE	52%		
FEMALE	48%		
URBAN	n/a	9.1% (76)	n/a
RURAL	n/a	90.9%	n/a
NET MIGRATION RATE	0		

	1995	1980	1965

IDENTITY

ETHNICITY

MELANESIAN	93%		
POLYNESIAN	4%		
MICRONESIAN	1.5%		
EUROPEAN	0.8%		
CHINESE	0.3%		

LANGUAGE

MELANESIAN PIDGIN	n/a		
ENGLISH	n/a		

RELIGION

ANGLICAN	34%		
ROMAN CATHOLIC	19%		
BAPTIST	17%		
UNITED METHODIST/PRESBYTERIAN	11%		
SEVENTH-DAY ADVENT	10%		
OTHER PROTESTANT	5%		
TRADITIONAL	4%		

VITAL STATISTICS

BIRTHS

BIRTH RATE	37.9	n/a	36.1 (69)
INFANT MORTALITY RATE	25.8	n/a	52.4
LIFE EXPECTANCY AT BIRTH	71.1	n/a	n/a

DEATHS

DEATH RATE	4.4	n/a	13 (69)

HOUSEHOLDS

NUMBER	n/a	43,842 (86)	
AVERAGE SIZE	n/a	6.5	

ECONOMICS AND LABOR

GDP PER CAPITA US$	$2,590		

LABOR FORCE (thousands)	26.8 (92)		
AGRICULTURE	6.4		

	1995	1980	1965
MINING	0		
MANUFACTURING	2		
UTILITIES	0.4		
CONSTRUCTION	1.1		
TRADE/FOOD/TOURISM	3.2		
TRANSPORT/COMMUNICATIONS	1.4		
FINANCE/INSURANCE/REAL ESTATE	1.2		
SOCIAL AND PERSONAL SERVICES	11.1		

TRANSPORT

JOURNEYS (by transport mode)

	1995	1980	1965
RAILROAD PASSENGER TRIPS	79 (94)		
(millions of miles/kilometers)			

HEALTH AND HEALTH CARE

	1995	1980	1965
RATE OF PHYSICIANS	n/a	n/a	0.2 (60)
RATE OF HOSPITAL BEDS	n/a	n/a	6.9

EDUCATION

	1995	1980	1965
SCHOOL AGE IN SCHOOL			
PRIMARY	n/a	n/a	93%
SECONDARY	n/a	n/a	3%
FEMALES IN SCHOOL			
PRIMARY	n/a	n/a	71%
SECONDARY	n/a	n/a	1%

COMMUNICATIONS

	1995	1980	1965
RATE OF RADIOS	121	88	48
RATE OF TELEVISIONS	6	0	0

Source: CIA, *The World Factbook, 1997*; ILO, *World Labour Report, 1997*; UN, *Demographic Yearbook, 1997*; UN, *Statistical Yearbook, 1996*; World Bank, *World Development Indicators, 1998*.

SOMALIA

Among the poorest countries in the world, Somalia has a per capita income of just $500 annually. A largely desert country, inhabited by nomads and subsistence farmers, Somalia is located on the Horn of Africa, at the easternmost extreme of the continent, with Djibouti to the north, Ethiopia to the north and west, and Kenya to the south. In fact, Somalia's borders have been a subject of much dispute. The country has fought several wars with Ethiopia over the Ogaden region of Ethiopia, which both governments claim as their own. Somalia also has a lengthy coastline of 1,891 miles along the Gulf of Aden and the Arabian Sea. Initially colonized by Italy and Great Britain, Somalia won its independence in 1960. After living for many years under the socialist dictatorship of Said Barre, Somalia descended into a brutal civil war when he was ousted in 1991. Despite the fact that the country, almost entirely composed of the Somali ethnic group, is one of the most homogenous in Africa, the fighting has fractured the population along clan lines. An international peacekeeping force was eventually driven out, after one of the clans killed a number of U.S. Marines in the early 1990s. Though strife-ridden, Somalia has one of the fastest rates of population growth in the world. In just 15 years, between 1980 and 1995, the population almost tripled from 3.25 to 9.64 million. The country's long-running war combined with rapid population growth has resulted in stunted social indexes. There is only one newspaper sold daily for every 1,000 citizens and life expectancy is just 55.5 years.

	1995	1980	1965
GEOGRAPHY			
AREA (square miles/kilometers)	246,201/637,660		
LAND AREA (square miles/kilometers)	242,216/627,340		
COASTLINE (miles/kilometers)	1,891/3,025		
CITIES			
CAPITAL	Mogadishu	n/a	n/a	230,000 (72)
POPULATION			
TOTAL	9,639,151	3,253,024 (75)	n/a
DENSITY (per square mile/square kilometer)	40/15	13/5	10/4
ANNUAL GROWTH	3.1%	3%	3.4%
AGE COHORTS			
0–14	44%		
15–64	52%		
65 AND OVER	4%		
MALE	51%		
FEMALE	49%		

	1995	1980	1965
URBAN	23.5% (86)		
RURAL	76.5%		
NET MIGRATION RATE	0		

IDENTITY

ETHNICITY
SOMALI	85%		
BANTU	n/a		
ARABS	n/a		

LANGUAGE
SOMALI (official)	n/a		
ARABIC	n/a		
ITALIAN	n/a		
ENGLISH	n/a		

RELIGION
SUNNI MUSLIM	n/a		

VITAL STATISTICS

BIRTHS
BIRTH RATE	44.2	47.9	
INFANT MORTALITY RATE	121.1	155	
LIFE EXPECTANCY AT BIRTH	55.5	40.9	

DEATHS
DEATH RATE	13.2	23.3	

ECONOMICS AND LABOR

GDP PER CAPITA US$	$500		

TRANSPORT

JOURNEYS (by transport mode)
RAILROAD PASSENGER TRIPS	90.0 (94)		
(millions of miles/kilometers)			

	1995	1980	1965
VEHICLES (thousands)			
CARS	10.5	n/a	5
COMMERCIAL VEHICLES	11.5	n/a	6.3

HEALTH AND HEALTH CARE

	1995	1980	1965
RATE OF PHYSICIANS	n/a	n/a	0 (60)
RATE OF HOSPITAL BEDS	n/a	n/a	1.7 (60)
AIDS/HIV CASES	13	13 (93)	

EDUCATION

	1995	1980	1965
SCHOOL AGE IN SCHOOL			
PRIMARY	n/a	30%	9%
SECONDARY	n/a	11%	2%
HIGHER	n/a	0.8% (75)	0%
FEMALES IN SCHOOL			
PRIMARY	n/a	22%	6%
SECONDARY	n/a	6%	1%
ADULT ILLITERACY M/F	n/a	81.6/93.5% (85)	n/a

COMMUNICATIONS

	1995	1980	1965
RATE OF NEWSPAPERS	1	1	2
RATE OF RADIOS	41	24	18 (70)
RATE OF TELEVISIONS	13	0	0

Source: CIA, The World Factbook, 1997; ILO, World Labour Report, 1997; UN, Demographic Yearbook, 1997; UN, Statistical Yearbook, 1996; World Bank, World Development Indicators, 1998.

SOUTH AFRICA

The economic giant of southern Africa, South Africa has a per capita income of $4,800, though this figure is distorted by the fact that the country's white minority is far richer than its black majority. Covering some 501,000 square miles at the southern end of Africa, South Africa has a population of 41.74 million. It is bordered by Namibia, Botswana, Zimbabwe, and Mozambique to the north and is surrounded by the Atlantic and Indian oceans to the west, south, and east. Until 1994, the country was governed by the white minority, who represent just 13.6 percent of the population. Descended from Dutch and English settlers, the whites ruled over a system known as apartheid, whereby Africans had no political rights and were kept economically impoverished.

Following decades of struggle, South Africa was transformed into a majority-ruled democracy in 1994, with the election of Nelson Mandela to the presidency. South Africa is the most industrialized country on the African continent, producing automobiles, electronics, chemicals, and other heavy and light industrial products. Still, the main pillar of the economy remains the country's mining industry. South Africa remains the world's largest producer of gold and diamonds. Its population also owns some 3.49 million cars, more than any other country in Africa. Its relatively high social indexes are slightly misleading, since there are major gaps between the levels of whites and those of blacks.

Identity

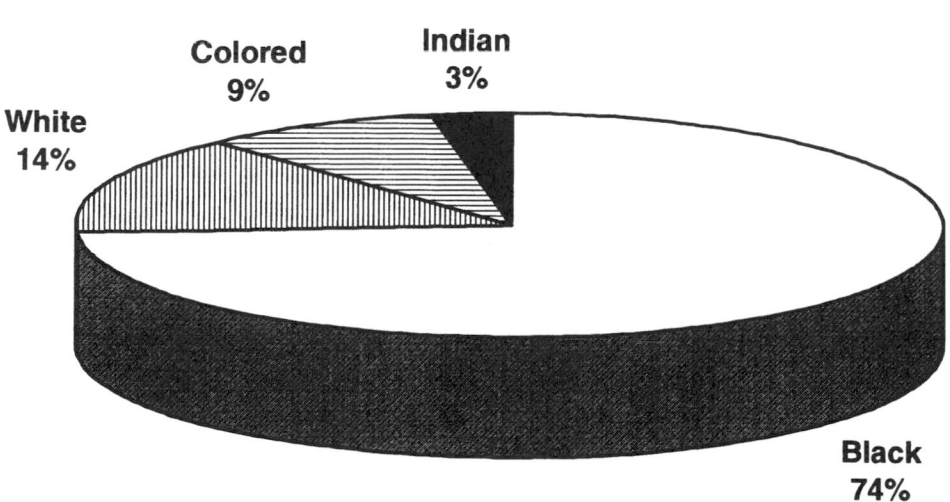

The political inequity of the old South African apartheid regime can be readily understood by observing the distribution of racial groups in the country. Constituting just 13.6 percent of the population, whites held virtually all political power.

Newspapers and Radios

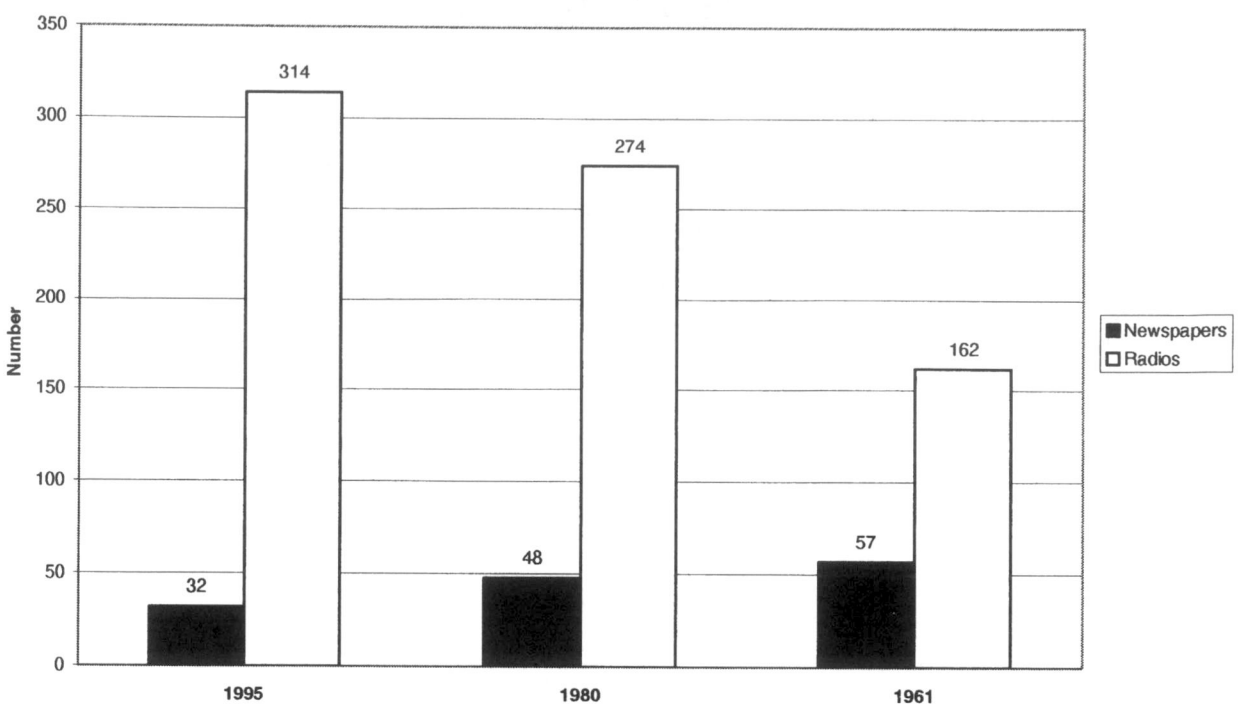

Note: Radios in 1,000s.

South Africa displays an odd pattern of newspaper readership and radio ownership over the years, a pattern explained in part by the oppressive political order. With newspapers heavily censored, much of the majority black population turned to radio to get information, since radios bring in stations from outside the country.

CHRONOLOGY

1960   Massacre of black protesters by white police in Sharpeville leads to international condemnation.

1961   South Africa severs ties with British Commonwealth; declares itself a republic.

1966   Prime Minister H. F. Verwoerd assassinated; is replaced by John Vorster.

1975   South Africa launches first invasion of Angola.

1977   Rioting breaks out in black township of Soweto.

1978   Vorster government implicated in scandal; Vorster resigns; P. W. Botha becomes prime minister.

1987   South Africa launches massive invasion of Angola.

1988   Defeated in Angola, South Africa also agrees to leave Namibia.

1989   F. W. de Klerk replaces Botha as prime minister.

1990   De Klerk frees African National Congress (ANC) leader Nelson Mandela from prison; legalizes ANC.

1991   Government begins negotiations with ANC in move toward majority rule; scraps apartheid laws.

1994   Mandela and ANC elected to power in first non-racial election in South African history.

		1995	1980	1965

GEOGRAPHY

		1995	1980	1965
AREA (square miles/kilometers)		501,510/1,219,912		
LAND AREA (square miles/kilometers)		501,510/1,219,912		
COASTLINE (miles/kilometers)		1,749/2,798		
CITIES				
CAPITAL	Pretoria	525,583 (91)	n/a	
MAJOR CITIES	Capetown	854,616	776,617 (85)	
	Durban	715,669	634,301	
	Johannesburg	712,507	632,369	
	Soweto	596,632	n/a	

POPULATION

	1995	1980	1965
TOTAL	41,743,459	25,016,525	16,002,797 (60)
DENSITY (per square mile/square kilometer)	83/34	50/21	32/13
ANNUAL GROWTH	1.76%	2.5%	2.4%
AGE COHORTS			
0–14	36%	n/a	40%
15–64	60%	n/a	56%
65 AND OVER	4%	n/a	4%
MALE	50%		
FEMALE	50%		
URBAN	56.6%	52.6%	
RURAL	43.4%	47.6%	
NET MIGRATION RATE	0	n/a	0.1

IDENTITY

	1995	1980	1965
ETHNICITY			
BLACK	75.2%		
WHITE	13.6%		
COLORED	8.6%		
INDIAN	2.6%		
LANGUAGE			
AFRIKAANS	n/a		
ENGLISH	n/a		
NDEBELE	n/a		

	1995	**1980**	**1965**
PEDI	n/a		
SOTHO	n/a		
SWAZI	n/a		
TSONGA	n/a		
TSWANA	n/a		
VENDA	n/a		
XHOSA	n/a		
ZULU	n/a		
RELIGION			
CHRISTIAN	n/a		
HINDU	n/a		
MUSLIM	n/a		

VITAL STATISTICS

	1995	**1980**	**1965**
BIRTHS			
BIRTH RATE	27.9	38.7	
INFANT MORTALITY RATE	48.8	83	
LIFE EXPECTANCY AT BIRTH	59.5	53.5	
MARRIAGES			
AVERAGE AGE AT MARRIAGE M/F	28.9/26.8 (91)		
DEATHS			
DEATH RATE	10.3	13.9	

HOUSEHOLDS

NUMBER	5,317,539 (91)
AVERAGE SIZE	5.8

ECONOMICS AND LABOR

GDP PER CAPITA US$	$4,800
LABOR FORCE (thousands)	4,950.5 (93)
AGRICULTURE	
MINING	561.7
MANUFACTURING	1,400.5
UTILITIES	42.5
CONSTRUCTION	374.5
TRADE/FOOD/TOURISM	764.4
TRANSPORT/COMMUNICATIONS	303.1

	1995	**1980**	**1965**
FINANCE/INSURANCE/REAL ESTATE	191.5		
SOCIAL AND PERSONAL SERVICES	1,312.4		

UNEMPLOYMENT
| TOTAL | 31.3% (93) | | |

UNION DENSITY
| | 21.8% | | |

POVERTY
| UNDER $1/DAY | 23.7% (93) | | |
| UNDER $2/DAY | 50.2% | | |

TRANSPORT

JOURNEYS (by transport mode)
RAILROAD PASSENGER TRIPS	71,573 (93)		
(millions of miles/kilometers)			
AIR PASSENGER TRIPS (thousands)	5,802 (94)		

VEHICLES (thousands)
| CARS | 3,488.6 | 2,333.10 | 1,117 |
| COMMERCIAL VEHICLES | 1,784.9 | 966.2 | 291 |

HEALTH AND HEALTH CARE

TOTAL DEATHS
| | 201,273 (93) | | |

HEALTH INDICATORS
PREGNANT WOMEN WITH ANEMIA	37%		
CHILD MALNUTRITION	9%		
SMOKING PREVALENCE M/F	52/17%		
TUBERCULOSIS INCIDENCE RATE	2.2		

HEALTH CARE
ACCESS TO SAFE WATER	70%		
ACCESS TO SANITATION	46%		
MEASLES IMMUNIZATION	77%		

AIDS/HIV CASES
| | 10,337 | 3,862 (93) | |

	1995	1980	1965

EDUCATION

SCHOOL AGE IN SCHOOL

PRIMARY	117%	85%	92%
SECONDARY	84%	n/a	30%
HIGHER	17%	n/a	3.3%

FEMALES IN SCHOOL

PRIMARY	49%	n/a	90%
SECONDARY	53%	n/a	28%

ADULT ILLITERACY M/F	18/18%

COMMUNICATIONS

RATE OF NEWSPAPERS	32	48	57 (61)
RATE OF RADIOS	314	274	162
RATE OF TELEVISIONS	101	69	0

Source: CIA, *The World Factbook, 1997;* ILO, *World Labour Report, 1997;* UN, *Demographic Yearbook, 1997;* UN, *Statistical Yearbook, 1996;* World Bank, *World Development Indicators, 1998.*

SPAIN

Encompassing the largest part of the Iberian peninsula at the southwestern extreme of Europe, Spain is separated from France by the Pyrenees Mountains. Occupying 194,884 square miles of territory—meaning it is roughly twice the size of Oregon—Spain has coastlines on the Mediterranean and the Atlantic. Spain's 39.18 million residents are ethnically quite diverse. Two distinctive linguistic minorities in the north—the Basques and the Catalans—have struggled for decades to achieve political and cultural autonomy. Spain once possessed one of the great empires of world history, and has left its linguistic and cultural imprint on a vast territory of the New World, from the Rio Grande River in north to the tip of South America. In the 1930s, Spain was torn by a devastating civil war that left a fascist dictatorship in power until 1975. Since then, the country has made a relatively smooth transition to democracy, becoming a member of NATO and the European Union in the past 20 years. Today, it has a per capita income of $14,300, though there are great differences in wealth between the prosperous north and the impoverished south. Still, the country has made enormous strides in the realm of social services. Between 1965 and 1995, the infant mortality rate dropped from 34.6 per 1,000 live births to just 6.3, which is comparable to the rates in much of the rest of Western Europe. During the same period, the percentage of young persons attending university climbed from just 4.8 percent to some 46 percent.

Cars and Commercial Vehicles

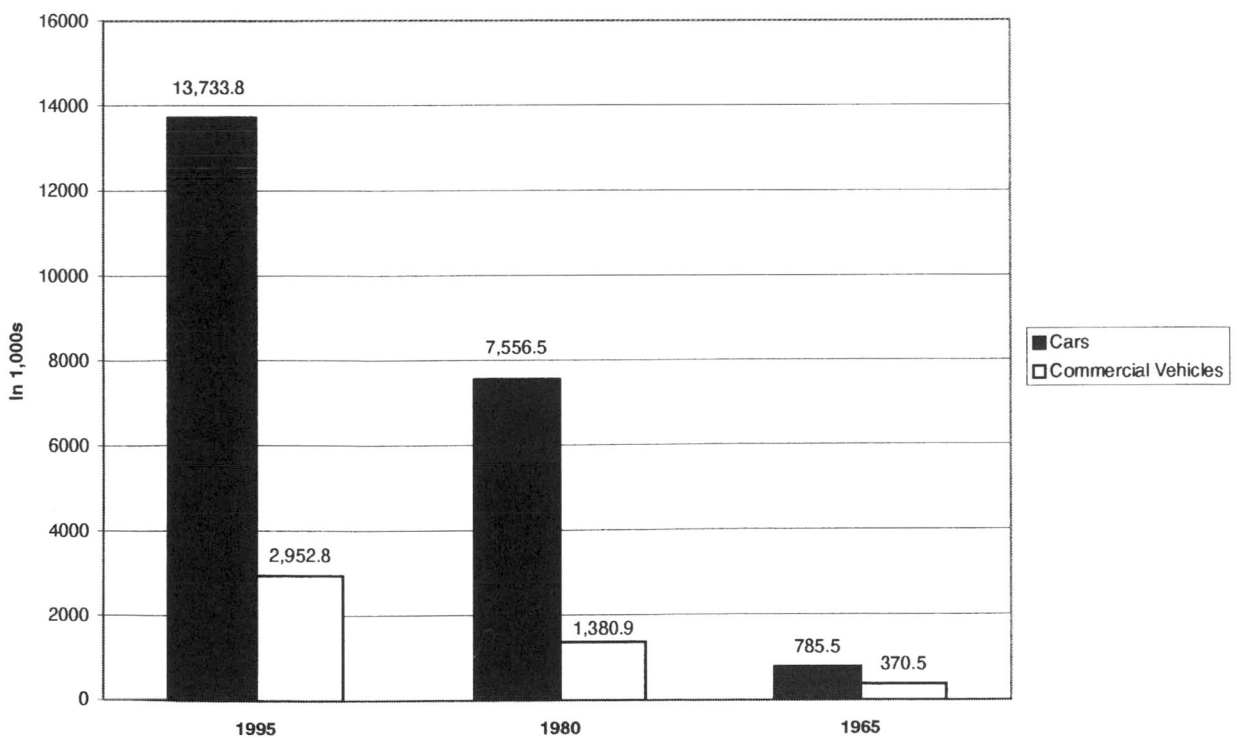

During the postwar era, Spain underwent a dramatic economic transformation, gradually pulling itself from developing-world levels to the lower rungs of the developed world. This transition can be seen in the ratio of private car ownership to commercial vehicles. In a poor country, there are usually more commercial vehicles in comparison to private autos than there are in developed countries, since few people can afford the latter.

Secondary and Higher Education

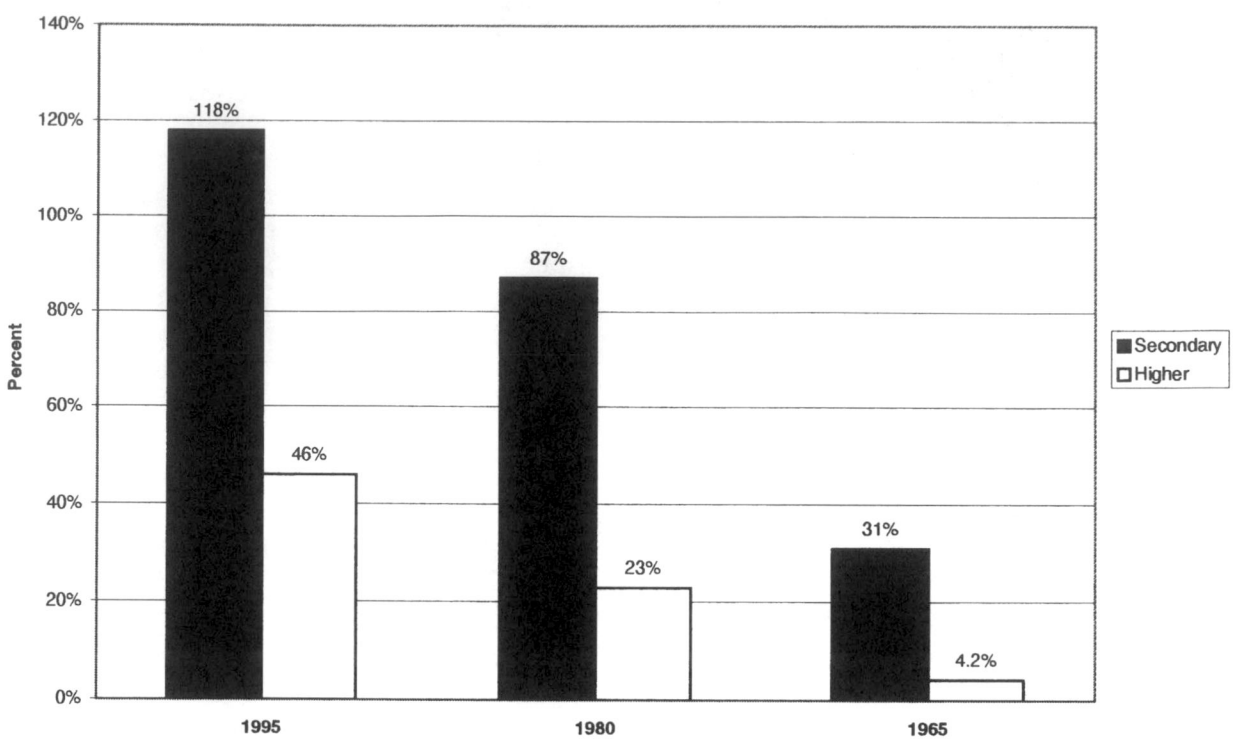

Educational levels and democracy are usually related, though which is cause and which effect is debatable. Do higher educational rates create the demand for democratic change or are democracies more willing to educate their populace? In either case, since the advent of democracy in Spain in the mid-1970s, education levels at the secondary and university levels have gone up significantly.

CHRONOLOGY

1969   Dictator Francisco Franco designates Prince Juan Carlos to become head of state following end of Franco regime.

1975   Franco dies after long illness.

1979   Prime Minister Adolfo Suarez grants autonomy to Catalonia and Basque region.

1981   Attempted military coup fails.

1982   Prime Minister Felipe Gonzalez and Socialist Party sweep to power in election.

1986   Spain is admitted to European Economic Community; votes to stay in North Atlantic Treaty Organization.

1996   Conservatives win nationwide election, replace Socialists as majority party in parliament.

1997   Gonzalez resigns as head of Socialist Party.

	1995	**1980**	**1965**

GEOGRAPHY

AREA (square miles/kilometers)	194,884/504,750	
LAND AREA (square miles/kilometers)	192,819/499,400	
COASTLINE (miles/kilometers)	3,102/4,964	

CITIES		
CAPITAL	Madrid (91)	2,976,064
MAJOR CITIES	Barcelona	1,596,190
	Valencia	749,361
	Seville	678,902
	Saragossa	598,078

POPULATION

	1995	**1980**	**1965**
TOTAL	39,181,114 (91)	37,746,260	30,430,698 (60)
DENSITY (per square mile/square kilometer)	203/78	196/76	158/61
ANNUAL GROWTH	0.16%	0.6%	0.8%
AGE COHORTS			
0–14	16%	n/a	27%
15–64	68%	n/a	65%
65 AND OVER	16%	n/a	8%
MALE	49%		
FEMALE	51%		
URBAN	64.1% (91)	91.4%	
RURAL	35.9%	8.6%	
NET MIGRATION RATE	0.4	n/a	−0.2

IDENTITY

	1995		
ETHNICITY			
MEDITERRANEAN AND NORDIC COMPOSITE	n/a		
LANGUAGE			
CASTILIAN SPANISH	n/a		
CATALAN	n/a		
GALICIAN	n/a		
BASQUE	n/a		

	1995	**1980**	**1965**
RELIGION			
ROMAN CATHOLIC	99%		

VITAL STATISTICS

	1995	**1980**	**1965**
BIRTHS			
BIRTH RATE	10	13.4 (82)	20.9
INFANT MORTALITY RATE	6.3	9.6	34.6
LIFE EXPECTANCY AT BIRTH	78.3	73.3	69.6
MARRIAGES			
MARRIAGE RATE	5	5 (82)	7.2
AVERAGE AGE AT MARRIAGE M/F	28.4/26 (91)		
DIVORCE RATE	0.6		
DEATHS			
DEATH RATE	8.9	7.4 (82)	8.6

HOUSEHOLDS

	1995	**1980**	**1965**
NUMBER	n/a	n/a	7,464,000 (50)
AVERAGE SIZE	n/a	n/a	3.7

ECONOMICS AND LABOR

GDP PER CAPITA US$	$14,300
LABOR FORCE M/F (thousands)	7,850.3/3,987.3 (93)
AGRICULTURE	869.7/328.1
MINING	55.6/2.6
MANUFACTURING	1,859.4/542.3
UTILITIES	73.5/6.5
CONSTRUCTION	1,046.1/42.3
TRADE/FOOD/TOURISM	1,596.5/1,095.5
TRANSPORT/COMMUNICATIONS	606.5/88.4
FINANCE/INSURANCE/REAL ESTATE	554.5/372.2
SOCIAL AND PERSONAL SERVICES	1,188.6/1,509.3
UNEMPLOYMENT	
TOTAL	24.2 (94)
UNION DENSITY	11.4%

	1995	1980	1965

TRANSPORT

JOURNEYS (by transport mode)

RAILROAD PASSENGER TRIPS	16,139 (94)		
(millions of miles/kilometers)			
AIR PASSENGER TRIPS (thousands)	21,992		

VEHICLES (thousands)

CARS	13,733.8	7,556.50	785.5
COMMERCIAL VEHICLES	2,952.8	1,380.90	370.5

HEALTH AND HEALTH CARE

RATE OF PHYSICIANS	4.1	2.8	1.2 (60)
RATE OF HOSPITAL BEDS	4	n/a	4
TOTAL DEATHS	343,965		

HEALTH INDICATORS

LOW-BIRTH-WEIGHT BABIES	1%		
SMOKING PREVALENCE M/F	48/25%		
TUBERCULOSIS INCIDENCE RATE	2.5		

HEALTH CARE

ACCESS TO SAFE WATER	99%		
ACCESS TO SANITATION	100%		
MEASLES IMMUNIZATION	90%		

AIDS/HIV CASES	37,847	25,559 (93)	

EDUCATION

SCHOOL AGE IN SCHOOL

PRIMARY	105%	109%	75%
SECONDARY	118%	87%	31%
HIGHER	46%	23%	4.2%

FEMALES IN SCHOOL

PRIMARY	48%	49%	75%
SECONDARY	51%	51%	25%
HIGHER	n/a	20.5%	4.8% (70)

ADULT ILLITERACY M/F	n/a	4.0/9.9% (81)	n/a

	1995	1980	1965
COMMUNICATIONS			
RATE OF NEWSPAPERS	104	93	153 (63)
RATE OF RADIOS	311	258	150
RATE OF TELEVISIONS	400	253	58

Source: CIA, The World Factbook, 1997; ILO, World Labour Report, 1997; UN, Demographic Yearbook, 1997; UN, Statistical Yearbook, 1996; World Bank, World Development Indicators, 1998.

SRI LANKA

Situated on the large island of Ceylon—the former name of the country—Sri Lanka is located off the southern tip of the Indian peninsula in South Asia. Covering some 25,332 square miles of territory, roughly the size of West Virginia, Sri Lanka has a population of 18.55 million, up from 10.59 million in 1965. The country has two main ethnic groups. The majority, at 74 percent of the population, are the Buddhist Sinhalese, natives of the island. A minority of some 18 percent, the Hindu Tamils, were imported as laborers by the colonial British rulers in the late nineteenth and early twentieth centuries to work on Sri Lanka's tea and other plantations. Since Sri Lanka's independence from England in 1948, the Tamils have felt discriminated against by the majority Sinhalese. Beginning in the 1970s, they rose up in rebellion, claiming the northern part of the island as an independent Tamil state. Brutal fighting between the rebels—known as the Tamil Tigers—and the Sinhalese government has left tens of thousands dead. Despite the fighting, the country has made significant progress in the realms of health and education. Between 1980 and 1995, the infant mortality rate dropped by a third, from 32.3 to 20.8 per 1,000 live births. Similarly, figures for education have improved dramatically. Between 1965 and 1995, the percentage of young persons attending secondary school rose from 45 percent to 75 percent.

		1995	1980	1965
GEOGRAPHY				
AREA (square miles/kilometers)		25,332/65,610		
LAND AREA (square miles/kilometers)		24,996/64,740		
COASTLINE (miles/kilometers)		838/1,340		
CITIES				
CAPITAL	Colombo	615,000 (90)		
MAJOR CITIES	Dehiwala	196,000		
	Moratuwa	170,000		
	Jaffna	129,000		
	Kotte	109,000		
POPULATION				
TOTAL		18,553,074	14,848,364 (81)	10,590,060 (60)
DENSITY (per square mile/square kilometer)		742/287	594/229	424/164
ANNUAL GROWTH		1.13%	1.4%	
AGE COHORTS				
0–14		28%	n/a	42%
15–64		66%	n/a	54%
65 AND OVER		6%	n/a	4%

	1995	1980	1965
MALE	51%		
FEMALE	49%		
URBAN	n/a	21.5%	n/a
RURAL	n/a	78.5%	n/a
NET MIGRATION RATE	−0.8	n/a	0 (64)

IDENTITY

ETHNICITY

SINHALESE	74%
TAMIL	18%
MOOR	7%
BURGHER, MALAY, AND VEDDA	1%

LANGUAGE

SINHALA	74%
TAMIL	18%

RELIGION

BUDDHIST	69%
HINDU	15%
CHRISTIAN	8%
MUSLIM	8%

VITAL STATISTICS

BIRTHS

BIRTH RATE	17.9	24.8 (84)
INFANT MORTALITY RATE	20.8	32.3
LIFE EXPECTANCY AT BIRTH	72.4	70.6

MARRIAGES

MARRIAGE RATE	9.2	7.9 (84)
DIVORCE RATE	0.2	0.2 (84)

DEATHS

DEATH RATE	5.8	6.5 (84)

HOUSEHOLDS

	1995	1980	1965
NUMBER	n/a	n/a	1,611,807 (53)
AVERAGE SIZE	n/a	n/a	5.0

	1995	1980	1965

ECONOMICS AND LABOR

GDP PER CAPITA US$ $3,600

LABOR FORCE M/F (thousands) 3,542.2/1,606.2 (94)
AGRICULTURE 1,445.2/746.4
MINING 30.3/0.5
MANUFACTURING 371.0/411.1
UTILITIES 19.7/0.0
CONSTRUCTION 171.6/0.0
TRADE/FOOD/TOURISM 560.4/105.9
TRANSPORT/COMMUNICATIONS 197.4/8.0
FINANCE/INSURANCE/REAL ESTATE 59.1/38.5
SOCIAL AND PERSONAL SERVICES 546.4/279.0

UNEMPLOYMENT
TOTAL 13.6% (94)

POVERTY
UNDER $1/DAY 4% (90)
UNDER $2/DAY 41.2%

TRANSPORT

JOURNEYS (by transport mode)
RAILROAD PASSENGER TRIPS 3,265.0 (94)
  (millions of miles/kilometers)
AIR PASSENGER TRIPS (thousands) 1,067

VEHICLES (thousands)

	1995	1980	1965
CARS	210.4	120.9	82.5
COMMERCIAL VEHICLES	175.3	78.2	36.3

HEALTH AND HEALTH CARE

	1995	1980	1965
RATE OF PHYSICIANS	0.1	0.1	0.2 (60)
RATE OF HOSPITAL BEDS	2.7	2.9	3.1
TOTAL DEATHS	93,752 (93)		

HEALTH INDICATORS
PREGNANT WOMEN WITH ANEMIA 39%
LOW-BIRTH-WEIGHT BABIES 17%
CHILD MALNUTRITION 38%

	1995	1980	1965
SMOKING PREVALENCE M/F	55/1%		
TUBERCULOSIS INCIDENCE RATE	0.4		
HEALTH CARE			
MEASLES IMMUNIZATION	88%		
AIDS/HIV CASES	58	33 (93)	

EDUCATION

	1995	1980	1965
SCHOOL AGE IN SCHOOL			
PRIMARY	113%	103%	110%
SECONDARY	75%	55%	45%
HIGHER	5%	3%	1.4%
FEMALES IN SCHOOL			
PRIMARY	48%	48%	98%
SECONDARY	51%	51%	42%
ADULT ILLITERACY M/F	13/7%	9.2/18.8% (81)	14.6/36.3% (63)

COMMUNICATIONS

	1995	1980	1965
RATE OF NEWSPAPERS	27	30	39
RATE OF RADIOS	201	98	41
RATE OF TELEVISIONS	49	2	

Source: CIA, The World Factbook, 1997; ILO, World Labour Report, 1997; UN, Demographic Yearbook, 1997; UN, Statistical Yearbook, 1996; World Bank, World Development Indicators, 1998.

SUDAN

The largest country in Africa, Sudan covers a territory of 967,492 square miles, an area roughly equal to the United States east of the Mississippi. Located in northeast Africa, the Sudan is bordered by Libya and Egypt to the north; Eritrea and Ethiopia to the east; Kenya, Uganda, and the Democratic Republic of the Congo to the south, and the Central African Republic and Chad to the west. It also has a 533-mile coastline on the Red Sea. Among the poorest countries in the world, Sudan has a per capita income of just $800 annually. Roughly three-quarters of its 31.55 million people—up from 10.26 million in 1965—live in rural areas. Agriculture is the main source of living in Sudan, with approximately 64 percent of men and 84 percent of women making their liv-

ing off the land as farmers and pastoralists. The low level of education and health is partially a reflection of the country's deep poverty. Just half the school-age children in the country attend primary institutions, and slightly over the half the population can neither read nor write. Another factor in these poor social indexes is war. For virtually all the three decades since Sudan won its independence from an Anglo-Egyptian condominium government, the country has been at war, with southern blacks—largely Christian or Animist—fighting against the dominant Arab government of the north. The rise of an Islamic fundamentalist government in Khartoum in the early 1990s has exacerbated the fighting.

	1995	1980	1965

GEOGRAPHY

AREA (square miles/kilometers)	967,494/2,505,810		
LAND AREA (square miles/kilometers)	917,374/2,376,000		
COASTLINE (miles/kilometers)	533/853		
CITIES			
CAPITAL	Khartoum	924,505 (93)	
MAJOR CITIES	Nyala	1,267,077	
	Sharg el Nil	879,105	
	Port Sudan	305,385	
	Kassala	234,270	

POPULATION

	1995	1980	1965
TOTAL	31,547,543	20,564,364 (83)	10,262,536 (56)
DENSITY (per square mile/square kilometer)	34/13	22/9	11/4
ANNUAL GROWTH	3.48%	2.9%	2.8%

	1995	**1980**	**1965**
AGE COHORTS			
0–14	46%		
15–64	52%		
65 AND OVER	2%		
MALE	50%		
FEMALE	50%		
URBAN	27.1%	23.7%	
RURAL	72.9%	76.3%	—
NET MIGRATION RATE	5.17		

IDENTITY

ETHNICITY	**1995**
BLACK	52%
ARAB	39%
BEJA	6%
FOREIGNERS	2%
LANGUAGE	
ARABIC	n/a
NUBIAN	n/a
TA BEDAWIE	n/a
NILOTIC DIALECTS	n/a
NILO-HAMITIC	n/a
SUDANIC LANGUAGES	n/a
ENGLISH	n/a
RELIGION	
SUNNI MUSLIM	70%
INDIGENOUS	25%
CHRISTIAN	5%

VITAL STATISTICS

	1995	**1980**	**1965**
BIRTHS			
BIRTH RATE	41.1	45.9	51.7
INFANT MORTALITY RATE	76	93.6	93.6
LIFE EXPECTANCY AT BIRTH	55.1	47.8	
DEATHS			
DEATH RATE	11.5	17.4	18.5

	1995	1980	1965

ECONOMICS AND LABOR

GDP PER CAPITA US$ $800

LABOR FORCE M/F
AGRICULTURE   64/84%
INDUSTRY   10/5%
SERVICES   26/11%

TRANSPORT

JOURNEYS (by transport mode)
RAILROAD PASSENGER TRIPS   1,183 (93)
  (millions of miles/kilometers)
AIR PASSENGER TRIPS (thousands)   432 (94)

VEHICLES (thousands)
CARS   116   87.7 (85)   20.5
COMMERCIAL VEHICLES   57   5.6   19.7

HEALTH AND HEALTH CARE

RATE OF PHYSICIANS   n/a   0.1 (60)   0
RATE OF HOSPITAL BEDS   1.1   0.9   1

HEALTH INDICATORS
PREGNANT WOMEN WITH ANEMIA   36%
LOW-BIRTH-WEIGHT BABIES   15%
CHILD MALNUTRITION   34%
TUBERCULOSIS INCIDENCE RATE   2.1

HEALTH CARE
ACCESS TO SAFE WATER   50%
ACCESS TO SANITATION   22%
MEASLES IMMUNIZATION   74%

AIDS/HIV CASES   1,341   883 (93)

	1995	1980	1965

EDUCATION

SCHOOL AGE IN SCHOOL

	1995	1980	1965
PRIMARY	54%	50%	29%
SECONDARY	13%	16%	4%
HIGHER		2%	0.6%

FEMALES IN SCHOOL

	1995	1980	1965
PRIMARY	44%	40%	21%
SECONDARY	n/a	37%	2%
ADULT ILLITERACY M/F	42/65%		

COMMUNICATIONS

	1995	1980	1965
RATE OF NEWSPAPERS	24	6	5 (62)
RATE OF RADIOS	257	187	22
RATE OF TELEVISIONS	80	43	1

Source: CIA, *The World Factbook, 1997;* ILO, *World Labour Report, 1997;* UN, *Demographic Yearbook, 1997;* UN, *Statistical Yearbook, 1996;* World Bank, *World Development Indicators, 1998.*

SURINAME

A former Dutch colony on the northern coast of South America, Suriname covers some 63,039 square miles of territory. Surrounded by the Caribbean to the north, French Guyana to the east, Brazil to the south and Guyana to the west, Suriname has a population of 436,418 persons, with a low density rate of just 7 persons per square mile. Indeed, much of the country is covered in thick bush or jungle, making agriculture difficult. Suriname has a relatively low rate of population growth, with its population increasing by just one-third over the past 30 years, one of the lowest growth rates in all of Latin America. In addition, it had a net migration rate of −2.4 per 1,000 citizens, as many young persons left for educational and job opportunities in the Netherlands. The country has a per capita income of $2,950 annually. Its population is quite mixed ethnically, reflecting its colonial past—which ended with independence in 1975—when laborers were imported first from Africa as slaves, and then from India and Java as indentured servants. In addition, the country has a significant minority—at some 10 percent of the population—of descendants of runaway African slaves who mixed with the indigenous Indian communities.

		1995	1980	1965
GEOGRAPHY				
AREA (square miles/kilometers)	63,039/163,270			
LAND AREA (square miles/kilometers)	62,344/161,470			
COASTLINE (miles/kilometers)	241/386			
CITIES				
CAPITAL	Paramaribo	n/a	n/a	110,867 (64)
POPULATION				
TOTAL		436,418	352,041	324,211 (64)
DENSITY (per square mile/square kilometer)		7/3	6/2	5/2
ANNUAL GROWTH		1.6%	1.1%	
AGE COHORTS				
0–14		34%	n/a	46%
15–64		62%	n/a	50%
65 AND OVER		4%	n/a	4%
MALE		49%		
FEMALE		51%		
NET MIGRATION RATE		−2.36		

	1995	1980	1965

IDENTITY

ETHNICITY

HINDUSTANI	37%		
CREOLE (European and African)	31%		
JAVANESE	15.3%		
"BUSH BLACK"	10.3%		
AMERINDIAN	2.6%		
CHINESE	1.7%		
EUROPEAN	1.0%		

LANGUAGE

DUTCH	n/a		
ENGLISH	n/a		
SRANANG TONGO	n/a		
HINDUSTANI	n/a		
JAVANESE	n/a		

RELIGION

HINDU	27.4%		
MUSLIM	19.6%		
ROMAN CATHOLIC	22.8%		
PROTESTANT	25.2%		
INDIGENOUS	5.0%		

VITAL STATISTICS

BIRTHS

	1995	1980	1965
BIRTH RATE	24.2	28	44.2
INFANT MORTALITY RATE	29.3	30.4	48
LIFE EXPECTANCY AT BIRTH	70	64.6	n/a

MARRIAGES

	1995	1980	1965
MARRIAGE RATE	4.7	6.7	2.8
DIVORCE RATE	4.2	1.1	0.7

DEATHS

	1995	1980	1965
DEATH RATE	5.8	7.9	8.1

ECONOMICS AND LABOR

	1995		
GDP PER CAPITA US$	$2,950		

	1995	1980	1965
LABOR FORCE M/F (thousands)	53.3/34.2 (93)		
AGRICULTURE	2.5/0.6		
MINING	2.3/0.0		
MANUFACTURING	6.8/1.0		
UTILITIES	1.4/0.2		
CONSTRUCTION	4.3/0.4		
TRADE/FOOD/TOURISM	7.2/0.6		
TRANSPORT/COMMUNICATIONS	4.1/0.2		
FINANCE/INSURANCE/REAL ESTATE	1.2/2.1		
SOCIAL AND PERSONAL SERVICES	20.7/22.6		
UNEMPLOYMENT			
TOTAL	16.3 (93)		

TRANSPORT

	1995	1980	1965
JOURNEYS (by transport mode)			
RAILROAD PASSENGER TRIPS	149.9 (94)		
(millions of miles/kilometers)			
VEHICLES (thousands)			
CARS	42.1	38.2 (78)	7.4
COMMERCIAL VEHICLES	17.2	13.6	2.1

HEALTH CARE

	1995	1980	1965
RATE OF PHYSICIANS	n/a	n/a	0.5 (60)
RATE OF HOSPITAL BEDS	n/a	n/a	6.6
TOTAL DEATHS	2,998 (93)		
AIDS/HIV CASES	209	169 (93)	

EDUCATION

	1995	1980	1965
SCHOOL AGE IN SCHOOL			
PRIMARY	n/a	115% (79)	126% (70)
SECONDARY	n/a	n/a	41%
FEMALES IN SCHOOL			
PRIMARY	n/a	n/a	122%
SECONDARY	n/a	n/a	45%
ADULT ILLITERACY M/F	n/a	10.0/10.0% (85)	16/16.7%

	1995	1980	1965
COMMUNICATIONS			
RATE OF NEWSPAPERS	105	127	51
RATE OF RADIOS	676	532	139
RATE OF TELEVISIONS	140	113	

Source: CIA, The World Factbook, 1997; ILO, World Labour Report, 1997; UN, Demographic Yearbook, 1997; UN, Statistical Yearbook, 1996; World Bank, World Development Indicators, 1998.

SWAZILAND

A mini-state of 6,700 square miles—roughly the size of New Jersey—Swaziland is tucked between South Africa and Mozambique in the southeastern corner of Africa. Swaziland has a population of 998,730 persons, most of whom make a living from subsistence farming. Of the 76,000 members of the official labor force, about one-third are employed in commercial agriculture. In addition, thousands of Swazis migrate to South Africa to work in that country's mines and factories. This outlet is shrinking as these sectors move to employ more native South African blacks since the fall of the apartheid regime in 1994. Returns from these migrant laborers helps boost the per capita income of the country to a relatively prosperous $3,700 annually. About one-quarter of the population of Swaziland lives in urban areas, largely in the capital, Mbabane. The largely rural makeup of the population helps to explain the relatively poor social indexes, since it is more difficult for the government to deliver services to a rural population. In 1995, the infant mortality rate was 88.4 per 1,000 live births and the life expectancy was just 57.3 years.

	1995	**1980**	**1965**
GEOGRAPHY			
AREA (square miles/kilometers)	6,703/17,360		
LAND AREA (square miles/kilometers)	6,641/17,200		
COASTLINE (miles/kilometers)	Landlocked		
CITIES			
CAPITAL	Mbabane	n/a	38,290 (86)	n/a
POPULATION			
TOTAL	998,730	494,534 (76)	374,697 (66)
DENSITY (per square mile/square kilometer)	150/58	74/29	56/22
ANNUAL GROWTH	3.24%	3.4%	n/a
AGE COHORTS			
0–14	46%	n/a	47%
15–64	52%	n/a	49%
65 AND OVER	2%	n/a	4%
MALE	47%		
FEMALE	53%		
URBAN	24.8%	15.2% (76)	n/a
RURAL	75.2%	84.8%	n/a
NET MIGRATION RATE	0		

	1995	1980	1965

IDENTITY

ETHNICITY
AFRICAN	97%		
EUROPEAN	3%		

LANGUAGE
ENGLISH	n/a		
SISWATI	n/a		

RELIGION
CHRISTIAN	60%		
INDIGENOUS	40%		

VITAL STATISTICS

BIRTHS
BIRTH RATE	42.9	47.3	
INFANT MORTALITY RATE	88.4	129	
LIFE EXPECTANCY AT BIRTH	57.3	48.5	

MARRIAGES
MARRIAGE RATE	4.2		
AVERAGE AGE AT MARRIAGE M/F	29.3/26 (91)		

DEATHS
DEATH RATE	10.6	17.4	

ECONOMICS AND LABOR

GDP PER CAPITA US$	$3,700		

LABOR FORCE M/F (thousands)	55.0/21.4 (86)		
AGRICULTURE	18.1/5.0		
MINING	2.3/0.1		
MANUFACTURING	7.5/3.4		
UTILITIES	1.3/0.1		
CONSTRUCTION	5.1/0.2		
TRADE/FOOD/TOURISM	4.3/3.1		
TRANSPORT/COMMUNICATIONS	4.9/0.7		
FINANCE/INSURANCE/REAL ESTATE	2.2/1.2		
SOCIAL AND PERSONAL SERVICES	9.2/7.6		

UNION DENSITY	19.1%		

	1995	1980	1965
TRANSPORT			
JOURNEYS (by transport mode)			
RAILROAD PASSENGER TRIPS	65.0 (94)		
(millions of miles/kilometers)			
VEHICLES			
PRIVATE CARS	22.0 92	13.3	
COMMERCIAL VEHICLES	16	12.6	
HEALTH AND HEALTH CARE			
RATE OF PHYSICIANS	n/a	n/a	0.1 (60)
RATE OF HOSPITAL BEDS	n/a	n/a	2
AIDS/HIV CASES	590	412 (93)	
EDUCATION			
SCHOOL AGE IN SCHOOL			
PRIMARY	n/a	106%	69%
SECONDARY	n/a	39%	8%
HIGHER	n/a	3.9%	0.2%
FEMALES IN SCHOOL			
PRIMARY	n/a	105%	65%
SECONDARY	n/a	38%	7%
ADULT ILLITERACY M/F	n/a	42.7/46.5% (76)	n/a
COMMUNICATIONS			
RATE OF NEWSPAPERS	15	15	n/a
RATE OF RADIOS	163	145	13
RATE OF TELEVISIONS	20	2	n/a

Source: CIA, *The World Factbook*, 1997; ILO, *World Labour Report*, 1997; UN, *Demographic Yearbook*, 1997; UN, *Statistical Yearbook*, 1996; World Bank, *World Development Indicators*, 1998.

SWEDEN

The largest country in Scandinavia in both territory and population, Sweden covers 173,731 square miles and has a population of 8.9 million. Located in northern Europe, Sweden is surrounded on the west and north by Norway, and is bordered by Finland on the northeast. Its eastern and southern flanks are bounded by the Gulf of Bothnia and the Baltic Sea. Its southwestern coastline is on the waterways known as the Kattegat and Skaggerak, which separates the country from Denmark to the south. One of the most prosperous countries in the world, Sweden has a per capita income of $20,100 annually. Of the country's 4-million–strong labor force, about 700,000 are involved in manufacturing—including electronics and shipbuilding—and some 1.6

million are engaged in services, reflecting the postindustrial composition of the Swedish economy. Perhaps best known for its comprehensive and inclusive social welfare system, Sweden has one of the most equitable wealth-distribution profiles in the world. It has one of the best set of social indexes as well. For example, fully 96 percent of all children under 12 years of age are immunized for measles, and the overall infant mortality rate is just 4.5 per 1,000 live births, and fully 43 percent of its young adult population attends university. Sweden is also one of the most ethnically homogenous countries in the world. While there is a tiny minority of pastoral Lapps in the north, the vast majority of the country is Swedish-speaking and of Nordic stock.

Hospital Beds

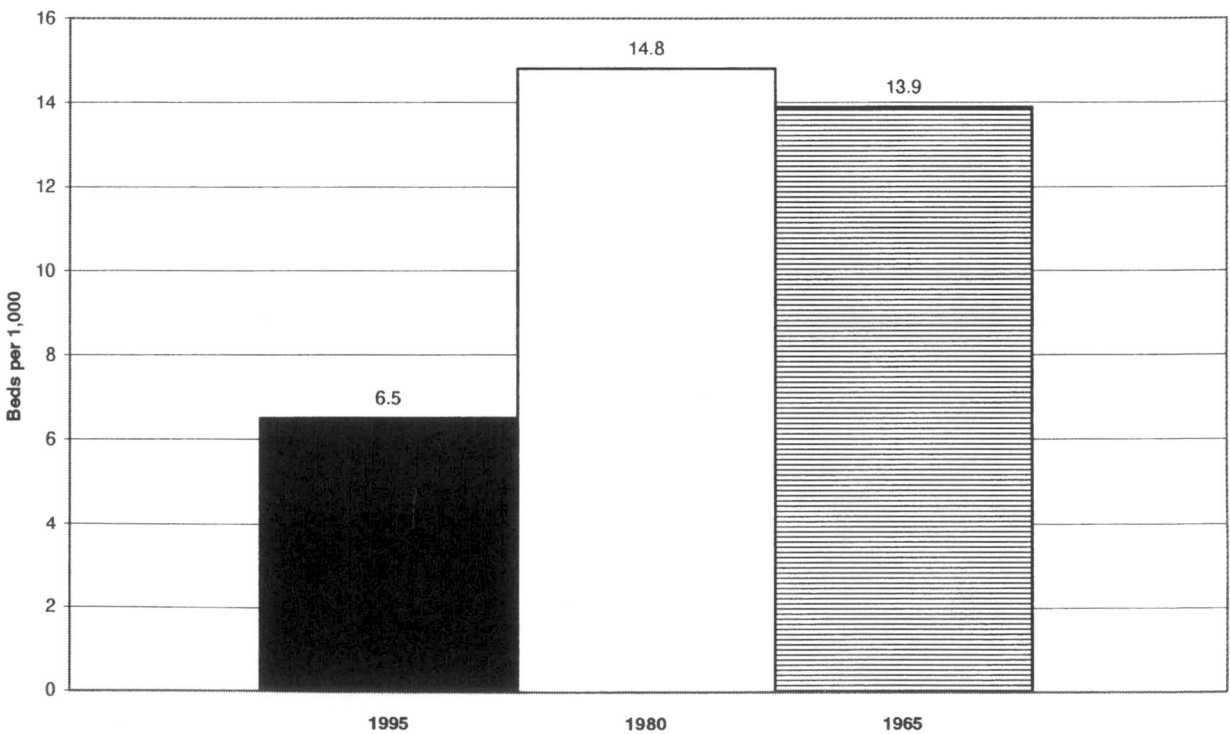

In a country with one of the finest national medical care services in the world, it would seem surprising to see the number of hospital beds decline. But this is understandable given modern medical technology, which allows many illnesses that were once treated in long hospital stays to be taken care of in shorter stays or on an outpatient basis. This reduces the needs for hospital beds.

Households

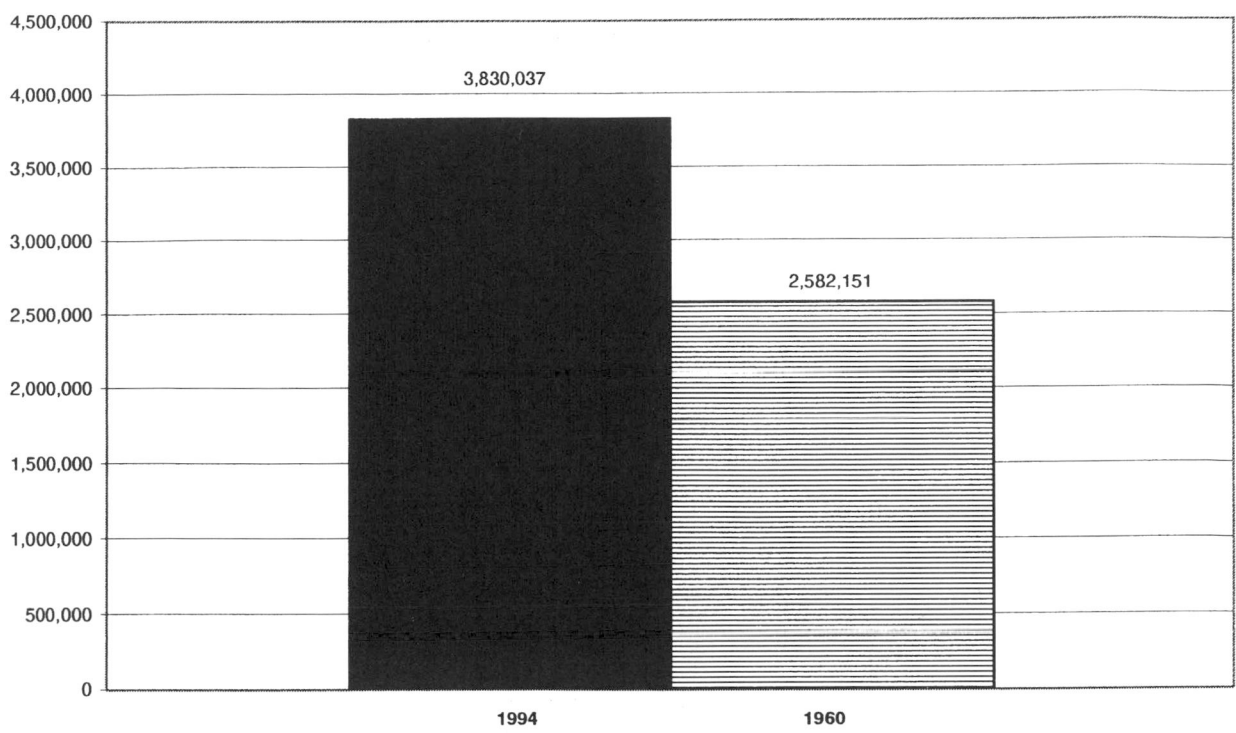

3,830,037

2,582,151

1994   1960

The number of households in Sweden has increased more rapidly than population over the past 30 years. This is due to the rise in single-person households or households headed by a single parent.

CHRONOLOGY

1967   New constitution replaces bicameral legislature with a single body.
1976   Forty-four years of Socialist Party rule ends in conservative coalition victory at polls.
1982   Olaf Palme and socialists return to power.
1986   Palme assassinated by unknown assailants.
1991   Socialists once again ousted from power.
1994   Voters agree to join European Union.

		1995	1980	1965

GEOGRAPHY

AREA (square miles/kilometers)	173,731/449,964
LAND AREA (square miles/kilometers)	158,659/410,928
COASTLINE (miles/kilometers)	2,011/3,218

CITIES		
CAPITAL	Stockholm	703,627(94)
MAJOR CITIES	Göteborg	440,533
	Malmö	242,706
	Uppsala	181,191
	Linköping	130,489

POPULATION

	1995	1980	1965
TOTAL	8,900,954	8,320,438	7,.495,316 (60)
DENSITY (per square mile/square kilometer)	56/22	52/20	47/18
ANNUAL GROWTH	0.56%	0.1%	0.7%
AGE COHORTS			
0–14	19%	n/a	21%
15–64	64%	n/a	66%
65 AND OVER	17%	n/a	13%
MALE	49%		
FEMALE	51%		
URBAN	83.4% (90)		
RURAL	16.6%		
NET MIGRATION RATE	5.5	n/a	4.5

IDENTITY

ETHNICITY	
WHITE	n/a
LAPP (Sami)	n/a
FOREIGN BORN AND FIRST	n/a
GENERATION	
IMMIGRANTS	n/a
LANGUAGE	
SWEDISH	n/a

	1995	1980	1965
RELIGION			
EVANGELICAL LUTHERAN	94%		
ROMAN CATHOLIC	1.5%		
PENTACOSTAL	1%		

VITAL STATISTICS

	1995	1980	1965
BIRTHS			
BIRTH RATE	11.6	11.8 (85)	15.8
INFANT MORTALITY RATE	4.5	6.7	13.3
LIFE EXPECTANCY AT BIRTH	78.1	77.9	73.6
MARRIAGES			
MARRIAGE RATE	3.9	4.6 (85)	7.8
AVERAGE AGE AT MARRIAGE M/F	33.3/31 (94)		
DIVORCE RATE	2.5	2.3 (85)	1.2
DEATHS			
DEATH RATE	11.4	11.3 (85)	10

HOUSEHOLDS

	1995	1980	1965
NUMBER	3,830,037 (90)	n/a	2,582,151 (60)
AVERAGE SIZE	2.1 (90)	n/a	2.8
TYPE OF HOUSEHOLD			
FEMALE HEADED	26.7%		
SINGLE	29.5%		
MARRIED	44.7%		
WIDOWED	13.2%		
DIVORCED/SEPARATED	12.6%		

ECONOMICS AND LABOR

	1995
GDP PER CAPITA US$	$20,100
LABOR FORCE M/F (thousands)	2,016/1,911 (94)
AGRICULTURE	101/35
MINING	8/1
MANUFACTURING	527/193
UTILITIES	26/6
CONSTRUCTION	202/18
TRADE/FOOD/TOURISM	292/276
TRANSPORT/COMMUNICATIONS	187/84

	1995	**1980**	**1965**
FINANCE/INSURANCE/REAL ESTATE	213/166		
SOCIAL AND PERSONAL SERVICES	457/1,131		
UNEMPLOYMENT			
TOTAL	8.0% (94)		
UNION DENSITY	77.2%		

TRANSPORT

	1995	**1980**	**1965**
JOURNEYS (by transport mode)			
RAILROAD PASSENGER TRIPS	5,975 (93)		
(millions of miles/kilometers)			
AIR PASSENGER TRIPS (thousands)	10,808 (94)		
VEHICLES (thousands)			
CARS	3,566	2,883.00	1,793.6
COMMERCIAL VEHICLES	643	194.4	118.6

HEALTH AND HEALTH CARE

	1995	**1980**	**1965**
RATE OF PHYSICIANS	3	2.2	1 (60)
RATE OF HOSPITAL BEDS	6.5	14.8	13.9
TOTAL DEATHS	96,910		
HEALTH INDICATORS			
LOW-BIRTH-WEIGHT BABIES	5%		
SMOKING PREVALENCE M/F	22/24%		
TUBERCULOSIS INCIDENCE RATE	0.07		
HEALTH CARE			
ACCESS TO SANITATION	100%		
MEASLES IMMUNIZATION	96%		
AIDS/HIV CASES	1,346	982 (93)	

EDUCATION

	1995	**1980**	**1965**
SCHOOL AGE IN SCHOOL			
PRIMARY	105%	97%	100%
SECONDARY	132%	88%	85%
HIGHER	43%	31%	8.9%

	1995	**1980**	**1965**
FEMALES IN SCHOOL			
PRIMARY	49%	49%	100%
SECONDARY	51%	51%	87%
HIGHER	n/a	35.7% (81)	18.5% (70)

COMMUNICATIONS

	1995	**1980**	**1965**
RATE OF NEWSPAPERS	511	528	505
RATE OF RADIOS	879	842	394
RATE OF TELEVISIONS	470	461	278

Source: CIA, The World Factbook, 1997; ILO, World Labour Report, 1997; UN, Demographic Yearbook, 1997; UN, Statistical Yearbook, 1996; World Bank, World Development Indicators, 1998.

SWITZERLAND

Arguably the richest country in the world, Switzerland has a per capita income of roughly $22,400 annually. Much of this wealth is generated by the large financial sector. Zurich, the country's largest city, is one of the great banking centers of the world. Tourism and manufacturing are also important sources of income for the country's 3.8-million–strong workforce. Located in the Alps of Western Europe, Switzerland's 15,942 square miles of territory are bordered by Germany to the north, Austria to the east, Italy to the south, and France to the west. This central location has made Switzerland a hodgepodge of ethnic and linguistic groups. Approximately 65 percent of the population is German speaking, 18 percent speak French, 10 percent are Italian speaking, and a tiny minority—largely rural persons—speak a native Swiss language known as Romansch. This ethnic melange resulted in one of the most decentralized governments in the world. Each of the country's 26 cantons has control over virtually all internal affairs, while the federal government in Bern handles only general finance and foreign policy issues. Switzerland is largely a neutral country, with membership in virtually none of the continent's or the world's multinational organizations, including the European Union and even the United Nations.

		1995	1980	1965
GEOGRAPHY				
AREA (square miles/kilometers)		15,942/41,290		
LAND AREA (square miles/kilometers)		15,355,39,770		
COASTLINE (miles/kilometers)		Landlocked		
CITIES				
CAPITAL	Bern	128,872 (94)		
MAJOR CITIES	Zurich	342,804		
	Bale	175,809		
	Geneva	172,138		
	Lausanne	116,917		
POPULATION				
TOTAL		7,207,060	6,365,960	5,429,061 (60)
DENSITY (per square mile/square kilometer)		469/181	415/160	354/137
ANNUAL GROWTH		0.59%	0%	1.9%
AGE COHORTS				
0–14		17%	n/a	30%
15–64		68%	n/a	62%
65 AND OVER		15%	n/a	8%

	1995	**1980**	**1965**
MALE	49%		
FEMALE	51%		
URBAN	67.8% (94)	57.1%	
RURAL	32.2%	42.9%	
NET MIGRATION RATE	4.2	n/a	0

IDENTITY

ETHNICITY	
GERMAN	65%
FRENCH	18%
ITALIAN	10%
ROMANSCH	1%

LANGUAGE	
GERMAN	65%
FRENCH	18%
ITALIAN	12%
ROMANSCH	1%

RELIGION	
ROMAN CATHOLIC	47.6%
PROTESTANT	44.3%

VITAL STATISTICS

BIRTHS	**1995**	**1980**	**1965**
BIRTH RATE	11.4 (94)	11.5	18.1
URBAN BIRTH RATE	11.3		
RURAL BIRTH RATE	13.1		
INFANT MORTALITY RATE	5.4	7.7 (84)	17.8
LIFE EXPECTANCY AT BIRTH	77.6	76.2 (84)	72.1

MARRIAGES			
MARRIAGE RATE	6.1	5.9 (84)	7.3
AVERAGE AGE AT MARRIAGE M/F	30/27.3		
DIVORCE RATE	2.1	1.8 (84)	0.8

DEATHS			
DEATH RATE	9.6	9.1 (84)	9.3

	1995	1980	1965

HOUSEHOLDS

NUMBER	2,841,850 (90)		1,581,000 (60)
AVERAGE SIZE	2.4		3.3

TYPE OF HOUSEHOLD

FEMALE HEADED	27.6%		
SINGLE	22.2%		
MARRIED	47.9%		
WIDOWED	11.6%		
DIVORCED/SEPARATED	8.3%		

ECONOMICS AND LABOR

GDP PER CAPITA US$	$22,400		

LABOR FORCE M/F (thousands)	2,248/1,525 (94)		
AGRICULTURE	93/50		
MINING	24/3		
MANUFACTURING	573/210		
CONSTRUCTION	243/35		
TRADE/FOOD/TOURISM	341/405		
TRANSPORT/COMMUNICATIONS	175/60		
FINANCE/INSURANCE/REAL ESTATE	302/179		
SOCIAL AND PERSONAL SERVICES	496/582		

UNEMPLOYMENT			
TOTAL	3.8% (94)		

UNION DENSITY	20%		

TRANSPORT

JOURNEYS (by transport mode)			
RAILROAD PASSENGER TRIPS	13.836 (94)		
(millions of miles/kilometers)			
AIR PASSENGER TRIPS (thousands)	9,338		

VEHICLES (thousands)			
CARS	3,165	2,246.80	919.1
COMMERCIAL VEHICLES	292.4	180.5	93.1

	1995	1980	1965

HEALTH AND HEALTH CARE

	1995	1980	1965
RATE OF PHYSICIANS	3.1	n/a	1.3 (60)
RATE OF HOSPITAL BEDS	20.8	n/a	12.7
TOTAL DEATHS	60,755		
HEALTH INDICATORS			
LOW-BIRTH-WEIGHT BABIES	5%		
SMOKING PREVALENCE M/F	36/26%		
TUBERCULOSIS INCIDENCE RATES	0.1		
HEALTH CARE			
ACCESS TO SAFE WATER	100		
ACCESS TO SANITATION	100		
AIDS/HIV CASES	5,094	4,150 (93)	

EDUCATION

	1995	1980	1965
SCHOOL AGE IN SCHOOL			
PRIMARY	107%	n/a	108%
SECONDARY	91%	n/a	50%
HIGHER	32%	18%	5.5%
FEMALES IN SCHOOL			
PRIMARY	49%	49%	n/a
SECONDARY	50%	49%	n/a
HIGHER	n/a	14.9%	4.9% (70)

COMMUNICATIONS

	1995	1980	1965
RATE OF NEWSPAPERS	377	393	376
RATE OF RADIOS	832	813	305
RATE OF TELEVISIONS	400	364	114

Source: CIA, *The World Factbook, 1997*; ILO, *World Labour Report, 1997*; UN, *Demographic Yearbook, 1997*; UN, *Statistical Yearbook, 1996*; World Bank, *World Development Indicators, 1998*.

SYRIA

Officially named the Syrian Arab Republic, the country is located in the heart of the Arab Middle East, sharing borders with Turkey to the north, Iraq to the east, Jordan to the south, and Israel and Lebanon to the west. It also has a 121-mile coastline along the eastern Mediterranean Sea. Of Syria's 71,998 square miles of territory, some 500 in the Golan Heights of the southwest have been illegally occupied by Israel since a 1967 war. (Israel illegally annexed the territory in 1981.) Syria had a population of 15.61 million in 1995, up from 4.57 million in 1965. With a growth rate of roughly 3.3 percent annually over the past 30 years, Syria has one of the fastest-growing populations in the world. The population is ethnically divided between an Arab majority of some 90 percent and several minorities—the largest of whom are the Kurds—who together make up the other 10 percent. A largely desert and semidesert land, Syria relies heavily on water from the Euphrates River, which runs through its northeast. Most of the country's people live in the western part of the country, where the capital, Damascus, is located. Having won its independence from a French mandate government in 1946, Syria has largely been ruled by military and single-party governments for much of its history. Syria and neighboring Israel have been in a virtual state of war since 1948.

Population Growth

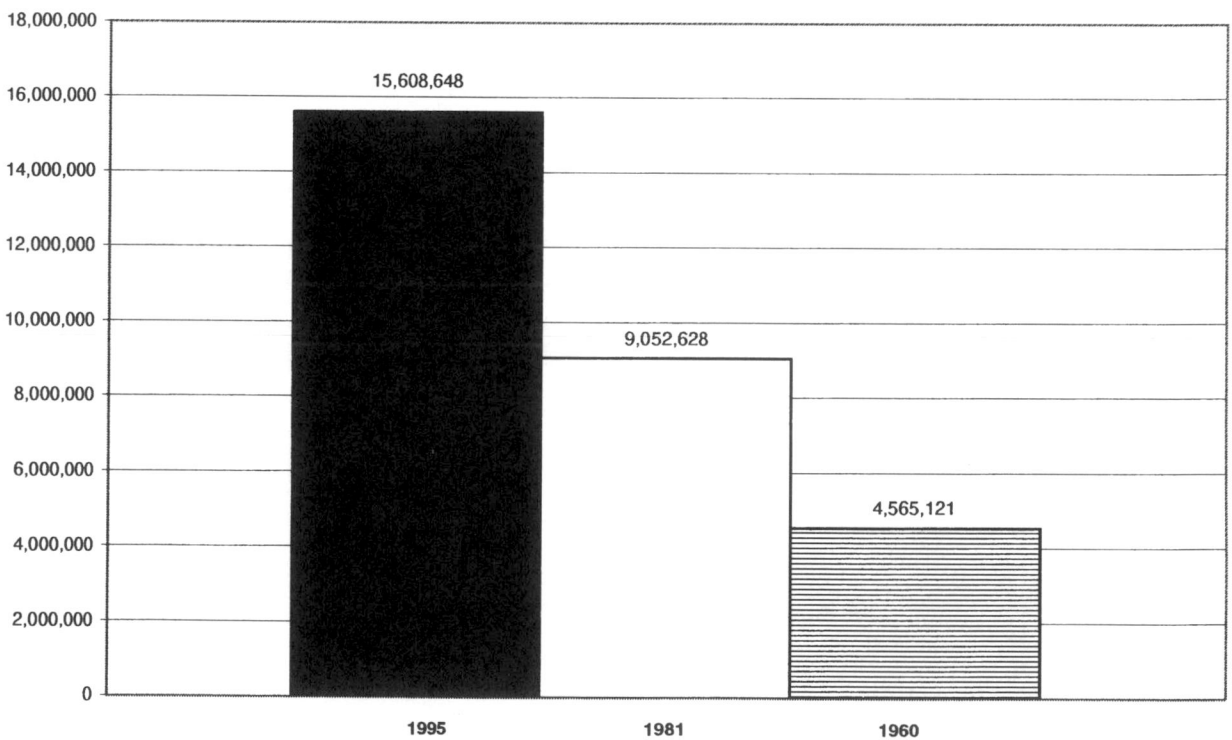

Like many Arab countries, Syria has one of the highest population growth rates in the world. Rising income levels and falling death rates—combined with a cultural propensity toward large families—lie behind this phenomenon.

Birth and Death Rates

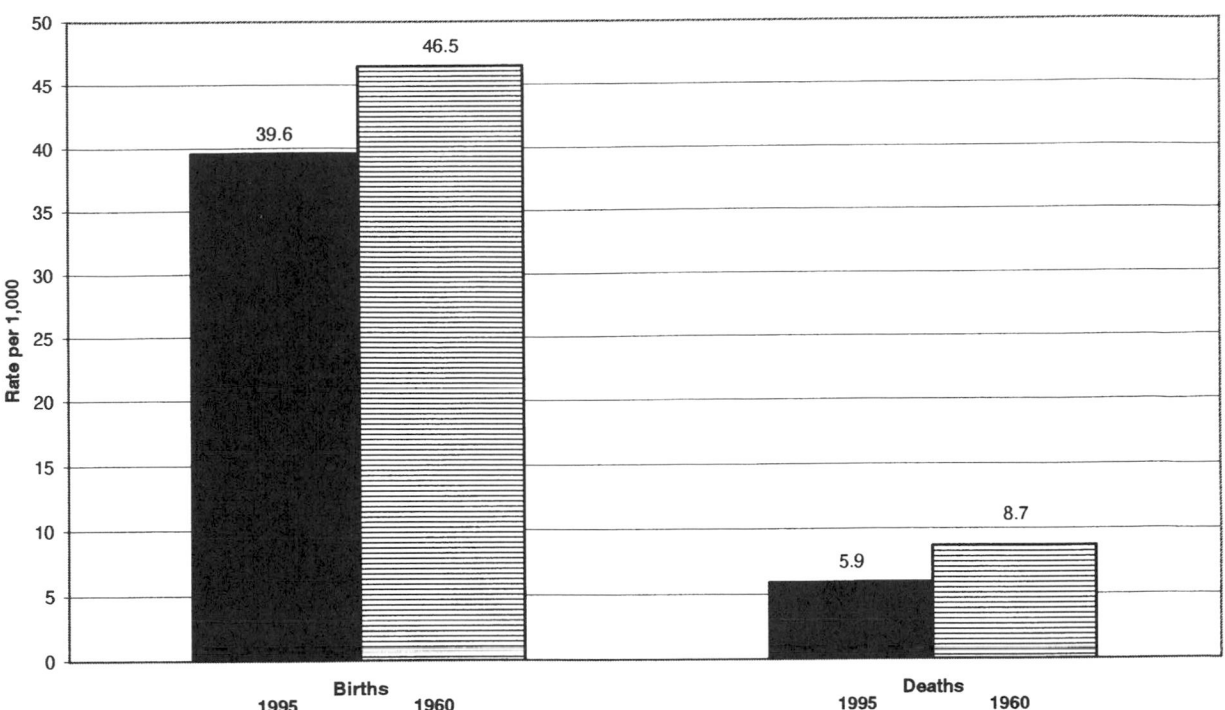

Falling death and birth rates in Syria reveal the problem of interpreting change in percentage versus absolute terms. If one were to state that birth rates in Syria fell by roughly 7 per 1,000 annually while death rates fell by about 3 per 1,000, it would seem that Syria was seeing a slowing growth rate. In fact, the opposite is true. In percentage terms, Syria's birth rate has fallen by 15 percent while its death rate has shrunk by nearly 33 percent, a different demographic picture altogether.

CHRONOLOGY

1961   Syria dissolves political union with Egypt.

1967   As member of coalition against Israel, Syria loses in Six-Day War; Israel occupies Golan Heights.

1973   Syria briefly regains control over Golan in October War.

1976   Syria sends peacekeeping troops to Lebanon.

1980   Military places surface-to-air missiles in Lebanon to defend against Israeli air attacks.

1990   President Hafez al-Assad rules out possibility of opposition parties; wins 99.98 percent of vote; joins allied coalition against Iraqi invasion of Kuwait.

1996   Israeli-Syrian talks concerning the Golan and Lebanon end in failure.

	1995	1980	1965

GEOGRAPHY

AREA (square miles/kilometers)	71,498/185,180¹	
LAND AREA (square miles/kilometers)	71,062/184,050	
COASTLINE (miles/kilometers)	121/193	

CITIES

CAPITAL	Damascus	1,549,000 (94)
MAJOR CITIES	Aleppo	1,542,000
	Homs	558,000
	Latakia	303,000
	Hama	273,000

POPULATION

	1995	1980	1965
TOTAL	15,608,648	9,052,628 (81)	4,565,121 (60)
DENSITY (per square mile/square kilometer)	220/85	127/49	64/25
ANNUAL GROWTH	3.37%	3.4%	3%

AGE COHORTS

	1995	1980	1965
0–14	47%	n/a	46%
15–64	50%	n/a	49%
65 AND OVER	3%	n/a	5%

	1995
MALE	51%
FEMALE	49%

	1995	1980
URBAN	51.7%	46.6%
RURAL	48.3%	53.4%

	1995
NET MIGRATION RATE	0

IDENTITY

ETHNICITY

	1995
ARAB	90.3%
KURD, ARMENIAN, AND OTHER	9.7%

LANGUAGE

	1995
ARABIC	n/a
KURDISH	n/a
ARMENIAN	n/a
ARAMAIC	n/a

	1995	**1980**	**1965**
CIRCASSIAN	n/a		
FRENCH	n/a		
RELIGION			
SUNNI MUSLIM	74%		
ALAWITE, DRUZE, AND OTHER MUSLIM	16%		
CHRISTIAN	10%		
JEWISH			

VITAL STATISTICS

	1995	**1980**	**1965**
BIRTHS			
BIRTH RATE	39.6	46.5	
INFANT MORTALITY RATE	40	59	
LIFE EXPECTANCY AT BIRTH	67.1	64.2	
MARRIAGES			
MARRIAGE RATE	8.6	8.4	
DIVORCE RATE	0.7	0.6	
DEATHS			
DEATH RATE	5.9	8.7	

HOUSEHOLDS

	1995	**1980**	**1965**
NUMBER	n/a	n/a	859,654 (62)
AVERAGE SIZE	n/a	n/a	5.9

ECONOMICS AND LABOR

	1995
GDP PER CAPITA US$	$5,900
LABOR FORCE M/F (thousands)	2,710.3/539.6 (91)
AGRICULTURE	625.0/292.0
MINING	6.7/0.0
MANUFACTURING	421.5/34.6
UTILITIES	7.9/0.6
CONSTRUCTION	334.3/6.4
TRADE/FOOD/TOURISM	369.0/9.3
TRANSPORT/COMMUNICATIONS	158.4/8.6
FINANCE/INSURANCE/REAL ESTATE	20.2/4.5
SOCIAL AND PERSONAL SERVICES	767.4/183.7

	1995	1980	1965
UNEMPLOYMENT			
TOTAL	6.8 (91)		

TRANSPORT

	1995	1980	1965
JOURNEYS (by transport mode)			
RAILROAD PASSENGER TRIPS	769 (94)		
(millions of miles/kilometers)			
AIR PASSENGER TRIPS (thousands)	464 (94)		
VEHICLES (thousands)			
CARS	159.1	71.5	27.2
COMMERCIAL VEHICLES	188.4	88.3	14.3

HEALTH AND HEALTH CARE

	1995	1980	1965
RATE OF PHYSICIANS	0.8	0.4	0.2 (60)
RATE OF HOSPITAL BEDS	1.1	1.1	1.1
TOTAL DEATHS	51,003 (94)		
HEALTH INDICATORS			
LOW-BIRTH-WEIGHT BABIES	8%		
TUBERCULOSIS INCIDENCE RATE	0.5		
HEALTH CARE			
ACCESS TO SAFE WATER	85		
ACCESS TO SANITATION	78		
MEASLES IMMUNIZATION	98		
AIDS/HIV CASES	36	26 (93)	

EDUCATION

	1995	1980	1965
SCHOOL AGE IN SCHOOL			
PRIMARY	101%	100%	80%
SECONDARY	44%	46%	28%
HIGHER	18%	17%	6.2%
FEMALES IN SCHOOL			
PRIMARY	47%	43%	52%
SECONDARY	44%	37%	12%
ADULT ILLITERACY M/F	14/44%	24.1/56.7% (85)	40.4/80.0% (70)

	1995	1980	1965
COMMUNICATIONS			
RATE OF NEWSPAPERS	22	13	21
RATE OF RADIOS	257	195	382
RATE OF TELEVISIONS	62	44	14

FOOTNOTE
1. Area does not include the Golan Heights that are occupied by Israel.

Source: CIA, *The World Factbook, 1997;* ILO, *World Labour Report, 1997;* UN, *Demographic Yearbook, 1997;* UN, *Statistical Yearbook, 1996;* World Bank, *World Development Indicators, 1998.*

TAIWAN

Taiwan (Republic of China) is located on a large island of 13,892 square miles about 150 miles off the southeastern coast of China, between the East and South China seas. It has a population of 21.47 million, up from 13.38 million in 1965. The country's political history is unique. Following his defeat in the Chinese civil war in 1949, nationalist Chinese leader Chiang Kai-shek led his forces and supporters to the offshore haven, as the communists took over the mainland. Heavily backed by the United States, Taiwan resisted efforts by Mainland China to reincorporate the island into the larger country by force or diplomatic means. At the same time, Taiwan rapidly advanced in the economic sphere, becoming one of the so-called tigers of Asia. Reliant on the export of electronics and other consumer goods, Taiwan saw its per capita income climb to $13,510 annually by 1995. By the late 1980s, this growing economic prosperity had led to popular demands for democracy. Despite the recent economic crisis in the region, Taiwan remains a prosperous democracy, though Mainland China is still committed to reincorporating it. Over the years, Beijing has won out over Taipei in the international arena. In 1971, the United Nations chose to recognize and seat China in the Security Council, ousting Taiwan. At the end of the decade, the United States followed suit, dropping formal recognition of Taiwan, though Washington remains committed to its military defense.

	1995	1980	1966
GEOGRAPHY			
AREA (square miles/kilometers)	13,892/35,980		
LAND AREA (square miles/kilometers)	12,456/32,260		
COASTLINE (miles/kilometers)	905,1,448		
CITIES			
CAPITAL	Taipei	n/a	
POPULATION			
TOTAL	21,465,881	n/a	13,383,357
DENSITY (per square mile/square kilometer)	1,723/665	n/a	1,074/415
ANNUAL GROWTH	0.89%	n/a	3.3%
AGE COHORTS			
0–14	23%	n/a	45%
15–64	69%	n/a	50%
65 AND OVER	8%	n/a	5%
NET MIGRATION RATE	−0.6	n/a	0 (60)

	1995	1980	1966

IDENTITY

ETHNICITY

TAIWANESE	84%		
MAINLAND CHINESE	14%		
ABORIGINE	2%		

LANGUAGE

MANDARIN CHINESE	n/a		
TAIWANESE	n/a		
HAKKA DIALECTS	n/a		

RELIGION

BUDDHIST, CONFUCIAN, AND TAOIST	93%		
CHRISTIAN	4.5%		

VITAL STATISTICS

BIRTHS

BIRTH RATE	15	n/a	32.5
INFANT MORTALITY RATE	7	n/a	22.2
LIFE EXPECTANCY AT BIRTH	76	n/a	63.4

MARRIAGES

MARRIAGE RATE	n/a	n/a	7.5
DIVORCE RATE	n/a	n/a	0.4

DEATHS

DEATH RATE	5.5	n/a	5.5

ECONOMICS AND LABOR

GDP PER CAPITA US$	$13,510		
UNION DENSITY	27.9%		

TRANSPORT

VEHICLES (thousands)

CARS	n/a	n/a	15.1
COMMERCIAL VEHICLES	n/a	n/a	17.5

	1995	1980	1966

EDUCATION

SCHOOL AGE IN SCHOOL

	1995	1980	1966
PRIMARY	n/a	n/a	101%
SECONDARY	n/a	n/a	39%

FEMALES IN SCHOOL

	1995	1980	1966
PRIMARY	n/a	n/a	99%
SECONDARY	n/a	n/a	31%

COMMUNICATIONS

	1995	1980	1966
RATE OF NEWSPAPERS	n/a	n/a	64
RATE OF RADIOS	n/a	n/a	95
RATE OF TELEVISIONS	n/a	n/a	3

Source: CIA, The World Factbook, 1997; ILO, World Labour Report, 1997; UN, Demographic Yearbook, 1997; UN, Statistical Yearbook, 1996; World Bank, World Development Indicators, 1998.

TAJIKISTAN[1]

One of the five former Central Asian republics of the former Soviet Union, Tajikistan is an amoeba-shaped country of 55,251 square miles—roughly the size of Wisconsin—bordered by Krgyzstan to the north, China to the east, Afghanistan to the south, and Uzbekistan to the west. The 5.92 million persons of Tajikistan are ethnically diverse. Approximately 65 percent of the country is of the Tajik ethnic group, while 25 percent are Uzbek, 3.5 percent are Russian, and the remainder of mixed backgrounds. Like many other parts of the former Soviet Union, Tajikistan has had a difficult time adjusting to a market economy. Lacking the oil reserves of its neighbors, Tajikistan has seen its per capita income fall to just $1,040 in 1995.

The collapsing economy has produced a migration rate of −9.9 per 1,000 citizens. At the same time, the country has suffered from intense political strife since 1991, when it broke free of the collapsing Soviet Union. Indeed, during much of the 1990s, the country has been gripped by a civil war between the government and Islamic militants. The strife and economic collapse have resulted in falling health indexes. The infant mortality rate of 113.1 per 1,000 live births is among the highest in Asia. Public health is also in jeopardy with less than two-thirds of the population living in residences with adequate sanitation facilities.

	1995	1980

GEOGRAPHY

AREA (square miles/kilometers)	55,251/143,100	
LAND AREA (square miles/kilometers)	55,097/142,700	
COASTLINE (miles/kilometers)	Landlocked	

CITIES		
CAPITAL	Dushanbe	528,600 (93)

POPULATION

TOTAL	5,916,373	
DENSITY (per square mile/square kilometer)	107/41	
ANNUAL GROWTH	1.54%	

AGE COHORTS		
0–14	43%	
15–64	53%	
65 AND OVER	4%	

MALE	49%	
FEMALE	51%	

	1995	**1980**
URBAN	29.1% (93)	
RURAL	70.9%	
NET MIGRATION RATE	−9.93	

IDENTITY

ETHNICITY		
TAJIK	64.9%	
UZBEK	25%	
RUSSIAN	3.5%	

LANGUAGE		
TAJIK	n/a	
RUSSIAN	n/a	

RELIGION		
SUNNI MUSLIM	80%	
SHI'A MUSLIM	5%	

VITAL STATISTICS

BIRTHS		
BIRTH RATE	33.8	
URBAN BIRTH RATE	24.5 (93)	
RURAL BIRTH RATE	36.6	
INFANT MORTALITY RATE	113.1	
ABORTION RATE	215.5 (93)	
LIFE EXPECTANCY AT BIRTH	64.4	

MARRIAGES		
MARRIAGE RATE	9.6	
AVERAGE AGE AT MARRIAGE M/F	23.2/20.9 (93)	
DIVORCE RATE	0.9	

DEATHS		
DEATH RATE	8.4	

HOUSEHOLDS

NUMBER	858,793 (89)	
AVERAGE SIZE	5.7	

	1995	**1980**	

ECONOMICS AND LABOR

GDP PER CAPITA US$ $1,040

LABOR FORCE M/F
AGRICULTURE   37/45%
INDUSTRY   28/17%
SERVICES   35/37%

TRANSPORT

JOURNEYS (by transport mode)
RAILROAD PASSENGER TRIPS   103.0 (92)
AIR PASSENGER TRIPS (thousands)   783.0 (94)

HEALTH AND HEALTH CARE

	1995	**1980**	
RATE OF PHYSICIANS	2.1	2.4	n/a
RATE OF HOSPITAL BEDS	8.8	10	n/a
TOTAL DEATHS	49,326 (93)		

HEALTH INDICATORS
PREGNANT WOMEN WITH ANEMIA   50%
TUBERCULOSIS INCIDENCE RATE   1.3

HEALTH CARE
ACCESS TO SANITATION   62%
MEASLES IMMUNIZATION   90%

EDUCATION

SCHOOL AGE IN SCHOOL
PRIMARY   89%
SECONDARY   82%
HIGHER   20%

FEMALES IN SCHOOL
PRIMARY   49%
SECONDARY   47%

	1995	1980

COMMUNICATIONS

RATE OF NEWSPAPERS   21

FOOTNOTE
1. Part of Soviet Union in 1980 and 1965.

Source: CIA, *The World Factbook, 1997;* ILO, *World Labour Report, 1997;* UN, *Demographic Yearbook, 1997;* UN, *Statistical Yearbook, 1996;* World Bank, *World Development Indicators, 1998.*

TANZANIA, UNITED REPUBLIC OF

Situated in East Africa, Tanzania is bordered by Uganda and Kenya on the north; Mozambique, Malawi, and Zambia to the south; and the Democratic Republic of the Congo, Burundi, and Rwanda to the west. To the east, the country has an 890-mile coastline on the Indian Ocean. Covering some 364,900 square miles—roughly twice the size of California—Tanzania has a population of 29.06 million people, up from 8.66 million in 1965. The growth rate, which peaked in 1980 at 3.2 percent annually, had fallen off to 1.2 percent by 1995. Still, some 45 percent of the population is under the age of 15, promising a large population growth into the near future. Originally two British colonies—Tanganyika on the mainland and the offshore island of Zanzibar—Tanzania came into being in 1964. During most of its independence years, Tanzania was ruled by Julius Nyerere. While Nyerere was extremely adept at creating political harmony out of the country's many ethnic groups, his experiments in socialist agriculture and industry nearly bankrupted Tanzania's economy. Today, Tanzania is one of the poorer countries in Africa, with a per capita income of $800 annually. Most of the population continues to practice subsistence farming and pasturage. Social indexes lag as well. Just two-thirds of the school-age population attended primary institutions in 1995, down from 93 percent in 1980. During the same period life expectancy at birth fell from 51 to 42.3.

	1995	1980	1965
GEOGRAPHY			
AREA (square miles/kilometers)	364,900/945,090		
LAND AREA (square miles/kilometers)	342,100/886,040		
COASTLINE (miles/kilometers)	890/1,424		
CITIES			
CAPITAL	Dar es Salaam n/a	1,096,000 (85)	n/a
MAJOR CITIES	Mwanza n/a	252,000	n/a
	Tabora n/a	214,000	n/a
	Mbeya n/a	194,000	n/a
	Tanga n/a	172,000	n/a
POPULATION			
TOTAL	29,058,470	17,512.611 (78)	8,663,000 (57)[1]
DENSITY (per square mile/square kilometer)	85/31	51/20	n/a
ANNUAL GROWTH	1.15%	3.2%	1.9%

	1995	1980	1965
AGE COHORTS			
0–14	45%	n/a	42.5%
15–64	52%	n/a	55%
65 AND OVER	3%	n/a	2.5%
MALE	49%		
FEMALE	51%		
URBAN	20.8% (90)	13.9%	
RURAL	79.2%	86.1%	
NET MIGRATION RATE	−10.36	n/a	0.12

IDENTITY

ETHNICITY			
AFRICAN	99%		
ASIAN, EUROPEAN, AND ARAB	1%		
LANGUAGE			
KISWAHILI	n/a		
RELIGION			
CHRISTIAN	45%		
MUSLIM	35%		
INDIGENOUS	20%		

VITAL STATISTICS

BIRTHS			
BIRTH RATE	41.3	50.4	46
INFANT MORTALITY RATE	105.9	160–165	190
LIFE EXPECTANCY AT BIRTH	42.3	51	35–40
DEATHS			
DEATH RATE	19.5	15.3	25

HOUSEHOLDS

NUMBER	4,377,288 (88)
AVERAGE SIZE	5.3

	1995	1980	1965

ECONOMICS AND LABOR

GDP PER CAPITA US$ $800

LABOR FORCE M/F
AGRICULTURE 78/91%
INDUSTRY 8/2%
SERVICES 14/7%

UNION DENSITY 17.4%

POVERTY
UNDER $1/DAY 10.5% (93)
UNDER $2/DAY 45.5%

TRANSPORT

JOURNEYS (by transport mode)
RAILROAD PASSENGER TRIPS 990 (91)
  (millions of miles/kilometers)
AIR PASSENGER TRIPS (thousands) 199 (94)

VEHICLES (thousands)			
CARS	44	45.4	33.1
COMMERCIAL VEHICLES	59.9	48.7	10

HEALTH AND HEALTH CARE

	1995	1980	1965
RATE OF PHYSICIANS	n/a	n/a	0.1 (60)
RATE OF HOSPITAL BEDS	0.9	1.4	1.5

HEALTH INDICATORS
LOW-BIRTH-WEIGHT BABIES 14%
CHILD MALNUTRITION 29%
TUBERCULOSIS INCIDENCE RATE 1.8

HEALTH CARE
ACCESS TO SAFE WATER 49%
ACCESS TO SANITATION 86%
MEASLES IMMUNIZATION 75%

	1995	1980	1965

EDUCATION

SCHOOL AGE IN SCHOOL

	1995	1980	1965
PRIMARY	67%	93%	35%
SECONDARY	5%	3%	2%
HIGHER	1%	0%	0%

FEMALES IN SCHOOL

	1995	1980	1965
PRIMARY	49%	47%	30%
SECONDARY	43%	33%	27% (70)

| **ADULT ILLITERACY M/F** | 21/43% | 37.8/68.6% (78) | n/a |

COMMUNICATIONS

	1995	1980	1965
RATE OF NEWSPAPERS	8	11	3 (62)
RATE OF RADIOS	26	16	13
RATE OF TELEVISIONS	2	0	n/a

FOOTNOTE

1. The 1957 date excludes Zanzibar.

Source: CIA, *The World Factbook, 1997;* ILO, *World Labour Report, 1997;* UN, *Demographic Yearbook, 1997;* UN, *Statistical Yearbook, 1996;* World Bank, *World Development Indicators, 1998.*

THAILAND

Until the economic collapse of 1997, Thailand had one of the fastest-growing economies in the world. By 1995, the per capita income had risen to $6,900 annually. Of its 31-million–strong labor force in 1991, some 19 million worked in the agricultural sector, while 3.4 million were involved in manufacturing, many in the assembly of electronic components at Japanese and American-owned factories. Covering some 198,456 square miles, Thailand is located in the heart of Southeast Asia, bordered by Laos to the north and east, Cambodia to the southeast, Malaysia to the south, and Myanmar (formerly Burma) to the west. The country—which remained an independent kingdom through the heyday of European colonialism in the late nineteenth and early twentieth centuries—also has a 2,012-mile-long coastline on the Gulf of Thailand. The nation has a population of 58.85 million, up from 26.26 million in 1965. Over the past 30 years, the country saw its growth rate gradually decline from 3 percent annually in 1965 to 1 percent in 1995. The percentage of the population under the age of 15 fell from 43 to 25 during those same years. Economic prosperity in the country can be measured by the steadily rising social indexes. Life expectancy, for example, climbed from 56.1 years in 1965 to 68.6 years in 1995. During the same period, the percentage of young persons attending secondary institutions rose from 12 to 55.

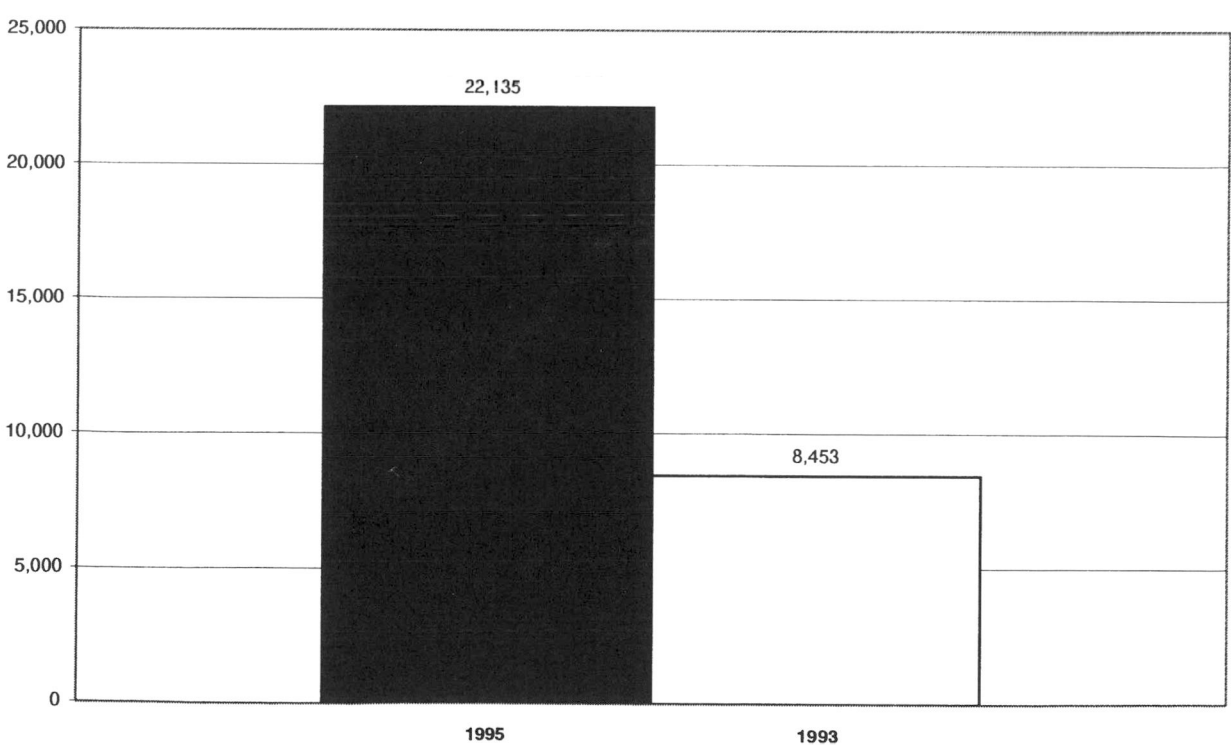

HIV Infection

Since the Vietnam War era, Thailand has been a haven for travelers seeking a liberal sexual order and easy access to heroin. The cost of that reputation is now being felt as Thailand experiences one of the fastest-growing rates of HIV infection in the world.

Radio and Television Ownership

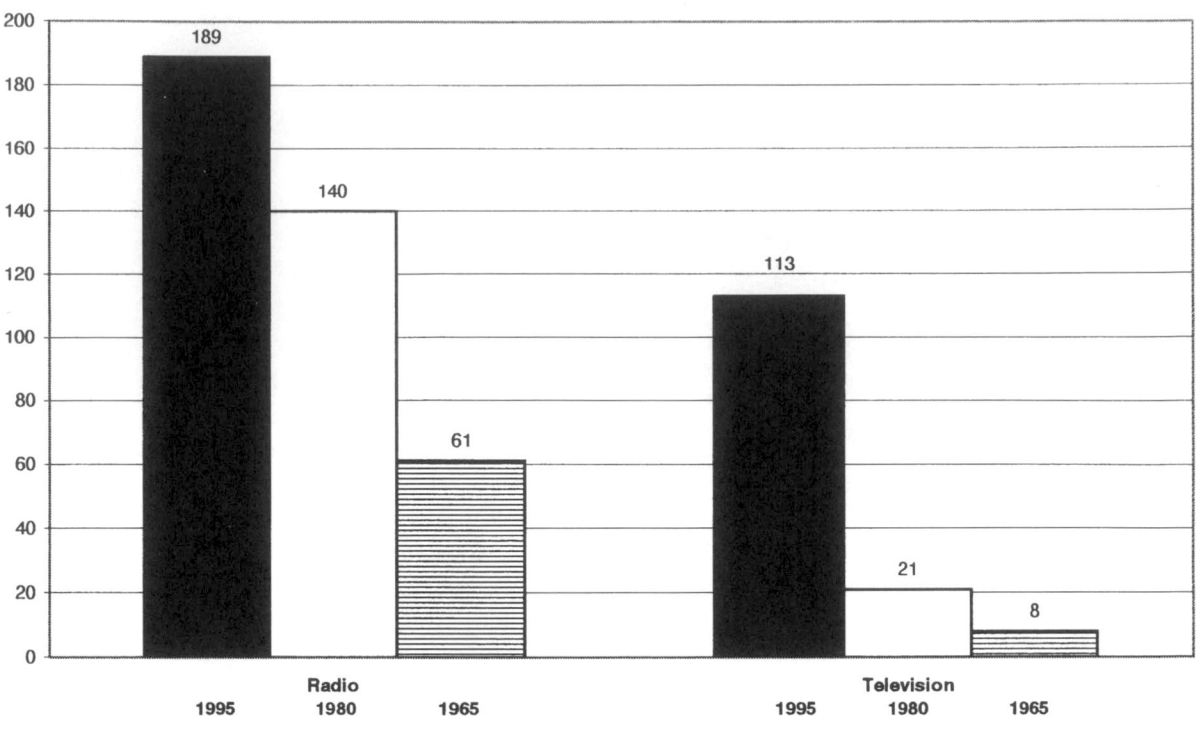

Note: Ownership in 1,000s.

Until the economic collapse of 1997, Thailand had one of the fastest-growing economies in the world, a fact reflected in the rapidly rising rates of media access.

CHRONOLOGY

1973   Experiment in civilian rule begins.
1975   Thailand recognizes Mainland China.
1976   Military overthrows civilian government; last U.S. troops leave.
1978   Refugees from Cambodian civil war and genocide pour into Thai refugee camps.
1980   Limited democracy permitted by military government.
1983   Election leads to civilian government.
1985   Coup attempt fails.
1991   Nonviolent military coup ends civilian government.
1992   Pro-military civilian government wins election.
1997   Economic crisis causes banks and other businesses to collapse.

	1995	1980	1965

GEOGRAPHY

AREA (square miles/kilometers)   198,456/514,000
LAND AREA (square miles/kilometers)   197,595/511,770
COASTLINE (miles/kilometers)   2,012/3,219

CITIES
CAPITAL

Bangkok	5,876,000 (90)
Nakhon Ratchasima	278,000
Songkhla	243,000
Nonthaburi	233,000
Khon Kaen	206,000

MAJOR CITIES (positioned with the list above)

POPULATION

	1995	1980	1965
TOTAL	58,851,357	44,824,540	26,257,916 (60)
DENSITY (per square mile/square kilometer)	298/115	227/88	133/51
ANNUAL GROWTH	1.03%	2%	3%
AGE COHORTS			
0–14	25%	n/a	43%
15–64	69%	n/a	54%
65 AND OVER	6%	n/a	3%
MALE	50%		
FEMALE	50%		
URBAN	18.7% (90)	17%	n/a
RURAL	81.3%	83%	n/a
NET MIGRATION RATE	0	n/a	0

IDENTITY

ETHNICITY

THAI	75%
CHINESE	14%

LANGUAGE

THAI	n/a
ENGLISH	n/a
REGIONAL DIALECTS	n/a

	1995	1980	1965
RELIGION			
BUDDHIST	95%		
MUSLIM	3.80%		
CHRISTIAN	0.50%		
HINDU	0.10%		

VITAL STATISTICS

	1995	1980	1965
BIRTHS			
BIRTH RATE	17.3	28	46 (60)
INFANT MORTALITY RATE	33.4	48	37.8
LIFE EXPECTANCY AT BIRTH	68.6	60.6	56.1
MARRIAGES			
MARRIAGE RATE	8.3	7.8	3.7
AVERAGE AGE AT MARRIAGE M/F	26/23.5 (90)		
DIVORCE RATE	0.7	0.6	0.1 (60)
DEATHS			
DEATH RATE	7	8	12.9 (60)

ECONOMICS AND LABOR

	1995
GDP PER CAPITA US$	$6,900
LABOR FORCE M/F (thousands)	16,850.9/14,287.5 (91)
AGRICULTURE	10,089.6/8,687.7
MINING	41.5/12.8
MANUFACTURING	1,717.5/1,747.5
UTILITIES	92.3/17.9
CONSTRUCTION	998.1/180.1
TRADE/FOOD/TOURISM	1,648.3/1,828.8
TRANSPORT/COMMUNICATIONS	739.0/94.9
SOCIAL AND PERSONAL SERVICES	1,515.0/1,710.6
UNEMPLOYMENT	
TOTAL	2.7% (91)
UNION DENSITY	3.10%
POVERTY	
UNDER $1/DAY	< 2% (92)
UNDER $2/DAY	23.5%

	1995	**1980**	**1965**

TRANSPORT

JOURNEYS (by transport mode)

	1995	**1980**	**1965**
RAILROAD PASSENGER TRIPS	14,496 (94)		
(millions of miles/kilometers)			
AIR PASSENGER TRIPS (thousands)	11,405 (94)		
VEHICLES (thousands)			
CARS	1,798.8	409.9	66.8
COMMERCIAL VEHICLES	2,384.1	140.8	87

HEALTH AND HEALTH CARE

	1995	**1980**	**1965**
RATE OF PHYSICIANS	0.2	0.1	0.1 (60)
RATE OF HOSPITAL BEDS	1.7	1.5	0.7 (60)
TOTAL DEATHS	305,526 (94)		
HEALTH INDICATORS			
PREGNANT WOMEN WITH ANEMIA	57%		
LOW-BIRTH-WEIGHT BABIES	13%		
CHILD MALNUTRITION	13%		
SMOKING PREVALENCE M/F	49/4%		
TUBERCULOSIS INCIDENCE RATE	1.7		
HEALTH CARE			
ACCESS TO SAFE WATER	81%		
ACCESS TO SANITATION	70%		
MEASLES IMMUNIZATION	86%		
AIDS/HIV CASES	22,135	8,453 (93)	

EDUCATION

	1995	**1980**	**1965**
SCHOOL AGE IN SCHOOL			
PRIMARY	87%	99%	80%
SECONDARY	55%	29%	12%
HIGHER	20%	15%	1.3%
FEMALES IN SCHOOL			
PRIMARY	49%	48%	76%
SECONDARY	50%	46%	10%
ADULT ILLITERACY M/F	8.0/4.0%	7.7/16.0%	

	1995	1980	1965
COMMUNICATIONS			
RATE OF NEWSPAPERS	85	57	13
RATE OF RADIOS	189	140	61
RATE OF TELEVISIONS	113	21	8

Source: CIA, *The World Factbook, 1997;* ILO, *World Labour Report, 1997;* UN, *Demographic Yearbook, 1997;* UN, *Statistical Yearbook, 1996;* World Bank, *World Development Indicators, 1998.*

TOGO

Located in West Africa, Togo is a narrow country bordered by Burkina Faso to the north, Benin to the east, and Ghana to the west. The nation of 21,154 square miles—roughly the size of West Virginia—has a 35-mile coastline on the Atlantic Ocean. Togo has a population of 4.57 million, up from 1.44 million in 1965. The rate of population growth has been going up, even as those of some of its West African neighbors have gone down. In the 1960s, the population grew at an annual average rate of 2.7 percent; by the 1990s, that figure was up to 3.5 percent. Not surprisingly, the cohort of citizens under the age of 15 has gone up from 39 to 49 percent. With a per capita in-come of just $900 annually, Togo is one of the poorest countries in the world. Still, only a small portion of its total population is involved in the commercial economy. Social indexes are low as well. Nearly half of all pregnant women suffer from anemia, while about one-quarter of the chil-dren under the age of 5 suffer from malnutrition. In addition, Togo, with nearly 6,500 sufferers, has one of the largest populations of AIDS and HIV victims per capita in West Africa. Educational op-portunities are limited as well. Just one-fourth of the young persons population attends secondary school.

	1995	1980	1965
GEOGRAPHY			
AREA (square miles/kilometers)	21,154/54,790		
LAND AREA (square miles/kilometers)	21,000/54,390		
COASTLINE (miles/kilometers)	35/56		
CITIES			
CAPITAL	Lome	n/a	n/a	148,486 (70)
POPULATION			
TOTAL	4,570,530	2,705,250 (81)	1,439,800 (60)
DENSITY (per square mile/square kilometer)	218/84	129/50	68/26
ANNUAL GROWTH	3.56%	3%	2.7%
AGE COHORTS			
0–14	49%	n/a	39%
15–64	49%	n/a	57%
65 AND OVER	2%	n/a	4%
NET MIGRATION RATE	0		

	1995	1980	1965

IDENTITY

ETHNICITY
NATIVE AFRICAN ETHNICITIES	99%		
EUROPEAN	n/a		
SYRIAN-LEBANESE	n/a		

LANGUAGE
FRENCH	n/a		
EWE	n/a		
MINA	n/a		
DAGOMBA	n/a		
KABYE	n/a		

RELIGION
INDIGENOUS	70%		
CHRISTIAN	20%		
MUSLIM	10%		

VITAL STATISTICS

BIRTHS
BIRTH RATE	46.2	45.2	55
INFANT MORTALITY RATE	84.3	127	127
LIFE EXPECTANCY AT BIRTH	57.9	35.1	35.1

MARRIAGES
MARRIAGE RATE	n/a	n/a	2.5

DEATHS
DEATH RATE	10.7	15.7	29

ECONOMICS AND LABOR

GDP PER CAPITA US$	$900		

LABOR FORCE (thousands)
LABOR FORCE (thousands)	60.7 (92)		
AGRICULTURE	4.4		
MINING	3.1		
MANUFACTURING	7.3		
UTILITIES	2.4		
CONSTRUCTION	2.3		
TRADE/FOOD/TOURISM	7.9		

	1995	1980	1965
TRANSPORT/COMMUNICATIONS	4.8		
SOCIAL AND PERSONAL SERVICES	28.5		

TRANSPORT

JOURNEYS (by transport mode)
	1995	1980	1965
RAILROAD PASSENGER TRIPS	117.0 (87)		
(millions of miles/kilometers)			
AIR PASSENGER TRIPS (thousands)	69.0 (94)		

VEHICLES
	1995	1980	1965
PRIVATE CARS	25.0 (93)	2	
COMMERCIAL VEHICLES	16.1	0.7	

HEALTH AND HEALTH CARE

	1995	1980	1965
RATE OF PHYSICIANS	0.1	0.1	0 (60)
RATE OF HOSPITAL BEDS	1.5	n/a	1.3

HEALTH INDICATORS
	1995	1980	1965
PREGNANT WOMEN WITH ANEMIA	48%		
LOW-BIRTH-WEIGHT BABIES	20%		
CHILD MALNUTRITION	25%		
TUBERCULOSIS INCIDENCE RATE	244		

HEALTH CARE

	1995	1980	1965
ACCESS TO SANITATION	22%		
MEASLES IMMUNIZATION	65%		
AIDS/HIV CASES	6,466	3,472 (93)	

EDUCATION

SCHOOL AGE IN SCHOOL
	1995	1980	1965
PRIMARY	118%	118%	59%
SECONDARY	27%	33%	5%
HIGHER	3%	2%	0%

FEMALES IN SCHOOL
	1995	1980	1965
PRIMARY	40%	38%	34%
SECONDARY	26%	24%	2%

	1995	1980	1965
ADULT ILLITERACY M/F	33/63%	53.3/81.5% (81)	

COMMUNICATIONS

	1995	1980	1965
RATE OF NEWSPAPERS	3	6	6
RATE OF RADIOS	211	203	21
RATE OF TELEVISIONS	7	4	

Source: CIA, *The World Factbook, 1997;* ILO, *World Labour Report, 1997;* UN, *Demographic Yearbook, 1997;* UN, *Statistical Yearbook, 1996;* World Bank, *World Development Indicators, 1998.*

TONGA

Tonga is a country of 106,466 persons scattered across numerous small islands in the South Pacific, about 2,000 miles northeast of New Zealand. With a total of 277 square miles of territory, Tonga has a density of 384 persons per square mile. The country won its independence from Britain in 1970. It has a per capita income of $2,160 annually, and its economy is largely reliant on fishing, tourism, and the production of tropical food products such as coconuts, bananas, vanilla, and coffee. Some 70 percent of the population is rural, with most of the urban population living in the capital of Nuku'alofa. Isolated and lacking in educational and job opportunities, Tonga has seen many of its young people leave for Britain, the United States, New Zealand, and Australia. The net migration rate in 1995 was −1.3 per 1,000 persons.

	1995	1980	1965
GEOGRAPHY			
AREA (square miles/kilometers)	277/718		
LAND AREA (square miles/kilometers)	277/718		
COASTLINE (miles/kilometers)	262/419		
CITIES			
CAPITAL	Nuku'alofa	n/a	18,312 (76)
POPULATION			
TOTAL	106,466	90,065 (76)	56,838 (56)
DENSITY (per square mile/square kilometer)	384/148	325/125	205/79
ANNUAL GROWTH	0.82%	0%	n/a
AGE COHORTS			
0–14	n/a	n/a	44%
15–64	n/a	n/a	49%
65 AND OVER	n/a	n/a	7%
MALE	50%		
FEMALE	50%		
URBAN	30.7% (86)		
RURAL	69.3%		
NET MIGRATION RATE	−1.29		

	1995	1980	1965

IDENTITY

ETHNICITY
POLYNESIAN n/a
EUROPEAN n/a

LANGUAGE
TONGAN n/a
ENGLISH n/a

RELIGION
CHRISTIAN n/a

VITAL STATISTICS

BIRTHS

	1995	1980	1965
BIRTH RATE	27.3	28.9 (85)	
INFANT MORTALITY RATE	40.3	5	
LIFE EXPECTANCY AT BIRTH	69		

MARRIAGES

	1995	1980	1965
MARRIAGE RATE	6.9	6.6 (85)	
AVERAGE AGE AT MARRIAGE M/F	n/a	27.1/24.8	
DIVORCE RATE	3.3	0.6 (85)	

DEATHS

	1995	1980	1965
DEATH RATE	6.3	3.5 (85)	

HOUSEHOLDS

	1995	1980	1965
NUMBER		15,065 (86)	
AVERAGE SIZE		6.3	

ECONOMICS AND LABOR

	1995	1980	1965
GDP PER CAPITA US$	$2,160		

TRANSPORT

JOURNEYS (by transport mode)

	1995	1980	1965
AIR PASSENGER TRIPS (thousands)	35.0 (94)		

	1995	1980	1965
VEHICLES			
PRIVATE CARS	3.3 (92)	1	
COMMERCIAL VEHICLES	3.7	1.3	

HEALTH AND HEALTH CARE

	1995	1980	1965
RATE OF PHYSICIANS	n/a	n/a	0.4 (60)
RATE OF HOSPITAL BEDS	n/a	n/a	2.5
TOTAL DEATHS	411 (91)		
AIDS/HIV CASES	5	4 (93)	

EDUCATION

	1995	1980	1965
SCHOOL AGE IN SCHOOL			
PRIMARY	n/a	n/a	145%
SECONDARY	n/a	n/a	78%
FEMALES IN SCHOOL			
PRIMARY	n/a	n/a	138%
SECONDARY	n/a	n/a	70%

COMMUNICATIONS

	1995	1980	1965
RATE OF NEWSPAPERS	72		
RATE OF RADIOS	560	217	70
RATE OF TELEVISIONS	15		

Source: CIA, The World Factbook, 1997; ILO, World Labour Report, 1997; UN, Demographic Yearbook, 1997; UN, Statistical Yearbook, 1996; World Bank, World Development Indicators, 1998.

TRINIDAD AND TOBAGO

Totaling some 1,981 square miles in territory and located at the southern end of the Lesser Antilles chain of islands in the eastern Caribbean, Trinidad and Tobago is just ten miles off the coast of Venezuela at its nearest point. Topographically and geographically, the two islands that make up the country are quite different. Trinidad, much larger in size, is actually an extension of the South American mainland, while Tobago is the last island in the Antilles. The populations of the two islands—totaling 1.27 million—are quite different as well. Trinidad's residents are an ethnic mix of descendants of African slaves and Indian laborers, the latter brought to the island by the British after the prohibition on slavery created labor needs on the island's commercial crop planta-

tions. The residents of Tobago, on the other hand, are almost entirely of African descent. Overall, Trinidad and Tobago have one of the healthier economies of the Caribbean basin, with a per capita income of $12,100 annually, but the two economies rely on different industries. Trinidad is a major oil producer and refiner, and Tobago largely depends on tourism for its income. Still, the relative wealth of the country as a whole is reflected in good public health statistics. For example, over 80 percent of the population has access to safe water. Similarly, the country's population is well educated, with some 72 percent of school-age children attending secondary institutions.

	1995	1980	1965
GEOGRAPHY			
AREA (square miles/kilometers)	1,981/5,130		
LAND AREA (square miles/kilometers)	1,981/5,130		
COASTLINE (miles/kilometers)	226/362		
CITIES			
CAPITAL	Port-of-Spain	46,222 (94)	
POPULATION			
TOTAL	1,272,385	1,079,791	974,722
DENSITY (per square mile/square kilometer)	642/248	545/210	492/190
ANNUAL GROWTH	n/a	1.8%	n/a
AGE COHORTS			
0–14	30%	n/a	43%
15–64	64%	n/a	53%
65 AND OVER	6%	n/a	4%
MALE	50%		
FEMALE	50%		

	1995	**1980**	**1965**
NET MIGRATION RATE	−8.6	n/a	−0.3

IDENTITY

ETHNICITY

BLACK	43%
EAST INDIAN (Northern Indian)	40%
MIXED	14%
WHITE	1%
CHINESE	1%

LANGUAGE

ENGLISH	n/a
HINDI	n/a
FRENCH	n/a
SPANISH	n/a

RELIGION

ROMAN CATHOLIC	32.20%
HINDU	24.30%
ANGLICAN	14.40%
PROTESTANT	14%
MUSLIM	6%

VITAL STATISTICS

BIRTHS

	1995	**1980**	**1965**
BIRTH RATE	16.2	28.5	37–39
INFANT MORTALITY RATE	18.2	15.9	35.3
LIFE EXPECTANCY AT BIRTH	70.3	68.3	64.2

MARRIAGES

	1995	**1980**	**1965**
MARRIAGE RATE	5.6	7.4	5.6
DIVORCE RATE	0.9	0.8	0.3

DEATHS

	1995	**1980**	**1965**
DEATH RATE	6.9	6.5	8

HOUSEHOLDS

	1995	**1980**	**1965**
NUMBER	274,846 (90)	n/a	180,846 (60)
AVERAGE SIZE	4.1	n/a	4.5

	1995	1980	1965

ECONOMICS AND LABOR

GDP PER CAPITA US$ | $12,100

	1995	1980	1965
LABOR FORCE M/F (thousands)	261.8/142.8 (93)		
AGRICULTURE	37.7/8.0		
MINING	13.1/1.9		
MANUFACTURING	28.1/12.2		
UTILITIES	6.2/0.9		
CONSTRUCTION	39.7/4.6		
TRADE/FOOD/TOURISM	35.5/35.6		
TRANSPORT/COMMUNICATIONS	25.2/4.8		
FINANCE/INSURANCE/REAL ESTATE	15.4/12.5		
SOCIAL AND PERSONAL SERVICES	60.5/62.2		

UNEMPLOYMENT
TOTAL | 19.8 (93)

TRANSPORT

JOURNEYS (by transport mode)
RAILROAD PASSENGER TRIPS | 1,642 (94)
  (millions of miles/kilometers)

VEHICLES (thousands)	1995	1980	1965
CARS	128.5	157	55.3
COMMERCIAL VEHICLES	33.6	49.1	16

HEALTH AND HEALTH CARE

	1995	1980	1965
RATE OF PHYSICIANS	0.7	0.7	0.4 (60)
RATE OF HOSPITAL BEDS	3.2	n/a	5.2 (60)
TOTAL DEATHS	8,807 (93)		

HEALTH INDICATORS	
PREGNANT WOMEN WITH ANEMIA	53%
LOW-BIRTH-WEIGHT BABIES	10%
CHILD MALNUTRITION	7%
SMOKING PREVALENCE M/F	42/8%
TUBERCULOSIS INCIDENCE RATE	0.2

	1995	**1980**	**1965**
HEALTH CARE			
ACCESS TO SAFE WATER	82%		
ACCESS TO SANITATION	56%		
MEASLES IMMUNIZATION	87%		
AIDS/HIV CASES	2,083	1,474 (93)	·

EDUCATION

	1995	**1980**	**1965**
SCHOOL AGE IN SCHOOL			
PRIMARY	96%	99%	133%
SECONDARY	72%	70%	24%
HIGHER	8%	4%	1.6%
FEMALES IN SCHOOL			
PRIMARY	49%	50%	131%
SECONDARY	51%	50%	25%
ADULT ILLITERACY M/F	3/1%	3.5/6.6%	n/a

COMMUNICATIONS

	1995	**1980**	**1965**
RATE OF NEWSPAPERS	138	143	102
RATE OF RADIOS	489	277	169
RATE OF TELEVISIONS	317	194	45

Source: CIA, *The World Factbook, 1997;* ILO, *World Labour Report, 1997;* UN, *Demographic Yearbook, 1997;* UN, *Statistical Yearbook, 1996;* World Bank, *World Development Indicators, 1998.*

TUNISIA

Tunisia is a medium-sized country, located on the Mediterranean coast of North Africa, bordering on Algeria and Libya. Totaling 63,170 square miles in territory—roughly the size of the state of Georgia—Tunisia has a population of 9.02 million. Dominated by Arab Muslims, it also has a significant minority of Berber-speaking people. Unlike its radical neighbors, Tunisia has had close relations with France—its former colonial ruler until 1956—and the Western world in general. This has given the country a leg up on winning Western investment, aid, and tourist dollars. These financial inputs are critical for the Tunisian economy because, unlike its neighbors, it does not have major hydrocarbon reserves. Still, Tunisia

has a moderate per capita income of $4,250 annually. Of its labor force, approximately one-third are involved in agriculture, one-third in manufacturing, and one-third in services. Over the past 30 years, Tunisia has made slow but steady gains in many social indexes. Its infant mortality rate dropped significantly from 110 per 1,000 live births in 1965 to 35.1 in 1995. Similarly, strides have been made in public health. The rate of physicians per resident has gone up by a factor of 6 since 1960. Educationally, the country has progressed as well. Whereas just 18 percent of the school-age population was attending secondary institutions in 1965, over 60 percent was doing so three decades later.

	1995	1980	1965
GEOGRAPHY			
AREA (square miles/kilometers)	63,170/163,610		
LAND AREA (square miles/kilometers)	59,985/155,360		
COASTLINE (miles/kilometers)	718/1,148		
CITIES			
CAPITAL	Tunis	n/a	596,654 (84)
POPULATION			
TOTAL	9,019,687	6,975,450 (84)	4,457,862 (66)
DENSITY (per square mile/square kilometer)	150/58	116/45	74/29
ANNUAL GROWTH	1.81%	2.1%	1.2%
AGE COHORTS			
0–14	34%	n/a	41% (56)
15–64	61%	n/a	52%
65 AND OVER	5%	n/a	6.8%¹
MALE	51%		
FEMALE	49%		

	1995	**1980**	**1965**
URBAN	n/a	52.8% (84)	
RURAL	n/a	47.2%	
NET MIGRATION RATE	−0.7	n/a	−0.6

IDENTITY

ETHNICITY

ARAB-BERBER	98%		
EUROPEAN	1%		
JEWISH	1%		

LANGUAGE

ARABIC	n/a		
FRENCH	n/a		

RELIGION

MUSLIM	98%		
CHRISTIAN	1%		
JEWISH	1%		

VITAL STATISTICS

BIRTHS

BIRTH RATE	24	32.8	47 (59)
URBAN BIRTH RATE	19.4 (94)		
RURAL BIRTH RATE	3.4		
INFANT MORTALITY RATE	35.1	125	110
ABORTION RATE	116.5		
LIFE EXPECTANCY AT BIRTH	72.6	60.6	n/a

MARRIAGES

MARRIAGE RATE	6.4	7.5	5.4
DIVORCE RATE	0.9	1.1	1.1

DEATHS

DEATH RATE	5.2	10	26

ECONOMICS AND LABOR

GDP PER CAPITA US$	$4,250		

	1995	1980	1965
LABOR FORCE M/F			
AGRICULTURE	22/42%		
INDUSTRY	33/32%		
SERVICES	44/26%		
UNION DENSITY	9.8%		
POVERTY			
UNDER $1/DAY	3.9% (90)		
UNDER $2/DAY	22.70%		

TRANSPORT

	1995	1980	1965
JOURNEYS (by transport mode)			
RAILROAD PASSENGER TRIPS	1,038 (94)		
(millions of miles/kilometers)			
AIR PASSENGER TRIPS (thousands)	1,391 (94)		
VEHICLES (thousands)			
CARS	325	n/a	51.2
COMMERCIAL VEHICLES	222	n/a	32.2

HEALTH AND HEALTH CARE

	1995	1980	1965
RATE OF PHYSICIANS	0.6	0.3	0.1 (60)
RATE OF HOSPITAL BEDS	1.8	2.1	2.7 (60)
TOTAL DEATHS	41,272 (94)		
HEALTH INDICATORS			
LOW-BIRTH-WEIGHT BABIES	10%		
CHILD MALNUTRITION	9%		
SMOKING PREVALENCE M/F	58/6%		
TUBERCULOSIS INCIDENCE RATE	0.5		
HEALTH CARE			
ACCESS TO SAFE WATER	n/a	72%	
ACCESS TO SANITATION	n/a	46%	
MEASLES IMMUNIZATION	89%		
AIDS/HIV CASES	270	166 (93)	

	1995	**1980**	**1965**

EDUCATION

SCHOOL AGE IN SCHOOL

PRIMARY	116%	102%	102%
SECONDARY	61%	27%	18%
HIGHER	13%	5%	1.5%

FEMALES IN SCHOOL

PRIMARY	47%	42%	73%
SECONDARY	47%	39%	13%

ADULT ILLITERACY M/F	21/45%	38.9/67.7%	53.6/82.4%

COMMUNICATIONS

RATE OF NEWSPAPERS	49	43	18
RATE OF RADIOS	198	157	69
RATE OF TELEVISIONS	81	47	1

FOOTNOTE
1. Age 60 or older

Source: CIA, *The World Factbook, 1997;* ILO, *World Labour Report, 1997;* UN, *Demographic Yearbook, 1997;* UN, *Statistical Yearbook, 1996;* World Bank, *World Development Indicators, 1998.*

TURKEY

Turkey's geographic location and situation has played a major role in the country's economic, political, and cultural history. With a tiny portion of its landmass in Europe and the vast bulk in Asia Minor, Turkey is a country with an element of Western ways laid over a largely Middle Eastern culture. The country is immense. Covering some 301,385 square miles of territory—about the size of Texas—Turkey bestrides the crossroads where Europe and the Middle East meet. Its population is ethnically divided, with about 80 percent of its 62.48 million citizens of Turkish descent and the remaining 20 percent largely consisting of persons of Kurdish heritage. Having lost its great empire in the wake of World War I,

the Turkish Republic—under the leadership of Kemal Mustafa "Ataturk"—struggled to retain its sovereignty against Western attacks. This led to a policy of repressing all non-Turkish cultural expression. Over the years, this repressive system led to numerous rebellions by the Kurdish minority, the most recent of which began in 1984 and continues to this day. Turkey has struggled between military dictatorships and democracy, and has experienced three coups since World War II. Despite this political turmoil, the country has come a long way in its efforts to develop an internal industrial base. With a per capita income of $5,500 annually, Turkey is one of the wealthier non-oil-producing nations in the Middle East.

Ethnicity

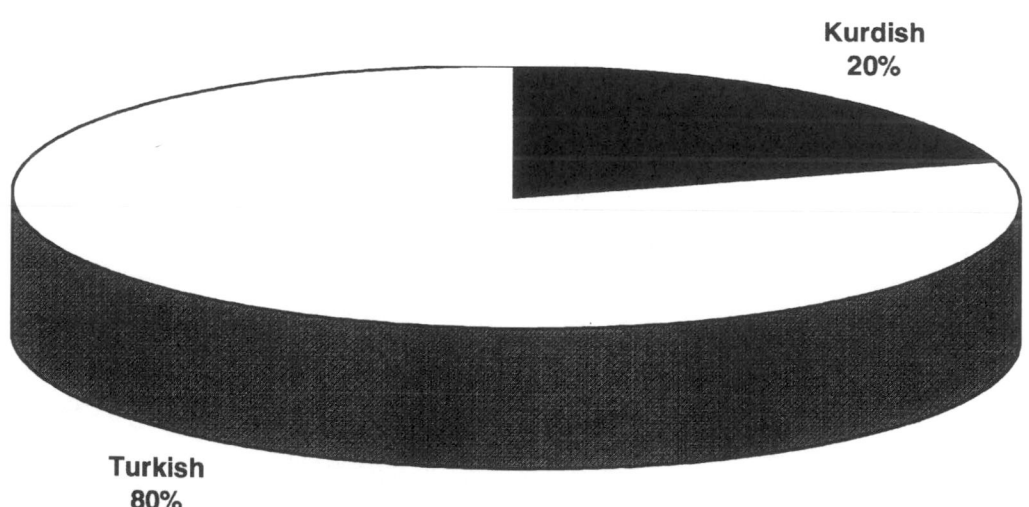

For the past 15 or so years, Turkey's military has been fighting against a Kurdish rebellion in the country's southeast. The Kurds, the largest minority in Turkey, once sought political independence but now demand cultural autonomy only.

Female Illiteracy and Birth Rates

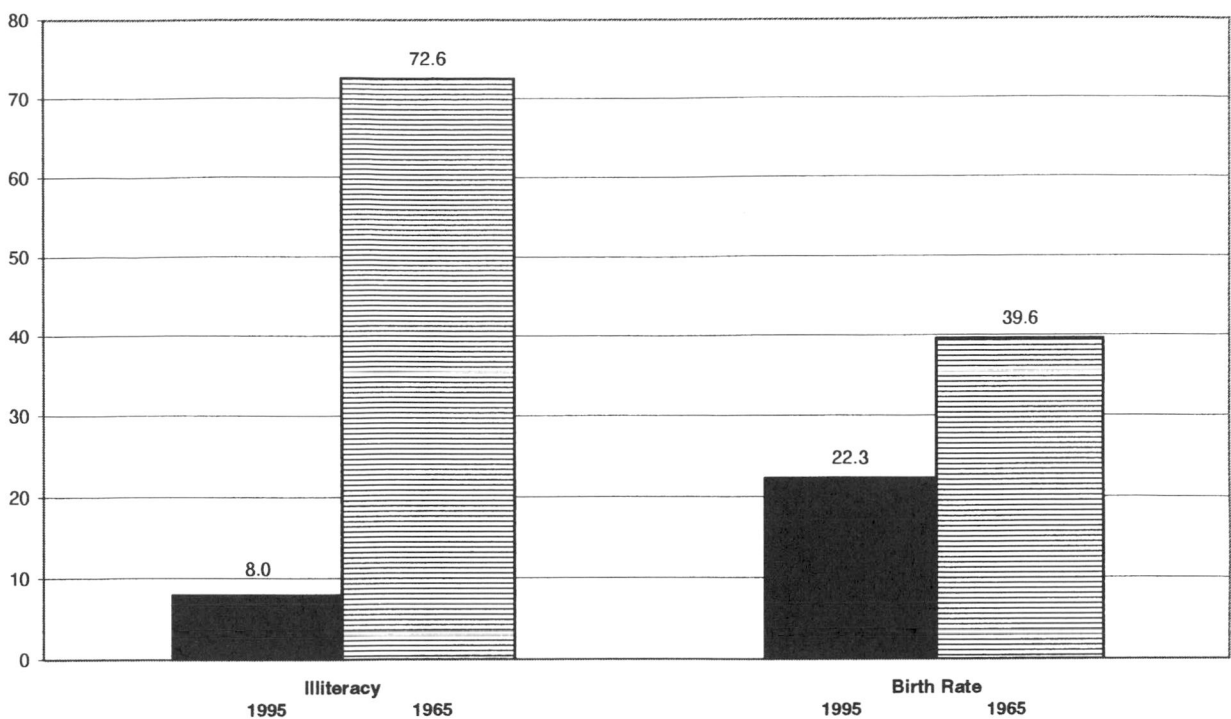

International agencies have come to recognize that increasing levels of female education mean declining birth rates because, with a larger worldview provided by learning, women can take more control over their bodies. Turkey provides an excellent case for this argument, as its declining birth rates and female illiteracy demonstrate.

CHRONOLOGY

1970   Following political unrest, military seizes power.

1974   Turkish military invades Cyprus to protect Turkish minority there.

1980   Military once again overthrows civilian government following widespread chaos.

1982   Turgut Ozal elected prime minister.

1984   Kurdish Workers Party launches guerrilla war; calls for independent Kurdistan.

1991   Hundreds of thousands of Kurdish refugees pour into Turkey following failed uprising after the Gulf War; Turkey agrees to allow allied warplanes to use bases to defend Kurdish "safe haven" in northern Iraq.

1993   Ozal dies; replaced by Suleyman Demirel.

1995   Turkey launches massive invasion of northern Iraq to root out Kurdish Workers Party bases there.

1996   Islamic Welfare Party takes power in Turkey.

1997   Islamic Welfare Party forced to surrender power after being warned by military about its pro-religious politics.

	1995	**1980**	**1965**

GEOGRAPHY

AREA (square miles/kilometers)	301,382/780,580	
LAND AREA (square miles/kilometers)	297,556/770,670	
COASTLINE (miles/kilometers)	4,500/7,200	

CITIES

CAPITAL	Ankara	2,782,200
MAJOR CITIES	Istanbul	7,774,169
	Izmir	2,017,699
	Adana	1,066,544
	Bursa	1,106,670

POPULATION

	1995	**1980**	**1965**
TOTAL	62,484,478	44,736,957	31,391,207
DENSITY (per square mile/square kilometer)	210/81	150/58	105/41
ANNUAL GROWTH	1.67%	2.1%	2.6%

AGE COHORTS

0–14	32%	n/a	42%
15–64	62%	n/a	54%
65 AND OVER	6%	n/a	4%

MALE	51%	
FEMALE	49%	

URBAN	62.6%	43.90%
RURAL	37.4%	56.1%

NET MIGRATION RATE	0	n/a	0

IDENTITY

ETHNICITY

TURKISH	80%
KURDISH	20%

LANGUAGE

TURKISH	n/a
KURDISH	n/a
ARABIC	n/a

	1995	1980	1965
RELIGION			
MUSLIM	99.80%		
CHRISTIAN	n/a		
JEWISH	n/a		

VITAL STATISTICS

	1995	1980	1965
BIRTHS			
BIRTH RATE	22.3	n/a	39.6 (67)
INFANT MORTALITY RATE	43.2	n/a	153 (67)
LIFE EXPECTANCY AT BIRTH	71.9	n/a	53.7 (67)
MARRIAGES			
MARRIAGE RATE	7.4		
AVERAGE AGE AT MARRIAGE M/F	25/22 (90)		
DIVORCE RATE	0.5	n/a	0.4 (67)
DEATHS			
DEATH RATE	5.5	n/a	14.6 (67)

HOUSEHOLDS

	1995	1980	1965
AVERAGE SIZE	5		
URBAN	4.6		
RURAL	6		

LABOR

	1995	1980	1965
GDP PER CAPITA $US	$5,500		
LABOR FORCE M/F (thousands)	3,570.6/405.6 (93)		
AGRICULTURE	65.7/4.5		
MINING	141.4/0.9		
MANUFACTURING	1,424.1/217.7		
UTILITIES	171.5/3.8		
CONSTRUCTION	566.3/10.2		
TRADE/FOOD/TOURISM	385.3/61.4		
TRANSPORT/COMMUNICATIONS	216.4/14.0		
FINANCE/INSURANCE/REAL ESTATE	39.3/9.1		
SOCIAL AND PERSONAL SERVICES	560.7/84.0		
UNEMPLOYMENT			
TOTAL	7.9% (93)		

	1995	1980	1965
UNION DENSITY	22%		

TRANSPORT

JOURNEYS (by transport mode)
	1995	1980	1965
RAILROAD PASSENGER TRIPS (millions of miles/kilometers)	6,335 (94)		
AIR PASSENGER TRIPS (thousands)	6,872 (94)		
VEHICLES (thousands)			
CARS	2,861.6	742.3	86.3
COMMERCIAL VEHICLES	530.4	304.2	101.3

HEALTH CARE

	1995	1980	1965
RATE OF PHYSICIANS	1.1	0.6	0.4 (60)
RATE OF HOSPITAL BEDS	2.5	2.2	1.7 (60)
TOTAL DEATHS	405,000		
HEALTH INDICATORS			
LOW-BIRTH-WEIGHT BABIES	8%		
CHILD MALNUTRITION	10%		
SMOKING PREVALENCE M/F	63/24%		
TUBERCULOSIS INCIDENCE RATE	0.5		
HEALTH CARE			
ACCESS TO SAFE WATER	92%		
ACCESS TO SANITATION	94%		
MEASLES IMMUNIZATION	65%		
AIDS/HIV CASES	188	131 (93)	

EDUCATION

	1995	1980	1965
SCHOOL AGE IN SCHOOL			
PRIMARY	105%	96%	74%
SECONDARY	56%	35%	20%
HIGHER	18%	5%	3.10%
FEMALES IN SCHOOL			
PRIMARY	47%	45%	61%
SECONDARY	39%	35%	12%
ADULT ILLITERACY M/F	28.0/8.0%	18.7/50.2%	35.5/72.6%

	1995	1980	1965
COMMUNICATIONS			
RATE OF NEWSPAPERS	71 (90)	56	45 (61)
RATE OF RADIOS	162	113	78
RATE OF TELEVISIONS	176	79	0.1

Source: CIA, *The World Factbook, 1997;* ILO, *World Labour Report, 1997;* UN, *Demographic Yearbook, 1997;* UN, *Statistical Yearbook, 1996;* World Bank, *World Development Indicators, 1998.*

TURKMENISTAN[1]

Located in central Asia, Turkmenistan is bordered by Kazakstan and Uzbekistan to the north, Afghanistan to the east, and Iran to the south. It also has a 1,105-mile-long coastline on the eastern shore of the Caspian Sea. Covering some 188,456 square miles of territory—about the size of California—the former Soviet Republic has a population of 4.15 million, and a density rate of 22 persons per square mile. Largely arid and semi-arid, Turkmenistan has a mild, subtropical climate in its west and a more frigid continental climate in its east. Since the breakup of the Soviet Union in 1991, the country has struggled in its efforts to transform itself into a market economy. With a per capita income of $2,820 annually, Turkmenistan's labor force is roughly equally divided between agricultural, industrial, and service sectors. Ethnically, the country is quite mixed. Approximately three-quarters of the population is of Turkmen background, while the rest of the population is divided among Russians, Uzbeks, and Kazaks. Some 87 percent of the population is Muslim, while most of the rest are members of the Eastern Orthodox church.

		1995	1980
GEOGRAPHY			
AREA (square miles/kilometers)		188,456/488,100	
LAND AREA (square miles/kilometers)		188,456/488,100	
COASTLINE (miles/kilometers)		1,105/1,768	
CITIES			
CAPITAL	Ashgabat	407,000 (90)	
MAJOR CITIES	Chardzhou	164,000	
	Tashauz	114,000	
POPULATION			
TOTAL		4,149,283	
DENSITY (per square mile/square kilometer)		22/9	
ANNUAL GROWTH		1.82%	
AGE COHORTS			
0–14		39%	
15–64		56%	
65 AND OVER		5%	
MALE		49%	
FEMALE		51%	

	1995	1980
URBAN	45.2% (89)	
RURAL	54.8%	
NET MIGRATION RATE	−2.08	

IDENTITY

ETHNICITY
TURKMEN	73.3%	
RUSSIAN	9.8%	
UZBEK	9%	
KAZAK	2%	

LANGUAGE
TURKMEN	72%	
RUSSIAN	12%	
UZBEK	9%	

RELIGION
MUSLIM	87%	
EASTERN ORTHODOX	11%	

VITAL STATISTICS

BIRTHS
BIRTH RATE	29.1	
INFANT MORTALITY RATE	81.6	
LIFE EXPECTANCY AT BIRTH	61.5	

MARRIAGES
MARRIAGE RATE	9.8	
DIVORCE RATE	1.4	

DEATHS
DEATH RATE	8.9	

ECONOMICS AND LABOR

GDP PER CAPITA US$	$2,820	

LABOR FORCE M/F
AGRICULTURE	34/41%	
INDUSTRY	30/14%	
SERVICES	36/44%	

	1995	1980
POVERTY		
UNDER $1/DAY	4.9% (93)	
UNDER $2/DAY	25.8%	

TRANSPORT

JOURNEYS (by transport mode)		
RAILROAD PASSENGER TRIPS	748 (94)	

HEALTH AND HEALTH CARE

	1995	1980
RATE OF PHYSICIANS	3.2	2.9
RATE OF HOSPITAL BEDS	11.5	10.6
TOTAL DEATHS	32,067 (94)	
HEALTH INDICATORS		
SMOKING PREVALENCE M/F	27/1%	
TUBERCULOSIS INCIDENCE RATE	0.7	
HEALTH CARE		
ACCESS TO SAFE WATER	85%	
ACCESS TO SANITATION	60%	
MEASLES IMMUNIZATION	90%	
AIDS/HIV CASES	1	1 (93)

EDUCATION

	1995	1980
SCHOOL AGE IN SCHOOL		
HIGHER	n/a	23

FOOTNOTE
1. Part of the Soviet Union in 1980 and 1965.

Source: CIA, The World Factbook, 1997; ILO, World Labour Report, 1997; UN, Demographic Yearbook, 1997; UN, Statistical Yearbook, 1996; World Bank, World Development Indicators, 1998.

TUVALU

One of the tiniest countries in the world, Tuvalu is a country of some 10 square miles located about 2,000 miles north of New Zealand in the southwest Pacific Ocean. Scattered across a number of tiny islands, Tuvalu has a population of 10,146 persons. Ethnically almost entirely Polynesian, the people of Tuvalu largely practice Protestant Christianity. Though a per capita income of $800 annually would make it seem that the country is among the poorest in the world, most of the population lives outside the commercial economy, working on tiny farms and fishing. The commercial economy is largely dependent on fishing and tourism.

	1995	**1980**	**1965**
GEOGRAPHY			
AREA (square miles/kilometers)	10.4/26		
LAND AREA (square miles/kilometers)	10.4/26		
COASTLINE (miles/kilometers)	15/24		
CITIES			
CAPITAL	Fongafane	n/a	
POPULATION			
TOTAL	10,146	7,300 (79)	
DENSITY (per square mile/square kilometer)	976/390	702/281	
ANNUAL GROWTH	1.51%		
AGE COHORTS			
0–14	36%		
15–64	59%		
65 AND OVER	5%		
NET MIGRATION RATE	0		
IDENTITY			
ETHNICITY			
POLYNESIAN	96%		
LANGUAGE			
TUVALUAN	n/a		
ENGLISH	n/a		

	1995	1980	1965
RELIGION			
CHURCH OF TUVALU (CONGREGATIONALIST)	97%		
SEVENTH DAY ADVENT	1.40%		
BAHA'I	1%		

VITAL STATISTICS

BIRTHS			
BIRTH RATE	24		
INFANT MORTALITY RATE	27.6		
LIFE EXPECTANCY AT BIRTH	63.3		
DEATHS			
DEATH RATE	8.9		

ECONOMICS AND LABOR

GDP PER CAPITA US$	$800		

COMMUNICATIONS

RATE OF RADIOS	307	206	

Source: CIA, *The World Factbook, 1997;* ILO, *World Labour Report, 1997;* UN, *Demographic Yearbook, 1997;* UN, *Statistical Yearbook, 1996;* World Bank, *World Development Indicators, 1998.*

UGANDA

Located astride the equator in the Great Lakes region of East Africa, Uganda is bordered by Sudan on the north, Kenya on the east, Tanzania and Rwanda on the south, and the Democratic Republic of the Congo on the west. It is also situated on the northwestern shore of Lake Victoria, Africa's largest lake. Covering some 91,000 square miles of territory—roughly the size of Oregon—Uganda is several thousand feet above sea level, making its climate less torrid than its position on the equator would indicate. Indeed, its moderate weather and lush landscape gave the country its nickname, the "Pearl of Africa." Once ruled by one of the most powerful royal houses in Africa, Uganda was conquered by the British, who ruled the country until 1962. In the years since independence, Uganda has experienced a great deal of political strife and governmental repression, a trend that reached its peak under the brutal dictatorship of Idi Amin in the 1970s. This troubled history set back progress in the social sectors. For example, the high infant mortality rate of 160 per 1,000 live births in 1965 failed to drop until after 1980. And while its population of 20.16 million is still relatively poor, with a per capita income of just $900 annually, stability under the Yuweri Museveni government has helped. The infant mortality rate, for example, had fallen to just under 100 by 1995.

	1995	1980	1965
GEOGRAPHY			
AREA (square miles/kilometers)	91,135/236,040		
LAND AREA (square miles/kilometers)	77,108/199,710		
COASTLINE (miles/kilometers)	Landlocked		
CITIES			
CAPITAL	Kampala		
Kampala	n/a	n/a	330,700 (69)
POPULATION			
TOTAL	20,158,176	9,548,847 (69)	6,536,616 (59)
DENSITY (per square mile/square kilometer)	261/101	124/48	85/33
ANNUAL GROWTH	2.24%	3.4%	2.5%
AGE COHORTS			
0–14	50%	n/a	41%
15–64	48%	n/a	57%
65 AND OVER	2%	n/a	2%
MALE	49%		
FEMALE	51%		

	1995	1980	1965
URBAN	11.3% (91)		
RURAL	88.7%		
NET MIGRATION RATE	−2.8	n/a	0

IDENTITY

ETHNICITY

BAGANDA	17%
KARAMOJONG	12%
BASOGO	8%
ITESO	8%
LANGI	6%
RWANDA	6%
BAGISU	5%
ACHOLI	4%
LUGBARA	4%
BUNYORO	3%
BATOBO	3%
EUROPEAN, ASIAN, ARAB	1%

LANGUAGE

ENGLISH	n/a
LUGANDA	n/a
SWAHILI	n/a
BANTU LANGUAGES	n/a
NILOTIC LANGUAGES	n/a

RELIGION

ROMAN CATHOLIC	33%
PROTESTANT	33%
MUSLIM	16%
INDIGENOUS	18%

VITAL STATISTICS

BIRTHS

	1995	1980	1965
BIRTH RATE	45.9	50.3	42
INFANT MORTALITY RATE	99.4	160	160
LIFE EXPECTANCY AT BIRTH	40.3	49	

MARRIAGES

AVERAGE AGE AT MARRIAGE M/F	23.7/19.4 (91)

DEATHS

	1995	1980	1965
DEATH RATE	20.7	16.8	20

	1995	1980	1965

HOUSEHOLDS

NUMBER	3,434,177 (91)		
AVERAGE SIZE	4.8		
TYPE OF HOUSEHOLD			
FEMALE HEADED	29%		

ECONOMICS AND LABOR

GDP PER CAPITA US$	$900		
LABOR FORCE M/F			
AGRICULTURE	81/88%		
INDUSTRY	7/2%		
SERVICES	12/10%		
UNION DENSITY	3.9%		
POVERTY			
UNDER $1/DAY	69.3% (90)		
UNDER $2/DAY	92.2%		

TRANSPORT

JOURNEYS (by transport mode)			
RAILROAD PASSENGER TRIPS	60.0 (91)		
(millions of miles/kilometers)			
AIR PASSENGER TRIPS	63.0 (94)		
VEHICLES (thousands)			
CARS	17.8	n/a	30.3
COMMERCIAL VEHICLES	25.3	n/a	5.9

HEALTH AND HEALTH CARE

RATE OF PHYSICIANS	n/a	0	0.1 (60)
RATE OF HOSPITAL BEDS	0.9	1.5	1.5 (60)
HEALTH INDICATORS			
PREGNANT WOMEN WITH ANEMIA	30%		
CHILD MALNUTRITION	26%		

	1995	1980	1965
SMOKING PREVALENCE M/F	10/1%		
TUBERCULOSIS INCIDENCE RATE	3		
HEALTH CARE			
ACCESS TO SAFE WATER	34%		
ACCESS TO SANITATION	57%		
MEASLES IMMUNIZATION	79%		
AIDS/HIV CASES	48,312	41,193 (93)	

EDUCATION

	1995	1980	1965
SCHOOL AGE IN SCHOOL			
PRIMARY	73%	50%	44%
SECONDARY	12%	5%	9%
HIGHER	2%	1%	0.2%
FEMALES IN SCHOOL			
PRIMARY	44%	43%	33%
SECONDARY	38%	29%	5%
ADULT ILLITERACY M/F	26/50%	30.3/54.7% (85)	

COMMUNICATIONS

	1995	1980	1965
RATE OF NEWSPAPERS	4	2	5
RATE OF RADIOS	107	30	31
RATE OF TELEVISIONS	11	6	0.8

Source: CIA, *The World Factbook, 1997;* ILO, *World Labour Report, 1997;* UN, *Demographic Yearbook, 1997;* UN, *Statistical Yearbook, 1996;* World Bank, *World Development Indicators, 1998.*

UKRAINE[1]

The second largest republic of the former Soviet Union by population—after Russia itself—Ukraine is a vast country situated in southeastern Europe, bordered by Belarus on the north; Russia on the east; and Moldova, Hungary, Slovakia, and Poland on the west. Ukraine encompasses 233,089 square miles of land area, roughly the area of Texas. It has an extensive, 1,739-mile coastline along the Black Sea to the south. Its population of 50.86 million, like several other former Soviet republics, has shrunk since the demise of the communist giant in 1991. In 1995, the population went down by 0.4 percent. This is largely explained by the dismal health statistics in the country. In 1965, Ukraine—as part of the Soviet Union—had a death rate of 7.5 per 1,000 persons. By 1995, the rate had more than doubled to 15.2. Concurrently, the birth rate had fallen from 15.5 in 1965 to 11.2 in 1995. The poor health profile is a reflection of the economic quagmire the country has been in since it began its shift to a market economy in the early 1990s. By 1995, its per capita income had fallen to just $3,370 annually. Other indexes are just as dismal. Life expectancy fell from 71 years in 1965 to just 66.8 in 1995, and the percentage of school-age children attending primary institutions fell from 100 percent in 1980 to 87 percent in 1995.

Marriage and Divorce Rates

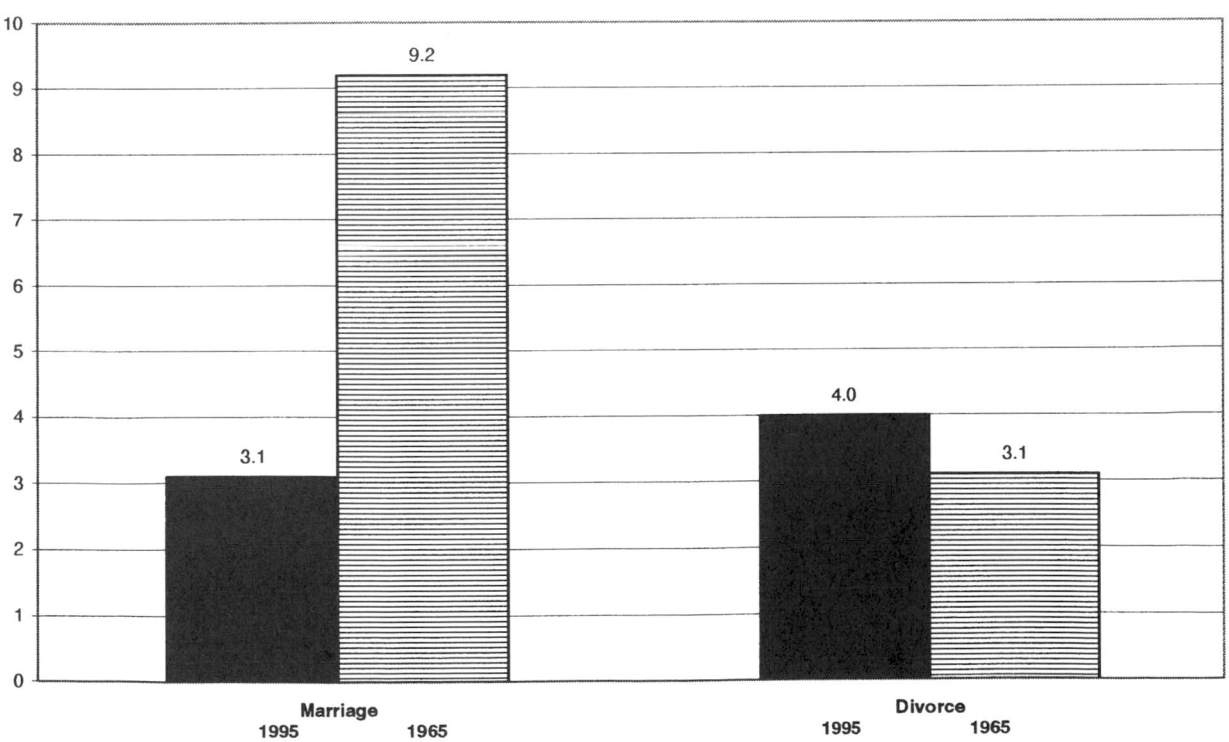

Like many countries of the former Soviet Union, Ukraine has experienced extreme economic dislocations in the 1990s. This helps explain the declining marriage rates, as young people forego starting families, and rising divorce rates, as marriages collapse under the tension of falling incomes.

Infant Mortality and Life Expectancy

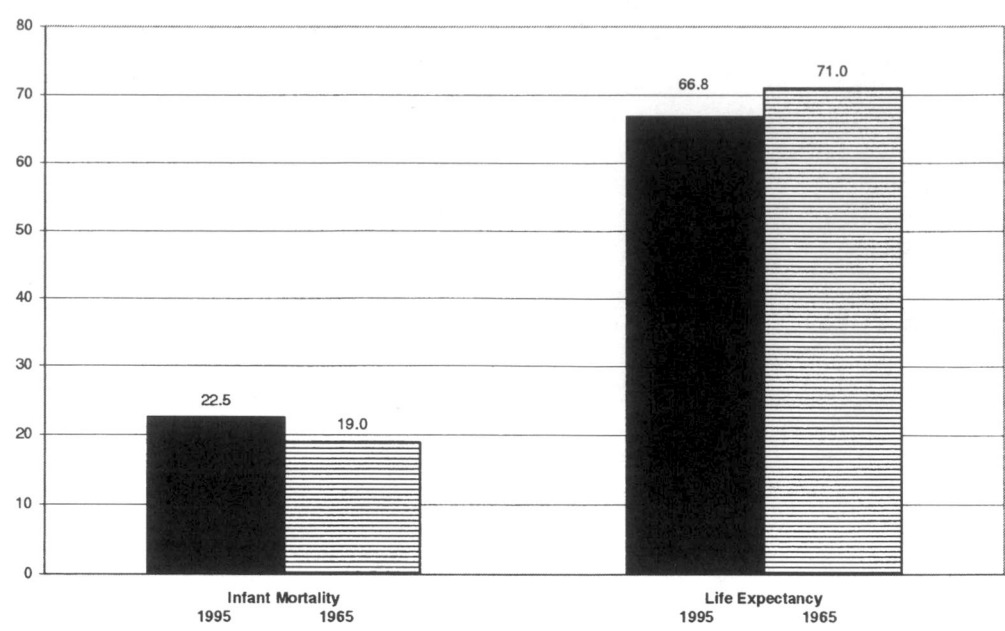

The economic collapse of the Ukraine economy since the collapse of communism is reflected in declining health indexes. While life expectancy has gone down, infant mortality has gone up.

	1995	1980	1965

GEOGRAPHY

AREA (square miles/kilometers)	233,116/603,770		
LAND AREA (square miles/kilometers)	233,089/603,700		
COASTLINE (miles/kilometers)	1,739/2,782		

CITIES

		1995	
CAPITAL	Kiev	2,646,100 (93)	
MAJOR CITIES	Kharkov	1,615,000	
	Dnepropetrovsk	1,185,500	
	Donetsk	1,121,200	
	Odessa	1,086,700	

POPULATION

	1995	1980	1965
TOTAL	50,864,009	49,754,642 (79)	41,869,046 (59)
DENSITY (per square mile/square kilometer)	218/84	213/82	180/69
ANNUAL GROWTH	−0.40%	n/a	1.2%

	1995	1980	1965
AGE COHORTS			
0–14	20%	n/a	34.3%[2]
15–64	66%	n/a	59%
65 AND OVER	14%	n/a	6.9%
MALE	46%		
FEMALE	54%		
URBAN	67.9% (93)	62.3%	
RURAL	32.1%	37.7%	
NET MIGRATION RATE	0.03		

IDENTITY

ETHNICITY	
UKRAINIAN	73%
RUSSIAN	22%
JEWISH	1%

LANGUAGE	
UKRAINIAN	n/a
RUSSIAN	n/a
ROMANIAN	n/a
POLISH	n/a
HUNGARIAN	n/a

RELIGION	
UKRAINIAN ORTHODOX	n/a
UKRAINIAN AUTOCEPHALOUS ORTHODOX	n/a
UKRAINIAN CATHOLIC	n/a
PROTESTANT	n/a
JEWISH	n/a

VITAL STATISTICS

BIRTHS			
BIRTH RATE	11.2	n/a	15.5
URBAN BIRTH RATE	10.1 (93)		
RURAL BIRTH RATE	12		
INFANT MORTALITY RATE	22.5	n/a	19
ABORTION RATE	1,517.2 (91)		
LIFE EXPECTANCY AT BIRTH	66.8	n/a	71

	1995	1980	1965
MARRIAGES			
MARRIAGE RATE	8.2	n/a	9.2
AVERAGE AGE AT MARRIAGE M/F	24.1/21 (89)	n/a	
DIVORCE RATE	4	n/a	3.1
DEATHS			
DEATH RATE	15.2	n/a	7.5

HOUSEHOLDS

NUMBER	14,057,509 (89)
AVERAGE SIZE	3.2

ECONOMICS AND LABOR

GDP PER CAPITA US$	$3,370

LABOR FORCE M/F	
AGRICULTURE	24/16%
INDUSTRY	46/34%
SERVICES	31/50%

TRANSPORT

JOURNEYS (by transport mode)	
RAILROAD PASSENGER TRIPS (millions of miles/kilometers)	70,882.0 (94)
AIR PASSENGER TRIPS (thousands)	769.0 (94)

VEHICLES	
RATE PER TYPE	4,384.1 (94)

HEALTH AND HEALTH CARE

	1995	1980
RATE OF PHYSICIANS	4.4	3.7
RATE OF HOSPITAL BEDS	12.2	12.5
TOTAL DEATHS	764,669 (94)	

HEALTH INDICATORS	
LOW-BIRTH-WEIGHT BABIES	5%
TUBERCULOSIS INCIDENCE RATE	0.5

	1995	**1980**	**1965**
HEALTH CARE			
ACCESS TO SAFE WATER	97%		
ACCESS TO SANITATION	49%		
MEASLES IMMUNIZATION	96%		
AIDS/HIV CASES	75	26 (93)	

EDUCATION

	1995	**1980**	**1965**
SCHOOL AGE IN SCHOOL			
PRIMARY	87%	102%	
SECONDARY	91%	94%	
HIGHER	41%	42%	15.2%
FEMALES IN SCHOOL			
PRIMARY	49%	49%	
SECONDARY	51%	n/a	

COMMUNICATIONS

	1995	**1980**	**1965**
RATE OF NEWSPAPERS	118		
RATE OF RADIOS	809	579	357
RATE OF TELEVISIONS	339	255	67

FOOTNOTES
1. Part of Soviet Union in 1980 and 1965.
2. Age 0–20.

Source: CIA, *The World Factbook, 1997;* ILO, *World Labour Report, 1997;* UN, *Demographic Yearbook, 1997;* UN, *Statistical Yearbook, 1996;* World Bank, *World Development Indicators, 1998.*

UNITED ARAB EMIRATES

Located on the southern Persian Gulf, bordered by Oman to the east and Saudi Arabia to the south and west, the United Arab Emirates (UAE) covers 29,182 square miles of territory. The largely desert domain is home to 3.06 million people. Formed out of a collection of emirates— or Arab principalities—under the British colonial regime, the UAE won its independence in 1971. Situated atop some of the largest oil reserves in the world, the people of the UAE enjoy one of the highest standards of living in the world. The per capita income in 1995 was $24,000, with much of the work in the country being performed by imported laborers. The tremendous wealth of the country—greatly augmented by the rapid rise in

oil prices in the 1970s—has allowed the government of the UAE to set up an inclusive public health care and educational system. Whereas most of the population lived in substandard conditions 30 years ago, fully 98 percent had access to safe water and some 95 percent lived in residences with adequate sanitation by 1995. Similarly, educational opportunities have expanded dramatically. Whereas just one-fourth of the school-age population attended secondary institutions in 1965, fully three-quarters did so by 1995, though the figures were significantly lower for girls than boys in both periods, reflecting the relatively conservative Islamic culture of the country.

		1995	1980

GEOGRAPHY

	1995	1980
AREA (square miles/kilometers)	29,182/75,581	
LAND AREA (square miles/kilometers)	29,182/75,581	
COASTLINE (miles/kilometers)	823/1,318	

CITIES			
CAPITAL	Abu Dhabi	n/a	242,975
MAJOR CITIES	Dubai	n/a	265,702
	Sharjah	n/a	125,149
	Al-Ain	n/a	101,663

POPULATION

	1995	1980	
TOTAL	3,057,337	1,043,225	
DENSITY (per square mile/square kilometer)	105/40	36/14	
ANNUAL GROWTH	4.33%	6.2%	2.5%

AGE COHORTS	
0–14	35%
15–64	64%
65 AND OVER	1%

	1995	1980
MALE	69%	
FEMALE	31%	
URBAN	n/a	80.9%
RURAL	n/a	19.1%
NET MIGRATION RATE	19.9	

IDENTITY

ETHNICITY

EMIRI	19%
ARAB AND IRANIAN	23%
SOUTH ASIAN	50%
OTHER EXPATRIATES (Westerner and East Asian)	8%

LANGUAGES

ARABIC	n/a
PERSIAN	n/a
ENGLISH	n/a
HINDI	n/a
URDU	n/a

RELIGION

MUSLIM	96%
CHRISTIAN	n/a
HINDU	n/a

VITAL STATISTICS

BIRTHS

	1995	1980
BIRTH RATE	26.4	29.8
INFANT MORTALITY RATE	20.4	38
LIFE EXPECTANCY AT BIRTH	72.7	67.6

MARRIAGES

MARRIAGE RATE	4
DIVORCE RATE	1.1

DEATHS

	1995	1980
DEATH RATE	3	4.3

	1995	1980	

ECONOMICS AND LABOR

GDP PER CAPITA US$	$24,000		
LABOR FORCE M/F			
AGRICULTURE	9/1%		
INDUSTRY	30/2%		
SERVICES	61/97%		

TRANSPORT

JOURNEYS (by transport mode)			
RAILROAD PASSENGER TRIPS	3,162.0 (94)		
(millions of miles/kilometers)			
VEHICLES (thousands)			
CARS	297.1	n/a	97.7
COMMERCIAL VEHICLES	72.8	n/a	26

HEALTH AND HEALTH CARE

RATE OF PHYSICIANS	0.8	1.1	
RATE OF HOSPITAL BEDS	3.1	2.8	
TOTAL DEATHS	4,597 (94)		
HEALTH INDICATORS			
PREGNANT WOMEN WITH ANEMIA	46%		
LOW-BIRTH-WEIGHT BABIES	8%		
CHILD MALNUTRITION	7%		
TUBERCULOSIS INCIDENCE RATE	0.3		
HEALTH CARE			
ACCESS TO SAFE WATER	98%		
ACCESS TO SANITATION	95%		
MEASLES IMMUNIZATION	90%		
AIDS/HIV CASES	8	8 (93)	

	1995	1980	

EDUCATION

SCHOOL AGE IN SCHOOL

	1995	1980	
PRIMARY	95%	89%	74%
SECONDARY	78%	52%	26%
HIGHER	9%	3%	5.9%

FEMALES IN SCHOOL

	1995	1980	
PRIMARY	48%	48%	59%
SECONDARY	51%	45%	15%

ADULT ILLITERACY M/F	21/20%	41.6/61.9% (75)

COMMUNICATIONS

	1995	1980	
RATE OF NEWSPAPERS	189	149	15 (63)
RATE OF RADIOS	311	236	54
RATE OF TELEVISIONS	106	88	11

Source: CIA, *The World Factbook, 1997;* ILO, *World Labour Report, 1997;* UN, *Demographic Yearbook, 1997;* UN, *Statistical Yearbook, 1996;* World Bank, *World Development Indicators, 1998.*

UNITED KINGDOM

Though it once possessed the greatest empire in world history—encompassing approximately one-fourth of the world's surface—the United Kingdom is now largely confined to the island of Britain and a corner of the island of Ireland, situated off the northwest coast of Europe between the North Sea and the Atlantic Ocean. (Britain continues to hold minor overseas possessions, largely in the form of small islands scattered across the globe.) Its geopolitical decline has been paralleled by its topple from economic prominence in the twentieth century. Still, this country of 94,525 square miles of territory, with a population in 1995 of 58.49 million, remains one of the world's largest economies and military powers.

Governed as a constitutional monarchy, Britain has one of the oldest living democracies in the world. Its economy, with a per capita income of $19,500 annually, is largely post-industrial in orientation, emphasizing services and trade. Indeed, trade accounts for about two-thirds of the jobs held by the 25.4-million–strong labor force. Until the post–World War II era, Britain was a relatively homogenous country ethnically. But in the past 50 years, it has seen an influx of people from its former colonies in Africa, Asia, and the Caribbean. Though a member of the European Union, Britain jealously guards its autonomy and has been hesitant to give up its currency for the Euro.

Major British Cities, 1995

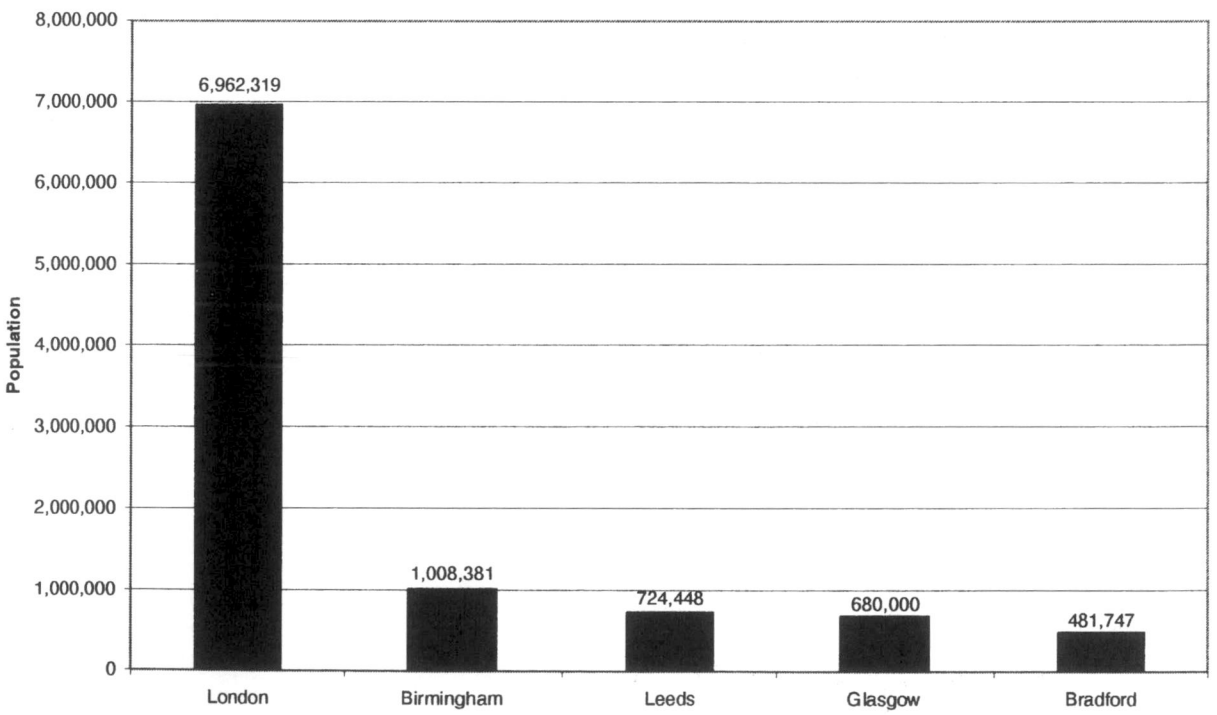

Like few other industrialized countries, Great Britain is dominated by its capital city, London, as these population statistics for the country's five largest cities indicate.

Population Growth and Shrinkage

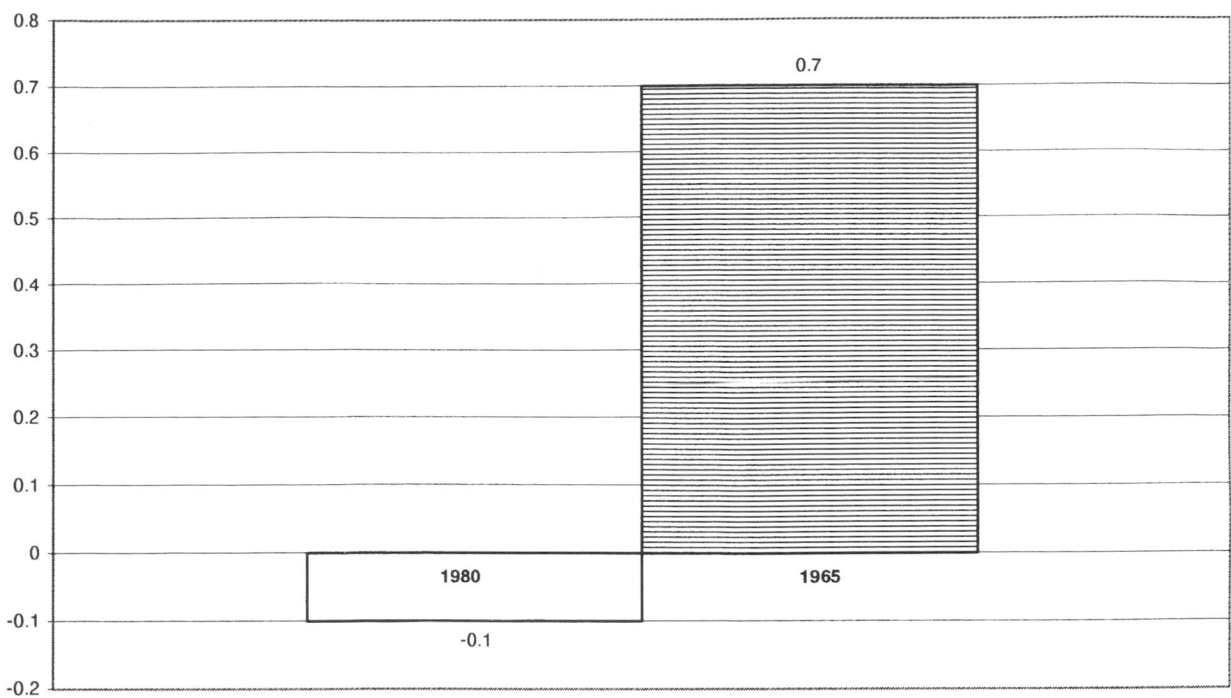

Like many other Western European countries, Great Britain has largely achieved population balance in the last 30 years, as evidenced by the annual growth rate rising and falling around zero.

CHRONOLOGY

1964   Harold Wilson leads Labour Party to victory in national election.

1969   Conflict breaks out in Northern Ireland between Catholics and Protestants; Britain sends troops.

1970   Flagging economy leads to Conservative Party victory.

1979   Hard-line Conservative Margaret Thatcher becomes prime minister.

1982   Britain goes to war with Argentina, after the latter occupies British-controlled Falkland Islands.

1990   John Major replaces Thatcher as prime minister.

1993   Britain signs Maastricht Treaty, calling for tighter European Union.

1997   Led by Tony Blair, Labour Party returns to power after 18 years.

	1995	1980	1965

GEOGRAPHY

AREA (square miles/kilometers)	94,525/244,820	
LAND AREA (square miles/kilometers)	93,278/241,590	
COASTLINE (miles/kilometers)	7,768/12,429	

CITIES

CAPITAL	London	6,962,319 (94)
MAJOR CITIES	Birmingham	1,008,381
	Leeds	724,448
	Glasgow	680,000
	Bradford	481,747

POPULATION

	1995	1980	1965
TOTAL	58,489,975	55,678,079 (81)	52,708,934 (61)
DENSITY (per square mile/square kilometer)	627/242	597/230	565/218
ANNUAL GROWTH	0.22%	−0.1%	0.7%

AGE COHORTS

	1995	1980	1965
0–14	20%	n/a	23% (66)
15–64	65%	n/a	65%
65 AND OVER	15%	n/a	12%

	1995	1980	1965
URBAN	n/a	87.7%	
RURAL	n/a	12.3%	

	1995	1980	1965
NET MIGRATION RATE	0.3	n/a	−0.2

IDENTITY

ETHNICITY

ENGLISH	81.5%
SCOTTISH	9.6%
IRISH	2.4%
WELSH	1.9%
ULSTER	1.8%
WEST INDIAN, INDIAN, PAKISTANI, OTHER	2.8%

LANGUAGE

ENGLISH	n/a
WELSH	n/a
SCOTTISH GAELIC	n/a

	1995	1980	1965
RELIGION			
ANGLICAN	n/a		
ROMAN CATHOLIC	n/a		
MUSLIM	n/a		
PRESBYTERIAN	n/a		
METHODIST	n/a		
SIKH	n/a		
HINDU	n/a		
JEWISH	n/a		

VITAL STATISTICS

	1995	1980	1965
BIRTHS			
BIRTH RATE	13.1		17.7
INFANT MORTALITY RATE	6.4		19
LIFE EXPECTANCY AT BIRTH	76.4		71.3
MARRIAGES			
MARRIAGE RATE	5.9	n/a	8
AVERAGE AGE AT MARRIAGE M/F	28.4/26.4 (91)		
DIVORCE RATE	3	n/a	0.7
DEATHS			
DEATH RATE	11.2	n/a	11.7

HOUSEHOLDS

	1995	1980	1965
NUMBER	n/a	n/a	16,622,612 (61)
AVERAGE SIZE	n/a	n/a	3.1

ECONOMICS AND LABOR

	1995	1980	1965
GDP PER CAPITA US$	$19,500		
LABOR FORCE M/F (thousands)	13,741/11,576 (93)		
AGRICULTURE	427/120		
MANUFACTURING	4,936/1,629		
TRADE/FOOD/TOURISM	8,125/9,809		
UNEMPLOYMENT			
TOTAL	7.9% (93)		
UNION DENSITY	26.2%		

	1995	1980	1965

TRANSPORT

JOURNEYS (by transport mode)

	1995	1980	1965
RAILROAD PASSENGER TRIPS (millions of miles/kilometers)	28,656.0 (94)		
AIR PASSENGER TRIPS (thousands)	55,475.0 (94)		

VEHICLES (thousands)

	1995	1980	1965
CARS	21,740	15,424.40	9245.8
COMMERCIAL VEHICLES	2,994	2,233.70	1795.8

HEALTH CARE

	1995	1980	1965
RATE OF PHYSICIANS	1.5	1.6	1.1 (60)
RATE OF HOSPITAL BEDS	4.9	9.3	10.5 (60)
TOTAL DEATHS	641,700		

HEALTH INDICATORS

	1995	1980	1965
SMOKING PREVALENCE M/F	28/26%		
TUBERCULOSIS INCIDENCE RATE	0.1		

HEALTH CARE

	1995	1980	1965
ACCESS TO SAFE WATER	100%		
ACCESS TO SANITATION	96%		
MEASLES IMMUNIZATION	92%		

	1995	1980	1965
AIDS/HIV CASES	12,416	9,397 (93)	

EDUCATION

SCHOOL AGE IN SCHOOL

	1995	1980	1965
PRIMARY	115%	103%	111%
SECONDARY	134%	83%	68%
HIGHER	48%	19%	6.2%

FEMALES IN SCHOOL

	1995	1980	1965
PRIMARY	49%	49%	110%
SECONDARY	49%	49%	65%
HIGHER	n/a	15%	9.5% (70)

	1995	**1980**	**1965**
COMMUNICATIONS			
RATE OF NEWSPAPERS	383	417	479
RATE OF RADIOS	1,146	950	307
RATE OF TELEVISIONS	435	401	256

Source: CIA, *The World Factbook, 1997;* ILO, *World Labour Report, 1997;* UN, *Demographic Yearbook, 1997;* UN, *Statistical Yearbook, 1996;* World Bank, *World Development Indicators, 1998.*

UNITED STATES OF AMERICA

Known colloquially as the "world's only remaining superpower," the United States has become, with the demise of the Soviet Union in 1991, the political, economic, and military colossus of the world. Located on the North American continent, between Mexico to the south and Canada to the north, the United States has expansive coastlines on the Atlantic and Pacific oceans, as well as on the Gulf of Mexico. (The United States also possesses several territories outside its borders in the Pacific and Caribbean.) Covering some 3,618,768 square miles of territory, the United States is the fourth-largest country in the world. Its 266.48 million residents make its population the third largest in the world, after those of China and India. With a per capita income of $27,500 annually, the United States has the largest gross national product of any nation, more than double that of its nearest rival, Japan. Its health and educational indexes are among the highest in the world; virtually all Americans attend primary and secondary school and most go on to college. About 90 percent of the population has access to safe water, and some 85 percent lives in residences with adequate sanitation. The population has a life expectancy of 75.9 years, up from 70.3 in 1965. The economic power and high standard of living attract numerous immigrants, causing a net migration rate of 3.1 per 1,000 persons in 1995. Still, the country faces enormous problems. Its minorities, consisting of citizens of African and Hispanic descent, earn an average of just two-thirds the income of whites. Overall, the country has one of the most skewed distributions of wealth of any industrialized country. In addition, nearly one-sixth of the country lacks health insurance.

Population Growth

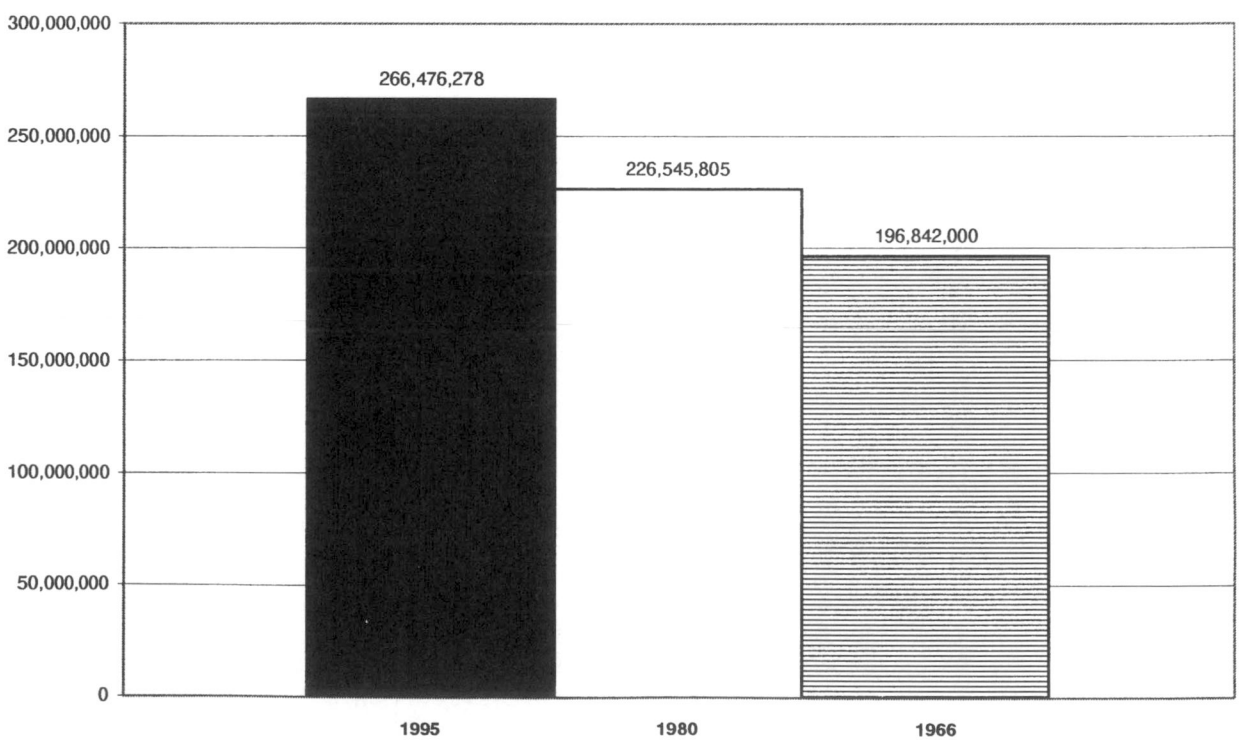

Of the industrialized countries in the world, the United States is practically the only one with a significantly rising population, which has more to do with immigration than with birth rates.

Cars

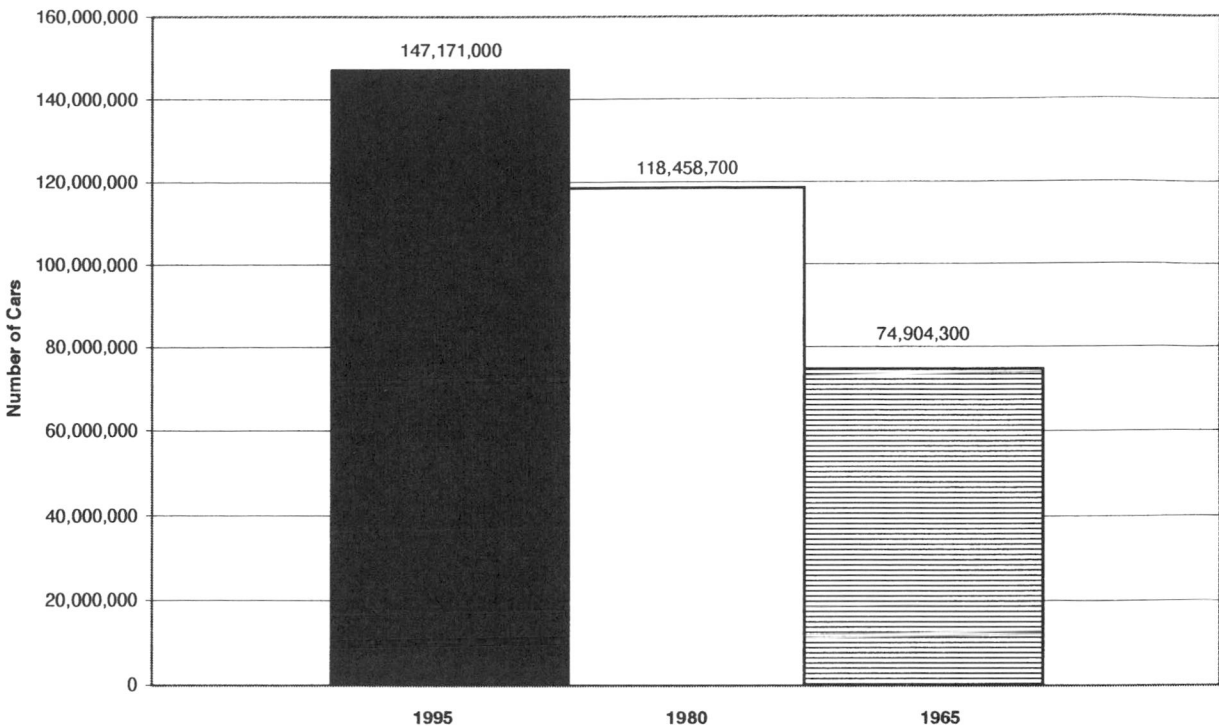

As many third-world countries complain, it is the consumption of first-world countries that remains the greatest threat to the global environment, not rising population levels. The sheer growth of private cars in the United States in the past 30 years would seem to back up that claim.

CHRONOLOGY

1965   United States sends troops to Vietnam.
1968   Civil rights leader Martin Luther King, Jr. is assassinated; Richard Nixon is elected president.
1969   United States puts first man on moon.
1973   War in Vietnam ends for United States.
1974   Nixon forced to resign because of Watergate scandal.
1980   Conservative Ronald Reagan elected president.
1982   Major recession hits economy.
1989   United States military invades Panama.
1991   United States leads allies in driving Iraq from Kuwait.
1992   Democrat Bill Clinton elected president; massive riots hit Los Angeles.
1994   Republicans win control of both houses of Congress for first time in 40 years.

	1995	1980	1965

GEOGRAPHY

AREA (square miles/kilometers)	3,618,768/9,372,610
LAND AREA (square miles/kilometers)	3,539,251/9,166,600
COASTLINE (miles/kilometers)	12,452/19,924

CITIES

CAPITAL	Washington	567,094 (94)
MAJOR CITIES	New York City	7,333,253
	Los Angeles	3,488,613
	Chicago	2,731,743
	Houston	1,702,086
	Philadelphia	1,524,249

POPULATION

	1995	1980	1965
TOTAL	266,476,278	226,545,805	196,842,000 (66)
DENSITY (per square mile/square kilometer)	75/29	64/25	56/21
ANNUAL GROWTH	n/a	1%	n/a
AGE COHORTS			
0–14	22%		31%
15–64	65%		60%
65 AND OVER	13%		9%
MALE	49%		
FEMALE	51%		
URBAN	75.2% (90)	73.7%	
RURAL	24.8%	26.3%	
NET MIGRATION RATE	3.1	n/a	3.2

IDENTITY

ETHNICITY

WHITE	83.4%
BLACK	12.4%
ASIAN	3.3%
NATIVE AMERICAN	0.8%

	1995	1980	1965
LANGUAGE			
ENGLISH	n/a		
SPANISH	n/a		
RELIGION			
PROTESTANT	56%		
ROMAN CATHOLIC	28%		
NONE	10%		
JEWISH	2%		

VITAL STATISTICS

	1995	1980	1965
BIRTHS			
BIRTH RATE	14.8	15.7 (85)	18.5
INFANT MORTALITY RATE	6.7	10.5 (85)	23.4
LIFE EXPECTANCY AT BIRTH	75.9	74.5 (85)	70.3
MARRIAGES			
MARRIAGE RATE	9	10.1 (85)	9.4
DIVORCE RATE	4.6	5 (85)	2.4
DEATHS			
DEATH RATE	8.8	8.7 (85)	9.5

HOUSEHOLDS

	1995	1980	1965
NUMBER	96,931,000 (93)	n/a	53,023,675 (60)
AVERAGE SIZE	2.6	n/a	3.3
TYPES OF HOUSEHOLDS			
FEMALE HEADED	35.9% (94)		
SINGLE	15.1% (92)		
MARRIED	54.8%		
WIDOWED	12.4%		
DIVORCED/SEPARATED	12.8%		

ECONOMICS AND LABOR

	1995
GDP PER CAPITA US$	$27,500
LABOR FORCE M/F (thousands)	66,450/56,610 (94)
AGRICULTURE	2,689/897
MINING	564/105
MANUFACTURING	13,686/6,471

	1995	1980	1965
UTILITIES	1,236/309		
CONSTRUCTION	6,775/718		
TRADE/FOOD/TOURISM	13,564/12,136		
TRANSPORT/COMMUNICATIONS	4,987/2,160		
FINANCE/INSURANCE/REAL ESTATE	6,352/7,213		
SOCIAL AND PERSONAL SERVICES	16,598/26,601		
UNEMPLOYMENT			
TOTAL	6.1% (94)		
UNION DENSITY	12.7%		

TRANSPORT

	1995	1980	1965
JOURNEYS (by transport mode)			
RAILROAD PASSENGER TRIPS	9,529.0 (94)		
(millions of miles/kilometers)			
AIR PASSENGER TRIPS (thousands)	513,756.0 (94)		
VEHICLES (thousands)			
CARS	147,171.0	118,458.70	74,904.3
COMMERCIAL VEHICLES	48,298.0	33,410.60	14,188.2

HEALTH AND HEALTH CARE

	1995	1980	1965
RATE OF PHYSICIANS	2.5	1.8	1.3 (60)
RATE OF HOSPITAL BEDS	4.2	5.9	9.2 (60)
TOTAL DEATHS	2,286,760 (94)		
HEALTH INDICATORS			
LOW-BIRTH-WEIGHT BABIES	7%		
SMOKING PREVALENCE M/F	28/23%		
TUBERCULOSIS INCIDENCE RATE	0.1		
HEALTH CARE			
ACCESS TO SAFE WATER	90%		
ACCESS TO SANITATION	85%		
MEASLES IMMUNIZATION	89%		
AIDS/HIV CASES	513,486	409,409 (93)	

	1995	**1980**	**1965**

EDUCATION

SCHOOL AGE IN SCHOOL

	1995	1980	1965
PRIMARY	102%	99%	104%
SECONDARY	97%	91%	96%
HIGHER	81%	56%	28.4%

FEMALES IN SCHOOL

	1995	1980	
PRIMARY	49%	49%	
SECONDARY	49%	49%	

COMMUNICATIONS

	1995	1980	1965
RATE OF NEWSPAPERS	236	273	310
RATE OF RADIOS	2,120	1,996	1,219
RATE OF TELEVISIONS	816	684	357

Source: CIA, *The World Factbook, 1997;* ILO, *World Labour Report, 1997;* UN, *Demographic Yearbook, 1997;* UN, *Statistical Yearbook, 1996;* World Bank, *World Development Indicators, 1998.*

URUGUAY

Tucked between its two giant neighbors—Brazil to the northeast and Argentina to the west—Uruguay faces onto the Rio de la Plata estuary and the Atlantic Ocean. Covering some 68,039 square miles of territory, Uruguay is dominated by prairies, which help support its vast cattle industry. Despite its vast ranches and farms, over 90 percent of the country's 3.24 million people live in urban areas, most of them in the metropolitan district of Montevideo, the capital. Ethnically dominated by descendants of European settlers, Uruguay has one of the smallest populations of mestizos—mixed white and Indian—in all of Latin America. Most of the country speaks Spanish, though Portuguese is widely understood, and virtually everyone is a member of the Roman Catholic Church. Though strife ridden during much of the 1960s and 1970s, Uruguay has remained prosperous throughout the postwar era. In 1995, its per capita income was $7,600, among the highest in Latin America and arguably the best distributed. The country also has one of the lowest growth rates in the region. In 1995, the population expanded by just 0.7 percent. Its relative prosperity and slow population growth have helped Uruguay achieve some of the best indexes of health and education in Latin America. Its infant mortality rate has fallen from 47.4 to 15.4 per 1,000 live births over the past 30 years, while the percentage of young persons attending secondary school has climbed from 45 to 82 over the same time period.

	1995	1980	1965
GEOGRAPHY			
AREA (square miles/kilometers)	68,039/176,220		
LAND AREA (square miles/kilometers)	67,035/173,620		
COASTLINE (miles/kilometers)	412/660		
CITIES			
CAPITAL	Montevideo 1,360,258 (91)		
POPULATION			
TOTAL	3,238,952	2,788,429 (75)	2,592,563 (63)
DENSITY (per square mile/square kilometer)	48/19	42/16	39/15
ANNUAL GROWTH	0.70%	0.7%	1.4%
AGE COHORTS			
0–14	24%	n/a	28%
15–64	63%	n/a	64%
65 AND OVER	13%	n/a	8%
MALE	49%		
FEMALE	51%		

	1995	**1980**	**1965**
URBAN	90.1%	83.8%	
RURAL	9.9%	16.2%	
NET MIGRATION RATE	−1	n/a	−0.4 (62)

IDENTITY

ETHNICITY

WHITE	88%
MESTIZO	8%
BLACK	4%

LANGUAGE

SPANISH	n/a
BRAZILERO (Portuguese-Spanish mix)	n/a

RELIGION

ROMAN CATHOLIC	66%
PROTESTANT	2%
JEWISH	2%
NONE OR OTHER	30%

VITAL STATISTICS

BIRTHS

BIRTH RATE	17	18.2 (82)	24–25 (63)
INFANT MORTALITY RATE	15.4	29.9	47.4
LIFE EXPECTANCY AT BIRTH	74.9	69	

MARRIAGES

MARRIAGE RATE	6.2	6.8 (82)	7.7 (63)
AVERAGE AGE AT MARRIAGE M/F	n/a	25.2/22.9 (85)	
DIVORCE RATE	3.1	1.3 (82)	0.5 (63)

DEATHS

DEATH RATE	9.1	9.2 (82)	9 (63)

HOUSEHOLDS

NUMBER	n/a	862,962 (85)
AVERAGE SIZE	n/a	3.3

TYPE OF HOUSEHOLD

FEMALE HEADED	23%
SINGLE	10.3%

	1995	1980	1965
MARRIED	62.4%		
WIDOWED	12.6%		
DIVORCED/SEPARATED	7.3%		

ECONOMICS AND LABOR

GDP PER CAPITA US$	$7,600		
LABOR FORCE M/F (thousands)	679.2/476.8 (93)		
AGRICULTURE	40.7/4.5		
MINING	1.9/0.1		
MANUFACTURING	149.2/89.9		
UTILITIES	13.1/2.9		
CONSTRUCTION	80.4/1.7		
TRADE/FOOD/TOURISM	126.5/90.7		
TRANSPORT/COMMUNICATIONS	55.2/9.1		
FINANCE/INSURANCE/REAL ESTATE	38.7/25.5		
SOCIAL AND PERSONAL SERVICES	173.5/252.3		
UNEMPLOYMENT			
TOTAL	8.3% (93)		
UNION DENSITY	11.6%		

TRANSPORT

JOURNEYS (by transport mode)			
RAILROAD PASSENGER TRIPS	140.0 (87)		
(in millions of miles/kilometers			
AIR PASSENGER TRIPS (thousands)	529.0 (94)		
VEHICLES (thousands)			
CARS	425.6	220.4	114
COMMERCIAL VEHICLES	44.4	42.7	82

HEALTH AND HEALTH CARE

RATE OF PHYSICIANS	3.2	n/a	2.1% (60)
RATE OF HOSPITAL BEDS	4.5	n/a	5.3 (60)
TOTAL DEATHS	29,784 (91)		
HEALTH INDICATORS			
PREGNANT WOMEN WITH ANEMIA	20%		
LOW-BIRTH-WEIGHT BABIES	8%		

	1995	1980	1965
CHILD MALNUTRITION	4%		
SMOKING PREVALENCE M/F	41/27%		
TUBERCULOSIS INCIDENCE RATE	0.2%		
HEALTH CARE			
ACCESS TO SAFE WATER	83%		
ACCESS TO SANITATION	82%		
MEASLES IMMUNIZATION	80%		

EDUCATION

	1995	1980	1965
SCHOOL AGE IN SCHOOL			
PRIMARY	111%	107%	116%
SECONDARY	82%	62%	45%
HIGHER	27%	17%	6.30%
FEMALES IN SCHOOL			
PRIMARY	49%	49%	
SECONDARY	58%	55%	
ADULT ILLITERACY M/F	3/2%	6.6/5.7% (75)	9.8/6.3% (63)

COMMUNICATIONS

	1995	1980	1965
RATE OF NEWSPAPERS	240	240	314
RATE OF RADIOS	604	559	351
RATE OF TELEVISIONS	232	126	77

Source: CIA, *The World Factbook, 1997;* ILO, *World Labour Report, 1997;* UN, *Demographic Yearbook, 1997;* UN, *Statistical Yearbook, 1996;* World Bank, *World Development Indicators, 1998.*

UZBEKISTAN[1]

One of the five former Soviet republics of Central Asia, Uzbekistan is bordered by Kazakstan on the west and north, Kyrgyzstan and Tajikistan to the east, and Afghanistan and Turkmenistan to the south. It also shares the shrinking Aral Sea with Kazakstan. Uzbekistan has an ethnically mixed population of 23.42 million. Of the 30 percent of the non-Uzbek population, the largest minorities include Russians, Tajiks, Kazaks, Tatars, and Karakalpaks, in that order. The country is roughly 88 percent Muslim and 9 percent Eastern Orthodox. Like other former Soviet republics, Uzbekistan has experienced a negative net migration rate, as Russians and others flee the economic and political chaos of the region. Still, unlike many of its Central Asian neighbors, Uzbekistan has avoided the worst of the transition to independence, and has avoided civil conflict. The country's economic situation, however, is another story. Since the breakup of the Soviet Union, the per capita income has fallen to just $2,370 annually. Health and educational indexes also lag. Just 18 percent of the population lives in housing with adequate sanitation and just 77 percent of children attend primary school, down from 81 percent in 1980.

	1995	**1980**

GEOGRAPHY

	1995	1980
AREA (square miles/kilometers)	172,741/447,400	
LAND AREA (square miles/kilometers)	164,247/425,400	
COASTLINE (miles/kilometers)	Landlocked	
CITIES		
CAPITAL	Tashkent	2,094,000 (90)
MAJOR CITIES	Chimkent	401,000
	Samarkand	370,000
	Namangan	312,000
	Andizhan	297,000

POPULATION

	1995	1980
TOTAL	23,418,381	
DENSITY (per square mile/square kilometer)	143/55	
ANNUAL GROWTH	1.87%	
AGE COHORTS		
0–14	40%	
15–64	55%	
65 AND OVER	5%	
MALE	49%	
FEMALE	51%	

	1995	1980
URBAN	40.6% (89)	
RURAL	59.4%	
NET MIGRATION RATE	−3.13	

IDENTITY

ETHNICITY

UZBEK	71.4%
RUSSIAN	8.3%
TAJIK	4.7%
KAZAK	4.1%
TATAR	2.4%
KARAKALPAK	2.1%

LANGUAGE

UZBEK	74.3%
RUSSIAN	14.2%
TAJIK	4.4%

RELIGION

MUSLIM	88%
EASTERN ORTHODOX	9%

VITAL STATISTICS

BIRTHS

BIRTH RATE	29.9
INFANT MORTALITY RATE	79.6
LIFE EXPECTANCY AT BIRTH	64.6

MARRIAGES

MARRIAGE RATE	7.8
DIVORCE RATE	1.5

DEATHS

DEATH RATE	8

ECONOMICS AND LABOR

GDP PER CAPITA US$	$2,370

	1995	1980
LABOR FORCE M/F		
AGRICULTURE	34/35%	
INDUSTRY	30/19%	
SERVICES	35/45%	

TRANSPORT

JOURNEYS (by transport mode)
RAILROAD PASSENGER TRIPS   2,217 (94)
  (millions of miles/kilometers)

HEALTH AND HEALTH CARE

	1995	1980
RATE OF PHYSICIANS	3.3	2.9
RATE OF HOSPITAL BEDS	8.7	11.5
TOTAL DEATHS	148,200 (94)	
HEALTH INDICATORS		
CHILD MALNUTRITION	4%	
SMOKING PREVALENCE M/F	40/1%	
TUBERCULOSIS INCIDENCE RATE	0.5	
HEALTH CARE		
ACCESS TO SANITATION	18%	
MEASLES IMMUNIZATION	71%	
AIDS/HIV CASES	3	2 (93)

EDUCATION

	1995	1980
SCHOOL AGE IN SCHOOL		
PRIMARY	77%	81%
SECONDARY	93%	105%
HIGHER	32%	29%
FEMALES IN SCHOOL		
PRIMARY	49%	49%
SECONDARY	48%	46%

	1995	1980

COMMUNICATIONS

RATE OF NEWSPAPERS | 21 |

FOOTNOTE
1. Part of Soviet Union in 1980 and 1965.

Source: CIA, *The World Factbook, 1997;* ILO, *World Labour Report, 1997;* UN, *Demographic Yearbook, 1997;* UN, *Statistical Yearbook, 1996;* World Bank, *World Development Indicators, 1998.*

VANUATU

Consisting of several dozen small and medium-sized islands scattered across roughly 120,000 miles of the South Pacific about 1,500 miles north of New Zealand, Vanuatu has a land area of 5,699 square miles and a population of 177,500 persons. It has a density of 31 persons per square mile. Ruled jointly by Britain and France until 1980, Vanuatu is an ethnically mixed country, dominated by Melanesians, most of whom practice one form of Protestant Christianity or another. With a per capita income of $1,220 annually, Vanuatu appears relatively poor, but many of its citizens exist outside the commercial economy, which is dominated by fishing and tourism. Approximately 80 percent of the people live in rural areas, with much of the urban population located in the capital of Port-Vila.

	1995	1980	1965
GEOGRAPHY			
AREA (square miles/kilometers)	5,699/14,760		
LAND AREA (square miles/kilometers)	5,699/14,760		
COASTLINE (miles/kilometers)	1,580/2,528		
CITIES			
CAPITAL Port-Vila	18,095 (89)		
POPULATION			
TOTAL	177,504	111,251 (79)	
DENSITY (per square mile/square kilometer)	31/12	20/8	
ANNUAL GROWTH	2.17%	4.3%	
AGE COHORTS			
0–14	40%		
15–64	57%		
65 AND OVER	3%		
MALE	52%		
FEMALE	48%		
URBAN	18.4% (89)	17.8%	
RURAL	81.6%	82.2%	
NET MIGRATION RATE	0		

	1995	**1980**	**1965**

IDENTITY

ETHNICITY
INDIGENOUS MELANESIAN	94%		
FRENCH	4%		
VIETNAMESE	n/a		
CHINESE	n/a		
PACIFIC ISLANDER	n/a		

LANGUAGE
ENGLISH	n/a		
FRENCH	n/a		
BISLAMA (Pidgin)	n/a		

RELIGION
PRESBYTERIAN	36.7%		
ANGLICAN	15%		
CATHOLIC	15%		
INDIGENOUS	7.6%		
SEVENTH-DAY ADVENT	6.2%		
CHURCH OF CHRIST	3.8%		

VITAL STATISTICS

BIRTHS
BIRTH RATE	30.6	n/a	45
INFANT MORTALITY RATE	64.6		
LIFE EXPECTANCY AT BIRTH	60.1		

MARRIAGES
AVERAGE AGE AT MARRIAGE M/F	25.3/22.6 (89)		

DEATHS
DEATH RATE	8.8	n/a	20

HOUSEHOLDS

NUMBER	28,252 (89)		
AVERAGE SIZE	5		

ECONOMICS AND LABOR

GDP PER CAPITA US$	$1,220		

	1995	1980	1965

TRANSPORT

JOURNEYS (by transport mode)

AIR PASSENGER TRIPS (thousands)	70.0 (94)		

VEHICLES

PRIVATE CARS	4.0 (93)	2.3	
COMMERCIAL VEHICLES	2.3	0.9	

HEALTH AND HEALTH CARE

RATE OF PHYSICIANS	n/a	n/a	0.3 (60)
RATE OF HOSPITAL BEDS	n/a	n/a	8.3 (60)

EDUCATION

ADULT ILLITERACY M/F	n/a	42.7/52.2% (79)	

COMMUNICATIONS

RATE OF RADIOS	292	197	120 (70)
RATE OF TELEVISIONS	12	0	0

Source: CIA, *The World Factbook, 1997;* ILO, *World Labour Report, 1997;* UN, *Demographic Yearbook, 1997;* UN, *Statistical Yearbook, 1996;* World Bank, *World Development Indicators, 1998.*

VENEZUELA

Venezuela is located at the northern end of South America, bordered by Guyana to the east, Brazil to the south and Colombia to the west. It has an extensive, 1,750-mile coastline along the Caribbean Sea, to the north. Its population was 21.98 million in 1995, having almost tripled in size from 7.52 million in 1965. The rapid rate of population growth has slowed somewhat over the past three decades. While the growth rate was 3.6 percent in 1965, that figure had dropped to 2.3 percent by 1995. At the same time, the percentage of the population under the age of 15 had declined from 46 percent to 35 percent. Venezuela is an ethnically mixed country, with one of the largest populations of people of African descent in all of Spanish-speaking Latin America. About 84 percent of the population is urban, and the country has a density of 65 persons per square mile. Most of the residents live in the northern third of the country, the southern part being dominated by thick rainforest. Venezuela has the highest per capita income in Latin America, at $9,300 annually. But this figure is distorted by the fact that the country remains the largest oil producer in South America. In fact, wealth is badly distributed and nearly one-third of the population subsists on incomes of $2 or less daily. The great wealth and poverty of the country can be seen by comparing private car ownership and sanitary housing rates. While the number of the former has grown from 384,900 in 1965 to 1,579,000 in 1995, the number of people living in homes with adequate sanitation is still below 60 percent.

Divorce Rates

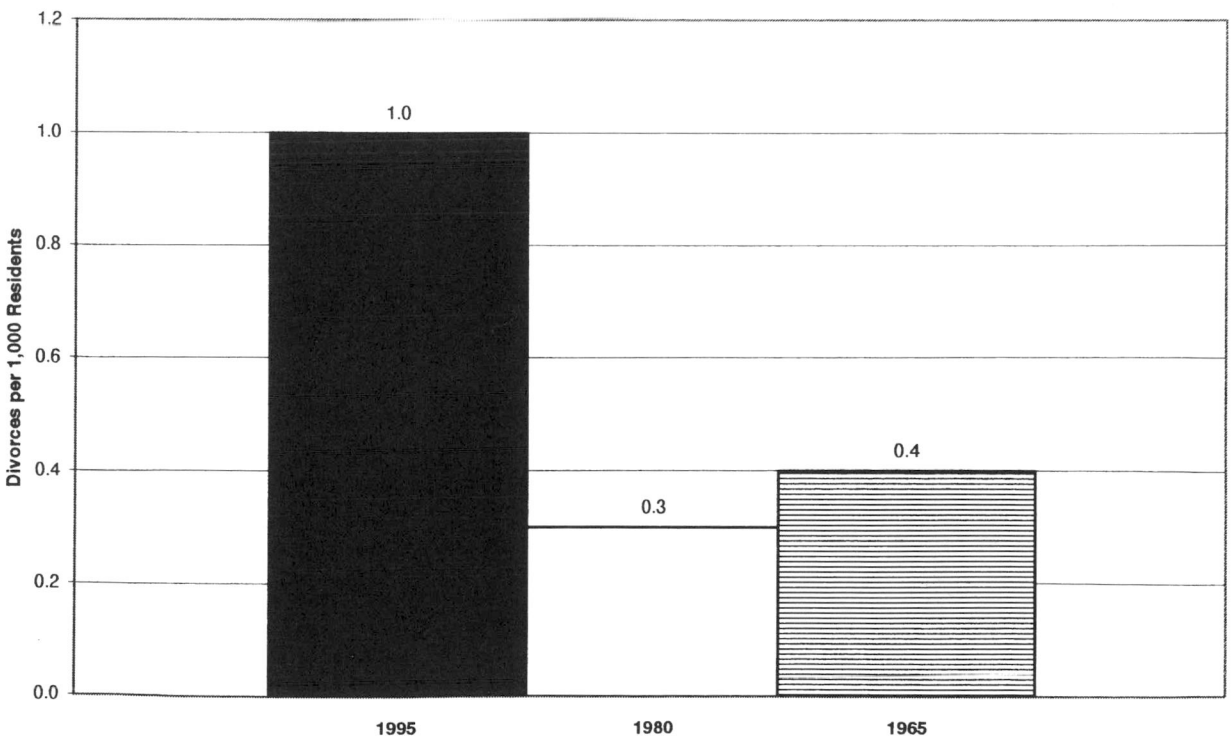

Urbanization and modernization tend to have strong effects on traditional values. A predominantly conservative Roman Catholic country, Venezuela has nevertheless seen its divorce rate triple over the past the past 30 years.

Poverty

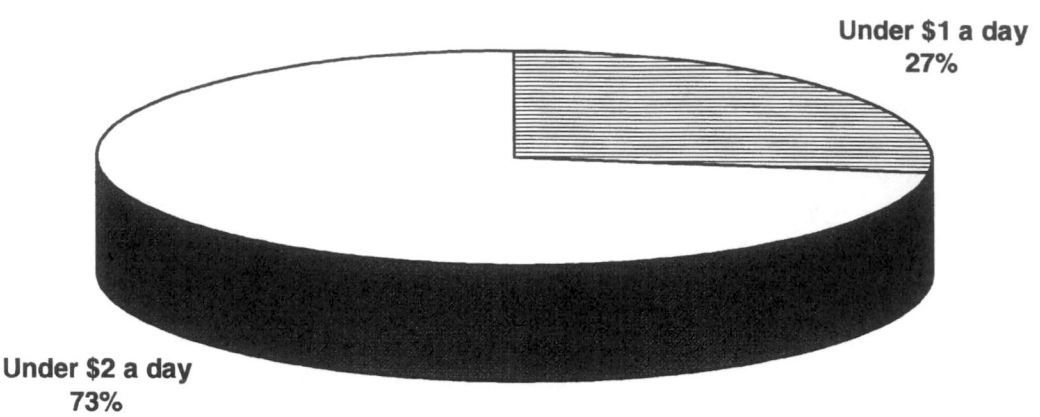

**Under $1 a day
27%**

**Under $2 a day
73%**

Though it is the largest oil producer in South America, Venezuela suffers from gross inequalities in wealth. Thus, while its per capita income is relatively high at $9,300 annually, significant portions of its population live in poverty and extreme poverty as defined by the United Nations.

CHRONOLOGY

1969   Leftist Rafael Caldera elected president; legalizes Communist Party; establishes relations with Moscow.

1974   Rise in oil prices quadruples government revenues.

1976   Venezuela nationalizes 21 oil companies.

1978   Conservative Luis Herrera elected president.

1988   Carlos Andres Perez reelected to presidency after being out of power for 10 years.

1993   Perez forced to resign under threat of impeachment for corruption.

1994   Half of country's banking sector collapses.

1995   Price increases of 20 percent lead to nationwide rioting.

	1995	1980	1965

GEOGRAPHY

AREA (square miles/kilometers) — 352,143/912,050
LAND AREA (square miles/kilometers) — 340,560/882,050
COASTLINE (miles/kilometers) — 1,750/2,800

CITIES

CAPITAL	Caracas	1,964,846		
MAJOR CITIES	Maracaibo	1,207,513 (90)		
	Valencia	1,034,033 (92)		
	Barquisimeto	692,599 (92)		
	Ciudad Guayana	523,578 (92)		

POPULATION

	1995	1980	1965
TOTAL	21,983,188	14,516,735 (81)	7,523,999 (61)
DENSITY (per square mile/square kilometer)	65/25	43/16	22/9
ANNUAL GROWTH	2.30%	2.9%	3.6%

AGE COHORTS

	1995	1980	1965
0–14	35%	n/a	46% (66)
15–64	61%	n/a	51%
65 AND OVER	4%	n/a	3%

	1995	1980	1965
MALE	50%		
FEMALE	50%		

	1995	1980	1965
URBAN	84.1% 90	76.10%	
RURAL	15.90%	23.90%	

	1995	1980	1965
NET MIGRATION RATE	−0.4	n/a	0.2 (64)

IDENTITY

ETHNICITY

	1995	1980	1965
MESTIZO	67%		
WHITE	21%		
BLACK	10%		
AMERINDIAN	2%		

LANGUAGE

	1995	1980	1965
SPANISH	n/a		
AMERINDIAN	n/a		

	1995	1980	1965
RELIGION			
ROMAN CATHOLIC	96%		
PROTESTANT	2%		

VITAL STATISTICS

	1995	1980	1965
BIRTHS			
BIRTH RATE	24.4	33	46–48
INFANT MORTALITY RATE	29.5	39	47.7
LIFE EXPECTANCY AT BIRTH	72.1	67.7	n/a
MARRIAGES			
MARRIAGE RATE	5.4	5.6	5.7
DIVORCE RATE	1	0.4	0.3
DEATHS			
DEATH RATE	5.1	5.5	9

HOUSEHOLDS

	1995	1980	1965
NUMBER	n/a	n/a	1,343,426 (61)
AVERAGE SIZE	n/a	n/a	5.3

ECONOMICS AND LABOR

GDP PER CAPITA US$	$9,300

LABOR FORCE M/F (thousands)	4,815.6/2,219.3 (93)
AGRICULTURE	719.8/36.3
MINING	60.4/8.8
MANUFACTURING	794.9/295.5
UTILITIES	47.2/9.7
CONSTRUCTION	611.5/25.0
TRADE/FOOD/TOURISM	989.1/576.6
TRANSPORT/COMMUNICATIONS	415.6/46.4
FINANCE/INSURANCE/REAL ESTATE	273.5/186.2
SOCIAL AND PERSONAL SERVICES	900.1/1,033.1

UNEMPLOYMENT	
TOTAL	6.4 (93)

UNION DENSITY	14.9%

	1995	**1980**	**1965**
POVERTY			
UNDER $1/DAY	11.8% (91)		
UNDER $2/DAY	32.2%		

TRANSPORT

	1995	**1980**	**1965**
JOURNEYS (by transport mode)			
RAILROAD PASSENGER TRIPS	44.0 (93)		
(millions of miles/kilometers)			
AIR PASSENGER TRIPS (thousands)	5,267.0 (94)		
VEHICLES (thousands)			
CARS	1,579	1,501.80	384.9
COMMERCIAL VEHICLES	460	718.3	165.9

HEALTH CARE

	1995	**1980**	**1965**
RATE OF PHYSICIANS	1.6	0.8	0.7 (60)
RATE OF HOSPITAL BEDS	2.6	0.3	3.5 (60)
TOTAL DEATHS	90,566 (92)		
HEALTH INDICATORS			
PREGNANT WOMEN WITH ANEMIA	29%		
LOW-BIRTH-WEIGHT BABIES	9%		
CHILD MALNUTRITION	5%		
TUBERCULOSIS INCIDENCE RATE	0.4		
HEALTH CARE			
ACCESS TO SAFE WATER	79%		
ACCESS TO SANITATION	58%		
MEASLES IMMUNIZATION	94%		
AIDS/HIV CASES	4,960	3,989 (93)	

EDUCATION

	1995	**1980**	**1965**
SCHOOL AGE IN SCHOOL			
PRIMARY	94%	93%	95%
SECONDARY	35%	21%	30%
HIGHER	29%	21%	5.3%
FEMALES IN SCHOOL			
PRIMARY	50%	50%	95%
SECONDARY	58%	43%	29%

	1995	**1980**	**1965**
ADULT ILLITERACY M/F	8/10%	13.5/17.0% (81)	32/41.6% (61)

COMMUNICATIONS

	1995	1980	1965
RATE OF NEWSPAPERS	205	195	70
RATE OF RADIOS	443	391	221
RATE OF TELEVISIONS	163	113	86

Source: CIA, *The World Factbook, 1997;* ILO, *World Labour Report, 1997;* UN, *Demographic Yearbook, 1997;* UN, *Statistical Yearbook, 1996;* World Bank, *World Development Indicators, 1998.*

VIETNAM

A long, narrow, S-shaped country on the coast of Southeast Asia, Vietnam is bordered by China on the north and by Laos and Cambodia to the west. Covering some 127,243 square miles of territory—roughly the size of New Mexico—Vietnam has a population of 73.98 million, most of whom live in the Red River valley of the north and the Mekong River delta of the south. Indeed, this bifurcated population pattern helps to explain the country's troubled history. Conquered by the French in the late nineteenth century, the northern half of Vietnam was able to win its independence after an 8-year-long anticolonial war in 1954. Expecting to be reunited shortly after, the communist northern half of the country soon went to war against the U.S.-supported, anticommunist southern half. By 1968, more than a half million U.S. troops were fighting indigenous South Vietnamese communists and North Vietnamese regulars. With the United States having pulled out by 1973, North Vietnam was able to unify the country militarily in 1975. This, however, did not bring peace, as a reunified Vietnam soon fought wars with China and Cambodia, which it invaded in the late 1970s. Altogether, the wars have cost the country greatly. While its Southeast Asian neighbors have prospered in recent years, Vietnam has lagged behind. Its per capita income of $1,300 annually is among the lowest in Asia.

Infant Mortality Rates

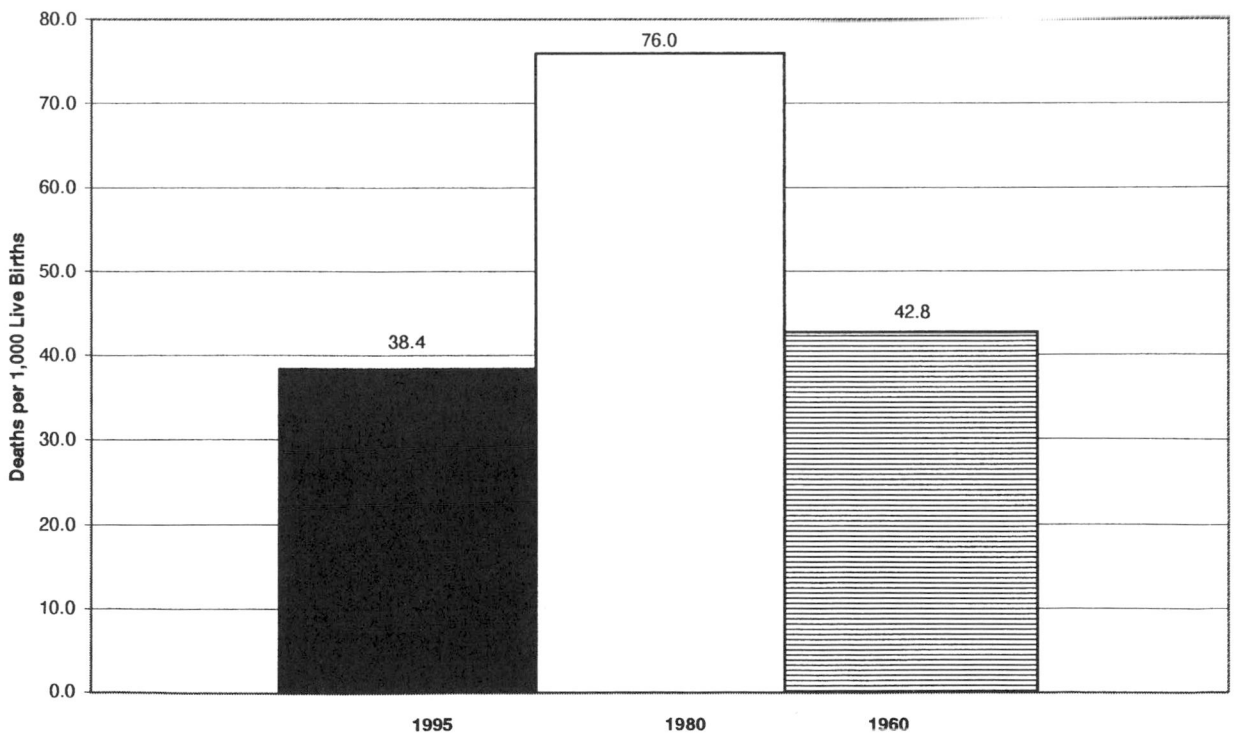

The Second Indochina War—or the Vietnam War, as Americans called it—had a significant impact on the country's ability to deal with social problems. For example, the infant mortality rate rose significantly between 1965 and 1980, during the heaviest period of U.S. involvement. It then fell off again during the postwar period.

Work Force

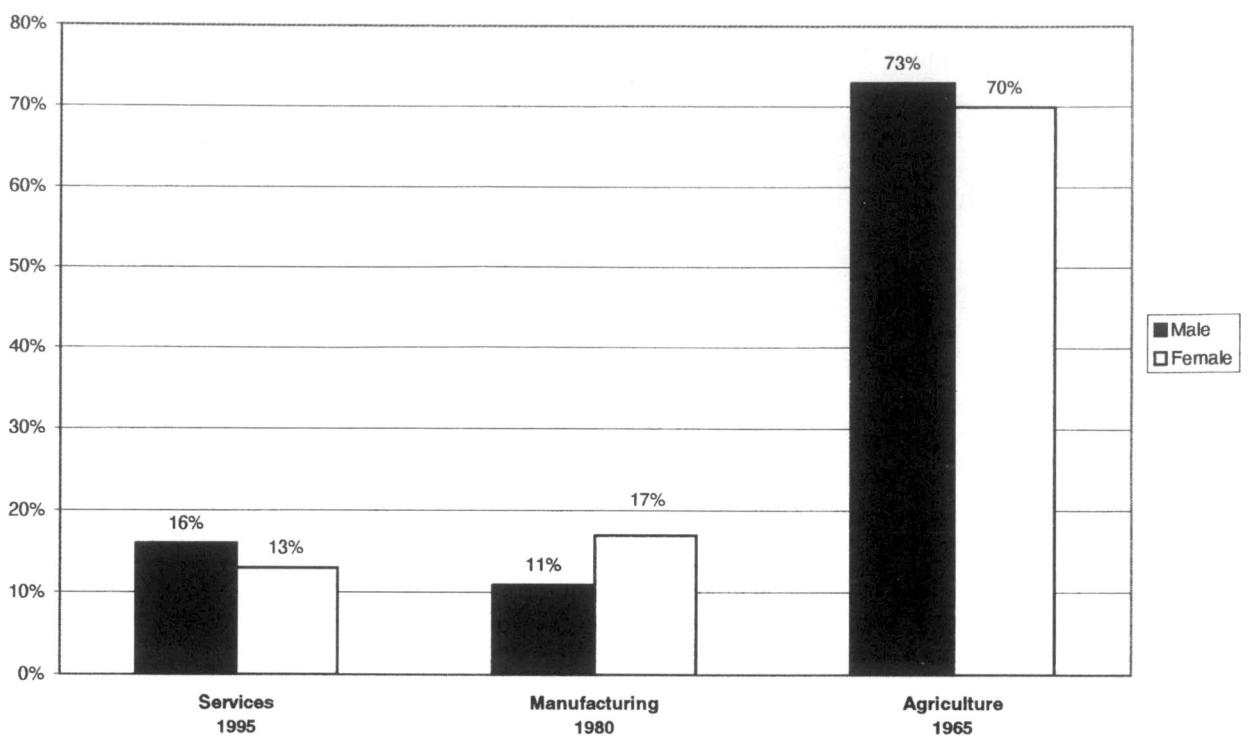

The near constant state of war in Vietnam from the end of World War II until about 1980 has retarded the economic growth of the country. While many of its neighbors have shifted to a more manufacturing-oriented economic base, Vietnam has remained primarily rural and agricultural.

CHRONOLOGY

1963   South Vietnam president Ngo Dinh Diem is overthrown and executed in United States-backed military coup.

1965   First U.S. troops arrive to support South Vietnam against communist Viet Cong guerrillas and North Vietnamese military.

1968   U.S. troop level hits 550,000; Tet offensive throws United States and South Vietnam off balance.

1969   United States begins troop withdrawal; North Vietnamese leader Ho Chi Minh dies.

1973   North Vietnam and United States sign peace treaty, ending U.S. involvement.

1975   South Vietnam falls in North Vietnamese invasion.

1978   Vietnam and China engage in border war.

1979   Vietnam invades Cambodia and overthrows Pol Pot regime.

1986   Government launches market reforms.

1994   United States lifts embargo against Vietnam.

1995   United States and Vietnam re-establish full diplomatic relations.

	1995	**1980**	**1965**

GEOGRAPHY

AREA (square miles/kilometers)	127,243/329,560			
LAND AREA (square miles/kilometers)	125,622/325,360			
COASTLINE (miles/kilometers)	2,152/3,444			

CITIES				
CAPITAL	Hanoi	1,073,760 (92)		
MAJOR CITIES	Ho Chi Minh City (Saigon)	3,015,743		
	Haiphong	783,133		
	Da Nang	382,674		
	Buon Ma Thuot	282,095		

POPULATION

	1995	**1980**	**1965**
TOTAL	73,976,973	52,741,766 (79)	n/a
DENSITY (per square mile/square kilometer)	589/227	412/162	
ANNUAL GROWTH	1.57%	2%	

AGE COHORTS			
0–14	36%		n/a
15–64	59%		n/a
65 AND OVER	5%		n/a

MALE	49%		
FEMALE	51%		

URBAN	19.5% (94)		
RURAL	80.5%		

NET MIGRATION RATE	−0.35		

IDENTITY

ETHNICITY			
VIETNAMESE	85–90%		
CHINESE	3%		
MUONG	n/a		
THAI	n/a		
MEO	n/a		
KHMER	n/a		
MAN	n/a		
CHAM	n/a		

	1995	1980	1965
LANGUAGE			
VIETNAMESE	n/a		
FRENCH	n/a		
CHINESE	n/a		
ENGLISH	n/a		
KHMER	n/a		
RELIGION			
BUDDHIST	n/a		
TAOIST	n/a		
ROMAN CATHOLIC	n/a		
INDIGENOUS	n/a		
ISLAM	n/a		
PROTESTANT	n/a		

VITAL STATISTICS

	1995	1980	1965
BIRTHS			
BIRTH RATE	23	31	35 (60)
INFANT MORTALITY RATE	38.4	76	42.8 (60)
LIFE EXPECTANCY AT BIRTH	67	58.9	
MARRIAGES			
MARRIAGE RATE	n/a	n/a	4 (60)
AVERAGE AGE AT MARRIAGE M/F	24.4/23.1 (89)		
DEATHS			
DEATH RATE	7	10.2	18 (60)

HOUSEHOLDS

NUMBER	12,958,041 (89)
AVERAGE SIZE	4.8

ECONOMICS AND LABOR

GDP PER CAPITA US$	$1,300

	1995	1980	1965
LABOR FORCE M/F			
AGRICULTURE	70/73%		
INDUSTRY	17/11%		
SERVICES	13/16%		

TRANSPORT

	1995	1980	1965
JOURNEYS (by transport mode)			
RAILROAD PASSENGER TRIPS	211 (94)		
(millions of miles/kilometers)			

HEALTH AND HEALTH CARE

	1995	1980	1965
RATE OF PHYSICIANS	0.4	0.2	
RATE OF HOSPITAL BEDS	3.8	3.5	
HEALTH INDICATORS			
PREGNANT WOMEN WITH ANEMIA	52%		
LOW-BIRTH-WEIGHT BABIES	17%		
CHILD MALNUTRITION	45%		
SMOKING PREVALENCE M/F	73/4%		
TUBERCULOSIS INCIDENCE RATE	1.6		
HEALTH CARE			
ACCESS TO SAFE WATER	36%		
ACCESS TO SANITATION	21%		
MEASLES IMMUNIZATION	95%		
AIDS/HIV CASES	315	108 (93)	

EDUCATION

	1995	1980	1965
SCHOOL AGE IN SCHOOL			
PRIMARY	114%	109%	
SECONDARY	47%	42%	
HIGHER	4%	2%	
FEMALES IN SCHOOL			
PRIMARY	n/a	47%	
SECONDARY	n/a	47%	
ADULT ILLITERACY M/F	9/4%	9.5/21.7% (79)	

	1995	1980	1965
COMMUNICATIONS			
RATE OF NEWSPAPERS	8	10	42
RATE OF RADIOS	104	93	
RATE OF TELEVISIONS	42	33 (85)	

Source: CIA, *The World Factbook, 1997;* ILO, *World Labour Report, 1997;* UN, *Demographic Yearbook, 1997;* UN, *Statistical Yearbook, 1996;* World Bank, *World Development Indicators, 1998.*

(WESTERN) SAMOA

Located on two small islands in the southwestern Pacific Ocean, about 2,000 miles to the northeast of New Zealand, Samoa has a land area of 1,104 square miles and a population of 214,384, making for a population density of 155 persons per square mile. The population is over 90 percent Samoan, a Polynesian ethnicity, with a minority of Euronesians—mixed European and Polynesian persons—and Europeans. This is a relatively healthy country; Samoans have a life expectancy of 68.7 years and an infant mortality rate of 34.3 per 1,000 live births. The per capita income of the island is $1,900, and the economy is largely dependent on fishing and tourism. Samoa won its independence from a New Zealand–administered U.N. trusteeship in 1962. The other half of the Samoan islands, American Samoa, remains a territory of the United States.

	1995	1980	1965
GEOGRAPHY			
AREA (square miles/kilometers)	1,104/2,860		
LAND AREA (square miles/kilometers)	1,100/2,850		
COASTLINE (miles/kilometers)	252/403		
CITIES			
CAPITAL	Apia	n/a	
POPULATION			
TOTAL	214,384	n/a	131,380
DENSITY (per square mile/square kilometer)	195/75	n/a	119/40
ANNUAL GROWTH	2.37%	n/a	2.8%
AGE COHORTS			
0–14	40%	n/a	50% (61)
15–64	56%	n/a	47%
65 AND OVER	4%	n/a	3%
NET MIGRATION RATE	−1.67		

	1995	1980	1965

IDENTITY

ETHNICITY
SAMOAN	92.6%		
EURONESIAN (European and Polynesian)	7%		
EUROPEANS	0.4%		

LANGUAGE
SAMOAN (Polynesian)	n/a		
ENGLISH	n/a		

RELIGION
CHRISTIAN	99.7%		

VITAL STATISTICS

BIRTHS
BIRTH RATE	31.1		
INFANT MORTALITY RATE	34.3		
LIFE EXPECTANCY AT BIRTH	68.7		

DEATHS
DEATH RATE	5.8		

HOUSEHOLDS

	1995	1980	1965
NUMBER	n/a	n/a	19,349 (61)
AVERAGE SIZE	n/a	n/a	5.8

ECONOMICS AND LABOR

	1995	1980	1965
GDP PER CAPITA US$	$1,900		

TRANSPORT

VEHICLES
PRIVATE CARS	5 (93)		
COMMERCIAL VEHICLES	1.8		

	1995	1980	1965
EDUCATION			
SCHOOL AGE IN SCHOOL			
PRIMARY	n/a	n/a	81% (67)
SECONDARY	n/a	n/a	30%
HIGHER	n/a	n/a	0.2%
FEMALES IN SCHOOL			
PRIMARY	n/a	n/a	79%
SECONDARY	n/a	n/a	29%
HIGHER	n/a	n/a	
ADULT ILLITERACY M/F	n/a	n/a	2.6/2.5%
COMMUNICATIONS			
RATE OF RADIOS	183	169	107
RATE OF TELEVISIONS	21	18	n/a

Source: CIA, *The World Factbook, 1997*; ILO, *World Labour Report, 1997*; UN, *Demographic Yearbook, 1997*; UN, *Statistical Yearbook, 1996*; World Bank, *World Development Indicators, 1998*.

YEMEN[1]

Once divided into a communist-dominated South Yemen and an anticommunist North Yemen, Yemen as a single political entity emerged with an accord of unity in 1990. Located on the southwestern corner of the Arabian Peninsula, Yemen covers an area of 203,849 square miles—making it roughly twice the size of Colorado—and has a population of 13.48 million. The population is expanding rapidly, with an annual growth rate of 3.6 percent annually in the mid-1990s. The percentage of the population under the age of 15 is 48 percent, promising rapid growth for the near-term future. A mountainous, desert country, Yemen is quite poor, with a per capita income of just $2,520 annually, a reflection of the fact that, unlike its Arabian Peninsula neighbors, Yemen has only moderate oil reserves. Thus, its economy remains largely agricultural, with well over half the workforce involved in farming and pasturage. At the same time, its health and health care indexes are quite poor. Nearly 20 percent of all babies are born underweight, and nearly one-third of all children under the age of 5 suffer from malnutrition. Only about half the population has access to safe water or live in houses with adequate sanitation. Similarly, Yemen has a low educational participation rate, with just 23 percent of all young persons attending secondary school.

1995

GEOGRAPHY

AREA (square miles/kilometers)	203,849/527,970
LAND AREA (square miles/kilometers)	203,849/527,970
COASTLINE (miles/kilometers)	1,190/1,906

CITIES

CAPITAL	Sanaa	926,595 (93)
MAJOR CITIES	Aden	400,783
	Taiz	290,107
	Hodeidah	246,068

POPULATION

TOTAL	13,483,178
DENSITY (per square mile/square kilometer)	66/26
ANNUAL GROWTH	3.56%

AGE COHORTS

0–14	48%
15–64	50%
65 AND OVER	2%

	1995
URBAN	26.4% (94)
RURAL	73.6%
NET MIGRATION RATE	0

IDENTITY

ETHNICITY
ARAB	n/a
AFRO-ARAB	n/a
SOUTH ASIAN	n/a
EUROPEAN	n/a

LANGUAGE
ARABIC	n/a

RELIGION
MUSLIM (Sha'fi, Sunni, and Shi'a)	n/a
JEWISH	n/a
CHRISTIAN	n/a
HINDU	n/a

VITAL STATISTICS

BIRTHS
BIRTH RATE	45.2
INFANT MORTALITY RATE	71.5
LIFE EXPECTANCY AT BIRTH	59.6

DEATHS
DEATH RATE	9.6

ECONOMICS AND LABOR

GDP PER CAPITA US$	$2,520

LABOR FORCE M/F
AGRICULTURE	50/88%
INDUSTRY	22/6%
SERVICES	29/7%

1995

TRANSPORT

JOURNEYS (by transport mode)
RAILROAD PASSENGER TRIPS   791.0 (94)
  (millions of miles/kilometers)

VEHICLES
PRIVATE CARS   176.1 (93)
COMMERCIAL VEHICLES   256.7

HEALTH AND HEALTH CARE

RATE OF PHYSICIANS   0.1
RATE OF HOSPITAL BEDS   0.8

HEALTH INDICATORS
LOW-BIRTH-WEIGHT BABIES   19%
CHILD MALNUTRITION   30%
TUBERCULOSIS INCIDENCE RATE   0.9

HEALTH CARE
ACCESS TO SAFE WATER   52%
ACCESS TO SANITATION   51%
MEASLES IMMUNIZATION   49%

AIDS/HIV CASES   22

EDUCATION

SCHOOL AGE IN SCHOOL
PRIMARY   79%
SECONDARY   23%
HIGHER   4%

FEMALES IN SCHOOL
PRIMARY   28%

1995

COMMUNICATIONS

RATE OF NEWSPAPERS	6/13 (90)
RATE OF RADIOS	30
RATE OF TELEVISIONS	28

FOOTNOTE
1. Yemen was divided between North Yemen and South Yemen in 1980 and 1965.

Source: CIA, *The World Factbook, 1997;* ILO, *World Labour Report, 1997;* UN, *Demographic Yearbook, 1997;* UN, *Statistical Yearbook, 1996;* World Bank, *World Development Indicators, 1998.*

ZAMBIA

Located in south-central Africa, Zambia is bordered by the Democratic Republic of the Congo to the north; Tanzania and Malawi to the east; Mozambique, Zimbabwe, and Namibia to the south; and Angola to the west. Originally called Northern Rhodesia under the British, Zambia won its independence in 1964. Ruled by the conservative president Kenneth Kaunda until the early 1990s, the country of 290,583 square miles—roughly the size of Texas—has avoided the political and ethnic strife that has plagued most of its neighbors in recent decades. Reliant on revenues from the country's vast copper mines, Kaunda tried to establish a system of cooperative farms and industries, but this program produced economic chaos. Following his fall from power, Kaunda was hounded by the democratically elected government that succeeded him, which feared that he was plotting to return to power. Zambia has a population of 9.16 million, up from 3.50 million in 1965. Though it has almost tripled in population over the past 30 years, its growth rate has slowed from 3 percent annually in 1965 to 2.1 percent in 1995. Still, some 49 percent of the population was under the age of 15 in the latter year, promising continued population growth into the near-term future. As noted above, Zambia's economy is dominated by mining. Of the roughly 360,000-strong workforce—in the commercial economy—approximately 15 percent labor in the mines. The country's per capita income had fallen to just $900 by 1995, significantly below that of the 1970s, largely as a consequence of falling prices for copper on the world market.

	1995	1980	1965
GEOGRAPHY			
AREA (square miles/kilometers)	290,583/752,610		
LAND AREA (square miles/kilometers)	285,992/740,720		
COASTLINE (miles/kilometers)	Landlocked		
CITIES			
CAPITAL	Lusaka	982,362 (90)	498,837
MAJOR CITIES	Ndola	376,311	250,490
	Kitwe	338,207	283,962
	Kabwe	166,519	127,422
	Chingola	162,954	130,872
POPULATION			
TOTAL	9,159,072	5,679,808	3,495,400 (63)
DENSITY (per square mile/square kilometer)	32/12	20/8	12/5
ANNUAL GROWTH	2.11%	2.7%	3%

	1995	1980	1965
AGE COHORTS			
0–14	49%		
15–64	48%		
65 AND OVER	3%		
MALE	49%		
FEMALE	51%		
URBAN	39.4% (90)	40.4%	
RURAL	60.6%	59.6%	
NET MIGRATION RATE	0	n/a	0.12

IDENTITY

ETHNICITY			
AFRICAN	98.7%		
EUROPEAN	1.1%		
LANGUAGE			
ENGLISH	n/a		
BEMBA, KAONDA, LOZI, LUNDA	n/a		
LUVALE, NYANJA, TONGA	n/a		
OTHER INDIGENOUS LANGUAGES	n/a		
RELIGION			
CHRISTIAN	n/a		
MUSLIM	n/a		
HINDU	n/a		
INDIGENOUS	n/a		

VITAL STATISTICS

BIRTHS			
BIRTH RATE	44.7	48.1	51.4
INFANT MORTALITY RATE	96.1	259	259
LIFE EXPECTANCY AT BIRTH	36.3	51.4	40
MARRIAGES			
AVERAGE AGE AT MARRIAGE M/F	25.9/21.2 (90)		
DEATHS			
DEATH RATE	23.6	15.1	19.6

	1995	1980	1965

HOUSEHOLDS

NUMBER	1,327,098 (90)		
AVERAGE SIZE	5.6		

TYPE OF HOUSEHOLD			
FEMALE HEADED	16.9%		
SINGLE	4.6%		
MARRIED	71.7%		
WIDOWED	6.9%		
DIVORCED/SEPARATED	8.7%		

ECONOMICS AND LABOR

GDP PER CAPITA US$	$900		

LABOR FORCE (thousands)	359.6 (89)		
AGRICULTURE	37.2		
MINING	54.2		
MANUFACTURING	50.9		
UTILITIES	8.7		
CONSTRUCTION	20.8		
TRADE/FOOD/TOURISM	26.6		
TRANSPORT/COMMUNICATIONS	26.1		
FINANCE/INSURANCE/REAL ESTATE	24.7		
SOCIAL AND PERSONAL SERVICES	110.2		

POVERTY			
UNDER $1/DAY	84.6% (93)		
UNDER $2/DAY	98.1%		

TRANSPORT

JOURNEYS (by transport mode)			
RAILROAD PASSENGER TRIPS	596.0 (89)		
(millions of miles/kilometers)			
AIR PASSENGER TRIPS (thousands)	235.0 (94)		

VEHICLES (thousands)			
CARS	96	68.7	43.7
COMMERCIAL VEHICLES	68	31.1	11.4

	1995	1980	1965
HEALTH AND HEALTH CARE			
RATE OF PHYSICIANS	0.1	0.1	0.1 (60)
RATE OF HOSPITAL BEDS	n/a	3.5	2.7 (60)
HEALTH INDICATORS			
PREGNANT WOMEN WITH ANEMIA	34%		
LOW-BIRTH-WEIGHT BABIES	13%		
CHILD MALNUTRITION	29%		
SMOKING PREVALENCE M/F	39/7%		
TUBERCULOSIS INCIDENCE RATE	3.4		
HEALTH CARE			
ACCESS TO SAFE WATER	43%		
ACCESS TO SANITATION	23%		
MEASLES IMMUNIZATION	78%		
AIDS/HIV CASES	34,000	32,308 (93)	
EDUCATION			
SCHOOL AGE IN SCHOOL			
PRIMARY	89%	90%	56%
SECONDARY	28%	16%	5%
HIGHER	3%	2%	0%
FEMALES IN SCHOOL			
PRIMARY	48%	47	49%
SECONDARY	38%	35	3%
ADULT ILLITERACY M/F	14/29%	15.8/32.6% (85)	
COMMUNICATIONS			
RATE OF NEWSPAPERS	8	19	7
RATE OF RADIOS	82	24	
RATE OF TELEVISIONS	27	10	

Source: CIA, *The World Factbook, 1997;* ILO, *World Labour Report, 1997;* UN, *Demographic Yearbook, 1997;* UN, *Statistical Yearbook, 1996;* World Bank, *World Development Indicators, 1998.*

ZIMBABWE

Formerly known as Rhodesia, Zimbabwe—a nation of 150,803 square miles—unilaterally declared its independence from Britain in 1965. From that year until 1979, the country was ruled by a white minority regime, much like that in apartheid South Africa to the south. During most of that time, members of the black majority fought a guerrilla war to overthrow the regime, leading eventually to a British-brokered peace settlement in 1979 and the election of the main guerilla leader—Robert Mugabe—to the presidency in the following year. Zimbabwe's 11.27 million citizens are moderately prosperous, with a per capita income of $1,620 annually, though this figure is distorted by the fact that the nation's quarter-million-strong white population have incomes comparable to first-world levels. Largely reliant on commercial agriculture and tourism for income, the country provides modest social services for its citizens, a fact reflected in the relatively high indexes for health and education. About three-quarters of the population has access to safe water, and a similar percentage of children are immunized against measles. Virtually all children also attend primary school and about half go on to secondary institutions.

	1995	1980	1965
GEOGRAPHY			
AREA (square miles/kilometers)	150,803/390,580		
LAND AREA (square miles/kilometers)	149,293/386,670		
COASTLINE (miles/kilometers)	Landlocked		
CITIES			
CAPITAL	Harare	1,189,103 (92)	
MAJOR CITIES	Bulawayo	621,742	
	Chitungwiza	274,912	
POPULATION			
TOTAL	11,271,314	7,550,000 (82)	
DENSITY (per square mile/square kilometer)	75/29	51/20	
ANNUAL GROWTH	1.41%	3.1%	
AGE COHORTS			
0–14	44%		
15–64	53%		
65 AND OVER	3%		
MALE	49%		
FEMALE	51%		

	1995	1980	1965
URBAN	n/a	19.3%	
RURAL	n/a	81.7%	
NET MIGRATION	n/a		

IDENTITY

ETHNICITY

AFRICAN (Shona, Nedebele, other)	98%		
WHITE	1%		
MIXED AND ASIAN	1%		

LANGUAGE

ENGLISH	n/a		
SHONA	n/a		
SINDEBELE	n/a		

RELIGION

SYNCRETIC (Christian/indigenous)	n/a		
CHRISTIAN	n/a		
INDIGENOUS	n/a		
MUSLIM	n/a		

VITAL STATISTICS

BIRTHS

BIRTH RATE	32.3	47.1	
URBAN BIRTH RATE	10.3 (92)		
RURAL BIRTH RATE	24.2		
INFANT MORTALITY RATE	72.8	122	
LIFE EXPECTANCY AT BIRTH	41.8	55.8	

MARRIAGES

AVERAGE AGE AT MARRIAGE M/F	26.1/21.3 (92)		

DEATHS

DEATH RATE	18.2	12.2	

HOUSEHOLDS

NUMBER	2,165,744 (92)		
AVERAGE SIZE	4.8		

	1995	1980	1965
TYPE OF HOUSEHOLD			
FEMALE HEADED	33.2%		
SINGLE	9.8%		
MARRIED	75.5%		
WIDOWED	8.6%		
DIVORCED/SEPARATED	6.1%		

ECONOMICS AND LABOR

	1995	1980	1965
GDP PER CAPITA US$	$1,620		
LABOR FORCE M/F (thousands)	1,018.0/252.2 (94)		
AGRICULTURE	228.7/94.8		
MINING	49.9/1.6		
MANUFACTURING	184.9/18.0		
UTILITIES	8.1/0.3		
CONSTRUCTION	82.8/6.1		
TRADE/FOOD/TOURISM	89.0/16.9		
TRANSPORT/COMMUNICATIONS	48.6/4.7		
FINANCE/INSURANCE/REAL ESTATE	15.7/7.0		
SOCIAL AND PERSONAL SERVICES	310.3/102.8		
UNION DENSITY	13.9%		
POVERTY			
UNDER $1/DAY	41 (91)		
UNDER $2/DAY	68.2%		

TRANSPORT

	1995	1980	1965
JOURNEYS (by transport mode)			
RAILROAD PASSENGER TRIPS	4,489.0 (94)		
(millions of miles/kilometers)			
AIR PASSENGER TRIPS (thousands)	605.0 (94)		
VEHICLES			
PRIVATE CARS	310.0 (92)	216.7	
COMMERCIAL VEHICLES	88		

HEALTH AND HEALTH CARE

	1995	1980	1965
RATE OF PHYSICIANS	0.1	0.2	0.2 (60)
RATE OF HOSPITAL BEDS	0.5	3.1	3.8 (60)
TOTAL DEATHS	98,808 (92)		

	1995	1980	1965
HEALTH INDICATORS			
LOW-BIRTH-WEIGHT BABIES	14%		
CHILD MALNUTRITION	16%		
SMOKING PREVALENCE M/F	36/15%		
TUBERCULOSIS INCIDENCE RATE	2		
HEALTH CARE			
ACCESS TO SAFE WATER	74%		
ACCESS TO SANITATION	58%		
MEASLES IMMUNIZATION (under 12)	77%		
AIDS/HIV CASES	41,298	27,905 (93)	

EDUCATION

	1995	1980	1965
SCHOOL AGE IN SCHOOL			
PRIMARY	116%	126% (82)	74% (70)
SECONDARY	47%	23%	7%
HIGHER	7%	1%	
FEMALES IN SCHOOL			
PRIMARY	48%	121% (82)	66% (70)
SECONDARY	44%	42%	6%
HIGHER	10/20%	1.8%	
ADULT ILLITERACY M/F		18.5/33.2% (85)	

COMMUNICATIONS

	1995	1980	1965
RATE OF NEWSPAPERS	19	19	16 (70)
RATE OF RADIOS	86	34	27 (70)
RATE OF TELEVISIONS	27	10	9 (70)

Source: CIA, *The World Factbook, 1997;* ILO, *World Labour Report, 1997;* UN, *Demographic Yearbook, 1997;* UN, *Statistical Yearbook, 1996;* World Bank, *World Development Indicators, 1998.*

Bibliography

Abernethy, Virginia. *Population Politics: The Choices That Shape Our Future.* New York: Insight Books, 1993.

Adepoju, Aderanti, ed. *Family, Population and Development in Africa.* London and Atlantic Highlands, NJ: Zed Books, 1997.

Appleman, Philip, ed. *Thomas Robert Malthus: An Essay on the Principle of Population.* New York: Norton, 1976.

Arizpe, Lourdes, Margaret Priscilla Stone, and David C. Major, eds. *Population and Environment: Rethinking the Debate.* Boulder, CO: Westview Press, 1994.

Bandarage, Asoka. *Women, Population and Global Crisis: A Political-Economic Analysis.* London and Atlantic Highlands, NJ: Zed Books, 1997.

Birg, Herwig. *World Population Projections for the Twenty-first Century: Theoretical Interpretations and Quantitative Simulations.* New York: St. Martin's Press, 1995.

Boserup, Ester. *The Conditions of Agricultural Growth: The Economics of Agrarian Change Under Population Pressure.* London: Allen and Unwin, and New York: Aldine, 1965.

———. *Economic and Demographic Relationships in Development.* Baltimore: Johns Hopkins University Press, 1990.

Clarke, Angus, and Evelyn Parsons, eds. *Culture, Kinship, and Genes: Towards Cross-Cultural Genetics.* London: Macmillan, and New York: St. Martin's Press, 1997.

Cohen, Joel E. *How Many People Can the Earth Support?* New York and London: Norton, 1995.

Corson, Stephen, Richard Derman, and Louise B. Tyrer, eds. *Fertility Control.* Boston: Little Brown, 1984; 2nd edition, London, Ontario: Goldin, 1994.

Coward, Harold G., ed. *Population, Consumption, and the Environment: Religious and Secular Responses.* Albany: State University of New York Press, 1995.

Donaldson, Loraine. *Fertility Transition: The Social Dynamics of Population Change.* Oxford and Cambridge, MA: Blackwell, 1991.

Driedger, Leo, and Neena L. Chappell. *Aging and Ethnicity: Toward an Interface.* Boston: Butterworths, 1987.

Dyson, Tim M. *Population and Food: Global Trends and Future Prospects.* London and New York: Routledge, 1996.

Dyson, Tim M., ed. *India's Historical Demography: Studies in Famine, Disease and Society.* London: Curzon, 1989.

Ehrlich, Paul. *The Population Bomb.* New York: Ballantine, 1968; London: Pan, 1971.

Ehrlich, Paul, and Anne Ehrlich. *The Population Explosion.* New York: Simon and Schuster, and London: Hutchinson, 1990.

Ehrlich, Paul, Anne Ehrlich, and Gretchen Daily. *The Stork and the Plow: The Equity Answer to the Human Dilemma.* New York: Putnam, 1995.

Eldredge, Niles. *Dominion.* New York: Holt, 1995.

Federici, Nora, Karen O. Mason, and Sylvia Sogner, eds. *Women's Position and Demographic Change.* New York: Oxford University Press, and Oxford: Clarendon Press, 1993.

Finkle, Jason, and C. Alison McIntosh, eds. *The New Politics of Population: Conflict and Consensus in Family Planning.* New York: Population Council, 1994.

Goldscheider, Calvin, ed. *Fertility Transitions, Family Structure, and Population Policy.* Boulder, CO: Westview Press, 1992.

———. *Population, Ethnicity, and Nation-Building.* Boulder, CO: Westview Press, 1995.

Grant, James P. United Nations. Department for Economic and Social Information and Policy Analysis. *The State of the World's Children 1993.* Oxford and New York: Oxford University Press for UNICEF, 1993.

Hardin, Garrett James. *Living Within Limits: Ecology, Economics, and Population Taboos.* New York: Oxford University Press, 1993.

Harkavy, Oscar. *Curbing Population Growth: An Insider's Perspective on the Population Movement.* New York: Plenum Press, 1995.

Hartmann, Betsy. *Reproductive Rights and Wrongs: The Global Politics of Population Control and Contraceptive Choice.* New York: Harper, 1987; revised as *Reproductive Rights and Wrongs: The Global Politics of Population Control,* Boston: South End Press, 1995.

Hobhouse, Henry. *Forces of Change: Why We Are the Way We Are Now.* London: Sidgwick and Jackson, 1989; as *Forces of Change: An Unorthodox View of History.* New York: Arcade, 1990.

Hornby, William F., and Melvyn Jones. *An Introduction to Population Geography.* Cambridge and New York: Cambridge University Press, 1980, 2nd edition, 1993.

Johnson, Stanley. *World Population, Turning the Tide: Three Decades of Progress.* Boston and London: Graham and Trotman, 1994.

Jones, Gawin W., ed. *The Continuing Demographic Transition.* New York: Oxford University Press, and Oxford: Clarendon Press, 1997.

Lancaster, Henry O. *Expectations of Life: A Study in the Demography, Statistics, and History of World Mortality.* New York: Springer-Verlag, 1990.

Lappé, Frances Moore, and Rachel Schurman. *Taking Population Seriously.* London: Earthscan, 1989; San Francisco: Institute for Food and Development Policy, 1990.

Lindahl-Kiessling, Kerstin, and Hans Landberg, eds. *Population, Economic Development, and the Environment.* Oxford and New York: Oxford University Press, 1994.

Lutz, Wolfgang. *Distributional Aspects of Human Fertility: A Global Comparative Study.* London: Academic Press, 1989.

———. *Future Demographic Trends in Europe and North America: What Can We Assume Today?* London and San Diego: Academic Press, 1991.

Lutz, Wolfgang, ed. *The Future Population of the World: What Can We Assume Today?* London: Earthscan, 1994, revised edition, 1996.

Mazur, Laurie Ann, ed. *Beyond the Numbers: A Reader on Population, Consumption, and the Environment.* Washington, DC: Island Press, 1994.

Menard, Scott W., and Elizabeth Moen Mathiot. *Perspectives on Population: An Introduction to Concepts and Issues.* New York: Oxford University Press, 1987.

Mink, Stephen Dorrance. *Poverty, Population, and the Environment.* Washington, DC: World Bank, 1993.

Moffett, George D. *Critical Masses: The Global Population Challenge.* New York: Viking, 1994; London: Penguin, 1995.

———. *Global Population Growth: Twenty-first Century Challenges.* New York: Foreign Policy Association, 1994.

Montgomery, Mark, and Barney Cohen, eds. *From Death to Birth: Mortality Decline and Reproductive Change.* Washington, DC: National Academy Press, 1998.

Myers, Norman. *Population, Resources, and the Environment: The Critical Challenges.* New York: United Nations Population Fund, 1991.

Neurath, Paul. *From Malthus to the Club of Rome and Back: Problems of Limits to Growth, Population Control, and Migrations.* Armonk, NY: Sharpe, 1994.

Niven, Catherine, and Anne Walker, eds. *Reproductive Potential and Fertility Control.* Boston and Oxford: Butterworth-Heinemann, 1996.

Piel, Gerard. *Only One World: Our Own to Make and to Keep.* New York: Freeman, 1992.

Preston, Samuel H., ed. *World Population: Approaching the Year 2000.* Newbury Park, CA: Sage, 1990.

Quale, G. Robina. *Families in Context: A World History of Population.* New York: Greenwood Press, 1992.

Razin, Assaf, and Efraim Sadka. *Population Economics.* Cambridge, MA: MIT Press, 1995.

Salk, Jonas. *World Population and Human Values: A New Reality.* New York: Harper, 1981.

Santos, Miguel A. *Managing Planet Earth: Perspectives on Population, Ecology, and the Law.* New York: Bergin and Garvey, 1990.

Schofield, Roger, and David S. Reher, eds. *Old and New Methods in Historical Demography.* New York: Oxford University Press, and Oxford: Clarendon Press, 1993.

Sen, Amartya, and Martha Nussbaum, eds. *The Quality of Life.* New York: Oxford University Press, and Oxford: Clarendon Press, 1993.

Simon, Julian Lincoln. *Population Matters: People, Resources, Environment, and Immigration.* New Brunswick, NJ: Transaction, 1990.

———. *The Ultimate Resource.* Princeton, NJ: Princeton University Press, and Oxford: Robertson, 1981; revised as *The Ultimate Resource 2.* Princeton, NJ, and Chichester, West Sussex: Princeton University Press, 1996.

Stein, Dorothy. *People Who Count: Population and Politics, Women and Children.* London: Earthscan, 1995.

Tarver, James D. *The Demography of Africa.* Westport, CT: Praeger, 1996.

Teitelbaum, Michael, and Jay Winter. *A Question of Numbers: High Migration, Low Fertility, and the Politics of National Identity.* New York: Hill and Wang, 1998.

Tobias, Michael. *World War III: Population and the Biosphere at the End of the Millenium.* Santa Fe, NM: Bear, 1994; 2nd edition, New York: Continuum, 1998.

United Nations. *The World's Women, 1995: Trends and Statistics.* New York: United Nations, 1995.

United Nations. Department for Economic and Social Information and Policy Analysis. *Population Policies and Programmes: Proceedings of the United Nations Expert Group Meeting on Population Policies and Programmes,* Cairo, Egypt, 12:16 April 1992. New York: United Nations, 1993.

United Nations. Department for Economic and Social Information and Policy Analysis, Population Division. *Levels and Trends of Contraceptive Use as Assessed in 1994.* New York: United Nations, 1996.

United Nations World Health Organization. *The AIDS Epidemic and Its Demographic Consequences.* New York: United Nations, 1991.

Valentei, D.I., ed. *The Theory of Population: Essays in Marxist Research.* Moscow: Progress, 1978.

Weeks, John R. *Population: An Introduction to Concepts and Issues.* Belmont, CA: Wadsworth, 1978; 7th edition, 1999.

Wolbarst, Anthony, ed. *Environment in Peril.* Washington, DC: Smithsonian Institution Press, 1991.

Wood, James W. *Dynamics of Human Reproduction: Biology, Biometry, Demography.* New York: Aldine de Gruyter, 1994.

Yaukey, David. *Demography: The Study of Human Population.* New York: St. Martin's Press, 1985.

Index

A

Afghanistan, 29
  communications, 137
  cultural identity, 136
  economy, 136
  education, 137
  geography, 135
  population, 135-36
  transport, 136-37
  vital statistics, 136
Africa, 67
  birth rates, 27
  boundaries of, 43
  death rates, 27
  geography, 106
  migration 67
  population density, 27-28
  population growth, 27
  population, 105-07
  poverty, 58
  vital statistics, 107
age structures
  Argentina, 40
  "balanced" societies, 40
  Brazil, 40
  China, 40
  definition of, 39-40
  Iran, 40
  Italy, 40
  Nigeria, 40
  "old" societies, 40
  Russia, 40
  and social problems, 41
  Thailand, 40
  "young" societies, 39-40
agricultural revolution, 17, 23
air transport
  impact on global culture, 77
  increases in, 76
    China, 77
    Ghana, 77
    Peru, 77
air-conditioning
  impact on environment, 5
Albania
  communications, 140
  cultural identity, 139
  economy, 139
  education, 140
  geography, 138
  health care, 140
  population, 138-39
  vital statistics, 139

Algeria
  communications, 145
  cultural identity, 143
  economy, 144
  education, 141, 145
  geography, 143
  health care, 145
  households, 144
  population, 143
  transport, 142, 144
  vital statistics, 144
Andorra
  communications, 147
  cultural identity, 146-47
  economy, 147
  geography, 146
  population, 146
  vital statistics, 147
Angola
  civil war, 21
  communications, 152
  cultural identity, 148, 150
  economy, 151
  education, 152
  geography, 150
  health care, 149, 151-52
  population, 150
  transport, 151
  vital statistics, 151
Antigua and Barbuda
  communications, 155
  cultural identity, 154
  economy, 154
  education, 155
  geography, 153
  health care, 155
  households, 154
  population, 153
  transport, 155
  vital statistics, 154
aquifer depletion
  United States, 15-16
  China, 16
  India, 16
Aquinas, St. Thomas, 7
Argentina
  communications, 160
  cultural identity, 158-59
  economy, 159
  education, 160
  geography, 156
  health care, 160
  households, 159
  population, 158
  transport, 159-60

Argentina *(continued)*
  vital statistics, 156-57, 159
Armenia
  communications, 163
  cultural identity, 162
  education, 163
  geography, 161
  health care, 161-62
  population, 161
  transport, 162
  vital statistics, 162
Around the World in Eighty Days, 74
Asia
  geography, 112
  population growth, 29
  population, 111-12
  vital statistics, 112-13
Australia
  colonization, 51-52
  communications, 168
  cultural identity, 52, 164, 166-67
  economy, 167
  education, 168
  geography, 131
  health care, 168
  households, 167
  immigration, 52
  population density of, 26
  population, 131, 165-66
  transport, 168
  vital statistics, 131, 167
Austria
  communications, 172
  cultural identity, 170
  economy, 170-71
  education, 172
  geography, 169
  health care, 171
  households, 170
  population, 169-70
  transport, 171
  vital statistics, 170
automobile industry, 55-56
automobiles. *See* motor vehicles
Azerbaijan
  communications, 175
  cultural identity, 174
  economy, 174
  education, 175
  geography, 173
  health care, 175
  population, 173-74
  transport, 175
  vital statistics, 174

B

baby boom, 37
Bahamas
    communications, 179
    cultural identity, 177
    economy, 178
    education, 178
    geography, 176
    health care, 178
    households, 177
    population, 176
    transport, 178
    vital statistics, 177
Bahrain
    communications, 183
    cultural identity, 181
    economy, 181-82
    education, 182
    geography, 180
    health care, 182
    households, 181
    population, 180-81
    transport, 182
    vital statistics, 181
Bangladesh
    communications, 188
    cultural identity, 186-87
    economy, 187
    education, 188
    geography, 186
    health care, 187-88
    organized labor, 58
    population density, 26
    population, 184-86
    transport, 187
    vital statistics, 187
Barbados
    communications, 192
    cultural identity, 190
    economy, 190-91
    education, 191
    geography, 189
    health care, 191
    households, 190
    population, 189
    transport, 191
    vital statistics, 190
Belarus
    communications, 196
    cultural identity, 194
    economy, 195
    education, 196
    geography, 193
    health care, 195
    households, 194
    population, 193-94
    transport, 195
    vital statistics, 194
Belgium
    communications, 200
    cultural identity, 198
    economy, 198-99

Belgium (continued)
    education, 199
    geography, 197
    health care, 199
    population, 197-98
    transport, 199
    vital statistics, 198
Belize
    communications, 204
    cultural identity, 202
    economy, 203
    education, 203-04
    geography, 201
    health care, 203
    households, 202
    population, 201-02
    transport, 203
    vital statistics, 202
Benin
    communications, 208
    cultural identity, 206
    economy, 207
    education, 207-08
    geography, 205
    health care, 207
    households, 206
    population, 205-06
    transport, 207
    vital statistics, 206
Bhutan
    communications, 211
    cultural identity, 210
    economy, 210
    education, 211
    geography, 209
    population, 209
    transport, 210
    vital statistics, 210
birth control and fertility, 35
    and Catholic Church, 28
    Kenya, 37
birth rates
    Kenya, 37
Bolivia
    communications, 215
    cultural identity, 213
    economy, 214
    education, 215
    geography, 212
    health care, 214-15
    households, 213-14
    population, 212-13
    transport, 214
    vital statistics, 213
Bosnia and Herzegovina
    civil war, 67
    communications, 218
    cultural identity, 217
    economy, 217
    ethnic composition, 50-51
    geography, 216
    health care, 218
    peacekeeping in, 11
    population, 216-17

Bosnia and Herzegovina (continued)
    religious composition, 51
    vital statistics, 217
Botswana
    communications, 222
    cultural identity, 220
    economy, 221
    education, 222
    geography, 219
    health care, 221-22
    households, 220
    population, 219-20
    transport, 221
    vital statistics, 220
Brazil
    communications, 228
    cultural identity, 225-26
    economy, 223, 226-27
    education, 227
    ethnic composition, 46-47
    geography, 225
    health care, 227
    households, 226
    population, 224-25
    poverty, 59
    slavery, 46
    transport, 227
    vital statistics, 226
Brown, Lester, 13
Brunei
    communications, 231
    cultural identity, 230
    economy, 230
    education, 231
    geography, 229
    health care, 231
    households, 230
    population, 229-30
    transport, 231
    vital statistics, 230
Bulgaria
    communications, 235
    cultural identity, 233
    economy, 234
    education, 235
    geography, 232
    health care, 234-35
    households, 233-34
    population, 232-33
    transport, 234
    vital statistics, 233
Burkina Faso
    communications, 238
    cultural identity, 237
    education, 238
    geography, 236
    health care, 238
    population, 236-37
    transport, 237
    vital statistics, 237
Burundi
    communications, 242
    cultural identity, 240
    economy, 240-41

Burundi *(continued)*
    education, 241
    geography, 239
    health care, 241
    population, 239-40
    transport, 241
    vital statistics, 240

C

Cambodia
    communications, 245
    cultural identity, 244
    economy, 244
    education, 245
    geography, 243
    health care, 245
    population, 243
    transport, 244
    vital statistics, 244
Cameroon
    communications, 249
    cultural identity, 247
    economy, 247
    education, 248
    geography, 246
    health care, 248
    population, 246-47
    transport, 248
    vital statistics, 247
Canada
    colonization, 47-48
    communications, 255
    cultural identity, 252
    economy, 253
    education, 254
    fishing disputes, 21
    geography, 252
    health care, 254, 258
    households, 253
    linguistic composition, 44, 48
    population, 258
    transport, 254
    vital statistics, 250-51, 253
Cape Verde
    communications, 259
    cultural identity, 257
    economy, 258
    education, 258
    geography, 256
    health care, 262
    households, 257
    population, 256-57
    transport, 258
    vital statistics, 257
carbon dioxide production, 20
    China, 20
    global, 20
    Malaysia, 20
    Nigeria, 20
    Turkey, 20
    United States, 20
Caribbean
    geography, 124

Caribbean *(continued)*
    migration, 67
    population, 124
    vital statistics, 125
Catholic Church
    birth-control views, 28
    economic views of, 10
Central Africa
    geography, 109
    population, 109-10
    vital statistics, 110
Central African Republic
    communications, 263
    cultural identity, 261
    economy, 262
    education, 263
    health care, 262
    households, 261-62
    geography, 260
    population, 260-61
    transport, 262
    vital statistics, 261
Central America
    geography, 124
    population, 125
    vital statistics, 125
Chad
    communications, 266-67
    cultural identity, 265
    economy, 265
    education, 266
    geography, 264
    health care, 266
    population, 264-65
    transport, 266
    vital statistics, 265
Chile
    communications, 271
    cultural identity, 268
    economy, 270
    education, 271
    geography, 268
    health care, 270-71
    households, 269
    population, 268-69
    transport, 270
    vital statistics, 269
China
    communications, 277
    cultural identity, 274-75
    economy, 275-76
    education, 273, 276
    geography, 274
    health care, 276
    households, 275
    migration, 65
    Mongol invasion, 24
    organized labor, 58
    population policy, 9, 11, 29, 37
    population, 272, 274
    transport, 276
    vital statistics, 275
climate change, 14-15, 19-20
    and flooding, 15

Cold War, 52
Colombia
    communications, 281
    cultural identity, 279
    economy, 279-80
    education, 281
    flower production, 5
    geography, 278
    health care, 280
    households, 279
    population, 278-79
    transport, 280
    vital statistics, 279
Communications
    Afghanistan, 137
    Albania, 140
    Algeria, 145
    Andorra, 147
    Angola, 152
    Antigua and Barbuda, 155
    Argentina, 160
    Armenia, 163
    Australia, 168
    Austria, 172
    Azerbaijan, 175
    Bahamas, 179
    Bahrain, 183
    Bangladesh, 188
    Barbados, 192
    Belarus, 196
    Belgium, 200
    Belize, 204
    Benin, 208
    Bhutan, 211
    Bolivia, 215
    Bosnia and Herzegovina, 218
    Botswana, 222
    Brazil, 228
    Brunei, 231
    Bulgaria, 235
    Burkina Faso, 238
    Burundi, 242
    Cambodia, 245
    Cameroon, 249
    Canada, 255
    Cape Verde, 259
    Central African Republic, 263
    Chad, 266-67
    Chile, 271
    China, 277
    Colombia, 281
    Comoros, 284
    Congo, Democratic Republic of (Zaire), 288
    Congo, Republic of, 292
    Costa Rica, 296
    Côte d'Ivoire, 300
    Croatia, 304
    Cuba, 309
    Cyprus, 313
    Czech Republic, 317
    Denmark, 321
    Djibouti, 324

Communications *(continued)*
  Dominica, 327
  Dominican Republic, 331
  Ecuador, 335
  Egypt, 341
  El Salvador, 345
  Equatorial Guinea, 348
  Estonia, 355
  Ethiopia, 361
  Fiji, 365
  Finland, 369
  France, 375
  Gabon, 378
  Gambia, 382
  Germany, 391
  Ghana, 395
  Greece, 399
  Grenada, 402
  Guatemala, 408
  Guinea, 412
  Guyana, 418
  Haiti, 421
  Honduras, 425
  Hungary, 429
  Iceland, 433
  India, 439
  Indonesia, 441, 445
  Iran, 451
  Iraq, 456
  Ireland, 460
  Israel, 466
  Italy, 472
  Jamaica, 478
  Japan, 484
  Jordan, 488
  Kenya, 499
  Kiribati, 501
  Korea, North, 504
  Korea, South, 510
  Kuwait, 514
  Laos, 521
  Latvia, 525
  Lebanon, 529
  Lesotho, 532
  Liberia, 535
  Libya, 539
  Liechtenstein, 542
  Lithuania, 547
  Luxembourg, 551
  Macedonia, 555
  Madagascar, 559
  Malawi, 563
  Malaysia, 567
  Maldives, 570
  Mali, 574
  Malta, 578
  Mauritania, 585
  Mauritius, 589
  Mexico, 595
  Moldova, 601
  Monaco, 604
  Mongolia, 607
  Morocco, 613
  Mozambique, 617

Communications *(continued)*
  Myanmar, 621
  Namibia, 625
  Nauru, 628
  Nepal, 632
  Netherlands, 638
  New Zealand, 642
  Nicaragua, 646
  Niger, 650
  Nigeria, 655
  Norway, 659
  Oman, 663
  Pakistan, 669
  Palau, 671
  Panama, 675
  Papua New Guinea, 679
  Paraguay, 683
  Peru, 689
  Philippines, 695
  Poland, 701
  Portugal, 705
  Puerto Rico, 709
  Qatar, 712
  Romania, 718
  Russian Federation, 724
  Rwanda, 728
  Saint Kitts and Nevis, 731
  Saint Lucia, 734
  Saint Vincent and the Grenadines, 737
  San Marino, 740
  Sao Tome and Principe, 743
  Saudi Arabia, 748
  Senegal, 754
  Serbia and Montenegro, 760
  Seychelles, 764
  Sierra Leone, 768
  Singapore, 774
  Slovakia, 778
  Slovenia, 782
  Solomon Islands, 785
  Somalia, 788
  South Africa, 790, 794
  Spain, 800
  Sri Lanka, 804
  Sudan, 808
  Suriname, 812
  Swaziland, 815
  Sweden, 821
  Switzerland, 825
  Syria, 831
  Taiwan, 834
  Tajikistan, 838
  Tanzania, 842
  Thailand, 844, 848
  Togo, 852
  Tonga, 855
  Trinidad and Tobago, 859
  Tunisia, 863
  Turkey, 869
  Tuvalu, 874
  Uganda, 878
  Ukraine, 883
  United Arab Emirates, 887
  United Kingdom, 893

Communications *(continued)*
  United States, 899
  Uruguay, 903
  Uzbekistan, 907
  Vanuatu, 910
  Venezuela, 916
  Vietnam, 922
  (Western) Samoa, 925
  Yemen, 929
  Zambia, 933
  Zimbabwe, 937
Comoros
  communications, 284
  cultural identity, 283
  economy, 284
  education, 284
  geography, 282
  health care, 284
  households, 283
  population, 282
  transport, 284
  vital statistics, 283
Congo, Democratic Republic of (Zaire)
  communications, 288
  cultural identity, 286
  economy, 287
  education, 287
  geography, 285
  health care, 287
  population, 285-86
  transport, 287
  vital statistics, 286
Congo, Republic of
  communications, 292
  cultural identity, 290
  economy, 290
  education, 291
  geography, 289
  health care, 291
  households, 290
  population, 289
  transport, 291
  vital statistics, 290
consumption
  developed world, 3, 5, 14, 52-53
Costa Rica
  communications, 296
  cultural identity, 294
  economy, 294-95
  education, 295-96
  geography, 293
  health care, 295
  population, 293-94
  transport, 295
  vital statistics, 294
Côte d'Ivoire
  communications, 300
  cultural identity, 298
  economy, 299
  education, 300
  geography, 297
  health care, 299
  households, 298
  population, 297-98

Côte d'Ivoire *(continued)*
   transport, 299
   vital statistics, 298
Croatia
   communications, 304
   cultural identity, 302
   economy, 302-03
   education, 303-04
   geography, 301
   health care, 303
   population, 301-02
   transport, 303
   vital statistics, 302
Cuba
   communications, 309
   cultural identity, 305, 307-08
   economy, 308
   education, 309
   geography, 307
   health care, 309
   population, 307
   transport, 308-09
   vital statistics, 306, 308
Cyprus
   communications, 313
   cultural identity, 311
   economy, 312
   education, 313
   geography, 310
   health care, 312
   population, 310
   households, 311-12
   transport, 312
   vital statistics, 311
Czech Republic
   communications, 317
   cultural identity, 315
   economy, 316
   education, 317
   geography, 314
   health care, 316
   households, 315
   population, 314-15
   transport, 316
   vital statistics, 315

D

debt, foreign, 57
   Africa, 57
   Caribbean, 57
   Latin America, 57
   South Asia, 57
decolonization, 67, 69
de Condorcet, Marquis, 7
deforestation
   Canada, 20
   United States, 20
demographic time lag, 26
demography
   uses of, 10
Denmark
   communications, 321

Denmark *(continued)*
   cultural identity, 319
   economy, 320
   education, 321
   geography, 318
   health care, 320
   households, 319
   organized labor, 58
   population, 318-19
   transport, 320
   vital statistics, 319
dependency ratio, 41
   Japan, 41
   Philippines, 41
devaluation, 62
Djibouti
   communications, 324
   cultural identity, 323
   economy, 323
   geography, 322
   health care, 323-24
   population, 322
   transport, 323
   vital statistics, 323
Dominica
   communications, 327
   cultural identity, 326
   economy, 326
   education, 327
   geography, 325
   health care, 327
   households, 326
   population, 325
   transport, 327
   vital statistics, 326
Dominican Republic
   communications, 331
   cultural identity, 329
   economy, 330
   education, 331
   geography, 328
   health care, 330
   households, 329
   population, 328-29
   transport, 330
   vital statistics, 329
droughts 19
   Midwest, 6
   Sahel, 6
Dubois, W.E.B., 52

E

East Africa
   geography, 106
   population, 108
   vital statistics, 108
East Asia
   age cohorts, 29
   birth rates, 29
   geography, 113
   organized labor, 58

East Asia *(continued)*
   population growth, 29
   population, 113
   vital statistics, 113
Eastern Europe, 69-70
   geography, 118
   migration, 69-70
   population, 118
   vital statistics, 118
"eco-tourism," 78
Economy
   Afghanistan, 136
   Africa, 61-62
   Albania, 139
   Algeria, 144
   Andorra, 147
   Angola, 151
   Antigua and Barbuda, 154
   Argentina, 159
   Australia, 167
   Austria, 170-71
   Azerbaijan, 174
   Bahamas, 178
   Bahrain, 181-82
   Bangladesh, 187
   Barbados, 190-91
   Belarus, 195
   Belgium, 198-99
   Belize, 203
   Benin, 207
   Bhutan, 210
   Bolivia, 214
   Bosnia and Herzegovina, 217
   Botswana, 221
   Brazil, 223, 226-27
   Brunei, 230
   Bulgaria, 234
   Burundi, 240-41
   Cambodia, 244
   Cameroon, 247
   Canada, 253
   Cape Verde, 258
   Central African Republic, 262
   Chad, 265
   Chile, 270
   China, 275-76
   Colombia, 279-80
   Comoros, 284
   Congo, Democratic Republic of (Zaire), 287
   Congo, Republic of, 290
   Costa Rica, 294-95
   Côte d'Ivoire, 299
   Croatia, 302-03
   Cuba, 308
   Cyprus, 312
   Czech Republic, 316
   Denmark, 320
   Djibouti, 323
   Dominica, 326
   Dominican Republic, 330
   Ecuador, 334
   Egypt, 339
   El Salvador, 344

Economy (*continued*)
Equatorial Guinea, 347
Eritrea, 350
Estonia, 353-54
Ethiopia, 356, 359
Europe, 62-63
Fiji, 363-64
Finland, 368
France, 373
Gabon, 377
Gambia, 380
Georgia, 384
Germany, 387, 389-90
Ghana, 393-94
Greece, 398
Grenada, 401
Guatemala, 403, 407
Guinea, 410
Guinea-Bissau, 414
Guyana, 417
Haiti, 420
Honduras, 423-24
Hungary, 428
Iceland, 431-32
India, 437-38
Indonesia, 443-44
Iran, 449
Iraq, 455
Ireland, 459
Israel, 464-65
Italy, 470
Jamaica, 476
Japan, 483
Jordan, 487
Kazakstan, 492-93
Kenya, 497
Kiribati, 501
Korea, North, 503
Korea, South, 57, 508-09
Kuwait, 513
Kyrgyzstan, 517
Laos, 520
Latvia, 524
Lebanon, 527-28
Lesotho, 531
Liberia, 534
Libya, 537
Liechtenstein, 541
Lithuania, 546
Luxembourg, 550
Macedonia, 554
Madagascar, 557-58
Malawi, 562
Malaysia, 566
Maldives, 569
Mali, 573
Malta, 577
Marshall Islands, 580
Mauritania, 583-84
Mauritius, 588
Mexico, 591, 593-94
Micronesia, 597
Moldova, 600
Monaco, 603

Economy (*continued*)
Mongolia, 606
Morocco, 611
Mozambique, 615-16
Myanmar, 619-20
Namibia, 624
Nauru, 627
Nepal, 631
Netherlands, 636
New Zealand, 641
Nicaragua, 644-45
Niger, 649
Nigeria, 651, 654
North America, 60
Norway, 658
Oman, 661
Pakistan, 667-68
Palau, 671
Panama, 674
Papua New Guinea, 677-78
Paraguay, 682
Peru, 687-88
Philippines, 693-94
Poland, 699-700
Portugal, 704
Puerto Rico, 708
Qatar, 711
Romania, 717
Russian Federation, 57, 722-23
Rwanda, 726-27
Saint Kitts and Nevis, 730
Saint Lucia, 733
Saint Vincent and the Grenadines, 736
San Marino, 740
Sao Tome and Principe, 742
Saudi Arabia, 747
Senegal, 750, 752
Serbia and Montenegro, 755, 758
Seychelles, 763
Sierra Leone, 766
Singapore, 770, 772
Slovakia, 777
Slovenia, 781
Solomon Islands, 784-85
Somalia, 787
South Africa, 792-93
South America, 60-61
Spain, 798
Sri Lanka, 803
Sudan, 807
Suriname, 810-11
Swaziland, 814
Sweden, 819-20
Switzerland, 824
Syria, 829-30
Taiwan, 832-33
Tajikistan, 837
Tanzania, 841
Thailand, 846
Togo, 850-51
Tonga, 854
Trinidad and Tobago, 858
Tunisia, 861-62
Turkey, 867-68

Economy (*continued*)
Turkmenistan, 871-72
Tuvalu, 874
Uganda, 877
Ukraine, 882
United Arab Emirates, 886
United Kingdom, 891
United States, 897-98
Uruguay, 902
Uzbekistan, 904-06
Vanuatu, 909
Venezuela, 912, 914-15
Vietnam, 918, 920-21
(Western) Samoa, 924
Yemen, 927
Zambia, 932
Zimbabwe, 936
Ecuador
border clashes with Peru, 21
communications, 335
cultural identity, 333
economy, 334
education, 335
geography, 332
health care, 334-35
households, 333
population, 332-33
transport, 334
vital statistics, 333
Education
Afghanistan, 137
Albania, 140
Algeria, 141, 145
Angola, 152
Antigua and Barbuda, 155
Argentina, 160
Armenia, 163
Australia, 168
Austria, 172
Azerbaijan, 175
Bahamas, 178
Bahrain, 182
Bangladesh, 188
Barbados, 191
Belarus, 196
Belgium, 199
Belize, 203-04
Benin, 207-08
Bhutan, 211
Bolivia, 215
Botswana, 222
Brazil, 227
Brunei, 231
Bulgaria, 235
Burkina Faso, 238
Burundi, 241
Cambodia, 245
Cameroon, 248
Canada, 254
Cape Verde, 258
Central African Republic, 263
Chad, 266
Chile, 271
China, 273, 276

Education *(continued)*
Colombia, 281
Comoros, 284
Congo, Democratic Republic of (Zaire), 287
Congo, Republic of, 291
Costa Rica, 295-96
Côte d'Ivoire, 300
Croatia, 303-04
Cuba, 309
Cyprus, 313
Czech Republic, 317
demographic influences on, 87
    Brazil, 87
    Côte d'Ivoire, 87
    India, 87
Denmark, 321
Dominica, 327
Dominican Republic, 331
economic influences on, 87
    Côte d'Ivoire, 87
    Malaysia, 87
Ecuador, 335
Egypt, 340
El Salvador, 345
Equatorial Guinea, 348
Eritrea, 351
Estonia, 354
Ehiopia, 360
Fiji, 364
Finland, 369
France, 374
Gabon, 378
Gambia, 381
Georgia, 385
Germany, 390
Ghana, 394
Greece, 399
Grenada, 402
Guatemala, 403, 407
Guinea, 411
Guinea-Bissau, 415
Guyana, 418
Haiti, 421
Honduras, 425
Hungary, 429
Iceland, 432
increases in female enrollment
    Eastern Europe, 88
    North Africa, 88
    South Asia, 88
    Western Europe, 88
increases in primary level enrollment
    Guinea, 88
    Mozambique, 88
increases in secondary level enrollment
    Jamaica, 88
    Thailand, 88
increases in tertiary level enrollment
    France, 88
    Portugal, 88
    Romania, 88
India, 438-39
Indonesia, 440, 444-45

Education *(continued)*
Iran, 450
Iraq, 453, 456
Ireland, 460
Israel, 462, 465
Italy, 471
Jamaica, 477
Japan, 484
Jordan, 488
Kazakstan, 493-94
Kenya, 498
Korea, North, 504
Korea, South, 506, 509-10
Kuwait, 513-14
Kyrgyzstan, 518
Laos, 521
Latvia, 525
Lebanon, 528
Lesotho, 532
Liberia, 535
Libya, 538
Liechtenstein, 541
Lithuania, 547
Luxembourg, 551
Macedonia, 555
Madagascar, 559
Malawi, 563
Malaysia, 567
Maldives, 570
Mali, 574
Malta, 577-78
Marshall Islands, 580
Mauritania, 584
Mauritius, 589
Mexico, 594-95
Micronesia, 597
Moldova, 601
Monaco, 603
Mongolia, 607
Morocco, 612
Mozambique, 616-17
Myanmar, 620-21
Namibia, 625
Nauru, 628
Nepal, 631
Netherlands, 637
New Zealand, 642
Nicaragua, 646
Niger, 650
Nigeria, 655
Norway, 659
Oman, 662
Pakistan, 669
Palau, 671
Panama, 675
Papua New Guinea, 678-79
Paraguay, 683
Peru, 688-89
Philippines, 690, 694-95
Poland, 701
Portugal, 705
Puerto Rico, 708-09
Qatar, 712
Romania, 718

Education *(continued)*
Russian Federation, 723
Rwanda, 727-28
Saint Kitts and Nevis, 731
Saint Lucia, 734
Saint Vincent and the Grenadines, 737
San Marino, 740
Sao Tome and Principe, 743
Saudi Arabia, 748
Senegal, 753
Serbia and Montenegro, 759
Seychelles, 763
Sierra Leone, 767
Singapore, 773
Slovakia, 778
Slovenia, 782
Solomon Islands, 785
Somalia, 788
South Africa, 794
Spain, 796, 799
Sri Lanka, 804
Sudan, 808
Suriname, 811
Swaziland, 815
Sweden, 820-21
Switzerland, 825
Syria, 830
Taiwan, 834
Tajikistan, 837
Tanzania, 842
Thailand, 847
Togo, 851
Tonga, 855
Trinidad and Tobago, 859
Tunisia, 863
Turkey, 865, 868-69
Turkmenistan, 872
Tuvalu, 874
Uganda, 878
Ukraine, 883
United Arab Emirates, 887
United Kingdom, 892
United States, 899
Uruguay, 903
Uzbekistan, 906
Vanuatu, 910
Venezuela, 915-16
Vietnam, 921
(Western) Samoa, 925
Yemen, 928
Zambia, 933
Zimbabwe, 937
Egypt
communications, 341
cultural identity, 338
economy, 339
education, 340
geography, 338
health care, 340
households, 339
population, 336-38
transport, 340
vital statistics, 339
Ehrlich, Anne and Paul, 3, 13

El Niño, 19
El Salvador
    communications, 345
    cultural identity, 343
    economy, 344
    education, 345
    geography, 342
    health care, 344-45
    households, 343
    population, 342-43
    transport, 344
    vital statistics, 343
employment, 55
    Brazil, 55
    China, 55
    Indonesia, 55
    Korea, South, 55
    Mexico, 55
energy consumption
    Africa, 16
    Asia, 16
    Europe, 16
    global, 16-17
    North America, 16
    Oceania, 16
    South America, 16
energy production
    Asia, 17
    Europe, 17
    global 17
    North America, 17
    Oceania, 17
    South America, 17
Engels, Friedrich, 9
Equatorial Guinea
    communications, 348
    cultural identity, 347
    economy, 347
    education, 348
    geography, 346
    health care, 348
    population, 346-47
    transport, 347
    vital statistics, 347
Eritrea
    cultural identity, 350
    economy, 350
    education, 351
    geography, 349
    health care, 351
    population, 349-50
    vital statistics, 350
Estonia
    communications, 355
    cultural identity, 353
    economy, 353-54
    education, 354
    geography, 352
    health care, 354
    population, 352
    transport, 354
    vital statistics, 353
Ethiopia
    communications, 361

Ethiopia *(continued)*
    cultural identity, 357-59
    economy, 356, 359
    education, 360
    geography, 358
    health care, 360
    households, 359
    population, 358
    vital statistics, 359
Europe
    birth rates, 30
    death rates, 30
    emigration, 29
    geography, 117
    immigration 29-30, 64
    population growth, 30
    population, 116-17
    vital statistics, 116, 118
exports, 60

F

families
    changes in, 33-34
    impact of industrial revolution on, 33
    impact of urbanization of, 33-34
fertility
    and birth control, 35
    and education, 35-36, 38, 89
        Caribbean, 89
        Latin America, 89
        North Africa, 89
        Southwest Asia, 89
        Sub-Saharan Africa, 89
    and prosperity, 38
        Asia, 89
    and urbanization, 35-36
    and women's status, 35-36, 38, 89
        Asia, 89
        Caribbean, 89
        Latin America, 89
        North Africa, 89
        Southwest Asia, 89
        Sub-Saharan Africa, 89
    Kenya, 37
    levels in United States, 34
    measurements of, 34
    Nazi Germany, 36
    North Korea, 36
    Palestine, 36
    reduction of, 36-38
    Tanzania, 37
fertilizer, 16, 18
Fiji
    colonization, 52
    communications, 365
    cultural identity, 363
    economy, 363-64
    education, 364
    ethnic composition, 52
    geography, 362
    health care, 364

Fiji *(continued)*
    labor force, 52
    population, 362
    transport, 364
    vital statistics, 363
Finland
    communications, 369
    cultural identity, 367
    economy, 368
    education, 369
    geography, 366
    health care, 368-69
    households, 367-68
    population, 366-67
    transport, 368
    vital statistics, 367
fisheries depletion of, 19
    China, 19
fishing disputes, 21
flooding
    Bangladesh, 15
    Florida, 15
    Netherlands, 15
    Nile Delta, 15
    Rio de la Plata, 15
"fourth world," 27
France
    communications, 375
    cultural identity, 372-73
    economy, 373
    education, 374
    export of language, 53
    geography, 372
    health care, 370, 374
    households, 373
    population, 371-72
    transport, 374
    vital statistics, 373
Franco, Francisco, 51

G

Gabon
    communications, 378
    cultural identity, 377
    economy, 377
    education, 378
    geography, 376
    health care, 378
    population, 376-77
    transport, 378
    vital statistics, 377
Gagarin, Yuri, 74
Gambia
    communications, 382
    cultural identity, 380
    economy, 380
    education, 381
    geography, 379
    health care, 381
    population, 379
    transport, 381
    vital statistics, 380

gasoline
    consumption in United States, 16
    prices in United States, 16
Gaza. *See* Palestine
gender ratios, 37
    China, 37
genetics and agriculture, 18-19
Geography
    Afghanistan, 135
    Africa, 106
    Albania, 138
    Algeria, 143
    Andorra, 146
    Angola, 150
    Antigua and Barbuda, 153
    Argentina, 156
    Armenia, 161
    Asia, 112
    Australia, 131, 166
    Austria, 169
    Azerbaijan, 173
    Bahamas, 176
    Bahrain, 180
    Bangladesh, 186
    Barbadoes, 189
    Belarus, 193
    Belgium, 197
    Belize, 201
    Benin, 205
    Bhutan, 209
    Bolivia, 212
    Bosnia and Herzegovina, 216
    Botswana, 219
    Brazil, 225
    Brunei, 229
    Bulgaria, 232
    Burkina Faso, 236
    Burundi, 239
    Cambodia, 243
    Cameroon, 246
    Canada, 252
    Cape Verde, 256
    Caribbean, 124
    Central Africa, 109
    Central African Republic, 260
    Central America, 124
    Chad, 264
    Chile, 268
    China, 274
    Colombia, 278
    Comoros, 282
    Congo, Democratic Republic of (Zaire), 285
    Congo, Republic of, 289
    Costa Rica, 293
    Côte d'Ivoire, 297
    Croatia, 301
    Cuba, 307
    Cyprus, 310
    Czech Republic, 314
    Denmark, 318
    Djibouti, 322
    Dominica, 325
    Dominican Republic, 328

Geography *(continued)*
    East Africa, 106
    East Asia, 113
    Eastern Europe, 118
    Ecuador, 332
    Egypt, 338
    El Salvador, 342
    Equatorial Guinea, 346
    Eritrea, 349
    Estonia, 352
    Ethiopia, 358
    Europe, 117
    Fiji, 362
    Finland, 366
    France, 372
    Gabon, 376
    Gambia, 379
    Georgia, 383
    Germany, 388
    Ghana, 392
    global, 103
    Greece, 396
    Grenada, 400
    Guatemala, 405
    Guinea, 409
    Guinea-Bissau, 413
    Guyana, 416
    Haiti, 419
    Honduras, 422
    Hungary, 426
    Iceland, 430
    India, 436
    Indonesia, 442
    Iran, 448
    Iraq, 454
    Ireland, 457
    Israel, 463
    Italy, 469
    Jamaica, 475
    Japan, 481
    Jordan, 485
    Kazakstan, 491
    Kenya, 496
    Kiribati, 500
    Korea, North, 502
    Korea, South, 507
    Kuwait, 511
    Kyrgyzstan, 515
    Laos, 519
    Latin America, 123
    Latvia, 522
    Lebanon, 526
    Lesotho, 530
    Liberia, 533
    Libya, 536
    Liechtenstein, 540
    Lithuania, 543
    Luxembourg, 548
    Macedonia, 552
    Madagascar, 556
    Malawi, 560
    Malaysia, 564
    Maldives, 568
    Mali, 571

Geography *(continued)*
    Malta, 575
    Marshall Islands, 579
    Mauritania, 582
    Mauritius, 586
    Melanasia, 131
    Mexico, 592
    Micronesia, 132, 596
    Moldova, 598
    Monaco, 602
    Mongolia, 605
    Morocco, 610
    Mozambique, 614
    Myanmar, 618
    Namibia, 622
    Nauru, 626
    Nepal, 629
    Netherlands, 635
    New Zealand, 131, 639
    Nicaragua, 643
    Niger, 647
    Nigeria, 653
    North Africa, 109
    North America, 128
    Northern Europe, 118
    Norway, 656
    Oceania, 130
    Oman, 660
    Pakistan, 664, 666
    Palau, 670
    Panama, 672
    Papua New Guinea, 676
    Paraguay, 680
    Peru, 684, 686
    Philippines, 692
    Poland, 698
    Polynesia, 132
    Portugal, 702
    Puerto Rico, 706
    Qatar, 710
    Romania, 715
    Russian Federation, 721
    Rwanda, 725
    Saint Kitts and Nevis, 729
    Saint Lucia, 732
    Saint Vincent and the Grenadines, 735
    San Marino, 738
    Sao Tome and Principe, 741
    Saudi Arabia, 746
    Senegal, 749
    Serbia and Montenegro, 757
    Seychelles, 761
    Sierra Leone, 765
    Singapore, 771
    Slovakia, 775
    Slovenia, 779
    Solomon Islands, 783
    Somalia, 786
    South Africa, 791
    South America, 125
    South Asia, 113
    Southeast Asia, 113
    Southern Africa, 109
    Southern Europe, 119

Geography *(continued)*
  Southwest Asia, 113
  Spain, 797
  Sri Lanka, 801
  Sudan, 805
  Suriname, 809
  Swaziland, 813
  Sweden, 818
  Switzerland, 822
  Syria, 828
  Taiwan, 832
  Tajikistan, 835
  Tanzania, 839
  Thailand, 845
  Togo, 849
  Tonga, 853
  Trinidad and Tobago, 856
  Tunisia, 860
  Turkey, 866
  Turkmenistan, 870
  Tuvalu, 873
  Uganda, 875
  Ukraine, 881
  Union of Soviet Social Republics (USSR),
    120
  United Arab Emirates, 884
  United Kingdom, 888, 890
  United States, 896
  Uruguay, 900
  Uzbekistan, 904
  Vanuatu, 908
  Venezuela, 913
  Vietnam, 919
  West Africa, 106
  Western Europe, 120
  (Western) Samoa, 923
  Yemen, 926
  Zambia, 930
  Zimbabwe, 934
Georgia
  cultural identity, 384
  economy, 384
  education, 385
  geography, 383
  health care, 385
  population, 383-84
  transport, 385
  vital statistics, 384
Germany
  communications, 391
  cultural identity, 388-89
  economy, 387, 389-90
  education, 390
  geography, 388
  health care, 390
  households, 389
  population, 388
  transport, 386, 390
  vital statistics, 389
Ghana
  communications, 395
  cultural identity, 392-93
  economy, 393-94
  education, 394

Ghana *(continued)*
  geography, 392
  health care, 394
  population, 392
  transport, 394
  vital statistics, 393
global warming, 6, 14-15, 19
Godwin, William, 7-8
grain production
  Argentina, 19
  Australia, 19
  Canada, 19
  United States, 19
Greece (ancient)
  population growth, 7
  desertification, 14
Greece
  communications, 399
  cultural identity, 397
  economy, 398
  education, 399
  geography, 396
  health care, 398-99
  households, 397-98
  population, 392-93
  transport, 398
  vital statistics, 397
Green Revolution, 16-18, 24
  Philippines, 18
Grenada
  communications, 402
  cultural identity, 400-01
  economy, 401
  education, 402
  geography, 400
  health care, 401-02
  households, 401
  population, 400
  transport, 401
  vital statistics, 401
Guatemala
  colonization, 47
  civil war, 47
  communications, 408
  cultural identity, 405
  economy, 403, 407
  education, 407
  ethnic composition, 47
  geography, 405
  health care, 407
  households, 406
  organized labor, 58
  population, 404-05
  poverty, 59
  religious composition, 47
  transport, 407
  vital statistics, 406
Guinea
  communications, 412
  cultural identity, 410
  economy, 410
  education, 411
  geography, 409
  health care, 411

Guinea *(continued)*
  population, 409
  transport, 411
  vital statistics, 410
Guinea-Bissau
  cultural identity, 414
  economy, 414
  education, 415
  geography, 413
  health care, 415
  population, 413
  poverty, 58
  transport, 415
  vital statistics, 414
Guyana
  communications, 418
  cultural identity, 417
  economy, 417
  education, 418
  geography, 416
  health care, 418
  households, 417
  population, 416-17
  transport, 418
  vital statistics, 417

H

Haiti
  communications, 421
  cultural identity, 420
  economy, 420
  education, 421
  geography, 419
  health care, 421
  population, 419-20
  transport, 421
  vital statistics, 420
Health care
  Albania, 140
  Algeria, 145
  and demography, 81
  and economic development 85-86
    International Monetary Fund, 84
    Thailand, 84
    World Bank, 84
    Zambia, 84
  and geography, 84-85
    India, 85
    Jamaica, 84
    Kazakstan, 84
    Kerala, 85
    Madhya Pradesh, 85
    Morocco, 85
    Mozambique, 85
    Uganda, 85
    Zambia, 85
  and poverty, 83
  and urbanization, 85
    Cuba, 85
    Mozambique, 85
    New York City, 85
  Angola, 149, 151-52
  Antigua and Barbuda, 155

Health care (*continued*)
Argentina, 160
Armenia, 161-62
Australia, 168
Austria, 171
Azerbaijan, 175
Bahamas, 178
Bahrain, 182
Bangladesh, 187-88
Barbados, 191
Belarus, 195
Belgium, 199
Belize, 203
Benin, 207
Bolivia, 214-15
Bosnia and Herzegovina, 218
Botswana, 221-22
Brazil, 227
Brunei, 231
Bulgaria, 234-35
Burkina Faso, 238
Burundi, 241
Cambodia, 245
Cameroon, 248
Canada, 254
Cape Verde, 258
Central African Republic, 262
Chad, 266 Chile, 270-71
China, 276 Colombia, 280
Comoros, 284
Congo, Democratic Republic of (Zaïre),
    287
Congo, Republic of, 291
Costa Rica, 295
Côte d'Ivoire, 299
Croatia, 303
Cuba, 309
Cyprus, 312
Czech Republic, 316
Denmark, 320
Djibouti, 323-24
Dominca, 327
Dominican Republic, 330
Ecuador, 334-35
Egypt, 340
El Salvador, 344-45
Equatorial Guinea, 348
Eritrea, 351
Estonia, 354
Ethiopia, 360
Fiji, 364
financing, 85-86
    United States, 82-83
    Mexico, 82-84
    Germany, 82-83
    Japan, 82
    Singapore, 82
Finland, 368-69
France, 370, 374
Gabon, 378
Gambia, 381
Georgia, 385
Germany, 390
Ghana, 394

Health care (*continued*)
Greece, 398-99
Grenada, 401-02
Guatemala, 407
Guinea, 411
Guinea-Bissau, 415
Guyana, 418
Haiti, 421
Honduras, 424
Hungary, 428-29
Iceland, 432
India, 438
Indonesia, 444
Iran, 450
Iraq, 452, 456
Ireland, 459-60
Israel, 465
Italy, 471
Jamaica, 477
Japan, 483
Jordan, 487-88
Kazakstan, 493
Kenya, 498
Kiribati, 501
Korea, North, 504
Korea, South, 509
Kuwait, 513
Kyrgyzstan, 518
Laos, 521
Latvia, 524
Lebanon, 528
Lesotho, 532
Liberia, 535
Libya, 538
Lithuania, 546
Luxembourg, 550
Macedonia, 554-55
Madagascar, 558
Malawi, 562
Malaysia, 567
Maldives, 570
Mali, 573
Malta, 577
Marshall Islands, 581
Mauritania, 584
Mauritius, 588-89
Mexico, 594
Micronesia, 597
Moldova, 601
Monaco, 604
Mongolia, 607
Morocco, 612
Mozambique, 616
Myanmar, 620
Namibia, 624-25
Nauru, 627
Nepal, 631
Netherlands, 637
New Zealand, 642
Nicaragua, 645
Niger, 649-50
Nigeria, 655
Norway, 659
Oman, 662

Health care (*continued*)
Pakistan, 665, 668
Palau, 671
Panama, 674-75
Papua New Guinea, 678
Paraguay, 682-83
Peru, 688
Philippines, 691, 694
Poland, 700-01
Portugal, 704-05
Puerto Rico, 708
Qatar, 712
Romania, 717-18
Russian Federation, 723
Rwanda, 727
Saint Kitts and Nevis, 730
Saint Lucia, 734
Saint Vincent and the Grenadines, 737
San Marino, 740
Sao Tome and Principe, 743
Saudi Arabia, 747-48
Senegal, 753
Serbia and Montenegro, 759
Seychelles, 763
Sierra Leone, 767
Singapore, 773
Slovakia, 778
Slovenia, 781-82
Solomon Islands, 785
Somalia, 788
South Africa, 793
Spain, 799
Sri Lanka, 803-04
Sudan, 807
Suriname, 811
Swaziland, 815
Sweden, 816, 820
Switzerland, 825
Syria, 830
Tajikistan, 837
Tanzania, 841
Thailand, 843, 847
Togo, 851
Tonga, 855
Trinidad and Tobago, 858-59
Tunisia, 862
Turkey, 868
Turkmenistan, 872
Uganda, 877-78
Ukraine, 882-83
United Arab Emirates, 886
United Kingdom, 892
United States, 898
Uruguay, 902-03
Uzbekistan, 906
Vanuatu, 910
Venezuela, 915
Vietnam, 921
Yemen, 928
Zambia, 933
Zimbabwe, 936-37
HIV/AIDS increases in, 86
    Africa, 86
    Cameroon, 86

HIV / AIDS increases (continued)
  Latin America, 86
  Southeast Asia, 86
  Uganda, 86
  United States, 86
  West Africa, 86
  Western Europe, 86
  Zimbabwe, 86
Holocaust, 49
Honduras
  communications, 425
  cultural identity, 423
  economy, 423-24
  education, 425
  geography, 422
  health care, 424
  households, 423
  population, 422-23
  transport, 424
  vital statistics, 423
Households
  Algeria, 144
  and industrialization, 38, 41-42
    Canada, 39
    Italy, 39
    Jamaica, 39
    Jordan, 38
    Namibia, 39
    New Zealand, 39
    South Korea, 38-39
    Turkey, 39
  and urbanization, 38
  Antigua and Barbuda, 154
  Argentina, 159
  Australia, 167
  Austria, 170
  Bahamas, 177
  Bahrain, 181
  Barbados, 190
  Belarus, 194
  Belize, 202
  Benin, 206
  Bolivia, 213-14
  Botswana, 220
  Brazil, 226
  Brunei, 230
  Bulgaria, 233-34
  Burundi, 240
  Canada, 253
  Cape Verde, 257
  Central African Republic, 261-62
  Chile, 269
  China, 275
  Colombia, 279
  Comoros, 283
  Congo, Republic of, 290
  Côte d'Ivoire, 298
  Cyprus, 311-12
  Czech Republic, 315
  definition of, 38
  Denmark, 319
  Dominica, 326
  Dominican Republic, 329
  Ecuador, 333

Households (continued)
  Egypt, 339
  El Salvador, 343
  Ethiopia, 359
  Finland, 367-68
  France, 373
  Germany, 389
  Greece, 397-98
  Grenada, 401
  Guatemala, 406
  Guyana, 417
  Honduras, 423
  Hungary, 427-28
  Iceland, 431
  India, 437
  Indonesia, 443
  Iran, 449
  Ireland, 458-59
  Israel, 464
  Italy, 470
  Jamaica, 476
  Japan, 483
  Jordan, 486
  Kazakstan, 490, 492
  Korea, South, 505, 508
  Kuwait, 512
  Kyrgyzstan, 517
  Latvia, 523-24
  Lebanon, 527
  Luxembourg, 549-50
  Macedonia, 554
  Malawi, 561
  Malaysia, 566
  Mali, 572
  Malta, 576
  Mauritius, 588
  Mexico, 593
  Moldova, 600
  Morocco, 611
  Namibia, 624
  Nepal, 630
  Netherlands, 636
  New Zealand, 640-41
  Nicaragua, 644
  Niger, 648-49
  Norway, 657-58
  Oman, 661
  Pakistan, 667
  Panama, 673
  Paraguay, 681
  Peru, 687
  Philippines, 693
  Poland, 699
  Portugal, 703-04
  Puerto Rico, 707-08
  Qatar, 711
  Romania, 714, 716
  Russian Federation, 720, 722
  Rwanda, 726
  Saint Kitts and Nevis, 730
  Saint Lucia, 733
  Saint Vincent and the Grenadines, 736
  San Marino, 739
  Sao Tome and Principe, 742

Households (continued)
  Serbia and Montenegro, 758
  Seychelles, 762
  Singapore, 770, 772
  Slovakia, 777
  Slovenia, 780-81
  Solomon Islands, 784
  South Africa, 792
  Spain, 798
  Sri Lanka, 802
  Sweden, 817, 819
  Switzerland, 824
  Syria, 827, 829
  Tajikistan, 836
  Tanzania, 840
  Tonga, 854
  Trinidad and Tobago, 857
  Turkey, 865, 867
  Uganda, 877
  Ukraine, 882
  United Kingdom, 891
  United States, 897
  Uruguay, 901-02
  Vanuatu, 909
  Venezuela, 911, 914
  Vietnam, 917, 920
  (Western) Samoa, 924
  Zambia, 932
  Zimbabwe, 935-36
Hungary
  communications, 429
  cultural identity, 427
  economy, 428
  education, 429
  geography, 426
  health care, 428-29
  households, 427-28
  population, 426-27
  transport, 428
  vital statistics, 427
Huntington, Samuel, 53-54
Hussein, Saddam, 20

I

Iceland
  communications, 433
  cultural identity, 431
  economy, 431-32
  education, 432
  fishing disputes, 21
  geography, 430
  health care, 432
  households, 431
  population, 430
  transport, 432
  vital statistics, 431
Identity, cultural
  Afghanistan, 136
  Albania, 139
  Algeria, 143
  Andorra, 146-47

Identity, cultural *(continued)*

Angola, 148, 150
Antigua and Barbuda, 154
Argentina, 158-59
Armenia, 162
Australia, 164, 166-67
Austria, 170
Azerbaijan, 174
Bahamas, 177
Bahrain, 181
Bangladesh, 186-87
Barbadoes, 190
Belarus, 194
Belgium, 198
Belize, 202
Benin, 206
Bhutan, 210
Bolivia, 213
Bosnia and Herzegovina, 217
Botswana, 220
Brazil, 225-26
Brunei, 230
Bulgaria, 233
Burkina Faso, 237
Burundi, 240
Cambodia, 244
Cameroon, 247
Canada, 252
Cape Verde, 257
Central African Republic, 261
Chad, 265
Chile, 268
China, 274-75
Colombia, 279
Comoros, 283
Congo, Democratic Republic of (Zaire), 286
Congo, Republic of, 290
Costa Rica, 294
Côte d'Ivoire, 298
Croatia, 302
Cuba, 305, 307-08
Cyprus, 311
Czech Republic, 315
Denmark, 319
Djibouti, 323
Domincan Republic, 329
Dominica, 326
Ecuador, 333
Egypt, 338
El Salvador, 343
Equatorial Guinea, 347
Eritrea, 350
Estonia, 353
Ethiopia, 357-59
Fiji, 363
Finland, 367
France, 372-73
Gabon, 377
Gambia, 380
Georgia, 384
Germany 388-89
Ghana, 393
Greece, 397

Identity, cultural *(continued)*

Grenada, 400-01
Guatemala, 405
Guinea, 410
Guinea-Bissau, 414
Guyana, 417
Haiti, 420
Honduras, 423
Hungary, 427
Iceland, 431
India, 436-37
Indonesia, 442-43
Iran, 448-49
Iraq, 454-55
Ireland, 458
Israel, 463-64
Italy, 469-70
Jamaica, 475
Japan, 481-82
Jordan, 486
Kazakstan, 489, 491-92
Kenya, 496-97
Kiribati, 500-01
Korea, North, 503
Korea, South, 507-08
Kuwait, 512
Kyrgyzstan, 516
Laos, 520
Latvia, 523
Lebanon, 527
Lesotho, 531
Liberia, 534
Libya, 537
Liechtenstein, 541
Lithuania, 545
Luxembourg, 549
Macedonia, 553
Madagascar, 557
Malawi, 561
Malaysia, 565
Maldives, 569
Mali, 572
Malta, 576
Marshall Islands, 580
Mauritania, 583
Mauritius, 587
Mexico, 592-93
Micronesia, 597
Moldova, 599
Monaco, 603
Mongolia, 606
Morocco, 610
Mozambique, 615
Myanmar, 619
Namibia, 623
Nauru, 626-27
Nepal, 630
Netherlands, 635
New Zealand, 640
Nicaragua, 644
Niger, 647
Nigeria, 652-54
Norway, 657
Oman, 661

Identity, cultural *(continued)*

Pakistan, 666-67
Palau, 670-71
Panama, 673
Papua New Guinea, 677
Paraguay, 681
Peru, 685-87
Philippines, 692-93
Poland, 698-99
Portugal, 703
Puerto Rico, 707
Qatar, 711
Romania, 715-16
Russian Federation, 721-22
Rwanda, 726
Saint Kitts and Nevis, 729-30
Saint Lucia, 733
Saint Vincent and the Grenadines, 736
San Marino, 739
Sao Tome and Principe, 742
Saudi Arabia, 746
Senegal, 749, 751-52
Serbia and Montenegro, 756-58
Seychelles, 762
Sierra Leone, 766
Singapore, 771-72
Slovakia, 776
Slovenia, 780
Solomon Islands, 784
Somalia, 787
South Africa, 789, 791-92
Spain, 797-98
Sri Lanka, 802
Sudan, 806
Suriname, 810
Swaziland, 814
Sweden, 818-19
Switzerland, 823
Syria, 828-29
Taiwan, 832-33
Tajikistan, 836
Tanzania, 840
Thailand, 845-46
Togo, 850
Tonga, 854
Trinidad and Tobago, 857
Tunisia, 861
Turkey, 864, 866-67
Turkmenistan, 871
Tuvalu, 873-74
Uganda, 876
Ukraine, 881
United Arab Emirates, 885
United Kingdom, 890-91
United States, 896-97
Uruguay, 901
Uzbekistan, 904
Vanuatu, 909
Venezuela, 913-14
Vietnam, 919-20
(Western) Samoa, 924
Yemen, 927
Zambia, 931
Zimbabwe, 935

Impact = population x affluence x technology
    (I = PAT), 3-4, 8-9
India
    caste system, 49
    civil war, 49
    colonization, 49
    communications, 439
    cultural identity, 436-37
    deforestation, 4
    economy, 437-38
    education, 438-39
    geography, 436
    health care, 438
    households, 437
    population, 434-36
    poverty, 59
    religious composition, 49
    transport, 438
    vital statistics, 437
Indonesia
    communications, 441, 445
    cultural identity, 442-43
    economy, 443-44
    education, 440, 444-45
    geography, 442
    health care, 444
    households, 443
    organized labor, 58
    population, 442
    rainforests in, 4
    transport, 444
    vital statistics, 443
industrial revolution, 17
    and birth rates, 26, 52
    and death rates, 24, 52
infant mortality
    Brazil, 82
    Bulgaria, 83
    Germany, 83
    Kenya, 37
    Rwanda, 82
    Thailand, 83
    United States, 83
inflation, 60
International Monetary Fund, 53, 84
internet growth in, 80
Iran
    communications, 451
    cultural identity, 448-49
    economy, 449
    education, 450
    geography, 448
    health care, 450
    households, 449
    population, 446, 448
    transport, 450
    vital statistics, 447, 449
Iraq
    communications, 456
    cultural identity, 454-55
    economy, 455
    education, 453, 456
    ethnic composition, 43
    geography, 454

Iraq (continued)
    health care, 452, 456
    oil disputes, 20-21
    population, 454
    transport, 455
    vital statistics, 455
Ireland
    communications, 460
    cultural identity, 458
    economy, 459
    education, 460
    geography, 457
    health care, 459-60
    households, 458-59
    population, 457-58
    transport, 459
    vital statistics, 458
Israel
    communications, 466
    cultural identity, 463-64
    economy, 464-65
    education, 462, 465
    ethnic composition, 49-50
    geography, 463
    health care, 465
    households, 464
    independence war, 49
    population, 461, 463
    religious composition, 49-50
    transport, 465
    vital statistics, 464
Italy
    communications, 472
    cultural identity, 469-70
    economy, 470
    education, 471
    geography, 469
    health care, 471
    households, 470
    population, 467-69
    transport, 471
    vital statistics, 470

J

Jamaica
    communications, 478
    cultural identity, 475
    economy, 476
    education, 477
    geography, 475
    health care, 477
    households, 476
    population, 473-75
    transport, 477
    vital statistics, 474, 476
Japan
    communications, 484
    cultural identity, 481-82
    economy, 483
    education, 484
    geography, 481

Japan (continued)
    health care, 483
    households, 483
    population, 481
    transport, 479, 483
    vital statistics, 480, 482
Jews migration, 67
Jordan
    communications, 488
    cultural identity, 486
    economy, 487
    education, 488
    geography, 485
    health care, 487-88
    households, 486
    population, 485-86
    transport, 487
    vital statistics, 486

K

Kazakstan
    cultural identity, 489, 491-92
    economy, 492-93
    education, 493-94
    geography, 491
    health care, 493
    households, 490, 492
    population, 491
    transport, 493
    vital statistics, 492
Kenya
    communications, 499
    cultural identity, 496-97
    economy, 497
    education, 498
    geography, 496
    health care, 498
    population, 494-96
    transport, 498
    vital statistics, 497
Keynes, John Maynard, 56
keynesianism, 56
Kiribati
    communications, 501
    cultural identity, 500-01
    economy, 501
    geography, 500
    health care, 501
    population, 500
    transport, 501
    vital statistics, 501
Korea, North
    communications, 504
    cultural identity, 503
    economy, 503
    education, 504
    geography, 502
    health care, 504
    population, 502
    transport, 503
    vital statistics, 503

Korea, South
  communications, 510
  cultural identity, 507-08
  economy, 57, 508-09
  education, 506, 509-10
  geography, 507
  health care, 509
  households, 505, 508
  organized labor, 58
  population, 505, 507
  transport, 509
  vital statistics, 508
Kuwait
  communications, 514
  cultural identity, 512
  economy, 513
  education, 513-14
  geography, 511
  health care, 513
  households, 512
  oil disputes, 20-21
  population, 511-11
  transport, 513
  vital statistics, 512
Kyrgyzstan
  cultural identity, 516
  economy, 517
  education, 518
  geography, 515
  health care, 518
  households, 517
  population, 515-16
  transport, 517
  vital statistics, 516

L

labor, organized, 57-58
  Bangladesh, 58
  China, 58
  Denmark, 58
  East Asia, 58
  Guatemala, 58
  Indonesia, 58
  Korea, South, 58
  Latin America, 58
  Mexico, 58
  Philippines, 58
  South Africa, 58
  Southeast Asia, 58
  Spain, 58
  Vietnam, 58
  Western Europe, 57-58
Laos
  communications, 521
  cultural identity, 520
  economy, 520
  education, 521
  geography, 519
  health care, 521
  population, 519-20
  transport, 520-21
  vital statistics, 520

Latin America
  age cohorts, 28
  birth rates, 28
  death rates, 28
  ethnic composition, 46
  geography, 123
  migration, 67
  organized labor, 58
  population density, 28
  population growth, 28
  population, 122-23
  poverty, 59
  vital statistics, 124
Latvia
  communications, 525
  cultural identity, 523
  economy, 524
  education, 525
  geography, 522
  health care 524
  households, 523-24
  population, 522
  transport, 524
  vital statistics, 523
League of Nations, 43
Lebanon
  communications, 529
  economy, 527-28
  education, 528
  geography, 526
  health care, 528
  households, 527
  identity, 527
  population, 526
  transport, 528
  vital statistics, 527
Lesotho
  communications, 532
  economy, 531
  education, 532
  geography, 530
  health care, 532
  identity, 531
  population, 530
  transport, 531-32
  vital statistics, 531
Liberia
  communications, 535
  economy, 534
  education, 535
  geography, 533
  health care, 535
  identity, 534
  population, 533
  transport, 534
  vital statistics, 534
Libya
  communications, 539
  economy, 537
  education, 538
  geography, 536
  health care, 538
  identity, 537
  population, 536-37

Libya (continued)
  transport, 538
  vital statistics, 537
Liechtenstein
  communications, 541
  economy, 541
  education, 541
  geography, 540
  identity, 541
  population, 540
  vital statistics, 541
literacy rates, 78
Lithuania
  communications, 547
  economy, 546
  education, 547
  geography, 544
  health care, 546
  households, 527
  identity, 545
  population, 544-45
  transport, 546
  vital statistics, 543, 545
Luxembourg
  communications, 551
  economy, 550
  education, 551
  geography, 548
  health care, 550
  households, 549-50
  identity, 549
  population, 549
  transport, 550
  vital statistics, 549

M

Macedonia, Former Yugoslav Republic of
  communications, 555
  economy, 554
  education, 555
  geography, 552
  health care, 554-55
  households, 554
  identity, 553
  population, 552-53
  transport, 554
  vital statistics, 553
Madagascar
  communications, 559
  economy, 557-58
  education, 559
  geography, 556
  health care, 558
  identity, 557
  population, 556-57
  poverty, 58
  transport, 558
  vital statistics, 557
Magellan, Ferdinand, 74
Malawi
  communications, 561
  economy, 561

Malawi *(continued)*
   education, 561
   geography, 560
   health care, 561
   households, 561
   identity, 561
   population, 560-61
   transport, 561
   vital statistics, 561
Malaysia
   colonization, 49
   communications, 567
   economy, 49
   economy, 566
   education, 567
   ethnic composition, 49
   geography, 564
   health care, 567
   households, 566
   identity, 565
   labor force, 49
   population, 564-65
   religious composition, 49
   transport, 566
   vital statistics, 565
Maldives
   communications, 570
   economy, 561
   education, 570
   geography, 568
   health care, 570
   identity, 569
   population, 568
   transport, 569
   vital statistics, 569
Mali
   communications, 574
   economy, 573
   education, 574
   geography, 571
   health care, 573
   households, 572
   identity, 572
   population, 571-72
   transport, 573
   vital statistics, 572
Malta
   communications, 577
   economy, 576
   education, 576-77
   geography, 575
   health care, 576
   households, 576
   identity, 576
   population, 575-76
   transport, 576
   vital statistics, 576
Malthus, Thomas, 8-9
Mao Zedong, 9
Marshall Islands
   economy, 580
   geography, 579
   health care, 580
   identity, 580

Marshall Islands *(continued)*
   population, 579
   transport, 580
   vital statistics, 580
Marx, Karl, 9
Mauritania
   communications, 585
   economy, 583-84
   education, 584
   geography, 582
   health care, 584
   households, 527
   identity, 583
   population, 582-83
   transport, 584
   vital statistics, 583
Mauritius
   communications, 589
   economy, 588
   education, 589
   geography, 586
   health care, 588-89
   households, 588
   identity, 587
   population, 586-87
   transport, 588
   vital statistics, 587
meat consumption, 19
Melanasia
   geography, 131
   population, 132
   vital statistics, 132
mercantilism, 7
Mexico
   communications, 595
   economy, 591, 593-94
   education, 594-95
   geography, 592
   health care, 594
   households, 593
   identity, 592-93
   organized labor, 58
   population, 590, 592
   poverty, 59
   transport, 594
   vital statistics, 593
Micronesia
   geography, 132
   population, 132
   vital statistics, 133
Micronesia, Federated States of
   economy, 597
   geography, 596
   health care, 597
   households, 527
   identity, 597
   population, 596
   vital statistics, 597
Middle Ages
   population growth, 7
Middle East. *See* Southwestern Asia
migration
   causes, 64-70
      Caribbean, 67

migration, causes *(continued)*
      China, 65
      Europe, 64
      Latin America, 67
      Southeast Asia, 67
      Southwest Asia, 67
      Western Europe, 67
   government policies, 10-11, 69-70
   patterns
      Africa, 72
      Asia, 70-71
      Europe, 72
      Latin America, 70
      North America, 70
Moldova
   communications, 601
   economy, 600
   education, 601
   geography, 598
   health care, 601
   households, 600
   identity, 599
   population, 598-99
   transport, 600
   vital statistics, 599
Monaco
   communications, 604
   economy, 603
   geography, 602
   health care, 604
   identity, 603
   population, 602
   transport, 603
   vital statistics, 603
Mongolia
   communications, 607
   economy, 606
   education, 607
   geography, 605
   health care, 607
   identity, 606
   population, 605
   transport, 607
   vital statistics, 606
Morocco
   communications, 613
   economy, 611
   education, 612
   geography, 610
   health care, 612
   households, 611
   identity, 610
   population, 608-10
   transport, 612
   vital statistics, 611
motor vehicles
   increase, 75-76
      France, 75
      Indonesia, 75
      Iran, 75
      Nigeria, 75-76
      United States, 75
   impact on environment, 76
      France, 76

motor vehicles, impact *(continued)*
    Poland, 76
Mozambique
    communications, 617
    economy, 615-16
    education, 616-17
    geography, 614
    health care, 616
    identity, 615
    population, 614-15
    transport, 616
    vital statistics, 615
Myanmar
    communications, 621
    economy, 619-20
    education, 620-21
    geography, 618
    health care, 620
    identity, 619
    population, 618-19
    transport, 620
    vital statistics, 619

N

Namibia
    communications, 625
    economy, 624
    education, 625
    geography, 622
    health care, 624-25
    households, 624
    identity, 623
    population, 622-23
    transport, 624
    vital statistics, 623
nation-state
    as measurement, 7
natural resources
    exploitation of, 13
        deforestation, 14
        desertification, 14
        groundwater depletion, 15-16
        land poisoning, 14
        land salinization, 14
        soil depletion, 14
        species depletion, 15
Nauru
    communications, 628
    economy, 627
    education, 628
    geography, 626
    health care, 627
    identity, 626-27
    population, 626
    transport, 627
    vital statistics, 627
neo-Malthusianism, 8-9
neo-liberalism, 56-57
neo-Marxism, 9-10
Nepal
    communications, 631

Nepal *(continued)*
    deforestation, 4
    economy, 630-31
    education, 631
    geography, 629
    health care, 631
    households, 630
    identity, 630
    population, 629-30
    transport, 631
    vital statistics, 630
Netherlands
    communications, 638
    economy, 636
    education, 637
    geography, 635
    health care, 637
    households, 636
    identity, 635
    population, 633-35
    transport, 637
    vital statistics, 636
New Zealand
    communications, 642
    economy, 641
    education, 642
    geography, 131, 639
    health care, 642
    households, 640-41
    identity, 640
    population, 131, 639-40
    transport, 641
    vital statistics, 131, 640
newly industrialized countries (NICs), 27
newspapers, 78
Nicaragua
    communications, 6
    economy, 645-46
    education, 646
    geography, 643
    health care, 645
    households, 644
    identity, 646
    population, 643-44
    transport, 645
    vital statistics, 644
NICs. *See* newly industrialized countries
Niger
    communications, 650
    economy, 649
    education, 650
    geography, 647
    health care, 649-50
    households, 648-49
    identity, 648
    population, 647-48
    poverty, 58-59
    transport, 649
    vital statistics, 648
Nigeria
    civil war, 45
    colonization, 45
    communications, 655
    economy, 651, 654

Nigeria *(continued)*
    education, 655
    ethnic composition, 45
    geography, 653
    health care, 655
    identity, 651, 653-54
    population, 653
    religious composition, 45
    transport, 654-55
    vital statistics, 654
North Africa
    geography, 109
    population, 109
    vital statistics, 109
North America
    age cohorts, 28
    birth rates, 28
    death rates, 28
    ethnic composition, 47
    geography, 128
    immigration, 28
    linguistic composition, 47
    population density, 28
    population growth, 28
    population, 127-28
    vital statistics, 128
North Atlantic Treaty Organization (NATO),
    51
Northern Europe
    geography, 118
    population, 119
    vital statistics, 119
Northern Ireland
    colonization, 51
    religious composition, 51
Norway
    communications, 659
    economy, 658
    education, 659
    geography, 656
    health care, 659
    households, 657-58
    identity, 657
    population, 656-57
    transport, 658
    vital statistics, 657
Nyerere, Julius, 43

O

Oceania
    geography, 130
    immigration, 30
    population growth, 30
    population, 129-30
    vital statistics, 129, 131
Oglalla aquifer, 15
Oman
    communications, 663
    economy, 661
    education, 662
    geography, 660

Oman *(continued)*
  health care, 662
  households, 661
  identity, 661
  population, 660
  transport, 662
  vital statistics, 661
Ottoman Empire, 50

P

Pakistan
  communications, 669
  economy, 667-68
  education, 669
  geography, 664, 666
  health care, 665, 668
  households, 667
  identity, 666-67
  population, 666
  transport, 668
  vital statistics, 667
Palau
  communications, 671
  economy, 671
  geography, 670
  health care, 671
  identity, 670-71
  population, 670
  vital statistics, 671
Palestine
  birth rates, 36
  fertility, 36
  population growth, 5
Panama
  communications, 675
  economy, 674
  education, 675
  geography, 672
  health care, 674-75
  households, 673
  identity, 673
  population, 672-73
  transport, 674
  vital statistics, 673
Papua New Guinea
  communications, 679
  economy, 677-78
  education, 678-79
  geography, 676
  health care, 678
  identity, 677
  population, 676
  transport, 678
  vital statistics, 677
Paraguay
  communications, 683
  economy, 682
  education, 683
  geography, 680
  health care, 682-83
  households, 681

Paraguay *(continued)*
  identity, 681
  population, 680-81
  transport, 682
  vital statistics, 681
pastoralists, 24
Persian Gulf, 15, 29
Persian Gulf War, 20-21, 62
Peru
  border clashes with Ecuador, 21
  communications, 689
  economy, 687-88
  education, 688-89
  geography, 684, 686
  health care, 688
  households, 687
  identity, 685-87
  population, 686
  transport, 688
  vital statistics, 687
pesticides, 18
Philippines
  communications, 695
  economy, 693-94
  education, 690, 694-95
  geography, 692
  health care, 691, 694
  households, 693
  identity, 692-93
  organized labor, 58
  population, 692
  transport, 694
  vital statistics, 693
Plato, 7
Poland
  communications, 701
  economy, 699-700
  education, 701
  geography, 698
  health care, 700-01
  households, 699
  identity, 698-99
  population, 698
  transport, 700
  vital statistics, 696-97, 699
Polynesia
  geography, 132
  population, 132
  vital statistics, 133
Population
  Afghanistan, 135-136
  Africa, 105-107
  Albania, 138-139
  Algeria, 143
  Andorra, 146
  Angola, 150
  Antigua and Barbuda, 153
  Argentina, 158
  Armenia, 161
  Asia, 111-112
  Australia, 131, 165-166
  Austria, 169-170
  Azerbaijan, 173-174
  Bahamas, 176

Population *(continued)*
  Bahrain, 180-181
  Bangladesh, 184-186
  Barbadoes, 189
  Belarus, 193-94
  Belgium, 197-98
  Belize, 201-02
  Benin, 205-06
  Bhutan, 209
  Bolivia, 212-13
  Bosnia and Herzegovina, 216-17
  Botswana, 219-20
  Brazil, 224-25
  Brunei, 229-30
  Bulgaria, 232-33
  Burkina Faso, 236-37
  Burundi, 239-40
  Cambodia, 243
  Cameroon, 246-47
  Canada, 258
  Cape Verde, 256
  Caribbean, 124
  causes of mortality, 8
  Central Africa, 109-110
  Central African Republic, 260-61
  Central America, 125
  Chad, 264-65
  Chile, 268-69
  China, 272, 274
  Colombia, 278-79
  Comoros, 282
  Congo, Democratic Republic of (Zaire),
    285-86
  Congo, Republic of, 289
  Costa Rica, 293-94
  Côte d'Ivoire, 297-98
  Croatia, 301-02
  Cuba, 307
  Cyprus, 310
  Czech Republic, 314-15
  Denmark, 318-19
  Djibouti, 322
  Dominica, 325
  Dominican Republic, 328-29
  East Africa, 108
  East Asia, 113
  Eastern Europe, 118
  Ecuador, 332-33
  Egypt, 336-38
  El Salvador, 342-43
  Equatorial Guinea, 346-47
  Eritrea, 349-50
  Estonia, 352
  Ethiopia, 358
  Europe, 116-117
  Fiji, 362
  Finland, 366-67
  France, 371-72
  Gabon, 376-77
  Gambia, 379
  Georgia, 383-84
  Germany, 388
  Ghana, 392-93
  global, 101-103

Population *(continued)*
    growth in, 3-4, 23-26
    government policies, 10-11
       Africa, 27
       and density, 26-28
       Asia, 28-29
       Europe, 29-30
       Latin America, 28
       North America, 28
       Oceania, 30
    Greece, 396-97
    Grenada, 400
    Guatemala, 404-05
    Guinea, 409
    Guinea-Bissau, 413
    Guyana, 416-17
    Haiti, 419-20
    Honduras, 422-23
    Hungary, 426-27
    Iceland, 430
    India, 434-36
    Indonesia, 442
    Iran, 446, 448
    Iraq, 454
    Ireland, 457-58
    Israel, 461, 463
    Italy, 467-69
    Jamaica, 473-75
    Japan, 481
    Jordan, 485-86
    Kazakstan, 491
    Kenya, 494-96
    Kiribati, 500
    Korea, North, 502
    Korea, South, 505, 507
    Kuwait, 511-12
    Kyrgyzstan, 515-16
    Laos, 519-20
    Latin America, 122-123
    Latvia, 522
    Lebanon, 526
    Lesotho, 530
    Liberia, 533
    Libya, 536-37
    Liechtenstein, 540
    Lithuania, 544-45
    Luxembourg, 548
    Macedonia, 552
    Madagascar, 556
    Malawi, 560
    Malaysia, 564
    Maldives, 568
    Mali, 571
    Malta, 575
    Marshall Islands, 579
    Mauritania, 582
    Mauritius, 586
    Melanesia, 132
    Mexico, 590-92
    Micronesia, 132, 596
    Moldova, 598-99
    Monaco, 602
    Mongolia, 605
    Morocco, 608-10

Population *(continued)*
    Mozambique, 614-15
    Myanmar, 618-19
    Namibia, 622
    Nauru, 626
    Nepal, 629-30
    Netherlands, 633-35
    New Zealand, 131, 639-40
    Nicaragua, 643-44
    Niger, 647-48
    Nigeria, 653
    Norway, 656-57
    North Africa, 109
    North America, 125
    North America, 127-128
    Northern Europe, 119
    Oceania, 129-130
    Oman, 660
    Pakistan, 666
    Palau, 670
    Panama, 672-73
    Papua New Guinea, 676-77
    Paraguay, 680-81
    Peru, 684, 686
    Philippines, 692
    Poland, 698
    Polynesia, 132
    Portugal, 702-03
    Puerto Rico, 706
    Qatar, 710
    Romania, 713, 715
    Russian Federation, 719, 721
    Rwanda, 725-26
    Saint Kitts and Nevis, 729
    Saint Lucia, 732
    Saint Vincent and the Grenadines, 735
    San Marino, 738
    Sao Tome and Principe, 741
    Saudi Arabia, 745-46
    Senegal, 751
    Serbia and Montenegro, 757
    Seychelles, 761-62
    Sierra Leone, 765-66
    Singapore, 769, 771
    Slovakia, 775-76
    Slovenia, 779
    Solomon Islands, 783
    Somalia, 786-87
    South Africa, 791
    Spain, 797
    Sri Lanka, 801-02
    Sudan, 805-06
    Suriname, 809
    Swaziland, 813
    Sweden, 818
    Switzerland, 822-23
    Syria, 826, 828
    Taiwan, 832
    Tajikistan, 835-36
    Tanzania, 839-40
    Thailand, 845
    Togo, 849
    Tonga, 853
    Trinidad and Tobago, 856-57

Population *(continued)*
    Tunisia, 860
    Turkey, 866
    Turkmenistan, 870-71
    Tuvalu, 873
    Uganda, 875-76
    Ukraine, 880-81
    United Arab Emirates, 884-85
    United Kingdom, 888-90
    United States, 894, 896
    Uruguay, 900-01
    Uzbekistan, 904-05
    Vanuatu, 908
    Venezuela, 913
    Vietnam, 919
    (Western) Samoa, 923
    Yemen, 926-27
    Zambia, 930-31
    Zimbabwe, 934-35
  poverty, 58-60
    Africa, 58
    Brazil, 59
    Guatemala, 59
    Guinea-Bissau, 58
    India, 59
    Latin America, 59
    Madagascar, 58
    Mexico, 59
    Niger, 58-59
    Senegal, 59
    Uganda, 58
    Zambia, 58
Portugal
  communications, 705
  economy, 704
  education, 705
  geography, 702
  health care, 704-05
  households, 703-04
  identity, 703
  population, 702-03
  transport, 704
  vital statistics, 703
preventive checks, 8
privatization, 60-61
projections, 30-32
  South Asia, 114
  Southeast Asia, 114
  Southern Africa, 110
  Southern Europe, 119
  Southwest Asia, 115
  Union of Soviet Socialist Republics (USSR), 121
  West Africa, 107-108
  Western Europe, 120
public health, 5
  Mali, 82
  Mexico, 82
  United Kingdom, 82
Puerto Rico
  communications, 709
  economy, 708
  education, 708-09
  geography, 706

Puerto Rico *(continued)*
  health care, 708
  households, 707-08
  identity, 707
  population, 706-07
  transport, 708
  vital statistics, 707

Q

Qatar
  communications, 711
  economy, 710
  education, 711
  geography, 710
  health care, 711
  households, 710
  identity, 710
  population, 710
  transport, 711
  vital statistics, 710
Quebec, 44, 48

R

radios
  increases in, 78-79
  foreign content of broadcasts, 79
rainforest depletion of, 4, 14, 19-20
refugees, 67
Romania
  communications, 718
  economy, 717
  education, 718
  geography, 715
  health care, 717-18
  households, 716
  identity, 715-16
  population, 713, 715
  transport, 717
  vital statistics, 714, 716
Rome (ancient)
  barbarian invasions, 24
  population growth, 7
Roosevelt, Franklin Delano, 15
Russian Federation
  communications, 724
  economy, 57, 722-23
  education, 723
  geography, 721
  health care, 723
  households, 722
  identity, 721-22
  population, 719, 721
  transport, 723
  vital statistics, 720, 722
Rwanda
  colonization, 45-46
  communications, 728
  economy, 726-27
  education, 727
  ethnic composition, 45-46

Rwanda *(continued)*
  genocide, 46
  geography, 725
  health care, 727
  households, 726
  identity, 726
  peacekeeping in, 11
  population density, 45
  population, 725-26
  transport, 727
  vital statistics, 726

S

Saint Kitts and Nevis
  communications, 731
  economy, 730
  education, 731
  geography, 729
  health care, 730
  househol ds, 730
  identity, 729-30
  population, 729
  transport, 730
  vital statistics, 730
Saint Lucia
  communications, 734
  economy, 733
  education, 734
  geography, 732
  health care, 734
  households, 733
  identity, 733
  population, 732
  transport, 734
  vital statistics, 733
Saint Vincent and the Grenadines
  communications, 737
  economy, 736
  education, 737
  geography, 735
  health care, 737
  households, 736
  identity, 736
  population, 735
  transport, 737
  vital statistics, 736
San Marino
  communications, 739
  economy, 739
  education, 739
  geography, 738
  health care, 739
  households, 739
  identity, 739
  population, 738
  vital statistics, 739
Sao Tome and Principe
  communications, 744
  economy, 742
  education, 743
  geography, 741

Sao Tome and Principe *(continued)*
  health care, 743
  education, 794
  geography, 791
  health care, 793
  households, 792
  identity, 789, 791—92
  organized labor, 58
  population, 791
  transport, 793
  vital statistics, 792
South America
  geography, 125
  population, 125
  vital statistics, 126
South Asia
  geography, 113
  population, 114
  population density, 29
  population growth, 29
  vital statistics, 114
Southeast Asia
  birth rates, 29
  death rates, 29
  geography, 113
  migration, 67
  organized labor, 58
  population, 114
  population growth, 29
  vital statistics, 115
Southwest Asia
  boundaries, 43
  geography, 113
  migration, 67
  population, 115
  population growth, 29
  vital statistics, 115
Southern Africa
  geography, 109
  population, 110
  vital statistics, 110
Southern Europe
  geography, 119
  population, 119
  vital statistics, 120
Spain
  communications, 800
  economy, 798
  education, 796, 799
  ethnic composition, 51
  geography, 797
  health care, 799
  households, 798
  identity, 797-98
  organized labor, 58
  population, 797
  transport, 795, 799
  vital statistics, 798
species depletion
  Cameroon, 15
  Canada, 15
  Chile, 15
  France, 15
  Haiti, 15

species depletion *(continued)*
    Madagascar, 15
    Tunisia, 15
Sri Lanka
    communications, 804
    economy, 803
    education, 8
    geography, 801
    health care, 803-04
    households, 802
    identity, 802
    population, 801-02
    transport, 803
    vital statistics, 802
St. Augustine, 7
Stanford University, 19
Sudan
    civil war in, 21, 46
    colonization, 46
    communications, 808
    economy, 807
    education, 808
    geography, 805
    health care, 807
    identity, 806
    population, 805-06
    religious composition, 46
    transport, 807
    vital statistics, 806
Suriname
    communications, 812
    economy, 810-11
    education, 811
    geography, 809
    health care, 811
    identity, 810
    population, 809
    transport, 811
    vital statistics, 810
Swaziland
    communications, 815
    economy, 814
    education, 815
    geography, 813
    health care, 815
    identity, 814
    population, 813
    transport, 815
    vital statistics, 814
Sweden
    geography, 818
    population, 818
    identity, 818-19
    vital statistics, 819
    households, 817, 819
    economy, 8819-20
    transport, 820
    health care, 816, 820
    education, 820-21
    communications, 821
Switzerland
    communications, 825
    economy, 824
    education, 825

Switzerland *(continued)*
    geography, 822
    health care, 825
    households, 824
    identity, 823
    population, 822-23
    transport, 824
    vital statistics, 823
Syria
    communications, 831
    economy, 829-30
    education, 830
    geography, 828
    health care, 830
    households, 829
    identity, 828-29
    population, 826, 828
    transport, 830
    vital statistics, 827, 829

T

Taiwan (Republic of China)
    communications, 834
    economy, 833
    education, 834
    geography, 832
    identity, 833
    population, 832
    transport, 833
    vital statistics, 833
Tajikistan
    economy, 837
    education, 837
    geography, 835
    health care, 837
    households, 836
    identity, 836
    population, 835-36
    transport, 837
    vital statistics, 836
    communications, 838
Tanzania (United Republic of)
    communications, 842
    economy, 841
    education, 842
    geography, 839
    health care, 841
    households, 840
    identity, 840
    population, 839-40
    transport, 841
    vital statistics, 840
telephones
    increase in, 79
        Canada, 79
        China, 79
        France, 79
        Ghana, 79
        Malaysia, 79
    mobile and cellular, 79
televisions
    foreign content of broadcasts, 79

televisions *(continued)*
    increase in, 78-79
Thailand
    communications, 844, 848
    economy, 846
    education, 847
    geography, 845
    health care, 843, 847
    identity, 845-46
    population, 845
    transport, 847
    vital statistics, 846
The Laws, 7
The Population Bomb, 3
The Population Explosion, 3, 8, 13
Tito, Marshal (Josef Broz), 51
Togo
    communications, 852
    economy, 850-51
    education, 851
    geography, 849
    health care, 851
    identity, 850
    population, 849
    transport, 851
    vital statistics, 850
Tonga
    communications, 855
    economy, 854
    education, 855
    geography, 853
    health care, 855
    households, 854
    identity, 854
    population, 853
    transport, 855
    vital statistics, 854
tourism, 77
    Maldives, 77-8
    "eco-tourism," 78
Transport
    Afghanistan, 136-37
    Algeria, 142, 144
    Angola, 151
    Antigua and Barbuda, 155
    Argentina, 159-60
    Armenia, 162
    Australia, 168
    Austria, 171
    Azerbaijan, 175
    Bahamas, 178
    Bahrain, 182
    Bangladesh, 187
    Barbados, 191
    Belarus, 195
    Belgium, 199
    Belize, 203
    Benin, 207
    Bhutan, 210
    Bolivia, 214
    Botswana, 221
    Brazil, 227
    Brunei, 231
    Bulgaria, 234

Transport *(continued)*
Burkina Faso, 237
Burundi, 241
Cambodia, 244
Cameroon, 248
Canada, 254
Cape Verde, 258
Central African Republic, 262
Chad, 266
Chile, 270
China, 276
Colombia, 280
Comoros, 284
Congo, Democratic Republic of (Zaire),
287
Congo, Republic of, 291
Costa Rica, 295
Côte d'Ivoire, 299
Croatia, 303
Cuba, 308-09
Cyprus, 312
Czech Republic, 316
Denmark, 320
Djibouti, 323
Dominica, 327
Dominican Republic, 330
Ecuador, 334
Egypt, 340
El Salvdor, 344
Equatorial Guinea, 347
Estonia, 354
Ethiopia, 360
Fiji, 364
Finland, 368
France, 374
Gabon, 378
Gambia, 381
Georgia, 385
Germany, 386, 390
Ghana, 394
Greece, 398
Grenada, 401
Guatemala, 407
Guinea, 411
Guinea-Bissau, 415
Guyana, 418
Haiti, 421
Honduras, 424
Hungary, 428
Iceland, 432
India, 438
Indonesia, 444
Iran, 450
Iraq, 455
Ireland, 459
Israel, 465
Italy, 471
Jamaica, 477
Japan, 479, 483
Jordan, 487
Kazakstan, 493
Kenya, 498
Kiribati, 501
Korea, North, 503

Transport *(continued)*
Korea, South, 509
Kuwait, 513
Kyrgyzstan, 517
Laos, 520-21
Latvia, 524
Lebanon, 528
Lesotho, 531-32
Liberia, 534
Libya, 538
Lithuania, 546
Luxembourg, 550
Macedonia, 554
Madagascar, 558
Malawi, 562
Malaysia, 566
Maldives, 569
Mali, 573
Malta, 577
Marshall Islands, 580
Mauritania, 584
Mauritius, 588
Mexico, 594
Moldova, 600
Monaco, 603
Mongolia, 607
Morocco, 612
Mozambique, 616
Myanmar, 620
Namibia, 624
Nauru, 627
Nepal, 631
Netherlands, 637
New Zealand, 641
Nicaragua, 645
Niger, 649
Nigeria, 654-55
Norway, 658
Oman, 662
Pakistan, 668
Panama, 674
Papua New Guinea, 678
Paraguay, 682
Peru, 688
Philippines, 694
Poland, 700
Portugal, 704
Puerto Rico, 708
Qatar, 712
Romania, 717
Russian Federation, 723
Rwanda, 727
Saint Kitts and Nevis, 730
Saint Lucia, 734
Saint Vincent and the Grenadines, 737
Sao Tome and Principe, 743
Saudi Arabia, 744, 747
Senegal, 753
Serbia and Montenegro, 759
Seychelles, 763
Sierra Leone, 767
Singapore, 773
Slovakia, 777
Slovenia, 781

Transport *(continued)*
Solomon Islands, 785
Somalia, 787-88
South Africa, 793
Spain, 795, 799
Sri Lanka, 803
Sudan, 807
Suriname, 811
Swaziland, 815
Sweden, 820
Switzerland, 824
Syria, 830
Taiwan, 832-33
Tajikistan, 837
Tanzania, 841
Thailand, 847
Togo, 851
Tonga, 855
Trinidad and Tobago, 858
Tunisia, 862
Turkey, 868
Turkmenistan, 872
Uganda, 877
Ukraine, 882
United Arab Emirates, 886
United Kingdom, 892
United States, 895, 898
Uruguay, 902
Uzbekistan, 906
Vanuatu, 910
Venezuela, 915
Vietnam, 921
(Western) Samoa, 924
Yemen, 928
Zambia, 932
Zimbabwe, 936
Trinidad and Tobago
colonization, 47
communications, 859
economy, 858
education, 859
ethnic composition, 47
geography, 856
health care, 858-59
households, 857
identity, 857
population, 856-57
religious composition, 47
slavery, 47
transport, 858
vital statistics, 857
Tunisia
geography, 860
population, 860-61
identity, 861
vital statistics, 861
economy, 861-62
transport, 862
health care, 862
education, 863
communications, 863
Turkey
communications, 869
economy, 867-68

Turkey *(continued)*
  education, 865, 868-69
  ethnic composition, 50
  geography, 866
  health care, 868
  households, 867
  identity, 864, 866-67
  population, 866
  transport, 868
  vital statistics, 865, 867
Turkmenistan
  economy, 871-72
  education, 872
  geography, 870
  health care, 872
  identity, 871
  population, 870-71
  transport, 872
  vital statistics, 871
Tuvalu
  communications, 874
  economy, 874
  geography, 873
  identity, 873-74
  population, 873
  vital statistics, 874
typhoid, 84

U

Uganda
  communications, 878
  economy, 876
  education, 878
  geography, 875
  health care, 876-78
  households, 876
  identity, 876
  population, 875-76
  poverty, 58
  transport, 876
  vital statistics, 876
Ukraine
  communications, 883
  economy, 882
  education, 883
  geography, 880
  health care, 882-83
  households, 882
  identity, 881
  population, 880-81
  transport, 882
  vital statistics, 879-82
Union of Soviet Socialist Republics (USSR)
  geography, 120
  migration, 69-70
  population, 121
  vital statistics, 121
  see also Russian Federation
unions. *See* organized labor
United Arab Emirates, 29
  communications, 887

United Arab Emirates *(continued)*
  economy, 886
  education, 887
  geography, 884
  health care, 886
  identity, 885
  population, 884-85
  transport, 886
  vital statistics, 885
United Kingdom
  communications, 893
  economy, 891
  education, 892
  export of language, 53
  geography, 888, 890
  health care, 892
  households, 891
  identity, 890-91
  population, 889-90
  transport, 892
  vital statistics, 891
United Nations Development Programme, 52-53
United Nations Food and Agriculture Organization, 19
United Nations Population Fund, 10
United States
  colonization, 48
  communications, 899
  economy, 897-98
  education, 899
  ethnic composition, 44
  ethnic composition, 48
  expansion, 48
  export of culture, 53
  fishing disputes, 21
  geography, 896
  health care, 898
  households, 897
  identity, 896-97
  immigration, 48
  population, 894, 896
  slavery, 48
  transport, 895, 898
  vital statistics, 897
Uruguay
  communications, 903
  economy, 902
  education, 903
  geography, 900
  health care, 902-03
  households, 901-02
  identity, 901
  population, 900-01
  transport, 902
  vital statistics, 901
Uzbekistan
  communications, 907
  economy, 905-06
  education, 906
  geography, 904
  health care, 906
  identity, 905
  population, 904-05

Uzbekistan *(continued)*
  transport, 906
  vital statistics, 905

V

Vanuatu
  communications, 910
  economy, 909
  education, 910
  geography, 908
  health care, 910
  households, 909
  identity, 909
  population, 908
  transport, 910
  vital statistics, 909
Venezuela
  communications, 916
  economy, 912, 914-915
  education, 915-16
  geography, 913
  health care, 915
  households, 914
  identity, 913-14
  population, 913
  transport, 915
  vital statistics, 911, 914
Verne, Jules 74
Vietnam, 29
  communications, 922
  economy, 918, 920-21
  education, 921
  geography, 919
  health care, 921
  households, 920
  identity, 919-20
  organized labor, 58
  population, 919
  transport, 921
  vital statistics, 917, 920
Vital statistics
  Afghanistan, 136
  Africa, 107
  Albania, 139
  Algeria, 144
  Andorra, 147
  Angola, 151
  Antigua and Barbuda, 154
  Argentina, 156-57, 159
  Armenia, 162
  Asia, 112-13
  Australia, 131, 167
  Austria, 170
  Azerbaijan, 174
  Bahamas, 177
  Bahrain, 181
  Bangladesh, 187
  Barbadoes, 190
  Belarus, 194
  Belgium, 198
  Belize, 202

Vital statistics (continued)
  Benin, 206
  Bhutan, 210
  Bolivia, 213
  Bosnia and Herzegovina, 217
  Botswana, 220
  Brazil, 224, 226
  Brunei, 230
  Bulgaria, 233
  Burkina Faso, 237
  Burundi, 240
  Cambodia, 244
  Cameroon, 247
  Canada, 250-51, 253
  Cape Verde, 257
  Caribbean, 124
  Central Africa, 110
  Central African Republic, 261
  Central America, 125
  Chad, 265
  Chile, 269
  China, 275
  Colombia, 279
  Comoros, 283
  Congo, Democratic Republic of (Zaire),
    286
  Congo, Republic of, 290
  Costa Rica, 294
  Côte d'Ivoire, 298
  Croatia, 302
  Cuba, 306, 308
  Cyprus, 311
  Czech Republic, 315
  Denmark, 319
  Djibouti, 323
  Dominica, 326
  Dominican Republic, 329
  East Africa, 108
  East Asia, 113
  Eastern Europe, 118
  Ecuador, 333
  Egypt, 339
  El Salvador, 343
  Equatorial Guinea, 347
  Eritrea, 350
  Estonia, 353
  Ethiopia, 359
  Europe, 116, 118
  Fiji, 363
  Finland, 367
  France, 373
  Gabon, 377
  Gambia, 380
  Georgia, 384
  Germany, 389
  Ghana, 393
  global, 103-04
  Greece, 397
  Grenada, 401
  Guatemala, 406
  Guinea, 410
  Guinea-Bissau, 414
  Guyana, 417
  Haiti, 420

Vital statistics (continued)
  Honduras, 423
  Hungary, 427
  Iceland, 431
  India, 437
  Indonesia, 443
  Iran, 447, 449
  Iraq, 455
  Ireland, 458
  Israel, 464
  Italy, 470
  Jamaica, 474, 476
  Japan, 480, 482
  Jordan, 486
  Kazakstan, 492
  Kenya, 497
  Kiribati, 501
  Korea, North, 503
  Korea, South, 508
  Kuwait, 512
  Kyrgyzstan, 516
  Laos, 520
  Latin America, 124
  Latvia, 523
  Lebanon, 527
  Lesotho, 531
  Liberia, 534
  Libya, 537
  Liechtenstein, 541
  Lithuania, 543, 545
  Luxembourg, 549
  Macedonia, 553
  Madagascar, 557
  Malawi, 561
  Malaysia, 565
  Maldives, 569
  Mali, 572
  Malta, 576
  Marshall Islands, 580
  Mauritania, 583
  Mauritius, 587
  Melanesia, 132
  Mexico, 593
  Micronesia, 133
  Micronesia, 597
  Moldova, 599
  Monaco, 603
  Mongolia, 606
  Morocco, 611
  Mozambique, 615
  Myanmar, 619
  Namibia, 623
  Nauru, 627
  Nepal, 630
  Netherlands, 636
  New Zealand, 131
  New Zealand, 640
  Nicaragua, 644
  Niger, 647
  Nigeria, 654
  North Africa 109
  North America, 128
  Northern Europe, 119
  Norway, 657

Vital statistics (continued)
  Oceania, 129, 131
  Oman, 661
  Pakistan, 667
  Palau, 671
  Panama, 673
  Papua New Guinea, 677
  Paraguay, 681
  Peru, 687
  Philippines, 693
  Poland, 699
  Polynesia, 133
  Portugal, 703
  Puerto Rico, 707
  Qatar, 711
  Romania, 714, 716
  Russian Federation, 720, 722
  Rwanda, 726
  Saint Kitts and Nevis, 730
  Saint Lucia, 733
  Saint Vincent and the Grenadines, 736
  San Marino, 739
  Sao Tome and Principe, 742
  Saudi Arabia, 747
  Senegal, 750, 752
  Serbia and Montenegro, 758
  Seychelles, 762
  Sierra Leone, 766
  Singapore, 770, 772
  Slovakia, 776
  Slovenia, 780
  Solomon Islands, 784
  Somalia, 787
  South Africa, 792
  South America, 126
  South Asia, 114
  Southeast Asia, 115
  Southern Africa, 110
  Southern Europe, 120
  Southwest Asia, 115
  Spain, 798
  Sri Lanka, 802
  Sudan, 806
  Suriname, 810
  Swaziland, 814
  Sweden, 819
  Switzerland, 823
  Syria, 827, 829
  Taiwan, 832-33
  Tajikistan, 836
  Tanzania, 840
  Thailand, 846
  Togo, 850
  Tonga, 854
  Trinidad and Tobago, 857
  Tunisia, 861
  Turkey, 865, 867
  Turkmenistan, 871
  Tuvalu, 874
  Uganda, 876
  Ukraine, 879-82
  Union of Soviet Socialist Republics, 121
  United Arab Emirates, 885
  United Kingdom, 891

Vital statistics *(continued)*
    United States, 897
    Uruguay, 901
    Uzbekistan, 904
    Vanuatu, 909
    Venezuela, 911, 914
    Vietnam, 917, 920
    West Africa, 108
    Western Europe, 120
    (Western) Samoa, 924
    Yemen, 927
    Zambia, 931
    Zimbabwe, 935

W

Wallerstein, Immanuel, 9
water pollution, 15-16
water shortages
    China, 16
West Africa
    geography, 106
    population, 107-08
    vital statistics, 108
West Bank. *See* Palestine
Western Europe
    geography, 120
    migration, 67
    organized labor, 57-58
    population, 120
    vital statistics, 120

(Western) Samoa
    communications, 925
    economy, 924
    education, 925
    geography, 923
    households, 924
    identity, 924
    population, 923
    transport, 924
    vital statistics, 924
wheat
    high yield variety (HYV), 18
World Bank, 53, 58, 84
World
    geography, 103
    population, 101-103
    vital statistics, 103-04

Y

yellow fever, 84
Yemen
    communications, 929
    economy, 927
    education, 928
    geography, 926
    health care, 928
    identity, 927
    population, 926-27
    transport, 928

Yemen *(continued)*
    vital statistics, 927
Yugoslavia
    collapse of, 51
    see also Serbia and Montenegro

Z

Zambia
    communications, 933
    economy, 931
    education, 933
    geography, 930
    health care, 933
    households, 931
    identity, 931
    population, 930-31
    poverty, 58
    transport, 931
    vital statistics, 931
Zimbabwe
    communications, 937
    economy, 936
    education, 937
    geography, 934
    health care, 936-37
    households, 935-36
    identity, 935
    population, 934-35
    transport, 936
    vital statistics, 935